To Katherine and William

who have brought joy and meaning into my life.

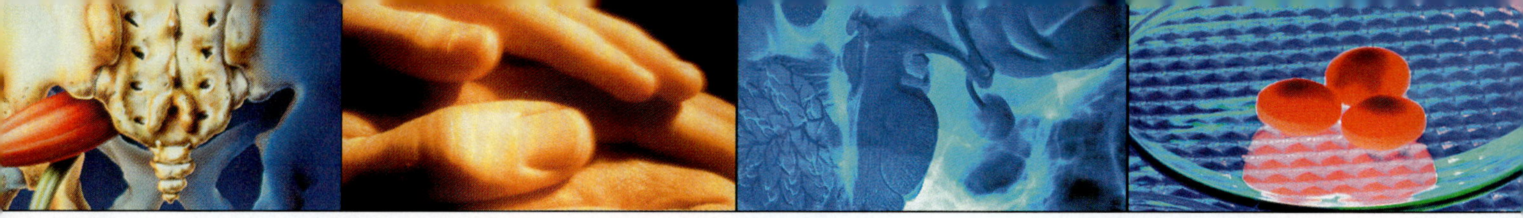

Brief Contents

Contents

PREFACE

Rationale and Goals

This text is intended to provide a general introduction to, and overview of, the structure of the nervous system and its role in determining behavior. My goal is to provide a biological psychology text that is thorough, yet can be understood by a student with little or no previous instruction in the biological sciences.

The decision to write such a text developed over several years of teaching biological psychology. The increasing public exposure to biological psychology, such as recent articles in major news magazines describing the neural bases of Alzheimer's disease, depression, and schizophrenia, among others, as well as the national focus on the consequences of illegal drug use, has produced an increasing need to provide the average student with a basic understanding of the biology of behavior.

The biggest challenge I faced was not developing lectures, but locating an appropriate textbook. I found a number of excellent, extremely detailed biological psychology texts, but students invariably had great difficulty getting through the complex material and relating it to their world. Their experiences led me to conclude that a biological psychology text needs to be pedagogically engaging and approachable as well as academically sound in order to be an effective teaching tool.

Content and Organization

I have found that all too often, beginning students are "turned off" by biological psychology because the terminology appears incomprehensible and the material seems irrelevant. I set out to write a text demonstrating the relationship between biological psychology and everyday behaviors that can be read and understood by individuals with little or no neuroscience background. My plan for accomplishing this goal has included a straightforward writing style, the incorporation of a number of pedagogical features (described in detail in the following section), and the judicious use of appropriate, interesting examples and research studies.

I wrote this text with the student in mind, who perhaps has not taken a science course since plowing through the requisites in high school. I have done my best to make the text readable, presenting even the most complex material clearly and concisely. The informal writing style, along with the inclusion of relevant examples, also helps students make connections between biological psychology and their everyday lives.

Among the relevant examples I have included are hypothetical case histories as well as actual situations reported in the popular press. It is my experience that students can grasp complex concepts much more readily if relevant applications are provided. For example, in Chapter 14 the famous case history of H. M., a man with brain damage that significantly affected his memory, is used to illustrate how a person's memory depends on the effective functioning of specific neural systems and how the quality of a person's life and the lives of those around him or her can be affected in a profound way by a neurological disorder.

I have included those research studies that best clarify the concepts being discussed, as well as demonstrate how neuroscientists gather information and solve problems. I have selected both classic experiments and recent major-impact studies to illustrate to the student that some ideas are enduring and some are brand new.

This text contains fifteen chapters. Chapter 1 describes the major historical discoveries in biological psychology; provides an overview of the major research perspectives in biological psychology; gives a brief overview of genetics; describes the development of the nervous system from simple invertebrate species to the complex vertebrate *homo sapiens*; and gives a brief presentation of the ethics of conducting research.

In Chapter 2 the student will learn about neuroanatomy, the organizational structure of the nervous system, as well as key structures within the nervous system that allow us to engage in many, varied activities. A description of research techniques used by neuroscientists to investigate the relationship between biology and behavior is also presented in this chapter.

Chapter 3 details the structural and cellular development of the nervous system. This discussion explains the wonder of the conversion of a single-celled embryo into a functional human, as well as the problems that ensue as a result of failures of neural development. The consequences of nerve damage and the treatments that are being developed to reverse the effects of this damage are also explored.

Chapter 4 discusses the events that lead to a neural message and the means by which this message is communicated to other neurons. The chapter also describes a number of neurotransmitters involved in that communication as well as communication by means of the circulatory system, i.e., hormones.

Chapter 5 describes the mechanisms by which psychoactive drugs affect the nervous system. The biology of reinforcement, the process that causes psychoactive drugs to have such a powerful influence on humans, is also explored in this chapter.

Chapters 6 and 7 explore how sensory systems detect environmental events. Chapter 6 describes the visual sensory system and explains how it enables us to recognize the shape and color of an object as well as its depth and movement. Chapter 7 discusses the auditory sensory system's recognition of sounds, the vestibular sensory system's detection of the head movements needed to maintain balance, the somatosensory system's recognition of touch, temperature, and pain, the gustatory system's detection of taste, and the olfactory system's detection of smell.

Chapter 8 describes how the nervous system produces movement. This discussion first explores the mechanism by which nerves cause muscles to move a body part, and then moves on to explain reflex control of movement and brain control of movement. Several degenerative neuromuscular disorders such as amyotrophic lateral sclerosis (ALS) and Parkinson's disease are used to illustrate what happens when one or more of these mechanisms goes awry. Possible treatments of these diseases are also explored.

Chapter 9 discusses biological rhythms and the processes by which the nervous system controls wakefulness and sleep. Chapter 9 also explains the biology of dreaming, and concludes with an examination of several sleep disorders.

Chapter 10 covers the biological basis of eating and drinking. The processes by which a person becomes hungry and thirsty are explored, as are the means for suppressing eating and drinking. Chapter 10 also discusses the causes and treatments of obesity and the eating disorders anorexia and bulimia.

Chapter 11 explores sexual development and behavior. The process responsible for the determination of gender and several possible bases for sexual preference are described, as are the mechanisms responsible for the initiation and suppression of sexual behavior. The chapter concludes with an application on treatment of sexual dysfunction.

Chapter 12 explores the physiology of emotional expression and the biology of aggressive behavior. Chapter 12 also describes the physiological changes that occur when a person encounters a stressor, how these physiological responses can be harmful, and what can be done to manage the stress response.

Chapter 13 examines lateralization and language. Split-brain studies in both animals and humans are used to explain differences in the function of the two hemispheres of the brain. Language is defined and broken down into its component parts, and the biological processes responsible for this uniquely human attribute as well as the causes and treatments of communicative disorders are explored.

Chapter 14 explores the biology of learning and memory. The anatomical changes in the nervous system that occur during learning, and that continue to allow recollections of past experiences, are described, as are several models of memory storage and retrieval. The chapter concludes with an application on the causes and treatment of Alzheimer's disease, a disorder with a devastating impact on memory.

Chapter 15 discusses the biological basis of mental disorders. The characteristics and physiology of the affective disorders and schizophrenia are described, as in the typical course of each disorder. Treatment approaches are also explored.

AN UNEXPECTED STROKE

John was in his room, engrossed in studying for finals, when the phone rang. John knew that something was wrong as soon as he heard his father's voice. John's grandmother, who was 74, had suffered a stroke and was in the hospital.

John was close to his grandmother, and the news of her illness was upsetting. She was expected to live, but she was paralyzed on the right side of her body and could not speak, although she seemed to understand what was said to her. Her doctor indicated that it might be weeks or even months before they knew whether the deficits would be permanent. Grandma was resting comfortably, and the doctors were hopeful that she would not suffer from another stroke.

During the next 5 days, John's thoughts turned often to his grandmother, making studying difficult. He started for home as soon as he finished his last exam, and he had plenty of time to think during the long drive. One friend had told him that his grandmother's disabilities might be permanent. Another friend, a premedical student, told him that his grandmother's stroke must have occurred on the left side of her brain; if it had occurred on the right, the left side of her body would have been paralyzed and her speech unaffected.

◄ The auditory receptors are sensitive enough to hear a pin drop to the ground.

As he neared the hospital, he wondered, would his grandmother recognize him? Would she understand him? Would she be able to speak? What awaited John behind the door to her room? ■

385

Pedagogical Features

I have incorporated a number of pedagogical features to heighten the students' interest and enhance their understanding of the text material.

Vignettes

A vignette is used to open each chapter, and some chapters include vignettes within the chapter as well. This pedagogical feature serves three purposes. First, it lets students know what type of material will be presented in the chapter and provides them with a frame of reference. Second, the vignette arouses the student's curiosity and enhances the impact of the text material. Third, references to the vignette have been incorporated into the text to give it a seamless quality. I have found that students like the chapter-opening vignettes, and I believe that their use solidifies the link between the text material and the students' lives.

Before You Begin

Why didn't the doctor prescribe any medication to alleviate her symptoms?

In this chapter, we will help you answer these and the following questions:

- How does the nervous system process information?
- How do neurons communicate with each other?
- What is myelin, and why is it so important?

"Before You Begin" and "Before You Go On" Sections

At the beginning of each chapter, in the Before You Begin sections, I have presented a list of questions that will be answered in that chapter. The questions in the Before You Begin sections serve as an outline of the topics that will be covered. I also have included one or

Before You Go On

Describe how diffusion, electrostatic pressure, and the sodium-potassium pump act on sodium and potassium ions. What is the cause of diffusion?

What is the purpose of the sodium-potassium pump?

two critical thinking questions in each of the Before You Go On sections, which appear throughout the chapter. The Before You Go On questions ensure that the students understand the material and allow them to apply this knowledge in original, creative ways. My students report that the use of this pedagogy is quite helpful in understanding what can be difficult concepts.

APPLICATION

Drug Treatment of Depression

Drugs can influence the activity of neurotransmitters in a variety of ways. One purpose of drug administration is to increase the levels of a depleted neurotransmitter in order to reinstate normal physiological and behavioral functioning. Drugs that elevate levels of norepinephrine, dopamine, and serotonin in the brain have been shown to decrease depressive symptoms (Baldessarini, 1995). Two classes of drugs that increase the activity of these three neurotransmitters have for many years been used to provide clinical relief for many depressed individuals.

"Application" Sections

Although applications of the text material are presented throughout each chapter, each chapter has at least one stand-alone application section. Many of the discoveries made by biological psychologists have been applied to solving real-world problems. These applications demonstrate that biological psychologists are interested in solving problems and not merely in accumulating knowledge. The application sections also enhance the relevance of the abstract ideas presented in the text, showing the student that the behaviors described do exist and are not just laboratory phenomena.

"Section Review"

I have presented section reviews in bulleted form at key points in each chapter, providing another tool with which students can check their understanding of the material that has just been covered. Although concise, the reviews are sufficiently inclusive to stand alone; that is, once the students have read the chapter, they can use the section reviews as a study tool in preparing for examinations.

Section Review

- The cell membrane of neurons is electrically charged.
- When the cell is at rest (not being acted upon by outside forces), the outside of the cell is positively charged relative to the inside of the cell, a difference in charge is referred to as the resting membrane
- Although the force of diffusion acts to push potassium ions out of the cell, electrostatic pressure and the sodium-potassium pump.

Illustration Program

Although illustrations cannot substitute for effective presentation of text material, they do provide an exciting and meaningful medium to enhance the student's attention to and understanding of the text. Photographs and line drawings are used throughout the text to illustrate significant concepts. In planning illustrations for the text, I have strived to present the relevant anatomical locations or physiological processes without an overwhelming level of detail.

"Critical Thinking Questions"

Critical thinking questions in the form of scenarios are presented at the end of each chapter. Answering these questions requires creative application of one or more of the major concepts presented in the chapter to further assist students in relating the principles presented in the text to situations that they may encounter in the real world.

"Vocabulary Questions" and "Review Questions"

A number of fill-in-the-blank vocabulary questions and multiple-choice review questions are included at the end of each chapter. Answers are provided in the Study Guide. These objective questions are intended as a self-test for students, giving them immediate feedback on their mastery of the concepts presented in each chapter.

"Suggested Readings"

Many students are excited by a particular topic and would like to know more about that area. I have carefully selected additional readings that describe important concepts presented in the text in greater detail. They range from the leading and most advanced studies to popular books and texts written by leading experts in a given area. This balance in the suggested readings will allow students to further pursue their individual interests in biological psychology.

Chapter Review

Critical Thinking Questions

1. Neuron A is a gustatory (taste) receptor. It is charged with determining whether or not a specific food is bitter. Explain how neuron A decides whether a food is bitter or not, using what you know about.

Vocabulary Questions

7. The brain structure that controls breathing and heart rate is the ________________.

Review Questions

11. The role of the thalamus is to
    a. detect hunger and thirst.
    b. relay sensory information.
    c. control release of pituitary hormones.
    d. control emotions.

Running Glossary and End-of-Text Glossary

I have included both a running glossary of the terms that appear on each page of the text and a complete glossary at the end of the text. The running glossary provides definitions of key terms as students read the chapter, and can be used as yet another study tool when preparing for examinations and quizzes. The comprehensive glossary at the end of the text allows students to efficiently access the meaning of terms that appear throughout the text.

Support Materials That Accompany the Book

Biological Psychology is accompanied by a superb set of teaching and learning materials. They include the following:

For the Instructor

Instructor's Resource Manual. This manual contains a wealth of teaching tips and creative ideas for new and experienced instructors alike. Each chapter includes Chapter Outlines, Lecture Suggestions, Classroom Discussion Topics, Classroom Demonstrations and Student Activities, and a complete listing of Prentice Hall and other Video Resources.

Prentice Hall Color Overhead Transparencies for *Biological Psychology*. Available in acetate form or as downloads from our *Companion Website*™, these transparencies will add visual appeal to your discussion of key concepts in *Biological Psychology*. They are designed in large format for use in lecture hall settings.

Test Item File. This test item file contains over 1,500 multiple choice, short answer, and essay questions in varying levels of difficulty.

Prentice Hall Custom Tests. Windows and Macintosh platforms allow instructors complete flexibility in building and editing their own customized tests. Advances in the most recent version of the software now allow online testing on a network and the World Wide Web.

Toll-Free Telephone Test Preparation. Prentice Hall offers a telephone test preparation service through which instructors can call a toll-free number and select up to 200 questions from the printed Test Item File available with the text. The test, an alternate version, and the answer key are mailed or faxed within hours of the initial request.

***Biological Psychology Companion Web Site*™ Faculty Module.** Providing online access to key instructor resources, this module contains resources for teaching including Lecture Outlines; Demonstrations, Handouts, and Activities; Power Point Presentation Slides; and an Online Graphics Archive of figures from the text that can be imported into any presentation software. This module is accessed via a password provided by your local Prentice Hall representative. Visit this site online at **www.prenhall.com/klein.**

For the Student

Study Guide. Designed to help students get the most out of the textbook, each chapter includes a Chapter Summary and Study Outline, Learning Objectives, Practice Tests, and Labeling Exercises.

***Biological Psychology Companion Web Site*™.** This online study guide provides unique tools and support that integrate the World Wide Web into your course. Tied specifically to this text, each chapter includes Multiple Choice, True/False, Fill-In, Labeling and Short Essay quizzes. Other activities include NetSearch, Web Destination, Chat Room, and Bulletin Board. Visit this site online at **www.prenhall.com/klein.**

Psychology on the Internet 1999-2000. This is a hands-on introduction and tutorial featuring web sites related to psychology. Designed to enhance the effectiveness of the text and *Companion Website*™, it guides students to resources on the World Wide Web. This supplement is free with every new book purchases. Contact your local Prentice Hall representative for information on how to order.

Acknowledgements

The textbook has had input from many people. I thank the students in my physiological psychology classes who read drafts of the chapters and pointed out which sections they liked, which they disliked, and which were unclear. The staff at Prentice Hall played an important role in the creation of this edition. Jennifer Gilliland, my editor at Prentice Hall, guided the development of the text from its inception to this final product. Karen Trost is a first-rate development editor. Her ideas and suggestions were right on target and my text is immeasurably better as a result of our collaboration. The production team, Mary Rottino and Lisa M. Guidone, ensured that the text was not only easy to read but also aesthetically appealing.

I also thank my colleagues who reviewed chapters of my text. I am especially grateful to Shawn Bachtler, Seattle University; Marie Banich, University of Illinois; Daniel Barth, University of Colorado at Boulder; Gary Bernston, Ohio State University; Mary Cassill, University of Texas; James Coleman, University of South

Carolina; Thomas B. Collins, Mankato State University; Allan Combs, UNC Asheville; Tom Cunningham, Seattle University; Steve Davis, Emporia State University Gary Dunbar, Central Michigan University; Terri Fetterman, Cabrillo College; June Foley, Clinton Community College; Jeffrey Greenspon, Hobart and William Smith Colleges; Leonard Hamilton, Rutgers University; Priscilla Kehoe, Trinity College; William F. McDaniel, Georgia College; Steven E. Meier, University of Idaho; Robert Mowrer, Angelo State University; Dean Murakami, American River College; Brady J. Phelps, South Dakota State University; Joseph Porter, Virginia Commonwealth University; Anthony Riley, The American University; Neil Rowland, University of Florida; Thomas Scott, University of Delaware; Michael Stoloff, James Madison University Rodney Swain, University of Wisconsin—Milwaukee; Susie Swithers, Purdue University; Richard Vadaris, Kent State University; Donald Vardiman, The William Patterson College of New Jersey; Paul Wellman, Texas A & M University for their detailed and constructive comments.

I wish to thank Barbara Butler and Cindy Cochran for their secretarial assistance, and my graduate assistant Wendy Williams for her technical support. Their help allowed the project to progress quite smoothly.

My family has been very supportive of my work on this text, and I am grateful for their help and understanding.

To The Student

I have always enjoyed teaching biological psychology, and have tried to convey this enjoyment as well as the conversational style of a lecture in my writing. There have been great advances in our understanding of the influence of biology on behavior. I hope that you become as excited by this material as I am and set out to learn more about biological psychology. In addition to the suggested readings in each chapter, you can learn a great deal from the Internet. I have suggested a number of fascinating sites on my homepage, which I hope you will visit: http://www.msstate.edu/dept/psychology/klein.html.

I would very much like to know what you think of my text. To help myself as well as future readers of the text, please send your thoughts to me at the Department of Psychology, Mississippi State University, Mississippi State, MS 39762. You can also reach me at my e-mail address: sbk1@ra.msstate.edu. I look forward to hearing from you.

Stephen B. Klein
Mississippi State University

About the Author

Stephen B. Klein is professor and head of the psychology department at Mississippi State University. He received a B.S. in psychology in 1968 from Virginia Polytechnic Institute and a Ph.D. in psychology in 1971 from Rutgers University. Professor Klein taught at Old Dominion University for twelve years and at Fort Hays State University for seven years prior to coming to Mississippi State University in 1990. He has written numerous articles for psychological journals in the area of the biological basis of learning and memory and is the author of *Motivation: Biosocial Approaches,* published by McGraw-Hill in 1982, and *Learning: Principles and Applications,* published by McGraw-Hill in 1987, 1991, and 1996. Dr. Klein coedited the two-volume text *Contemporary Learning Theories,* which was published in 1989 by Lawrence Erlbaum and Associates. His family includes his wife, Marie, and five children, Dora, David, Jason, Katherine, and William. In his spare time, he enjoys sports, most passionately baseball, and science fiction, especially Star Trek and Star Wars.

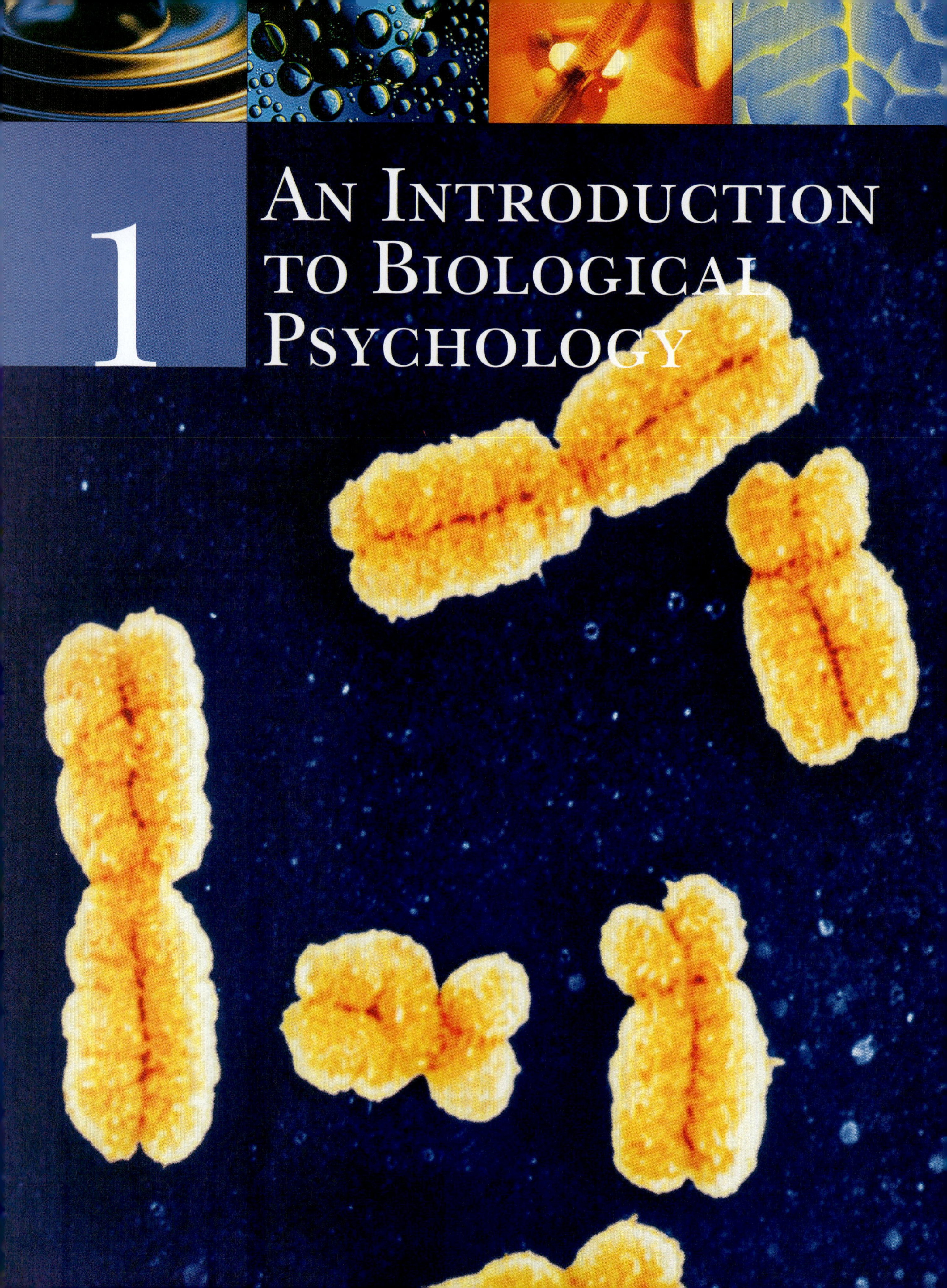

1 An Introduction to Biological Psychology

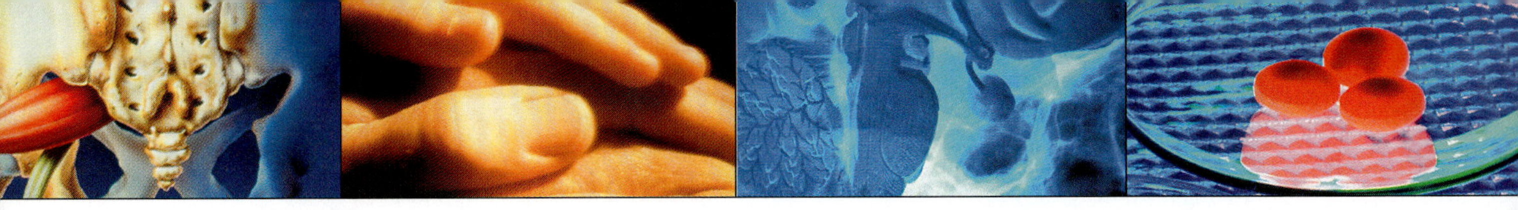

The Joy of Discovery

When Laura entered college 2 years ago she was sure that she would become a journalist. During the past year, though, she took an introductory psychology course to satisfy a distribution requirement and found it to be more exciting and challenging than her journalism classes. Laura especially enjoyed learning about how biology influences behavior and now wonders what careers this interest could lead her to pursue.

Laura's interest in psychology has been enhanced by the discovery that her mother has Huntington's disease, an incurable disease characterized by involuntary movements and progressive central nervous system degeneration. Laura chose to undergo genetic testing, and to her relief she discovered that she had not inherited the disease.

Because of her interest in the biology of behavior, Laura decided to switch majors; however, her advisor recommended that she take a biological psychology course before she made a final decision. Laura had already taken several courses in the biology department and wondered why the psychology department had its own course. She soon found out. The course taught her how biological systems control such basic actions as sensing, learning, remembering, and thinking. She also learned how dysfunctions in specific biological systems can lead to many disorders. Laura thoroughly enjoyed the course, except for the discussion of research. She knows that animal experimentation is necessary to advance the science, but it still makes her somewhat uncomfortable. ■

◀ Humans have between 60,000 and 150,000 genes located on 23 pairs of chromosomes.

Before You Begin

What are the various fields of biological psychology Laura has to choose from?

What causes Huntington's disease?

How would genetic testing help predict whether Laura would develop Huntington's?

In this chapter we will help you answer these and the following questions:

- What is biological psychology?
- How does an understanding of biological processes help us to understand how behavior is controlled?
- How are Huntington's disease and other genetic disorders inherited?
- Which members of the animal kingdom have nervous systems? How are theirs different from ours?
- Why is the use of animal subjects in biological psychology research sometimes necessary?

Definition of Biological Psychology

Laura is thinking of going home this weekend to see how her mom is doing. Laura's trip home involves deciding that she wants to go, thinking about how she will get there, and planning what she needs to bring (some laundry, perhaps?). Deciding, thinking, and planning are all behaviors, or activities of the mind.

Biological psychology is the study of the influences of biological systems, especially the nervous system, on behavior. In the context of biological psychology, **behavior** is anything that an organism does involving action and response to stimulation (Webster, 1995). Thus, the jerky, involuntary movements that Laura's mother suffers because of her disease are behaviors, as is Laura's decision to go home for the weekend. Wait a minute, you might say. Involuntary movements are obviously caused by some biological flaw, but Laura just has to make up her mind to go home. Did you say "mind"? You have just stumbled onto one of the biggest philosophical debates in history—where in the body is the mind located?

biological psychology The discipline that investigates the influence of biological systems on behavior.

behavior A response of an organism.

Historical Origins of Biological Psychology

Throughout history, there has been considerable speculation as to the physical location in the body of the human mind, a controversy often referred to as the mind-body problem. Early philosophers, such as the Greek philosopher Aristotle (384–322 B.C.), thought that the mind resided in the heart. Aristotle reasoned that the location of the origin of blood must be the place of the origin of life—or the soul. In Aristotle's view, the brain merely served to cool the blood. The Egyptians also believed that the heart was the source of life. When the Egyptians embalmed a person, the heart was preserved and the brain discarded.

Most Greek philosophers, however, believed the brain, not the heart, to be the locus of the mind. Hippocrates (460–377 B.C.) speculated some 50 years earlier than Aristotle that the brain gives rise to human actions. Plato (428–348 B.C.), who was Aristotle's teacher, also believed that the mind resided in the brain. Because the sphere is a perfect geometrical shape, Plato reasoned that the mind must be located in the spherical head (or the summit) of the human body.

During the Middle Ages (400–1350), the Christian church was considered the absolute authority on all intellectual matters. The church proposed that nutrients absorbed from the intestines were converted by the liver into natural spirits. Upon reaching the heart, natural spirits were converted to vital spirits, which were carried by blood vessels to the base of the brain and then converted to animal spirits. Animal spirits were stored in three fluid-filled chambers or ventricles at the base of the brain. The first ventricle analyzed sensory input, the second ventricle was responsible for reason and thought, and the third ventricle stored memories. The church's view was widely accepted until the Renaissance period (1350–1650).

The French philosopher René Descartes (1596–1650) rejected the church's view, offering a different conceptualization of mind (brain)-body interaction. Descartes' (1637/1956) hydraulic model envisioned the nervous system as a group of hollow tubes containing delicate threads that connected sensory receptors to the brain. Other hollow tubes led to the muscles, which contained empty bladders. When a sensory organ was stimulated, the threads to the brain were tightened, opening a "pore" in the brain. Animal spirits, released from the brain when the "pore" opened, flowed through the hollow tubes, filled the bladders, and moved the muscle. Descartes' conception of the nervous system was similar to the operation of the animated statues, or automata, seen in the gardens of St. Germain in the court of Louis XIV; the limbs of these statues could be started by stepping on a plate connected to the statues' hydraulic system.

In *Les Passions de L'ame* (*Passions of the Soul*) Descartes (1650/1911) proposed that the mind communicated with the body via the pineal gland (see **Figure 1.1**). He based his belief on the fact that the pineal gland is located in the center of the brain and that it is not paired as are other brain structures. (Descartes was wrong about the pineal gland; its removal does not significantly alter a person's mental functioning.)

Luigi Galvani (1737–1798) provided convincing evidence against Descartes' theory. Galvani (1791/1953) observed that when electrical stimulation was applied to a frog's leg, the leg muscle twitched. If Descartes' hydraulic model was valid, removal of the frog's leg from its body would cause the animal spirits to stop flowing from the brain to the muscle; stimulation of the frog's leg muscle after amputation should no longer produce a muscle twitch. However, the frog's muscle did indeed continue to twitch after removal from the frog's body. Galvani's observations suggested that electricity was an essential element in the functioning of the nervous system.

Descartes' speculation that the brain was the locus of the mind was not confirmed until the classic research of Pierre Jean Marie Flourens (1794–1867). Flourens (1824/1965) used the ablation technique to remove parts of the brain of a number of animal species. (An **ablation** is the surgical removal of a part of the body.) Flourens thought that perception, intellect, and will, all considered activities of the mind, were functions of the **cerebrum**, which is the uppermost portion of the brain. To demonstrate that the cerebrum determined mental functions, Flourens removed this area of the brain and then nursed the animal back to health. After the animal recovered from surgery, Flourens noted any changes in the animal's behavior. He found that a pigeon without a cerebrum, kept alive by force feeding, never showed either voluntary movements or responses to lights or sounds. Flourens concluded from these observations that the cerebrum controlled voluntary movements and perception.

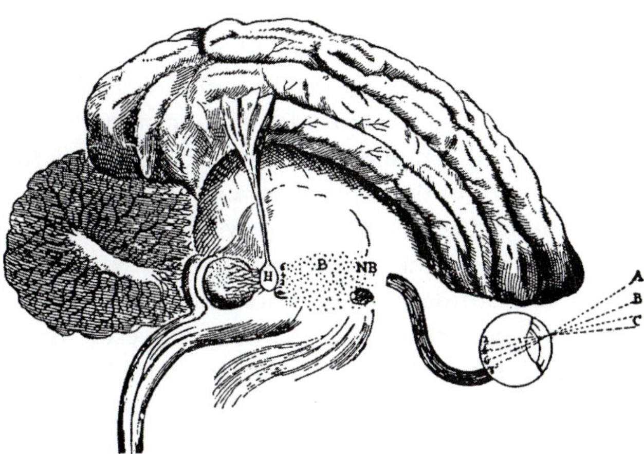

Figure 1.1 Drawing of the human brain by René Descartes. Descartes believed that the pineal gland (labeled H in the drawing) was the location where the mind and the body interacted.
➤ *How do we know that the pineal gland is not the location of the mind? (p. 5)*

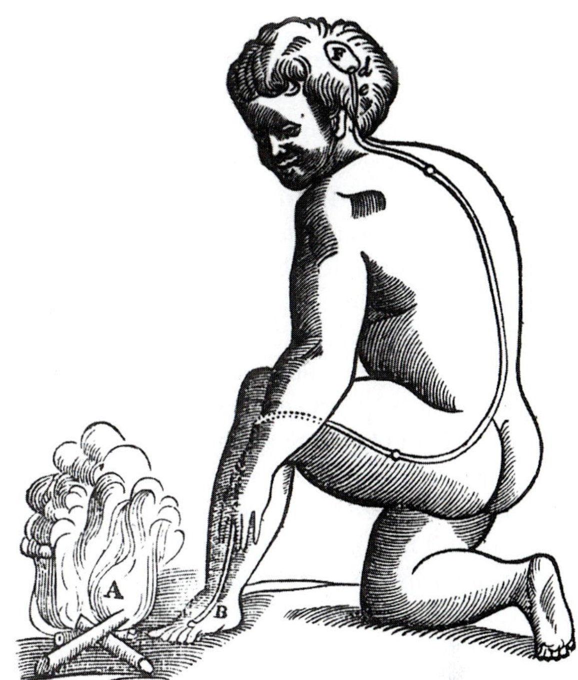

Figure 1.2 Illustration of Descartes' view of reflex action. Detection of heat (A) on the skin (B) tightens nerve threads that open "pores" (F) in the brain, causing the release of animal spirits into the hollow tube that travels to the muscles. Inflation of appropriate bladders by the animal spirits causes movement in the muscles that pulls the foot away from the fire.
➤ *What is the origin of the term reflex? (p. 6)*

The Reflex

Another facet of Descartes' theory was that external events could cause muscle movements. For example, as seen in **Figure 1.2**, Descartes (1662/1972) believed that the heat of the fire stimulates sensory spots on the person's skin and results in the movement of the foot away from the fire. Descartes envisioned the external envi-

ablation The surgical removal of a part of the body.
cerebrum The uppermost portion of the brain.

ronmental stimulation being *reflected* by the muscles, and thus coined the term **reflex**. Descartes' general concept of a reflex has been accepted by modern scientists, although the mechanism is radically different from the one he proposed (see Chapter 2).

Robert Whytt (1714–1766) did not accept Descartes' idea that muscle movements are simply reflections of external stimulation. He observed that reflex movements occur too rapidly to be dependent on mental processes. Instead, Whytt (1751) proposed that reflexes are controlled by the spinal cord. Whytt found that movement could be produced by electrical stimulation of a small segment of a frog's spinal cord.

The classic research of English physiologist Sir Charles Bell (1774–1842) provided new insights into the sensory and motor systems. (Sensory refers to the detection of environmental events and motor refers to actions.) In 1811, Bell reported that spinal nerves, the fibers that enter and exit the spinal cord and carry sensory and motor information, divide into two roots: a dorsal ("toward the back") root and a ventral ("toward the belly") root. He observed that touching the ventral root with a probe produced muscle contractions in rabbits. Touching the dorsal root did not produce movement. On the basis of these observations, Bell concluded that sensory and motor nerves were separate, with sensory information entering the spinal cord through the dorsal root and motor information leaving the spinal cord through the ventral root. Bell published 100 copies of a pamphlet describing his research and gave them to his friends.

Eleven years after Bell distributed his 100 pamphlets, French physiologist François Magendie (1783–1855) published his studies of spinal nerves, in which he used dogs as subjects. Dog's feet are very sensitive. If you pinch a dog's leg or prick it with a pin, the dog will normally jerk the leg away (wouldn't you?). Magendie found that after he cut the dorsal root of the nerves of one limb, pinching or pricking produced no movement, but the dog could still move the limb. When the ventral root was cut, complete paralysis was observed. Magendie concluded from these

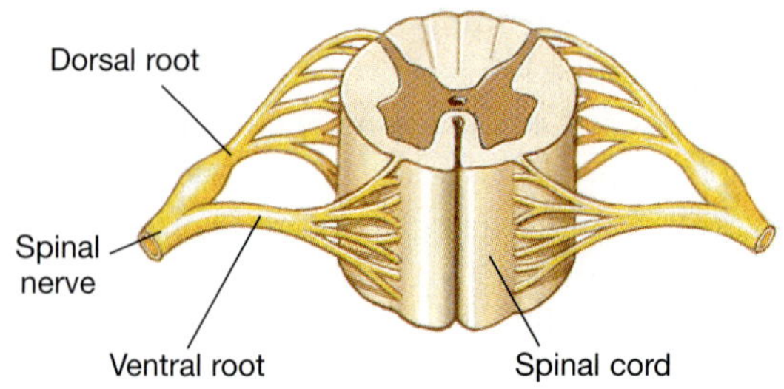

Figure 1.3 Cross sectional view of the spinal cord. The sensory nerves enter the spinal cord through the dorsal root and exit the spinal cord via the ventral root.

➤ *What was the significance of the Bell-Magendie law? (p. 6)*

observations that the dorsal root carries sensory information, whereas the ventral root carries motor messages (see **Figure 1.3**). This finding is today known as the **Bell-Magendie law**, recognizing the initial importance of Bell's research and the more thorough and convincing evidence of Magendie.

Johannes Müller (1801–1858) went a step further, suggesting that each sensory nerve carries specific information about the quality and location of sensory events. For example, touching a flame with the index finger of your right hand will activate a pain receptor on that finger. The pain receptor will send a message through the sensory nerve that pain is being detected at the top of the index finger of your right hand. If this same pain receptor was activated by electrical stimulation, the signal sent by the pain receptor would be the same; that is, that pain is being experienced in the top of the index finger of the right hand. If Müller was right, stimulation of this particular sensory nerve anywhere along its path to the brain would cause the same message to be sent. According to Müller's theory, activation of the optic nerve would produce visual sensations, whereas activation of the auditory nerve would produce auditory sensations. The idea that the event detected by the brain depends on which nerve carries the message is known as Müller's (1838) **doctrine of specific nerve energies**.

You can demonstrate the doctrine of specific nerve energies on yourself. Gently press the right side of your right eye. The pressure on your eye will activate the optic nerve and cause you to perceive a shower of light. The brain detects stimulation of the optic nerve as light even though the nerve is being activated by pressure from your finger rather than actual light.

We will have more to say about the doctrine of specific nerve energies when we discuss the various senses—vision, audition, vestibular, somatosensory, gustatory, and olfactory—in Chapters 6 and 7.

reflex An involuntary response to a stimulus caused by a direct connection between the sensory receptor and muscle.

Bell-Magendie law The principle that the dorsal root carries sensory information to the spinal cord and the ventral root conveys commands to the muscles.

doctrine of specific nerve energies The theory that the message detected by the nervous system is determined by the nerve carrying the message.

Before You Go On

Using the Bell-Magendie law, explain what happens when someone tickles your foot.

Someone taps you on the shoulder to get your attention. Using the doctrine of specific nerve energies, explain how you know which direction to turn in response.

Section Review

- Biological psychology is the study of the influence of biological systems, especially the nervous system, on behavior.
- Aristotle believed that the heart was the locus of the human mind.
- Hippocrates and Plato proposed that the mind resided in the brain.
- The church's view was that the brain contained three ventricles, filled with animal spirits, where mental activities were conducted.
- Descartes' hydraulic system described the nervous system as a group of hollow tubes connecting the sensory organs to the brain and the brain to the muscles.
- Galvani's research disproved Descartes' hydraulic model by showing that a frog's muscle twitched in response to stimulation even when the leg had been removed from the body.
- Flourens found that various abilities associated with the mind were eliminated following removal of the cerebrum or the uppermost part of the brain, demonstrating that the brain is the locus of the mind.
- Descartes coined the term *reflex*, suggesting that muscle movements reflect external stimulation.
- Whytt proposed that reflex movements are controlled by the spinal cord, and showed that stimulation of small segments of the spinal cord elicited motor responses.
- The Bell-Magendie law states that spinal nerves divide into two roots: a dorsal root containing a sensory nerve entering the spinal cord and a ventral root containing a motor nerve exiting the spinal cord.
- Müller's doctrine of specific nerve energies states that the particular message detected by the brain depends on which nerve carries the message.

Localization of Function

Many scientists in the 19th century proposed that a specific function was localized to a particular area within the nervous system. The Bell-Magendie law provided support for a localization view, as did the doctrine of specific nerve energies.

Further support for the idea that different functions were localized in different brain areas came from an unlikely source. German physician and anatomist Franz Joseph Gall (1758–1828), who founded the pseudoscience known as **phrenology**, meaning "science of the mind," concluded from examinations of the brains of many different animal species, and of humans of different ages and capacities, that mental functioning, or the strength of mental functioning, was related to the size and integrity of the brain. He argued that mental character could be divided into a number of moral and intellectual facilities, which, according to Gall, were localized in different places in the brain. Gall believed that an individual who demonstrated an above-average faculty had a corresponding brain area that was larger than normal, whereas a person with a below-average faculty had a corresponding brain area that was smaller than normal. Furthermore, Gall argued that an enlarged brain area produced a bump on the skull above that area, whereas an indentation in the skull resulted from a diminished brain area.

The examination of these bumps (check your own "bumps") and indentations, called *cranioscopy*, revealed the strength of an individual's mental faculties. According to Gall, there are 27 highly specific faculties, including acquisitiveness, amativeness, benevolence, firmness, mirthfulness, secretiveness, and veneration, that reside in different areas of the brain (see **Figure 1.4**).

Gall's phrenology was quite popular in the 19th century. Unfortunately, many people's skulls did not match their mental character. As discrepancies accumulated, people became disillusioned with phrenology. Its influence began to wane early in the 20th century, and it was soon replaced by other means of measuring personality.

Even though phrenology proved to be an inaccurate measure of mental functioning, Gall's general concept that mental faculties are localized in specific brain areas has proved to be generally valid. We will next briefly examine evidence collected by several 19th century scientists that indicates that language functioning is localized in several brain areas. A more thorough discussion of the role of the brain in determining language will be presented in Chapter 13. Evidence of localization of other mental functions will be discussed shortly.

phrenology Gall's "science of the mind" assumed that mental functioning is related to the size and the integrity of specific areas of the brain.

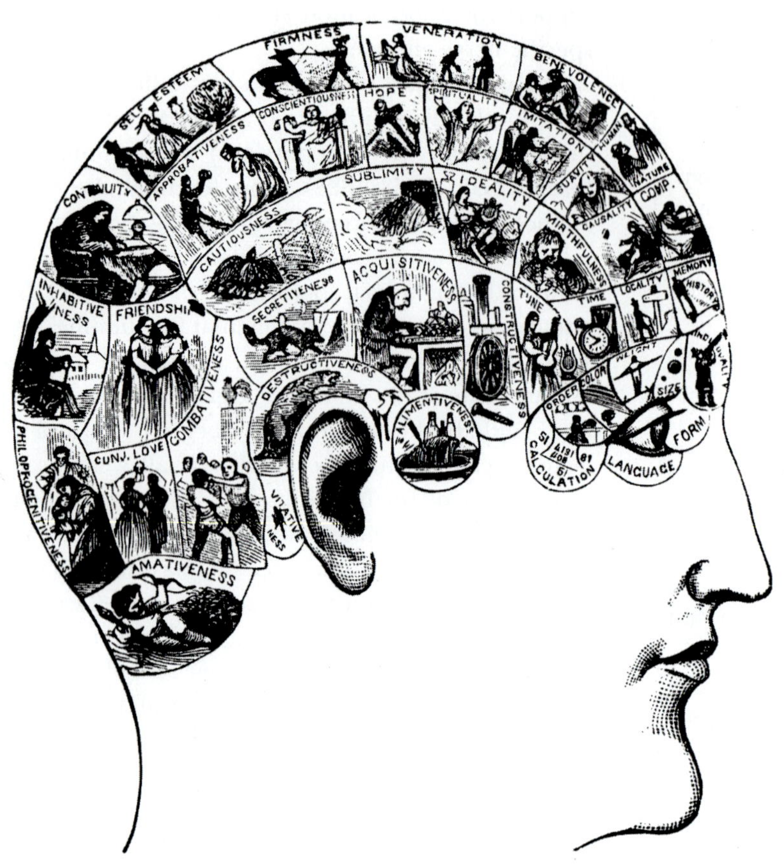

Figure 1.4 Example of phrenology map. Faculties are located in specific areas of the cortex, and personality could be revealed by measuring the bumps and indentations on a person's head.
➤ *What caused phrenology to no longer be considered a valid theory of human nature? (p. 7)*

In 1825, Jean Baptiste Bouilland (1796–1881) suggested that a language "organ" was located in the frontal area of the brain. Ernest Aubertin (1825–1893), Bouilland's son-in-law, provided some evidence to support this idea. One of Aubertin's patients had fully recovered from a gunshot wound to the front left side of his head except for a soft spot in his skull over the wound. When Aubertin pressed the spot, the man could no longer speak. Another of Aubertin's patients had lost his speech but otherwise retained mental functioning. Aubertin predicted that an autopsy of the patient, who was near death, would reveal damage to the frontal lobes.

Before Aubertin could test his hypothesis (the patient lived longer than expected!), French physician Pierre Paul Broca (1824–1880) successfully identified a language area in the frontal lobes. In 1861, Broca treated a 51-year-old man named Leborgne who had been transferred to his ward with gangrene in his right leg, a life-threatening condition in those days, before the discovery of antibiotics. Leborgne could understand everything said to him, but, despite having the ability to speak due to intact vocal cords, could only say "*tan, tan*," or, when extremely frustrated because of his inability to communicate, would say the curse words "*Sacré nom de Dieu.*" Broca actually asked Aubertin if Leborgne would be a suitable test of Aubertin's hypothesized language area. Aubertin concurred that Leborgne provided a good test, and when Leborgne died 6 days later, Broca performed an autopsy that revealed a tumor about the size of an egg located in the third convolution in the frontal lobe on the left side of the brain. Shortly after the autopsy, Broca reported his findings to the *Société d'Anthropologie* (Paris Anthropological Society), beating Aubertin to the finish line in the race for language area fame and a place in the history books. Broca continued to accumulate evidence from other patients, providing additional documentation of the existence of a language area in the left frontal lobe. Damage to this brain area, today called **Broca's area** (see **Figure 1.5**), produces a language deficit called nonfluent aphasia. (Aphasia refers to a deficit in lan-

Broca's area An area in the frontal lobe of the left hemisphere of the brain that programs and sequences speech production.

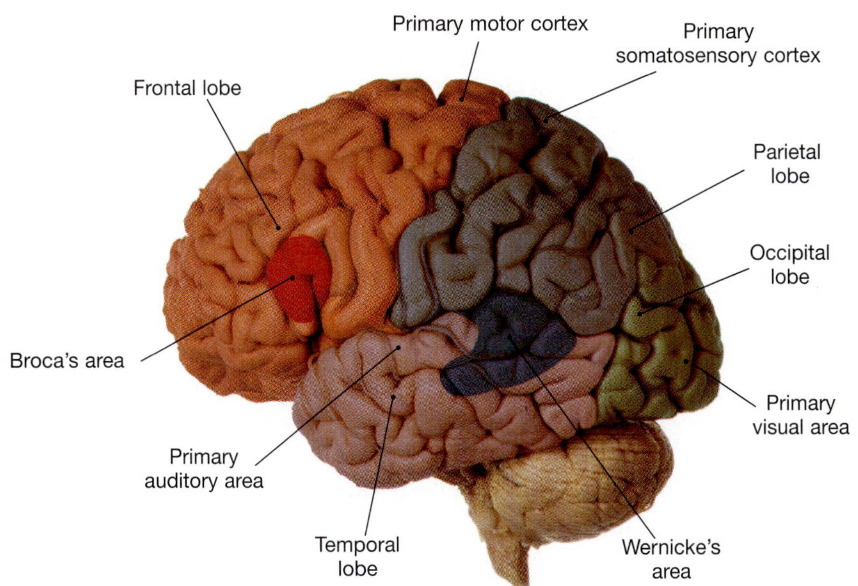

Figure 1.5 Illustration showing the four lobes of the cerebral cortex. Broca's and Wernicke's areas are shown as well as the areas of the cerebral cortex that control skin senses (somatosensory cortex) and movement (motor cortex).

➤ *What might happen if Broca's area or Wernicke's area were damaged? (p. 9)*

guage.) A person like Leborgne with nonfluent aphasia has great difficulty speaking, but can understand the speech of others. We will look more closely at Broca's area and nonfluent aphasia in Chapter 13.

In 1874, German neurologist Carl Wernicke (1848–1905) identified a second language area in the brain. Some of Wernicke's patients could verbalize clearly, but were unable to speak either intelligibly to others or to understand the speech of others. Wernicke found that this type of language deficit was associated with damage to the upper portion of the left temporal lobe. Damage to this area of the brain, now called **Wernicke's area** (see **Figure 1.5**), produces fluent aphasia. A patient with fluent aphasia can speak easily, but his or her speech is meaningless. The patient also has poor language comprehension. In Chapter 13, we will look more closely at Wernicke's area and fluent aphasia. We also will examine the roles of Wernicke's area in speech comprehension and Broca's area in speech production.

Other research has provided evidence for the localization of motor behavior and sensory perception (see **Figure 1.5**). In 1870, the German scientists Gustav Fritsch (1838–1927) and Edward Hitzig (1838–1907) demonstrated that direct electrical stimulation of a dog's motor cortex produced muscle action on the opposite side of the body (see **Figure 1.5**). They also showed that increasing the intensity of the electrical current increased the number of muscle groups that became active. Further, they observed that moving the electrical stimulation to different areas of the cortex produced different movements. We will have much more to say about the brain's control of movement in Chapter 8.

Scottish neurologist David Ferrier (1843–1928) and German physiologist Herman Munk (1839–1912) used electrical stimulation, as well as ablation, with monkey subjects to identify areas in the brain controlling specific sensory systems (see **Figure 1.5**). Their work showed that vision is controlled by areas in the occipital lobe, audition by areas in the temporal lobe, and skin senses (e.g., touch, temperature) in the parietal lobe (see **Figure 1.5**). We will have more to say about the brain's detection of environmental events in Chapters 6 and 7.

The Neuron

We have learned that certain brain functions are controlled by specific areas of the brain. Evidence for localization of function came from the development of two experimental techniques: electrical stimulation of specific nervous system structures, which elicits specific behaviors, and ablation of these structures, which eliminates these behaviors. The last great discovery of the 19th century involved identifying the structure responsible for these functions. Scientists of the last century assumed that the nervous system consisted of a net of connected nerves. We know today that the nervous system is made up of individual nerve cells, called **neurons**

Wernicke's area An area in the temporal lobe of the left hemisphere of the brain that understands language and produces intelligible speech.

neuron An individual nerve cell.

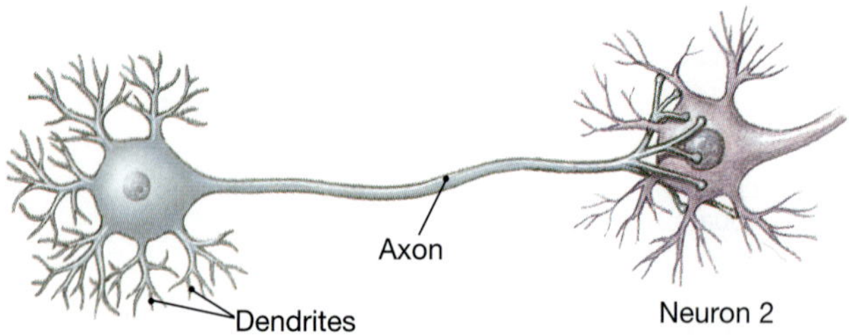

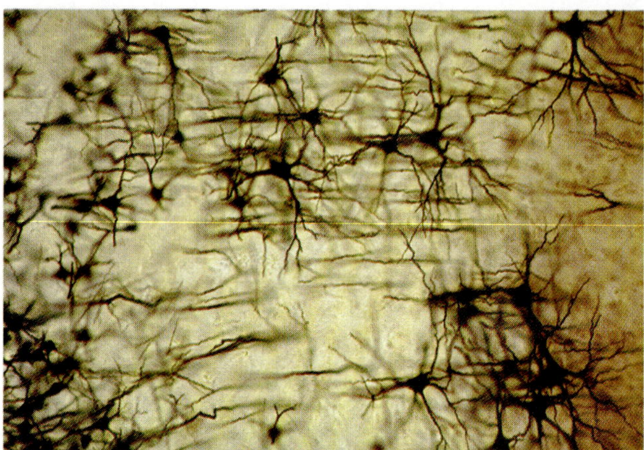

Figure 1.6 The neuron. The structure of a neuron and the synapse connecting neurons, as revealed by the Golgi stain method.

➤ *Why was Cajal's use of the Golgi stain on a slice of neural tissue so important? (p. 10)*

(**Figure 1.6**). The development of a third technique to investigate the nervous system—staining of cells—was responsible for the discovery of the neuron.

Italian histologist and physician Camillo Golgi (1843–1926) developed the stain, called in his honor the Golgi stain, that led to this momentous discovery. (Histology is the study of the cellular structure of tissues.) Joseph von Gerlach (1820–1896) and Johannes Müller (1801–1858) had developed methods for hardening and staining tissues. Using these methods, Golgi found that black stains provided the best microscopic view of tissue. Osmic acid stained cells black, but was scarce and expensive. Searching for a substitute for osmic acid, Golgi discovered that tissue could be stained black by first exposing it to potassium dichromate and then to silver nitrate. The chemical reaction between the potassium dichromate and silver nitrate created silver chromate, which invaded only a few cells of a slice of tissue. The invaded cells were stained entirely black, whereas the other cells were not at all affected by the silver chromate. Using the Golgi stain, Spanish histologist and neurologist Santiago Ramón y Cajal (1852–1934) found that nervous system tissue consisted of independent cells with tiny gaps between each cell (see **Figure 1.6**). For their discoveries, Golgi and Cajal shared the Nobel Prize for physiology or medicine in 1906.

synapse The point of contact between neurons.

The Synapse

Cajal's discovery of independent neurons within the nervous system raised the question of how information was transmitted across the gaps between the individual neurons. The research of English physician and physiologist Sir Charles Scott Sherrington (1857–1952) helped answer that question.

Sherrington called the point of contact between neurons the **synapse**, which means binding (-apse) together (syn-). His understanding of synaptic transmission came from his studies of spinal reflexes in dogs. (Remember Magendie's work described earlier in this chapter?) This spinal reflex consisted of three neurons: a sensory neuron, a motor neuron, and a third neuron (an interneuron) that connects the sensory and motor neurons. Sherrington measured the amount of time it took for an electrical current to travel along a neuron, and then compared it to the amount of time it took for a spinal reflex to occur. Sherrington found that the spinal reflex (with its three synapses) took longer, suggesting that transmission across the synapse was not as fast as transmission along the neuron. Sherrington also observed that following each spinal reflex, there was a period of time during which the sensory neuron would not respond to further stimulation. For his work, Sherrington shared the 1932 Nobel Prize for physiology or medicine.

How is information communicated across the synapse? Sherrington thought that an electrical wave spread from one neuron across the synapse to the next neuron. However, the classic research of Otto Loewi (1873–1961), a German physiologist, led him to conclude that communication across the synapse is chemical, not electrical. Because stimulation of certain nerves decreased rather than increased the functioning of an organ, Loewi did not believe that synaptic transmission could be electrical. Loewi believed that nerves might contain chemicals that were released into the synapse and acted to stimulate the target neuron, but how to prove it? The answer came to Loewi while he was sleeping on the night before Easter Sunday in 1920. Loewi awakened in the middle of the night with a plan to test his hypothesis. He wrote his idea down on a piece of paper and then went back to sleep. Loewi could not read his writing the next day, but remembered his plan the following night, and upon awakening on Monday, went into his laboratory and conducted the following experiment.

Loewi (1921) removed the hearts of two frogs. He left the nerves of the first heart attached while removing the nerves of the second. Both hearts were attached to tubes filled with Ringer's solution. (Ringer's solution is physiological saline containing chemicals that preserve tissue functioning; for reasons that are beyond the scope of this text, this treatment allowed the frog hearts to continue beating.) Loewi electrically stimulated the vagus nerve of the first heart for a few minutes, which caused that heart rate to decrease. He then removed the Ringer's solution from the first heart and transferred it to the second heart. Loewi noted that the heart rate of the second heart slowed following infusion of the Ringer's solution from the first heart. Loewi reasoned that the neurons of the first heart had released into the Ringer's solution chemicals responsible for slowing down the heart; when those chemicals acted on the second heart, its heart rate decreased also. To confirm these observations, Loewi stimulated the accelerator nerve of the first heart, which increased heart rate in the first heart and again upon infusion of the Ringer's solution from the first heart, in the second heart. Loewi called the chemical that decreased heart rate **vagusstoff**, literally, "vagus stuff." Otto Loewi shared the Nobel Prize for physiology or medicine in 1936 for his discovery that communication between neurons is a chemical process. Later it was learned that there are also electrical synapses that operate in the heart muscle artery. We will have more to say about both chemical and electrical synapses in Chapter 4.

Mass Action and Equipotentiality

Our discussion thus far has focused on the localization of function within specific neural structures. The research of Karl Lashley, however, indicates that not all functions are localized. Karl Spencer Lashley (1890–1958) received his formal training in biology at Johns Hopkins University, where he developed an interest in behavior while studying under the noted psychologist John Watson. Lashley also worked with Shepard Ivory Franz (1874–1933), who argued that the return of partial functioning after brain damage contradicted the localization of function theory. Lashley's own research, published in *Brain Mechanisms and Intelligence* in 1929, involved testing brain-damaged rats on several different tasks. This research allowed Lashley to develop two ideas regarding the nonlocalization of brain functioning: mass action and equipotentiality.

Lashley found that the amount of damage to cortical tissue rather than the exact location of the damage influenced the level of impairment, but only on complex learning tasks. (A complex learning task presents many different cues and requires many different motor responses for successful learning of the task. Learning a maze would be an example of a complex learning task.) Lashley reported that all neurons of a particular area of the brain are involved in the acquisition of a complex learning task, a process that Lashley called **mass action**. According to Lashley, the mass action of neurons in cortical areas of the brain causes the level of impairment in functioning following an injury to the brain to be determined by the degree of damage to cortical tissue rather than the exact location of the damage: the greater the damage, the greater the impairment.

Lashley recognized that some localization of function does exist in the brain, but he argued that other functional units were not localized, but were distributed within a particular brain area, an idea he called **equipotentiality**. Lashley proposed that equipotentiality exists only in cortical association areas (those areas of the cerebral cortex that are not entirely involved in sensation or movement). In Lashley's view, equipotentiality is responsible for the mass action process; all neurons of a particular area of the brain are involved in a complex learning task because each neuron in that area has the same function. Equipotentiality explains why partial functioning is retained following brain damage, provided some part of the functional unit is intact. Further, Lashley's view explains the recovery of functioning following damage.

Before You Go On

What is phrenology? What was its lasting contribution to biological psychology?

Where is Broca's area? Where is Wernicke's area? Explain the importance of the discoveries of these two areas.

Describe the nervous system using what you have learned about the discoveries by Golgi, Cajal, Sherrington, and Loewi. Now imagine that you are an 18th-century biologist. Try to describe the nervous system without mentioning the neuron, the synapse, or chemical communication across the synapse.

---

vagusstoff Loewi's term for the chemical that acts to decrease heart rate.

mass action The idea that a specific function is shared by all the neurons of a particular region of the brain.

equipotentiality The idea that all neurons within a particular brain area share equally in determining a specific function.

Section Review

- Gall suggested that mental functioning could be divided into 27 moral and intellectual faculties localized in different areas in the brain. According to Gall, personality could be assessed by examining the bumps and indentations on the skull.
- Broca successfully identified the language area responsible for speech as the third convolution in the frontal lobe on the left side of the brain. Damage to this area, now called Broca's area, produces a language deficit characterized by great difficulty in speaking called nonfluent aphasia.
- Wernicke identified a second language area in the upper portion of the left temporal lobe. Damage to this area, now called Wernicke's area, produces articulate but meaningless speech and an inability to understand the speech of others, a disorder called fluent aphasia.
- Fritsch and Hitzig electrically stimulated the motor cortex of a dog and observed movement of the limbs on the opposite side of the body, providing support for the localization of motor behavior.
- Ferrier and Munk reported that vision is controlled by areas in the occipital lobe, audition in the temporal lobe, and skin senses in the parietal lobe, supporting the localization of sensory perception.
- Golgi discovered a cell-staining technique that stained selected cells completely black.
- Cajal used the Golgi stain to show that nervous system tissue consists of independent cells with tiny gaps between each cell.
- Sherrington called the point connecting two neurons a synapse. His research showed that transmission of impulses across the synapse was not as fast as electrical transmission along the neuron, and that a period of unresponsiveness followed each stimulation.
- Loewi showed that communication across the synapse was a chemical process. He called the chemical released into the synapse vagusstoff.
- Lashley suggested that functioning is not localized in complex learning tasks that are governed by the association areas of the brain's cortex. He proposed two concepts: mass action, which assumed that all neural tissue in these association areas shares equally in the acquisition of complex learning, and equipotentiality, which proposed that all neurons within a functional unit contribute equally to that function.

neuroscience Study of the nervous system.

Current Approaches to Biological Psychology

Do you know what you want to be when you grow up? Perhaps you, like Laura in the vignette opening this chapter, are trying to decide what career to pursue. Biological psychology offers the both of you a multitude of choices. To further complicate matters, biological psychology can and should be considered part of a larger discipline, **neuroscience**, the study of the nervous system. A neuroscientist can study the anatomy of the nervous system or can investigate the chemical basis of neural activity. **Table 1.1** presents a listing of specializations within neuroscience, among them, behavioral neuroscience, which as you can see from the description, is a major part of the discipline of biological psychology. Biological psychology, because of its interdisciplinary nature, also relies heavily on knowledge from the other disciplines of neuroscience. For example, the drug Xanax can be used therapeutically to reduce anxiety levels. Our understanding of the effect of Xanax on behavior comes from neurochemistry (how does the drug influence the chemical balance in the nervous system?) and neuroanatomy (which nervous system structures are affected by the drug?). Throughout the text, information related to the physiology (function) and anatomy (structure) of the nervous system will be presented

Table 1.1 ■ Specializations within Neuroscience

Specialization	Area of Investigation
Behavioral neuroscience	The impact of the nervous system on behavior.
Developmental neurobiology	The development of the nervous system.
Neuroanatomy	The structure of the nervous system.
Neurochemistry	The chemical basis of neural activity.
Neuroendocrinology	The influence of hormones on the nervous system and of the nervous system on endocrine function.
Neuropathology	The disorders of the nervous system.
Neuropharmacology	The effects of drugs on the nervous system.
Neuropsychology	The behavioral consequences of disorders of the nervous system.

because it adds to our understanding of how the nervous system controls behavior.

Now that you understand how biological psychology fits in the big picture of neuroscience, we will narrow our focus to five different areas of study within biological psychology that sound similar but are, in fact, very different from one another: physiological psychology, psychophysiology, psychopharmacology, neuropsychology, and comparative psychology.

Physiological Psychology

Physiological psychology is the investigation of the relationship between the nervous system and behavior by surgically, electrically, or chemically influencing specific nervous system functions and then observing the effects on behavior. For example, a physiological psychologist might electrically stimulate a specific structure in the brain of a rat and then observe any changes in the rat's maternal care of her offspring.

Research in physiological psychology is conducted under tightly controlled conditions primarily with nonhuman animal subjects (see **Figure 1.7**), because most investigations would be unethical to conduct with human subjects (for more on the ethics of animal research see page 25). Strict laboratory control provides scientifically valid results, but the application of the results to our understanding of human behavior can be somewhat limited. As we will learn shortly, the knowledge gained from physiological psychology research can be combined with findings from other areas of biological psychology to better understand the relationship between the nervous system and behavior.

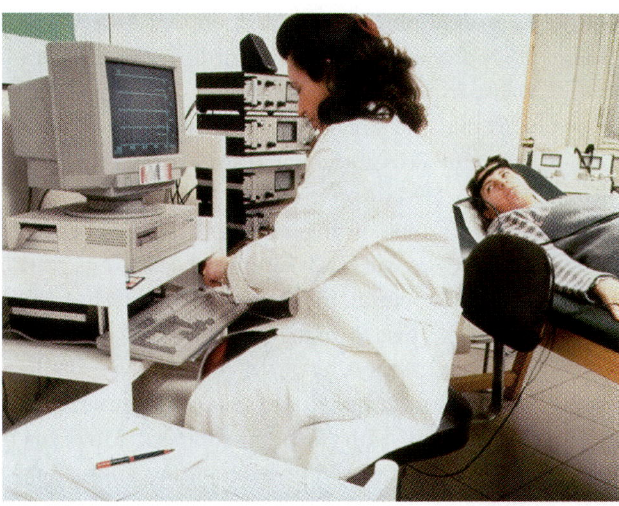

Figure 1.8 Research in psychophysiology. The psychophysiologist notes any changes in nervous system activity.

➤ *What are the limitations of psychophysiological research? (p. 14)*

Figure 1.7 Research in physiological psychology. Any changes in maternal behavior can be recorded by this physiological psychologist.

➤ *How is the research of physiological psychology different from that of psychophysiology? (p. 13)*

Psychophysiology

Psychophysiology is the study of the relationship between physiology and behavior through analysis of the physiological responses of human subjects engaged in various activities (see **Figure 1.8**). The psychophysiologist measures changes in brain activity, heart rate, and other bodily functions and correlates the measurements with observed changes in behavior. These correlations are used to establish potential physiology-behavior relationships. (A correlation does not equal causation; that is, the fact that two measurements are correlated does not mean that one causes

---

physiological psychology The study of the relationship between the nervous system and behavior by surgically, electrically, or chemically influencing specific nervous system structures.

psychophysiology The study of the relationship between behavior and physiology through the analysis of the physiological responses of human subjects engaged in various activities.

the other.) For example, if heart rate increases as stress levels increase (as revealed in an electrocardiogram), the psychophysiologist hypothesizes that there is a relationship between heart rate and stress level. This hypothesis is later confirmed or refuted by additional tests.

Research in psychophysiology has focused on enhancing our understanding of the physiology of psychological processes such as emotion, learning, and memory. Unlike research in physiological psychology, psychophysiologists use human subjects and measure nervous system functioning with noninvasive techniques. Until recently, psychophysiology research was conducted primarily with normal subjects. However, recent studies have measured physiological responses in clinical populations (populations of persons with particular psychological disorders). For example, individuals with anxiety disorders show greater physiological reactions to stressors than do normal subjects (Sarason & Sarason, 1993). But does this greater physiological responsivity contribute to the anxiety disorder or result from it? Remember that research in psychophysiology is correlational; only controlled experimentation can establish direct causal relationships. Combining the highly controlled research of physiological psychology and the correlational studies of psychophysiology can provide significant insight into the relationship between nervous system and behavior.

Psychopharmacology

Psychopharmacology is the study of the effects of drugs on behavior. Investigations focus mostly on **psychoactive drugs**; that is, drugs that affect mental functioning. For example, a psychopharmacologist might administer cocaine directly into a specific structure in a rat's brain and then observe whether the rat's memory of the place in a maze where a reward was previously located is enhanced or impaired as the result of cocaine exposure.

Research in psychopharmacology attempts not only to establish the relationship between a drug and behavior, but also to determine the neural mechanism by which the drug influences behavior. Thus, the psychopharmacologist in our cocaine example would also want to know what neural circuits in the rat's brain are being affected by the drug.

Figure 1.9 Neuropsychological research. This neuropsychologist measures the mental functions in a child suspected of having a neurological impairment.

➤ *Why is it difficult to generalize the results of neuropsychological research? (p. 14)*

Most psychopharmacological research uses nonhuman animals as subjects; however, the therapeutic value of a drug can only be established by examining its effect in humans. We will look closely at the effects of drugs on behavior in Chapter 5.

Neuropsychology

Neuropsychology is the study of the behavioral effects of brain damage in humans. Research in neuropsychology uses subjects who have suffered brain damage as a result of disease, accident, or surgery, because it is obviously unethical to expose humans to any treatment that might cause damage to the nervous system.

The goal of research in neuropsychology is to better understand the structure and function of the nervous system and how alterations to the nervous system can lead to behavioral impairment (see **Figure 1.9**). For example, a head trauma caused by an automobile accident may leave a person unable to speak. (Remember Broca and Wernicke? Which area of the brain do you think was damaged?) Studying patients with this type of brain damage helps us understand how the human brain produces and comprehends speech, and how damage to a particular area of the brain can lead to language deficits.

This type of research does have limitations. As you may already have noted, unlike physiological psychology, where a specific area of the brain can be damaged and the results studied, the damage cannot be controlled—a bullet to the brain rarely causes damage to a specific, limited area. And the damage will vary from subject to subject (the trajectory of that bullet will most likely be different in different vic-

psychopharmacology The study of the effects of psychoactive drugs on behavior.

psychoactive drugs Drugs that influence mental functioning.

neuropsychology The study of the behavioral effects of brain damage in humans.

tims), so the research is by nature very individualized. However, combining the results of research studies in physiological psychology and neuropsychology can help clarify the role of a specific nervous system structure in behavior.

Comparative Psychology, Ethology, and Behavior Genetics

As the name implies, in **comparative psychology**, scientists compare the behavior of different species of animals focusing on the influence of genetics and evolution on behavior (we will learn more about genetics and evolution shortly). For example, a comparative psychologist's research might examine the differences in aggressive behavior in a chimpanzee and in a human. Observed differences, along with knowledge of anatomical and physiological differences, can reveal important information about the biological basis of aggression.

Research in comparative psychology is generally conducted under controlled, seminatural laboratory settings. For example, a setting that resembles a primate's natural environment might be used to study its social behaviors (see **Figure 1.10**). In a related field, **ethology**, the behavior of animals is observed in their natural environments. In another related field, **behavior genetics**, selective breeding is used to determine how inheritance (the genetic kind, not the monetary kind) affects the behavior of a specific species. The observational research of comparative psychology and ethology, like the correlational studies of psychophysiology, can only suggest possible relationships between genetics and behavior. However, when considered with the controlled laboratory research of the behavior geneticist, the reports of comparative psychologists can establish the impact of biology on behavior.

Figure 1.10 Comparative psychology. The primates' social interactions are observed in a seminatural environment.

➤ *Name two fields of research closely related to comparative psychology. (p. 15)*

Before You Go On

How is biological psychology related to neuroscience?

What are the five major areas of specialization within biological psychology? How do they differ?

Section Review

- Biological psychology, the study of the influences of biological systems on behavior, can be considered part of a larger discipline, neuroscience, which is the study of the nervous system.
- Physiological psychology is the study of the neural control of behavior through invasive experimentation on nonhuman subjects.
- Psychophysiology is the study of the physiology of human psychological processes through noninvasive tests.
- Psychopharmacology is the study of the effects of drugs on behavior.
- Neuropsychology is the study of the behavioral effects of brain damage.
- Comparative psychology is the study of the influence of genetics and evolution on behavior through comparisons of the behavior of different animal species in a laboratory setting.
- Ethology is the study of the behavior of species in their natural environments.
- Behavior genetics involves the selective breeding of animals to determine the effects of inherited biological characteristics on behavior.

The Genetic Basis of Behavior

To understand how Laura came to her decision to go home for the weekend and how she will choose one of the many fields of biological psychology, we first need to

comparative psychology The comparative study of the behavior of different species of animals, generally in a laboratory setting.

ethology The study of the behavior of animals in their natural environments.

behavior genetics The study of how inheritance affects the behavior of a specific species.

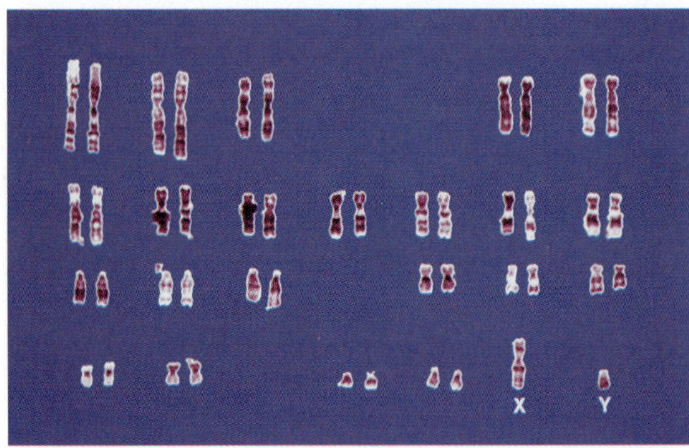

Figure 1.11 Human male chromosomes. This enlarged photograph shows the 46 chromosomes (23 pairs) of a normal human male.
➤ *Which chromosome pair would differ in a human female?* *(p. 16)*

learn the basics. In this section we will start with molecules (remember your high school biology?). Specifically, we will consider how **genetics**, the science of heredity, provides the molecular building blocks that will form the cells that will in turn form the systems that control behavior.

We all inherit characteristics from our parents. Laura may be said to have her mother's eyes, her father's hair, her grandmother's nose, etc. But it is not just visible characteristics that we inherit. Every cell in our bodies is determined by the combination of our parents' genes in the fertilized egg. These **genes**, or units of heredity, are located on structures called **chromosomes**, which are contained within the nucleus of each cell in our bodies. A gene is a portion of **deoxyribonucleic acid (DNA)**, which is a large, two-stranded molecule consisting of the sugar deoxyribose and the bases adenine, guanine, cytosine, and thymine. DNA is the principal active compound of each chromosome.

Each somatic (nonsexual) human cell contains 46 chromosomes, or 23 pairs (see **Figure 1.11**). One chromosome of each pair is received from the father and the other chromosome from the mother. Wait a minute—if each cell contains 23 pairs, how can one chromosome of each pair come from the father, and one from the mother? The answer is that the sperm and the egg are not somatic cells, but gametes, the only cells in the human body that have a different number of chromosomes, exactly half that of somatic cells (23 or 23 "half pairs"). It makes sense, if you think about it—once the sperm and the egg fuse at the moment of fertilization we are back to 46 chromosomes (23 full pairs). The gametes are formed in a complex process called **meiosis**, a series of two cell divisions preceded by a single round of replication of the genetic material, so that a single diploid cell (one with 46 replicated chromosomes—actually 92 individual chromosomes because of replication) is converted into four haploid cells (with 23 chromosomes each). During meiosis some exchange of genetic material can occur, through a process called **crossing over**. Crossing over allows pieces of genetic material to be transferred from one chromosome of a pair to another (see **Figure 1.12**) which actually mixes our two parents' original genes. This exchange increases the genetic variation among offspring. Genetic variation is responsible for differences among species as well as individual differences within a species.

You may have already figured out that if chromosomes occur in pairs, the genes on the chromosomes must also occur in pairs. This is true for all but the sex chromosomes, those that determine whether a child will be a boy or a girl. (Remember the Xs and Ys from your high school biology class where boys (XY) did not have a true pair, but girls do (XX)?) For now, let's consider the 44 human chromosomes that are paired in both

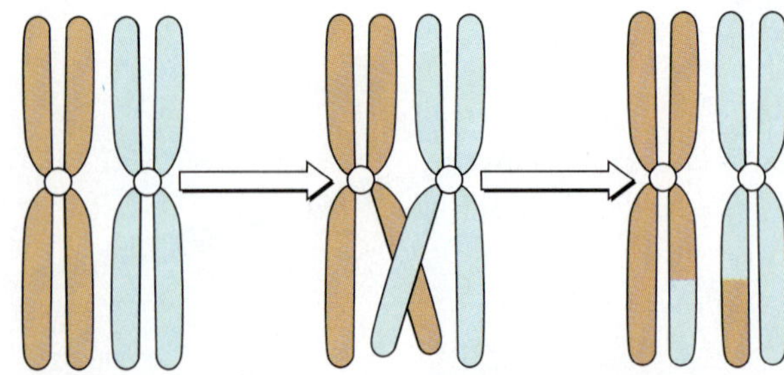

Figure 1.12 Crossing over. During meiosis, the pair members of replicated chromosomes sometimes exchange pieces of genetic material.
➤ *What effect would crossing over have on the genetic makeup of siblings?* *(p. 16)*

genetics Study of heredity or inheritance.

gene The structure that provides the blueprint for the development and function of the physical and psychological characteristics of a species. A region of DNA.

chromosome The structure in a cell containing genes or the units of inheritance.

deoxyribonucleic acid (DNA) A large, two-stranded molecule that consists of the sugar deoxyribose and the bases adenine, guanine, cytosine, and thymine.

meiosis The formation of gametes, with the reduction of chromosomes to the haploid state.

crossing over The process of exchange of genetic material between chromosomes during meiosis.

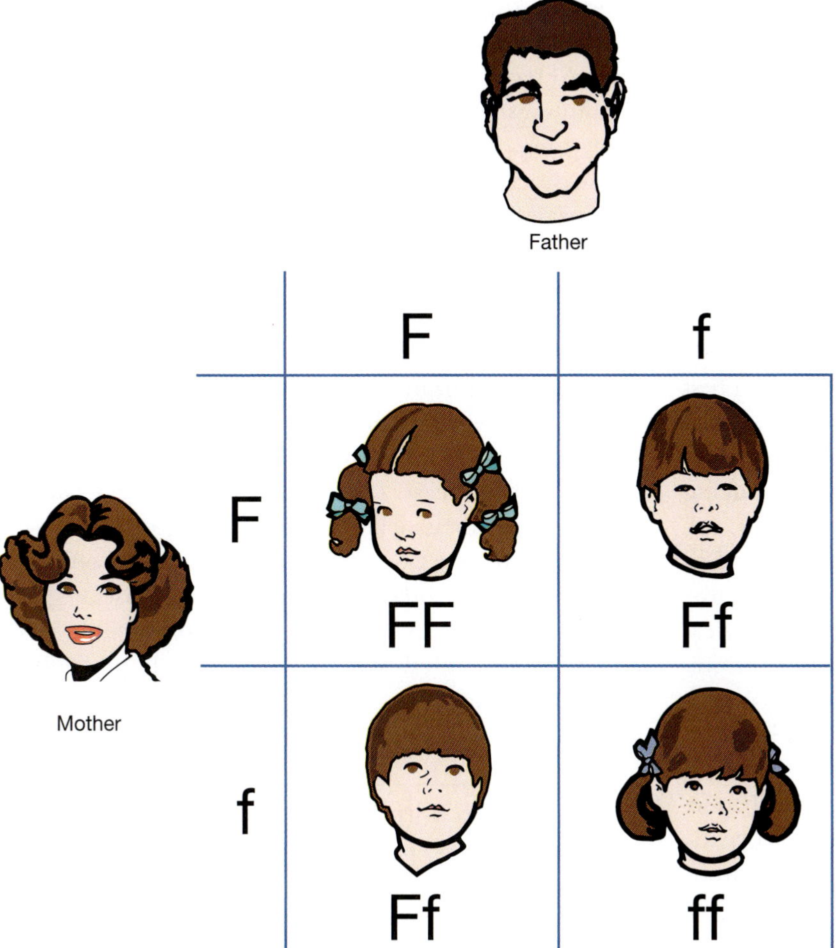

Figure 1.13 The inheritance of freckles. In this illustration, both parents carry one gene for nonfreckles (F) and one gene for freckles (f). On average, three-fourths of the offspring of this couple will not have freckles and one-fourth will have freckles. This box is called a Punnett square.

➤ *If the father were homozygous for nonfreckles (FF), could any of the children have freckles? (p. 17)*

males and females (sexual development and the sex hormones will be covered in Chapter 11).

Two main types of genes occur in pairs: **dominant genes** and **recessive genes**. If a gene is dominant, the expression of that gene will dominate that of the other gene in the pair; in other words, the dominant characteristic will be expressed in the offspring regardless of the characteristic carried by the other gene. A characteristic controlled by a recessive gene will be expressed only when both members of the gene pair are recessive.

Consider the characteristic of freckles to illustrate the action of dominant and recessive genes (see **Figure 1.13**). A lack of freckles is the dominant gene. If a child inherits a lack of freckles gene from either parent (remember—a child receives one chromosome of each pair—and thus one gene from each pair—from each parent), the child will not have freckles. A child will have freckles only when two freckle genes have been inherited (i.e., the gene pair is **homozygous** for freckles [homo = same]). (A gene pair can obviously also be homozygous for a lack of freckles.) A child can have freckles even if both parents do not have freckles as long as each parent carries one recessive freckles gene (i.e., the parent's gene pairs are **heterozygous** [hetero = different]). See the ff pair in **Figure 1.13** to show how two nonfreckled parents can have a freckled child. However, two parents with freckles cannot have a child without freckles, as they do not have the dominant nonfreckles gene (if they did, they would not have freckles!). Similarly, if one of the parents in the example shown in **Figure 1.13** were homozygous for nonfreckles,

---

dominant gene A gene that determines the expression of a physical or behavioral characteristic, regardless of whether it is present in one or both members of a gene pair.

recessive gene A gene that can determine the expression of a specific physical or behavioral characteristic only when that gene is present in both members of a gene pair.

homozygous A term describing a gene pair in which the two members of the gene pair are alike.

heterozygous A term describing a gene pair in which the two members of the gene pair are different.

none of the children could have freckles as they would all have at least one dominant gene (F). Other single dominant genes include normal skin pigment, free ear lobes, and curly hair.

Unlike the freckles example above, most human traits are governed by the action of several genes. Huntington's disease, controlled by a single dominant gene, is another exception (Chase, Wexler, & Barbeau, 1979). As we described at the beginning of the chapter, Huntington's disease is a progressive neurological disorder characterized by slow deterioration of muscle control and of mental functioning (Young, 1995). The first symptom of this devastating disease is often a facial twitch. As the disease progresses, tremors occur in other parts of the body. Voluntary movements such as walking and speaking become slow and clumsy; eventually, voluntary motor movements become impossible. (See Chapter 8 for a detailed description of the motor dysfunction associated with this disorder.) These physical symptoms are accompanied by a progressive deterioration of memory and general mental functioning.

The onset of Huntington's disease is usually between the ages of 30 and 40, although onset in childhood or old age has been reported. Mental and physical functioning deteriorates over the course of 10 to 15 years, until the person dies. Currently there is no treatment or cure for Huntington's disease.

The gene for Huntington's disease is located on human chromosome 4 (Wexler, Rose, & Housman, 1991). The non-Huntington form of this gene contains a sequence of three bases (cytosine, adenine, quanine) that are normally repeated from 11 to 24 times, but can be repeated up to 34 times. However, if the molecule sequence is repeated more than 37 times, Huntington's disease will occur. Further, the more base repetitions, the earlier the onset of the disease (Claes et al, 1995; Perischetti et al, 1994). Thus, a person with around 40 repeats will likely show symptoms after age 40, whereas those with more than 50 repetitions will generally begin to show symptoms before 30. The identification of the exact gene causing Huntington's disease and the abnormal sequence of bases that are associated with it has enabled professionals to predict whether or not a person will get Huntington's disease and if they are going to get it, the likely age that symptoms will begin to appear.

You will recall that Laura, whom we discussed at the beginning of the chapter, decided to undergo genetic testing for Huntington's disease, and the discovery that she does not have the gene for Huntington's disease can allow her to have children and live a normal life without wondering whether she or the children will develop this disorder. However, if she had discovered that she inherited the Huntington's disease gene, she would have to live with the knowledge that debilitating symptoms of Huntington's disease could develop at any time. Because stress may hasten the onset of this disease, a positive test result can actually add to the damage from this disease.

One unfortunate aspect of Huntington's disease is that symptoms of the disease usually do not develop until after the child-bearing years. Recognizing prior to having children that the gene for Huntington's disease has been inherited may lead to a decision not to have children, because on average half of the offspring of a Huntington's disease gene carrier will inherit the disease (assuming that only one copy of the gene form associated with Huntington's disease is present; to have two copies of the gene, the offspring would have to inherit a Huntington's disease gene from both parents, which is highly improbable given that in the United States only 50 people per million have the disease).

Before You Go On

You have free ear lobes, and your spouse has attached ear lobes. Your father has attached ear lobes, and your mother has free ear lobes. What are the chances that you will have attached ear lobed children? (Hint: Use Punnett squares like the one shown in Figure 1.13, starting with your parents' generation.) Why are the ear lobes of your spouse's parents unimportant?

Explain how discovery of the exact location of the Huntington's gene on chromosome 4 has proven valuable for individuals with a family history of Huntington's disease.

Section Review

- Genetics, the science of heredity, involves the study of genes, the units of heredity, which are located on chromosomes in the nucleus of each cell of the human body.
- Humans have 23 pairs of chromosomes, or 46 chromosomes.
- A gene is said to be dominant if the characteristic that it produces (such as nonfreckles) is expressed regardless of the characteristic produced by the other gene of the pair (such as freckles).
- A gene is said to be recessive if its characteristic (such as freckles) is expressed only when two copies of the recessive gene are present.

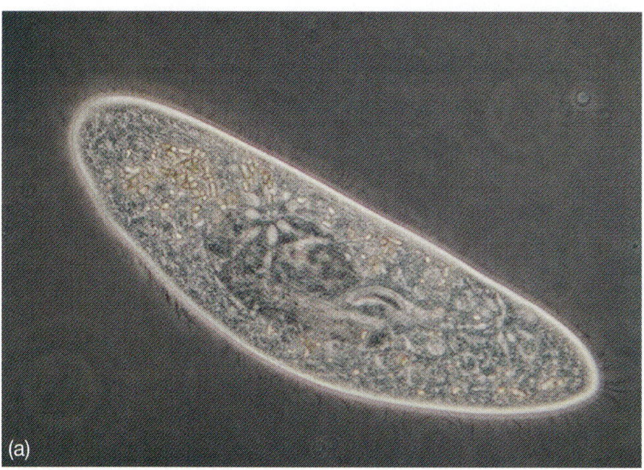

Figure 1.14 Examples of primitive organisms. (a) The well-known protozoan *Paramecium caudatum*. (b) A sponge.
➤ *Do protozoans and sponges have nervous systems? (p. 19)*

- A gene pair is homozygous if both genes produce the same characteristic (FF or ff), and heterozygous if the genes produce different characteristics (Ff).
- Huntington's disease is a genetically determined neurological disorder characterized by progressive deterioration of muscle control and mental functioning, with onset usually between the ages of 30 and 40.
- The dominant gene for Huntington's disease is located on human chromosome 4. Individuals with 37 or more repetitions of the base sequence cytosine, adenine, and quanine will develop Huntington's disease, which is used as a test for the presence of this disease. Further, the greater the number of base sequences above 37, the earlier the symptoms of Huntington's disease are likely to appear.

The Evolution of the Nervous System

We explained earlier in the chapter that differences in genetic makeup are responsible for individual differences. Genetic makeup also is responsible for differences among species as well as individual differences. Have you ever asked yourself why we have a nervous system? Some species survive perfectly well without one, and have for hundreds of millions of years. Primitive forerunners of animals such as single-celled protozoa (**Figure 1.14a**) or multicellular organisms such as sponges (**Figure 1.14b**) do not have specialized nerve cells or an organized nervous system to respond to environmental stimulation. How did we humans come to possess a complex system that allows us to laugh, cry, throw a ball, and appreciate a painting (preferably by not throwing the ball at it!) The answer lies in the study of the **evolution** of the nervous system. Evolution is defined as the process by which succeeding generations of organisms change in both physical appearance, function, and behavior. The changes in physical appearance, function, and behavior begin with increases or decreases in the frequency with which specific genes are represented in the population over successive generations. And these changes occur as species adapt to changing environmental circumstances.

The Emergence of the Nervous System in Invertebrates

Most of the animals on Earth are **invertebrates**, or animals without backbones (in = without, vertebra = backbones). For example, for every human, there are a billion insects. Most invertebrates have much simpler nervous systems than vertebrates, but are nevertheless able to adapt to a large number of situations. For example, many invertebrates have elaborate sensory systems that allow them to be extremely sensitive to certain types of environmental events such as tactile or light stimuli. The following examples demonstrate the variations in nervous system complexity among various invertebrate species.

evolution The process by which succeeding generations of animals change in both physical appearance, function, and behavior.

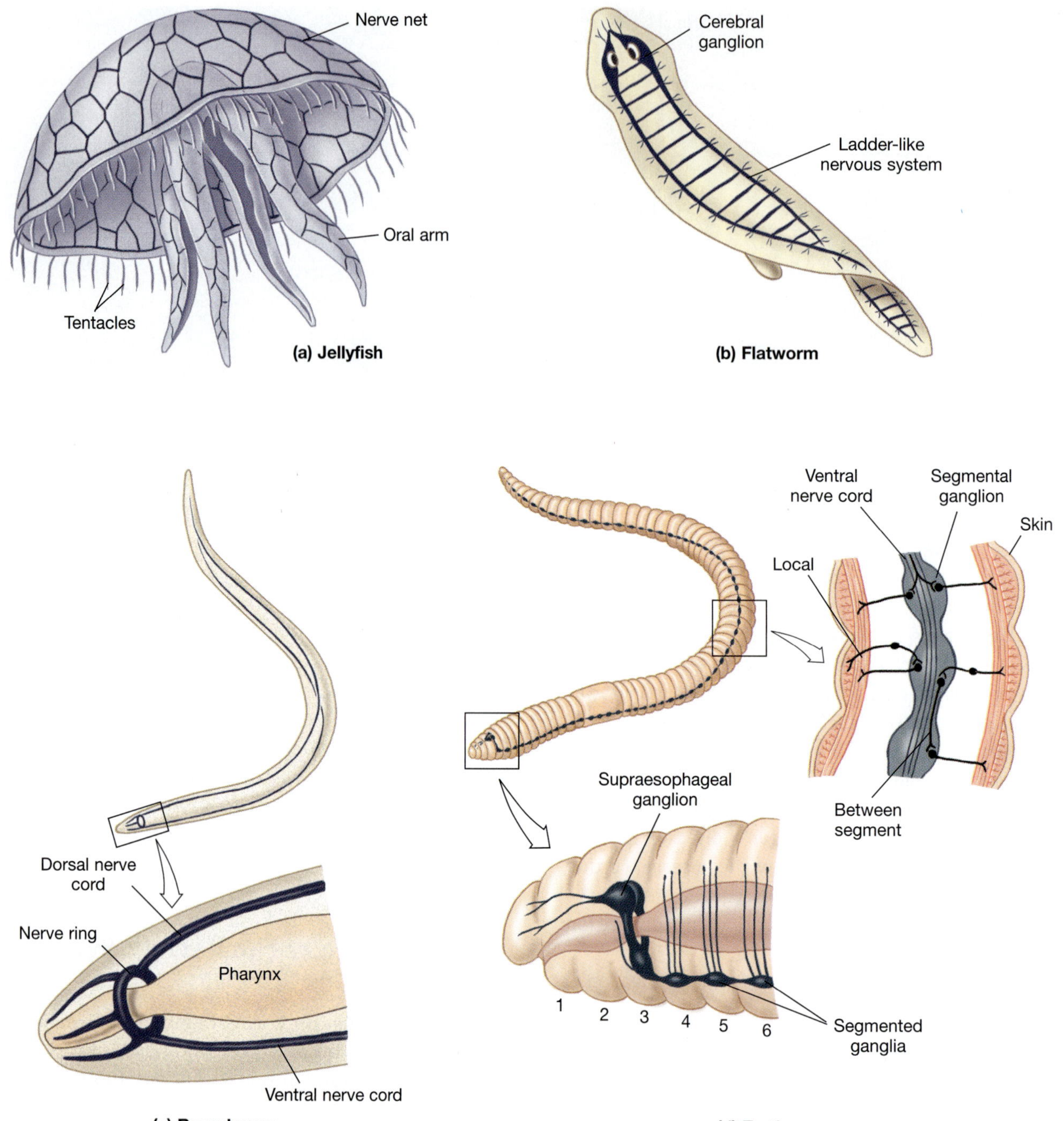

Figure 1.15 Nervous systems of various invertebrate species. Schematic representation of the nervous system of a (a) jellyfish, (b) planaria or flatworm, (c) roundworm, and (d) earthworm.

➤ *What is the difference between the nerve net of the jellyfish and the ganglia of the flatworm? (p. 20–21)*

The jellyfish (see **Figure 1.15a**) has specialized nerve cells that respond to touch, light, and chemicals in the environment, but no true nervous system. By reacting to these stimuli, the jellyfish can capture food and escape from danger. The nerve cells of the jellyfish are interconnected in a nerve net, with individual nerve cells having either a sensory or a motor function.

ganglia Nerve cells that are grouped together and that show specialization of function.

In more complex organisms such as the planaria, or flatworm, nerve cells become grouped together into clusters called **ganglia**. In the flatworm, two ganglia

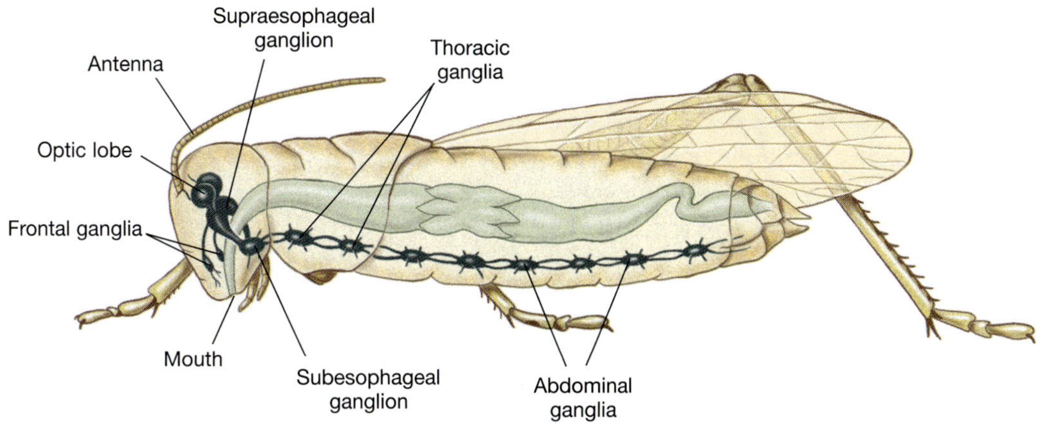

Figure 1.16 A schematic representation of the nervous system of an insect. Many neurons have combined to form a large supraesophageal ganglia (brain) and paired ganglion in each body segment below the brain, with nerve fibers connecting each ganglion to the brain.

➤ *Why is the insect considered a more advanced invertebrate than the earthworm? (p. 21)*

formed in the head region (see **Figure 1.15b**) are connected by a bridge of nerve fibers called nerve cords, forming a true nervous system with a ladderlike appearance. Each ganglion receives information from one side of the body and controls the functioning on that side. This specialization of function is what makes the flatworm nervous system more complex than anything in the jellyfish. The nerve cords also allow for information received on one side of the flatworm to be relayed to neurons on the flatworm's other side.

The "brain" of the roundworm is actually a simple ring of nerves around the pharynx, the *circumphayngeal nerve ring* or "the nerve ring around the pharynx"; see **Figure 1.15c**), which controls action throughout the roundworm's nervous system, and can be considered a primitive brain. The evolutionary process of concentrating neurons around the head region is called **cephalization.** As you move from primitive invertebrates to more advanced invertebrates and then to the vertebrates, the level of cephalization increases, with greater fusion and bigger and larger, more complex brains.

The flatworm and roundworm's nervous systems are unsegmented; that is, their nervous system acts as a singular system. By contrast, the earthworm's nervous system is segmented; that is, segments of its nervous system may act separately from other segments. The earthworm's belly contains a series of segmented paired ganglia (see **Figure 1.15d**). The ganglion pairs consist of joined neurons. Sensory neurons convey information from the outside world to the ganglion in a particular segment, and motor neurons control the responses of that segment. Interneurons connect the sensory and motor neurons in a local segment. The segments communicate with each other by means of other interneurons that connect adjacent local segments.

The fusion of neurons that started in the flatworms increases in the earthworm. Some local segments are fused in the earthworm's abdomen and thorax; increasingly greater fusion of the neurons is observed in the **supraesophageal ganglia** (supra = above, esophageal = esophagus).

As those of us who have been outside at dusk on a warm summer night well know, there are over one million different species of insects. The insect has no rival in the animal kingdom in terms of variety of color, structure, and habitat. Yet, despite this diversity among insect species, the central nervous system of all insects is quite similar (Edwards & Palka, 1991). The nervous system of the adult insect consists of a relatively larger supraesophageal ganglion (there's that tongue twister again!) than is seen in the earthworm. Further, the insect, like the earthworm, has paired ganglia in each body segment located behind its brain (see **Figure 1.16**).

The brain of the insect is divided into three vesicles: the protocerebrum, the deutercerebrum, and the tritocerebrum. The protocerebrum is divided into a right lobe and a left lobe, each connected in turn to a large optic lobe. Nerve cells in the optic lobe receive input from both the insect's compound eye and its brain.

The existence of different parts of the protocerebrum would seem to imply that function is localized in different

cephalization The fusion of many ganglion pairs to form an increasingly larger and more complex brain.

supraesophageal ganglia A primitive brain above the esophagus, formed by the fusion of several ganglion pairs.

parts of the insect brain. Also, the difference in the relative size of the parts of the protocerebrum appears to be related to behavioral variations among insects (Edwards & Palka, 1991). For example, the corpus pedunculatum, which is a part of the protocerebrum, is larger in social insects such as bees than in solitary insects such as roaches.

The Vertebrate Nervous System

The nervous systems of invertebrates like the flatworm and the insect are much simpler than those of vertebrates. A **vertebrate** has a protective covering over its spinal cord and brain. The protective covering is the bony skull and vertebral column and represents one major difference in the nervous systems of invertebrate and vertebrate animals. The cell bodies of vertebrate neurons tend to be located inside these bony coverings and the axons tend to be on the outside; in invertebrates, the axons are in the inner core of ganglia and cell bodies are in an outer ring. (Axons are elongated projections away from the cell bodies of neurons that transmit messages along the length of the neuron [see **Figure 1.6**].)

The spinal cord and brain of vertebrates are located on the back, or dorsal surface of the body; the nerve cord of invertebrates is on the belly, or ventral surface (see **Figure 1.16**). Motor responses on each side of the body are controlled by the same side of the invertebrate brain. The vertebrate brain controls motor responses on the opposite side. In other words, instructions from the left side of the brain control actions on the right side of the body, and those from the right side of the brain control actions on the left side. (Have you ever heard the expression "Only left-handed people are in their right minds"?)

Sensory information from one side of the body is transmitted to the opposite (contralateral) as well as the same (ipsilateral) side of the vertebrate brain. Invertebrates have a few giant axons to transmit neural messages rapidly; by contrast, many axons of mammalian vertebrates are encased in a substance called myelin (see Chapter 2) which conduct impulses even more quickly.

The vertebrate brain has a much larger number of nerve cells than the invertebrate brain. As we learned earlier, the more extensive grouping or incorporation of neurons into the brain, or cephalization, represents a major step in the evolution of the nervous system. Much of the evolution of the nervous system among vertebrates takes place within the brain. In the vertebrate, there are

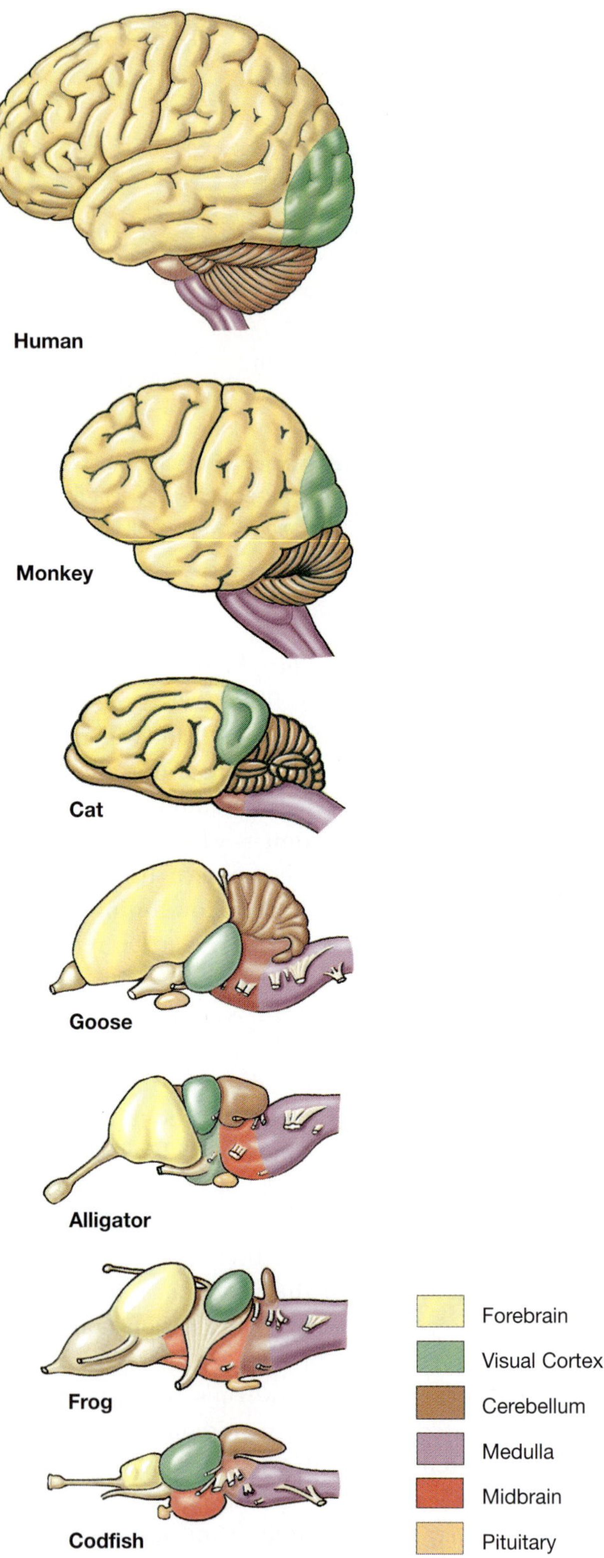

Figure 1.17 Differences in the brains of seven vertebrate species. The size of the forebrain relative to the hindbrain and the midbrain increases with more advanced vertebrates. The midbrain and part of the hindbrain are surrounded by the forebrain in humans. In the cat, monkey, and human, the visual cortex is part of the forebrain.

➤ *Why can't an alligator use the phrase "You silly goose!"? (p. 23)*

---

vertebrate An animal with a protective covering over its spinal cord and brain.

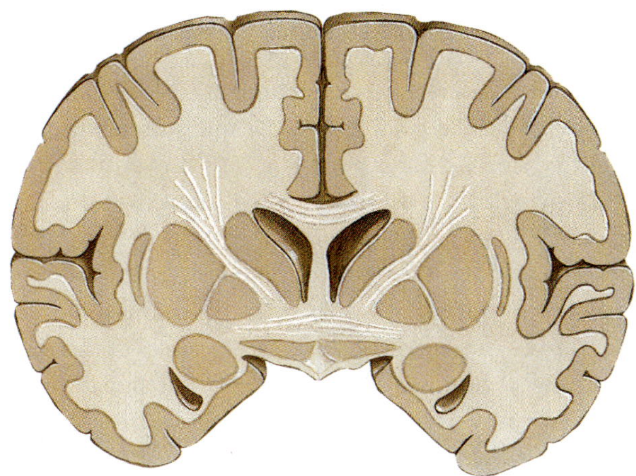

Figure 1.18 Cross section of the human brain. This view of the human brain reveals the extensive folding of the cerebral cortex.
➤ *What is the significance of this folding? (p. 23)*

three distinct major divisions of the brain: the hindbrain, the midbrain, and the forebrain. These three main parts of the brain are present in the codfish, as shown in **Figure 1.17**. Note the larger midbrain and hindbrain as compared to the smaller forebrain. In a more advanced vertebrate such as a frog (see **Figure 1.17**), the forebrain relative to the other two segments of the brain is greatly increased in size. Development of the forebrain continues to increase with more evolutionarily advanced vertebrate species. In humans, for example, the midbrain and much of the hindbrain are surrounded by the much larger forebrain (see **Figure 1.17**).

Size of the forebrain is not the only difference in the nervous systems of different vertebrate species. The cerebral cortex, a part of the forebrain associated with conscious thought and intellectual functioning in humans, is first seen in reptiles as a three-layer structure. Interestingly, part of the cerebral cortex in reptilian species is analogous to the hippocampus in mammals, which also is a three-layer structure. The cerebral cortex in mammals is a six-layer structure. The percentage of brain volume represented by the cerebral cortex increases in mammals, with the cerebral cortex accounting for more than half of the volume in more advanced mammalian species.

In mammalian species, the cerebral cortical structure becomes deeply folded, which provides greater surface area; the greater the surface area, the larger the number of nerve cells (see **Figure 1.18**). As a matter of fact, two-thirds of the surface of the cerebral cortex in humans is hidden in the grooves (Kolb & Whishaw, 1996). The total surface area of the human cerebral cortex is roughly equivalent to 2.5 square feet of flat surface (Martini, 1998); the only way to fit that much brain into your skull is to crumple it up like your last surprise quiz.

As the brain evolves, there are changes in function as well as structure. For example, the processing of visual information takes place in the midbrain in fish, amphibians, and reptiles and in the cerebral cortex in birds and mammals. The function of the midbrain in birds and mammals is to relay neural impulses to higher brain structures.

As you may already have guessed, as the forebrain increases in size, the size of its nerve cells and the number of synaptic connections between nerve cells increase (the forebrain is, after all, composed of nerve cells, as is most of the rest of the nervous system; see Chapter 2). For example, the pyramidal nerve cells of the motor cortex play a significant role in the initiation of fine motor responses (see Chapter 8); the size and number of the dendrites and the size and number of axon projections of pyramidal neurons increase in more advanced mammalian species (see **Figure 1.19**).

One specific difference between humans and other mammals is that larger sensory and motor areas of the cerebral cortex are devoted to the hands, related to the greater ability of humans to use their hands to manipulate the environment. Humans also have larger cortical areas devoted to speech recognition and production, which is associated with the significant role that language plays in human life (see Chapter 13). There also are

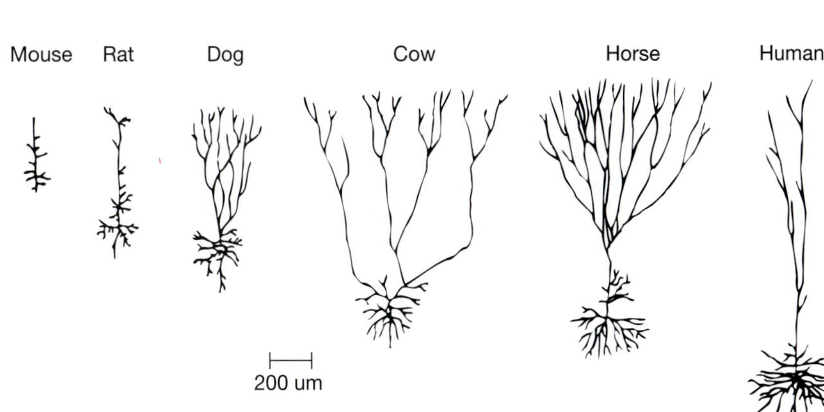

Figure 1.19 Pyramidal neurons of the motor cortex in different mammalian species. The size of the neuron and the number of dendrites in the forebrain increases in more advanced mammalian species.
➤ *What is the role of the pyramidal neurons of the motor cortex? (p. 23)*

larger areas of the cerebral cortex devoted to nonsensory and nonmotor processes, allowing for greater analysis of information and for more varied behavioral responses to environmental stimuli. For example, the prefrontal cortex in humans is involved in the planning and coordination of activities rather than the recognition of environmental events or the initiation of motor responses.

Before You Go On

What is the advantage of having the neural cell bodies protected by a bony skull and vertebral column? (Hint: See the section in Chapter 3 on redevelopment of the nervous system.)

Compare and contrast the nervous systems of a butterfly and a rabbit.

Section Review

- Specialized nerve cells are first seen in simple invertebrates such as the jellyfish.
- Nerve cells are grouped into systems in more advanced invertebrates such as the planaria.
- The primitive brain, or supraesophageal ganglion, is first seen in the earthworm.
- The segmented nervous system is first seen in the earthworm.
- Localization of function within the primitive brain is first seen in insects such as the grasshopper.
- The central nervous system of vertebrates is encased in a bony skull and vertebral column, with the cell bodies generally on the inside and the axons generally extending outward.
- The spinal cord and brain are on the dorsal or back surface of vertebrates, unlike the ventral or belly orientation of the nerve cord in invertebrates.
- In mammalian species, the axons of nerve cells are covered in a protective substance called myelin which increases the speed of neural impulses.
- In vertebrates, the brain is divided into the forebrain, midbrain, and hindbrain.
- In more advanced species, the forebrain becomes larger relative to the other two divisions.
- Sensory functions controlled by the midbrain in fish, amphibians, and reptiles are taken over by the cerebral cortex in birds and mammals.
- Nonsensory and nonmotor functions such as planning and coordination of activities are also controlled by the cerebral cortex in humans.

The Ethics of Conducting Research

Now that we understand some of the differences between our nervous system and that of the mosquitoes trying to use us "higher" animals as lunch, let's move on to how this information was obtained—research—and how research is conducted on human and animal subjects. You will recall that this part of the course material made Laura rather uneasy, as it does many of us, but it is a necessary part of the scientific search for answers to the question of why we humans behave as we do. Further, far more animals are sacrificed for food, hunting, or furs than for research and education (Nichols & Russell, 1990).

Conducting Research with Humans

When a biological psychologist plans a study using human subjects (see **Figure 1.20**), an ethics committee decides whether that research is permissible under guidelines provided by the American Psychological Association (APA, 1992). The researcher must demonstrate that the planned study maximizes potential gain in knowledge and minimizes the potential risks to the subjects.

Also, subjects *must* participate of their own free will. In the past, students at many universities were required to participate in psychological experiments as a course requirement in general psychology. Such a requirement is now considered a form of coercion and is no longer permissible. Students can volunteer to participate, but failing to volunteer cannot be counted against the student.

The biological psychologist enters into a written agreement with each human subject, explaining the general

Figure 1.20 Research with a human subject. This woman is participating in a study on sleep (see Chapter 9).

➤ *If your roommate pushed you into participating in a sleep study for her psychology class, could you get out of it? (p. 24–25)*

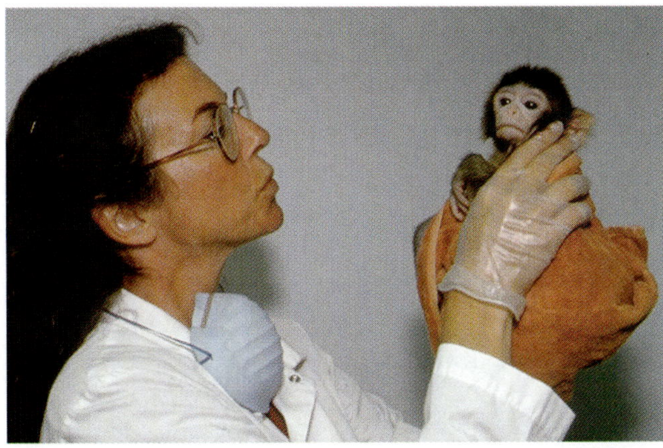

Figure 1.21 Research with a nonhuman subject. Strict guidelines determine what research can be done with this young primate.
➤ *What are the reasons for conducting research on animal rather than human subjects? (p. 25)*

purpose of the study and potential risks of participating. Further, the anonymity and confidentiality regarding the subject's behavior in the study must be maintained.

As part of this agreement, the subject may be informed that he or she will receive tangible rewards (e.g., money), personal help (e.g., counseling), and/or information regarding the study (e.g., results). This agreement is considered a contract between the researcher and subject. After the study is completed, information about the results must be made available to the subject. The subject must sign this agreement to indicate consent but is free to withdraw from a study at any time.

Conducting Research with Nonhuman Subjects

Many of the studies that will be described in this text have used as subjects nonhuman animals, including mice, rats, birds, cats, dogs, and monkeys (see **Figure 1.21**). Why do psychologists use animals in their research? One reason is the problem of documenting the cause of human behavior. The wide variations in human behavior makes it difficult to obtain a representative sample. Because the behavior of nonhuman animals is less variable, causal relationships are easier to demonstrate.

Another reason for using nonhuman animals is that it would be unethical to conduct some types of research with humans. For example, suppose a biological psychologist suspects that a certain area of the brain is responsible for memory storage. The researcher came up with this idea from studying case histories of individuals with memory disorders who have a tumor in this brain area. But just because these individuals have memory disorders does not mean that the area occupied by the tumor is responsible for memory storage. The only way to demonstrate causality is to damage this area of the brain and then observe whether memory storage problems result. Obviously, we cannot do this type of research with humans; as discussed earlier in the chapter, it would be unethical to expose a person to any treatment that could lead to a behavior pathology. Using nonhuman animals as subjects circumvents this difficulty, although it does introduce the issue of whether it is ethical to conduct this type of research with nonhuman animals.

Several arguments have been offered in defense of the use of nonhuman animals in psychological research. Humans suffer from many different behavior disorders, and animal research can provide knowledge about the causes of these disorders, as well as about how to prevent or cure these disorders. As the noted psychologist Neal Miller (1985) points out, animal research has led to a variety of treatment programs, including rehabilitation for neuromuscular disorders and drug and behavioral therapies for phobias, depression, and schizophrenia. When it can be demonstrated that human suffering may be prevented or alleviated by a study using animal subjects, such research is certainly appropriate (Feeney, 1987). Animal research also had led to significant advances in veterinary medicine. Currently, animal research is conducted only when approved by a committee, such as an Institutional Animal Care and Use Committee (IACUC), that acts to ensure that animals are used humanely and in strict accordance with local, state, and federal regulations.

Before You Go On

Would you volunteer to participate in a biological psychology study? Explain why or why not.

Why do psychologists use animals in their research?

Section Review

- Ethical principles established by the American Psychological Association govern what kind of research is permissible using humans as subjects.
- A researcher must demonstrate to an ethics committee that the planned study both maximizes the potential gain in psychological knowledge and minimizes the costs and potential risks to human subjects.
- Causal relationships can be demonstrated more readily in animals, using certain experimental designs that cannot be used ethically with humans.
- Animal research must be approved by a committee such as the IACUC, which ensures that animals are used in accordance with local, state, and federal regulations.

Chapter Review

Critical Thinking Questions

1. Laura and her boyfriend are studying for a test in her dorm room. As a break from reading *Biological Psychology*, Laura observes her boyfriend concentrating on his accounting textbook. His breathing is deep and even (she checked, and his eyes are open!), he is resting his head in his left hand and rubbing his forehead with his right (it looks as though he needs a break too!), and sighing occasionally as he turns a page. Which of these activities is behavior according to the definition in this chapter?
2. As we discussed at the beginning of the chapter, Laura's mother has Huntington's disease. What is her prognosis? What is the likelihood that Laura would inherit the disease? Recall that Laura tested negative. Should Laura's siblings be tested to determine whether they have Huntington's disease? Explain the reasons for your answers.
3. Michael is opposed to the use of animals in biological psychological research. What might be some of his objections? What are some reasons for using animals in research? Is there room for compromise in this debate?

Vocabulary Questions*

1. The study of the influence of biological systems on behavior is called ________________.
2. The debate over the physical location of the human mind is called the ________________ problem.
3. Flourens used the ________________ technique to show that mental processes are controlled by the brain.
4. Whytt proposed that reflex movements are controlled by the ________________.
5. Cajal used the Golgi stain to discover the ________________.
6. The point connecting two neurons is called the ________________.
7. Lashley's concept of ________________ assumes that functioning is distributed equally throughout all parts of the association areas of the cerebral cortex.
8. In ________________, the nervous system is influenced surgically, electrically, or chemically, and the effect on behavior is observed.
9. ________________ is the comparison of the behavior of different species of animals in a laboratory setting; ________________ is the study of animals in their natural habitats.
10. ________________ is the science of heredity and ________________ are the units of heredity.
11. A gene pair is ________________ if both members of the pair control the same characteristic; a gene pair is ________________ if each member of the pair control different characteristics.
12. ________________ are animals without backbones; ________________ are animals with backbones.
13. The ________________ of the roundworm can be considered a primitive brain.
14. The spinal cord and brain of vertebrates are located on the ________________ surface of the body.
15. The three vesicles of the vertebrate brain are the ________________, the ________________, and the ________________.

Review Questions

1. The Christian church in the Middle Ages assumed that the mind is located in the ________________, whereas Descartes suggested that the mind is located in the ________________.
   a. heart, brain
   b. ventricles, heart
   c. ventricles, brain
   d. brain, heart
2. The Bell-Magendie law asserts that spinal nerves enter the spinal cord in the ________________ root and motor nerves leave the spinal cord in the ________________ root.
   a. anterior, posterior
   b. posterior, anterior
   c. dorsal, ventral
   d. ventral, dorsal

* After completing the Vocabulary and Review Questions at the end of each chapter, refer to the Study Guide for answers.

3. The doctrine of specific nerve energies assumes that stimulation of the optic nerve would produce a ________________ sensation.
   a. tactile
   b. auditory
   c. olfactory
   d. visual

4. Gall's phrenology suggests that intellectual faculties are determined by ________________.
   a. the strength of a person's character
   b. a person's weight
   c. the size of one's brain
   d. the size of specific locations in the brain

5. ________________ is the study of the nervous system; ________________ is the study of the influence of the nervous system on behavior.
   a. Neuroscience, neuroanatomy
   b. Neuroscience, biological psychology
   c. Neurophysiology, neuropsychology
   d. Neuroanatomy, neuropsychology

6. A ________________ analyzes the physiological responses of human subjects engaged in various activities.
   a. neuropsychologist
   b. physiological psychologist
   c. neurophysiologist
   d. psychophysiologist

7. ________________ is the study of the behavioral effects of brain damage in humans.
   a. Neuropsychology
   b. Neuroanatomy
   c. Neuropathology
   d. Psychophysiology

8. In ________________, selective breeding is used to determine how inheritance affects behavior.
   a. artificial selection
   b. natural selection
   c. developmental neurobiology
   d. behavior genetics

9. ________________ are located on ________________ contained in the nucleus of every cell (except red blood cells) of the human body.
   a. Chromosomes, genes
   b. Genes, mitochondria
   c. Genes, chromosomes
   d. Chromosomes, Golgi bodies

10. If a gene is ________________, the characteristic controlled by the gene will be present regardless of the characteristic carried by the other member of the gene pair.
   a. recessive
   b. sex-linked
   c. paternal
   d. dominant

11. Clusters of nerve cells are called ________________.
   a. ganglia
   b. nerve cords
   c. neurons
   d. brains

12. The brain of the insect is divided into the ________________.
   a. protocerebrum, deuterocerebrum, and cerebellum
   b. protocerebrum, diencephalon, and tritocerebrum
   c. protocerebrum, deuterocerebrum, and tritocerebrum
   d. protocerebrum, cerebellum, and pituitary gland

13. Instructions from the ________________ side of the vertebrate brain control action on the ________________ side of the body.
   a. left, left
   b. right, right
   c. left, right
   d. right, left

14. The processing of visual information takes place in the ________________ in fish and in the ________________ in birds.
   a. hindbrain, forebrain
   b. midbrain, hindbrain
   c. forebrain, midbrain
   d. midbrain, forebrain

Suggested Readings

Fearing, F. (1970). *Reflex action: A study in the history of physiological psychology.* Cambridge, MA: M.I.T. Press.

Miller, N. E. (1985). The value of behavioral research on animals. *American Psychologist, 40,* 423–440.

Plomin, R. (1990). The role of inheritance in behavior. *Science, 248,* 183–188.

Sasnat, H. B., & Netsky, M. G. (1974). *Evolution of the nervous system.* New York: Oxford University Press.

Thorne, B. M., & Henley, T. B. (1997). *Connections in the history and systems of psychology.* Boston: Houghton Mifflin.

2 Exploring the Nervous System

Anatomy and Research Techniques

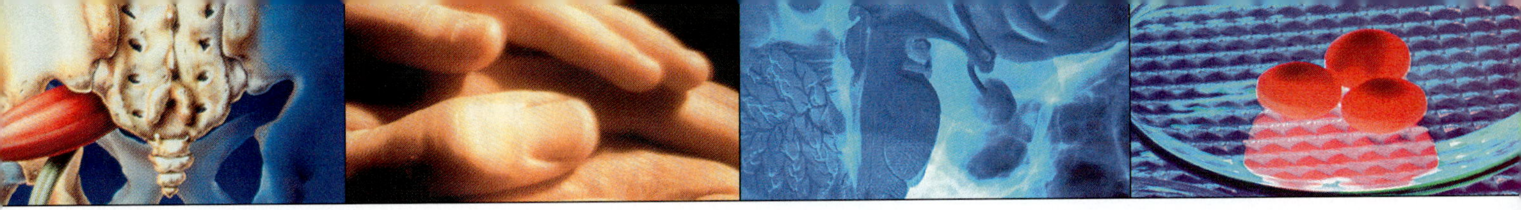

One too Many Shots

The first time I saw John Moore fight, he was an unknown middleweight just out of high school. Still, I knew even then that Moore would become a great boxer. Moore was tall for a middleweight, but lightning quick. With his long arms, Moore could use his sharp jab to keep his opponent at a distance. Moore's reflexes were superb: again and again, his opponent's best-aimed punches met thin air. Moore's opponent that night was an experienced boxer, but it took Moore only two rounds to take him out.

I continued to follow Moore's career as he rocketed through the middleweight ranks. After winning his first 21 fights, 19 by knockout, Moore was ready to fight for the title. The title fight generated much interest: Tim Weathers had been champ for 5 years, which is a long time for a fighter, but most experts predicted a Moore victory. Moore's prefight interview on television revealed that he was articulate and smart. If he won, John Moore certainly would be a positive reflection on the somewhat-tarnished world of boxing. And Moore did win that title fight. It was not quite as easy as his previous fights, but he decisively beat the champ.

Over the next several years, I watched many of Moore's fights. His early challengers were no match for him and he won easily. However, as Moore aged, his fights became tougher. After 16 successful defenses, Moore was defeated by Sam Dugan. Moore regained his title in a rematch and remained champion for several more fights before retiring from boxing after losing a vicious bout with Jose Gonzalez.

Ten years passed before I saw John Moore again. As a famous middleweight ex-champion, he was visiting my town for a promotion to open a sporting goods store. When Moore arrived, I was shocked by his appearance. He had a difficult time walking, his head bobbed, and his arms trembled. It was clear that he was not the same man I had seen 20 years earlier. ■

◀ The human brain contains about 100 billion neurons.

Before You Begin

What part(s) of John Moore's brain was (were) damaged during his boxing career?

How did the injury to his brain affect his body's functioning?

In this chapter, we will help you answer these and the following questions:

- What are the primary functions of the nervous system?
- What are the two major divisions of the nervous system?
- How do these two divisions work together to perform its primary functions?
- What types of cells make up the structures in the nervous system? What are their functions?
- What are the functions of the two divisions of the peripheral nervous system?
- What are the functions of the two divisions of the central nervous system?
- What structures and features protect the central nervous system? How do they function?
- What is the structure of the spinal cord?
- What is a spinal reflex? What is its major function?
- What are the divisions of the brain? What are their major functions?
- What major techniques do researchers use for studying the brain? Which are most invasive? What are the circumstances in which each technique is used?

The Importance of the Nervous System

As we go about our daily lives, we encounter an enormous amount of information. Some of this information relates to pleasant events, and some to events that are not so pleasant. For example, John Moore walks into the cafeteria expecting to eat lunch all alone, and a friend is seated at a table several feet away. Detecting this information will allow John to enjoy lunch with his friend. In a less appealing scenario, it is 20 degrees below zero and John's car battery is weak. Recognizing that his car may not start in the extreme cold may cause John to stay inside and thereby enable him to avoid experiencing the frustration of trying and failing to start his car.

In each of the two above examples, John must first *detect* the relevant information from among the multitude of stimuli present in the environment (his friend or the low outside temperature). Once the relevant stimuli have been detected, he must *recognize* their significance. For example, he remembers past good times he has spent with the person he sees in the cafeteria, or understands that his weak car battery may not start his car today.

He must next *decide* how to respond to the significant event. In some instances, the decision is relatively straightforward: once he remembers past positive encounters with his friend, the decision to sit with him or her is an easy one. Other decisions are more difficult: John may recognize that his weak battery may fail, but having no other transportation, he must decide whether to stay stuck at home or try to start the car. Finally, he needs to execute the appropriate behaviors after the decision process is completed. In our first example, execution involves John's act of sitting down next to his friend. In the second example, it involves trying to start the car or sitting on the couch watching "I Love Lucy" reruns, depending on the result of the previous step.

As our above discussion suggested, there are four stages to our reaction to environmental events. How are we able to detect, recognize, decide, and execute? The answer lies in the nervous system. But to understand how the nervous system accomplishes these functions, we must first understand its structure. In the remainder of this chapter, we describe the nervous system as a whole, and each of its components, focusing on how the

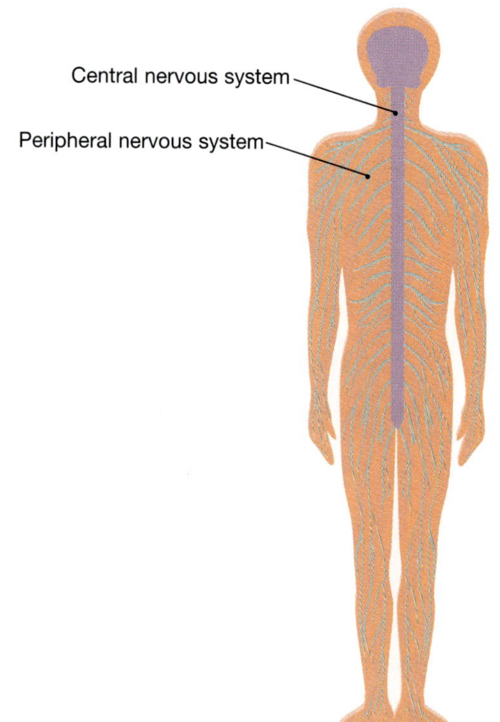

Figure 2.1 The nervous system. The central and peripheral nervous systems are seen in this illustration.

➤ *What are the two divisions of the central nervous system? (p. 31)*

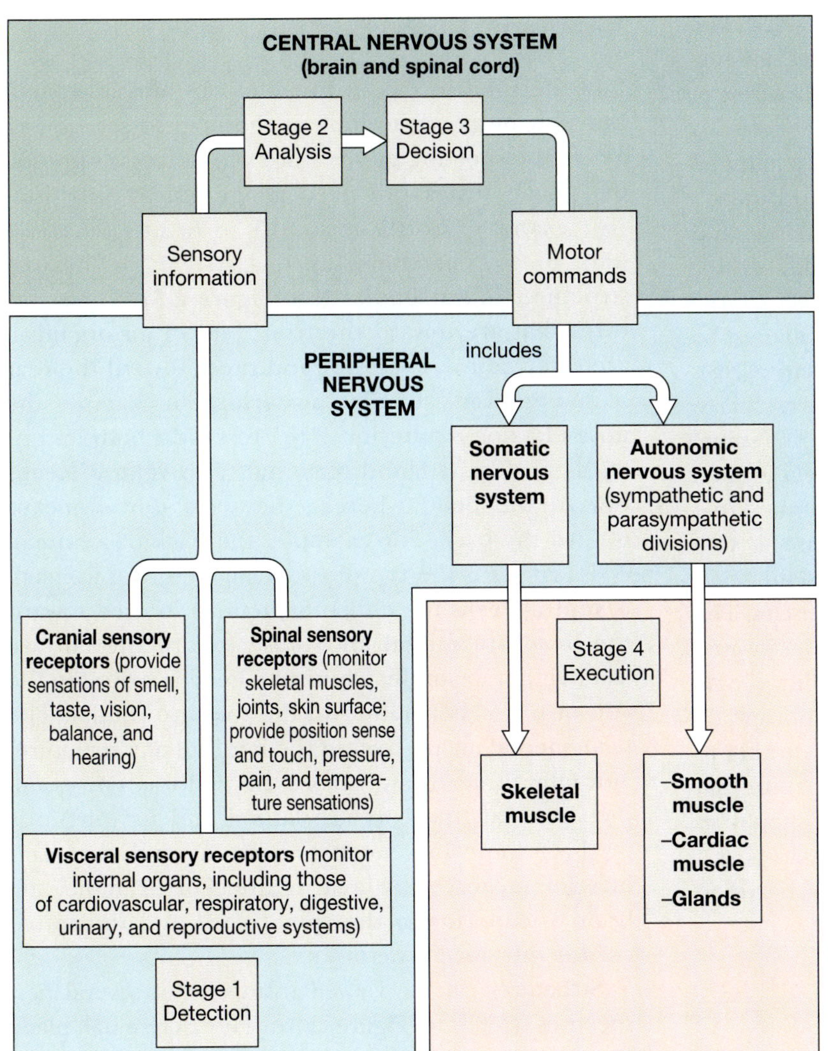

Figure 2.2 The functions and organization of the nervous system. Sensory receptors detect stimuli in Stage 1. The central nervous system analyzes the stimuli for meaning in Stage 2 and then decides on an appropriate response in Stage 3. A muscle response is executed in Stage 4.
➤ *Which division of the nervous system is responsible for detection and execution? Which is responsible for recognition and decision? (pp. 31–32)*

nervous system carries out these four basic functions. In the last section of this chapter, we discuss some of the techniques researchers use to analyze the functioning of various parts of the nervous system.

The Organization of the Nervous System

The vertebrate nervous system is divided into two major divisions: the peripheral nervous system and the central nervous system (refer to **Figure 2.1**). The **peripheral nervous system (PNS)** has two main functions: detecting environmental information and transmitting it to the central nervous system for analysis and decision and then transmitting that decision to the muscles, glands, and organs for its execution (see **Figure 2.2**). Sensory receptors located in the peripheral nervous system detect environmental events, and sensory nerves carry the information detected by the sensory receptors to the central nervous system. For example, the sensory receptors in John's peripheral nervous system allow him to detect his friend's presence and send that information via his sensory nerves to his central nervous system. The peripheral nervous system also consists of motor nerves that convey orders to the muscles. Thus, John's motor nerves carry the orders to the muscles that allows him to sit by his friend.

The peripheral nervous system has two major divisions: the somatic nervous system and autonomic nervous system (refer to **Figure 2.2**). The **somatic nervous system** contains both the sensory receptors that detect environmental (external and internal) stimulation

peripheral nervous system (PNS) The division of the nervous system that detects environmental information, transmits that information to the central nervous system, and executes decisions by the central nervous system.

somatic nervous system The division of the peripheral nervous system containing sensory receptors that detect environmental stimuli and motor nerves that activate skeletal muscles.

and the nerves that activate the skeletal muscles. The **autonomic nervous system** includes the nerves that regulate the functioning of our internal organs. In terms of our example, John's somatic nervous system detects his friend's presence and conveys the orders to the muscles that move John to sit down next to his friend. John's autonomic nervous system increases his heart rate and respiration rate in response to seeing his friend.

If detection and execution are controlled by the peripheral nervous system, analysis and decision must be the responsibility of the **central nervous system (CNS)**. The central nervous system is also divided into two parts: the spinal cord and the brain (see **Figure 2.2**). The **spinal cord**, the portion of the central nervous system located within the vertebrate spinal column, plays a limited role in analysis and decision; it either responds directly to a sensory stimulus or carries a sensory message to the brain or a motor command from the brain to the muscles. The **brain**, the portion of the central nervous system located within the vertebrate skull, has the responsibility of analyzing sensory information and deciding the appropriate behavioral responses to the sensory input. Returning to our example, John's brain allows him to recognize that his friend is present and to decide that he should sit down next to his friend, and his spinal cord serves as a conduit for the sensory message from his spinal nerves to his brain and from his brain to his motor nerves.

Before You Go On

Illustrate the four functions of the nervous system by using an example of an activity you perform every day, such as crossing a street or getting dressed.

Anatomical Directions

John decided to try starting the car, and it started! But now he needs to look at the map to see how to get to the sporting goods store where he is supposed to appear. Just as we need geographical directions (for example, north or south) to locate places we want to go, anatomists need a system for locating structures in our bodies (see **Figure 2.3**). The structures that are toward the front end of an organism are referred to as **anterior** and those toward the rear of an organism are called **posterior**. For example, the nose of a dog is anterior to the rest of its body and its tail is posterior. The directional term **ventral** means toward the belly, whereas the term **dorsal** means toward the back. For example, the back of a human is dorsal (as is the top of the head) and the stomach is ventral (as is the chin). Structures located toward the head are **rostral** and those toward the tail are **caudal**. For example, a human's head is rostral to the rest of his or her body and the toes are caudal. The term **medial** means toward the midline of a structure, and **lateral** means away from the midline. For example, in a cat, the ears are lateral and its tongue is medial. **Superior** means above a structure and **inferior** means below a structure. For example, the brain is superior to the spinal cord and the spinal cord is inferior to the brain.

Structures can be viewed from one of several perspectives (refer to **Figure 2.3**). The **horizontal plane** shows structures as they would be viewed from above. **Sagittal plane** is one that divides the subject into the left and right parts, and a **coronal plane** presents structures as viewed from the front.

---

autonomic nervous system The division of the peripheral nervous system containing the nerves that regulate the functioning of internal organs.

central nervous system (CNS) The division of the nervous system that analyzes the significance of sensory information, decides how to respond to that information, and sends the message to execute that response to the peripheral nervous system.

spinal cord The division of the central nervous system located within the vertebrate spinal column that receives sensory messages from and sends motor commands to the peripheral nervous system. Most sensory messages are sent to the brain and most motor commands originate in the brain.

brain The division of the central nervous system located within the vertebrate skull that interprets sensory messages and determines the appropriate behavioral response to that sensory message.

anterior Toward the front end.

posterior Toward the rear end.

ventral Toward the belly.

dorsal Toward the back.

rostral Toward the head.

caudal Toward the tail.

medial Toward the midline.

lateral Away from the midline.

superior Above a structure.

inferior Below a structure.

horizontal plane A view of a structure from above.

sagittal plane A view that divides a structure into left and right parts.

coronal plane A view of a structure from the front.

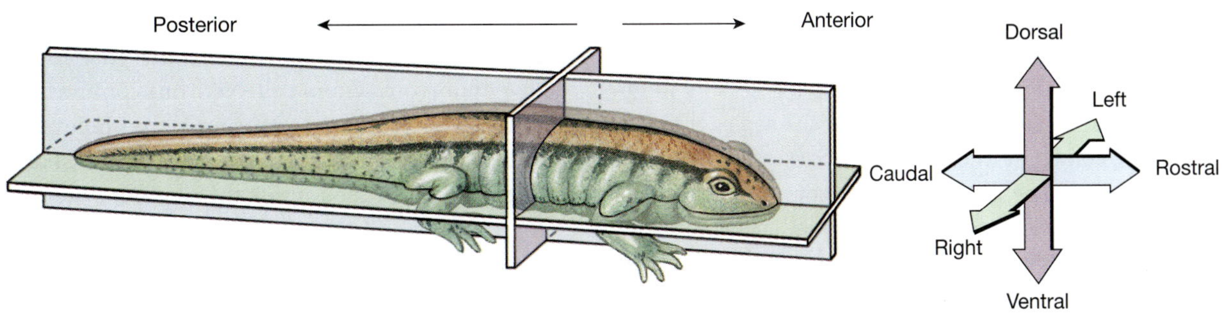

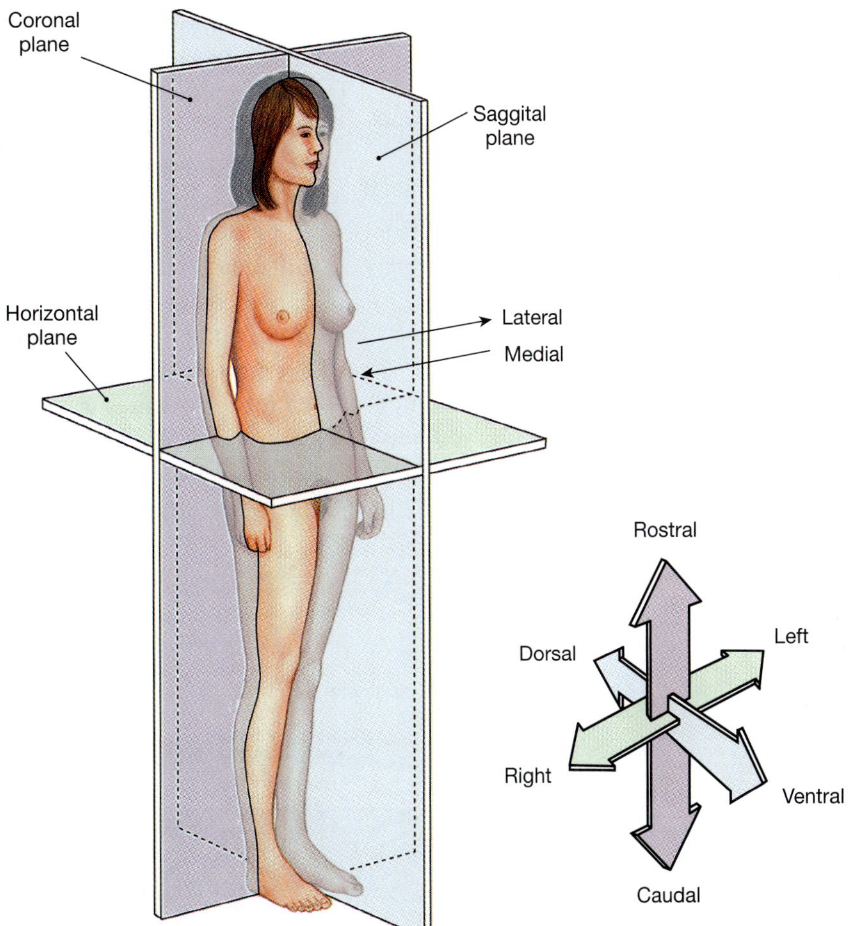

Figure 2.3 Anatomical directions and perspectives. The relative location of structures is indicated by anatomical directions and perspectives.
➤ *What features are on the anterior surface of your head? What brain structure is posterior to the spinal cord? (p. 32)*

Before You Go On

What part of your nervous system is primarily in control when you are reading? When you are digesting food? When you are running?

What part of your body is caudal to your chest? What would a dorsal view of your head show?

Section Review

- The nervous system regulates the body's internal state and integrates the body's functioning with that of the external environment.
- The four major functions of the nervous system are detection, analysis, decision, and execution.

- The peripheral nervous system is divided into the somatic nervous system and autonomic nervous system.
- The somatic nervous system contains the sensory receptors that detect external stimuli and the nerves that execute the activity of the skeletal muscles.
- The autonomic nervous system includes the nerves that regulate the functioning of our internal organs.
- The central nervous system is divided into the spinal cord and brain.
- The spinal cord carries sensory messages to the brain and motor commands from the brain to the muscles.
- The brain interprets, or recognizes, the significance of sensory information and determines, or decides, the appropriate behavioral responses to sensory input.
- All of the components of the nervous system must work together to perform its major functions smoothly.
- A system of anatomical directions allows researchers and physicians to describe the location of parts of the body.

Cells of the Nervous System

To understand how the various components of the nervous system work together to produce behavior, you must first understand the workings of the nervous system at the cellular level. We introduced the neuron briefly in Chapter 1. In this chapter, you will become much better acquainted with the neuron and the glial cell, a second type of nervous system cell. Neurons communicate information within the nervous system and between the nervous system and other systems in the body. Glial cells provide a support function for the nervous system.

Neurons: The Building Blocks of the Nervous System

A computer can perform a variety of functions: it can receive information from a keyboard, interpret the data, make decisions, and execute the decisions. The computer chip, the central element of a computer, processes the information, breaks it down into its simplest form, and relays messages to different parts of the computer. The neuron is to the nervous system what the computer chip is to the computer. A neuron can communicate with other neurons, muscles, or glands. A typical neuron is shown in **Figure 2.4**. Neurons are cells that perform the information-processing and communication functions of the nervous system. **Nerves**, or bundles of neurons that connect structures to each other within the nervous system, also control muscles, thereby enabling us to interact with the environment. The nervous system contains many neurons; although we do not have an exact figure, it is

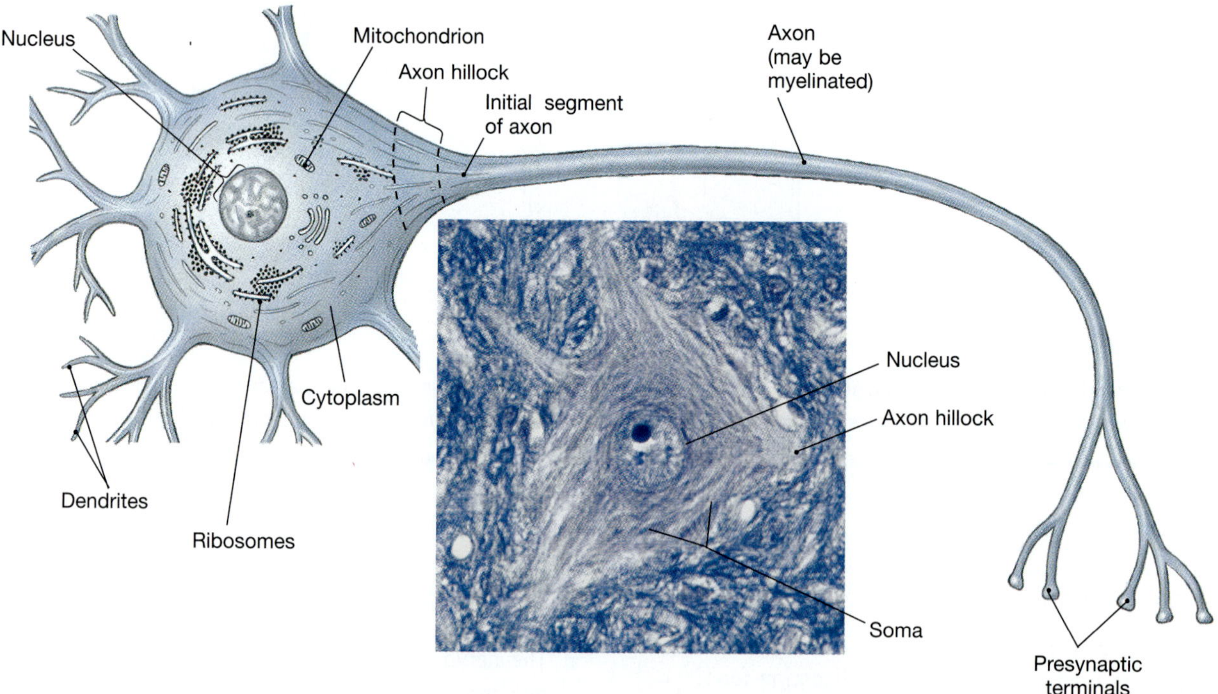

Figure 2.4 A typical neuron. Identified are the principal structures (dendrites, soma, axon hillock, axon, presynaptic terminal) that are related to the neural transmission of information.

➤ *Which part(s) of the neuron receive(s) information from other neurons? Which part(s) transmit(s) information to other neurons? (pp. 35–36)*

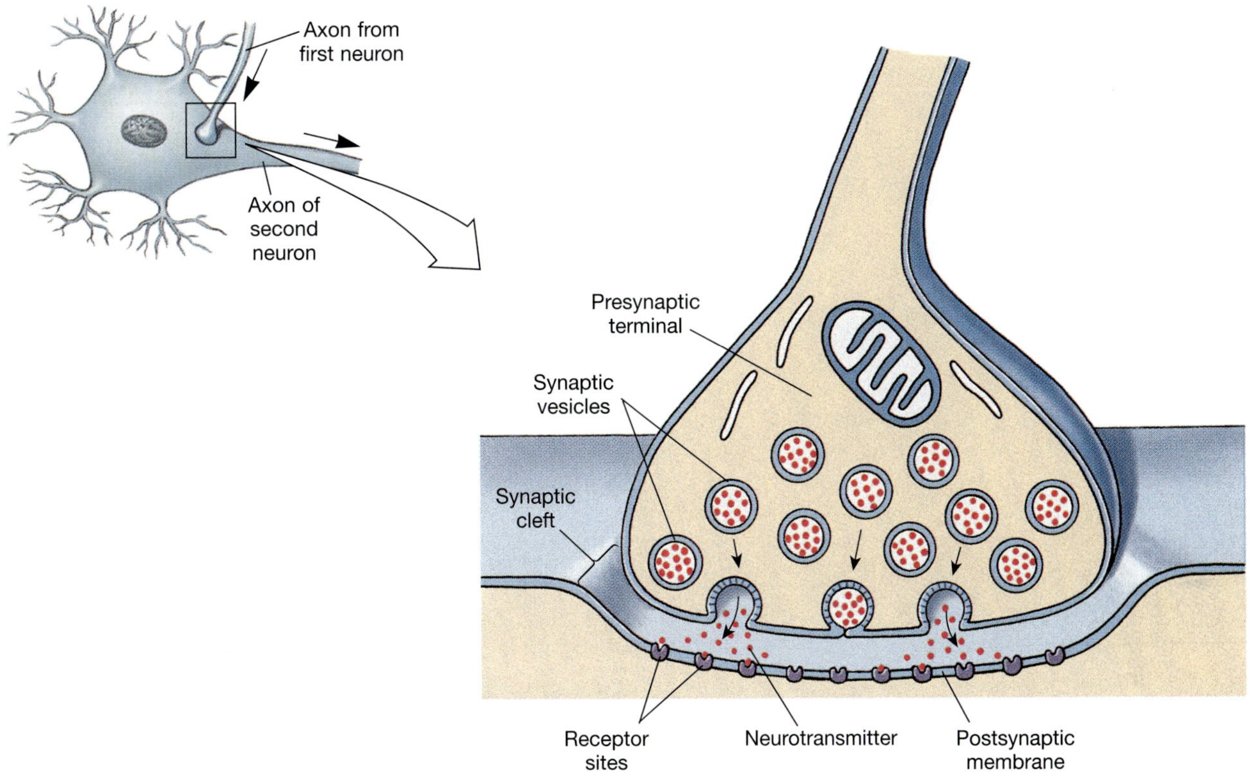

Figure 2.5 Significant structures involved in the transmission of information between neurons. Neurotransmitter substance, stored in synaptic vesicles, is released at the presynaptic membrane, where it diffuses across the synaptic cleft and affects the receptors of the next neuron.

➤ *Where are neurotransmitters stored? Where are they released? (p. 36)*

estimated that the human nervous system has about 100 billion neurons (Williams & Herrup, 1988).

Like other cells, each neuron contains a nucleus, cytoplasm, and cell membrane. The **nucleus** of the neuron, like the nuclei of all cells, contains the chromosomes which are made up of deoxyribonucleic acid (DNA), a large, two-stranded molecule consisting of the sugar deoxyribose and the bases adenine, guanine, cytosine, and thymine. The sequence of the nucleotides comprise the genes, so it can be said to contain the genetic blueprint of the entire organism (see Chapter 1). DNA controls the production of **ribonucleic acid (RNA)**, a large single-stranded molecule that governs the manufacture of proteins, which in turn regulate cell functioning. (As you will see later on, a "nucleus" can also refer to the cell body of a neuron.) The **cytoplasm** is the jellylike semiliquid substance inside the cell that contains structures involved in cell functioning. Key structures in the cytoplasm are the *mitochondria*, which extract useful energy from foods, and the *ribosomes*, which synthesize new proteins. The **cell membrane** surrounds the neuron and controls the flow of substances into and out of the cell, allowing some substances entry, and keeping other substances out of the cell.

Neurons have several unique structures that enable them to perform their information-processing and communication functions. One of these is the **dendrites**, which are thin, widely branching projections from the cell body, or **soma**. (The Greek root word for tree is *dendr*, and the shape of dendrites definitely resembles a tree.) The dendritic spines or small buds on the surface of the

nerve A bundle of neurons.

nucleus The part of a cell containing DNA, the genetic blueprint; group of neural cell bodies in the central nervous system.

ribonucleic acid (RNA) A large, single-stranded molecule that controls the manufacture of proteins, which in turn regulates cell functioning.

cytoplasm The jellylike semiliquid substance inside the cell.

cell membrane Structure that controls the flow of substances into and out of the neuron.

dendrites Thin, widely branching projections from the cell body of a neuron that receive neural impulses.

soma Cell body of the neuron.

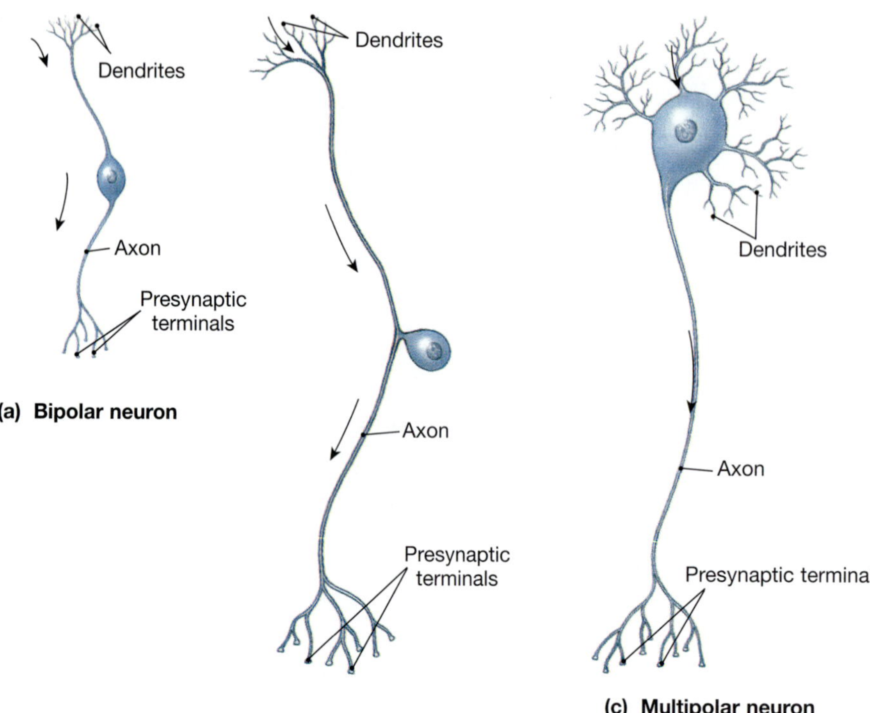

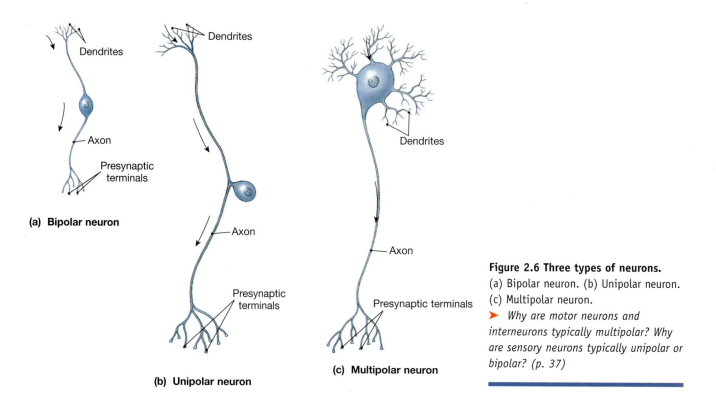

Figure 2.6 Three types of neurons. (a) Bipolar neuron. (b) Unipolar neuron. (c) Multipolar neuron.

➤ *Why are motor neurons and interneurons typically multipolar? Why are sensory neurons typically unipolar or bipolar? (p. 37)*

dendrites contain specialized junctions, called receptor sites, where information is received from other neurons.

Neural messages can also be transmitted directly to receptor sites on the soma. Information received by the dendrites and the soma is then transmitted away from the soma by a single long, relatively thick (as compared to dendrites) fiber called an **axon**. (The term *axon* comes from the Greek word *axis*; the axon resembles an axis projecting from one pole of the neuron.) The axon is joined to the soma at the **axon hillock** (refer to **Figure 2.4**). A single axon projects from the soma, but it may have many branches (telodendria) at its end.

Located at the end of the axon is a swelling called the **presynaptic terminal** (see **Figures 2.4** and **2.5**). Within the presynaptic terminal are sacs, called **synaptic vesicles**, which contain chemical substances called **neurotransmitters**. Neurotransmitters are chemicals that transmit information between neurons, or from neurons to muscles or glands. The small space that separates the presynaptic terminal from the dendrites or soma of a neighboring neuron or from its target gland or muscle is called the **synaptic cleft**.

When a message reaches the end of the axon, the synaptic vesicles move to the outer surface or **presynaptic membrane** of the presynaptic terminal and release the neurotransmitter into the synaptic cleft. The neurotransmitter then diffuses, or flows, across the synaptic cleft, where it affects the **postsynaptic membrane** of the target. Thus, the function of the axon is to relay information to another neuron, to a muscle, or to a gland. We will examine communication between two neurons in Chapter 4 and between neurons and muscles in Chapter 8.

Together, the presynaptic terminal, synaptic cleft, and postsynaptic membrane are considered the synapse, or point of contact between a neuron and its target, whether the target is another neuron, a muscle, or a gland. Another name for the synapse between a neuron and a muscle is the **neuromuscular junction**.

---

axon The long, relatively thick fiber that transmits neural impulses away from the neural cell body.

axon hillock The area between the soma and axon of a neuron where neural impulses are generated.

presynaptic terminal A swelling at the end of the axon.

synaptic vesicles Sacs within the presynaptic terminal that contain neurotransmitters.

neurotransmitters Chemicals stored in the synaptic vesicles that are released into the synaptic cleft and transmit messages to other neurons.

synaptic cleft The space between the presynaptic and the postsynaptic membranes.

presynaptic membrane The outer surface of the presynaptic terminal, which is the site of release of neurotransmitters into the synaptic cleft.

postsynaptic membrane The outer surface of a target cell that receives messages from the presynaptic membrane.

neuromuscular junction The point of contact between a neuron and a muscle.

As we have discussed, the axon of one neuron usually synapses with, or meets, the dendrites or the soma of the next neuron. However, in some cases, the dendrites of one neuron synapse with the dendrites of another neuron; in other cases, the axons of one neuron synapse with the axons of another neuron. We will have more to say about the reasons for the varied forms of connections between neurons in Chapter 4.

There are many structural forms of neurons; we will look at the three major ones next. Bipolar neurons have one dendritic tree and one axon at opposite ends of the soma (see **Figure 2.6a**). The unipolar neuron has a single projection from the soma that divides into two branches. The top branch is a single dendritic tree, and the bottom branch is the axon (see **Figure 2.6b**). A multipolar neuron has many dendritic trees extending from the soma (see **Figure 2.6c**).

Neurons are also classified into three functional types. **Sensory neurons** detect information from the outside world and carry the information to the central nervous system. A sensory neuron is usually unipolar or bipolar. **Motor neurons** carry information from the central nervous system to the muscles to control their functioning. **Interneurons** connect sensory and motor neurons or communicate with other interneurons. Interneurons and motor neurons are typically multipolar. The shape of multipolar neurons can vary dramatically. **Figure 2.7** presents several examples of multipolar neurons.

Before You Go On

What cellular structures are unique to neurons? What is the function of these unique structures?

What are the three main structural types of neurons? Describe the three functional types of neurons.

Glial Cells

The second type of cells found in the nervous system is the **glial cell**. Glial cells serve a support function in the nervous system. (The term *glia* comes from the Greek word meaning glue, as it was once thought that glial cells were like glue holding the neurons together.) Glial cells are about one-tenth the size of a neuron, but approximately 10 times as numerous, perhaps one trillion, which means that they occupy approximately the same volume in the nervous system as neurons.

There are a variety of different types of glial cells (see **Figure 2.8**). The **astrocytes**, the largest of the glial cells, are star-shaped (astr = star) and provide physical support for neurons by protecting them and holding them in place. The astrocytes also isolate neurons from one another, thereby preventing accidental transmission of neural messages. In addition, astrocytes transport nutrients into the neuron, remove waste products from the neuron, regulate the flow of blood in the central nervous system, and guide neuron development in

sensory neuron Specialized neuron that detects information from the outside world.

motor neuron Specialized neuron that carries messages from the central nervous system to muscles.

interneuron A neuron that connects a sensory and a motor neuron or communicates with other neurons.

glial cell A type of nervous system cell that provides a support function.

astrocyte The star-shaped glial cell that provides physical support for a neuron, transports nutrients into and waste products out of the neuron, regulates blood flow, and guides neural development.

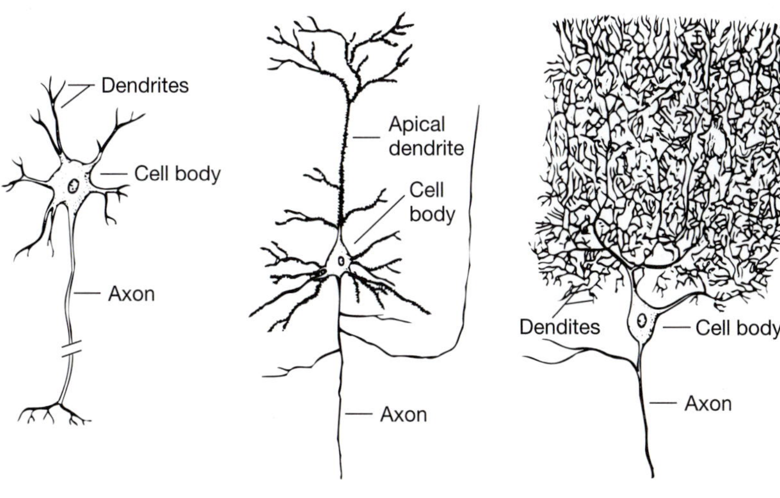

Figure 2.7 Three examples of multipolar neurons. The extent of dendrite projections of a multipolar neuron varies from few in a spinal motor neuron to many in a Purkinje cell of the cerebellum.

Adapted from Kandel et al., 1991.

➤ *Why do neurons have so many shapes? (p. 37)*

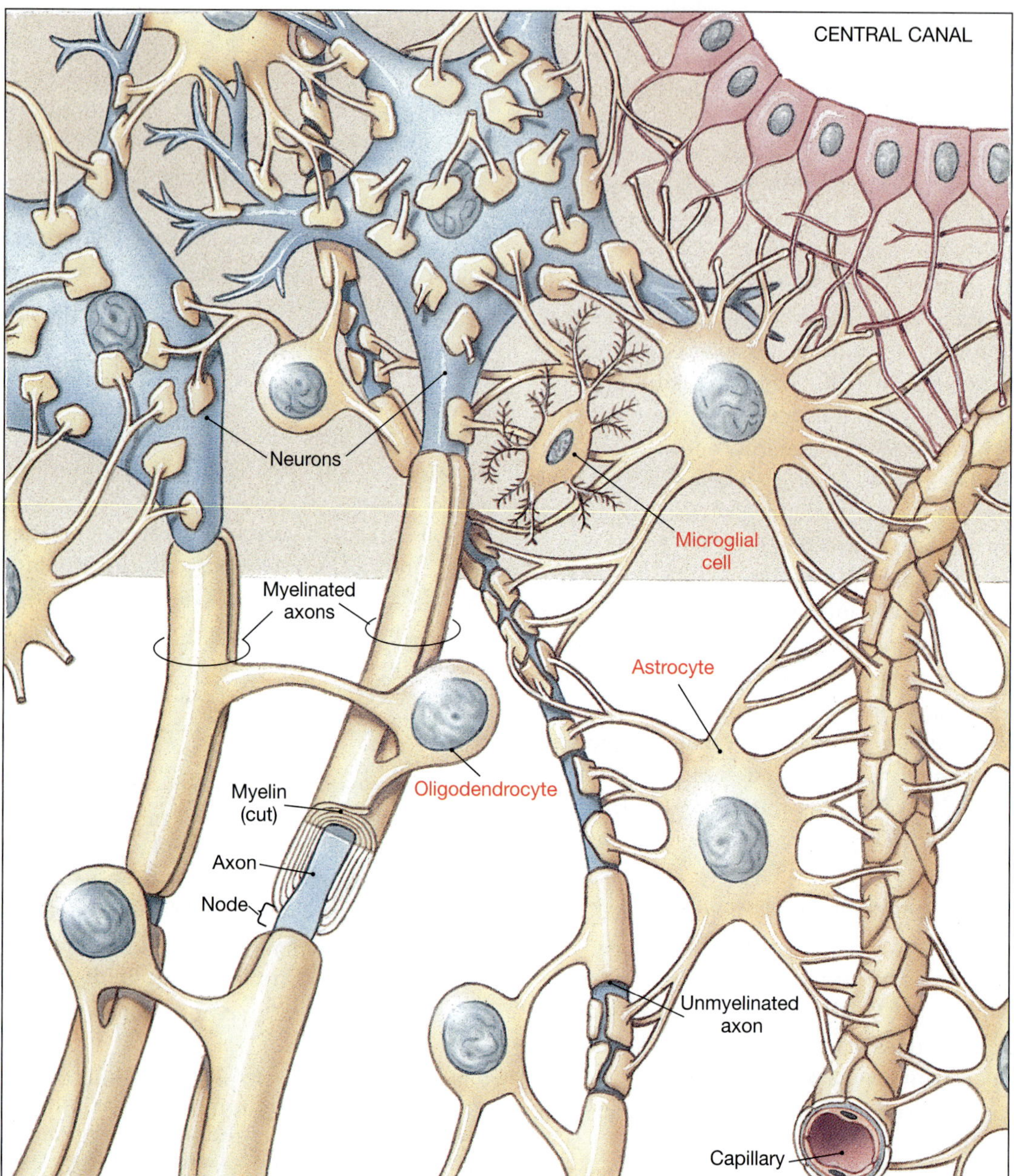

Figure 2.8 Types of glial cells. Glial cells of the central nervous system include astrocytes, microglia, and oligodendrocytes. (Schwann cells are not shown, as they are found in the peripheral nervous system.)

➤ *What is the function of each type of glial cell? (pp. 37–39)*

the embryo and fetus. Traditionally, it has been thought the astrocytes only performed these support functions, but recent evidence suggests that astrocytes may also relay their own chemical messages between different parts of the brain (Travis, 1994).

microglia A type of glial cell that removes dead neurons.

myelin A fatlike substance that surrounds and insulates certain neurons.

Some astrocytes and another type of glial cell, called **microglia**, remove debris from neurons that have died. These astrocytes and microglia travel through the nervous system, locate the tissue of dead neurons, and digest the debris. They leave behind a network of astrocytes to form scar tissue, walling off the vacant area of the nervous system. (See also the section on recovery from damage in Chapter 3.)

Two other types of glial cells produce a complex, fatlike substance called **myelin** that surrounds and insulates certain axons to speed the transmission of neural messages. The **oligodendrocytes** or oligodendroglia protect and insulate the axons of certain neurons in the brain and spinal cord, and **Schwann cells** serve the same function in the peripheral nervous system. As we will see in Chapter 4, the myelination of axons increases the speed of information transmission within the nervous system.

Before You Go On

What is the function of glial cells?

What types of glial cells myelinate neurons?

Section Review

- The nervous system is composed of two types of cells, neurons and glial cells.
- Neurons carry neural messages throughout the body. Their specialized structure, with long, branching projections, allows them to transmit messages from cell to cell over long distances.
- Sensory neurons detect outside information and transmit it to the central nervous system.
- Motor neurons transmit messages from the central nervous system to the muscles and glands.
- Interneurons connect sensory and motor neurons.
- Glial cells include astrocytes, microglia, oligodendrocytes, and Schwann cells.
- Astrocytes support and protect neurons.
- Microglia remove debris of dead neurons.
- Oligodendrocytes and Schwann cells produce a protective substance called myelin.

The Peripheral Nervous System

Remember the four functions of the nervous system—detection, analysis, decision, and execution? As we saw earlier, the peripheral nervous system detects information about external events and internal states and executes the decision made by the central nervous system in response to that input. The sensory receptors of our sense organs detect a variety of environmental events. For example, the eyes detect light waves, and the ears react to sound waves. Other specialized receptors respond to events within the body; for example, proprioceptive receptors detect the stretch and tension of a muscle. (These receptors let you know how much force to exert when you lift your backpack full of books!) The peripheral nervous system not only carries sensory information to the central nervous system but also conveys signals from the central nervous system to peripheral organs and muscles. For example, the central nervous system can send a message to the peripheral nervous system that causes John Moore to duck when his opponent throws a punch. The peripheral nervous system can also activate the skeletal muscles that allow John to reach up and block the punch.

The Somatic Nervous System

As we mentioned earlier, the peripheral nervous system has two subsystems: the somatic nervous system and the autonomic nervous system (refer to **Figure 2.2**). The somatic nervous system contains the neurons that allow us to interact with the physical environment. Within the somatic nervous system, **afferent neurons** send messages from the sensory receptors to the central nervous system, and **efferent neurons** send messages from the central nervous system to the skeletal muscles. *Afferent* means toward, and *efferent* means away, always with the central nervous system as the referent.

The somatic nervous system has two main types of nerves. **Spinal nerves** send messages to and from the brain through the spinal cord. **Cranial nerves** directly link the sensory receptor to the brain, and the brain to certain muscles. Both spinal and cranial nerves have afferent sensory input nerves and efferent motor output nerves.

There are 31 sets of spinal nerves and 12 pairs of cranial nerves. **Table 2.1** shows the sensory and motor information conveyed by the 12 pairs of cranial nerves.

oligodendrocyte The type of glial cell that myelinates certain neurons in the central nervous system.

Schwann cell The type of glial cell that myelinates certain neurons in the peripheral nervous system.

afferent neuron A neuron that sends messages from the sensory receptors to the central nervous system.

efferent neuron A neuron that sends messages from the central nervous system to the muscles, glands, and organs.

spinal nerve A group of neurons that sends messages to and from the brain through the spinal cord.

cranial nerve A group of neurons that directly links sensory receptors to the brain, and the brain to certain muscles.

Table 2.1 ■ Type and Function of the 12 Cranial Nerves

Number and Name	Type	Function
I Olfactory	Sensory	Smell
II Optic	Sensory	Vision
III Oculomotor	Motor	Eye movement
IV Trochlear	Motor	Eye movement
V Trigeminal	Motor	Masticatory movements
	Sensory	Sensitivity of face
VI Abducens	Motor	Eye movement
VII Facial	Motor	Muscles of facial expression
	Sensory	Taste from anterior two-thirds of tongue
VIII Auditory	Sensory	Hearing, balance
IX Glossopharyngeal	Motor	Movement of pharynx, salivary secretion
	Sensory	Taste from posterior one-third of tongue
X Vagus	Sensory, motor	Sensitivity and movement of heart, lungs, gastrointestinal tract, larynx
XI Spinal accessory	Motor	Movement of neck muscles and viscera, swallowing
XII Hypoglossal	Motor	Tongue movement

All but four cranial nerves have a single function, either sensory or motor. **Figure 2.9** shows the 31 pairs of spinal nerves and the area each pair serves.

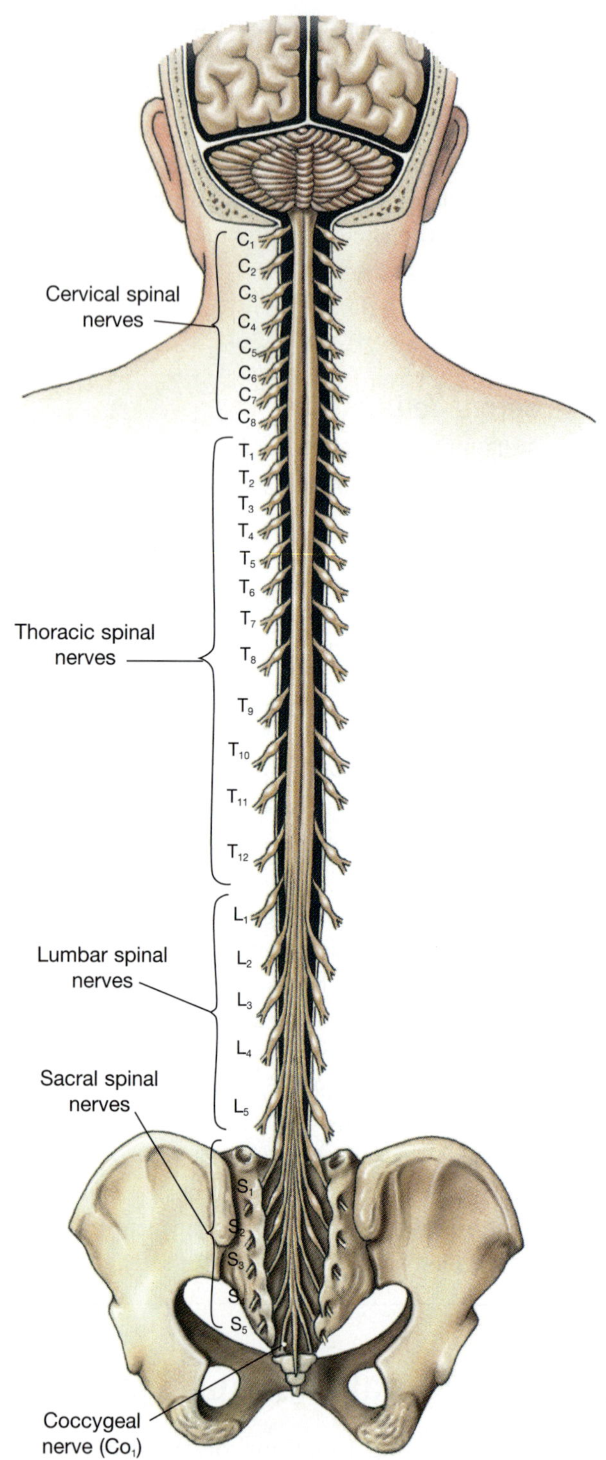

Figure 2.9 The 31 sets of spinal nerves. This figure indicates the general area of the body that each spinal nerve serves.

➤ *Why are there so many different spinal nerves? What is the effect of damage to sensory or motor nerves? (pp. 39–40)*

The Autonomic Nervous System

We learned earlier that the nerves of the autonomic nervous system regulate the functioning of our internal organs. The autonomic nervous system contains efferent neurons that control gland activity and internal organ functioning. Like the somatic nervous system, the autonomic nervous system is composed of two divisions: the sympathetic division and the parasympathetic division (refer to **Figure 2.10**). The actions of these two parts of the autonomic nervous system are typically antagonistic, or opposite in effect. The **sympathetic nervous system** is activated by conditions that promote arousal, particularly those involving emotional reactions to stressors (Berry & Pennebaker, 1993). Thus, stimulation of the sympathetic nervous system prepares you to respond to challenging or

sympathetic nervous system A division of the autonomic nervous system that is activated by challenging or dangerous situations.

dangerous conditions. For example, John Moore steps into the ring. Anticipation of the match will stimulate his sympathetic nervous system to a state of arousal, which may be manifested by an increased heart rate and sweating palms. The sympathetic nervous system also is stimulated by challenging, yet nonthreatening situations, such as taking a test or working on a paper. In contrast, the **parasympathetic nervous system** is activated by conditions of recovery, or the termination of stressors, and it allows you to replenish energy-depleted stores. For example, after the fight, John Moore walks into the locker room, lies on a bench, and turns on the radio, leading to stimulation of the parasympathetic nervous system. His heart rate decreases and his respiratory rate slows, allowing him to recover enough to talk to the media and be congratulated on his victory. The activation of the parasympathetic nervous system after sympathetic nervous system activation ends, a process called *parasympathetic rebound,* helps to ensure that John is ready to respond to further fights.

Although the actions of the sympathetic and parasympathetic nervous systems are typically antagonistic, there is some cooperative functioning between the two systems. An example of this cooperation occurs with sexual activity. Suppose a man sees an attractive woman. Seeing the woman might stimulate his sympathetic nervous system, leading to an increase in his heart rate and his rate of respiration. At the same time, the parasympathetic nervous system might become activated, causing penile erection. Parasympathetic innervation of the penile

parasympathetic nervous system A division of the autonomic nervous system that is activated by conditions of recovery or termination of stressors.

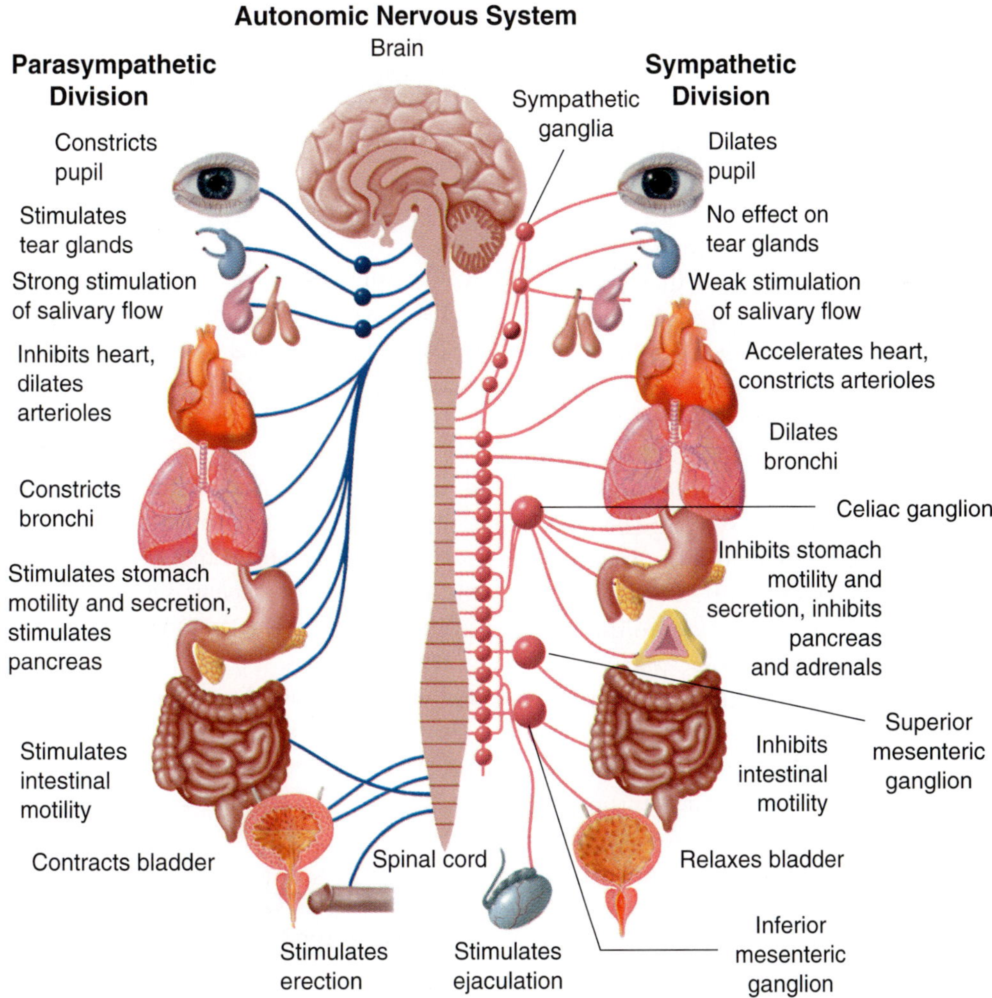

Figure 2.10 The autonomic nervous system. This figure presents the major organs whose actions are controlled by the sympathetic and parasympathetic divisions of the autonomic nervous system.

➤ *What is the major function of the parasympathetic nervous system? What is the major function of the sympathetic nervous system? (pp. 40–41)* arteries causes these arteries to dilate, which increases the blood flow to the genital area, causes the erectile tissue to become engorged with blood, and produces penile erection. (There is a similar parasympathetic engorgement in the clitoris, which is the female equivalent of the penis.) Continued sympathetic nervous system arousal may lead to ejaculation.

Have you noticed that the effects of exposure to a stressful event, such as participation in a boxing match, can last long after the event is over, but the recuperative effects of a pleasant event, like listening to music, seem short-lived? One reason for the differences in the duration of physiological effects is that the sympathetic and parasympathetic nervous systems have quite different structures. Both contain ganglia (singular: ganglion), which are groupings of neurons with a common function in the peripheral nervous system. (Recall from **p. 35** that neural cell bodies with a common function in the central nervous system are called **nuclei**.) The difference lies in where within the peripheral nervous system the ganglia occur. (The following discussion can be confusing because of the similarity and length of the terms. To make it easier, keep the word roots in mind: preganglionic means before the ganglion, and postganglionic means after the ganglion. I leave it up to you to keep sympathetic and parasympathetic straight.)

The axons of the preganglionic sympathetic neurons that leave the spinal cord are short, and they synapse with the postganglionic sympathetic neurons in the sympathetic ganglia (see red circles in **Figure 2.10**). The axons of the postganglionic sympathetic neurons are long, and they synapse directly on the target organ (for example, the heart). By contrast, the axons of the preganglionic parasympathetic neurons are long, and they synapse with the postganglionic parasympathetic neurons at the parasympathetic ganglia close to the target organ (see blue circles in **Figure 2.10**). Because the parasympathetic ganglia are located so close to the target organ, the axons of the postganglionic parasympathetic neurons are much shorter than those of the postganglionic sympathetic neurons.

Because the sympathetic ganglia are so far from the target organs, one preganglionic sympathetic neuron can activate up to 20 or 30 postganglionic neurons, which can, in turn, stimulate several different target organs. By contrast, because the parasympathetic ganglia are so much closer to the target organ, the activation of a preganglionic parasympathetic neuron produces a more specific effect. One preganglionic parasympathetic neuron only activates a few postganglionic parasympathetic neurons, which, in turn, activate only a single target organ. This makes sense if you think about it—the body needs to respond much more quickly to sympathetic stimulation, such as the avoidance of a punch, so it is an advantage that the short preganglionic sympathetic neurons can activate more organs in a shorter time. John Moore has all the time in the world for his parasympathetic division to counteract the effect of sympathetic stimulation after the stress of the bout has passed (although his interviews with the press may reactivate his sympathetic division!); recovery proceeds more slowly because each preganglionic parasympathetic neuron affects a single organ.

nuclei Groupings of neurons with a common function in the central nervous system.

Before You Go On

Explain the difference between afferent and efferent nerve fibers.

Give an example of the antagonistic effects of the sympathetic and parasympathetic divisions of the autonomic nervous system.

Section Review

- The two divisions of the peripheral nervous system are the somatic and autonomic nervous systems.
- The somatic nervous system consists of the spinal and cranial nerves, receives input from sensory receptors located throughout the body, and activates the skeletal muscles.
- The autonomic nervous system, which consists of the sympathetic and parasympathetic nervous systems, activates the glands and organs that control body functioning.
- The sympathetic nervous system, which is activated by arousing conditions, prepares the body to cope with challenge or danger.
- The parasympathetic nervous system is stimulated by conditions of rest. It allows recovery from arousal and replenishment of energy stores.

The Protective Features of the Central Nervous System

A blow from his opponent catches John Moore by surprise and sends him flying across the ring, where he hits his head on the corner post. In all likelihood, the most serious consequences of his fall will be a headache and maybe a bump on the head. Why? The answer lies in three protective features of the central nervous system: (1) the skull and vertebral column, or backbone, (2) the meninges, and (3) the ventricular system.

The Skull and Vertebral Column

The brain is protected from injury by a set of bones that comprise the **skull**; the bones of the **vertebral column** (sometimes called the spine or backbone) protect the spinal cord. Within the vertebral column, there are 24 individual vertebrae (cervical, thoracic, and lumbar), as well as the fused vertebrae of the sacral and coccygeal portions (see **Figure 2.11**). The hard, bony composition of the vertebral column provides important protection for the soft tissue of the spinal cord. The skull gives the brain similar protection.

skull The outer bony covering that protects the brain.

vertebral column The outer bony covering that protects the spinal cord; also called the spine or backbone.

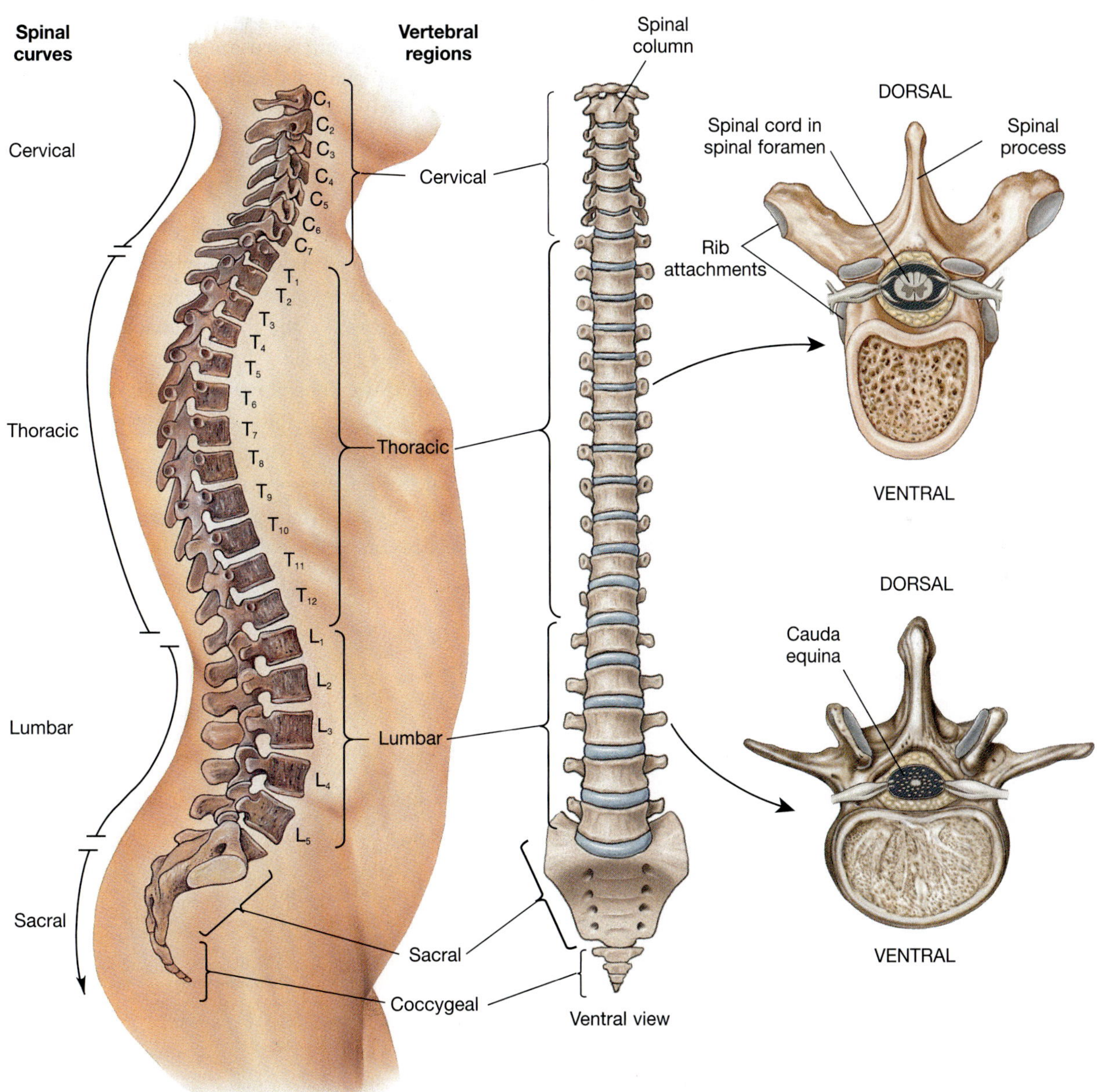

Figure 2.11 The human spinal column. There are 24 individual vertebrae (cervical, thoracic, and lumbar) and the fused vertebrae of the sacral and coccygeal regions. The spinal cord passes through the middle of the upper two-thirds of the spinal column; the bottom third of the spinal column is filled with a mass of spinal root nerves called the cauda equina. Note that the numbering of the spinal column corresponds to the numbering of the spinal nerves in Figure 2.9.

➤ *What are the consequences of damage to the cervical vertebrae? What consequences follow damage to the lumbar region? (p. 40)*

The Meninges

Between the skull and the brain, and between the spinal cord and the vertebral column, there are three layers of tissue called the **meninges** (singular: meninx, from the Greek word for membrane). The outermost layer of the meninges is the dura mater (see **Figure 2.12**). The **dura mater** is thick, tough, and flexible. The term *dura mater* comes from the Latin words meaning "hard mother." The dura mater actually consists of two layers of closely united tissue, except for the open areas (venous sinuses) where blood is returned from the brain to the heart.

The **arachnoid mater** is the middle layer of the meninges. This layer is a very thin weblike sheet of tissue, which gets its name from the Greek word meaning "spider track."

The **subarachnoid space**, filled with cerebrospinal fluid (see next section), lies between the arachnoid membrane and the pia mater. The **pia mater**, or innermost layer, comes from the Latin words meaning "soft or tender mother." The pia mater is a thin membrane that adheres closely to the surface of the brain and has a rich blood supply.

meninges The three layers of tissue between the skull and the brain and the vertebral column and the spinal cord.

dura mater The thick, tough, and flexible outermost layer of the meninges.

arachnoid mater The thin weblike sheet of tissue, which is the middle layer of meninges.

subarachnoid space Space between arachnoid mater and pia mater that is filled with cerebrospinal fluid.

pia mater The thin membrane that adheres closely to the surface of the brain and is the innermost layer of the meninges.

ventricular system A series of hollow, interconnected chambers in the brain and spinal cord that contain cerebrospinal fluid.

ventricles The four chambers of the ventricular system in the brain.

central canal The chamber of the ventricular system that runs through the spinal cord.

cerebrospinal fluid The clear fluid contained in the ventricular system and arachnoid space that supports and protects the CNS and provides it with nutrients.

The Ventricular System

The **ventricular system** consists of a series of hollow, interconnected chambers in the brain and spinal cord. The four chambers or **ventricles** in the brain consist of two lateral ventricles, the third ventricle, and the fourth ventricle. The chamber that runs through the spinal cord is called the **central canal** (see **Figure 2.13**).

Like the subarachnoid space of the meninges, the chambers of the ventricular system contain **cerebrospinal fluid**. Cerebrospinal fluid, which is clear and resembles blood plasma, cushions and protects the brain and spinal cord from injury. It also provides buoy-

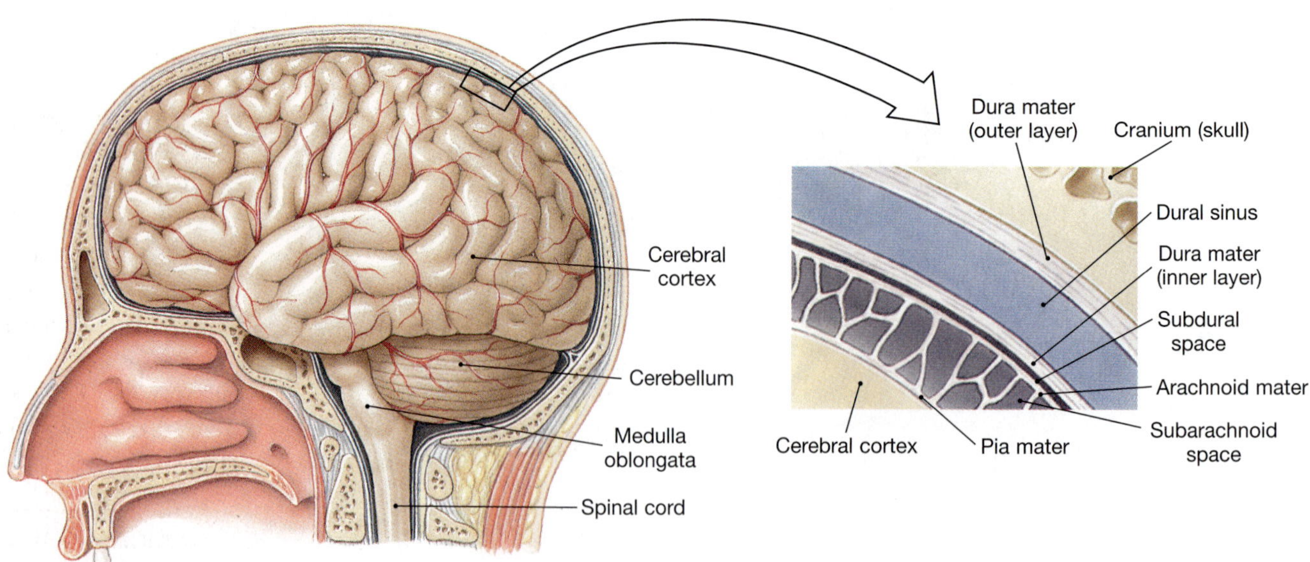

Figure 2.12 Illustration of the three layers of the meninges between the skull and the brain. The dura mater is the outermost layer; the arachnoid mater is the middle layer; and the pia mater is the innermost layer. The subarachnoid space lies between the arachnoid membrane and the pia mater and is filled with cerebrospinal fluid.

➤ *Why are there so many layers of tissue between the brain and the skull? (p. 44)*

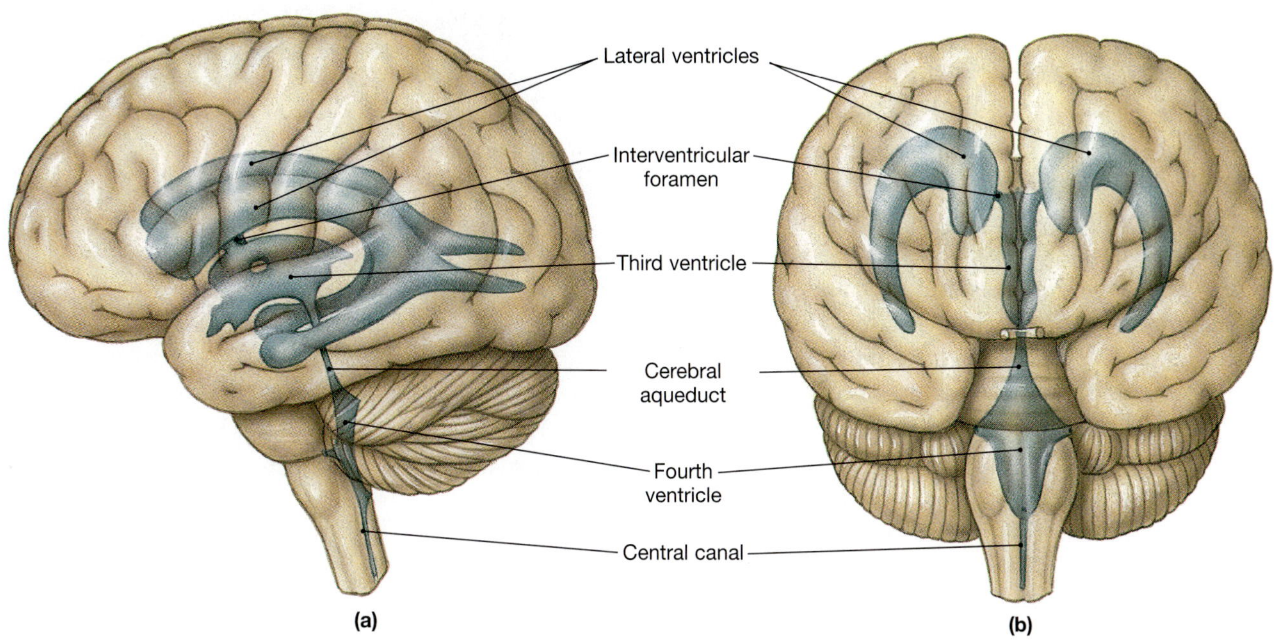

Figure 2.13 Ventricular system. (a) Sagittal view and (b) coronal view.
➤ *What functions does the cerebrospinal fluid serve? (pp. 44–45)*

ancy to support the brain against the force of gravity and contains nutrients needed by the central nervous system. Each ventricle contains a rich network of blood vessels called the **choroid plexus**, which includes a covering of cells that manufacture the cerebrospinal fluid.

Cerebrospinal fluid from the two lateral ventricles travels to the third ventricle through the interventricular foramen, the opening that permits cerebrospinal fluid to flow between the lateral and third ventricles (inter = between; foramen = opening). The fluid then flows into the fourth ventricle through the cerebral aqueduct. The fourth ventricle tapers into a canal that becomes the central canal of the spinal cord. The cerebrospinal fluid flows from the fourth ventricle into the central canal. There is a steady production of cerebrospinal fluid in the ventricular system, and the absorption of cerebrospinal fluid into the bloodstream prevents the accumulation of excess levels.

Before You Go On

Explain how the skull, the meninges, and the ventricular system protect your brain if you fall and hit your head.

Brain Damage

John Moore's current motor impairments, described at the beginning of the chapter, are likely a result of brain damage caused by repeated blows to his head. In this section, we will examine several major causes of brain damage. Later in the chapter, we will discuss the specific areas of the brain that were most likely to have been damaged during John Moore's career in boxing.

Trauma is one major source of brain damage (Davis, 1993). Trauma can occur not only as a result of injuries sustained during sports such as boxing, but also as a result of blows to the head from accidents such as automobile and motorcycle crashes or gunshot wounds. There are two classes of *trauma*: penetrating head injury and closed head injury. The damage to the brain caused by boxing is an example of a closed head injury, whereas a gunshot wound (such as that suffered by President John F. Kennedy) is an example of a penetrating head injury.

Trauma is not the only cause of brain damage. Other causes of brain damage include congenital disorders, vascular disorders, infections, tumors, and degenerative diseases (Davis, 1993). Some damage to the brain is **congenital** or present at birth. Congenital disorders include conditions such as cerebral palsy, which involves defects in motor behavior and coordination, and Down syndrome, which involves mental retardation and particular physical characteristics.

Vascular problems can also lead to brain damage. One major category of vascular disorders is cerebral vas-

---

choroid plexus The rich network of blood vessels in the ventricles that manufactures the cerebrospinal fluid.

congenital Present at birth.

cular accidents (CVAs) or *strokes.* A cerebral vascular accident can result from an obstruction of a blood vessel by a clot or from bleeding in the brain caused by the rupture of an artery. Other vascular disorders include transient ischemic attacks, which are temporary disruptions of the blood supply that produce specific neurological problems such as blurring of vision or speech difficulty, and pseudobulbar palsy, which is a permanent muscular paralysis in the head and neck area.

Brain damage can result from a variety of infections, such as encephalitis or meningitis. Other examples of brain damage due to infections are those that result from abscesses in the brain or those that are associated with syphilis, a sexually transmitted disease caused by a microorganism that attacks the nervous system.

A **tumor**, an abnormal proliferation of cells, is another cause of brain damage. Within the brain, the tumor arises from excessive glial cell duplication. As the tumor grows, there is increasing pressure on neural tissue, which adversely affects its function. Malignant Grades 3 and 4 astrocytomas (or the proliferation of astrocytes) are the most common primary brain tumors in adults. These tumors primarily occur in the frontal and temporal lobes of the cerebral cortex and grow quite rapidly. A person with this type of tumor will survive for about a year. Less common tumors are Grades 1 and 2 astrocytomas, oligodendrogliomas, and meningiomas. Grades 1 and 2 astrocytomas and oligodendrogliomas develop more slowly than Grades 3 and 4 astrocytomas. The average survival rate with these types of tumors is 5 to 6 years. Meningiomas are benign tumors arising from the arachnoid cells of the meninges. These tumors usually do not invade the brain and the prognosis is favorable.

Finally, brain damage can be caused by degenerative neurological diseases, which involve progressive deterioration of function due to the death of neurons. Examples are Parkinson's disease, Huntington's disease, multiple sclerosis, and Alzheimer's disease. Parkinson's disease, Huntington's disease, and multiple sclerosis are primarily disorders of movement, whereas Alzheimer's disease is primarily a disorder of mental functioning. We will discuss briefly Parkinson's disease and Huntington's disease later in this chapter (in addition, see coverage of Huntington's disease in Chapter 1); multiple sclerosis is discussed in Chapter 4. A detailed discussion of Alzheimer's disease is found in Chapter 14.

An understanding of the causes and consequences of brain damage can tell us much about how the brain functions as well as contribute to the development of effective methods of preventing or curing neurological disorders. In this text, we discuss the known causes and treatments for a number of neurological disorders that can affect us. Sadly, there are a number of disorders, such as multiple sclerosis and Alzheimer's disease, for which the cause and/or treatment is as yet undiscovered. Research in these areas is continuing, and sometime in the near future we hope to have cures for these devastating diseases.

tumor An abnormal proliferation of glial cells and meninges cells.

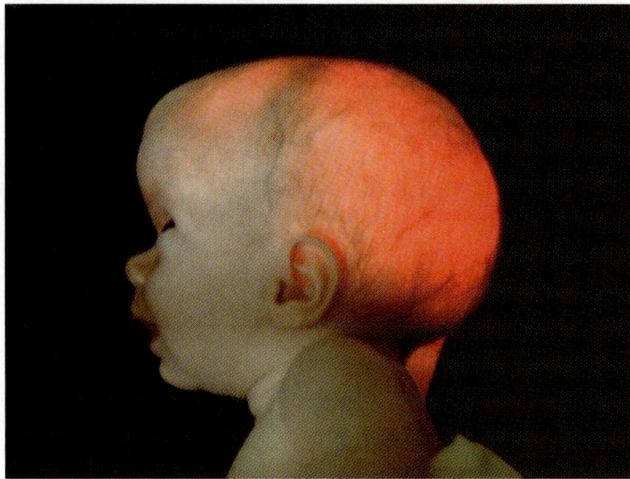

Figure 2.14 Hydrocephalus. This photograph vividly shows the distortion of the brain and the enlargement of the skull of an infant following the build-up of fluid due to blockage of the cerebral aqueduct or the constriction of the subarachnoid spaces when left untreated.

➤ *What might be done to prevent the development of hydrocephalus? (p. 47)*

APPLICATION

Detecting Brain Damage

Damage to the brain can sometimes be detected by a medical procedure called a spinal tap, which involves removing a small amount of cerebrospinal fluid from the subarchnoid space. When infection is present in the central nervous system, the white blood cell count and the protein content in the cerebrospinal fluid are much higher than normal. Chemicals in the cerebrospinal fluid can provide information about brain disorders, such as *encephalitis,* which is an inflammation of the brain, and *meningitis,* which is an inflammation of the meninges of the brain or the spinal cord. Cerebrospinal fluids can also provide information about behavior pathology. For example, low levels of the metabolite 5-HIAA (5-hydroxyindoleacetic acid) of the neurotransmitter serotonin is a marker for suicide among people with depression, and thus is a warning sign for a clinical psychologist or psychiatrist (Roy, DeJong, & Linnoila, 1989).

The flow of cerebrospinal fluid from the brain is sometimes blocked, a condition known as **hydrocephalus** (see **Figure 2.14**). In adults, this condition is life-threatening unless the pressure is relieved. In young children, whose skull bones have not yet fused completely, this condition can cause the skull bones to spread, causing an overgrown head and mental retardation. ■

Before You Go On

Describe the function of cerebrospinal fluid. What happens if the flow of cerebrospinal fluid is blocked?

Describe several causes of brain damage. How does a spinal tap reveal possible causes of brain damage?

Section Review

- The central nervous system is protected by the skull and vertebral column, the meninges, and the ventricular system.
- The meninges are three layers of tissue that separate the central nervous system structures from the skull and vertebrae. The layers are the dura mater, the arachnoid mater, and the pia mater.
- The subarachnoid space lies between the arachnoid mater and pia mater and contains cerebrospinal fluid.
- The ventricular system is a series of interconnected hollow spaces in the brain and spinal column including four chambers in the brain called the ventricles, and the central canal, which runs through the spinal cord.
- The chambers of the ventricular system are filled with cerebrospinal fluid, which cushions and protects the brain and spinal cord.
- Cerebrospinal fluid flows continuously throughout the ventricular system. Blockage of the flow of cerebrospinal fluid is a life-threatening condition.
- Damage to the brain can result from trauma, congenital disorders, vascular disorders, infections, tumors, and degenerative diseases.

The Central Nervous System: The Spinal Cord

We have discovered that the peripheral nervous system, consisting of the sensory motor nerves and the motor nerves of the somatic nervous system and the motor nerves of the autonomic nervous system, detects the presence of environmental events and internal state and activates the muscles that produce movement in the external environment and control internal organs. Many afferent nerves enter the central nervous system through the spinal cord, and many efferent nerves exit through the spinal cord. In some cases, a response to environmental input is controlled solely by the spinal cord, in other cases, however, the spinal cord is merely a conduit for information to and from the brain. In the next section, we will examine the structure and function of the spinal cord to discover how it influences our actions.

Structure and Function

The spinal cord is a long, cylindrical structure that runs through the vertebral column. The main function of the spinal cord is to carry sensory input to and motor input from the brain (Heimer, 1995). Thirty-one pairs of spinal nerves enter and exit the spinal cord. There are 8 pairs of cervical nerves, 12 pairs of thoracic nerves, 5 pairs of lumbar nerves, 5 pairs of sacral nerves, and 1 pair of coccygeal nerves. For each pair of spinal nerves, the incoming sensory input from the peripheral nervous system enters through the dorsal or back side of the cord and outgoing motor neurons exit through the ventral or belly side (remember the Bell-Magendie law). **Figure 2.15** shows a cross-sectional view of the spinal cord. The sensory nerves that enter the spinal cord through the dorsal root are axons of sensory neurons, and the motor nerves that exit through the ventral root are axons of motor neurons. Each spinal nerve pair receives sensory input from and sends motor output to a specific part of the body, although there is some overlap in the nerves controlling certain areas, such as the spinal nerves controlling respiration. Because respiration is controlled by several spinal nerves (cervical nerves C3 through C5), respiration may be compromised by damage to one cervical nerve, but it can continue due to the continuing activity of the other two cervical nerves.

In cross-section, two kinds of material are visible in the spinal cord: **gray matter**, consisting of neural cell bodies, and **white matter**, consisting of groups of nerve fibers. The axons of these nerves appear white because they are *myelinated*. Myelination is important because it

hydrocephalus A blockage of the flow of cerebrospinal fluid.

gray matter The cell bodies of neurons.

white matter Myelinated axons of nerve fibers.

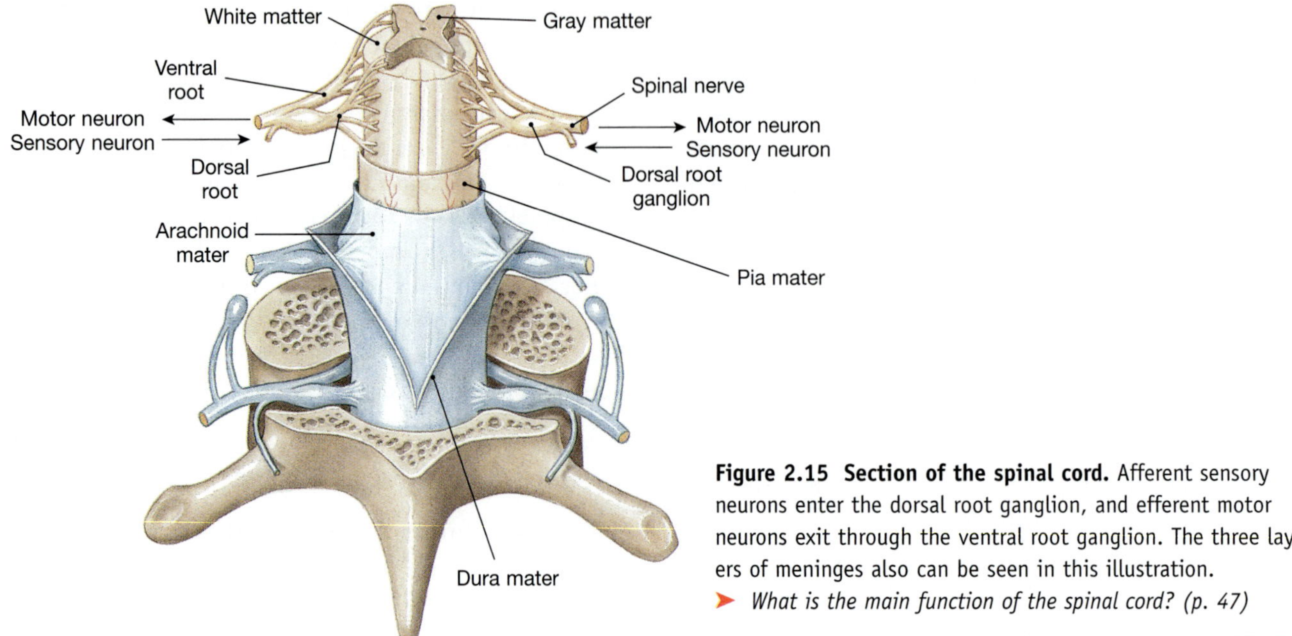

Figure 2.15 Section of the spinal cord. Afferent sensory neurons enter the dorsal root ganglion, and efferent motor neurons exit through the ventral root ganglion. The three layers of meninges also can be seen in this illustration.

➤ *What is the main function of the spinal cord? (p. 47)*

enhances the rate of transmission of neural information. We will discuss the reason myelinated neurons transmit messages faster than unmyelinated neurons in Chapter 4.

Spinal Reflexes

Remember Descartes' model of the reflex (**p. 5–6**). Although our brain controls most of our behavior, some reflexes occur without the intervention of the brain. In **spinal reflexes**, afferent sensory input enters the spinal cord and directly activates the appropriate efferent motor neuron.

Why are spinal reflexes important? Spinal reflexes allow rapid reactions to environmental events, when minimal analysis of information is sufficient to produce an appropriate response. Further responses, or adjustments to the initial response, can occur later, after information has been processed by higher brain structures. Spinal reflexes also play an important role in posture and postural adjustments.

One example of a spinal reflex is the withdrawal reflex, which causes the rapid removal of a limb from the source of stimulation. This is what happens when you jerk your hand away from a hot stove. The patellar reflex is another example of a spinal reflex. To visualize the patellar reflex, imagine being in your doctor's office for a physical exam. The doctor takes out a rubber mallet and strikes you below the kneecap (refer to **Figure 2.16**). Without conscious effort, you extend your leg. Your leg extension is entirely reflexive; that is, the receptors in the extensor muscle of the leg react to the sudden stretching that occurs when the tendon below your kneecap is stimulated by a blow from the mallet. The sensory message is carried to the spinal cord by sensory neurons that synapse on the motor neurons in the spinal cord that control the same leg extensor muscle. Sudden stretching of this muscle, by the hammer in this case, causes your leg to extend. The patellar reflex plays an important role in maintaining posture and allowing you to stay upright. It also can be used to reveal some motor disorders. For example, a hyperactive patellar reflex would suggest spasticity, a motor disorder characterized by a slow, limited range of movement.

Penile erection is another example of a spinal reflex. Penile erection is a reflex involving the lower part of the spinal cord. Stimulation by a touch to the genitals can elicit an erection in men with injuries to the upper part of the spinal cord, but not in men with injuries to the lower spinal cord.

spinal reflex A reflex in which afferent sensory input enters the spinal cord and then directly innervates an efferent motor neuron.

Before You Go On

What is the difference between white matter and gray matter in the spinal cord? What function does each type perform?

Describe a spinal reflex. What benefit is provided by the spinal reflex bypassing the brain?

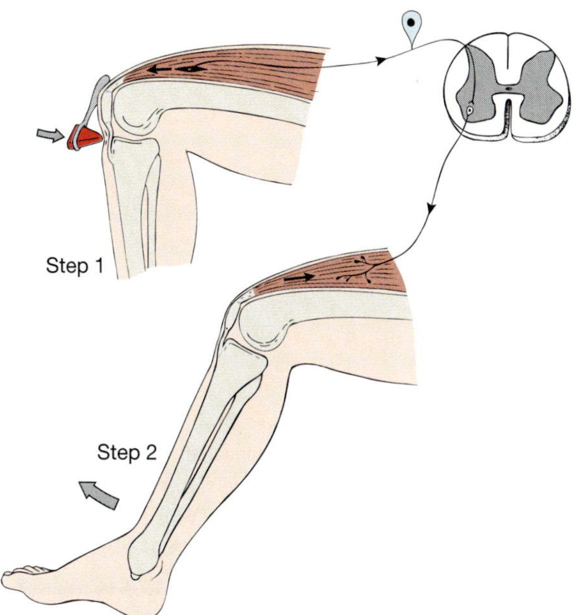

Figure 2.16 The patellar or knee-jerk reflex. When your doctor strikes your knee (Step 1), a sensory neuron is activated that carries the message to the spinal cord. The sensory nerve synapses on a motor neuron in the spinal cord. Activation of the motor neuron carries the message to a muscle in your thigh. Contraction of this muscle causes you to extend your leg (Step 2).

➤ *Describe how the knee-jerk reflex illustrates your body's reaction to sensory information. (p. 48)*

Section Review

- The spinal cord carries sensory input to the brain and motor input away from the brain. The spinal cord consists of 31 sets of spinal nerves.
- The spinal cord is composed of gray matter, or neural cell bodies, and white matter, or axons. The axons appear white because they are myelinated.
- Spinal reflexes allow sensory input to directly affect motor neurons without entering the brain for processing.
- Examples of spinal reflexes are the withdrawal reflex, the patellar (knee-jerk) reflex, and penile erection.

The Central Nervous System: Functions of the Brain

The brain serves a critical role in our interaction with the environment. We can think of the brain as having three main functions. Recall our four-stage model of the behavioral functions of the nervous system described earlier in the chapter (refer to **Figure 2.2**). The detection of events (Stage 1) is the function of the peripheral nervous system. After the peripheral nervous system detects sensory input, the information is sent to specific parts of the brain for analysis (Stage 2).

The significance of an event to you depends not only on your brain's recognition of the event's physical characteristics, but also on your ability to recall past experiences related to the event and on the detection of the emotional and motivational states that exist when the present event is experienced. For example, suppose a friend asks you to go to John Moore's latest match. The question is detected by the ear and transmitted to the brain. Your brain recognizes the meaning of the question, then allows you to remember previous trips to the fights, and considers these memories along with information about whether you feel like going today (your emotional and motivational states).

This analysis yields a decision (Stage 3) to go or not go to the bout. After the brain decides how to respond to a specific sensory input, it then executes the decision (Stage 4) by controlling the specific muscles that will produce the desired motor response (which is formation by the mouth of the word *yes* or *no* and activation of the vocal cords).

Our discussion thus far of the brain's main functions by no means describes all that the brain does. Some activities, such as dreaming and remembering, do not always occur in response to sensory input, and may or may not lead to a motor response. Think about it (there's another brain function!)—the brain is a complex, fascinating organ that has inspired entire disciplines and multitudes of books; throughout this one we will discuss its various functions, some more easily explained than others.

One or Three Brains

Recall our discussion in Chapter 1 of cephalization or the continuing fusion of ganglion pairs to form an increasingly larger and more complex brain. Paul MacLean (1977) proposed that humans actually have three interconnected brains (see **Figure 2.17**). Each of the brains evolved at different times and served different functions in our evolutionary past. According to MacLean, an ancient reptile brain can be found deep within our present brain. (Evolutionary theorists maintain that mammals arose from a certain line of ancient reptiles.) This reptilian brain contains behavioral programs that are not modified by experience and that elicit rigid, instinctive reactions such as flinching when you are startled.

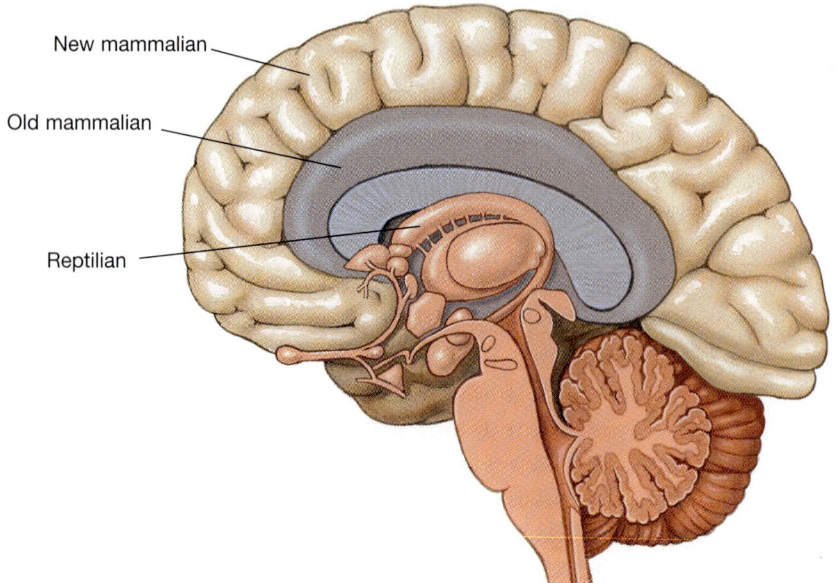

Figure 2.17 Three brains in one. The reptilian brain, old mammalian brain, and new mammalian brain are shown.
➤ *How do you control your old mammalian and reptilian brains? (pp. 49–50)*

An old mammalian brain, first seen in mammals such as cats, rats, and rabbits, surrounds the reptilian brain. This old mammalian brain is survival oriented. The actions controlled by this part of the brain include feeding, fighting, fleeing, and sexual behavior.

Above these two primitive brains is the new mammalian brain, or neocortex (neo = new). According to MacLean, this most recent mammalian brain is responsible for our intelligence and creativity.

MacLean called the old mammalian brain a "sleeping animal," suggesting that at times "the primitive needs of mice may mess up the rational plans of man and woman." Basically, MacLean argued that primitive instincts and emotions lie just below our efforts to behave rationally. Although the neocortex allows humans to engage in higher mental processes, the older two parts of the brain can also exert some control over behavior. Thus, we may often be affected by our primitive brains despite our attempts to control them. For example, although boxing requires skill and intellect, it is for the most part a behavior controlled by instinct.

Now that we have covered the major functions of the brain, let's move on to discuss the brain's structure and how its various components work together to analyze and decide. The three major divisions of the brain are the hindbrain, the midbrain, and the forebrain, each of which includes a number of important structures (see **Table 2.2**). The hindbrain and midbrain constitute the reptilian brain, and the forebrain contains both the old and the new mammalian brains.

Before You Go On

What are the brain's most important functions? Give an example of each.

Section Review

- The primary functions of the brain are to store information, to process and interpret sensory messages, and to control motor functioning.
- MacLean proposed that humans have three interconnected brains: the reptilian brain, the old mammalian brain, and the new mammalian brain.

The Central Nervous System: The Hindbrain and the Midbrain

Hindbrain

Just above the spinal cord is the **hindbrain**, which contains four important structures: the medulla oblongata, the pons, the cerebellum, and the raphe system (see **Figure 2.18**).

The **medulla oblongata**, whose name means "oblong marrow," is located rostral to the spinal cord. This vital

hindbrain The division of the brain just above the spinal cord that contains the medulla oblongata, the pons, the cerebellum, and the raphe system.

medulla oblongata Hindbrain structure located just rostral to the spinal cord that controls functions such as respiration and heart rate that are essential to life.

structure controls functions essential to life, such as respiration and heart rate. It also stimulates reflexive responses (via cranial nerves) such as coughing, sneezing, vomiting, and salivation. Information from the cranial nerves is received in the medulla oblongata and then relayed to higher structures, such as the thalamus. Sensory information from the spinal cord is also relayed through the medulla oblongata, and motor information passes back through this area on its way to the spinal cord. The result of damage to the medulla oblongata is death, due to the loss of the ability to activate vital internal organs. President Kennedy died as the result of massive damage to this area of the brain caused by the invasive trauma of a gun shot wound to the back of his head.

The **pons** is superior to the medulla. Pons is the Latin word for bridge, and many neurons pass through the pons on their way from the sensory receptors via cranial nerves and the spinal cord and from the areas of the cerebral cortex controlling

pons Hindbrain structure located superior to the medulla that relays sensory information to the cerebellum and thalamus.

Table 2.2 ■ Major Structures of the Human Brain and Their Primary Functions

Structure	Major Function
Hindbrain	
Cerebellum	Coordinates complex motor responses
Medulla oblongata	Controls essential functions; relays sensory information to thalamus
Pons	Relays sensory information to cerebellum and thalamus
Raphe system	Controls sleep-wake cycle
Midbrain	
Tectum	Controls simple reflexes and orients eye and ear movements
Inferior colliculi	Relays auditory information
Superior colliculi	Relays visual information
Tegmentum	
Red nucleus	Controls basic body and limb movements
Reticular formation	Controls arousal and consciousness
Substantia nigra	Integrates voluntary movements
Forebrain	
Basal ganglia	Integrates voluntary movement; maintains posture and muscle tone
Caudate nucleus	
Globus pallidus	
Putamen	
Cerebral cortex	Processes sensory information;
Frontal lobe	controls thinking and decision
Occipital lobe	making; stores and retrieves
Parietal lobe	memory; initiates motor responses
Temporal lobe	
Hypothalamus	Detects need states; controls pituitary hormone production and release
Limbic system	
Amygdala	Controls anger and fear
Cingulate gyrus	Elicits positive and negative emotional responses
Hippocampus	Stores and retrieves memory
Thalamus	Relays information from sensory receptors to cerebral cortex

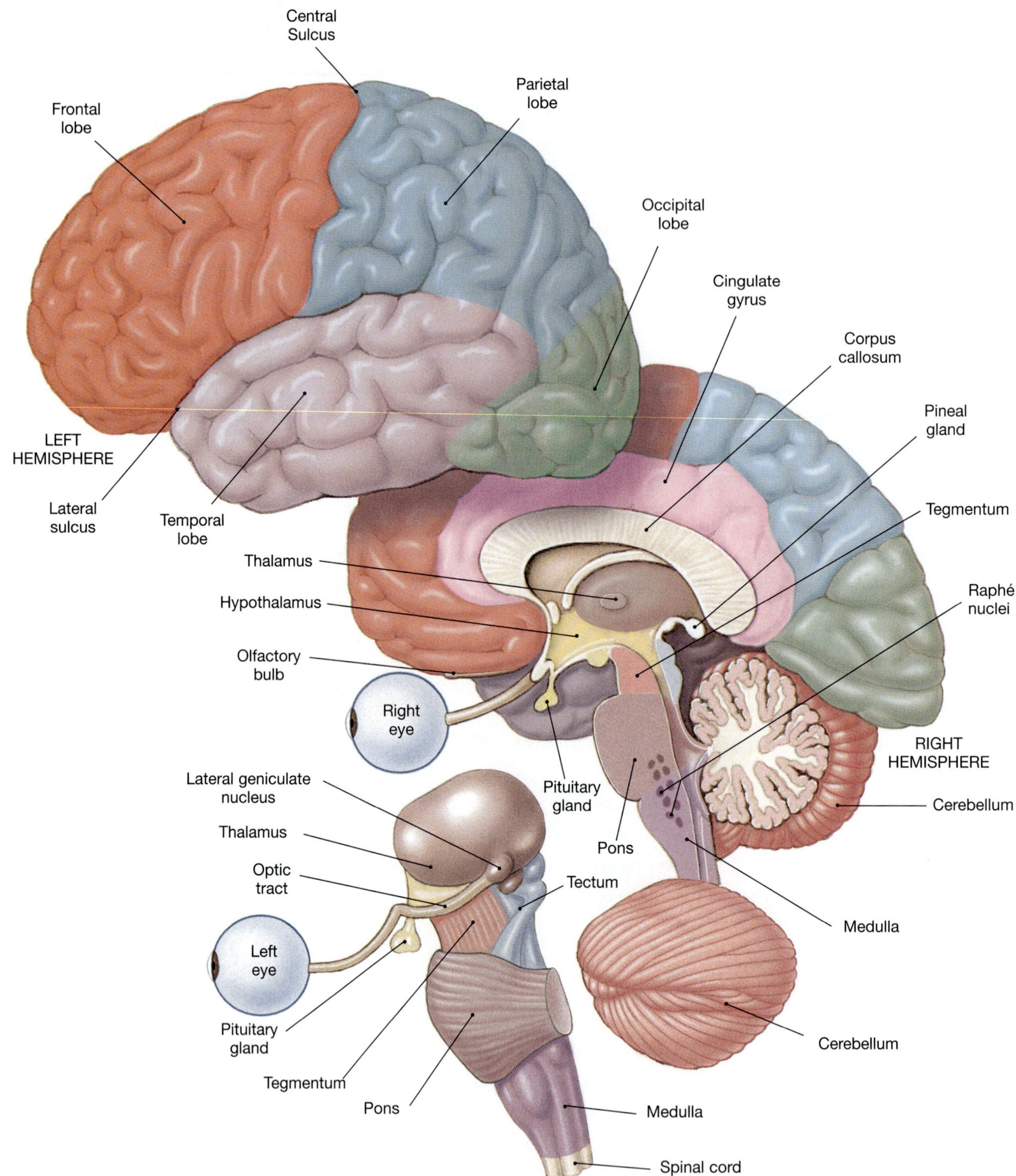

Figure 2.18 The hindbrain structures. Key structures in the hindbrain are medulla, pons, cerebellum, and the raphe system. Other structures seen are part of the spinal cord, midbrain, thalamus, hypothalamus, corpus callosum, and cerebral cortex.

➤ *Describe the hindbrain's location in relation to the spinal cord and the midbrain using the anatomical directions you learned earlier in the chapter. What deficits would be seen following damage to the hindbrain? (p. 50–53)*

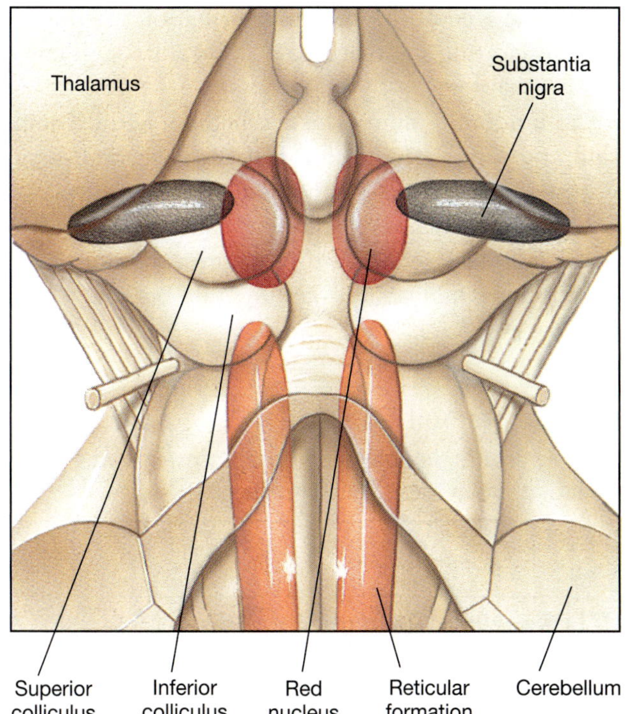

Figure 2.19 The midbrain. Key structures in the tectum (the inferior colliculus, the superior colliculus) and tegmentum (the red nucleus, the reticular formation, the substantia nigra).
➤ *What is the function of the reticular formation? (p. 53)*

movement to the cerebellum. Additional neurons travel through the pons to relay information related to arousal, sleep, and dreaming to higher brain structures, such as the thalamus.

The **cerebellum**, meaning "little brain" in Latin, is involved in the development and coordination of movement (Kolb & Whishaw, 1996). This structure provides information relating to body and limb position. It receives information about intended movement from other brain structures and about actual motor responses from sense organs. The cerebellum compares actual and intended movements and makes adjustments to correct errors in movements. Through the influence of the cerebellum, awkward movements become fluid, skilled actions. We will have much more to say about the important role that the cerebellum plays in movement in Chapter 8 and in motor learning in Chapter 14.

The **raphé system** is a group of nuclei (sing. nucleus) that is located along the midline of the hindbrain between the medulla and the midbrain. As we discussed on **p. 42**, in addition to being the name for the part of the cell containing DNA, a nucleus can also refer to a group of cell bodies in the central nervous system that have a common function (not to be confused with individual cell nuclei!). The raphe system plays a crucial role in the sleep-wake cycle (Lovick, 1997). We will look more closely at the raphe system's role in sleep-wake cycles in Chapter 9.

Before You Go On

Explain this statement: "A person would probably survive considerable damage to the cerebral cortex, but could not survive extensive damage to the medulla oblongata."

Describe how the cerebellum coordinates activity with the sensory receptors and with other brain structures. Why is this coordination important?

Midbrain

Located above the pons, the **midbrain** has two parts: the tectum and the tegmentum (see **Table 2.2** and **Figures 2.18** and **2.19**). The **tectum** contains neurons that relay visual and auditory information and control simple reflexes such as blinking. Visual information is relayed through the **superior colliculi** of the tectum, and auditory information is relayed through the **inferior colliculi**. The tectum also controls eye and ear movements that orient an animal to external stimuli. The **tegmentum** contains three main structures: the **substantia nigra** and the **red nucleus**, which are important parts of the motor system, and the **reticular formation**. The substantia nigra is involved in the inte-

cerebellum Hindbrain structure located posterior to the medulla that develops and coordinates complex movement.

raphé system A group of nuclei located along the midline of the hindbrain between the medulla and midbrain that controls the sleep-wake cycle.

midbrain A division of the central nervous system that contains the tectum and the tegmentum.

tectum Structure in the midbrain that controls simple reflexes and orients eye and ear movements.

superior colliculi Structure in the tectum that relays visual information.

inferior colliculi Structure in the tectum that relays auditory information.

tegmentum Division of the midbrain that contains the substantia nigra, the red nucleus, and the reticular formation.

substantia nigra Structure in the tegmentum that is involved in the integration of voluntary movements.

red nucleus Structure in the tegmentum that controls basic body and limb movements.

reticular formation Network of neurons that controls arousal and consciousness.

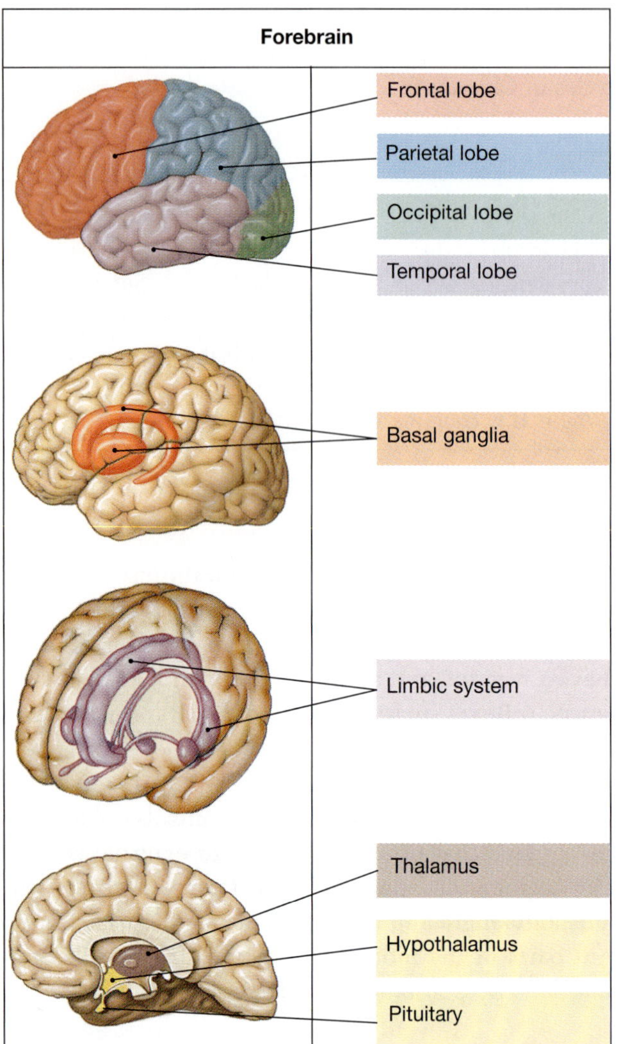

Figure 2.20 Major structures of the forebrain. The location of the thalamus, the hypothalamus, the pituitary, the limbic system, the basal ganglia, and the cerebral cortex.

➤ *What types of messages does the thalamus transmit? (p. 55)*

gration of voluntary movements, such as driving to John Moore's fight, and the red nucleus is involved in controlling basic body movements, such as John's postural adjustments in the chair at his corner of the ring, and corresponding limb movements. The reticular formation (sometimes called the reticular activating system) is a diffuse, interconnected network of neurons that begins in the hindbrain and extends through the midbrain, and then continues into higher brain structures. It maintains consciousness and plays an important role in arousal (Steriade, 1996). The role of the reticular formation in controlling consciousness and arousal will be addressed more fully in Chapter 9.

The hindbrain, minus the cerebellum, and the midbrain are often referred to together as the brainstem, because these structures contain all of the connections between the spinal cord and cerebral cortex (refer to **Figure 2.18**). These structures also form the stem from which the two hemispheres of the brain branch.

Before You Go On

What structures are included in the brainstem? Why do scientists group these structures together?

Section Review

- The three major divisions of the brain are the hindbrain, the midbrain, and the forebrain.
- The hindbrain contains the medulla oblongata, the pons, the cerebellum, and the raphé system.
- The medulla oblongata controls breathing and heart rate and stimulates basic reflexive responses.
- The pons brings information to the cerebellum and relays messages to higher brain structures.
- The cerebellum develops and coordinates complex movements.
- The raphe nuclei influences sleep-wake cycles.
- The midbrain contains the tectum and tegmentum.
- The tectum, which includes the superior colliculus and the inferior colliculus, receives and relays visual and auditory information and controls simple reflexes.
- The tegmentum includes the substantia nigra, the red nucleus, and the reticular formation.
- The substantia nigra is involved in integrating voluntary motor movements.
- The red nucleus controls basic body and limb movements.
- The reticular formation, which connects with higher brain structures, maintains consciousness and produces arousal.

The Central Nervous System: The Forebrain

The **forebrain** is the final major division of the brain, located rostral to and surrounding the midbrain. Much of what you would see if the top of your skull were removed is the cerebral cortex, one of the five structures of the forebrain; the other four are the thalamus, the hypothalamus, the limbic system, and the basal ganglia (refer to **Table 2.2** and **Figure 2.20**).

forebrain The division of the brain containing the basal ganglia, the cerebral cortex, the hypothalamus, the limbic system, and the thalamus.

Thalamus

The **thalamus** is the main relay station for most sensory messages—visual, auditory, somatosensory, gustatory—(refer to **Figures 2.18**, **2.19**, **2.20**, and **2.21**). This structure receives information from sensory receptors in the peripheral nervous system and transmits this information to the appropriate higher brain structures for analysis. Some of the neurons in the thalamus receive information from specific sensory receptors, via the medulla and pons. The thalamus is made up of a number of nuclei, and different sensory receptors carry information to different nuclei within the thalamus. The nuclei in the thalamus that receive information from a specific sensory receptor connect to the sensory areas of the cerebral cortex that recognize that sensory message.

Consider the following example. John Moore hears the bell ending the third round. The sensory receptors in John's auditory system detect the ringing. This message is sent through the hindbrain and midbrain structures to the medial geniculate nucleus of the thalamus, which transmits the neural record of the bell ring to the area of the cortex that can recognize the meaning of the sound and motivate John to cease trouncing his opponent. If the stimulation were visual instead of auditory (e.g., the referee waved a flag), the sensory receptors in the visual system would send the message to the lateral geniculate nucleus of the thalamus, which would relay the information to a different part of the cortex. As we will see shortly, each sensory modality is understood by a different brain structure. Of the sensory modalities, only the olfactory system is not connected to the thalamus, a fact that we will explore in greater detail in Chapter 7.

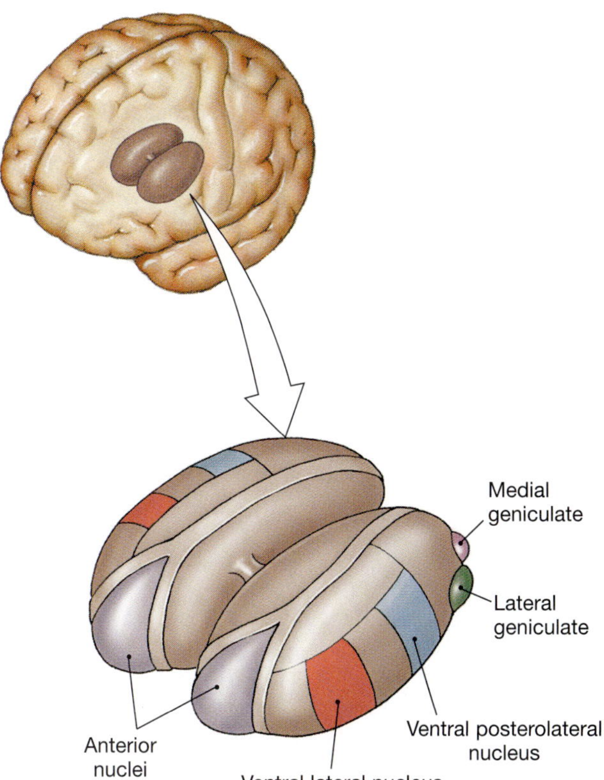

Figure 2.21 The thalamus. Neural messages about visual stimuli travel to the lateral geniculate nuclei, about auditory stimuli to the medial geniculate nuclei, about somatosensory stimuli to the ventral posterolateral nuclei, and about the state of the motor system to the ventrolateral nuclei. The anterior nuclei is concerned with emotions and memory.

➤ *Describe the significance of the structure of the thalamus to Muller's doctrine of specific nerve energies. (p. 6, 55)*

As indicated previously, some neurons in the thalamus send sensory messages to the appropriate higher cortical structures. Other neurons in the thalamus connect to cortical areas of the brain not related to reception of sensory information. For example, the ventral lateral nucleus of the thalamus receives information from the cerebellum. The thalamus relays this information to the motor cortex to allow the brain to determine whether its decision, or intended movement, corresponds to the actual movement executed. This information allows the cortex to make adjustments to ensure that the message from the motor cortex is executed smoothly by the motor neurons of the peripheral nervous system. For example, the motor cortex might execute a message for you to reach out and grab your pen from the top of your desk, but your hand starts heading away from the pen. Your cerebellum recognizes that your movement is off target and sends a message to your motor cortex via the thalamus so that you change the course of your movement and get the pen. The thalamus is also an important area for processing certain pain sensations (Parrent et al., 1992) and organizing the sleep-wake cycle (McCormick & Bal, 1994).

Hypothalamus

The **hypothalamus** is about the size of a peanut and makes up only .3 percent of the brain (Hoffman & Swaab, 1994). Yet, it has sensors capable of detecting internal conditions throughout the body (e.g., glucose level, testosterone level, or estrogen level) that are used as internal stimuli for "basic" motives, such as hunger or

---

thalamus Structure in the forebrain that relays information from the sensory receptors to the cerebral cortex.

hypothalamus Structure in the forebrain that detects need states and controls pituitary hormone production and release.

sex (Siddiqui & Shah, 1997; refer to **Figures 2.20** and **2.22**). Stimulation of specific neurons in the hypothalamus by these internal states leads to the motivation to respond to those needs.

The following example illustrates the influence of the hypothalamus on behavior. You walk by a bakery and smell bread baking. The smell of the bread makes you hungry, and you go inside the bakery and buy several loaves of bread. You eat half a loaf of bread immediately. Why did you feel hungry when you smelled the bread? Generally, smelling food stimulates the lateral part of the hypothalamus. Stimulation of the lateral hypothalamus produces sensations of hunger and motivates eating (Klein, 1982). Chapter 10 discusses further the important influence that the hypothalamus plays in eating, and the role of the hypothalamus in sexual behavior is described in Chapter 11.

The hypothalamus has a second important function: it controls the production and release of pituitary hormones from the **pituitary gland**, located just ventral to the hypothalamus. The pituitary gland has two parts: the anterior pituitary and the posterior pituitary. The hypothalamus influences the **anterior pituitary gland** through an arterial capillary link, called the **hypophyseal portal system** (see **Figure 2.22**). (A *portal system* is a vessel that connects two capillary beds.) Hormones produced in the hypothalamus are released into the hypophyseal portal system and travel to the anterior pituitary. These hormones, appropriately called *releasing hormones*, act on the

pituitary gland A gland located just ventral to the hypothalamus; it is divided into two segments: the anterior pituitary gland and the posterior pituitary gland.

anterior pituitary gland The part of the pituitary that manufactures and secretes releasing hormones.

hypophyseal portal system The arterial capillary link from the hypothalamus to the anterior pituitary gland.

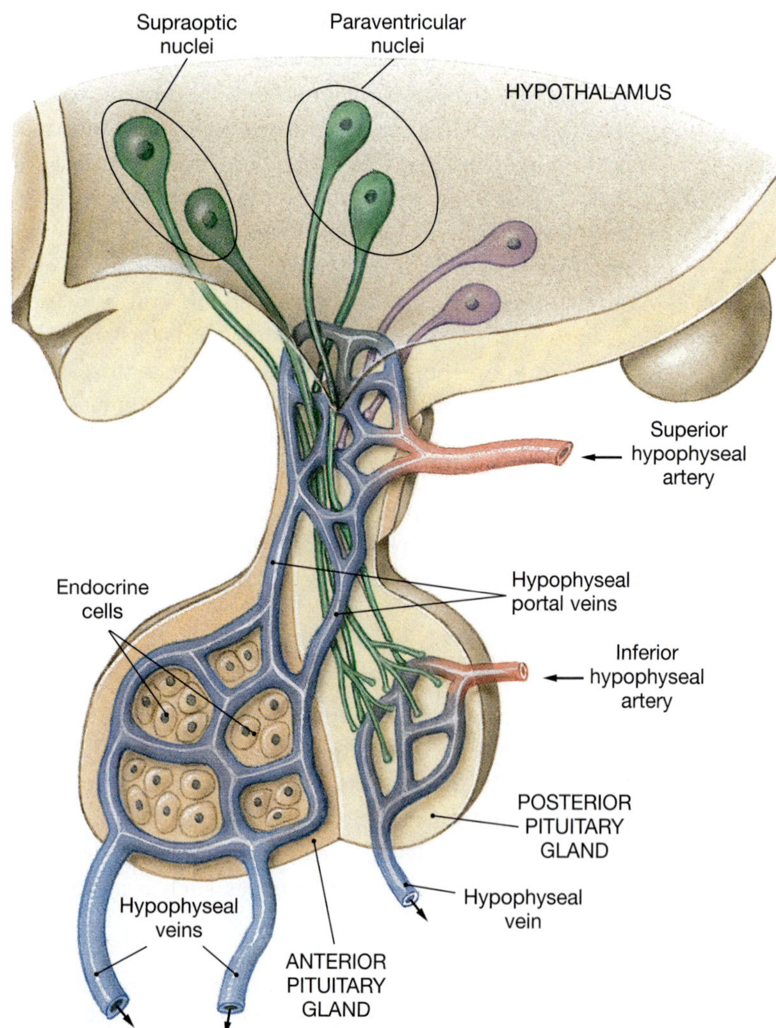

Figure 2.22 Hypothalamus-pituitary connection. The hypothalamus and anterior pituitary are linked by the hypophyseal portal system, and the posterior pituitary are axons of the supraoptic and paraventricular nuclei of the hypothalamus.

➤ *What is the significance of the connection between the hypothalamus and pituitary gland? (pp. 56–57)* anterior pituitary to stimulate the production and release of six anterior pituitary gland hormones.

The hypothalamus influences the **posterior pituitary gland** more directly. The posterior pituitary is actually an extension of the hypothalamus, consisting of axons of the supraoptic and paraventricular nuclei of the hypothalamus (see **Figure 2.22**). The posterior pituitary is also called the neurohypophysis, indicating that it is a part of the nervous system. (The anterior pituitary is part of the endocrine system, but is affected by hormones released by the hypothalamus.) The two posterior pituitary hormones, oxytocin and antidiuretic hormone, are produced in the aforementioned supraoptic and paraventricular nuclei of the hypothalamus and released into the capillaries that surround the posterior pituitary. As you will learn in Chapter 4, oxytocin stimulates labor contraction in the uterus and milk secretion by the mammary glands or contractions by the prostate gland, and antidiuretic hormone (ADH) stimulates reabsorption of water by the kidneys and elevates blood volume and pressure.

Limbic System

Athletes like John Moore speak of the thrill of victory and the agony of defeat. The emotional impact of these two experiences is related to activity in the **limbic system**. Other emotions, such as anger, frustration, and fear, are also governed by limbic system structures. The limbic system is not a single brain structure but a group of structures surrounding the brainstem. Some important limbic system structures include the amygdala, the cingulate gyrus, and the hippocampus (see **Figure 2.23**).

The **amygdala**, which is located at the base of the temporal lobe, plays a central role in the experience of the emotions of anger and fear (Adamec, 1991; Koolhaas et al., 1990). Destruction of the amygdala can produce either heightened defensiveness or extreme passivity, depending on the particular part of the amygdala that is destroyed. This observation indicates that certain parts of the amygdala elicits anger or fear, whereas other sections inhibit these emotions.

The **cingulate gyrus** also plays a significant role in the control of emotional behavior (refer to **Figure 2.23**). It receives input from many structures, including the decision-making centers of the cerebral cortex, the limbic system structures that elicit specific emotions, and the neural systems controlling movement. Activity in the cingulate gyrus elicits positive or negative emotional responses and plays an important role in attention. Damage to cingulate gyrus causes a person to stop talking and walking (Amyes & Nielsen, 1955).

The **hippocampus** plays an important role in memory processes (see **Figure 2.23**; Gluck & Myers, 1995; Zola-Morgan & Squire, 1993). Hippocampal damage is linked to an inability to store and later recall previously acquired information. For example, John Moore might forget who his opponent was last night due to damage to his hippocampus suffered in prior fights. Chapter 14 describes in detail the role of the hippocampus in memory storage and retrieval.

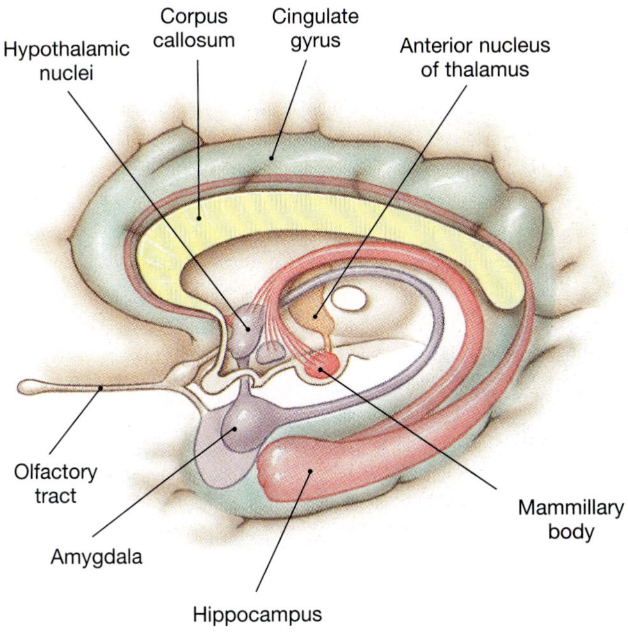

Figure 2.23 The limbic system. The limbic system includes the amygdala, the cingulate gyrus, and the hippocampus.

➤ *Why did MacLean refer to the limbic system as the old mammalian brain? (p. 50)*

posterior pituitary gland The part of the pituitary gland, considered an extension of the hypothalamus, that produces and releases oxytocin and antidiuretic hormone; also called the neurohypophysis.

limbic system The part of the forebrain, consisting of a group of structures surrounding the brainstem, that controls emotional expression and the storage and retrieval of memories.

amygdala A structure in the limbic system located at the base of the temporal lobe that controls the emotions of anger and fear.

cingulate gyrus A structure in the limbic system involved in positive and negative emotional response.

hippocampus A structure in the limbic system that controls memory storage and retrieval.

Before You Go On

Explain the role of the thalamus in transmitting visual signals.

Why would obesity researchers be interested in studying the functions of the hypothalamus?

Why would damage to the cingulate gyrus stop a person from talking or walking?

Basal Ganglia

The **basal ganglia** consists of three large nuclei: the caudate nucleus, the putamen, and the globus pallidus (refer to **Figure 2.24**). This area of the brain plays a crucial role in integrating voluntary movements and maintaining posture and muscle tone. The basal ganglia receive input from the substantia nigra and the cerebral cortex and send messages to the midbrain and cerebral cortex. Degeneration of the neurons with dopamine as the neurotransmitter that link the substantia nigra to the basal ganglia leads to Parkinson's disease, which is characterized by difficulty integrating movement, rigidity, and tremors at rest. Damage to this fiber tract system, like that described in the chapter opening vignette, or that of real-life boxers like Muhammed Ali, produces Parkinson's-like symptoms (Parkinson's disease represents degeneration of the neurons in this tract due to organic causes, whereas the death of neurons in Muhammed Ali was the result of repeated blows to his head. Thus, Muhammed Ali has parkinsonian symptoms). By contrast, damage to the caudate nucleus and putamen leads to Huntington's disease. Recall from Chapter 1 that Huntington's disease is characterized by uncontrollable, jerky limb movements. These movements appear to be pieces of normally purposeful actions.

basal ganglia A structure in the forebrain that integrates voluntary movement, consisting of three nuclei: the caudate nucleus, the putamen, and the globus pallidus.

Before You Go On

What would be the effects of a lack of input from the substantia nigra to the basal ganglia?

Describe the results of damage to the connections between the basal ganglia and the substantia nigra of the tegmentum.

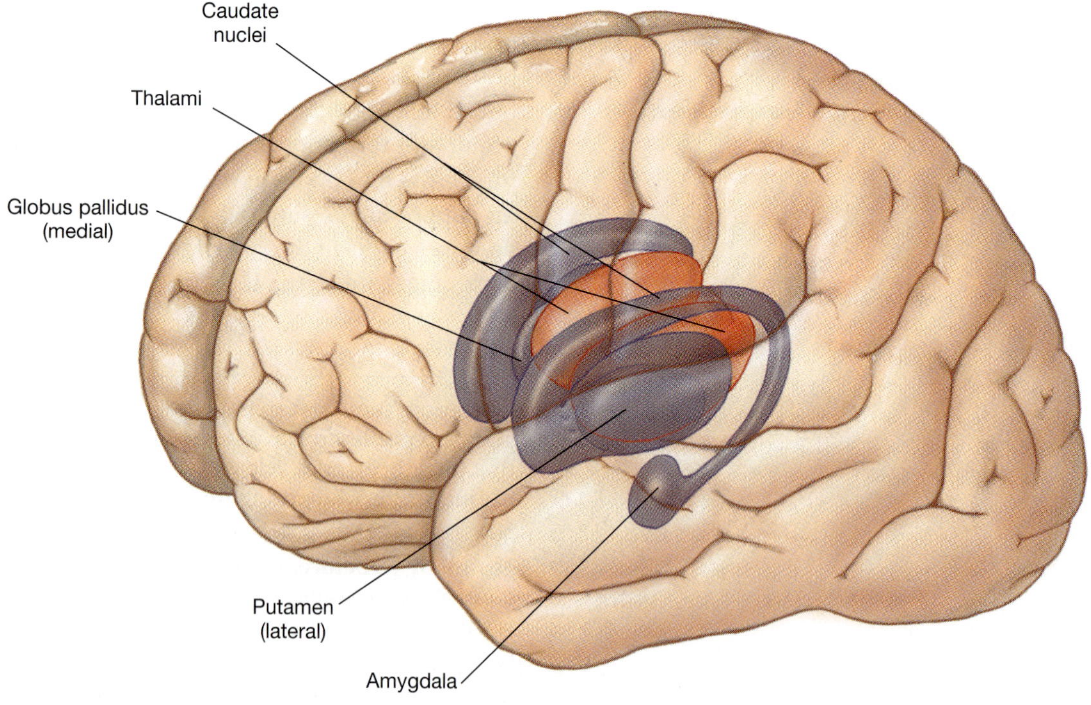

Figure 2.24 The basal ganglia. The basal ganglia consists of three large nuclei—the caudate nucleus, putamen, and the globus pallidus—and has widespread connections to the cerebral cortex and midbrain.

From Nieuwenhuys et al., 1988.

➤ *How is the basal ganglia involved in Parkinson's disease and Huntington's disease? (p. 58)*

Cerebral Cortex

The **cerebral cortex** is the outer layer of the brain that is responsible for higher mental processes (see **Figures 2.18** and **1.4**). The cerebral cortex is divided into sensory, motor, and association areas. Certain areas of the cerebral cortex are responsible for the perception of sensory events (sensory detection areas). Other structures within the cerebral cortex control motor movements (motor execution areas). Still other areas allow us to think, reason, and communicate (analysis and decision areas).

The cerebral cortex contains up to six layers of cell bodies that run parallel to its surface. Some regions of the cerebral cortex contain six layers, others contain fewer than six and still others comprise only a single layer. The layers are separated by fibers that come to or from the cell bodies. The thickness of each layer is determined by the function of that region of the cerebral cortex. For example, the thickness of cortical layers III and IV is greatest in the motor cortex (where the large pyramidas cells originate). By contrast, the thickness of cortical layer IV is greatest in the primary sensory areas for vision, audition, taste, and somatosenses (where the axons from sensory nuclei in the thalamus are received).

The cerebral cortex consists of the right and the left hemispheres, which are separated by the **longitudinal fissure** (see **Figure 2.25**). The two hemispheres are connected by axons that cross over and synapse with neurons in the other hemisphere. The axons connecting the two hemispheres are grouped into **cerebral commissures**, the largest of which is the **corpus callosum**.

Recall from the discussion of the evolution of the vertebrate brain (Chapter 1) that the left hemisphere of the cerebral cortex controls motor responses on the right side of the body and the right hemisphere controls motor movement in the left side of the body, an arrangement known as **contralateral control**. (Chapter 8 will provide a more detailed discussion of the control of movement.) Considerable evidence indicates that, for most people, the left hemisphere has a greater role in verbal or language functions, whereas the right hemisphere has a greater influence on nonverbal, visual-spatial functions (Gazzaniga & LeDoux, 1978; Sperry, 1982). This differentiation or **lateralization of function** between the two hemispheres has been referred to as *hemispheric asymmetries*. We will have much more to say about lateralization of function in Chapter 13.

Each hemisphere is divided into four lobes: occipital, temporal, parietal, and frontal (see **Figure 2.18**). As its name implies, the frontal lobe is the most anterior of the four lobes of the cerebral hemisphere. The parietal lobe is dorsal and posterior to the frontal lobe. The temporal lobe is lateral, or more to the side (picture where your temples are), and the occipital lobe is the most posterior of the four lobes. The lobes are divided by two deep grooves, or sulci (singular form is sulcus). The **lateral sulcus** separates the temporal lobe from the frontal and parietal lobes. The **central sulcus** is a vertical groove that separates the anterior

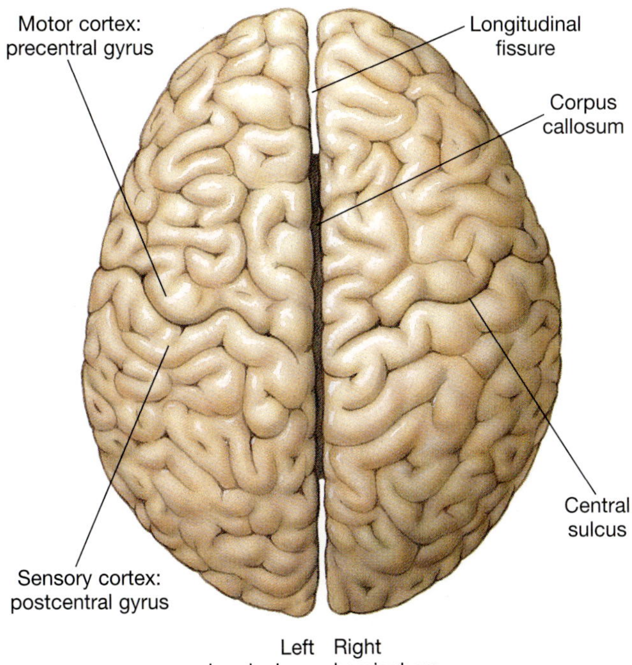

Figure 2.25 A dorsal view of the cerebral cortex. This illustration shows the two cerebral hemispheres separated by the longitudinal fissure and connected by the cerebral commissures (the largest of which is the corpus callosum).
➤ *What is lateralization of function? (p. 59)*

cerebral cortex A structure in the forebrain that processes sensory information, controls thinking and decision making, stores and retrieves memories, and initiates motor responses.

longitudinal fissure The deep groove that separates the right and left hemispheres.

cerebral commissures The fiber tracts that connect the two hemispheres of the brain.

corpus callosum The largest of the cerebral commissures.

contralateral control The process by which one side of the brain controls the movement on the opposite side of the body.

lateralization of function The differentiation of the functions of the two hemispheres of the brain.

lateral sulcus The deep groove that separates the temporal from the frontal and parietal lobes of the cerebral cortex.

central sulcus The deep groove that separates the anterior and posterior halves of the cerebral cortex.

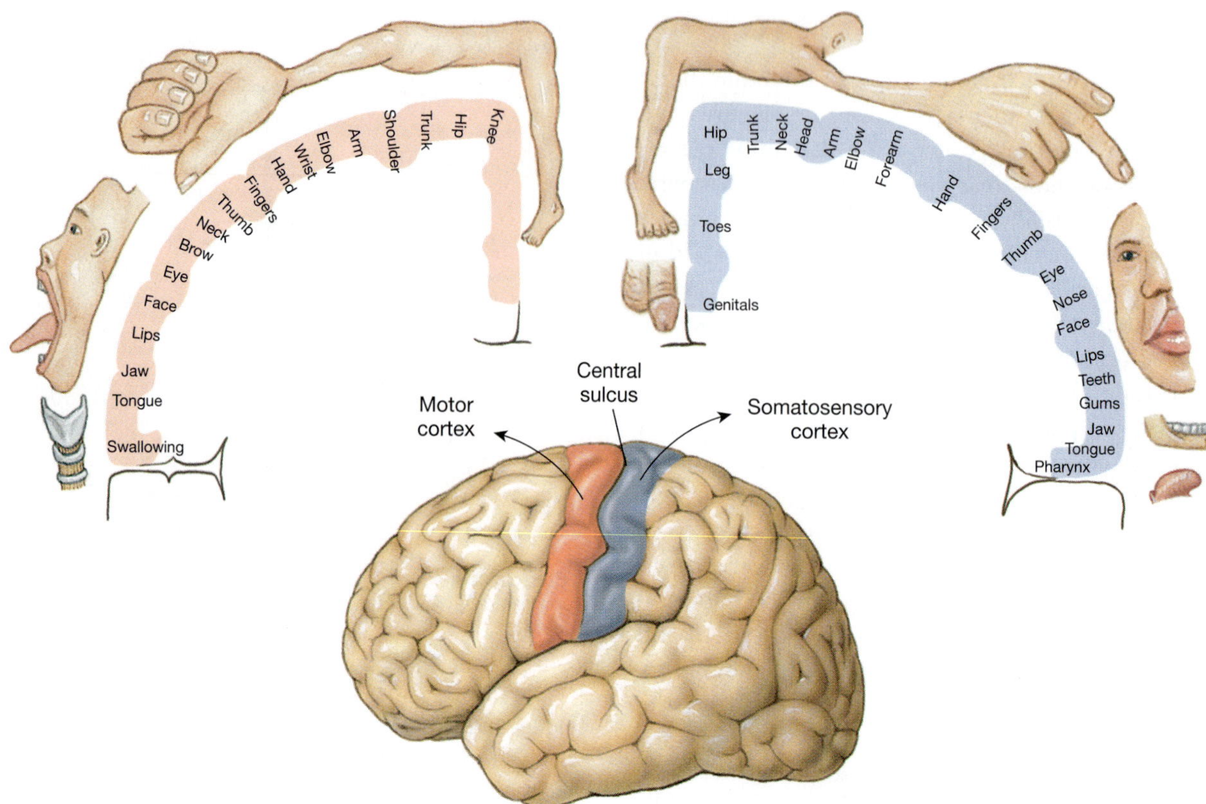

Figure 2.26 The sensory homunculus and the motor homunculus. The areas of the somatosensory cortex where sensory information from various parts of the body are received and the areas of the motor cortex that send messages to various muscles of the body are shown. Notice the unequal representation of the face, hands, and feet in both the motor cortex and somatosensory cortex.
➤ *Why is the face overrepresented in both the motor cortex and somatosensory cortex? (pp. 60–61)*

and posterior halves of the cerebral cortex. The cerebral cortex is very convoluted; the wrinkles of the cerebral cortex allow more surface area and a correspondingly greater number of neurons to carry out its functions.

Occipital Lobe. The primary function of the **occipital lobe** (see **Figure 2.18**) is the analysis of visual information. Information from the visual sensory receptors arrives at the **primary visual cortex** in the occipital lobe via pathways from the thalamus. Destruction of the primary visual cortex in both hemispheres will lead to cortical blindness (Aldrich et al., 1987). A person with cortical blindness would be able to see light but unable to recognize patterns of visual stimuli (for example, recognize that an object is a triangle) in that part of the occipital lobe that is damaged (for example, damage to the left occipital lobe would produce cortical blindness for visual stimuli in the right visual field).

Parietal Lobe. The **parietal lobe** is located between the central sulcus and the occipital lobe (see **Figure 2.18**). The anterior portion of the parietal lobe consists of the **somatosensory cortex**. Sensory information about touch, pain, pressure, temperature, and body position is analyzed in this area of the parietal lobe. The posterior portion of the parietal lobe receives visual information from the occipital lobe and is involved in spatial perception.

The neurons of the somatosensory cortex are organized in such a way that the body is represented in an orderly, but upside-down fashion; that is, information from the toes is transmitted to the top of the parietal lobe, whereas sensory information from the mouth travels to the bottom of the lobe (see **Figure 2.26**). Sensory infor-

occipital lobe The lobe located in the posterior most part of the cerebral cortex responsible for the analysis of visual stimuli.

primary visual cortex Area in the occipital lobe that receives visual information from the thalamus.

parietal lobe The lobe in the cerebral cortex located between the central sulcus and the occipital lobe responsible for the analysis of somatosensory stimuli.

somatosensory cortex Area in the anterior part of the parietal lobe that receives information about touch, pain, pressure, temperature, and body position from the thalamus.

mation from the face and hands is overrepresented in the human somatosensory cortex, reflecting the relative significance of information coming from the facial area of the body. In humans, facial stimulation provides significant information. We can feel happy or sad depending on feedback provided by our facial muscles, which are differentially reactive to environmental circumstances. In other species, different parts of the body are overrepresented. Calford et al. (1985) found that bats, which use their feet to hang from trees, have a relatively greater area of the parietal lobes devoted to the representation of their feet.

Damage to the parietal lobe has several significant effects (Lynch, 1986). Individuals with parietal lobe damage often show clumsiness or neglect of the side of their body opposite the damage, experience difficulty identifying objects by touch, and cannot draw or follow maps, or describe how to get from one place to another.

Temporal Lobe. The **temporal lobe**, located below the lateral sulcus and bounded posteriorly by an imaginary line that forms the anterior border of the occipital lobe, contains the **primary auditory cortex** (see **Figure 2.18**). Information from the auditory receptors (the ears) is sent to the auditory cortex via the thalamus.

Destruction of the primary auditory cortex to both hemispheres leads to cortical deafness, which is an inability to recognize sounds (for example, the inability to recognize a baby's cry; Brookshire, 1997). Auditory messages are sent from the primary auditory cortex to an adjacent part of the left temporal lobe for analysis. If the auditory stimulus is verbal, it is interpreted, as we learned in Chapter 1, in Wernicke's area (refer to **Figure 1.4**). An individual will have difficulty comprehending language if this portion of the temporal lobe on the left hemisphere is damaged.

The visual recognition of objects is also a function of the temporal lobes, as is the processing of information from the vestibular organs of the inner ear about balance and equilibrium. The temporal lobe may also be involved in our emotional reaction to events. Klüver and Bucy (1939) observed that destruction of the temporal lobes, which included the amygdala located below the temporal lobes, caused male monkeys to exhibit dramatic behavioral changes, including placidity (even extremely annoying events elicited no reaction) and bizarre sexual behavior (attempts to mate with other species). Comparable results have been observed in human males who have sustained temporal lobe damage, which may be the cause of fetishes in human males (Terzian & DalleOre, 1955). We will have more to say about the role of the temporal lobes and the amygdala in the control of aggressive behavior in Chapter 12 and of sexual behavior in Chapter 11.

Frontal Lobe. The **frontal lobe** is the largest of the lobes of the cerebral cortex (see **Figure 2.18**). Just adjacent to the central sulcus in the frontal lobe is the **motor cortex**. The motor cortex controls voluntary body movements. Like the somatosensory cortex, the motor cortex is organized upside down (see **Figure 2.26**); that is, the top of the motor cortex controls movements in the feet and toes, whereas the facial muscles are controlled by the lower regions.

As with the somatosensory cortex, the facial muscles are overrepresented in motor cortex. The overrepresentation allows the production of the precise movements characteristic of different facial expressions as well as the intricate oral motor movements needed for speech.

The frontal lobe in the left hemisphere also contains Broca's area (see **Figure 1.4**). This area controls the programming and sequencing for speech production. As we mentioned in the previous chapter, damage to Broca's area leads to difficulty with expressive language.

The **prefrontal cortex**, the part of the frontal lobe that lies anterior to the motor cortex, controls complex intellectual functions such as the planning and sequencing of behavior (Winn, 1995). Damage to this area of the brain is associated with a diminished ability to effectively plan future action, such as the steps needed to assemble a swing set (Eslinger & Grattan, 1993).

Before You Go On

John Moore picks up a boxing glove with his right hand. Which side of his cerebral cortex is controlling this behavior?

Describe the connection between the primary visual cortex and the thalamus.

Why is sensory information from the face overrepresented in the human somatosensory cortex?

Distinguish the functions of Wernicke's area and Broca's area in the perception and production of language.

---

temporal lobe The lobe of the cerebral cortex that is ventral to the lateral sulcus and is responsible for the analysis of auditory stimuli.

primary auditory cortex Area in the temporal lobe that receives auditory information from the thalamus.

frontal lobe The lobe in the anterior most part of the cerebral cortex that is responsible for higher mental processes and the control of movement.

motor cortex Area in the frontal lobe that controls voluntary body movements.

prefrontal cortex Area in the anterior part of the frontal lobe that controls complex intellectual functions.

Section Review

- The forebrain contains the hypothalamus, thalamus, limbic system, basal ganglia, and cerebral cortex.
- The thalamus receives sensory messages and relays them to the proper part of the cortex for processing. It also works with the cerebellum to coordinate and evaluate movement.
- The hypothalamus detects need states, such as hunger and thirst. It also controls the production and release of pituitary hormones.
- The limbic system is a set of interconnected structures that control basic emotions, such as anger and fear, and the storage and retrieval of memories.
- The basal ganglia are a set of three nuclei that are important in integrating voluntary movements and maintaining posture and muscle tone.
- The cerebral cortex consists of two hemispheres, each of which is composed of four primary lobes. Each hemisphere controls motor functions on the opposite side of the body.
- The primary function of the occipital lobe is to analyze visual information.
- The somatosensory cortex, located in the parietal lobe, analyzes sensory information about touch, pain, pressure, temperature, and body position.
- The temporal lobe contains the primary auditory cortex, which receives auditory information from the ears via the thalamus. It also is involved in visual object recognition, in balance, and in emotional response.
- Wernicke's area, which is responsible for the interpretation of language, is located in the left temporal lobe.
- The frontal lobe contains the motor cortex, which controls voluntary body movement.
- Broca's area, which controls the programming and sequencing of speech production, is located in the left frontal lobe.

APPLICATION

The Tragedy of a Prefrontal Lobotomy

In the 1940s and 1950s, about 40,000 people in the United States underwent a surgical operation called a **prefrontal lobotomy** (Shutts, 1982). In this operation, intended to decrease episodes of aggressive behavior, the neural connections of the prefrontal cortex (the anterior part of the frontal lobe) were severed. One justification for conducting this operation was evidence indicating that damage to the prefrontal cortex in chimpanzees made them tamer without influencing sensory or motor functions (Fultan & Jacobsen, 1935). However, the early research that provided this evidence did not accurately measure prefrontal lobe functions, and many prefrontal lobotomies performed on humans were unsuccessful in producing the intended effect, produced unintended side effects, or both.

Subsequent research has shown that the prefrontal cortex plays a central role in thinking, memory, emotional expression, and social inhibition. Individuals with prefrontal damage often show the following effects: (1) apathy, (2) lack of motivation to plan and initiate behavior, (3) memory deficits, (4) distractibility, (5) lack of facial expressions, and (6) a blunted emotionality. Further, sometimes prefrontal damage causes a person to lose social inhibitions and thereby to act in a callous and rude fashion. Not all of the symptoms are present in all people with prefrontal damage, and the severity of symptoms varies among individuals.

Interestingly, patients with prefrontal lobotomies did not always show timidity or lessened hostility. In fact, in a rather ironic twist of fate, Egas Moniz, the originator of the operation, was rendered paraplegic by a gunshot wound from a patient who had undergone a prefrontal lobotomy. Because the amygdala lies directly below the frontal lobe, the occurrence of emotional changes following this operation likely depended on whether the functioning of the amygdala was affected by the surgery. Prefrontal lobotomy is rarely performed today, although it has not completely disappeared (Valenstein, 1986). ■

prefrontal lobotomy Surgical procedure that severs the connections of the prefrontal cortex to the rest of the brain.

You have now learned the major divisions of the brain and their functions. For a review of this material, please see **Table 2.2**. But how do we know that the occipital lobe is responsible for analysis of visual information? How do we know that the cerebellum coordinates complex motor responses? In the following section, we will discuss some of the research techniques used to help answer these questions.

Before You Go On

What actor made famous the following quotation: "I'd rather have a bottle in front of me than a frontal (sic) lobotomy"?

For what reason might a prefrontal lobotomy be performed today?

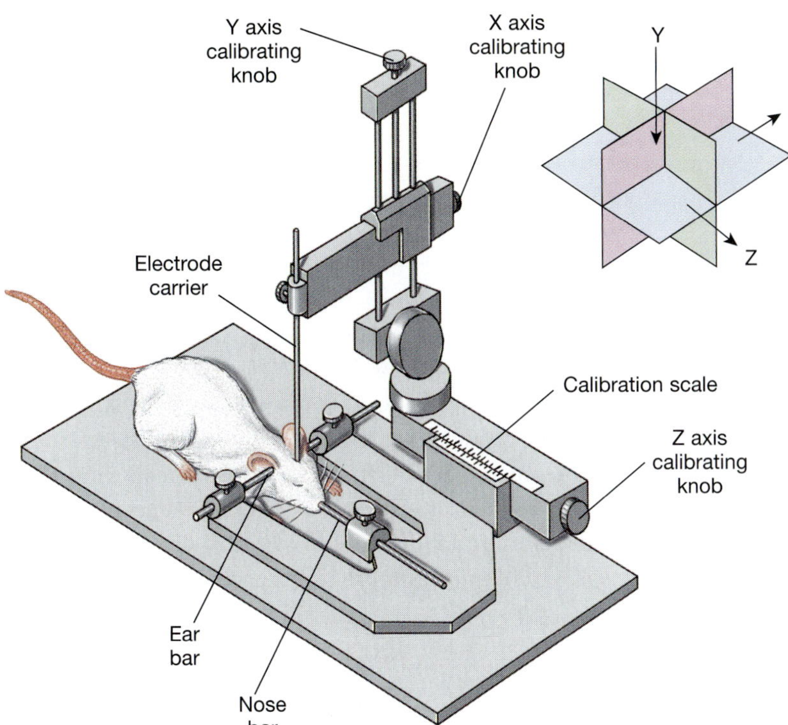

Figure 2.27 A stereotaxic apparatus. A stereotaxic apparatus is used to permanently implant an electrode into an animal's brain. After surgery, an electrical current can be passed through the tip of the electrode to stimulate a specific site in the animal's brain through the cannula.

➤ *What information about the brain can be obtained from the use of stereotaxic apparatus? (pp. 63–64)*

Techniques for Studying Brain Function

Throughout this chapter, we have listed specific functions of the nervous system: The primary visual cortex controls sight, the autonomic nervous system controls gland activity and internal organ functioning, and so on. But how exactly do neuroscientists determine the specific function of a particular area of the nervous system? In this section, we will look briefly at several of the tools used by neuroscientists to unlock the mysteries of the nervous system.

Ablation of Neural Tissue

One technique for identifying the behavioral function of a particular area involves the experimental destruction, or ablation, of the neurons in that area, a technique sometimes referred to as lesioning. This technique is typically carried out on nonhuman subjects for obvious ethical reasons (see Chapter 1), although the ablation technique has been used in humans to treat neurological disorders. For example, destruction of the neural locus of epilepsy or the area of the brain where the seizure begins, represents a potentially effective treatment for this disorder (Penfield & Jasper, 1954). Ablation is carried out most frequently on the brain. An animal is first anesthetized and then placed in a special surgical instrument, called a **stereotaxic apparatus** (refer to **Figure 2.27**), to confine the ablation to a particular region of the brain. There are three methods for producing a brain lesion. In the first method, the brain's outer cover (dura mater) is cut away and the underlying cortical tissue is removed by cutting or suction. In the second method, a small stainless steel or platinum wire, insulated except for the tip, is inserted into the desired area, and electric current is passed through it. The current carries enough intensity to destroy the targeted neurons. The amount of brain tissue destroyed depends on the intensity and duration of the electrical current. In the third method, toxic chemicals such as Kainic acid are injected to destroy specific areas of the brain. The toxic chemical is administered through a small tube called a cannula, which is implanted in the selected area of the brain.

A stereotaxic atlas is used to locate the area to be lesioned. Using a skull feature called bregma—the junction of the sagittal and coronal *sutures,* or the fibrous joint between flat bones of the skull (see **Figure 2.28**)—as a guide, the atlas indicates where and how deep the electrode or cannula should be placed. By observing the behavioral changes that occur after lesioning, a biological psychologist can infer the influence of a particular area of the brain on behavior.

At the end of an experiment, the researcher will examine the cell structure of the animal's brain to determine whether the ablation was performed on the correct area. After the animal is euthanized, its brain is frozen or other-

stereotaxic apparatus A surgical instrument that allows a neuroscientist to lesion a specific region of the brain.

Figure 2.28 A dorsal view of a skull. The sagittal and coronal sutures, or joints between flat bones of the skull, meet at a point called bregma.

➤ *Describe the value of bregma in ablation studies. (p. 63)*

wise hardened and then cut into small slices with a device called a *microtome*. The tissue slices are stained to reveal the site of the ablation. As we noted in Chapter 1, the Golgi stain will cause entire neurons to become dark black. Other stains reveal only cell bodies, and still other stains show fiber tracts. By using different stains, researchers can identify the ablated area of the brain (see **Figure 2.29**).

computerized axial tomography (CT) A technique that produces a static image of the brain by shooting a narrow beam of x-rays from all angles to produce a cross-sectional view of the brain; the resulting image is commonly referred to as a CT scan.

Inferior colliculus
Superior colliculus
Hippocampus
Cerebellum
Neocortex
Olfactory bulb
Thalamus
Midbrain
Striatum
Hindbrain
Hypothalamus
Pons
Substantia nigra
Subthalamic nucleus

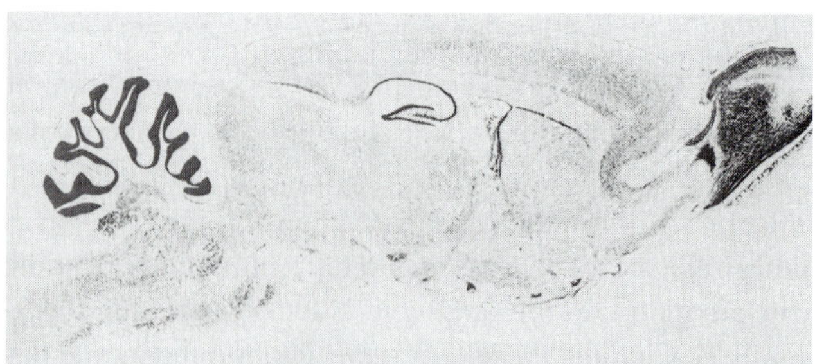

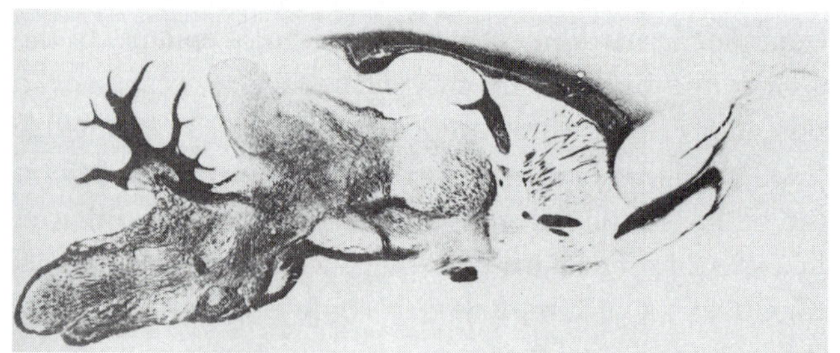

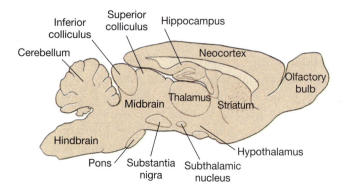

Figure 2.29 Two histological views of the rat brain. The photo on the top right uses a stain to show cell bodies and the photo on the bottom right uses a stain to show axons. The illustration above shows brain structures seen in the two photos on the right.

➤ *What are the limitations of the histological method? (p. 64)*

The ablation techniques cannot by themselves establish the function of a particular area of the nervous system. Consider the following example to illustrate the limitations of this method. After a particular area of a rat's brain is destroyed, the animal no longer becomes aggressive when frustrated. Does this mean that the destroyed area motivates aggressive behavior? Although reduced aggression after lesioning could be the result of lessening of aggressive emotional states, other interpretations are possible. A motor deficit could have caused the behavior change following the lesion; that is, the destroyed area may have controlled the ability to engage in aggressive behavior rather than the experience of aggressive emotional states.

How can we establish the function of a specific area? Ablation can provide some evidence, but to more fully understand functioning, information from other, less invasive, techniques must also be considered.

Static Images of the Nervous System

Recent technological advances have allowed neuroscientists to observe the nervous systems of living subjects. Two of these techniques are computerized axial tomography (CT scan) and magnetic resonance imaging (MRI).

Computerized Axial Tomography. People often suffer damage to specific areas of their brains as a result of tumors or strokes. This damage can lead to significant behavioral impairments. One way to identify the area of damage is to use **computerized axial tomography** or **CT scan**. A CT scanner shoots a narrow beam of x-rays to take pictures of the person's head from all angles and thus to produce a cross-sectional view (**Figure 2.30a** is a

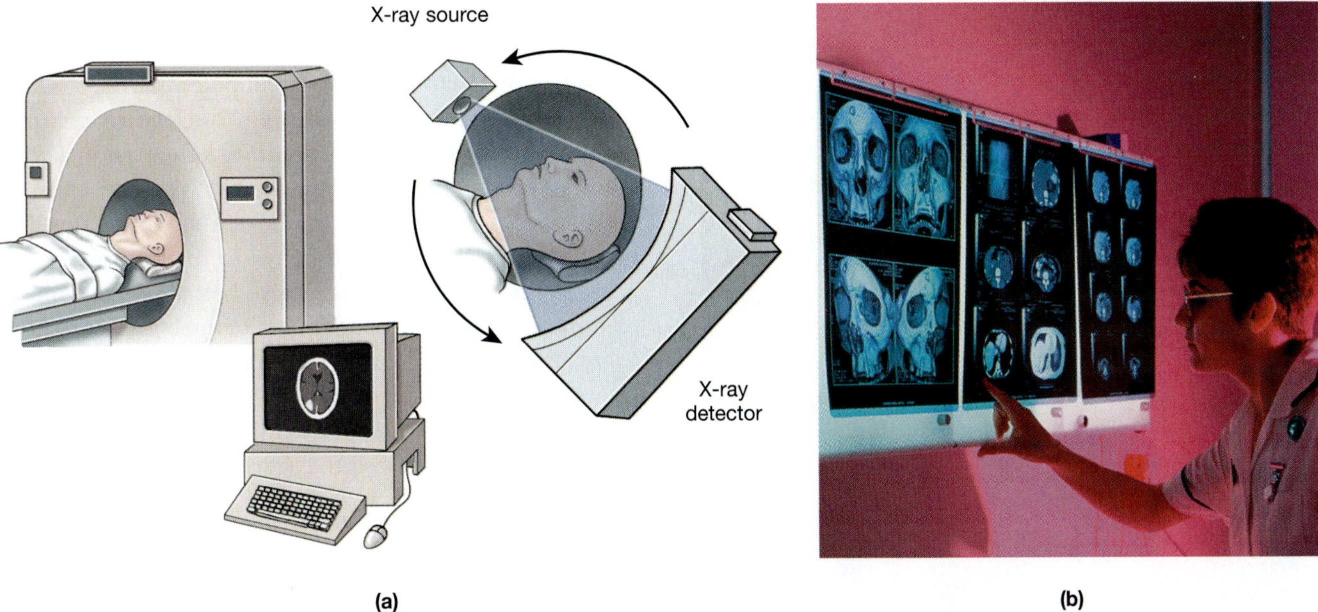

Figure 2.30 Computerized axial tomography. (a) The process of viewing the brain using the computerized axial tomography equipment. (b) The resulting CT scan reveals a tumor in the occipital lobe.

➤ *Describe the value of a CT scan for identifying damage to the brain. What are the limitations of a CT scan? (p. 64–65)*

diagram of how the CT scanner works). The person's head is placed inside the CT scanner, which slowly rotates over 180 degrees (a half circle) while passing the narrow beam of x-rays through the head. When the half-rotation is completed, the computer constructs a cross-sectional image from the pictures. As **Figure 2.30b** shows, the resulting image indicates the precise locations of damage to the brain. Once the area of damage is identified, appropriate treatment(s) can be prescribed.

Magnetic Resonance Imaging. In **magnetic resonance imaging (MRI)**, radio waves (instead of potentially harmful radiation used in a CT scan) are used to obtain a picture of the brain. A strong magnetic field is first passed through the patient's head. This magnetic field causes the nuclei of some molecules in the brain to spin with a particular orientation. When a radio wave is then passed through the brain, these nuclei will emit radio waves. The MRI scanner measures the radiation emitted from hydrogen molecules. Because the hydrogen molecules are present in different concentrations in different parts of the brain, the MRI scanner can use this information to provide an extremely clear three-dimensional view of the brain (see **Figure 2.31**).

Although information provided by either the CT scan or MRI is considerable, both techniques suffer from the same limitations as the studies using the ablation technique. Both the CT scan and the MRI are static images and, therefore, do not provide images of the brain at work. Further, any behavioral changes produced by brain damage could be the result of a variety of causes. Therefore, specific functioning of particular brain areas cannot be ascertained solely from the use of these techniques.

Recording Nervous System Activity

Biological psychologists have developed several methods for recording ongoing activity in the nervous system, especially the brain, to better ascertain function. One of these methods measures electrical activity, a second method infers neural activity from metabolic functioning, and a third measure infers the level of neural activity from cerebral blood flow.

Electrical Recording. One method for studying the function of a particular area of the nervous system involves recording the electrical activity of that area during the performance of a particular behavior. The potential changes that occur during neural transmission can be recorded in two ways. In the first method, electrodes are placed on the scalp and cortical activity recorded (see **Figure 2.32**). The

magnetic resonance imaging (MRI) A technique that produces a static image of the brain by first passing a strong magnetic field through the brain, followed by a radio wave, and measuring the radiation emitted from hydrogen molecules.

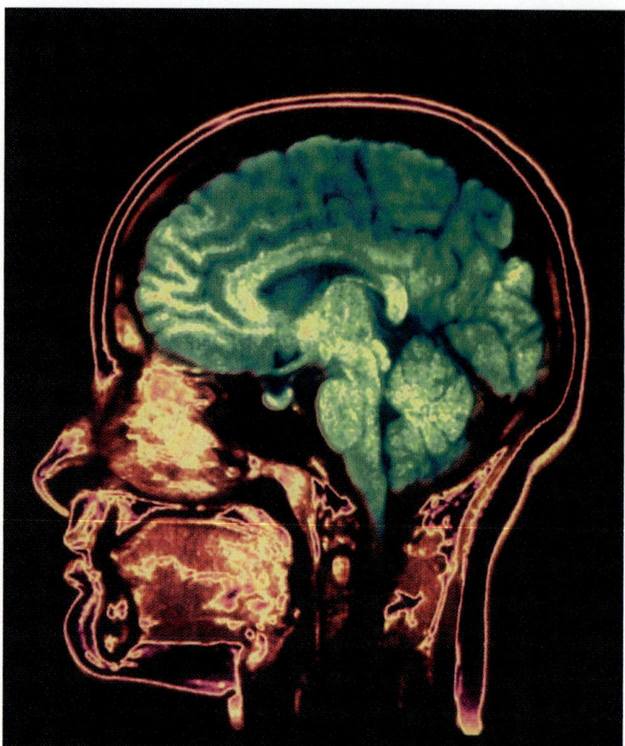

Figure 2.31 Magnetic resonance imaging (MRI). This photograph shows the human brain with magnetic resonance imaging technology.
➤ *What is the advantage of using MRI rather than a CT scan? (p. 65)*

electroencephalograph measures electrical potentials in the cerebral cortex and provides a record of this activity, called an **electroencephalogram (EEG)**.

In the second, more invasive method (used typically on nonhuman subjects), a small stainless steel or platinum wire that records the activity of one or several neurons can be inserted into the nervous system. This procedure is employed when the area of interest is too deep in the nervous system for surface electrodes to detect activity. The wire, insulated except at the tip, records neural activity occurring in the neuron(s) surrounding the tip. After the wire has been inserted and is in place, an electric socket, attached to the electrode, is cemented to the animal's skull with dental plastic. After surgery, the psychologist can "plug" the animal into the recording system and detect the occurrence of electrical activity while the animal is engaged in various behaviors (see **Figure 2.33**). An oscillograph, or polygraph, amplifies the electrical activity and creates a record of the changes in electrical potential.

How can the information provided by electrical recording be used? Suppose that we notice that neurons in a certain area of the brain show increased activity just before a rat engages in aggressive behavior, but when the aggressive behavior ends, the activity decreases to the level observed prior to the onset of the aggressive behavior. This information would suggest that this area of the brain motivates aggressive activity. Or would it? Although the evidence shows that a correlation exists between electrical activity in this area and aggression, we cannot conclude that activity in this area actually caused the aggressive behavior.

Positron Emission Topography. Rather than directly measuring electrical activity, **positron emission topography (PET)** infers neural activity by measuring metabolic activity in the nervous system, especially the brain. Glucose is used by neurons as an energy source for metabolism. Because little glucose is stored in the neurons, increased neural activity causes increased absorption of glucose from the bloodstream. How might one measure glucose absorption in the brain? One way to measure glucose utilization is to inject a chemical called 2-deoxyglucose (2-DG) into the bloodstream. Brain cells absorb 2-DG but cannot metabolize it. If 2-DG molecules are made radioactive, a record of 2-DG absorption into the neurons of the brain will provide information regarding neural activity in the brain.

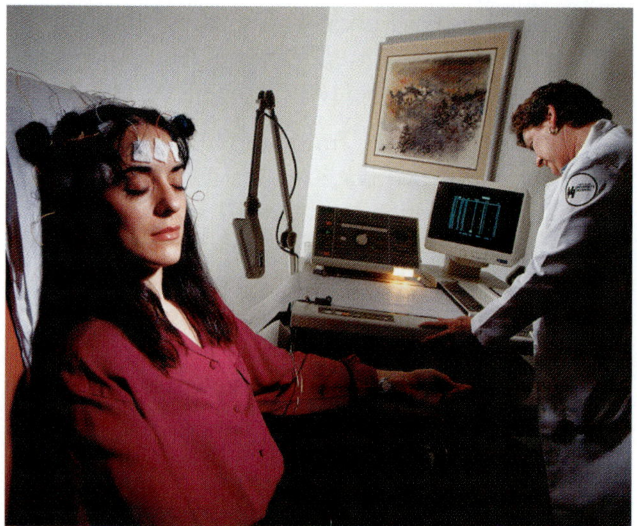

Figure 2.32 The electroencephalograph (EEG). Recording electrodes are attached to the surface of the individual's scalp. The EEG records the level of activity in the brain, which is recorded in the form of line tracings called brain waves.
➤ *How might an EEG suggest that a person is not telling the truth? (p. 65–66)*

electroencephalogram (EEG) A graphical record of the electrical activity of the cerebral cortex.

positron emission topography (PET) Measurement of metabolic activity of a specific structure in the nervous system in order to determine neural functioning.

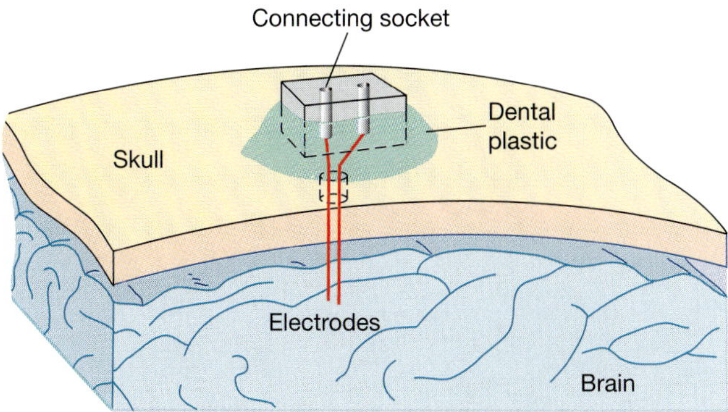

Figure 2.33 The permanent implantation of an electrode in an animal's brain. After surgery, the animal can be plugged into a recording system that detects the occurrence of electrical activity in the brain.
➤ *Why must the implantation technique rather than surface electrodes be used in some cases? (p. 66)*

The PET scanner is a device that measures the stream of positrons (positively charged electrons) that are emitted from the nuclei of the radioactive carbon atoms of 2-DG. A computer combines the signals into a record of neural activity called a PET scan.

How can information provided by the PET scanner be used? Suppose a PET scan is taken while John Moore is speaking to the press or thinking about his strategy for his next bout. As seen in **Figure 2.34**, the PET scan reveals that during such activities as speaking and thinking, certain areas of the brain are more active than other areas. Normal resting levels of cortical activity are represented by the green areas of the PET scan. Yellow and red areas indicate a higher-than-normal level of cortical activity, whereas blue areas indicate lower-than-normal cortical activity. Thus, the prefrontal lobe is bright red when John is thinking, whereas the Broca's area is bright red when John is speaking. Note from **Figure 2.34** that the occipital lobe would be bright red when John is viewing a video of his last bout (seeing), and the temporal lobe would be bright red when he is listening to another person.

The PET scan technology can be modified to provide a measure of cerebral blood flow. In this procedure, called a *regional cerebral blood flow (rCBF)*, a person injects or inhales a radioactive form of the gaseous chemical xenon. Because xenon accumulates in areas of the brain in which blood flow is high, it can be assumed to reflect those brain areas that are most active.

PET scans have proved especially valuable to cognitive neuroscience, or the study of the relationship between the nervous system and mental processes. This technology has allowed cognitive neuroscientists to investigate the workings of the nervous system while an animal is engaged in mental processes. We will see the results of this investigation at many places throughout the text.

Functional Magnetic Resonance Imaging (fMRI). Just as the PET technology can be modified to provide a measure of cerebral blood flow, so can the MRI technology. This modified MRI procedure, called a **functional MRI (fMRI)** utilizes high-powered, rapidly oscillating magnetic fields and powerful computation to measure the cerebral blood flow in the brain and thereby obtain a measure of neural activity in the brain. This image of neural activity is accomplished by setting the fMRI to detect the energy released from hemoglobin, which is a protein in vertebrate red blood cells that contains oxygen. The more oxygen in

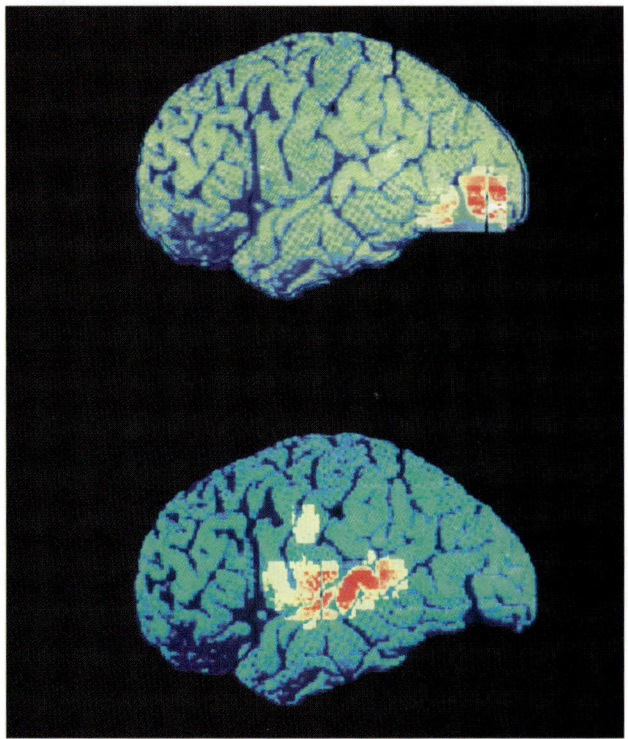

Figure 2.34 PET scans. PET scans are taken while a person is seeing (top scan) or listening (bottom scan). The colors indicate the level of activity in specific areas of the cortex. Green areas indicate average cortical activity, the yellow and red show higher-than-average cortical activity, and blue areas show lower-than-average cortical activity.
➤ *How does the PET scan differ from the CT scan and the MRI? What are its advantages? (p. 65–66)*

functional MRI (fMRI) The fMRI utilizes high-powered, rapidly oscillating magnetic fields and powerful computation to measure cerebral blood flow in the brain and obtain an image of the neural activity in a specific area of the brain.

the hemoglobin, the more energy that is released and detected by the fMRI. Areas of the brain with more energy release are assumed to be more active.

Measuring Chemical Activity in the Nervous System

What if a neuroscientist wanted to identify the neurotransmitters found in a particular area of the brain or wished to discover which neural structure is affected by a specific drug? We will next look briefly at two approaches that can measure the chemical activity in the nervous system.

Autoradiography. One method of determining the area of the nervous system where a particular chemical is found is a technique called **autoradiography**. In this method, a neuroscientist injects a particular radioactive chemical into the bloodstream and then waits several minutes for the chemical to reach the nervous system. The animal is then euthanized and the target neural tissue, most likely an area of the brain, is sliced into thin sections. Each slice of tissue is placed against a piece of x-ray film and a record taken of the radioactivity emitted. This record will show exactly what neural areas absorb this specific radioactive chemical and, thereby, indicate the chemical activity that occurs in these areas.

Microdialysis. With autoradiography, the animal must be euthanized so that tissue samples can be obtained. Chemical analysis also can be made using a living animal. One technique for identifying chemical activity is **microdialysis**. With this technique, a fine tube is passed through the neural tissue. A short semipermeable section of the tube is placed in a specific area of the nervous system and neurochemicals in that area diffuse into the tube. An automated chromatograph, which is an instrument that can measure the chemical constituents of blood and other liquids, determines which neurotransmitters are present in that specific neural area. Another method for assessing chemical activity is to inject a chemical directly into a specific neural area and then evaluate the chemical's effect on behavior; we will look at this chemical stimulation method in the last section of this chapter.

autoradiography Injection of radioactive chemicals into the bloodstream and subsequent analysis of neural tissue to determine where a specific chemical is found in the nervous system.

microdialysis A technique for identifying the neurotransmitter in a specific area of the nervous system by measuring the chemical constituents of blood and other liquids.

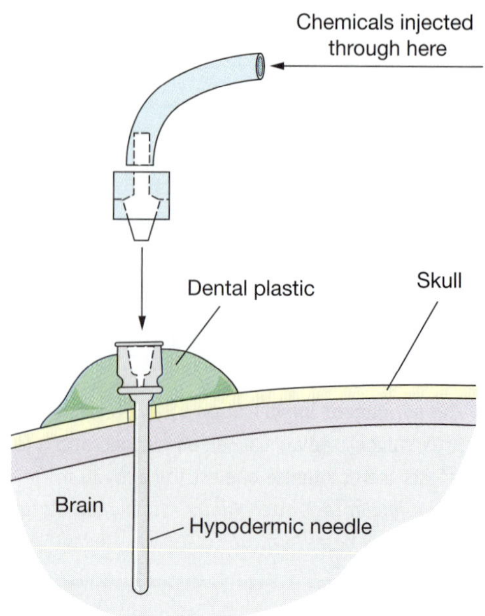

Figure 2.35 The permanent implantation of a cannula into an animal's brain. After surgery, chemicals can be injected into the brain through the cannula.

➤ *What information can be obtained by chemically stimulating a specific brain structure? What are the limitations of this technique? (p. 68–69)*

Direct Stimulation of the Nervous System

Rather than destroying a particular area of the nervous system or recording its activity indirectly, an experimenter can assess the function of the area by stimulating its neurons directly. An area can be stimulated either by passing a weak electric current through a small wire or, as we have just mentioned, by administering a chemical through a cannula (see **Figure 2.35**). The behavior produced by direct stimulation provides yet another source of information concerning the influence of the area on behavior. This type of chemical stimulation can also be used to identify which neurotransmitter affects a particular brain area.

Like the other research methods that we have discussed, stimulation studies yield results that must be viewed with caution. Suppose that we stimulate a certain brain area and the animal then becomes aggressive. Although this observation indicates that the stimulated area is somehow involved in aggressive behavior, it does not indicate that activity in this area directly causes aggression. It is possible that stimulation of the area inhibits another brain structure that had been preventing aggression. Thus, the stimulation may have caused a release of neural inhibition of aggression rather than directly eliciting aggressive behavior.

Why are so many different methods needed to study brain functioning? Because of the complexity of the information-processing tasks performed by the nervous system, the results of different techniques must be considered together in order to get a complete picture. Suppose that a lesion of a particular area causes no change in a behavior of interest. You might conclude that this area is not crucial to motivating a particular behavior. However, electrical stimulation of the area could activate the behavior by releasing it from inhibition. Or perhaps one area of the brain is active when a specific behavior occurs as measured by a PET scan, but stimulation of that area alone does not elicit the behavior because other areas must also be activated for the behavior to occur. Only by using a combination of techniques can the function of a specific area of the nervous system be identified.

Before You Go On

What information about the brain can be provided by ablation? What information can ablation *not* provide?

Describe which techniques you would use to determine which parts of your brain are active as you read this question.

Section Review

- Methods used to study brain functioning include ablation, static imaging (CT scans and MRI), recording nervous system activity (EEG, oscillograph, PET scan, or fMRI), measurement of chemical activity (autoradiography and microdialysis), and direct stimulation.
- Ablation is the experimental destruction of specific neurons in the nervous system; also called lesioning.
- Computerized axial tomography (CT) is a technique that produces a static image of the brain by shooting a narrow beam of x-rays from all angles to produce a view of the brain; the resulting image is commonly referred to as a CT scan.
- Magnetic resonance imaging (MRI) is a technique that produces a static image of the brain by first passing a strong magnetic field through the brain, followed by a radio wave, and measuring the radiation emitted from hydrogen molecules.
- Electroencephalogram (EEG) is a graphical record of the electrical activity of the cerebral cortex.
- Positron emission topography (PET) is a technique for measuring metabolic activity of a specific structure in the nervous system in order to determine neural functioning.
- Functional MRI (fMRI) utilizes high-powered, rapidly oscillating magnetic fields to measure cerebral blood flow in the brain and obtain an image of neural activity in the brain.
- Autoradiography is a technique that injects radioactive chemicals into the bloodstream; subsequent analysis of neural tissue determines where a specific chemical is found in the nervous system.
- Microdialysis is a technique for identifying the neurotransmitter in a specific area of the nervous system by measuring the chemical constituents of blood and other liquids.
- Evaluation of the results of various methods must be considered together to give an accurate picture of the function of a particular area of the nervous system.

Chapter Review

Critical Thinking Questions

1. Describe the organizational structure of the nervous system. Indicate the key differences between the functions of the peripheral and central nervous systems. How does the differentiation allow the nervous system to carry out its varied functions?
2. Using what you have learned about the functions of the various areas of the brain, including those of Broca's area and Wernicke's area, explain why there is lateralization of function in the human brain. Would lateralization of function differ in right-handed and left-handed people?
3. Biological psychologists use various methods to study how the nervous system influences behavior. Suppose that you are interested in identifying the neural structures responsible for depression. Describe the various methods you would use to reveal the involvement of the nervous system in depression.

Vocabulary Questions

1. The part of the nervous system that analyzes the significance of events and decides how to respond is the ________________.

2. The location where messages are transmitted between two neurons is a ________________.
3. ________________ are neurons that send messages from the sensory receptors to the central nervous system.
4. The layers of tissue that protect the brain and spinal cord are called the ________________.
5. The hollow interconnected chambers within the brain are the ________________.
6. An afferent sensory neuron enters the spinal cord and directly synapses with an efferent neuron in a ________________.
7. The brain structure that controls breathing and heart rate is the ________________.
8. The hindbrain, minus the cerebellum, and the midbrain are referred to as the ________________.
9. The part of the forebrain that detects hunger and sex is the ________________.
10. The ________________ is a vertical groove that separates the anterior and posterior halves of the cerebral cortex.
11. The part of the left frontal lobe that controls the planning of speech production is ________________.
12. A scan that measures metabolic activity in the brain is ________________.

Review Questions

1. The four main functions of the nervous system are
   a. seeing, hearing, tasting, and movement.
   b. balance, movement, language, and memory.
   c. detection, analysis, decision, and execution.
   d. storage, processing, integration, and motor control.
2. The two main divisions of the nervous system are the
   a. central nervous system and peripheral nervous system.
   b. sympathetic nervous system and parasympathetic nervous system.
   c. autonomic nervous system and the somatic nervous system.
   d. brain and spinal cord.
3. A neuron receives information from other neurons through the
   a. nucleus, cytoplasm, and cell membrane.
   b. receptor sites at the end of the dendrites.
   c. myelinated sheath of its axon.
   d. axon hillock where the axon projects from the soma.
4. Sensory neurons carry information from the
   a. central nervous system to the muscles.
   b. motor neurons to other sensory neurons.
   c. outside world to the central nervous system.
   d. central nervous system to the peripheral nervous system.
5. A major function of astrocytes is to
   a. provide physical support for neurons.
   b. remove debris from dead neurons.
   c. produce myelin.
   d. connect motor and sensory neurons.
6. The cranial nerves directly connect the
   a. spinal cord and brain.
   b. sympathetic and parasympathetic nervous systems.
   c. sensory receptors and brain.
   d. brain and muscles.
7. Which of the following is *not* a function of cerebrospinal fluid?
   a. provides nutrients to the brain
   b. carries messages to the brain
   c. cushions and protects the brain
   d. provides buoyancy and support to the brain
8. The gray matter in the spinal cord consists of
   a. cerebrospinal fluid.
   b. myelinated axon sheaths.
   c. dendrites.
   d. neural cell bodies.
9. Which hindbrain structure coordinates rapid motor movement?
   a. medulla oblongata
   b. pons
   c. cerebellum
   d. reticular formation
10. Which midbrain structure controls simple reflexes such as blinking?
    a. tectum
    b. substantia nigra
    c. red nucleus
    d. tegmentum
11. The role of the thalamus is to
    a. detect hunger and thirst.
    b. relay sensory messages.
    c. control release of pituitary hormones.
    d. control emotions.
12. Which part of the limbic system plays a part in memory functions?
    a. septum
    b. amygdala
    c. cingulate gyrus
    d. hippocampus

13. Huntington's disease results from damage to the
    a. cerebral commissures.
    b. basal ganglia.
    c. hippocampus.
    d. cerebral cortex.
14. The two hemispheres of the cerebral cortex are connected at the
    a. basal ganglia.
    b. central fissure.
    c. cerebral commissures.
    d. somatosensory cortex.
15. For most people, the left hemisphere has more control than the right hemisphere over
    a. sensory perception.
    b. language functions.
    c. motor functions.
    d. memory.
16. The primary visual cortex is located in the
    a. occipital lobe.
    b. parietal lobe.
    c. temporal lobe.
    d. frontal lobe.
17. Which parts of the human body are overrepresented in the somatosensory cortex?
    a. feet and legs
    b. reproductive organs
    c. face and hands
    d. mouth and eyes
18. Primary functions of the temporal lobe relate to
    a. seeing and speaking.
    b. hearing, object recognition by sight, and balance.
    c. movement, following maps or charts, and sight.
    d. smell and taste.
19. A stereotaxic atlas is used to
    a. locate the region of the brain to be lesioned.
    b. obtain cross-sectional images of the brain.
    c. create slides of brain tissue for examination.
    d. pass electric current through the brain.
20. A technique for determining the neurotransmitter(s) found in a specific brain structure is:
    a. MRI.
    b. CT scan.
    c. EEG.
    d. autoradiography.

Suggested Readings

HAINES, D. E. (1991). *Neuroanatomy: An atlas of structures, sections and systems* (3rd ed.). Baltimore: Urban and Schwarzenberg.

HEIMER, L. (1995). *The human brain and spinal cord* (2nd ed.). New York: Springer-Verlag.

MARTIN, J. H. (1989). *Neuroanatomy: Text and atlas.* New York: Elsevier.

NAUTA, W. J. H., & FEIRTAG, M. (1986). *Functional neuroanatomy.* New York: Freeman.

3 The Development and Redevelopment of the Nervous System

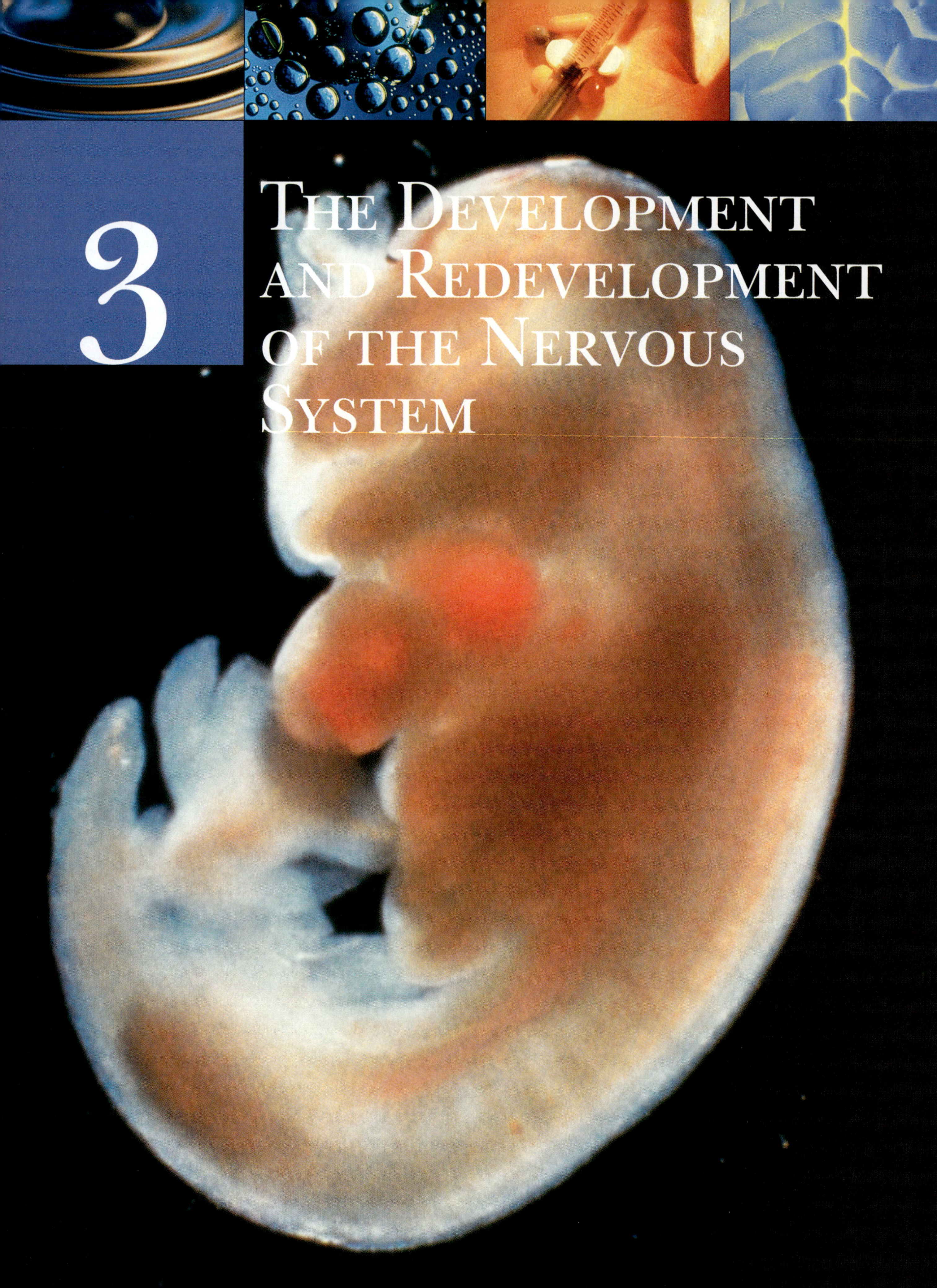

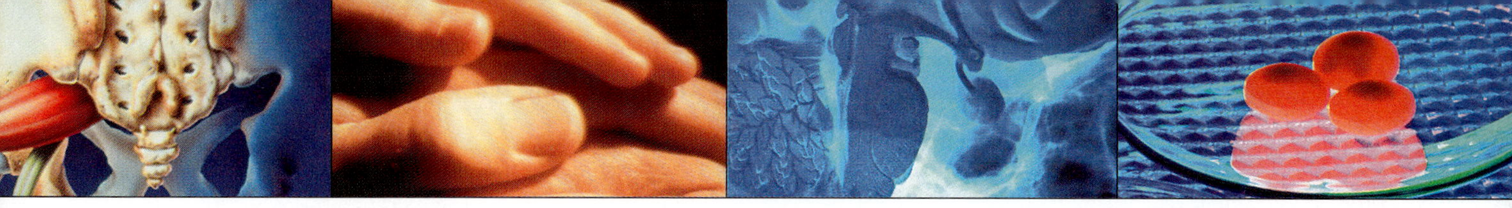

A Need to Know

Anne, 38, and Nathan, 42, have been married for 11 years. Early in their marriage they discussed having children, but they decided to wait until they were more financially secure. Although they have enjoyed the material benefits of their success, they have begun to feel that something is missing in their lives.

They decided several months ago that the time was right to have a child, and Anne became pregnant quickly. Because the risks of having a child with Down syndrome or other birth defects increases substantially for women over 35, Anne's obstetrician recommended testing for birth defects. Along with the triple screen test, which measures alpha-fetoprotein, human chorionic gonadotrophic, and estradiol levels and is a standard prenatal blood test for women of any age, Anne had two choices: she could have the chorionic villus sampling (CVS) test or the amniocentesis test. She could also opt to have no testing at all. Her obstetrician recommended amniocentesis ("amnio"). After discussing the obstetrician's recommendation with Nathan, Anne decided to go ahead with the amniocentesis.

At the Medical Center, a genetics counselor asked about family history, which revealed no apparent genetic defects in either Anne's or Nathan's families. A technician then took the blood sample for the alpha-fetoprotein test and did an ultrasound test. Anne and Nathan were excited as the technician pointed out the features of their baby revealed by the ultrasound. Now it was time for the amnio. The physician guided a slender needle through Anne's abdomen into her amniotic sac and withdrew about an ounce of amniotic fluid. The amniotic fluid and the fetal cells contained in the amniotic fluid would be examined for genetic defects and metabolic abnormalities. The physician told Anne and Nathan that it would take 3 or 4 weeks for the tests to be interpreted and a diagnosis made. As Anne left the Medical Center, she wondered whether her baby was all right. ■

◀ Approximately 250,000 new neurons develop each minute in the human fetus.

Before You Begin

Why did Anne's physician recommend amniocentesis?

If you were in her position, would you have had the testing done?

In this chapter, we will help you answer these and the following questions:

- What happens during the development of the human nervous system?
- How do neurons develop?
- How do neurons form the millions of connections that allow us to live and behave?
- What causes birth defects?
- When does the development of the nervous system end?
- Can the nervous system recover from injury after development ends?

Structural Development of the Human Nervous System

Remarkable changes will occur during the development of the nervous system of Anne and Nathan's baby. We begin our discussion of the development of the human nervous system at **conception**, the moment of **fertilization** of an egg by a sperm.

The Human Embryo

After a sperm successfully penetrates the egg's wall and conception occurs, a **zygote** is formed. The single-cell zygote has 46 chromosomes (23 from the sperm and 23 from the egg), which contain the genetic blueprint for embryonic and fetal development (see discussion of genetics in Chapter 1). After the zygote divides, which takes about 12 hours, the developing human is called an **embryo** for the first 8 weeks after conception, and then a **fetus** for the remainder of the pregnancy. The division of the cells of the embryo continues, and after 3 days, the embryo has divided into a mass of homogeneous cells that looks like a cluster of grapes.

Cell division continues, and within two weeks after conception, the embryo has divided into three distinct layers of cells (see **Figure 3.1**). The **endoderm**, the innermost layer (endo = inside), will form many of the body's linings, including those of the gut, lungs, and liver. The middle layer, the **mesoderm** (meso = middle), will form the connective tissue, such as muscle, bone and cartilage, and the blood and blood vessel linings. The layer of most

conception The moment of fertilization of an egg by a sperm.

fertilization The fusion of the egg and the sperm.

zygote A single cell formed when the sperm fertilizes the egg.

embryo The developmental stage for the first 8 weeks after conception.

fetus The developmental stage beginning at 8 weeks and continuing for the remainder of the pregnancy.

endoderm The innermost layer of the embryo, which will form linings of the gut, lungs, and liver.

mesoderm The middle layer of the embryo, which will form the connective tissue, muscle, and blood and blood vessels.

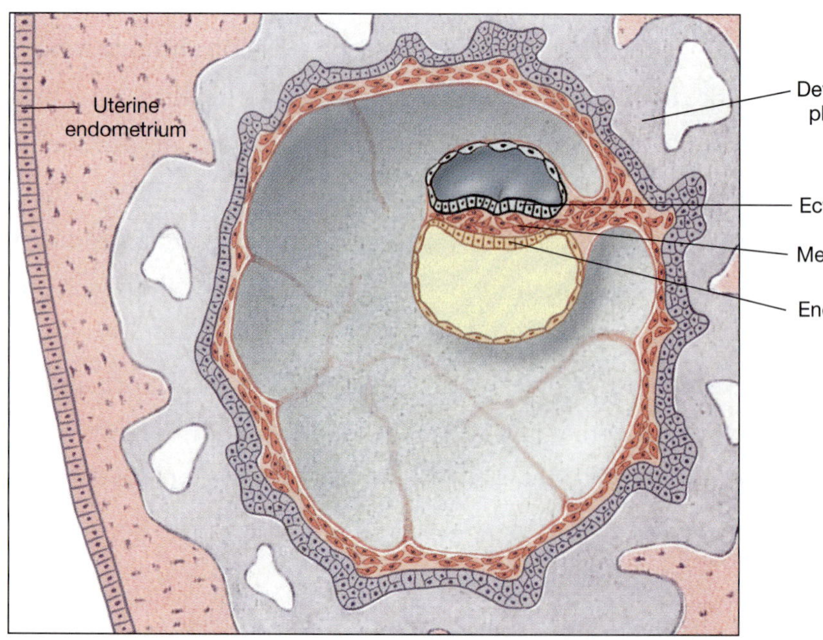

Figure 3.1 Cell layers of two-week-old embryo. The three cell layers of the two-week-old embryo include the ectoderm, mesoderm, and endoderm. ➤ *Which layer will give rise to the spinal cord? (p. 75)*

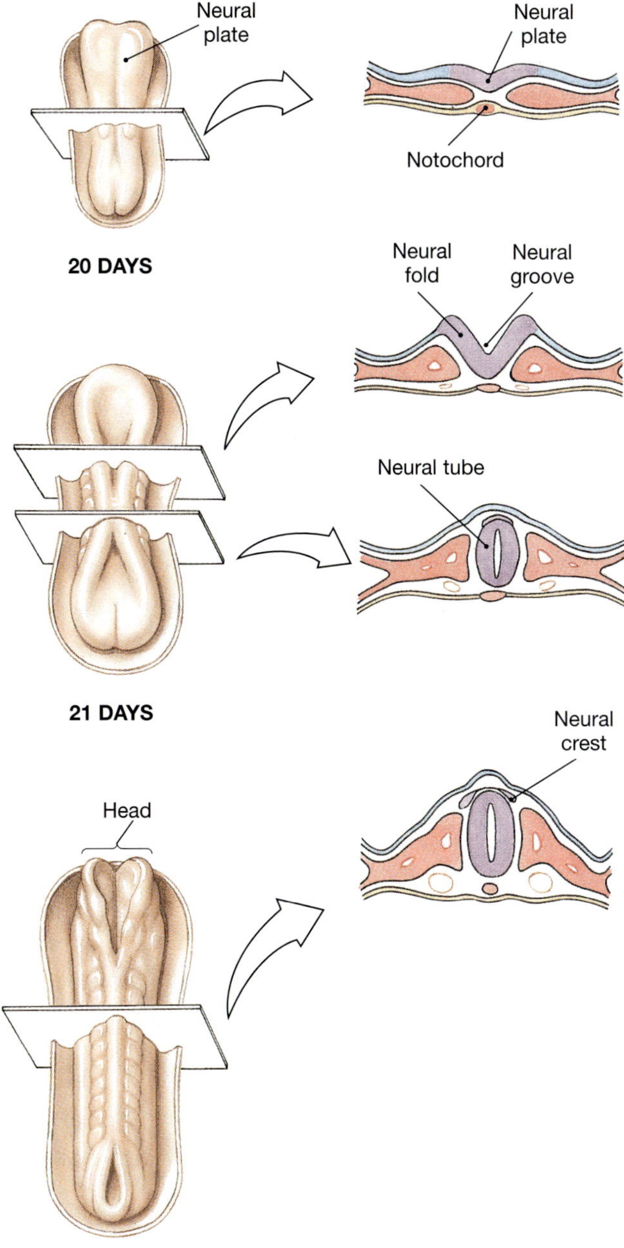

Figure 3.2 The formation of the neural tube and central nervous system in the human embryo. The neural groove begins to form at 20 days. At 21 days the neural folds begin to fuse, forming the neural tube. At 23 days the neural tube is completely formed and the brain begins to emerge.

➤ *What happens if the neural folds do not meet? (p. 75)*

interest to us in this course is the **ectoderm**, the outermost layer (ecto = outside), which will become the nervous system along with the epidermis, and parts of the eye and ear. **Differentiation**, the creation of different cell types, continues throughout development in the amazing process that produces a human being from a single fertilized egg cell. The rest of our discussion will focus on the differentiation of the nervous system into the structures that allow us to walk, talk, and otherwise behave.

The Emergence of the Nervous System

As cell division proceeds, the three layers of the embryo thicken into three flat oval plates. The thickened ectoderm layer is called the **neural plate** (see **Figure 3.2**). The lateral edges of the neural plate, the **neural folds**, push up to form a space called the **neural groove**. The groove begins to develop by day 20; the neural folds continue to move toward one another for the next 3 days. Under normal circumstances, by day 23 the neural folds have met along the length of the embryo, and the neural groove has become the **neural tube**. The brain and spinal cord then develop from the walls of the enclosed neural tube.

However, in some embryos, the neural folds fail to close, producing what is called a neural tube defect. Two common neural tube defects are spina bifida and anencephaly. **Spina bifida** results when some part of the neural folds fails to close. A small opening may lead to minor problems, which can in some cases be corrected surgically. A large opening, especially one high in the spinal cord, can produce profound impairments, such as paralysis, limb deformities, and mental retardation. Some fetuses with spina bifida do not survive, but one of every thousand live births exhibits this neural tube defect. **Anencephaly** (literally, "no brain") is a defect that results when the brain or a major part of it fails to develop. Fetuses with this neural tube defect are usually stillborn. Infants born with anencephaly die shortly after birth.

Anne's obstetrician recommended that she undergo amniocentesis in the 16th or 17th week of pregnancy because, in addition to the genetic defects that chorionic villus sampling can reveal, such as Down syndrome, amniocentesis can detect neural tube defects such as spina bifida and anencephaly. The danger of miscarriage is also

---

ectoderm The outermost layer of the embryo, which will become the nervous system.

differentiation The creation of different cell types.

neural plate The thickened ectoderm layer of embryo.

neural folds The lateral edges of the neural plate.

neural groove The space formed when the neural folds push up.

neural tube The closed space that is formed when the neural folds meet and close the neural groove.

spina bifida A neural tube defect that results when some part of the neural folds fails to close.

anencephaly A neural tube defect that results when the brain or a major part of it fails to develop.

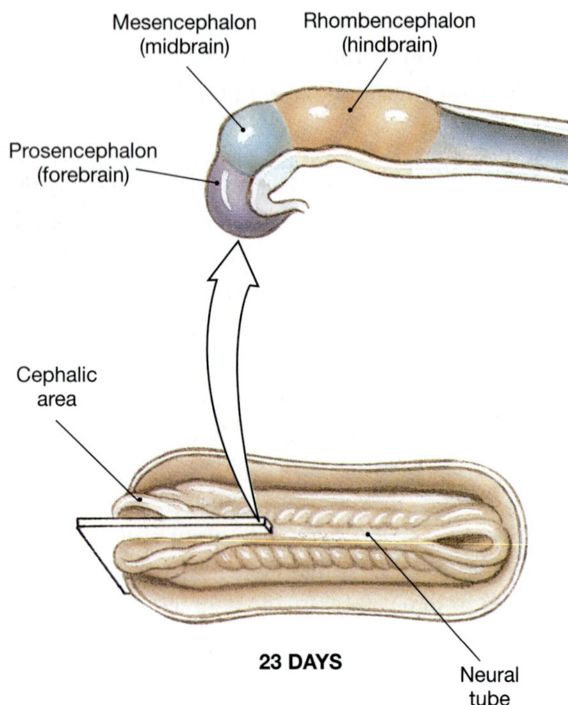

Figure 3.3 The development of the neural tube into the spinal cord and brain. The brain has differentiated into three separate structures at 23 days: the forebrain, the midbrain, and the hindbrain.

➤ *Which of these three structures will develop into the cerebral cortex? The hypothalamus? (p. 77)*

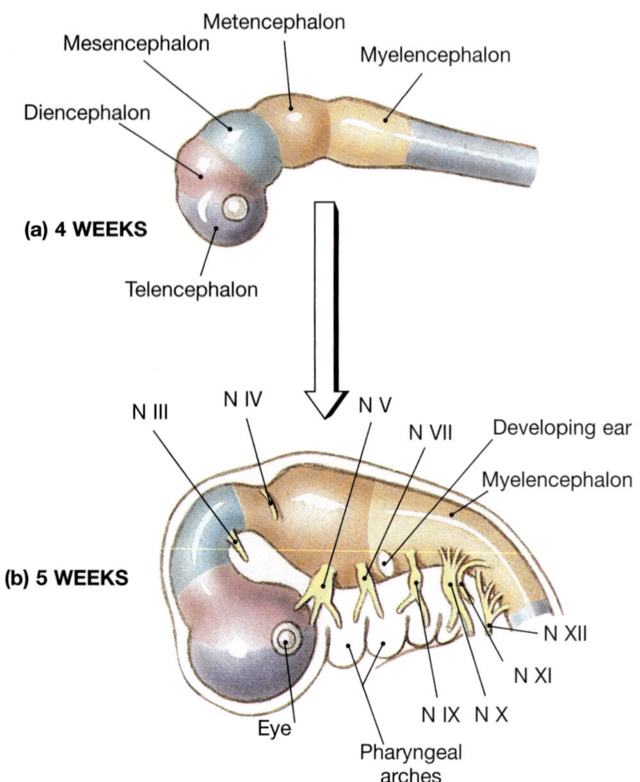

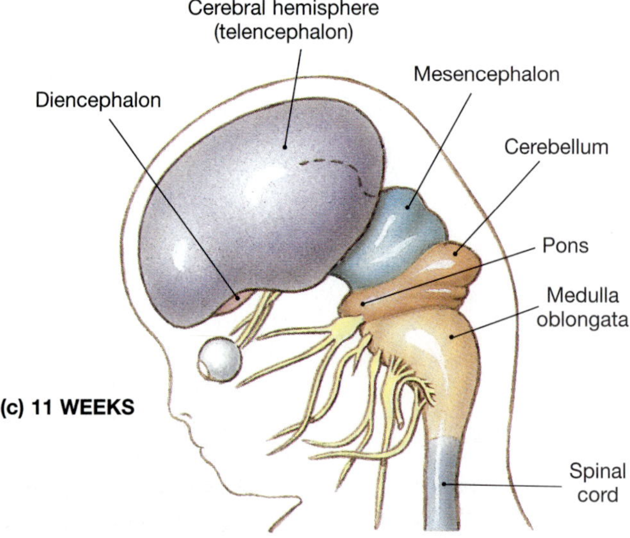

Figure 3.4 Nervous system of the human embryo. A sagittal view of the nervous system of the human embryo is shown at 4 weeks (a) and 5 weeks (b). The major divisions of the brain are apparent at 11 weeks (c).

➤ *Which structures does the telencephalon form? The mesencephalon? (p. 77)*

lesser with amniocentesis because chorionic villus sampling is done earlier in the pregnancy (between the 10th and 12th weeks), when the fetus is less well established.

The neural tube cavity becomes the ventricular system, whereas the cells that line the walls of the neural tube will produce the neurons and glial cells of the central nervous system. These cells also produce a specialized group of migratory cells, called the **neural crest** (see **Figure 3.2**). Shortly after formation, the neural crest cells leave the dorsal region of the neural tube, migrating away from the neural tube to form several types of tissue, including the sensory and autonomic neurons of the peripheral nervous system.

The Developing Brain. The structural development of the nervous system proceeds rapidly beginning at about the 3rd week of embryonic development (Martin & Jessell, 1991). The rostral (toward the head) part of the neural tube becomes the brain, and the caudal (toward the tail) part becomes the spinal cord. The brain initially differentiates into three parts: the forebrain (prosencephalon), the midbrain (mesencephalon), and the hindbrain (rhombencephalon; see **Figure 3.3**).

neural crest A specialized group of cells that migrate away from the neural tube to form several types of tissue, including the sensory and autonomic neurons of the peripheral nervous system.

At about the 4th week of embryonic development, the forebrain and the hindbrain divide again (refer to **Figure 3.4** and to Chapter 2 for a review of the anatomy of the mature brain). The forebrain (**prosencephalon**) subdivides into the **telencephalon**, which includes the cerebral cortex, the basal ganglia, the hippocampus, the amygdala, and the olfactory bulb, and the **diencephalon**, which includes the thalamus, the hypothalamus, and several visual structures. The midbrain or the **mesencephalon** does not divide in the embryonic brain. The hindbrain (**rhombencephalon**) divides into the **metencephalon**, which includes the pons and the cerebellum, and the **myelencephalon**, which includes the medulla. By the 11th week of embryonic development, many of the key brain structures have developed and are clearly visible. **Figure 3.5** provides a flow chart illustrating the differentiation of the brain.

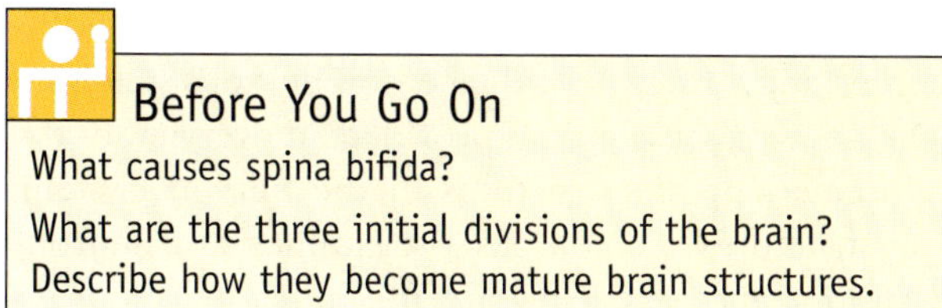

Before You Go On

What causes spina bifida?

What are the three initial divisions of the brain? Describe how they become mature brain structures.

The Developing Spinal Cord. As we learned in the last chapter, the mature spinal cord is divided into a dorsal root that receives sensory input and a ventral root that controls motor responses (refer to **Figure 2.15** for review of spinal cord). This organization of the spinal cord emerges in the embryonic period of development and is complete when a baby is born. Two major zones of cells appear in the developing spinal cord (see **Figure 3.6**).

prosencephalon The embryonic division that becomes the forebrain.

telencephalon The embryonic division of the forebrain that becomes the cerebral cortex, the basal ganglia, the hippocampus, the amygdala, and the olfactory bulb.

diencephalon The embryonic division of the forebrain that becomes the thalamus, the hypothalamus, and several visual structures.

mesencephalon The embryonic division that becomes the midbrain.

rhombencephalon The embryonic division that becomes the hindbrain.

metencephalon The embryonic division of the hindbrain that becomes the pons and the cerebellum.

myelencephalon The embryonic division of the hindbrain that becomes the medulla.

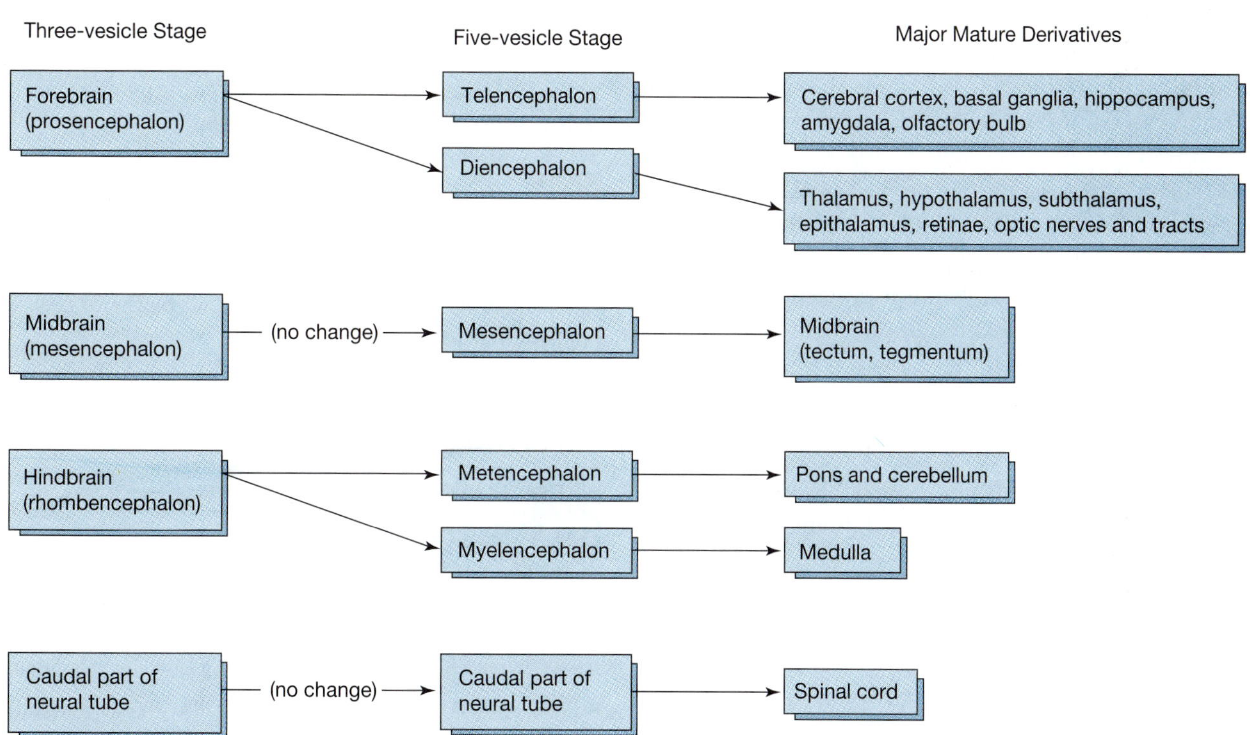

Figure 3.5 Differentiation of the brain. The main subdivisions of the embryonic central nervous system are shown at the three-vesicle and five-vesicle stages, and the mature adult forms.

➤ *What brain functions would be impaired if the hindbrain failed to develop into the metencephalon and myelencephalon? (p. 51–52, 54)*

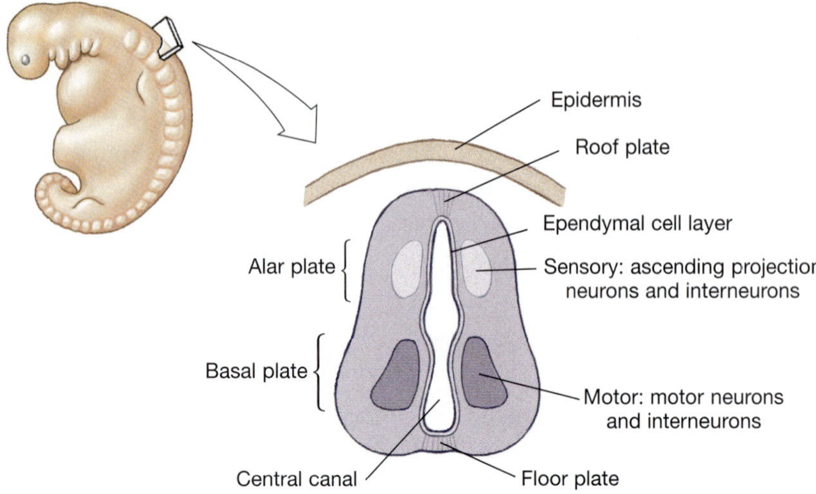

Figure 3.6 A coronal plane view of the developing spinal cord at 28 days. The dorsal root of the spinal cord emerges from the alar plate, and the ventral root emerges from the basal plate.
Adapted from Kandel et al., 1991.

➤ *What portion of the spinal cord contains the sensory neurons? The motor neurons? (p. 78)*

From the **alar plate**, the dorsal portion of the neural tube, sensory neurons project to the brain and interneurons of the dorsal horn of the spinal cord develop. From the **basal plate**, the ventral portion of the spinal cord, motor neurons and interneurons of the ventral root of the spinal cord develop. The sympathetic and parasympathetic nervous systems also develop from the basal plate of the spinal cord.

The spinal cord of the 3-month-old fetus runs the entire length of the vertebral column. As the fetus develops, the vertebral column lengthens more than the spinal cord. As a result of the longer vertebral column, the spinal cord in the newborn only extends to the level of the third lumbar vertebra. In the adult, the spinal cord only extends to the first lumbar vertebra, which causes the spinal nerves that extend to and from the lumbar and sacral segments of the vertebra to be quite long. Think about it: nerves have to run from the middle of your back all the way down to your toes! The spinal nerves are covered with meninges for protection, with additional protection provided by the cerebrospinal fluid. Despite all of this protection, because of their length these nerves are still subject to damage, as any among you who has suffered from sciatica or other lower back ailments know well.

The Developing Ventricular System. Recall that the ventricular system develops in the space inside the neural tube and that the ventricles contain the cerebrospinal fluid that will protect and provide nutrients to the central nervous system. The four ventricles of the brain (the two lateral ventricles, the third ventricle, and the fourth ventricle) and the central canal of the spinal cord all develop during the embryonic stage of development. The form of the ventricular system is affected by the emerging structure of the central nervous system.

The above discussion has provided an overview of the development of the structures of the nervous system. These structures are composed of millions of neurons and supporting cells. How are the individual neurons formed? And how do they make the billions of connections that will enable Anne's baby to smile for the first time, take her first steps, and speak her first words? The answer lies in the cellular development of the nervous system (remember, despite their unique appearance, neurons are simply specialized cells!).

Before You Go On

What would happen if the dorsal horn of the spinal cord did not develop properly from the alar plate? Or the ventral horn from the basal plate?

What are the four components of the ventricular system? What is its function?

Section Review

- During embryonic development, the nervous system emerges from the ectoderm layer to form the neural plate and then the neural tube.
- The ventricular system forms in the cavity of the neural tube.
- The inner cells of the neural tube give rise to the central nervous system and to neural crest cells.
- The brain initially forms into three vesicles: the forebrain, the midbrain, the hindbrain.

---

alar plate A zone of cells of the dorsal portion of the neural tube that develops into the sensory neurons and interneurons of the dorsal horn of the spinal cord.

basal plate A zone of cells of the ventral portion of the neural tube that develops into motor neurons and interneurons of the ventral horn of the spinal cord and the sympathetic and parasympathetic nervous systems.

- The hindbrain develops into the metencephalon, which becomes the pons and cerebellum, and the myelencephalon, which becomes the medulla.
- The forebrain develops into the telencephalon, which becomes the cerebral cortex, basal ganglia, hippocampus, and amygdala, and the diencephalon, which becomes the thalamus and hypothalamus.
- The dorsal horn of the spinal cord develops from the alar plate and receives sensory input from the peripheral nervous system.
- The ventral horn of the spinal cord develops from the basal plate and controls motor responses.
- The ventricular system consists of four ventricles—the two lateral ventricles, the third ventricle, and the fourth ventricle—and the central canal.

The Cellular Development of the Nervous System

The Formation of Neurons and Glial Cells

Amazingly, the nervous system, with its extensive capacity for thought, memory, action, and simple reflexes begins as a single layer of ectoderm cells that lie along the inner surface of the neural tube (refer to **Figure 3.1**). These cells divide to eventually form a closely packed layer of cells called the **ventricular layer** (not to be confused with the ventricular system). These cells divide into "daughter cells," which then migrate initially to the outer surface or **marginal layer** and later to the **intermediate layer** of the neural tube. Some of these daughter cells are destined to become either neurons or glial cells (see **Figure 3.7**). Other cells return to the ventricular layer and divide into new daughter cells. These new daughter cells then migrate to the marginal or intermediate layers, where they will either form neurons or glial cells or again return to the ventricular layer. Over time, the intermediate layer thickens. When this layer is well-established, two new layers are formed. Some daughter cells migrate to a layer between the intermediate and marginal layers. This new layer of daughter cells is called the **cortical plate**, which eventually develops into the neurons and glial cells of the cerebral cortex. Daughter cells also migrate to form a layer between the intermediate and ventricular layer, called the subventricular layer. The daughter cells that migrate to the **subventricular layer** become either glial cells or interneurons. The daughter cells that remain in the ventricular layer after the migration is completed will develop into *ependymal cells*, which form the lining of the ventricles of the brain and the central canal of the spinal cord.

ventricular layer The innermost layer of the developing nervous system whose cells divide to become daughter cells.

marginal layer The outermost layer of the developing nervous system to which daughter cells migrate.

intermediate layer The layer of cells that forms between the ventricular and marginal layers of the developing nervous system.

cortical plate A layer of daughter cells between the intermediate and marginal layers that develops into the neurons and glial cells of the cerebral cortex.

subventricular layer A layer of daughter cells between the intermediate and marginal layers that becomes either glial cells or interneurons.

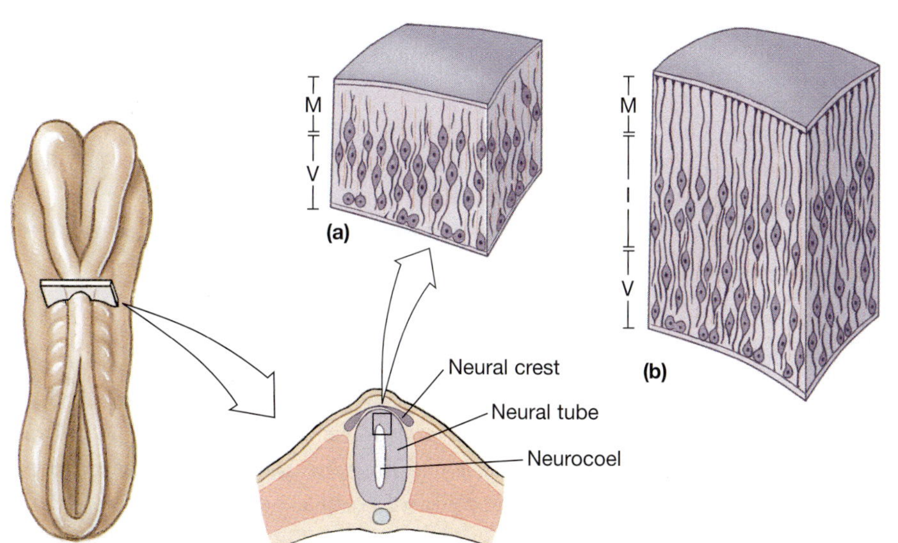

Figure 3.7 The proliferation of neurons and glial cells on the inner surface of the neural tube. At an early stage of embryonic development, only the inner ventricular layer (V) and outer marginal layer (M) are seen (a). As the embryo develops, the intermediate layer (I) emerges as the neural tube thickens (b). Daughter cells migrate from the ventricular layer to outer layers. Some daughter cells become neurons, and others return to the ventricular layer where they divide again; these new cells then return to the outer layer.

➤ *From which of the three layers of cells do neurons and glial cells develop? (p. 79)*

The division of daughter cells continues throughout embryonic and fetal development. The formation of new neurons, referred to as **neurogenesis** (neuro = neuron; genesis = birth), continues until birth in most mammalian species (Jacobson, 1991). In humans, few neurons are formed after birth. Exceptions include cerebellum cells that form for several months after birth, olfactory receptor neurons that are replaced throughout your lifetime, although olfactory thresholds do increase with age, and hippocampal neurons, whose birth may be important for learning and memory (see Chapter 14).

Some daughter cells become neurons as they migrate from the inner to the outer surface of the developing nervous system. The migration of these newly formed neurons is not random. Throughout embryonic development of the nervous system, neural migration is guided by specialized glial cells, called **radial glial cells** (see **Figure 3.8**). These radial glial cells radiate outward from the inner to the outer surface of the developing nervous system, like the spokes on a bicycle wheel. A newly formed neuron, with short extensions at the "head" and "tail" ends, creeps along the surface of the radial glial cell as if it were shinnying up a rope. The radial glial cells act like guide wires, enabling the new neurons to migrate to the appropriate locations. Once these initial neurons have migrated along the radial glial cells, the axons of these neurons can serve as guides for the migration of additional neurons. Thus, later-migrating cells can use as guides either radial glial cells or the axons of previously migrated neurons (Hatten, 1991).

In addition to the structural help provided by radial glial cells and other neurons, neurons are aided by **glycoprotein** molecules, which is a class of compounds in which a protein is combined with a carbohydrate group (Jessell, 1991). Neural cell adhesion molecules and cadherins (two types of glycoprotein molecules) that are present on the surfaces of neurons and radial glial cells allow neurons to bind to other neurons or radial glial cells by providing sticky neuron-to-glial-cell or neuron-to-neuron handholds to help shinny up that rope. In a similar fashion, integrins (another type of glycoprotein molecule) that are present on the surface of the neuron bind with integrins on the extracellular matrix. If these glycoprotein molecules fail to guide neuron migration properly, the result can be either a reduced number of neurons or a disorganized arrangement of neurons. In either case, neurological disorders are the likely consequence of glycoprotein failure.

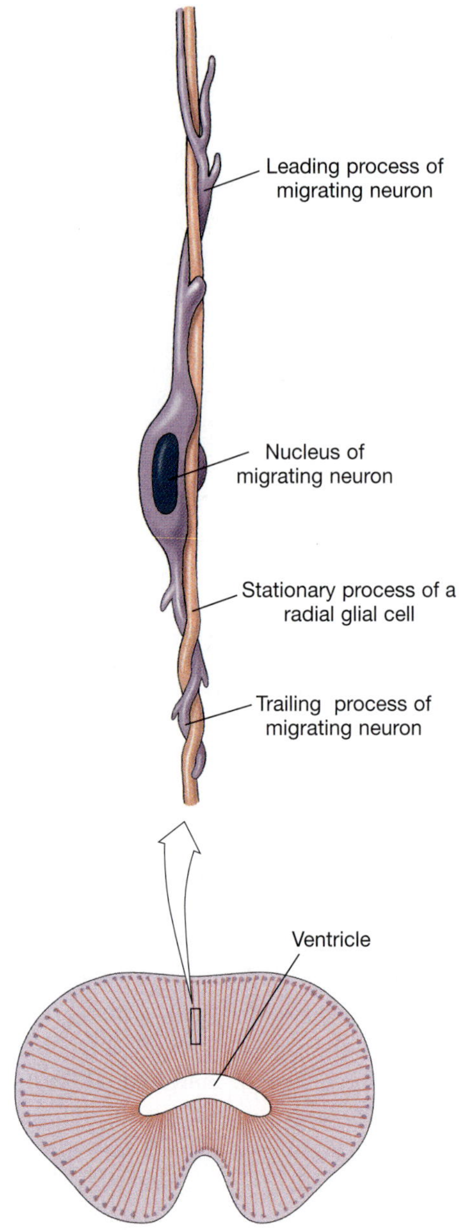

Figure 3.8 The migration of a neuron along a radial glial cell. The radial glial cells fan outward like the spokes of a bicycle wheel. The neuron creeps along radial glial cells to its predetermined location in the emerging nervous system.

Adapted from Rakic, 1972.

➤ *What chemical substance helps the neuron to creep along the radial glial cell? (p. 80)*

Caviness and Sidman (1973) described the effects of a failure of normal cell migration in a genetic mutant mice strain. In the normal mouse, cortical neurons form from the inside out. By contrast, in the genetic mutant mouse, the first generation of cortical neurons lie near the surface, and the last generation of neurons lie deepest, which

neurogenesis The formation of new neurons.

radial glial cells The glial cells that guide the migration of daughter cells during the embryonic development of the nervous system.

glycoprotein A class of compounds in which a protein is combined with a carbohydrate group.

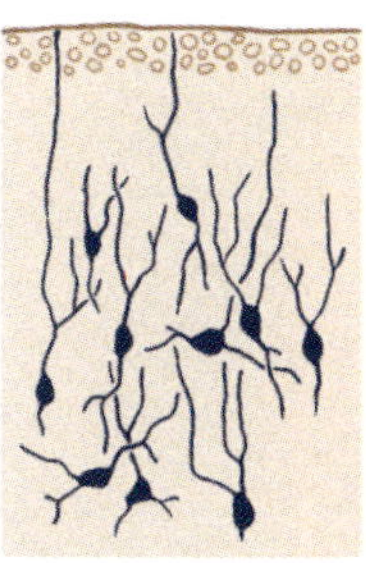

Figure 3.9 Purkinje cells. The Purkinje cells of the cerebellum are shown at 12 fetal weeks, at birth, and in the adult. The Purkinje cells develop extensive dendritic trees.

Adapted from Zecevic & Rakic, 1976.

➤ *In what way would the nervous system be affected if the Purkinje cells did not develop these extensive dendritic trees? (p. 53)*

creates an abnormally inverted cortex. One consequence of this failure of normal cell migration is abnormal, reeling movements exhibited by the genetic mutant mouse.

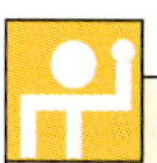

Before You Go On

What is neurogenesis?

Describe the migration of daughter cells among the cell layers of the neural tube.

How do radial glial cells and glycoproteins differ in guiding neural migration?

Cell Differentiation

The cells that migrate from the inner ventricular layer to the outer marginal layer of the developing nervous system do not look like neurons; instead, their appearance is much like other cells in the body. The neuron takes on its distinctive appearance (see **Figure 2.4** in Chapter 2) once it reaches its intended location in the nervous system.

As we noted in Chapter 2, not all neurons look alike. Spinal motor neurons are large, multipolar cells (refer to **Figure 2.6c**), whereas sensory neurons can be unipolar or bipolar (**Figure 2.6a&b**). How do neurons achieve these variations in final form?

Cell differentiation in the nervous system can be of two types. Many neurons contain genetic programming that causes them to develop in a particular way. Thus, **cell-autonomous differentiation** occurs when neurons develop without outside influence.

The Purkinje cell provides an example of cell-autonomous differentiation (see **Figure 3.9**). The Purkinje cells are found in the cerebellum which, as you will recall from Chapter 2, is involved in developing and coordinating skilled movement motor functions. A Purkinje cell will develop properly into its final distinctive form even when it is extracted from its natural environment and grown in a Petri dish (Seil, Kelly, & Leiman, 1974). Thus, the Purkinje cell must contain sufficient genetic instructions and self-activated control genes to allow it to develop its distinctive branching without any connections with other cells.

In the second type of differentiation, neurons rely on the influence of other cells to determine their final form. When neurons rely on such influences, they are said to develop through **induction**. Consider once again the spinal motor neuron. Just ventral to the developing nervous system is a structure called the notochord that somehow influences some, but not all, cells in the spinal cord to become spinal motor neurons (Roelink et al., 1994). It is thought that the notochord releases a chemical that directs certain neurons to become spinal motor neurons.

---

cell-autonomous differentiation A process whereby neurons develop without outside influence.

induction A process whereby neurons rely on the influence of other cells to determine their final form.

Glial Cell Development

Glial cells develop in the ventricular layer from the same group of daughter cells that produce neurons. But what determines whether a daughter cell will differentiate into a neuron or a glial cell? We do not know.

The production of glial cells from immature cells in the ventricular layer starts in the embryonic period and continues through the fetal period and into the postnatal period. In fact, the most intense period of glial cell production occurs after birth.

Myelination, the wrapping of the nerve axon with a protective myelin sheath, is an important function of glial cells (see **Figure 2.8**). Myelination of the cranial and spinal nerves begins at about 24 weeks. In the central nervous system, myelination begins in the fiber tracts within the spinal cord, spreads to the hindbrain, then to the midbrain, and finally to the forebrain. The sensory areas of the cerebral cortex are myelinated prior to the motor areas, which is why sensory functions mature prior to motor functions. Thus, Anne's baby's sense of smell, taste, and hearing will be well developed before he or she learns to walk.

Before You Go On

Compare and contrast the two types of neural cell differentiation.

Why do you think the most intense period of glial cell production occurs after birth?

The Formation of Neural Connections

Once a neuron has migrated to its destination and has developed the form characteristic of that location, through either induction or cell-autonomous differentiation, it is ready to establish the connections that will allow it to function as an effective part of the nervous system. These connections are established by the growth of axons toward their **target cells**, which can be other neurons, muscles, glands, or organs such as the liver. The axon emerges from the **growth cone**, which is the swollen end of the developing neuron. Extending from the growth cone of the neuron are spinelike extensions called **filopodia** (see **Figure 3.10**). The filopodia continually extend out from and retract back toward the growth cone as if they are looking for something. Once they find it, the filopodia appear to adhere to the extracellular environment and pull the growth cone in a particular direction. This activity does not move the cell body of the neuron, but instead elongates the developing axon along with the growth cone.

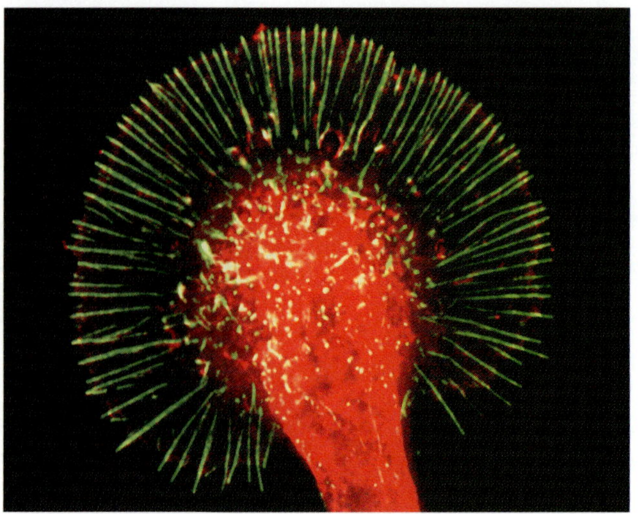

Figure 3.10 The growth cone. This micrograph, a photograph taken by an electron microscope at extremely high magnification, shows the growth cone of a developing neuron with its many filopodia.
➤ *What guides the filopodia toward the target cell? (p. 82)*

What is it that the filopodia are looking for? Remember Ramón y Cajal, who discovered the neuron (see Chapter 1)? In 1911, he proposed that chemicals guide the direction of axon growth in a process called **chemotropism** (from the Greek word tropos meaning "turn"). The target cell releases chemicals, called **neurotrophins**, that attract the filopodia and guide the axon to its appropriate location in the nervous system (Tessier-Laviqne & Goodman, 1996). Several well known neurotrophins include nerve growth factor (NGF), brain-derived neurotrophic factor (BDNF), neurotrophin 3 (NT3), and neurotrophin 4 (NT4). It is believed that the filopodia use the concentration gradient of the chemicals released by the target cell as a guide. In other words, they move toward the area with the highest concentration of chemicals much like a fox hunts down a rabbit by the strength of its scent. **Figure 3.11** illustrates the movement of the filopodia and growth cone toward the target cell.

Rita Levi-Montalcini and Stanley Cohen (Cohen, 1960; Levi-Montalcini, 1951) discovered the first neurotrophin, nerve growth factor (NGF). NGF is produced by target cells in the sympathetic nervous system. When

target cells The cells with which neurons establish synaptic connections.

growth cone The swollen end of the developing neuron from which an axon emerges.

filopodia Spinelike extensions from the growth cone that pull the axon to the target cell.

chemotropism The process by which the target cell releases chemicals that attract the filopodia and guide the axon to its appropriate location in the nervous system.

neurotrophins The chemicals released by target cells that attract the filopodia of a developing neuron.

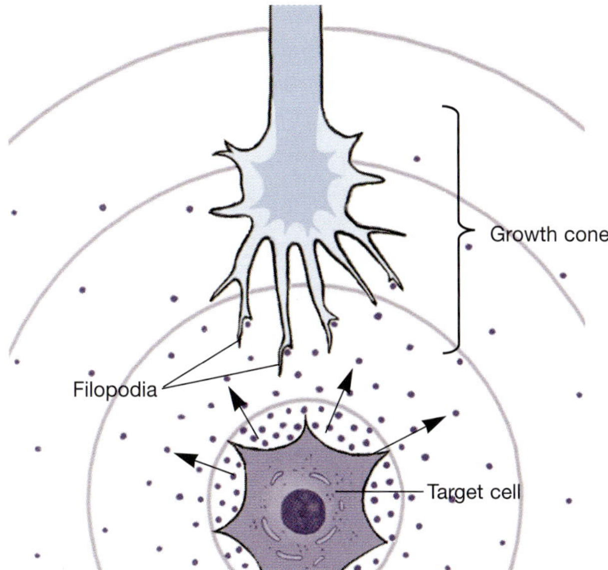

Figure 3.11 Movement of filopodia and growth cone. The movement of filopodia pulls the growth cone toward target neurons releasing a particular chemical. This allows the axon to establish new neural connections.

Adapted from Kandel et al., 1991.

➤ *How do the filopodia pull the growth cone to its destination? (p. 82)*

Levi-Montalcini and Cohen injected antibodies to NGF into newborn mice, total degeneration of sympathetic ganglia was observed. (An antibody is a protein produced by blood cells that binds to a specific antigen and destroys it; an antibody for NGF would destroy it.) These results indicate that the presence of NGF is necessary for the development of the sympathetic nervous system. The 1986 Nobel Prize in physiology or medicine was awarded to Levi-Montalcini and Cohen for their discovery of NGF.

Different neurotrophins are involved in the development of different parts of the nervous system. For example, NGF is involved in the development of sympathetic and sensory nerves in the PNS, whereas brain-derived neurotrophic factor (BDNF) is involved in the development of visual pathways in the CNS (Bothwell, 1995).

Chemical signals may not only attract the growth cone of some cells but also repel those of other cells (Keynes & Cook, 1995). This repulsion may act to ensure that only the appropriate axon moves toward a particular target cell.

The path that an axon takes to reach its target cell may be long, and there may be abrupt changes in direction along the way, much like those we must make when the roads that we must use to travel between point A and point B do not exactly follow the path that the crow flies. The map that guides the axon in making these changes in direction is composed of cells appropriately called **guidepost cells** (Jessell, 1991). When the filopodia reach a guidepost cell, the growth cone adheres to it; the guidepost cell then redirects the growth of the axon toward the target cell (see **Figure 3.12**).

Once an axon reaches its target cell, a synaptic connection is formed between the migrating axon and the target cell. As the synapse is formed, the neurotransmitters that are to be used in communications between the two neurons are also established. Chemicals released by the target cell determine which neurotransmitter is released by the presynaptic membrane into the synaptic cleft. Schotzinger and Landis (1988) provide evidence for this role of the target cell. Norepinephrine is the neurotransmitter found in most sympathetic neurons in the autonomic nervous sys-

guidepost cells Cells that redirect the growth of the axon toward the target cell.

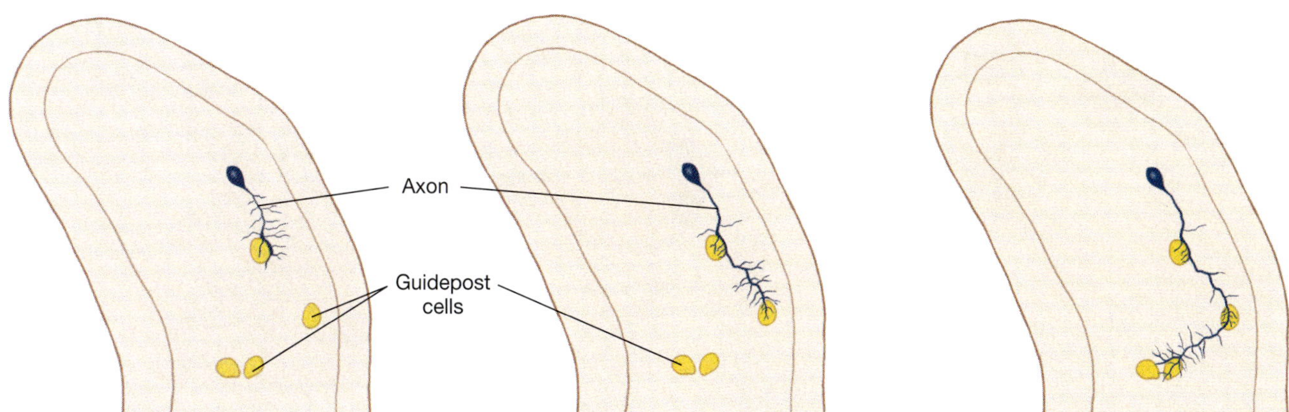

Figure 3.12 The migration of the axon of a sensory neuron. The growth of the axon of a sensory neuron (blue circles) to its predetermined location in the nervous system of a grasshopper embryo. The guidepost cells (yellow circles) direct the axon on its long and circuitous route.

➤ *How are the filopodia guided toward the target cell? (p. 82–83)* tem. The sympathetic neurons that innervate sweat glands in the foot pads are the exception; here, acetylcholine is the neurotransmitter. Newly differentiated sympathetic neurons destined for the sweat glands initially have the same properties as other sympathetic neurons; as the axon of the sympathetic neuron approaches the sweat gland, however, these neurons adopt acetylcholine as the neurotransmitter that they will release.

The Importance of Neural Activity

You might have the impression that only the final neural connections are established during neural development. If so, you have gotten the wrong impression. During the course of axon growth, many side branches emerge. Some of these branches are lost, whereas others form elaborate branches. These branches eventually form synaptic connections to the appropriate areas of the brain. Shatz (1992) suggests that adult neural connections emerge during development by a process that she calls axonal remolding. According to Shatz, axons grow to many different "addresses"; some of these addresses are correct and others are not. The correct addresses remain, and the incorrect addresses are eliminated.

How are the correct addresses established? Consider the development of the visual system to illustrate the complexity of this developmental process. The axons of the ganglion cells of the retina migrate to specific sites in the thalamus, where they synapse with specific neurons in the lateral geniculate nucleus of the thalamus (see **Figure 3.13**). The axons of these neurons migrate to specific sites in the occipital lobe of the cerebral cortex, where they synapse with specific neurons in the occipital lobe. The axons of ganglion neurons do not migrate to just any lateral geniculate neuron; instead, the axons of adjacent ganglion neurons synapse with the dendrites of adjacent neurons in the lateral geniculate nucleus, which then synapse with adjacent neurons in the cerebral cortex. Thus, neurons in the visual system not only develop to specific target sites, but also do so in alignment with adjacent cells. As we will discover in Chapter 6, this alignment is necessary as neural activity in the visual system is not random, but temporally and spatially defined; that is, specific patterns of activity of neurons in the visual system allow us to perceive accurately the characteristics of our visual environment.

Shatz (1992) suggested that neurons that fire together in temporal and spatial sequences get wired together, which is why adjacent ganglion neurons synapse with adjacent lateral geniculate neurons. How does this adjacent wiring occur? We learned earlier that axon growth is controlled by chemicals that attract or repulse the growth cone to the target neuron. However, the presence of a specific neurotrophin is not sufficient for neural development. Neurons must also respond, or a neural impulse be conducted, for axon growth to progress to the target neuron. Without neural activity, the neuron will connect to both correct and incorrect addresses. Shatz (1992) reported that the administration of a drug (tetrodotoxin) that blocks neural impulses from ganglion neurons to the lateral geniculate nucleus neurons resulted in more extensive rather than more restricted neural connections. Apparently neural activity is in part responsible for ensuring that the correct wiring takes place in the nervous system.

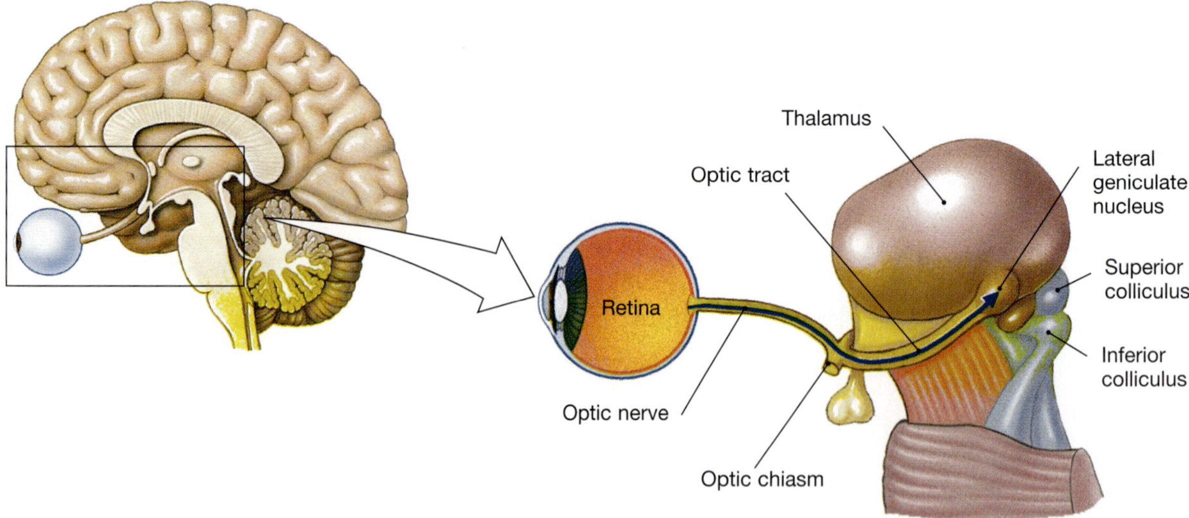

Figure 3.13 Development of the visual system. The neural circuit between the retina and primary visual cortex begins when the growth cones from ganglion cell bodies grow toward their target cells, the neurons in the lateral geniculate nucleus.

➤ *What is the significance of the cell migration process? (p. 83–84)*

You might be wondering how neural activity could occur in a fetus. Galli-Resta and Maffli (1988) reported that there were spontaneous bursts of neural activity from fetal ganglion cells, and this spontaneous neural activity occurred in the darkness of the developing eye. Further, Galli-Resta and Maffli found that such activity was not random, but occurred in predictable and rhythmic bursts. They found that these bursts lasted several seconds and were followed by 30 seconds to 2 minutes of inactivity. The activities of these ganglion cells were highly correlated; that is, simultaneous activity was much more likely to occur in neighboring cells than in ganglion neurons distant from one another. It appears that patterns of neural activity in the developing fetus lead to the wiring of the nervous system that enables environmental events, in this case, visual stimuli, to produce similar patterns of neural activity.

We have seen that almost all neuron formation and growth occurs during prenatal development. At birth, Anne's baby's brain will weigh approximately 350 grams (Purves & Lichtman, 1985). The baby's brain will increase in size to approximately 800 grams by his or her first birthday and will weigh approximately 1,350 grams by adulthood. The increase in brain weight that occurs after birth is mainly the result of the increasing size of existing neurons rather than the formation of new neurons (with the exception of the rose-smelling olfactory receptor neurons that we discussed earlier in the chapter). Thus, the brain becomes bigger following birth because (1) neurons increase in size, (2) the number of axons and dendrites increase, and (3) the number of synaptic connections between those axons and dendrites increases (Shatz, 1992).

New synaptic connections are formed after birth as well as during the prenatal period. These new neural connections allow for the increasingly sophisticated analysis of information and the many varied behavioral responses to environmental circumstances that develop during infancy and childhood. For example, at birth Anne's baby will be able to see approximately 30 inches, just far enough to see Mom's face when Anne is cradling or nursing her. By 6 months, the baby will be able to see approximately 300 inches, and when he or she is an adult, will be able to read a road sign from several hundred feet. We will examine the formation of the new synaptic connections that develop as a result of postnatal experience, a topic that may be more familiar to you by its common name, learning, in Chapter 14.

Neural Cell Death

Cell death is not a topic that usually comes to mind in a discussion of neural development, but neural cell death is a natural developmental process. The extent of cell death during neural development is quite large (Oppenheim, 1991). In fact, in some regions of the brain and spinal cord, most neurons die. Viktor Hamburger (1958), who first described neural cell death, reported that half of the spinal motors die in chicks before they hatch.

Why do neurons die during prenatal development? One theory about why neural cell death occurs is that neurons compete for connections to target cells; those neurons that establish adequate connections survive, and those that fail to form connections die. A second theory is that neurons receiving a certain quantity of the chemical released by the target cells survive, and those neurons that do not receive enough of these chemical messages die. (Picture the filopodia of different neurons competing against one another to acquire the most molecules of the desired chemical like children on an egg hunt trying to get the most eggs.)

We have already mentioned that some synaptic connections are lost during development. This process has been likened to the pruning of a tree or a bush. Redfern (1970) recorded the synaptic responses from skeletal muscle fibers in newborn rats. He observed a decline in the number of synaptic inputs to a single muscle fiber over the course of the first weeks after birth. This reduction is due to a withdrawal of some presynaptic terminals from the muscle fiber and not to a decrease in the number of motor neurons. Because of this type of withdrawal, over the course of development, the number of muscles activated by a motor neuron declines. However, the strength of the muscle fiber reaction does not decline. Instead, the one remaining presynaptic terminal acquires more presynaptic terminals and postsynaptic receptor sites, which allows that single motor neuron to produce a stronger synaptic input to the muscle fiber and, thereby, replace the influence of innervation from several different motor neurons.

Synaptic elimination also can be found in the central nervous system (Jessell, 1991). For example, over the course of development, the number of climbing fibers that innervate a Purkinje neuron in the cerebellum declines from three or four to a single climbing fiber that synapses with the Purkinje neuron in the adult cerebellum.

Brain growth slows by late childhood or young adulthood and begins to reverse at about age 40. The brain decreases in weight because of a reduction in the size of brain cells as well as the increasing death of brain cells. This normal change in the number and size of brain cells does not significantly affect a person's intellect. Disease processes, such as those that produce Alzheimer's disease, involve a very substantial death of brain cells and are thus very different from the normal aging process.

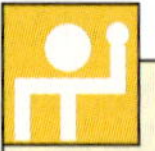

Before You Go On

Describe the physical and chemical means used by the filopodia to reach the target cell.

Why do some neurons die during development?

Why are some synaptic connections lost during development?

Section Review

- The nervous system begins as a single layer of cells along the inner surface of the neural tube that divides into a closely packed ventricular layer of cells.
- Daughter cells migrate from the ventricular level to predetermined locations on the marginal or intermediate layers of the neural tube to become either neurons or glial cells.
- Radial glial cells and previously formed neurons guide migration of neurons by allowing the newly formed neurons to creep along their surface.
- Neural cell differentiation is of two types: cell-autonomous processes and induction.
- Glial cells emerge from the immature cells of the ventricular layer during both the prenatal and postnatal periods to myelinate neurons of the peripheral nervous system, the spinal cord, and the brain.
- Axons grow toward target cells to establish neural connections.
- Filopodia, which extend from the growth cones of the axons, pull the growing axons toward their target cell.
- Neurotrophins, chemicals released by target cells, attract the filopodia. Different neurotrophins guide the development of different parts of the nervous system.
- Guidepost cells also direct the axons along a sometimes long and circuitous route to their target cells.
- Neurotrophins released by the target cell also influence the type of neurotransmitter that is released by the axon.
- Neural development occurs by selectively strengthening appropriate synaptic connections and eliminating inappropriate ones.
- Spontaneous neural activity in the developing fetus is responsible for wiring the nervous system so that environmental events produce patterns of neural activity from adjacent neurons.
- Some neurons die during prenatal development, perhaps because of a failure to establish adequate connections with other neurons, and some synaptic connections are lost.

Down syndrome A genetic disorder caused by the presence of three copies of chromosome 21; characterized by altered facial features, decreased mental functioning, and abnormalities in several internal organs.

phenylketonuria (PKU) A genetic disorder involving the absence of an enzyme needed to break down phenylalanine; the resulting dangerous buildup of phenylalanine can lead to mental retardation.

APPLICATION

Failures of Neural Development

Normal development leads to a nervous system that can detect environmental events, analyze their significance, decide on a response, and execute that response. As we have already seen in our discussions of spina bifida and anencephaly, failure of the nervous system to develop properly can lead to failures in any of these areas. In some cases the failures are preventable, but in others they are not.

Genetic defects represent one source of impaired neural development. An altered gene leads to altered cellular proteins, which results in a change in the neurons controlled by those proteins. The resulting change in neural process will affect the behavior controlled by these neurons. For example, earlier in the chapter we mentioned that Anne's amniocentesis could detect the occurrence of Down syndrome. **Down syndrome**, characterized by altered facial features, decreased mental functioning, and abnormalities in several internal organs, is caused by a defect that produces three copies of chromosome 21 instead of the usual two (it is sometimes called trisomy 21; see **Figure 3.14**). The incidence of Down syndrome is much higher in babies born to women over age 35, presumably due to aging of the eggs in the ovary (Purdy, 1993).

The disorder **phenylketonuria (PKU)** is caused by a deficit in an enzyme necessary to break down phenylalanine, an amino acid present in many foods. The consequence is a dangerous buildup of phenylalanine in the body. PKU is caused by a recessive gene carried by approximately 1 in 50 persons and occurs in about one in ten thousand births. Fortunately, early screening of phenylalanine levels allows detection of this disorder; before Anne's baby even leaves the hospital a PKU test will be done. A diet low in phenylalanine for the early years, especially the first two, can prevent the impairment of the nervous system and the mental retardation typically associated with phenylketonuria. You may have wondered what the warning on your soda can "phenlyketonurics: contains phenylalanine" means—now you know! (A phenylketonuric is someone who has PKU.)

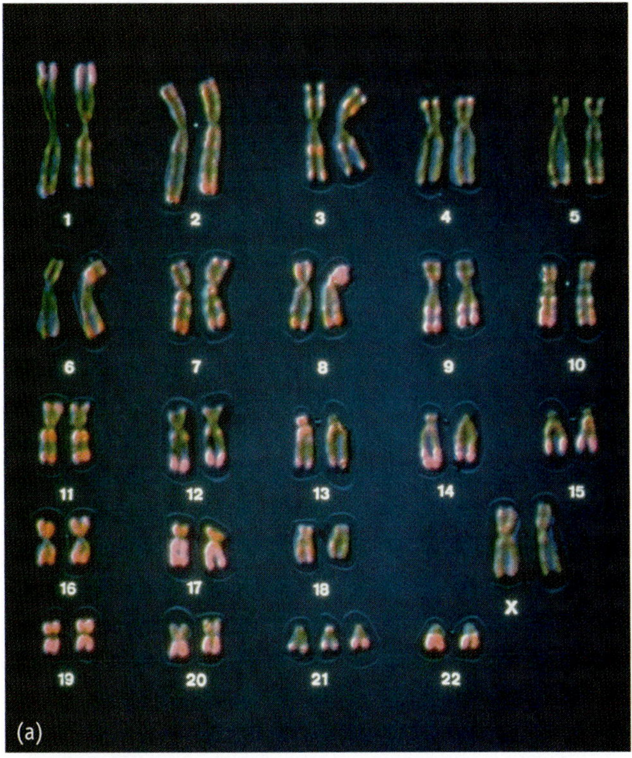

Figure 3.14 Down syndrome. The extra copy of chromosome 21 is shown in part (a). Part (b) shows the altered facial features typical of an individual with Down syndrome, most strikingly the extra folds of skin over the eyes.

➤ *What are the other characteristics of this disorder? (p. 86)*

Individuals with **fragile X syndrome** have an abnormal facial appearance (long narrow face, large prominent ears, and prominent forehead and jaw) and mental retardation that varies from mild to severe (Baumgardner, Green, & Reiss, 1994). After Down syndrome, fragile X syndrome is the leading cause of mental retardation in the United States (McEvoy, 1992). Hyperactivity and attention deficits are also associated with fragile X syndrome. As its name implies, this disorder is caused by a fragile gene at one site on the large arm of the X chromosome that can actually cause the X chromosome to break. Normally, the gene is responsible for producing a particular protein, called FMR-1, but the fragile gene produces drastically reduced levels of FMR-1 (Paulson & Fischbisk, 1996). It is because FMR-1 protein is widely distributed in fetal tissue, especially in differentiating and migrating neurons, that the consequences of reduced FMR-1 protein are so widespread (Dykens, Hodapp, & Leckman, 1994).

Genetic disorders cause deficits in the developing nervous system. As we have seen, some of these deficits can be treated, but it is not possible to prevent them. Many external factors also can influence the developing nervous system. We will next look at two external factors to demonstrate how sensitive the developing nervous system is to disruption.

You may have heard advertisements urging pregnant women to seek medical care during their pregnancy. One important aspect of this medical care is ensuring that a pregnant woman consumes a nutritionally sound diet. The failure to provide sufficient nutrients to the developing brain of the fetus can have a number of negative consequences. Malnutrition has been shown to have extremely detrimental effects on the developing brain (Sigman, 1995), causing such problems as decreased birth weight and increased infant mortality (Susser & Lin, 1992). Further, early malnutrition lowers performance on a variety of tests of mental capacity (Udani, 1992). The damaging effects of malnutrition can sometimes be reversed, but only with early and prolonged intervention (Gunston et al., 1992). However, malnutrition can be prevented by the nutritional counseling included in prenatal medical care. Even if an expectant mother thinks that

fragile X syndrome A disorder caused by a fragile gene at one site on the large arm of the X chromosome that can cause the X chromosome to break; individuals with this disorder have an abnormal facial appearance and mental retardation.

she is eating properly, a deficiency in even a single nutrient can cause irreversible damage to the developing fetus. An inadequate supply of the nutrient folic acid can cause neural tube defects such as spina bifida and anencephaly in the first few weeks of development, possibly before the woman even realizes she is pregnant. For this reason, the FDA has proposed that folic acid be added to a number of food staples, such as bread, just as vitamin D is added to our milk.

Toxins such as alcohol and drugs cause severe damage to the developing nervous system. For example, consumption of even moderate amounts of alcohol during pregnancy can cause significant physical and behavioral problems (Colangelo & Jones, 1982). Individuals with **fetal alcohol syndrome** have low birth weight and diminished height; distinctive facial features (sunken nasal bridge, altered shape of nose and eyelids; see **Figure 3.15**); and behavioral problems (mental retardation, hyperactivity, and irritability). The threshold of alcohol consumption during pregnancy that will produce fetal alcohol syndrome has not been established, so pregnant women are generally advised to avoid any consumption of alcohol. ■

Before You Go On

Give two examples of genetic failures of neural development.

Why is what a pregnant woman eats and drinks important to the development of the nervous system?

fetal alcohol syndrome A disorder produced by exposure to alcohol during prenatal development; characterized by low birth weight and diminished height, distinctive facial features, mental retardation, and behavioral problems (hyperactivity and irritability).

Section Review

- Neural development can be impaired by defective genes, causing such disorders as Down syndrome, in which there are three copies of chromosome 21; phenylketonuria, in which there is a deficit in the enzyme necessary to breakdown phenylalanine; and fragile X syndrome, in which there are reduced levels of FRM-1 protein.
- External factors that can adversely affect nervous system development include malnutrition during pregnancy, which can lead to low birth weight, increased infant mortality, and neural tube defects, and consumption of alcohol during pregnancy, which can lead to fetal alcohol syndrome.

Redevelopment of the Nervous System

We have seen some of the ways damage can be done to the nervous system during development. But what happens if the nervous system is damaged after development is completed? In 1995, the actor Christopher Reeve fell off his horse and was paralyzed from the neck down. As discussed earlier in the chapter, at birth almost all neurons have been formed. What will happen to Reeve's damaged neurons? How much function can he expect to recover? We will answer these questions in this section.

The nervous system can suffer damage in many ways, including blunt trauma from a blow, invasive trauma from an injury such as a gunshot wound, tumors, infections, drugs and other toxic substances, exposure to radiation, and degenerative conditions such as Parkinson's disease (see Chapter 2 for a detailed discussion of the causes of damage to the nervous system). If the damage to a neuron occurs to the cell body, the neuron will die, because the cell body is the metabolic center of the neuron. Damage to the axon also leads to degenerative changes in the neuron that may or may not cause cell death. When an axon is damaged, the part between the break and the presy-

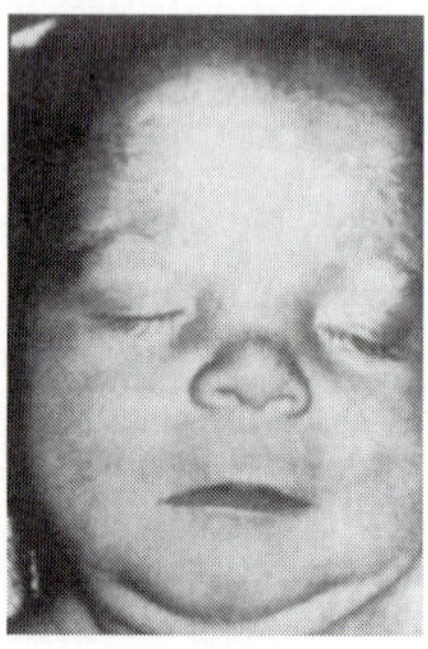

(a)

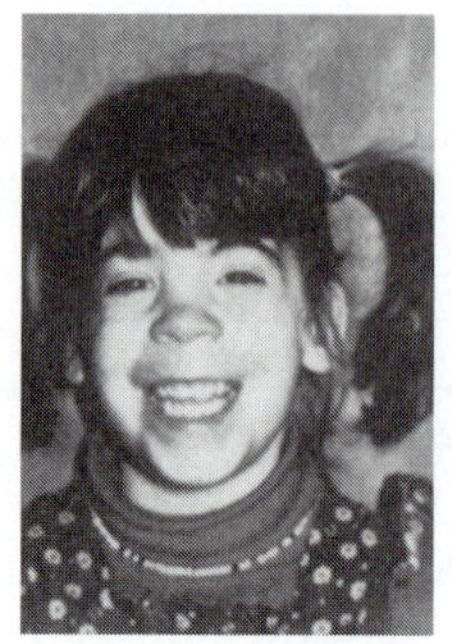

(b)

(c)

Figure 3.15 Fetal alcohol syndrome. You can see the altered facial features caused by the mother's consumption of alcohol during pregnancy.

➤ *What are the other characteristics of this disorder? (p. 88)*

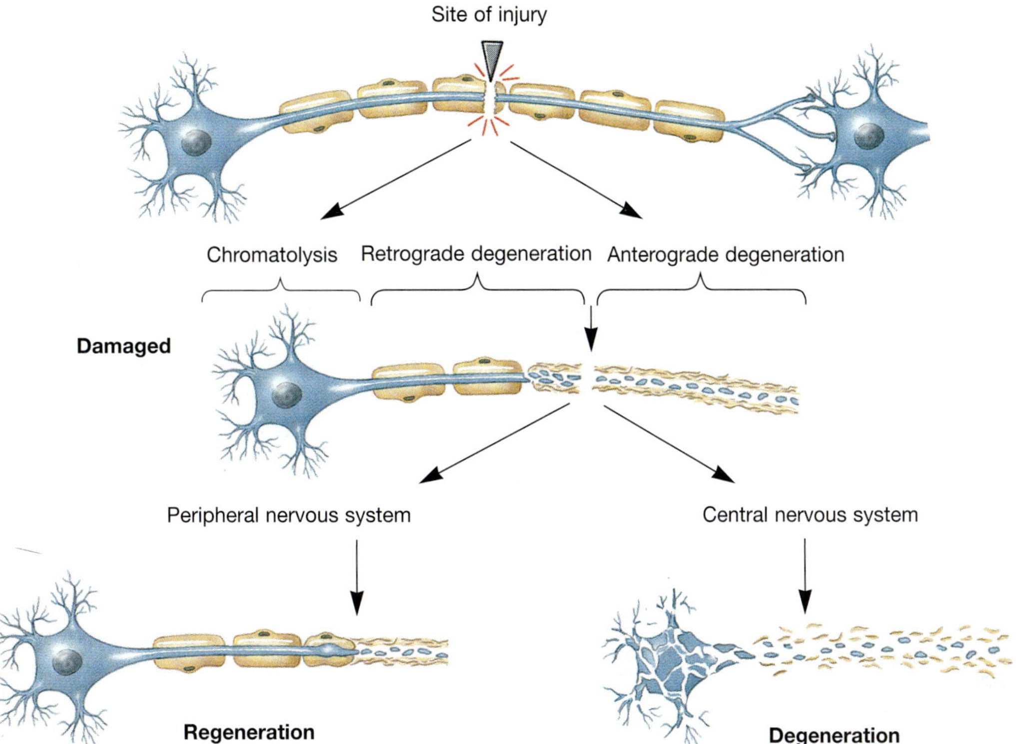

Figure 3.16 The degeneration of a neuron following axon damage. Regeneration of the axon can occur in the peripheral nervous system, but not in the central nervous system.

Adapted from Schneider & Tarshis, 1995.

➤ *Why does regeneration occur in the peripheral nervous system but not in the central nervous system? (p. 90)*

naptic terminals breaks down through a process called **anterograde degeneration** (see **Figure 3.16**). Damage to the part of the axon between the break and the cell body deprives the cell body of life-sustaining substances, which leads to the progressive breakdown of the undamaged part of the axon attached to the cell body, a process called **retrograde degeneration**, and the cell body itself, a process called **chromatolysis** (refer to **Figure 3.16**). It is easy to remember the difference between anterograde and retrograde degeneration if you recall that transmission of neural messages is a one-way process from the cell body, down the axon, and to the synapse (see Chapter 2). Antero- or anterior means toward the front or forward, and retro- means backward, so anterograde degeneration is forward (toward the synapse) from the damage, and retrograde degeneration is backward (toward the cell body).

A degenerating neuron may in turn damage those neurons with which it has synaptic connections, a process called **transneuronal degeneration**. Transneuronal degeneration may produce mild changes in connecting neurons, or the changes may be severe enough to lead to the degeneration of those affected neurons. This degeneration can occur in neurons that receive synaptic input from the degenerating neuron (called anterograde transneuronal degeneration) and to neurons that synapse onto the degenerating neuron (called retrograde transneuronal degeneration).

Transneuronal degeneration can lead to widespread damage to the nervous system (Jessell, 1991). For example, suppose the axons of some retinal ganglion cells that comprise the optic nerve are severed. Degeneration of these ganglion cells will lead to anterograde degeneration of the neurons of the lateral geniculate nucleus. The degeneration may spread from the lateral geniculate nucleus to the connecting neurons in the visual cortex, to adjacent neurons in the visual cortex, and then back to the lateral geniculate nucleus and retinal ganglion layer. The end result of this degeneration is severe damage to the visual system. The

---

anterograde degeneration The breakdown of the axon from the site of damage to the presynaptic terminals.

retrograde degeneration The progressive breakdown of the axon between the site of the break and the cell body.

chromatolysis The breakdown of the cell body following damage to the axon.

transneuronal degeneration Damage to neurons with which a degenerating neuron has synaptic connections.

consequences of damage to the visual system would be a loss of some or all ability to process visual information. A more detailed discussion of the visual system and the effects of damage to the visual system will be presented in Chapter 6.

Is degeneration inevitable? The answer to this question depends on where in the nervous system the damage occurs. If the axon that is damaged is in the peripheral nervous system, the neuron can regrow and reestablish its connections to other neurons. However, such **regeneration** does not occur if the damaged axon is in the central nervous system (refer to **Figure 3.16**).

Why does regeneration occur in the peripheral nervous system but not in the central nervous system? Damaged central nervous system neurons will regenerate if transplanted into the peripheral nervous system, but regeneration does not occur if damaged peripheral nervous system neurons are transplanted into the central nervous system (Bray et al., 1987; Cotman & Nieto-Sampedro, 1984). These data indicate that factors external to the damaged neuron are somehow responsible.

Jessell (1991) has identified two likely factors. First, two glycoproteins that promote cone growth, laminin and fibronectin, are present in the mature mammalian peripheral nervous system, but absent from the central nervous system. The presence of these glycoproteins enables the regeneration of damaged axons in the peripheral nervous system, whereas their absence from the central nervous system makes regeneration unlikely. Second, the oligodendrocytes of the central nervous system synthesize a glycoprotein that inhibits axon growth, but no such inhibitory glycoprotein is found in the Schwann cells of the peripheral nervous system.

Although the neurons of the central nervous system cannot regenerate after damage, neighboring neurons can sometimes compensate for the loss of neural connections through a process called **collateral sprouting**. When a neuron degenerates, neighboring neurons sometimes sprout new axonal endings to connect to the receptor sites left vacant by the degenerated neuron (see **Figure 3.17**). Can these new connections serve the same function as the original ones? Some neuroscientists (Reeves & Smith, 1987) believe that the new connections could reinstate normal functioning. In support of this view, Kolb (1995) reported that following hippocampal damage in rats, collateral sprouts developed between the hippocampus and the cerebral cortex at the same time as the recovery of behaviors following the brain damage. At this time, researchers are investigating the experimental application of collateral sprouting as a means of restoring function following nerve damage.

We learned earlier in this chapter that chemical signals can repel as well as attract axon growth toward a target cell during the development of the nervous system. What might happen if these axon growth-inhibiting chemicals were suppressed following damage to neurons in the central nervous system? Would this treatment lead to regeneration of neurons in the central nervous system? A number of researchers have investigated this possibility in adult rats following damage to the corticospinal motor system. Some of these studies (Bregman et al., 1995; Cadelli & Schwab, 1991; Schnell & Schwab, 1993: Weibel, Cadelli, & Schwab, 1994) looked at regeneration of corticospinal motor axons following spinal cord lesions in adult rats exposed to antibodies that neutralize the activity of axon growth-inhibitory proteins. Exposure to these antibodies leads to significant long-distance regeneration of the axons of corticospinal motor neurons.

Other studies (Bregman et al., 1993; Bregman et al., 1995; Kunkel-Bagden & Bregman, 1990; Kunkel-Bagden, Dai, & Bregman, 1993) examined the recovery of motor functions in similarly treated rats. These studies report recovery of some, but not all, motor functions. For example, recovered stride length was equal to animals whose spinal cord was not damaged. (Nontreated spinal cord-damaged adult rats show shorter stride lengths.) Other motor functions remained impaired despite the administration of the antibodies. For example, these researchers found contact placing (the lifting of a limb and placing it on a surface for support following light skin contact such as a pin prick) by the spinal cord-damaged animal was not improved when antibodies for axon growth-inhibitory proteins were administered. Contact placement is a more precise sensory-motor response than is stride length, which may explain the difference. Research continues on the use of antibodies that suppress axon growth-inhibitory proteins as a means of producing regeneration of axons in the central nervous system. The usefulness of this approach to help individuals like Christopher Reeves with spinal cord injury is promising, but will require much more investigation.

A final area of active research is the transplantation of fetal tissue to the damaged area of the central nervous system. Fetal tissue is thought by some to be the ideal treatment because the lack of cell differentiation at this stage of neural development allows for the flexibility needed to reestablish critical neural circuits, and thereby, allow for recovery of function following neuronal damage. However, others have strong beliefs that the use of fetal tissue is unethical for this or any other reason.

---

regeneration The regrowth of a neuron and the reestablishment of its connections to other neurons.

collateral sprouting A process by which neighboring neurons of a degenerating neuron sprout new axonal endings to connect to the receptor sites left vacant by the degenerated neuron.

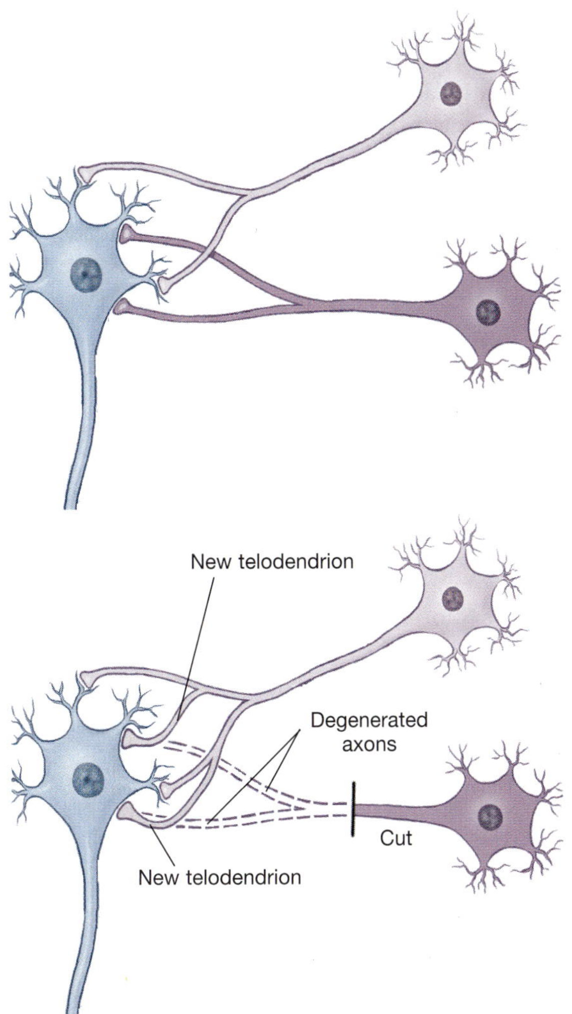

Figure 3.17 Illustration of collateral sprouting. Degeneration of one neuron leads to collateral sprouting of another neuron so that the new axons synapse with the receptor sites formerly occupied by the degenerating neuron.

➤ *What is the purpose of collateral sprouting? (p. 90)*

In Chapter 2, we learned that damage to the dopaminergic neurons that connect the substantia nigra to basal ganglia leads to Parkinson's disease, which is characterized by rigidity and extreme difficulty integrating voluntary motor responses. In a number of studies, fetal tissue has been transplanted into the brains of adult rats with substantia nigra lesions (Dunnett & Bjorklund, 1987; Gage & Fisher, 1991; Labbe et al., 1983; Wictorin et al., 1990). These transplants have restored movement following lesioning of substantia nigra neurons that project to the basal ganglia and maze-learning ability after brain grafting to lesioned cortical areas. Fetal tissue implants have also been shown to improve motor function in primates with damage to the dopaminergic neurons of the substantia nigra (Redmond et al., 1988). Movement has been reported to improve following fetal tissue implants in humans with Parkinson's disease (Freed et al., 1992; Kordower et al., 1995; Lindvall et al., 1994), although this experimental treatment has only been tried on a relatively small number of persons.

Research studies (Clarke et al., 1988; Stromberg et al., 1989) that have examined the brains of rats with substantia nigra lesions following fetal tissue implants have reported that fetal dopaminergic neurons replaced synapses that were damaged, indicating that brain microcircuitry was repaired following fetal tissue implantation. Several recent studies (Deacon et al., 1997; Kordower et al., 1996) have reported that fetal tissue implantation into the caudate-putamen area resulted in the growth of dopaminergic neurons from the graft site and the establishment of synaptic connections to neurons in this area of the brain. These results suggest that the improvement in motor function in patients with Parkinson's disease following fetal tissue implants is due to the establishment of new dopaminergic synapses in the basal ganglia. At this point, only very preliminary studies have been done with humans, and the jury is still out regarding the effectiveness of such transplants in treating Parkinson's disease.

Certain kinds of experiences may allow individuals who have suffered nerve damage to develop compensatory behaviors that substitute for lost functions, a process called **rehabilitation**. For example, speech-language pathologists use a number of treatment approaches to help patients regain language abilities following a stroke or other brain injury. We will have more to say about various rehabilitation approaches throughout the text.

Before You Go On

What is the difference in response to damage of neurons in the central and peripheral nervous systems?

Why would implantation of fetal tissue help in the treatment of nervous system damage?

Section Review

- Damage to the cell body of a neuron leads to the breakdown or degeneration of the entire neuron.
- Axonal damage causes degeneration toward the presynaptic terminal called anterograde degeneration. Degeneration of the axon toward the cell body is called retrograde degeneration.
- Chromatolysis is the degeneration of the cell body.

rehabilitation The process of developing compensatory behaviors that substitute for lost functions.

- Transneuronal degeneration by the damaged neuron causes the death of neurons that have synaptic connections with the damaged neuron and can be quite widespread.
- An axon in the peripheral nervous system can regenerate after damage because of the presence of laminin and fibronectin, glycoproteins that promote cone growth.
- The absence of laminin and fibronectin and the presence of inhibitory glycoproteins synthesized by oligodendrocytes prevent the regeneration of neurons in the central nervous system.
- Collateral sprouting is the generation of new axons by neighboring neurons to occupy receptor sites left vacant by degenerating neurons.
- The experimental application of collateral sprouting, administration of antibodies of axon growth-inhibitory proteins, and the implantation of fetal tissue are all procedures currently being investigated as treatments for damaged neurons in the central nervous system.
- Rehabilitation can sometimes compensate for lost function.

Chapter Review

Critical Thinking Questions

1. Miscarriage is not an uncommon occurrence during a pregnancy. Using your knowledge of the processes responsible for the developing nervous system, suggest several reasons an embryo or fetus might not survive.
2. As we have discussed, development of new neurons in the nervous system ceases shortly after birth with a few minor exceptions. Why doesn't the nervous system continue to generate new neurons throughout the life cycle?
3. Many individuals become paralyzed as a result of accidents. Describe what might be done to enable victims of spinal cord damage to regain the use of their limbs. Your answer should make use of your understanding of nerve migration and the formation of synaptic connections.

Vocabulary Questions

1. The three distinct layers of cells formed by the week-old embryo are the ________________, the ________________, and the ________________.
2. A ________________ defect such as ________________ or ________________ occurs when some portion of the neural folds fails to close to form the neural tube.
3. The forebrain divides into the ________________ and the ________________.
4. The ________________ subdivision of the forebrain will become the cerebral cortex, basal ganglia, hippocampus, amygdala, and the ________________.
5. The ________________ subdivision of the forebrain will become the thalamus and ________________.
6. The hindbrain divides into the ________________, which includes the ________________ and cerebellum, and the ________________, which includes the ________________.
7. ________________ cells and ________________ cells develop in the ventricular layer and migrate to the ________________ layer.
8. The ________________ cells guide the migration of the daughter cells from the inner to the outer surface of the developing nervous system.
9. The two types of cell differentiation are ________________ differentiation and ________________.
10. ________________ is the guidance of axon growth by chemical signals.
11. ________________, or trisomy 21, is a genetic disorder caused by an extra copy of chromosome 21.
12. ________________ is a genetic disorder caused by an abnormality in a gene on the X chromosome that causes the X chromosome to break.
13. Consumption of alcohol during pregnancy can cause ________________ syndrome.
14. Degeneration of the cell body is called ________________.
15. Damage to neighboring neurons by a degenerating neuron is called ________________ degeneration.
16. Neural regrowth and reestablishment of synaptic connections is called ________________.
17. The growth of new axons by neurons adjacent to degenerating neurons is called ________________.

Review Questions

1. The cell layer that forms the various parts of the nervous system is the
   a. endoderm.
   b. mesoderm.
   c. ectoderm.
   d. marginal layer.
2. The brain initially differentiates into the
   a. forebrain, midbrain, and hindbrain.
   b. forebrain, medulla, and hypothalamus.
   c. pons, medulla, and cerebellum.
   d. thalamus, hypothalamus, and cerebral cortex.
3. The four ________________ of the ________________ system protect and provide nutrients to the brain.
   a. divisions, peripheral nervous
   b. ventricles, ventricular
   c. ganglia, peripheral
   d. cell layers, limbic
4. The formation of new neurons is called
   a. chemotropism.
   b. chromatolysis.
   c. regeneration.
   d. neurogenesis.
5. Newly formed neurons are guided toward their destinations by glycoproteins such as
   a. neural cell adhesion molecules, cadherins, and integrins.
   b. adherins, radial glial cells, and daughter cells.
   c. Purkinje cells, glial cells, and cadherins.
   d. neural cell adhesion molecules, daughter cells, and glial cells.
6. The ________________ extend from the ________________ to guide the developing axon toward its proper destination.
   a. growth cones, axon
   b. filopodia, growth cone
   c. growth cones, synapse
   d. filopodia, axon
7. The growth cone may be redirected toward its destination by
   a. daughter cells.
   b. glial cells.
   c. target cells.
   d. guidepost cells.
8. One important function of ________________ cells is ________________, the wrapping of the nerve axon with myelin.
   a. daughter, chemotropism
   b. glial, neurogenesis
   c. daughter, myelination
   d. glial, myelination
9. The particular neurotransmitter that will be used at the developing synapse is determined by the
   a. filopodia.
   b. growth cone.
   c. target cell.
   d. cell body.
10. A dangerous buildup of the amino acid phenylalanine is the cause of a genetic disorder called
    a. chromatolysis.
    b. neurogenesis.
    c. phenylketonuria.
    d. anterograde degeneration.
11. Malnutrition can cause problems such as
    a. decreased mental function and increased hyperactivity.
    b. decreased birth weight and increased infant mortality.
    c. decreased bone density and increased attention deficits.
    d. decreased mental function and increased amino acid levels.
12. The neuron degenerates toward the synapse in ________________ degeneration and toward the cell body in ________________ degeneration.
    a. retrograde, anterograde
    b. anterograde, retrograde
    c. transneuronal, anterograde
    d. retrograde, transneuronal
13. Regeneration occurs in the ________________ system but not in the ________________ system.
    a. central nervous, peripheral nervous
    b. limbic, digestive
    c. peripheral nervous, central nervous
    d. vertebral, cranial
14. Experimental approaches to recovery of function after nervous system damage include
    a. collateral sprouting and fetal tissue transplants.
    b. rehabilitation and neurogenesis.
    c. induction and chemotropism.
    d. regeneration and collateral sprouting.

Suggested Readings

BROWN, M. C., HOPKINS, W. G., & KEYNES, R. J. (1991). *Essentials of neural development.* Cambridge University Press: Cambridge.

GILBERT, S. F. (1991). *Developmental biology.* Sunderland, MA: Sinauer Associates.

PURVES, D., & LICHTMAN, J. W. (1985). *Principles of neural development.* Sunderland, MA: Sinauer Associates.

SHATZ, C. J. (1992). The developing brain. *Scientific American, 267,* 61–67.

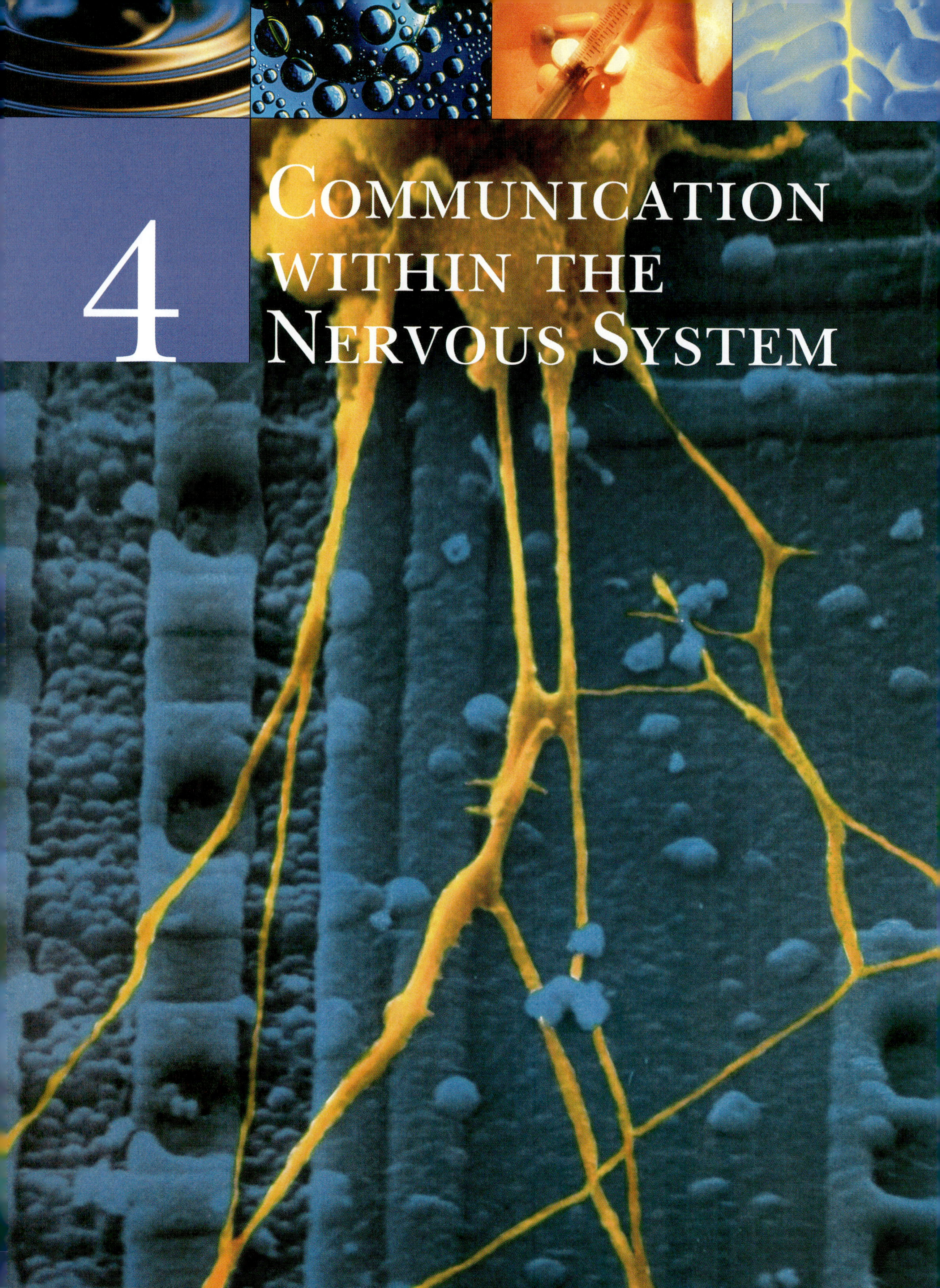

4 Communication within the Nervous System

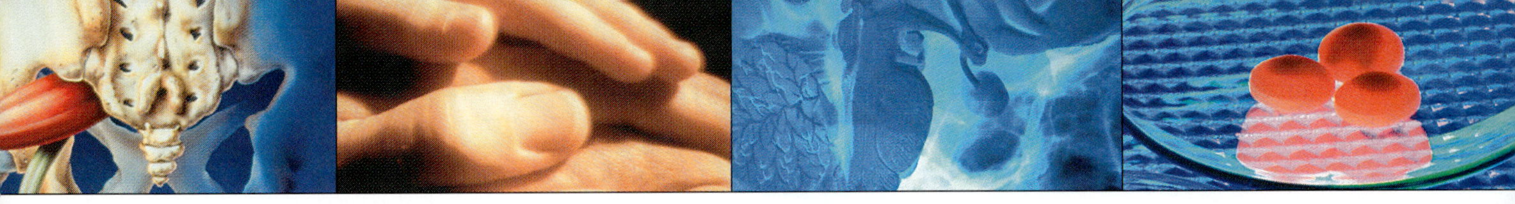

A Feeling of Doom

Michele had been feeling out of sorts for some time, weak and easily fatigued. At times, she became dizzy and her vision blurred. At first, Michele thought that she had the flu. The symptoms lasted only a few days, and when they were gone, she quickly forgot about them. When the symptoms returned, they were much worse. The weakness in her muscles was so profound that Michele had difficulty walking. And then she found herself slurring words and forgetting the names of people she had known all of her life.

Michele postponed going to the doctor, mostly because she was afraid of what she would learn. The symptoms finally became so disturbing that Michele dragged herself to the doctor. The doctor listened patiently as Michele described her symptoms, did a physical examination, and conducted a battery of tests. When Michele met the doctor in her office, the news was not good: The tests revealed that she had multiple sclerosis. Michele did not know much about multiple sclerosis except that it was a serious illness. The doctor tried to reassure Michele that the disease progression can be quite varied. Some people become rapidly incapacitated, whereas others experience a slow progression of the illness with periods of remission, or absence of symptoms. The remissions may last for years, during which time the individual can live a perfectly normal life. Even during times when the symptoms are present, a person can continue to function in a productive way.

Michele might need physical therapy if her symptoms worsened, but at this time she should just get enough sleep and not try to do too much. She also started Michele on methylprednisone, with the hope that this drug would reduce or eliminate her symptoms. The physician told Michele that she might need to get some psychological help if she became too fearful or depressed, but she did not think counseling was necessary now. The doctor wanted to see Michele regularly to monitor her condition. Michele was very upset when she left the doctor's office. She did not know how long she could continue to work, and she dreaded the thought of becoming an invalid. ■

◀ A neuron can receive input from up to 100,000 different sources.

Before You Begin

What caused Michele to develop multiple sclerosis?

What is the effect of multiple sclerosis on the nervous system? Why did her physician prescribe methylprednisone?

In this chapter, we will help you answer these and the following questions:

- How does the nervous system process information?
- How do neurons communicate with each other?
- What is myelin, and why is it so important? What happens when the immune system destroys the myelin covering?
- Why do drugs influence the function of the nervous system?
- How do hormones work? Why are hormonal effects more profound than those of neurotransmitters?
- What causes the "runner's high"? Why does the body manufacture an opiate-like substance?

Exchange of Information

As we saw in Chapter 2, neurons receive information from other neurons as well as from the external and internal environments. We will discuss the process responsible for the exchange of information between neurons in this chapter. The site of this information exchange, the synapse, usually involves transmission from the axon of one neuron to the dendrite or soma of another neuron, but in some cases, the transmission is from the axon of one neuron to the axon of another neuron or from the dendrite of one neuron to the dendrite of another neuron. The process by which information is transferred from the axon of one neuron to the dendrite or soma of another neuron is described next. Later in the chapter, the process by which information is transmitted from the axon of one neuron to the axon of another neuron and from the dendrite of one neuron to the dendrite of another neuron is discussed. The process by which neurons detect external and internal stimulation is discussed in Chapters 6 and 7.

To paraphrase the words of William Shakespeare, one of Michele's favorite authors, "to fire or not to fire, that is the question." And the end result of information exchange between neurons is essentially answering a yes or no question. For example, suppose that Michele steps on a tack. A neuron in Michele's brain "asks" the question, Is the stimulus painful? If the answer is yes, the most likely one in this case, the neuron will convey this answer, in the form of a neural impulse, to other neurons by means of the release of neurotransmitters that travel across the synapse and bind to receptor sites on the postsynaptic membrane. Michele will feel the tack, probably verbalize some response, and remove it from her foot. By contrast, no neural impulse will be conveyed by the neuron if the answer is no. For example, neurons in Michele's pain detection system might not respond to the tack stimulus if she had recently consumed several glasses of wine. The mechanism responsible for the effects of alcohol on pain detection will be discussed in Chapter 5. (The first step in detection is the pain receptor. A pain receptor, like other receptors such as the visual and auditory receptors, detects the presence of external stimuli. By contrast, the receptor sites on nonsensory neurons detect neurotransmitter molecules.)

How did Michele's pain detection system recognize the presence of the tack? Or fail to detect it? In what form was that information conveyed to the other neurons in the nervous system? The way in which sensory receptors detect environmental stimuli differs from the way in which neurons detect information from other neurons. We will focus on the communication between neurons in this chapter and have more to say about the detection of sensory information by sensory receptors in Chapters 6 and 7.

The Resting Membrane Potential

The cell membrane of a neuron, like the cell membranes of all cells, lets some substances into the neuron and keeps other substances out. However, the neural cell membrane has a unique quality that it does not share with nonneural cell membranes: The entire membrane of a neuron is electrically charged, or polarized. You might envision this membrane charge as being similar to the positive and negative charges on a battery. In the neuron, the fluid inside the cell is more negatively charged than the fluid outside the cell. When the neuron is at rest, not receiving information from other neurons, this difference in polarity is called the **resting membrane potential**.

Unlike that of a battery, the difference in polarity between the inside and the outside of the cell membrane is quite small. The typical polarization of the cell membrane is 70 mV (a millivolt is one thousandth of a volt). (By contrast, the difference in a 9-volt battery is 9,000 mV.) The fluid inside the cell is always used as the reference point. The typical resting membrane potential is –70 mV, mean-

resting membrane potential The difference in polarity between the inside and the outside of the cell membrane when the neuron is at rest.

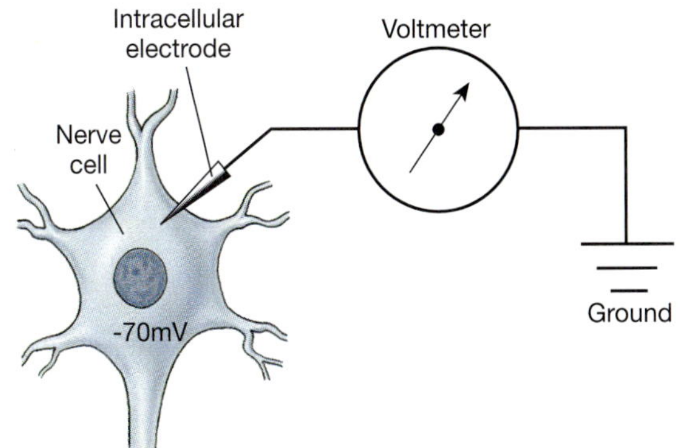

Figure 4.1 Recording a neuron's resting membrane potential. The neuron's resting potential can be recorded by inserting a micropipette (filled with a liquid that conducts electricity) connected to a voltmeter into the cell. Recordings from the voltmeter show that the inside of the cell is 70 mV more negatively charged than outside of the cell.

➤ *What ion differences exist across the resting neural cell membrane? (p. 97)*

ing that the fluid inside the cell is 70 mV more negatively charged than the fluid outside of the cell (see **Figure 4.1**).

What causes the cell membrane of a neuron to be charged? This difference in charge is caused by the greater concentration of positive ions outside the cell as compared with their concentration inside the cell. An **ion** is a charged particle of an element such as sodium (Na), potassium (K), or chloride (Cl). Some ions such as sodium and potassium are positively charged; other ions, such as chloride, are negatively charged.

When the neuron is at rest, sodium (Na^+), potassium (K^+), and chloride (Cl^-) ions enter and exit the neuron through gates (or channels) in the cell membrane (see **Figure 4.2**). However, the ions do not exist inside and outside the cell in equal concentrations: more Na^+ and Cl^- ions are found outside the cell and more K^+ ions and A^- (large protein molecules) are found inside the cell.

Why are there differences in ion concentrations? The protein ions (A^-) are relatively large and cannot leave the cells. The other three ions (Na^+, K^+, Cl^-) enter and leave the cell through the ion channels, although the cell membrane is much more permeable to K^+ and Cl^- ions than to Na^+ ions. Two passive forces, diffusion and electrostatic pressure, and one active process, the sodium-potassium pump, affect the movement of the other three ions across the neural cell membrane.

ion A charged particle of an element.

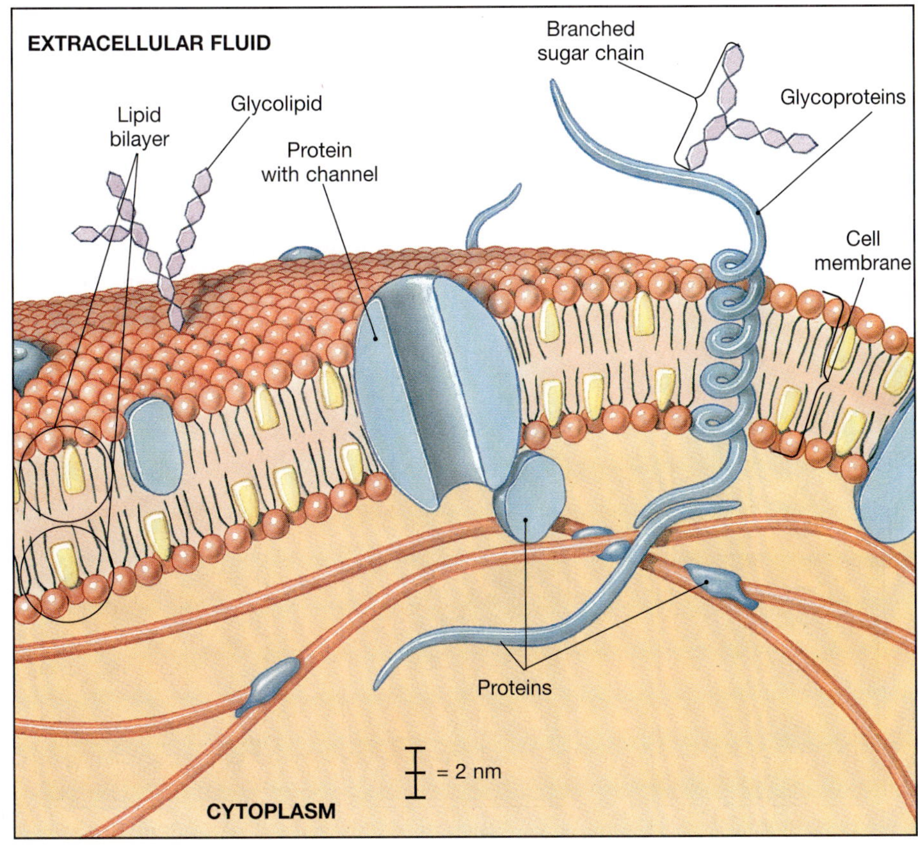

Figure 4.2 Diagram of the cell membrane. The cell membrane is a double layer of lipid molecules with imbedded proteins. The ions move in and out of the cell through channels in the protein molecules. Movement of ions can be controlled by opening or closing the ion channels.

➤ *What is the function of the protein molecules embedded in the neural cell membrane? (p. 97)*

Diffusion and Electrostatic Pressure

Diffusion refers to the tendency of molecules to move from areas of higher concentration to areas of lower concentration. The result of diffusion, if it is the only force at work, will be an even distribution of molecules (see **Figure 4.3**). Consider the following example to illustrate the effect of diffusion. Have you ever been at a really crowded party, where the people are so packed in that there is barely enough room to turn around? Your natural tendency is to try to find the area where there are the fewest people, or at least not so many people that someone bumps your arm and spills your drink.

The movement of ions across the membrane is affected by electrical charges as well as by chemical concentrations. Do you know the old saying "opposites attract"? If you place two bar magnets end to end, they will either attach to one another or push away from one another. **Electrostatic pressure** refers to the attraction of opposite-polarity molecules (the two magnets that are attached) and the repulsion of same-polarity molecules (the two magnets that push away from one another). Electrostatic pressure would tend to even out the number of ions on either side of the membrane based on electrical charge rather than on concentration. Thus, if electrostatic pressure were the only force at work, there would be equal numbers of chloride ions inside and outside the neural cell membrane, as well as equal numbers of sodium and potassium ions, and the resting membrane potential would be 0 mV, not –70 mV.

diffusion The tendency of molecules to move from areas of higher concentration to areas of lower concentration.

electrostatic pressure The attraction of opposite-polarity (+/-) molecules and the repulsion of same-polarity (+/+ or -/-) molecules.

To simplify matters, we have described what the forces of diffusion and electrostatic pressure would do if they acted alone. However, as the following discussion will show, they do not act alone, but together, to influence the movement of ions across the neural cell membrane. Diffusion would normally act to move Cl^- ions into the cell because there are more of these ions found outside of the cell. However, the force of diffusion is counteracted by the electrostatic pressure created by the greater negative charge inside (remember those negatively charged proteins that cannot exit the cell); that is, repulsion of like charges prevents many Cl^- ions from entering the cell. As seen in **Figure 4.4**, the opposing forces of diffusion and electrostatic pressure act to keep the Cl^- ion concentration higher outside the cell.

The opposing forces of diffusion and electrostatic pressure also act to keep most K^+ ions inside the cell (refer to **Figure 4.4**). The force of diffusion works to move K^+ ions out of the cell, but because of electrostatic pressure, the greater positive charge outside as compared to inside the cell acts to keep most K^+ ions inside the cell.

Although the forces of diffusion and electrostatic pressure have opposing effects on Cl^- and K^+ ions, both forces act to bring Na^+ ions into the cell (see **Figure 4.4**). Because many more Na^+ ions are found outside the cell than inside the cell, the force of diffusion acts to push Na^+ ions into the cell. Electrostatic pressure caused by the negative charge on the inside of the cell acts to attract the positively charged Na^+ ions. With the push to the inside of the cell by both of the forces, our neurons should be filled to the brim with sodium ions. Why then are more Na^+ ions found outside than inside the cell? One reason is that the ion channels are typically closed to Na^+ ions, which makes it quite difficult for Na^+ ions to enter the cell. The sec-

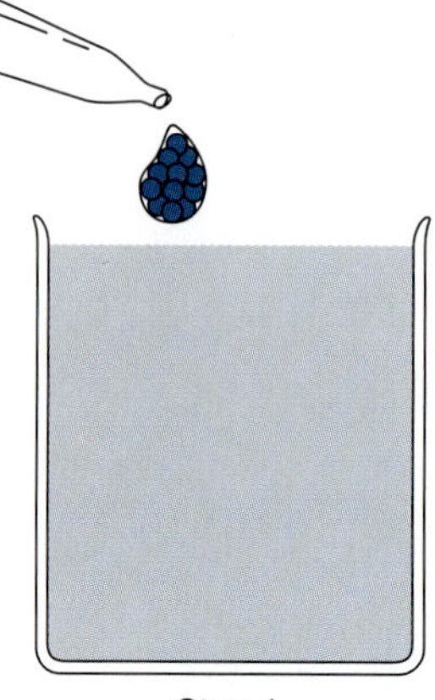

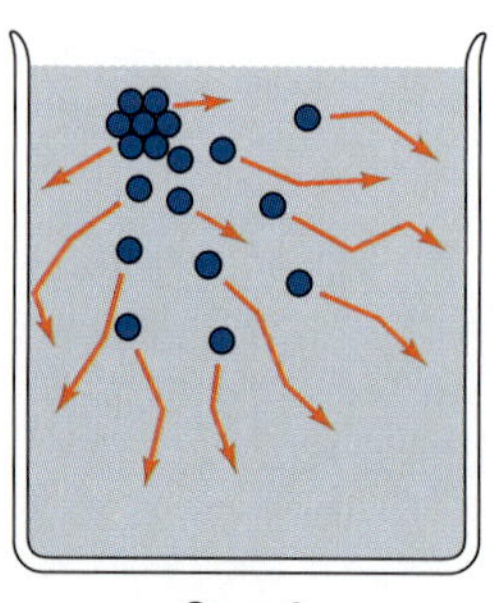

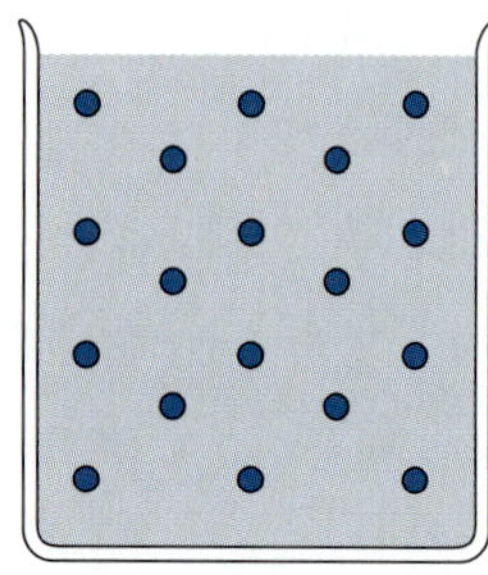

Figure 4.3 Diffusion. In step 1, a drop of ink is placed into a glass of water. As diffusion occurs in step 2, the molecules move from the area of higher concentration (the drop) to the area of lower concentration (the surrounding water). Eventually, diffusion results in an even distribution of molecules (step 3).

➤ *What are the other two forces affecting movement of ions across the cell membrane? (p. 98–99)*

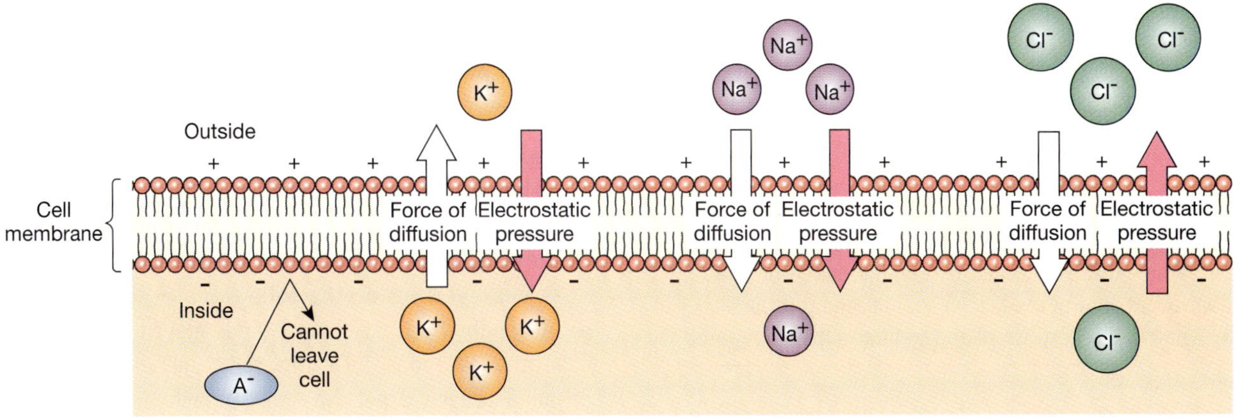

Figure 4.4 The influence of diffusion and electrostatic pressure on the movement of ions into and out of cell. The force of diffusion acts to move K^+ ions out of the cell and Na^+ and Cl^- ions into the cell, whereas electrostatic pressure acts to move Cl^- ions out of the cell and K^+ and Na^+ ions into the cell.

➤ *What forces affect the level of sodium, potassium, and chloride ions inside the cell? (p. 98–100)*

ond reason is that the third factor in the movement of ions across the cell membrane, the sodium-potassium pump, actively expels any Na^+ ions that do happen to get into the cell.

The Sodium-Potassium Pump

In contrast to the two passive forces described above, the **sodium-potassium pump** is an active process. The sodium-potassium pump actively transports sodium ions out of the cell and potassium ions into the cell, expelling three Na^+ ions for every two K^+ ions that it brings back into the cell (see **Figure 4.5**). The difference in the rate of Na^+ ion expulsion and the rate of K^+ ion entry maintains the polarization of the cell membrane; that is, the larger number of Na^+ ions on the outside than K^+ ions on the inside causes the fluid outside of the cell to be more positively charged than the fluid inside the cell.

The process of expelling Na^+ ions from the cell and bringing K^+ ions back into the cell requires a lot of energy. This energy is provided by adenosine triphosphate (ATP), which is a high-energy compound consisting of adenosine and three phosphate groups (the third of which is attached with a high-energy bond), and manufactured by the mitochondria (see Chapter 2 and **Figure 2.4**). The sodium-potassium pump converts ATP to ADP (adenosine diphosphate), which releases the energy needed to operate the sodium-potassium pump.

Once the resting potential of the membrane is established by the sodium-potassium pump, the passive forces of diffusion and electrostatic pressure keep most Cl^- ions out of the cell and most K^+ ions in the cell. Any K^+ ions that escape the cell are retrieved by the sodium-potassium pump. As discussed above, the forces of diffusion and electrostatic pressure act to bring Na^+ ions

sodium-potassium pump A process that actively transports sodium ions out of the cell and potassium ions into the cell, expelling three Na^+ ions for every two K^+ ions that it brings back into the cell.

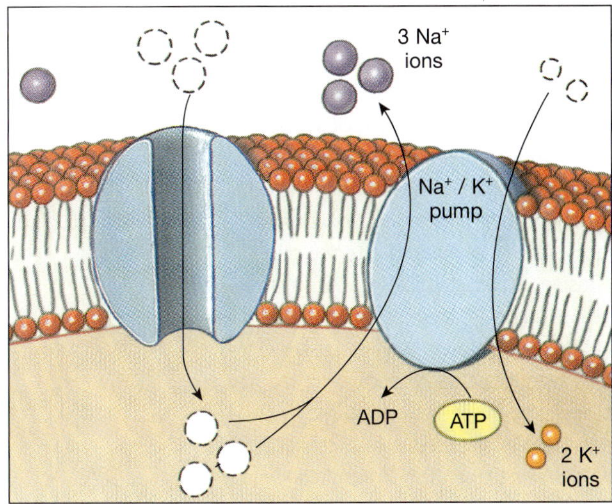

Figure 4.5 The influence of the sodium-potassium pump. The sodium-potassium pump actively expels three Na^+ ions from the cell for every two K^+ ions that are brought back into the cell. The sodium-potassium pump requires a lot of energy, which is provided by the conversion of ATP into ADP.

➤ *How does the sodium-potassium pump establish the cell's resting membrane potential? (p. 99–100)* into the cell, but the continued activity of the sodium-potassium pump expels Na^+ ions and, thereby, maintains the membrane's resting potential. For a summary of the neuron at rest, see **Figure 4.6**.

Before You Go On

Describe how diffusion, electrostatic pressure, and the sodium-potassium pump act on sodium and potassium ions. What is the purpose of the sodium-potassium pump?

Section Review

- The cell membrane of neurons is electrically charged.
- When the cell is at rest (not being acted on by outside forces), the inside of the cell is negatively charged relative to the outside of the cell, a difference in charge referred to as the resting membrane potential.
- More protein ions (A^-) are found on the inside than on the outside of the cell because they are large molecules and cannot pass through the cell membrane.
- More chloride ions (Cl^-) are found outside than inside the cell because, although the force of diffusion acts to move Cl^- ions into the cell, this force is counteracted by electrostatic pressure, which pushes Cl^- ions out because of the presence of negatively charged molecules inside the cell.
- Although the force of diffusion acts to push potassium ions out of the cell, electrostatic pressure and the sodium-potassium pump act together to maintain high K^+ ion levels inside the cell.
- Although both diffusion and electrostatic pressure attract Na^+ ions into the cell, the sodium-potassium pump actively expels Na^+ ions. In fact, the sodium-potassium pump expels three Na^+ ions for every two K^+ ions that are brought back into the cell, which establishes and maintains the membrane's resting potential.

action potential The changes that occur within the neuron on receipt of information about a stimulus.

The Action Potential

We have learned what is involved in maintaining the resting membrane potential, the distribution of ions when the neuron is at rest. But what happens to this balance when the neuron receives information about a stimulus? The changes that occur within the neuron on receipt of information about a stimulus consist of a series of events, collectively referred to as the **action potential**. The neuron is said to "fire" when an action

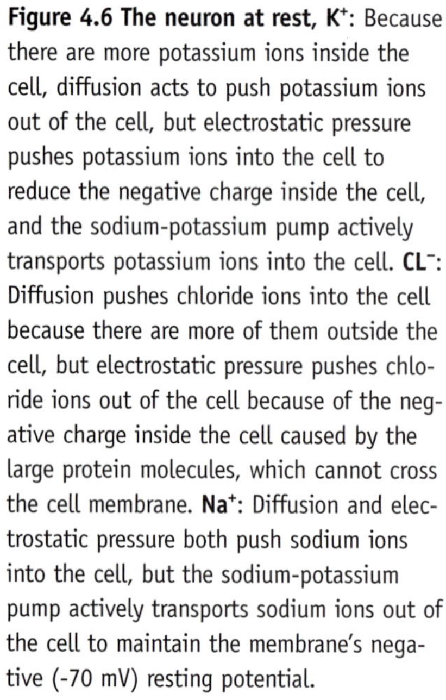

Figure 4.6 The neuron at rest, K^+: Because there are more potassium ions inside the cell, diffusion acts to push potassium ions out of the cell, but electrostatic pressure pushes potassium ions into the cell to reduce the negative charge inside the cell, and the sodium-potassium pump actively transports potassium ions into the cell. **CL^-:** Diffusion pushes chloride ions into the cell because there are more of them outside the cell, but electrostatic pressure pushes chloride ions out of the cell because of the negative charge inside the cell caused by the large protein molecules, which cannot cross the cell membrane. **Na^+:** Diffusion and electrostatic pressure both push sodium ions into the cell, but the sodium-potassium pump actively transports sodium ions out of the cell to maintain the membrane's negative (-70 mV) resting potential.

➤ *What happens to the levels of these ions when the neuron is transmitting a message?* *(p. 101)*

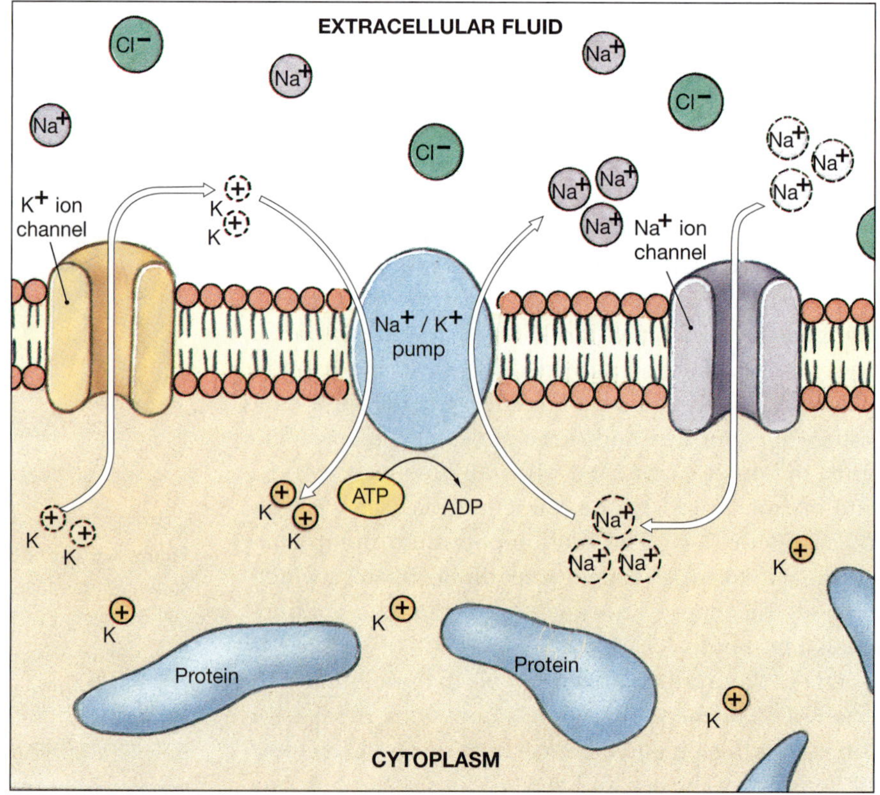

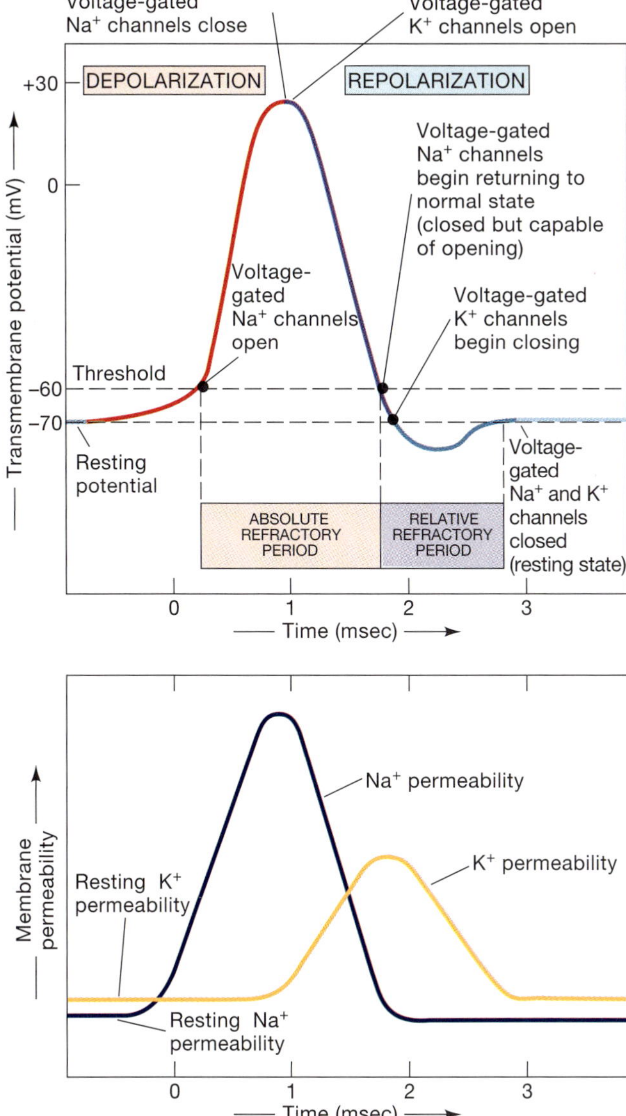

Figure 4.7 Changes in the membrane potential once the level of depolarization reaches threshold. At the threshold level, depolarization causes Na^+ ion channels to open, allowing more Na^+ ions to enter the cell and changing the polarity so that the inside of the cell is positively charged in relation to the outside of the cell. Soon after threshold is reached, the Na^+ ion channels close. The K^+ ion channels open, causing K^+ ions to leave the cell, which causes the cell membrane potential again to become more negatively charged inside relative to the outside of the cell. For a brief time, the cell is slightly more polarized than normal, but quickly returns to the resting membrane potential.

➤ *How is the original ion distribution restored after depolarization? (p. 102)*

potential occurs. We will describe each of the events involved in producing an action potential in turn: depolarization to threshold, reversal of the membrane potential, repolarization to the resting potential, and the refractory period.

Depolarization and Threshold

Although the entire cell membrane is polarized, the detection of neural messages occurs at specific receptor sites. The result of stimulation of a neuron by another neuron is a change in the polarization of the cell membrane at that point: The inside of the cell becomes more positively charged. The opening of Na^+ ion channels and the resulting increased entry of Na^+ ions into the cell cause the increase in positive charge inside the cell. Remember that the resting membrane potential is –70 mV (the inside of the cell is 70 mV more negative than the outside), so any influx of positive ions into the cell will reduce the negative charge (make it less negative, or more positive). This reduction in the charge across the membrane is called **depolarization.**

Remember Michele stepping on the tack? As we learned earlier, neurons only respond when the answer to the question being asked (Is the stimulus painful?) is an affirmative one. How does the neuron determine whether the answer is yes or no? The decision depends on whether the stimulation reaches a crucial level, called the threshold. The **threshold** is the level of cell membrane depolarization that is required for the neuron to determine that the answer is yes, and to respond appropriately. In another example, one of Michele's auditory neurons may be asked the question, "Do you hear something?" If the stimulation created by the sound is sufficient to reach the threshold of this neuron, then the sound will be detected, and the neuron will communicate this conclusion to the next neuron in the information-processing chain. However, the auditory neuron will not transmit any information if the membrane potential depolarization does not reach threshold. In this case, the sound is not detected.

Once threshold is reached (at about –60 mV as shown in **Figure 4.7**), the cell membrane undergoes a more radical change in polarization. The Na^+ ion channels now open and Na^+ ions pour in, causing the inside of the cell to become positive relative to the outside of the cell (about +30 mV, refer to **Figure 4.7**). Why do the Na^+ ion channels open? They open because of the sensitivity of ion channels to changes in membrane potential, a process referred to as **voltage-gated ion channels.** Voltage-gated ion channels are opened or closed by changes in membrane potential. The Na^+ ion channels are especially sensitive to changes in

depolarization The reduction in the charge across the neural cell membrane by a stimulus.

threshold The level of cell membrane depolarization that is required for an action potential to occur.

voltage-gated ion channels Ion channels that are sensitive to changes in the cell membrane potential.

membrane potential. The decreased membrane potential caused by a depolarizing stimulus opens Na^+ voltage-gated ion channels, which allows Na^+ ions to pour into the cell and results in the inside of the cell now being more positively charged than the outside of the cell.

Repolarization and the Refractory Period

Next, the Na^+ ion channels close and Na^+ ions stop entering the cell. Shortly after the Na^+ channels close, the K^+ ion channels open and K^+ ions exit the cell. (The K^+ ion channels are less sensitive to changes in membrane potential than are Na^+ ion channels and therefore open later than do the Na^+ ion channels.) The exit of K^+ ion channels from the cell causes the inside of the cell to again become more negatively charged than the outside of the cell. During the time from when the membrane potential is depolarized to threshold until the membrane potential returns to threshold, called the **absolute refractory period**, the cell is insensitive to further stimulation (see **Figure 4.7**). For a brief time, the cell membrane actually becomes slightly more polarized, or hyperpolarized, than its normal resting state. During this time, a **relative refractory period** occurs (see **Figure 4.7**) during which time the neuron can be stimulated only by an event of greater intensity than is normally required to activate the neuron. As you can see from **Figure 4.7**, during the relative refractory period the membrane potential dips below the resting membrane potential of –70 mV to about –80 mV, so that to reach threshold a stimulus must be 10 mV stronger than normal. The distribution of Na^+ and K^+ ions has changed as the result of depolarization, but the distribution of ions quickly returns to normal. This process of recovery of the resting membrane potential, which begins when the Na^+ channels close, is called **repolarization**. As soon as the resting membrane potential is fully restored, the sodium-potassium pump acts to maintain the ion concentration differences until it is changed by a depolarizing stimulus.

absolute refractory period The time following the repolarization of the membrane potential that the neuron is insensitive to further stimulation.

relative refractory period The time following the absolute refractory period that the neuron can be stimulated only by an event of greater intensity than is normally required to activate the neuron.

repolarization The process of recovery of the resting membrane potential.

rate law The principle stating that the greater the stimulus intensity, the faster rate of neural firing (up to the maximum rate possible for that neuron).

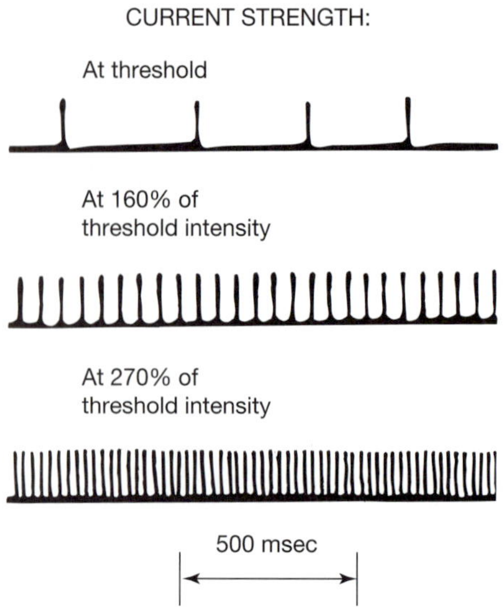

Figure 4.8 The neuron's firing rate as a function of stimulus intensity. The figure shows the firing rate of the crab axon in response to three different intensities of stimuli. The action potential appears as a spike, because the time scale is slow. The rate of firing increases with more intense stimuli.

Adapted from Eccles, 1977.

➤ *Why isn't the action potential higher for the more intense stimuli? (p. 102–103)*

The Intensity of a Stimulus

Information about stimulus intensity is not provided by a single action potential, because once threshold is reached, the strength of the action potential is independent of the intensity of the stimulus. Yet, information about stimulus intensity can be quite important. Take light, for example. Failing to wear sunglasses on a very bright day could cause a baseball player to drop a fly ball ("I lost it in the sun!"). However, the player should not wear sunglasses on a cloudy day, for example, when the light stimulus is less intense, because the sunglasses could limit his or her vision.

So how can a player detect different intensities of sunlight to distinguish between a bright, sunny day and an overcast day? The rate at which a neuron fires, as measured by the number of action potentials per unit of time, provides information about the intensity of a particular stimulus (see **Figure 4.8**). An intense stimulus will cause a neuron to fire more often than a weak stimulus. Thus, bright sunlight on a clear day produces a high rate of firing in the neurons in the visual system. By contrast, sunlight dimmed by clouds produces a lower firing rate in the visual neurons. The information provided by the rate of firing in visual neurons allows the baseball player to decide whether or not to wear sunglasses. The **rate law** describes this relationship between the rate of firing and the intensity of a stimulus. The rate law states that the greater the stimulus intensity, the faster the rate of neural firing (up to the maximum rate possible for that neuron).

How does a more intense stimulus cause a neuron to fire more rapidly than a weaker one? A strong stimulus can produce an action potential during the relative refractory period and will produce a higher rate of firing than will a weaker stimulus, which may only be able to activate a neuron after the relative refractory period has ended and the resting membrane potential has been restored.

One further point deserves mentioning. You may have the impression that neurons exist in one of two states; that is, they are either at rest or firing. As it turns out this is true for neurons in the peripheral nervous system, but not for neurons in the central nervous system. Neurons in the central nervous system are typically active all the time. How then is information detected by neurons in the central nervous system? The answer lies in changes in a neuron's firing rate. Some neurons have faster rates of firing than others. The length of the absolute refractory period affects the firing rate of a neuron. A neuron with a short absolute refractory period can fire at a more rapid rate than can a neuron with a long absolute refractory period. Some input may lead to an increased firing rate, whereas other input might decrease the rate of action potentials in a specific neuron. For example, a bright light might increase the rate at which a specific neuron fires, whereas a dim light decreases its firing rate. It is the challenge of the central nervous system to recognize the meaning of a specific change in the firing rate.

Now you have seen each of the events that comprise the action potential: depolarization to threshold, reversal of membrane polarity, repolarization to the resting potential, and the refractory period. The result of the "firing" of the action potential is the transmission of a neural impulse along the axon and then on to another neuron or to a target organ such as a muscle. In the next section, we will discuss the details of transmission of the neural impulse along the axon.

Before You Go On

Describe what happens during an action potential, using the terms resting membrane potential, depolarization, threshold, repolarization, Na^+ ions, K^+ ions, and the sodium-potassium pump.

Section Review

- Stimulation of a neuron by another neuron causes a reduction in the electrical charge across the membrane called depolarization.
- Depolarization is caused by the opening of Na^+ ion channels and the increased flow of some Na^+ ions into the cell.
- If the level of depolarization reaches a particular threshold, depolarization proceeds rapidly: many Na^+ ion channels open and Na^+ ions rapidly flow into the cell, causing the inside of the cell to become positive relative to the outside.
- Repolarization follows depolarization: the Na^+ channels close and then K^+ ion channels open, allowing increased exit of K^+ ions from the cell and causing the inside of the cell to again be more negatively charged than the outside of the cell. During the time from when the membrane potential reached threshold until it returns to threshold, the neuron is insensitive to further stimulation (absolute refractory period).
- For a brief time, the cell membrane is hyperpolarized. During this time, the neuron is less sensitive to further stimulation (relative refractory period).
- The distribution of ions quickly returns to normal, and the sodium-potassium pump maintains the ion concentration differences until it is changed by a depolarizing stimulus.
- The process of depolarization to threshold, reversal of the membrane polarity, repolarization, and restoration of the resting membrane potential is referred to as an action potential, which leads to the transmission of the neural impulse along the axon.
- Perceived stimulus intensity is the result of the neuron's firing rate. The rate law states that the greater the stimulus intensity, the higher the firing rate.

The Neural Impulse

Once the action potential is generated, the message or **neural impulse** needs to be transmitted to other neurons. In most cases, communication occurs within the nervous system by means of an axon projecting from each neural cell body. As described earlier, a message is received by the dendrites or soma; it is then passed on to the axon hillock, where all input is summed up and, if threshold is reached, the action potential is generated. Once threshold is reached, the strength of the

neural impulse The transmission of a message by means of an axon projecting from each neural cell body.

action potential that is propagated along the entire length of the axon will be the same regardless of the intensity of the original stimulus, a phenomenon known as the **all-or-none law**. The message must then be transmitted to the next neuron or to the target organ. (Recall that impulse transmission along a neuron occurs in just one direction, away from the cell body, much like water released from a dam.)

How is the message propagated, or carried along the axon? Although the axon is a continuous structure, to understand impulse propagation it is simpler to visualize the axon as a series of segments, one stimulating the next to create a flow of Na^+ ions entering the cell along the length of the axon (**Figure 4.9**). At the same time that the ion channels in the first segment close to Na^+ ions, Na^+ ions flow down the inside of the axon and enter the next segment, attracted by its lack of Na^+ ions (its negative charge). The resulting depolarization brings the second segment of the axon to threshold and continues the action potential.

This process of Na^+ influx followed by closure of Na^+ ion channels continues as the neural impulse is propagated down the entire length of the axon. When depolarization reaches the end of the axon, the presynaptic terminal (see Chapter 2), neurotransmitter molecules are released, and the message is transmitted to the next neuron.

The speed of impulse transmission is not the same for all neurons. Transmission rate is affected by the thickness of the axon; the thicker the axon, the faster the propagation of the action potential. As we learned earlier, when an action potential occurs and the neuron fires, there is a flow of Na^+ ions along the axon, which depolarizes the segment of the axon cell membrane that lies just ahead. The thicker the axon, the further down the axon cell membrane the local membrane depolarization will occur. And the further apart the initial and subsequent depolarizations, the faster the neural impulse will travel along the axon cell membrane.

Why is the flow of Na^+ ions further for thicker than thinner axons? Consider the following example to illustrate why thickness affects rate of transmission. Water flows more quickly through a thick hose than a thin one: the reason being, in part, because there is less resistance to the flow of water in the thicker hose, and thereby, the water flows faster. Similarly, Na^+ ions flow faster along the axon cell membrane of a thick axon than a thin axon. As we will learn next, the speed of transmission also is influenced by whether or not the neuron is myelinated.

Saltatory Conduction

The axons of many neurons are covered with myelin, a complex, fatty substance produced by some glial cells (see Chapter 2). Although the axon is a continuous structure, for reasons that will soon become clear, myelin occurs in segments along the axon. The myelinated segments (collectively called the myelin sheath) are separated by small spaces, known as **nodes of Ranvier** (see **Figure 4.10**), between adjacent myelin segments. The cell membrane is exposed to the extracellular fluid only at the nodes of Ranvier. Recall that the membrane is where the ion channels are located, and that the action potential is generated by the movement of ions into and out of the cell through the ion channels. Thus, only the nodes can respond to a depolarizing stimulus such as the flow of Na^+ ions. In this way, the action potential is propagated; it can be said to "jump" from node to node along a myelinated axon, a process called **saltatory conduction**, from the Latin word *saltare*, "to jump."

The process of saltatory conduction increases the speed at which information is transmitted. Picture Michele and her dog: If Michele is walking the dog, she is most likely taking normal steps (unless, of course, her dog sees a cat!). If the dog gets off the leash to go after the cat and Michele has to chase him, she will run, taking longer strides. The speed with which she travels depends not only on how fast she moves her legs, but also on the length of her stride, or how much ground she covers with each step. An action potential has to "walk" down an unmyelinated axon from segment to segment, whereas it can "run" (or "jump") down a myelinated axon.

You might be wondering how the action potential "runs" down a myelinated axon, but only "walks" down an unmyelinated one. The myelin sheath acts like a cable conducting an electrical current. The ability of the myelin sheath to conduct electrical current, or its cable properties, allows the current to flow through myelinated regions of the axon from one node of Ranvier to the next. Although the level of the depolarizing current diminishes along the length of a myelin segment, there is still sufficient current to generate another action potential. The depolarizing stimulus resulting from an action potential is then transmitted through the myelinated segment to the next node. Thus, because Na^+ ions can only enter the axon

---

all-or-none law The principle that once threshold is reached, an action potential will be the same regardless of the intensity of the original stimulus.

node of Ranvier The unmyelinated space between the myelinated segments (collectively called the myelin sheath) of an axon.

saltatory conduction The propagation of an action potential from node to node of myelinated axons.

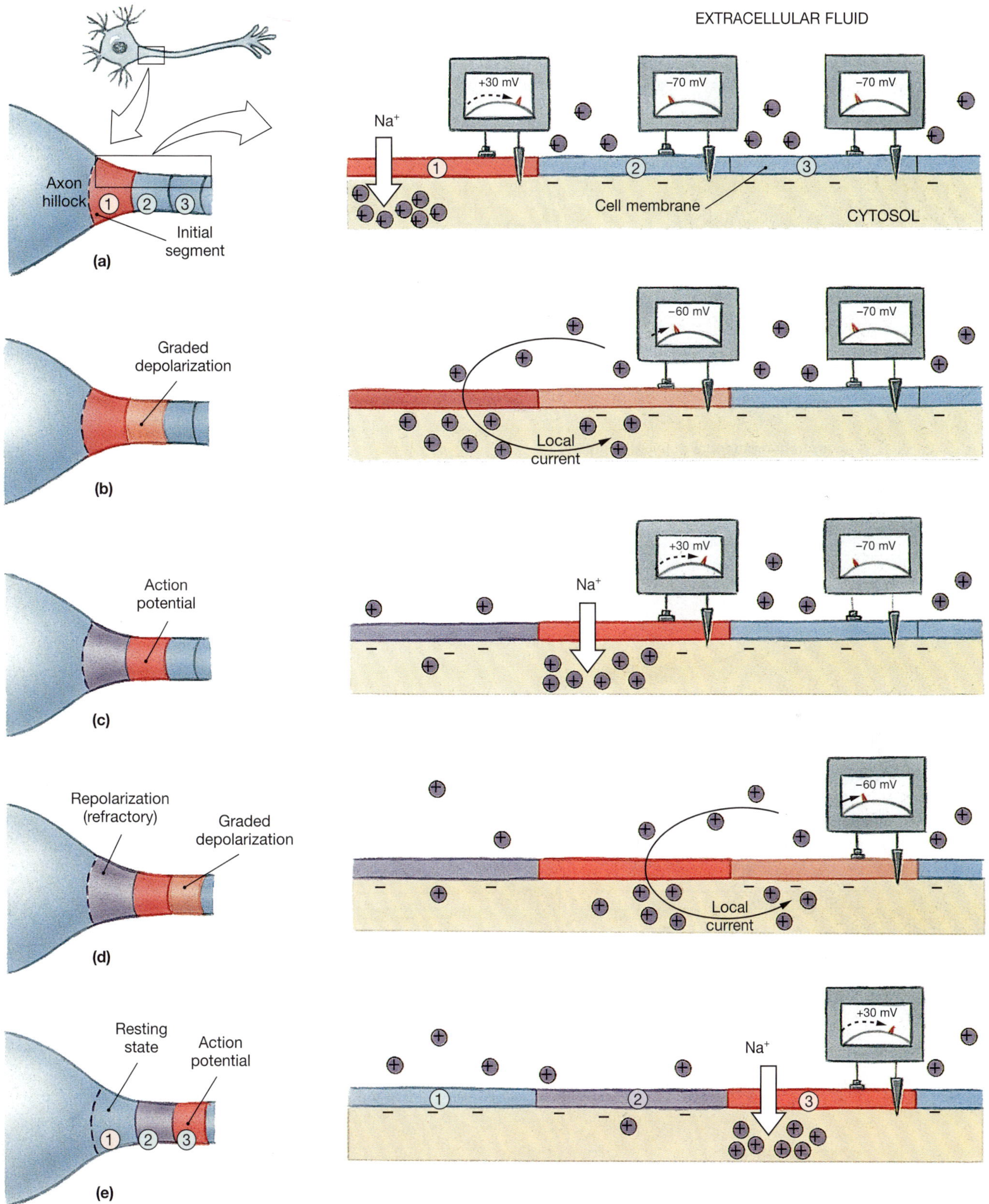

Figure 4.9 The flow of depolarization Na^+ ions along the axon. The influx of Na^+ ions into one segment of the axon causes a change in the polarity at that segment. The polarity in the first segment returns to normal as K^+ ions leave the cell. The movement of Na^+ ions into the next segment causes the polarity of the second segment to change, with the inside becoming positively charged. These changes in polarity continue along the axon until reaching the presynaptic terminals.

➤ *What attracts the Na^+ ions to flow from one segment of the axon to the next? (p. 104)*

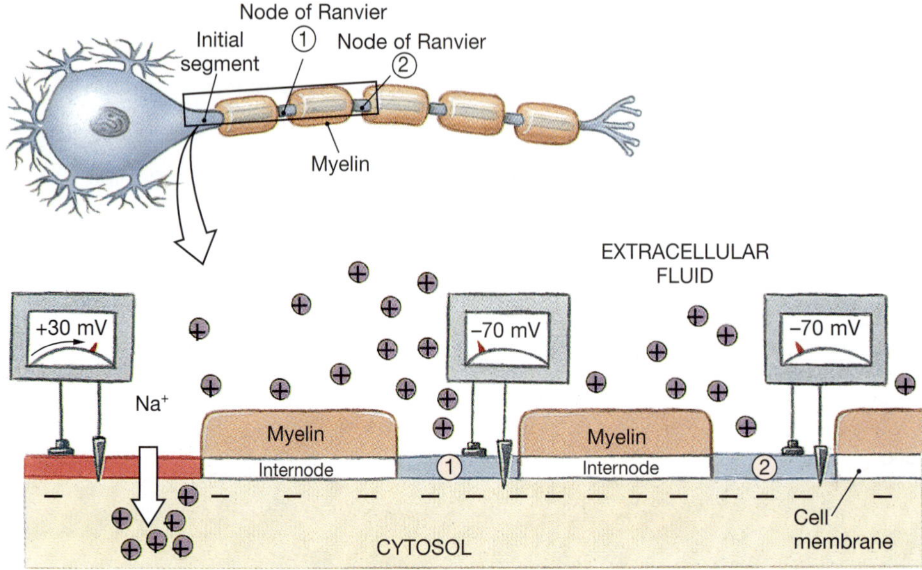

(a) Action potential at initial segment

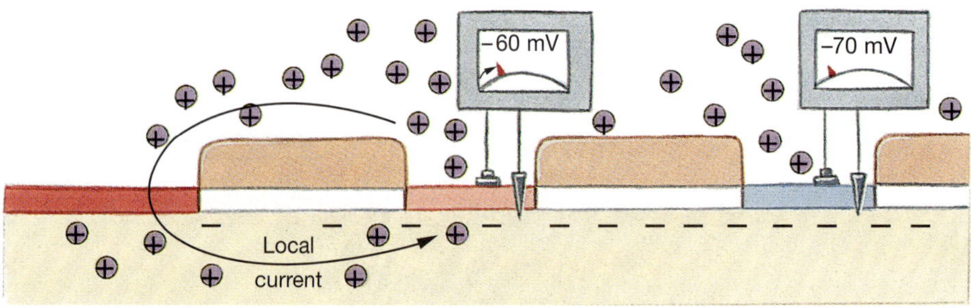

(b) Depolarization to threshold at node of Ranvier 1

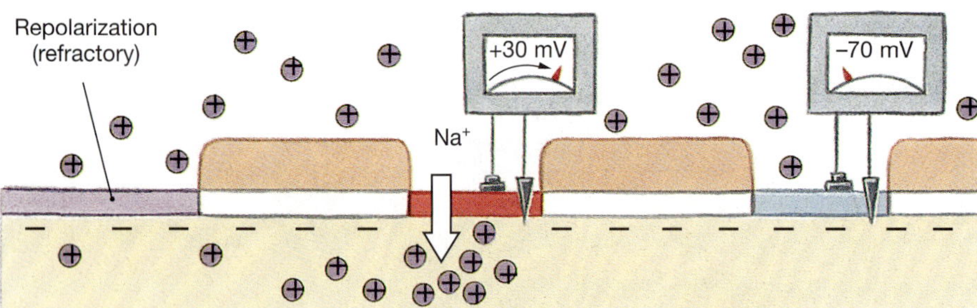

(c) Action potential at node of Ranvier 1

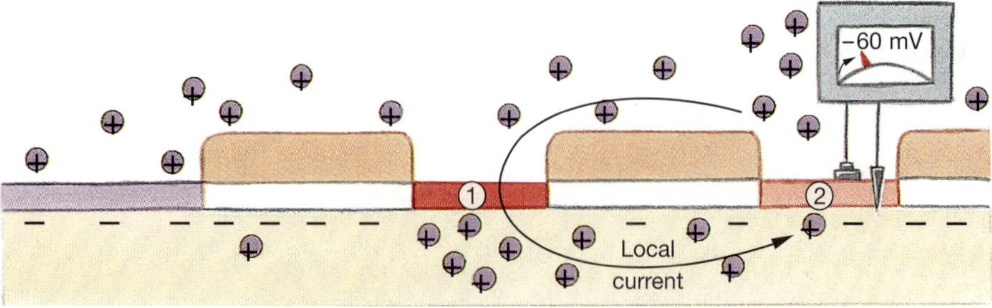

(d) Depolarization to threshold at node of Ranvier 2

Figure 4.10 The transmission of a neural impulse along a myelinated neuron. The action potential that develops at the axon hillock is propagated as the flow of deplorarizing Na^+ ions move along the axon between nodes of Ranvier, first to node one and then to node two.
➤ *Why is transmission faster along a myelinated than along an unmyelinated axon? (p. 104)*

at each node, the action potential is propagated much more readily along a myelinated axon than in an unmyelinated one, where Na^+ ions must flow into the cell along the entire unmyelinated axon.

But just how much faster is transmission of the neural impulse along a myelinated than unmyelinated axon? The difference in the rate of transmission in myelinated as compared to unmyelinated neurons is striking. For example, a myelinated mammalian neuron with a diameter of 1.5μm can conduct information at speeds up to 100 meters per second. By contrast, an unmyelinated neuron of the same size can conduct action potentials at a rate of only about 1 meter per second.

Myelinization provides other benefits. It prevents the leakage of ions and, thereby, the reduction in cell membrane potential. It also takes considerable energy for the sodium-potassium pump to expel Na^+ ions that enter the neuron during an action potential. Because Na^+ ions enter myelinated neurons only at the nodes of Ranvier, rather than along the entire axon as with unmyelinated neurons, far less energy is expended by the myelinated neuron pumping out the excess Na^+ ions.

A Failure of Saltatory Conduction

Remember Michele's diagnosis? **Multiple sclerosis (MS)** is a progressive neurological disorder caused by the degeneration of the myelin covering the axons of the nervous system by the body's own immune system. The immune system destroys myelin in localized areas of the nervous system, treating it as a foreign substance. This localized demyelination impairs the capacity of the affected nerve cells to function effectively. Because the location of the central nervous system damage varies among individuals, the symptoms of patients with multiple sclerosis are variable. Multiple sclerosis usually begins in young adulthood, but symptoms may be present for months or even years before the disease is diagnosed. Some individuals are immediately incapacitated, whereas others experience periods of remissions and relapses. There is at present no cure for this debilitating illness although several new treatments look promising. We will discuss these treatments later in the chapter.

Before You Go On

Compare the propagation of the action potential down an unmyelinated axon and a myelinated axon. Describe the target (immune system? myelin? glial cells?) of a hypothetical medication used to treat multiple sclerosis.

Section Review

- The action potential is propagated along the axon through a continuous process of Na^+ influx and K^+ exit until it reaches the presynaptic terminal.
- Once an action potential has been generated, the strength of the action potential that is propagated along the entire length of the axon will be the same regardless of the intensity of the original stimulus, a phenomenon known as the all-or-none law.
- The axons of some neurons are covered by a myelin sheath, a segmented fatty covering produced by some glial cells.
- Ion channels occur only at the spaces between myelinated segments, called nodes of Ranvier.
- The propagation down a myelinated axon, or the jumping of the action potential from one node of Ranvier to the next is called saltatory conduction.
- Neural transmission in myelinated neurons is faster than in unmyelinated neurons.
- Multiple sclerosis is a progressive neurological disorder that occurs when, for some unknown reason, the body's immune system attacks the myelin covering the neurons' axons.

Synaptic Transmission

Recall from Chapter 2 that, although each neuron can have only one axon, the axon may have many branches at the end, called telodendria. At the end of each of these axon projections, there is a swelling called the presynaptic terminal. Inside the presynaptic terminal there are sacs, or vesicles, that contain chemical substances called neurotransmitters. Because there is no direct physical connection between neurons, neurotransmitters provide one means of communication among neurons throughout the nervous system.

Neurotransmitter Release

When the action potential reaches the presynaptic terminals (see **Figure 4.11a**), calcium ion channels open and calcium (Ca^{++}) ions enter the cell. The entry of Ca^{++} ions into the cell causes the synaptic vesicles to move to the release sites on the presynap-

multiple sclerosis A progressive neurological disorder caused by the degeneration of the myelin covering the axons of the nervous system by the immune system.

tic membrane (see **Figure 4.11b**). The neurotransmitter is then released from the vesicles into the synaptic cleft. Neurotransmitter molecules are not always released when an action potential reaches the presynaptic terminals: many action potentials fail to release any neurotransmitter molecules (Sudhof, 1995). Further, the same amount of neurotransmitter is not released each time, although neurotransmitter molecules are released in a fixed amount, called a quantum. Thus, the neuron may release few, many, or even no quantum, of neurotransmitter molecules. The factors that influence how much neurotransmitter is released will be discussed later in the chapter.

Diffusion allows the neurotransmitter to be carried across the synaptic cleft. Once the neurotransmitter molecules have crossed the synaptic cleft, they attach to receptor sites on the postsynaptic membrane specific to that particular neurotransmitter (refer to **Figure 4.11c**).

We learned earlier that some ion channels are sensitive to changes in membrane potential. Other ion channels are sensitive to the presence of specific neurotransmitter molecules. These ion channels are referred to as **transmitter-gated ion channels**. The action of neurotransmitter molecules on the receptor sites on the postsynaptic membrane is to open or close the transmitter-gated ion channels, which might result in either depolarization or hyperpolarization, depending on which ion channels opened or closed. Let's next look at how ion channels are affected by the presence of neurotransmitter molecules and what would be the effect of these ion channel changes.

The neurotransmitter can have one of two influences on the postsynaptic membrane: excitatory or inhibitory. If the influence of the neurotransmitter is excitatory, then the neurotransmitter produces depolarization at the postsynaptic membrane. Depolarization, as we noted earlier, is caused by the increased opening of some of the Na^+ ion channels, thereby allowing more Na^+ ions to enter the cell. The depolarization of the postsynaptic membrane is called an **excitatory postsynaptic potential** (**EPSP**; see **Figure 4.12a**).

Neurotransmitters can also have an inhibitory effect on the postsynaptic membrane. Inhibition is caused by

transmitter-gated ion channels Ion channels that are sensitive to the presence of a specific neurotransmitter.

excitatory postsynaptic potential (EPSP) The depolarization produced by neurotransmitter molecules acting on the receptor sites on the postsynaptic membrane.

hyperpolarization The increase in the charge across the cell membrane.

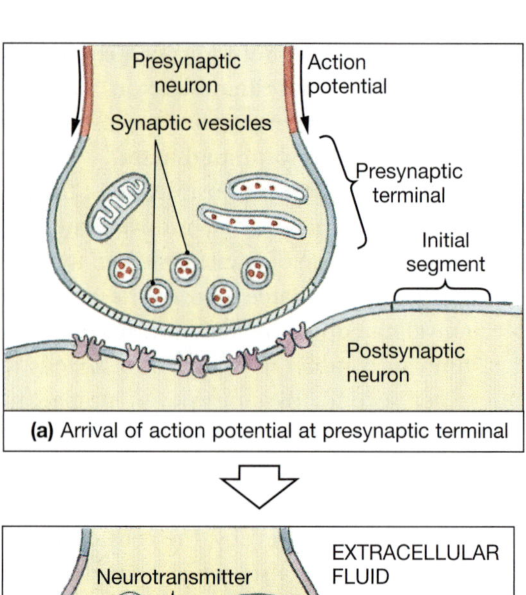

(a) Arrival of action potential at presynaptic terminal

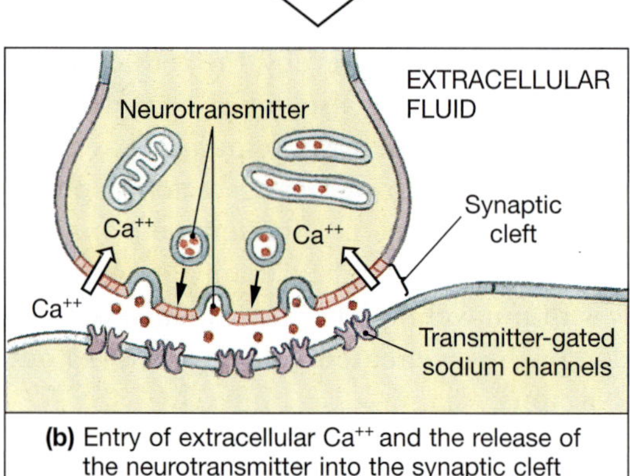

(b) Entry of extracellular Ca^{++} and the release of the neurotransmitter into the synaptic cleft

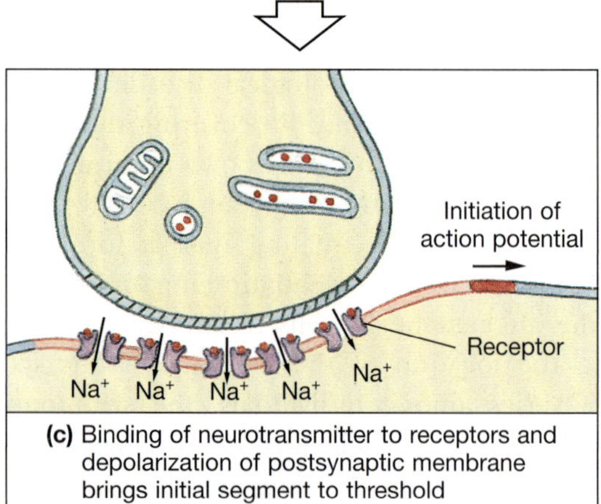

(c) Binding of neurotransmitter to receptors and depolarization of postsynaptic membrane brings initial segment to threshold

Figure 4.11 Synaptic transmission. (a) When the action potential reaches the presynaptic terminals, the synaptic vesicles move to the presynaptic membrane and release their neurotransmitters. (b) The neurotransmitters diffuse across the synaptic cleft (c) and attach to receptor sites on the postsynaptic membrane. The influence of the neurotransmitter causes depolarization (excitation) in this figure but can also hyperpolarize (inhibit) the postsynaptic membrane.

➤ *What causes the synaptic vesicles to move to the presynaptic membrane? (p. 107–108)*

the increased exit of K^+ ions from the cell or the increased entry of Cl^- ions into the cell, both of which hyperpolarize the cell membrane, or cause the differ-

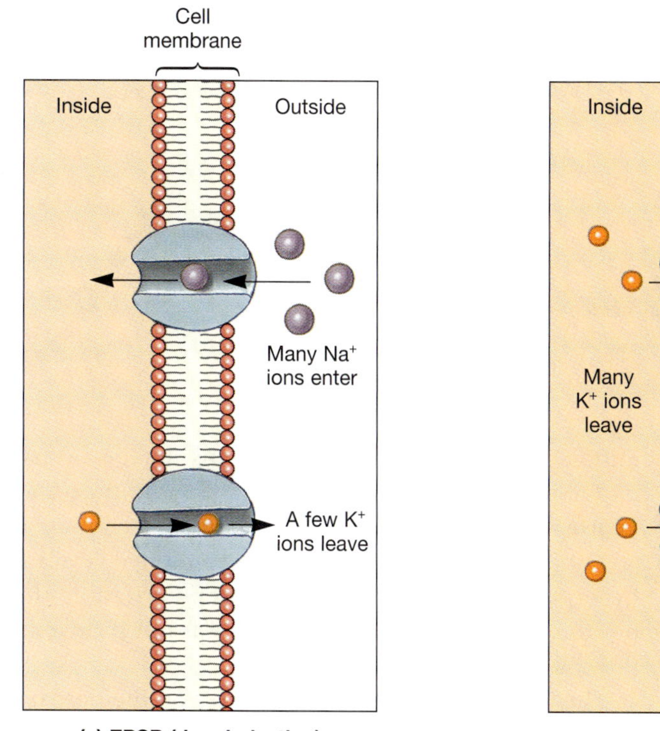

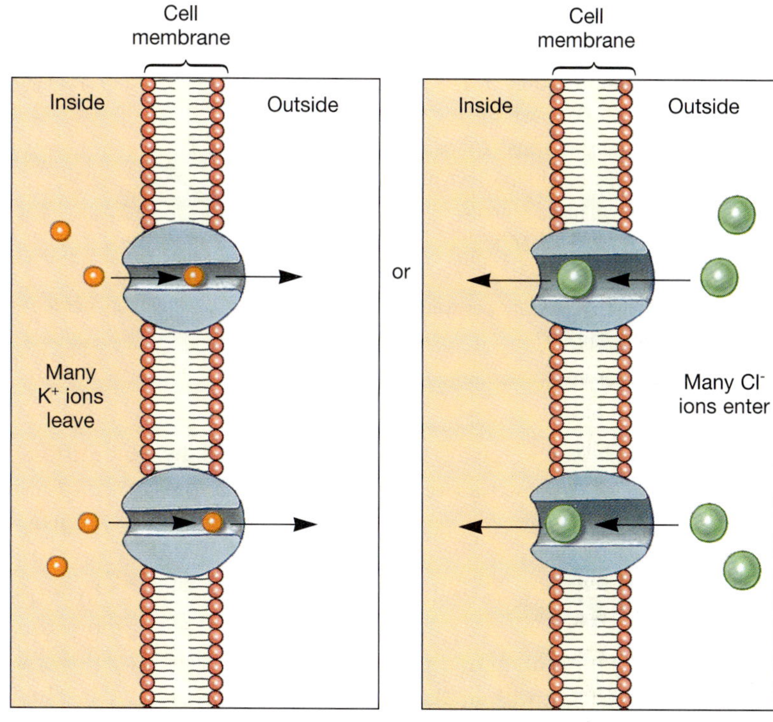

(a) EPSP (depolarization) **(b) IPSP (hyperpolarization)**

Figure 4.12 Ion changes at the postsynaptic membrane caused by neurotransmitters. (a) When the neurotransmitter causes depolarization, more Na^+ ions enter the cell (excitatory postsynaptic potential or EPSP). (b) Hyperpolarization by the neurotransmitter causes increased K^+ ions to leave the cell or increased Cl^- ions to enter the cell (inhibitory postsynaptic potential or IPSP).

➤ *What is the value of neural inhibition caused by the IPSP? (p. 108–109)*

ence in charge across the membrane to increase. The **hyperpolarization** of the cell membrane by the neurotransmitter is called an **inhibitory postsynaptic potential** (**IPSP**; refer to **Figure 4.12b**).

Hyperpolarizing the cell membrane increases the difference between the resting membrane potential and the threshold required to produce an action potential. Therefore, a higher level of excitation is required to activate an inhibited neuron than is required to activate an uninhibited one. Thus, neural inhibition impairs and in some cases prevents detection of stimuli by decreasing the neuron's sensitivity to stimulation.

Why does one neuron act to inhibit the activity of another neuron? The following two examples illustrate the importance of neural inhibition. Suppose that Michele wants to do some research on multiple sclerosis, but can find no quiet place to concentrate. Although she might just decide not to study, her nervous system does have the ability to inhibit environmental sounds from being perceived, so if she were really determined, she could study even amid the chatter in the cafeteria, unaware of any distracting noises. This process, called selective attention, is possible because of neural inhibition. Consider another example. Some biological psychologists believe that the brain has stored memories of all our experiences. What if we were unable to inhibit the recall of our memories, and all memories entered consciousness at the same time? If this were to happen to you, you would be unable to focus your attention on learning about the action potential, how neurons communicate with each other, or any other single activity.

Do not confuse neural inhibition with behavioral inhibition. Neural inhibition can even lead to behavior if the inhibited system normally suppresses behavior. Consider the following example. Michele's nephew has been punished for crossing the street. In this case, the threat of punishment is suppressing the behavior of crossing the street. Seeing an attractive toy on the other side of the street leads the child to ignore the prospect of punishment and cross the street by himself. In this case, the punishment system, which

---

inhibitory postsynaptic potential (IPSP) The hyperpolarization produced by neurotransmitter molecules acting on the receptor sites on the postsynaptic membrane.

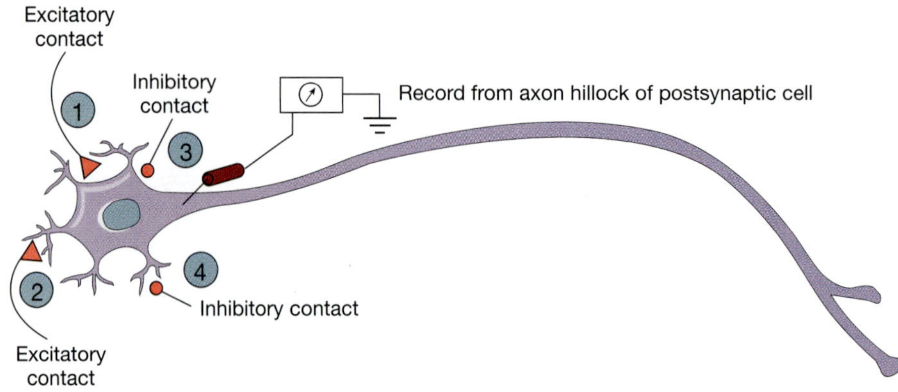

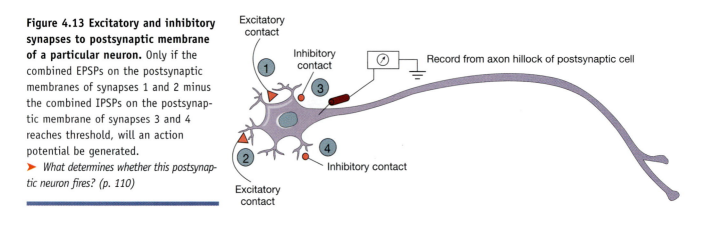

Figure 4.13 Excitatory and inhibitory synapses to postsynaptic membrane of a particular neuron. Only if the combined EPSPs on the postsynaptic membranes of synapses 1 and 2 minus the combined IPSPs on the postsynaptic membrane of synapses 3 and 4 reaches threshold, will an action potential be generated.

➤ *What determines whether this postsynaptic neuron fires? (p. 110)*

normally suppresses behavior, has been inhibited by the presence of the attractive toy, which leads the child to cross the street.

Summation Effects

Will an EPSP lead to an action potential at the postsynaptic membrane? Or, will an IPSP prevent the postsynaptic membrane from reaching threshold? Recall from the beginning of this chapter that most neurons continually receive multiple inputs; some are excitatory, and others are inhibitory (see **Figure 4.13**). The net effect of excitation and inhibition will determine whether the neuron is activated (remember the axon hillock, the accountant of the neuron).

Unlike action potentials, which are all-or-none, EPSPs and IPSPs are graded; that is, they can have different values at different times. As we have discussed, each EPSP causes a depolarization of the postsynaptic membrane and each IPSP causes a hyperpolarization of the postsynaptic membrane. The various EPSPs received by the postsynaptic membrane can be added together to produce a combined level of depolarization. Similarly, the various IPSPs received by the postsynaptic membrane can be added together to produce a combined level of hyperpolarization. If the combined level of depolarization minus the combined level of hyperpolarization reaches threshold, an action potential will be generated and the neuron will fire; otherwise, the neuron will not fire.

This process of adding and subtracting postsynaptic potentials is known as summation. **Spatial summation** refers to the combined influence of many neurotransmitters released at different locations on the postsynaptic membrane at a particular moment in time (see **Figure 4.14a**). As indicated above, if the combined level of depolarization minus the combined level of hyperpolarization causes sufficient depolarization, the neuron will fire. If the depolarization is not sufficient, the cell will not fire.

The influence of a neurotransmitter on the postsynaptic membrane is brief; that is, the depolarization of an EPSP or the hyperpolarization of an IPSP is short-lived. When the excitatory or inhibitory effects are over, the cell membrane quickly returns to its resting state. However, summation can also occur across time if the stimuli occur close enough. **Temporal summation** refers to the combined effects of depolarizing or hyperpolarizing stimuli over time. For example, a neuron may receive a depolarizing stimulus several times in succession. If the postsynaptic membrane is still depolarized from the first stimulus when the neuron is activated again, the combined level of depolarization from both stimuli will be greater than the level would have been from a single stimulus. If temporal summation causes the postsynaptic membrane to reach threshold, an action potential will be generated and the neuron will fire (see **Figure 4.14b**). Consider the following example to illustrate temporal summation. Michele's husband asks her how she is feeling two times. Michele does not hear the question the first time, but does the second. Although there are other explanations for Michele's hearing the question only after it is repeated a second time, temporal summation, in which sufficient depolarization of Michele's auditory neurons occurred only after two auditory messages, is a likely explanation of her hearing the message after it was presented a second time.

If hyperpolarizing stimuli occur in quick succession, temporal summation also occurs; in this case the membrane potential is removed further from threshold, making it more difficult for the postsynaptic membrane to reach threshold.

spatial summation The combined influence of many neurotransmitter releases at different locations on the postsynaptic membrane at a particular moment in time.

temporal summation The combined effects of neurotransmitter release over time.

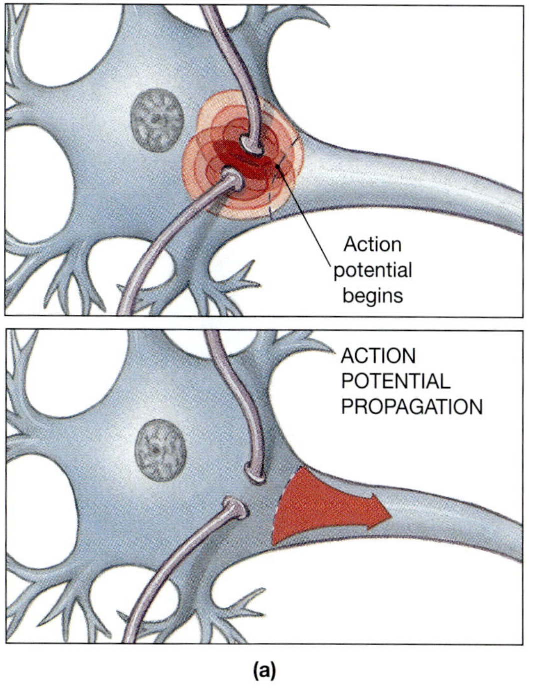

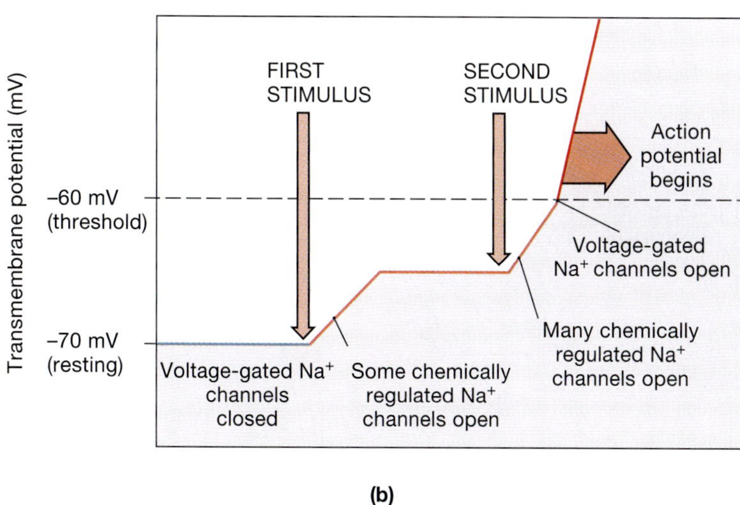

Figure 4.14 Spatial and temporal summation. (a) Spatial summation occurs when stimuli exert their effects at the same time on different receptor sites on the postsynaptic membrane. (b) Temporal summation occurs when stimuli occur close enough in time that their effects are additive.

➤ *Why do the stimuli have to occur close together for temporal summation to occur? (p. 110)*

Before You Go On

What is the advantage of not having direct physical connections between neurons?

What is the difference between EPSPs and IPSPs?

A postsynaptic membrane received EPSPs that, when combined, equal 40 mV and IPSPs that, when combined, equal –30 mV. Will the postsynaptic neuron fire an action potential?

Presynaptic Effects

As was just mentioned, when a neuron fires, the neurotransmitter from its presynaptic terminals is not released automatically. Several processes influence the amount of neurotransmitter released. One such process is presynaptic inhibition. **Presynaptic inhibition** is the prevention of the release of a normal amount of neurotransmitter despite the occurrence of an action potential in the presynaptic neuron. Presynaptic inhibition is caused by the release of a neurotransmitter from another neuron (see **Figure 4.15a**) and is an example of the **axoaxonic transmission** of a neural impulse. The binding of a neurotransmitter from the inhibitory neuron to the receptor sites on the presynaptic neuron can cause depolarization of the presynaptic membrane. This decreased polarity blocks some Ca^{++} ion channels, which reduces the amount of neurotransmitter released (see **Figure 4.15a**). The greater the depolarization of the presynaptic membrane, the smaller the number of neurotransmitter molecules that are released. If, on the other hand, the binding of the neurotransmitter to the presynaptic membrane causes hyperpolarization, more neurotransmitter molecules are released from the presynaptic terminal, a process called **presynaptic facilitation** (see **Figure 4.15b**).

A neuron can also be inhibited by its own neurotransmitter. In some cases, a neurotransmitter not only affects the postsynaptic membrane but also binds to receptor sites on its own presynaptic membrane. Inhibition of

---

presynaptic inhibition The prevention of the release of a normal amount of neurotransmitter from the presynaptic membrane, despite the occurrence of an action potential, caused by the action of another neuron.

axoaxonic transmission Communication between the axon of one neuron with the axon of another neuron.

presynaptic facilitation The enhanced release of neurotransmitters from the presynaptic membrane caused by the action of another neuron.

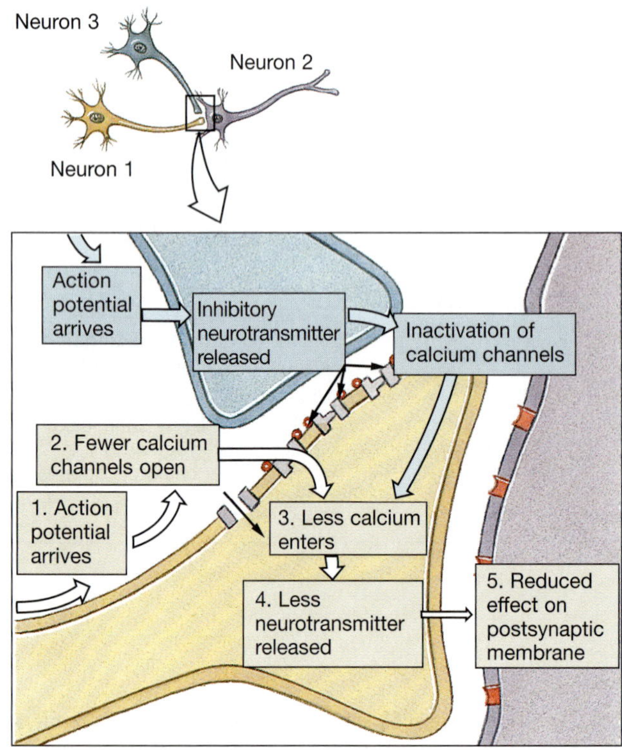

(a) Presynaptic inhibition

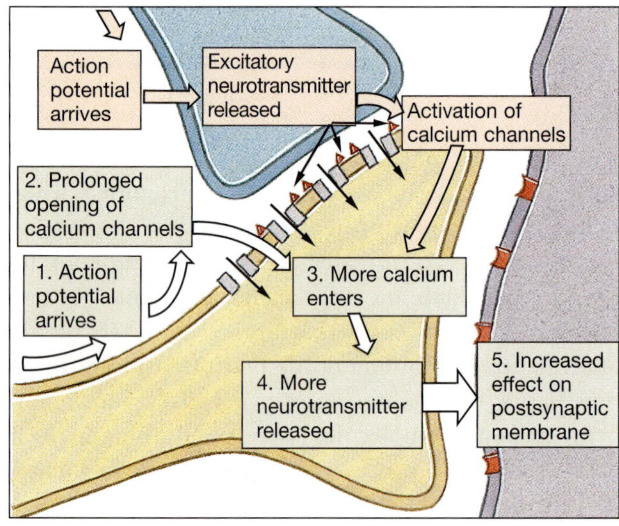

(b) Presynaptic facilitation

Figure 4.15 Two means of regulating neurotransmitter release. (a) Presynaptic inhibition decreases neurotransmitter release, whereas (b) presynaptic facilitation enhances the release of the neurotransmitter.

➤ *What is the advantage to the neuron of presynaptic facilitation? (p. 111)*

autoreceptors The inhibitory action of a neurotransmitter on the receptor sites on the presynaptic membrane, which acts to decrease further neurotransmitter release.

enzymatic degradation Deactivation of neurotransmitter molecules by an enzyme in the synapse.

neurotransmitter reuptake Return of the neurotransmitter to the vesicles in the presynaptic membrane.

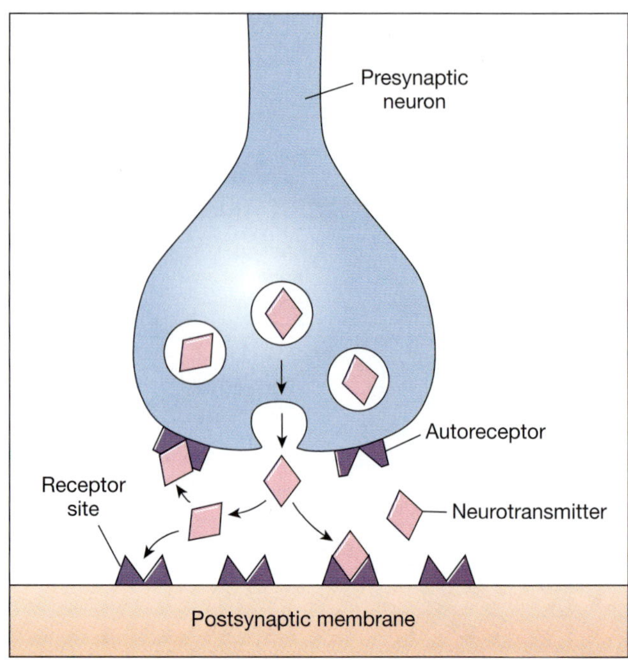

Figure 4.16 Autoreceptor. Released neurotransmitter can act on an autoreceptor to inhibit subsequent neurotransmitter release.

➤ *What is the advantage of having autoreceptors on the presynaptic membrane? (p. 111–112)*

these presynaptic receptors or **autoreceptors** (auto = self) decreases the number of neurotransmitter molecules released by the presynaptic neuron. This process allows the neuron to regulate the release of its neurotransmitter (refer to **Figure 4.16**).

The Cessation of Neurotransmitter Effects

The influence of the neurotransmitter on the postsynaptic membrane is very short-lived. In some instances, once the neurotransmitter has bound to the receptor sites on the postsynaptic membrane, the neurotransmitter is deactivated by an enzyme in the synapse, an event called **enzymatic degradation**. In other cases, the neurotransmitter is returned to the presynaptic membrane, a process called **neurotransmitter reuptake**. Both enzymatic degradation and neurotransmitter reuptake occur within a fraction of a second after the neurotransmitter acts on the postsynaptic membrane. In neurotransmitter reuptake, a pump-like mechanism in the presynaptic membrane sends the released neurotransmitter molecules to the reuptake site and then into the cytoplasm where they are again stored in synaptic vesicles (refer to **Figure 4.17**).

Once the neurotransmitter molecules have been restored to the synaptic vesicles, the presynaptic neuron can fire again. The very rapid reuptake of neurotransmitter allows neurons to transmit many messages each second. The ability to produce an almost continuous flow of impulses is what allows the nervous system to process the enormous amount of information necessary for survival.

Before You Go On

What is the advantage of presynaptic inhibition?

How does enzymatic degradation differ from neurotransmitter reuptake?

Section Review

- Once the flow of depolarizing Na^+ ions reaches the presynaptic terminals, Ca^{++} ions move into the cell, causing the synaptic vesicles to move to the presynaptic membrane and release the neurotransmitter into the synaptic cleft.
- The neurotransmitter diffuses across the synaptic cleft, binds to receptor sites located on the surface of the postsynaptic membrane, and depolarizes or hyperpolarizes the postsynaptic membrane.
- Depolarization (excitation) of the postsynaptic membrane, called an excitatory postsynaptic potential (EPSP), can cause the postsynaptic neuron to fire by bringing it closer to the threshold potential.
- Hyperpolarization (inhibition) of the postsynaptic membrane, called an inhibitory postsynaptic potential (IPSP), can prevent the neuron from firing by moving the potential farther from threshold.
- The increased membrane potential produced by hyperpolarization occurs as a result of more K^+ ions leaving the cell or more Cl^- ions entering the cell.
- The various EPSPs occurring at the postsynaptic membrane can be added together to produce a combined level of depolarization.
- The various IPSPs occurring at the postsynaptic membrane can be added together to produce a combined level of hyperpolarization.
- If the combined depolarizations (EPSPs) minus the combined hyperpolarizations (IPSPs) reaches threshold, the postsynaptic neuron will fire.
- The combined influence of EPSPs and IPSPs occurring on different parts of the postsynaptic membrane at a particular moment in time is called spatial summation.
- The combined effects of EPSPs and IPSPs over time is referred to as temporal summation.
- In presynaptic inhibition, an inhibitory neuron synapses with the axon of the presynaptic neuron releasing neurotransmitter molecules that close some Ca^{++} ion channels in the presynaptic membrane, and thereby depolarizing the cell membrane and reducing the amount of neurotransmitter released by the presynaptic neuron.
- Presynaptic facilitation increases the amount of neurotransmitter released by hyperpolarizing the presynaptic membrane.
- Neurotransmitter molecules can bind to receptors, called autoreceptors, that are located on the presynaptic membrane, causing the inhibition of further neurotransmitter release.
- In enzymatic degradation, neurotransmitter molecules are deactivated by an enzyme in the synapse. In neurotransmitter reuptake, neurotransmitter molecules are returned to the vesicles in the presynaptic membrane.

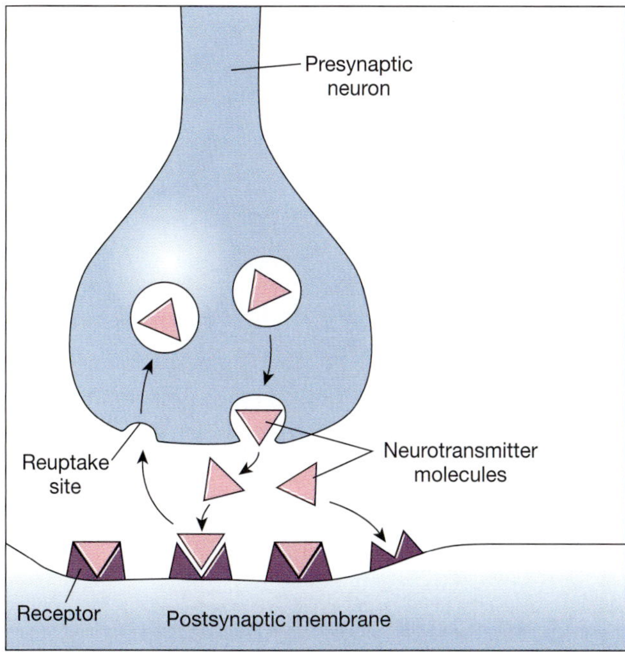

Figure 4.17 Neurotransmitter reuptake. Released neurotransmitter molecules are moved to the reuptake site by a pump-like mechanism and then into the cytoplasm where they are stored in synaptic vesicles.

➤ *What advantage does the neurotransmitter reuptake have over enzymatic degradation? (p. 112–113)*

Electrical Transmission

While our discussion has focused on axon transmission, you will recall from Chapter 2 that many neurons in the mammalian nervous system do not have axons (**anaxonic**). These neurons are components in the

anaxonic A neuron with no axons.

complex interneuronal circuits in which neural impulses can move in either direction (if they had axons, the impulses could move in only one direction down the axon). These circuits are found primarily in brain areas that control complex activities such as learning or memory. Because there are no axons, communication among these neurons occurs from the dendrites of one neuron to the dendrites of another neuron, hence the name **dendrodendritic transmission**.

dendrodendritic transmission Communication between anaxonic neurons from the dendrites of one neuron to the dendrites of another neuron.

electrical synapses The junction between the dendrites of one neuron and the dendrites of another neuron where localized depolarization or hyperpolarization moves across the gap junction.

gap junction The narrow space between the dendrite of one neuron and the dendrite of another neuron.

connexons Specialized protein channels that allow ions to move across gap junctions.

How do neurons without axons communicate? Unlike neurons that have axons, which produce action potentials and communicate by means of chemical transmission, neurons with only dendrites and somas produce small localized depolarizations and hyperpolarizations on the dendrites of adjacent neurons (Kandel, Siegelbaum, & Schwartz, 1991). This communication occurs across **electrical synapses**, where ions move across a space called a **gap junction** from the dendrites of one neuron to the dendrites of adjacent neurons (see **Figure 4.18**). (It should be mentioned that electrical synapses also are found in cardiac and smooth muscle.) The gap junction is quite small, with only 3 nm separating the dendrites (by contrast, the synaptic cleft is 30 to 50 nm). Ions move across the gap junctions through specialized protein channels called **connexons**. The transfer of ions from one dendrite to another dendrite results in a localized depolarization or hyperpolarization, which moves to adjacent areas of the stimulated (or inhibited) dendrite and then through gap junctions to other neurons. As the localized depolarization or hyperpolarization moves to adjacent areas, the strength

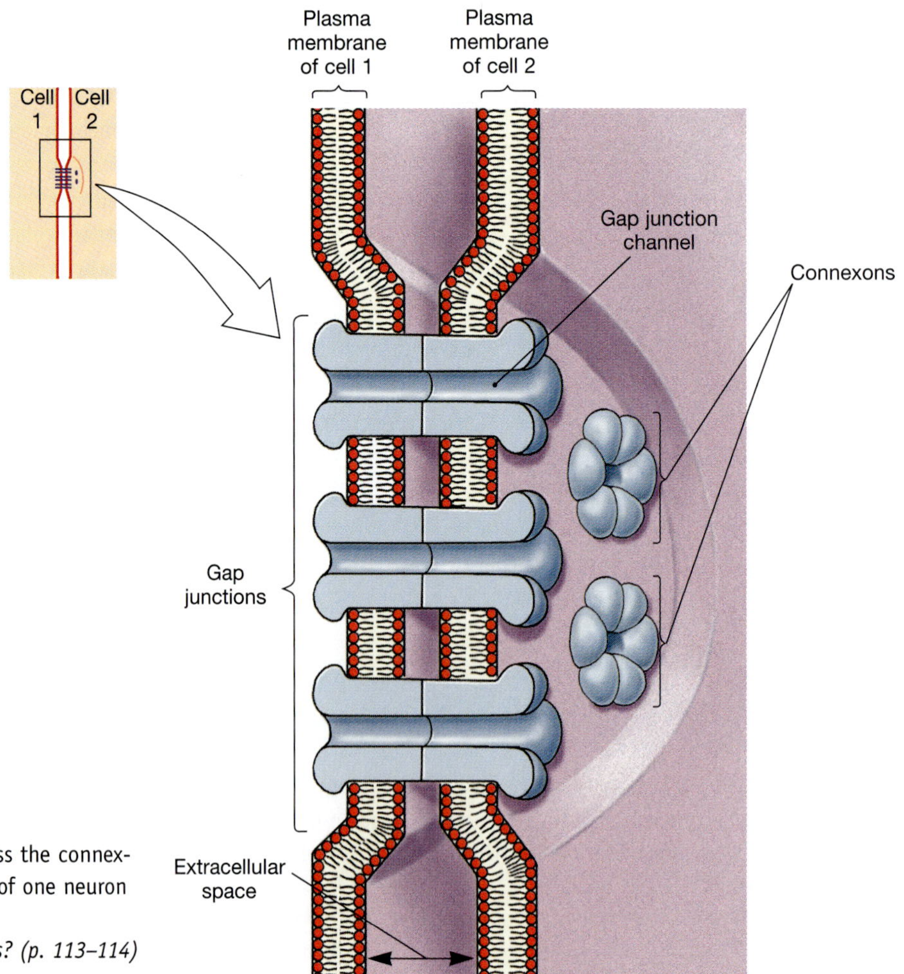

Figure 4.18 Gap junction. Ions travel across the connexons of the gap junction from the dendrites of one neuron to the dendrites of another neuron.

➤ *What is the value of neurons without axons? (p. 113–114)*

of the change in a cell's membrane potential diminishes, until it reaches the resting potential.

Recall that with axodendritic or axoaxonic transmission, the action potential is controlled by the all-or-none law and stimulus intensity is determined either by the number of neurons that fire and/or by the rate of neural firings. With dendrodendritic transmission, there are no action potentials and the level of depolarization or hyperpolarization varies: The intensity of the stimulus determines the level of depolarization or hyperpolarization, with a more intense stimulus causing greater depolarization or hyperpolarization of the dendrite's cell membrane.

Before You Go On

How does the transmission of a neural impulse differ across electrical and chemical synapses?

What is the advantage of having dendrodendritic transmission?

Section Review

- Some neurons do not have axons (anaxonic), so impulse transmission occurs from the dendrite of one neuron to the dendrite of another neuron, a process known as dendrodendritic transmission.
- Communication between the dendrite of one neuron to the dendrite of another neuron occurs across an electrical synapse, where ion charges move across the gap junction through protein channels called connexons. Upon reaching the dendrite of the next neuron, the transferred ion charges produce either depolarization or hyperpolarization of the postsynaptic membrane.
- Anaxonic neurons can be found in complex interneuronal circuits in the brain areas that control activities such as learning and memory.

Agents of Synaptic Transmission

Now that you have learned the basic mechanism of transmitter action, it's time to look at some specific neurotransmitters. Although dozens of different neurotransmitters are found throughout the nervous system (Snyder, 1984), we will focus our discussion to five: acetylcholine, norepinephrine, dopamine, serotonin, and gamma-aminobutyric acid. By studying the action of these representative neurotransmitters, we can discover much about how neurons work and how neurotransmitters affect our behavior.

Acetylcholine

One important neurotransmitter is **acetylcholine (ACh)**, which is distributed throughout the nervous system. ACh is synthesized from acetyl CoA and choline in the presence of the enzyme choline acetyltransferase. Synaptic transmission involving ACh is said to be **cholinergic** (see **Figure 4.19**).

There are two types of cholinergic receptors, named for the drugs that can also stimulate them. The nicotinic receptors are also activated by the drug nicotine, which as you probably know is the addictive component of cigarettes. The second type, muscarinic receptors are also stimulated by muscarine, a poison found in mushrooms.

acetylcholine (ACh) A neurotransmitter that is synthesized from acetyl CoA and choline; occurs only in the presence of the enzyme choline acetyltransferase.

cholinergic Synaptic transmission involving ACh as the neurotransmitter.

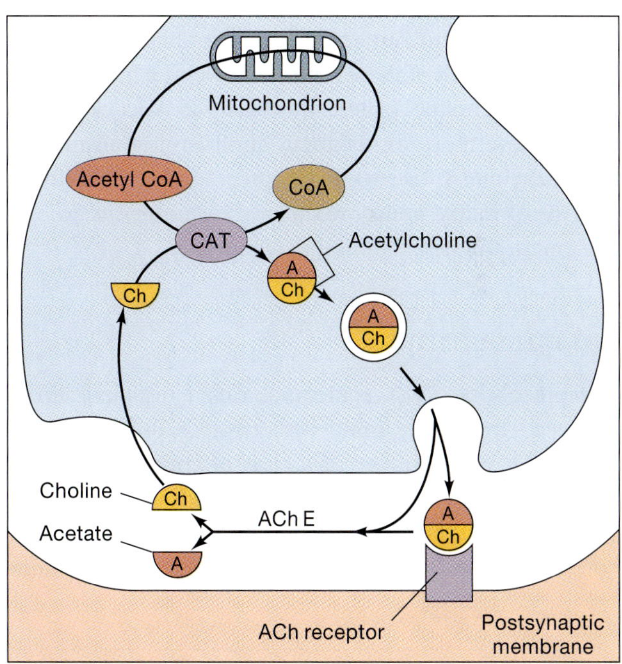

Figure 4.19 Cholinergic synapse. Acetylcholine (ACh) is synthesized from acetyl CoA and choline in the presence of the choline acetyltransferase (CAT) and stored in the synaptic vesicles. When released into the synaptic cleft, ACh diffuses across the synaptic cleft and binds to the receptor site on the postsynaptic membrane. A few milliseconds after binding to the receptor site, ACh is deactivated by the acetylcholinesterase (AChE) by splitting ACh into choline and acetate. Choline molecules are taken up by the presynaptic membrane for reconversion into ACh.

➤ *How is the process of ending cholinergic transmission different from other neurotransmitters? (p. 116)*

Research in this area has also identified four subtypes of nicotinic receptors and five subtypes of muscarinic receptors (McCormick, 1989).

Once ACh is released and binds to the postsynaptic membrane, it is quickly deactivated by the enzyme **acetylcholinesterase (AChE)**, which is present in the synaptic cleft waiting for acetylcholine to be released. (Some acetylcholine molecules obviously do make it to the receptor sites on the postsynaptic membrane; they are quickly deactivated, but only after producing an EPSP or IPSP.) AChE splits ACh into acetate and choline, neither of which is effective by itself (this is an example of the process of enzymatic degradation). After deactivation, most of the choline is taken up by the presynaptic membrane and stored in the presynaptic terminal, where it can be reused to synthesize new ACh (remember neurotransmitter reuptake).

Acetylcholine has a variety of important behavioral functions. One important action of ACh is related to the processes of learning and memory. Research (Coyle, Price, & DeLong, 1983) indicates that the death of cholinergic neurons occurs with Alzheimer's disease, a devastating disorder characterized by severe memory loss, including an inability to remember even familiar people and places. The death of these neurons leaves the brain depleted of acetylcholine (Allen, Dawbarn, & Wilcock, 1988). We will have more to say about cholinergic transmission and Alzheimer's disease in Chapter 14. Acetylcholine is also the primary neuromuscular transmitter; its role in movement will be examined in Chapter 8.

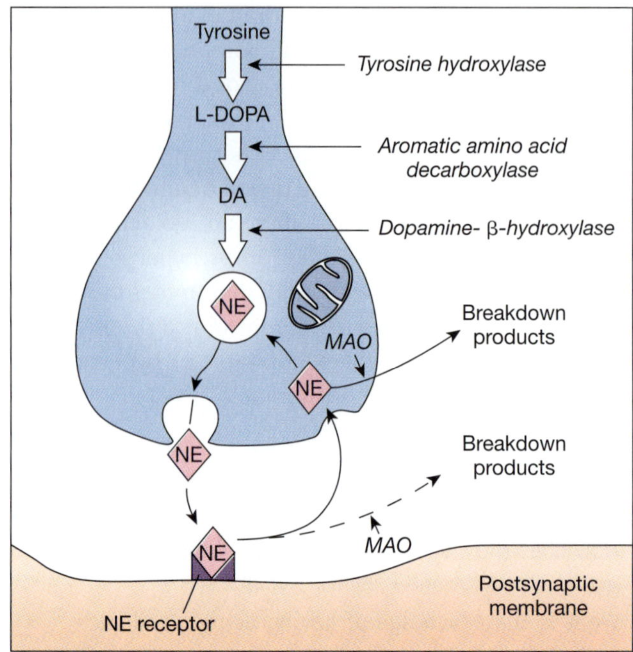

Figure 4.20 Noradrenergic synapse. Norepinephrine (NE) is synthesized from the amino acid tyrosine, which is first converted by the enzyme tyrosine hydroxylase to L-DOPA and then by the enzyme acromatic amino acid decarboxylase to dopamine (DA). Dopamine is converted to NE by the enzyme dopamine-β-hydroxylase. Norepinephrine diffuses across the synaptic cleft and binds to the receptor site on the postsynaptic membrane. A few milliseconds after binding to the receptor site, NE is deactivated by the enzyme monoamine oxidase or returned by reuptake transport to the presynaptic membrane.
➤ *How does noradrenergic transmission differ from cholinergic transmission? (p. 115–116)*

Norepinephrine

Norepinephrine (NE), sometimes called noradrenalin, is produced from the amino acid tyrosine in the adrenal medulla. It is a member of a class of compounds called **monoamines**, which are amine compounds with one amine group (NH_2). When transmission is at a synapse involving norepinephrine, the transmission is referred to as **noradrenergic** (see **Figure 4.20**). There are four major types of noradrenergic receptors. Some noradrenergic transmission stops with the reuptake of norepinephrine by the presynaptic membrane; in other cases, the enzyme **monoamine oxidase** deactivates norepinephrine and, thereby, prevents further remaining noradrenergic transmission.

Like acetylcholine, norepinephrine is widely distributed throughout the nervous system and has a number of important behavioral functions. Norepinephrine appears to have a prominent role in regulating arousal level (Panksepp, 1986). It also has a role in the development of depression. Schildkraut in 1965 proposed that a deficiency in norepinephrine in certain brain areas caused depression. Subsequent studies (Depue & Evans, 1976) have reported lower-than-normal levels of norepinephrine metabolites in the urine of depressed people. More recent research (Schildkraut, Green, & Mooney, 1985) suggests that changes in receptor sensitivity to norepinephrine is more important than the amount of neurotransmitter released. We will look again at the role of noradrenergic transmission in arousal in Chapter 9 and in depression in Chapter 15.

---

acetylcholinesterase (AChE) An enzyme present in the synaptic cleft that quickly deactivates ACh after it is released and binds to the postsynaptic membrane.

norepinephrine (NE) A neurotransmitter, sometimes called noradrenalin, that is produced from the amino acid tyrosine.

monoamine A class of neurotransmitters that contains an amine group (NH_2); includes norepinephrine, dopamine, and serotonin.

noradrenergic Synaptic transmission involving norepinephrine as the neurotransmitter.

monoamine oxidase An enzyme that acts to deactivate norepinephrine, dopamine, and serotonin.

Before You Go On

Why doesn't acetylcholinesterase degrade acetylcholine in the synaptic cleft *before* acetylcholine binds to its postsynaptic receptors?

Nerve poisons such as pesticides block acetylcholinesterase activity. Describe the deadly impact on the nervous system, using what you have learned about enzymatic degradation and neurotransmitter reuptake.

Why might the neurotransmitter norepinephrine be involved in the regulation of arousal level?

Dopamine

Like norepinephrine, **dopamine (DA)** is produced from the amino acid tyrosine. Norepinephrine and dopamine are close chemical relatives (both are classified as monoamines); in fact, when the enzyme dopamine ß-hydroxylase attaches a hydroxyl group to dopamine, it becomes norepinephrine. Synaptic transmission involving dopamine are referred to as **dopaminergic** (see **Figure 4.21**). There appear to be at least five types of dopamine receptors (Schwartz et al., 1992). Of these five, two types (D_1 and D_2 dopamine receptors) have been the most studied. The D_1 dopamine receptors are found only on the postsynaptic membrane, whereas the D_2 dopamine receptor can be found on both presynaptic and postsynaptic membranes. Dopaminergic transmission ends when dopamine molecules are either taken up by the presynaptic membrane or deactivated by monoamine oxidase.

Dopamine has been implicated in several neurological disorders. Dopamine is the neurotransmitter in the synapses between the substantia nigra and the basal ganglia, which acts to integrate voluntary movements (see Chapter 2). The degeneration of dopaminergic neurons in the substantia nigra has been implicated in Parkinson's disease (Youdin & Riederer, 1997), which, as we discussed in Chapter 2, is characterized by severe tremors, muscular rigidity, and decreased control of voluntary movements.

Dysfunction in the activity of dopaminergic transmission also may be involved in the development of schizophrenia. Schizophrenia is a severe mental illness marked by irrational thought, hallucinations, poor contact with reality, and deterioration of adaptive behavior. Some investigators have proposed that schizophrenia is caused by overactivity of dopaminergic synapses. Drugs that block normal dopaminergic transmission have been shown in many cases to be effective in reducing the symptoms of schizophrenia (Snyder, 1986). However, among the possible side effects of these drugs

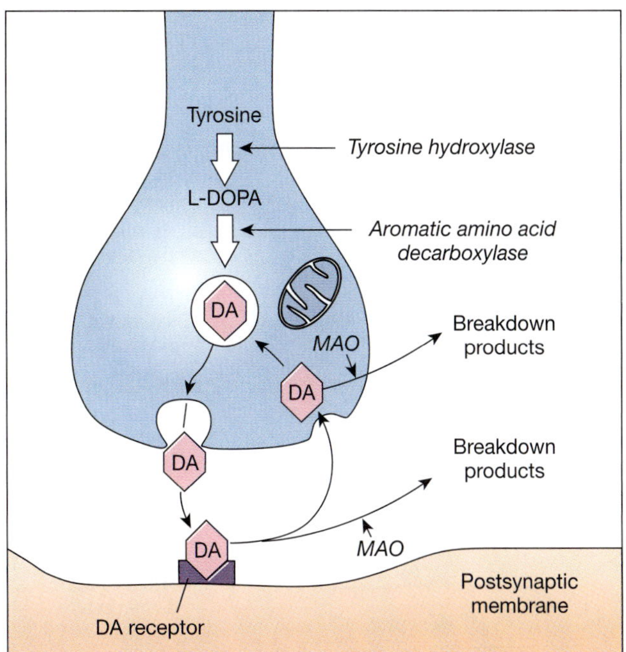

Figure 4.21 Dopaminergic synapse. Dopamine (DA) is synthesized from the amino acid tyrosine. The enzyme tyrosine hydroxylase first converts tyrosine into L-DOPA and then the enzyme aromatic amino acid decarboxylase converts L-DOPA into DA. Dopamine diffuses across the synaptic cleft and binds to the receptor site on the postsynaptic membrane. A few milliseconds after binding to the receptor site, DA is deactivated by the enzyme monoamine oxidase or returned by reuptake transport to the presynaptic membrane.
➤ *How does dopaminergic transmission differ from noradrenergic transmission? (p. 116–117)*

are Parkinson's symptoms. We will discuss the role of dopamine in Parkinson's disease in Chapter 8 and in schizophrenia in Chapter 15.

Serotonin

A third monoamine neurotransmitter is commonly known as **serotonin (5-HT)**, or less commonly, as 5-hydroxytryptamine. Widely distributed throughout the central nervous system, serotonin is synthesized from the amino acid tryptophan. Synaptic transmission involving serotonin is referred to as **serotonergic**

---

dopamine (DA) A neurotransmitter that is produced from the amino acid tyrosine.

dopaminergic Synaptic transmission involving dopamine as the neurotransmitter.

serotonin (5-HT) A neurotransmitter that is synthesized from the amino acid tryptophan.

serotonergic Synaptic transmission that involves serotonin as the neurotransmitter.

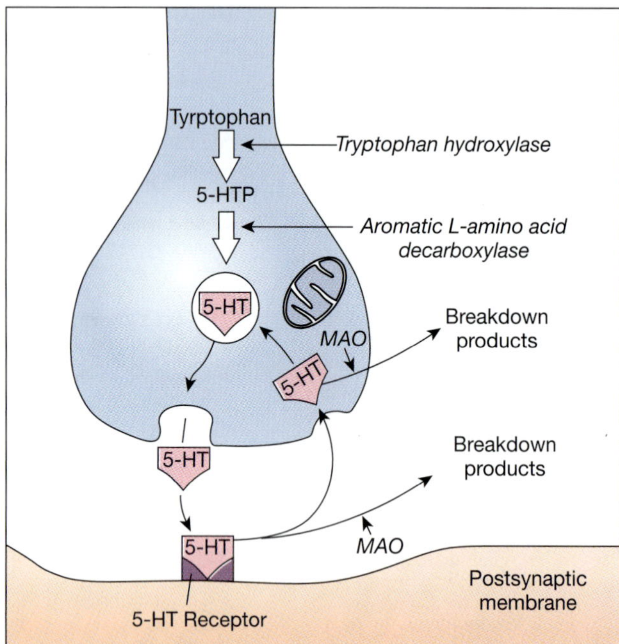

Figure 4.22 Serotonergic synapse. Serotonin (5-hydroxytryptamine; 5-HT) is synthesized from the amino acid tryptophan. The enzyme tryptophan hydroxylase first converts tryptophan into 5-hydroxytryptophan (5-HTP) and then the enzyme aromatic L-amino acid decarboxylase converts 5-HTP into 5-HT. Serotonin diffuses across the synaptic cleft and binds to the receptor site on the postsynaptic membrane. A few milliseconds after binding to the receptor site, 5-HT is deactivated by the enzyme monoamine oxidase or returned by reuptake transport to the presynaptic membrane.

➤ *How does serotonergic transmission differ from dopaminergic transmission? (p. 117–118)*

(see **Figure 4.22**). There appear to be at least 10 types of serotonergic receptors (Humphrey, Hartig, & Hoyer, 1993). Some serotonergic receptors are found on both presynaptic and postsynaptic membranes. One, the 5-HT_2 receptor, is found only on the postsynaptic membrane. Some serotonin molecules are recycled via neurotransmitter reuptake; others are deactivated by monoamine oxidase.

Serotonergic neurons play an important role in a variety of behaviors, including the regulation of sleep (Bloom & Lazerson, 1988). Depletion of serotonin decreases the duration of sleep (Laguzzi & Adrien, 1980), whereas ingestion of the amino acid L-tryptophan, which can be converted to serotonin, seems to help some people go to sleep (Schneider-Helmert & Spinweber, 1986). Serotonin also has been implicated in depression; individuals with severe depression have decreased levels of serotonin metabolites (Träskmann et al., 1981). Drugs, such as fluoxetine (Prozac), that increase the activity of serotonergic neurons have been reported to improve mood and alleviate depression (Feighner et al., 1991). The role of serotonin in mood disorders will be examined further in Chapter 15.

Gamma-aminobutyric Acid

Neurons releasing **gamma-aminobutyric acid (GABA)** are located throughout the central nervous system; as many as one-third of all neurons in the CNS may be **GABAergic** (see **Figure 4.23**) (Enna & Gallagher, 1983). GABA is produced from glutamic acid when the enzyme glutamic acid decarboxylase removes a carboxyl group. The main effect of GABA neurons is to suppress or inhibit the action of other neurons. The action of GABA terminates as a result of its deactivation by the enzyme GABA transaminase and then its reuptake by the presynaptic membrane.

gamma-aminobutyric acid (GABA) A neurotransmitter that is synthesized from glutamic acid when the enzyme glutamic acid decarboxylase removes a carboxyl group.

GABAergic Synaptic transmission that involves GABA as the neurotransmitter.

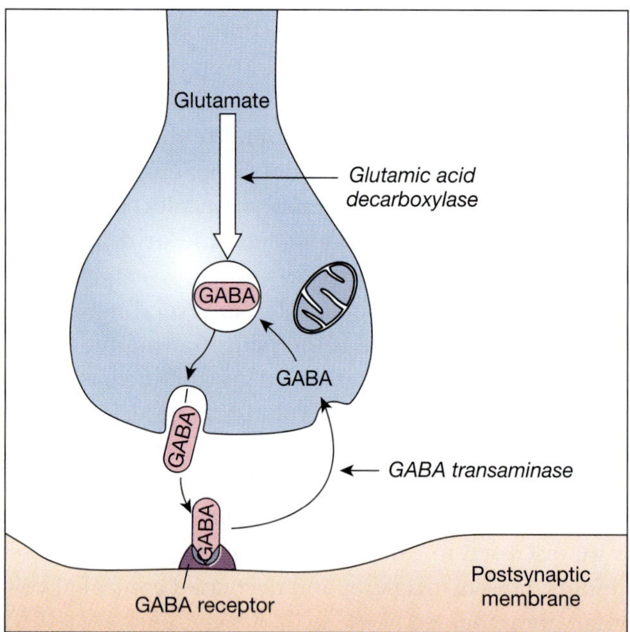

Figure 4.23 GABAergic synapse. Gamma aminobutyric acid (GABA) is synthesized from the amino acid glutamic acid. The enzyme glutamic acid decarboxylase converts glutamic acid into GABA. Gamma aminobutyric acid diffuses across the synaptic cleft and binds to the receptor site on the postsynaptic membrane. A few milliseconds after binding to the receptor site GABA is deactivated by the enzyme GABA transaminase and then returned by reuptake transport to the presynaptic membrane.

➤ *How does GABAergic transmission differ from serotonergic transmission? (p. 118)*

The primary role of the inhibitory action of GABA neurons is to keep the brain from becoming excessively aroused. There are at least five types of GABA receptors (Kerr & Ong, 1995). $GABA_A$ and $GABA_B$ are the most studied, with $GABA_A$ receptors believed to control Cl^- ion movement and $GABA_B$ receptors believed to control K^+ ion movement. With both types of receptors, GABA acts to hyperpolarize the postsynaptic cell membrane by opening ion channels to either increase Cl^- ion movement into the cell at the $GABA_A$ receptor or increase K^+ ion movement out of the cell at the $GABA_B$ receptor.

Deficiencies in GABA have been linked to a number of behavior disorders. For example, a decrease in GABA neurons appears to be involved in Huntington's disease, an inherited neurological disorder that is characterized, as we noted in Chapter 1, by progressive dementia and by jerky, uncoordinated movements of the face and body that reflect a failure to inhibit motor movements. We will discuss this disease again in greater detail in Chapter 8.

Extreme anxiety, which is characterized by intense physiological arousal and strong feelings of apprehension, guilt, and a sense of impending doom, has also been linked to lowered levels of GABA (Hollander, Simeon, & Gorman, 1994). People are likely to be very anxious when GABA levels in the brain decline, and drugs that increase GABA activity, such as Valium and alcohol, decrease anxiety levels (Ballinger, 1991).

In addition to acetylcholine, norepinephrine, dopamine, serotonin, and gamma-aminobutyric acid, there are other neurotransmitters that have important influences on behavior. For example, several amino acids—aspartate, glutamate, and glycine—have been suggested as neurotransmitters (Hall, 1992). Glutamate is distributed widely throughout the brain and its effects are excitatory. Activation of glutamate receptors produces increased alertness, attention, and cortical arousal (Silinsky, 1989). People who are especially sensitive to monosodium glutamate, which is the sodium salt of glutamate acid, will experience temporary dizziness. Both aspartate and glycine appear to be inhibitory neurotransmitters.

Second Messengers

Our discussion has suggested that the effect of neurotransmitter molecules is to directly act on the receptor site to open or close ion channels. This is one action of a neurotransmitter. A neurotransmitter can also produce ion channel changes indirectly. When the effects are indirect, the neurotransmitter produces chemical changes within the cell. These chemicals, called **second messengers**, then act to produce ion channel changes on the postsynaptic membrane. One example of a second messenger is cyclic adenosine monophosphate (cyclic AMP). Cyclic AMP is produced from adenosine triphosphate (ATP), which we learned earlier is a prime source of energy for cellular metabolism. Another secondary message is nitrous oxide, which as we will discover in Chapter 14, has an important role in memory storage.

When a neurotransmitter directly acts to change ion channels, it is acting on an **ionotrophic receptor**, whereas if it changes ion channels indirectly, it is acting on a **metabotrophic receptor**. The same neurotransmitter can act on both ionotrophic and metabotrophic receptors, which is a process called divergence. The divergence process allows a neurotransmitter to have multiple effects. For example, the effect of serotonin on both mood and sleep is but one example of divergence.

You might wonder why there are so many different neurotransmitters. In many parts of the nervous system, especially in the brain, neurons serving different behavioral functions are in close physical proximity to each other. One explanation for the existence of varied neurotransmitters for different functions is that they are needed to prevent undesired or inadvertent communication between neurons. For example, the neurons controlling eating and sexual behavior are located in the same general area of the brain, yet because the chemical transmitters controlling each behavior are different (norepinephrine for eating and dopamine for sex), we can engage in each behavior separately. Another possibility is that these different neurotransmitter systems evolved separately, and just happen to occupy the same space (or nearly the same space).

APPLICATION

Drug Treatment of Depression

Drugs can influence the activity of neurotransmitters in a variety of ways. One purpose of drug administration is to increase the levels of a depleted neurotransmitter in order to reinstate normal physiological and behavioral functioning. Drugs that elevate levels of norepinephrine, dopamine, and serotonin in the brain have been shown to decrease depressive symptoms (Baldessarini, 1995). Two classes of drugs that increase the activity of these three neurotransmitters have for many years been used to provide

---

second messenger Chemical changes produced inside the cell by a neurotransmitter that lead to ion channel changes.

ionotrophic receptor A receptor whose ion channels are changed directly by the action of the neurotransmitter.

metabotrophic receptor A receptor whose ion channels are changed by a second messenger.

clinical relief for many depressed individuals. The **tricyclic compounds** increase levels of norepinephrine in the brain, and to a lesser extent dopamine and serotonin, by interfering with neurotransmitter reuptake. The **monoamine oxidase (MAO) inhibitors** increase levels of norepinephrine, dopamine, and serotonin by preventing enzymatic degradation (recall that these three neurotransmitters are degraded by monoamine oxidase in the synapse).

Biochemically, what we call depression is probably a collection of different disorders with similar symptoms. One line of evidence pointing to this conclusion is that people who are classified as depressed vary in their responsivity to drugs. For instance, some people with depression, particularly those who are agitated, tend to respond well to the sedating action of the tricyclic drug amitriptyline. Other people with depression are withdrawn, and they tend to respond well to the stimulating effect of the tricyclic compound protriptyline (Frazer & Winokur, 1977). Tricyclics are generally more effective than MAO inhibitors in most depressed individuals, but MAO inhibitors are helpful for many depressed individuals who do not respond to tricyclics (Thase, Trivedi, & Rush, 1995).

The reason for the differential responsivity to different drug treatments is not entirely clear, but it is likely that a number of brain structures and specific systems are involved in producing depression. The success of any drug treatment may depend on whether the neurotransmitter chemical neurotransmitter in the specific structure altered by a drug is involved in a particular individual's depression. We will look at the biological structures involved in mood disorders and the use of drugs to influence these structures, especially those that have more specific neurotransmitter effects, in more detail in Chapter 15.

Before You Go On

Name the five major neurotransmitters and their functions. What would happen if GABA release were suddenly inhibited?

Would the effects of inhibiting the release of norepinephrine or serotonin be different from the effect of inhibiting GABA? Why?

tricyclic compounds A class of drugs that increase brain norepinephrine, and to a lesser extent dopamine and serotonin, by interfering with neurotransmitter reuptake.

monoamine oxidase (MAO) inhibitors A class of drugs that increases levels of norepinephrine, dopamine, and serotonin by preventing enzymatic deactivation.

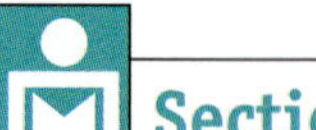

Section Review

- Acetylcholine (ACh) plays an important role in learning and memory; lowered levels of ACh are associated with Alzheimer's disease.
- After ACh acts on the postsynaptic membrane, it is deactivated by the enzyme acetylcholinesterase.
- Norepinephrine is involved in the control of arousal and mood, with lowered levels implicated in depression.
- After binding to the postsynaptic membrane, norepinephrine is taken back into the presynaptic vesicles and deactivated by monoamine oxidase.
- Dopamine is involved in the integration of voluntary behavior, with the degeneration of dopamine neurons in the substantia nigra associated with Parkinson's disease; hyperactivity of dopaminergic synapses has been identified as a possible cause of schizophrenia.
- The binding of dopamine to the postsynaptic receptors is followed by reuptake by the presynaptic membrane and deactivation by monoamine oxidase.
- Serotonin is involved in the regulation of sleep; depletion of serotonin has been associated with decreased sleep and depression.
- Serotonin is both returned to the presynaptic vesicles and deactivated by monoamine oxidase.
- Gamma-aminobutyric acid (GABA) acts to inhibit other neurons and, thereby, helps prevent the brain from being excessively aroused. Deficiencies of GABA have been linked to Huntington's disease and to excessive anxiety.
- GABA action is terminated by deactivation by the enzyme GABA transaminase and then by reuptake by the presynaptic membrane.
- Other neurotransmitters include the amino acids glutamate, which is an excitatory neurotransmitter, and aspartate and glycine, which are inhibitory neurotransmitters.
- A neurotransmitter can bind to ionotrophic receptors and directly change ion channels.
- A neurotransmitter can bind to metabotrophic receptors and produce metabolic changes in the cell, called secondary messengers, that lead to ion channel changes. Examples of secondary messages include cyclic AMP and nitrous oxide.

The Blood-Brain Barrier

The ability of the nervous system to process and then to respond to environmental stimuli effectively depends on the maintenance of a delicate electrolyte balance between the fluid that surrounds the neuron (extracellular) and the fluid inside the neuron (intracellular). Any disruption in this balance jeopardizes the functioning of the nervous system. This balance is maintained by a structure called the **blood-brain barrier**, which prevents the free flow of substances from the bloodstream into the brain.

Structure and Function of the Blood-Brain Barrier

Substances entering the body quickly find their way into the bloodstream. Many of the substances entering our body are essential to our survival. For example, the brain needs oxygen and glucose to fuel metabolic processes but is unable to store even moderate amounts of either substance. The circulatory system provides the brain with these essential resources. Other substances entering the bloodstream, such as alcohol, can disrupt the functioning of the nervous system and therefore are a source of potential harm.

Several major arteries provide blood to the brain. These large arteries branch into many smaller arteries and then into very fine channels called capillaries. It is the capillaries that actually deliver nutrients to the neurons of the brain. Endothelial cells line the outside surface of the capillaries. The endothelial cells form the protective lining of the thin capillaries. In most capillaries found in the human body, gaps between the endothelial cells allow relatively large molecules to pass from the bloodstream into the cells. However, in the brain the endothelial cells are closely joined. The smaller gaps between endothelial cells in the capillaries of the brain prevent the free flow of substances from the blood into the neurons of the brain (Rapoport & Robinson, 1986; see **Figure 4.24**).

The small gaps between endothelial cells are not the only means of preventing substances from entering the brain through the bloodstream. Access to the brain is also limited by the astroglia (see Chapter 2 and **Figure 4.24**) surrounding the capillaries. For example, astroglia keep certain blood-borne toxic substances from entering neurons.

The blood-brain barrier is not perfect. Small uncharged molecules, such as oxygen and carbon dioxide, can pass readily through the capillaries and endothelial cells. In addition, any substance that is soluble in lipids can pass from the bloodstream into the brain. (Recall from Chapter 2 that cell membranes are composed of a lipid bilayer.) For example, heroin and nicotine can enter the brain by first attaching to the lipids in the capillary walls.

The blood-brain barrier is not uniformly effective throughout the brain. Several regions of the brain are more vulnerable than others. For example, the blood-brain barrier is relatively weak in the area postrema, a region of the medulla oblongata that controls vomiting. The greater permeability of this area increases the chances that an ingested poison will be vomited: Toxic substances can leave the bloodstream in the area postrema, stimulating the neurons in this area to produce vomiting. However, the same toxic substances cannot cross the barrier in other areas of the brain, protecting the brain from their dangerous effects.

The blood-brain barrier works both ways—it also prevents many substances from leaving brain cells and entering the bloodstream. Although waste products are removed from the neuron by active transport systems, large molecules, such as proteins, remain within the neuron. When such proteins are lost, through various disease processes, the result can be damage to the brain. Remember Michele? Failure of the blood-brain barrier to prevent protein molecules from leaving brain cells may play a role in the development of multiple sclerosis.

---

blood-brain barrier A barrier formed by the tight joints in the endothelial walls that surround the capillaries and by astroglia cells that limits the flow of certain substances between the bloodstream and the brain.

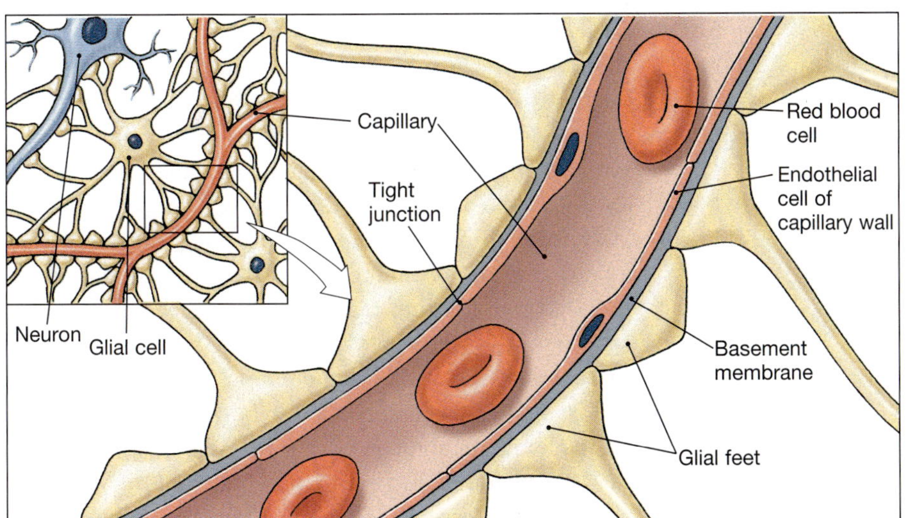

Figure 4.24 The transport of substances into and out of the capillaries surrounding the brain. Notice the tight joining of endothelial cells that limits the movement of large molecules. Some substances enter the brain by passing freely through the walls of the capillaries. Other substances enter the brain by attaching to the lipids in the capillary walls or by being pumped out of the bloodstream.

➤ *How does nicotine cross the blood-brain barrier? (p. 121)*

The Blood-Brain Barrier and Multiple Sclerosis

As we learned earlier, multiple sclerosis is a neurological disorder caused by the progressive degeneration of the myelin covering the axons of the nervous system, which leads to serious sensory impairment and loss of motor control. What causes the loss of myelin in individuals with multiple sclerosis? The body's own immune system. For some as yet unknown reason, the immune system attacks myelin as if it were a foreign substance. The destruction of myelin impairs the propagation of the action potential in the affected neurons. Without the ability to transmit impulses along myelinated neurons, the nervous system can no longer function effectively. Currently, the most frequently employed treatment for multiple sclerosis is corticosteroids, such as methylprednisone, that act to suppress the immune system (National Multiple Sclerosis Society, 1998). Clinical trials are presently being conducted to determine the effectiveness of immune system suppressant drugs such as the interferons Betascron or Avonex. (Interferons are peptides released by virus-infected cells, which make other cells more resistant to that virus.) Another experimental treatment is the monoclonal antibody drug Antegren. (Monoclonal antibodies are genetically engineered antibodies.) It is hoped that these new classes of treatments will reduce the severity and duration of acute attacks experienced by multiple sclerosis patients.

Why does the immune system attack neural myelin? One theory is that damage to the blood-brain barrier allows myelin proteins to enter the bloodstream. Because of its usual isolation from the nervous system, the immune system does not recognize these proteins and therefore reacts to the myelin as it would any foreign substance.

What evidence supports this explanation of multiple sclerosis? **Experimental allergic encephalomyelitis** is a neurological disorder with symptoms that resemble multiple sclerosis. Experimental allergic encephalomyelitis is produced when myelin proteins are injected into the bloodstream of laboratory animals (Schwartz, 1991). This research finding suggests that the immune system can be triggered to attack and destroy myelin in reaction to the presence of myelin protein in the bloodstream. So if this model is correct, people like Michele with multiple sclerosis should have myelin protein in their blood. Sure enough, myelin protein is indeed present in the bloodstream of individuals with multiple sclerosis.

Before You Go On

Name three substances that can cross the blood-brain barrier, and describe how they gain entry into the brain.

Section Review

- The blood-brain barrier restricts the flow of substances from the bloodstream into the brain.
- The blood-brain barrier is formed by the close joining of the endothelial cells lining the outside surface of the capillaries of the brain.
- Astroglia also control the flow of substances into the brain.
- Uncharged small molecules and substances that are soluble in lipids can pass from the bloodstream into the brain.
- According to one theory, multiple sclerosis is caused by damage to the blood-brain barrier that allows myelin proteins to leak into the bloodstream.

Hormones and Neuromodulators

The Endocrine System

Earlier in the chapter, we discussed the action of neurotransmitters that transmit impulses from one neuron to the next. However, there are many cases in which communication must be more widespread. In these circumstances, the glands of the **endocrine system** release chemical transmitters into the bloodstream. The bloodstream then carries the transmitter to distant target areas (see **Figure 4.25**). Such transmitters are called **hormones**. In Chapter 2, we discussed the production and release of hormones by the pituitary gland, sometimes called the "master gland"; as you can see from **Figure 4.25**, however, endocrine glands are located throughout the body. Although hormones are a slower means of communication than neurotransmitters, they can transmit information more widely. For example, testosterone is produced by the testes, but can have profound effects as far away as the brain.

Like neurotransmitters, specific hormones stimulate the postsynaptic membranes of specific target cells. **Table 4.1** lists the major endocrine glands and some of the hormones they release. For example, activation of the adrenal

---

experimental allergic encephalomyelitis A neurological disorder with symptoms resembling multiple sclerosis that is produced when myelin proteins are injected into the bloodstream of laboratory animals.

endocrine system A system consisting of cells that release hormones into the bloodstream, where they are carried to distant target areas.

hormones Chemicals produced by the endrocrine glands that are circulated widely throughout the body via the bloodstream.

glands causes the release of **epinephrine** and norepinephrine into the bloodstream. Stimulation of the neurons sensitive to epinephrine and norepinephrine produces intense internal arousal. You will note that one of the five major neurotransmitters that we discussed earlier in the chapter, norepinephrine, is listed in **Table 4.1** as a hormone released from the adrenal medulla. Confusing, you say? And norepinephrine is not the only one like this! Norepinephrine is considered a neurotransmitter when it is communicating from neuron to neuron, and a hormone when it is distributed by the bloodstream. So it is *distribution* that differentiates neurotransmitters from hormones.

Hormones carry messages to neurons, muscles, and organs, and can also stimulate development of these targets. For example, as we saw in Chapter 3, the hormone testosterone controls the maturation of the male's reproductive system. As we will see throughout the text, hormones often have important influences on our behavior.

Many hormones are controlled by the brain through feedback loops, which can be either positive or negative. In one example of a **positive feedback loop**, release of a hormone acts to promote further release of the hormone. For example, consider the process of labor, which once it begins needs to be completed quickly. The stimulus for beginning labor is the secretion of oxytocin initiated by the distortion of the uterus by the growing fetus (Martini, 1998).

epinephrine A hormone produced by the adrenal medulla and released into the bloodstream.

positive feedback loop The release of a substance acts to promote its further release.

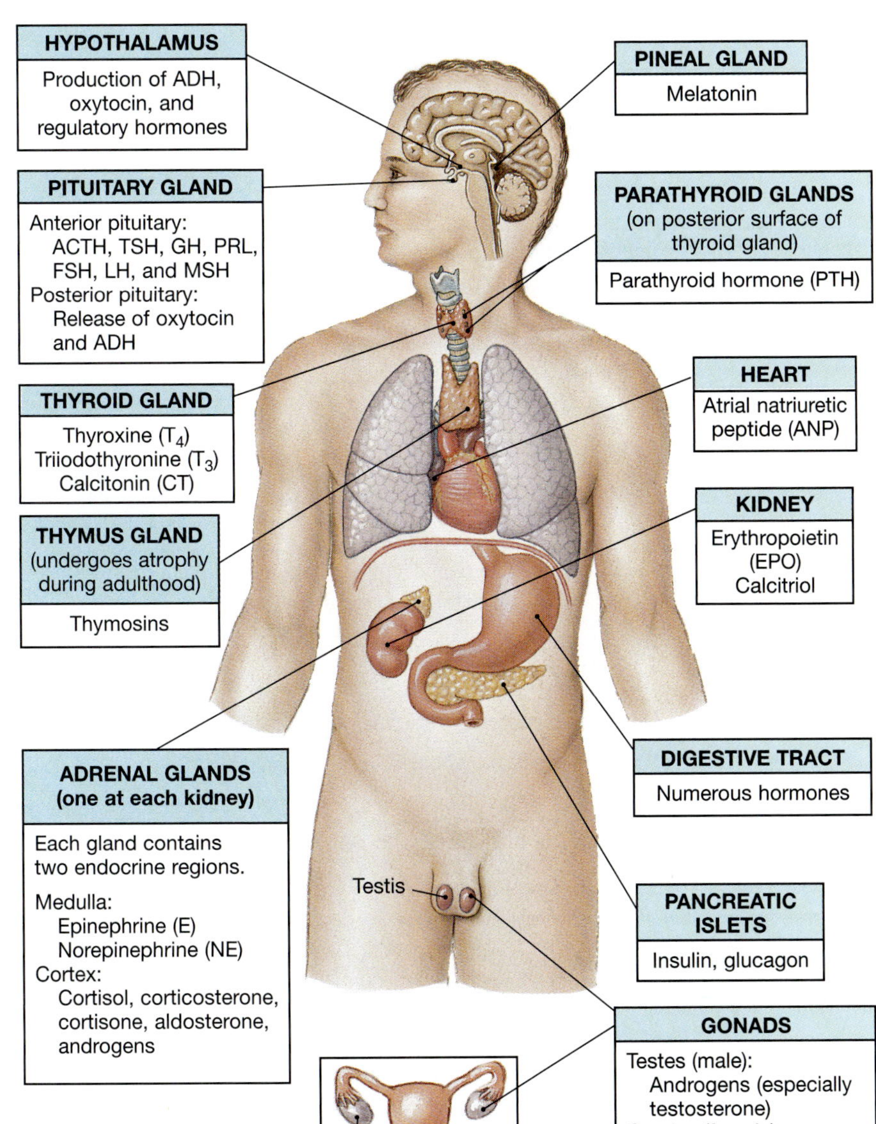

Figure 4.25 Location of major endocrine glands. These glands have an important influence on biological processes and behavior.

➤ *How do hormones travel from the gland in which they are produced to the target organs? (p. 122–123)*

Table 4.1 ▪ Major endocrine glands, the hormones they secrete, and their principal functions

Gland	Hormone	Function
Adrenal gland		
Cortex	Aldosterone	Retention of sodium and excretion of potassium
	Androstenedione	Growth of pubic and underarm hair, sex drive (women)
	Cortisone	Metabolism; response to stress
Medulla	Epinephrine, norepinephrine	Metabolism; response to stress
Hypothalamus*		
	Releasing hormones	Control of anterior pituitary hormone secretion
Kidneys		
	Renin	Control of aldosterone secretion; blood pressure
Ovaries		
	Estrogen	Maturation of female reproductive system; secondary sex characteristics
	Progesterone	Maintenance of lining of uterus; promotion of pregnancy
	Inhibin	Control of FSH release
Pancreas		
	Insulin, glucagon	Regulation of glucose utilization and storage
Pineal		
	Melatonin	Regulation of circadian cycle
Pituitary Gland		
Anterior	Adrenocorticotropic hormone	Control of adrenal cortex
	Gonadotropic hormones (FSH,LH)	Control of testes and ovaries
	Growth hormone	Growth; control of metabolism
	Prolactin	Milk production
	Thyroid-stimulating hormone	Control of thyroid gland
Posterior	Antidiuretic hormone**	Retention of water
	Oxytocin**	Release of milk, contraction of uterus
Testes		
	Androgens	Maturation of male reproductive system; sperm production; secondary sex characteristics; sex drive (men)
	Inhibin	Control of FSH release
Thyroid gland		
	Thyroxine, triodothyronine	Energy metabolism; growth and development
	Calcitonin	Uptake of calcium by bones
Parathyroids		
	Parathyroid hormone	Breakdown of bone calcium to blood

*The hypothalamus, although it is part of the brain, secretes hormones; thus it can be considered to be an endocrine gland.

**These hormones are produced by the hypothalamus but are transported to and released from the posterior pituitary gland.

Source: Adapted from Carlson, N. R. (1988). *Foundations of physiological psychology*. Boston: Allyn & Bacon.

Stretch receptors on the uterine wall detect contractions and activate the hypothalamus to continue the release of oxytocin (see **Figure 4.26**). A positive feedback loop increases the level of oxytocin release and the strength of uterine contractions until the delivery release of the newborn.

In some cases, the release of a hormone acts to inhibit its subsequent release, one example of a cycle called a

negative feedback loop. The release of the hormone estrogen is controlled by negative feedback (see **Figure 4.27**). Stimulation of the basal tuberal region of the hypothalamus in females causes the anterior pituitary to release the follicular-stimulating hormone (FSH). One effect of this follicular-stimulating hormone is to cause the ovary to secrete estrogen. When estrogen is carried by the bloodstream to the hypothalamus, one of its actions is to inhibit FSH release, which causes estrogen levels to fall. The lowered level of estrogen acts to remove this inhibition and results in resumed production of FSH.

Certain hormones, called **pheromones**, are released into the air rather than into the bloodstream. The odors of these hormones can have a powerful effect on behavior. When Michele's dog was in heat, Michele had a hard time keeping the many male dogs from her neighborhood at bay. This attraction is produced by the pheromones that are released by female dogs when they are sexually responsive (Gleason & Reynierse, 1969).

Neuromodulators: Chemical Transmitters or Hormones?

Jerry, Michele's dad, wonders why he enjoys running so much. He has run at least 10 miles a day more days than not, for as long as he can remember. As a child, he enjoyed running on the playground; in high school he was a member of the track team. Jerry ran in several marathons when he was younger, but now, at age 50, he just runs by himself. He lives in Vermont, where it is not easy being a runner. Many times, especially in the winter, he has been tempted to stay inside his comfortable house rather than venture out into the rain, sleet, or snow. Yet, if he can get out of his house, Jerry runs. He is sure that many of his neighbors feel that he is crazy to run in such bad weather, but he just has to run. As he has gotten older, aches and pains have meant some discomfort at the beginning of a run, and the pain is greater if the weather is bad. He starts running slowly and then picks up his speed about half a mile into his run. After about one mile, Jerry starts to feel better. After several miles, he feels really good. Jerry has a hard time describing the feeling to Michele, but it is a feeling of great exhilaration. All of his body tingles, and he feels as though he is floating rather than running and, if only for a while, he forgets his worries about Michele's condition. However, the intensely good feeling he has after several miles lasts for only a few minutes. He then settles into a relaxed, comfortable feeling for the rest of his run. Jerry is tired at the end of a run, but he still feels good. In fact, the excitement and pleasure of running lasts for several hours. Jerry always runs early in the morning, and he goes to bed each night looking forward to that high he will experience the next morning. ■

Why does Jerry feel compelled to run every day? Why does he get a jolt of pleasure from running? Why does his pleasure last for so long? We will provide some answers to these questions in the following paragraphs.

negative feedback loop The release of a substance acts to inhibit its subsequent release.

pheromones Hormones that are released into the air rather than into the bloodstream.

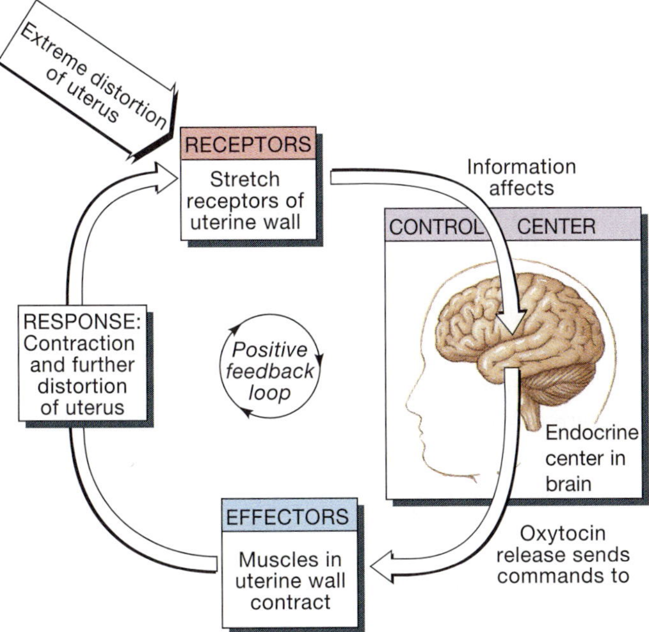

Figure 4.26 Positive feedback loop involved in the birth of a newborn. Uterine contractions initiated by oxytocin release caused by distortion of uterus by growing fetus leads to continued oxytocin release and increasing greater uterine contractions.

➤ *Why is the positive feedback loop important in childbirth? (p. 123–124)*

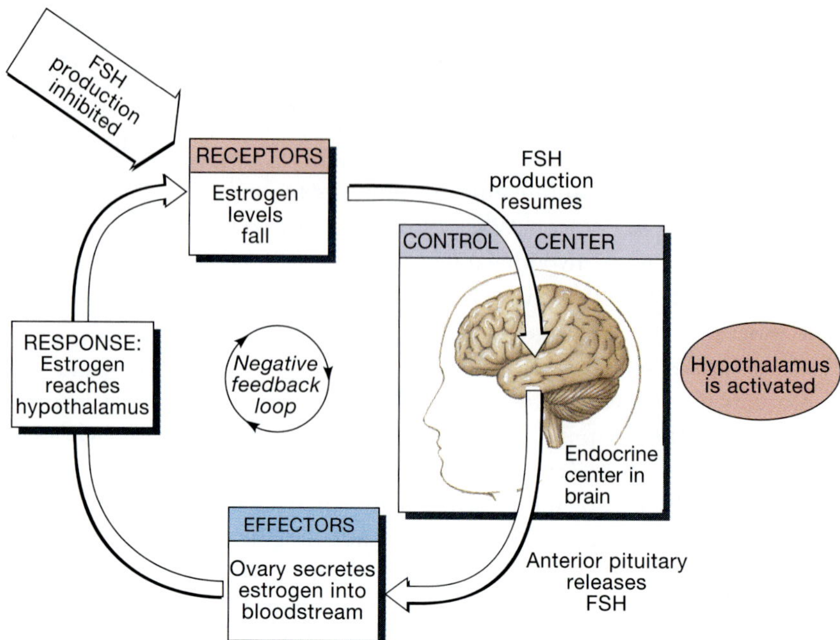

Figure 4.27 Negative feedback loop involved in regulation of estrogen levels. Increases in estrogen result in the activation of processes that lead to reduced estrogen levels, which then results in processes that elevate estrogen levels. ➤ *Does the negative feedback loop maintain a consistent level of estrogen? (p. 124–125)*

Opiates, such as heroin and morphine, have a powerful effect on people. These drugs produce analgesia, a decreased perception of pain. Opiates also provide a strong sense of emotional well-being, a phenomenon that we will explore further in Chapter 5. How do opiate drugs influence pain perception and elicit strong positive feelings? Abram Goldstein (1976) proposed that chemicals resembling opiates are normally produced by the body, and that these naturally occurring chemicals stimulate specific neurons. Further, Goldstein suggested that opiate drugs affect behavior by mimicking the naturally occurring opiates and activating the same neurons.

Why did Goldstein believe that the brain produces natural opiates? He discovered that when opium was ingested, it ended up concentrated in specific areas of the brain. In fact, most of the opium was most active in the areas of the brain associated with the perception of pain and with emotions. Goldstein reasoned that this pattern of opium concentration in the brain meant that the brain contains a natural opiate substance.

opiates Drugs, such as heroin and morphine, that produce decreased perception of pain and a strong sense of emotional well-being.

endorphins Naturally occurring peptides with opiate-like effects.

substance P Neurotransmitter released by sensory pain receptors when an animal is exposed to a painful event.

neuromodulators A class of chemicals, including the endorphins, that controls the amount of neurotransmitter released at the presynaptic membrane.

At around the same time, John Hughes and Hans Kosterlitz, two researchers at the University of Aberdeen in Scotland, discovered two naturally occurring peptides in the brain that were strongly attracted to the same neurons stimulated by the synthetic opiates. Hughes and Kosterlitz (Hughes et al., 1975) named these two peptides leu-enkephalin and met-enkephalin (from the Greek word meaning "in the head"). Today, **endorphin** is the general term for all peptides with opiate-like effects.

How do both endorphins and opiates work? Sensory pain receptors contain an excitatory neurotransmitter, called **substance P**, which is released when a person is exposed to a painful event. Both endorphins and opiates act to inhibit the release of substance P and thereby act to reduce sensations of pain (Fernandez & Turk, 1992).

Running can be a painful experience. The experience of pain causes the release of endorphins, which reduce Jerry's sensitivity to pain (Miczeck, Thompson, & Shuster, 1986). Jerry's great exhilaration, or "runner's high," is also caused by the release of endorphins.

Recall our discussion of presynaptic inhibition, in which a reduced amount of neurotransmitter is released because of depolarization of presynaptic receptor sites by neurotransmitter molecules from an inhibitory neuron. The endorphins have a similar mode of action (refer to **Figure 4.28**). The endorphins belong to a class of chemicals called **neuromodulators** (modulate = change). They work by affecting the amount of neurotransmitter released at the presynaptic membrane. However, the endorphins are not neurotransmitters. Rather than influencing the action of a single neuron as a neurotransmitter does, the endorphins have a more general effect, traveling throughout the brain. This general effect of endorphins is similar to hormonal action. Yet, the endorphins are not hormones; hormones act directly on postsynaptic membranes, whereas endorphins merely modulate neurotransmitter release. Thus, although endorphins have some qualities in common with both neurotransmitters and hormones, the neuromodulators are chemicals that act differently than neurotransmitters and hormones. Thus, neuromodulators are considered chemical transmitters, but are neither hormones nor neurotransmitters.

You might wonder what purpose is served by modulation of pain sensitivity. Suppose that you are exposed to a painful event such as an electric shock. The pain causes the release of endorphins, reducing your pain sensitivity. This allows you to react to the danger (escape from the source of the shock) without being so overwhelmed by pain that you cannot cope with the danger. On the other hand, if you are exposed to an extraordinarily painful event, so much endorphin may be released that you may go into shock and thus be unable to respond to the painful stimulus. In these extreme situations, the reduction in pain is profound; however, such drastically lowered response to painful events has the effect of reducing rather than enhancing the likelihood of survival. We will look more closely at the sensory reception of pain in Chapter 7.

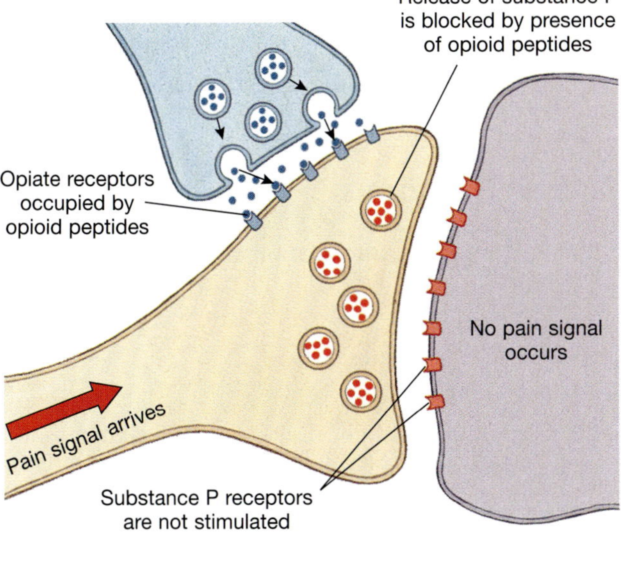

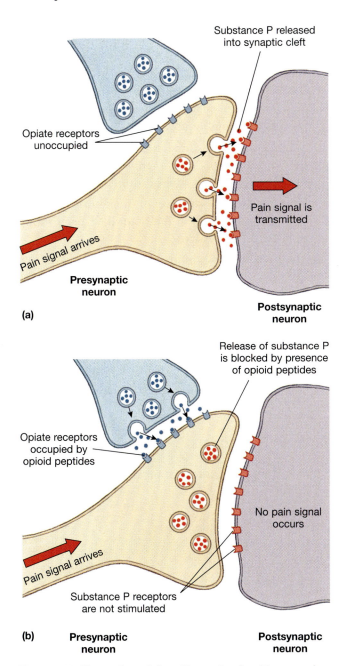

Figure 4.28 Illustration of the effects of endorphins on pain perception. In (a) the neurotransmitter substance P is released and neuron signaling pain stimulation is activated. As seen in (b), the presence of endorphins (opioid peptides) in opiate receptor sites inhibits the release of substance P, which results in analgesia or a lack of pain detection by postsynaptic membrane.
➤ *What other presynaptic effect is similar to neuromodulation? (p. 126–127)*

Before You Go On

Compare the effects of neuromodulators and hormones.

Describe a possible mechanism for the experience of physiological shock.

Section Review

- The endocrine glands of the endocrine system release hormones into the bloodstream, which can affect distant target organs.
- Although a slower means of communication than neurotransmitters, hormones allow more widespread transmission of information.
- In a positive feedback loop, release of a hormone acts to promote further release of that hormone.
- In a negative feedback loop, the release of a hormone inhibits its release.
- Pheromones are hormones, released into the air, that affect the behavior of other members of the same species.
- Neuromodulators are chemicals that affect neuronal functioning by controlling the amount of neurotransmitter released at the presynaptic membrane.
- Endorphins, one type of neuromodulator, are released in reaction to painful events and reduce sensitivity to painful events.
- Opiate substances, such heroin and morphine, suppress pain responses and produce feelings of euphoria by mimicking the body's natural endorphins.

Chapter Review

Critical Thinking Questions

1. Neuron A is a gustatory (taste) neuron. It is charged with determining whether a specific food is bitter. Using what you know about the functioning of neurons, explain how neuron A decides whether a food is bitter. Use the terms *synapse, postsynaptic membrane, threshold, summation,* and *action potentials.*
2. On two occasions, June asked her friend Michele how she was feeling. Michele did not hear June's question the first time, but did when June asked a second time. Suggest several possible reasons why Michele was able to hear the question the second time, but not the first, using what you have learned about temporal and spatial summation.
3. Describe a possible treatment for multiple sclerosis, using what you have learned about the destruction of myelin and the leakage of myelin proteins through the blood-brain barrier. Would it be best to target the immune system? The blood-brain barrier?

Vocabulary Questions

1. The net effect of all input to a particular neuron is added up at the ________________.
2. The difference in polarity between the outside and inside of the neural cell membrane at rest is called the ________________.
3. An ________________ is a charged particle of an element such as sodium, potassium, or chloride.
4. ________________ is the tendency of molecules to move from areas of higher concentration to areas of lower concentration; ________________ refers to the attraction of opposite-polarity molecules.
5. Reduction in the charge across the neural cell membrane is called ________________.
6. Depolarization past threshold causes the occurrence of an ________________.
7. The action potential moves down the ________________ from the axon hillock to the presynaptic terminal.
8. The rate law states that the ________________ the stimulus intensity, the ________________ the rate of neural firing.
9. The depolarization of the postsynaptic membrane is called an ________________, and the hyperpolarization of the postsynaptic membrane is called an ________________.
10. A decrease in the neuron's sensitivity to stimulation because of an increased difference between the resting membrane potential and threshold is called ________________.
11. The prevention of the release of a normal amount of neurotransmitter despite the occurrence of an action potential is called ________________; the release of a greater-than-normal amount of neurotransmitter caused by hyperpolarization of the presynaptic membrane is called ________________.
12. Transmission from the dendrites of one neuron to the dendrites of another is called ________________ transmission.
13. Drugs that elevate the level of the neurotransmitter ________________ in the brain have been shown to decrease depression.
14. The prevention of the free flow of substances from the bloodstream into the brain is called the ________________.
15. In ____________ feedback, release of a hormone promotes further release; in ____________ feedback, release of a hormone inhibits further release.
16. Naturally occurring chemicals with opiate-like effects are called ________________.

Review Questions

1. Neurons receive information at
   a. the synapse.
   b. the nucleus.
   c. the chromosomes.
   d. the axon projections.
2. Unlike those of other cells, the neural cell membrane
   a. is composed of a lipid bilayer.
   b. contains protein channels.
   c. allows nothing to pass into or out of the cell.
   d. is polarized.
3. The three forces that affect the movement of ions across the cell membrane are
   a. diffusion, electrolysis, and the chloride pump.
   b. diffusion, electrostatic pressure, and the sodium-potassium pump.
   c. diversion, electrostatic pressure, and the sump pump.
   d. diversion, ion charges, and the sodium-potassium pump.

4. Sodium and potassium are ________________ charged; chloride is ________________ charged.
   a. not, negatively
   b. positively, not
   c. positively, negatively
   d. negatively, positively

5. The sodium-potassium pump expels ____________ sodium ions from the cell for every ________________ potassium ions that it brings into the cell.
   a. three, two
   b. two, three
   c. one, two
   d. two, one

6. For an action potential to occur, the membrane must be depolarized to
   a. belief.
   b. the resting membrane potential.
   c. threshold.
   d. the excitatory postsynaptic potential.

7. An action potential consists of
   a. depolarization to threshold, hyperpolarization, and recovery.
   b. hyperpolarization, inhibition, and return to the resting potential.
   c. hyperpolarization, repolarization, and recovery.
   d. depolarization to threshold, repolarization, and return to the resting potential.

8. The propagation of an action potential from node to node along a myelinated axon is called
   a. saltatory conduction.
   b. an inhibitory postsynaptic potential.
   c. nodes of Ranvier.
   d. an excitatory postsynaptic potential.

9. Neurotransmitters are released from synaptic vesicles into the ________________, where they attach to receptor sites on the ________________.
   a. inhibitory neuron, presynaptic membrane
   b. presynaptic membrane, axon
   c. synaptic cleft, postsynaptic membrane
   d. synaptic cleft, inhibitory neuron

10. ________________ is the combined influence of many neurotransmitters released at different locations on the postsynaptic membrane at a particular moment in time; ________________ is the combined effects of neurotransmitter effects over time.
   a. Temporal summation, spatial summation
   b. Temporal summation, synaptic transmission
   c. Spatial summation, synaptic transmission
   d. Spatial summation, temporal summation

11. A neurotransmitter that binds to its own presynaptic membrane as well as to receptor sites on the postsynaptic membrane is called
   a. an autoreceptor.
   b. an inhibitory neuron.
   c. presynaptic facilitation.
   d. an automatic neuron.

12. The breakdown of a neurotransmitter in the synapse is ________________; the recycling of a neurotransmitter into synaptic vesicles in the presynaptic neuron is ________________.
   a. neurotransmitter reuptake, enzymatic degradation
   b. enzymatic degradation, autoreception
   c. enzymatic degradation, neurotransmitter reuptake
   d. neurotransmitter reuptake, presynaptic inhibition

13. The glands of the ________________ produce hormones that are circulated by the bloodstream to targets throughout the body.
   a. circulatory system
   b. nervous system
   c. digestive system
   d. endocrine system

14. Hormones that travel through the air rather than the bloodstream are called
   a. aerial hormones.
   b. pheromones.
   c. neuromodulators.
   d. autoreceptors.

15. Neuromodulators are
   a. hormones.
   b. neurotransmitters.
   c. chemical transmitters that modulate neurotransmitter release.
   d. pheromones.

Suggested Readings

Cooper, J. R., Bloom, F. E., & Roth, R. H. (1996). *The biochemical basis of neuropharmacology* (7th ed.). New York: Oxford University Press.

Kandel, E. R., Schwartz, J. H., & Jessell, T. M. (2000). *Principles of neural science* (4th ed.). New York: McGraw-Hill.

Levitan, I. B., & Kaczmarck, C. K. (1996). *The neuron* (2nd ed.). New York: Oxford University Press.

Nicolls, J. G., Martin, A. R., Wallace, B. G., & Kuffer, S. W. (1993). *From neuron to brain* (3rd ed.). Sutherland, MA: Sinauer Associations.

Shepard, G. M. (1988). Neurobiology (2nd ed.). New York: Oxford University Press.

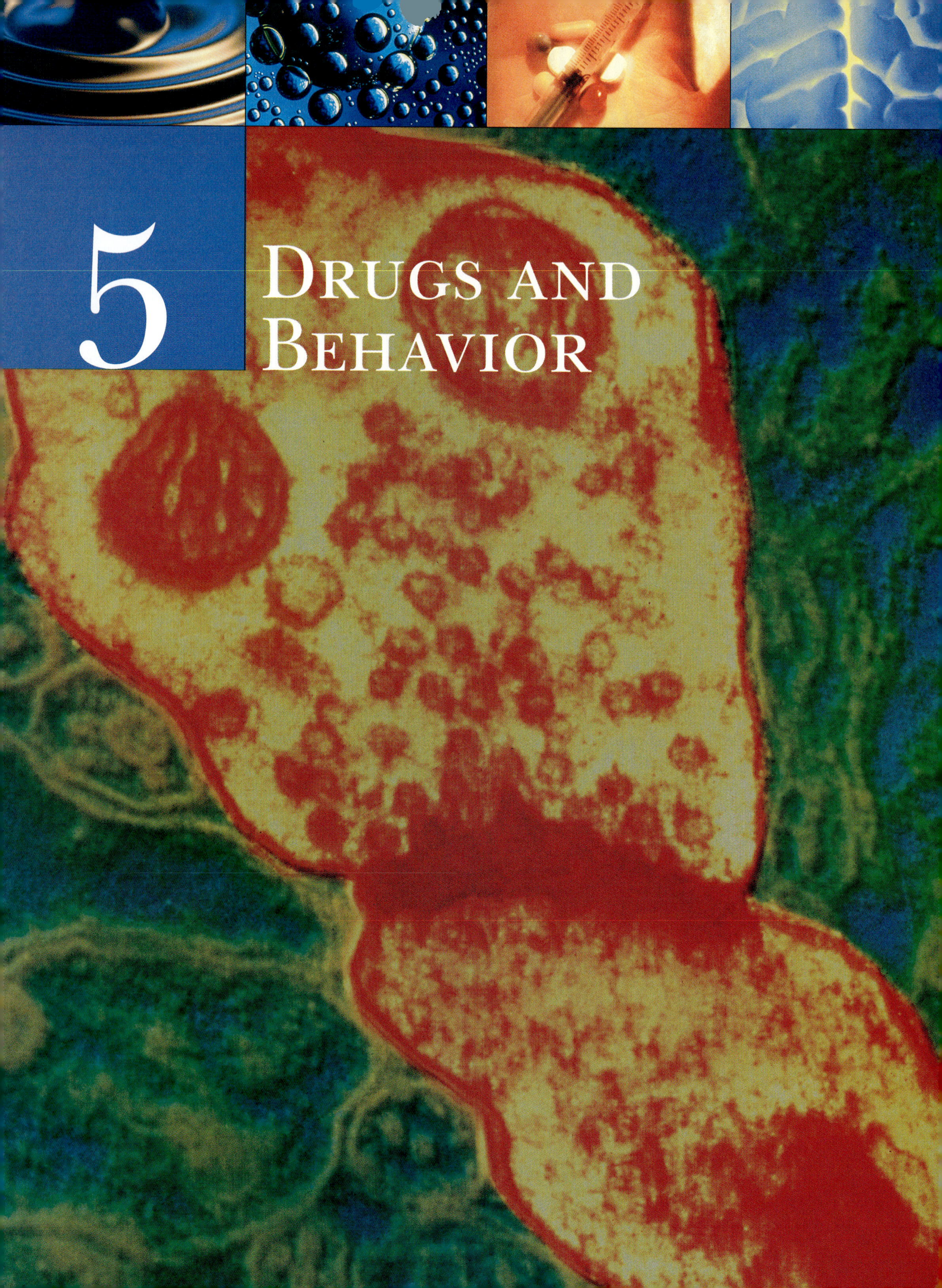

5 Drugs and Behavior

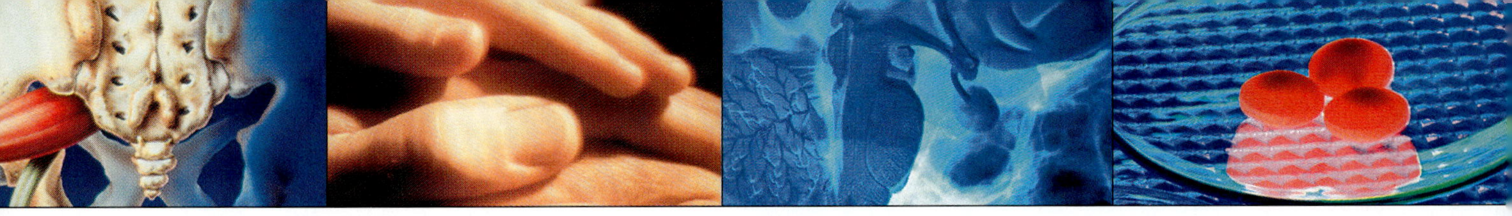

The High Cost of Crack

The most important thing in Evelyn's life is smoking crack. Nothing else seems to matter. All of her thoughts revolve around the next high, how she will get the money, who she will buy it from, and where she will smoke it. It has not always been this way. Evelyn had a good job as a software analyst and an active social life with many friends. It was some of these "friends" who introduced her to cocaine at a party just last year. She was reluctant at first, but after some encouragement, she inhaled a line of cocaine. Her intense high lasted for what seemed forever. The positive glow lasted for much of that night. Evelyn did not use cocaine again for several weeks, but she thought about her experience often.

Her second experience with cocaine was also incredible, almost as great as the first. Over the next few weeks, Evelyn snorted cocaine often. At first, she used cocaine only at parties with friends. Then she met a man who offered to get cocaine for her. She bought her first gram for $100, and it lasted her several days.

For a while, Evelyn was able to hold on to her job, maintain her lifestyle, and occasionally use cocaine, too. As she began using more often, her habit increased from one gram every few days to several grams a day, and the costs increased, too.

Evelyn sold her possessions to get money. Then she borrowed money from family and friends. When these sources dried up, Evelyn started stealing jewelry from friends, and lately from stores. She has been arrested for shoplifting several times. Her urge to get high, and to get money for drugs, overwhelmed any embarrassment about getting caught. She lost her job after her second arrest, her friends now avoid her, and she is so far behind in her rent that she is about to be evicted from her apartment.

Lately, she has started using crack cocaine. It is cheaper than powdered cocaine and the feelings it produces are still pleasurable. The man who had been supplying her with crack has been arrested. She has heard of several places where crack is sold, all in a dangerous, unfamiliar part of town. Evelyn has pawned some stolen jewelry and has $100 in her pocket. She is frightened but determined to go, for getting high is all she has left. She just hopes that she can find a new source quickly. ■

◀ The distance between the presynaptic and postsynaptic membrane is between 30 and 50 nanometers.

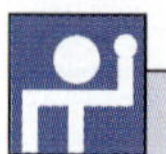

Before You Begin

What caused Evelyn to become addicted to cocaine?

What is addiction, anyway?

In this chapter, we will help you answer these and the following questions:

- What is a psychoactive drug? What are the different classes of psychoactive drugs?
- How does a person become addicted to a drug? What happens inside the body when addiction occurs?
- How do different kinds of psychoactive drugs affect the brain? What effects do drugs have on synapse functioning?
- How do drugs affect mood and behavior?

Definition of a Drug

According to Carroll (1989), a drug is "any substance that enters the human body and can change either the function or the substance of the human organism." This definition is quite broad and includes such substances as foods, vitamins, air pollutants, and pesticides as well as medicines that are taken for therapeutic purposes. This chapter will focus only on one particular class of drugs, the psychoactive drugs.

Cocaine in its many forms is just one example of a **psychoactive drug**, a drug that changes the way a person like Evelyn thinks, feels, perceives, or acts. Psychoactive drugs vary widely in their effects on the body and brain. The pain-inhibiting effects of heroin contrast sharply with the arousing effects of the amphetamines. In this chapter, we will first examine the biological and psychological influences of psychoactive drugs, such as the cocaine that is ruining Evelyn's life. We will also examine the biological basis of addiction to find out why drugs like cocaine are so addictive that people like Evelyn are willing to risk their lives for that next high.

Mechanisms of Drug Action

As we learned in Chapter 4, drugs can either facilitate or inhibit transmission of neural impulses (see the Application on Drug Treatment of Depression in Chapter 4). Drugs that mimic or enhance the activity of a neurotransmitter are called **agonists** (from the Greek for competitor). You can think of agonists as competing with neurotransmitters to produce similar effects; runners, for example, compete for the same goal—the finish line. Drugs that block the activity of a neurotransmitter are called **antagonists** (ant = against). You can think of antagonists as competing with neurotransmitters to produce opposite effects; for example, opposing soccer teams have opposite goals.

Drug Agonists

There are a number of different mechanisms by which a drug can act as an agonist (see **Figure 5.1**). In one mechanism (see #1 in **Figure 5.1**), the drug attaches to a receptor site and produces the same effect on the postsynaptic membrane as the neurotransmitter, either an excitatory postsynaptic potential (EPSP) or an inhibitory postsynaptic potential (IPSP) (see Chapter 4 to review these concepts if necessary). For example, heroin activates receptor sites for the endorphins (remember Jerry's runner's high in Chapter 4?) to produce its analgesic (pain suppressing) effects.

A drug can also bind to the receptor site and produce its agonist effect by increasing the effect of the neurotransmitter on the postsynaptic membrane rather than directly affecting the receptor site. For example, the sedating effect of alcohol is produced by enhancement of the influence of the neurotransmitter GABA on one type of GABA receptor.

Drugs can affect synaptic transmission less directly. A drug can block either enzymatic degradation or neurotransmitter reuptake (see #2 in **Figure 5.1**). With what you learned about enzymatic degradation and neurotransmitter reuptake in Chapter 4, can you guess how blocking these activities would produce agonist action? Because the neurotransmitter is around for a longer time, its effects on the postsynaptic membrane last longer. Evelyn's nemesis, cocaine, blocks the reuptake of norepinephrine and dopamine, allowing these neurotransmitters to produce the enhanced alertness and pleasure characteristic of a cocaine high.

In another indirect mechanism, a drug can increase the amount of neurotransmitter that is stored in the synaptic vesicles. This agonist action occurs in one of two ways: the synthesis of neurotransmitter can be increased (see #3 in **Figure 5.1**) or the reuptake degrading enzymes can be destroyed (see #4 in **Figure 5.1**). An example of #3 is the drug L-DOPA decreasing the symptoms of Parkinson's disease by increasing the synthesis of the neurotransmitter dopamine (recall

---

psychoactive drug A drug that changes the way a person thinks, feels, perceives, or acts.

agonists Drugs that mimic or enhance the activity of a neurotransmitter.

antagonists Drugs that block the activity of a neurotransmitter.

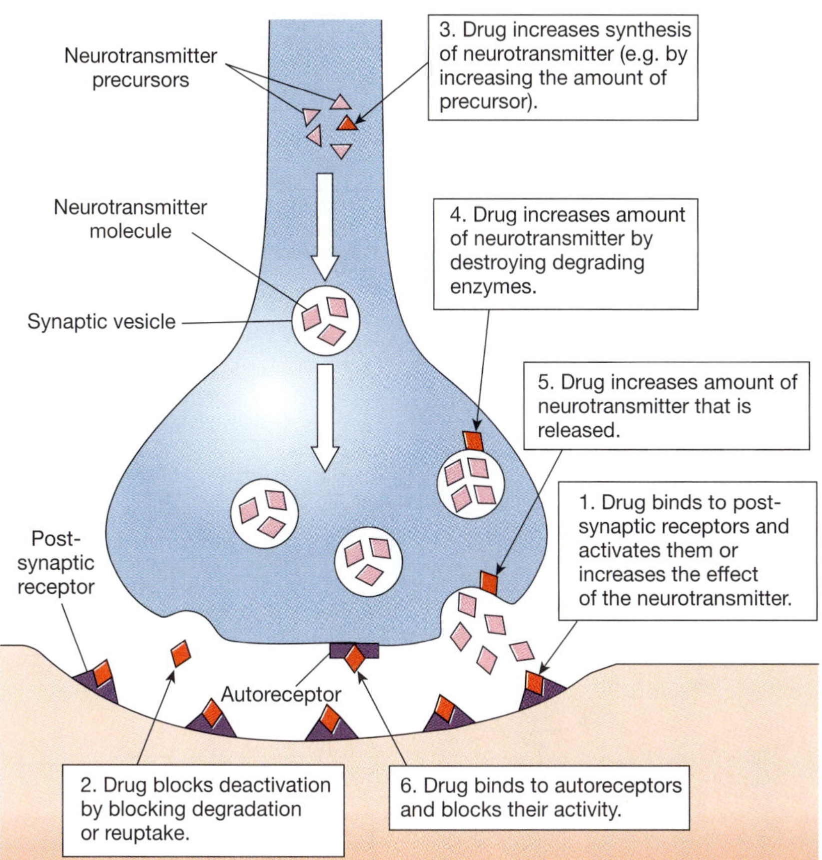
Neurotransmitter precursors
3. Drug increases synthesis of neurotransmitter (e.g. by increasing the amount of precursor).
Neurotransmitter molecule
4. Drug increases amount of neurotransmitter by destroying degrading enzymes.
Synaptic vesicle
5. Drug increases amount of neurotransmitter that is released.
1. Drug binds to post-synaptic receptors and activates them or increases the effect of the neurotransmitter.
Post-synaptic receptor
Autoreceptor
2. Drug blocks deactivation by blocking degradation or reuptake.
6. Drug binds to autoreceptors and blocks their activity.

Figure 5.1 Agonist drug effects. Drugs can enhance synaptic transmission in one or more of the six ways shown in this figure.

➤ *Which of these mechanisms is used by heroin to produce its analgesic effects? (p. 127 & 133–134)*

from Chapter 2 that in Parkinson's disease, the individual has difficulty integrating voluntary movements and these movements, when they occur, are much slower than normal).

An agonist drug can also enhance the release of the neurotransmitter from the presynaptic membrane (see #5 in **Figure 5.1**) or prevent the inhibition of continued neurotransmitter release by binding to and suppressing the neuron's autoreceptors (see #6 in **Figure 5.1**). One example of the first type of agonist effect is the increased arousal produced by the drug amphetamine. Amphetamine binds to the norepinephrine and dopamine autoreceptors on the presynaptic membrane; this delay in the signal to decrease the release of these neurotransmitters increases the number of neurotransmitter molecules that are active at the postsynaptic membrane receptor sites.

A specific drug may utilize only one of the mechanisms described above or its agonist action may reflect a combination of several. For example, the arousing effect of nicotine is due to the direct activation of postsynaptic cholinergic receptors along with increasing the release of the neurotransmitters dopamine and serotonin by stimulating cholinergic receptors that are on the presynaptic membrane of dopamergic and serotonergic neurons (Julien, 1998).

Before You Go On

Describe two different mechanisms of agonist drug action including examples of each.

Drug Antagonists

Drugs can also act to antagonize or impair synaptic transmission, via several mechanisms, many of which are similar to those employed by the agonists (see **Figure 5.2**). A drug can attach to the postsynaptic membrane without having the effect of the neurotransmitter. The presence of the drug acts to prevent the neurotransmitter from binding to the receptor sites and thereby blocks the neurotransmitter from acting on the postsynaptic membrane. A drug that impairs synaptic transmission in this way is called a **false transmitter** (see #1 in **Figure 5.2**). Synaptic transmission remains blocked as long as the drug occupies the receptor sites. Consider the schizophrenic who experiences hallucinations and delusions. The major tranquilizers reduce

---

false transmitter A drug that prevents the neurotransmitter from binding to the receptor sites by attaching to the receptor sites on the postsynaptic membrane.

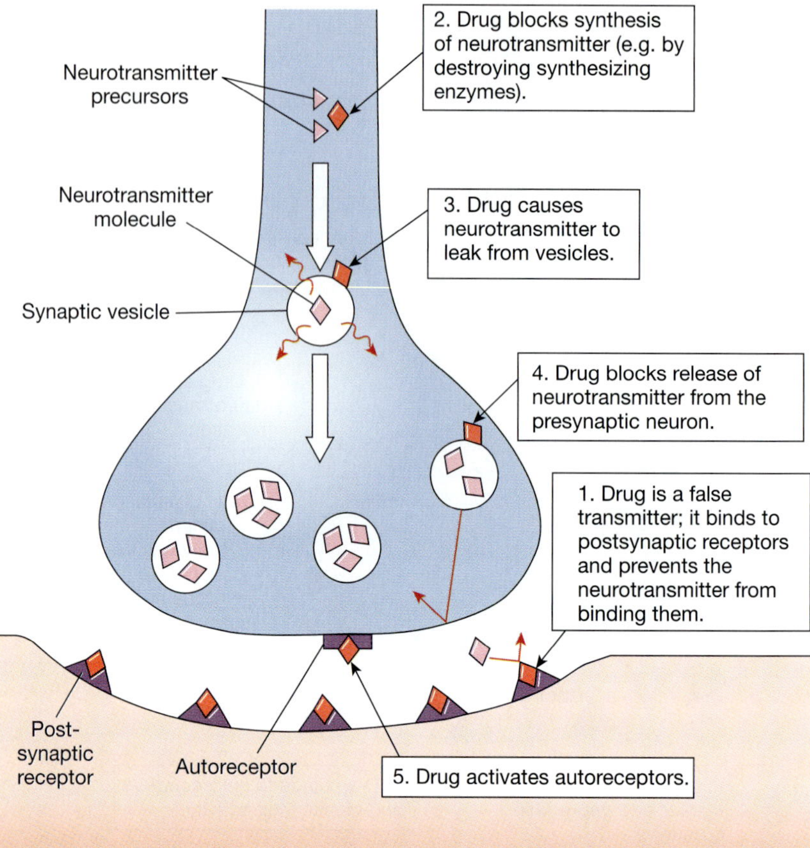

2. Drug blocks synthesis of neurotransmitter (e.g. by destroying synthesizing enzymes).
Neurotransmitter precursors
Neurotransmitter molecule
3. Drug causes neurotransmitter to leak from vesicles.
Synaptic vesicle
4. Drug blocks release of neurotransmitter from the presynaptic neuron.
1. Drug is a false transmitter; it binds to postsynaptic receptors and prevents the neurotransmitter from binding them.
Post-synaptic receptor
Autoreceptor
5. Drug activates autoreceptors.

Figure 5.2 Antagonistic drug actions. Drugs can reduce synaptic transmission in one or more of the five ways shown in this figure.
➤ *Which of these mechanisms is used by tranquilizers to alleviate the symptoms of schizophrenia? (p. 133–134)*

these symptoms of schizophrenia by binding to dopaminergic receptor sites and blocking the effects of dopamine.

Drugs need not bind to the receptor site to have an antagonistic action. A drug may decrease the level of available neurotransmitter by causing either a decrease in the synthesis of the neurotransmitter (see #2 in **Figure 5.2**) or a loss of neurotransmitter from the synaptic vesicles (see #3 in **Figure 5.2**).

A drug also can inhibit the release of the neurotransmitter from the presynaptic membrane (see #4 in **Figure 5.2**) or enhance the inhibition of neurotransmitter release by activating the neuron's autoreceptors (see #5 in **Figure 5.2**). The arousing effect of caffeine is due to the inhibition of the release of the neurotransmitter adenosine. (As we will discover later in this chapter, adenosine is an inhibitory neurotransmitter for glutamate receptors, see Chapter 2.) As with drug agonists, a specific drug may impair synaptic transmission in only one way or its antagonistic influence may reflect several of the above mechanisms.

addiction A pattern of behavior characterized by an overwhelming involvement with securing and then using a drug despite adverse consequences of drug use, and with a significant likelihood of relapse after quitting or withdrawal.

Before You Go On

Explain how a drug can have an antagonistic effect without binding to a receptor site. Give an example.

Section Review

- Drugs can function as agonists or as antagonists.
- Agonists enhance neural transmission. They can attach directly to receptor sites, block neurotransmitter degradation or reuptake, increase neurotransmitter synthesis and release, or decrease autoreceptor activity.
- Antagonists decrease neural transmission. They can block the neurotransmitter from binding to receptor sites, inhibit the release of the neurotransmitter, block the synthesis of the neurotransmitter, cause neurotransmitter leakage from the synaptic vesicles, or activate autoreceptors.

Long-Term Effects of Drug Use

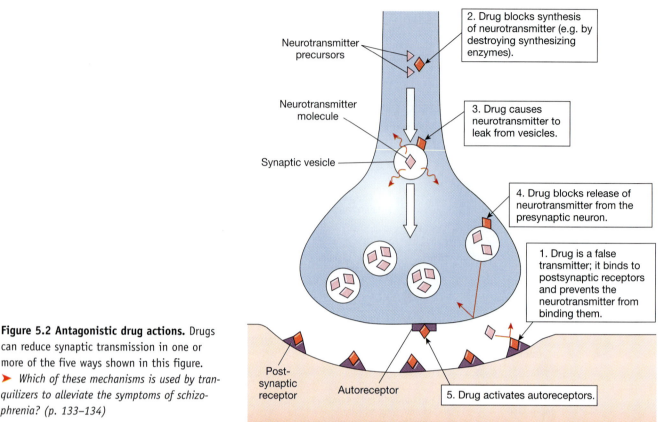

The long-term effects of drug use include addiction, tolerance, withdrawal, physical dependence, and psychological dependence. Carroll (1989) defines **addiction** as

Table 5.1 ■ The Physical and Psychological Effects of Psychoactive Drugs

Category	Typical Effects	Tolerance/Dependence
Narcotics		
Codeine, heroin, morphine, meperidine, opium	Analgesia, euphoria, drowsiness, "rush" of pleasure, little impairment of psychological functions	Tolerance, physical and psychological dependence, severe withdrawal symptoms
Depressants		
Alcohol	**low doses:** decreased alertness, feelings of relaxation **moderate doses:** mild sedation, impairment of sensory-motor functions **high doses:** severe motor disturbances, unconsciousness, coma, death	Tolerance, physical and psychological dependence, withdrawal symptoms
Sedative-hypnotic drugs Barbiturates and nonbarbiturate sedative-hypnotics	Calming effect, relaxation of muscles, reduction of tension, anxiety, and irritability; induces sleep; anesthetic; anticonvulsant	Tolerance, psychological and physical dependence, withdrawal symptoms
Antianxiety drugs	Reduction in nervousness, anxiety, or fear	Tolerance, low physical and high psychological dependence, withdrawal symptoms
Antipsychotic drugs	Alleviates hallucinations and delusions in psychotic patients; calming of stroke patients	No tolerance or psychological or physical dependence
Stimulants		
Amphetamine, cocaine	Increased alertness, sense of well-being, sleeplessness, appetite suppression	Tolerance, psychological and physical dependence, withdrawal symptoms
Caffeine, nicotine	Increased alertness, euphoria, sleeplessness, more rapid reaction times, increased metabolism	Tolerance, physical and psychological dependence, withdrawal symptoms
Psychedelics		
Marijuana, hashish	Euphoria, relaxed inhibitions, increased vividness of experiences, increased appetite, mild hallucinations, possible disorientation, impaired motor coordination, decreased reaction time, distortions in time perception	Psychological dependence
LSD	Illusions, hallucinations, distortions in time perception, loss of contact with reality	None known
PCP	Illusions, hallucinations, distortions in time perception, loss of contact with reality	Psychological dependence
Peyote	Visual hallucinations	None known
Psilocybin, psilocin	Illusions, hallucinations, distortions in time perception, loss of contact with reality	None known

"a pattern of behavior characterized by an overwhelming involvement with using a drug and securing its supply, despite adverse consequences associated with use of the drug, and with a significant tendency to relapse after quitting or withdrawal." In other words, like Evelyn's, the addict's life revolves around either taking the drug or trying to obtain it, even if it means risking personal safety.

Tolerance refers to the reduced effects of a drug as a result of repeated use. As tolerance develops, the pleasurable effects of the drug diminish. To compensate for these reduced effects, the individual will take higher doses of the drug.

When the effects of the drug end, users undergo **withdrawal**, a variety of unpleasant, sometimes painful symptoms signaling the end of the "high." The symptoms of withdrawal vary depending on the drug. An intense craving for the drug (see psychological dependence below) often accompanies these unpleasant physiological symptoms, giving the addict an even greater incentive to get more of the drug.

Two other signs besides tolerance and withdrawal that a person is addicted to a drug are physical dependence and psychological dependence. **Physical dependence** refers to a state of physical need for the drug. **Psychological dependence** refers to the aforementioned craving for the drug. Psychological dependence can develop independently of physical dependence. For example, even a single experience with a drug that produces intense euphoria, such as cocaine, can lead to a psychological dependence on that drug. Physical dependence, on the other hand, is linked to the development of tolerance for a drug. In general, tolerance leads to the experience of withdrawal symptoms when the drug is not taken, and continued use of a drug to avoid withdrawal symptoms leads to physical dependence.

As you might have guessed, the psychoactive drugs, also referred to as psychotropic or mind-altering drugs, are included in this text because they exert their influence through their action on the nervous system, particularly the brain and spinal cord, although they affect many other biological systems as well. They either produce pleasant feelings or relieve unpleasant ones by modifying synaptic transmission in critical nervous system structures; the resulting affective, or emotional, reactions alone can often lead to addiction.

There are four main classes of psychoactive drugs: narcotics, depressants, stimulants, and psychedelics (see **Table 5.1**). In the following sections, we will describe the effects of each class of psychoactive drugs and present several examples of each.

Narcotics

In her flight from some crazed drug dealers in that unsafe part of town, Evelyn falls and breaks her arm. At the hospital, she is in extreme pain, and the physician gives her a shot of Demerol, the trade name commonly used to refer to the narcotic meperidine. When the drug takes effect, her pain goes away.

Why did Demerol eliminate Evelyn's pain? Demerol is a narcotic drug whose main effect is pain relief, or **analgesia**. The term *narcotic* is often used in law enforcement and by the media to refer to all illegal drugs, but we will use a narrower definition here. **Narcotics**, frequently called opioids or opiates, are drugs that are derived from the opium poppy plant (see **Figure 5.3**) or that have an action comparable to drugs from the opium poppy.

Analgesia is not the only defining feature of the narcotic drugs. To qualify as a narcotic, the drug also must

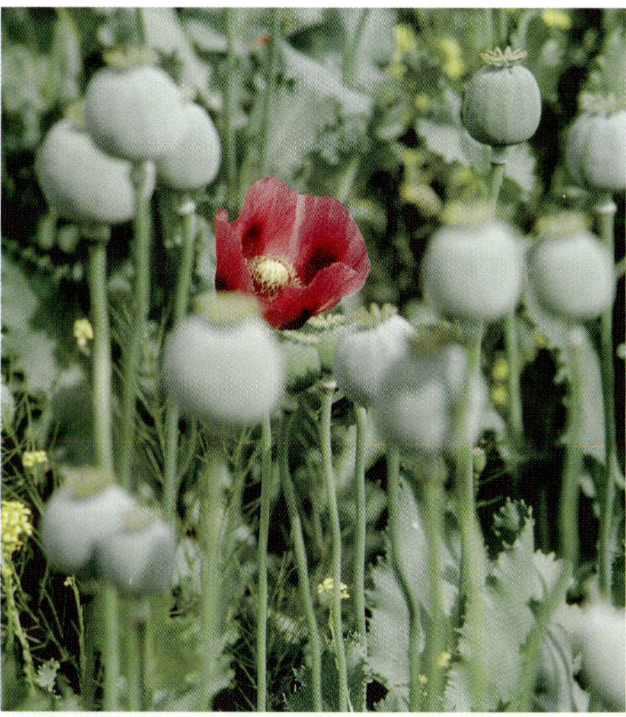

Figure 5.3 A field of opium poppies, showing seedpods. The opium poppy plant is the source of the narcotic drugs heroin and morphine.

➤ *What drugs come from opium poppies? What are the effects of the opiate drugs?* *(p. 137)*

---

tolerance The reduced effects of a drug as a result of repeated use.

withdrawal The unpleasant, sometimes painful symptoms that occur when the effects of a drug end.

physical dependence A state of physical need for a drug.

psychological dependence The intense craving for a drug.

analgesia Pain relief.

narcotics Opiate drugs that produce analgesia, sedation, and a sense of well-being.

act on the central nervous system to produce stupor or have sleep-inducing actions. Returning to our broken arm example, the Demerol will not only eliminate Evelyn's pain, but also make her drowsy. The narcotic drugs also induce a feeling of well-being or euphoria. Narcotics are also the most effective cough suppressant and antidiarrheal medications. The three main classes of narcotics are based on their origins: natural, semisynthetic, and synthetic.

Narcotics of Natural Origin

Opium, or "the mother drug," comes directly from the opium poppy, a lovely, seemingly innocent red flower (see **Figure 5.3**). (That was some spell the Wicked Witch of the West cast on Dorothy and her friends—"Poppies! Poppies!") When the unripe seedpod is slit with a knife, a milky fluid oozes out. When allowed to dry, the brownish gum becomes crude or raw opium. Although crude opium is sometimes eaten, inhaling the vapors of smoked opium is the typical method of experiencing its analgesic effects.

Opium contains several *alkaloid* compounds, which are nitrogen compounds containing an organic base. The main alkaloid compound in opium is **morphine**. Depending on the plant, morphine makes up 4 to 21 percent of the opium seedpod. An extremely potent drug, morphine has a bitter taste when taken orally; it is usually administered intravenously. It not only reduces pain but induces powerful feelings of well-being. Morphine is used in patients with severe pain, such as that caused by terminal cancer. Another alkaloid found in opium is *codeine*. Less potent than morphine, codeine is often combined with aspirin and cough suppressants as a prescription analgesic. Tylenol III, which contains codeine, can only be obtained by prescription due to codeine's potential for abuse (Julien, 1998).

Semisynthetic Narcotics

Some opiates are combinations of natural opiates and other chemicals. The most common semisynthetic narcotic is *heroin*. According to Carroll (1989), 90 percent of opiate abuse involves heroin.

Heroin is made by adding acetic anhydride to morphine to create a compound with the rather daunting chemical name *diacetylmorphine*. The drug was introduced as a cough suppressant in 1898, and its name comes from the German word meaning "long" or "powerful." Heroin is an exceptionally potent narcotic and, like morphine, has a bitter taste. When injected into the bloodstream, heroin induces an intense euphoric response that lasts from 3 to 6 hours.

Synthetic Narcotics

Drugs with opiate properties can also be manufactured in the laboratory. Meperidine (Demerol) is one of these synthetic narcotics. In fact, Demerol was the first synthetic narcotic, and this powerful *analgesic* can eliminate even intense pain. A synthetic narcotic with weaker action than Demerol is propoxyphene (Darvon). An estimated 30 million prescriptions for Darvon are written in the United States each year (Carroll, 1989). Other examples of synthetic narcotics that are widely prescribed include oxycodone (Percodan) and hydromorphone (Dilaudid).

Mechanisms of Narcotic Action

In Chapter 4, we learned that the brain contains neuromodulators called *endorphins* that have opiate-like properties. Endorphins suppress the pain induced by negative events and allow us to cope with such events. The narcotic drugs are endorphin agonists that work by binding to the endorphin receptor sites and activating the same neurons in the brain as do the endorphins (see #1 in **Figure 5.1**).

Long-Term Effects of Narcotic Use

Narcotic drugs are exceptionally dangerous. Although short-term use of narcotics to alleviate pain can be beneficial, long-term use can be severely addictive.

When narcotics are taken frequently, tolerance develops quickly, especially to the powerful opiates. Withdrawal from narcotics can be extremely intense. Symptoms include chills, diarrhea, nausea, and sweating, with tremors and intense cramps occurring with extremely intense withdrawal. Withdrawal symptoms may persist for some time. For example, heroin withdrawal may last for 2 to 3 days.

Physical dependence on narcotics occurs as a result of the suppression of the production of endorphins that occurs with repeated use of narcotic drugs. The psychological dependence of the narcotic addict is strong; this intense craving for the drug is the mind's attempt to reduce the negative physical and psychological effects of withdrawal and reinstate the pleasurable effects of the drug by encouraging the addict to resume drug use.

---

opium A natural opiate that comes directly from the opium poppy.

morphine An extremely potent natural narcotic that is the main alkaloid compound found in opium.

heroin (diacetylmorphine) A powerful semisynthetic narcotic that is made by adding acetic anhydride to morphine.

Before You Go On

What distinguishes narcotics from other pain killers and other classes of psychoactive drugs?

Why are the narcotics so addictive? Explain their effects on the nervous system.

Section Review

- Narcotics, including opium, codeine, heroin, and morphine, are a strongly addictive type of psychoactive drug that reduces pain and induces sleep and feelings of well-being.
- Narcotics act as endorphin agonists that directly stimulate endorphin receptors.
- Long-term use of narcotics can lead to tolerance, withdrawal, psychological dependence, and physical dependence.

Depressants

You have a major examination next week. This test is extremely important and you are nervous about taking it. As the date of the test approaches, your level of nervousness intensifies. Your fear is preventing you from concentrating, and your preparation for the examination is suffering. You visit a doctor, who gives you a prescription for Valium. Shortly after taking the medication, you no longer feel nervous, and you are able to study.

For many years, Valium was the most frequently prescribed psychoactive drug (Long, 1984). It belongs to a class of drugs called **depressants**, which act on the central nervous system to slow down mental and physical functioning. At low doses, depressants reduce anxiety, tension, or irritability; at higher doses, depressants produce drowsiness and sleep.

There are two major types of depressants: alcohol and sedative-hypnotic drugs. Alcohol includes wine, beer, and distilled spirits (the so-called hard liquors, such as vodka or scotch); the sedative-hypnotic drugs include the barbiturates, nonbarbiturates, antianxiety drugs, and antipsychotic drugs. (Narcotics have some effects that are similar to alcohol and sedative-hypnotics, but they also produce analgesia.) Because alcohol and the sedative-hypnotics are so different, we will describe them separately in the following sections.

Alcohol

Alcohol is so widely consumed in our society that many do not consider it a drug, thinking of it instead as a social beverage. However, **alcohol** is a powerful depressant that has a significant influence on consciousness and on the ability to respond effectively to the environment. Consumption of even a small amount of alcohol results in reduced effectiveness at school or work. Alcohol abuse, in addition to the damage it does to the central nervous system and other parts of the body, dramatically increases the probability of having a motor vehicle accident (see **Figure 5.4**).

Types of Alcohol. The alcohol that we drink is *ethyl alcohol*, a clear, colorless fluid with a mild, aromatic odor and pungent taste. Ethyl alcohol is produced by the fermentation of certain grains and fruits. Fermentation

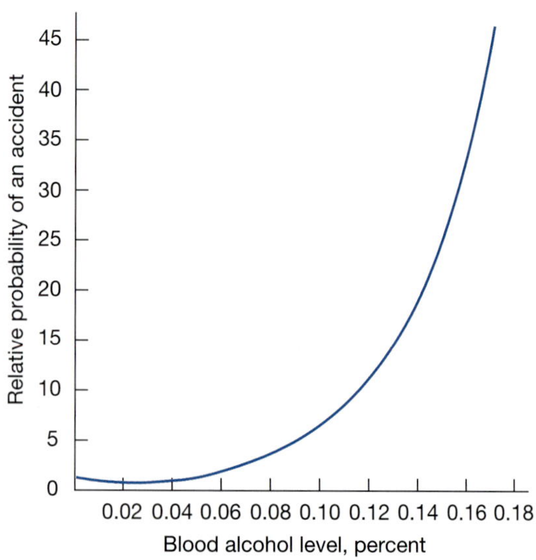

Figure 5.4 Alcohol and driving are not a good idea. This illustration shows the detrimental effect of drinking on driving; the higher the alcohol level, the higher the probability of an accident.

➤ *What is the probability of an accident at 0.10 percent blood alcohol level? (p. 140) At what level do you think the legal limit should be set?*

depressants A class of psychoactive drugs that act on the central nervous system to slow down mental and physical functioning.

alcohol (ethyl alcohol) A powerful depressant produced by the fermentation of certain grains and fruits; allows the neurotransmitter GABA to bind more readily or more tightly to the GABA receptor sites.

Figure 5.5 Alcohol content. A 1.00-ounce shot of 80-proof whiskey, a 4-ounce glass of light wine, and a 12-ounce can of 3.2 beer all contain the same amount of alcohol.
➤ *Why do people perceive "hard" liquor to be more dangerous than wine or beer? (p. 139)*

occurs when yeast cells convert the sugar in grain or fruit to carbon dioxide and alcohol. Wine is made by fermenting grapes or other fruits and has an alcohol content of 10 to 14 percent. Beer is made in two stages: converting the starch in cereal grains to sugar by a process called *brewing*, and then fermenting the sugar. This process yields beer with an alcohol content between 3.6 and 6 percent. Distilled spirits are produced by heating fermented cereal grains or fruits. Because ethyl alcohol boils at a lower temperature than the other products of fermentation, it can be collected by cooling and condensing the vapors. The ethyl alcohol concentration of distilled spirits is typically 40 to 50 percent.

Alcohol Intoxication. As with all drugs, the magnitude of the effects of alcohol depends on dose level. Although distilled spirits have a higher concentration of alcohol than beer, people typically drink more beer at a sitting than they do liquor. In fact, a 1.00-ounce shot of 80-proof whiskey, a 4-ounce glass of light wine, and a 12-ounce can of 3.2 beer contain about the same amount of alcohol (see **Figure 5.5**). The behavioral effects of alcohol vary from person to person. Although one or two beers will typically make me drowsy, I have a friend who can drink a six-pack in less than an hour without showing any behavioral signs of intoxication.

Because the ethyl alcohol concentration of drinks varies so widely, and because of the variations in behavioral changes, blood alcohol level provides an objective measure for examining the effects of alcohol. Low blood alcohol levels (.05 percent or .05 milligrams of alcohol per 100 milliters of blood) produce lowered alertness and feelings of relaxation (see **Table 5.2**). Modest levels (.10 percent) lead to mild sedation and some impairment in sensory-motor functions. Even this relatively mild impairment can be quite dangerous; the likelihood of having an automobile accident with a blood alcohol content of .10 percent is six to seven times the likelihood when blood alcohol level is zero (see **Figure 5.4**), primarily because of the decreased reaction time caused by sensory-motor impairment. A blood alcohol level of .10 percent is considered legally intoxicated in most states, although eight states now use .08 percent as the definitive value. Mental and physical functions decline further with greater blood alcohol levels, causing more substantial impairments (see **Table 5.2**). At blood alcohol levels of .35 percent, alcohol acts as anesthetic, causing unconsciousness. Higher blood alcohol levels will result in coma, substantial unconsciousness, or eventually death due to respiratory failure.

Why does alcohol produce relaxation at low doses, but lead to unconsciousness at high doses? As we saw in Chapter 2, higher levels of stimulation of the reticular formation lead to greater cortical activity. Alcohol depresses activity in the reticular formation. Therefore, a small amount of alcohol-induced depression will lead to relax-

Table 5.2 ■ Blood Alcohol Levels and Behavioral Effects for People with Moderate Drinking Experience

Level of Alcohol in the Blood	Behavioral Effects
0.05%	Lowered alertness; increased relaxation
0.10%	Mild sedation; impairment in sensory-motor functions causes decrease in reaction time
0.15%	Reaction time is greatly decreased
0.20%	Marked suppression of sensory-motor abilities
0.25%	Severe motor disturbances, such as staggering; perception is greatly impaired
0.30%	Semistupor
0.35%	Level for surgical anesthesia; death is possible
0.40%	Death is likely (usually because of respiratory failure)

Source: Adapted from O. S. Ray & C. Ksir. (1996). *Drugs, society and human behavior* (7th ed.). St. Louis: Mosby.

ation and feelings of well-being; however, if the reticular formation is depressed too much, cortical activity will be lowered to a point at which mental and physical functioning is impaired. Very high levels of suppression of cortical activity can result in sleep, coma, or death.

Mechanisms of Action of Alcohol. Alcohol exerts its major effects on three activities of the nervous system: movement of Na^+ ions across the cell membrane, binding of GABA to its receptors, and activity at the opiate receptors.

Alcohol inhibits the movement of Na^+ ions across the cell membrane (refer to Chapter 4, **Figure 4.2**). This reduced Na^+ ion movement interferes with activity in the central nervous system. The higher the dose of alcohol, the greater the general reduction in central nervous system functioning. And decreased nervous system functioning leads to the diminished judgment and impaired sensory-motor coordination characteristic of alcohol intoxication.

Alcohol also influences one type of GABA receptor. (As we saw in Chapter 4, certain GABA receptors control Cl^- ion movement.) Alcohol attaches to the GABA receptor but does not directly influence activity in GABA neurons; instead, alcohol allows the neurotransmitter to bind more tightly to its receptor sites and, thereby increases the effect of GABA on the postsynaptic membrane (Sudzak et al., 1986). The enhanced influence of GABA produces relaxation and decreased anxiety.

The consumption of alcohol is also pleasurable. The pleasurable effects of alcohol are due to its agonist effect on opiate receptors, which is to increase the effects of endorphin stimulation of opiate receptors (see #1 in **Figure 5.1**; Linseman & Harding, 1990).

Long-Term Effects of Alcohol Use. We learned earlier that tolerance, withdrawal, and physical and psychological dependence characterize addiction. These attributes certainly describe the consequences of repeated alcohol consumption. The development of tolerance allows a person to consume larger and larger amounts of alcohol. Withdrawal from alcohol can produce symptoms ranging from restlessness to tremors, insomnia, anxiety, mental confusion, and hallucinations. Long-term alcohol consumption can lead to both physical dependence, as evidenced by the symptoms of withdrawal, and psychological dependence, as indicated by intense craving. **Alcoholism** or alcohol dependence is a major problem in the United States. Approximately 10 percent of adult drinkers abuse alcohol, or deliberately use alcohol to the degree that physical, mental, emotional, and/or social impairment occurs (Carroll, 1989).

Sedative-Hypnotic Drugs

The drug diazepam, or Valium, described at the beginning of this section, belongs to a class of drugs referred to as **sedative-hypnotic drugs**. At low doses, these drugs have a calming (sedative) influence, whereas higher doses have a sleep-inducing (hypnotic) effect. ("Hypnotic" in this case refers only to sleep-inducing properties and not to a hypnotic trance.) Sedatives are used to induce a calming effect, relax muscles, and reduce tension, anxiety, and irritability.

Types of Sedative-Hypnotic Drugs. There are several classes of sedative-hypnotic drugs. These drugs differ in their chemical nature as well as their use. Some of the sedative-hypnotic drugs are used primarily for their sedative action; others are typically employed as surgical anesthetics.

One major class of sedative-hypnotic drugs is the **barbiturates**, the derivatives of barbituric acid. A barbiturate can be assigned to one of the following subclasses, depending on how long it takes the drug's actions to begin and end: ultrashort-acting barbiturates, short-intermediate-acting barbiturates, and long-acting barbiturates. The ultrashort-acting barbiturates, such as thiopental (Pentothal) and thiamylal (Surital), take effect within 1 minute after the drug is consumed and last up to 3 hours. These types of barbiturates are frequently used as *anesthetics* during surgery. Short-intermediate-acting barbiturates begin to be effective after about 15 to 40 minutes and act for up to 6 hours. Some of the short-intermediate-acting barbiturates include pentobarbital (Nembutal) and secobarbital (Seconal), which are widely used as *sedatives*. The long-acting barbiturates, such as phenobarbital (Luminal) begin to have an effect after 1 hour and can be effective for as long as 16 hours. Because of the long stretch of time they are effective, these drugs are used as *anticonvulsants* in the treatment of epilepsy.

A second class of sedative-hypnotic drugs is called **nonbarbiturate sedative-hypnotic drugs**. This type of

---

alcoholism A dependence on alcohol.

sedative-hypnotic drugs A class of drugs that at low doses have a calming (sedative) influence; higher doses have a sleep-inducing hypnotic effect.

barbiturates A class of sedative-hypnotic drugs that are derivatives of barbituric acid, which acts by enhancing the binding of GABA neurotransmitter on certain GABA receptor sites.

nonbarbiturate sedative-hypnotic drugs A class of sedative-hypnotic drugs that are not derived from barbituric acid, but have the same mode of action as barbiturates.

drug includes sedative-hypnotics that are not derived from barbituric acid, but have the same mode of action as the barbiturate sedative-hypnotics. These drugs are frequently used to treat insomnia. Chloral hydrate is one of the drugs in this group. First synthesized in 1862, chloral hydrate, with street names such as "Mickey Finn" or "knockout drops," produces sleep shortly after being taken. The sleep produced by chloral hydrate lasts for up to 5 hours. Another nonbarbiturate sedative-hypnotic drug is methaqualone (Quaalude). Quaaludes were once prescribed for insomnia, but are now considered to have a high potential for abuse and are no longer prescribed.

The third class of sedative-hypnotic drugs, the **antianxiety drugs** or **minor tranquilizers**, are extremely powerful drugs that are often used to reduce nervousness, anxiety, or fear. The first antianxiety drug, meprobamate (Miltown) was introduced in the mid-1950s. Meprobamate produces rapid anxiety relief and was once widely used. In 1960, chlordiazepoxide (Librium) was marketed as an antianxiety drug, followed by diazepam (Valium) 3 years later. Librium and Valium belong to a class of drugs called **benzodiazepines**, which are widely prescribed minor tranquilizers. In fact, Valium was the most frequently used antianxiety drug for almost 20 years (Koch, 1982). During the past decade, alprazolam (**Xanax**) has replaced Valium as the most frequently used benzodiazepine. Xanax is a faster acting and more powerful drug than Valium, but it also has more potential for abuse (Julien, 1998).

The fourth class of sedative-hypnotic drugs, the **antipsychotic drugs** or **major tranquilizers**, are used in the treatment of schizophrenia and to calm stroke victims and other agitated individuals (Ray & Ksir, 1996). (Schizophrenia is a serious behavior disorder characterized by hallucinations or false sensory experiences; delusions or false systems of belief; motor disturbances, which range from complete immobility to wild excitement; and affective disturbances, which include flat or inappropriate affect.) The chemical name for some members of this class of sedative-hypnotics is **phenothiazine**. In 1952, the French researcher H. Laborit found that promethiazine (the first phenothiazine) produced deep anesthesia. Later that year, other French researchers found that another phenothiazine, chlorpromazine (Thorazine) produced calmness and sedation when given prior to surgery. Soon after the sedating effects of Thorazine were noticed, it was introduced as a treatment for schizophrenia (Goldman, 1955). In 1967, a second class of antipsychotic drugs, the *butyrophenones*, which includes haloperidol (Haldol), was introduced as an antipsychotic medication. The phenothiazines are more sedating than the butyrophenones and the drug selected depends, in part, on how much sedation is needed (Ray & Ksir, 1996). A third class of antipsychotic drugs was introduced in the 1990s and include clozapine (Clozaril) and risperidine (Risperdal). One of the dangers (side effects) of the phenothiazines and butyrophenones is *tardive dyskinesia,* which is a movement disorder with Parkinson-like symptoms (see Chapter 2). The new generation of antipsychotic drugs have fewer movement-related problems, but some can have serious physical side effects. Further, although the phenothiazines and butyrophenones reduce hallucinations and delusions (positive symptoms of schizophrenia), the new generations of antipsychotic drugs effectively treat both the positive (hallucinations and delusions) and negative (movement and affective disturbances) symptoms. We will look more closely at the causes and treatments of schizophrenia in Chapter 15.

Mechanisms of Action of Sedative-Hypnotics. All of the sedative-hypnotic drugs produce some general depression of activity in the central nervous system. Other effects are specific to a particular drug. As we learned earlier, alcohol attaches to certain GABA receptors and enhances the binding of the neurotransmitter to these receptor sites. Many sedative-hypnotic drugs appear to have a similar influence on GABA receptors.

Barbiturate and Nonbarbiturate Sedative-Hypnotics. The barbiturate and nonbarbiturate sedative-hypnotics bind to one kind of GABA receptor site (different ones than alcohol) and enhance the binding of a GABA transmitter to those receptor sites and,

---

antianxiety drugs (minor tranquilizers) A class of sedative-hypnotic drugs that are often used to reduce nervousness, anxiety, or fear.

benzodiazepines A class of antianxiety drugs that includes Librium, Valium, and Xanax; acts by facilitating the binding of GABA neurotransmitter to specific GABA receptor sites.

Xanax (alprazolam) The most frequently used benzodiazepine.

antipsychotic drugs (major tranquilizers) A class of sedative-hypnotic drugs that are used in the treatment of psychosis, and to calm stroke victims and other agitated individuals, by blocking postsynaptic dopamine and serotonin receptors.

phenothiazine A class of antipsychotic drugs that includes chlorpromazine (Thorazine).

thereby, increase GABA action on the postsynaptic membrane (see #1 in **Figure 5.1**; Majewska et al., 1986). At low doses, this activity results in a calming effect. At higher doses, these drugs produce greater central nervous system depression, which causes drowsiness and sleep.

Antianxiety Drugs. Specific sites on the postsynaptic membrane of another type of GABA receptor (different ones than alcohol and barbiturate/nonbarbiturate sedative-hypnotics) are sensitive to the antianxiety drugs (Guidotti et al., 1986). The antianxiety drugs attach to the GABA receptor sites without directly activating GABA neurons. Instead, the antianxiety drugs facilitate the binding of GABA neurotransmitter to its receptor sites (see #1 in **Figure 5.1**; Macdonald, Weddle, & Gross, 1986). The increased influence of GABA enhances activity of the GABA neurons and leads to decreased anxiety. Although the antianxiety drugs also produce central nervous system depression, they are safer than the barbiturates because they are less toxic and less sleep-inducing.

Antipsychotic Drugs. The phenothiazines and butyrophenones have an antagonistic effect on dopaminergic neurons. These drugs act in two ways: they block postsynaptic membrane dopamine receptors (see #1 in **Figure 5.2**; Snyder et al., 1974) and impair the release of dopamine neurotransmitter from the presynaptic membrane (see #5 in **Figure 5.2**; Seeman & Lee, 1975). The new generation of antipsychotic drugs acts to block serotonin as well as dopamine receptors (Richelson, 1996).

People sometimes mix alcohol and many sedative-hypnotic drugs. Because alcohol and sedative-hypnotic drugs act on the same GABA neurons, a considerable risk of overdose is created when sedative-hypnotic drugs and alcohol are taken together. The untimely death of the actress Judy Garland points to the potentially lethal effect of mixing alcohol and sedative-hypnotic drugs.

Long-Term Effects of Sedative-Hypnotic Drugs. The calming effect of the sedative-hypnotic drugs is pleasurable and leads to repeated use. Repeated use of sedative-hypnotic drugs leads to tolerance, withdrawal, and dependence, with the exception of the antipsychotic drugs (Julien, 1998). As tolerance develops, increasingly greater doses are required to maintain the same level of sedative effect, increasing the risk of overdose. Withdrawal from sedative-hypnotic drugs can be severe. The person will feel extremely tense, anxious, and irritable, and may suffer from prolonged insomnia. Withdrawal from the sedative-hypnotic drugs also can produce convulsions and seizures, which can be fatal. Because of the rapid development of tolerance and the severity of withdrawal symptoms, sedative-hypnotic drugs have a high potential for addiction. Repeated use of sedative-hypnotic drugs produces both physical and psychological dependence. As noted above, tolerance, withdrawal, and dependence are not observed with the antipsychotic drugs. However, the discontinuance of medication can lead to a return of the symptoms of schizophrenia (Gilbert et al., 1995).

Before You Go On

Can a person become as drunk from drinking beer as from drinking whiskey? Explain your answer.

Why is it particularly dangerous to mix alcohol and sedative-hypnotic drugs?

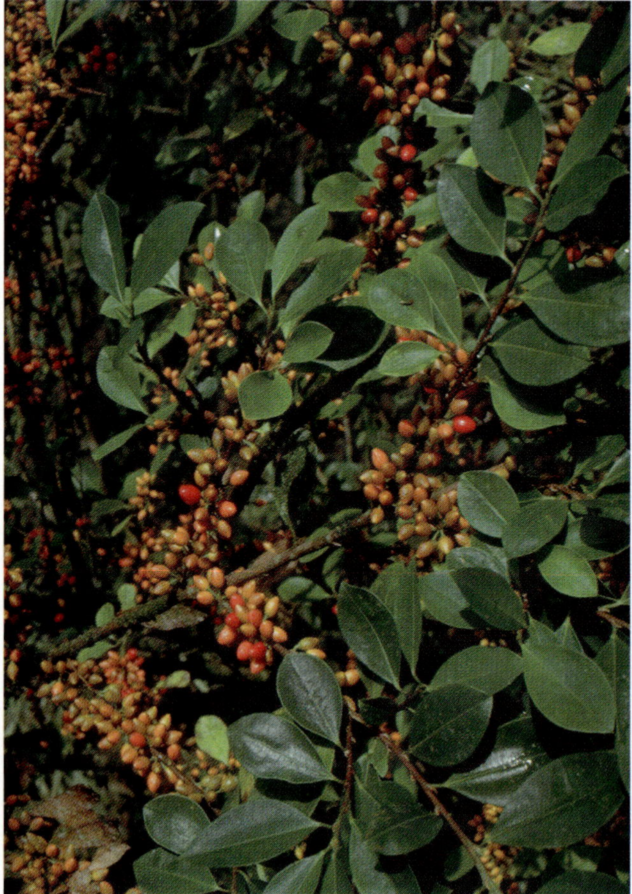

Figure 5.6 Coca plant. Cocaine is found in the leaves of the coca plant.

➤ *What is the most common form of cocaine use? (p. 144)*

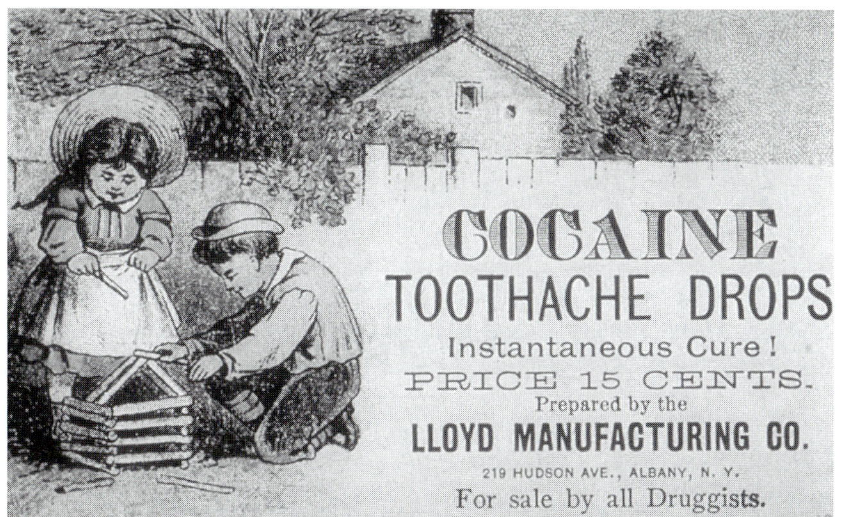

Figure 5.7 Cocaine and Toothaches. Cocaine was not always considered a dangerous drug. In this ad, the benefit of cocaine as a cure for ailments was touted.

➤ *What are the effects of cocaine? (p. 144)*

Section Review

- Depressants slow down mental and physical functions. They include alcohol and sedative-hypnotics.
- At low doses, depressants produce relaxation and decreased anxiety. At higher doses, they produce drowsiness and sleep.
- Alcohol, barbiturate sedative-hypnotics, nonbarbiturate sedative-hypnotics, and antianxiety drugs function as GABA agonists. Alcohol also reduces Na^+ ion movement across the cell membrane.
- Antipsychotic drugs act as dopaminergic and serotonergic antagonists.
- Long-term depressant use can lead to tolerance, withdrawal, and physical and psychological dependence.

Stimulants

Evelyn awakened after a night's sleep feeling very tired. With difficulty, she managed to stagger to the kitchen and pour herself a cup of coffee. After finishing a second cup, she feels awake and ready to start her day.

Why did two cups of coffee make Evelyn feel alert even after a lousy night's sleep? Coffee contains a drug called caffeine. Caffeine belongs to a class of drugs called **stimulants**. A stimulant produces alertness by enhancing the functioning of the sympathetic nervous system and the reticular activating system. Thus, the caffeine in Evelyn's two cups of coffee produced sufficient alertness to enable her to begin her day, which unfortunately will probably revolve around another search for crack.

Types of Stimulants

There are four types of stimulants: amphetamine, cocaine, caffeine, and nicotine (Julien, 1998).

Amphetamine. The term **amphetamine** actually is a collective term for three closely related drugs: amphetamine or levoamphetamine (Benzedrine), dextroamphetamine (Dexedrine), and methamphetamine or "speed." Speed is the most commonly abused amphetamine. Although amphetamines are usually taken orally, crystalline amphetamine can be smoked or, after being diluted, injected intravenously. Amphetamines are typically used to prevent sleep or to suppress appetite and thus control weight. After taking amphetamine, an individual experiences greater energy, decreased need to sleep, reduced appetite, and positive affect (mood).

Cocaine. The stimulant **cocaine**, extracted from the leaves of the coca plant (see **Figure 5.6**), is an alkaloid compound of white, odorless crystals or crystalline powder. Although its medical use is now rare, when it was first introduced, cocaine was used to treat a number of ailments in both children and adults (see **Figure 5.7**).

---

stimulants A class of drugs that produce alertness by enhancing the functioning of the sympathetic nervous system and the reticular activating system.

amphetamine A class of stimulant drugs typically used to prevent sleep or to suppress appetite that increase the release of norepinephrine and dopamine by blocking their reuptake.

cocaine A stimulant extracted from the leaves of the coca plant that produces increased alertness and decreased fatigue by triggering the release and blocking the reuptake of norepinephrine and dopamine.

Figure 5.8 A Cup of Coffee. The energizing effects of caffeine are clearly depicted in this Garfield cartoon.

➤ *In what circumstances do you use stimulants like caffeine and nicotine? (p. 144–145)*

When applied to the mucous membranes of the nose, throat, larynx, and lower respiratory passages, cocaine can act as a local anesthetic. It also stops bleeding during intranasal (nose) surgery due to its ability to constrict the blood vessels (vasoconstriction). Like amphetamine, cocaine produces increased alertness, greater energy, and decreased need for sleep. It also produces an extremely pleasurable emotional state.

Until recently, snorting, or sniffing through the nose, was the most common method of using cocaine. Cocaine can also be taken orally by chewing the coca leaves, or changed into a smokeable form, called a freebase, by mixing cocaine with a strong alkali compound and with ether. The cocaine freebase is then smoked in a pipe. This method of using cocaine can be quite dangerous because of the combustability of ether. Comedian Richard Pryor's clothes once caught fire and he received third-degree burns over most of the upper-half of his body while freebasing cocaine.

Crack cocaine, introduced in 1985, has become a popular way of using cocaine, as the effects are similar to the effects produced by freebasing. Crack is made by mixing cocaine hydrochloride with ammonia or baking soda and water. The resulting crack crystals are smoked in a pipe. Crack is a potent form of cocaine, and as we have seen in Evelyn's case, can lead to addiction very quickly.

Caffeine. A third type of stimulant drug is **caffeine** (see **Figure 5.8**). Caffeine is a bitter-tasting, odorless compound found in various plants. Coffee, an extract from the fruit of the *Coffee arabica* plant and related species, contains caffeine. In this country, the majority of caffeine is consumed in coffee. In fact, it is estimated that the average American drinks about 1,000 cups of coffee each year (Carroll, 1989). Caffeine is also found in cola-flavored drinks as well as in cocoa, chocolate, and tea (see **Table 5.3**). Although mostly consumed in drinks or foods, caffeine can also be taken in pill form, usually as appetite-suppressant nonprescription diet pills. Caffeine's effects are similar to, though milder, than those of amphetamine and cocaine. It leads to clearer thought processing, reduced drowsiness, more rapid reaction times, enhanced intellectual functioning, and an overall positive feeling.

caffeine A stimulant found in various plants that increases alertness and decreases fatigue by increasing glutamate release.

Table 5.3 ■ Caffeine Content of Some Frequently Used Products

Product	Amount	Milligrams of Caffeine
Brewed coffee	5 fl. oz.	90–150*
Instant coffee	5 fl. oz.	14–93*
Decaffeinated coffee	5 fl. oz.	1–6
Tea	5 fl. oz.	30–70**
Cola beverages	12 fl. oz.	30–50
Chocolate bar	1 oz.	20–22***
No-Doz	one tablet	100
Anacin	one tablet	32

*Amount depends on type of coffee, strength, and brewing method.

**Tea also contains the related stimulant *theophylline*.

***Chocolate also contains the related stimulant *theobromine*.

Source: C. O. Byer & L. W. Shainberg. (1995). *Living well: Health in your hands* (2nd ed.). New York Harper Collins.

Nicotine. The fourth type of stimulant is **nicotine**, found in the leaves of the tobacco plant (see **Figure 5.9**). Nicotine is most commonly ingested by smoking cigarettes, cigars, or pipes. It can also be ingested orally as chewing tobacco or by chewing nicotine gum. The newest method of taking nicotine is absorption through the skin via the nicotine patch; the patch and nicotine gum are methods people use to stop the other, more dangerous, methods of nicotine consumption.

Increased alertness and reduced fatigue are the two primary effects of nicotine consumption. It is perhaps surprising to nonsmokers that smoking a cigarette has the same "pick-me-up" effect as drinking a cup of coffee. Nicotine also increases metabolism, with the result that people gain weight when they stop smoking. However, the weight gain after the cessation of smoking is usually less than 10 pounds (Perkins, Epstein, & Pastor, 1990). Given the considerable physical dangers of smoking, a few extra pounds is a small price to pay for not smoking.

Mechanisms of Action of Stimulants

Although all of the stimulants produce arousal, the mechanisms responsible for this effect differ. Amphetamine acts by increasing the release of norepinephrine and dopamine from the presynaptic membrane (see #5 in **Figure 5.1**) and by blocking the reuptake of both neurotransmitters (see #2 in **Figure 5.1**; King & Ellinwood, 1992), whereas cocaine stimulates noradrenergic and dopaminergic neurons by blocking the reuptake of norepinephrine and dopamine (see #2 in **Figure 5.1**; Dichiara, Acquas, & Tanda, 1996). The result of this agonist action of amphetamine and cocaine is increased activity of the noradrenergic and dopaminergic neurons in the areas of the brain controlling arousal and pleasure.

Caffeine's stimulating effect results from increased activity in neurons where glutamate is the neurotransmitter. The release of glutamate is increased following caffeine consumption; however, caffeine does not directly increase glutamate release (see **Figure 5.10**). Instead, caffeine blocks the release of the inhibitory neurotransmitter adenosine, which normally blocks the release of glutamate. By preventing adenosine release, caffeine indirectly increases the activity in glutamate neurons (Silinsky, 1989). There is also evidence that caffeine has an agonist action on dopaminergic neurons (see #1 in **Figure 5.1**; Wise, 1988).

The arousing effects of nicotine result from two agonist processes. Nicotine activates cholinergic receptors (called, appropriately, nicotinic receptors; see #1 in **Figure 5.1**), and it also increases the release of dopamine from the presynaptic membrane (see #5 in **Figure 5.1**; Jarvik & Schneider, 1992), resulting in increased activity of dopaminergic neurons.

The Dangers of Stimulant Abuse

The stimulants are powerful drugs that are widely used and often abused in our society. The dangers of cocaine use have become quite evident in the past several years, especially since the widely publicized death of University of Maryland star basketball player Len Bias. Yet, there was a

---

nicotine A stimulant found in the leaves of the tobacco plant that produces increased alertness and decreased fatigue by activating cholinergic receptors and by increasing the release of dopamine.

Figure 5.9 Tobacco leaves. Nicotine is found in the leaves of the tobacco plant.

➤ *What is the most common form of consumption of nicotine? (p. 145)*

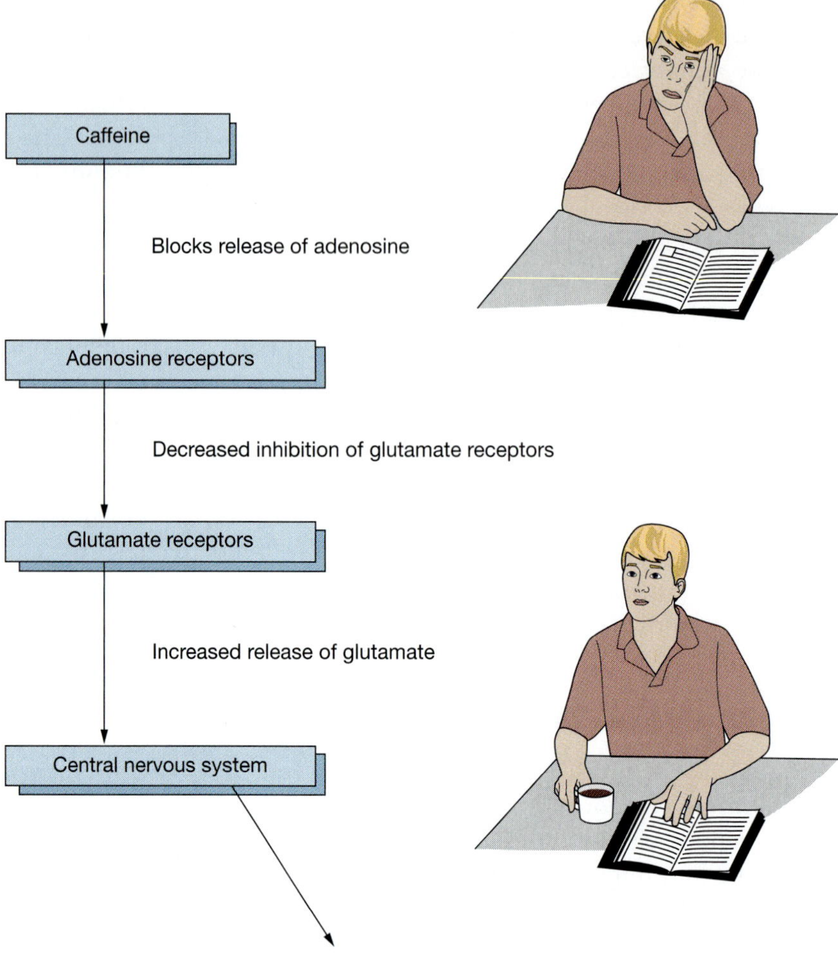

Figure 5.10 The mechanism by which caffeine produces behavioral alertness, attention, and arousal. Caffeine blocks the release of adenosine, which releases the inhibition of glutamate receptions and, thereby, produces CNS arousal.

➤ *How are the physiological effects of caffeine different from those of amphetamine and cocaine? (p. 145)*

time when cocaine was thought to be a safe drug with little danger of abuse (Demarest, 1981). The dangers of amphetamine, caffeine, and nicotine are also becoming more widely recognized. Among these stimulants, only cocaine is illegal; other stimulants are readily available, either with or without a prescription. For example, the amphetamines are still available for short-term weight control (Ray & Ksir, 1996) and caffeine and nicotine can obviously be obtained easily in many different forms. The age restrictions set on cigarettes and related sources of nicotine do not appear to work, as many begin this damaging habit as teenagers and preteens.

Tolerance to all stimulants develops rapidly. The development of tolerance to nicotine is the reason some individuals smoke two or three packs of cigarettes each day. Similarly, some people drink eight to ten cups of coffee daily because their tolerance to caffeine is so high.

Symptoms of withdrawal from stimulants range from mild to severe. Mild withdrawal from a stimulant will be experienced as a lack of alertness and feelings of lethargy. Intense withdrawal symptoms include sleeping for up to 48 hours followed by depression lasting for several days or weeks (Wilford, 1981). The withdrawal from a stimulant drug can be so severe that it is often known as "crashing," and the depression resulting from withdrawal may be so intense as to present a suicide risk.

Physical dependence occurs with all of the stimulant drugs (Julien, 1998). The physical dependence to the stimulants is evident from the withdrawal that occurs once drug use stops.

Psychological dependence is common with repeated use of stimulants. Cravings in individuals with a psychological dependence can occur even after the drug has not been used for a long time. I have a friend who has not smoked for 7 years but still has a desire to smoke, especially when he is around others who are smoking or when he is in situations in which he smoked in the past. For example, he still sometimes reaches into his shirt pocket for a pack of cigarettes after finishing his meal.

Another serious consequence of stimulant abuse, particularly to amphetamine and cocaine, is *stimulant-induced psychosis.* Frequent use of amphetamine can lead to paranoia, or feelings of persecution, as well as delusions and hallucinations. These symptoms can also be produced by excessive cocaine use. Stimulant-induced psychosis can even lead to violent behavior. We will look more closely at the nature of amphetamine and cocaine psychoses in Chapter 15.

Before You Go On

Describe the effects of stimulants on the brain and body.

Linda must drink at least four cups of coffee before she can start work in the morning. Explain the effect of caffeine on her brain.

Section Review

- Stimulants produce increased alertness, reduced appetite, and increased energy. They include amphetamines, cocaine, nicotine, and caffeine.
- Amphetamine and cocaine are noradrenergic and dopaminergic agonists. Caffeine is an adenosine antagonist, whereas nicotine is a cholinergic and dopaminergic agonist.
- Users of stimulants quickly develop tolerance; withdrawal symptoms can range from mild to severe, and physical and psychological dependence result from long-term use.

Psychedelics

> I lost all count of time. . . . everything appeared deformed as in a faulty mirror. Space and time became more and more disorganized and I was overcome by a fear that I was going out of my mind. The worst part of it being that I was clearly aware of my condition. . . . Occasionally, I felt as if I were out of my body. I thought that I had died. My ego seemed suspended somewhere in space, from where I saw my dead body lying on the sofa. . . . Acoustic perceptions, such as the noise of water gushing from a tap or the spoken word, were transformed into optical illusions. (Quoted in Julien, 1998, p. 361)

The preceding story is not a dream, but the description of an experience by Swiss chemist Albert Hofmann in 1938 with a drug called lysergic acid diethylamide or LSD. LSD belongs to a class of drugs called psychedelic drugs.

The **psychedelics**, sometimes called **hallucinogens**, produce profound alterations in a person's state of consciousness (Cohen, 1985). A psychedelic drug alters a person's sensory experiences. For example, vivid but

Figure 5.11 Peyote cactus. Peyote (mescal buttons) and mescaline are derived from this cactus.

➤ *What effects do the Mexican Indians experience smoking peyote?* *(p. 148)*

unreal images, called illusions, or "pseudohallucinations," may occur. Perceptual changes that may be induced by psychedelics include increased sensory awareness; heightened clarity of a sensory experience; perception of the routine elements of environment as novel, beautiful, or harmonious; and lessened capacity to distinguish between the self and the environment. For example, a person under the influence of a psychedelic drug may believe that he or she is talking to a long-deceased relative. Emotional changes that may be produced by psychedelic drugs include reduced control over reaction to environmental circumstances and assignment of profound meaning to even the slightest of sensations.

Even for the same individual, each experience with a psychedelic drug will be different. In one case, a person may perceive that objects are moving in slow motion, whereas at another time, the same individual may perceive an ordinary object as being especially beautiful.

Types of Psychedelics

Some psychedelic drugs are obtained from plants, and others are manufactured in the laboratory. For thousands of years, Native American Indians of southwestern United States and northern Mexico have experienced powerful psychedelic experiences, primarily visual hallucinations, after ingesting part of the peyote cactus as part of their

psychedelics (hallucinogens) A class of drugs that produce profound alterations in a person's state of consciousness.

religious rituals. **Mescaline** is the psychoactive ingredient in this drug, called **peyote**. The tips of the fleshy green peyote cactus (see **Figure 5.11**), called mescal buttons, are removed from the cactus and dried. The buttons taste bitter, so instead of eating them, the Mexican Indians smoke the ground-up peyote or drink it in tea. The psychedelic experience produced by peyote lasts 6 to 10 hours. In pure form, mescaline is an extremely powerful psychedelic with effects resembling those produced by LSD (see below).

Marijuana, another drug with psychedelic properties, is obtained from a mixture of crushed leaves, flowers, stems, and seeds of the hemp plant, *Cannabis sativa* (see **Figure 5.12**). The resinous secretions of *Cannabis sativa* can be dried into a solid called *hashish*. The psychoactive ingredient in both hashish and marijuana is *delta-9-tetrahydrocannabinol*, or THC. At low doses, both marijuana and hashish have a weak sedative effect, but at higher doses, a psychedelic experience is produced. Because of these dual effects, many classify marijuana and hashish separately from other psychedelic drugs.

Although the U.S. Drug Enforcement Administration (DEA) still considers marijuana to be a drug "without medical usefulness," its active ingredient, THC, has been used medically to treat nausea and stimulate appetite (Levine, 1993; Nahas, 1984). The drug dronabinol, which contains THC, has helped cancer patients gain weight (Nahas, 1984) and has stimulated appetite in AIDS patients (Levine, 1993). Dronabinol has also been used to reduce muscle spasms and pain in persons with multiple sclerosis and to reduce intraocular pressure in people with glaucoma (Julien, 1998).

The primary psychedelic effect of both hashish and marijuana is perceptual. After taking either drug, a person's experiences seem more vivid. Food tastes better or worse, and odors seem more intense. Visual and auditory sensations seem more powerful. A notable effect is a change in time perception: time seems to move very slowly. Hallucinations sometimes occur and thought processes are occasionally fragmented by these drugs. Also, motor coordination is impaired and reaction times slowed so that driving after smoking marijuana or hashish is similarly dangerous to driving while intoxicated by alcohol (Murry, 1986).

Figure 5.12 Marijuana plant. Delta-9-tetrahydrocannabinol (THC) is the psychoactive ingredient of the marijuana plant.
➤ *What are the effects of smoking marijuana? (p. 148)*

Other psychedelic drugs found in plants include *psilocybin* and *psilocin*, found in at least 15 different species of mushrooms belonging to the genera *psilocybe*, *panaeolus*, and *conocycbe*. Mushrooms containing psilocybin and psilocin are found throughout the world. The mushroom *psilocybe mexicana* is used as an integral part of religious ceremonies by Indians in Central America. The effects of these two psychedelic drugs are similar to, but weaker than, those of LSD, and the duration of action is much shorter (2 to 4 hours compared with 10 to 12 hours).

Some psychedelic drugs are synthesized in the laboratory. **Lysergic acid diethylamide (LSD)**, sometimes referred to as "acid," is one widely used synthetic psychedelic drug. **Figure 5.13** provides a vivid example of the hallucinogenic effect of LSD. When it was first synthesized, LSD was thought to provide a mechanism to study serious mental disorders because it seemed to mimic psychoses. The value of the LSD experience was widely touted by Timothy Leary and Richard Alpert of Harvard University during the late 1950s. Leary and Albert were dismissed by Harvard in 1963 for drug use and advocacy of drug use, yet LSD has remained a widely used psychoactive drug (Julien, 1998). LSD is consumed orally in tablets or tiny squares of gelatin.

Another synthetic psychedelic drug is **phencyclidine (PCP)**. PCP was first introduced as a surgical anesthetic in the 1950s. Although taken off the market in 1965, PCP remains a popular hallucinogenic drug (Crider, 1986). PCP, sometimes referred to as "angel dust," is a white powder that can be injected, smoked, inhaled, or sniffed.

mescaline The hallucinogenic ingredient found in peyote that acts by stimulating serotonergic receptors.

peyote A psychedelic drug obtained from the peyote cactus plant.

marijuana A psychedelic drug obtained from a mixture of crushed leaves, flowers, stems, and seeds of the hemp plant (*Cannabis sativa*) that acts by stimulating THC receptors.

lysergic acid diethylamide (LSD) A powerful synthetic hallucinogenic drug that acts by stimulating serotonergic receptors.

phencyclidine (PCP) Another powerful synthetic hallucinogenic drug sometimes known as angel dust that, when used for long periods of time, can lead to permanent neurological damage.

Mechanisms of Action of Psychedelics

The hallucinogens produced by LSD are thought to be caused by agonist action on one type of serotonergic receptor. LSD attaches to the serotonin receptor site and directly stimulates the serotonergic neuron (see #1 in **Figure 5.1**; Jacobs, 1987). The psychedelic properties of mescaline, psilocin, and psilocybin appear to be due to the same mechanism as LSD (Julien, 1998).

Studies have suggested that marijuana binds with specialized receptors for its active ingredient, THC, found in the basal ganglia, cerebellum, hippocampus, and cerebral cortex (Howlett et al., 1990). Why would the brain have receptors sensitive to THC if it is not naturally produced in the body? It was not until after the discovery of THC that a chemical endogenous to the brain called anandamide was found; anandamide attaches to these same receptors (DiMarzo et al., 1994). Because the THC receptor was discovered first, the family of chemicals of which anandamide is a member is called, in somewhat backward fashion, the endogenous (naturally occurring) cannabinoids (you will recall that *Cannabis* is the botanical name for marijuana). Although their actual function remains unclear, the endogenous cannabinoids most likely are involved in interpreting sensory imput.

Dangers of the Use of Psychedelics

Perhaps the biggest danger of the use of psychedelic drugs is the unpredictability of their effects. Individuals who take hallucinogenic drugs can experience panic reactions, or "bad trips," characterized by extreme distress and in some cases paranoia or feelings of persecution.

Another danger is the occurrence of flashbacks. A *flashback* is a hallucination experienced long after the original "trip" has ended. It may be a recurrence of the original hallucinogenic experience or it may be a totally new hallucinogenic experience. It can occur spontaneously or be elicited by an environmental stressor. The physical danger of such events is quite obvious; the spontaneous flashbacks can occur at any time, so the person could be driving or performing other activities that could be disrupted by the episode. Such unexpected events can be quite frightening, leaving the drug user unsure of what has happened and fearful of additional episodes.

With repeated use of marijuana and hashish, tolerance develops. Withdrawal symptoms include restlessness, irritability, insomnia, and nausea. Because marijuana is smoked, users are vulnerable to the same types of cancers as cigarette smokers. Further, marijuana users experience craving for the drug, indicating psychological dependency.

Tolerance is observed with most other psychedelic drugs, with no evidence of withdrawal after the drugs are no longer used (Carroll, 1989). However, more serious permanent damage is seen in users of PCP; long-term PCP use can lead to psychological dependence and neurological problems including memory lapses, speech difficulty, and visual impairment (Olney, 1994).

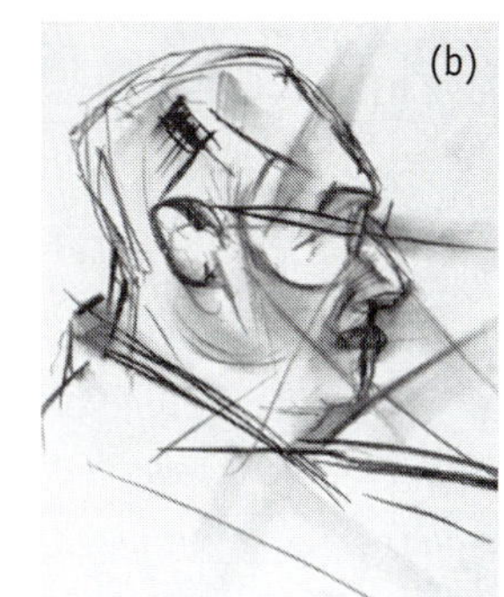

Figure 5.13 Drawings done by a man under the influence of LSD. There was no effect seen 20 minutes after first dose (a), but some alterations in the perception of a model 25 minutes after second dose (b). The most intense effects of the drug can be seen after 2 hours and 45 minutes (c). The drug's effects began to wear off after 5 hours and 45 minutes (d), and were almost gone by 8 hours after taking LSD (e).

➤ *What are your impressions from these drawings of the changes in perception produced by LSD? (p. 148)*

Before You Go On

Describe the effects that psychedelic drugs have on the brain and body.

Evan has unknowingly taken LSD. Explain the effects that LSD might have on him. How long might these effects last?

Section Review

- Psychedelic drugs, which include LSD, peyote, marijuana, and PCP, induce substantial changes in the way a person thinks, feels, or perceives.
- LSD, mescaline, psilocin, and psilocybin act as agonists, attaching to serotonergic receptors and directly stimulating serotonergic neurons. THC, the active ingredient in marijuana, binds with specialized receptors found in the basal ganglia, cerebellum, and cerebral cortex, affecting the interpretation of sensory input.
- Marijuana use can result in tolerance and psychological dependence. Other psychedelic drugs can produce flashback experiences after the drug is no longer used, and psychological dependence and permanent neurological damage can result from extended use of PCP.

Addiction: The Biology of Reinforcement

The last thing Sam remembered after the explosion was being carried on a stretcher by two medics. His Marine unit had been in a fire fight with the Viet Cong. A mortar exploded in front of him and as the shrapnel entered his body, he felt horrible pain. Sam lay on the ground for what seemed like days. After the fighting stopped and the Viet Cong withdrew, medics found Sam. A quick injection eased his pain and he fell asleep on the stretcher. He awoke to an intense pain in his legs. He opened his eyes, realized that he was in the hospital bed, and asked a nearby nurse if he was okay. The nurse reassured Sam that he would be going home in a few weeks, and she gave him another injection, which caused the pain to fade and a warm glow to take its place. Sam felt intense pleasure. Sam asked what drug he had been given. "Morphine" was the reply.

Sam's thoughts then turned to his parents, and he hoped they wouldn't be worried, since he felt just fine. He decided that morphine was a super drug.

Morphine, like other opiates, has two main effects: it acts as an analgesic to eliminate pain, and it produces pleasurable feelings. Because a person who feels these effects will attempt to experience them again, the drug is

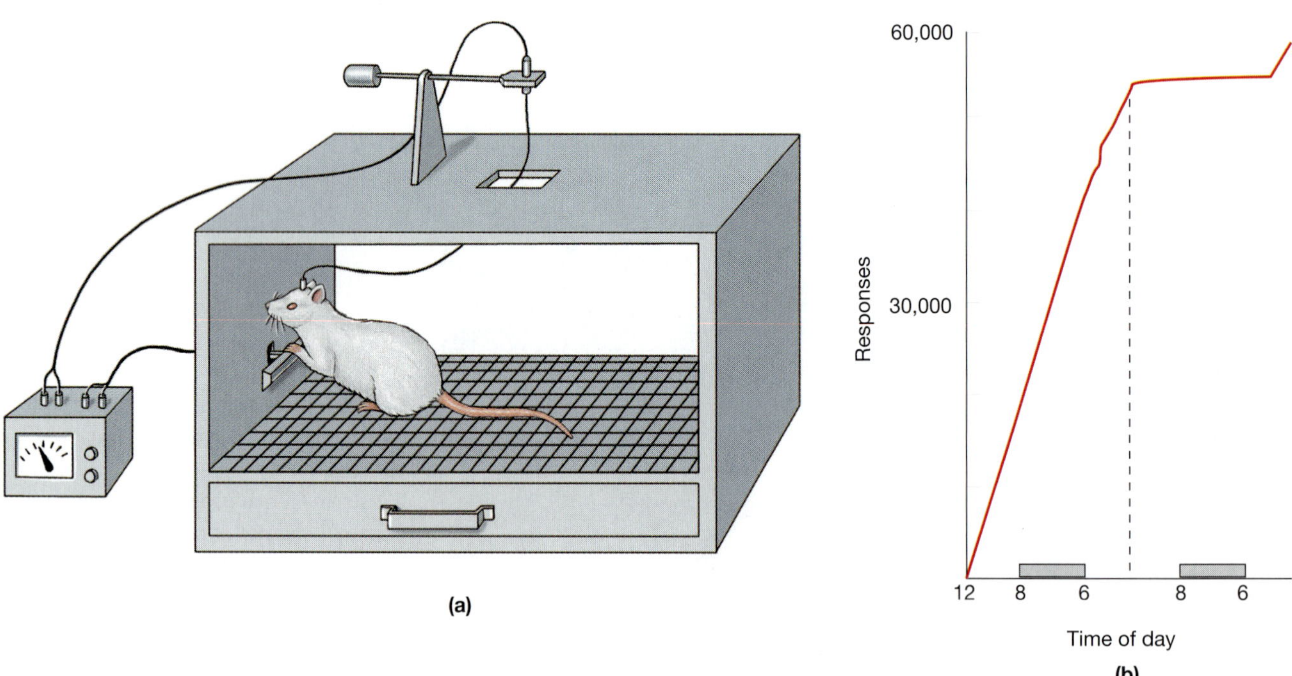

Figure 5.14 (a) Rat pressing a bar for electrical stimulation of the brain (ESB). (b) Sample cumulative record. Note the extremely high rate of responding (over 2,000 bar presses per hour) that occurred for more than 24 hours and was followed by a period of sleep.

➤ *Why did the rate of bar presses increase over time? (p. 151)*

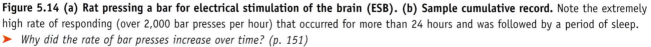

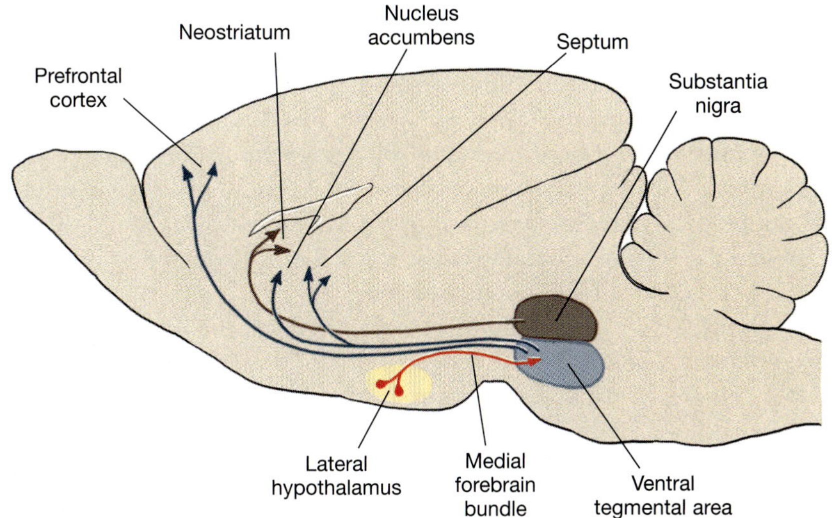

Figure 5.15 Sagittal plane view showing the structures in the mesotelencephalic reinforcement system of the rat brain. The tegmentostriatal pathway begins in the lateral and preoptic areas of the hypothalamus and travels through the medial forebrain bundle to the ventral tegmental area. Fibers from the ventral tegmental area extend to the nucleus accumbens, septum, and prefrontal cortex. The nigrostriatal pathway begins in the substantia nigra and projects to the caudate nucleus and putamen (neostriatum).

➤ *How are these structures involved in the experience of pleasure produced by cocaine or heroin? (p. 151–155)*

considered a powerful reinforcer. A reinforcer is an event or an activity that increases the frequency of the behavior preceding that event or activity (Klein, 1996). In this case, morphine and its pleasurable effects act as a reinforcer of subsequent attempts to obtain the drug. In this section, we will discuss the biology of reinforcement, focusing on the central nervous system structures that allow us to experience the affective state of pleasure, as well as the influence of reinforcers on our actions. Read on to learn why drugs such as cocaine and heroin are so reinforcing and thus have such an impact on our society. Our discussion will also provide a better understanding of how drug use can lead to addiction.

The Discovery of Reinforcement

Our knowledge of the effects of reinforcement began like so much of scientific knowledge, with a lucky accident. In 1954, James Olds and Peter Milner were trying to determine the effects of activation of the reticular formation of the brain of a rat. The electrode they used to activate the rat's brain was misplaced and ended up in the rat's hypothalamus. When this area was stimulated, the rat behaved as if the stimulation were desirable; the rat subsequently showed a strong preference for the particular location on the long table where it had received the stimulation. In other words, stimulation of this particular area of the brain was highly reinforcing.

To confirm these observations, Olds and Milner implanted electrodes into many different areas of the brain and made brain stimulation dependent on pressing a bar in a Skinner box (see **Figure 5.14**); stimulation would only occur if the rat pressed the bar. They found that rats quickly learned to press the bar to receive brain stimulation. Subsequent studies have demonstrated that many species, including pigeons (Goodman & Brown, 1966), rats (Olds & Milner, 1954), cats and dogs (Stark & Boyd, 1963), primates (Brady, 1961), and humans (Ervin, Mark, & Steven, 1969), experience stimulation of particular areas of the brain as reinforcing.

Before You Go On

Why would stimulation of the hypothalamus be reinforcing?

The Influence of the Medial Forebrain Bundle

In the 1960s, researchers suggested that a group of nerve fibers, the **medial forebrain bundle (MFB)** located in the limbic system, was the physical location of the reinforcement mechanism, a sort of reinforcement center (see **Figure 5.15**; Margules & Stein, 1967; Stein, 1969; Stein & Wise, 1969, 1973).

They based this suggestion on the fact that stimulation of the MFB has four characteristics: (1) it is highly reinforcing; (2) it motivates behavior; (3) its functioning is stimulated by the presence of reinforcers; and (4) its reinforcing effects are enhanced by deprivation. Each of these characteristics will be discussed in the following sections.

The Reinforcing Effect of MFB Stimulation. Sam places a dollar in a video poker machine and pulls the lever. When the machine stops spinning, he has four

medial forebrain bundle (MFB) A group of nerve fibers located in the limbic system considered part of the brain's reinforcement system.

aces and wins $200. Not surprisingly, Sam shouts in joy. Why was Sam so overjoyed after he won $200? The research on MFB stimulation provides a likely answer.

Valenstein and Beer's 1964 study of reinforcing properties of stimulation on the brains of rats found that for weeks, rats would press a bar delivering stimulation of the MFB up to 30 times per minute, stopping for only a short time to eat and groom. These rats responded until exhausted, fell asleep for several hours, and awoke to resume bar pressing. But would such *electrical stimulation of the brain (ESB)* have a more powerful effect on behavior than conventional reinforcers such as food, water, or sex? Routtenberg and Lindy (1965) constructed a situation in which pressing one lever initiated brain stimulation and pressing another lever produced food. The rats in this experiment were placed in this situation for only 1 hour a day and had no other food source. Still, all of the rats spent the entire hour pressing for brain stimulation, eventually starving themselves to death. Obviously, ESB has greater reinforcing value than food, at least to rats.

The seemingly pleasurable aspect of brain stimulation has also been demonstrated in humans. For example, Ervin, Mark, and Steven (1969) reported that MFB stimulation not only eliminated pain in cancer patients but also produced a euphoric feeling (approximately equivalent to the effect of two strong alcoholic drinks) that lasted several hours. Sem-Jacobson (1968) found that brain stimulation was experienced as pleasurable by patients suffering intense depression, fear, or physical pain; patients who felt well prior to ESB experienced only mild pleasure.

The Motivational Influence of MFB Stimulation. Sam goes to the bank and cashes a $50 check that he received for his birthday. The cashier hands him two twenties and one ten-dollar bill. How does this make him feel? In all likelihood, he would experience a little pleasure from feeling the bills in his palm. Now what might he do next? He could set the money in a drawer for a rainy day or take it to the casino and play video poker. What do you think Sam will do? Of course, he goes to the casino. Spending the money demonstrates that reinforcers have both pleasurable and motivating properties. The pleasurable property is the feeling that Sam experiences when he receives the reinforcer (money). The motivating property is that, upon receipt of the reinforcer, Sam is motivated to perform another behavior (spend it).

The research of Elliot Valenstein and his associates (Valenstein, Cox, & Kakolewski, 1969) demonstrated that activation of the medial forebrain bundle motivates behavior. The researchers found that the specific response motivated by brain stimulation depends on the prevailing environmental conditions: Brain stimulation motivates eating when food is available and drinking when water is present. This phenomenon is called **stimulus-bound behavior**.

To this point we have discussed the reinforcing and motivational effects of direct MFB stimulation. Yet, we do not have electrodes implanted in our MFB; these neurons must be activated by naturally occurring processes. The next two sections explain how reinforcement and deprivation naturally stimulate the MFB and increase our search for reinforcement.

The Influence of Reinforcers on MFB Function. Sam finds sexual intercourse more pleasurable after watching an erotic film. Based on our discussion to this point, do you think it is possible that the movie activates the MFB, which then increases the reinforcing quality of sex? A number of studies have demonstrated that a reinforcing activity (for example, sexual activity) or stimuli associated with a reinforcing activity (for example, an erotic film) enhances the functioning of the MFB.

Mendelson (1967) demonstrated the effect of water on the reinforcement value of ESB. Mendelson compared how often rats in his study pressed a bar to obtain brain stimulation when water was available to how often they pressed the bar in the absence of water. His results showed that rats exhibited a significantly higher rate of bar pressing when water was present than they did when it was not. Coons and Cruce (1968) found that the presence of food increased the number of attempts to obtain brain stimulation, and Hoebel (1969) reported that a peppermint odor or a few drops of sucrose in the mouth had the same effect. These results suggest that the presence of reinforcement enhances the functioning of the MFB. The effect of this enhanced MFB functioning is the increased responding for reinforcers. Further, reinforcers will be more pleasurable due to the higher level of MFB activity. Returning to our example, watching an erotic film activates Sam's MFB, which motivates him to engage in sexual activity, which he finds highly reinforcing (pleasurable).

The Influence of Deprivation on the MFB. Sam goes the ballpark on a very hot day and drinks several beers. It is cold the next time he goes to the ballpark and he drinks only one beer. Why does Sam drink

---

stimulus-bound behavior The motivation of behavior by prevailing environmental conditions.

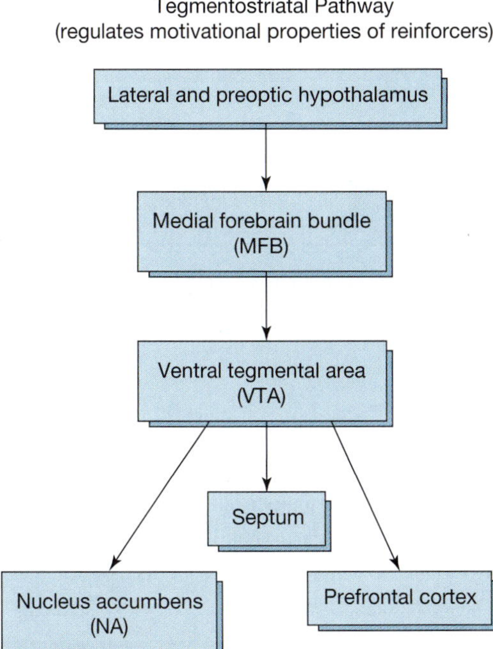

Figure 5.16 The mesotelencephalic reinforcement system. This system consists of two brain pathways: (a) the tegmentostriatal pathway mediates the influence of motivation on reinforcement and (b) the nigrostriatal pathway is involved in memory consolidation. ➤ *Which portions(s) of the tegmentostriatal pathway is (are) dopaminergic? (p. 154–155)*

more beers on a hot than a cold day? The effect of deprivation on MFB functioning gives us an answer to this question.

Deprivation is a restriction in the access to a reinforcer. Drinking ice water is very satisfying on a hot day, yet on a cold day ice water has little incentive value. This example illustrates one characteristic of deprivation: a physiological need increases the incentive value of reinforcers. In this example, the presence of thirst on a hot day enhances the reinforcement value of ice water. Increased activity in the brain's reinforcement system is one probable mechanism of this enhancement.

Brady (1961) showed that the rate of a rat's self-stimulation varies depending on the level of hunger; the longer the rats were deprived of food, the more intense was the rate at which they pressed the bar to obtain brain stimulation. Similarly, Olds (1962) found an enhanced value of brain stimulation in rats that had been deprived of water, as compared to nondeprived rats.

Our discussion has indicated that MFB activity is pleasurable. Environmental reinforcers, such as food or drink, and internal needs, such as hunger, thirst, or desire for sex, activate the MFB, and the effect of stimulating this system is to motivate the behavior necessary to obtain reinforcers. In the next section, we will discover that psychoactive drugs, such as cocaine or heroin, act on the same brain reinforcement system, with craving for a drug acting on this system in the same manner as hunger or thirst.

Before You Go On

Explain how scientists discovered the effect of the medial forebrain bundle on reinforcement.

How might money act on the medial forebrain bundle? Would the need for money or the amount of money affect the influence of the medial forebrain bundle on the pleasurable and motivating qualities of money?

Mesotelencephalic Reinforcement System

In the late 1980s, Wise and Rompre concluded that the medial forebrain bundle is only part of the brain's reinforcement system. Wise and Rompre (1989) suggest that the **mesotelencephalic reinforcement system** contains two neural pathways. One of these neural pathways is the **tegmentostriatal pathway**, which begins in the lateral and preoptic areas of the hypothalamus (see **Figures 5.15** and **5.16**). Neurons in

mesotelencephalic reinforcement system The brain reinforcement system that contains the tegmentostriatal pathway and the nigrostriatal pathway.

tegmentostriatal pathway A group of nerve fibers that detects reinforcement-related stimuli in the lateral and preoptic areas of the hypothalamus and transmits the information through the MFB to the ventral tegmental area (VTA). Neural impulses from the VTA are then sent to the nucleus accumbens (NA), septum, and prefrontal cortex.

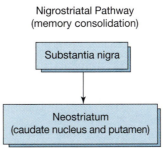

these areas of the hypothalamus detect reinforcement-related stimuli and transmit the information through the MFB to the ventral tegmental area (VTA). Neural impulses from the VTA are then sent to the nucleus accumbens (NA), septum, and prefrontal cortex.

The second pathway is the **nigrostriatal pathway** (refer to **Figures 5.15** and **5.16**). This pathway begins in the substantia nigra (nigro-) and projects to the neostriatum (-striatal), consisting of the caudate nucleus and putamen. In Chapter 8, we will discuss the involvement of the nigrostriatal pathway in the elicitation of voluntary behavior, such as going to the refrigerator to get an apple. In Chapter 10, we will examine its role in the control of eating that apple.

Function of the Two Reinforcement Pathways. Why would the brain have two separate reinforcement pathways? It is likely that the two pathways regulate two different aspects of reinforcement (Vaccarino, Schiff, & Glickman, 1989). The tegmentostriatal pathway detects whether sufficient motivation is present for voluntary behavior to occur. For example, a rat will not bar press for food if it is not deprived or if the value of the reinforcer is insufficient. Deprivation and reinforcer value in this context are called motivational variables. The behavioral effects of stimulating structures in the tegmentostriatal pathway other than the MFB are also affected by motivational variables (Evans & Vaccarino, 1989). In contrast, motivational variables do not influence the behavioral effects of stimulation of structures in the nigrostriatal pathway (Winn, Williams, & Herberg, 1982).

In addition to motivating behavior, reinforcers facilitate the storage of experiences, commonly known as memory. Memory allows past experiences to influence future behavior—the rat has to be able to remember that it was the bar press that delivered the ESB. Although structures in the nigrostriatal pathway are not involved in the motivational aspect of reinforcement, they do play a role in the consolidation, or the permanent storage, of a memory. Evidence for this influence of reinforcers is that memory is significantly enhanced when an animal is exposed to a positive reinforcer for a short time following training (Coulombe & White, 1982; Major & White, 1978). Other studies have

nigrostriatal pathway A group of nerve fibers beginning in the substantia nigra and projecting to the neostriatum; these nerve fibers play a role in the consolidation of a memory.

ventral tegmental area (VTA) Structure in the tegmentostriatal reinforcement system that projects to the nucleus accumbens.

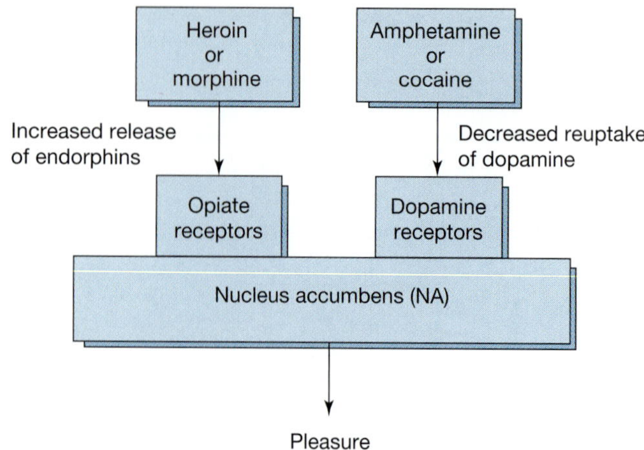

Figure 5.17 Diagram showing the separate mechanisms by which heroin and cocaine activate the nucleus accumbens. Activity in the NA is highly pleasurable.

➤ *Why do cocaine and heroin have separate mechanisms to activate nucleus accumbens? (p. 154–155)*

shown that stimulation of the nigrostriatal pathway, but not the tegmentostriatal pathway, increases the consolidation of the memory of a reinforcing experience (Carr & White, 1984). To summarize, activity in the tegmentostriatal pathway regulates the motivational properties of reinforcers and activity in the nigrostriatal pathway is responsible for memory consolidation.

Dopaminergic Control of Reinforcement. The neurotransmitter dopamine plays a significant role in regulating the behavioral effects of reinforcement (Vaccarino, Schiff, & Glickman, 1989; Wise & Rompre, 1989). Only part of the tegmentostriatal system is regulated by dopamine (refer to **Figure 5.16a**). The fibers from the lateral hypothalamus to the ventral tegmental area (VTA) are not dopaminergic (Gallistel, Shizgal, & Yeomans, 1981). The neurons in this tract that motivate self-stimulation are heavily myelinated (dopaminergic neurons are not) and thus conduct neural impulses very rapidly. Dopamine does, however, govern the activity of the neurons that connect the **ventral tegmental area (VTA)** to the nucleus accumbens, septum, and prefrontal cortex, and several lines of evidence indicate that dopamine plays an important role in mediating the effect of reinforcement on behavior.

One indication of dopaminergic influence is the effect of the dopamine agonists amphetamine and cocaine, which have powerful reinforcing properties (see **Figure 5.17**). (Recall that an agonist stimulates or enhances the activity of a naturally occurring chemical. Thus, cocaine and amphetamine actions increase the level of dopamine activity at dopaminergic receptors.) As we saw from our description of Evelyn, people are highly motivated to obtain substances such as amphetamine or cocaine. The reinforcing property of these drugs results in part from their ability to activate the dopaminergic tegmentostriatal pathway. Many researchers have shown that animals will quickly learn a behavior enabling them to self-administer amphetamine and cocaine (Bozarth & Wise, 1983; Koob & Bloom, 1988). They also will learn, and will emit at a high rate, a behavior that triggers injections of cocaine or amphetamine into the **nucleus accumbens (NA)** (Carr & White, 1986; Guerin et al., 1984). Further, elevation of dopamine levels in the nucleus accumbens has been found after administration of amphetamine (Hurd & Ungerstedt, 1989; Westerink et al., 1987) and cocaine (Church, Justice, & Byrd, 1987; Hurd, Kehr, & Ungerstedt, 1988).

A variety of reinforcers other than cocaine and amphetamine initiate the release of dopamine, providing support for dopaminergic involvement in the neural control of reinforcement. For example, electrical stimulation of the MFB (Blaha & Phillips, 1990; Moghaddam & Bunney, 1989) and of the VTA (Phillips, Blaka, & Fibinger, 1989) causes the release of dopamine in the NA. When animals perform a behavior in order to receive stimulation of the MFB or VTA, dopamine is also released. Natural reinforcers, such as food and water, also elicit NA release of dopamine, probably due to the reinforcing properties of drinking or eating in water- or food-deprived animals (Chang et al., 1988). Researchers have found increased dopamine levels following administration of alcohol (Gessa et al., 1985), cannabis (Chen, Paredes, & Gardner, 1994), and nicotine (Clarke et al., 1985; Mereu et al., 1987).

Further support for dopaminergic control of reinforcement comes from studies in which the functioning of dopaminergic neurons in the tegmentostriatal pathway is impaired. Destruction of dopaminergic neurons in this pathway weakens the reinforcing properties of both electrical stimulation and dopamine agonists such as amphetamine or cocaine (Roberts & Koob, 1982; Spryaki, Fibiger, & Phillips, 1982). In another study, the administration of drugs that block dopamine receptors caused animals to cease performing a behavior that had previously been used to receive cocaine or amphetamine (Roberts & Zito, 1987).

Opiate Activation of the Tegmentostriatal Pathway. The opiate drugs also appear to be capable of stimulating the tegmentostriatal pathway (Vaccarino, Schiff, & Glickman, 1989). Animals will learn to self-administer opiate drugs such as heroin or morphine just as they learn to self-administer amphetamine and cocaine (Koob et al., 1984; Mucha et al., 1982). Animals will also bar press to receive injections of heroin or morphine into the VTA (Bozarth & Wise, 1981) or NA (Goeders, Lane, & Smith, 1984). Injection of opiate antagonists into the VTA or NA causes rats to stop bar pressing (Britt & Wise, 1983).

Do the narcotics stimulate the same dopaminergic receptors in the NA and VTA as amphetamine and cocaine? Studies suggest that the opiate drugs activate opiate-sensitive receptors and not dopaminergic receptors (refer to **Figure 5.17**). (Although we learned that the endorphins were neuromodulators in the last chapter, their mode of action is to excite opiate-sensitive receptors). Drugs that antagonize dopamine receptors reduce self-administration of amphetamine or cocaine but do not affect self-stimulation for opiate drugs (Ettenberg et al., 1982). Also, destruction of dopaminergic neurons in the tegmentostriatal pathway decreases consumption of cocaine but has no influence on narcotic use. An opposite pattern is found when opiate receptors are blocked. Vaccarino, Bloom, and Koob (1985) reported that administration of opiate antagonists causes animals to stop self-administering morphine but not cocaine. On the basis of these findings, Koob (1992) suggested that the tegmentostriatal pathway contains two separate types of receptors, and that dopaminergic agonists activate the dopamine receptors and opiates stimulate the opiate receptors with the same result—activation of the nucleus accumbens (see **Figure 5.17**).

Before You Go On

Describe the two pathways of the mesotelencephalic reinforcement system.

What is the role of dopamine in amphetamine and cocaine addiction? In opiate addiction?

APPLICATION

Drug Treatment of Heroin and Alcohol Addiction

We have learned several significant facts about the narcotic drug heroin in this chapter. Heroin is an endor-

nucleus accumbens (NA) Structure in the tegmentostriatal reinforcement system containing dopamine and opiate receptors; the NA produces pleasurable feelings.

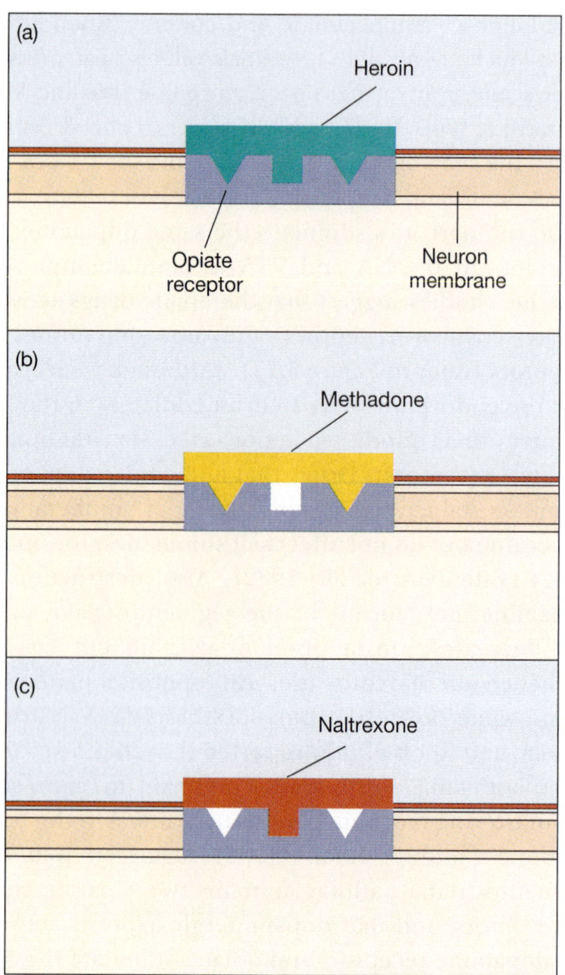

Figure 5.18 The effects of heroin, methadone, and naltrexone on opiate receptors. (a) Attachment of heroin to opiate receptors. (b) Methadone also binds to the opiate receptors, but not as closely, and (c) naltrexone attaches to opiate receptors less strongly.

➤ *How does naltrexone prevent heroin from producing pleasurable effects? (p. 157)*

phin agonist, binding to opiate receptors and mimicking the effects of naturally occurring endorphins (see **Figure 5.18**). Heroin also produces feelings of pleasure by activating the tegmentostriatal pathway. Repeated use of heroin leads to physical and psychological dependence; the addiction produced by heroin use can have devastating consequences.

Can the heroin addict overcome his or her dependence? Until recently, it was generally assumed that the answer was a sorrowful "no." Now, heroin addiction can in many cases be treated with a combination of intense psychological counseling and administration of a drug called methadone (Julien, 1998).

Methadone is an endorphin agonist that, like heroin, binds to opiate receptor sites (see **Figure 5.18**). In fact, **methadone** is a narcotic drug with pleasurable effects similar to heroin. However, unlike heroin, methadone can be taken in pill form (the digestive tract breaks down heroin and little enters the bloodstream). Taken as a pill, the effects of methadone develop gradually over several hours. The individual taking methadone in this form does not experience the reinforcing "rush" associated with intravenous injection of heroin and other opiates. Methadone administration alleviates the craving for heroin and prevents the withdrawal symptoms that otherwise would result from not taking heroin.

The user of methadone thus actually substitutes a less powerful narcotic for heroin. The aim of methadone treatment is to stop the addict from taking heroin and, after the addict has avoided heroin use for some time, to decrease the dosage of methadone over a period of several weeks. The withdrawal symptoms that result from this gradual weaning from methadone are less severe than those that result from discontinuing the use of heroin. Weaning an addict off of heroin through the use of methadone also is thought to be safer physiologically than simply stopping heroin use "cold turkey."

Early studies evaluating the success of methadone programs suggested that heroin addicts receiving methadone did stop taking heroin (Schlaadt & Shannon, 1990) and eventually stopped using methadone. The incidence of criminal activity also diminished. However, more recent research suggests that these early evaluations were unreasonably optimistic. It has proven difficult to get many heroin addicts to seek treatment. Also, individuals who receive methadone treatment often switch from heroin to other drugs, such as alcohol, barbiturates, cocaine, or amphetamine. Further, methadone has itself become an illicit street drug. Methadone use on the street has had the same harmful consequences as heroin use. However, methadone treatment should not be abandoned. According to Schlaadt and Shannon (1990), methadone can help rehabilitate an addict if combined with "a large and dedicated staff, adequate facilities, sufficient funding, various diversified therapy programs (group and individual), educational-improvement opportunities, vocational training and job-placement services, and health care."

methadone A narcotic drug that binds to opiate receptor sites, alleviates the craving for heroin, and prevents the withdrawal symptoms that otherwise would result from not taking heroin.

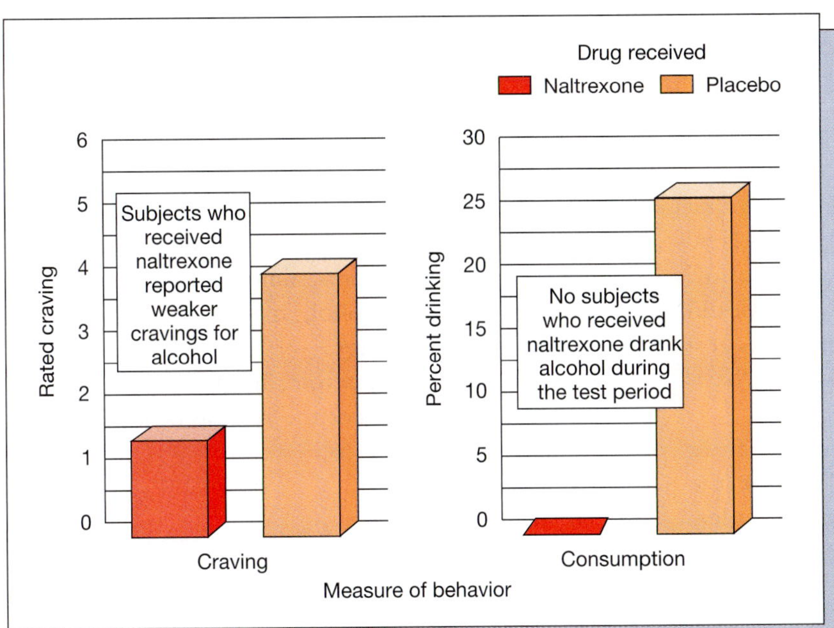

Figure 5.19 The effects of naltrexone on alcohol craving and consumption. Administration of naltrexone to individuals with a history of alcohol abuse reduced the craving for alcohol and stopped its consumption.

➤ *Why does naltrexone reduce the craving for alcohol? (p. 157)*

Some of the difficulty with methadone treatment is that although the effects of methadone are less intense than those of heroin, it is nevertheless an addictive drug. An alternative to methadone treatment may be the use of opiate antagonists like **naltrexone**. As seen in **Figure 5.18**, naltrexone binds to the same opiate receptor sites as heroin and methadone and blocks the action of heroin and other opiates, preventing the experience of the pleasurable aspects of heroin use. Without the rush and high from heroin use, it is believed that drug craving will decline, along with the destructive behaviors associated with drug use. As one might expect, Gerra, Marato, and Caccacari (1995) found that naltrexone reduces the cravings for heroin and other opiates.

Naltrexone also blocks a craving for alcohol in alcoholics (Volpicelli et al., 1990). Volpicelli and his colleagues gave two groups of subjects who abused alcohol either naltrexone or a placebo for 12 weeks. **Figure 5.19** shows that the subjects receiving naltrexone reported weaker cravings for alcohol than did subjects receiving a placebo. Further, the level of alcohol consumption was significantly lower in the naltrexone treatment group than in the control group. O'Malley, Jaffe, Chang, and Scottenfeld (1996) also reported a weaker craving for alcohol and reduced consumption of alcohol during naltrexone treatment.

Why does naltrexone act to reduce craving and decrease alcohol use? As we learned earlier, alcohol, like the opiates, is an opiate agonist that increases the stimulation of endorphin receptors. The pleasurable effects of alcohol are probably the result of this stimulating action on the opiate receptors in the brain's reinforcement system. By blocking alcohol's effect on this system, naltrexone reduces the craving for and consumption of alcohol. ■

Section Review

- The mesotelencephalic system mediates the influence of reinforcement on behavior.
- The mesotelencephalic system includes the tegmentostriatal pathway, which governs motivational properties of reinforcers, and the nigrostriatal pathway, which governs memory consolidation.
- The pleasurable effects of both amphetamine and cocaine result from the activation of dopaminergic receptors in the tegmentostriatal pathway.
- The pleasurable effects of opiate agonists such as heroin and morphine result from stimulation of opiate receptors in the tegmentostriatal pathway.
- Opiate agonists and dopamine agonists activate different receptors in the tegmentostriatal pathway, with the same end result: activation of the nucleus accumbens.
- Methadone and naltrexone are two drugs used to treat heroin addiction. Naltrexone has also been shown to be effective in treating alcoholism.

naltrexone An opiate antagonist that binds to opiate receptor sites and blocks the action of heroin and other opiates.

Chapter Review

Critical Thinking Questions

1. Neal enjoys a few beers after work. He claims that it calms him after a hard day at the office. Is Neal correct about the calming effect of alcohol? Describe the physiological action of alcohol. Could Neal substitute another drug for alcohol? Suggest several possible alternatives and explain the basis of your suggestions.
2. As we saw earlier in the chapter, Evelyn finds cocaine to be extremely pleasurable. Describe the neural system that allows Evelyn to experience pleasure from cocaine. Indicate why cocaine is such a powerful reinforcer.
3. Discuss why heroin is such a powerful reinforcer. Are the brain structures that produce the reinforcing effects of heroin the same as or different from cocaine? Give a possible explanation for the common or differing effects of these two drugs based on what you have learned about their mechanisms of action and their mechanisms of reinforcement.

Vocabulary Questions

1. A person who has developed ________________ will require ever-larger amounts of a drug to feel the same effect.
2. Chemicals that change the way a person thinks, feels, perceives, or behaves are ________________.
3. Drugs that impair synaptic transmission of a specific neurotransmitter are referred to as ________________.
4. Drugs that both reduce pain and induce sleep are ________________.
5. Drugs that act on the central nervous system to slow down mental and physical functioning are ________________.
6. ________________ are used to prevent sleep or suppress appetite.
7. A drug obtained from cactus tips used in Native American Indian religious ceremonies is ________________.
8. The part of the brain that mediates the effect of deprivation on brain stimulation is the ____________.
9. The part of the brain that mediates the influence of reinforcement on brain stimulation is the ________________.

Review Questions

1. The four main types of psychoactive drugs are
   a. heroin, speed, alcohol, and cocaine.
   b. narcotics, depressants, stimulants, and psychedelics.
   c. barbiturates, alcohol, major tranquilizers, and minor tranquilizers.
   d. LSD, marijuana, peyote, and PCP.
2. A drug that enhances the release of a neurotransmitter is referred to as
   a. an antagonist.
   b. an agonist.
   c. a synapse.
   d. a hallucinogen.
3. One way that a drug can have an antagonistic effect is by
   a. increasing neurotransmitter release.
   b. blocking neurotransmitter degradation.
   c. producing the same effect on the postsynaptic membrane as the neurotransmitter.
   d. preventing the neurotransmitter from binding to the receptor sites.
4. Morphine is an example of a
   a. semisynthetic narcotic.
   b. narcotic of natural origin.
   c. hallucinogen.
   d. central nervous system depressant.
5. At low doses, depressants act to
   a. produce drowsiness.
   b. relieve pain.
   c. reduce tension.
   d. create hallucinations.
6. What blood alcohol level is considered to constitute legal intoxication in most states?
   a. .01 percent
   b. .05 percent
   c. .10 percent
   d. .40 percent
7. The effect of high doses of sedative-hypnotic drugs is to
   a. reduce pain.
   b. induce sleep.
   c. relieve tension.
   d. suppress appetite.
8. Alcohol, antianxiety drugs, and barbiturates work by attaching to receptor sites on
   a. dopamine neuron.
   b. acetylcholine neuron.
   c. GABA neurons.
   d. serotonin neuron.

9. Which drug has few or no medical uses?
   a. morphine
   b. codeine
   c. Valium
   d. LSD

10. Amphetamine acts by increasing the release of
   a. glutamate.
   b. acetylcholine.
   c. norepinephrine and dopamine.
   d. GABA and glycine.

11. Intense withdrawal symptoms from stimulants include
   a. wakefulness and appetite suppression.
   b. prolonged sleeping and depression.
   c. hallucinations.
   d. increased alertness.

12. Cocaine causes an increased level of dopamine in the
   a. hippocampus.
   b. nucleus accumbens.
   c. pons.
   d. ventral tegmental area.

13. Naltrexone blocks the craving for
   a. amphetamine.
   b. caffeine.
   c. cocaine.
   d. alcohol.

Suggested Readings

JULIEN, R. M. (1998). *A primer of drug action* (8th ed.). New York: Freeman.

OLDS, J., & MILNER, P. M. (1954). Positive reinforcement produced by electrical stimulation of septal area and other regions of rat brain. *Journal of Comparative and Physiological Psychology, 47,* 419–427.

VACCARINO, F. J., SCHIFF, B., & GLICKMAN, S. E. (1989). Biological view of reinforcement. In S. B. Klein & R. R. Mowrer (Eds.), *Contemporary learning theories: Instrumental conditioning theory and the impact of biological constraints on learning* (pp. 111–142). Hillsdale, NJ: Erlbaum.

WISE, R. A. (1996). Addictive drugs and brain stimulation reward. *Annual Review of Neuroscience, 19,* 319–340.

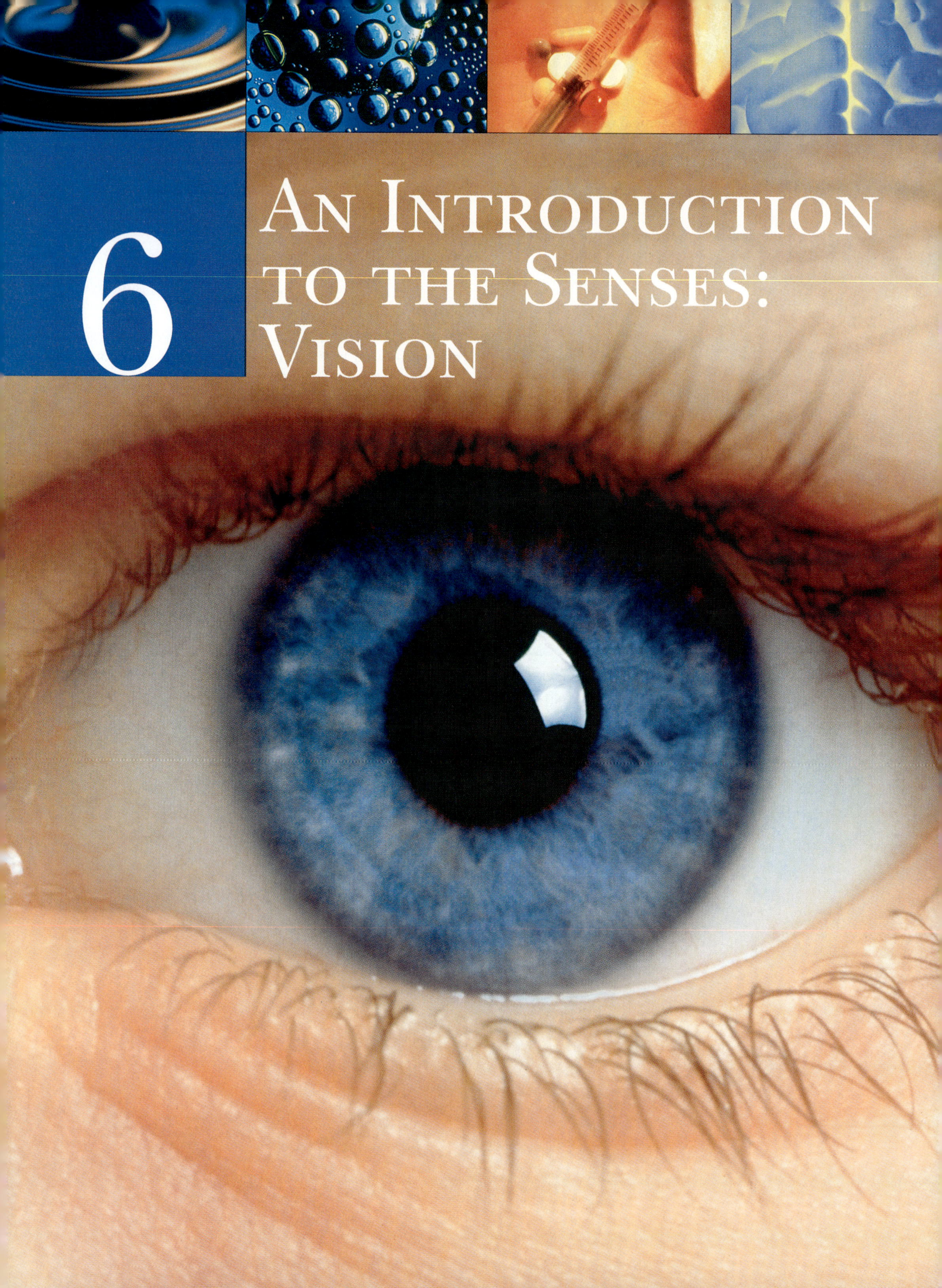

6 An Introduction to the Senses: Vision

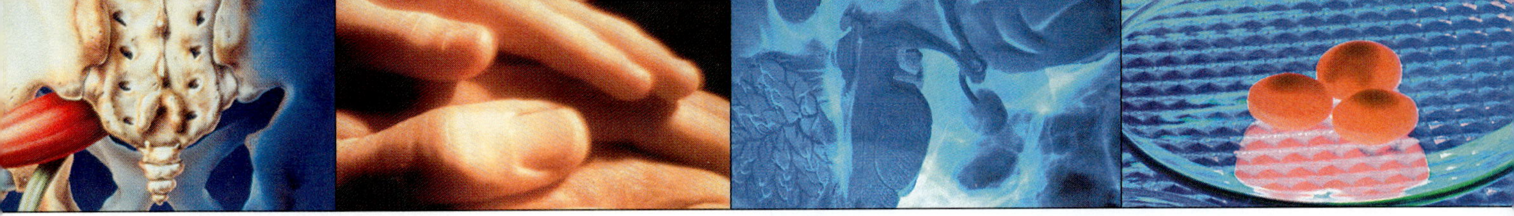

A Loss of Vision

Reading is one of Alan's greatest joys. He reads several books a week. Mysteries, spy novels, and legal thrillers are among his favorites. He was halfway through John Grisham's *The Testament* when he noticed that his vision seemed blurry. When Alan called for an appointment with the ophthalmologist, the receptionist said that the next available appointment was in three weeks.

During this time, Alan's vision grew worse. By the time he saw the doctor, Alan could not recognize anything further than a few feet away and he was becoming quite concerned. He could not read his beloved books, watch the evening news, drive, or even shave properly. When the doctor examined his eyes, she noticed a buildup of fluid behind his eyes that was causing his visual problems.

His family history pointed to diabetes as the cause of this fluid accumulation. The ophthalmologist told Alan that when blood sugar levels rise, as in diabetics, fluid accumulates behind the cornea of the eye, causing blurred vision. She suggested that he make an appointment with his family doctor to have his blood sugar levels checked. She stressed that if his blood sugar was high, treatment for diabetes would need to be started immediately, or Alan would be at risk for developing glaucoma, an excessive accumulation of fluid that can lead to blindness. She reassured him that proper treatment of diabetes can lower blood sugar levels and return vision to normal. The ophthalmologist told Alan that she would confer with his family doctor after he had been tested. Alan called his family doctor right from the eye doctor's office and left relieved to know that his vision problems could be treated but still somewhat anxious to get his vision back so that his life could return to normal. ■

◀ The human retina contains about 120 million rods and 6 million cones.

Before You Begin

How does the visual system recognize the letters and words in the books that Alan reads?

What is the nature of the fluid of the eye, and why should a fluid buildup cause blurred vision?

In this chapter, we will help you answer these and the following questions:

- What path does light take through the visual system?
- What is light, and how is it converted into a neural signal?
- Where in the visual system is light converted into a neural signal?
- Which photoreceptors enable Alan to read? To see his dog in the backyard at night?
- What processes make it possible to visually recognize objects?
- How do we perceive our world in three dimensions?
- What is the neurological basis of color vision?

The Detection of Environmental Events

Alan's concern about the possible loss of his vision reflects the importance of the visual sense. Try to imagine what it would be like to lose your vision—you could never see another sunrise or drive down the open highway, and you would have to learn to read this book using your fingers. Several years ago, I traveled to Lake Tahoe. The view of the crystal clear blue lake surrounded by white snow-capped mountains was breathtaking. If my visual sense had been impaired, I would still have been able to feel the cool breeze and smell the wildflowers, but not see the reflection of the mountains in the waters on the lake or the eagle in flight above. In this chapter, we will discuss how the visual system enables us to perceive these beautiful aspects of our environment, as well as those that are more routine or definitely not beautiful.

Is the sky blue? Is the song loud? Is the ball smooth? Is the orange sweet? The function of our senses is to answer these and many other questions about environmental events.

Webster's Dictionary (Webster's New Dictionary, 1995) defines a **sense** as "the ability of the nerves and the brain to receive and react to stimuli, as light, sound, impact, constriction, etc; specifically, any of the five faculties of receiving impressions through specific bodily organs and the nerves associated with them (sight, touch, taste, smell, and hearing)." Thus, the senses allow the nervous system to connect us with the outside world. We are able to detect the presence of significant events in our physical environment and then decide whether or not (and how) to respond to them. We will first discuss the general process by which sensory receptors detect environmental stimuli and communicate these data to other parts of the nervous system. Later in this chapter, we will examine how the visual system detects light and processes visual information. Chapter 7 describes the auditory sense (hearing), the vestibular sense (balance), the somatosenses (touch, temperature, pain), the olfactory sense (smell), and the gustatory sense (taste).

In Chapter 4, we learned that neurotransmitters released into the synaptic cleft can bind to the receptor sites of the postsynaptic membrane and produce a localized depolarization of the postsynaptic membrane (an EPSP). If the combined level of depolarization of the EPSPs reaches threshold, an action potential will be generated. This action potential reflects an affirmative response of the postsynaptic neuron to the question of whether the sky is blue or the song is loud.

But how does this process begin? How does "blue" or "loud" translate into a neural impulse that can be communicated to the postsynaptic neuron? The process by which a specific type of neuron, the sensory receptor, responds to such environmental events is one focus of this chapter and the next. We will also discuss how sensory receptors communicate their message to other neurons.

Although the type of information detected by sensory receptors differs, all sensory receptors perform three basic functions. First, sensory receptors must absorb physical energy from the environment. As we shall see shortly, the particular kind of physical energy that is absorbed is different for each type of sensory receptor—the sensory receptors in the visual system absorb light energy from which they detect blue, and the sensory receptors in the auditory system absorb energy from moving air molecules beating against the ear drum which enables you to hear sounds.

After a sensory receptor absorbs the energy from an environmental stimulus, it must then convert that energy into a neural impulse. This process of the **transduction**, which is the conversion of physical energy into a neural impulse, differs for different sensory systems. Some sensory receptors follow the all-or-none law; that is, the sensory receptor will fire and a neural impulse will be generated only if the level of depolarization is sufficient to reach

sense The ability of the nervous system to receive and react to environmental stimuli.

transduction The process of converting physical energy into a neural impulse.

theshold. Other sensory receptors do not respond according to the all-or-none law. For these sensory receptors, the level of response is determined by the intensity of the stimulation; that is, the greater the intensity of stimulation, the higher the level of receptor response. In this chapter, our discussion will focus on how light is transduced into a neural message in the visual system; the next chapter will describe the processes for other sensory systems.

The sensory receptors generate a specific pattern of neural activity, a process referred to as **coding**. Coding allows the nervous system to construct a representation of the physical world; that is, the coded message contains information about stimuli in the physical environment.

How does the brain recognize that a certain neural impulse from the visual receptors means that the sky is blue, or that a certain neural impulse from the auditory receptors means that a sound is loud? Recall from Chapter 1 our discussion of Muller's doctrine of specific nerve energies, which states that the particular event that is detected by the brain depends on which nerve carries the message. One reason that the brain recognizes the different meanings of different neural impulses is that different messages are carried by different neurons; that is, certain neurons transmit messages about things that are blue, whereas other neurons transmit messages about things that are loud. Sensory receptors transmit specific information about the environment through different neural connections to different parts of the cerebral cortex for analysis and decision making.

We can also detect differences in stimuli within a particular sensory system. For example, our visual system can detect that a car is either maroon or purple. Similarly, the gustatory system can detect that a food is sweet or bitter.

The differences between maroon and purple and between sweet and bitter are detected via two very different types of coding.

In **labeled-line coding**, different receptors within a sensory system react to different stimulation. This type of coding takes place in the gustatory system. Separate taste receptors detect sweet and bitter. If a food is bitter, certain taste receptors are activated and transmit an action potential to the cerebral cortex; the cerebral cortex recognizes that the food is bitter because of the activity in the particular cortical neurons that are activated only by bitter foods.

Although different tastes activate different neurons, we do not have different sensory receptors for every color. Instead, the cerebral cortex recognizes a particular pattern of responses from a number of visual receptors to determine whether a color is orange or purple. The process that allows us to distinguish colors such as orange and purple is referred to as **across-fiber pattern coding**.

Our discussion to this point suggests that labeled-line coding is used by the gustatory system and across-fiber pattern coding is used by the visual system. Pretty straightforward, you say? The process of coding sensory information is of course more complex than this. The gustatory system uses across-fiber pattern coding when two types of flavors are combined; the taste of bittersweet candy, for example, is produced by across-fiber coding. Labeled-line coding is used in the visual system when a primary color, such as blue, activates a single type of visual sensory receptor. The rest of this chapter will deal with how the visual sensory system receives and interprets the physical energy of light; the auditory, vestibular, somatosenses, olfactory, and gustatory sensory systems will be discussed in Chapter 7.

Before You Go On

What type of physical energy is absorbed by the sensory receptors of the visual system to allow Allan to read his beloved books?

What type of coding is used in the visual perception of a bouquet of red roses? (Hint: Remember the green leaves!)

Section Review

- A sense is the ability of the nervous system to detect a specific set of stimuli.
- The function of a sense is to absorb a specific physical energy from the environment by means of a sensory receptor.
- Each sensory system absorbs a different type of physical energy and then transduces that energy into a neural impulse.
- Coding is the generation of a specific pattern of neural activity by a sensory receptor.
- In labeled-line coding, different receptors within a sensory system react to different stimuli.
- In across-fiber pattern coding, a particular pattern of neural activity is produced by each kind of stimulus.

coding A specific pattern of neural activity that contains information about stimuli in the physical environment.

labeled-line coding Type of coding in which information about the stimulus is determined by the nerve carrying that message.

across-fiber pattern coding Type of coding in which information about a stimulus is determined by the pattern of neural impulses carried by two or more neurons.

The Visual Sense: Structure

The physical energy to which visual receptors respond is light, which is a form of electromagnetic radiation. Other parts of the electromagnetic spectrum include television and radio broadcast bands, infrared rays, ultraviolet rays, radar, x-rays, and gamma radiation. We will return to the physical characteristics of light shortly. To understand how the eye detects light, we must first understand its structure.

The Eyes

For us to see a stimulus, it must be detected by the receptor cells that are located at the back of the eyes. These receptor cells, called **photoreceptors** (photo = light), transmit information about the detected stimulus to the primary visual cortex, located in the occipital lobe of the cerebral cortex.

Figure 6.1 presents a cross-sectional view of one eye and the path of light. Light passes through the **cornea**, the transparent outer layer of the eye, and then through the clear fluid, similar to blood plasma, of the **aqueous humor** contained in the anterior chamber of the eye. Behind the aqueous fluid is the **iris**, which consists of bands of muscles covered by the colored portion of the eye (blue, green, brown). Light passes through an opening in the iris called the **pupil**. In bright light the muscles of the iris cause the pupil to constrict (decrease in size), limiting the amount of light allowed into the eye. The pupil dilates (becomes larger) when the light is dim, allowing more light to enter the eye.

After passing through the pupil, light reaches the **lens**. The lens consists of a series of transparent, onion-like layers of tissue. The shape of the lens, which changes to focus particular images, is controlled by the contraction of the **ciliary muscles** pulling on the suspensory ligaments. The lens becomes more convex (rounded) to focus on nearby objects and less convex (flattened) to focus on objects that are distant. The

---

photoreceptors The receptors located at the rear of the eye that transduce light into a neural impulse.

cornea Transparent outer layer of the eye.

aqueous humor A clear fluid, similar to blood plasma, that fills the anterior cavity of the eye.

iris Bands of muscles covered by the colored portion of the eye.

pupil Opening in the iris through which light passes.

lens A series of transparent, onion-like layers of tissue that change shape to focus images.

ciliary muscles The muscles that control the shape of the lens.

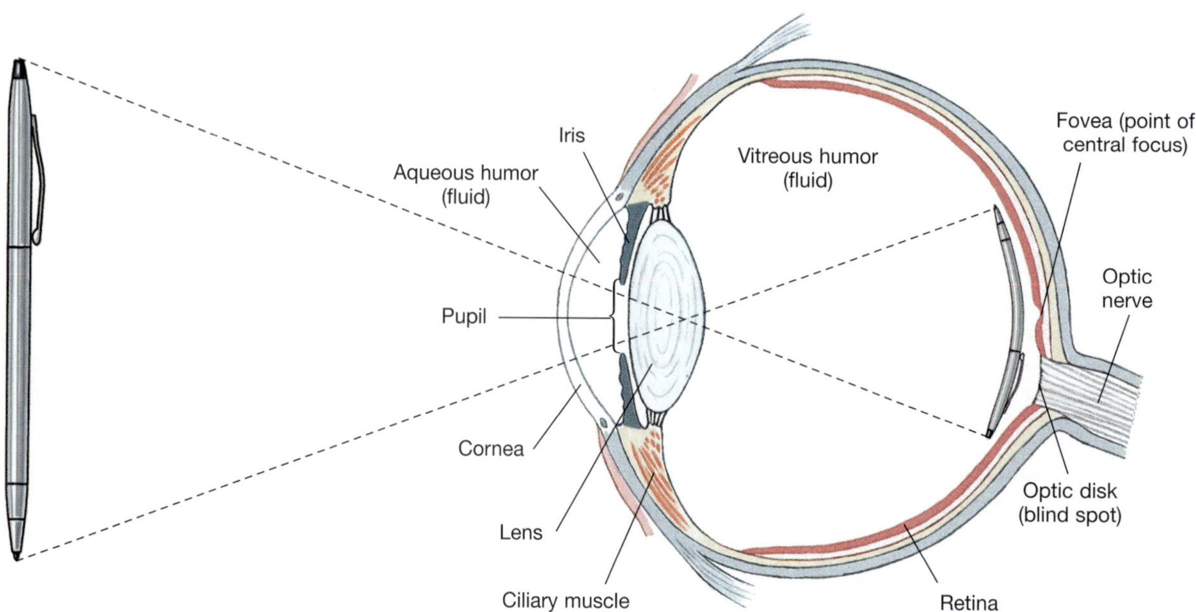

Figure 6.1 A cross-sectional view of the human eye. This illustration shows the projection of the image of the pen onto the retina at the back of the eye.

➤ *At what point is the image turned right side up? (p. 165)*

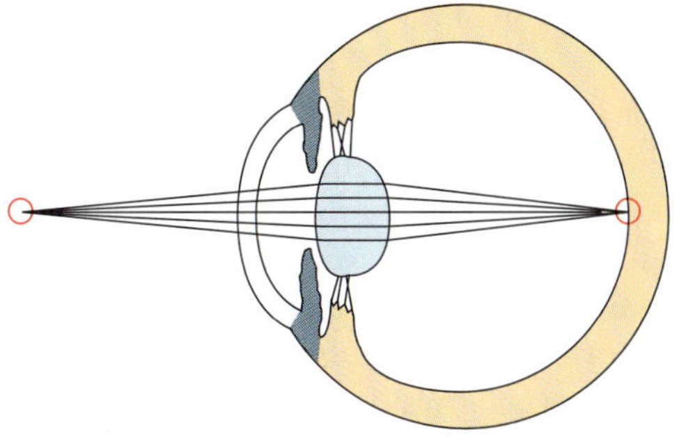

(a) Ciliary muscle contracted, lens rounded for close vision

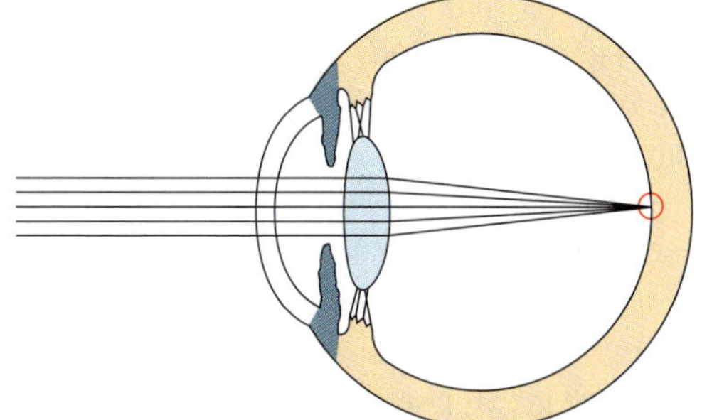

(b) Ciliary muscle relaxed, lens flattened for distant vision

Figure 6.2 Accommodation. The lens becomes more convex (rounded) when focusing on a close object and becomes less convex (flattened) when focusing on a distant object.

➤ *Where does the light go after it passes through the lens? (p. 164–165)*

change of the shape of the lens to focus on particular images is called **accommodation** (see **Figure 6.2**). After passing through the lens and a clear, jelly-like fluid, here called **vitreous humor**, light reaches the **retina**, the interior lining at the back of the eye.

The image focused on the retina is not exactly like the stimulus that exists in the environment. First, the focused image is upside down (refer to **Figure 6.1**). Second, the focused image is reversed; that is, the right side of the image is focused on the left part of the retina, and the left side of the image is focused on the right part of the retina. This upside-down, backwards image is encoded by the nervous system as neural activity and is sent to the cerebral cortex where it is transformed so that it is right side up and in the correct position in the visual field.

Before You Go On

Describe the path of light through the eye from the cornea to the retina.

The Retina

The recognition of a visual stimulus begins in the retina of the eye. The retina is composed of three layers of neurons: the aforementioned photoreceptors, the **bipolar cells**, and the **ganglion cells** (see **Figure 6.3**). The focused light passes through the transparent layers of ganglion and bipolar cells before reaching the photoreceptors.

The photoreceptors are the cells of the nervous system that detect light stimulation. There are two types of photoreceptors: **rods** and **cones** (refer to **Figure 6.3**). The human retina contains approximately 120 million rods and 6 million cones. The cones are most concentrated in the central region of the retina, called the **fovea** (see **Figure 6.1**), whereas the rods are most concentrated at the periphery of the retina.

Perhaps you have noticed that you can see the features of an object more clearly in the daytime than at night; that is, visual acuity is greater in the daytime than at night. The reason for this difference is that cones, which are able to detect small features in visual stimuli, operate more effectively in bright light. Rods are more sensitive to light than cones and are able to detect visual stimuli even in dim lighting conditions, but less able than cones to detect small features of visual stimuli.

But what makes cones better able to detect small features and rods better adapted to night vision? The answer lies in the relative number of receptor cells that

accommodation The change of the shape of the lens to focus a particular image.

vitreous humor A clear, jelly-like fluid that fills the posterior cavity of the eye.

retina The interior lining at the back of the eye comprised of three layers of neurons.

bipolar cells Neurons that form the middle layer of the retina.

ganglion cells Neurons that form the outermost layer of the retina.

rod Type of photoreceptor concentrated at the periphery of the retina that is responsible for night vision.

cone Type of photoreceptor concentrated in the central region of the retina that is responsible for the acuity of daytime vision.

fovea The central region of the retina where a light stimulus is focused.

synapse with a particular ganglion cell, called convergence (see **Figure 6.4**). Only a few cones synapse with a particular ganglion cell, allowing the brain to better detect the input from each cone. Recall that the cones are concentrated in the central region of the retina; the visual acuity is thus greater for objects in the center of the field of vision. The greater number of rods converging on ganglion cells reduces the detected detail of objects, but the greater sensitivity of the rods allows the detection of objects at night. The fact that rods are more concentrated in the periphery of the retina means that we are better able to detect dimly lit stimuli in the periphery of the visual field.

Not all animals have the same arrangement of rods and cones in the fovea as humans. For example, many bird species have two foveas in each eye (Wallman & Petigrew, 1985). In these bird species, one fovea is pointed forward and the other pointed to the side. This anatomy allows the bird to see clear images in the periphery as well as toward the front. Predatory bird species, such as hawks, have more densely concentrated visual receptors in the top of their retinas than in the bottom (Waldvogel, 1990). This arrangement allows predatory birds to see fine detail when looking down and thus to detect their prey more easily. (Confused? Remember that images are represented upside down on the retina, so the top of the retina detects the lower portion of visual field.)

Bipolar and ganglion cells are not merely conduits for neural messages about light stimuli between the photoreceptors and the primary visual cortex. Although most of the analysis of light stimuli occurs in the cerebral cortex, the initial processing begins in the retina. For example, the detection of the edges of objects that is crucial for the separation of a figure from its background occurs in the retina. We will have more to say about the important role that bipolar and ganglion cells play in the analysis of light stimuli throughout this chapter.

Before You Go On

Why are rods better adapted to night vision?

Why are cones better able to detect small details?

Pathways to the Primary Visual Cortex

The photoreceptors transduce light into a neural message that is passed on to the ganglion cells. But how does the neural message get to the cerebral cortex for analysis? The axons from the ganglion cells

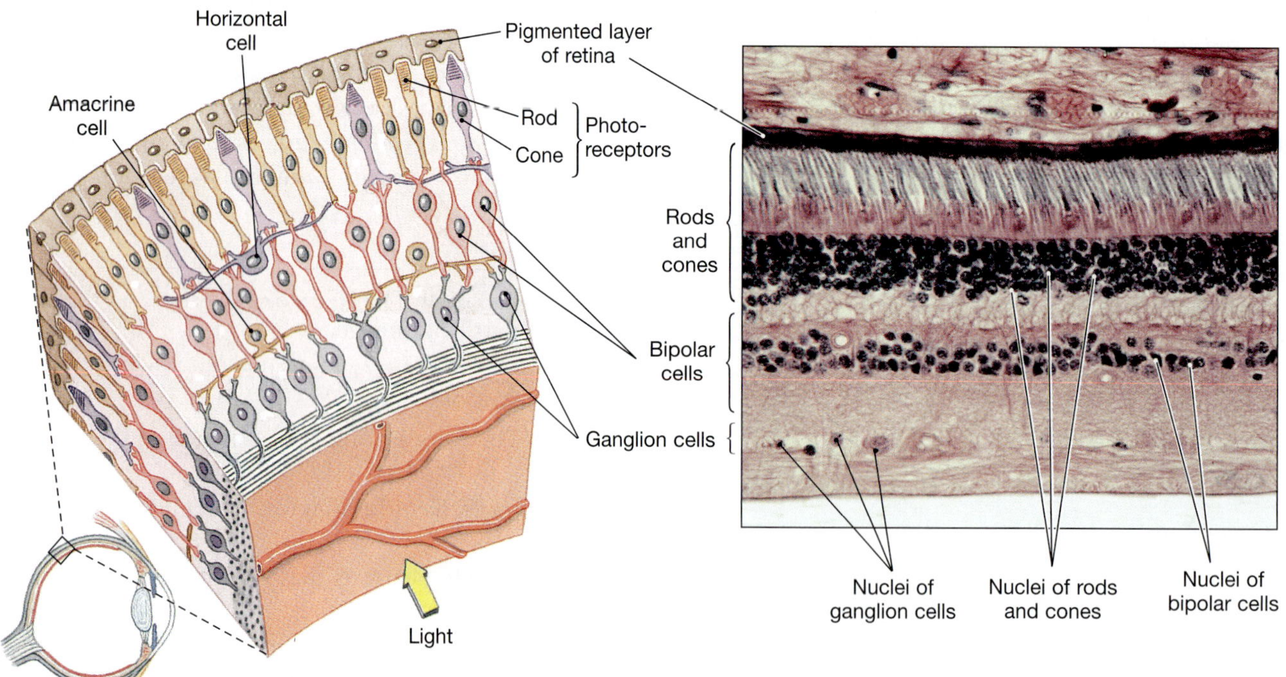

Figure 6.3 Cellular organization of the retina. Light passes through ganglion and bipolar cells before reaching photoreceptors (rods and cones) at the back of the eye.

➤ *What type of cell detects a light stimulus? (p. 165)*

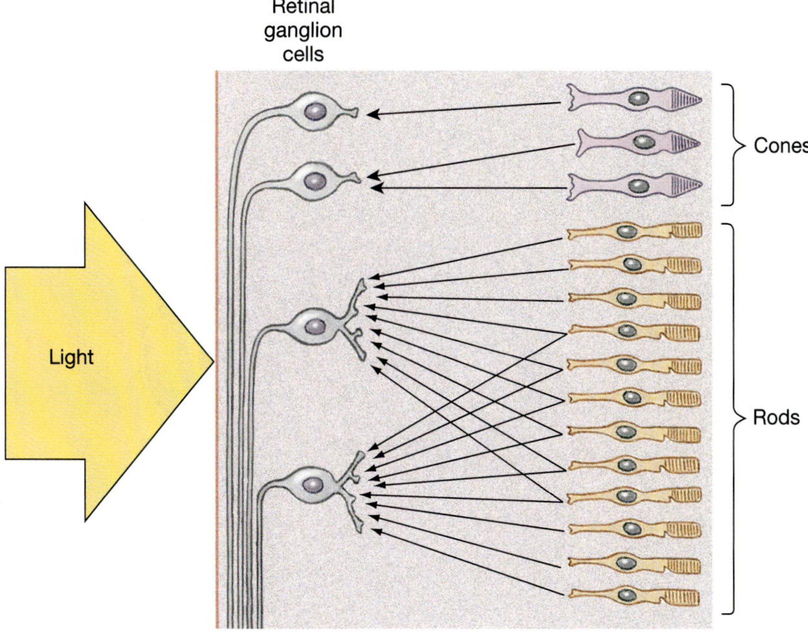

Figure 6.4 Convergence of cones and rods onto ganglion cells. Notice that there is less convergence of cones than of rods onto a ganglion cell, which leads to greater acuity of vision mediated by cones than rods.

➤ *Are the rods and cones part of the peripheral nervous system or the central nervous system? (p. 165–166)*

come together at the **optic disk**, the blind spot at the back of the eye. The arteries enter and the veins exit the eye at this point. The **blind spot** is approximately 16 mm to the lateral side of the fovea or fixation point (refer to **Figure 6.1**). An object focused only on this area of the eye would not be seen. However, because objects are focused on large parts of the retina, we are not aware of our blind spot. Although our visual system fills in the gap created by the blind spot, an isolated stimulus such as a cross will disappear in the blind spot. **Figure 6.5** presents a vivid demonstration of the blind spot.

Figure 6.5 Blind spot. To demonstrate the existence of the blind spot, you should close your right eye and keep the cross in the center of your left eye's visual field. Start by having the page a few inches from your left eye. Slowly move your book away from you. The image of the cross will disappear when it is focused on your blind spot.

➤ *Why do we have a blind spot? (p. 166–167)*

Although ganglion cells differ in their distance from the optic disk, the neural messages about a particular visual stimulus coming from all the ganglion cells are conveyed to higher neural structures at the same time. This synchrony of input allows us to see an entire visual stimulus as a complete whole, rather than as separate stimuli. Synchrony of input is made possible because of differential propagation of neural impulses along the ganglion axon; the further a ganglion cell is from the optic disk, the faster an action potential is propagated along its axon (Stanford, 1987).

After leaving the optic disk, the ganglion cells form one **optic nerve** from each eye, for a total of two (in most animals that I know of, with the exception of the mythical cyclops who would have only one). The two optic nerves meet at the **optic chiasm**. In some vertebrates, such as amphibians and reptiles, all of the fibers in each optic nerve cross over to the opposite side of the brain at the optic chiasm (see **Figure 6.6a**). (Recall from Chapter 2 that the cerebral cortex is divided into two hemispheres.) This arrangement means that each hemisphere has a totally different view of the world with the coordination of vision requiring communication

optic disk The point at the back of the eye where the axons from the ganglion cells come together.

blind spot Lack of photoreceptors at optic disk creates a place on retina where object cannot be seen.

optic nerves The two nerves formed by the axons of ganglion after leaving the optic disk.

optic chiasm The place where the two optic nerves meet.

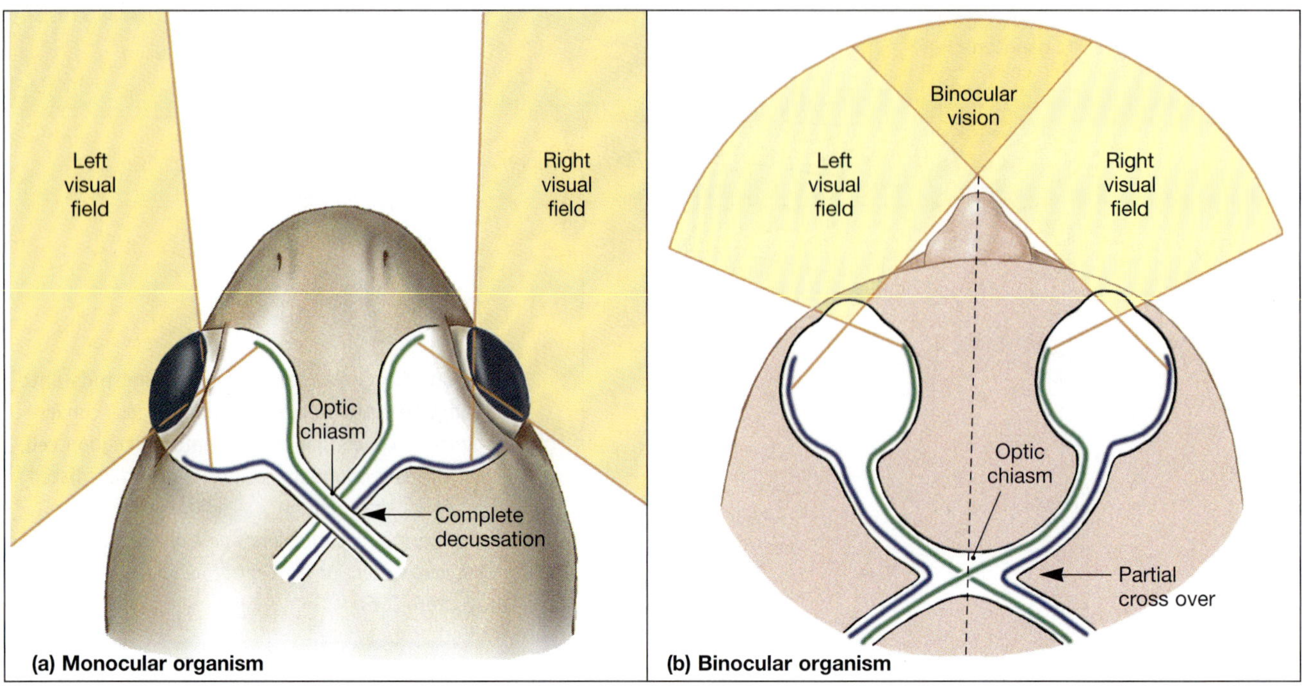

Figure 6.6 Visual fields. The visual fields of a monocular animal (a) and a binocular animal (b).

➤ *How does the view of the world differ in a monocular and binocular animal? (p. 167–168)*

between hemispheres through the cerebral commissures. Such organisms are said to have monocular vision. In most mammals, some fibers cross over to the opposite side of the brain, whereas others project to the same side of the brain. **Figure 6.6b** shows the visual pathways to the primary visual cortex in binocular organisms. As seen in this figure, the optic nerve fibers that originate in the nasal half (closest to the nose) of each retina cross over to the contralateral side of the brain (contra = against), whereas the optic nerve fibers that originate in the lateral half of each retina stay on the ipsilateral side of the brain (ipsi = same). This arrangement means that input from the right visual field is transmitted to the left hemisphere and from the left visual field to the right hemisphere. Unlike the monocular organism, there is some overlap of the visual field seen by both hemispheres. We will learn later in the chapter that the organization found in a binocular organism provides additional information about depth.

The **optic tracts**, or second cranial nerves, are formed by the fibers leaving the optic chiasm. Most (approximately 80 percent) of these fibers project to the **lateral geniculate nucleus** of the thalamus (see **Figure 6.7**). The term *genu* means "bent" and refers to the bent knee appearance of this area. Each lateral geniculate nucleus is composed of six layers. Adjacent areas of the retina activate adjacent regions of the lateral geniculate nucleus. This organization of the lateral geniculate nucleus allows the form of the visual stimulus to remain intact as it is processed by the visual system (so that we can see the pen in **Figure 6.1** instead of a mishmash of colors and lines).

The nerve fibers that reach the lateral geniculate nucleus are composed of the axons of the retinal ganglion cells. Thus, the first synapse in the visual analysis of information within the central nervous system occurs at the level of the thalamus. The nerve fibers that leave the lateral geniculate nucleus project to the primary visual cortex (Area V1) in the occipital lobe of the cerebral cortex (refer to **Figure 6.7**). The primary visual cortex is also called the striate cortex because of its striped appearance in a cross-sectional view. Like the lateral geniculate nucleus, the primary visual cortex is organized spatially like a map of the retina, so that the pen remains intact from the beginning to the end of its journey through the visual system.

Recall our discussion of the convergence of rods and cones on ganglion cells. We learned that there is less convergence of cones—which are more concentrated at

optic tracts The fiber tracts, or second cranial nerves, that are formed by the axons of the ganglion cells leaving the optic chiasm.

lateral geniculate nucleus The neurons of the thalamus that receive neural impulses via synapses from the axons of the ganglion cells of the retina.

the fovea—than of rods—which are more concentrated at the periphery. This causes a disproportionately greater representation of the fovea than of other retinal areas in the primary visual cortex. Approximately 25 percent of the primary visual cortex receives input from the fovea even though the fovea is only a small part of the retina. The greater representation of the fovea is one reason why details of objects seen in the daylight are so much clearer than details of objects seen at night.

Where do the 20 percent of fibers of the mammalian optic tract that do not project to the lateral geniculate nucleus go? Many of these fibers go to a structure in the tectum of the midbrain called the superior colliculus. The superior colliculus projects to parts of the parietal and temporal lobes and is responsible for attention to visual stimuli and coordination of eye movements. Other projections of the optic tract go to the ventral lateral geniculus nucleus of the thalamus, which sends messages to other subcortical areas; the accessory optic nuclei of the midbrain, which influence saccadic (side to side) eye movements; the suprachiasmatic nucleus of the hypothalamus, which regulates circadian rhythms; and the pretectum area of the midbrain, which influences the size of the pupil.

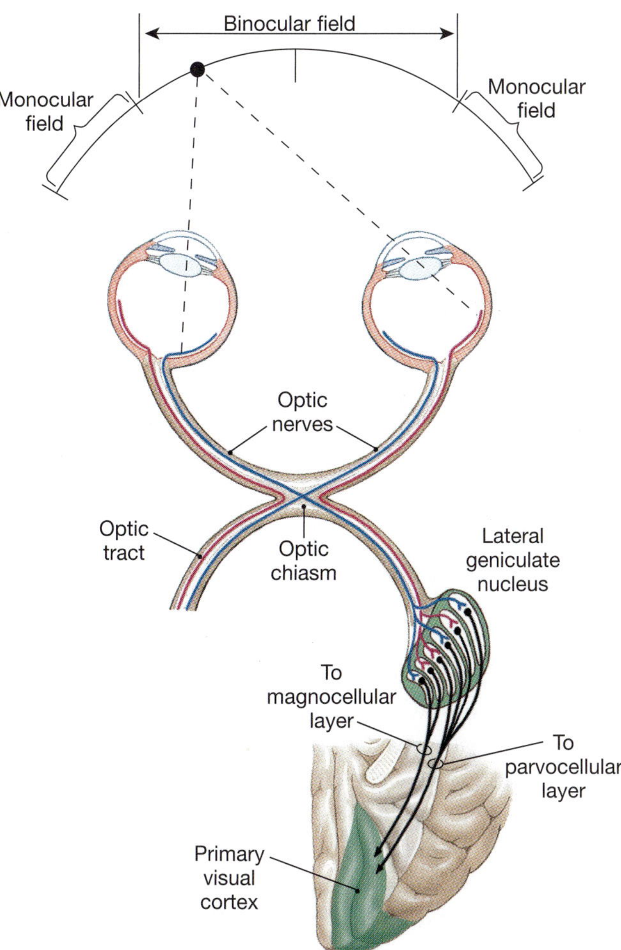

Figure 6.7 Visual pathways. Visual pathways to the primary visual cortex.

➤ *Where does the first synapse in the visual portion of the central nervous system occur? (p. 168–169)*

Before You Go On

What would happen to the vision of an amphibian or reptile if you severed the connections between the two hemispheres of its brain?

Describe the path of a visual image from the photoreceptors to the primary visual cortex.

The Structure of the Primary Visual Cortex

Like the lateral geniculate nucleus, the primary visual cortex is composed of six layers. The top four layers are called **parvocellular layers** (parvo = small), and the bottom two layers are called the **magnocellular layers** (magno = large). The reason for the names of these layers makes sense when we learn that the parvocellular layers are composed of the projections of small retinal ganglion cells called **X ganglion cells**, and the magnocellular layers are composed of projections of large retinal ganglion cells called **Y ganglion cells**. The cell bodies of X cells are located mostly in and around the fovea, whereas those of the Y cells are distributed equally throughout the retina.

In 1979, Margaret Wong-Riley discovered that the parvocellular pathways of the primary visual cortex contain blob-shaped clusters of neurons, which she gave the descriptive, if not especially elegant, name **blobs**. These blob-shaped clusters of neurons can be distinguished from other neurons in the primary visual cortex by staining with the chemical cytochrome oxidase. The blobs are sensitive to specific colors (Livingstone & Hubel, 1988). We will discover how our blobs allow us to recognize the color of an object later in this chapter. Other neurons in the parvocellular pathways are sensitive to stationary objects and detect stimulus boundaries,

parvocellular layers The top four layers of the primary visual cortex.

magnocellular layers The bottom two layers of the primary visual cortex.

X ganglion cells Small retinal ganglion cells that project to the parvocellular layers of the primary visual cortex.

Y ganglion cells Large retinal ganglion cells that project to the magnocellular layers of the primary visual cortex.

blobs Blob-shaped clusters of neurons in the primary visual cortex that are sensitive to specific colors.

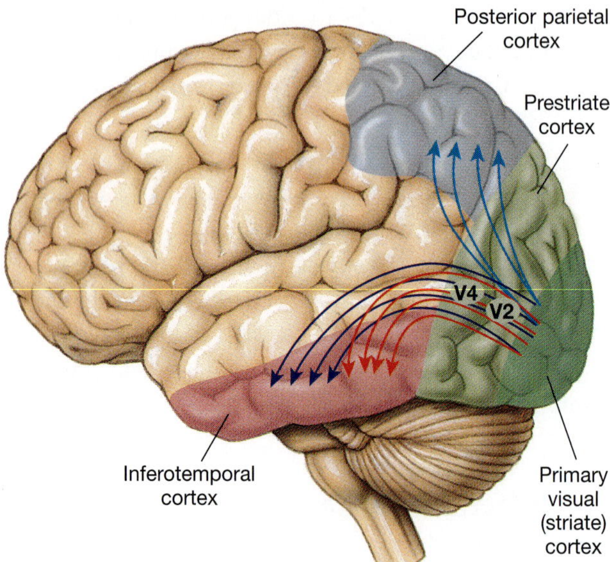

Figure 6.8 The visual cortex. The locations of the primary visual (striate) cortex and the secondary visual cortex (the prestriate cortex [Areas V2 and V4], the inferotemporal cortex, and the posterior parietal cortex).

➤ *What are the three pathways that relay information to the secondary visual cortex? (p. 170)*

whereas the neurons in the magnocellular pathways are responsive to moving objects and detect movement as well as stimulus orientation and retinal disparity.

Why is the visual system divided into parvocellular and magnocellular layers? According to Livingstone and Hubel (1988), the magnocellular layers are more primitive evolutionarily and are found in all mammalian species. The fact that there are neurons in this pathway that are selectively sensitive to a specific stimulus moving in a particular direction is consistent with the view that these neurons provide the basic visual information needed to move around in the environment, to locate prey, and to avoid predators. Livingstone and Hubel suggest that the parvocellular layers have evolved more recently to allow the detection of smaller detail and of color.

Pathways to the Secondary Visual Cortex

The function of the primary visual cortex is to detect features of the visual environment (the lines and colors that make up the pen in **Figure 6.1**); the **secondary visual cortex** puts the visual features back together in a recognizable visual perception (the pen). The visual pathway that detects the shape of objects begins in Area V1 of the primary visual cortex, travels to Area V2 in the prestriate cortex, and ends at the inferotemporal cortex (see purple arrows in **Figure 6.8**). The visual pathway that detects color begins in Area V1, travels to Areas V2 and then V4 in the prestriate cortex, and finally ends at the posterior inferotemporal cortex (refer to red arrows in **Figure 6.8**). The visual pathway that detects movement and depth begins in Area V1, travels to Area V2, then proceeds to the middle-temporal (MT) cortex (Area V5) and the medial superior temporal (MST) cortex, and finally ends at the posterior parietal cortex (see blue arrows in **Figure 6.8**). How do these visual pathways allow us to detect the shape, color, distance, and movement of objects in our environment? We will address these questions later in the chapter.

secondary visual cortex The area that detects the shape, color, movement, and depth of a light stimulus.

visual field deficit An inability to see objects placed in a particular part of the visual field caused by damage to a portion of one of the cerebral hemispheres.

APPLICATION

Testing for Visual Field Deficits

Following a recent stroke, Alan's mother, Sadie, has had difficulty naming objects presented visually. Her physician is having a therapist test for a number of possible causes. One of the most likely causes is aphasia, which is a language impairment, especially if one consequence of the stroke was damage to the left frontal lobe (Broca's area). Another possibility is amnesia, which is a memory loss, for the names of all objects learned prior to the stroke. A third possible reason is a **visual field deficit**, an inability to see objects placed in a particular part of the visual field caused by damage to a portion of one of the nerve fibers to the cerebral hemispheres (Brookshire, 1997).

The visual field deficit will be contralateral to the site of the damage if the damage is posterior to the optic chiasm (remember the crossover of nerve fibers at the optic chiasm). If upper nerve fibers are damaged, the visual field deficit will be in the opposite lower quadrant (see **Figure 6.9a**), whereas the visual field deficit will be in the opposite upper quadrant if lower nerve fibers are damaged (see **Figure 6.9b**). If both upper and lower nerve fibers are damaged, a condition called homonymous hemianopsia will result. The term *hemianopsia* refers to the fact that half the visual field is affected (hemi = half, an = not, opsia = visual); the term *homonymous* refers to the fact that the same part of the visual field is affected in each eye (homo = same; see **Figure 6.9c**).

The therapist tests Sadie very carefully to rule out aphasia or amnesia. She places objects in different quadrants of space and asks Sadie to point to them. Sadie consistently

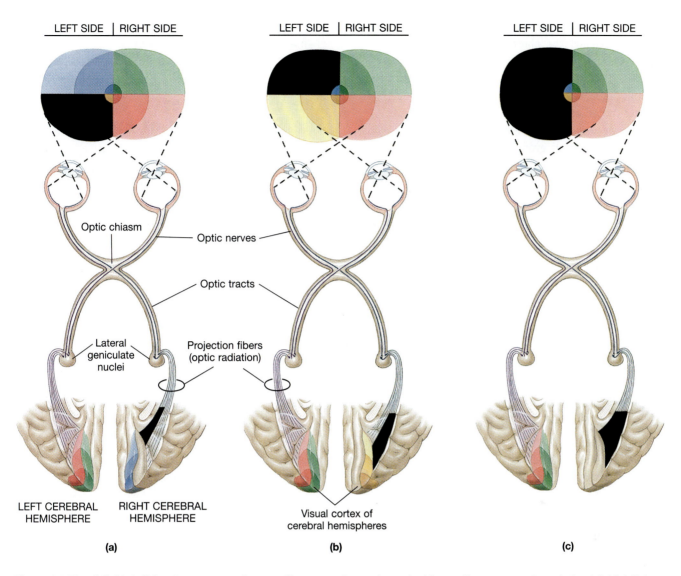

Figure 6.9 Visual field deficits. Damage to optic nerve fibers posterior to the optic chiasm will cause contralateral visual field deficits. (a) Damage to nerve fibers connecting to the upper right visual hemisphere will cause a visual field deficit in the lower left quadrant (the area shown in black). (b) Damage to nerve fibers connecting to the lower right visual hemisphere will cause a visual field deficit in the upper left quadrant. (c) Damage to nerve fibers connecting to both the upper and lower portions of the right hemisphere will cause homonymous hemianopsia, in which there is a deficit in the left half of the visual field of each eye.

➤ *What would be the deficit if the nerve fibers connecting to the lower left visual field and the right hemisphere were damaged? (p. 170–171)*

fails to detect objects only when they appear in the upper right quadrant. To confirm this, the therapist then presents objects only to those portions of Sadie's visual field that are not impaired. Because objects presented in the left visual field and the lower right visual fields can be named, Sadie's physician concluded that she does not suffer from either aphasia or amnesia but instead from a visual field deficit of the upper right quadrant. The therapist can help Sadie compensate for this deficit by training her to move so that objects can be detected by the intact portions of the visual field; most patients quickly learn to compensate for visual field deficits. ■

Section Review

- The form of energy that the visual system detects is light, electromagnetic radiation reflected by stimuli in the environment.
- Light passes through the transparent cornea, the clear aqueous humor, and the pupil before reaching the lens.
- The lens focuses the image of the object on the retina.
- The image on the retina is upside down and reversed.
- The retina contains three layers of neurons: the photoreceptors, the bipolar cells, and the ganglion cells.

- Light passes through the ganglion and bipolar layers before reaching the photoreceptors, which then transduce the light into neural impulses.
- There are two types of photoreceptors: rods and cones. Cones are most concentrated in the fovea; rods are most concentrated at the periphery of the retina.
- Cones are responsible for the details of daytime vision; rods detect stimuli even under dim lighting conditions such as those that occur at night.
- Cones synapse with bipolar cells, which then synapse with ganglion cells.
- Ganglion cells converge at the optic disk to form the optic nerve.
- In binocular organisms, such as humans, the optic nerve fibers that originate in the nasal half of each retina cross over to the contralateral side of the brain at the optic chiasm, whereas the optic nerve fibers that originate in the lateral half remain on the ipsilateral side.
- The optic tract, or second cranial nerve, is a continuation of ganglion cell axons.
- Most of the fibers of the optic tract project to the lateral geniculate nucleus, where they synapse with neurons projecting to the primary visual cortex (Area V1).
- The remaining optic tract fibers extend to other subcortical structures, including the superior colliculus, ventral lateral geniculate nucleus, the accessory optic nuclei, the suprachiasmatic nucleus, and the pretectum area.
- The X ganglion cells are small, found mostly in and around the fovea, and project to the top four parvocellular layers of the primary visual cortex.
- The Y ganglion cells are large, distributed equally throughout the retina, and project to the bottom two magnocellular layers of the primary visual cortex.
- Information from the primary visual cortex is sent by three pathways to the secondary visual cortex for analysis.
- One pathway projects to Area V2 of the prestriate cortex, and then to the inferotemporal cortex; it is involved in shape recognition.
- The second pathway projects to Area V2, then on to Area V4 of the prestriate cortex, and finally to the posterior inferotemporal cortex; it provides information related to color.
- The third pathway projects to Area V2, then to the middle-temporal (MT) cortex and the medial superior temporal (MST) cortex, and finally to the posterior parietal cortex; it is involved in the detection of spatial location (depth) and movement.
- A visual field deficit is an inability to see objects placed in a particular part of the visual field.

hue Wavelength of light stimulus measured in nanometers (nm or billionth of a meter).

brightness Intensity of light stimulus.

saturation The purity of a light stimulus.

The Visual Sense: The Transduction of Energy

So now we know that physical energy, light, travels through the eye to the photoreceptor cells (rods and cones), and a neural message of the light through the optic nerve to the cerebral cortex. But what are the characteristics of light, and how exactly do rods and cones detect light and tranduce it into a neural message that can be passed on to the visual cortex?

Characteristics of Light

The light that we see (or to be more accurate, the light reflected off objects) varies according to three dimensions. Light can vary in terms of its wavelength or **hue**. Wavelength is measured in nanometers (nm or billionth of a meter), and humans can see wavelengths from 380 to 760 nanometers (see **Figure 6.10**). When our visual system detects a particular wavelength, we perceive that wavelength as a specific hue, or color. Light of a short wavelength (such as 419 nm) is perceived as blue; light of a middle wavelength (such as 531 nm) is perceived as green; light of a middle to long wave length (such as 580 nm) is seen as yellow and light of a long wavelength (such as 660 nm) is seen as red. These wavelengths of light are considered the primary colors.

Humans can detect only a small part of the total range of the electromagnetic spectrum. Many insects can detect ultraviolet rays, which are shorter wavelengths than we can see, and many fish and reptiles are sensitive to infrared rays, which are longer wavelengths than we can detect.

Light also varies in terms of its intensity or **brightness**. Some stimuli, such as aluminum foil, reflect a great deal of light and are perceived as bright, whereas other stimuli, such as coal, reflect little light and are perceived as dark.

The third dimension is the purity or **saturation** of the visual stimulus. A pure light contains only light of one wavelength and is thus highly saturated. A light containing all wavelengths is perceived as white—think of daylight. A mixture of wavelengths is perceived as a nonprimary color such as orange or purple. (The primary colors are red, blue, green, and yellow.)

The Detection of Visual Stimuli

The process by which photoreceptors transduce light into neural signals was first described by George Wald, who was awarded the Nobel Prize in 1967 for this dis-

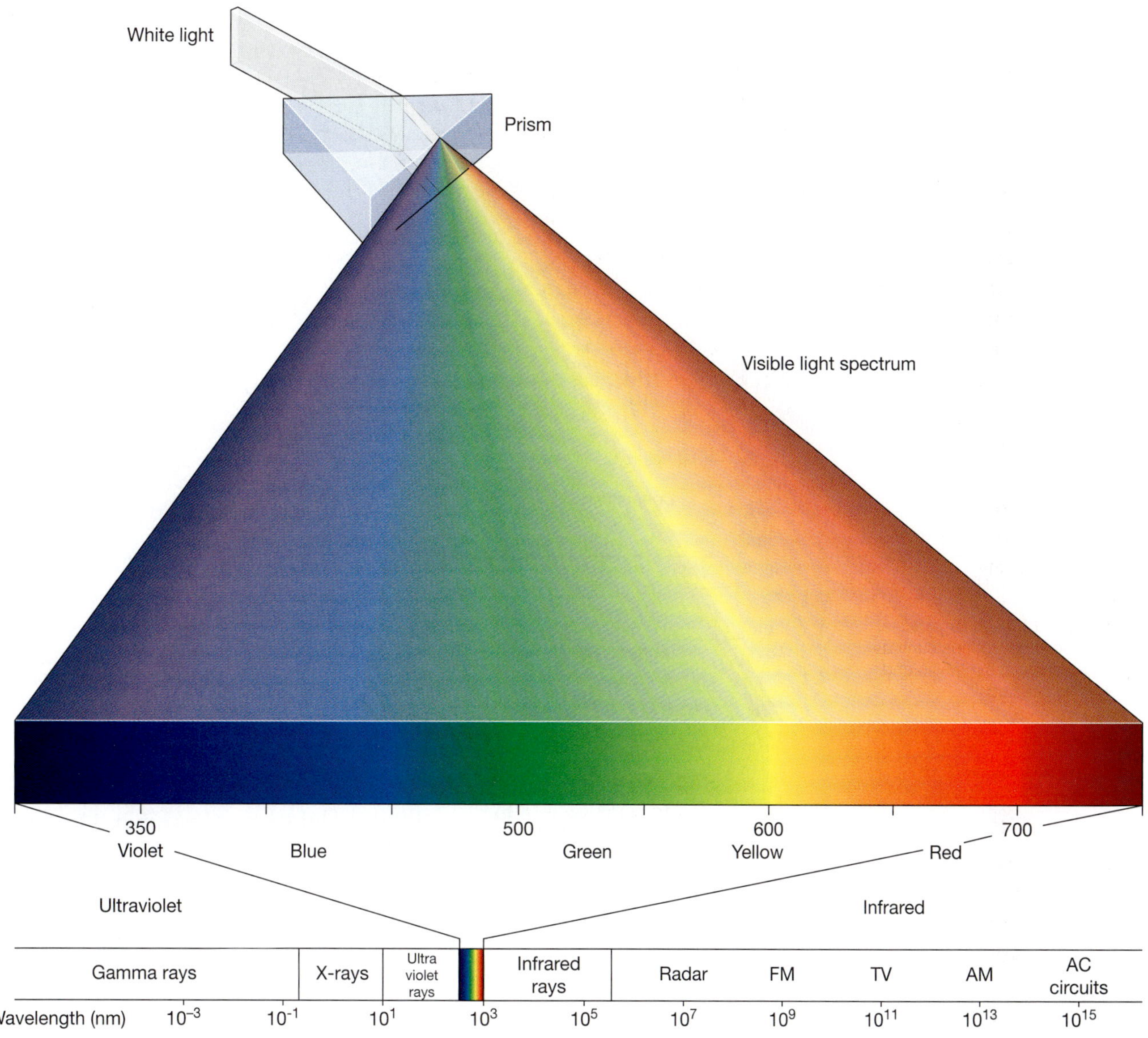

Figure 6.10 The electromagnetic spectrum. Humans are only able to detect a small portion of the electromagnetic spectrum as different colors.
➤ *If a light contains all wavelengths, what color is it perceived to be? (p. 172)*

covery. He found that a photoreceptor contains an outer segment that is connected to an inner segment by cilia (or hairlike extensions; refer to **Figure 6.11a**). The inner segment contains the cell nucleus, whereas the outer segment contains several hundred thin membranes that form disks, called **lamellae**.

Embedded in the lamellae are the chemical molecules called **photopigments,** responsible for the detection of light. Photopigments contain two parts: a protein **opsin** and a lipid **retinal** (see **Figure 6.11b**). There are several different forms of opsin. The type of opsin found in rods is called, sensibly enough, **rod opsin**. Three forms of opsin exist in cones, corresponding to three different types of cones. The three types of cones are involved in the recognition of color, which will be discussed later in this chapter on **p. 185**. Retinal is synthesized from Vitamin A, a vitamin commonly found in vegetables such

lamellae The thin membranes contained in the outer segment of a photoreceptor.

photopigment The chemical molecules embedded in the lamellae that are responsible for the detection of light.

opsin The protein component of photopigment.

retinal The lipid component of photopigment that is synthesized from Vitamin A.

rod opsin The form of opsin found in rods.

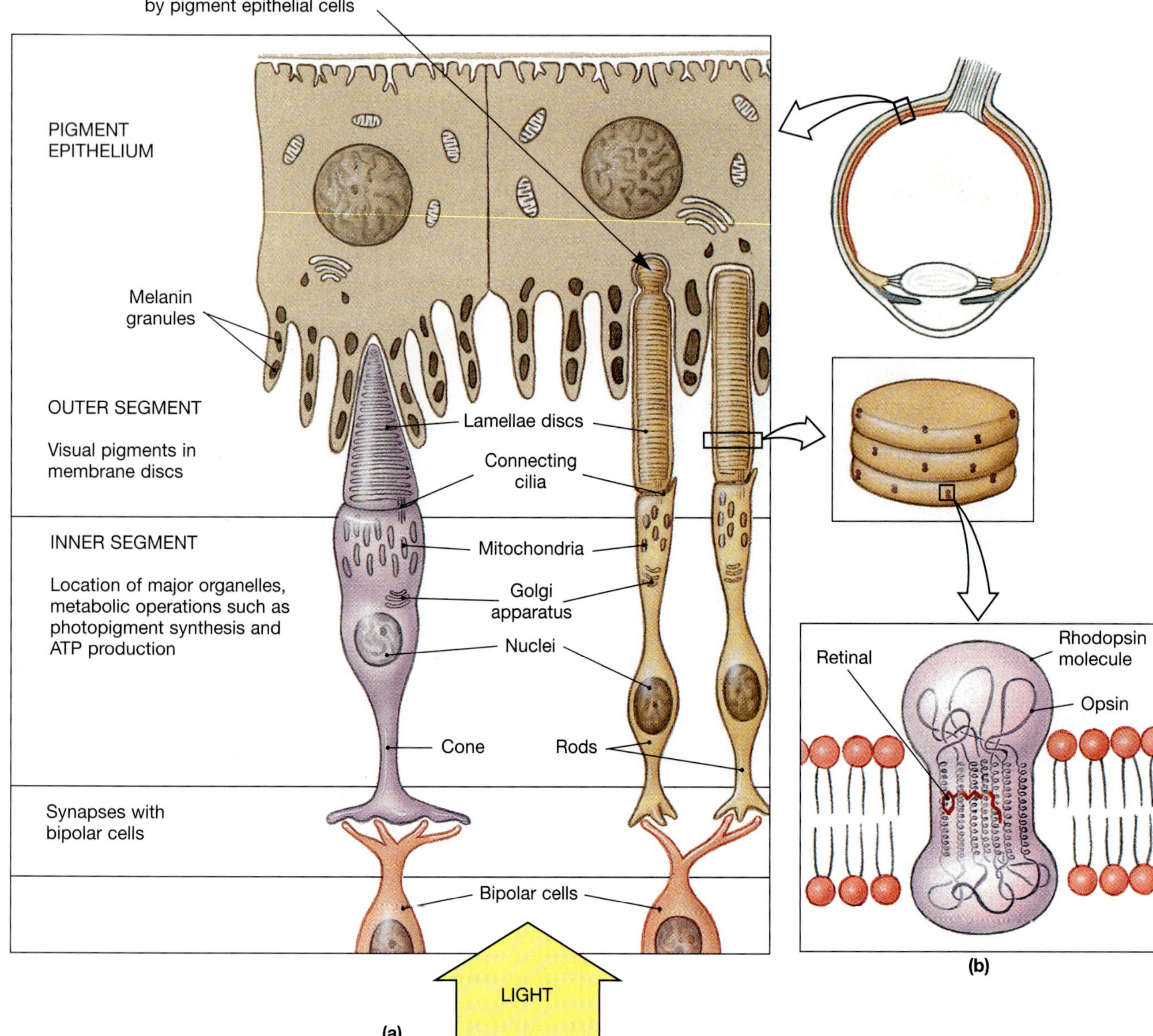

Figure 6.11 Photoreceptors. Main structural components of rods and cones.
➤ *Where in the eye are the rods and cones located? (p. 173–174)*

as carrots (so your mother was right when she told you to eat your carrots to keep your eyesight sharp!). **Rhodopsin** (not to be confused with rod opsin) is the photopigment found in rods, which consists of rod opsin and retinal. There are many photopigment molecules, perhaps as many as 10 million, in each receptor cell.

Rhodopsin has a rosy or pink color before it is exposed to light. (The term *Rhod* comes from the Greek word *rhodon,* meaning "rose.") When rhodopsin is exposed to light, it breaks down into rod opsin and retinal, and has a pale yellow color. When light is removed, the rod opsin and retinal recombine into rhodopsin, and the rosy color returns (see **Figure 6.12**). It can be said that light bleaches the photopigment in receptor cells. The bleaching of rhodopsin is an extremely rapid chemical reaction, occurring in 200 femtoseconds (200×10^{-15}; Schoenlein et al., 1991).

The splitting of rhodopsin into rod opsin and retinal by a light stimulus is the key to the photoreceptor's detection of light. Photoreceptor cells continuously release

rhodopsin The photopigment found in rods, which consists of rod opsin and retinal.

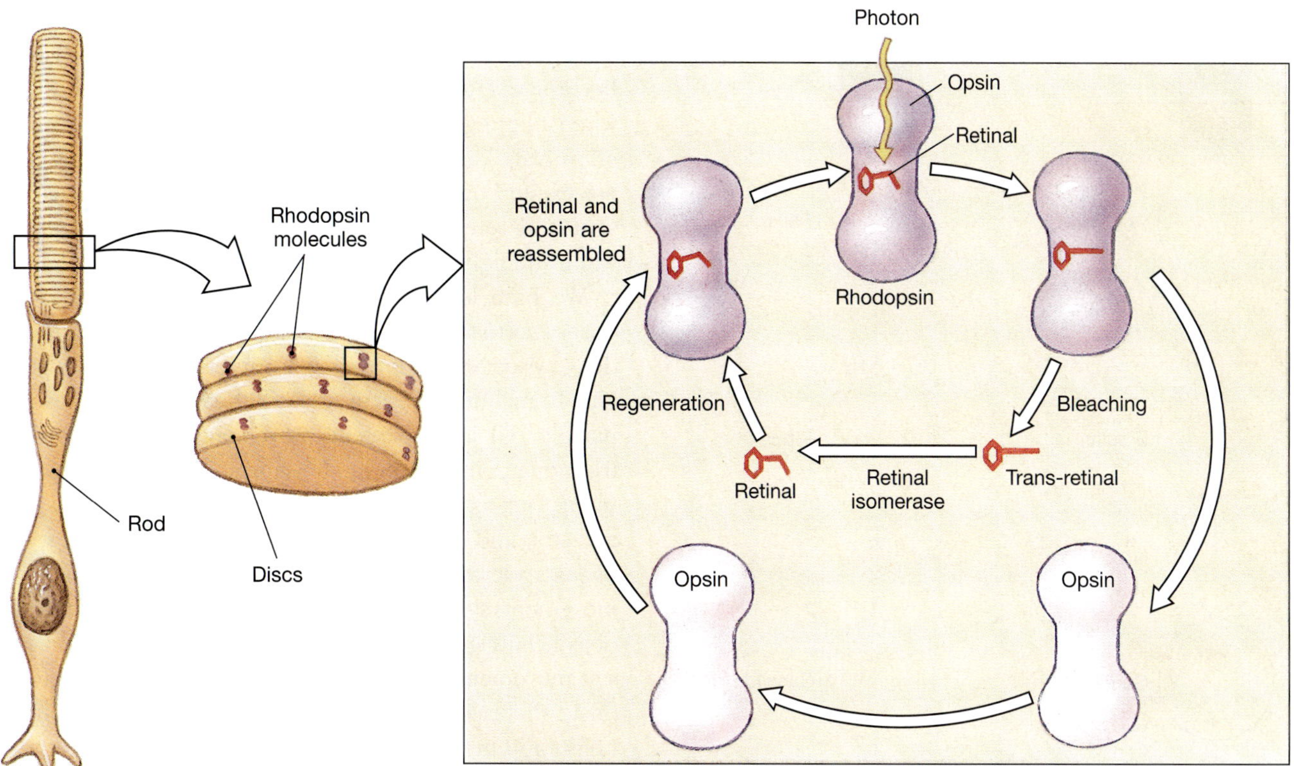

Figure 6.12 The bleaching and regeneration of visual pigments in the rods. Light breaks rhodopsin down into its components, rod opsin and retinal; when light is removed, rod opsin and retinal recombine into rhodopsin.

➤ *How does the splitting of rhodopsin stimulate the rod cell? (p. 174–175)*

neurotransmitter molecules that inhibits the bipolar cells, the layer of retinal cells located just in front of the receptors (refer to **Figure 6.3**). Thus, a photoreceptor that is not stimulated by light will inhibit (hyperpolarize) a bipolar cell. When light splits rhodopsin, a number of chemical reactions occur that cause the Na^+ ion channels in the photoreceptor to close (O'Brien, 1982). When the Na^+ ion channels close, the polarity of the photoreceptor's membrane increases (Schnapf & Baylor, 1987).

This hyperpolarization of the photoreceptor membrane decreases the release of neurotransmitters (Yau, 1991), which reduces the inhibition of the bipolar cells. As a result, the bipolar cell's membrane becomes depolarized. Bipolar cells have a graded depolarization, with the level of depolarization influencing the amount of neurotransmitter released by the cell; that is, the greater the level of depolarization, the more neurotransmitter molecules that are released into the synaptic cleft between the bipolar and ganglion cells. The bipolar cells have an excitatory influence on the ganglion cells, which transmit information about visual events to the cerebral cortex via the optic nerves.

The retina also contains two other types of neurons that run parallel to the surface of the retina: **horizontal cells** and **amacrine cells**. As seen in **Figure 6.3**, the photoreceptors synapse with the horizontal cells as well as with the bipolar cells. The horizontal cells in turn synapse with and have an inhibitory influence on the bipolar cells. Similarly, the amacrine cells synapse with and inhibit both bipolar and ganglion cells. The effect of this inhibitory influence of the horizontal and amacrine cells on adjacent bipolar and ganglion cells will become clear when we describe the action of three types of ganglion cells below.

Some ganglion cells respond when a light stimulus is presented. These ganglion cells, called **on ganglion cells**, are excited by bipolar cells in response to a light stimu-

---

horizontal cell Type of retinal neuron that receives neural messages from the photoreceptors and synapses with and has an inhibitory influence on the bipolar cells.

amacrine cell Type of retinal neuron that receives neural messages from the bipolar cells and synapses with and inhibits both bipolar and ganglion cells.

on ganglion cell Type of ganglion neuron that is excited by bipolar cells in response to a light stimulus.

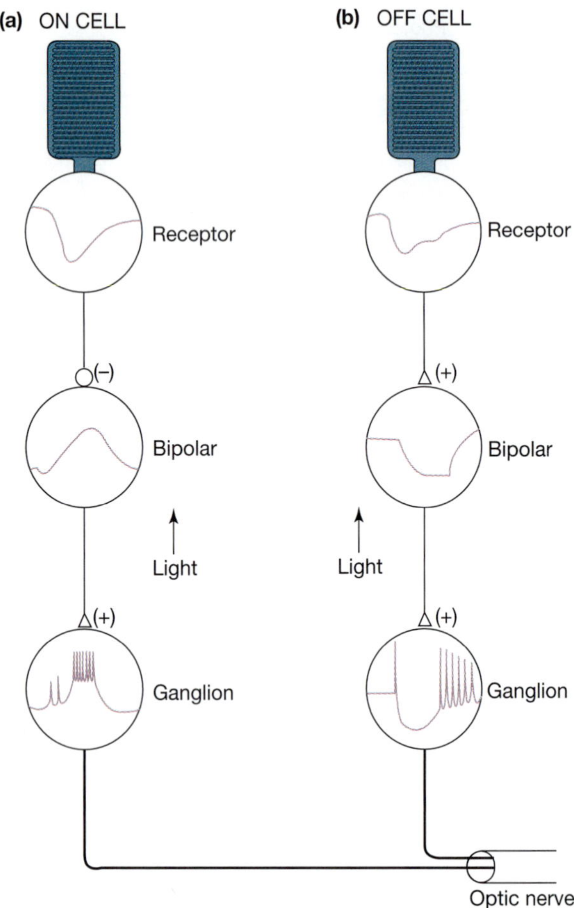

Figure 6.13 The excitatory (triangles) and inhibitory (circles) influences on (a) an on ganglion cell and (b) an off ganglion cell. The onset of a light leads to activation of on ganglion cells; the onset of a light inhibits and the termination of a light leads to activation of off ganglion cells.

Adapted from Kandel et al., 1991.

➤ *What type of cell inhibits an off cell? (p. 176)*

lus (see **Figure 6.13**). Other ganglion cells are excited when a light stimulus is removed. These ganglion cells, called **off ganglion cells**, are inhibited by amacrine cells in the presence of light. When the light stimulus ends, inhibition is released, enabling the ganglion cells to become excited. Still other ganglion cells respond both when a light goes on and when a light goes off. Such ganglion cells, called (you guessed it!) **on-off ganglion cells**, are excited by a bipolar cell when a light stimulus is present and released from inhibition by an amacrine cell when the light stimulus is removed.

We have learned that ganglion cells respond to the onset and to the termination of light. Yet, we continuously detect visual events in our environment. How is that possible? To maintain the activation of photoreceptors, our eyes make rapid jerky **saccadic movements**, shifting abruptly from one point to another as we scan the physical environment. During this scanning process, eye movements start and stop and then start again. The occurrence and speed of a saccade cannot be consciously controlled. Saccadic eye movements slow down when we attempt to follow a moving object. This smoother type of eye movement is called **pursuit movement**. When the object stops and our eyes focus on it, the saccadic movements again begin scanning the object and maintain the stimulation of the visual system.

off ganglion cell Type of ganglion neuron that is inhibited by amacrine cells in the presence of light and excited by the termination of light stimulus due to removal of inhibition from amacrine cells.

on-off ganglion cells Type of ganglion neurons that are excited by a bipolar cell when a light stimulus is present and released from inhibition by an amacrine cell when the light stimulus is removed.

saccadic movements The rapid jerky movements of the eye from one point to another as the physical environment is scanned.

pursuit movement The smooth eye movements that occur when the eyes follow a moving object.

Before You Go On

Why is it important to be able to recognize when a light goes off as well as when it is turned on?

Section Review

- Light varies in terms of wavelenth (hue), intensity (brightness), and purity (saturation).
- Photoreceptors (rods and cones) transduce light into neural impulses.
- Photoreceptors contain photopigments, which consist of a protein opsin and a lipid retinal. Light acts to break down the photopigment into two separate molecules. When light is removed, the protein opsin and lipid retinal recombine.
- Photoreceptors continually release neurotransmitter molecules that inhibit bipolar cells.
- When light splits the photopigment, Na^+ ion channels close, the photoreceptor membrane becomes hyperpolarized, and less neurotransmitter is released.
- The reduced release of inhibitory neurotransmitters from the photoreceptors leads to depolarization of the bipolar cells, which, if sufficient, causes the bipolar cells to fire.
- The bipolar cells have an excitatory influence on the ganglion cells, whereas the horizontal cells and amacrine cells have an inhibitory influence.
- On-center ganglion cells respond when a light is turned on, due to the excitatory influence of bipolar cells.

- Off ganglion cells respond when a light is turned off, due to the removal of the inhibitory influence of the amacrine cells.
- On-off ganglion cells respond when a light stimulus is present as well as when the light stimulus ends.

The Visual Sense: Function

Alan is feeling much better. His ophthalmologist's hunch was right—he does have diabetes, which is now under control via daily insulin injections. He is sitting in a chair reading a new book, when out of the corner of his eye he sees a flash of red; a cardinal has come to visit the bird feeder in the backyard. The cardinal is just one of a multitude of objects in Alan's environment. The visual system allows him to recognize such objects and to distinguish them from one another (Alan could see that it was a cardinal, not a bear, at his bird feeder). He also sees colors, such as the bright red of the male cardinal's feathers, and movement—the streak of red as the cardinal flew to the feeder. And he perceived the cardinal in three dimensions. In the following sections, we will examine the discrete functions of the visual system in the recognition of these four features of an object: its form, depth, movement, and color.

Vision: The Recognition of an Object

Alan is now looking at a picture of a sailboat. How can he tell that it is a sailboat and not a cruise ship? The answer to this question is quite complex, but we will begin by describing lateral inhibition, which allows Alan to sense the edges of an object in order to distinguish the sails of the sailboat from the smokestacks of a cruise ship.

Lateral Inhibition

The white sails of the sailboat are surrounded by a dark blue sky. Based on our previous discussion, you would expect that the white sail would activate Alan's photoreceptors to a greater degree than the dark blue sky. Although this differential photoreceptor activity would allow him to recognize that an object is being viewed, the object would merely appear as a light blur against the dark background; that is, the object would appear out of focus and could not be recognized. To see where the sailboat ends and the sky begins, he must be able not only to sense the brightness differences between an object and the surround, but also to sense the edges of the object (where, for example, the sails end and the sky begins).

We have learned that when light reaches the retina, photoreceptors are hyperpolarized, causing a decreased release of neurotransmitter molecules. This decreased release of neurotransmitters not only activates the bipolar cell—by releasing the inhibition of the bipolar cell—but also excites the horizontal cells (see **Figure 6.13**). Activation of the horizontal cells has an inhibitory effect on bipolar cells adjacent to the one that was activated. The inhibition of surrounding bipolar cells is called **lateral inhibition.** Lateral inhibition allows us to sense edges by enhancing the contrast between an object and its surround. Thus, the white sails are clearly focused against the dark blue sky because of

lateral inhibition The enhancement of the contrast between a light stimulus and its surround by the inhibition of the bipolar cells adjacent to the active photoreceptors, which allows the detection of the edges of a light stimulus.

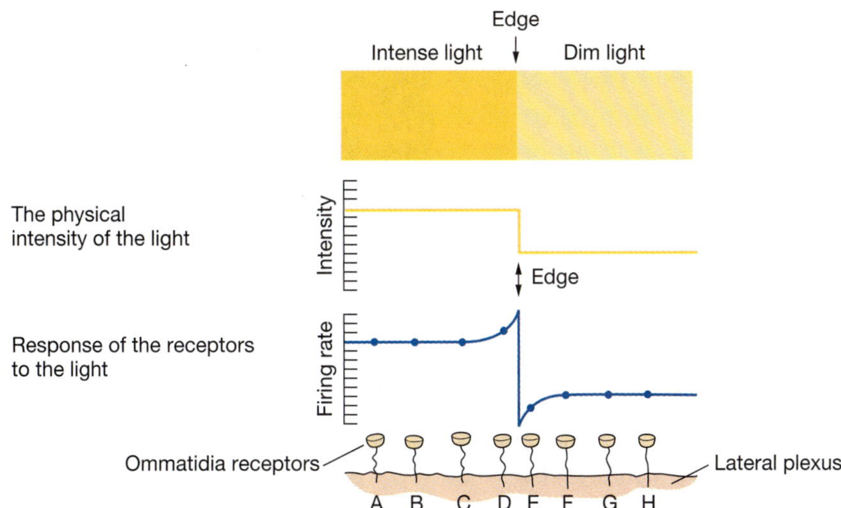

Figure 6.14 Firing rate of ommatidium receptors A through H of the horseshoe crab, *Limulus*, when adjacent intense and dim lights are projected to the retina. The increased firing rate of receptor D and decreased firing rate of receptor E create an edge between the intense and dim lights.

➤ *To what vertebrate structure is the lateral plexus of the horseshoe crab analogous? (p. 178)*

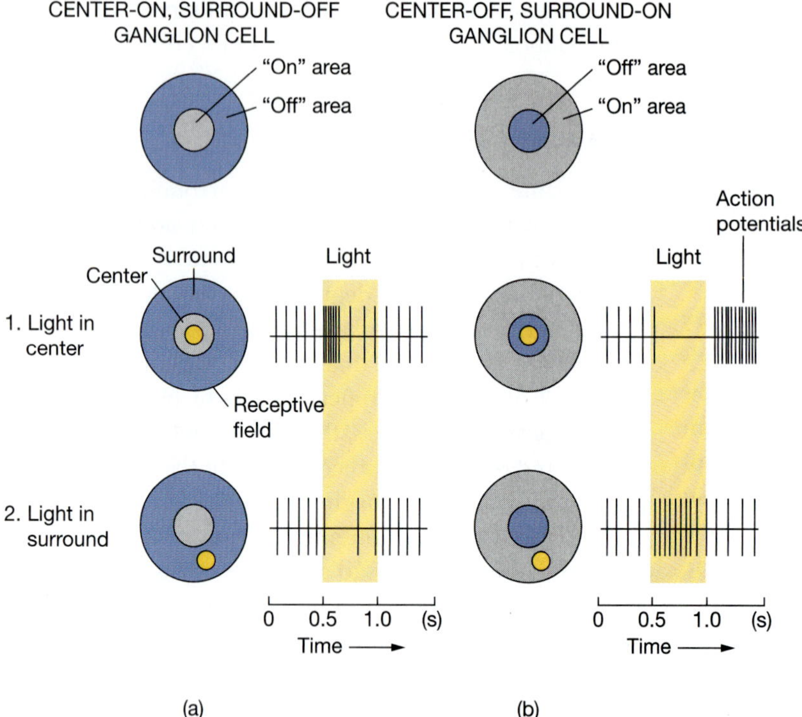

Figure 6.15 The receptive fields of center-on, surround-off and center-off, surround-on ganglion cells. A spot of light in the center of field increases the activity in center-on, surround-off cell and decreases activity in center-off, surround-on cell, whereas a spot of light in surround of field decreases activity in center-on, surround-off cell and increases activity in center-off, surround-on cell.

➤ *How many receptive fields does each ganglion cell contain? (p. 179)*

the inhibition of the bipolar cells adjacent to the photoreceptors stimulated by the white sails.

How exactly does lateral inhibition contribute to the perception of the contrast between the edge of an object and the background? **Figure 6.14** illustrates how lateral inhibition enhances contrast and creates the perception of edges in a horseshoe crab, the subject of a classic study (Hartline, 1949). The eye of a horseshoe crab consists of many little eyes, called ommatidia, each of which has a lens and a receptor cell. The ommatidia synapse with a single large neuron called the eccentric cell, and also relay information to each other via a connection called the lateral plexus. The lateral plexus is analogous to the horizontal cells of vertebrates; activation of the lateral plexus by an ommatidium inhibits ommatidia adjacent to the one that stimulated the lateral plexus. Suppose that an intense light is presented against a dimly lit background. The ommatidia receptors A, B, and C are inhibited by adjacent receptors via the lateral plexus. Because receptor D is next to receptors exposed to a dimly lit background as well as those exposed to the intense light, it is inhibited less than receptors A, B, and C. The ommatidia receptors F, G, and H are only acted on by receptors exposed to the dimly lit background. By contrast, receptor E is inhibited by receptor D as well as receptors F, G, and H. The lateral inhibition of receptors E by receptor D results in less response of receptor E than receptors F, G, and H. This greater activation of receptor D and greater inhibition of receptor E enhances the contrast between the intense light and dimly lit background and is responsible for the perception of the edge between the two different light stimuli.

Receptive Fields

Lateral inhibition is only part of the process that allows us to recognize objects. Recognition of objects such as a

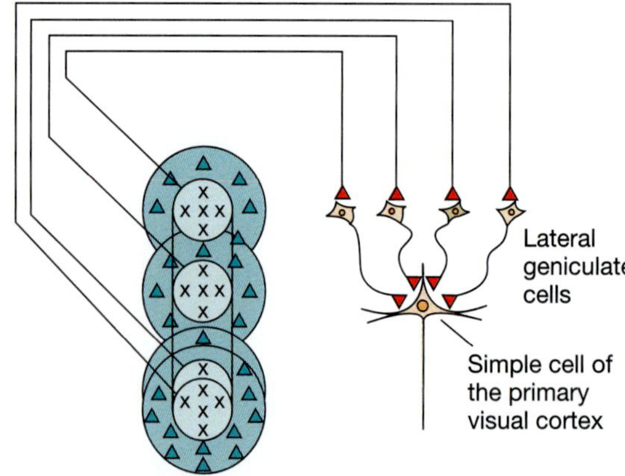

Figure 6.16 The receptive field of a simple cell of the primary visual cortex. Simple cell activity reflects a combination of the receptive fields of several lateral geniculate nucleus (LGN) cells, and reacts to line orientation shown.

➤ *How may types of cells are there in the primary visual cortex? (p. 179–180)*

sailboat also involves the operation of a process called a receptive field. In a classic study, Kuffler (1953) found that a particular ganglion cell responded to a small light stimulus only when the light stimulus was presented to a limited, circular area of the retina. He called this limited area of the retina activated by the light the **receptive field** of that ganglion cell. (A receptive field is that part of the visual field, or field of vision, to which a particular neuron is sensitive. So the visual field contains many receptive fields.)

Remember the three types of ganglion cells described earlier in the chapter (see **p. 175–176**)? There are actually two receptive fields for each type of ganglion cell (see **Figure 6.15**). Suppose that the environment contains a dark object against a light background. Kuffler found that some ganglion cells respond when the center of the receptive field is dark and the periphery of the receptive field, called the surround, is light, whereas other cells respond when the center is light and the surround is dark. Ganglion cells stimulated when the center of the receptive field is illuminated are called **center-on, surround-off ganglion cells**, whereas those stimulated when the surround is illuminated are called **center-off, surround-on ganglion cells**.

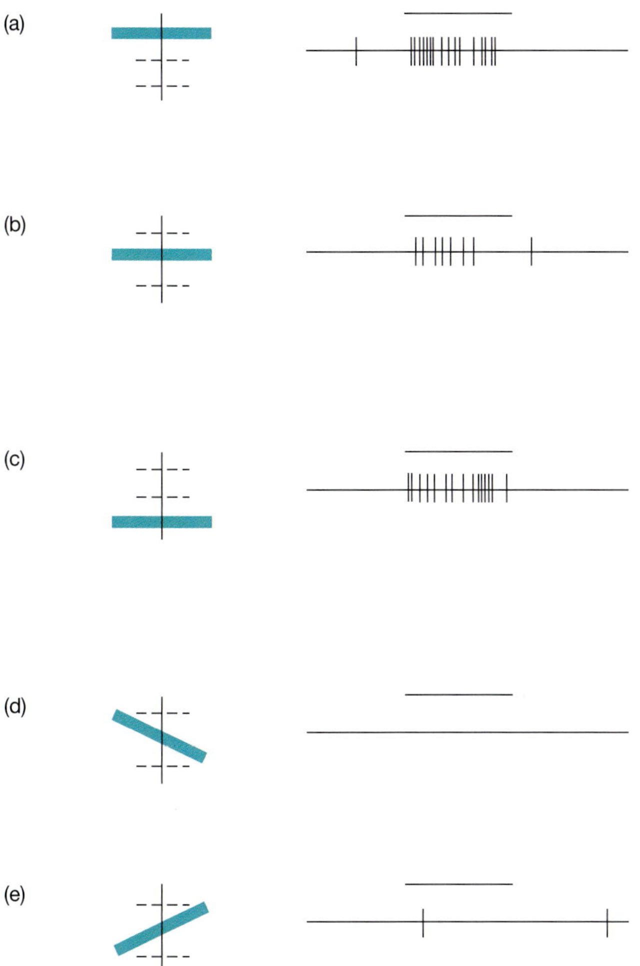

Figure 6.17 Complex cells in the primary visual cortex. The response of a complex cell is not restricted to a specific location within the receptive field (a, b, and c), but is restricted by stimulus orientation (d and e).

➤ *What is the difference between simple cells and complex cells? (p. 179–180)*

Information from both center-on, surround-off and center-off, surround-on ganglion cells is relayed to the lateral geniculate nucleus. Neurons in the lateral geniculate nucleus also differentially respond to the physical environment; that is, some are excited by stimulation of the center of the receptive field and inhibited by stimulation of the surround, and others are inhibited by stimulation of the center of the receptive field and excited by stimulation of the surround. Thus, cells in the lateral geniculate nucleus detect information about objects and their surround, and relay this information to the primary visual cortex for analysis.

How does the primary visual cortex assemble the input from the lateral geniculate nucleus to detect form? David Hubel and Torsten Wiesel studied how the primary visual cortex analyzes the information needed to detect the form of objects. Hubel and Wiesel (1965) reported that there are receptive fields in the primary visual cortex. However, these receptive fields are not like the center-surround fields found in the ganglion cells and in the neurons of the lateral geniculate nucleus. Instead, a receptive field in the primary visual cortex reflects a combined influence of the receptive fields of cells in the lateral geniculate nucleus (see **Figure 6.16**).

Hubel and Wiesel identified four types of cells in the primary visual cortex. **Simple cells** respond to lines (edges) that have a specific orientation (line-tilt; refer to **Figure 6.16**). A particular simple cell will respond to a particular line that is presented in a specific part of the visual field. If either the orientation of the line or the location of the line in the visual field is changed, that particular simple cell will not respond. As seen in **Figure 6.16**, only a specific line will activate the simple cell. Further, the simple cell responds

---

receptive field The part of the visual field to which a particular neuron is sensitive.

center-on, surround-off ganglion cells Type of ganglion neurons that are stimulated when the center of the receptive field is illuminated.

center-off, surround-on ganglion cells Type of ganglion neurons that are stimulated when the surround is illuminated.

simple cells Neurons in the primary visual cortex that respond to lines (edges) in a specific part of the visual field that have a specific orientation (line-tilt).

based on input from several lateral geniculate nucleus cells. The combined input from these receptive fields determines whether the simple cell will respond.

Complex cells are very sensitive to a line stimulus oriented in a particular direction; this line, however, can appear anywhere in the receptive field (see **Figure 6.17**). Because the receptive fields of complex cells are larger than those of simple cells, the stimulus can appear in many different locations and still activate the complex cell. (Some complex cells also will respond when the line moves in a specific direction; other complex cells will react to line movement in any direction. We will discuss the process responsible for the detection of movement later in this chapter.)

Hypercomplex cells, like complex cells, respond to visual stimuli of a particular orientation (line-tilt) and a specific length (see **Figure 6.18**). However, as can be seen from **Figure 6.18d**, the stimulus must appear in a particular location within the receptive field in order for the hypercomplex cell to be activated.

The fourth type of cell in the primary visual cortex, the **higher-order hypercomplex cells**, responds to stimuli of specific sizes and shapes. The research of Hubel and Wiesel greatly enhanced our understanding of how the primary visual cortex works. For their efforts, they were awarded the Nobel Prize in 1981.

Hubel and Wiesel proposed that cells in the primary visual cortex respond to straight lines and construct our perception by combining straight lines of different orientation. The three straight lines of a sail are one example of this construction. But, how does the visual cortex recognize stimuli such as faces that are not easily broken down into straight lines? Russell De Valois and Karen De Valois (De Valois, Albrecht, & Thorell, 1982; De Valois & De Valois, 1988) argue that neurons in the primary visual cortex are more likely to respond to **sine-wave gratings** of light and dark (curved lines) rather than to straight lines. **Figure 6.19** illustrates a sine-wave grating of a visual stimulus. Notice that the intensity of light varies

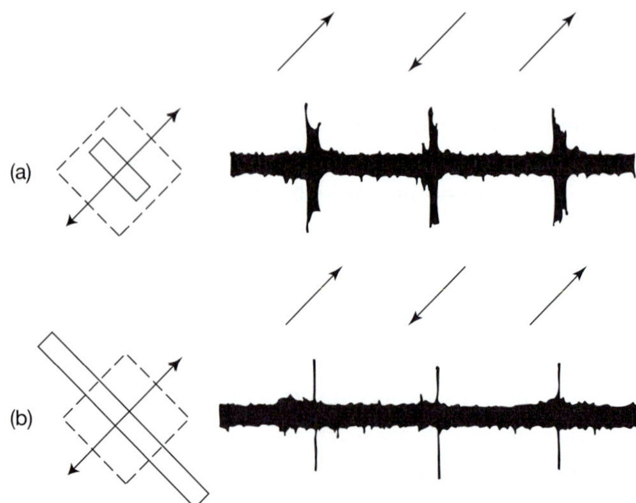

Figure 6.18 Hypercomplex cells in the primary visual cortex. Reaction of a hypercomplex cell is limited to a stimulus in a specific location within its receptive field; this cell will not respond to the same stimulus in a different location.

➤ *What is the difference between complex cells and hypercomplex cells? (p. 180)*

in the sine-wave grating, becoming alternately lighter and then darker. No two sine waves are alike; sine waves can differ in terms of frequency (the width of the light and dark bars), amplitude (the intensity difference between light and dark bars), and angle.

The complex pattern of light and dark seen in **Figure 6.19** actually consists of many simple sine waves. A complex mathematical procedure called fourier analysis can break down any sine-wave grating into its constituent sine waves (see **Figure 6.20**). De Valois, Albrecht, and Thorell (1982) found that each neuron in the primary visual cortex responds best to one particular sine-wave pattern. In other words, different neurons in the primary visual cortex respond to different sine-wave patterns. At this time it is not clear whether neurons in the primary visual cortex respond to both straight lines and sine-wave gratings or just sine-wave gratings. Researchers (He, Cavanaugh, & Intilgator, 1996; Hughes, Nozawa, & Kitterle, 1996) are attempting to answer this question, as well as the question of how the visual system reconstructs straight lines and/or sine-wave gratings into the perception of a specific object.

The Role of the Secondary Visual Cortex in Object Recognition

As we learned earlier in the chapter, three pathways relay information from the primary visual cortex to the secondary visual cortex (see **p. 170**). Of these, the pathway extending from the primary visual cortex through the prestriate cortex to the inferotemporal cortex appears to be involved in the recognition of objects.

---

complex cells Neurons in the primary visual cortex that are very sensitive to a line stimulus oriented in a particular direction, which can appear anywhere in the receptive field.

hypercomplex cells Neurons in the primary visual cortex that respond to visual stimuli of a particular orientation and a specific length in a particular location within the receptive field.

higher-order hypercomplex cells Neurons in the primary visual cortex that respond to stimuli of specific sizes and shapes.

sine-wave gratings The alternating lighter and then darker intensities found in a light stimulus.

Remember Sadie's visual field deficit? She was unable to detect objects in the upper quadrant of her visual field because of damage to some of the fibers to her optic nerve. Her visual field deficit is an example of a sensory problem, in which the path from the sensory organ to the cerebral cortex is damaged. With an inability to name objects, a perceptual problem, the pathway from the sensory organ to the cerebral cortex is intact, but there is damage within the cerebral cortex. In one such perceptual problem, **visual agnosia**, a person is unable to name an object when it is presented visually, but can identify it when it is presented in another modality (e.g., a cube cannot be identified visually, but can be identified when it is felt with the hands). Visual agnosia occurs following damage, usually bilateral damage, to the inferotemporal cortex (Pohl, 1973). The person with visual agnosia is not blind, and can respond to some, especially visually familiar, objects in the environment.

Perhaps you have heard of the term *grandmother cell*? This term implies that you have a neuron in your brain that becomes active when you see your grandmother. Although the brain does not appear to contain a "grandmother cell" per se (if you had only one neuron that responded to grandma, you would not be able to recognize grandma if that neuron was damaged), it does contain neurons that respond to some faces and not others. Puce, Allison, Gore, and McCarthy (1995) measured brain activity with an fMRI (see Chapter 2) when individuals were exposed to familiar and unfamiliar faces. When they saw a face they recognized, activity increased in the inferotemporal cortex, whereas activity did not change when they saw an unfamiliar face. Also, Gross and Sergent (1992) reported that specific neurons responded intensely to some faces, less intensely to other faces, and hardly at all to still other faces. Further, Courtney et al. (1996) used PET scans to reveal that general information about facial features and gender are provided by the posterior parts of this pathway, whereas the identification of specific faces is the function of anterior parts of the pathway. These results suggest that as the neural impulses flow through this system, more specific identification of the features of the light stimulus is extracted until the light stimulus (in this case, a face) is identified.

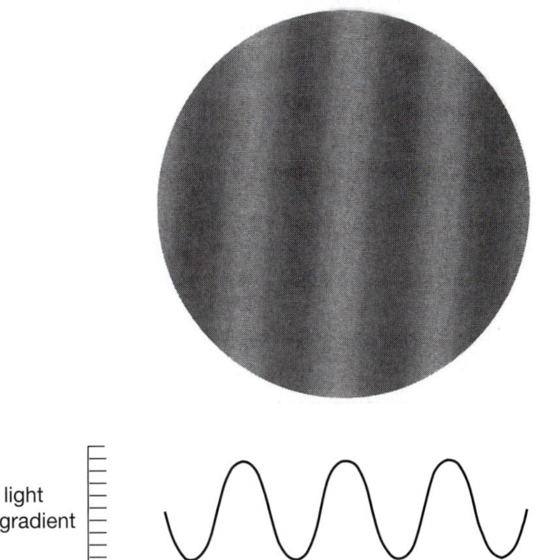

Figure 6.19 A sine-wave grating. The increasing and decreasing brightness of light seen within the circle is depicted as the sine-wave grating seen above.

From DeValois & DeValois, 1988.

➤ *In what three ways can sine waves differ from one another? (p. 180)*

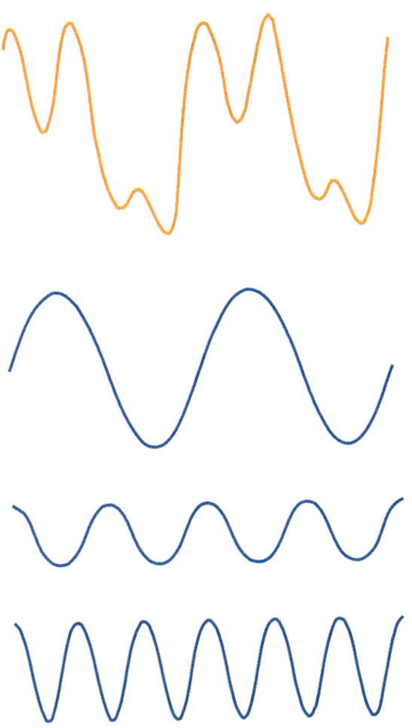

Figure 6.20 Sine-wave grating. Fourier analysis shows that the sine-wave grating seen at the top is composed of the three sine waves shown below.

From DeValois & DeValois, 1988.

➤ *How many different neurons would be needed to respond to the sine-wave pattern at the top of this figure? (p. 180)*

How do we learn to recognize grandma's face? The research of Keiji Tanaka (Kobatake & Tanake, 1994) provides us with a likely mechanism. Kobatake and Tanaka (1994) trained monkeys to discriminate between

visual agnosia Following bilateral damage to the inferotemporal cortex, the inability to name an object when it is presented visually but not when it is presented in another modality.

Figure 6.21 Object recognition. Examples of complex shapes that inferotemporal cortical neurons can learn to respond to. What effect would damage to the inferotemporal cortex have on the recognition of these shapes? *(p. 182)*
Figure courtesy of Keiji Tanaka.

28 moderately complex shapes (see **Figure 6.21**). (In a discrimination task, the monkey is presented two stimuli and reinforced if it picks one stimulus, but not if it selects the other stimulus.) After one year of discrimination training, 39 percent of the neurons in the anterior part of the inferotemporal cortex responded to some of these shapes. By contrast, only 9 percent of neurons in the inferotemporal cortex of monkeys that had not received the discrimination training responded to any of these shapes. As discrimination training increases so does the ability to respond differently to different stimuli (Klein, 1996). The results of Kobatake and Tanake (1994) indicate that experience allows neurons in our inferotemporal cortex to recognize complex light stimuli, such as grandma's face. What would happen if these neurons in the inferotemporal cortex were damaged? We look at the effects of just such damage next.

One rather curious type of impairment in object recognition is called **prosopagnosia**, or a difficulty recognizing faces (*prosopon* is Greek for "person"). A person with prosopagnosia has problems distinguishing among the faces of different individuals; for example, he or she might be unable to recognize a close family member in a shopping mall full of people. Autopsies of people with prosopagnosia have revealed damage to the inferior prestriate area and adjacent portions of the inferotemporal cortex (Damasio, 1990). The importance of the inferotemporal cortex for object recognition is not limited to humans; recordings of activity in the inferotemporal cortex have identified neurons that selectively respond to faces in both sheep (Kendrick & Baldwin, 1987) and nonhuman primates (Young & Yamane, 1992).

Damasio (1990) has suggested that prosopagnosia reflects an impairment in the ability to distinguish between similar members of complex classes of visual stimuli rather than merely an inability to recognize faces. A person with prosopagnosia can recognize an object as a face but is unable to identify the face. There is some evidence that people with prosopagnosia also have difficulty distinguishing among other objects. For example, Damasio reports a case of a farmer who, after he became prosopagnosic, could no longer distinguish among his cows. In another case, a bird watcher who became prosopagnosic could no longer identify different bird species.

Recall that there is another major pathway from the primary visual cortex to the secondary visual cortex, extending through the prestriate cortex to the posterior parietal cortex, which is responsible for detecting the location of objects in space and their movement through that space. You may perhaps recognize the concept of spatial location by its more commonly used name, depth perception. The recognition of depth and movement are the subjects covered in the next two sections.

prosopagnosia An impaired ability to recognize faces following damage to the inferior prestriate area and adjacent portions of the inferotemporal cortex.

Before You Go On

Explain how a person with visual agnosia could recognize a batch of freshly baked cookies.

Section Review

- The recognition of objects in our environment is made possible by lateral inhibition, which creates the perception of edges between an object and its surround.
- If the object is brighter than the surround (or vice versa), the activity of ganglion cells at the boundary of the object and its surround increases or decreases depending on the presence or absence of lateral inhibition from adjacent receptors.
- The enhanced contrast in ganglion cell activity produces the perception of the edge of the object.

- Ganglion cells respond to light presented to a limited area called a receptive field.
- Some ganglion cells are excited by a light presented to center and inhibited by light in the surround (center on, surround off), whereas other ganglion cells are inhibited by light in the center and excited by light in the surround (center off, surround on).
- Information about light in the receptive field is sent by a particular ganglion cell to the lateral geniculate nucleus.
- The cells of the lateral geniculate nucleus also have receptive fields and send information about objects and their surround to the primary visual cortex.
- There are four types of cells in the primary visual cortex.
- Simple cells respond to lines that have a specific orientation and location in the visual field.
- Complex cells are sensitive to a specific line stimulus that moves in a particular direction anywhere in the visual field.
- Hypercomplex cells respond to visual stimuli of specific orientation and length.
- Higher-order hypercomplex cells react to visual stimuli of specific sizes and shapes.
- Neurons in the primary visual cortex respond to sine waves or bands of lighter and darker light, as well as to straight lines, with different neurons reacting to different sine-wave patterns.
- Damage to the pathway from the primary visual cortex to the prestriate cortex and then to the inferotemporal cortex leads to visual agnosia, or an inability to visually recognize objects.
- Prosopagnosia is a form of visual agnosia in which the person has difficulty recognizing faces.

Vision: The Perception of Depth, Movement, and Color

The Detection of Depth

On the shelf of my bookcase is a photograph that my eldest son, David, took on a trip to Alaska with his grandparents. The picture was taken around sunset in British Columbia, and is of two wild horses grazing near a lake with snow-capped mountains in the background. The mountains are reflected in the lake, and the sky is beautiful shades of red and purple. Although the picture is two dimensional, I perceive the horses to be located in the foreground against the background of the lake and mountains. My visual system allows me to perceive depth in this two-dimensional picture. Similarly, my visual system allows me to perceive depth in the physical world around me. Without depth perception, we would have great difficulty doing many things that we want to do. We could not, for example, recognize how far our hand is from a pen that we want to pick up and would be unable to reach for it successfully.

How does our visual system allow us to perceive depth? We use a number of cues to recognize depth (see **Figure 6.22**). **Monocular depth cues** are provided by each eye individually (mono = one; ocular = eye). Relative size is one example of a monocular depth cue: objects that produce a larger image on the retina are usually closer to us than objects that produce a smaller image. Other monocular cues include overlap (an object that covers another object is perceived as closer), relative texture (coarser objects are perceived as closer than fine-grain objects), relative height (objects higher in our visual field are perceived as farther away), linear perspective (the greater the convergence, the farther away the object), relative brightness (brighter objects are perceived as closer than dimmer objects), and relative motion (when we move, objects that are stationary appear to move in the opposite direction to the way we are moving).

Binocular depth cues are those provided by both eyes (bi = two; refer to **Figure 6.7**). Because our eyes are approximately $2\frac{1}{2}$ inches apart, each eye has a slightly different view of the world. Our brain compares these two images, with the difference, or retinal disparity, providing an important depth cue: the greater the disparity in the two images, the farther away the object.

So our brains detect differences such as retinal disparity and linear perspectives and use these differences to create a perception of depth. But how? In the preceding section, we learned that different cells in the primary visual cortex respond to different straight lines and sine-wave patterns. The responses of the cells of the primary visual cortex are communicated to the secondary visual cortex to detect the form of objects. Evidence suggests that cells in the primary visual cortex also react to depth cues. For example, Heydt, Peterhans, and Dürsteler (1992) found that some cells in the primary visual cortex respond to one texture but not to another. Similarly, Poggio and Poggio (1984) reported that other cells in the primary visual cortex respond when each eye sees an object in a slightly different position; that is, when retinal disparity exists. Further, Poggio (1986) found that some neurons are sensitive to slight differences in retinal disparity, whereas others are sensitive to greater differences in the input from each eye.

monocular depth cues Depth cues provided by each eye individually including relative size, overlap, relative texture, relative height, linear perspective, relative brightness, and relative motion.

binocular depth cues Depth cues provided by comparing the images received by each of the two eyes.

Figure 6.22 Four examples of monocular depth cues. (a) Overlap, (b) relative brightness, (c) linear perspective, and (d) relative texture.
➤ *What area(s) of the brain are responsible for depth perception? (p. 184)*

Input from the neurons in the primary visual cortex is sent to Area V2, then to the middle-temporal (MT) cortex and the medial superior temporal (MST) cortex, and finally to the posterior parietal lobe. Neurons in this pathway respond to depth cues, where input is perceived as differences in depth.

The Detection of Movement

Recall that information about movement, like information about depth, is first sent to neurons in the magnocellular layers of the primary visual cortex from the Y ganglion cells (via the lateral geniculate nucleus). This information is then transmitted to Area V2 of the prestriate cortex, then to the MT cortex, and MST cortex, and finally on to the posterior parietal cortex (refer to **Figure 6.8**). As is the case with the detection of shape and depth, the neurons in the pathway from Area V1 to the posterior parietal lobe are selectively sensitive to movement (Movshon, 1990). Research using fMRIs reveals that neurons in the MT or MST cortex become active when people look at moving objects (Tootell, 1995).

The neurons in the primary visual cortex in this system are not responsive to any movement, but are selectively sensitive to one of three types of movement; specifically, they are selectively sensitive to motion that is perpendicular to one axis of orientation, which can be horizontal, vertical, or oblique. Thus, some neurons in Area V1 are responsive to movement that is horizontal to their plane of axis, whereas other Area V1 neurons react to vertical motion.

Each motion-sensitive neuron of Area V1 detects movement in only one plane—horizontal, vertical, or oblique. For example, a specific neuron in the primary visual cortex can detect whether an object is moving right or left, but not up or down. The research of Movshon and his colleagues (Movshon, 1990; Movshon et al., 1985; Newsome, Britten, & Movshon, 1989) refers to the neurons in Area V1 that detect movement as **component direction-selective neurons**. To illustrate the functioning of these neurons, suppose an object is moving up and to the left. One type of Area V1 neuron detects the "up" (vertical) movement and another detects the "to the left" (horizontal) movement. Yet another type of neuron located in the MT cortex, called **pattern direction-selective neurons**, combines the information coming from the primary visual cortex to recognize that the object is moving both up and to the left.

What about the speed of movement? Neurons in the MST cortex can detect the speed at which an object is moving (Movshon, 1990). This information is extracted from the firing pattern of neurons in the MT cortex, with a higher rate of firing signaling a faster moving object.

These motion-sensitive neurons respond only to movement and are insensitive to the identity of the object (Lague, Raiguel, & Orban, 1993). For example, a motion-sensitive cell would respond equally to a small or large object that is moving in the same direction. Further, people with damage to this area of the brain cannot identify the speed or direction of an object, but can identify the object that is moving (Greenlee et al., 1995).

How is information about the movement of objects in our environment used? Neural impulses from the MT and MST cortex travel directly to the brainstem and then on to the cerebellum, where pursuit eye movements, or eye movements that track a moving object, can be controlled. Thus, information from motion-sensitive neurons in the visual system allows us to follow moving objects in our environment. This magnocellular pathway detecting movement also projects to the posterior parietal cortex, often referred to as the visual motor area, which guides body movements toward objects in the environment. For example, information from this part of the visual system can be used by a batter in a baseball game to swing a bat at the time when the batter is most likely to hit the ball. This visual pathway can also allow a person to shake hands with another person. These examples, swinging a bat and shaking hands, are but two of the many ways that movement information guides our behavior.

Before You Go On

What might happen following damage to the posterior parietal cortex?

The Detection of Color

How are we able to sense the blue color of the sky or the green of grass or the red of a sunset? Recall that the photoreceptors responsible for the perception of color are the cones. But how exactly is color perceived? Two different theories of color vision have been proposed: the Young-Helmholz trichromatic theory and Hering's opponent-process theory.

Young-Helmholz Trichromatic Theory. English physicist Thomas Young proposed in 1802 that there are three types of receptors in the eye, and that different patterns of stimulation of these receptors result in the perception of different colors. Herman von Helmholz in 1852 modified Young's earlier theory, suggesting that there are three different sets of fibers (receptors) in the eye: one that responds to blue, a second to green, and a third to red. Activation of those fibers in different combinations allows us to perceive colors other than blue, green, and red. For example, a yellow object would activate both the green and red fibers, creating the perception of the color yellow. To recognize the contribution of both researchers, this view of color vision is now known as the **Young-Helmholz trichromatic theory**.

Hering's Opponent-Process Theory. In 1878, German physiologist Ewald Hering suggested that there are four primary colors—blue, green, yellow, and red—and two noncolor visual stimuli—white and black. According to Hering, these six stimuli operate in opposing pairs: blue-yellow, green-red, and white-black. A different receptor cell exists for each member of an opponent pair, so there are six types of color receptors. The activity of a particular receptor cell is increased by the detection of one color of the pair and decreased by the detection of the other color of the pair. For example, detection of the color red increases activity of the red-green receptor cell, whereas green decreases activity. Similarly, blue increases activity of the blue-yellow receptor and yellow decreases activity. This view of color vision is now known as Hering's **opponent-process theory**.

---

component direction-selective neurons Neurons in the primary visual cortex (Area V1) that detect the movement of an object in one plane—horizontal, vertical, or oblique.

pattern direction-selective neurons Neurons located in the middle-temporal (MT) cortex that combine the information coming from the primary visual cortex to recognize the exact direction in which an object is moving.

Young-Helmholz trichromatic theory The view that there are three different sets of fibers (receptors) in the eye: one that responds to blue, a second to green, and a third to red.

opponent-process theory The view that there are six stimuli that operate in opposing pairs: blue-yellow, green-red, and white-black. A different receptor cell exists for each member of an opponent pair, so there are six types of color receptors.

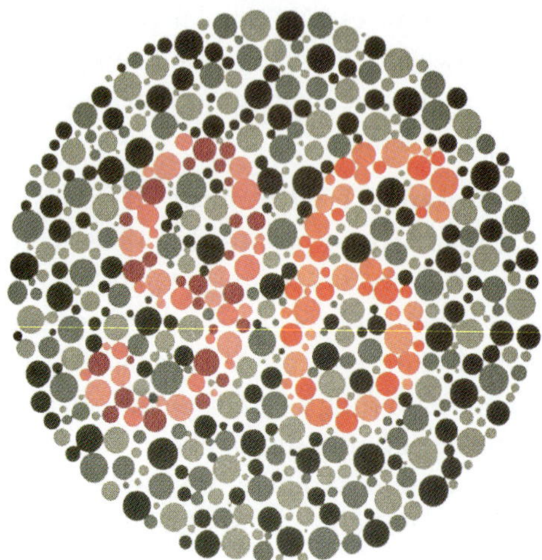

Figure 6.23 A test of color vision. If you cannot see the number in the figure, you are red-green color blind.

➤ *What area(s) of the brain recognize colors? (p. 186)*

But who is right, Hering or Young and Helmholz? Several lines of evidence indicate that the visual system is indeed composed of receptors for opposing pairs of colors, not for independent colors as Young-Helmholz suggested. According to the trichromatic theory, any combination of colors is possible; however, an object can be reddish yellow or bluish green, but not reddish green or bluish yellow. This observation is consistent with Hering's opponent-process theory; because red and green (or blue and yellow) have opposing effects on the same receptor, they cannot be combined.

According to trichromatic theory, yellow is a combination of red and green. But people with red-green color blindness have no trouble seeing yellow, another strike against the trichromatic theory. The observation that color blindness seems to exist for pairs of colors, red-green (see **Figure 6.23**) and blue-yellow (which is quite rare), lends support to the opponent-process theory.

The existence of negative afterimages presents another stumbling block for the trichromatic theory. A **negative afterimage** is a lingering sensation of a color experienced after a person has stared at its complementary color for some time. Thus, you may see red after looking at a green object for a while or see blue after looking at a yellow object. To illustrate a negative afterimage, stare at the rather unusual flag on the left in **Figure 6.24** for a minute. Now look at the blank rectangle on the right. What colors do you see? The process of negative afterimages would cause you to see a flag with a blue field and red and white stripes.

You might have concluded at this point that opponent-process theory presents the more accurate view of color vision. However, several investigators (Brown & Wald, 1964; Marks, Dobelle, & MacNichol, 1964) have studied the responsivity of cones to various wavelengths of light and have found that sensitivity to light is clustered into three categories: some cones are maximally sensitive to blue, others to green, and still others to red. The differences in responsivity result from different rates of absorption of different wavelengths of light by the three types of cones and rods in humans (see **Figure 6.25**). This evidence indicates that there are three kinds of cones, supporting the trichromatic theory.

negative afterimage The lingering sensation of a color that is experienced after staring at its complementary color for some time.

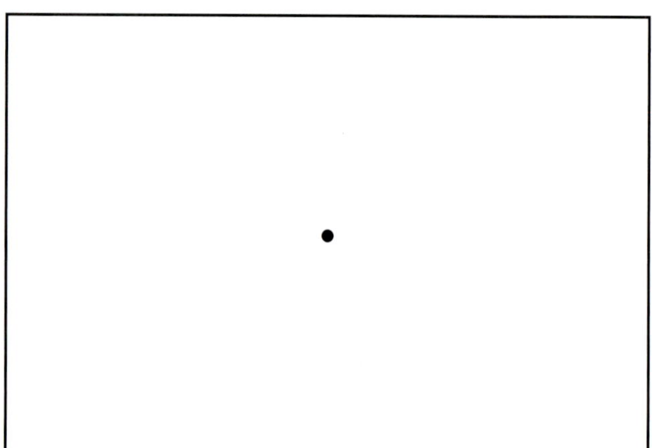

Figure 6.24 Negative afterimages. A demonstration of negative afterimages is found by staring at the flag for a minute. Now look at the white rectangle. You should see a blue flag with a blue field and red and white stripes.

➤ *What would be the negative afterimage of a blue flower with green leaves? (p. 186)*

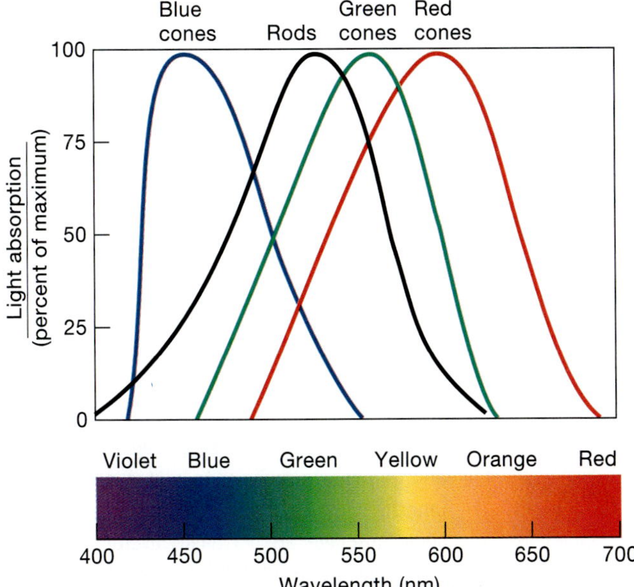

Figure 6.25 The relative absorption of different wavelengths of light by three types of cones and by rods. "Blue" cone is maximally responsive to a 419-nm light; "green" cone maximally responds to a 531-nm light; and a "red" cone is maximally responsive to a 559-nm light.

➤ *The existence of three types of cones supports which theory of color vision? (p. 185)*

Still other evidence indicates that colors are detected by opposing pairs of ganglion cells. Several researchers (Daw, 1968; Gouras, 1968) have reported evidence that there are ganglion cell pairs that are differentially sensitive to neural messages about red-green and blue-yellow (see **Figure 6.26**). In the red-green ganglion cell pair, one ganglion cell responds to red in the center of its receptive field and green in its surround (called a red-green ganglion cell), and the other (called a green-red ganglion cell) responds to green in the center of the receptive field and red in the surround. Similarly, a ganglion cell that reacts to blue in the center and yellow in the surround (blue-yellow) will be opposed by a ganglion cell that responds to yellow in the center and blue in the surround (yellow-blue).

It would appear that there are three types of cones as predicted by trichromatic theory (red, green, blue) and two pairs of ganglion cells as predicted by opponent-process theory (red-green and blue-yellow). How does our visual system perceive the color yellow if cones are not sensitive to yellow? As shown in **Figure 6.27**, yellow stimulates both the red and green cones. Activation of a red cone will excite a red-green ganglion cell. However, the simultaneous activation of a green cone excites a green-red ganglion cell, and thus the net excitation of red-green and green-red ganglion cells is zero. However, the excitation of the yellow-blue ganglion cells by both the red and green cones creates the perception of the color yellow.

Differential responding to the four colors (blue, green, yellow, red) also seems to involve specific cells

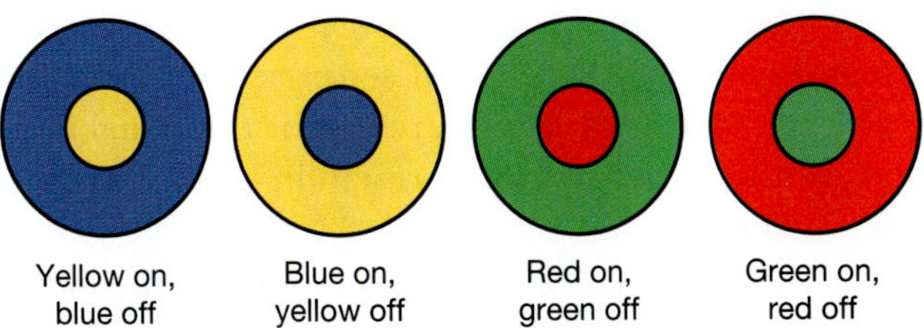

Figure 6.26 Four types of ganglion cells. Each ganglion cell is stimulated in the center by one color and in the surround by its opponent color.

➤ *The existence of ganglion cell pairs supports which theory of color vision? (p. 187)*

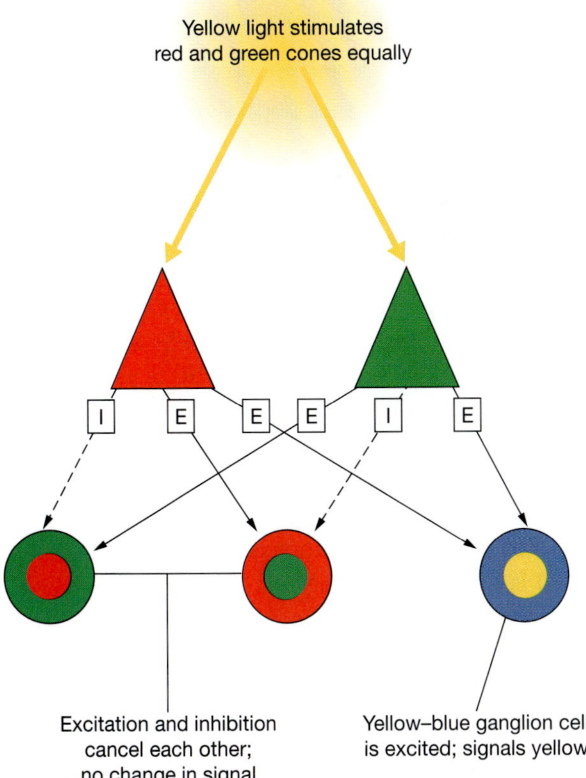

Figure 6.27 How yellow light produces perception of yellow. Yellow light stimulates red and green cones. Activation of the red-green ganglion cell is offset by stimulation of the green-red ganglion cell. The only input signaled is the activation of yellow-blue ganglion cell. (I = inhibition; E = excitation.)

➤ *Where are the cones located? (p. 187)*

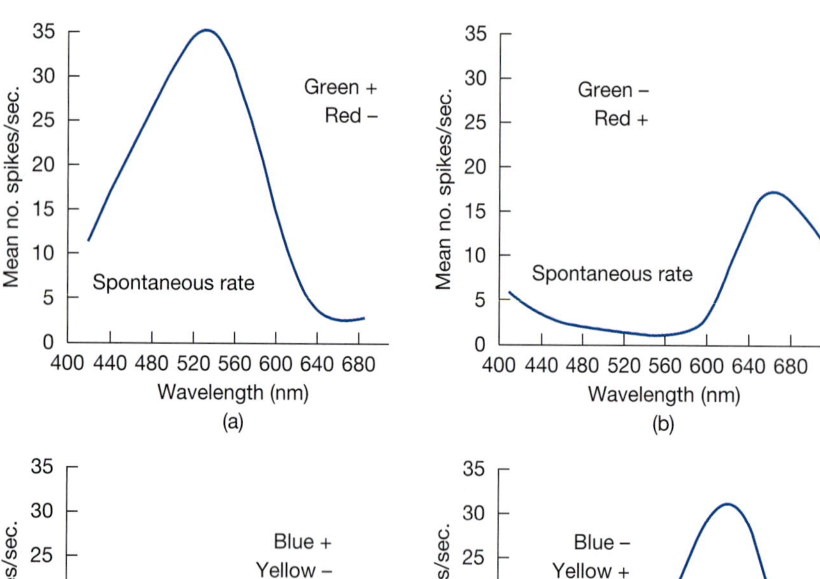

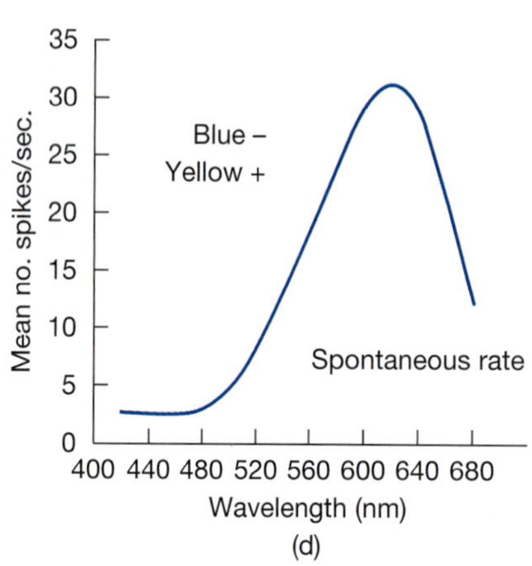

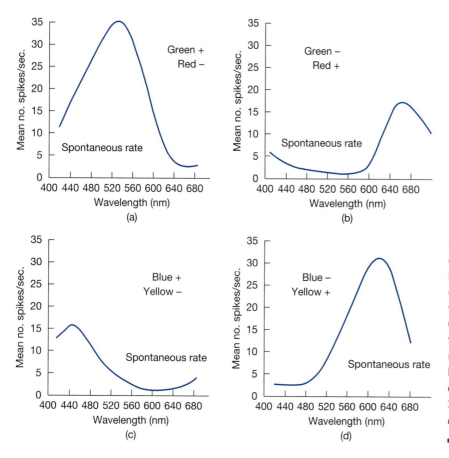

Figure 6.28 The response of cells in the lateral geniculate nucleus to different wavelengths of light. (a) Green+, Red- lateral geniculate cells are maximally excited by green wavelengths and inhibited by red; (b) Red+, Green- cells are maximally excited by red and inhibited by green; (c) Yellow+, Blue- cells are maximally excited by yellow and inhibited by blue; (d) Blue+, Yellow- cells are maximally excited by blue and inhibited by yellow.

➤ *How are colors other than green, red, blue, and yellow perceived? (p. 188)*

farther down the visual pathway in the lateral geniculate nucleus of the thalamus (see **Figure 6.28**). DeValois and DeValois (1975) reported that some lateral geniculate cells are excited by a red stimulus and inhibited by a green stimulus (Red+, Green-), whereas other lateral geniculate nucleus cells are excited by a green stimulus and inhibited by a red stimulus (Green+, Red-), or are excited by a blue stimulus and inhibited by a yellow stimulus (Blue+, Yellow-), or are excited by a yellow stimulus and inhibited by a blue stimulus (Yellow+, Blue-).

Perception of colors other than blue, green, yellow, or red is believed to reflect the combined activation of nonopposing color cells. For example, the color orange activates both red and yellow lateral geniculate nucleus cells. Similarly purple reflects the combined activation of blue and red cells.

Information about color is sent from the lateral geniculate nucleus to the visual cortex. Area V1 of the primary visual cortex contains cells sensitive to color (Zeki, 1993). The cells in Area V1 react in a manner similar to ganglion and lateral geniculate cells; that is, activity in these cells is increased by one color and decreased by its opposing color. By contrast, cells in Area V4 of the secondary visual cortex respond only to very specific colors or to a narrow wavelength of light.

We know that the way in which a color is perceived is affected by the context in which it is presented. To illustrate this effect, look at the painting shown in **Figure 6.29**. The lines on the right look yellow and the ones on the left appear gray. However, the color is the same (gold), but appears to be different because of the different contexts. The action of cells in Area V4 is believed to be responsible for this contrast effect. For example, one cell sensitive to green may react one way if red is also present in the visual field and another way if yellow is present in another part of the visual field.

There is much that we still do not understand about the neural mechanisms responsible for color vision. For example, an object is generally perceived as being the same color even under different lighting conditions. This phenomenon, called **color constancy**, allows us to perceive a leaf as green in the bright light of the afternoon as well as in the dim light of dusk, and is not yet understood. Also, no current theory of color

---

color constancy The perception that the color of an object remains the same even under different lighting conditions.

vision can explain how we detect such colors as brown or gold. Future research will undoubtedly seek to answer these questions.

Why Three Pathways in the Visual Sensory System?

One question that remains to be answered is how the visual system incorporates the information detected by each of the three visual pathways that detect shape, color, and motion and depth. Merigan and Maunsell (1993) suggest that there are extensive connections among the three pathways throughout the visual system. These connections begin in the primary visual cortex (Area V1) and increase as the three pathways move anterior in the cerebral cortex. The interconnections of the three pathways provide for a singular perception of a light stimulus; that is, a visual stimulus that has a specific shape, color, and movement and depth. Not all neuroscientists (Orban et al., 1996; Schiller, 1996), however, believe that there are separate pathways for the analysis of shape, color, and motion and depth. Instead, these neuroscientists assume that many visual areas perform several different functions rather than identifying one attribute of a visual stimulus. Research is currently continuing to explore the mechanisms responsible for the combination of the attributes of a light stimulus into a perceived visual stimulus.

In the next chapter, we move on to the other senses that allow us to fully experience the wonders of the world around us: the hearing of a bell signaling the start of class, the dizziness we feel if we sit down too quickly, the smoothness of the writing surface of our desk, the smell of perfume on the student sitting next to us, and the taste of the gum we are chewing.

Figure 6.29 Contrast effects. This painting by Josef Albers shows the influence of context on color. The gold lines appear gray on the left and yellow on the right (photo courtesy of the Josef Albers Foundation).

➤ *Which area of the brain is believed to be responsible for such contrast effects? (p. 188)*

Before You Go On

Explain a possible neurological basis for red-green color blindness.

Section Review

- Several types of cues provide information about the spatial location of a stimulus, or depth perception.
- Monocular cues include relative size, overlap, texture, relative height, linear perspective, and relative motion.
- The difference in visual images from the two eyes, called retinal disparity, provides a binocular depth cue.
- Specific neurons in the primary visual cortex react to texture and retinal disparity.
- Component direction-selective neurons in Area V1 of the primary visual cortex respond to movement in one of three planes—horizontal, vertical, or oblique.
- Pattern direction-selective neurons in the middle-temporal (MT) cortex combine information from separate component direction-selective neurons to recognize the actual direction an object is moving.
- The magnocellular visual pathway controls pursuit eye movements and body movements toward objects in the environment.
- The Young-Helmholz trichromatic theory suggests that there are three different sets of fibers (receptors) in the eye: one that responds to blue, a second to green, and a third to red.
- Hering's opponent-process theory proposes that six stimuli operate in opposing pairs: blue-yellow, green-red, and white-black. A different receptor cell exists for each member of an opponent pair, so there are six types of color receptors.
- Cones are classified into three categories depending on the color to which they respond: some are maximally sensitive to blue, others to green, and the third kind to red.
- Ganglion cells are found in opposing pairs: red-green, yellow-blue, and white-black.
- Each ganglion cell responds to one color in its center and to the opposing color in the surround.
- Perception of colors other than the primary colors (blue, green, yellow, and red) reflects the combined activation of nonopposing color cells.
- Cells in the lateral geniculate nucleus are excited by one color and inhibited by the opponent color.
- Cells in Area V1 react in a manner similar to ganglion and lateral geniculate nucleus cells, whereas cells in Area V4 respond only to a narrow wavelength of light.
- Activity in Area V4 cells is affected by the presence of other colors in the visual field, so that the perception of a color is determined by the context in which it is viewed.

Chapter Review

Critical Thinking Questions

1. Donna looked out of her hotel window to the beauty of Mobile Bay. The water moved gently to the shore, and in the distance, a yellow sailboat approached. Explain the mechanism responsible for Donna's ability to recognize the moving object as being a yellow sailboat.
2. Sheila mistakenly approached a stranger at the mall thinking that the stranger was her friend Heather. The unfamiliar woman looked like Heather, but was not her. Suggest several possible reasons for Sheila's failure to distinguish between Heather and the other woman.
3. The Hall of Fame baseball player Ted Williams claimed that he could see the seams rotating on a baseball that had been thrown to him. (Before you say "so what?", remember that major league pitchers can hurl a fastball at speeds close to 100 mph.) Trace the image of the baseball through Ted Williams' visual sensory system and explain a possible mechanism for the super acuity of his visual perception.

Vocabulary Questions

1. The transformation of physical energy into a neural impulse is called ________________.
2. The separate taste receptors for bitter and sweet are an example of ________________ coding.
3. The recognition of a particular pattern of response from a number of visual receptors to detect a particular color is an example of ________________ coding.
4. The retina contains three layers of neurons: the ________________, the ________________ cells, and the ________________ cells.
5. The central region of the retina is called the ________________.
6. ________________ operate more effectively in bright light and are responsible for vision in dim light.
7. The optic nerves meet at the ________________, where many of the fibers cross over to the opposite side of the brain.
8. An inability to see objects placed in a particular part of the visual field is called a ________________.
9. ________________, the photopigment found in rods, consists of a protein ________________ and a lipid ________________.
10. The process that allows the detection of edges in order to recognize an object is called ________________.
11. The four types of cells in the primary visual cortex are ________________, ________________, ________________, and ________________.
12. ________________ is a difficulty in the recognition of faces.
13. The layers of the primary visual cortex responsible for the detection of movement are the ________________ layers.
14. According to the ________________ theory, visual stimuli operate in three opposing pairs: blue-yellow, green-red, and white-black.
15. The phenomenon called ________________ allows us to perceive objects as being the same color under different lighting conditions.

Review Questions

1. The functions of the sensory receptors are
   a. absorption of physical energy and conversion of energy into a neural impulse.
   b. seeing, tasting, and smelling.
   c. seeing, sensing touch, and tasting.
   d. absorption of physical energy and transmission of neural impulses.
2. Light passes through the ____________, then the __________ and the ____________ before it reaches the ________________ of the eye.
   a. retina and iris, cornea, pupil, blind spot
   b. cornea, pupil, lens, retina
   c. pupil, iris, retina, optic nerve
   d. blind spot, optic tectum, cornea, lens
3. The two types of photoreceptors are the
   a. ganglion cells and the amacrine cells.
   b. horizontal cells and the bipolar cells.
   c. rods and bipolar cells.
   d. rods and cones.
4. The rods are more concentrated in the ____________ of the retina, and cones are more concentrated in the __________ of the retina.
   a. periphery, center
   b. center, periphery
   c. center, surround
   d. surround, center

5. The blind spot at the back of the eye is also called the
   a. retina.
   b. optic nerve.
   c. optic disk.
   d. optic tectum.
6. Most fibers of the optic tract project to the
   a. primary visual cortex.
   b. lateral geniculate nucleus.
   c. secondary visual cortex.
   d. opposite side of the brain.
7. Light can vary in terms of
   a. wavelength, frequency, and depth.
   b. wavelength, brightness, and saturation.
   c. length, depth, and height.
   d. brightness, depth, and movement.
8. The chemical molecules responsible for the detection of light are called
   a. photopigments.
   b. photoreceptors.
   c. photographers.
   d. opsins.
9. Ganglion cells that are excited in response to a light stimulus are called
   a. off cells.
   b. on-off cells.
   c. on cells.
   d. center cells.
10. The limited, circular area of the retina to which a ganglion cell is responsive is called the
    a. receptive field.
    b. visual field.
    c. on-center field.
    d. center field.
11. When a person cannot identify an object presented visually but can identify it by touching it, that person is said to suffer from
    a. a visual field deficit.
    b. visual agnosia.
    c. amnesia.
    d. blindness.
12. ________________ is a monocular depth cue, and ________________ is a binocular depth cue.
    a. Retinal disparity, texture
    b. Retinal disparity, relative size
    c. Relative height, texture
    d. Relative size, retinal disparity
13. According to the trichromatic theory, the three types of receptors in the eye are
    a. blue, green, and red.
    b. horizontal cells, ganglion cells, and bipolar cells.
    c. ganglion cells, amacrine cells, and photoreceptors.
    d. yellow, blue, and red.
14. Neurons in the lateral geniculate nuclei respond to colors as predicted by
    a. trichromatic theory.
    b. specific nerve theory.
    c. opponent process theory.
    d. color code theory.

Suggested Readings

De Valois, R. L., & De Valois, K. K. (1988). *Spatial vision.* New York: Oxford University Press.

Hubel, D. H. (1988). *Eye, brain, and vision.* New York: Seventh American Library.

Kaiser, P. K., & Boynton, R. M. (1996). *Human color vision.* Washington, DC: Optical Society of America.

Merigan, W. H., & Maunsell, J. H. B. (1993). How parallel are the private visual pathways? *Annual Review of Neuroscience, 16,* 369–402.

Wandell, B. A. (1995). *Foundations of vision.* Sutherland, MA: Sinauer.

Zeki, S. (1992). The visual image in mind and brain. *Scientific American, 267* (3), 69–76.

7 BEYOND VISION

THE AUDITORY, VESTIBULAR, SOMATOSENSORY, AND CHEMICAL SENSES

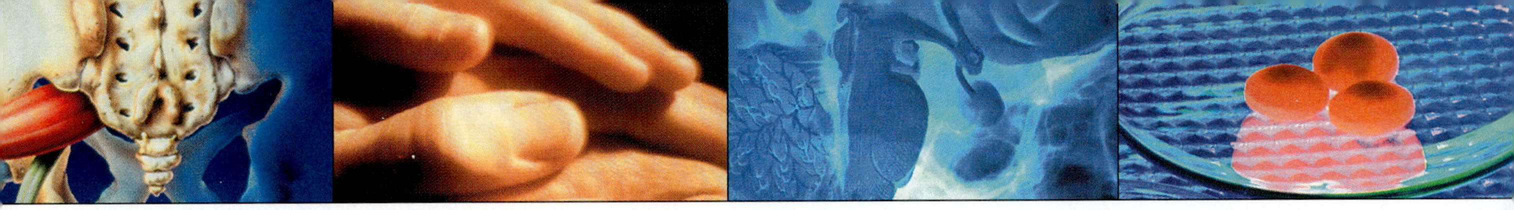

A Welcomed Call

Heather and her daughter Kathy live several hours away from each other, but talk on the telephone several times a week. Their conversations mostly center on Sarah, Heather's only grandchild, who just turned four. Each call brings exciting news about Sarah's latest exploits. Yesterday, Sarah wrote her name in preschool and was quite proud of herself.

Sarah also likes to talk with grandma on the telephone. She becomes very excited upon learning that grandma is on the phone. Sarah was waiting to tell grandma the latest news about their neighbor's new puppy, Buddy. Buddy is black with white spots and loves to jump and lick her. Sarah also tells grandma that they are having spaghetti for dinner, which is her favorite food, and about a new song she has learned, "Three Blind Mice." Sarah then proceeds to sing for grandma.

◀ There are approximately 12,000 outer hair cells and 3,400 inner hair cells in each ear.

After Sarah's telephone performance, Heather smiles and tells her that she enjoyed the song. She also tells Sarah that she loves her very much and that she will see her in a few weeks. After she stands up to hang up the phone, Heather wipes a tear from her cheek. Sarah is a great joy and she can't wait to see her. ■

Before You Go On

How was Heather able to hear Kathy and Sarah's voices on the telephone?

Which sense enabled Heather to feel the tear on her cheek and Sarah to feel the dog licking her face?

Which sense(s) allowed Heather to stand up and hang up the telephone and Sarah to keep from falling over when Buddy jumped up on her?

In this chapter, we will help you answer these and the following questions:

- What is sound, and how are sounds such as the notes that make up "Three Blind Mice" received and processed by the auditory system?
- Which sense helps us orient our bodies in space?
- How many types of touch receptors are there, and what happens if one or more of them malfunctions?
- What is the olfactory system, and how does it allow us to detect the delicious smell of Kathy's spaghetti sauce simmering on the stove?
- Which sense allows us to taste the sauce?

Table 7.1 ■ Sound Amplitude and Perceived Loudness

Typical Decibel Level	Example	Dangerous Time Exposure
0	Lowest audible sound	
30	Quiet library; soft whisper	
40	Quiet office; living room; bedroom away from traffic	
50	Light traffic at a distance; refrigerator; gentle breeze	
60	Air conditioner at 20 feet; conversation; sewing machine in operation	
70	Busy traffic; noisy restaurant	Some damage if continuous
80	Subway; heavy city traffic; alarm clock at 2 feet; factory noise	More than 8 hours
90	Truck traffic; noisy home appliances; shop tools; gas lawnmower	Less than 8 hours
100	Chain saw; boiler shop; pneumatic drill	2 hours
120	"Heavy metal" rock concert; sandblasting; thunderclap nearby	Immediate danger
140	Gunshot; jet plane	Immediate danger
160	Rocket launching pad	Hearing loss inevitable

Source: Martini, F. H. (1998). *Fundamentals of Anatomy and Physiology* (4th ed.). Upper Saddle River, NJ: Prentice-Hall.

The Auditory Sense

In the opening vignette, the auditory sense, or sense of hearing, was the one most actively used by Heather as she strained to hear her granddaughter's every word. If you have found a quiet place to study, your auditory sense is not distracting you from using your visual sense to read these pages. But have you ever thought about how important hearing is? About how you would have to modify your behavior if you lost your hearing? You wouldn't be able to talk on a regular telephone, listen to your favorite music, or hear the words accompanying a television show or movie, and you would have to learn how to read lips and/or use sign language to communicate. In this section of the chapter, we will explain how a normally functioning auditory system is able to detect sounds and recognize their meaning.

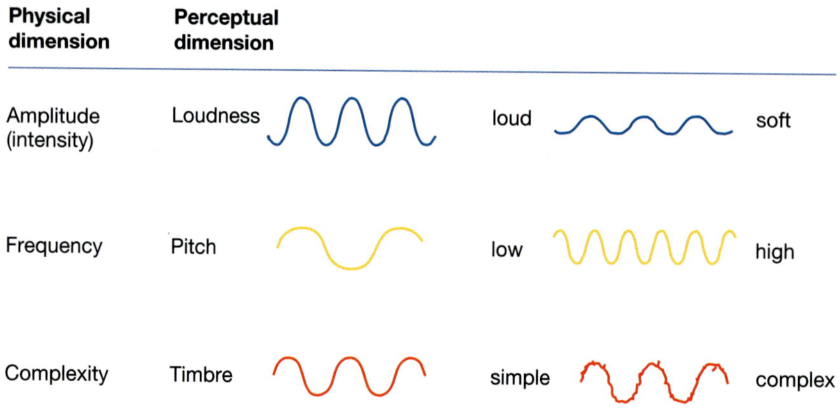

Physical dimension	Perceptual dimension		
Amplitude (intensity)	Loudness	loud	soft
Frequency	Pitch	low	high
Complexity	Timbre	simple	complex

Figure 7.1 Wave forms for the three timbre dimensions of sounds. The three perceptual qualities of a sound, loudness, pitch, and timbre, correspond to the amplitude, frequency, and complexity of the sound wave.

➤ *Which dimension(s) is (are) used to differentiate Sarah's rendition of "Three Blind Mice" from a version by the Boston Pops Orchestra? (p. 195)*

When objects in the environment such as Sarah's vocal cords vibrate, they set molecules in the air in motion, alternately condensing them (pushing them together) and rarefying them (pulling them apart), and creating waves of movement that travel away from the vibrating object. These waves are detected by auditory receptors in the ear and are ultimately perceived as particular sounds.

Sound waves, like waves of light, vary along three dimensions (see **Figure 7.1**). One dimension is the frequency of a sound wave, which we perceive as **pitch**. Frequency refers to the number of vibrations per second and is measured in hertz (Hz). Humans can hear only sounds that vary from 20 Hz (low pitch) to 20,000 Hz (high pitch). Some species, such as elephants and whales, can hear sounds as low as 15 Hz (infrasounds), whereas other animals, such as dogs, can hear sounds as high as 40,000 Hz (ultrasounds).

Sound waves, like ocean waves, also differ in terms of their amplitude or height, which we perceive as **loudness**. The more intensely that an object vibrates, the greater the amplitude, or change in condensation and rarefaction of the air molecules. Objects that produce small changes (small ripples) are perceived as soft sounds; objects that produce large changes (large ripples) are perceived as loud sounds. The amplitude of a sound wave is measured in decibels (dB); the higher the decibel level, the louder the sound. **Table 7.1** presents examples of sounds of differing loudness.

Some sounds are pure, consisting of a single frequency. Other sounds are complex, consisting of multiple frequencies. The combination of frequencies gives each sound its characteristic quality, which we perceive

pitch Perception of the frequency of a sound wave, measured in hertz (Hz).

loudness Perception of the amplitude of a sound wave, measured in decibels (dB).

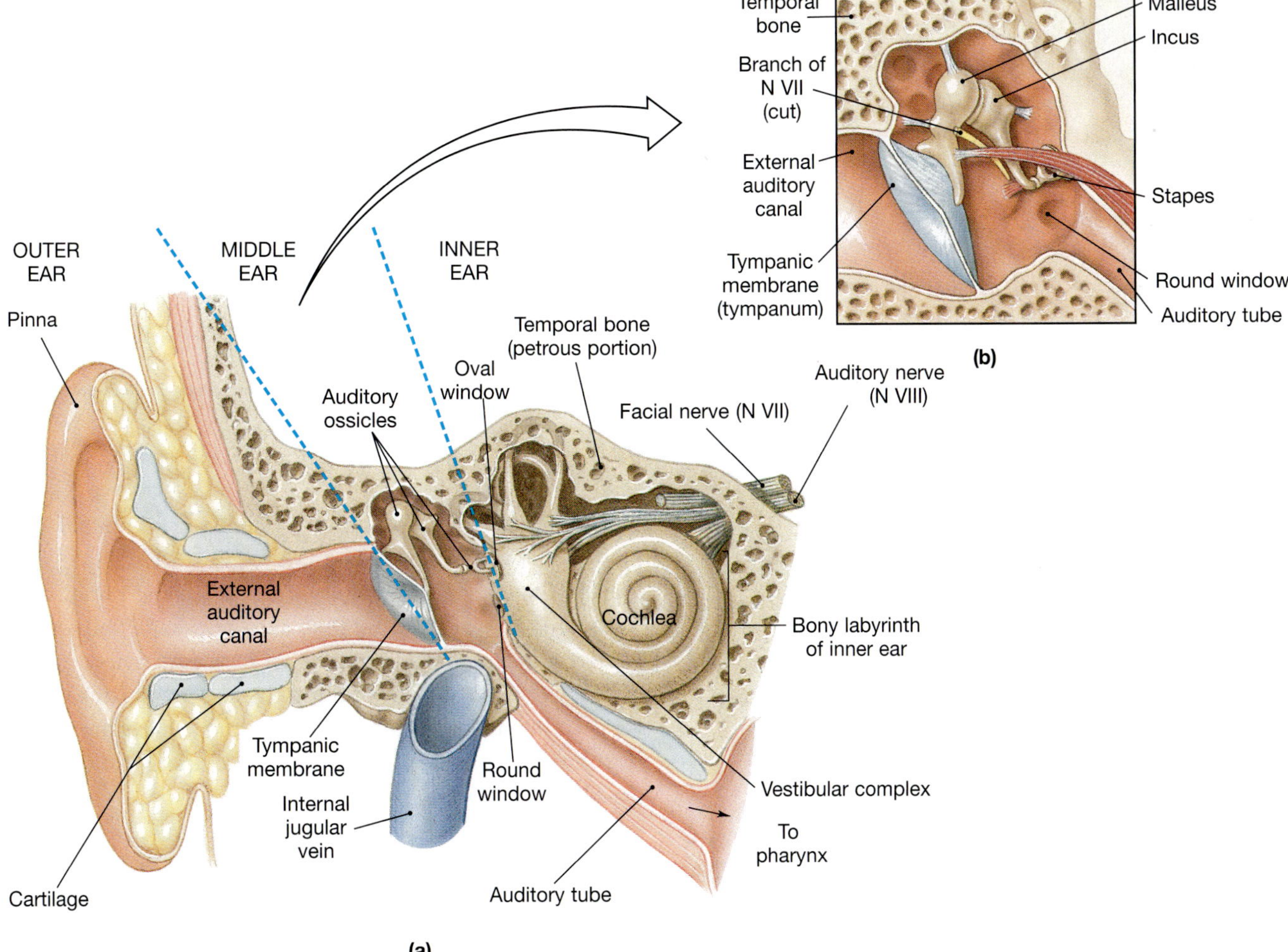

Figure 7.2 The ear. (a) Cross-sectional view of the main structures of the ear. (b) Detail of the structure of the middle ear.

➤ *What causes the increased force of the vibrations through the middle ear? (p. 197)*

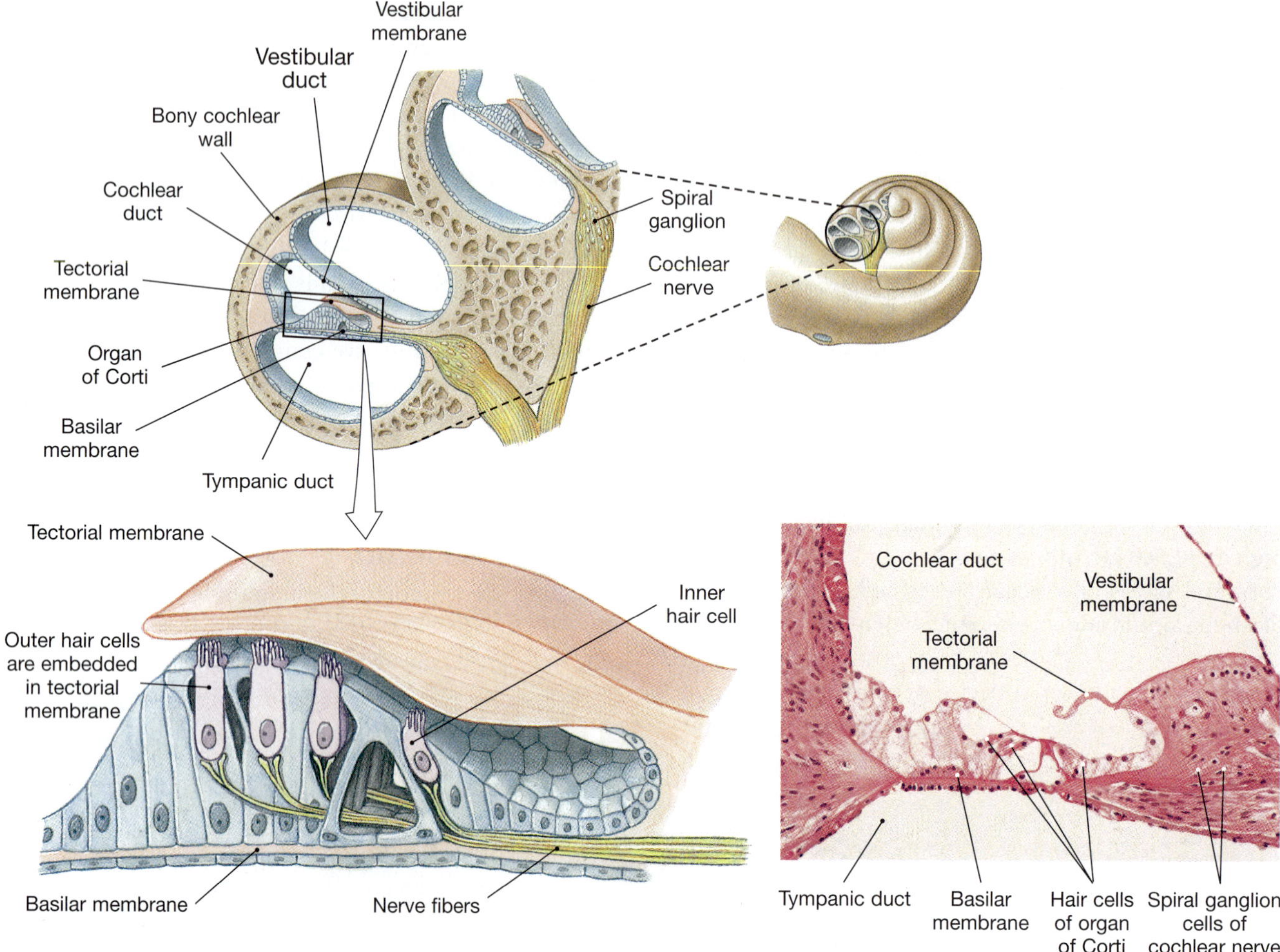

Figure 7.3 The organ of Corti. Cross-sectional view of main structures of the organ of Corti. The basilar and tectorial membranes vibrate in response to sound waves, and the inner and outer hair cells transduce these vibrations into neural impulses.

➤ *How are the hair cells attached to the basilar membrane? (p. 197)*

as **timbre**. A violin has a different sound than a trumpet because the combinations of frequencies produced by each instrument are different.

Frequency, amplitude, and complexity are physical qualities of a given sound. The auditory receptors of the nervous system detect these qualities and transduce them into neural activity. The auditory cortex then interprets the neural messages so that we perceive a sound of a certain pitch, loudness, and timbre.

timbre The purity of a sound; the combination of frequencies that gives each sound its characteristic quality.

pinna The outer, visible portion of the ear.

tympanic membrane The membrane that divides the outer and middle parts of the ear; also called the eardrum.

malleus (hammer) The bone of the middle ear that is attached to the tympanic membrane and the incus.

The Ear

The ear is much more than the visible portion that Sarah puts earrings on when she plays dress-up. The biological name for the visible portion of the ear is the **pinna**, and strangely enough, although its unusual shape helps us to detect where sound is coming from, it is not needed for hearing. The ear is divided into three sections, the outer ear (pinna to ear drum), middle ear (the eardrum to the oval window), and the inner ear (including the cochlea and the vestibular system; see **Figure 7.2**).

Sound waves enter the pinna and travel down the external (see **Figure 7.2**) auditory canal until reaching the **tympanic membrane** (eardrum; see **Figure 7.2**). The sound waves cause the eardrum to vibrate, and the vibrations are transmitted by the three small bones, or auditory ossicles of the middle ear—the **malleus**, the **incus**, and the **stapes**—which are also known as the hammer, the anvil, and the stirrup, respectively based (very loosely!) on their shapes. The malleus, or hammer, is attached to the tympanic membrane and conducts the vibrations through the incus and stapes to the **oval window**.

The tympanic membrane has a surface approximately 20 times larger than the stapes (see **Figure 7.2**). This difference causes the force of the vibrations to increase as sound is transmitted by the three bones of the middle ear. This increased force enables the sound wave to be transmitted through the oval window and through the fluid contained in the inner ear.

Inside the oval window is the snail-shaped structure called the **cochlea** (from the Greek word meaning "land snails"). The cochlea contains three long, fluid-filled chambers: the vestibular duct, the cochlear duct, and the tympanic duct (refer to **Figure 7.3**). The vibrations of the oval window create changes in pressure in the fluid of the cochlea; these changes are transmitted through the cochlea to the round window. When the vibrations reach the **round window**, the window is pushed out. The fluid then reverses direction and the round window is pushed in, causing the pressure to move through the cochlea until the fluid bounces back against the oval window. The fluid inside the cochlea continues to move as long as the stapes vibrates in response to the presence of a sound wave.

Within the cochlear duct is the **organ of Corti**, which contains the basilar membrane, the hair cells, and the tectorial membrane (refer to **Figure 7.3**). The **hair cells** are the auditory receptors that initially detect moving fluid (sound waves). There are approximately 12,000 outer hair cells and 3,400 inner hair cells in each ear. Both the outer and the inner hair cells are attached to the **basilar membrane** by Deiter's cells (see **Figure 7.4**). The inner hair cells come into close contact with the **tectorial membrane**, but do not actually touch it, whereas the outer hair cells are embedded in the tectorial membrane.

---

incus (anvil) The bone of the middle ear that is attached to the malleus and stapes.

stapes (stirrup) The bone of the middle ear that is attached to the incus and the oval window.

oval window The membrane that divides the middle and inner parts of the ear.

cochlea The snail-shaped structure in the inner ear, composed of the vestibular duct and the tympanic duct, that contains the auditory receptors.

round window The membrane that, along with the oval window, maintains the movement of fluid of the inner ear through the cochlea as long as the stapes vibrates in response to sound waves.

organ of Corti The structure within the cochlea that contains the basilar membrane, the hair cells, and the tectorial membrane.

hair cells Auditory receptors.

basilar membrane A membrane in the organ of Corti to which the auditory receptors are attached by Deiter's cells.

tectorial membrane A membrane in the organ of Corti in which the outer hair cells are embedded that comes in close contact with inner hair cells.

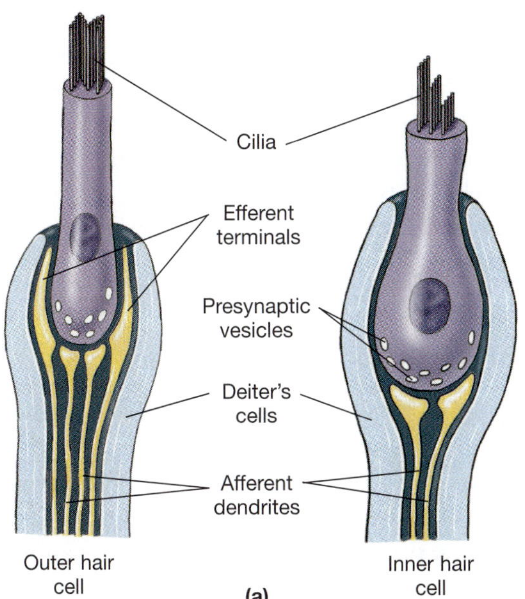

Figure 7.4 Auditory receptors. (a) A cross-sectional view of the structure of inner hair cells (right) and outer hair cells (left) and (b) photomicrograph of the inner and outer hair cells.

➤ *What is the difference between outer hair cells and inner hair cells? (p. 197)*

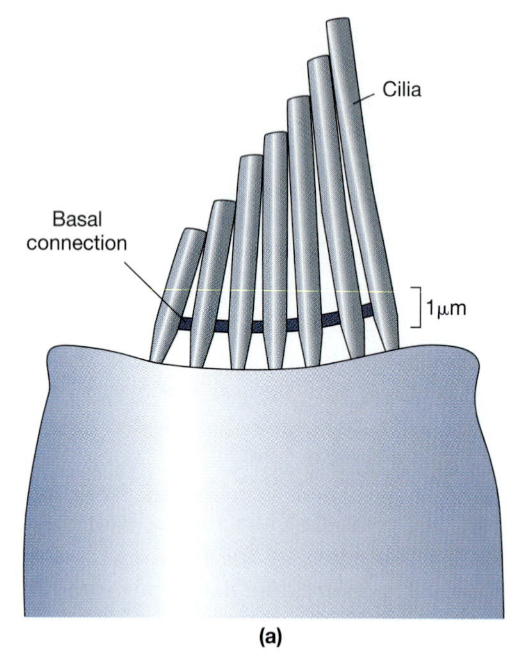

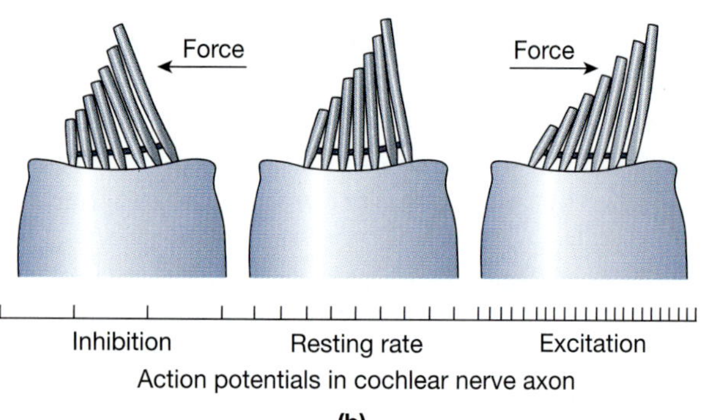

Figure 7.5 Activation of auditory receptors. (a) The cilia of auditory receptors in resting state. (b) As a result of sound stimulus, the movement of basilar and tectorial membranes increases the firing rate of the auditory receptors. The firing rate decreases when the sound ends and the hair cells are moved in the opposite direction. Adapted from Hudspeth, 1988.

➤ *What causes the movement of the outer hair cells? Of the inner hair cells? (p. 198)*

The movement of fluid through the cochlea produces movement of the basilar and tectorial membranes, which leads to activation of the auditory hair cell receptors. The movement of the tectorial membrane bends the cilia of the outer hair cells. The inner hairs do not touch the tectorial membrane, but the fluid movement acts to bend the cilia of the inner hair cells (see **Figure 7.5**).

spiral ganglion cells Neurons that receive neural messages from auditory receptors.

cochlear nerve Nerve formed by neurons that synapse with the afferent dendrites of the auditory receptors.

Before You Go On

Describe the path of the sound of Sarah's voice from the telephone to her grandmother's inner ear.

Transduction of Sound Waves into Neural Impulses

The bending of the cilia excites the auditory receptors (the inner and outer hair cells). The auditory receptors have a resting potential of –60 mv (Hudspeth, 1997). The bending of the cilia leads to an opening of the K^+ ion channels. As the ion channels open, K^+ ions flow into the cell, resulting in membrane depolarization. The depolarization of the auditory receptor membrane leads to a rapid influx of Ca^{++} ions into the hair cell, which results in the release of the neurotransmitter glutamate (Hudspeth, 1997). As the cilia move back to their original position, the K^+ ion channels close, the membrane becomes temporarily hyperpolarized, and neurotransmitter release decreases.

The outer hair cells are more sensitive to sound amplitude than are the inner hair cells. Outer hair cells respond to very soft sounds as well as louder sounds, and inner hair cells react only to sounds of 50 to 60 db or louder (Scharf, 1975). This differential sensitivity is thought to result from different mechanisms activating the inner and outer hair cells: outer hair cells are bent by the movement of the tectorial membrane, whereas inner hair cells are bent by fluid movement. For a summary of the steps involved in producing an auditory sensation, see **Figure 7.6**.

Pathways to the Auditory Cortex

Unlike the visual system with its single major pathway (retina-lateral geniculate nucleus-primary visual cortex—sound familiar? If not, see **pp. 165–170**), several interconnected pathways extend from the auditory receptors in the organ of Corti to the primary auditory cortex. The hair cells synapse with the **spiral ganglion cells**. The afferent axons of the spiral ganglion cells merge to form the **cochlear nerve**. These cochlear nerve fibers join with fibers from the vestibular (balance) system (to be discussed later in this chapter) to form the **auditory nerve**, also called the vestibulocochlear nerve or the eighth cranial nerve (see **Figure 7.7**).

The eighth cranial nerve synapses with the **cochlear nuclei** of the medulla (see **Figure 7.7**). Some of the axons leaving the cochlear nuclei cross over at the hindbrain and synapse with the **superior olivary nucleus** of the medulla on the contralateral side of the brain, whereas other fibers synapse with the superior olivary nucleus on the ipsilateral side of the brain (see **Figure 7.7**). Still other axons extend from the cochlear nuclei directly to **inferior colliculus** of the tectum of the midbrain (see **Figure 7.7**), which is also the destination of the fibers from the superior olivary nuclei.

The inferior colliculus is adjacent to the superior colliculus. As we learned in Chapter 6, some fibers of the optic nerve project to the superior colliculus. The superior and inferior colliculi together make up the corpora quadrigemina and coordinate the visual and auditory senses, so that as she watches Sarah sing to grandma on the telephone, Kathy's auditory input ("Three Blind Mice") is coordinated with the visual input (the movement of Sarah's mouth).

Fibers from the inferior colliculus extend to the **medial geniculate nucleus** of the thalamus (see **Figure 7.7**). Some of these fibers cross over on their way from the inferior colliculus to the medial geniculate nucleus,

---

auditory nerve (vestibulocochlear or eighth cranial nerve) The nerve formed when fibers from the cochlear nerve and vestibular nerve merge.

cochlear nuclei Neurons in the medulla that receive neural messages from the auditory receptors via the auditory nerve.

superior olivary nucleus Group of neurons in the medulla that receives neural messages from the cochlear nuclei.

inferior colliculus Area of the tectum of the midbrain that receives neural messages from both the cochlear nuclei and superior olivary nucleus; responsible, with the superior colliculus, for coordination of the visual and auditory senses.

medial geniculate nucleus Group of neurons in the thalamus that receives neural impulses from the inferior colliculus.

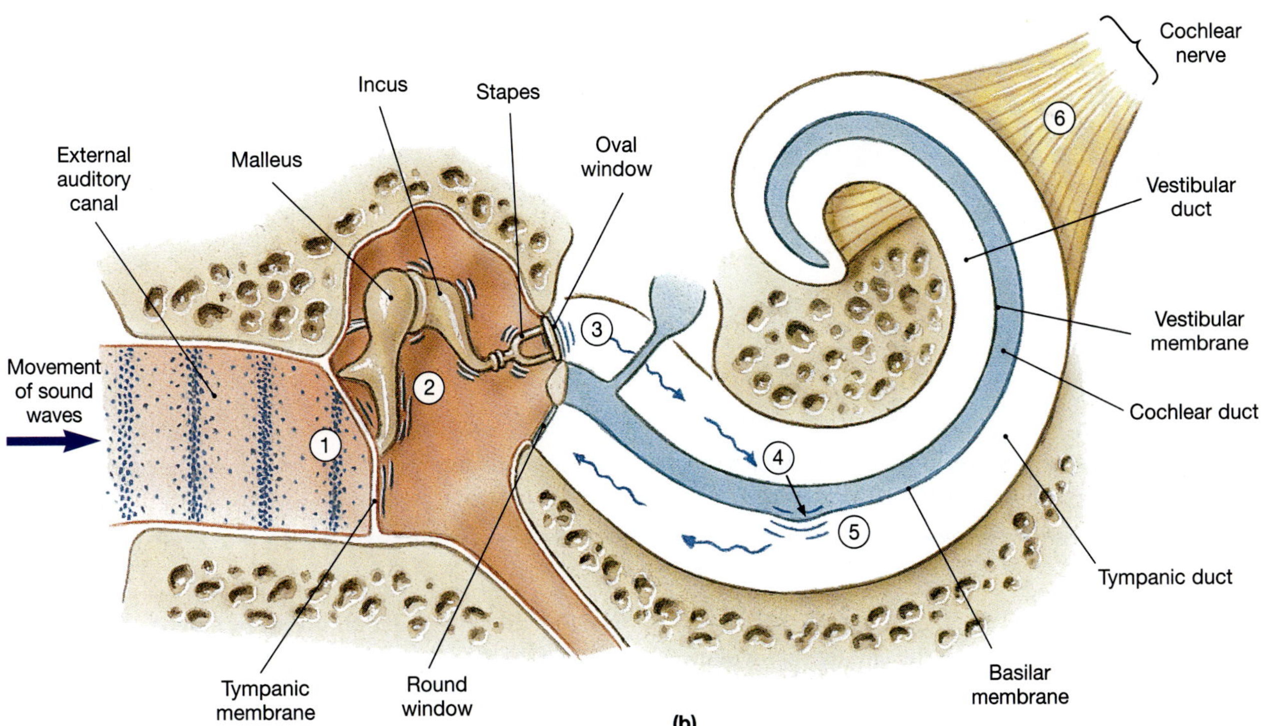

Figure 7.6. Steps in the production of an auditory sensation. (1) Sound waves arrive at the tympanic membrane; (2) movement of the tympanic membrane causes displacement of bones of the middle ear; (3) movement of the stapes at the oval window establishes pressure waves in the vestibular duct; (4) the pressure waves distort the basilar membrane on their way to the round window of the tympanic duct; (5) vibration of the basilar membrane causes the auditory receptors to be activated; (6) information about the sound is transmitted to the central nervous system via the cochlear nerve.

➤ *At which point in this pathway are sound waves converted into a neural impulse? (p. 198)*

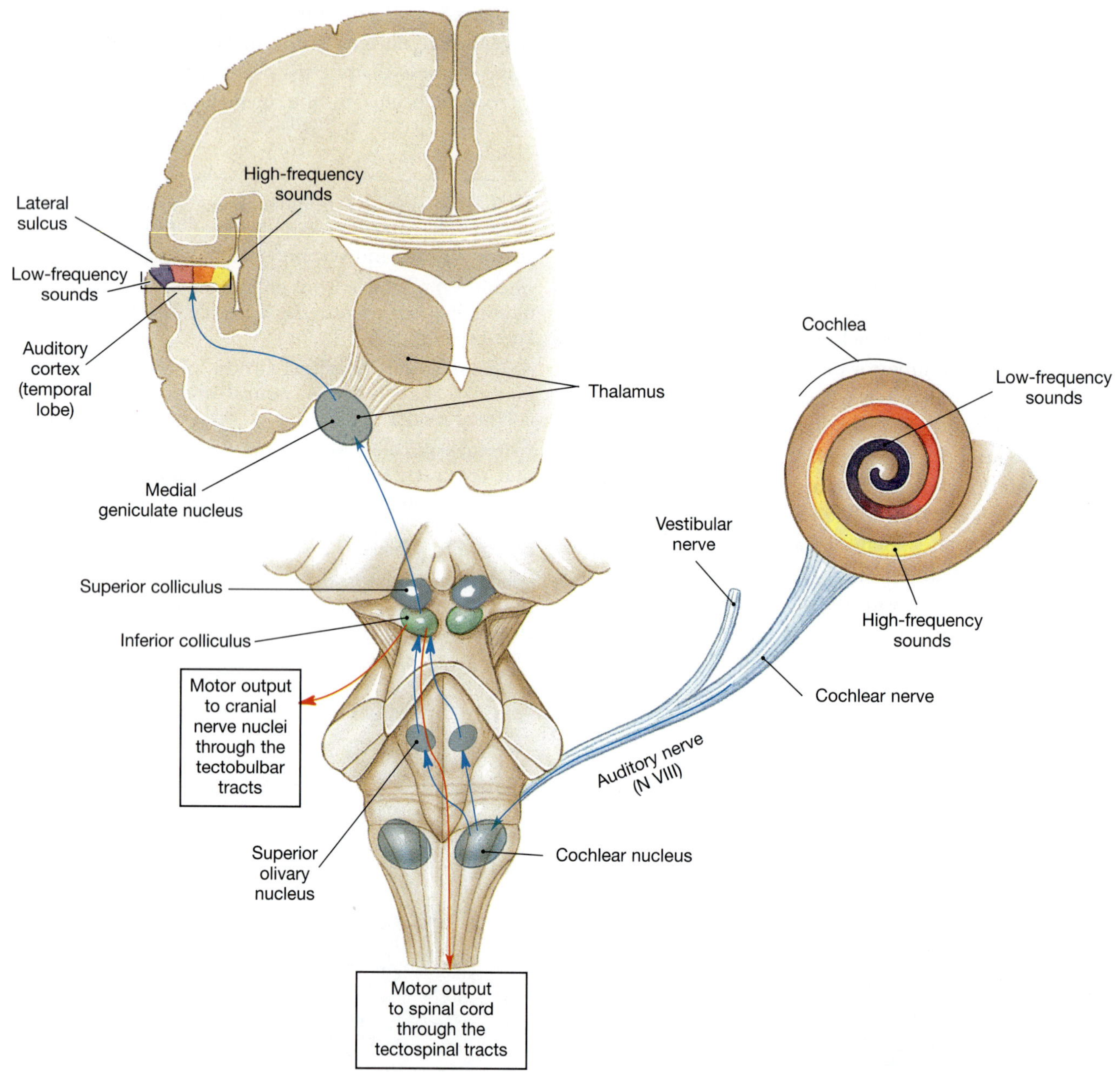

Figure 7.7 Auditory pathway. Routes of sound information from hair cells through cochlear nerve to the primary auditory cortex.
➤ *What structure controls the coordination of the visual and auditory senses? (p. 199)*

whereas others remain on the same side of the brain. Finally, the axons of neurons of the medial geniculate nucleus extend to the primary auditory cortex. Because of the crossover of some but not all of the neurons in the auditory system, each primary auditory cortex receives information from both ears. In other words, although Heather holds the telephone to her right ear, both the right and left halves of her auditory cortex receive neural input from Sarah's voice.

secondary auditory cortex The area of the temporal lobe surrounding the primary auditory cortex where the perception of pitch, loudness, and timbre is made.

The primary auditory cortex is located in the temporal lobe on the inside of the lateral sulcus (see **Figure 7.7**). The primary auditory cortex detects characteristics of sounds (frequency, amplitude, complexity) from the neural impulses originating from the auditory receptors and transmits this information to the **secondary auditory cortex**, which surrounds the primary auditory cortex and where the perception of pitch, loudness, and timbre is made. In the next sections, we will examine how the primary auditory cortex detects the frequency, intensity, and purity of sounds, and then how the secondary auditory cortex recognizes specific sounds.

Before You Go On

Construct a flow chart depicting the path of auditory input from the organ of Corti to the primary auditory cortex.

Why is it possible to still hear sounds from all around you if you lose the hearing in one ear?

The Detection of Frequency

How can Heather distinguish the different notes of Sarah's song? As we discussed at the beginning of the chapter, how low or high we perceive a sound to be has to do with the frequency of the sound, which we perceive as pitch.

Remember the basilar membrane of the middle ear, in which the hair cells are anchored? In the 19th century, Herman von Helmholz, a German physiologist, proposed that different parts of the basilar membrane respond to different frequencies of sound waves. Helmholz envisioned the basilar membrane as a piano, with the fibers (hair cells) of the basilar membrane analogous to the strings of a piano. According to Helmholz's theory, the activation of a nerve fiber located at a specific place on the basilar membrane produces the sensation of a sound of a specific pitch. Helmholz's **place theory of pitch** suggested that high-pitch sounds, such as Sarah's voice, activate the nerve fibers at the basal end of the basilar membrane closest to the oval window, whereas low-pitch sounds, such as the rumbling of a passing truck, stimulate nerve fibers at the apex end of the basilar membrane.

Some evidence supports the place theory of pitch. Exposure to damaging, high-intensity sounds of a particular frequency can impair a subject's ability to detect that frequency in subsequent trials (Smith, 1947). As the frequency of the damaging sound becomes higher, damage to the basilar membrane moves closer to the basal end of the membrane.

Further support for the place theory of pitch is observed in the pattern of damage caused by antibiotic drugs. Damage to hair cells from high doses of antibiotic drugs such as kanamiun and neomycin is not random; rather, the death of hair cells begins at the basal end of the basilar membrane and progresses toward the apex. Stebbins, Miller, Johnsson, and Hawkins (1969) found that a monkey given high does of antibiotics progressively lost the ability to detect pitch, matching the progressive death of hair cells: the ability to detect highest frequencies was lost first, and the ability to detect low frequencies was the last to be lost.

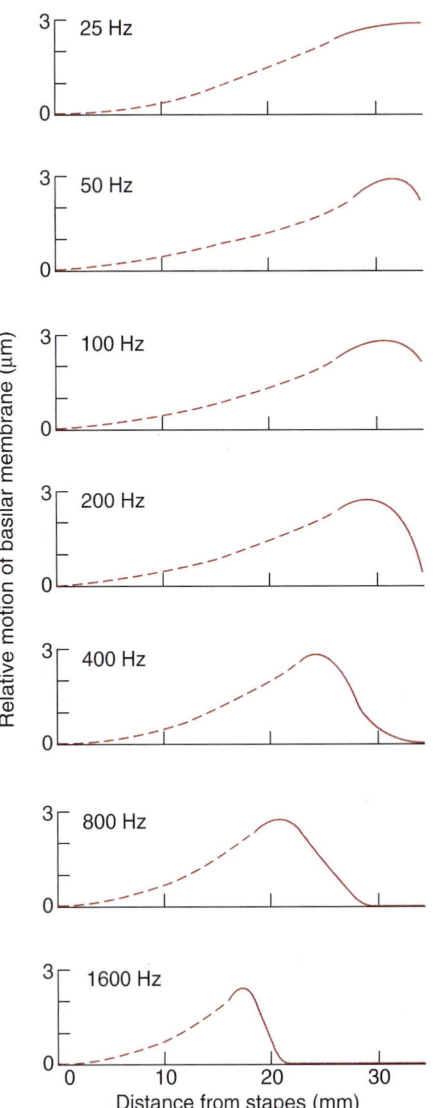

Figure 7.8 Data supporting the place theory of pitch perception. The location of maximum vibration on basilar membrane moves closer to the oval window as the frequency of sound increases.
Adapted from Von Békésy, 1960.

➤ *What evidence supports the place theory of pitch perception? (p. 201–202)*

Perhaps the strongest support for place theory of pitch came from the work of Hungarian physiologist George Von Békésy. Békésy (1947) studied the movement of the basilar membrane of recently deceased humans and other animals in response to sounds of different frequencies. After drilling a small "observation window" into the

place theory of pitch The view that different sounds activate the nerve fibers at different locations on the basilar membrane

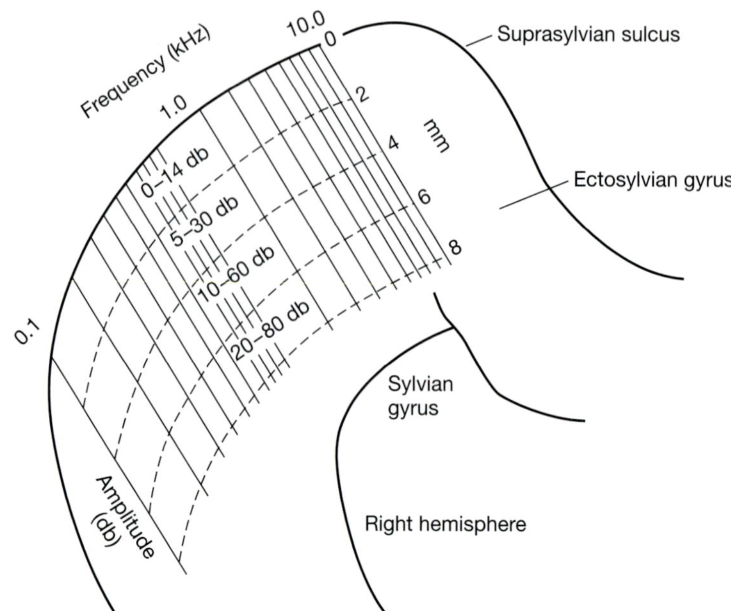

Figure 7.9 The tonotopic distribution of the primary auditory cortex. The neurons in the primary auditory cortex are differentially sensitive to sounds of different amplitude (loudness, db) and frequency (pitch, KHz).
➤ *How is the loudness of high-frequency sounds perceived? (p. 203)*

cochlea, Békésy sprinkled tiny silver particles onto the basilar membrane to make the basilar membrane visible through a microscope. Békésy then flashed stroboscobic light of varying frequencies through the "observation window" and found that the point of maximal vibration of the basilar membrane varied according to the frequency of the stimulation: low-frequency stimulation produced maximum vibrations near the apex end of the basilar membrane, whereas high-frequency stimulation produced maximum vibrations near the basal end of the membrane (see **Figure 7.8**). Békésy won the Nobel Prize in physiology in 1961 for his work.

How else might the nervous system detect the pitch of a sound? There is another theory. (You didn't think we'd let you get away with learning just one! Got to keep those neurons firing!) In 1886, physicist William Rutherford suggested that in response to a sound of a given frequency, the entire basilar membrane vibrates at that same frequency. According to Rutherford, a 2,000 Hz tone would cause the basilar membrane to vibrate at the rate of 2,000 times per second. In addition, with each vibration, the hair cells would fire, causing the basilar membrane to send 2,000 impulses per second through the auditory nerve in response to a 2,000 Hz tone. Rutherford's theory has been referred to as the **frequency theory of pitch**.

American psychologist Ernest Wever (1949) provided some evidence in support of the frequency theory. Wever implanted recording electrodes into the auditory nerve and recorded the firing rate of auditory fibers in response to sounds of various frequencies. He found that the rate of firing of auditory fibers matched the frequency of the sound, but only up to a maximal firing rate of 4,000 times per second (4,000 Hz). Recall that humans can hear up to 20,000 Hz. Puzzled? Read on!

A single auditory receptor cannot actually fire 4,000 times per second. The maximum response rate for a single auditory receptor is 100 times per second (Corso, 1973). You might be wondering how the frequency theory could be valid if an individual auditory receptor cannot respond more than 100 times per second. The answer is that auditory receptors can fire in unison. It is the combined response of auditory receptors that corresponds to the actual frequency of a sound up to 4,000 Hz; that is, the rate of auditory nerve responding as a single unit is equal to the frequency of a sound (Rose et al., 1967).

But what accounts for pitch detection of sounds above 4,000 Hz? The most likely answer is provided by place theory. The pitch of sounds above 4,000 Hz is detected by the place on the basilar membrane at which maximum vibration occurs. So the detection of pitch is accurately explained by a combination of the place theory and the frequency theory.

There is also evidence that individual neurons in the auditory pathway respond selectively to sounds of particular frequencies. The spiral ganglion cells have been found to respond to a particular frequency of sound (Kelly, 1991). Further, a specific spiral ganglion cell is most responsive to the frequency of sound that activates the hair cell auditory receptor that synapses with the spiral ganglion cell.

---

frequency theory of pitch The view that the entire basilar membrane vibrates at the frequency of a given sound.

Other neurons in the auditory pathway also show a frequency specificity. Katsuki (1961) measured the response of neurons in the cochlea, inferior colliculus, and medial geniculate nucleus and found that individual cells in these structures responded only to a narrow range of frequencies of sound. A similar selectivity of responding has been observed in the primary auditory cortex (Merzenich, Knight, & Roth, 1975).

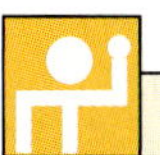

Before You Go On

Compare and contrast the place theory and the frequency theory of pitch. How do they complement one another?

The Detection of Amplitude

The auditory system is sensitive to sounds even softer than a whisper. Wilska (1935) found that our ear drum will respond to a sound that causes it to vibrate the distance of less than the diameter of a hydrogen atom. More recent studies (Corwin & Warchol, 1991; Hudspeth, 1983) have indicated that the hair cells respond when they are moved less than 100 picometers (100 trillionths of a meter). In fact, in a very quiet environment, the auditory receptors can even detect the sound of blood rushing through the arteries of the ear.

How is the amplitude or intensity of a sound encoded by the auditory receptors? For high-frequency sounds, the rate at which hair cells respond indicates loudness; high-intensity sounds produce a greater rate of responding than low-intensity sounds. For low-frequency sounds, it is pitch, not loudness, that is determined by the rate of responding. Loudness of low-frequency sounds is determined by the number of neurons that are firing—the more neurons firing, the louder the sound.

Tunturi (1953) found that neurons in different areas of the primary auditory cortex react to sounds of different loudness. **Figure 7.9** shows the location of neurons in the primary auditory cortex that Tunturi observed to respond to sounds of different frequencies and amplitudes. The neurons in the primary auditory cortex apparently are distributed according to both frequency (pitch) and amplitude (loudness).

Before You Go On

Why do you think that the rate of hair cell firing indicates the loudness of high-frequency sounds and the pitch of low-frequency sounds?

The Detection of Complexity

Pure tones consist of a sound of only one frequency. Complex sounds are sounds made up of two or more frequencies. The particular combination of frequencies produces what we perceive as the timbre or quality of a particular sound. It enables us to distinguish, for example, between two different instruments playing the same pitch. We are able to distinguish the C played by a flute from the C played by a trumpet because of the differences in sound quality. Most of the sounds in our environment are complex rather than simple sounds.

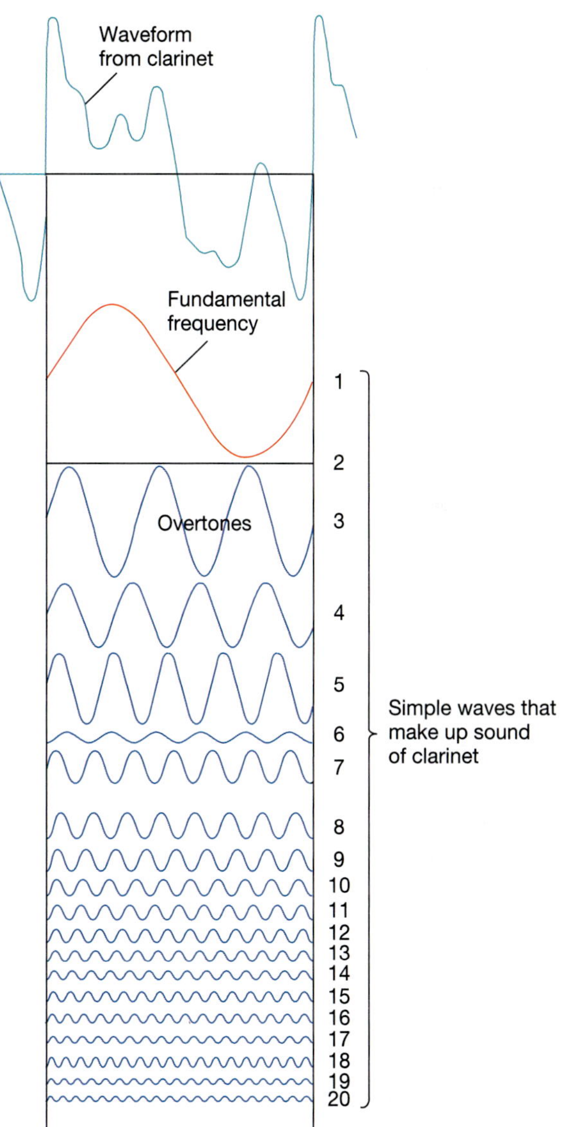

Figure 7.10 A sound wave from a clarinet. The clarinet produces a distinctive fundamental frequency and overtones.

➤ *How many waves would be shown in the Fourier analysis of a pure tone? (p. 204)*

How are we able to recognize the timbre of a particular sound? Each complex sound has a fundamental frequency (or the rate of vibration of an object set in motion) and many harmonics (overtones), or multiples (2 times, 3 times, etc.) of the fundamental frequency. And it is the complexity of the sounds of a musical instrument that gives it its particular sound quality. **Figure 7.10** presents the sound wave from a clarinet playing a specific note. Fourier analysis, like the one shown in **Figure 6.20** on **p. 180** in the discussion of the visual detection of objects, indicates that the sound produced by the clarinet consists of a fundamental frequency and many harmonics.

The particular area of the basilar membrane that is activated by a complex sound is determined by the fundamental frequency and the overtones of that frequency. According to the place theory, because each sound frequency activates a specific area of the basilar membrane, a complex sound produces a unique pattern of neural activity, enabling us to distinguish between the notes of the aforementioned flute and trumpet based on the particular basilar membrane activity generated by each sound. The area of the primary auditory cortex that is responsible for detecting timbre remains a mystery (a good topic for your graduate research!).

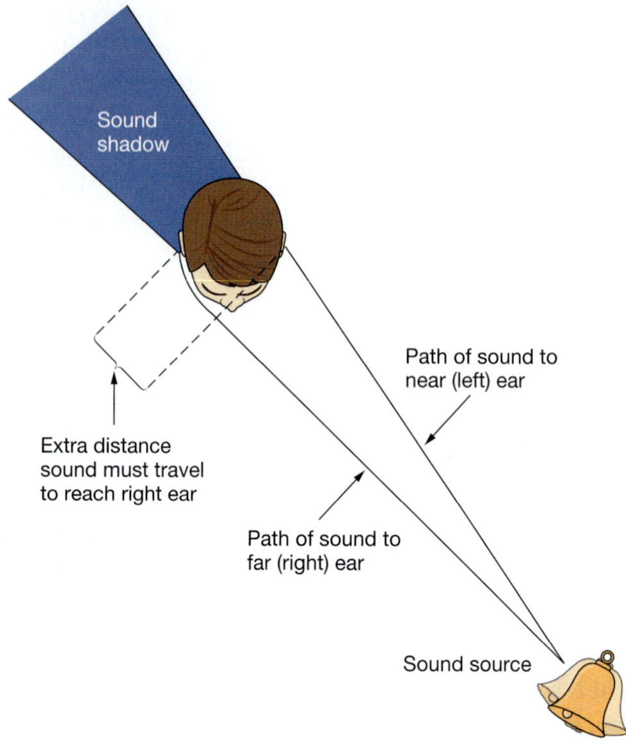

Figure 7.11 The use of timing and intensity cues in the location of a sound. Sound first reaches the ear closest to the source, and sound intensity is greater in the ear closest to the sound source.

➤ *Which structures of the brain detect the differences in arrival time of input from the two ears? (p. 204)*

The Location of a Sound

Sarah's mother calls to her from across the playground. Sarah looks over her left shoulder and frowns as she sees Kathy gesturing that it is time to go. How could Sarah tell that the sound of her mother's voice was coming from the left? The auditory system uses several types of cues to identify the location of a sound. Timing cues are one source of information about location. As noted in **Figure 7.11**, a sound coming from the right reaches the right ear before it reaches the left ear. As a result of differential activation of the basilar membrane of the two ears, the sound message reaches the medial superior olives (see **Figure 7.7**) at different times. Cells in the medial superior olives are sensitive to even the slightest differences in the time of arrival of input from the two ears (Heffner & Masterton, 1990).

The differential intensity of input from the ears is another cue used to locate the source of a sound. The intensity of the sound experienced in the ear farther away from the source is less than the intensity experienced by the ear closer to the source (see **Figure 7.11**). This differential intensity is detected by neurons in the lateral superior olives (Heffner & Masterton, 1991).

Information from the medial and lateral superior olives is transmitted to the inferior colliculus (Ivarson, de Ribauprene, & de Ribauprene, 1988; see **Figure 7.7**). Neurons in the inferior colliculus are sensitive to both timing and intensity cues, and they function to detect the location of the sound source.

Role of the Auditory Cortex in Sound Recognition

We're back at the playground. Sarah urgently shouts "Mommy!" Only Kathy looks up; how can she tell that it is her child calling her, and how can each of the other mothers tell that it is not the voice of her child?

We have learned that auditory receptors record the frequency, intensity, and timbre of a sound and then send this information to the primary auditory cortex (see **Figure 7.12**), and that neurons in the primary auditory cortex respond selectively to the various aspects of sounds. For example, Saitoh, Maruyama, and Kudoh (1981) found that neurons in the primary auditory cortex of cats responded only to complex sounds that were made up of certain frequencies. Similarly, Sutter and Schreiner (1991) observed that a specific combination of two or more tones of particular frequencies activated specific neurons in the primary auditory cortex of cats. These observations indicate that neurons in the primary auditory cortex react to the whole pattern of a complex sound rather than to its individual features.

Information from the primary auditory cortex is transmitted to the secondary auditory cortex (see **Figure 7.12**). Damage to Wernicke's area and surrounding areas, which are part of the secondary auditory cortex in the hemisphere controlling language (usually the left hemisphere as we will discuss in Chapter 13), produces Wernicke's aphasia or an inability to understand language (Brookshire, 1997). This observation indicates that Wernicke's area and the surrounding areas are responsible for detecting the combination of sounds that we recognize as specific words. Bilateral damage to the secondary auditory cortex can lead to **auditory agnosia**, or an inability to recognize sounds (both language and nonlanguage sounds). If Kathy had this type of damage, she might not be able to recognize Sarah's voice or the sound of a car's horn. These observations suggest that the secondary auditory cortex is responsible for determining the meaning of the wide range of sounds detected by the auditory receptors and transmitted to the primary auditory cortex.

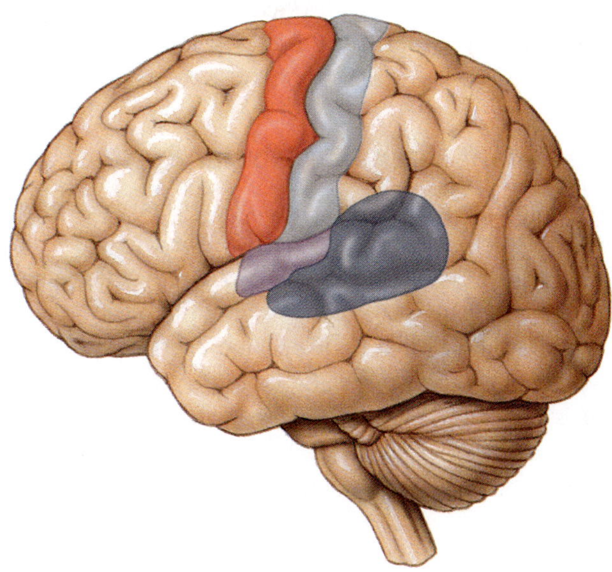

Figure 7.12 Auditory cortex. The primary auditory cortex and secondary auditory cortex are located almost entirely in the temporal lobe, but the secondary auditory cortex also extends into the parietal lobe.

➤ *What would be the behavioral consequences of damage to the secondary auditory cortex? (p. 205)*

Before You Go On

Give an example from your own experience of (a) a simple sound and (b) a complex sound.

Section Review

- The auditory system detects sound waves produced by vibrating objects.
- Sound waves differ in three ways: frequency (perceived as pitch), which is measured in compressions per second or hertz (Hz); intensity (perceived as loudness), which is measured by the amplitude of the wave or decibels (db); and complexity of the sound (perceived as timbre).
- Sound waves enter the outer ear and travel down the auditory canal, where they cause the tympanic membrane (eardrum) to vibrate.
- The vibrations of the tympanic membrane are transmitted by the three bones of the middle ear to the oval window, which vibrates and causes the fluid in the cochlea to move from the oval window to the round window.
- The fluid movement produces movement of the basilar and tectorial membranes, which acts to bend the cilia of the hair cells, which function as auditory receptors.
- The bending of the hair cell cilia opens the K^+ ion channels, resulting in the influx of K^+ ions and the depolarization of the auditory hair cells.
- The depolarization of the auditory receptor leads to a rapid influx of Ca^{++} ions into the hair cell, which results in the release of the neurotransmitter glutamate.
- The auditory receptors synapse with neurons of the cochlear nerve (the eighth cranial nerve), which project to the cochlear nuclei of the medulla.
- Most axons leaving the cochlear nuclei cross over and synapse with the superior olivary nucleus of the medulla, but some of the axons remain on the ipsilateral side of the brain.
- Information from the cochlear nuclei and superior olivary nucleus is then transmitted to the inferior colliculus of the tectum, the medial geniculate nucleus of the thalamus, and the primary auditory cortex.
- The place theory of pitch suggests that different sounds activate the nerve fibers at different locations on the basilar membrane.

auditory agnosia An inability to recognize language and nonlanguage sounds due to bilateral damage to the secondary auditory cortex.

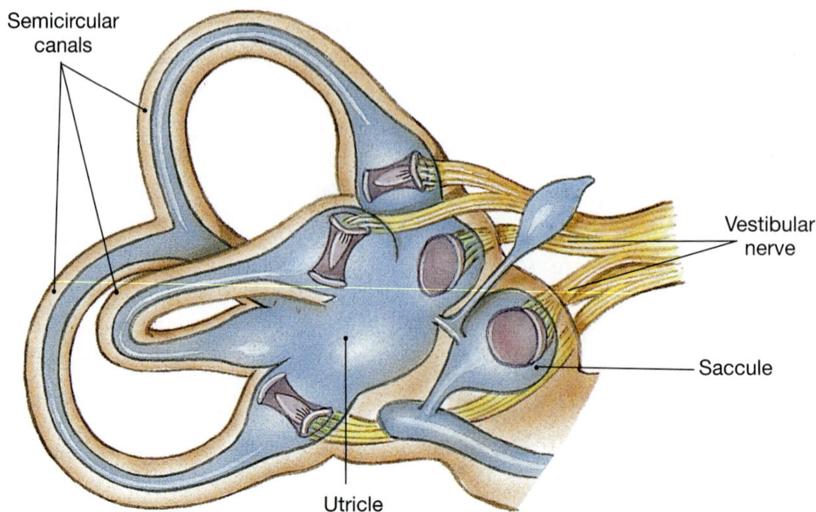

Figure 7.13 The major structures of the vestibular system. The hair cells in the vestibule are stimulated by passive movement of the head, and the hair cells of the semicircular canals by any rotation of the head.

➤ *Where are the vestibular receptor cells located? (p. 207)*

- The frequency theory of pitch suggests that the entire basilar membrane vibrates at the frequency of a given sound.
- For low-frequency sounds, pitch seems to be determined by the rate of responding, and loudness encoded by the number of neurons firing.
- For high-frequency sounds, pitch is detected by the place on the basilar membrane that maximum vibration occurs, and loudness is determined by the rate of firing, with high-intensity sounds producing a greater rate of responding than low-intensity sounds.
- Each complex sound has one fundamental frequency and many overtones (multiples of the fundamental frequency).
- The auditory system identifies a sound, such as the sound of a specific instrument, on the basis of the unique pattern of basilar membrane activity produced by that source.
- The recognition of the location and the direction of a sound is determined by timing cues and intensity cues.
- Neurons in the primary auditory cortex respond selectively to frequency, intensity, and complexity.
- The recognition of the meaning of a sound is the function of the secondary auditory cortex.
- Bilateral damage to the secondary auditory cortex leads to auditory agnosia, which is an inability to recognize sounds.

vestibule (or vestibular sacs) Structures in the inner ear that detect passive head movement.

utricle Sacs in the vestibule that contain vestibular receptors.

saccule Sacs in the vestibule that contain vestibular receptors.

otoliths Calcium carbonate crystals located atop a gelatinous mass in the vestibular sacs.

semicircular canals Three fluid-filled structures in the cochlea that detect rotation of the head.

The Vestibular Sense

After Heather and Sarah have said their goodbyes, Heather gets up from her chair to hang up the telephone and momentarily loses her balance. But what exactly do we mean when we say "I lost my balance"? What exactly is balance? How does your body maintain its orientation in space? The sense responsible for maintaining balance is the vestibular sense, from the Latin word *vestibulum*, which means "cavity." (This time the word origin is not very helpful, is it?) It is our highly developed vestibular sense that allows humans to walk on two feet, keep our heads in an upright position, and adjust eye movements to compensate for head movements.

The Organs of the Vestibular System

The vestibular system is composed of two parts: the vestibule (or vestibular sacs) and the semicircular canals (see **Figure 7.13**). The vestibular sacs provide information about the static sense of head position with regard to gravity, which occurs when body position changes (for example, when bending over). By contrast, the semicircular canals provide information related to actual head movement or rotation of the head. These structures are located in the inner ear and are attached to the cochlea of the auditory system.

The **vestibule** occur in two sac-like structures: the **utricle** and the **saccule**, that contain the vestibular receptor cells or hair cells. Some vestibular receptor cells are located on the "floor" of the utricle and others on the "wall" of the saccule. These receptor cells are imbedded in a gelatinous mass. Located on top of the gelatinous mass are small crystals of calcium carbonate, called **otoliths** (see **Figure 7.14**).

In each vestibular system, there are three **semicircular canals**. Each canal is filled with fluid and contains an enlarged area called the **ampulla**. Within the ampulla is a structure called the **crista**, and within the crista are vestibular receptors, or the hair cells, embedded in a gelatinous mass called the **cupula**. The semicircular canals are oriented in three major planes—sagittal, coronal, and horizontal planes (see **Figure 2.3** on **p. 33** for a review of these planes).

The Vestibular Receptor Cells

The receptor cells of the vestibular system look much like the hair cells of the auditory system (compare **Figures 7.4** and **7.14**). The hair cells in the vestibular sacs are stimulated by passive movement of the head, which causes the gelatinous mass to shift in position and results in the otoliths, or calcium carbonate crystals, bending the hairs or cilia located within the gelatinous mass. The bending of the hairs causes either depolarization or hyperpolarization of the cell membrane of these vestibular receptors, depending on the direction that the cilia move (see **Figure 7.15**). Depolarization increases neurotransmitter release, whereas hyperpolarization decreases neurotransmitter release from these vestibular receptors.

Any rotation of the head stimulates the vestibular receptors in the cristae of the semicircular canals. A shift in the flow of the fluid in the semicircular canals, occurring in response to a change in the orientation (or rotation) of the head, causes the gelatinous mass to bend the hairs of the hair cells in the semicircular canals, which depolarizes or hyperpolarizes the cell membrane, depending on the direction of the movement of the hairs. Depolarization causes more neurotransmitter release from the vestibular receptors, whereas less neurotransmitter molecules are released when the hair cells are hyperpolarized. The vestibular receptor cells convert information about the passive movement of the head and any active rotation of the head into an increase or decrease in neurotransmitter release. But where do the neurotransmitter molecules go?

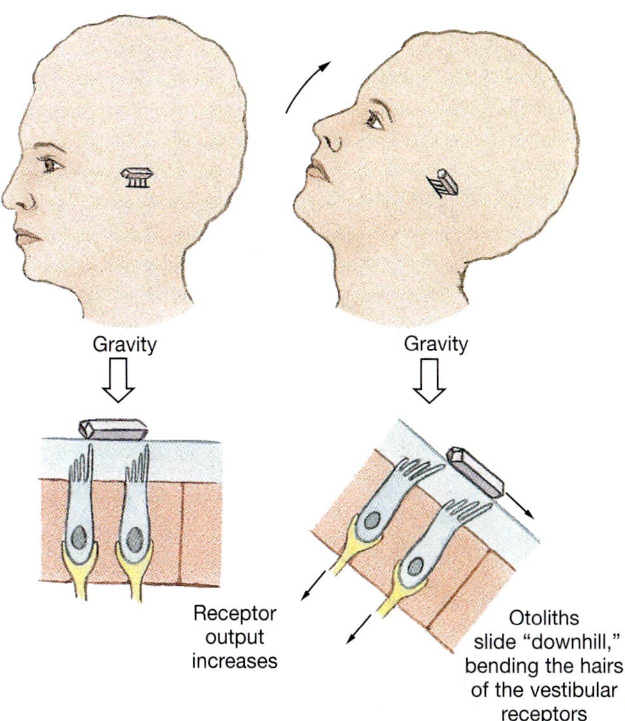

Figure 7.15 Head movement. Movement of the head causes the otoliths to shift, which bends the cilia of the hair cell vestibular receptors. Depending on the direction of head movement, the cell membrane of the vestibular receptor will be either depolarized or hyperpolarized.

➤ *How does passive head movement affect one's balance? (p. 207)*

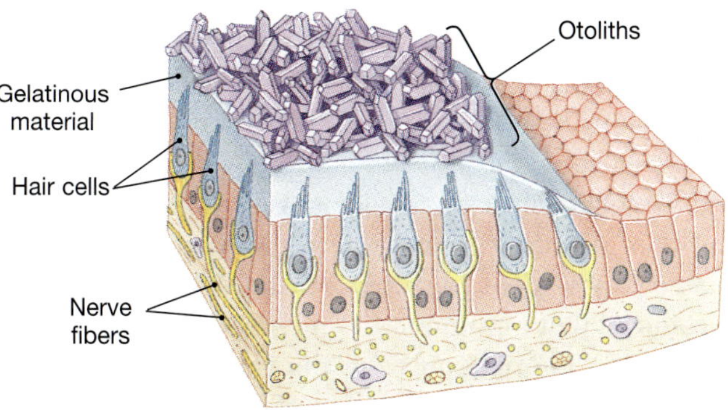

Figure 7.14 The vestibular receptor cells embedded in the gelatinous material of the vestibule (saccule and utricle). The hair cells in the saccule and utricle are stimulated by passive movement of the head.

➤ *What causes the otoliths to move? (p. 207)*

The Vestibular Pathways

The vestibular receptors synapse with afferent vestibular nerve fibers (as shown in **Figure 7.16**). The afferent axons of the vestibular nerve fibers are bipolar. The cell bodies of these bipolar cells form the **vestibular ganglion**, several

ampulla Enlarged area in each semicircular canal.

crista Structure in the ampulla that contains vestibular receptor cells.

cupula Gelatinous mass in the crista in which the vestibular receptor cells are embedded.

vestibular ganglion The bipolar neurons that receive input from the vestibular receptors.

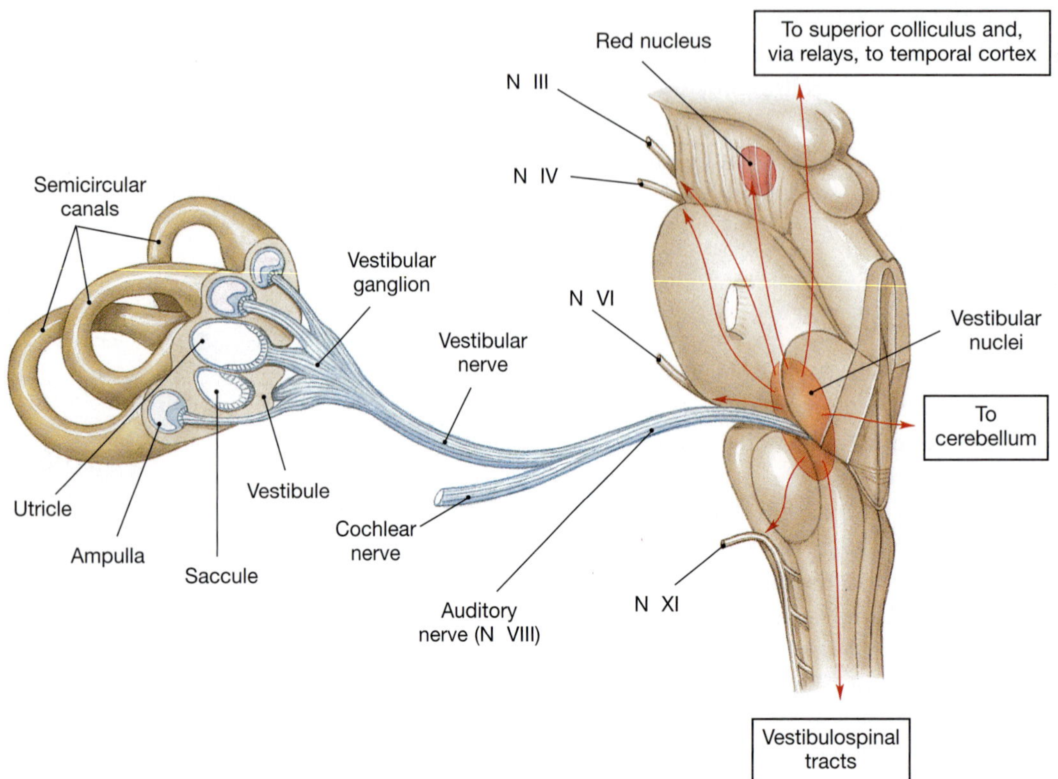

Figure 7.16 Vestibular pathways. The major pathways of the vestibular system from vestibular receptors to the cerebral cortex.
➤ *What parts of the brain receive vestibular input? (p. 208)*

of which are clustered together to become the **vestibular nerve**. These vestibular fibers combine with cochlear nerve fibers from the hair cells of the auditory receptors (see **p. 197**) to form the auditory or eighth cranial nerve.

The majority of vestibular nerve fibers synapse with the **vestibular nuclei** located in the medulla (see **Figure 7.16**). Other vestibular nerve fibers connect directly with neurons in the cerebellum. The vestibular nuclei project to other areas of the medulla, as well as to the pons, the cerebellum, the spinal cord, the red nucleus, the superior colliculus, and the temporal cortex. The projections of the vestibular nuclei to the spinal cord and to the cerebellum influence the coordination of balance, changes in body position, and body movement. Vestibular nuclei that project to other areas of the medulla and to the pons coordinate head and eye movements. These neurons act to move the eyes to compensate for movements of the head.

Several years ago I went on a cruise. The back and forth rocking of the boat caused me to feel dizzy and nauseous, especially when the boat's movements were strong. My dizziness and nausea were symptoms of **motion sickness**. There are two main kinds of motion sickness, both of which occur when the body is moved passively without motor input, such as when riding in an airplane, car, or boat or when hurling down a seemingly impossible decline in a roller coaster. The first kind of motion sickness occurs when the vestibular system detects movement, but motor action that could have produced that movement has not occurred. The inconsistency in information from the vestibular and motor systems produces the symptoms of motion sickness.

The second kind of motion sickness occurs when the vestibular system senses movement that is inconsistent with the information about movement sensed by the eyes: passive movement causes the vestibular system to report motion while the eyes register no motion. This inconsistency produces **nystagmus**, or rapid side-to-side movements

---

vestibular nerve The axons of the vestibular ganglion cell bodies.

vestibular nuclei That part of the medulla that synapse with most vestibular nerve fibers.

motion sickness Feelings of dizziness and nausea that occur when the body is moved passively without motor input.

nystagmus Rapid side-to-side movements of the eyes caused by inconsistent information from the visual and vestibular systems.

of the eyes. The nystagmoid movements represent an attempt by the visual system to compensate for the report of movement by the vestibular system. The inconsistency of motion cues from the vestibular and the visual systems can lead to the symptoms of motion sickness. It is thought that brainstem structures produce the nausea and vomiting that occur with motion sickness, whereas stimulation of the temporal cortex causes the awareness of dizziness.

If you have a strong desire to experience the second kind of motion sickness, close your eyes and spin yourself around on a swivel chair. Stop the chair and open your eyes. When your eyes open, you should experience nystagmus and symptoms of motion sickness.

Before You Go On

What element(s) of the vestibular system must be especially fine-tuned in a tightrope walker?

Compare the hair cells of the auditory system with the vestibular receptor cells.

Section Review

- The vestibular system, comprised of the vestibule (the saccule and utricle) and the semicircular canals, maintains balance, helps keep the head in an upright position, and adjusts eye movements to compensate for head movements.
- Head movement caused by changes in body position causes the calcium carbonate crystals located on top of the gelatinous mass in the utricle and saccule of the vestibular sacs to shift, which in turn causes the cilia of these vestibular receptors to bend.
- Vestibular receptors are embedded in the cristae, a gelatinous mass within the fluid of the three semicircular canals, and the hairs of these receptors are bent by rotation of the head in one of three planes (sagittal, coronal, and horizontal).
- The vestibular receptors synapse with afferent vestibular nerve fibers, which combine with cochlear nerve fibers to form the auditory or eighth cranial nerve.
- Vestibular nerve fibers project to the medulla and pons, which coordinate head and eye movements; to the spinal cord and cerebellum, which coordinate balance, body position, and body movement; and to the temporal cortex.

The Somatosenses

Kathy reaches down and wipes the snow off the windshield of her car; although she'd rather stay inside and have another cup of coffee on a morning like this, she has to get Sarah to preschool. Her hands feel frozen as she finishes clearing the windshield. She wonders where she left her gloves. Opening the car door and starting the car only makes her hands feel colder. As she waits for the car to become warm, she runs into her apartment to collect Sarah and search for gloves.

The feeling of cold is one example of a skin sensation, or **somatosense**. Lowering temperature is the stimulus that produces the sensation of cold. Another example of a somatosense is the feeling of warmth, which occurs in response to an increase in temperature. Touch and pain are other examples of somatosenses. Touch is actually a response to two different stimuli: pressure, which is caused by a deformation of the skin, and vibration, which is caused by skin moving across a rough surface. Many different stimuli can produce pain. Each of these pain-inducing stimuli has the common attribute of causing at least some tissue damage to the skin. The senses of cold, warmth, touch, and pain have been referred to as cutaneous senses.

The **proprioceptive system** is another example of a somatosense. This system monitors body position and movement, acts to maintain body position, and ensures the accuracy of intended movements. The receptors of the proprioceptive system are located in the muscles, tendons, and joints. The receptors located in skeletal muscles report changes in muscle length, and receptors located in the tendons measure the force exerted by the muscles of the tendons. Receptors in the joints, the junction of two or more bones, record the magnitude and duration of limb movement. Information from the proprioceptive receptors is essential to the control of movement. For example, if the receptors in your elbows (the joint between the single upper arm bone and the two bones of your forearm) were not working, you would have trouble holding this book and turning its pages. Our discussion in this chapter will focus on the cutaneous senses of warmth, cold, touch, and pain. We will describe the role of the proprioceptive system in the control of movement in Chapter 8.

The Skin Receptors

The skin consists of two layers: the dermis and the epidermis (see **Figure 7.17d**). The appearance of the skin can vary from very hairy to smooth and hairless

somatosense Skin sensations of touch, pain, temperature, and proprioception.

proprioceptive system Somatosense that monitors body position and movement, acts to maintain body position, and ensures the accuracy of intended movements.

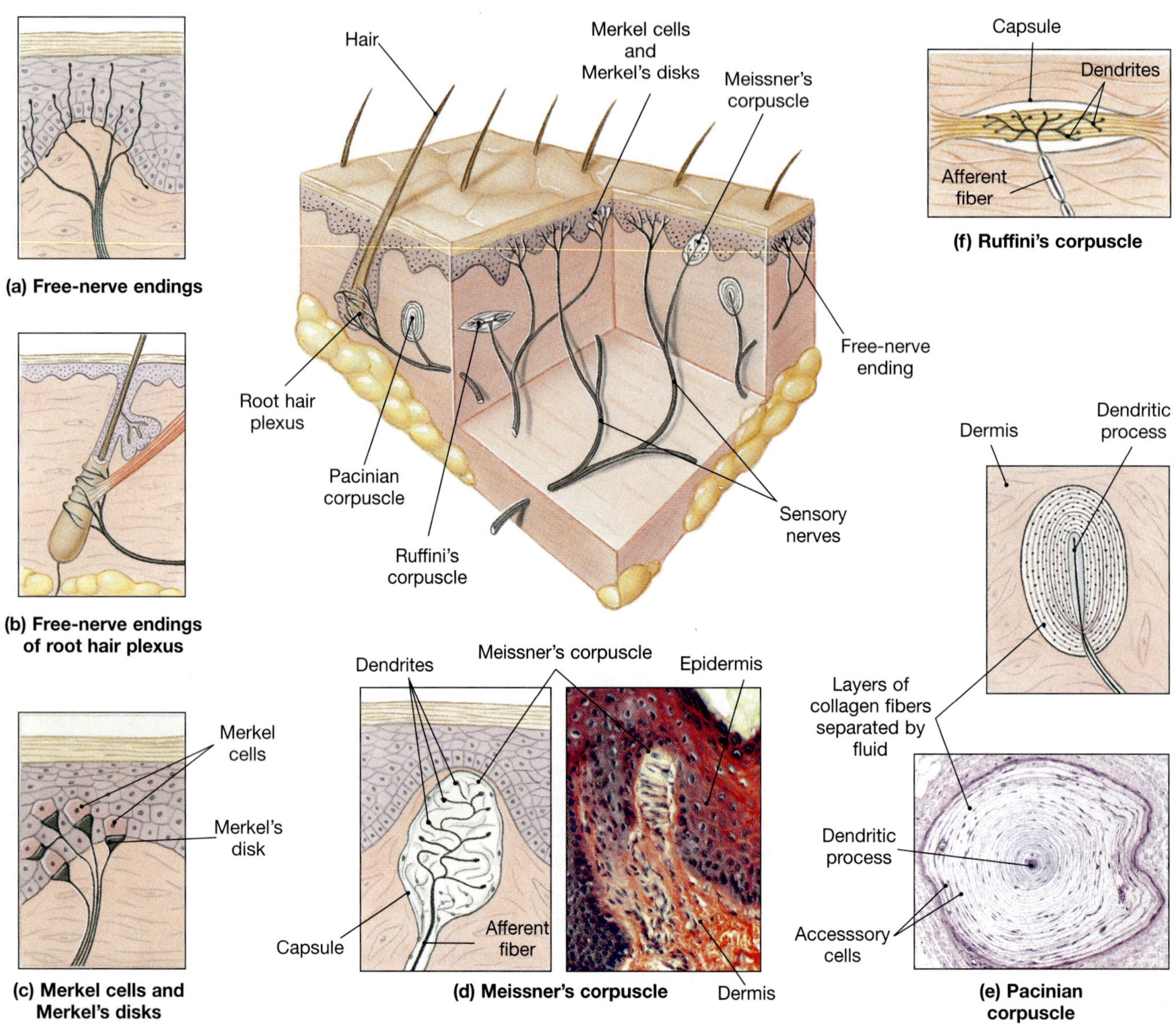

Figure 7.17 Skin receptors. (a & b) Free-nerve endings, (c) Merkel's cells and disks, (d) Meissner's corpuscle, (e) Pacinian corpuscle, and (f) Ruffini's corpuscle.

➤ *To what types of stimuli is the Pacinian corpuscle sensitive? (p. 210)*

(glabrous). The skin serves several important functions. It protects the internal organs from injury. It also helps to regulate body temperature by producing sweat, which cools the body when it becomes too hot, and is a first line of defense against invading microorganisms.

Several different types of somatosensory receptors are located in the skin. The largest of these receptors are **Pacinian corpuscles**, which are found in both hairy and hairless skin (see **Figure 7.17e**). These receptors also are located in the joints, tendons, muscles, external genitalia, mammary glands, and some internal organs. Pacinian corpuscles are approximately 0.5 × 1.0 mm, which makes them the largest sensory receptor in the body and visible to the naked eye. A Pacinian corpuscle receptor consists of a terminal button of a single myelinated axon enclosed within seventy layers of onion-like tissue. These receptors are sensitive to touch stimulation, primarily high-frequency vibrations (200 to 300 Hz) such as those caused by running your fingers across a rough surface such as a towel. The vibrations cause the tip of the axon contained in the corpuscle to bend. When the axon bends, the Na^+ ion channels in the membrane open, allowing Na^+ ions to enter and depo-

Pacinian corpuscles The largest of the skin receptors found in dermis layer of both hairy and hairless skin that detects high-frequency vibrations.

larize the cell. If sufficient depolarization occurs to reach threshold, an action potential is generated. The receptive fields of Pacinian corpuscles are quite large; that is, stimulation of a small part of the hand will be felt in a much wider area (see **Figure 7.18c**). For example, a tactile stimulus applied to the tip of your middle finger will feel like your entire finger is being touched.

A second type of receptor found in the skin is the **free-nerve ending** (see **Figure 7.17a, b**). Free-nerve endings are located just below the skin in both hairy and hairless skin. Changes in temperature are one stimulus detected by free-nerve endings. A change in temperature, whether it be from touching a cold or hot object or from a change in air temperature, acts to increase the firing rate of free-nerve ending receptors. The greater the increase in firing rate, the greater the sensation of coolness or warmth. The specific free-nerve endings that detect warmth and coolness differ: receptors for coolness seem to be close to the surface of the skin, and those that detect warmth seem to be located deeper in the skin (Sinclair, 1981). This is why it took Kathy's hands so much longer to feel warm (once she found her gloves) than it took for them to feel cold while clearing the windshield. Interestingly, sensations of warmth and coolness are relative. A temperature of 30° F might feel quite cold to someone from Florida, but not cold to a person from Alaska. Similarly, 90° F might be sensed as quite warm by an individual from Minnesota but not by someone living in Arizona.

The free-nerve endings also serve as receptors for pain stimuli. Direct pressure stimulation of high threshold free-nerve endings signals the presence of a painful stimulus (the lower threshold free-nerve endings detect touch rather than pain). This type of pain, referred to as **fast pain** or **prickling pain,** is produced by experiences such as an injection or a deep cut. The sensations of pain are carried over myelinated Type A fibers and quickly reach the spinal cord (Martini, 1998). From the spinal cord, the neural messages are carried to the primary somatosensory cortex,

---

free-nerve ending Skin receptor located just below the skin in both hairy and hairless skin that detect temperature and pain stimuli.

fast pain (prickling pain) Type of pain carried over myelinated Type A fibers that quickly reaches the spinal cord.

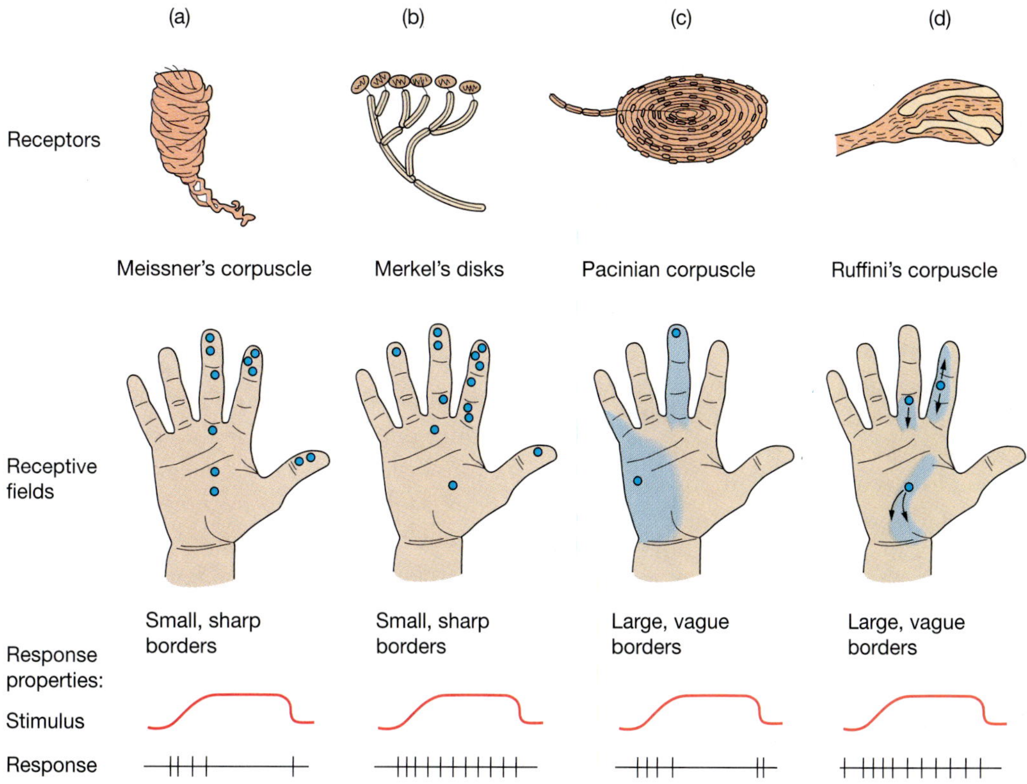

Figure 7.18 Receptive fields and adaptation rates of touch receptors. (a) Meissner's corpuscles, (b) Merkel's disks, (c) Pacinian corpuscle, and (d) Ruffini's corpuscle.

Adapted from Vallbo & Johnson, 1984.

➤ *Why do the receptive fields and adaptation rates of the skin receptors differ? (p. 210–212)* where a conscious perception of localized pain is experienced. A second, more roundabout way, in which painful sensations are produced is as a result of cell damage. Damaged or injured cells synthesize prostaglandin, a hormone that increases the sensitivity of free-nerve endings to histamine. Histamine, also released by cells that are injured, activates the free-nerve endings, producing the sensation of pain. This type of pain, referred to as **slow pain** or **burning and aching pain**, is propagated by unmyelinated Type C fibers. Sensations are of an awareness of pain with only a general awareness of the area damaged.

Several other types of receptors are found in skin cells. **Meissner's corpuscles**, found only in hairy skin cells, are located in the elevations, called papillae ("nipples"), of the dermis into the epidermis (see **Figure 7.17d**). These receptors respond to pressure on the skin and to low-frequency vibrations (50 Hz), such as might be produced by a smooth cotton shirt, and produce touch sensations. Unlike Pacinian corpuscles, Meissner's corpuscles have small receptive fields (see **Figure 7.18a**). Thus, a tactile stimulus applied to the tip of your middle finger will only be felt on your fingertip.

Merkel's disks, which are receptors located at the base of the epidermis near the sweat ducts (see **Figure 7.17c**), are sensitive to pressure and not vibrations, and have small receptive fields (see **Figure 7.18b**). **Ruffini's corpuscles**, which are located just below the skin (see **Figure 7.17f**), respond to low-frequency vibrations but not to pressure, and have large receptive fields (see **Figure 7.18d**). Both Merkel's disks and Ruffini's corpuscles respond to vibrations of even lower frequency than do Meissner's corpuscles, such as might be produced by the very smooth surface of your pen.

Some touch receptors (Meissner's corpuscles, Pacinian corpuscles) adapt quickly to stimulation and react only to the onset or termination of stimulation (see stimulus response column in **Figure 7.18**). Moderate, constant stimulation of the skin does not produce sensations in these touch receptors. Consider what happens when you put on a shirt. You will feel the pressure on the skin when you first put on the shirt, but after a few seconds, you no longer notice the sensation produced by the shirt. The advantage of touch receptor adaptation is obvious; if they did not adapt, you would be constantly sensing the clothes that you are wearing, and as a result, you would have difficulty attending to other aspects of your environment. The fact that touch receptors of the skin adapt means that for an object to be identified by the skin senses, the object must be moved along the skin. Movement causes vibrations and allows the object to be identified by those touch receptors (Pacinian corpuscles, Meissner's corpuscles) that adapt quickly to touch sensations. Other touch receptors (Merkel's disks, Ruffini's corpuscles) do not adapt quickly, but instead, continue to respond while the stimulus remains present. Thus, you will continue to feel the pen while holding it, but not the shirt you are wearing.

Somatosensory Pathways

Axons of the skin receptors project to the central nervous system either through the cranial nerves of the face and head (See **Table 2.1** on **p. 40**) or through the spinal nerves of the rest of the body (see **Figure 2.9** on **p. 40**). Once information from the skin reaches the central nervous system, the neural message travels through one of three somatosensory systems: the dorsal column-medial lemniscal system, the anterolateral system, or the spinocerebellar system (see **Figure 7.19**).

The **dorsal column-medial lemniscal system**, which transmits information about touch and proprioception, projects to the medulla, where it synapses with the **dorsal column nuclei** (refer to **Figure 7.19a**). There are two dorsal column nuclei in the medulla. The medial nucleus gracilis receives dorsal column projections from the lower body and the lateral nucleus cuneatus receives projections from the upper body. At this point, the two dorsal columns cross over to the other side of the brain and form a ribbon-like band of fibers called the **medial lemniscus** (from the Greek

slow pain (burning and aching pain) Type of pain propagated by unmyelinated Type C fibers that slowly reaches the spinal cord.

Meissner's corpuscles Skin receptors located in the elevations (papillae) of the dermis found only in hairy skin cells into the epidermis that detects low-frequency vibrations.

Merkel's disks Skin receptors located in the base of epidermis near the sweat ducts that are sensitive to pressure.

Ruffini's corpuscles Skin receptors located just below the skin that detect low-frequency vibrations.

dorsal column-medial lemniscal system Somatosensory pathways which begin in the spinal cord and project information about touch and proprioception to the primary somatosensory cortex.

dorsal column nuclei (DCN) Neurons in the medulla that receive neural messages about touch and proprioception via the dorsal column-medial lemniscal system.

medial lemniscus A ribbon-like band of fibers in the dorsal column-medial lemniscal system that convey neural messages from the dorsal column nuclei to the ventral posterolateral thalamic nuclei.

ventral posterolateral thalamic nuclei Neurons in the thalamus that receive information about touch and proprioception via the dorsal column-medial lemniscal system and about temperature and pain via the anterolateral system.

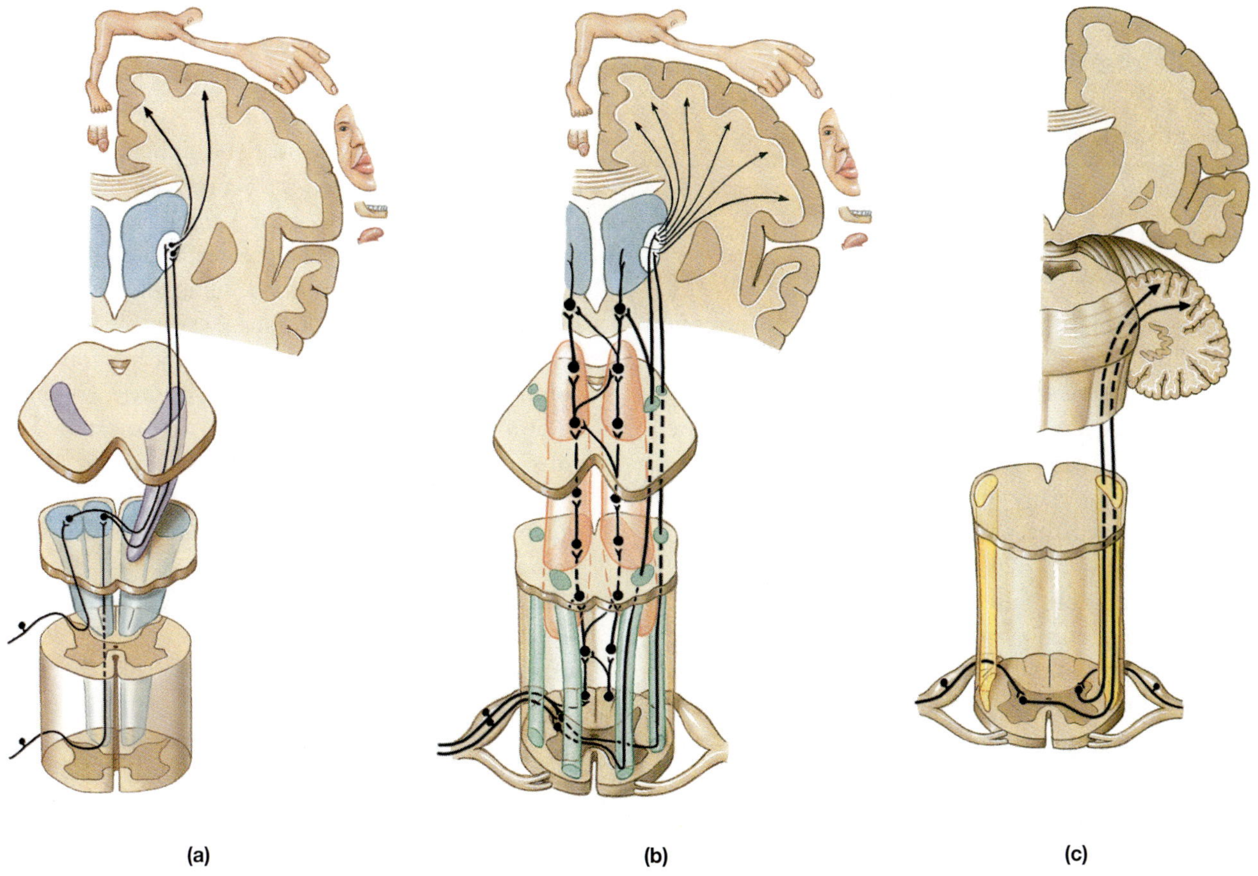

Figure 7.19 Somatosensory pathways. The three major somatosensory pathways from the sensory receptors to the cerebellum somatosensory cortex.

➤ *Information about which type of somatosensation is transmitted via the dorsal column-medial lemniscal system? (p. 212)*

word *lemniskos,* which means "ribbon"). Both the dorsal columns synapse with the **ventral posterolateral nucleus**. Information about touch and proprioceptive stimulation is then transmitted from the thalamus to the **primary somatosensory cortex**.

After crossing over at the spinal cord, many of the fibers of the **anterolateral system**, which transmits information about temperature and pain, project to the ventral posterolateral thalamic nucleus and the **posterior nuclei** of the thalamus (see **Figure 7.19b**). Other fibers terminate in the brainstem reticular formation. From the thalamus, some fibers of the anterolateral system extend to primary somatosensory cortex and others travel to the **secondary somatosensory cortex**, an area of the cortex that is lateral and slightly posterior to the primary somatosensory cortex.

Fibers of the **spinocerebellar system**, which transmit information about proprioception, enter the central nervous system through the dorsal root ganglia and synapse with the interneurons in the spinal cord (refer to **Figure 7.19c**). Some axons of these interneurons cross over at the spinal cord level (anterior spinocerebellar tract), while others do not (posterior spinocerebellar tract). These fibers then project directly to the cerebellar cortex.

---

primary somatosensory cortex Area in the anterior part of the parietal lobe that detects characteristics of tactile stimulation (touch, temperature, pain, and proprioception).

anterolateral system Somatosensory pathways which begin in the spinal cord and project information about temperature and pain to the brainstem reticular formation and the primary somatosensory cortex.

posterior nuclei Group of neurons in the thalamus that receive information about temperature and pain via the anterolateral pathway.

secondary somatosensory cortex An area of the cortex that is lateral and slightly posterior to the primary somatosensory cortex and is responsible for the perception of touch, temperature, pain, and proprioception.

spinocerebellar system Somatosensory pathways that begin in the spinal cord and project proprioceptive information to the cerebellum.

Before You Go On

Describe the path of touch sensation from your fingertips to the primary somatosensory cortex.

The Location of Input to the Somatosensory System

We learned in the previous chapter that information about visual stimulation of adjacent photoreceptors in the retina is transmitted to adjacent neurons in the lateral geniculate nucleus and then on to adjacent neurons in the primary visual cortex. A similar organization exists for the somatosensory system. In 1973, Wilder Penfield mapped the primary somatosensory cortex in humans (see **Figure 7.20**). Penfield found that when he stimulated areas of the postcentral gyrus or the primary somatosensory cortex in conscious patients prior to surgery, the patients reported feeling sensations from various parts of the body. Penfield observed that, like the visual system, the somatosensory system is topographically organized. Adjacent places on the skin activate adjacent neurons in the primary somatosensory cortex, but the organization of the primary somatosensory cortex is upside down, with sensory input from the feet going to the top of the primary somatosensory cortex and information from the head going to the bottom of the primary somatosensory cortex. As seen in the somatotopic map or somatosensory homunculus ("little man in the brain") presented in **Figure 7.20**, not all parts of the body are equally represented in the primary somatosensory cortex. The greatest representation is for areas such as hands, lips, and tongue that are involved in fine tactile discrimination.

The primary somatosensory cortex has four parallel columns (Kaas et al., 1981). Each of these columns has its own topographic organization, with most of the neurons of each column being sensitive to different somatosensory input. For example, neurons in one column respond to touch, whereas neurons in another column respond to temperature.

Like the primary somatosensory cortex, the secondary somatosensory cortex is topographically organized. It receives most of its input from the primary somatosensory cortex (Pons et al., 1987). Further, there appear to be separate somatotopic maps for each type of somatosense; that is, separate areas in the secondary somatosensory cortex have been found to receive neural impulses from rapidly adapting touch

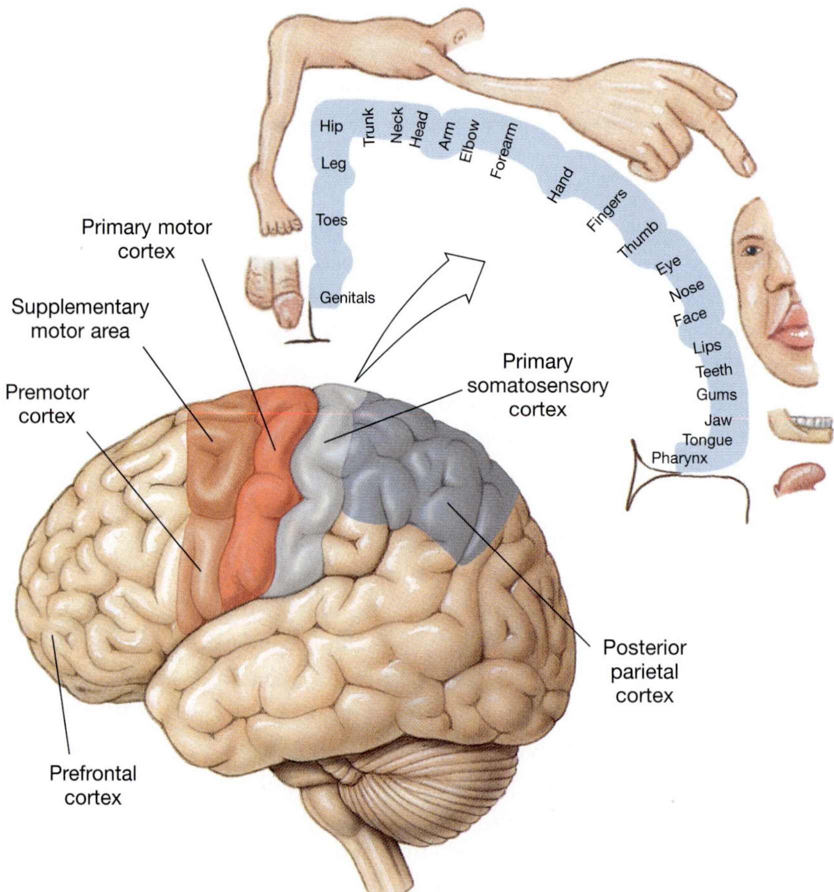

Figure 7.20 The somatosensory cortex. Figure at the top presents the somatosensory homunculus, or somatotopic map of human primary somatosensory cortex. Cortical structures receiving somatosensory input are seen in the lower figure.

➤ *What parts of the body are the most important in fine tactile discrimination? (p. 214)*

receptors, from slow-adapting touch receptors, from temperature receptors, from pain receptors, and from proprioceptive receptors (Dykes, 1983).

APPLICATION

The Control of Pain

As Kathy listens to Sarah talk to her grandmother on the telephone, she is preparing dinner (the spaghetti sauce that Sarah is so enthusiastic about); suddenly she feels pain in her right hand and realizes that it is brushing up against the hot saucepan. She pulls her hand away quickly and runs it under cold water. Meanwhile on the other end of the line, Heather switches the telephone from her left hand to her right hand, as she feels her arthritis acting up.

The perception of pain is an important somatosensory message. Pain can be beneficial; it alerts Kathy to her injury, enabling her to act to prevent further damage and then treat her injury. Chronic pain, such as that caused by Heather's arthritis, can be debilitating. In extreme cases, we can become so preoccupied by the pain itself that we are unable to deal with the source of the pain.

How do our bodies manage pain so that we are aware of an injury or illness but are not incapacitated? In 1965, Ronald Melzack and Patrick Wall proposed a **gate-control theory of pain**. According to Melzack and Wall, the sensory input from pain receptors produce the perception of pain only if the message first passes through a "gate" located in the spinal cord and lower brainstem structures. Melzack and Wall identified a descending fiber tract that begins in the **periaqueductal gray (PAG)** of the midbrain and synapses with inhibitory interneurons in the spinal cord and lower brainstem (see **Figure 7.21**). These inhibitory neurons synapse with ascending sensory neurons carrying messages about pain. Activity in the periaqueductal gray activates the inhibitory interneurons, which then block the pain message from entering the central nervous system.

How can the "gate" be closed to prevent the experience of pain? Recall our discussion of endorphins in Chapter 2. Researchers (Basbaum & Fields, 1984; Watkins & Mayer, 1982) believe that endorphins, which are released in response to a painful stimulus, stimulate neurons in the PAG, and thereby close the "gate" to incoming pain messages. In support of this view, Basbaum and Fields (1984) reported that small amounts of the opiate drug morphine injected into the PAG relieve pain (recall from Chapter 5 that endorphins are endogenous opiates and that opiates have an agonist action on endorphin receptors), whereas the same amounts of morphine injected into other areas of the brain did not produce any analgesic effect. In another study, electrical stimulation of the PAG allowed

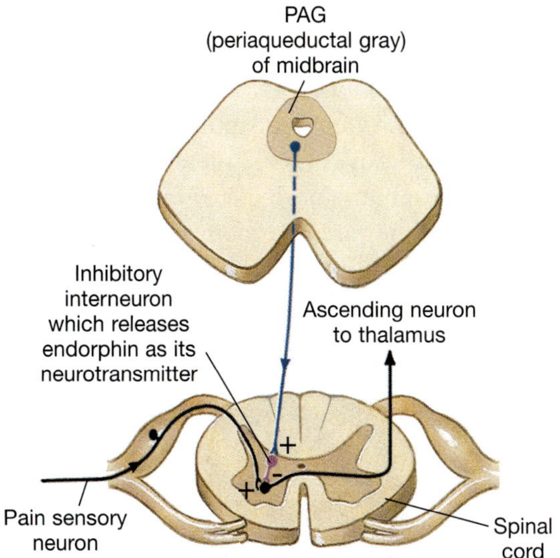

Figure 7.21 The periaqueductal gray fiber tracts. The descending fibers from periaqueductal gray inhibit sensory pain messages at the spinal cord and lower brainstem.

➤ *What substance stimulates the neurons of the periaqueductal gray to "close the gate" to pain messages? (p. 215)*

Reynolds (1969) to do abdominal surgery in animals without any drugs. These observations suggest that opiates such as morphine block pain by stimulating the PAG.

Opiate drugs are not the only treatment that can stimulate the PAG and block incoming pain messages. Acupuncture is a pain control technique that has been used in China for over 2,000 years. Fine needles are inserted into the skin over different parts of the body (see **Figure 7.22**). The acupuncture technique has been used successfully in a variety of medical procedures including tooth extractions, tonsillectomies, and childbirth (Yang, 1979).

How does acupuncture relieve pain? It is likely that the acupuncture needles stimulate the release of endorphins, thereby closing the "gate" to incoming pain messages. The points that the acupuncture needles are inserted are very close to the somatosensory pathways that conduct sensations of pain (Chen, Li, & Jiang, 1986). Further, Lipton, Brewington, and Smith (1993) found that administration of naloxone, a drug that antagonizes the influence of endorphins, blocked the analgesic effect of acupuncture.

Distraction is another method of reducing pain. Researchers (Lavine, Buchshaum, & Poncy, 1976; McCaul

---

gate-control theory of pain The view that sensory input from pain receptors will produce the perception of pain only if the message first passes through a "gate" located in the spinal cord and lower brainstem structures.

periaqueductal gray (PAG) An area of the midbrain that is the origin of a descending fiber tract that synapses with inhibitory interneurons in the lower brainstem and spinal cord to block messages about pain.

& Malott, 1984) report that the perception of pain is lessened when people listen to music, play a game, or even just remember a pleasant experience; Kathy uses the technique of distraction whenever Sarah is about to receive a shot at the pediatrician's office. Patients have been found to recover from surgery more quickly and complain less about pain when they are in a room with a pleasant view than in a room with a poor view or no window (Ulrich, 1984). So when you are troubled by pain, try to distract yourself by doing something pleasant. ■

Before You Go On

Describe the role of the periaqueductal gray in the inhibition of pain perception.

Section Review

- Somatosenses, or skin senses, include detection of touch, temperature, and pain as well as proprioception.
- The cutaneous or skin receptors detect touch, temperature, and pain.
- The largest of the skin receptors are Pacinian corpuscles, which are embedded in the dermis of the skin and are sensitive to touch stimulation, particularly high-frequency vibrations.
- Free-nerve endings are located just below the skin and detect changes in temperature and painful stimulation.
- Other cutaneous receptors are Meissner's corpuscles, which are sensitive to pressure and low-frequency vibrations; Merkel's disks, which are sensitive to pressure; and Ruffini's corpuscles, which are sensitive to low-frequency vibrations.
- Skin receptor fibers project either through the cranial nerves of the face and head or through the spinal nerves to the central nervous system. Information from the skin receptors travels along one of three pathways: the dorsal column-medial leminiscal system, the anterolateral system, and the spinocerebellar system.
- The dorsal column-medial lemniscal system carries information about touch and proprioceptive sensations to the dorsal column nuclei, then to the ventral posterolateral thalamic nuclei and the primary somatosensory cortex.
- The anterolateral system carries information about temperature and pain sensations to the brainstem reticular formation, or the ventral posterolateral thalamic nuclei and the posterior nuclei of thalamus, and then to the primary somatosensory cortex.
- The spinocerebellar system carries information about proprioception to the cerebellar cortex.

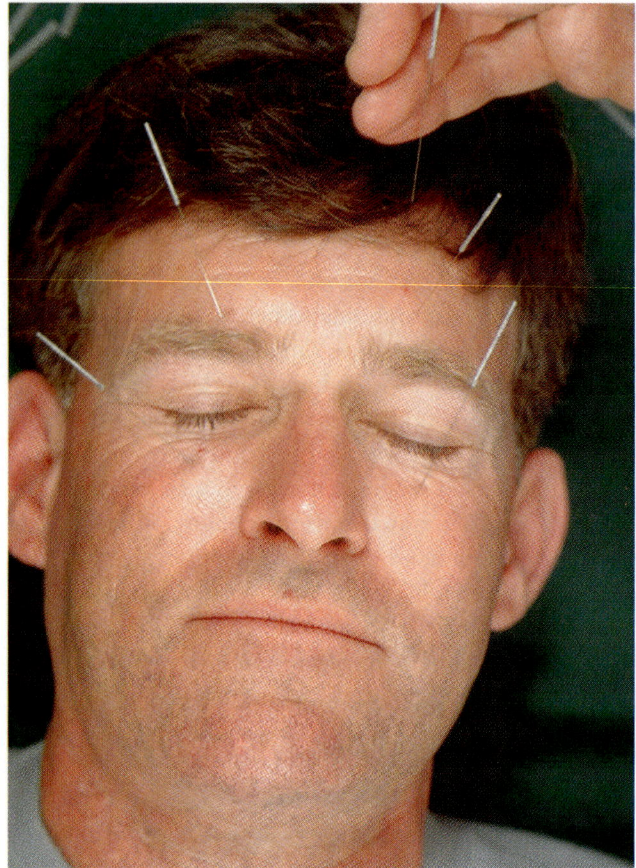

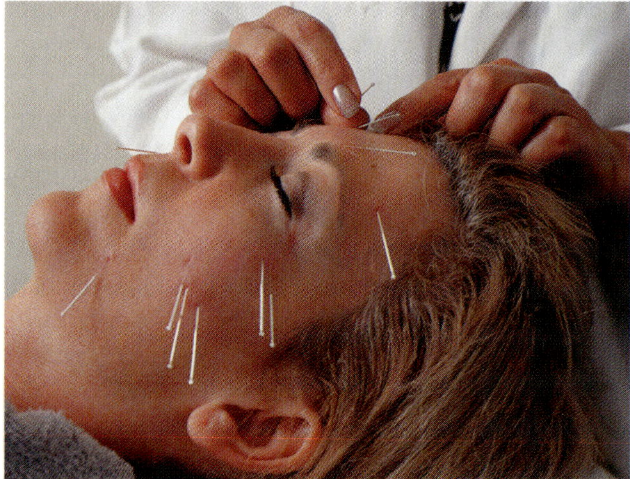

Figure 7.22 Acupuncture. Photographs show the insertion of fine needles in acupuncture treatment for pain.

➤ *What structure of the central nervous system is acupuncture believed to stimulate? (p. 215)*

- The somatosensory cortex is organized topographically, with adjacent areas of the skin represented by adjacent areas of somatosensory cortex.
- Input from the feet is transmitted to the top of the somatosensory cortex, and input from the head is transmitted to the bottom of the somatosensory cortex.

- Gate-control theory of pain assumes that sensory input from pain receptors will produce the perception of pain only if the message first passes through a "gate" located in the spinal cord and lower brainstem structures.
- The periaqueductal gray (PAG) is a midbrain structure that synapses with inhibitory interneurons in the lower brainstem and spinal cord to block messages about pain.

The Chemical Senses

When Kevin arrived home from school, he knew immediately that his next door neighbor, Kathy, was cooking. From the aroma, he guessed that she was cooking spaghetti. Kevin was sure that Kathy made the best spaghetti sauce in the world. The aroma of the sauce simmering on the stove made his mouth water. He snuck through her back door into the kitchen and took a sip of the sauce with the spoon sitting beside the pan. If he got caught, Kathy would yell at him for tasting the sauce, but it was just irresistible. He hoped Kathy would send over some sauce, as she often did.

The aroma and the taste of food are what make eating such an enjoyable activity. Similarly, it would be hard to imagine enjoying a glass of iced tea that did not have a pleasant fragrance and taste. Our senses of smell and taste play significant roles in our lives. In the next two sections, we will examine the biology of the gustatory (taste) and olfactory (smell) systems.

The Gustatory Sense

You eat one piece of candy and it tastes sweet. Another piece tastes sour. A peanut might taste salty, but it also might taste bitter. Although the quality of tastes may differ, there are only four basic tastes: sweet, sour, bitter, and salty. The tastes of an apple and a pear obviously differ, but both taste sweet. Our sense of taste is referred to in clinical terms as our gustatory sense, from the Latin *gustare*, "to taste."

To taste sweetness, bitterness, or any other flavor, the molecules in the food must dissolve in the saliva in the mouth and then stimulate the taste receptors on the tongue. Each taste receptor in the tongue is sensitive to all four tastes, but maximally sensitive to just one taste. For example, the taste receptors that respond most to the hydrogen ions (H^+) found in all acids are maximally responsive to sour tastes. Those receptors most sensitive to sodium chloride molecules detect salty tastes. A bitter taste is detected by receptors that are maximally responsive to alkaloid compounds, and a sweet taste is detected by receptors maximally sensitive to sugars.

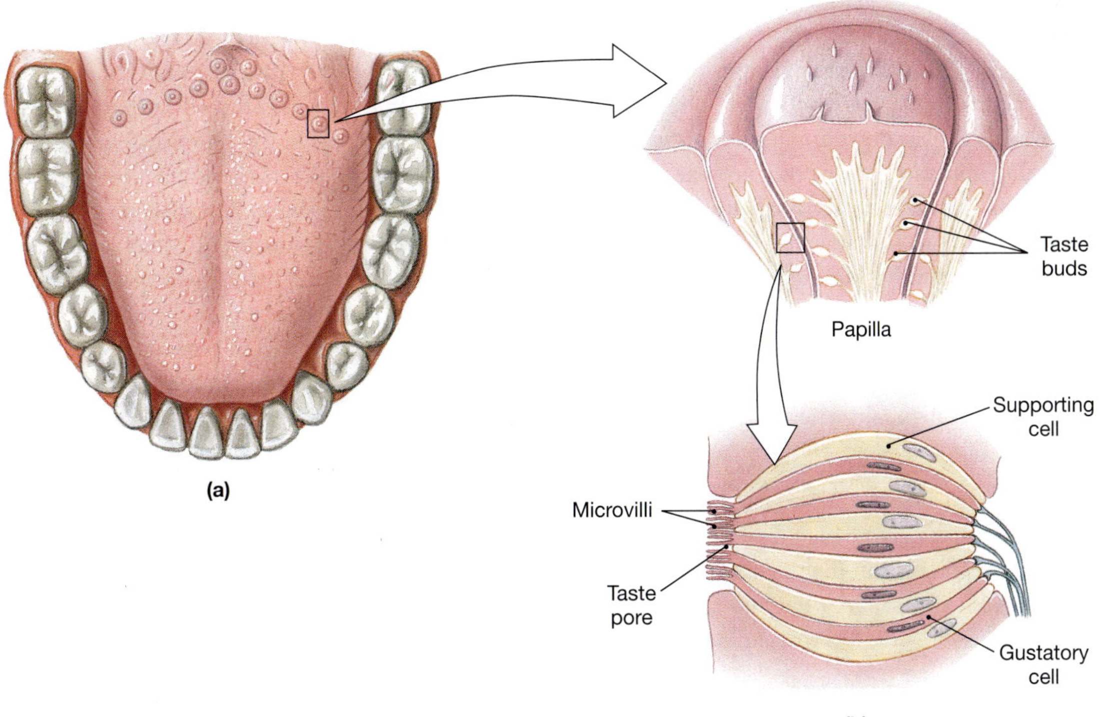

Figure 7.23 Gustatory receptors. (a) Location of taste buds in the papillae of the tongue, and (b) major structures of the taste bud.
➤ *How are the taste receptors stimulated? (p. 219)*

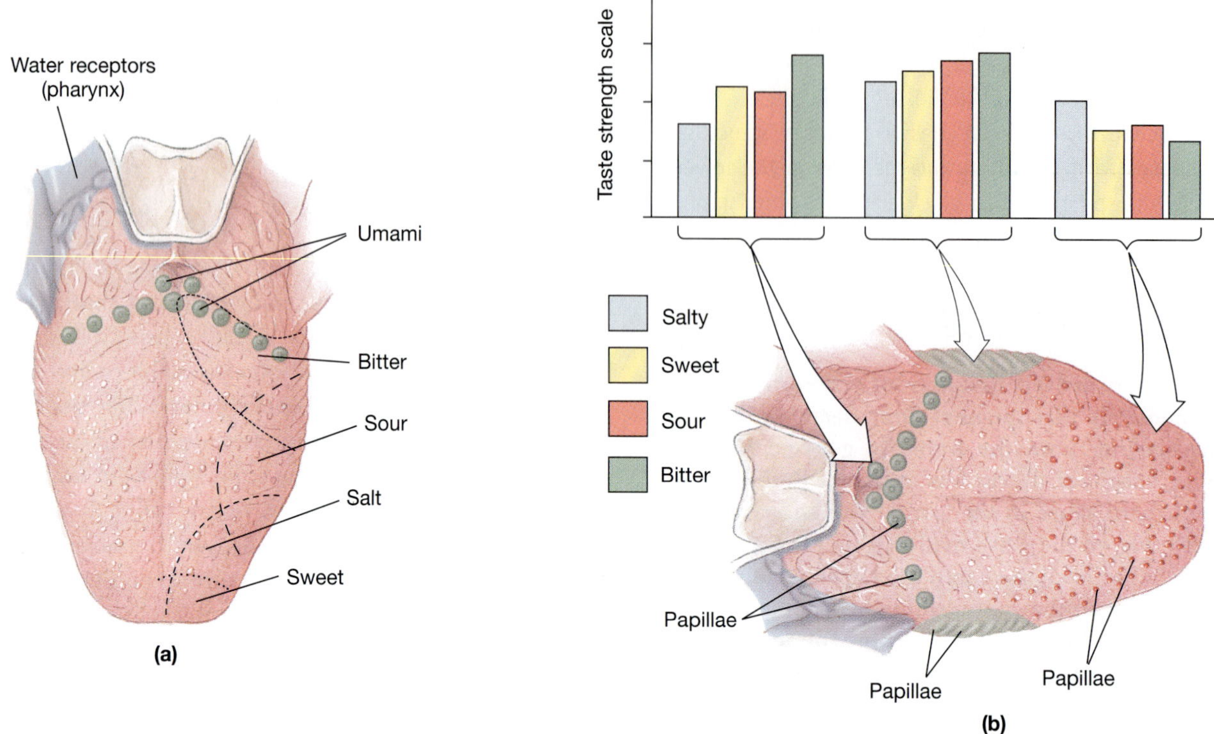

Figure 7.24 Taste receptor distribution. (a) The hypothetical distribution of receptors for the basic tastes (salty, sweet, sour, and bitter) on the tongue. (b) The actual distribution of taste receptors is basically the same at various places on the tongue.

➤ *How does a salty food activate its taste receptor? (p. 219)*

Enjoying food and drink is pleasurable, but what is so important about taste? You may not think of it this way, but the ability to detect different tastes is important to our survival. Because many foods become acidic when they spoil, avoiding sour foods can prevent illness. Many plants contain bitter-tasting alkaloid poisons that are dangerous to eat. Loss of fluids can deplete sodium chloride from the blood; a sensitivity to salt (salt craving) allows us to eat food or drink fluids containing salt, and thereby replenish our depleted sodium chloride. Sweet foods usually contain sugars needed for cell metabolism. Thus, humans and nonhuman animals generally avoid bitter and sour tastes and seek out sweet and salty ones.

Taste Receptors. The tongue contains many small bumps, called **papillae**. (To see them, you can look at your roommate's tongue with a magnifying glass, if you dare!) **Taste buds** lie either near or within the papillae (see **Figure 7.23**). The tongue, with the palate, pharynx, and larynx, contain about 10,000 taste buds. Taste receptors are individual cells located in the taste buds. A taste bud contains from 20 to 50 taste receptors. At the end of each receptor are microvilli that protrude through the opening or pore of the taste bud and into the saliva that coats the tongue. Molecules contained in the saliva stimulate the receptors.

Take a look at the drawing of the tongue in **Figure 7.24a**. The drawing shows that the tip of the tongue contains receptors most sensitive to sweet and salty tastes, the sides of the tongue contain receptors that are maximally sensitive to sour tastes, and the receptors at the back of the tongue are most sensitive to bitter tastes. Many of my students report having learned in high school or college biology that the tongue contains the distribution of taste receptors described above. Unfortunately, as Linda Bartoshuk, a noted researcher on taste, eloquently put it "The (usual) tongue map has become an enduring scientific myth" (Bartoshuk, 1993). Neuroscientists (Bartoshuk, 1993; Yanagisawa et al., 1992) have found that taste receptors for the four basic tastes can be found anywhere on the tongue and that the areas do not differ greatly in sensitivity to the four basic tastes (see **Figure 7.24b**).

You might have noted the term *umami* in **Figure 7.24a**. Umami comes from the Japanese word meaning "good taste." Researchers (Kurihara, 1987; Scott & Plata-Salaman, 1991) noted a sensitivity to monosodium glu-

---

papillae Small, visible bumps on the tongue that contain taste buds.

taste buds A cluster of 20 to 50 taste receptors that lie either near or within the papillae.

tamate (MSG) and suggested the existence of **umami receptors** that detect the presence of glutamate as well as other amino acids. Why might there be amino acid receptors in your tongue? Although glutamate tastes salty, other amino acids (for example, leucine) taste bitter. So it is not likely that taste quality is the reason for umami receptors. Most likely it is because amino acids are the building blocks of proteins, which are excellent sources of energy. Thus, the ability to detect amino acids, such as glutamate, would have adaptive value.

Perhaps you really enjoy eating bitter-tasting foods. Or have a sweet tooth. Research by Bartoshuk and her colleagues (Bartoshuk & Beauchamp, 1994; Bartoshuk et al., 1992; Reedy et al., 1993) has found that people differ in their sensitivity to bitter and some sweet tastes, such as saccharin. And these differences appear to be related, at least in part, to the number of taste buds that a person has on his or her tongue. Supertasters, which comprise about 25 percent of the population, have the most taste buds (averaging 425 per square centimeter on the tongue tip). By contrast, medium tasters, which comprise 50 percent of the population, have approximately 184 taste buds per square centimeter, and nontasters, which comprise the remaining 25 percent of the population, have approximately 96 taste buds per square centimeter.

The differences in taste sensitivity appear to be genetically determined. For example, nontasters cannot taste two bitter tastes—phenylthiocarbamide (PTC) and 6-n-propylthiouracil (PROP). The gene for tasting PTC and PROP has been identified, and in order to taste these two bitter substances, the T form of this gene must be present. Nontasters do not have this form of the gene, whereas people who can taste both PTC and PROP do.

Mechanisms of Taste Reception. The mechanism by which a food activates a taste receptor differs for each of the four basic tastes. A salty food activates a taste receptor by causing the Na^+ ions to move through the sodium channels in the cell membrane of the taste receptor. The increased entry of Na^+ ions causes the receptor membrane to depolarize, which leads to neurotransmitter release (Avenet & Lindemann, 1989). The more salty the food, the greater the entry of Na^+ ions into the cell, resulting in greater depolarization and neurotransmitter release.

Hydrogen ions in sour foods and the sugar molecules in sweet foods close the K^+ ion channels, reducing the exit of K^+ ions from the cell. The accumulation of K^+ ions depolarizes the taste receptors, which leads to neurotransmitter release (Avenet & Lindemann, 1989; Kinnamon, Dionne, & Beam, 1988). As was true of salty foods, the sweeter or more sour the food, the greater the level of cell membrane depolarization and neurotransmitter release.

Alkaloid compounds that give bitter foods their bite trigger the movement of Ca^{++} ions into the cytoplasm from storage sites within the taste receptor. The increased level of Ca^{++} ions inside the receptor causes more neurotransmitters to be released (Akabas, Dodd, & Al-Awqati, 1988). And the more bitter the food, the more Ca^{++} ions will enter the cell and the greater the neurotransmitter molecules that are released.

Taste Pathways. Axons of taste receptors become branches of three cranial nerves (cranial nerves 7, 9, and 10) and transmit neural impulses about taste to the central nervous system (see **Figure 7.25**). Taste sensations originating in the anterior two-thirds of the tongue are carried by the **chorda tympani**, a branch of the seventh cranial nerve. Branches of the ninth and tenth cranial nerves convey taste information from the posterior tongue and the palate and throat.

The nerve fibers carrying information from the taste receptors synapse with the **nucleus of the solitary tract**, an area located in the medulla. Axons that project to the nucleus of the solitary tract synapse with neurons in the **ventral posteromedial thalamic nucleus**. These neurons then project to and synapse with neurons in the **primary gustatory cortex**, located just ventral and rostral to the area representing the tongue in the somatosensory cortex.

What Taste Is It? Life would be pretty boring if all we could taste were sweet, sour, bitter, and salty. How do we distinguish a particular taste? How can we tell a McIntosh apple from a Golden Delicious apple?

We have learned that taste receptors react maximally to one of the four basic tastes, and that axons of the taste receptors synapse with the nucleus of the solitary tract, which then synapses in the ventral posteromedial thalamic nucleus. Like the taste receptors, the neurons in these two structures are differentially sen-

---

umami receptor A taste receptor sensitive to the presence of glutamate and other amino acids.

chorda tympani A branch of the seventh cranial nerve that conveys taste information from the posterior tongue and the palate and throat to the nucleus of the solitary tract.

nucleus of the solitary tract A group of neurons in the medulla that receives information from the taste receptors.

ventral posteromedial thalamic nucleus A group of neurons that receives taste information from the nucleus of the solitary tract and then projects that information to the primary gustatory cortex.

primary gustatory cortex An area located just ventral and rostral to the area representing the tongue in the somatosensory cortex that recognizes the qualities of a taste stimulus.

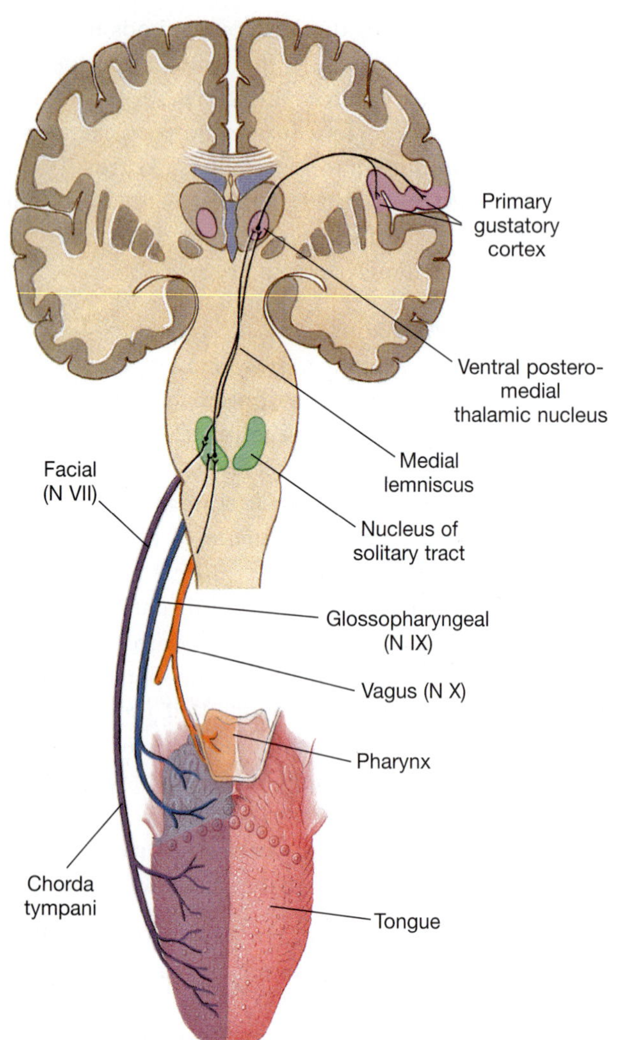

Figure 7.25 Gustatory pathways. Pathways from taste receptors to primary gustatory cortex.

Adapted from Kandel et al., 1991.

➤ *Which nerves carry taste information from the posterior tongue, palate, and throat? (p. 219)*

sitive to a particular taste (Beckstead, Morse, & Norgren, 1980). Further, these neurons are organized into clusters of taste-sensitive neurons; that is, neurons that are sensitive to a particular taste are grouped together. A similar clustering of neurons is found in the primary gustatory cortex. Activity in neurons of the primary gustatory cortex is thought to be the source of the perception of a specific taste.

Our taste perception is not determined solely by the molecules acting on the tongue at the moment we ingest a food. Past experiences also influence our taste sensations. For example, a wine that may seem bitter to a novice might be tasted as sweet by an expert.

Sarah cannot stand the taste of carrots, because once "when she was little," she ate carrots when she had a stomach virus and vomited orange. She now associates the taste of carrots with being sick. Although Kathy had to clean up the mess, she does not suffer from the same association and hopes that Sarah's will wear off as she gets older. We will learn more about this type of association in Chapter 14 on learning and memory.

Some foods can alter the taste experience of other foods. Such context effects are similar to the visual aftereffects described in Chapter 6 (remember the negative afterimage of the American flag?), but occur via a different mechanism. Drinking orange juice after brushing your teeth, for example, will leave a bitter taste in your mouth; normally, orange juice tastes sweet, but the sodium lauryl sulfate in most toothpastes increases the perceived bitterness of orange juice and decreases its sweetness (DeSimone, Heck, & Bartoshuk, 1980). The sodium lauryl sulfate in the toothpaste prevents the sugar molecules from binding to sweet receptors and inhibits the perception of the orange juice's sweetness. Artichokes, which contain the chemical theophylline, reduce the perceived bitterness of foods (Bartoshuk, 1988). Many people report that water and most other liquids taste much sweeter after eating artichokes. So if you need to drink orange juice after brushing your teeth, eat an artichoke first!

Another instance in which taste perception can be altered involves the miracle berry, a plant native to West Africa. The miracle berry itself is tasteless, but it contains a protein called miraculin that causes acids to stimulate sweetness receptors (Bartoshuk et al., 1974). After a miracle berry is chewed, acids, which normally taste sour, will taste sweet. This effect of the miracle berry lasts about half an hour, and during this time all acids tasted will seem sweet.

So you don't have any miracle berries on hand and you can't make it to West Africa before the next quiz? You can still experience the context effects of taste by performing the following simple experiment. You will need a lemon, a cube of sugar, and a glass of water. (No, we're not going to make lemonade!) Suck on a lemon for a few seconds and then take a sip of water. The water should taste sweet. Now eat a cube of sugar. A sip of water should now taste sour. Now you can see for yourself that the taste of a particular food or drink is affected by more than just the activity of the taste receptors on the tongue.

Before You Go On

Describe the pathway of the taste of a nectarine from the moment you bite into it to the perception of taste by the primary gustatory cortex.

Why do you think that your roommate likes the taste of broccoli and you hate it?

Olfactory Sense

As a young child, I can remember driving past the saw mills on the Rappohannock River in Virginia and experiencing a quite unpleasant pungent odor. Most of the time, I held my breath until the saw mills were far behind me. We are able to detect many different odors, some of them pleasant (like the fragrances of flowers or perfumes) and others unpleasant (like the saw mill). The olfactory sense plays a significant role in our everyday lives. For example, we use odor to detect and avoid eating rotting food. The smell of smoke can alert us to danger. In nonhuman animals, odors are used to detect predators or track prey. Odors also are a crucial stimulus in many species in the recognition of potential mates.

The stimuli detected by the olfactory system, **odors** or smells, are molecules of volatile substances in the air. Humans are quite sensitive to these molecules, although not quite as sensitive as nonhuman animals. For example, people can detect the unpleasant smell of ethyl mercaptan even in concentrations as small as 1 part per 50 billion parts of air (Engen, 1982). Our extreme sensitivity to mercaptan is why it is added to odorless natural gas so that we may be able to detect gas leaks.

We are apparently quite sensitive to odors. In fact, humans can detect more than 1,000 different odors (Ressler, Sullivan, & Buck, 1994). But can we describe odors the way colors (blue, green, yellow, red, etc.) are described? The following study addresses this question. Cain (1982) presented 80 relatively common odors to college students. Most were able to identify correctly the odors of coffee, peanut butter, and chocolate, but few could identify soy sauce, prune juice, or cough syrup. Despite our sensitivity to odor, our language contains few words to describe what we smell. Although we can distinguish between two brands of perfume, determining why one brand is more fragrant than the other is difficult. We have developed an extensive vocabulary for describing what we see or hear, but find describing what we smell more difficult.

The Olfactory Receptors. The olfactory receptors line the mucous membrane, called the **olfactory epithelium**, located in the top rear of the nasal passage (see **Figure 7.26**). Odor molecules sometimes passively reach the olfactory receptors. At other times, a sniff is needed to move the air to the back of the nasal passage, or you might not detect the odor. Proteins present in the fluids of the olfactory epithelium transport the odor molecules

odors Molecules of volatile substances in the air that are detected by olfactory receptors.

olfactory epithelium The mucous membrane located in the top rear of the nasal passage that is lined by olfactory receptors.

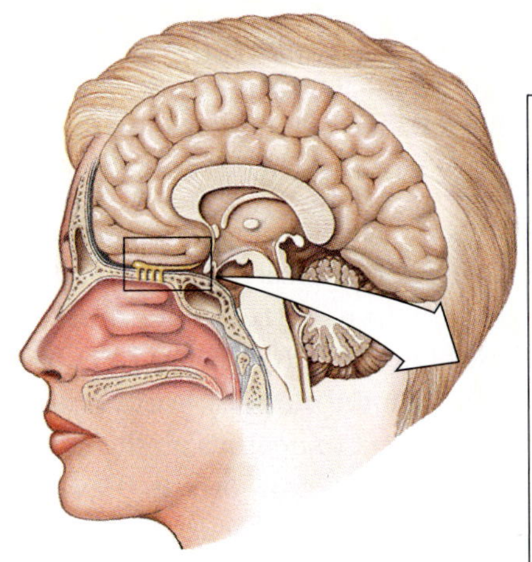

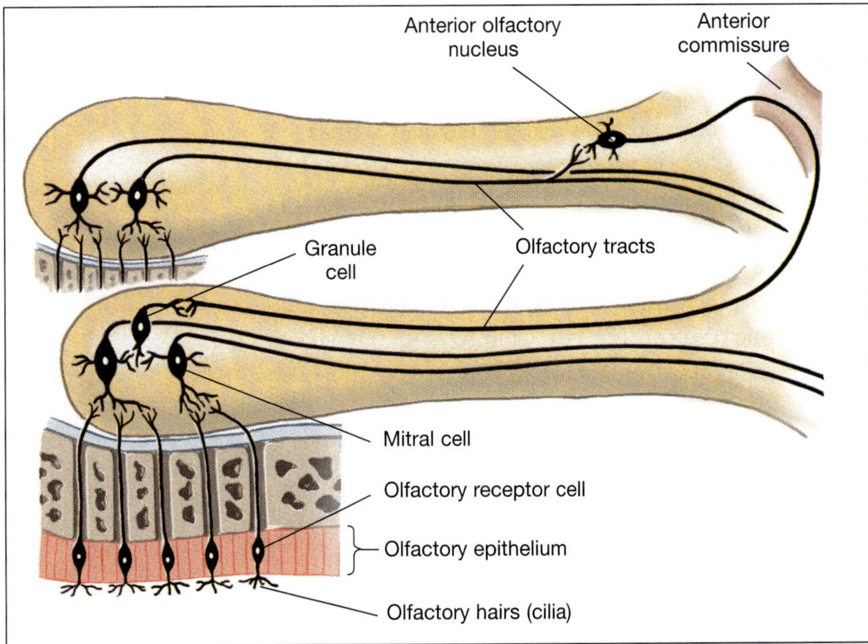

Figure 7.26 Olfactory receptors. Illustration showing the structure of the olfactory receptors and the location of olfactory receptors.
➤ *Why do you sometimes need to sniff to smell odors and other times you don't? (p. 221)*

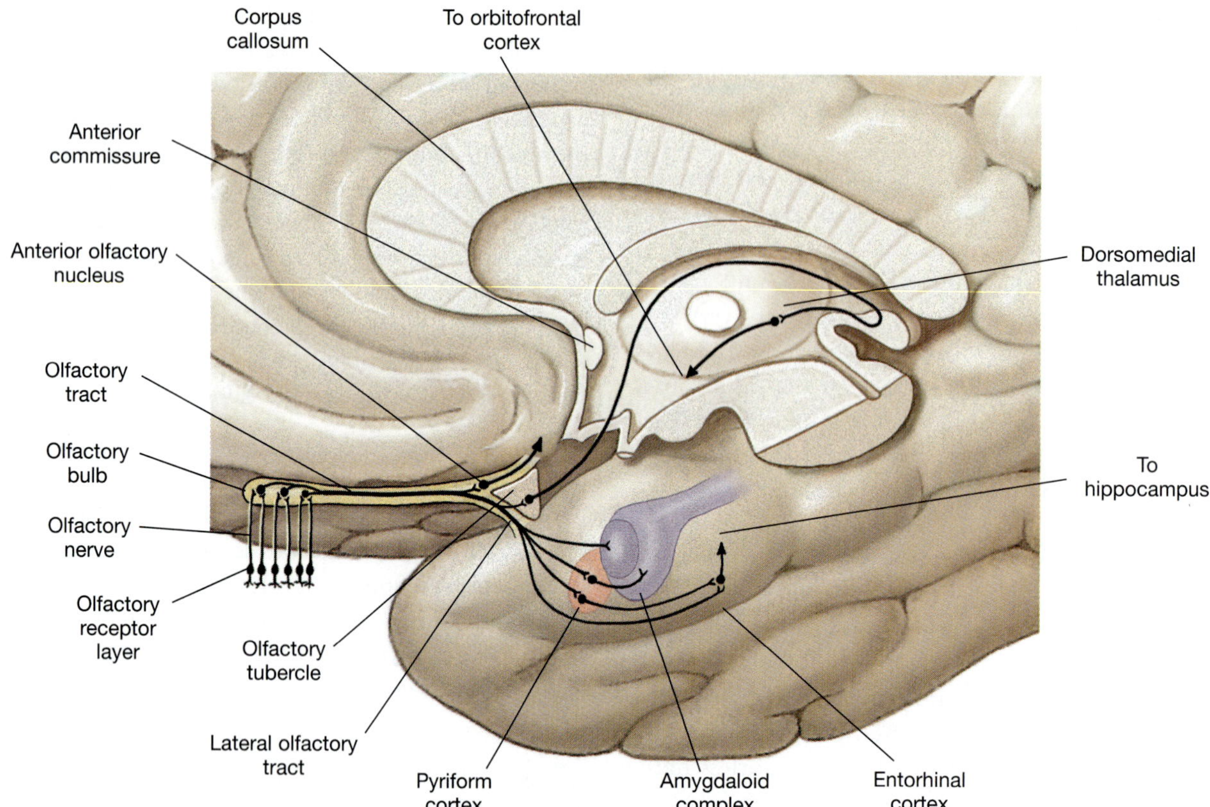

Figure 7.27 Olfactory pathways. Pathways from the olfactory receptors to the primary olfactory cortex (located in the pyriform cortex) and then on to limbic system, the dorsomedial thalamus, and orbitofrontal cortex.

➤ *How is the olfactory system different from the other sensory systems? (p. 222–223)*

to olfactory receptors (Farbman, 1994). Each olfactory receptor contains cilia or olfactory hair cells that extend into the olfactory epithelium. You have approximately 50 million olfactory receptors that detect smell.

Odor molecules dissolve in the fluid covering the mucous membrane and activate the olfactory receptors. A protein, called G_{olf}, is present in the olfactory receptors (Menco et al., 1992). The odor molecules stimulate the G_{olf} protein, which then activates an enzyme that catalyzes the synthesis of cyclic adenosine monophosphate, or cyclic AMP. Cyclic AMP is a second messenger that influences synaptic transmission (see Chapter 4 for a review of second messengers). In olfactory receptors, the presence of cyclic AMP opens the Na^+ ion channels and depolarizes the receptor membrane. Sufficient depolarization of the membrane causes the message to be transmitted along the axon of the olfactory receptor directly to the brain.

The Olfactory Pathway. The axons of the olfactory receptors enter the skull through small holes in the cribriform plate and synapse with the mitral cells of the **olfactory bulbs** that lie at the base of the brain (see **Figure 7.27**). The axons of the mitral cells form the **olfactory tract**. Some of the olfactory tract fibers project to neurons on the ipsilateral side of the brain, and others cross over to the other side of the brain and synapse with the olfactory bulb on the contralateral side of the brain. Fibers from the olfactory bulb extend to the primary olfactory cortex (see **Figure 7.27**). The **primary olfactory cortex** is located in the pyriform cortex, an area of the limbic system.

The primary olfactory cortex is the only primary cortex located outside of the cerebral cortex. The location of the primary olfactory cortex in the limbic system gives odors an emotional component, which can explain our strong response to particular smells. Thus, when Kevin walks into Kathy's kitchen and smells spaghetti sauce simmering, his initial reaction to this stimulus is not only a sensation of

olfactory bulbs Paired structures at the base of the brain that contain mitral cells, which receive information about odor from the olfactory receptors.

olfactory tract Fiber bundles formed by axons of the mitral cells of the olfactory bulb, which project to the primary olfactory cortex.

primary olfactory cortex Area in the pyriform cortex of the limbic system that detects the emotional character of an odor.

odor but also a strong emotional response. It is no wonder, then, he finds it so hard to stop from tasting the sauce.

Olfactory messages are transmitted from the primary olfactory cortex to the hypothalamus. These messages are important in motivating approach or avoidance behavior toward food or drink, as well as toward potential mates. Other messages are transmitted to the dorsomedial thalamus and then to the orbitofrontal cortex (see Figure 7.27). The orbitofrontal cortex also receives input from the gustatory system, and may act to combine the taste and the odor of a food into its perceived flavor. (Try to taste your favorite candy bar while holding your nose and you will understand the difference between taste and flavor.)

What Odor Is It? Axel (1995) suggested that an odor molecule is shaped like a "key" that fits into a specific receptor "lock." According to this theory, one type of olfactory molecule activates one type of olfactory receptor, and another odor molecule stimulates another type of olfactory receptor. As we learned earlier, olfactory receptors contain a protein (G_{olf}) that is activated by odor molecules. Buck and Axel (1991) have identified 18 different receptor proteins, which suggests at least 18 different odor receptors. Raming and colleagues (1993) have found still further olfactory receptor proteins. The olfactory receptors show clustering in the nose, with receptors that respond to a particular odor grouped together (Ressler, Sullivan, & Buck, 1994).

Differential responding to odors is also observed in neurons in the olfactory bulb. Kauer (1988) observed that different odors activated different neurons of the olfactory bulbs of salamanders. Similarly, Tanabe, Iino, and Takagi (1975) reported that half of the neurons in the olfactory area of the orbitofrontal cortex of monkeys responded to a single odor. Other neurons reacted to two, three, or four odors, but none responded to five or more odors. Our recognition of a specific odor may be the result of the combined activity of specific neurons in the olfactory system.

One further point deserves mentioning. As we learned in Chapter 6, our visual system can combine different wavelengths of light to form synthetic colors from the three primary colors. By contrast, our auditory systems distinguish different sounds even when presented at the same time. The olfactory system does both. The smell of coffee alone is actually a mixture of several hundred different odor molecules. When coffee is brewing and eggs are frying, our olfactory system combines these hundreds of molecules so that we can smell the coffee, yet we can still distinguish the smell of eggs. These observations suggest that some of our sensory systems operate by combining stimuli (vision), others by detecting individual stimuli (audition), and still others by a combination of both (olfaction). In the next chapter, we will discuss the biological basis of movement, which enables us to pour the coffee and flip the eggs.

Before You Go On

Describe how the odor and taste of Kathy's spaghetti sauce are combined to form its flavor.

Section Review

- The gustatory system distinguishes among four basic tastes: sweet, sour, bitter, and salty.
- Taste receptors are found in taste buds located near or within the papillae in the tongue, the palate, pharynx, and larynx, and respond to molecules dissolved in the saliva.
- Umami receptors detect the presence of glutamate (in monosodium glutamate; MSG) as well as other amino acids in foods.
- Salty foods open Na^+ ion channels.
- Hydrogen ions in acidic foods (sour taste) and sugar molecules (sweet taste) close K^+ ion channels.
- Alkaloid compounds (bitter taste) increase Ca^{++} ion levels inside the receptor cell.
- Taste receptors send neural messages through the seventh, ninth, and tenth cranial nerves, which synapse with the nucleus of the solitary tract of the medulla.
- Projections of the nucleus of the solitary tract connect to the ventral posteromedial thalamic nucleus and to the primary gustatory cortex located just ventral and rostral to the area representing the tongue in the somatosensory cortex.
- Neurons in both the ventral posteromedial thalamic nucleus and the primary gustatory cortex respond differentially to each of the four basic tastes.
- The olfactory receptors are sensitive to airborne molecules of volatile substances.
- Each olfactory receptor contains cilia that extend into the mucous membrane of the olfactory epithelium that lines the nasal passage.
- Odor molecules dissolve in the mucous and activate the olfactory receptors, causing Na^+ ion channels to open, the cell membrane to depolarize, and an odor message to be sent.
- The axons of the olfactory receptors synapse with the mitral cells of the olfactory bulbs.
- Mitral cell fibers form the olfactory tracts, which project to the primary olfactory cortex, an area of the limbic system.
- Olfactory messages from the primary olfactory cortex are transmitted to the hypothalamus and the dorsomedial thalamus.
- The orbitofrontal cortex receives information from the dorsomedial thalamus as well as the gustatory system and may be responsible for combining input about the taste and odor of food into its perceived flavor.

Chapter Review

Critical Thinking Questions

1. Bill was awakened to the sound of his daughter's crying. It was his turn to feed the baby and he struggled to get out of bed. He picked up his daughter and she stopped crying as the bottle went into her mouth. How was Bill able to hear his daughter crying? What process allowed him to distinguish her crying from other sounds in the night?
2. Janis felt the reassuring touch of her dad's hand on her shoulder as she fine-tuned her résume. His touch made her feel confident that she would do well on her interview. Trace the neural circuit from the sensory receptors to the primary somatosensory cortex that allowed Janis to feel her father's reassuring touch.
3. Tim is looking forward to his trip. The sights and sounds of New Orleans are always quite exciting, but the best part of New Orleans is the food. His first stop would be the Cafe DuMonde for a beignet and a cup of coffee. Tim also is looking forward to the spicy taste of jambalaya, or seafood gumbo. Explain the process that allows Tim to experience the culinary delights of New Orleans. How is the taste and odor of gumbo combined into its flavor?

Vocabulary Questions

1. The visible portion of the ear, which does not actually receive auditory input, is called the ________________.
2. Sound waves cause the ________________ to vibrate.
3. The middle ear is the section of the auditory system from the ________________ to the ________________.
4. The auditory receptors synapse with neurons that form the ________________ nerve.
5. According to the ________________ theory of pitch, sounds of high frequency activate the basal end of the basilar membrane and sounds of low frequency activate the apex end.
6. According to the ________________ theory of pitch, the entire basilar membrane vibrates at the same frequency as the perceived sound.
7. The particular combination of frequencies produces what we perceive as the ________________ of a sound.
8. Two types of cues the auditory system uses to identify the location of a sound are ________________ and ________________.
9. The vestibular system consists of the ________________ and the ________________ canals.
10. The ________________ are calcium carbonate crystals that respond to the change in fluid flow when we shift position.
11. The largest type of skin receptor is the ________________.
12. The three pathways from the skin receptors to the central nervous system are the ________________, the ________________, and the ________________.
13. ________________ and ________________ combine for the perception of flavor.
14. Taste receptors are located in the ________________ on the tongue.
15. Taste sensations originating in the anterior two-thirds of the tongue are carried by the ________________, a branch of the seventh cranial nerve.
16. Odor molecules dissolve in the ________________ of the ________________, or mucous membrane.
17. The primary olfactory cortex is the only primary cortex located outside the cerebral cortex; it is located in the ________________ of the limbic system.

Review Questions

1. The three dimensions along which sound waves vary are
   a. frequency, amplitude, and complexity.
   b. Moe, Larry, and Curly.
   c. frequency, pitch, and timbre.
   d. loudness, amplitude, and pitch.
2. The three bones, or ossicles, of the middle ear are the
   a. frequency, amplitude, and complexity.
   b. humerus, radius, and ulna.
   c. malleus, incus, and stapes.
   d. cochlea, semicircular canals, and vestibule.
3. The ossicles of the middle ear transmit vibrations to the
   a. round window.
   b. cochlea.
   c. semicircular canals.
   d. oval window.

4. The _______________ of the hair cells respond to movement of fluid through the organ of Corti.
   a. nerves
   b. membranes
   c. nuclei
   d. cilia
5. The cochlear nerve fibers join with fibers from the vestibular system to form the
   a. auditory nerve.
   b. vestibular nerve.
   c. primary visual cortex.
   d. organ of Corti.
6. A complex sound consists of the _______________ and its _______________.
   a. fundamental frequency, amplitude
   b. amplitude, overtones
   c. pure tone, frequency
   d. fundamental frequency, overtones
7. The _______________ is responsible for the analysis of the meaning of sounds.
   a. secondary auditory cortex
   b. primary auditory cortex
   c. vestibular system
   d. auditory agnosia
8. The area of the brain responsible for detecting the combinations of sounds that we recognize as specific words is
   a. Broca's area.
   b. Wernicke's area.
   c. the primary auditory cortex.
   d. the medulla.
9. The vestibular sacs consist of the
   a. cochlea and semicircular canals.
   b. ampulla and cupula.
   c. utricle and saccule.
   d. utricle and stapes.
10. When the vestibular system detects movement, but motor action has not occurred, you experience
   a. euphoria.
   b. motion sickness.
   c. nystagmus.
   d. food cravings.
11. The detection of _______________, _______________, _______________, and _______________ are all examples of somatosenses.
   a. cold, heat, sound, pressure
   b. cold, vision, sound, olfaction
   c. heat, pressure, vision, olfaction
   d. cold, heat, pressure, pain
12. Meissner's corpuscles respond to _______________ and _______________, whereas Ruffini's corpuscles respond only to _______________.
   a. pressure, vibration, vibration
   b. pain, pressure, pressure
   c. pain, pressure, vibration
   d. pressure, vibration, pressure
13. Fibers from the _______________ act to reduce the perception of pain.
   a. primary somatosensory cortex
   b. medial lemniscus
   c. secondary somatosensory cortex
   d. periaqueductal gray
14. The four basic tastes are
   a. sweet, sour, bitter, and salty.
   b. meat, dairy, vegetables, and fruits.
   c. salt, sugar, flour, and pepper.
   d. salt, alkaloid, sugar, and hydrogen.
15. Supertasters are most sensitive to _______________ and _______________ tastes.
   a. sour, bitter
   b. bitter, sweet
   c. sweet, salty
   d. salty, sour
16. The stimulus detected by the olfactory system is
   a. light.
   b. sound.
   c. odor.
   d. pressure.
17. The axons of the olfactory receptors synapse with the
   a. mitral cells of the olfactory bulbs.
   b. olfactory tract.
   c. primary olfactory cortex.
   d. pyriform cortex.

Suggested Readings

BARTOSHUK, L. M., & BEAUCHAMP, G. K. (1994). Chemical senses. *Annual Review of Psychology, 19*, 419–449.

EDELMAN, G. M., GALL, W. E., & COWAN, W. M. (1988). *Auditory functions.* New York: Wiley.

FARBMAN, A. I. (1992). *The cell biology of olfaction.* Cambridge, England: Cambridge University Press.

GOLDSTEIN, E. B. (1999). *Sensation and perception* (5th ed.). Belmont, CA: Wadsworth.

IGGO, A., & ANDRES, K. H. (1982). Morphology of cutaneous receptors. *Annual Review of Neuroscience, 5*, 1–32.

MCLAUGHLIN, S., & MARGOLSKEE, R. F. (1994). The sense of taste. *American Scientist, 83*, 538–545.

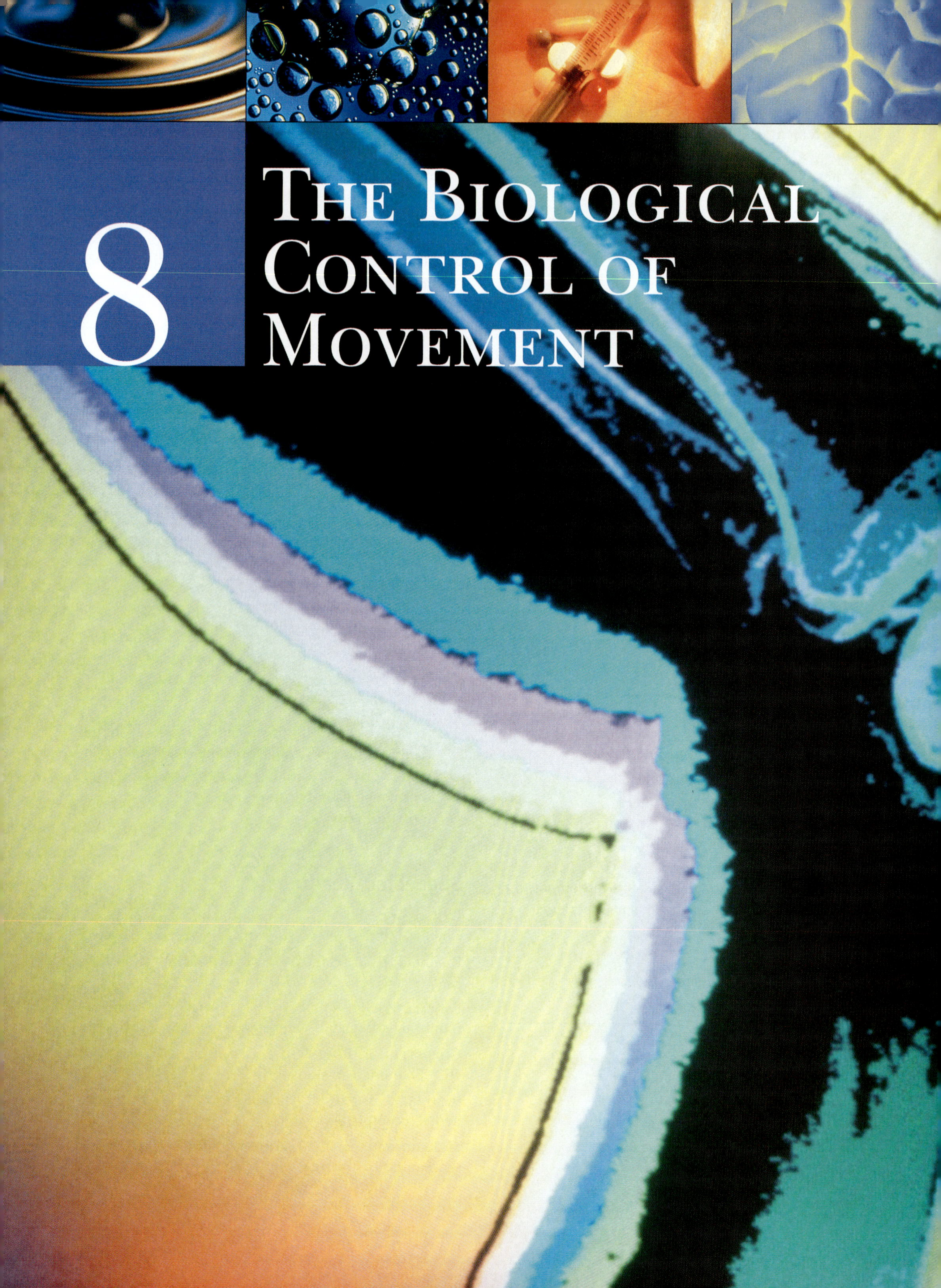

8 The Biological Control of Movement

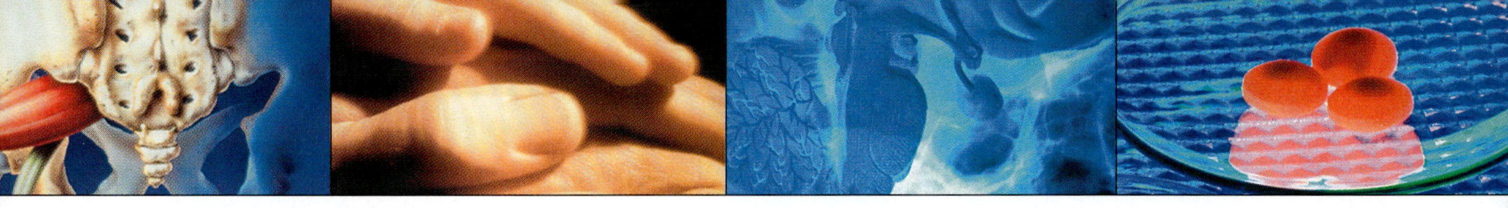

An Uncomfortable Feeling

Tanya gave Sam a NordicTrack exerciser for his birthday. He had gained some weight in the past couple of years and knew he was definitely out of shape, but his talk of exercising was just talk; he had gone to a neighborhood gym off and on but had never stuck with it. Tanya had seen an ad for the NordicTrack and thought that having an exercise machine at home might motivate Sam to work out.

When it arrived, Sam complained about how much it cost, but agreed to give it a try. On his first encounter, Sam found it impossible to move his feet and his arms simultaneously without losing his balance, an uncomfortable feeling similar to one most of us have experienced—learning to ride a bike. Instead of calling it quits once again, he decided to start by just moving his feet. At first, his movements were slow and jerky; after a while, he began to feel comfortable and was able to move his feet more quickly in a smooth, continuous motion. After 10 minutes, Sam was exhausted. He vowed to try it again the following day.

When the following day came, Sam did not feel like exercising, but with Tanya's urging, he got back on. At first he experienced that same awkwardness, but within a few minutes he was moving his legs smoothly and easily. After a few more minutes, Sam decided to try to move both his arms and legs. Again, he felt awkward and off balance, but his coordination slowly improved until he was able to move his arms and legs faster and in a coordinated fashion. At the end of his second session, Sam felt tired, but he looked forward to continuing to improve his newly learned skill and his health and fitness. ■

◀ The patellar reflex can be elicited in approximately 50 milliseconds.

Before You Begin

Why were Sam's initial movements on the NordicTrack so awkward?

What neural changes allowed Sam to become proficient on this type of exercise equipment?

In this chapter, we will help you answer these and the following questions:

- What nervous system mechanisms control Sam's muscle movement?
- How does the nervous system prevent Sam from moving too quickly and falling off the NordicTrack?
- What structures in Sam's brain allow him to start and stop muscle movements on the NordicTrack?
- What brain structure converts Sam's initial clumsiness on the NordicTrack into a skilled action?
- What neurological problems might cause Sam's movement on the NordicTrack to return to its original awkwardness?

Overview of Neurological Control of Movement

This chapter discusses the biological control of **movement**, a change in one's place or position. Sam's gradual transition from awkward, slow movements to coordinated, rapid movements is typical of many experiences, including learning to walk, swim, tie a shoe, or play the piano. In this chapter, we will examine the neural structures that control movement and the neural process responsible for Sam's transition from hesitant and clumsy to rapid and coordinated. Sometimes neural control of movement fails; several resulting disorders of movement—apraxia, Huntington's chorea, Parkinson's disease, myasthenia gravis, amyotrophic lateral sclerosis (ALS, or Lou Gehrig's disease)—illustrate the importance of nervous system control of the arm and leg movements required to operate a NordicTrack and do a number of other things.

Not all movements are as complex as operating a NordicTrack, an acquired skill involving the coordination of many different muscles. The simplest movements are reflexive reactions such as sneezing when a speck of dust activates a sensory receptor in your nasal passage or blinking your eyes when an object approaches. Other movements, which can be more complex than simple reflexes but less complex than acquired skills, include posture and postural changes (e.g., standing, sitting), locomotion (e.g., walking, running), sensory orientation (e.g., eye movement, head turning), and species-typical fixed action patterns (e.g., courtship or grooming behaviors).

Movement is executed by the motor neurons of the central nervous system. The neural control of a particular movement operates on several different levels (see **Figure 8.1**). The most basic level involves the spinal cord. In some cases, the spinal cord alone controls movement; one example of such a reflex (see Chapter 2) is removing a hand from a hot stove. In other instances, higher neural structures operate through the cranial or spinal nerves to produce movement; one example is turning off the stove.

The next level of control involves brainstem (hindbrain and midbrain) structures. Movement can originate in brainstem structures and be transmitted via the cranial and spinal nerves. One example of such movement is visual pursuit of a light stimulus (see Chapter 6). Brainstem structures also receive input from higher brain structures and transmit commands to the spinal cord.

The highest level of the control of movement involves the cerebral cortex. One area of the cerebral cortex, the primary motor cortex, initiates movement through the brainstem structures and the spinal cord. The input received from other cortical structures is crucial to the functioning of the primary motor cortex. The secondary motor cortex provides the data needed for planning and sequencing voluntary movements. The posterior parietal cortex gives the primary motor cortex the visual, auditory, and somatosensory information needed to guide movement. Feedback from the muscles and tendons through the somatosensory cortex provides the primary motor cortex with information about the current state of the motor system.

The cerebellum and the basal ganglia are two other structures important to the control of movement. As seen in **Figure 8.1**, both structures can influence the activity of the brainstem structures and the primary motor cortex. The basal ganglia integrates movement by smoothing out and refining movement. In other words, the basal ganglia gets rid of extraneous movement and acts to ensure that the selected movement occurs with sufficient, but not too much force. It is also responsible for muscle tone and postural adjustments so that normal movement can occur. Maybe you have seen a person with **cerebral palsy**, which is a congenital neurological motor disor-

---

movement A change in place or position.

cerebral palsy A congenital motor disorder characterized by postural instability and extraneous movement.

Somatosensory cortex (feedback from muscles and tendons)

Secondary motor cortex (planning and sequencing information)

Primary motor cortex (controls voluntary movements)

Posterior parietal cortex (visual, auditory,and somatosensory information)

Basal ganglia (integrates movement)

Brainstem

Cerebellum (coordinates skilled action)

Cranial nerves

Spinal cord (spinal nerves)

Movement

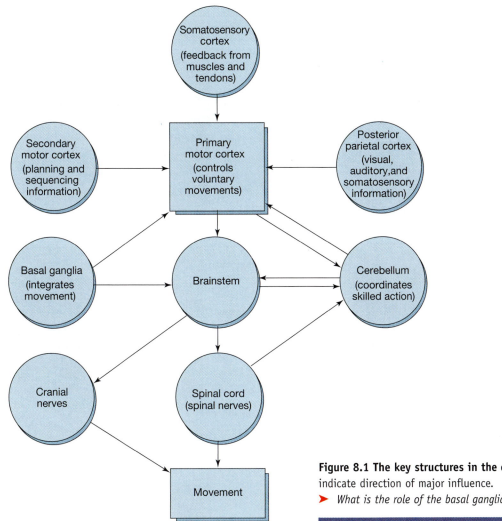

Figure 8.1 The key structures in the control of movement. Arrows indicate direction of major influence.

➤ *What is the role of the basal ganglia in movement? (p. 228)*

der, struggle to perform acts that you easily perform. The difficulty that person demonstrated with postural instability and extraneous movement reflects damage to the basal ganglia.

The cerebellum plays a central role in translating an otherwise uncoordinated movement into a skilled action. (Sam's cerebellum was hard at work when he first hopped on that NordicTrack!) This development of skilled actions is accomplished through the cerebellum's control of the learning of neural motor programs. The cerebellum also receives feedback from the sensory receptors monitoring movement and the brainstem structures initiating movement. This dual input allows the cerebellum to compare intended movement (brainstem) to actual movement (sensory neurons) and to make adjustments to ensure that intent and action coincide.

The control of movement is a complex process. To understand the "big picture" we've just presented, we need to learn how muscles work and how neural control of movement occurs at the cellular level.

Before You Go On

Using Figure 8.1 as a guide, describe what happens when Sam decides to step off the NordicTrack at the end of his workout, beginning with the initiation of movement by the primary motor cortex.

Section Review

- Types of movement include simple reflexes, posture and postural changes, locomotion, sensory orientation, fixed action patterns, and complex learned behaviors such as operating a NordicTrack or riding a bicycle.
- In some cases, the spinal cord alone controls movement; in others, higher neural structures are involved.
- Movement can originate in brainstem structures, or information from higher brain structures can be passed through the brainstem to the spinal cord.

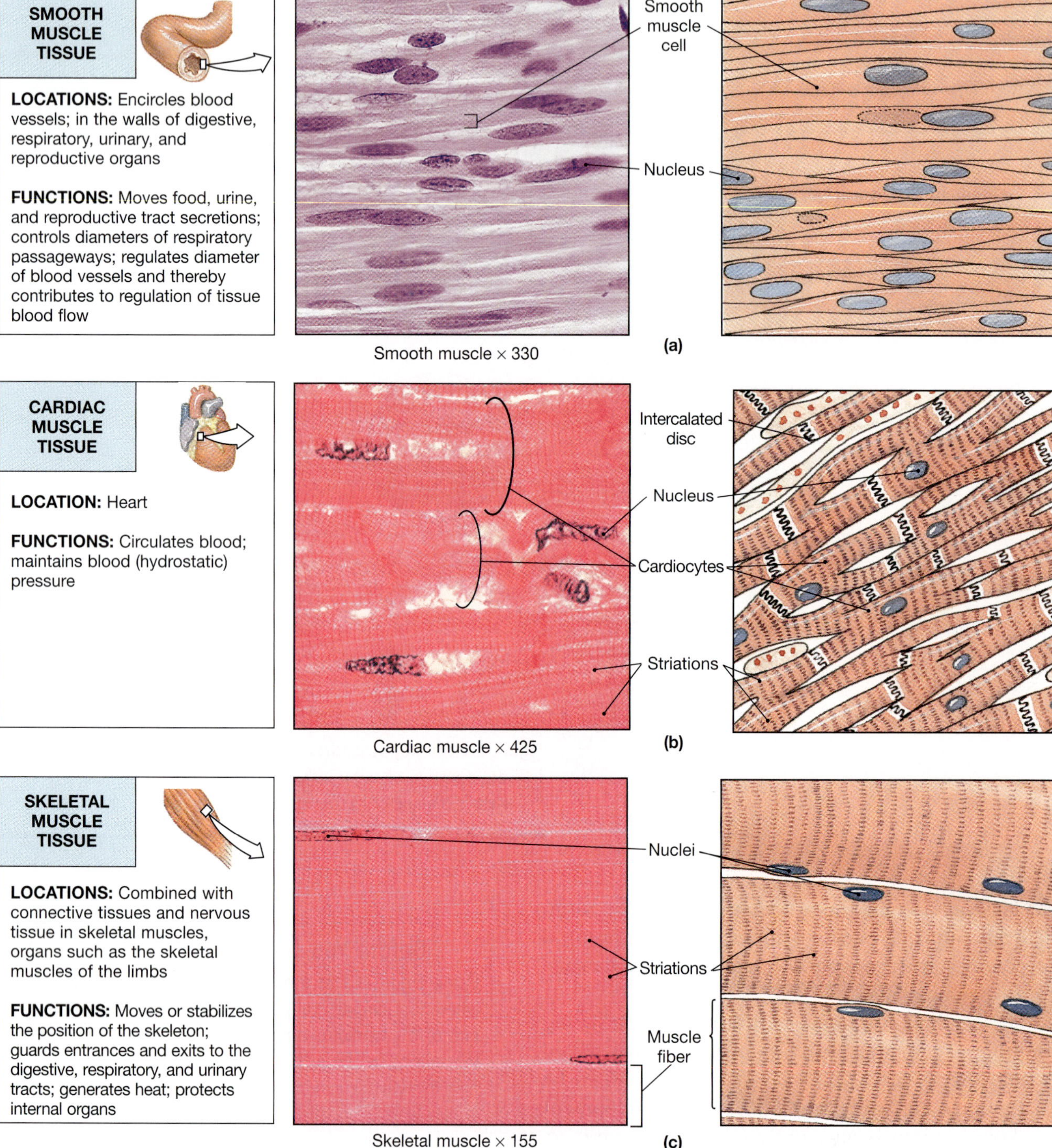

Figure 8.2 Muscle tissue. The three types of muscle tissue include: (a) smooth muscle tissue, (b) cardiac muscle tissue, and (c) skeletal muscle tissue.

➤ *Which type of muscle tissue helps Sam to digest his after-workout snack? (p. 230)*

- The primary motor cortex initiates movement through the brainstem and spinal cord.
- The posterior parietal cortex guides movement by providing the primary motor cortex with visual, auditory, and somatosensory information.
- The somatosensory cortex gives the primary motor cortex information about the current state of the motor system.
- The secondary motor cortex provides signals for planning and sequencing voluntary movements.
- The basal ganglia integrates movement and regulates posture adjustments.
- The cerebellum coordinates movement and receives feedback from sensory neurons and brainstem structures.

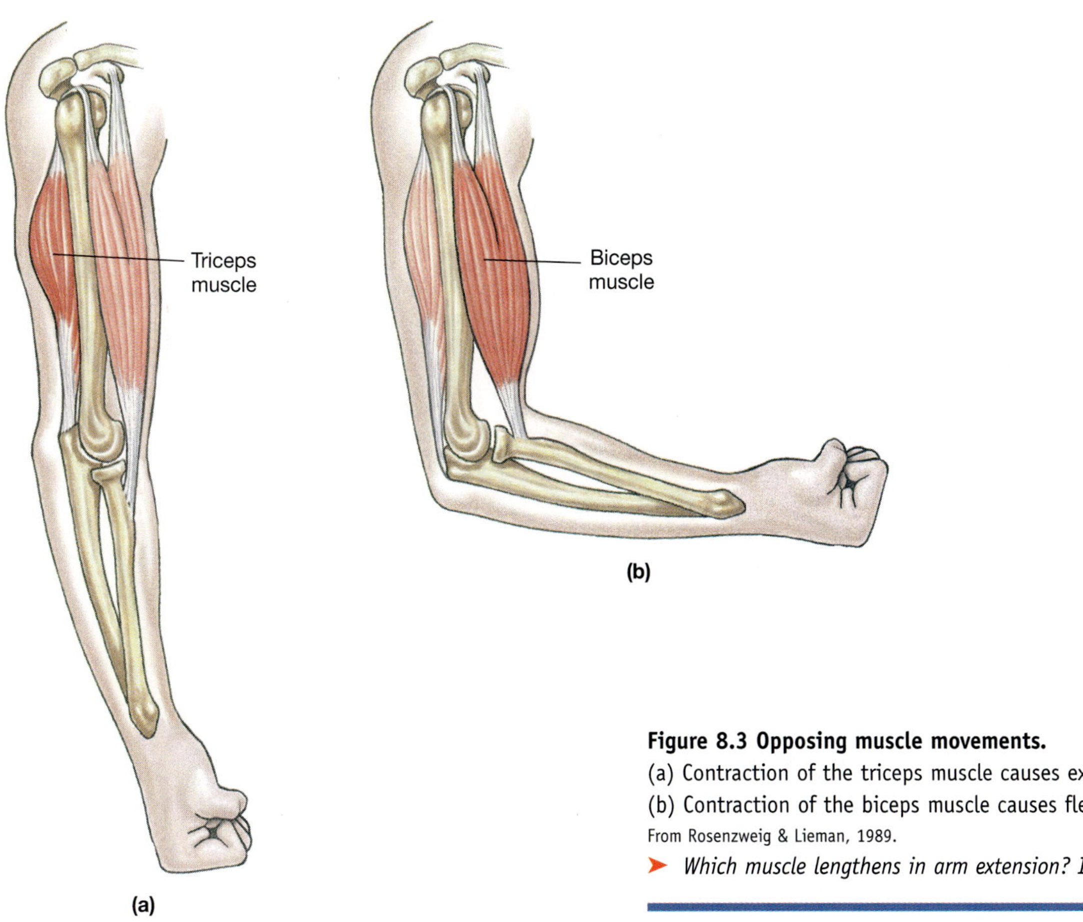

Figure 8.3 Opposing muscle movements.
(a) Contraction of the triceps muscle causes extension of the arm.
(b) Contraction of the biceps muscle causes flexion of the arm.
From Rosenzweig & Lieman, 1989.

➤ *Which muscle lengthens in arm extension? In arm flexion? (p. 231)*

The Mechanics of Movement Control

When Sam is on the NordicTrack, he is using all three types of muscles in his body. Without him even noticing, his **smooth muscles** are controlling the movement of his internal organs (see **Figure 8.2a**). His **cardiac muscles** are actively working to help pump blood through his circulatory system (see **Figure 8.2b**). The third type of muscle, and the one he is probably most aware of as he is working out, is **skeletal muscle** (see **Figure 8.2c**). The contraction of skeletal muscles allows us to move around in our environment. Skeletal muscles are attached to bones by **tendons**, which are strong bands of connective tissue. It is our muscles that cause the movements of our bones, and many work in opposing pairs. When one muscle of a pair contracts or shortens, the other must relax (lengthen) or there will be no movement of the bone.

One example of opposing action is the extension and flexion of our limbs. The contraction of an **extensor muscle** produces **extension**, the movement of a limb away from the body. For example, the triceps (the extensor muscles) contract and the biceps lengthen, producing the movement of an arm away from the body (see **Figure 8.3a**). **Flexion**, the drawing of a limb toward the body, is produced by the contraction of **flexor muscles**, such as the biceps, while the triceps lengthen, bringing an extended arm back toward the body (see **Figure 8.3b**).

Complex movements such as walking require coordinated sequences of excitation and inhibition of different flexor and extensor muscles. When you walk, you extend one leg while flexing the other and then flex the first leg and extend the second, and so on. The coordination by the central nervous system is so efficient that we are unaware of it, for the most part.

---

smooth muscle Muscle that controls internal organs.

cardiac muscle Heart muscle that pumps blood through the circulatory system.

skeletal muscle Muscle that produces movement in the physical environment.

tendon Strong band of connective tissue linking muscle to bone that causes the movement of bones.

extensor muscle Muscle that produces movement of a limb away from the body.

extension Movement of a limb away from the body.

flexion Movement of a limb toward the body.

flexor muscle Muscle that produces movement of a limb toward the body.

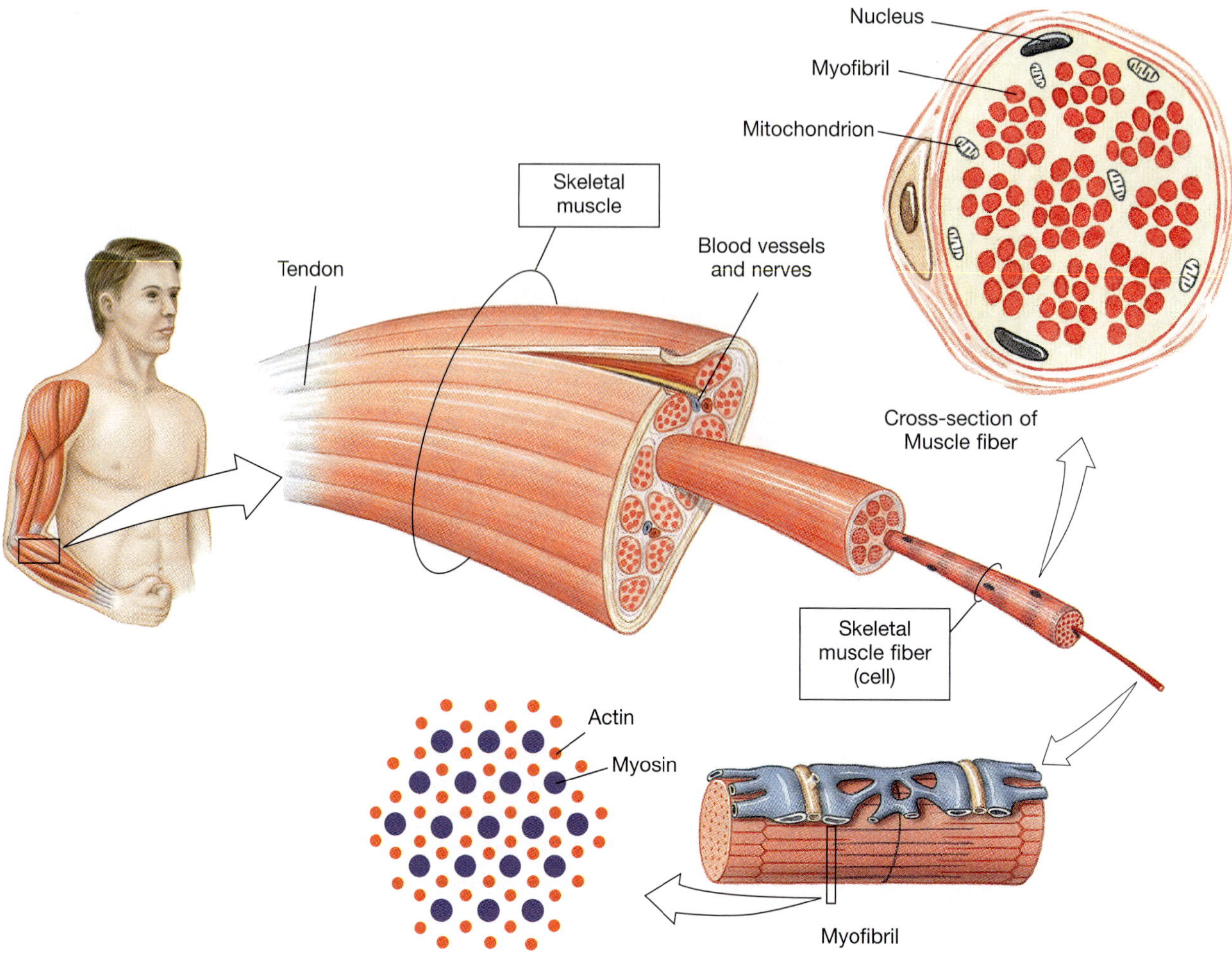

Figure 8.4 The major parts of a striated muscle. Skeletal (or striated) muscle consists of many individual muscle fibers, which are composed of myosin and actin myofilaments.

➤ *Which type of protein is found in thick myofilaments? (p. 232)*

Try this—have your roommate watch as you walk from one end of the room to the other. Now, do it again but try to consciously flex and extend your leg muscles. If your roommate can stop laughing long enough, ask him or her to describe the difference. To understand how the central nervous system provides the coordination you need to walk across the room without being followed by gales of laughter, we need first to understand the anatomy of the muscle and how it works.

muscle fiber Long and slender muscle cell that produces movement.

myofibril Cylindrical structure within a muscle fiber.

myofilament The two components of myofibrils, myosin and actin.

myosin The thick protein myofilament found in muscle fiber.

actin The thin protein myofilament found in muscle fiber.

The Anatomy of a Muscle

A skeletal muscle consists of many individual **muscle fibers** (see **Figure 8.4**). Each muscle fiber is about 10 to 100 microns in diameter and is in turn composed of many **myofibrils** (myo = muscle), cylindrical structures about 1 to 2 microns in diameter. A myofibril contains two kinds of **myofilaments**, one is made of a protein called **myosin**, and the other is made of the protein **actin**. Myosin myofilaments are thicker than actin myofilaments, and each myosin molecule has a distinct head end and tail end (see **Figure 8.5b**); because of the differences in diameter, myosin myofilaments are also called thick myofilaments and actin myofilaments are also known as thin myofilaments. The myosin heads are also called cross bridges; the reason for this will become clear shortly. Within the myofibrils, the actin and myosin molecules are organized into functional units called **sarcomeres** (see **Figure 8.5**). In each sarcomere, the overlapping bands of thick myosin myofilaments and thin actin myofilaments give skeletal muscles a striated or striped appearance. The alternate name for skeletal muscles, **striated muscles**, comes from this striped appearance.

Neural Control of Muscle Contraction

As we learned earlier, it is the motor neurons of the peripheral nervous system that control the skeletal muscles. The cell bodies of motor neurons are located in the gray matter of the ventral horn of the spinal cord and in different parts of the brainstem. Most motor neurons have long axons that leave the ventral root of the spinal cord or the brainstem and synapse with individual muscle fibers. Such motor neurons are called **alpha motor neurons** and are among the largest neurons in the body. The axons of alpha motor neurons can conduct information very rapidly, often at a speed of more than 220 meters/second.

The muscle fiber controlled by an alpha motor neuron is called an **extrafusal muscle fiber**. The alpha motor neuron and the extrafusal muscle fiber connect at a highly specialized synapse called the neuromuscular junction (see **Figure 8.6**). The extrafusal muscle fiber flattens out to form the **motor end plate** at the point where the motor neuron and muscle fiber synapse.

In Chapter 4, we discussed transmission of neural impulses from neuron to neuron. The transmission of a neural impulse from a motor neuron to a muscle fiber at the neuromuscular junction is very similar. The presynaptic neuron (the motor neuron) releases neurotransmitter into the synaptic cleft. The neurotransmitter, in this case

---

sarcomere Functional unit of the myofibril, consisting of overlapping bands of thick myosin myofilaments and thin actin myofilaments.

striated muscle Another name for skeletal muscle originating from its striped appearance caused by the overlapping bands of thick myosin myofilaments and thin actin myofilaments.

alpha motor neuron Motor neuron with a long axon that leaves the ventral root of the spinal cord or brainstem and synapses with individual muscle fibers.

extrafusal muscle fiber Muscle fiber that is controlled by an alpha motor neuron.

motor end plate The flattened area of the extrafusal muscle fiber where the motor neuron and muscle fiber synapse.

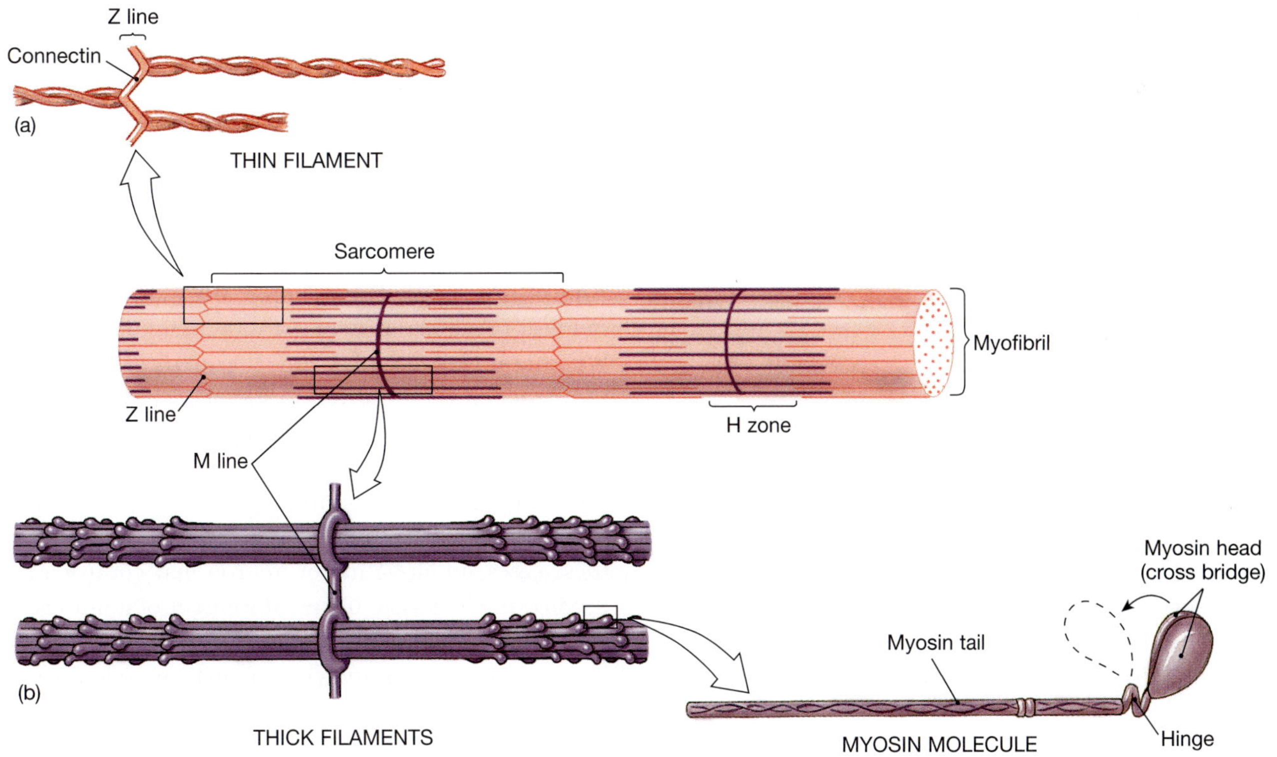

Figure 8.5 Thin and thick myofilaments. (a) Gross structure of a thin (actin) myofilament. (b) Structure of a thick (myosin) myofilament and the myosin molecule, with its distinct head and tail ends.

➤ *Which end of the myosin molecule is responsible for muscle contraction? (p. 233–234)*

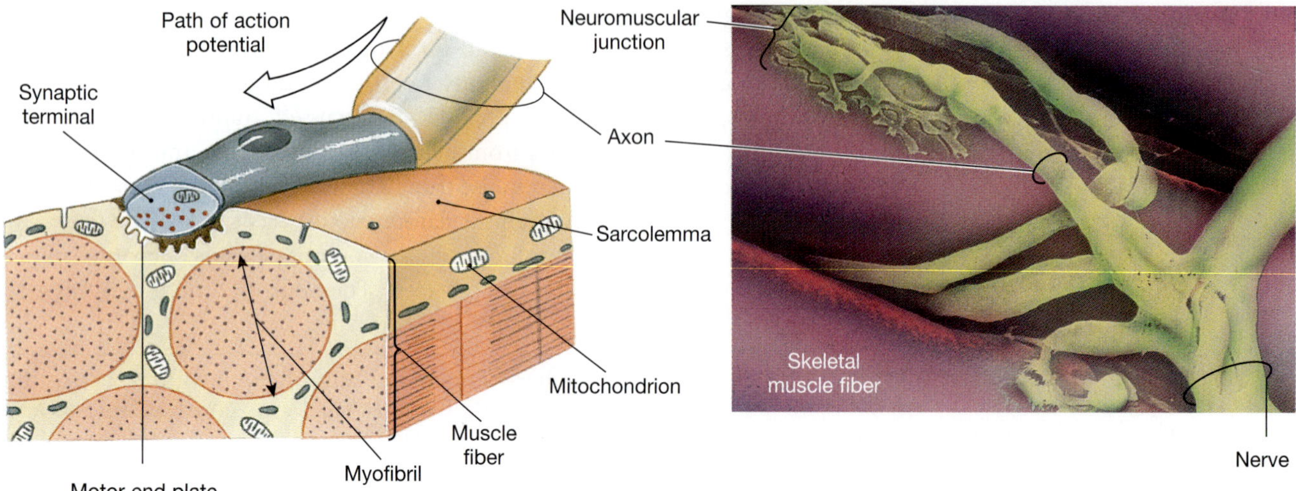

Figure 8.6 The neuromuscular junction. The diagram on the left shows the motor neuron and muscle as well as the location of the neuromuscular junction, and the photo on the right shows the flattening of the presynaptic membrane on the motor end plate.

➤ *Which neurotransmitter is released by the motor neuron? (p. 233–234)*

acetylcholine, then binds to and has an excitatory effect on the postsynaptic membrane (the muscle fiber).

With sufficient excitation, an action potential is generated at the postsynaptic membrane. As the action potential travels down the muscle fiber, it increases the fiber membrane's permeability to calcium ions. Remember the overlapping myosin and actin myofilaments of the sarcomere? The influx of calcium ions causes the myosin heads to form cross bridges with the actin filaments. The myosin heads then pivot, causing the myosin and actin filaments to move past one another. The cross bridges then break and reattach, in a sort of rowing motion, causing the sarcomere, and thus the entire muscle fiber, to shorten. The shortening of the muscle causes the attached bone(s) to move, producing movement. When the muscle relaxes, the myosin and actin myofilaments slide back to their initial positions, and the muscle fiber is returned to its original length (see **Figure 8.7**).

Before You Go On

The flexor muscles of the knee, located in your thigh, are the hamstrings and the sartorius; the knee extensors are collectively known as the quadriceps. Describe what happens to these muscles when you bend your knee, using the terms *alpha motor neuron, extrafusal muscle fiber,* and *neuromuscular junction*.

motor unit The alpha motor neuron and all the muscle fibers that it controls.

The Motor Unit

Some motor neurons have axons with only a few branches. Others have axons with many branches. Each branch of the axon of a motor neuron synapses with a single muscle fiber, so some motor neurons control just a few muscle fibers, and others control many muscle fibers.

Collectively, a motor neuron and all the muscle fibers that it controls are known as a **motor unit**. Why do some motor units contain a few muscle fibers whereas others contain many fibers? The answer is that some movements require very fine motor control, while others do not. When the axon of an alpha motor neuron has a few branches and controls only a few muscle fibers, precise control is possible. For example, the grasping of a pen requires precise control of the movement of our fingers. We might fail to pick up the pen or drop it if the fingers are not moved in just the right manner. To achieve this precise control, an alpha motor neuron activates only a few muscle fibers. By contrast, moving a limb does not require such precise control; instead, many muscle fibers need to be contracted to move a limb. In these cases, an alpha motor neuron may control a hundred or more muscle fibers. Movement of a limb is possible because the axons of some alpha motor neurons have many branches and control many muscle fibers.

Adaptation of Muscles

A sprinter must move exceptionally quickly but for only a short time. By contrast, a long-distance runner needs to run steadily for a long time. How does the nervous sys-

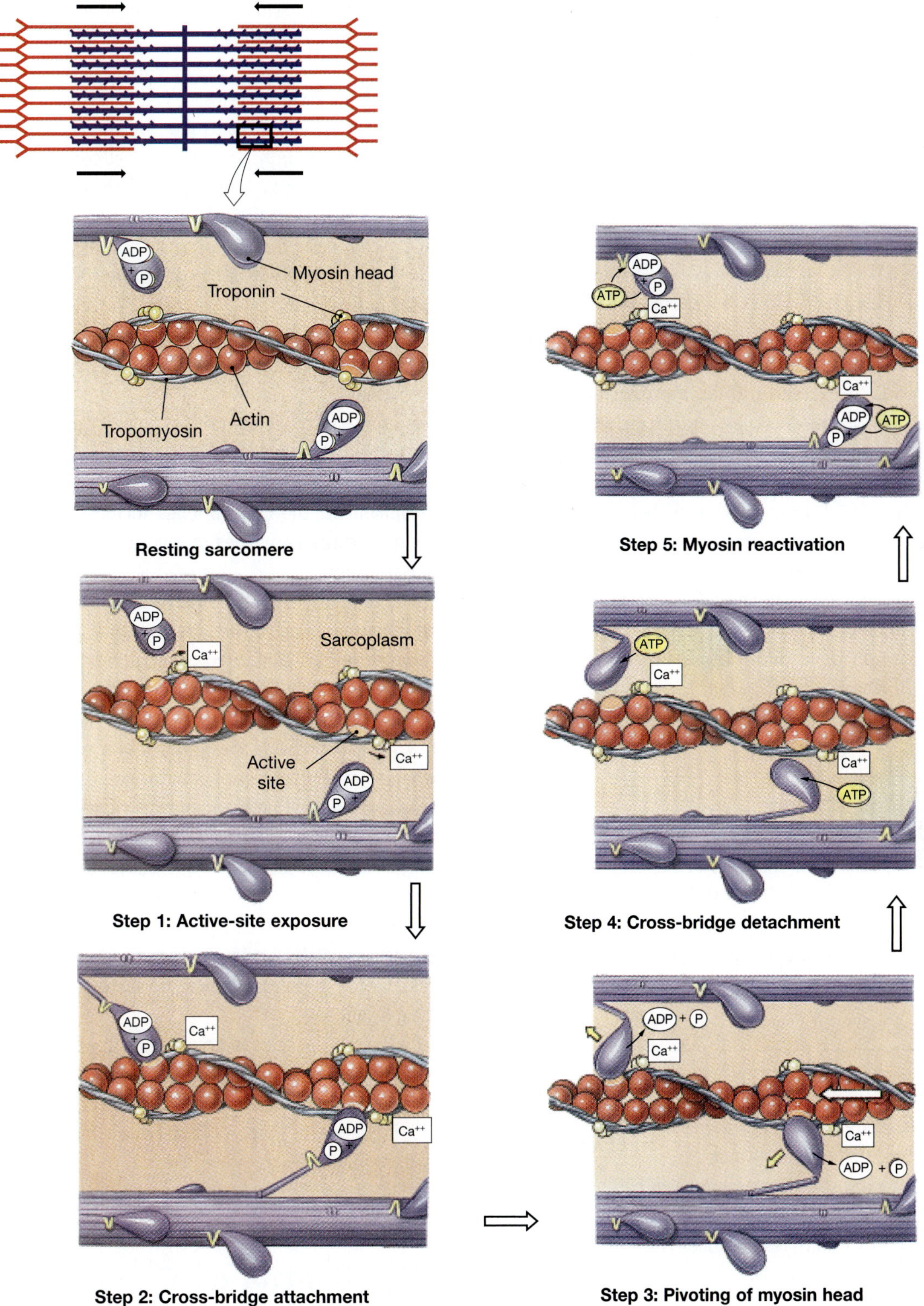

Figure 8.7 Movement of actin and myosin myofilaments during muscle contraction. Prior to contraction, the sarcomere is at rest. It cannot shorten because the troponin molecules are blocking actin's active sites and the myosin bridges cannot attach. Then, when an action potential spreads over the muscle fiber, stored calcium ions are released into the sarcomere. They divert the troponin from the active sites, permitting the myosin bridges to attach to the actin (steps 1 and 2). Each bridge attachment uses up an ATP (ATP—> energy + ADP), which supplies the energy for the pivoting action and new bridge attachment. How is contraction stopped? Once the action potential ceases, the calcium ions are actively transported out of the sarcomeres, bridge formation is once more inhibited by troponin, and the muscle comes to rest.

➤ *How does movement of myofilaments lead to muscle contraction? (p. 234)* tem adapt to the needs of both the sprinter and the long-distance runner? There are three main categories of muscles. The **fast-twitch muscles** produce the fastest contractions, but tire quickly. The **slow-twitch muscles** produce the slowest contractions, which can be maintained for longer periods without fatiguing. In an unusual display of common sense, the fibers with contractions intermediate between those of fast-twitch muscles and slow-twitch muscles were named **intermediate-twitch muscles**.

The different types of muscles serve different purposes. We use primarily slow- or intermediate-twitch muscles when we stand or walk. When we run at full speed, we use fast-twitch muscles. Some individuals possess great speed or great endurance; the distribution of the different types of muscles plays an important role in determining the success of world-class sprinters and long-distance runners. One type of muscle, be it fast or slow, can be developed. The world-class Swedish marathon runner Bertis Järlaker built up an enormous amount of slow-twitch muscle (Sjostrom, Friden, & Erkblom, 1987). However, he had few fast-twitch muscles and thus he was not particularly fast. By contrast, world-class sprinters have many more fast-twitch fibers than slow-twitch fibers.

Before You Go On

Continuing the process you described on page 229, explain what happens when Sam decides to step on the NordicTrack, beginning at the level of the motor neuron.

Describe the effect on the target muscle of acetylcholine release at the neuromuscular junction.

Section Review

- Skeletal muscles are attached to bones by tendons; bones move when these muscles contract.
- Contraction of extensor muscles produces extension, the movement of a limb away from the body.
- Contraction of flexor muscles produces flexion, the drawing of a limb toward the body.
- Each muscle contains many muscle fibers, which are composed of many myofibrils.
- A myofibril consists of sarcomeres, overlapping bands of myosin and actin proteins.
- Skeletal muscles are controlled by the action of efferent alpha motor neurons from the spinal cord.
- Alpha motor neurons synapse with extrafusal muscle fibers at the neuromuscular junction.
- Acetylcholine is the neurotransmitter in the neuromuscular junction, and it has an excitatory influence on extrafusal muscle fibers.
- As the action potential travels down the muscle fiber, it causes the permeability of the cell membrane to Ca^{++} ions to increase.
- The increased movement of Ca^{++} ions into the cell permits cross bridges from the myosin to the actin myofilaments to form, break, and reform, further along. This rowing movement of the cross bridges increases the amount of overlap of the two types of myofilament, shortening the muscle fiber.
- When the muscle relaxes, the overlap decreases, the muscles lengthen, and the bone returns to its original position.
- A motor unit is composed of an alpha motor neuron and all of the muscle fibers that it controls.
- Some motor units consist of a motor neuron with only a few axon branches controlling only a few muscle fibers, whereas others consist of a motor neuron with many axon branches controlling many muscle fibers.
- Precise control of movement demands smaller motor units, and gross limb movements depend on larger motor units.
- There are three main categories of muscle: fast-twitch muscles, slow-twitch muscles, and intermediate-twitch muscles.
- Fast-twitch muscles produce the fastest contractions but fatigue quickly.
- Slow-twitch muscles produce the slowest contractions, which can be maintained for long periods of time.
- Intermediate-twitch muscles produce contractions that fall in between those of fast-twitch muscles and slow-twitch muscles.

fast-twitch muscle Muscle fiber that contracts rapidly, but tires quickly.

slow-twitch muscle Muscle fiber that contracts slowly, but fatigues slowly.

intermediate-twitch muscle Muscle fiber that contracts at a rate somewhere between that of fast-twitch and slow-twitch muscles.

Reflex Control of Movement

Sam is seated on the examination table in his doctor's office. (He has decided, very sensibly, that if he is serious about getting in shape, he needs a physical to determine his current condition.) She taps the tendon just below his kneecap with a small rubber hammer. The tap causes him to kick his leg outward. This movement is an example of a reflex. A reflex is a simple, automatic response to a sensory stimulus. The reflex experienced by Sam is called the **patellar tendon reflex** (patella is the clinical term for the knee cap).

The patellar tendon reflex is an example of a **monosynaptic stretch reflex**, the contraction of a muscle in response to the stretching of that muscle. The term *monosynaptic* means that only one synapse exists between the sensory receptor (in Sam's knee) and muscle effector (muscles of his leg) (mono = one) (see **Figure 8.8**). The hammer tap on the tendon stretches one of the muscles that extends the leg. The resulting contraction of this muscle causes the leg to kick outward. Other reflexes involve more than one synapse and are called **polysynaptic reflexes** (poly = many). Although the brain controls many movements, reflexes are usually produced by the spinal cord without brain involvement. In other words, the spinal cord usually mediates the reflexive reaction to the input from sensory receptors.

Monosynaptic Stretch Reflex

Suppose that Sam wants to get off the examination table and stand up. To stand, he must extend his legs away from his body. When he stands, the force of gravity will exert pressure on his legs. If the force of gravity were not counteracted, his legs would eventually buckle and he would fall down.

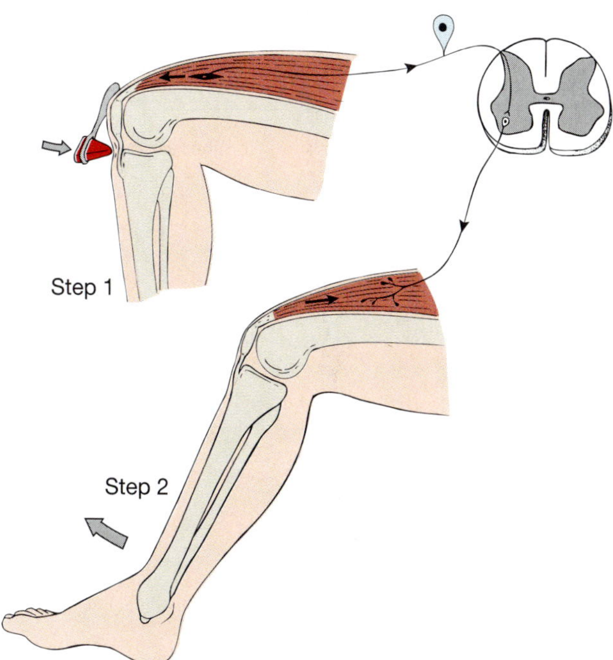

Figure 8.8 Monosynaptic stretch reflex. The patellar tendon reflex is one example of a monosynaptic stretch reflex.
➤ *Can you find the synapse in the figure? (p. 237)*

How does Sam's body enable him to stand when the force of gravity acts in favor of falling? The stretching of the muscles that extend our legs when we stand produces an opposing muscle contraction like the one experienced by Sam when the doctor tapped his knee. The monosynaptic stretch reflex allows us to remain standing rather than fall.

How does the nervous system know when a muscle has been stretched? What mechanism allows the nervous system to contract a muscle to counteract the muscle's stretching? Embedded within the extrafusal muscle fiber is a structure called the **muscle spindle** (see **Figure 8.9**). The muscle spindle contains muscle fibers known as **intrafusal muscle fibers**. The intrafusal muscle fibers extend the entire length of the muscle spindle. The center portion of the intrafusal muscle fiber is a modified muscle fiber that lacks myofibrils. The central part of the intrafusal muscle fiber also has a sensory receptor, called **annulospiral endings**, wrapped around it. When the extrafusal muscle fibers are stretched, so are the intrafusal fibers. The stretching of the intrafusal muscle fibers stimulates the annulospiral endings. (The sensory annulospiral endings are actually always active. As we will see shortly, the continuous activity is responsible for muscle tone.) The stretching of the intrafusal muscle fibers causes the annulospiral endings to fire more rapidly. This increased neural activity is carried along the axons, called **Ia fibers**, of the annulospiral endings. The Ia fibers enter the dorsal root of the spinal cord and synapse with alpha motor neurons. The Ia fiber have an excitatory influence on alpha motor neurons. Stimulation of alpha motor neurons causes the extrafusal muscle fibers to contract.

---

patellar tendon reflex A type of reflex in which a tap on the tendon of the knee stretches the muscles that extend the leg, causing the leg to kick outward.

monosynaptic stretch reflex A reflex in which only one synapse exists between the sensory receptor and motor neuron.

polysynaptic reflex A reflex with more than one synapse between the sensory receptor and motor neuron.

muscle spindle A structure embedded within the extrafusal muscle fiber that enables the central nervous system to contract a muscle to counteract the stretching of the extrafusal muscle fiber containing the muscle spindle.

intrafusal muscle fiber Muscle fiber within muscle spindle surrounded by annulospiral endings.

annulospiral endings Sensory receptors that surround the central part of the intrafusal muscle fiber.

Ia fibers Axons from the annulospiral endings that enter the dorsal root of the spinal cord and synapse alpha motor neurons.

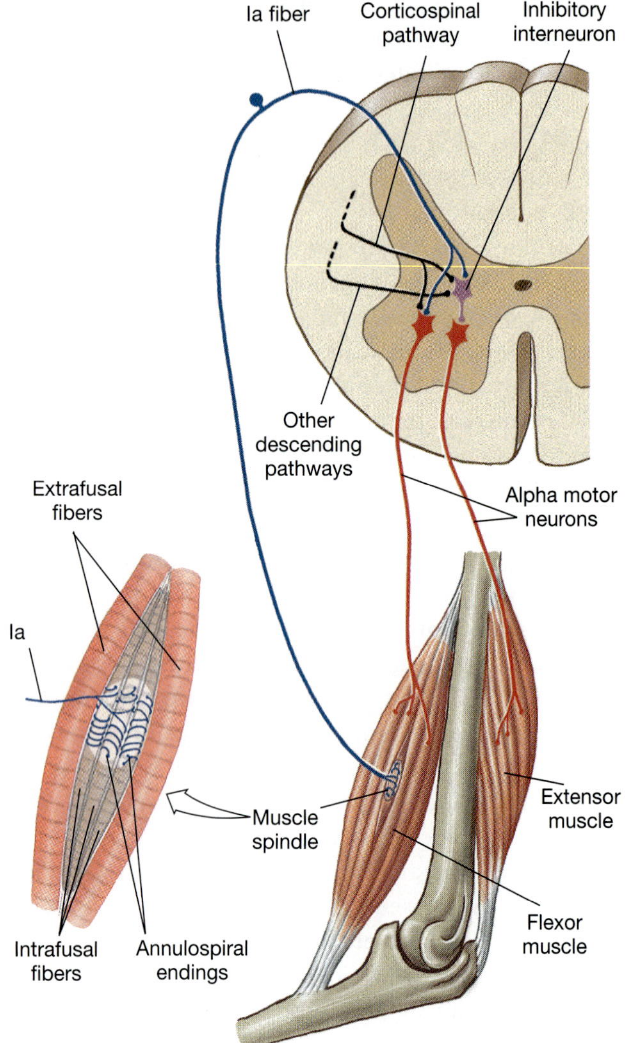

Figure 8.9 Components of the monosynaptic stretch reflex. Stretching the muscle spindle activates the annulospiral endings of the muscle spindle. Axons from the annulospiral endings (Ia fibers) enter the dorsal root of the spinal cord and synapse with alpha motor neurons. Stimulation of the alpha motor neurons causes the extrafusal muscle fiber to contract.

Adapted from Kandel et al., 1991.

➤ *What causes the intrafusal muscle fibers to stretch? (p. 238)*

Let's see how this process works to keep a person standing despite the force of gravity. The force of gravity stretches both the extrafusal and intrafusal muscle fibers of the leg. The stretching of the intrafusal muscle fibers is detected by the annulospiral endings and conveyed to the spinal cord by the Ia fibers. The Ia fibers stimulate the alpha motor neurons that contract the extensor muscles that straighten the legs and, thereby, allow us to remain standing.

The contraction of the extrafusal muscle fibers also causes the intrafusal muscle fibers to contract. The contraction of the intrafusal muscle fibers decreases the firing rate of the annulospiral endings, unless the conditions that lead to the stretching of the intrafusal muscle fibers continue, which would be the case as long as we remain standing.

The process of responding to the stretching of extrafusal muscle fibers is almost instantaneous. Like alpha motor neurons, the speed at which Ia fibers transmit information is quite rapid; for example, a patellar reflex can be elicited in approximately 50 milliseconds.

Polysynaptic Reflex

Most reflexes involve more than one synapse. Such polysynaptic reflexes vary greatly in complexity. Some are relatively simple reflexes in which the sensory neuron enters the spinal cord at the same level that the motor neuron exits the spinal cord; within the spinal cord, the two are connected by one or more interneurons. Other polysynaptic reflexes are quite complex, with neurons entering and exiting the spinal cord at different levels with connections to many interneurons.

Consider the following example. Suppose that you are walking barefoot and step on a nail (see **Figure 8.10**). You would not only reflexively withdraw your foot from the nail

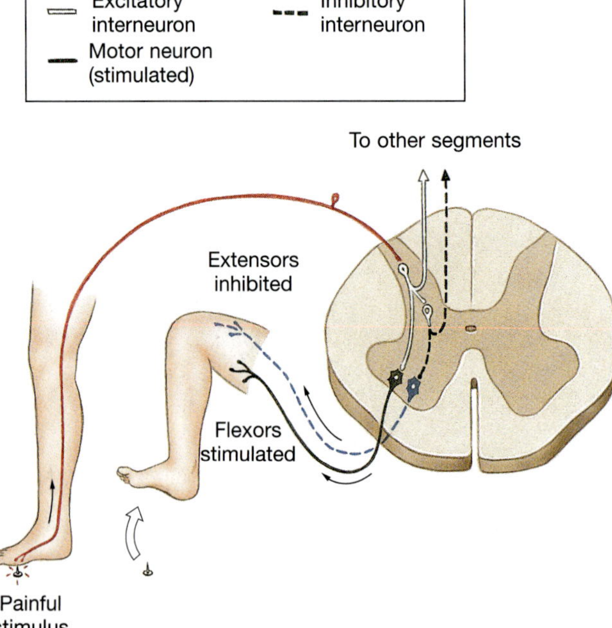

Figure 8.10 Polysynaptic reflex. The withdrawal reflex is one example of a polysynaptic reflex.

➤ *Describe the path of the polysynaptic reflex from the time you step on the nail to the time you remove your foot. (p. 238–239)*

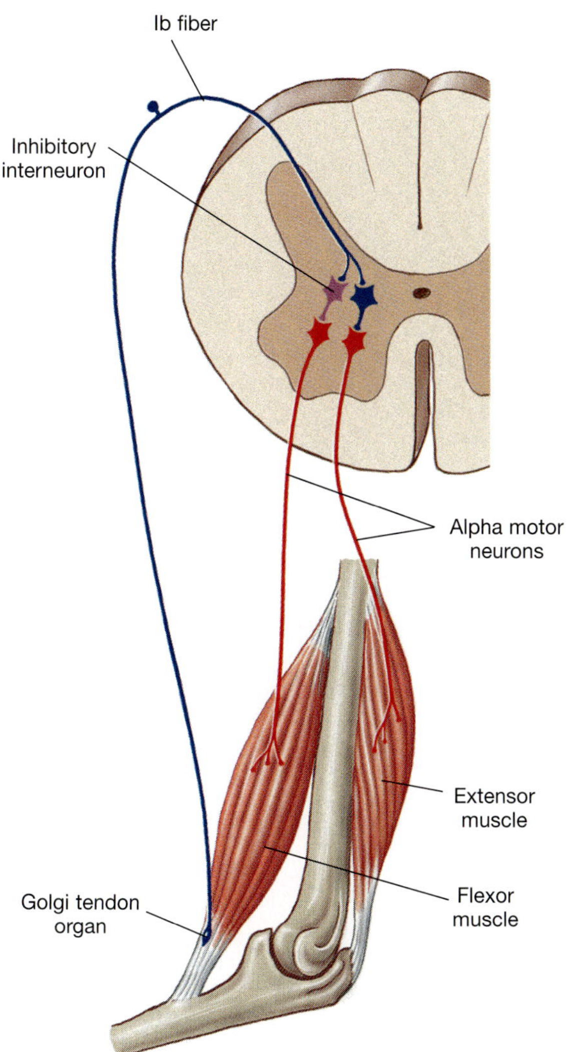

Figure 8.11 The Golgi tendon organs. Excessive firing of extrafusal muscle fibers activates Golgi tendon organs. Axons from Golgi tendon organs enter the dorsal root of the spinal cord where they synapse with an inhibitory interneuron. Activation of these interneurons, which synapse with alpha motor neurons, inhibits the alpha motor neurons.

Adapted from Kandel et al., 1991.

➤ *What is the other name for the axons of the Golgi tendon organs? (p. 239)*

(a phenomenon sensibly called the **withdrawal reflex**), but also make some postural changes to control your balance, such as extending your arms or reaching out for something to keep from falling. You might even utter some words that your mother never heard you use. (Quick—which of these is not a polysynaptic reflex? If you guessed !#?@, you are correct!)

As we learned earlier, reflexes usually occur without any mediation from brain structures. However, the brain can influence the execution of polysynaptic reflexes. What if the object you reached out for to maintain your balance was a tree with a snake coiled around it? In this instance, you would probably not use the tree to keep your balance; your brain would inhibit this reflex to prevent you from touching the snake. But how, you ask? The brain activates interneurons that inhibit the alpha motor neurons responsible for executing the reflex. In our example, the brain sends a message to the interneuron in the part of the spinal cord where the alpha motor neurons leading to arm extension are located, inhibiting them from letting you reach out and grab the tree with the snake in it. The spinal cord can also cause the inhibition of reflexes, in some cases to prevent damage to our muscles, the subject of the next section.

The Golgi Tendon Organs

My eldest son broke a bone in his arm while pitching in a Little League baseball game. In all likelihood, he exerted so much force throwing the ball that the muscles in his arm contracted too much, snapping the bone in his arm. Many pitchers, both amateur and professional, have damaged their muscles, tendons, and bones by throwing a baseball, a very unnatural motion. Of course, pitchers do not break bones every time they throw the ball, thanks to a mechanism that allows the motor system to control the extent to which muscles contract.

This mechanism is a set of receptors known as **Golgi tendon organs** (see **Figure 8.11**), neurons located among the fibers of the tendon, the tissue that connects muscle to bone. These receptors measure the total amount of force exerted by the muscle on the bone to which the tendon is attached. The strength of contraction of the muscle reflects the degree of force exerted by the muscle on the bone: the greater the contraction of the muscle fibers, the greater the force on the bone.

When too much force is exerted by the muscles, the Golgi tendon organs are activated. A neural message travels along axons of the Golgi tendon organs, known as **Ib fibers**, to the spinal cord, where they synapse with small interneurons. These interneurons in turn synapse with and inhibit the alpha motor neurons, reducing the con-

withdrawal reflex The automatic withdrawal of a limb from a painful stimulus.

Golgi tendon organs Receptors located among the fibers of tendons that measure the total amount of force exerted by the muscle on the bone to which the tendon is attached.

Ib fibers Axons of the Golgi tendon organs that extend to the spinal cord, where they synapse with small interneurons that inhibit alpha motor neurons.

traction of extrafusal muscle fibers. As a result, less pressure is exerted by the muscle on the tendon and bone.

The Golgi tendon organ receptors do not have the same threshold as do the sensory receptors located in the muscle spindle. The higher threshold of the Golgi tendon organs enables the muscles to contract normally; it is only when the force exerted is too great that the Golgi tendon organs are activated and the extrafusal muscle fibers inhibited. But what if you want to exert more force than your muscles (and Golgi tendon organs) will allow? Weight lifters, for example, need to lift enormous amounts of weight to be successful in competition. Lifting such tremendous amounts of weight is dangerous to the body, and the Golgi tendon organ receptors resist the actions of the weight lifter. Weight lifters have been known to inject local anesthetics into their tendons to block the action of the Golgi tendon organs. Although the weight lifter may be able to lift more weight, he or she is also likely to damage the muscle, tear the tendon, or break a bone.

Renshaw Cells

Muscles can also become damaged by fatigue; that is, if they contract too often they can no longer work properly and may become injured. The nervous system mechanism that prevents fatigue is a set of cells called **Renshaw cells**. Each alpha motor neuron has a collateral branch that turns back within the spinal cord to synapse with its Renshaw cell, an inhibitory interneuron. The axon of the Renshaw cell circles around to the dendrites of that same alpha motor neuron, forming a circuit (see **Figure 8.12**).

The more an alpha motor neuron fires, the more the Renshaw cell fires. When the level of inhibitory influence of the Renshaw cell on the alpha motor neuron reaches a threshold level, the alpha motor neuron will stop firing, preventing excessive contraction of the muscle fiber.

As we have learned, a muscle contains many muscle fibers. The alpha motor neurons innervating those fibers will be firing at different rates. Only those that exceed the threshold for Renshaw cell inhibition will stop firing. Other alpha motor neurons will continue to fire and to contract some muscle fibers. The inhibition of some but not all alpha motor neurons means that a muscle can maintain prolonged muscle contraction without becoming fatigued or damaged.

The inhibition of the alpha motor neuron by a Renshaw cell is short-lived; it is controlled by a negative feedback loop described in Chapter 4. As soon as the alpha motor neuron stops firing, its excitatory influence on its Renshaw cell ceases. This in turn ends the inhibitory effect of the Renshaw cell on the alpha motor neuron, allowing the alpha motor neuron to resume firing.

Renshaw cell An inhibitory interneuron excited by a collateral branch of an alpha motor neuron that causes an alpha motor neuron to stop firing, preventing excessive contraction of the muscle fiber.

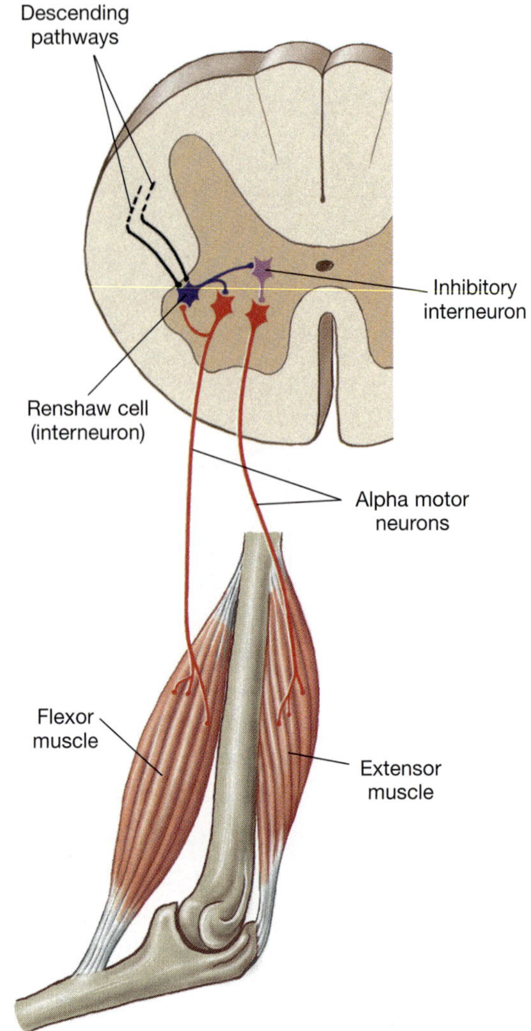

Figure 8.12 Renshaw cell. The Renshaw cell prevents muscle fatigue by inhibiting the alpha motor neuron once it reaches a certain rate of firing.
Adapted from Kandel et al., 1991.

➤ *Is the inhibition of the alpha motor neuron long term or short term? (p. 240).*

Before You Go On

Compare and contrast the roles of the Golgi tendon organ and the Renshaw cell in preventing muscle fatigue and injury.

The Neural Control of Opposing Muscle Pairs

Remember the flexor and extensor muscles? We have learned that muscles occur in pairs and that for one muscle of the pair to contract, the opposing extensor muscle must relax, or lengthen. Contraction of the opposing muscle must be actively inhibited for this to occur. As we will see shortly, the process by which one muscle is excited and its opposing muscle inhibited is similar to the action of the Golgi tendon organ receptors.

Suppose that your right foot steps on a sharp object such as a nail. To withdraw your right foot, you must contract your flexor muscles in your right leg and relax your extensor muscles in that leg. Further, you need to contract the extensor muscles in your left leg and relax your flexor muscles in that leg in order to not fall down. How are you able to accomplish this movement? Sensory pain receptors in your right foot provide one stimulus for this action. Axons from the pain receptors form four branches in the spinal cord (see **Figure 8.13**). One branch synapses with the alpha motor neurons that contract the flexor muscles

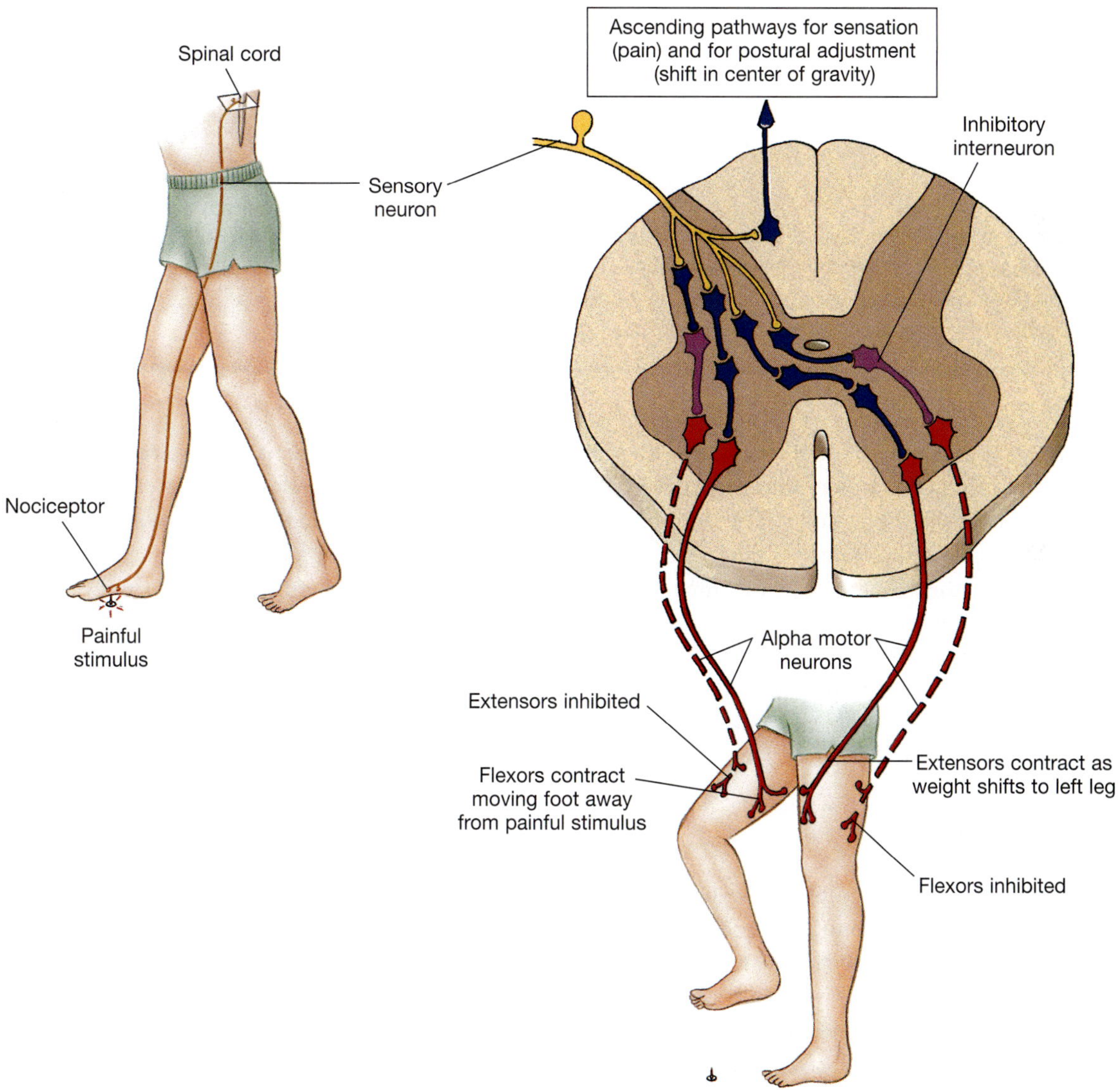

Figure 8.13 Neural control of opposing muscle pairs. One branch of the axon from the pain receptors in the right foot synapses with the alpha motor neurons that contract the flexor muscles in the right leg. A second branch goes to interneurons that inhibit the alpha motor neurons connected to the extensor muscles in the right leg. A third branch synapses with the alpha motor neurons that contract the extensor muscles in the left leg, and the fourth branch synapses with interneurons that inhibit the alpha motor neurons connected to the flexor muscles in the left leg.

➤ *Why is it important to inhibit one member of an opposing muscle pair when exciting its opposing muscle? (p. 241–242)*

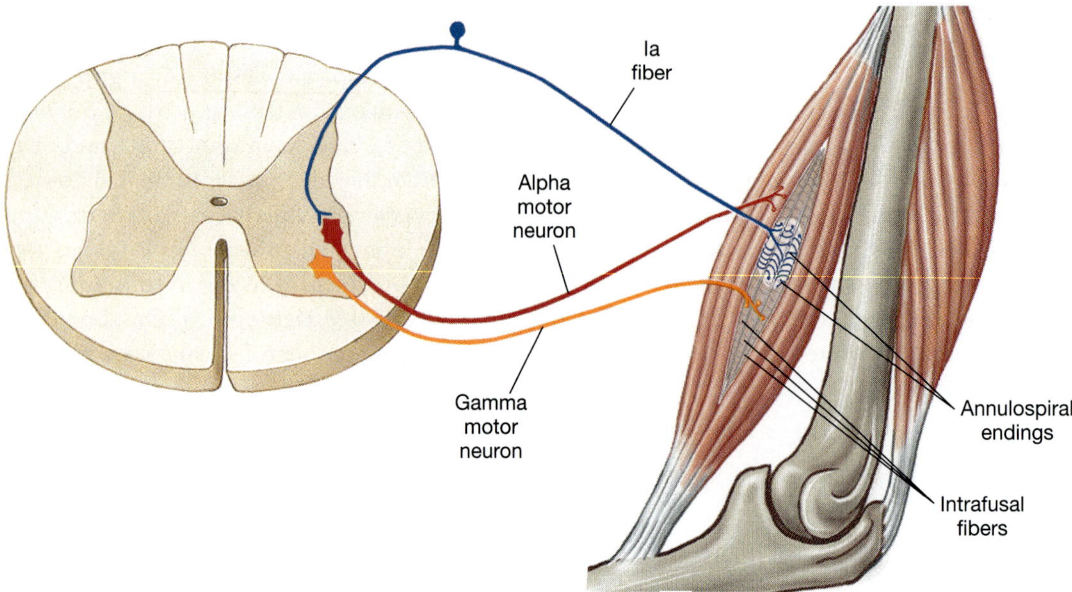

Figure 8.14 Gamma motor neuron. Gamma motor neurons produce muscle tension by contracting intrafusal muscle fibers, which stretches the middle of the muscle spindle. Stretching the muscle spindle activates the annulospiral endings, which leads to the contraction of the extrafusal muscle fibers and muscle tension.

➤ *Why is it important for the muscles to be tense when at rest? (p. 242–243)*

in the right legs. A second branch synapses with the interneurons that inhibit the alpha motor neurons going to the extensor muscles in the right leg. The third branch synapses with the alpha motor neurons that contract the extensor muscles of the left leg, and the final branch synapses with the interneurons that inhibit the alpha motor neuron going to the flexor muscles in the left leg. Activation of this polysynaptic reflex allows you to lift your right leg while maintaining your balance by straightening your left leg.

Gamma Motor System

So far we have described how stimulation by alpha motor neurons causes a muscle to contract, producing movement. But muscle contraction does not always lead to movement. All of our muscles remain tense (or contracted) even when no movement is occurring. Because the initiation of a movement starts from a contracted rather than relaxed muscle, this continuous tension allows for the rapid movement characteristic of spinal reflexes. This continuous muscle tension is due to the operation of a set of neurons called **gamma motor neurons**, collectively known as the gamma motor system (see **Figure 8.14**).

Gamma motor neurons originate in the spinal cord, exit the ventral root of the spinal cord, and synapse with the intrafusal muscle fibers of the muscle spindle (see **Figure 8.9**). (Recall that alpha motor neurons innervate extrafusal muscle fibers.) Gamma motor neurons are smaller than alpha motor neurons, and thus conduct neural impulses more slowly. The intrafusal muscle fibers contract when activated by gamma motor neurons. Contraction of the intrafusal muscle fibers stretches the middle of the muscle spindle, which activates the annulospiral endings and results in the contraction of the extrafusal muscle fibers.

The gamma motor neurons are usually active. This continuous activity of gamma motor neurons produces the constant contraction of the extrafusal muscle fibers. Therefore, our muscles are rarely inactive, but instead are almost always tensed; this resting tension of skeletal muscle is called **muscle tone**. As we will learn in Chapter 9, muscle tone is lost when we go into a particular stage of sleep called REM.

The gamma motor system serves several functions other than maintaining muscle tone. One of these functions is the ability to anticipate certain movements and react quickly. For example, a batter needs to be ready to swing

gamma motor neuron A neuron that synapses with the intrafusal muscle fibers to produce continuous muscle tension.

muscle tone The resting tension of skeletal muscle caused by activity of gamma motor neurons.

the bat at a ball that is over the plate (and *not* swing if the ball is outside the plate). The extensor muscles in the arms and legs need to be primed for action if a ball is thrown in the strike zone. This readiness is accomplished by an increase in activity in the gamma motor neurons controlling the muscles that swing the bat and move the front leg to stride toward the ball. Increasing activity in these gamma motor neurons increases contraction of the appropriate muscles and allows the batter to be ready to hit the ball.

We learned how reflexive movement occurs, and how the muscle is readied for the instruction to swing or not to swing at the ball. But how does the brain communicate the instruction to the muscle; in other words, how does voluntary movement occur? In the next section, we will examine the neural mechanisms in the brain that translate intention into action.

Before You Go On

Why is it important for muscles to exist in a resting state of tension?

Section Review

- A reflex is a simple, automatic response to sensory stimulation.
- In the monosynaptic stretch reflex, the simplest type of reflex, a muscle contracts in response to the stretching of that muscle.
- When intrafusal muscle fibers are stretched, the annulospiral endings are activated, causing a neural message to be sent to the spinal cord through axons called Ia fibers.
- The Ia fibers synapse with alpha motor neurons, which in turn cause the contraction of the extrafusal muscle fibers.
- Polysynaptic reflexes, reflexes consisting of more than one synapse, can be quite simple, involving only a sensory neuron and a motor neuron at the same level of the spinal cord connected by only one or a few interneurons, or quite complex, with sensory and motor neurons entering and exiting the spinal cord at different levels and involving many interneurons.
- Some polysynaptic reflexes occur without input from the brain; others are controlled by higher neural structures.
- The brain or the spinal cord can inhibit spinal reflexes.
- When too much force is exerted by a muscle, the Golgi tendon organ is activated.
- Axons from the Golgi tendon organs, known as Ib fibers, extend to the spinal cord and synapse with interneurons that in turn synapse with the alpha motor neurons.
- The inhibitory effect of these interneurons on the alpha motor neurons reduces the contraction of the extrafusal muscle fibers, decreasing the force exerted by the muscle on the tendon and bone.
- A collateral branch of each alpha motor neuron synapses with an inhibitory Renshaw cell, which in turn synapses with the dendrites of the alpha motor neurons.
- Activity in the alpha motor neuron produces activity in the Renshaw cells.
- When alpha motor neuron activity reaches a threshold level, the alpha motor neuron will be inhibited by the Renshaw cell and excessive contraction of the muscle fiber prevented.
- Ia fibers from the sensory annulospiral endings form two branches: one branch has an excitatory influence on one muscle of an opposing pair, and the other branch has an inhibitory influence on the other muscle of the pair.
- The gamma motor system produces muscle tone by keeping the muscles continually active.
- Gamma motor neurons activate intrafusal muscle fibers, stimulating the annulospiral endings and causing the contraction of extrafusal muscle fibers.

Brain Control of Movement

Rhea loves to play golf. She only learned to play a few years ago, and now wonders why she waited so long. Rhea feels great when she gives it all she has and drives the little ball 250 yards straight down the fairway; using precise aim and just enough force to sink a 20-foot putt is equally satisfying. When she first started playing golf, Rhea, like Sam on his NordicTrack, felt like a child learning to ride a bike. Mastering her swing took a lot of work; she would hit the top of the ball, hitting it only a few feet, or even miss the ball completely, sometimes taking out big chunks of sod. Over time and with a lot of practice, the number of slices, hooks, and divots decreased. Rhea now feels good about her drives and approach shots to the greens, but has some work to do on her putting. She still finds it difficult to hit the ball just hard enough to get it in the hole. Rhea guesses she just needs more experience.

Golf involves both powerful movements (the drive) and controlled movements (the putt). The brain has the amazing capacity to direct both of these movements, as well as the thousands of others that we perform each day. We will next look at the brain structures that direct our bodies to produce drives and putts, as well as our various other voluntary movements.

Primary Motor Cortex

The **primary motor cortex** is the area of the brain that controls voluntary movements, such as swinging a golf club. The control center for movement is located in the **precentral gyrus** of the frontal lobe (see **Figure 8.15a**). As seen in the somatotopic map in **Figure 8.15b**, the movement of different parts of the body is controlled by different sections of the primary motor cortex. As you can see from the unusual proportions of the little man, not every part of the body is equally represented in the primary motor cortex. Most of the primary motor cortex acts to control parts of the body, such as the hands or mouth, that produce precise movements. A smaller proportion of the primary motor cortex is used to control parts of the body, such as the arms and legs, that produce gross movements.

There are significant differences between the primary motor cortex and other areas of the cerebral cortex. The small granular (or seedlike) cells found in Layer IV of other cortical areas are virtually absent in the primary motor cortex. By contrast, Layers III and IV of the primary motor cortex contain large neurons,

primary motor cortex Area in the precentral gyrus of the frontal lobe that initiates voluntary movements.

precentral gyrus Area in the posterior part of the frontal lobe that contains the primary motor cortex, the control center for movement.

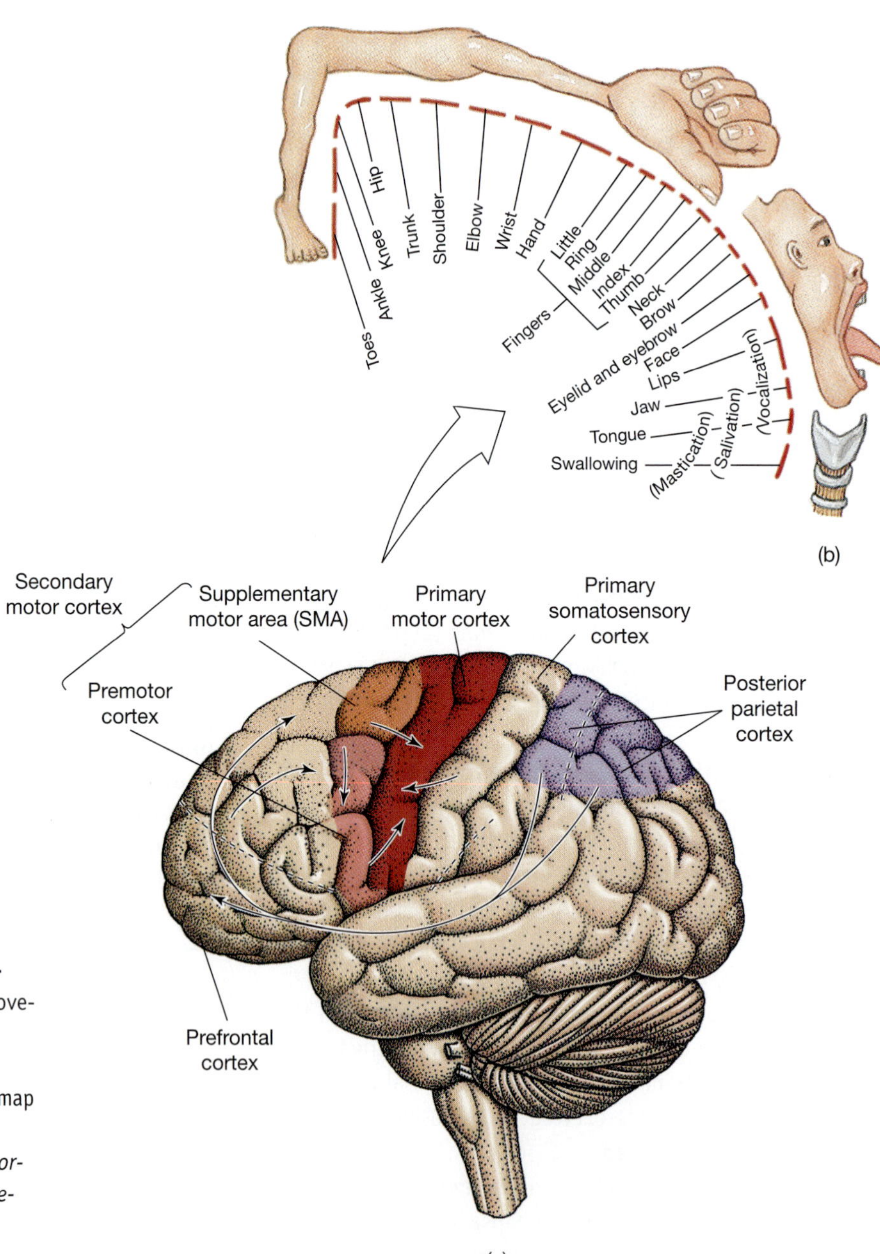

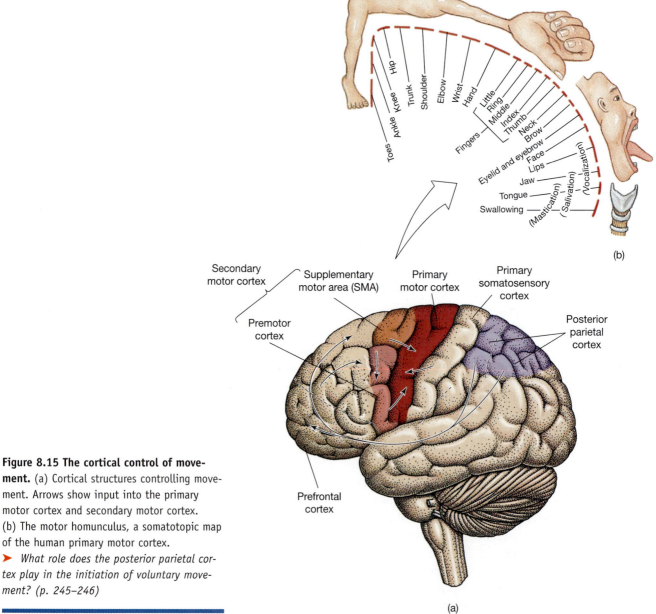

Figure 8.15 The cortical control of movement. (a) Cortical structures controlling movement. Arrows show input into the primary motor cortex and secondary motor cortex. (b) The motor homunculus, a somatotopic map of the human primary motor cortex.

➤ *What role does the posterior parietal cortex play in the initiation of voluntary movement? (p. 245–246)* called **pyramidal cells** because of the pyramid-like shape of their cell bodies. Because of the presence of the large pyramidal cells, the primary motor cortex is much thicker than other cortical tissue. For example, the primary motor cortex in humans is 3.5 to 4.0 mm thick compared to the 1.5- to 2.0-mm thickness of the primary visual cortex.

The axons of the pyramidal cells leave the primary motor cortex in a columnar organization. The columns are perpendicular to the cortical surface and are organized into *colonies* of motor cortex neurons (Ghez, Hening, & Gordon, 1991). The neurons in each colony control a specific movement. Activation of one motor neuron in a colony acts to excite the other neurons in that colony. This mutual excitation is thought to amplify the output from the primary motor cortex to ensure that sufficient neural activity is established to elicit a specific movement (Asanuma, 1989).

The activation of one colony of motor cortex neurons also has the effect of inhibiting adjacent colonies (Asanuma, 1989). This inhibition of neighboring colonies serves to prevent competing motor responses, and, thereby, further ensures that the desired movement occurs.

Colonies of motor cortex neurons also control the direction of a specific movement. To demonstrate this specificity in motor control, Georgopoulous, Taira, and Lukashin (1993) trained monkeys to reach for objects with their arms in eight different directions. These researchers then measured the activity of hundreds of individual motor cortex neurons during each different movement. They observed that although each motor cortex neuron responded to a particular direction, the activity of no single motor cortex neuron corresponded to the exact direction of arm movement. By contrast, a strong relationship was found between the activity of several hundred motor cortex neurons and the specific direction that a monkey's arm moved. Further, the activity of different colonies of neurons corresponded to different movement directions. In other words, neural activity in a specific colony increased when the arm moved in one direction, but not for the other directions.

The primary motor cortex does not operate independently of other areas of the cerebral cortex. It receives three types of information from three different cortical structures; this information allows Rhea's primary motor cortex to initiate successful movements (refer to **Figure 8.15a**). One type of information, the amount of force that Rhea must exert on her arms to produce a particular swing, such as a putt, is provided by the primary somatosensory cortex. A second type of information, the present position of the golf ball, is needed so that she can move the club to hit the golf ball; this information is provided by the posterior parietal cortex. The final type of information, the planning and sequencing of Rhea's swing, is provided by the secondary motor cortex.

Primary Somatosensory Cortex

The sensory receptors in the muscles and in the joints send information about the physical environment to the somatosensory cortex; this information is then passed on to the primary motor cortex. This input allows the primary motor cortex to be aware of the status of the muscles that must be activated and the location of the body parts that must be moved, so that the right amount of force can be exerted.

Suppose Rhea wants to hit a 50-foot pitch shot to the green. If she hits the ball with too much force, it may sail 100 yards; but if she hits it with too little force, it may go only a few feet. Her arms must not be too tight against her body, but they cannot be too far away either. Feedback from the muscles and joints allows the primary motor cortex to send the correct message to her muscles so that she will move her arms with sufficient force to hit the ball and land it on the green, preferably near the hole.

Posterior Parietal Cortex

Suppose that Rhea finds her golf ball under a tree rather than in the fairway. She must limit the backhand extension of her arms so as to hit the ball without also hitting the tree with the club. Input from the visual system allows her to swing her arms just enough to hit the ball but not the tree.

Obviously, visual sensory information is necessary if Rhea is to avoid hitting the tree with her golf club. As we discussed in Chapter 6, we rely heavily on our visual sense to guide our movements. Yet, other senses also play important roles in directing movement. Suppose that you walk into a dark room and need to turn on the light switch at the opposite end of the room. Input from your tactile sense can be used to guide you to the light switch, unless of course you walk into the coffee table, in which case the tactile input will only make you angry. You can also locate the light switch by following the ticking of the grandfather clock next to it.

The **posterior parietal cortex** integrates input from the visual, auditory, and skin senses (see **Figure 8.15a**) and relays it to the primary motor cortex (Cheney, 1985;

---

pyramidal cells Large pyramid-shaped neurons in the primary motor cortex.

posterior parietal cortex Area in the posterior part of the parietal cortex that integrates input from the visual, auditory, and somatosensory systems and relays it to the primary motor cortex.

Ghez, 1985). The primary motor cortex then uses this information to guide our movements.

The specific area of the posterior parietal lobe that becomes active during movement depends on the type of movement (Bushnell, Bowers, & Robinson, 1981). Certain neurons in the posterior parietal cortex become active when Rhea reaches for a golf ball. Different neurons become active when she is holding it.

Damage to the posterior parietal cortex produces movement deficits. Patients with damage to the posterior parietal cortex have difficulty responding to visual, auditory, or somatosensory stimuli presented to the contralateral side of the body (Heilman, Bowers, & Valenstein, 1985). This disturbance in the ability to respond is called **contralateral neglect**. The following case history of Mrs. S., who suffered damage to the posterior parietal lobe of her right hemisphere after a stroke, illustrates the impairment associated with contralateral neglect:

> She has totally lost the idea of 'left,' with regard to both the world and her own body. Sometimes she complains that her portions are too small, but this is because she only eats from the right half of the plate—it does not occur to her that it has a left half as well. Sometimes, she will put on lipstick and make up the right half of her face, leaving the left half completely neglected: it is almost impossible to treat these things, because her attention cannot be drawn to them. (Sachs, 1985, p. 73)

Returning once again to the golf example, feedback from somatosensory receptors to the posterior parietal cortex allows Rhea to swing the golf club just enough to hit the ball and not the tree. However, swinging a golf club is not a single movement, but instead is several movements: gripping the club, moving the arms backward, and then moving the arms forward to make contact with the ball. These movements require the planning and sequencing of all the various muscles involved in the swing. The planning and sequencing of voluntary movements is the function of the secondary motor cortex.

Secondary Motor Cortex

The **secondary motor cortex** includes two brain areas: the **supplementary motor area** and the **premotor cortex** (see **Figure 8.15a**). Both of these areas are involved in the planning and sequencing of voluntary movements. The supplementary motor area receives input from the posterior parietal cortex and the somatosensory cortex, and the premotor cortex receives input mostly from the visual cortex. A considerable number of neural connections exists between the supplementary motor area and the premotor cortex, which allows for the integration of information arriving from other areas of the cerebral cortex.

There do appear to be differences in the movements planned and sequencing by the premotor cortex and the supplementary motor area (Larsson, Gulyas, & Roland, 1996). The supplementary motor area appears to plan and sequence movements guided by internally generated stimuli (or intentions), whereas the premotor cortex plans and sequences movements guided by external stimuli. Because most movements are guided by both intention and external stimuli, the connections between the supplementary motor area and the premotor cortex provide for coordinated planning of these movements.

The role of the secondary motor cortex in sequencing movement is evident in monkeys trained to push a peanut through a hole with the finger of one hand and retrieve the peanut with the palm of the other hand (see **Figure 8.16**). Although a normal monkey has no difficulty with this task, a monkey with damage to the supplementary motor area or premotor cortex generally fails to get the peanut (Brinkman, 1984). This failure occurs because monkeys with damage to these areas of the brain must push the peanut with the nonpreferred hand through the hole and have the preferred hand underneath ready to catch it. Unfortunately the peanut generally falls because the monkeys cannot catch it.

Before You Go On

Describe how the posterior parietal cortex, the somatosensory cortex, and the secondary motor cortex work to allow Rhea to hoist her golf bag onto her shoulder.

Motor Tracts Controlling Movement

We have learned that several cortical structures—the posterior parietal cortex, somatosensory cortex, and sec-

---

contralateral neglect A disturbance in the ability to respond to visual, auditory, or somatosensory stimuli on one side of the body due to damage to the contralateral posterior parietal cortex.

secondary motor cortex Area in the frontal lobe that plans and sequences voluntary movements; includes the supplementary motor area and the premotor cortex.

supplementary motor area An area in the frontal lobe that receives input from the posterior parietal cortex and the somatosensory cortex and is involved in the planning and sequencing of voluntary movements.

premotor cortex An area in the frontal lobe that receives input mostly from the visual cortex and is involved in the planning and sequencing of voluntary movements.

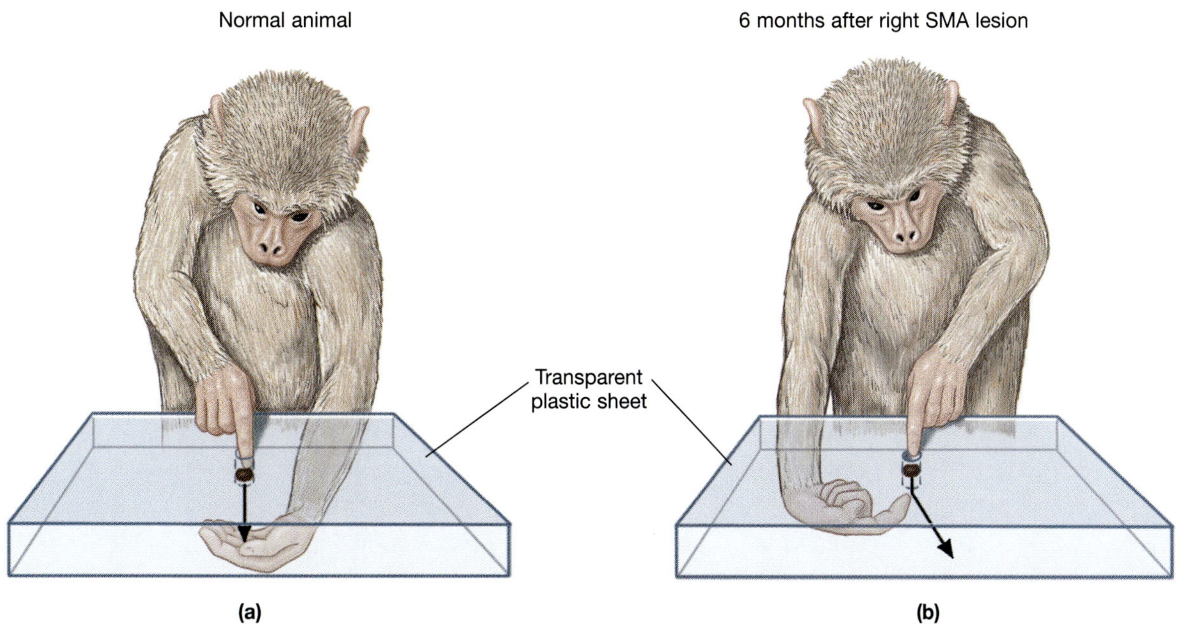

Figure 8.16 Secondary motor cortex and planning and sequencing of voluntary movement. Damage to secondary motor cortex impairs coordinated movement. The normal monkey (a) is able to obtain food using both hands, whereas the monkey with damage to secondary motor cortex (b) generally loses the food due to inability to sequence movement of its two hands.

➤ *Describe another action you would be unable to perform if your secondary motor cortex were damaged. (p. 246)*

ondary motor cortex—provide information to the primary motor cortex, and that the primary motor cortex uses this input to initiate movement. Several fiber tracts originate in the primary motor cortex and travel through the midbrain and hindbrain before connecting with the peripheral nervous system, where movement is produced. Other fiber tracts begin in subcortical areas (midbrain and hindbrain) and descend to the peripheral nervous system.

Tracts Originating in the Motor Cortex. Two major motor fiber tracts originate in the primary motor cortex: the corticospinal tract and the corticobulbar tract. The corticospinal tract controls movement of the fingers, hands, and arms as well as the trunk, legs, and feet. The corticobulbar tract controls movement of the face and tongue.

Most of the neurons in the **corticospinal tract** originate in large pyramidal cells of the motor cortex. The remaining cell bodies in this tract originate in the premotor cortex and somatosensory cortex. The axons of neurons in the corticospinal tract are quite long, typically 3 to 4 feet. After leaving the cerebral cortex, the axons in the corticospinal tract travel through the midbrain and hindbrain to the spinal cord (see **Figure 8.17**).

Most axons in the corticospinal tract cross over in the medulla to connect to the opposite side of the spinal cord. Axons that cross over comprise the **lateral corticospinal tract**. These axons synapse with those alpha motor neurons in the spinal cord that control movement of the fingers, hands, arms, lower legs, and feet. Because the axons of the lateral corticospinal tract cross over, axons originating in the right side of the brain control movement of the left fingers, hand, arm, lower leg, and foot, whereas axons from the left side of the brain control movement of the right fingers, hand, arm, lower leg, and foot. The axons that do not cross over comprise the **ventral corticospinal tract**. These axons synapse with those alpha motor neurons that control the movement of the trunk and upper legs.

The importance of the corticospinal tract in the control of precise movements can be seen when this motor pathway is damaged. In one study (Lawrence & Kuypers, 1968), both the lateral and ventral corticospinal tracts in

corticospinal tracts Two motor pathways that originate in the pyramidal cells of the primary motor cortex and are involved in the control of precise voluntary movements of the fingers, hands, and arms as well as the trunk, legs, and feet.

lateral corticospinal tract Group of neurons originating in the primary motor cortex whose axons cross over to synapse with those alpha motor neurons in the spinal cord that control movement of the fingers, hands, arms, lower legs, and feet.

ventral corticospinal tract Group of neurons originating in the primary motor cortex whose axons do not cross over; synapse with those alpha motor neurons that control the movement of the trunk and upper legs.

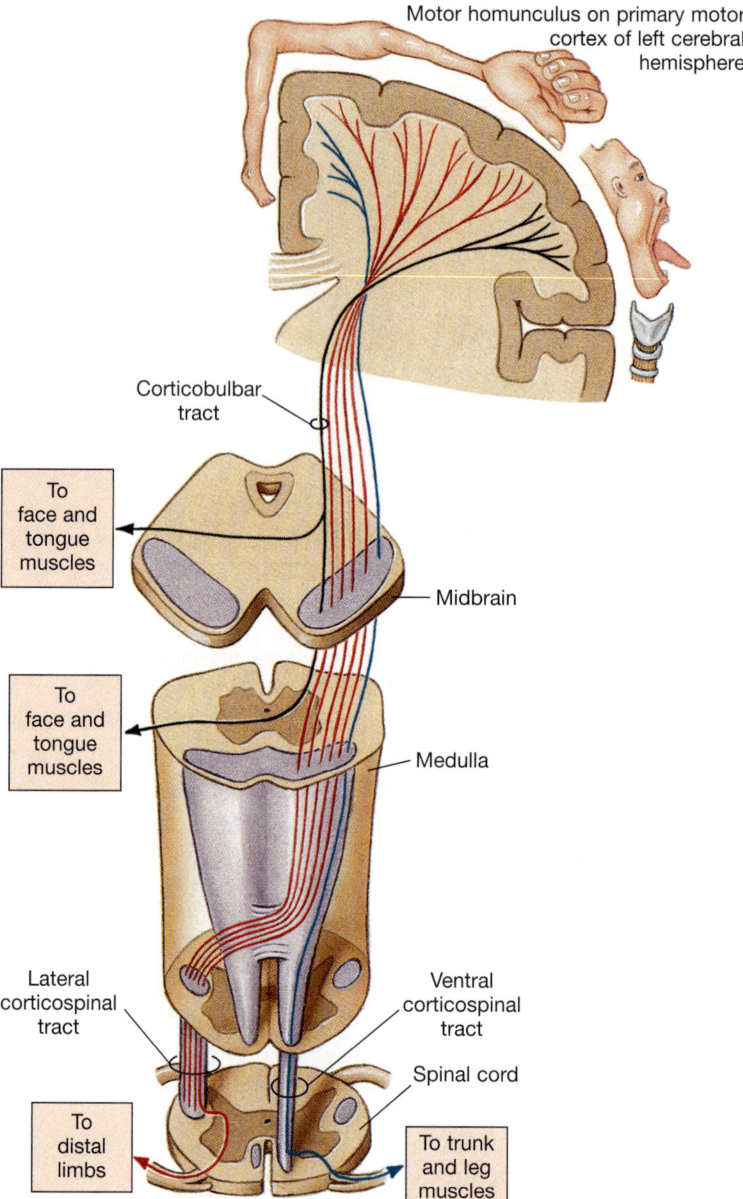

Figure 8.17 Illustration of motor tracts that originate in the primary motor cortex. Notice how the lateral corticospinal tract fibers cross over in the medulla prior to entering the spinal cord, whereas ventral corticospinal tract fibers do not cross over. Corticobulbar tract fibers synapse with cranial nerves and extend to the face and tongue.

➤ *Describe the path of the lateral corticospinal tract from the motor cortex to the spinal cord. (p. 247)*

monkeys were severed. These monkeys quickly regained the ability to reach for and then grasp an object, and there were no impairments in posture or locomotion, but they showed permanent deficits in the ability to use their fingers independently to pick up small pieces of food or to release food once they were holding it.

corticobulbar tract Group of neurons originating mostly in the primary motor cortex involved in the control of the movement of the face and tongue.

ventromedial tracts Four motor pathways originating in different parts of the subcortex that control movements of the trunk and limbs; includes the vestibulospinal, tectospinal, lateral reticulospinal, and medial reticulospinal tracts.

The second motor tract that originates in the cerebral cortex is the **corticobulbar tract**. The cell bodies of neurons in this tract are located in the motor cortex; their axons descend through the subcortex (midbrain and hindbrain) to synapse with the motor neurons of the cranial nerves that control the movement of the facial and tongue muscles (see **Figure 8.17**).

Tracts Originating in the Subcortex. Two major motor tracts originate in the subcortex: the ventromedial tracts and the rubrospinal tracts. The **ventromedial tracts** consist of four separate fiber tracts that originate in different parts of the subcortex and control movements of the trunk and limbs (see **Figure 8.18**): the vestibulospinal tract, the tectospinal tract, the lateral reticulospinal tract, and the medial reticulospinal tract. The **vestibulospinal tract** begins in the vestibular nuclei of the brainstem and synapses with those alpha motor neurons in the spinal cord that produce lower trunk and leg movement. This fiber tract plays a central role in the control of posture. The **tectospinal tract** originates in the superior colliculi and synapses with those spinal alpha motor neurons that control upper trunk (shoulder) and neck movement. The coordination of head and trunk movements, especially the visual tracking of stimuli, is the main function of this fiber tract. The **lateral reticulospinal tract** originates in the medullary reticular formation and synapses with those alpha motor neurons of the spinal cord that activate the flexor muscles of the legs. The **medial reticulospinal tract** begins in the pontine reticular formation and synapses with those spinal alpha motor neurons that activate the extensor muscles of the legs. The coordinated activity of the lateral and medial reticulospinal tracts controls walking and running.

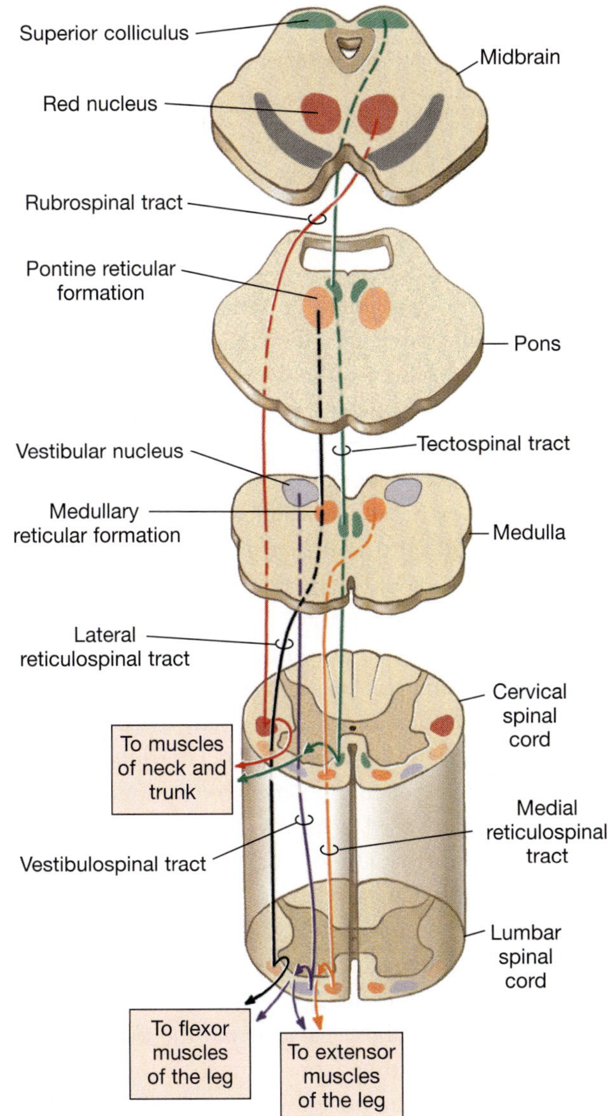

Figure 8.18 Illustration of motor tracts originating in subcortical areas. Ventromedial tracts control movements of trunk and limbs, and rubrospinal tract controls movement of lower arms and legs.
➤ *What are the four separate tracts of the ventromedial tracts? (p. 248–249)*

As you have guessed from the descriptions of their functions, damage to the ventromedial tracts impairs posture and leg movements. In one study (Lawrence & Kuypers, 1968), the fibers of the ventromedial tracts in monkeys were severed. Monkeys with damage to the ventromedial tracts had great difficulty standing and could not take more than a few steps without falling.

The **rubrospinal tract** originates in the red nucleus and synapses in the spinal cord with those alpha motor neurons that control movement of the hands (but not the fingers), as well as the lower arms, lower legs, and feet (see **Figure 8.18**). Axons in this fiber tract cross over completely, and thus control movement in the contralateral side of the body. The effect of damage to the rubrospinal tract is impairment of arm and leg movement. In the same study described in the last paragraph, Lawrence and Kuypers (1968) cut the rubrospinal tract of other monkeys and observed that these monkeys had difficulty reaching for and holding food. **Table 8.1** lists the major motor tracts with their points of origins and the muscles they control.

In the past, biological psychologists viewed the motor pathways as two independent motor systems: the pyramidal motor system and the extrapyramidal motor system. It was

---

vestibulospinal tract Motor pathway that originates in the vestibular nuclei of the brainstem, synapses with those alpha motor neurons in the spinal cord that produce lower trunk and leg movement, and plays a central role in the control of posture.

tectospinal tract Motor pathway that originates in the superior colliculi, synapses with those spinal alpha motor neurons that control upper trunk (shoulder) and neck movement, and coordinates head and trunk movements, especially the visual tracking of stimuli.

lateral reticulospinal tract Motor pathway that originates in the medullary reticular formation and synapses with those alpha motor neurons of the spinal cord that activate the flexor muscles of the legs.

medial reticulospinal tract Motor pathway that originates in the pontine reticular formation and synapses with those spinal alpha motor neurons that activate the extensor muscles of the legs.

rubrospinal tract Motor pathway that originates in the red nucleus and crosses over to synapse in the spinal cord with those alpha motor neurons that control movement of the hands (but not the fingers), as well as the lower arms, lower legs, and feet.

Table 8.1 ■ Major Motor Pathways Controlling Movement

Motor Tract	Point of Origin	Muscles Controlled
Corticospinal Tracts		
Lateral corticospinal tract	Finger, hand, and arm region of the motor cortex	Fingers, hands, arms, lower legs, and feet
Ventral corticospinal tract	Trunk and upper leg region of motor cortex	Trunk and upper legs
Corticobulbar Tract	Face region of the motor cortex	Face and tongue
Ventromedial Tracts		
Vestibulsopinal tract	Vestibular nuclei of the brainstem	Lower trunk and legs
Tectospinal tract	Superior colliculi	Neck and upper trunk
Lateral reticulospinal tract	Medullary reticular formation	Flexor muscles of legs
Medial reticulospinal tract	Pontine reticular formation	Extensor muscles of legs
Rubrospinal Tract	Red nucleus	Hands (not fingers), lower arms, feet, and lower legs

thought that the pyramidal motor system originated in the primary motor cortex and mediated voluntary movements, whereas the extrapyramidal motor system began in the subcortical areas and controlled involuntary movements. This separation of the control of movement into two distinct motor systems is no longer believed to be accurate. Instead, evidence has indicated that there is extensive interaction between the tracts that originate in the motor cortex and those that originate in subcortical areas. This interaction is the result of the collateral axons of neurons of the corticospinal tracts synapsing with the ventromedial and rubrospinal tracts. These connections allow the coordination of functions required for everyday activities.

With much practice, Rhea has learned to execute the same swing each time she is faced with a particular shot. Her swing has become faster and more confident with experience. We next turn our attention to two subcortical structures—the cerebellum and basal ganglia—that play key roles in the development of a successful golf swing.

Before You Go On

Using what you know about the various motor circuits, describe which parts of the body would be affected by a stroke occurring in the right motor cortex.

ballistic movement Movement that occurs rapidly and is not dependent on sensory feedback.

deep cerebellar nuclei Group of neurons that project to the ventral lateral thalamus, the red nucleus, the descending reticular formation, and the alpha motor neurons of the spinal cord to correct movements in progress.

Cerebellum

Rhea's consistent swing is an example of a **ballistic movement**—a movement that is a well-practiced habit, occurring rapidly, and not dependent on sensory feedback. Ballistic movements are governed by the cerebellum, the area of the brain responsible for the development of rapid, coordinated responses or habits (Leiner, Leiner, & Dow, 1989).

The cerebellum is located behind and beneath the cerebral cortex. It consists of two hemispheres, with an outer surface that is extremely convoluted (see **Figure 8.19**). You might have noticed that the wrinkled appearance of the cerebellum looks a lot like that of the cerebrum. The term *cerebellum* is from the Latin for "little brain." The cerebellum represents only 10 percent of the mass of the brain, but contains more than half of its neurons. These neurons provide the cerebellum with the ability to control movement and enable us to develop rapid, coordinated habits.

Input to the cerebellum comes from a number of neural structures, conveyed by means of large bundles of axons known as peduncles. These axons pass through the pons (see **pp. 51–53** in Chapter 2) into the white matter of the cerebellum and then into the cerebellar cortex (see **Figure 8.19**). Some of these axons come from the primary motor cortex. Other axons come from the vestibular system, providing information about balance and the position of the head in space. Still other axons come from the spinal cord, providing data about the position of the limbs and the extent of muscle contraction. The cerebellum integrates all of this information and determines whether ongoing movements are deviating from the intended course.

If movements do begin to deviate, the cerebellum can correct them by sending signals to other structures involved in movement. Located within the white matter of the cerebellum are **deep cerebellar nuclei** (see **Figure 8.19**). Axons from these deep cerebellar nuclei project to the ventral lateral thalamus, which in turn projects to the primary motor cortex. Axons of the deep cerebellar nuclei also project to the red nucleus and to the descending reticular formation. As we have already discussed, both of these structures are connected to the alpha motor neurons of the spinal cord.

The process by which the cerebellum produces coordinated ballistic movements is quite complex. There are a number of different types of cells in the cerebellar cortex (see **Figure 8.20**). Input into the cerebellar cortex comes from neurons called **climbing fibers** and **mossy fibers**. These neurons have an inhibitory influence on the cerebellar cortex, allowing the cerebellum to reset quickly and to respond to new incoming information. Output from the cerebellar cortex is transmitted by the **Purkinje cells**. When one Purkinje cell is active, it inhibits surrounding Purkinje cells, as well as surrounding **basket cells**. As basket cells have an inhibitory influence on a Purkinje cell, inhibition of the basket cells allows the Purkinje cell to remain active. By inhibiting surrounding Purkinje cells and maintaining its own activity, the Purkinje cell produces continuous movement in a specific muscle and prevents movement in opposing muscles. The Purkinje cell will remain active until the movement is completed. In this way, the cerebellum ensures that Rhea's golf swing is rapid and continuous rather than halting or hesitant.

Learning appears to be an important part of the cerebellum being able to establish skilled movements. It has

climbing fibers Neurons that have an inhibitory influence on the cerebellum, allowing it to reset quickly and to respond to new incoming information.

mossy fibers Neurons that have an inhibitory influence on the cerebellum, allowing it to reset quickly and to respond to new incoming information.

Purkinje cells Neurons in the cerebellum that remain active until a movement is completed.

basket cells Neurons that inhibit surrounding Purkinje cells to produce continuous movement in a specific muscle and prevent movement in opposing muscles.

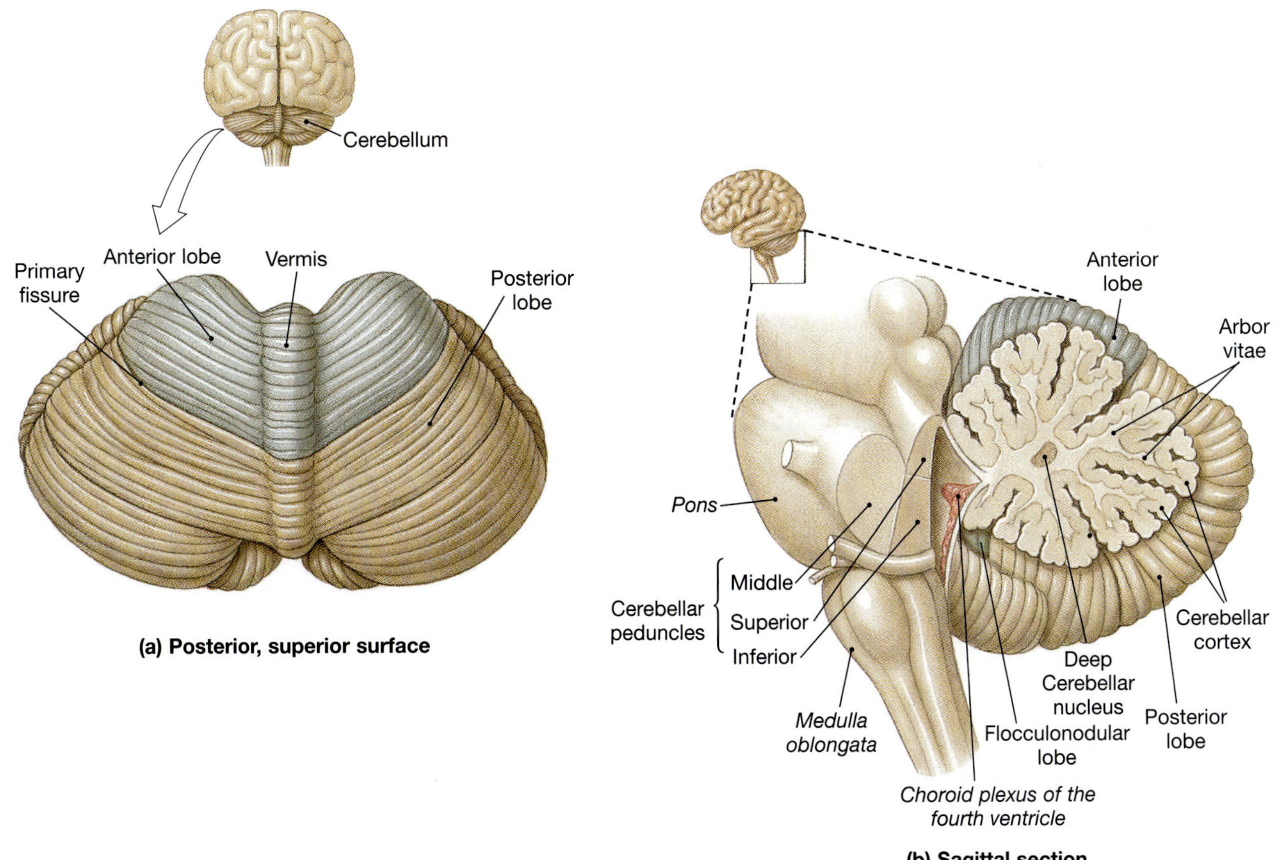

Figure 8.19 Key structures of the cerebellum. (a) The coronal view shows the anterior and posterior divisions of the cerebellum. (b) The sagittal view shows the relation to pons and medulla oblongata.

➤ *What types of movement are controlled by the cerebellum? (p. 250)*

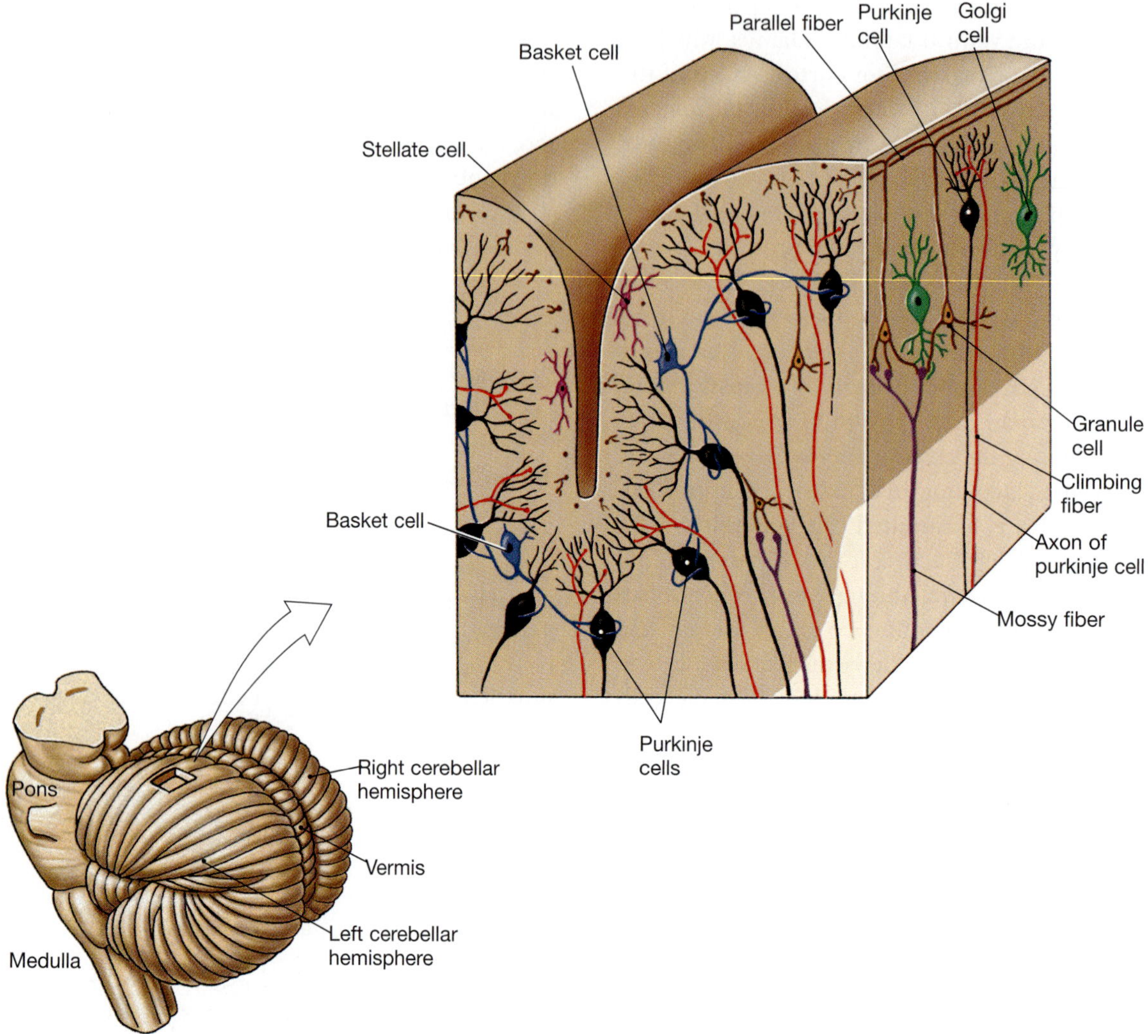

Figure 8.20 Cellular structure of the cerebellar cortex. Input enters the cerebellar cortex through climbing and mossy fibers and exits through Purkinje cells. Other cells in the cerebellar cortex (granule cell, Golgi cell, basket cell, and stellate cell) act to moderate the input and output of the cerebellum.

➤ *Are the mossy fibers inhibitory or excitatory? (p. 251)*

been suggested that the cerebellum establishes skilled movements by creating neural motor programs. Activation of these neural circuits allows Rhea's swing to become automatic. As we will discover in Chapter 14, learning involves the establishment of new or more efficient neural circuits. The important role that the cerebellum plays in motor learning will be evident from the discussion of learning in Chapter 14.

Damage to the cerebellum leads to difficulty performing well-established habits (Dichgans, 1984; Ghez & Fahn, 1985). Movement is still possible, but is not rapid or coordinated. There can be impairment of movement in direction, force, velocity, aim, and/or timing of movement.

Individuals with cerebellar damage also can have difficulty maintaining a stable posture, so movements such as walking can be unsteady. Speech can be slurred and eye movements uncoordinated. Recall that the position of the lens of the eye is controlled by fine ciliary muscles (see Chapter 6). A person with cerebellar damage can have difficulty focusing on an object because of problems in coordinating the angle and position of the lens. The cerebellum controls the saccadic eye movements that shift our eyes from one fixation point to the next and maintain stimulation of the visual system (see Chapter 6). Damage to the cerebellum can impair saccadic eye movements, another way that the ability to focus on objects can be disrupted.

A person suspected of driving while intoxicated may be asked by a police officer to hold one arm straight out and then to touch his or her nose (see **Figure 8.21**). A normal, noninebriated person has no difficulty with this finger-to-nose test. Someone with damage to the cerebellum may move the finger not far enough, hitting his or her eye with the finger or may move the finger too far, bashing the nose with the wrist or forearm. This response is characteristic of alcohol intoxication and may lead to the false arrest of someone with damage to the cerebellum. Neurons in the cerebellum are quite sensitive to alcohol, and alcohol intoxication can lead a person to show signs of cerebellar damage.

Basal Ganglia

The basal ganglia, which integrates movement and controls postural adjustments and muscle tone, is actually composed of three subcortical structures located close to the thalamus (see **Figure 8.22**). The **caudate nucleus**, from the Latin word meaning "tail" (recall from Chapter 2 that caudal means toward the tail) is a long curving structure. Adjacent to the caudate nucleus is the **putamen**, from the Latin word meaning the part of a fruit that remains as waste, which is an oval-shaped structure (think of a peach pit). The third structure is the **globus pallidus**, which is shaped like a globe with very pale markings. (For once, these names actually make sense!) In cross section, these structures appear striped because of the presence of both cell bodies and axons. The caudate nucleus and putamen are often referred to as the **neostriatum**, meaning "new striped body," because these structures are phylogenetically newer than the

Figure 8.21 A test of cerebellar function. Damage to the cerebellum will leave this young man unable to walk a straight line, which may lead the police officer to conclude that he is drunk.

➤ *Why might cerebellar damage be confused for alcohol intoxication? (p. 252–253)*

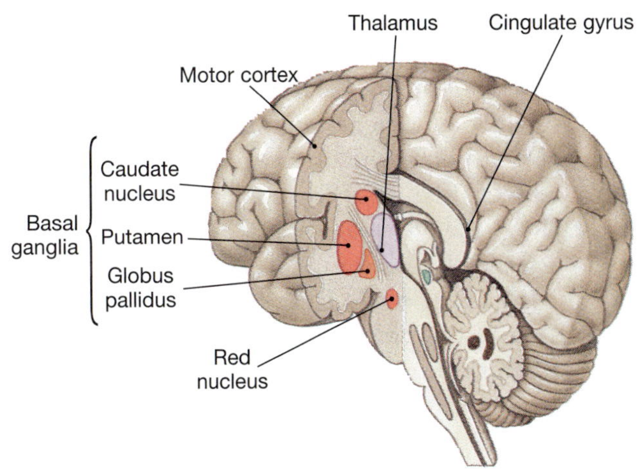

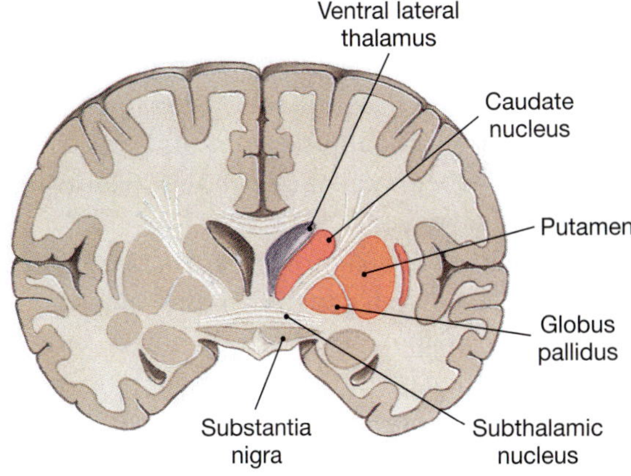

Figure 8.22 The basal ganglia. The structures of the basal ganglia as well as other structures shown here are involved in the control of movement.

➤ *What are the structures of the basal ganglia? (p. 253–254)*

caudate nucleus A long curving structure that is part of the basal ganglia.

putamen An oval-shaped structure that is part of the basal ganglia.

globus pallidus An area shaped like a globe with very pale markings that is part of the basal ganglia.

neostriatum Phylogenetically newer part of basal ganglia that contains the caudate nucleus and putamen, which receive sensory input from the thalamus, the substantia nigra, and the primary motor cortex and sends messages to the paleostriatum.

globus pallidus, which is referred to as **paleostriatum**, meaning "old striped body."

The structures of the basal ganglia receive input from a number of other brain structures and send information to other brain structures (see **Figure 8.23**). The neostriatum receives sensory input from the thalamus, the substantia nigra, and the primary motor cortex, which passes the message to paleostriatum, which in turn sends messages to the thalamus and then on to the primary motor cortex and brainstem structures controlling movement.

We learned earlier that the cerebellum coordinates rapid, smoothly executed movements; the basal ganglia is responsible for the integration of movement and the control of posture and muscle tone (Kolb & Whishaw, 1996). The basal ganglia integrates movement through its interconnections with the primary motor cortex, the cerebellum, and other motor centers in the brain (substantia nigra, red nucleus, etc.). It controls postural adjustments and muscle tone through the subcortical motor tracts (ventromedial and rubrospinal tracts).

The effects of damage provide further evidence for the role of the basal ganglia in the integration of movement (Marsden, 1984). Individuals with basal ganglia damage may show poor muscle tone, postural instability, and poorly integrated movements, and may experience considerable difficulty performing voluntary movements such as standing or walking. You may recognize these symptoms as those of Parkinson's disease. As we learned in Chapter 4, Parkinson's patients show abnormally low levels of dopamine in the circuit connecting the substantia nigra to the basal ganglia and degeneration of dopaminergic synapses in the basal ganglia. The resulting impairment in basal ganglia functioning is responsible for the symptoms of Parkinson's disease. We will look more closely at Parkinson's disease in a later section of this chapter.

Huntington's disease is another disorder resulting from damage to the basal ganglia. We learned in Chapter 1 that Huntington's disease is a degenerative neurological disorder characterized by rapid, uncontrolled movements of the limbs and facial muscles. As the disease progresses, individuals with Huntington's disease become unable to walk or speak, and show a deterioration of cognitive functioning. We will discuss the role of the basal ganglia in Huntington's disease in more detail in a later section.

paleostriatum Phylogenetically older part of basal ganglia that contains the globus pallidus, which receives information from the neostriatum and sends messages to the thalamus and then on to the primary motor cortex and brainstem structures controlling movement.

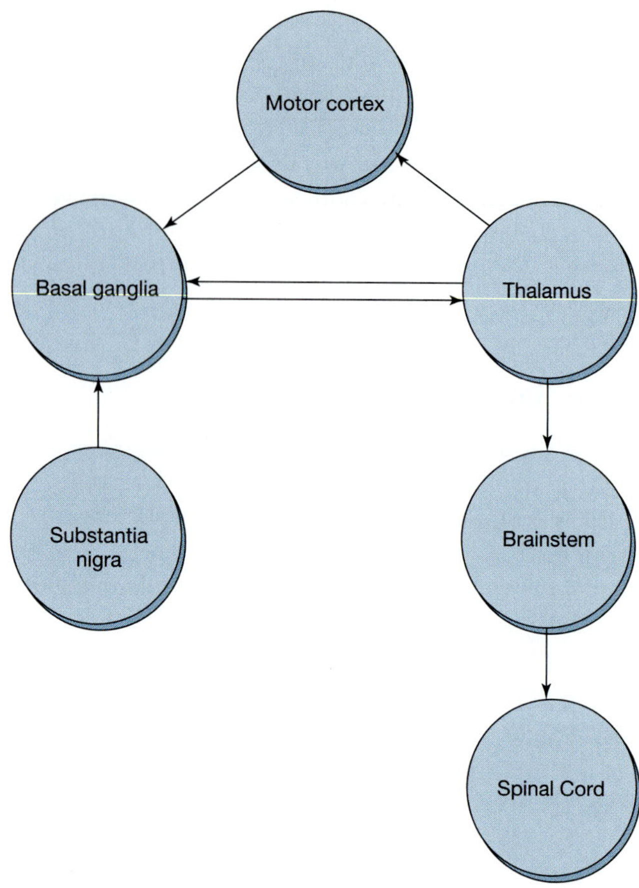

Figure 8.23 Basal ganglia and voluntary movement. The basal ganglia receives and sends information to and from several brain structures. The direction of the arrows shows the relationship of the basal ganglia to other brain structures involved in the control of movement.

➤ *What part of the basal ganglia receives sensory input from the thalamus, substantia nigra, and the primary motor cortex? (p. 254)*

Before You Go On

Describe the role of Purkinje cells in the control of movement.

Section Review

- The primary motor cortex, located in the precentral gyrus of frontal lobe, controls voluntary movements.
- The largest part of the primary motor cortex is devoted to the control of the precise movement of the hands and mouth.

- The primary motor cortex receives information about the status of muscles to be activated and the location of body parts to be moved from the primary somatosensory cortex.
- The posterior parietal lobe integrates input from the visual, auditory, and skin senses, and relays it to the primary motor cortex.
- The secondary motor cortex (supplementary motor area and premotor cortex), which plans and sequences voluntary movements, receives information from the posterior parietal lobe, somatosensory cortex, and visual cortex, and relays information to the primary motor cortex.
- Two motor tracts that originate in the primary motor cortex are the corticospinal tract and the corticobulbar tract.
- The corticospinal tract, especially important in the control of fine movements, controls the movement of the fingers, hands, and arms as well as the trunk, legs, and feet.
- Lateral corticospinal tract fibers cross over in the medulla, whereas ventral corticospinal tract fibers do not cross over.
- The corticobulbar tract controls movements of the face and tongue.
- The ventromedial tracts and rubrospinal tract originate in the subcortex. There are four ventromedial fiber tracts: (1) the vestibulospinal tract, which begins in vestibular nuclei, controls lower trunk and leg movement, and plays a central role in posture; (2) the tectospinal tract, which begins in the superior colliculi, controls the upper trunk and neck, and coordinates head and trunk movements, especially visual tracking; (3) the lateral reticulospinal tract, which begins in the medullary reticular formation and activates the flexor muscles of the legs; and (4) the medial reticulospinal tract, which begins in the pontine reticular formation and controls the extensor muscles of the legs.
- The rubrospinal tract originates in the red nucleus and controls movements of the hands, but not the fingers, as well as the lower arms, legs, and feet.
- The cerebellum, located behind and beneath the cerebral cortex, contains more than half the neurons in the brain, enabling the cerebellum to produce rapid, coordinated, skilled movements. The cerebellum establishes skilled movements by creating neural motor programs.
- The cerebellum receives information from the primary motor cortex (about motor activity), the vestibular system (about balance and the position of the head in space), and the spinal cord (about position of the limbs and extent of muscle contraction).
- The cerebellum sends information first to the ventral lateral thalamus and then to the primary motor cortex, as well as to the red nucleus and the descending reticular formation.
- The basal ganglia, which integrates movement and controls postural adjustments and muscle tone, contains three structures: the caudate nucleus, the putamen, and the globus pallidus.
- Sensory input from the thalamus, the substantia nigra, and the primary motor cortex is received by the neostriatum (caudate nucleus, putamen).
- The paleostriatum (globus pallidus) sends information to the thalamus and then onto the primary motor cortex or to the brainstem structures involved in movement.

Causes and Treatment of Disorders of Movement

This chapter concludes with a brief discussion of the causes and treatment for five disorders. Amyotrophic lateral sclerosis, apraxia, Huntington's disease, myasthenia gravis, and Parkinson's disease are among the most prevalent and best understood disorders of movement. Three of these disorders were introduced in earlier chapters. Now that you understand the neurological basis of movement, you can more fully appreciate how damage to the motor system can lead to severe impairments of movement. We begin by looking at amyotrophic lateral sclerosis (ALS), or Lou Gehrig's disease. ■

Amyotrophic Lateral Sclerosis

The first time I had heard of amyotrophic lateral sclerosis was when I watched the Lou Gehrig story on television as a child. I remember being very moved by the devastating effect that this disease had on Lou Gehrig, the Iron Man. One of the greatest baseball players of all time, Lou Gehrig played in 2,130 consecutive games before becoming incapacitated by this terrible disease. Gehrig died in 1941 at the age of 37.

Amyotrophic lateral sclerosis is a degenerative neuromuscular disease. Approximately 6,000 persons in the United States will be diagnosed with ALS this year. This disease is caused by the degeneration of the corticospinal and corticobulbar tracts, and the anterior (ventral) horns of the spinal cord (Caroscio et al., 1987). Control of most voluntary muscles is affected by this disease. The initial symptoms are feelings of weakness in a limb or problems in speaking or swallowing. Over time, the extent and severity of symptoms intensifies. Amyotrophic lateral sclerosis is a terminal disease, with most patients dying within 3 to 5

amyotrophic lateral sclerosis A degenerative neuromuscular disease that impairs the control of most voluntary muscles and is caused by the degeneration of the corticospinal and corticobulbar tracts and the anterior horns of the spinal cord.

years after diagnosis. However, some patients die within a few months, whereas others live for many years.

At this time, the cause of ALS is unknown. Theories regarding the cause of ALS include exposure to toxins, slow viral infection, trauma, or immunological abnormalities (Tandan & Bradley, 1985). Although there are currently no known effective treatments for ALS, some researchers (McDonald et al., 1994) have found that the length of survival is related to psychological well-being. Patients who felt depressed or hopeless survived significantly less time than did patients who had a more positive outlook.

Apraxia

At the "19th hole," Rhea picks up a glass and takes a drink of soda from the glass. What if she could not perform this same task when asked by someone else to do so? In that case, she would be said to suffer from apraxia. The term **apraxia**, which literally means "no action," refers to missing or inappropriate actions that are not the result of paralysis or any other motor impairment. Persons with apraxia have problems organizing purposeful movements. They can sometimes spontaneously perform a movement, but they are then unable to do the same movement when requested to do it. A person might answer the phone spontaneously but be unable to pick up the phone in response to a verbal request, or a person might say hello to a friend but not be able to respond verbally when asked to say hello.

The history of this disorder dates back to 1866 when Hughlings-Jackson observed that some of his patients were unable to perform some voluntary movements even though there was no evidence of muscle weakness. A detailed investigation of apraxia was conducted by Liepmann early in this century. In 1920, Liepmann proposed that apraxia is caused by damage to the left cerebral hemisphere or to the corpus callosum. According to Liepmann's theory, the left frontal lobe plans voluntary movements that are executed by the left parietal lobe. Damage to the left frontal lobe would produce apraxia of the limbs on the right side of the body.

However, a person with apraxia can show impairment of movement on both sides of the body. Liepmann accounted for this result by proposing that the left parietal cortex controls motor behavior on the left or ipsilateral side of the body by sending a message to the left frontal cortex and then on to the right frontal cortex through the corpus callosum. In this way, apraxia could occur on both sides of the body.

Kolb and Whishaw (1996) identified several problems with Liepmann's model. There are several different motor systems, not all of which are located in the left frontal lobe; damage to each motor system produces a different subtype of apraxia. For example, damage to the right parietal lobe produces **constructional apraxia**, in which individuals have difficulty drawing pictures or assembling objects. However, they show no impairment of other skilled movements of their arms or hands; a person with constructional apraxia could pick up a cup when requested but could not draw a cup. Impairment in the voluntary use of a limb, **limb apraxia**, can be caused by damage to the left parietal lobe or the corpus callosum. Persons with **apraxia of speech** have great difficulty speaking clearly, but do not have a language impairment (aphasia). Their language is grammatically correct and only the production of speech is impaired. Apraxia of speech is generally thought to be due to damage limited to Broca's area of the left frontal lobe.

The second problem with Liepmann's model is that he ignored the role of subcortical areas in movement. As we learned earlier, the basal ganglia and thalamus are the major routes for conveying messages from the primary motor cortex to the muscles. Damage to both subcortical motor areas and cortical motor areas produces more severe impairments than does damage restricted to the cortical areas. Severe apraxia appears to involve the entire motor system, not only the left frontal lobe.

The goal of treatment of any type of apraxia is to restore volitional control of the muscles (Hodge, 1991). This treatment can be provided by a speech language pathologist for apraxia of speech and by a physical or occupational therapist for the other types of apraxia. Treatment involves the establishment of a planned sequence of movements. For example, a speech-language pathologist utilizes a series of exercises to produce a sequenced production of speech sounds in a person with apraxia of speech. As the apractic person learns simple sounds and words, more difficult sounds and words are attempted. Treatment can be long and arduous, but with much effort, most persons with apraxia can regain voluntary control of the affected movement.

apraxia A disorder of movement that is characterized by problems in performing purposeful movements.

constructional apraxia A difficulty drawing pictures or assembling objects.

limb apraxia A difficulty purposefully moving a limb caused by damage to the left parietal lobe or the corpus callosum.

apraxia of speech A great difficulty speaking clearly, without language impairment (aphasia), caused by damage limited to Broca's area of the left frontal lobe.

Before You Go On

What is the cause of Lou Gehrig's disease?

Differentiate between constructional apraxia and limb apraxia.

Huntington's Disease

As we discussed in Chapter 1, **Huntington's disease** is a genetic neurological disorder caused by a defect in a gene on the short arm of chromosome 4. This defect is characterized by 37 or more repetitions of the base sequence cytosine, adenine, and guanine; the greater the number of repetitions, the earlier the onset of symptoms. Individuals with Huntington's disease show a slow, progressive deterioration of motor control, cognition, and emotion (Young, 1995). George Huntington first observed the symptoms of this disorder when as a child he accompanied his physician father on rounds; two tall, thin women who were twisting and grimacing made a big enough impression on him that, when he later became a physician himself, Huntington chose to study this disorder. In 1872, at the age of 22, Huntington published the first complete description of this disorder.

The onset of Huntington's disease is usually between the ages of 30 and 50. The initial symptoms are a decline in activity and loss of interest in worldly activities (apathy). The individual soon starts showing involuntary movements of whole limbs or parts of a limb. At first, these involuntary movements are slight and inconsistent, but over time they become more pronounced and constant. Eventually, the involuntary movements involve the head, face, trunk, and limbs, and interfere with such voluntary movements as walking, writing, swallowing, and speech. Initially, voluntary movements are slow and clumsy; as the disease progresses, voluntary movements become impossible. Cognitive deficits produced by Huntington's disease include impaired storage and later retrieval of information, deficits in visuospatial problem solving, poor abstract reasoning, and diminished cognitive flexibility. Anxiety and depression are also common in individuals with Huntington's. There is a gradual reduction in the ability to carry out daily living activities; affected individuals experience difficulties in social communication and judgment and tend to withdraw from social activities.

Autopsy studies of persons with Huntington's disease show massive pathology (Roos, 1986). There is shrinkage and thinning of the cerebral cortex as well as substantial decreases in the number of small neurons of the caudate nucleus and putamen and the large neurons of the globus pallidus. The loss of neurons in the basal ganglia leads to gross atrophy of this structure (see **Figure 8.24**).

How does damage to the basal ganglia lead to the involuntary movements characteristic of Huntington's disease? The neurotransmitters in the basal ganglia are GABA and ACh (Kolb & Whishaw, 1996). These neurotransmitters normally act on the excitatory dopaminergic neurons in the nigrostriatal tract that extend from the substantia nigra to the basal ganglia to inhibit involuntary movement. However, the death of neurons in the basal ganglia causes a significant decrease in GABA and ACh levels, resulting in increased activity in the nigrostriatal dopaminergic pathway.

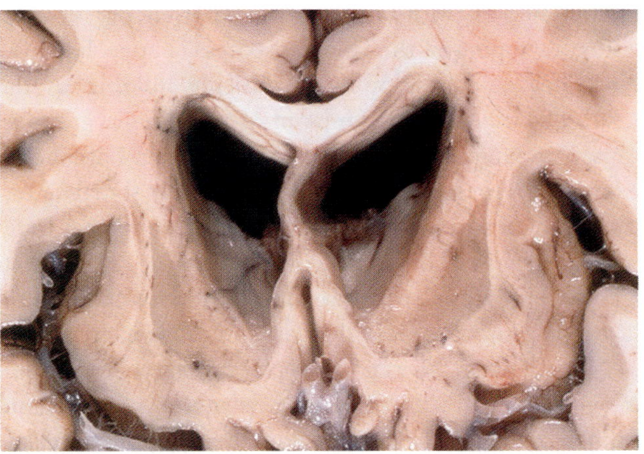

Figure 8.24 The neostriatum and Huntington's disease. The death of neurons in the caudate nucleus and putamen of a person with Huntington's disease leads to substantial enlargement of the lateral ventricles, which can be seen clearly in this coronal section of the brain.

➤ *Why does neuron death in the neostriatum (caudate nucleus and putamen) lead to enlargement of lateral ventricles? (p. 253)*

In support of this model, high levels of dopamine are found in the brain tissue of persons with Huntington's (Kolb & Whishaw, 1996). Large doses of the tranquilizer haloperidol (Haldol) and fluphenazine (Permitil, Prolixin), which inhibit dopaminergic neurons, are quite helpful in managing the motor impairments caused by Huntington's disease (Chusid, 1985). By contrast, drugs such as amphetamines that stimulate dopaminergic neurons aggravate the symptoms of Huntington's.

The symptoms of Huntington's disease worsen over a period of about 15 years (Chase, Wexler, & Barbeau, 1979). Eventually, death occurs as a result of loss of muscle control.

Myasthenia Gravis

Myasthenia gravis is a neuromuscular disorder in which, for some unknown reason, the immune system produces antibodies that destroy the cholinergic receptors at the neuromuscular junctions (Drachman, Adams, & Josifer, 1982). The first signs of the disease usually involve the

---

Huntington's disease A neurological disorder caused by a defect in a gene on the short arm of chromosome 4 that destroys neurons in the cerebral cortex and basal ganglia and is characterized by a slow, progressive deterioration of motor control, cognition, and emotion.

cranial nerves, with the patient experiencing double vision, drooping of the voice, weakness of speech, problems chewing or swallowing, or difficulty holding up the head, but the primary symptom of myasthenia gravis is muscular fatigue that occurs after muscles have been exercised. The muscle weakness may occur shortly after the muscle exercise begins or toward the end of a long muscle exercise. This disease differs from the fatigue that all of us experience when we exercise too much because it can develop early as well as late in muscle exercise.

Myasthenia gravis can develop at any age but its onset is typically in the thirties, and it is more often seen in women than men. In some persons, the symptoms are relatively mild, whereas in others, symptoms can be quite severe or even life threatening due to respiratory paralysis (Kolb & Whitshaw, 1996). Most or all of the muscles of the body can be affected. Myasthenia gravis is a rare disorder, affecting about 3 people per 100,000 each year in the United States. There is no actual muscle pathology associated with myasthenia gravis. Instead, because of the destruction of the cholinergic receptors, few messages come to the muscles from the cranial or the spinal nerves. Myasthenia gravis also involves a reduction in the responsiveness of the remaining cholinergic receptors (Albuquerque et al., 1976). The reason that the antibodies form or how they attack the receptor sites has not been established. Muscle weakness does not occur equally in all muscles; the reason for this is also unknown.

Treatment for myasthenia gravis employs two strategies (Kolb & Whishaw, 1996). First, patients are given drugs to suppress the immune system and the thymus is removed to reduce antibody production. Although this surgical procedure reduces the attack on cholinergic receptors, it leaves the patient more susceptible to illness. The second strategy is to administer drugs such as physostigmine (eserine) that block the action of acetylcholinesterase (AChE). We learned in Chapter 4 that AChE terminates cholinergic transmission by splitting acetylcholine into acetyl and choline. Drugs that block the breakdown of acetylcholine prolong the action of ACh at the postsynaptic membrane receptor sites. Symptoms of muscle weakness are reduced when cholinergic transmission is thus enhanced. The combination of immune system suppression and AChE therapy has proved to be an effective means of relieving the symptoms of myasthenia gravis, resulting in a lower mortality rate.

Parkinson's Disease

We introduced Parkinson's disease in Chapter 4. English physician James Parkinson described **Parkinson's disease** in an essay published in 1817, observing that affected individuals show "involuntary tremulous motion, with lessened motor power, in parts not in action and even when supported with a propensity to bend the trunks forward and to pass from a walking to a running pace, the senses and intellect being unimpaired." These tremors, the most visible symptom of Parkinson's disease, are intermittent and worsen when a limb is resting. One type of tremor that occurs is called pin-rolling; that is, movement as if a pin were being rolled between two fingers. These tremors involve the thumb, index finger, or wrist.

Another symptom of Parkinson's disease is increasing rigidity of the limbs caused by increased muscle tone. When the limbs are moved passively, there is considerable resistance to movement; continued attempts to move will lead to some movement and then returned resistance. The term *cogwheel rigidity* refers to the continuous stop-start movements characteristic of Parkinson's disease.

The posture and locomotion of the patient with Parkinson's disease is also impaired. When sitting, the head is dropped forward, and the body is usually stooped when standing (see **Figure 8.25**). People with this disease show a slowness of movement called **bradykinesia** and have great difficulty taking the first step from a stationary position. Once walking, footsteps are short. Balance is impaired, with a need for support to keep from falling, and changing direction is quite difficult. Movements like brushing one's hair, buttoning a coat, or even adjusting a tie take more and more effort. Difficulty in speech is also observed, with the voice becoming weak, low in volume, and monotonous.

Most patients do not show all of the above symptoms of Parkinson's disease, and there are individual differences in the symptoms of Parkinson's disease experienced. For example, one person experiences tremors as the predominate symptom, whereas rigidity and bradykinesia are the symptoms experienced by another person. In fact, 25 percent of persons with Parkinson's disease experience very slight tremor or none at all (Parkinson's Disease Foundation, 1998).

Parkinson's disease usually begins at around age 50 or 60. However, the disease can appear much earlier. The

---

myasthenia gravis A neuromuscular disorder in which the body produces antibodies that destroy the cholinergic receptors at the neuromuscular junctions; the major symptom is muscular fatigue that occurs after muscles have been exercised.

Parkinson's disease A degenerative neurological disorder characterized by difficulty integrating voluntary movement, rigidity of the limbs caused by increased muscle tone, and muscle tremors, due to degeneration of those dopamine-producing cells of the substantia nigra that synapse with the basal ganglia.

bradykinesia A movement disorder where a person shows a slowness of movement.

Figure 8.25 Stooped posture and Parkinson's disease. The stooped posture of a person with Parkinson's disease is vividly portrayed in this drawing by Paul Richter, who was a late 19th and early 20th century physician and artist.

➤ *Damage to what area of the brain results in the stooped posture of a person with Parkinson's disease? (p. 258)*

actor Michael J. Fox was diagnosed with Parkinson's disease when he was in his early thirties. The first sign of Parkinson's disease may be a tremor in one hand or some stiffness in the muscles of a leg. Over time, the rigidity and tremors worsen and movement becomes more and more impaired. The motor disturbances are due to degeneration of those dopamine-producing cells of the substantia nigra that synapse with the basal ganglia. This nigrostriatal dopaminergic system normally has an excitatory influence on the basal ganglia. Removal of this excitatory influence causes the bradykinesia described above. The rigidity and tremors are thought to be due to excessive activity in a neural loop that extends from the ventrolateral thalamus to the primary motor cortex and then back again.

Cognitive deficits are also observed in approximately 40 to 60 percent of Parkinson's disease patients (Alloy, Acocella, & Bootzin, 1996). These cognitive deficits include problems with learning, memory, attention, judgment, apathy, and social withdrawal.

There are a variety of causes of Parkinson's disease (Chusid, 1985). An attack of encephalitis can lead to Parkinson's disease. Other causes include cerebral arteriosclerosis, carbon monoxide or manganese poisoning, trauma to the head, neurosyphilis, or a cerebrovascular accident.

Exposure to toxic substances can also be a cause of Parkinson's disease (Jenner, 1990). An important environmental toxicology study observed several young adults who had used heroin contaminated with two chemicals: MPPP and MPTP (Ballard, Tetrud, & Langston, 1985). The consequences were severe: all of the young people developed permanent symptoms of Parkinson's disease.

Why did exposure to MPPP and MPTP produce symptoms of Parkinson's disease? The answer lies in the fact that MPTP is converted to MPP^+, a chemical that is selectively toxic to dopaminergic neurons in the substantia nigra (Snyder & D'Amato, 1986). Subsequent studies have reported the development of symptoms of Parkinson's disease following administration of MPTP to monkeys.

The dangers of exposure to MPTP are not limited to adults ingesting contaminated heroin. Many pesticides, such as paraquat, contain chemicals similar to MPTP. Epidemiological studies have found significantly greater rates of Parkinson's disease in regions where paraquat was used as a pesticide (Snyder & D'Amato, 1986).

As was mentioned earlier, the actor Michael J. Fox was diagnosed with Parkinson's disease when he was in his early thirties. What treatment did Michael J. Fox receive? He has been taking Sinemet, which is a combination of levodopa (dihydroxyphenylalanine) or L-dopa and carbidopa. **Levodopa**, or **L-dopa**, is used in the treatment of Parkinson's disease because it is a precursor of dopamine that can be converted by dopaminergic neurons into dopamine, increasing the dopamine levels depleted by the disease. However, if L-dopa was administered by itself, it would not reach the brain (Standaert & Young, 1996). Most of the L-dopa would be destroyed by enzymes in the intestine and plasma. The remaining L-dopa would be converted to dopamine in the peripheral nervous system, which would lead to nausea. How to get L-dopa into the brain to be converted to dopamine has been solved by combining L-dopa with carbidopa. **Carbidopa** prevents the conversion of L-dopa in the PNS, but not in the CNS. The use of L-dopa has proved to be highly effective in decreasing rigidity and improving movement, but it is less effective in reducing the tremors (Julien, 1998). Side

levodopa (L-dopa) Precursor of dopamine that is converted by dopaminergic neurons into dopamine.

carbidopa Drug that prevents the destruction of L-dopa by enzymes in the intestine and plasma and conversion of L-dopa in the PNS.

effects from the use of L-dopa include nausea and vomiting, hypotension, and cardiac dysrhythmia.

The success of L-dopa treatment of Parkinson's disease declines during the later stages of the disease as dopaminergic neurons in the substantia nigra continue to degenerate (Kolb & Whishaw, 1996). The dose of L-dopa can be increased, but this approach has risks, such as the occurrence of schizophrenic symptoms. The drugs bromocriptine mesylate (Pavlodel) and pergolide (Permax) can be substituted for L-dopa when tolerance to L-dopa develops. Both drugs are dopaminergic agonists that directly stimulate striatal dopaminergic receptors. Unfortunately, both drugs also appear to be less effective than L-dopa and have more adverse side effects (Hughes, 1997).

Michael J. Fox noticed that his symptoms, especially the tremors, increased over the 7 years since he was diagnosed with Parkinson's disease, despite his taking Sinemet. What can be done for people like Michael J. Fox who find drug treatment becoming less effective? The answer for Michael J. Fox was a psychosurgery procedure called a **thalamotomy**. Hassler and Riechert introduced thalamotomy as a surgical treatment for Parkinson's disease in 1954. In a thalamotomy treatment, the ventrolateral thalamus is lesioned. This procedure was found effective in relieving tremors and improving rigidity, but not to change the bradykinesia (Hassler & Riechert, 1954).

The thalamotomy was a common surgical intervention for Parkinson's disease in the 1950s and 1960s. Another psychosurgery was a **pallidotomy**. This procedure was introduced by Meyers in the late 1930s (Meyers, 1942). The pallidotomy treatment, like the thalamotomy, was found to reduce tremors and rigidity, but also reduced bradykinesia or the slowness of movement (Svennilson, Torvik, Lowe, & Leksell, 1960). In a pallidotomy, selected areas of the globus pallidus are lesioned. The initial sites targeted were the anterodorsal part of the globus pallidus, but later studies (Svennilson, 1960) showed that lesions of the posterior and ventral globus pallidus were most effective.

The use of these two psychosurgical procedures—thalamotomy and pallidotomy—was all but abandoned in the late 1960s by the introduction of drug treatments for Parkinson's disease (Cosgrove & Eskander, 1998). However, as the limitations of L-dopa and other dopaminergic agonists became apparent, psychosurgery has reemerged as a viable treatment for Parkinson's disease. There is considerable evidence of the effectiveness of both thalamotomy (Burchiel, 1995; Goldman & Kelly, 1992; Tasker & Kiss, 1995) and pallidotomy (Baron et al., 1996; Iacono et al., 1995; Johansson et al., 1997) as a treatment for patients with Parkinson's disease. Both of these psychosurgical procedures involve risk—speech difficulties and concentration problems being the most likely risks—and are recommended only as the effectiveness of drug treatments diminish. At this time, thalamotomy is the psychosurgery of choice when the predominant complaint is tremor, with the pallidotomy being recommended for other patients with Parkinson's disease (Cosgrove & Eskandler, 1998).

Unfortunately, psychosurgery does not cure Parkinson's disease. Cosgrove and Eskander (1998) described the psychosurgical treatments for Parkinson's disease as "turning the clock back four or five years." Is there any hope for a cure of Parkinson's disease? Although certainly controversial, transplantation of fetal tissue, implanted in the caudate nucleus–putamen area of the brain, offers promise of such a cure (see **Figure 8.26**). Preliminary results have been encouraging, with an observed growth of dopaminergic neurons and enhanced synaptic connections, as well as an improvement in motor function (Deacon et al., 1997; Kordower et al., 1996). However, these results are only preliminary and further research is needed to demonstrate that this is a viable treatment of Parkinson's disease.

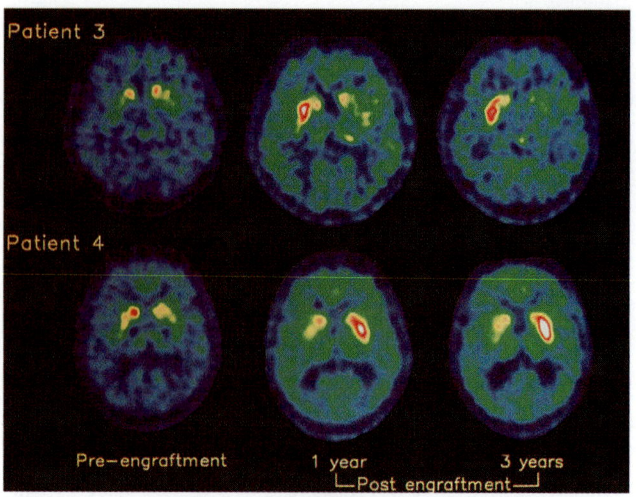

Figure 8.26 Fetal tissue implants and Parkinson's disease. The increased activity in the basal ganglia of two persons with Parkinson's disease after an injection of human fetal cells can be seen in the PET scans taken one and three years after treatment.
➤ *What is the implication of the increased activity in the basal ganglia of a person with Parkinson's disease following fetal tissue implantation? (p. 260)*

thalamotomy Psychosurgery treatment for Parkinson's disease that lesions the ventrolateral thalamus and relieves tremors and improves rigidity, but not bradykinesia.

pallidotomy Psychosurgery treatment for Parkinson's disease that lesions the posterior and ventral globus pallidus and reduces tremors, rigidity, and bradykinesia.

Now that you understand how the brain controls movement, it is time to move on (no pun intended!) to learn how the brain controls two other, related behaviors, wakefulness and sleep. So get another cup of coffee, and read on!

Before You Go On

Contrast the effects on the nigrostriatal pathway of Huntington's disease and Parkinson's disease.

Speculate on why the immune system might destroy the cholinergic receptors to produce myasthenia gravis.

Section Review

- In amyotrophic lateral sclerosis, a neuromuscular disease caused by degeneration of the corticospinal and corticobulbar tracts and anterior horns of the spinal cord, control of most voluntary movement is lost, with the extent and severity of disease intensifying over time.
- A person with apraxia, a neurological disorder producing impairments in purposeful movements, may spontaneously perform a movement, but not be able to do the same movement when requested.
- Limb apraxia is the impairment in voluntary movement of a limb and is caused by damage to the left parietal lobe or corpus callosum.
- Persons with constructional apraxia, caused by damage to the right parietal lobe, have difficulty drawing pictures or assembling objects.
- Apraxia of speech involves difficulty speaking clearly, and is caused by damage limited to Broca's area.
- In Huntington's disease, a degenerative neuromuscular disorder linked to a gene on the short arm of chromosome 4, atrophy of the cerebral cortex and basal ganglia causes an inability to control voluntary movements.
- The death of inhibitory GABA and ACh neurons in the basal ganglia caused by Huntington's disease increases activity in the nigrostriatal dopaminergic pathways.
- The primary symptom of myasthenia gravis, a neuromuscular disorder in which the immune system destroys the cholinergic receptors at the neuromuscular junction, is muscular fatigue that occurs after the muscles are exercised, either early or late in exercise.
- Treatment for myasthenia gravis involves removal of the thymus and administration of drugs that block the action of acetylcholinesterase.
- Symptoms of Parkinson's disease include muscle rigidity, tremors that worsen when a limb is resting, impairment in posture, and slowness of movement.
- The motor impairments characteristic of Parkinson's are caused by degeneration of those dopaminergic cells of the substantia nigra that synapse with the basal ganglia, whereas damage to the neural circuit between the ventral thalamus and the motor cortex causes the rigidity and tremors.
- Treatments for Parkinson's disease include the drugs levodopa (L-dopa), which is converted by dopaminergic neurons into dopamine, and carbidopa, which prevents the destruction of L-dopa by enzymes in the intestine and plasma and the conversion of L-dopa in the PNS; thalamotomy, a lesioning of the ventrolateral thalamus that relieves tremors and improves rigidity, but not bradykinesia; pallidotomy, a lesioning of the posterior and ventral globus pallidus that reduces tremors, rigidity, and bradykinesia; and fetal tissue implantation, which reestablishes neural connections in the basal ganglia.

Chapter Review

Critical Thinking Questions

1. Sonja is about to run the most important race of her life. She moves up to the starting block, her left foot almost touching the line, and her right knee bent so that her right foot rests on the block. As she kneels and waits to run, Sonja can feel her muscles tense. When the gun goes off, Sonja lurches forward and starts down the track. Discuss the neural process that allows Sonja to be ready to run this race. What neural mechanism is responsible for the initiation of Sonja's movements down the track?
2. John has tried to learn to play the piano but even with many lessons, he does not play very well. Sybil plays the piano well, but has not been able to master tennis. John is quite envious of the quality of Sybil's piano playing, but glad that he is a much better tennis player than Sybil. What neural systems control movements such as playing the piano and playing tennis? Why do John and Sybil differ in their ability to play the piano and to play tennis?
3. Dennis has difficulty moving his arms, and walking has become quite a chore. Theresa experiences involuntary movements of her arms, and severe muscle contractions. What neurological disorders are likely causing Dennis's and Theresa's symptoms? Explain the neurological deficits responsible for their motor impairments.

Vocabulary Questions

1. Movement is executed by the ________________ neurons of the peripheral nervous system.
2. The three types of muscle are ________________, ________________, and ________________.
3. The contraction of ________________ muscles allows Sam to operate the NordicTrack.
4. The muscle fiber controlled by an alpha motor neuron is called an ________________.
5. The ________________ is the part of the extrafusal muscle fiber where the muscle fiber synapses with the motor neuron.
6. A motor neuron and all the muscle fibers that it controls are known as a ________________.
7. The ________________ muscles produce the fastest contractions, the ________________ muscles produce the slowest contractions, and the ________________ muscles produce contractions that fall in between.
8. The muscle spindle contains muscle fibers known as ________________.
9. A reflex involving two or more synapses is called a ________________.
10. The ________________ measure the total amount of force exerted by the muscle on the bone to which a tendon is attached.
11. Each alpha motor neuron has a collateral branch that turns back within the spinal cord to synapse with its ________________, which prevents muscle fatigue.
12. The resting tension of skeletal muscle is called ________________.
13. The sensory receptors in the muscles and joints send information about the physical environment to the ________________ cortex.
14. The two areas of the secondary motor cortex are the ________________________ and the ________________________.
15. The two major motor pathways originating in the subcortex are the ________________ and the ________________.
16. The basal ganglia is composed of three subcortical structures: ________________, ________________, and ________________.
17. The degeneration of the corticospinal and corticobulbar tracts and the anterior horns of the spinal cord causes a disease called ________________, or Lou Gehrig's disease.
18. Apraxia, once thought to be caused by damage to the left frontal lobe, is now thought to be caused by damage to the ________________.
19. In ________________ the immune system produces antibodies that destroy the cholinergic receptors at neuromuscular junctions.

Review Questions

1. Movement can be controlled at the
   a. spinal cord, brainstem, or cerebral cortex.
   b. spinal cord, muscles, or bones.
   c. brainstem, muscles, or cerebral cortex.
   d. brainstem, spinal cord, or bones.
2. The contraction of a ________________ muscle produces extension; the contraction of a ________________ muscle produces flexion.
   a. skeletal, cardiac
   b. skeletal, smooth
   c. extensor, flexor
   d. flexor, extensor
3. The two proteins that make up muscle fibers are
   a. myofibril and myofilament.
   b. actin and myosin.
   c. actin and micron.
   d. myosin and ribonucleic acid.
4. The alpha motor neuron and the extrafusal muscle fiber synapse at the
   a. neurotransmitter receptor site.
   b. myofibril.
   c. neuromuscular junction.
   d. motor end plate.
5. When an action potential occurs in a motor neuron, the influx of calcium ions causes the ________________ to form cross bridges with the ________________.
   a. myosin heads, actin filaments
   b. actin filaments, myosin heads
   c. myofibrils, sarcomeres
   d. myofilaments, flexors
6. The shortening of a muscle during muscle contraction is caused by the pivoting of the ________________, causing the entire ________________ to shorten.
   a. actin filaments, myofibril
   b. myosin heads, flexor
   c. myosin heads, sarcomere
   d. actin filaments, sarcomere
7. The reflex experienced when a doctor taps your knee with a rubber hammer is called the
   a. patellar tendon reflex.
   b. polysynaptic stretch reflex.
   c. muscle spindle reflex.
   d. fast-twitch reflex.

8. The sensory nerve endings surrounding the central part of the intrafusal muscle fiber are called
   a. extrafusal muscle fibers.
   b. intrafusal endings.
   c. Ia fibers.
   d. annulospiral endings.
9. Continuous muscle tension is due to the operation of the
   a. Renshaw cells.
   b. Parkinje cells.
   c. Golgi tendon organs.
   d. gamma motor system.
10. The part of the brain that initiates movement is the
    a. primary motor cortex.
    b. cerebellum.
    c. pons.
    d. medulla.
11. The ______________ and the ______________ are overrepresented in the homunculus of the primary motor cortex.
    a. hands, feet
    b. hands, face
    c. chest, face
    d. chest, feet
12. The visual system and other sensory systems send information to the
    a. somatosensory cortex.
    b. secondary motor cortex.
    c. posterior parietal cortex.
    d. primary motor cortex.
13. The two major motor circuits originating in the primary motor cortex are the
    a. corticospinal tract and the corticobulbar tract.
    b. corticospinal tract and the cerebellar tract.
    c. neurospinal tract and the corticobulbar tract.
    d. Washington, D.C. "Loop" and the Los Angeles freeway.
14. Ballistic movements are governed by the
    a. primary motor cortex.
    b. secondary motor cortex.
    c. Senate.
    d. cerebellum.
15. The ______________ of the cerebellum produce continuous movement in a specific muscle and prevents movement in an opposing muscle.
    a. mossy fibers
    b. climbing fibers
    c. Purkinje cells
    d. basket cells
16. Difficulty performing voluntary movement that is not the result of paralysis is a manifestation of
    a. apraxia.
    b. Lou Gehrig's disease.
    c. Parkinson's disease.
    d. Huntington's disease.
17. Damage to the right parietal lobe produces ______________, in which individuals have difficulty drawing pictures or assembling objects.
    a. limb apraxia
    b. constructional apraxia
    c. amyotrophic lateral sclerosis
    d. Huntington's disease
18. The motor disturbances of ______________ are due to decreased production of dopamine; those of ______________ are due to increased dopamine levels.
    a. Parkinson's disease, Huntington's disease
    b. Huntington's disease, Parkinson's disease
    c. myasthenia gravis, Huntington's disease
    d. Parkinson's disease, amyotrophic lateral sclerosis

Suggested Readings

CHUSID, J. G. (1985). *Correlative neuroanatomy and functional neurology* (19th ed.). Los Alto, CA: Lange Medical Publications.

KANDEL, E. R., SCHWARTZ, J. H., & JESSELL, T. M. (2000). *Principles of neural science* (4th ed.). New York: McGraw-Hill.

KOLB, B., & WHISHAW, I. Q. (1996). *Fundamentals of human neuropsychology* (4th ed.). New York: W. H. Freeman.

ROTHWELL, J. (1994). *Control of human voluntary movement* (2nd ed.). London: Chapman and Hall.

SCHNEIDER, J. S., & LIDSKY, T. I. (1987). *Basal ganglia and behavior: Sensory aspects and motor functioning*. Bern: Hans Huber.

9 Wakefulness and Sleep

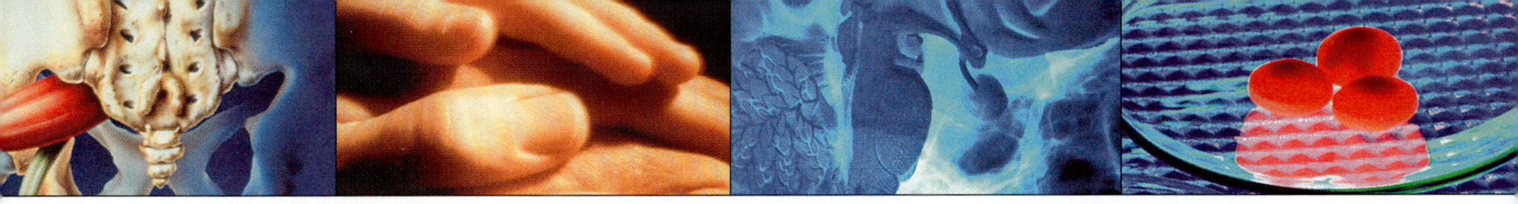

A Trying Trip

Sheila had been excited for weeks about her trip to Paris, her first outside the continental United States. Most of the travel in her job, selling computer systems to small companies, involved the New England area. Although she was only going for a few days, Sheila was determined to see as much of Paris as she could. She scheduled her flight from Boston on Friday evening so that she could spend the weekend sightseeing before her Monday and Tuesday meetings. She planned to leave Paris by Wednesday afternoon.

Sheila's flight left Boston at 8 P.M., and it lasted 7 hours. She had hoped to be able to get some sleep, but she was too excited and the flight was extremely crowded and noisy. When she arrived in Paris, at 3 A.M. Boston time, the clock in the baggage claim area showed 9 A.M. Getting through customs and finding a cab seemed to take forever, but Sheila's excitement grew as her cab neared the city. After getting settled in her room in a small hotel near the Champs Elysées, Sheila set off to see the sights, tired but determined.

The coffee she had with lunch at a sidewalk café helped ease her fatigue and perked her up for her walk down the Champs Elysées to the Louvre. She spent several exhilarating hours in this wonderful art museum and found each world-famous work of art more breathtaking "in person" than she had ever dreamed. She arrived back at the hotel around 4 P.M., exhausted, and decided to take a short nap before dinner.

Although she had planned to sleep only for an hour, when she awakened, she noticed that it was dark outside; her newly reset watch read 2 A.M. Sheila still felt tired and attempted to go back to sleep, but her efforts failed. She tried to read her travel guide, but found herself reading the same sentence over and over again. As she lay in bed, her head spinning, Sheila hoped that she would adjust to the time difference by the time her meetings rolled around. ■

◀ Broad-spectrum light from the sun resets our biological clock everyday.

Before You Begin

Why was Sheila unable to go back to sleep yet able to function well enough to find out where the Louvre was located?

What caused the disruption of her sleep schedule?

In this chapter, we will help you answer these and the following questions:

- What are the physiological changes that regulate our sleeping and waking?
- What is jet lag, and why does it occur?
- How did that cup of coffee help Sheila to get through the afternoon?
- How do people eventually adjust to new time zones?
- What purpose does sleep serve?
- What are dreams, and when do they happen?
- Why do we dream?
- Does everyone dream?
- We all know that there is such a thing as too little sleep; is there such a thing as too much sleep?

Biological Rhythms

We all have biological rhythms that cause us to sleep and awaken at certain times; the disruption of these rhythms that is experienced when a person travels across several time zones is called jet lag. In her flight from Boston to Paris, Sheila crossed several time zones, so the local time did not match her biological clock. Sheila will probably need several days to adjust to the new time; unfortunately, this adjustment will probably occur just when she is scheduled to return home. In the next section, we will discuss the biological patterns of wakefulness and sleep and how adjustments to them will enable Sheila to function in her new time zone.

Humans and nonhuman animals experience regular fluctuations in the timing of bodily processes. Some of these fluctuations occur over several minutes, whereas others occur over hours or days. For example, there is a 90-minute cycle of activity and drowsiness in humans (Coleman, 1986). Another example is the 28-day menstrual cycle seen in human females and a similar, but less obvious, cycle of sex hormone secretions in human males (Parlee, 1982). Cycles can even be as long as one year. In some extreme cases people experience significant mood changes based on the seasons during the course of the year (Nelson, Badura, & Goldman, 1990). Assuming they live in the northern hemisphere, these individuals feel good in the summer and depressed in the winter (the opposite is true for persons living in the southern hemisphere). This pattern of mood changes, called seasonal affective disorder (SAD), will be discussed later in the chapter.

The 90-minute, 28-day, or yearly cycles generally have only a modest effect on behavior. By contrast, daily or 24-hour cycles have a profound influence on human endeavors. The fluctuations in biological processes that occur during a 24-hour period are governed by circadian rhythms, the subject of the next section.

The Circadian Cycle

A **circadian cycle** is a change in biological and behavioral functioning that occurs over a 24-hour period (circa = about, dies = day). For example, we experience different levels of activity (or movement in the environment) throughout the day, with activity levels typically increasing until midday and then declining until sleep. Our level of alertness (or attention to stimuli in the environment) also fluctuates (see **Figure 9.1a**). When we are awake, we are sometimes very alert and at other times we are less attentive to our environment. Alertness (or attentiveness) levels usually increase and then decrease during the course of a day. An endogenous (or intrinsic) rhythm, or **circadian rhythm**, controls the biological and behavioral changes that occur during a circadian cycle.

Some people are active and alert in the morning and become drowsy and inattentive in the evening. Akerstedt and Froberg (1976) referred to individuals with this activity and alertness pattern as **larks**. By contrast, **owls** are drowsy and inattentive in the morning, and active and alert in the evening. About 10 percent of the population are extreme larks and another 10 percent extreme owls. The rest of us unnamed birds fall somewhat in the middle, functioning best during the middle of the day. Research has shown that these patterns of alertness correspond with changes in levels of epinephrine (Akerstedt & Froberg, 1976). Larks have been shown to have peak epinephrine levels in the morning, whereas levels in owls are highest in the evening. For the rest of us, levels peak in the middle of the day.

Does being a lark or owl affect one's behavior? It apparently does. A study by Guthrie, Ash, and Bendapudi (1995) reported that larks did better (obtained higher grades) on examinations taken in morning courses than evening

---

circadian cycle A change in biological and behavioral functioning that occurs over a 24-hour period.

circadian rhythm The intrinsic process that controls the 24-hour cycle.

lark Individual who is active and alert in the morning and becomes drowsy and inattentive in the evening.

owl Individual who is drowsy and inattentive in the morning and active and alert in the evening.

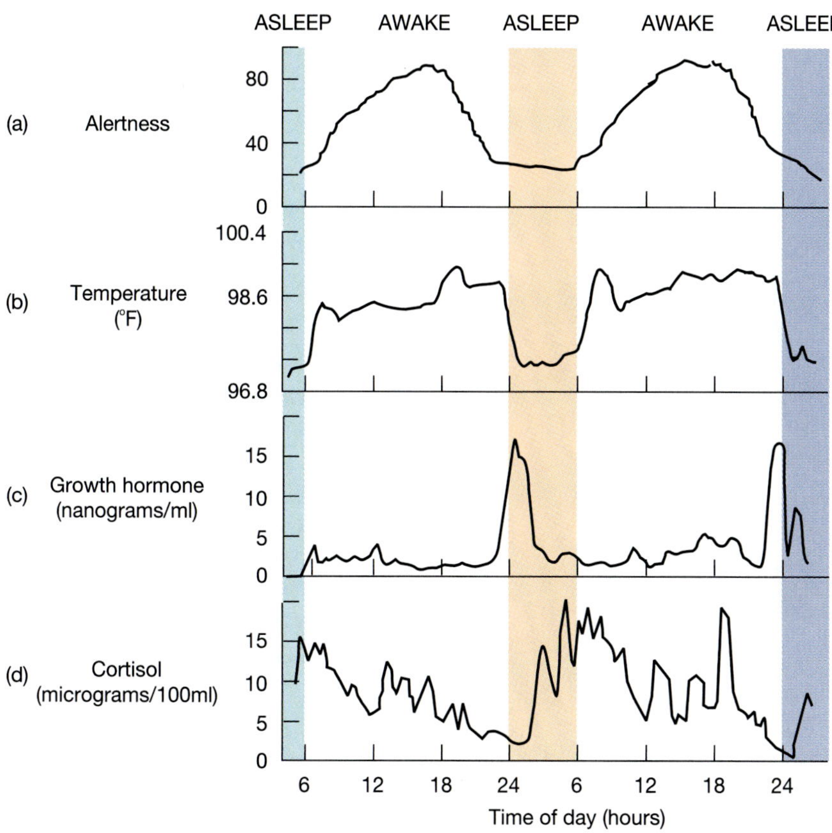

Figure 9.1 Illustration of changes in alertness, body temperature, growth hormone secretion, and cortisol secretion in humans during two successive 24 hour periods. Alertness and body temperature are highest during the day and lowest at night. By contrast, the secretion of growth hormones and cortisol is lowest during the day and highest at night. ➤ *What is the difference between a lark and an owl (the human kind, not the birds!)? (p. 266–267).*

courses. By contrast, students classified as owls did better on examinations in evening courses than morning courses. Curious whether you are a lark or an owl? See **Table 9.1**.

Table 9.1 ■ Are You a Lark or an Owl?

Respond to each of the following items by circling either "Day" or "Night."

1.	I feel most alert during the	Day	Night
2.	I have most energy during the	Day	Night
3.	I prefer to take classes during the	Day	Night
4.	I prefer to study during the	Day	Night
5.	I get my best ideas during the	Day	Night
6.	When I graduate, I would prefer to find a job during the	Day	Night
7.	I am most productive during the	Day	Night
8.	I feel most intelligent during the	Day	Night
9.	I enjoy leisure-time activities most during the	Day	Night
10.	I prefer to work during the	Day	Night

Note: If you answer "Day" to eight or more of these questions, you are probably a lark. If you answer "Night" to eight or more, you are probably an owl.

From Wallace, B. (1993). Day persons, night persons, and variability in hypnotic susceptibility. *Journal of Personality and Social Psychology*, *64*, 827–833.

Body temperature also changes over a 24-hour period. For most people, body temperature is lowest during the early hours of the morning and highest in the late afternoon or early evening (see **Figure 9.1b**; Aschoff & Wever, 1976). Not surprisingly, larks have higher body temperatures in the morning, and owls in the evening (Luce, 1971).

Hormone levels also change over the course of a day. As you can see in **Figure 9.1c**, growth hormone secretion is highest in the middle of the night. The level of cortisol, secreted by the adrenal gland, and melatonin, a hormone secreted by the pineal gland, also is highest at night (see **Figure 9.1d** for cortisol changes over a two-day period).

Role of the Suprachiasmatic Nucleus

In 1967, Curt Richter reported that large medial hypothalamic lesions in rats disrupted activity-related changes in the circadian cycle. Two research teams, Moore and Eichler (1972) and Stephan and Zucker (1972) identified the **suprachiasmatic nucleus (SCN),**

suprachiasmatic nucleus (SCN) An area located above the optic chiasm in the medial hypothalamus that is responsible for the circadian control of circadian cycle.

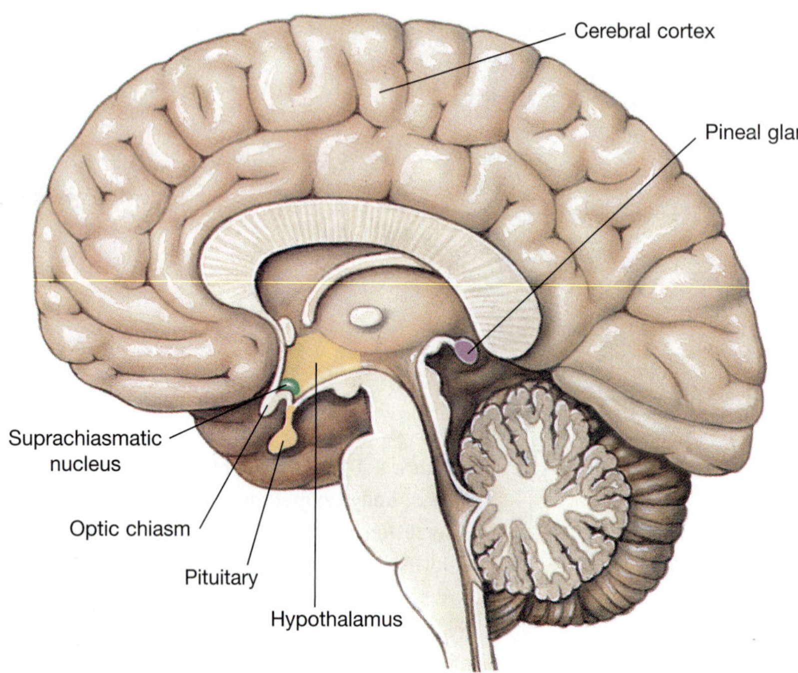

Figure 9.2 A sagittal plane view of the suprachiasmatic nucleus (SCN) and the pineal gland in the human. Suprachiasmatic nucleus controls the circadian cycle, while the pineal gland secretes the hormone melatonin, which reduces activity and produces fatigue. Adapted from Kalat, 1998.

➤ *What is the significance of the location of the SCN in the brain? (p. 267–269)*

located above the optic chiasm in the medial hypothalamus, as the area responsible for the circadian cycle (see **Figure 9.2** for a look at the SCN in humans). These researchers reported that SCN lesions eliminated activity changes over a 24-hour cycle. Damage to the SCN also affected hormone-release cycles and sleep-wake cycles.

diurnal animals Animals that are awake during the day and sleep at night.

nocturnal animals Animals that sleep during the day and are awake at night.

In 1982, Moore reported that neurons in the SCN of rats show circadian cycles of electrical, metabolic, and biochemical activity. Activity in the SCN was significantly greater during the day than at night. To observe activity in the SCN, Schwartz and Gainer (1977) administered radioactive 2-deoxyglucose (2-DG); they found that the SCN absorbs more 2-DG during the day than at night (see **Figure 9.3**). Curiously, this finding has been observed for both nocturnal and diurnal animals. Except for the real owls among us and some shift workers, humans are **diurnal animals**; we are awake during the day and sleep at night. Rats are **nocturnal animals**; that is, they sleep during the day and are awake at night.

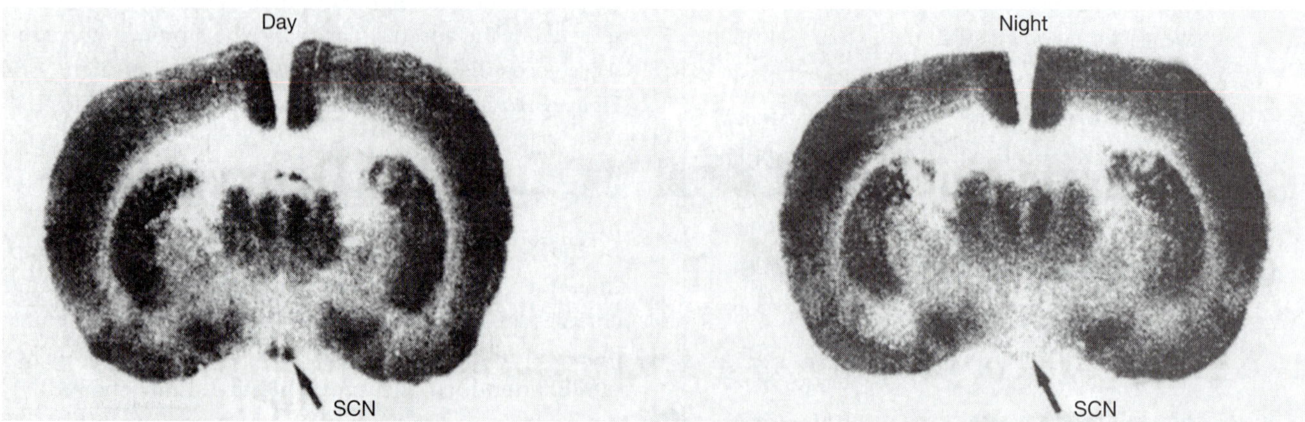

Figure 9.3 Autoradiographic records of the uptake of radioactive 2-deoxyglucose (2-DG) by the SCN of a rat during the day and the night. The pattern of absorption of 2-DG indicates greater SCN activity during the day than at night.

➤ *Does the SCN control circadian activity directly? (p. 269)*

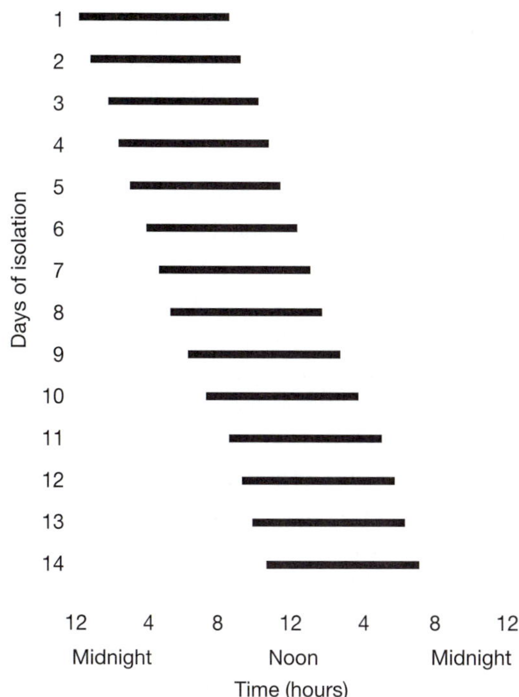

Figure 9.4 Sleep-wake cycle in the absence of external time cues. Most subjects went to sleep 1 hour later each day, producing the 25-hour circadian cycle.

➤ *Why do we usually maintain a 24-hour cycle? (p. 267–268)*

Wouldn't you think that SCN activity in nocturnal animals would be highest at night, when the animals are most active? The observation that SCN activity is highest during the day and lowest at night for both nocturnal and diurnal animals suggests that the SCN keeps track of day and night but does not directly control activity. Instead, the monitoring of day and night by the SCN affects the functioning of other neural structures; those structures in turn produce changes in observed activity levels. In other words, the SCN is responsible for establishing the length of the circadian cycle, but other structures are responsible for the activities during that cycle.

Is SCN activity independent on the activity of other brain structures? Researchers have found that lesions that isolate the SCN from other CNS structures did not affect cyclical changes in SCN activity (Groos & Hendricks, 1982; Inouye & Kawamura, 1979), but did cause the 24-hour cycle to increase to a 25-hour cycle. (The reason for this change from a 24-hour to a 25-hour cycle will be apparent shortly.) Other studies provide more evidence of autonomous SCN activity levels. In another study, Ralph, Foster, Davis, and Menaker (1990) found that transplanting the SCN from a strain of mice that shows a 20-hour cycle into mice with a 24-hour cycle produced a 20-hour cycle in the 24-hour mice. The opposite was observed when the SCN from mice with a 24-hour cycle was transplanted into mice with a 20-hour cycle; the 20-hour mice showed a 24-hour circadian cycle. These results suggest that the SCN is genetically programmed to have a specific circadian rhythm and that the particular rhythm is unaffected by other structures.

How does the SCN control the circadian cycle in other brain structures? The SCN in a rat contains approximately ten thousand small neurons packed closely together (Meijer & Rietveld, 1989). These neurons, which contain a large amount of rough endoplasmic reticulum (a network of channels involved in intracellular transport) are clustered around capillaries (Moore, Card, & Riley, 1980). The SCN releases hormones into the capillaries, and then these hormones are transported throughout the body by the circulatory system. The SCN also projects to other areas of the hypothalamus, the brainstem, the pineal gland, and the pituitary gland, which are the areas of the brain that produce the biological and behavioral changes that occur during the circadian cycle (Moore-Ede, Sulzman, & Fuller, 1982).

A 25-Hour Day?

What would happen if you lived in a cave? In such an environment, you would not experience the change from the darkness of night to the light of day. How would you know when to go to sleep and when to wake up? Moore-Ede, Sulzman, and Fuller (1982) studied a group of people who volunteered to live in an environment without any external time cues—no windows, no clocks, no radios, no televisions—and only artificial light to see. Living in this environment caused most of the individuals in this study to shift from a 24-hour day to a 25-hour day during the first days or weeks of the study. They would wake up and go to sleep an hour later each day (refer to **Figure 9.4**). Other bodily functions, such as activity and temperature, also shifted to the 25-hour cycle. After several days or weeks, the cycle may increase to as much as 36 hours. The 25-hour (or more) sleep-wake cycle that occurs in the absence of natural light is referred to as a **free-running rhythm**.

Why did the circadian cycle of the cave dwellers become 25 (or more) hours? How is the 24-hour cycle maintained for those of us who do not choose to live in caves? Many conditions in nature, such as the position of the sun and the outdoor temperature, operate according to a 24-hour cycle. These 24-hour conditions, called **zeitgebers** (pronounced tsite-gay-burs), which in German means "time giver," reset an animal's biological clock

---

free-running rhythm A 25-hour (or more) sleep-wake cycle that occurs in the absence of external time cues.

zeitgebers The external time cues that reset an animal's biological clock every 24 hours.

every 24 hours. Although many zeitgebers exist in nature, studies have suggested that intense broad-spectrum light is the critical stimulus that resets our circadian rhythm.

As we learned in Chapter 6, light is detected by the photoreceptors in the eye, where it is transduced into a neural impulse. The vertebrate eye actually contains two classes of photoreceptors (Foster, 1992). One class of photoreceptor, which was discussed in Chapter 6 and is called a **visual photoreceptor**, codes features of a light stimulus that are later detected by the primary visual cortex and analyzed by the secondary visual cortex. The other class of photoreceptor, called a **nonvisual photoreceptor**, detects the daily dawn-dusk cycle. Several lines of evidence support the view that there are two types of photoreceptors, visual and nonvisual. Argamaso, Boggs, and Foster (1992) reported that in the C3Hf strain of mice, all visual rods and cones develop normally until the end of the first postnatal week. After this time, these visual rods and cones degenerate and the mice become blind. However, this strain of mice, although blind, shows circadian cycles identical to other strains of mice. Further, Martens, Klein, Rizzo, Shanahan, and Czeisler (1992) reported that although the majority of totally blind humans fail to show 24-hour cycles, some blind persons show normal circadian cycles to a 24-hour light-dark cycle.

Where is the information detected by the nonvisual photoreceptors sent? As we learned in Chapter 6, most information detected by the visual photoreceptors is transmitted by the optic nerve to the lateral geniculate nucleus and on to the primary visual cortex. The visual stimulation is processed, and objects in our environment are identified. The nonvisual photoreceptors send information to the suprachiasmatic nucleus via the **retinohypothalamic tract**. Neural messages about the light-dark cycle are detected by the nonvisual photoreceptors and act to reset the biological clock. Several lines of evidence support the view that information from the nonvisual photoreceptors resets the SCN. Damage to the connections from the retina to the SCN produces a 25-hour biological cycle (Moore & Eichler, 1972). Electrical stimulation of the SCN has an effect similar to the action of pulses of light (Rusak & Groos, 1982). Injections of glutamic acid also mimic the effect of light stimuli (Meijer, van der Zee, & Dietz, 1988), suggesting that light activates SCN cells by releasing the neurotransmitter glutamate.

Exposure to intense broad-spectrum light does more than just reset the body's biological clock. The SCN influences the secretion of the hormone **melatonin** from the pineal gland (see **Figure 9.2**). Activity in the SCN, caused by exposure to light, inhibits melatonin release, whereas a lack of SCN activity, ordinarily experienced under dim lighting conditions, results in increased melatonin release. Melatonin has a sedative effect (Moore & Card, 1985); high levels of melatonin reduce activity and produce fatigue.

During the winter months in the northern hemisphere, fewer hours of daylight occur than during the other seasons. This reduced exposure to light produces **seasonal affective disorder (SAD)** in some individuals. Affected individuals have elevated levels of melatonin (Rosenthal et al., 1985) and feel tired no matter how much sleep they get. As you might have guessed, increased exposure to intense broad-spectrum light during the winter months through the use of artificial light, called **light therapy**, reduces melatonin release and produces increased activity and enhanced mood.

The SCN does not control all circadian cycles. For example, damage to the SCN does not affect daily changes in body temperature (Turek, 1985). The structure controlling the circadian cycle for body temperature has not yet been identified.

visual photoreceptor Type of photoreceptor that codes the features of a light stimulus.

nonvisual photoreceptor Type of photoreceptor that detects the daily dawn-dusk cycle.

retinohypothalamic tract Fiber tract that conveys information about the daily dawn-dusk cycle to the SCN.

melatonin Hormone secreted from the pineal gland that has a sedative effect; high levels of melatonin reduce activity and produce fatigue.

seasonal affective disorder (SAD) An affective (emotional) disorder characterized by elevated levels of melatonin, fatigue, and depression as a result of fewer hours of daylight during winter.

light therapy The use of intense, broad-spectrum light to reduce melatonin release and produce increased activity and enhanced mood in individuals with seasonal affective disorder.

Before You Go On

Are you a lark or an owl? (See **Table 9.1**.)

Explain the mechanism by which exposure to bright light might help Sheila overcome her jet lag in time for her Monday morning meeting.

Phase-Sequence Problems

We usually experience few disturbances in circadian cycles; we are able to go to sleep when tired and awaken after a restful night's sleep. However, for some people the biological clock can, under certain circumstances, get out of sync with natural day-night fluctuations in activity. This forces people like Sheila to try to stay awake when their bodies say it is time to sleep and try to sleep when their bodies indicate it is time to stay awake. Jet lag is one example; another is shift work. Shift work involves an individual working different hours on different weeks (or rotating shifts).

People who work the late shift, usually midnight to 8 A.M., are required to be awake when they normally would be asleep. Many workers rotate shifts, sometimes working at night and at other times working during the day. Moorcroft (1987) found that 20 percent of the workers in the United States are on rotating shift schedules. Most individuals experience considerable problems with shift work. Coleman (1986) reported that 62 percent of shift workers complained of sleep disturbances, including difficulty going to sleep, fewer hours of sleep, and poor quality of sleep.

Shift workers are prone to fall asleep on the job, often with dire consequences (Akerstedt, 1991). Industrial accidents and automobile accidents occur more frequently among shift workers than among nonshift workers (Meijmann, van der Meer, & van Dormolen, 1993). Other adverse effects of shift work include higher rates of stress-related diseases such as coronary disease and ulcers and greater use of alcohol, sleeping pills, and other drugs (Liddell, 1982). Bickford (1985) estimated that the economic loss from the adverse effects of shift work in the United States is $70 billion a year.

Can anything be done to ease the problems of shift work? A study by Czeisler, Moore-Ede, and Coleman (1982) suggested one approach to reducing the adverse effects of shift work. The standard shift rotation requires a worker to start on the late shift and then rotate to an earlier shift. This schedule, called a **phase-advance shift**, acts to shorten the day. Czeisler, Moore-Ede, and Coleman studied a group of industrial workers on the phase-advance shift whose first week's shift was midnight to 8 A.M., the second week's shift was 4 P.M. to midnight, and the third week's shift was 8 A.M. to 4 P.M. (see **Figure 9.5a**). This shift rotation shortens the day because the worker starts to work on the third shift when he or she would still have been sleeping on an earlier shift. Another group of workers, who were placed on a **phase-delay shift**, rotated to a later shift

---

phase-advance shift A schedule that requires a worker to start on the late shift and then rotate to an earlier shift, which acts to shorten the day.

phase-delay shift A schedule in which a worker is rotated to a later shift each week, which acts to lengthen the day.

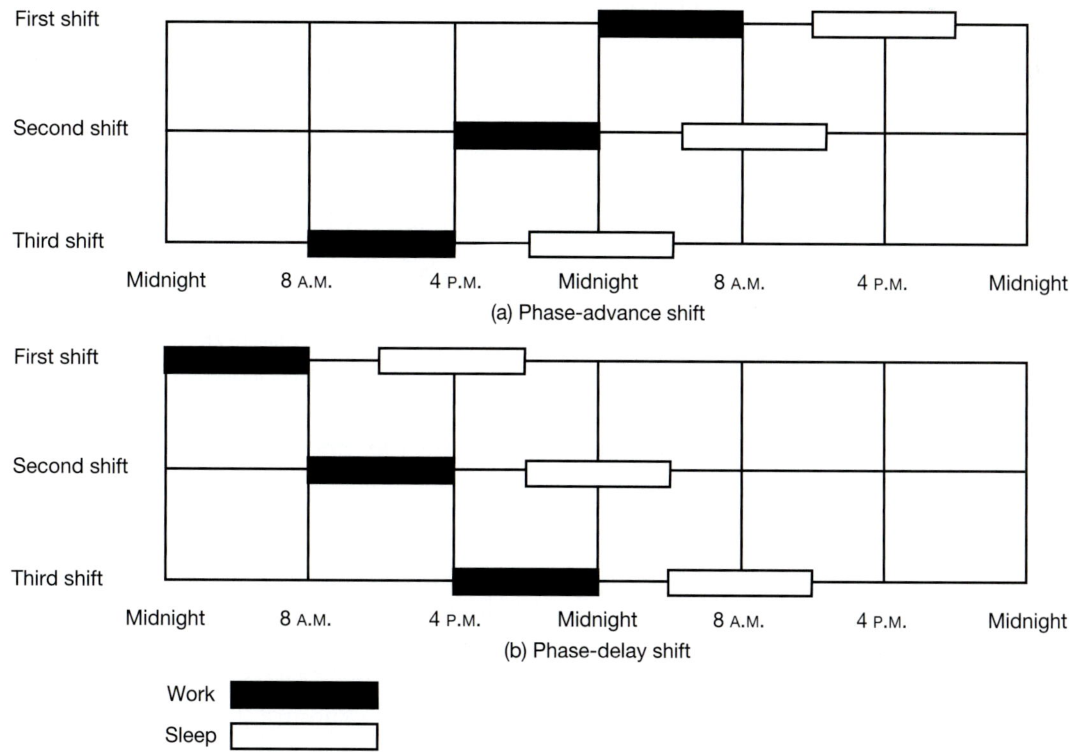

Figure 9.5 Easing of the burden of shift work. (a) Phase-advance shift. (b) Phase-delay shift.

➤ *To which type of shift do workers respond better? (p. 271–272)* each week. These workers started at midnight, then shifted to an 8 A.M. start, and finally a 4 P.M. start (see **Figure 9.5b**). This shift rotation lengthens the day because the worker starts to work on the second or third shifts after he or she had been awake for longer than on an earlier shift. Czeisler, Moore-Ede, and Coleman reported that the workers on the phase-delay shift reported greater satisfaction with their jobs, had fewer health problems, and experienced a lower turnover rate than phase-advance shift workers.

You might wonder why the phase-delay rotation is so much better for the shift worker. Remember the 25-hour (or longer) day? The body's natural tendency is to extend the circadian cycle to 25 (or more) hours. The typical phase-advance shift rotation works against the circadian rhythm, because the worker must shorten his or her day (go to sleep earlier); whereas the phase-delay rotation works with the circadian rhythm, because the worker must lengthen his or her day (go to sleep later).

The chapter-opening vignette described the fatigue and sleep problems that Sheila experienced after traveling eastward across five time zones from Boston to Paris. These symptoms are typical of **jet lag**, another phase-sequencing problem. There are other symptoms that Sheila is probably not even aware of. Athletes, for example, have been found to have diminished anaerobic power and capacity, as well as diminished dynamic strength (Hill et al., 1993). These effects eased after several days, an observation consistent with earlier reports (Tepas, 1982) that people's circadian rhythm can adjust to a new time zone.

What will happen when Sheila returns to Boston? She again will experience jet lag, although the time needed for her body to adjust will be shorter. As with shift work, it is easier to lengthen your day by flying westward (phase delay) than it is to shorten your day by flying eastward (phase advance). Moore-Ede, Sulzman, and Fuller (1982) reported that flyers generally adjusted more readily to westward than to eastward travel (see **Figure 9.6**).

What can Sheila do to ease the disruptive effects of jet lag? First, it's too late now, but she should have shifted to the new time zone several days prior to the trip. For her west to east trip from Boston to Paris, Sheila should have gone to bed earlier and gotten up earlier each day. To prepare for her flight home, the opposite is true; she should go to bed later and get up later (kind of tough when she's working!). Second, high-protein foods help you stay awake, whereas high-carbohydrate foods can hasten sleep, so a diet consisting of a high-protein breakfast and lunch and a high-carbohydrate dinner should have been started in advance of the trip. (Reserve those delicious croissants for dinnertime!). Third, Sheila is doing the right thing by spending some time outdoors sightseeing. Time in the bright sunlight will help reset her biological clock (Shanahan & Czeisler, 1991). The timing of exposure to sunlight is important: The suprachiasmatic nucleus is insensitive to light in the middle of the day, and exposure to light at this time will have little effect (Moore-Ede, 1993)—so the timing of Sheila's trip to the Louvre was just right!

jet lag The fatigue and sleep disturbance caused by traveling across several time zones.

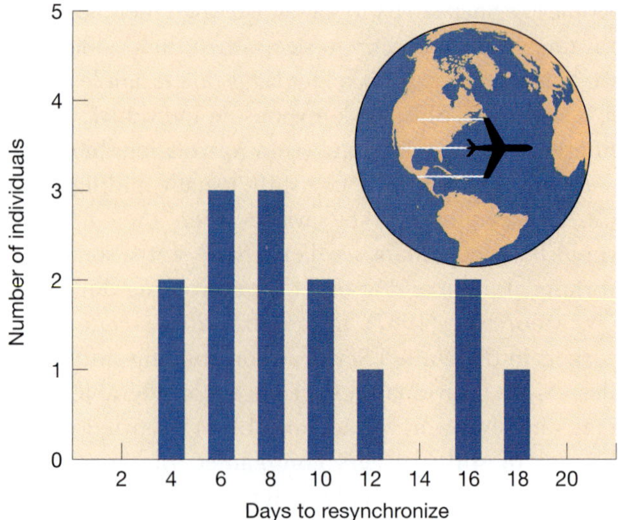

(a) Eastbound (phase advance)

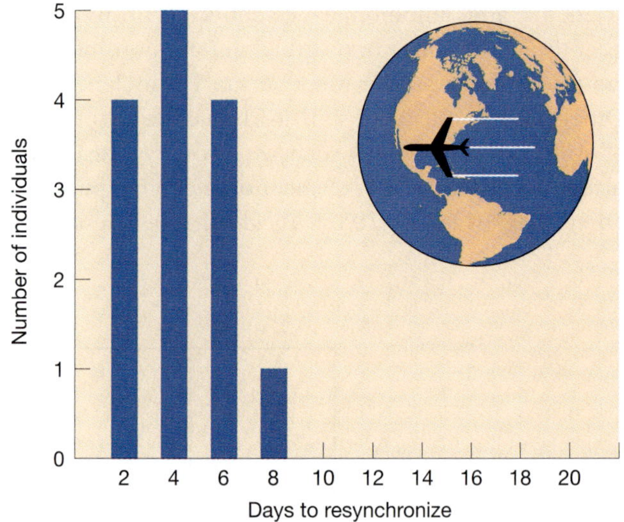

(b) Westbound (phase delay)

Figure 9.6 Disturbances in sleep-wake cycle caused by jet lag. Air travelers generally experience greater difficulty adjusting to (a) eastbound travel than to (b) westbound travel.

➤ *Do flyers adapt more easily to eastward travel or westward travel? (p. 272)*

Recall that the hormone melatonin, secreted by the pineal gland in the absence of SCN activity, has a sedative effect. Several studies (Arendt, Aldhous, English, & Marks, 1987; Lino et al., 1993; Nickelsen, 1991) have reported that taking synthetic melatonin can reduce or prevent the symptoms associated with jet lag when taken in the late afternoon or early evening of the day of arrival in a new time zone. Arendt (1994) suggested that a combination of bright light and melatonin may be the best way of avoiding jet lag.

So now you know all about the circadian cycle. But how does the central nervous system control our levels of activity and alertness? Why are we so much more alert for a 10:00 A.M. class than a 4:00 P.M. class?

Before You Go On

Describe a phase-advance shift and a phase-delay shift with regard to air travel and shift work.

What can Sheila do on Sunday, Monday, and Tuesday to ease the jet lag she will experience when she returns to Boston on Wednesday?

Section Review

- A circadian cycle is one that occurs over 24 hours.
- Activity is one process governed by the circadian rhythm, with activity generally increasing up to midday and then decreasing until sleep.
- Changes in alertness also occur over the course of the day; people who are most active and alert in the morning are called larks; those most active and alert in the evening are called owls.
- Body temperature and hormone release also change over a 24-hour period.
- The suprachiasmatic nucleus (SCN), located above the optic chiasm in the medial hypothalamus, controls the circadian cycle.
- Without any external light cues, the circadian cycle set by the SCN is 25 (or more) hours.
- Dim lighting conditions lead to an increased release of melatonin from the pineal gland and to reduced activity and increased fatigue.
- Intense broad-spectrum light activates the SCN through a branch of the optic nerve and can reset the biological clock.
- The biological clock of people who work the late shift or do rotating shift work is out of sync with the natural day-night fluctuations in available light, causing fatigue and sleep problems as well as higher rates of accidents and stress-related diseases.
- Fatigue and sleep disturbance also are caused by jet lag, or traveling across several time zones.
- Adjusting to phase-sequence discontinuity is easier when the day is lengthened (phase-delay shift) than when it is shortened (phase-advance shift).

Wakefulness

Levels of Arousal

Two distinct patterns of cortical arousal occur during the time that we are awake (refer to **Figure 9.7**). When we are awake and active, as measured by an electroencephalogram (EEG), our brain-wave patterns show a rapid desynchronized pattern of small voltage changes (approximately 18 to 24 Hz or cycles/sec; see Chapter 2). The active EEG pattern is called **beta activity** (or **beta waves**). Another EEG pattern, called **alpha activity** or (**alpha waves**), is observed while we relax with our eyes closed. The frequency of alpha

beta activity (or **beta waves**) A rapid desynchronized EEG pattern of small voltage changes (18 to 24 Hz) that occurs when an individual is awake and active.

alpha activity (or **alpha waves**) An EEG pattern of waves that are larger and more synchronized (8 to 12 Hz) than those of beta activity, that occurs when an individual is relaxed with eyes closed.

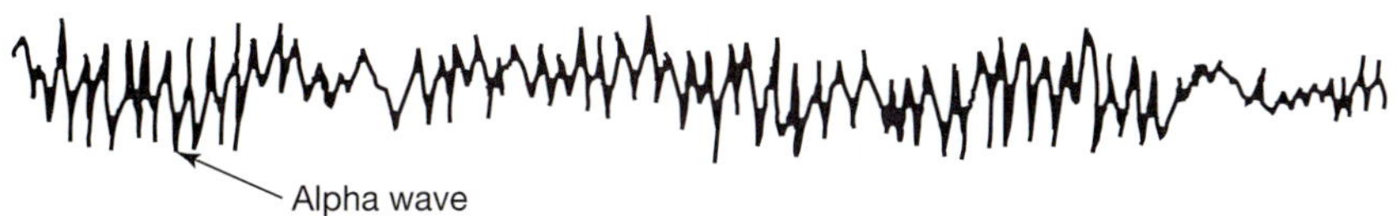

Figure 9.7 Two distinct EEG patterns of waking state. Beta activity (18 to 24 Hz) is associated with being awake and active, while alpha waves (8 to 12 Hz) occur when a person is relaxing with eyes closed.

➤ *Describe the awake state in which alpha waves are observed. (p. 273–274)*

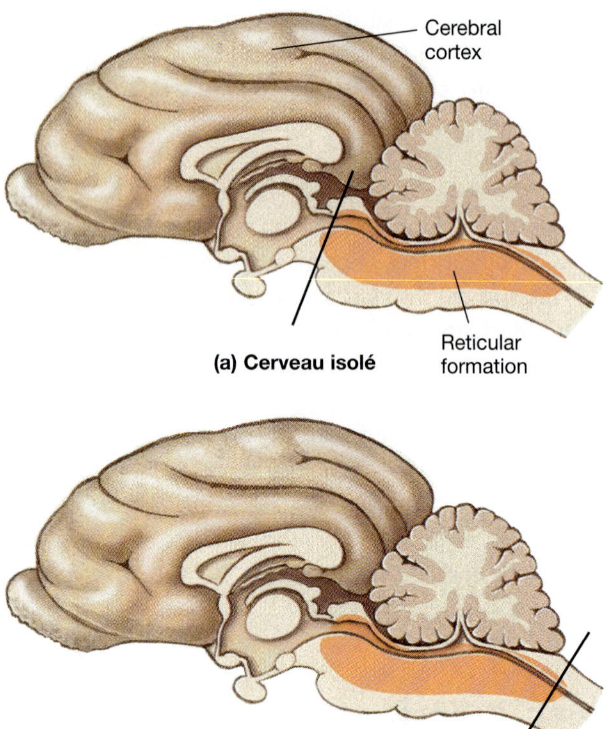

Figure 9.8 The cerveau isolé and encephalé isolé preparations of the cat. (a) Animals receiving the cerveau isolé preparation sleep continuously. (b) By contrast, normal sleep-wake cycles are found in animals receiving the encephalé isolé preparation.
➤ *What important connection does the cerveau isolé preparation serve? (p. 274–275)*

activity decreases to between 8 and 12 Hz, and the waves are larger and more synchronized than those of beta activity. Alpha activity stops when we open our eyes and resume normal activity, or when we become so relaxed that we drift off to sleep.

You might think of the different EEG patterns as different kinds of water on a lake. Beta waves correspond to small choppy waves with high frequency and low amplitude, and alpha waves correspond to large waves that are more spread out. But what causes these different kinds of ripples in the water? What structure in the central nervous system controls wakefulness? How? In the following section we will try to answer these questions, if we can keep those alpha waves away!

Brain Mechanisms Controlling Arousal

Recall from Chapter 2 that the reticular formation is a diffuse, interconnected network of neurons that begins in the hindbrain and extends through the midbrain. Studies using two different surgical procedures have provided strong evidence that output from the reticular formation, also called the **reticular activating system (RAS)**, produces cortical arousal and behavioral alertness. Fredrick Bremer (1937) performed an operation on cats called a **cerveau isolé preparation** (pronounced ser-voe ees-o-lay). In the cerveau isolé preparation, the cerebral cortex is isolated from the rest of the brain by a transection between the inferior colliculus and superior colliculus (see **Figure 9.8a**). Cats on which this procedure had been performed sleep continuously and cannot be awakened. Because the brain receives little sensory input following this procedure, Bremer concluded that sleep was produced by the absence of sensory input to the cerebral cortex.

The results of studies using a second kind of operation, the **encephalé isolé preparation** (pronounced on-

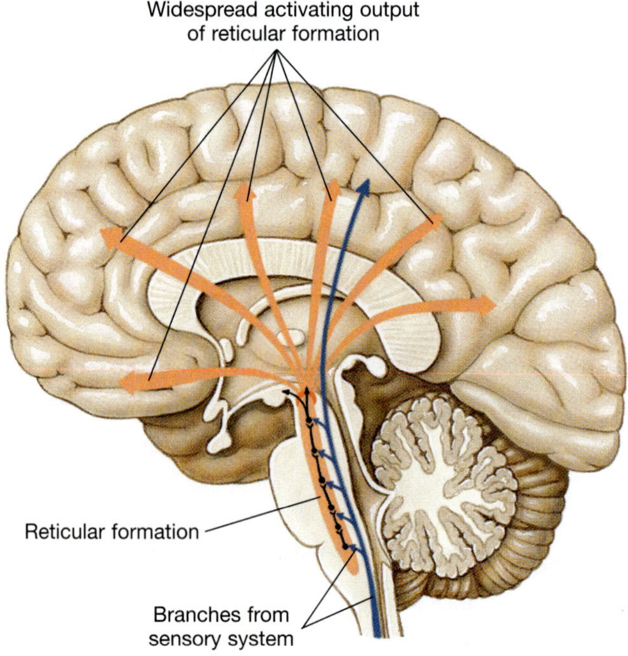

Figure 9.9 The reticular activating system. The dark arrows represent input from specific sensory systems. The light arrows indicate the general activating effect of output from the reticular formation.
➤ *What are the two main functions of the reticular activating system? (p. 274)*

reticular activating system (RAS) A diffuse, interconnected network of neurons originating in the hindbrain and extending through the midbrain that produces cortical arousal and behavioral alertness.

cerveau isolé preparation Surgical procedure in which the cerebral cortex is isolated from the rest of the brain by a transection between the inferior colliculus and superior colliculus, which produces continuous sleep and an inability to be awakened.

encephalé isolé preparation A surgical procedure that transects the brain at the level of the spinal cord and has no effect on normal sleep-awake cycles.

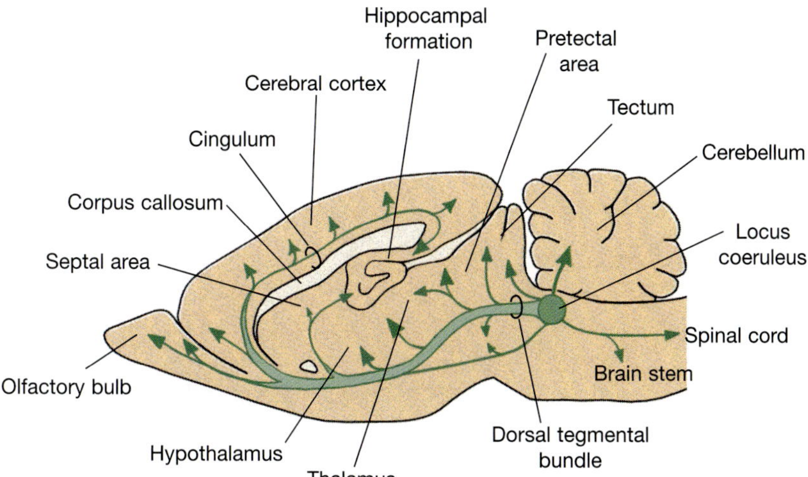

Figure 9.10 Sagittal plane view of a rat's brain. This view shows the location of the locus coeruleus, a key structure in determining the level of alertness, and its projections throughout the brain.
Adapted from Moore, 1979.

➤ *In what structure is the locus coeruleus located? (p. 275)*

say-fell ees-o-lay), provide evidence that the disconnection between the RAS and the cerebral cortex was responsible for the effects of the cerveau isolé damage, not a lack of sensory input as Bremer suggested. The encephalé isolé surgical procedure transects the brain at the level of the spinal cord. (refer to **Figure 9.8b**) Although cats receiving the cerveau isolé preparation showed continuous sleep, cats with the encephalé isolé preparation had normal sleep-awake cycles. The difference in behavior produced by these two surgical procedures supports the view that the area in the brain that produces wakefulness lies between the superior colliculus and the brainstem, where the RAS is located.

Confirmation of the role of the RAS in arousal was provided by Giuseppe Moruzzi and H. W. Magoun (1949), who reported that direct electrical stimulation of the RAS produced beta-wave EEG arousal and behavioral alertness similar to the effects of environmental stimuli. They also found that disruption of RAS functioning produced large-wave synchronized EEG recordings characteristic of sleep (see **p. 277**) and a low level of alertness. When the RAS was damaged, stimuli reached the sensory cortex but produced neither EEG arousal nor behavioral alertness. These observations indicate that unless an environmental event activates the RAS, we will not attend to it.

Donald Lindsley's research in the 1940s and 1950s (Lindsley, 1951, 1958; Lindsley, Bowden, & Magoun, 1949) provided further support for the role of the RAS in producing both cortical arousal and behavioral alertness. Stimulation of the RAS in rats by environmental events produced the EEG beta-wave pattern seen during cortical arousal as well as high levels of behavioral alertness. In Lindsley's view, the degree of alertness is highly correlated with the level of cortical arousal.

How does the RAS affect cortical arousal and behavioral alertness? Both the cerebral cortex and the RAS receive input from all sensory systems (refer to **Figure 9.9**). If the level of depolarization of the neurons in the RAS, produced by external input, reaches threshold, the RAS acts to stimulate the cerebral cortex, and the environmental event will be noticed. The RAS also maintains the muscle tone necessary for responding behaviorally to environmental stimuli.

The following example illustrates the influence of the RAS. You are listening to a dull lecture; your environment is devoid of perceptually arousing stimulation. (It's certainly not a biological psychology lecture!) Under these conditions, the RAS will not be activated, no beta-wave EEG activity will occur, and drowsiness will be experienced. Sensory information (the sound of words from the lecture) is being transmitted to the cerebral cortex, but because the RAS is not activated, you are not aware of the information.

Now you are listening to a fascinating biological psychology lecture. Stimulated by the content of the lecture, the RAS will arouse your cerebral cortex. You sit up in your seat and attend to the instructor's every word. However, an exciting lecture produces only a moderate level of RAS activation. Considerably greater RAS activation will be induced if your instructor mentions an impending examination. This information produces intense cortical arousal and behavioral alertness, and perhaps some anxiety.

The Locus Coeruleus. The **locus coeruleus** is a group of neurons within the reticular formation that appears to be central to determining levels of cortical activity and behavioral alertness. The locus coeruleus has widespread connections to other areas in the central nervous system, including the thalamus, hippocampus, and cerebral cortex (see **Figure 9.10**), and several lines of evidence support its role in producing cortical activity and behavioral

---

locus coeruleus The group of neurons within the reticular formation that appears to play a central role in determining the levels of cortical activity and behavioral alertness.

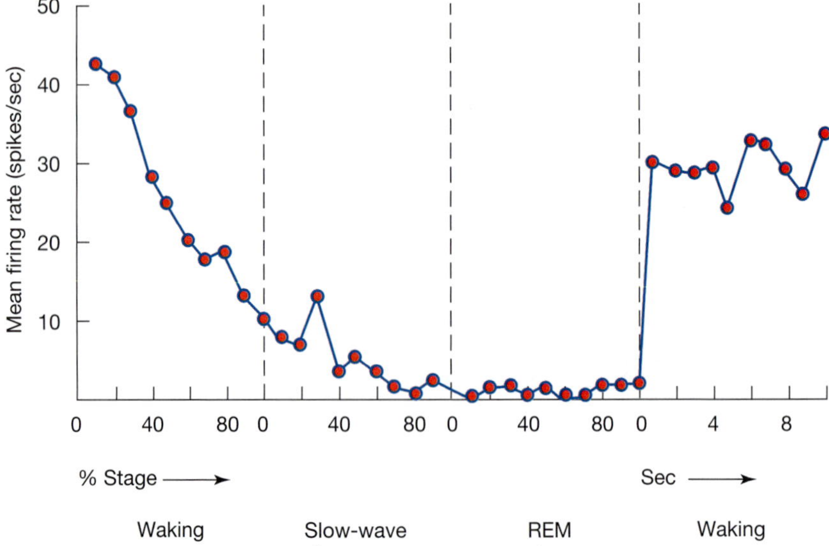

Figure 9.11 The activity in the locus coeruleus during wakefulness and sleep in the rat. The level of activity decreases as an animal goes to sleep and increases when it awakens.

➤ *In what stage of the sleep-wake cycle does the lowest level of locus coeruleus activity occur? (p. 276)*

alertness. First, its destruction produces increased sleep and decreased wakefulness (Jones, Bobillier, & Jouvet, 1969). Also, activity in the locus coeruleus is highly correlated with the level of wakefulness (Aston-Jones & Bloom, 1981; Hobson, 1988): the higher the level of activity in the locus coeruleus, the higher the level of behavioral activity. Aston-Jones and Bloom (1981) found that the rate of firing of neurons increases as an animal awakens and declines when an animal goes to sleep (see **Figure 9.11**). The longer the animal is awake, the higher the activity in the locus coeruleus, whereas activity declines to almost zero when the animal goes to sleep.

Aston-Jones (1985) suggests that the locus coeruleus influences an animal's attention to environmental stimuli. She observed that when animals are grooming or drinking sweetened water, activity level in the locus coeruleus is low; by contrast, when animals are attending to environmental events, activity in the locus coeruleus is high.

The neurotransmitter that acts in the locus coeruleus is norepinephrine. Injections of norepinephrine or drugs that activate adrenergic neurons in the locus coeruleus (e.g., amphetamines) produce wakefulness and increased attention to environmental stimulation (Waterhouse et al., 1988).

The material we have just examined indicates that RAS activity influences levels of cortical arousal and behavioral functioning and that cortical arousal serves a vital function in the effectiveness of our behavior when we are awake. Sleep also serves a valuable function. Disruption of the sleep-wake cycle, such as with sleep deprivation, can have severe consequences. The next section describes the stages of sleep and how they affect us, and examines the brain systems that control our ability to sleep.

Before You Go On

When do you experience alpha activity? Beta activity?

What are the consequences of RAS stimulation by the sensory systems? (Hint: There are two.)

Section Review

- Beta activity, the awake EEG pattern, is characterized by rapid (18 to 24 Hz), desynchronized, small voltage changes.
- During the relaxed state, alpha waves of 8 to 12 Hz are recorded.
- Activation of the reticular activating system (RAS) by environmental stimuli produces cortical arousal and behavioral alertness.
- The more stimulating the environment, the greater the activation of the RAS, the higher the level of cortical arousal, and the greater the degree of behavioral alertness.
- The locus coeruleus, an area in the reticular formation with widespread connections throughout the brain, is the particular structure that determines the level of cortical activity and behavioral alertness.
- Activity in the locus coeruleus is highly correlated with behavioral activity, and damage to the locus coeruleus produces increased sleep and decreased wakefulness.

Sleep

Many researchers have investigated the sleep process by observing subjects in a laboratory setting whose sleep is monitored by an electroencephalogram (see **Figure 9.12**). Like the awake state, sleep is characterized by different

EEG patterns. During light sleep, **theta activity** (or **theta waves**; 4 to 7 Hz) occurs, while **delta activity** (or **delta waves**; 1 to 4 Hz) occurs during deep sleep. The theta and delta waves are synchronized, are larger in amplitude than are beta and alpha activity, and are referred to as **slow-wave sleep (SWS)**. A third pattern, called **rapid eye movement (REM) sleep** because our eyes move rapidly behind their closed lids, resembles our awake state (compare the EEG beta waves and REM sleep shown in **Figure 9.13**). REM sleep is the phase of sleep during which most dreaming occurs. For a comparison of the EEGs of the different sleep-wake states, see **Figure 9.13**.

Levels of Sleep

Our brain activity varies during the course of a night's sleep. When we first fall asleep (Stage 1), the EEG shows theta waves (see **Figure 9.13**). During the next 90 minutes, the theta and delta waves become larger and slower as we progress into deeper sleep—through Stage 2, on to Stage 3, and finally to Stage 4.

Two distinct EEG patterns—sleep spindles and K complexes—are observed during Stage 2 sleep (refer to **Figure 9.13**). **Sleep spindles** are 1- to 2-second bursts of activity of 12 to 14 Hz, and **K complexes** are comprised of a single large negative wave (upward spike) followed by a single large positive wave (downward spike).

What causes sleep spindles and K complexes? As we go to sleep, brain activity slows down, then increases, then slows down again, and so on. This transition, from being awake to being asleep, is thought to be responsible for sleep spindles and K complexes.

As sleep deepens, the bursts of increased activity stop and the brain remains relatively calm. Delta waves occur very infrequently in Stage 2, more frequently in Stage 3,

theta activity (or **theta waves**) An EEG pattern during light sleep that is characterized by synchronized waves that are larger in amplitude (4 to 7 Hz) than beta and alpha waves.

delta activity (or **delta waves**) An EEG pattern during deep sleep that is characterized by synchronized waves that are larger in amplitude (1 to 4 Hz) than theta waves.

slow-wave sleep (SWS) The phase of sleep in which theta and delta activity occurs.

rapid eye movement (REM) sleep The phase of sleep in which the EEG pattern resembles the awake state, the eyes move rapidly behind their closed lids, and muscle tone is absent.

sleep spindle A 1- to 2-second burst of activity of 12 to 14 Hz that occurs during Stage 2 of sleep.

K complex A single large negative wave (upward spike) followed by a single large positive wave (downward spike) seen during Stage 2 sleep.

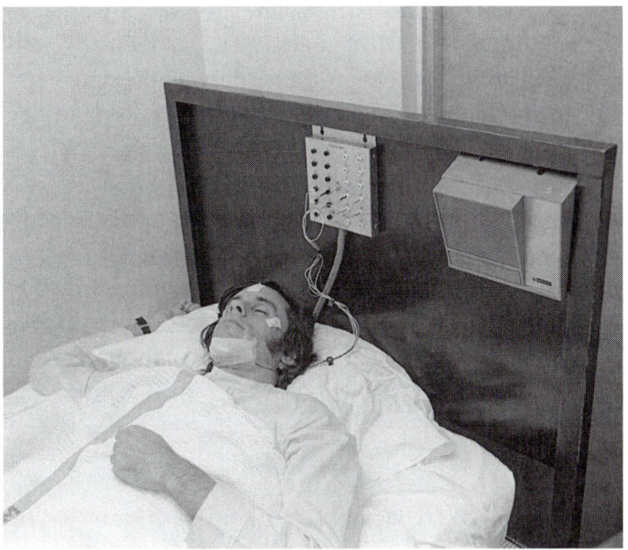

Figure 9.12 Sleep researcher William Dement is seen monitoring the sleep of a subject. His studies and those of other sleep researchers have revealed much about the nature of sleep.

➤ *What type of recording is used to monitor sleep? (p. 276–277)*

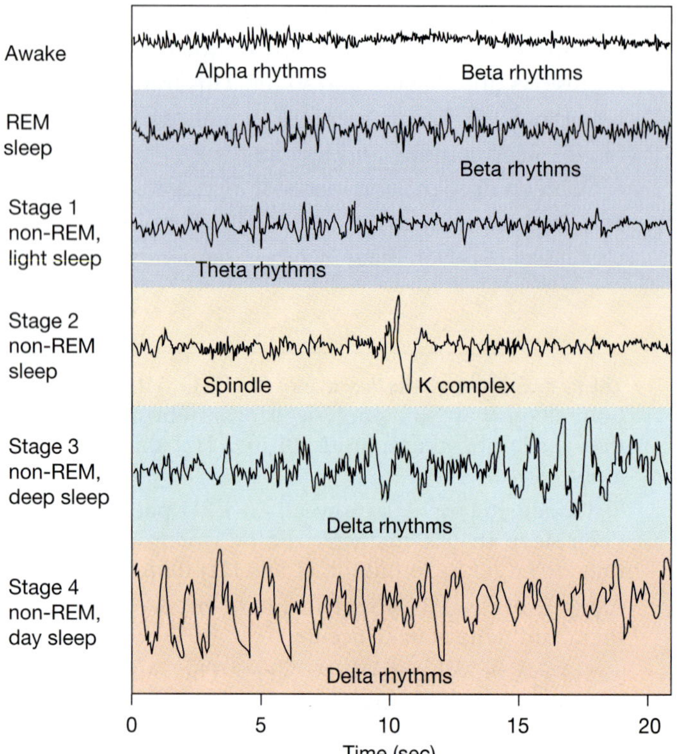

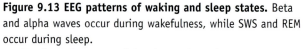

Figure 9.13 EEG patterns of waking and sleep states. Beta and alpha waves occur during wakefulness, while SWS and REM occur during sleep.

➤ *To what other stage of the sleep-wake cycle is the REM sleep wave pattern similar? (p. 278).*

and predominate in Stage 4. Deepening sleep renders us increasingly more difficult to awaken. Interestingly, if you are able to awaken a person in Stage 4, which usually occurs about 45 minutes into the first or second sleep cycle, the person will report (probably rather grumpily) that he or she just fell asleep. Try it on your roommate!

Approximately 90 minutes after we fall asleep (see **Figure 9.14**), our cortical activity changes radically, with EEG indicating low voltage, rapid, desynchronized waves that resemble those of our waking state. This sleep stage is called REM sleep because of the rapid eye movements that occur; it is sometimes called paradoxical sleep because of the awake pattern of EEG activity observed in a sleeping state. (Webster's defines "paradox" as "a statement that is seemingly contradictory or opposed to common sense and yet is perhaps true.") Most of our dreams occur during REM sleep, although dreams have been reported in other stages of sleep (not to mention the daydreaming taking place in the awake state, usually during the aforementioned boring lecture).

Until the early 1950s, biological psychologists assumed that sleep consisted entirely of SWS. The phenomenon of REM sleep was discovered by a graduate student named Eugene Aserinsky while he was observing a subject in the sleep laboratory of Nathaniel Kleitman. Aserinsky noted that every 90 minutes or so, the EEG patterns would change from the slow waves characteristic of sleep to fast, low-amplitude waves characteristic of an awake state. Even though the EEG patterns indicated an awake state, the subject was clearly asleep. Aserinsky also noticed that during these periods of awake EEG activity, the eyeballs made rapid lateral movements under the eyelids. The term *REM sleep* was coined following Aserinsky's observations (Aserinsky & Kleitman, 1953).

Figure 9.14 A typical night's sleep. Over the course of the night, the depth of sleep lessens, but the length of time in light sleep increases. Also, the duration of an REM sleep cycle increases as the night progresses.

➤ *What are the two major types of sleep? (p. 277)*

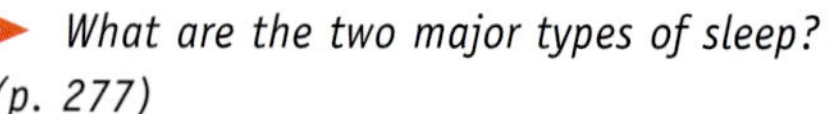

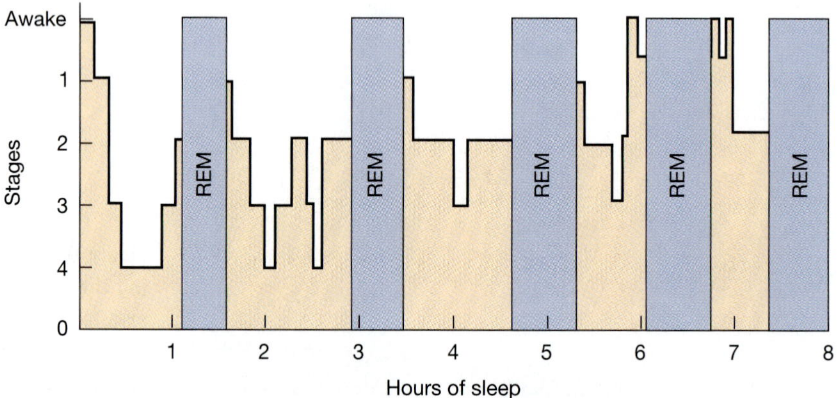

SWS and REM sleep differ in ways other than cortical EEG pattern. Our internal regulatory processes such as heart rate and blood pressure slow down during SWS, but we maintain muscle tone. By contrast, heart rate and blood pressure increase during REM sleep, but we lose muscle tone (Dement & Kleitman, 1957). This very deep relaxation of large muscle groups prevents us from acting out the dreams that occur during REM sleep.

> **Before You Go On**
>
> Why is REM sleep sometimes called paradoxical sleep?
>
> What is the difference in brain activity between Stage 1 sleep and Stage 4 sleep? Between Stage 4 and REM sleep?

Why Do We Sleep?

Certainly all of us have stayed up several hours, if not many hours, past our usual bedtime. Tired and irritable by the end of the following day, we fall asleep early and feel rested the next morning, having "made up" for the lost sleep. Because of this type of experience, it is generally assumed that the function of sleep is to restore biological resources consumed while we are awake. There is another view, one based on evolutionary theory, which holds that sleep enhances the survival of a species by keeping animals inactive when food is scarce and there is less danger from predators.

A Restorative Function. Remember the Greek philosopher Aristotle, who thought that the mind resided in the heart? (See Chapter 1.) Another of his theories was that poisonous substances accumulate in the body during the day and are then eliminated by sleep. Although scientists have discovered no poisonous buildup during the day (wrong again, Aristotle!), sleep researchers have determined that valuable substances are manufactured during sleep (Arch et al., 1988). For example, the highest levels of growth hormone secretions occur during slow-wave sleep, and protein synthesis in the brain is greatest during REM sleep. This suggests that we need sleep for our bodies to grow and our nervous systems to develop.

Additional evidence has been provided by studies of individuals who engage in unusually high levels of activity during wakefulness. Studies of individuals who have performed strenuous exercises (e.g., running in a marathon) found increased sleep time after the performance (Hartmann, 1973; Shapiro, 1982). Interestingly, the increase occurred in the amount of time spent in SWS; individuals who engaged in strenuous physical exercise showed no change in REM sleep time.

Further support for a restorative view is provided by a study by Horne and Wilkinson (1985). These researchers found that individuals who reduced their sleep time reported increased feelings of fatigue and fell asleep faster than nondeprived individuals, but once allowed to sleep, recovered quickly. Sleep Stages 3 and 4 appear especially important for restoring depleted biological systems. Agnew, Webb, and Williams (1967) found that people deprived of only Stage 4 sleep are physically lethargic but display no other behavioral changes. Webb and Agnew (1970) reported that people whose overall sleep time was reduced, a technique called partial deprivation, engaged in as much Stage 3 and Stage 4 sleep as the control group, which was allowed normal sleep time. Further, Mistlberger, Bergmann, and Rechtschaffen (1987) observed increased SWS EEG recordings following sleep deprivation.

Other effects of partial deprivation depend on the circumstances surrounding the deprivation. Johnson (1982) found that an overnight reduction in sleep to 4 to 5 hours impaired performance on difficult, boring, or long-lasting tasks. However, Friedmann and colleagues (1977) found that if sleep time was reduced slowly, by a half hour each night to 4 to 5 hours, performance was not impaired. In fact, people can experience partial sleep deprivation for years without any lasting effect by taking a few nights to catch up on their sleep and by taking an occasional nap (Mullaney et al., 1983). For example, college students experience many nights of reduced sleep and still manage to survive, although they would probably learn more if they got more sleep!

Sleep researchers have also examined the effects of the selective deprivation of REM sleep (Dement, 1974). Selective REM sleep deprivation is accomplished by awakening a subject whenever his or her EEG indicates REM sleep. After a brief time, the subject is allowed to go back to sleep and is reawakened when REM begins again. This procedure is continued throughout the night's sleep. Control subjects are awakened from SWS sleep the same number of times as their REM-deprived counterparts. The effects of REM sleep deprivation are relatively mild, with subjects reporting feeling tired, experiencing impaired concentration, and showing increased irritability. Also, REM-deprived subjects showed more and more attempts at REM sleep with continued deprivation. Further, subjects deprived of REM sleep will spend a greater proportion of sleep time in REM sleep when they are no longer being deprived, a process called REM rebound. Increased REM time may last for several days or even weeks following REM deprivation (Hobson, 1989). This observation provides indirect evidence that REM sleep is regulated separately from SWS. More direct evidence is provided later in the chapter when we describe the neural structures controlling REM sleep and SWS.

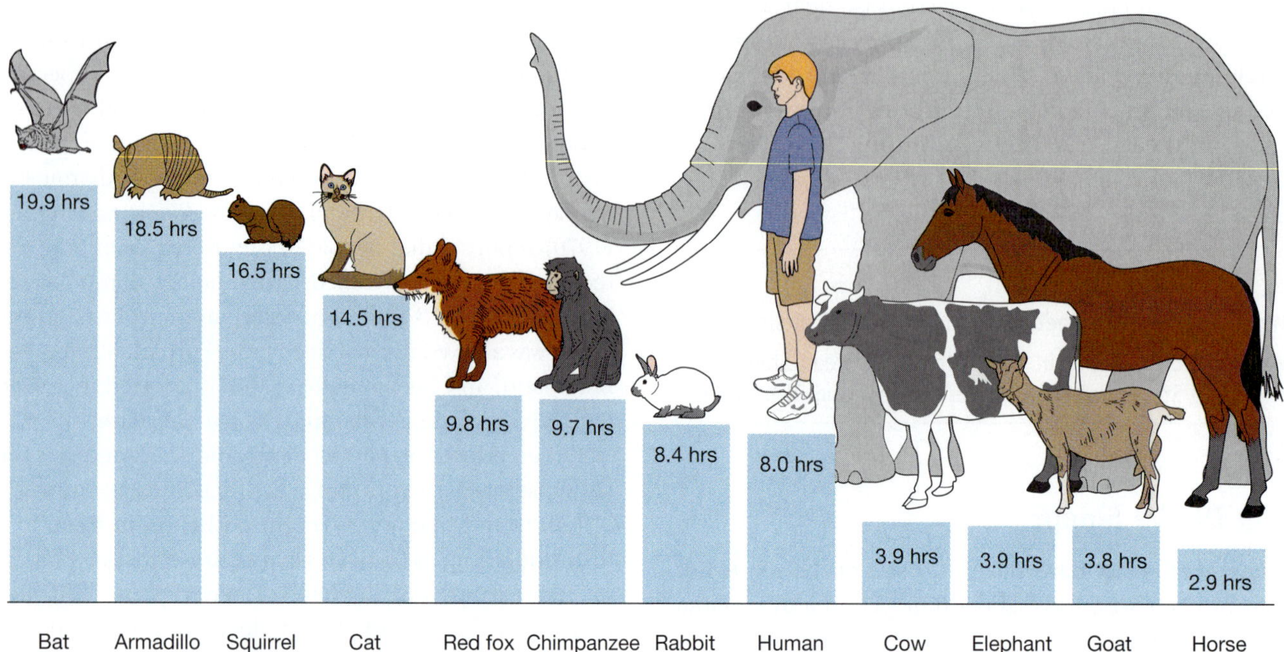

Figure 9.15 The number of hours per day that various animals sleep. Animals such as goats that have many predators sleep very little; by contrast animals such as cats with few predators sleep a lot.

➤ *Would owls sleep more or less than rabbits? (p. 280–281)*

In 1965, Randy Gardner, a high school student from San Diego, California, stayed awake for 264 hours (11 days) in order to break the world record for sleeplessness. He accomplished this feat by watching television, talking to family and friends, and playing pinball. He became very tired and was sometimes confused, but showed no severe or permanent impairment from 11 days of sleep loss. Randy's recovery from his sleep loss was quite rapid: he slept for 15 hours the first night, and his sleep time returned to normal on the second night.

Sleep researchers (Johnson, 1982; Webb & Cartwright, 1978) have more systematically examined the effects of complete sleep deprivation. The negative effects of complete sleep deprivation are surprisingly mild, and include feelings of fatigue, poor concentration, increased irritability, and decreased motivation. Subjects in a sleep laboratory have great difficulty staying awake beyond 3 or 4 days. Further, after 72 hours, subjects exhibit periods of **microsleep** in which they look like they are awake but their EEG patterns resemble Stage 1 sleep. Look around you during your next boring lecture and see if you can tell who is just daydreaming and who is in microsleep. (The notebook crashing to the floor is a dead giveaway!)

microsleep A very brief period of sleep in which subjects are awake but EEG patterns resemble Stage 1 sleep.

One might be tempted to conclude that sleep does not serve any critical function because people can, at least temporarily, function despite its absence. However, the effects of sleep deprivation can be quite serious, especially for those with occupations such as a truck driver, airline pilot, or surgeon. For those of us living in metropolitan areas, the "overturned tractor-trailer" may be a commonplace annoyance preventing us from reaching our destination, but for that driver or those driving nearby, it could be deadly.

An Evolutionary Perspective. In a second theory about sleep, Wilse Webb (1975, 1988) suggested that sleep evolved simply to keep us quiet at night. He argued that animals sleep when food is scarce and when there is less danger from predators.

If this evolutionary perspective is valid, the amount of time that a particular animal sleeps should depend on the degree of danger faced by its species: species that have few predators should sleep more than species with many predators. Animal species do differ in the amount of time that they sleep (see **Figure 9.15**). Some animals sleep most of the day, others sleep little. The comparison of animals that fall into each category is consistent with the evolutionary theory. Animals such as sheep and goats, which have many predators, sleep very little. By contrast, animals such as cats and armadillos, which have few predators, sleep a lot. Further, animals such as horses or cows that graze most of the day sleep very little, whereas predatory animals such as cats that eat one meal a day sleep a lot. However, Hauri (1979) suggested that this evolutionary perspective has some problems. One unanswered question is why sheep and goats sleep at all, considering that they are constantly in danger. The evolutionary perspective does not explain the occurrence of sleep in these highly preyed-upon species.

Developmental Changes in Sleep

Do children sleep as much as adults? Is the percentage of sleep time in SWS and REM sleep the same in children as in adults? Sleep researchers have also investigated these questions.

Roffwarg, Muzio, and Dement (1968) reported that the amount of time humans spend in REM sleep decreases steadily from infancy to adulthood (refer to **Figure 9.16**). On the other hand, SWS increases slightly from infancy to the age of 6 years and then declines slightly until adulthood. Adults' SWS time is only slightly less than that of infants. These observations suggest that the significance of REM sleep decreases as we get older, yet SWS continues to provide an important restorative function throughout our lives.

What is the adaptive significance of REM sleep time for young children? It is likely that REM sleep functions to enhance brain development. Recall from Chapter 3 that neural activity is essential to neural development; REM sleep may be a source of brain stimulation that prevents babies' brains from remaining inactive for many hours a day. Two lines of evidence support this view. First, infants born prematurely show even greater amounts of REM sleep than do normal newborns. The brains of premature infants are developing at a rapid rate, and higher levels of cortical activity during REM sleep may facilitate this process. As expected, newborn cats and dogs experience greater REM sleep time than do newborn cows and horses, because cows and horses have well-developed brains at birth, whereas those of dogs and cats are less developed at birth.

Before You Go On

Explain how partial sleep deprivation might have helped Sheila to reduce the effects of jet lag.

Why do you think that rabbits sleep so much more than goats?

Section Review

- There are two distinct phases of sleep: slow-wave sleep (SWS) and rapid eye movement (REM) sleep.
- SWS is characterized by large-amplitude, slow-wave, synchronized EEG patterns.
- REM sleep is characterized by low-amplitude, fast-wave EEG patterns.
- In the first stage of sleep, EEG patterns show theta waves (Stage 1).
- Over the next 45 minutes, the waves become slower and slower as sleep deepens.
- In Stage 2, theta activity (4 to 7 Hz) as well as sleep spindles and K complexes are observed.
- Delta waves (1 to 4 Hz) are found in Stages 3 and 4.

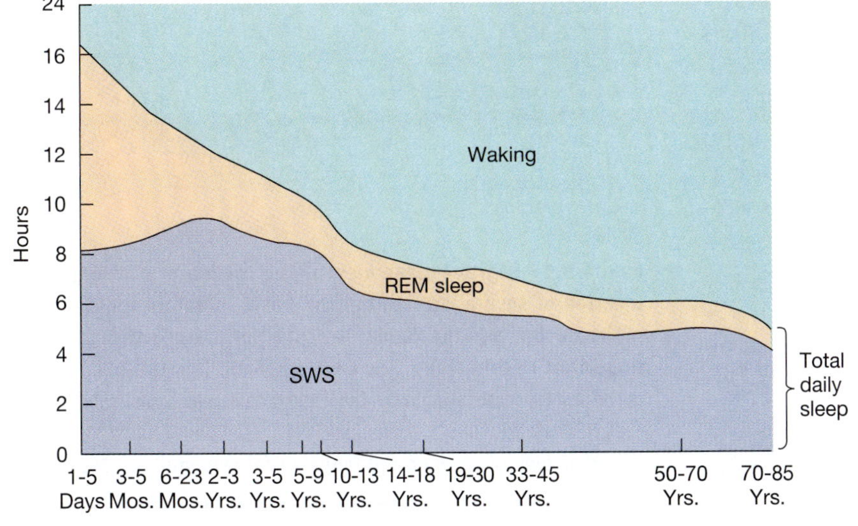

Figure 9.16 The amount of time that people of various ages spend in SWS and REM sleep. Although the amount of SWS time remains relatively constant throughout life, the length of time spent in REM each night decreases as we get older.

Adapted from Roffwarg et al., 1966.

➤ *Why do infants spend more time in REM sleep than do adults? (p. 281)*

- After about 90 minutes, REM sleep begins.
- During REM sleep, EEG activity resembles the waking state, the eyeballs make rapid lateral movements, and muscle tone is lost.
- The restorative view of sleep argues that biological reserves depleted during the day are restored during sleep.
- Sleep deprivation results in feelings of fatigue, reduced concentration, greater irritability, and decreased motivation; the symptoms of sleep deprivation are usually alleviated by a few extra hours of sleep.
- The evolutionary view argues that sleep evolved in response to the scarcity of food and the absence of danger from predators.
- The length of REM sleep time decreases as people become older; the amount of SWS time remains relatively constant throughout life.

Brain Mechanisms Controlling Sleep

In the first part of the chapter, we discussed the mechanisms within the central nervous system that control arousal. But what are the mechanisms controlling sleep? Is there a single mechanism, or more than one? The phenomenon of REM rebound (selective recovery of lost REM sleep—see **p. 279**) suggests that REM sleep is regulated separately from slow-wave sleep, and Michael Jouvet (1967, 1969) conducted research confirming this. Jouvet (1967) electrically stimulated the raphé nuclei of cats and observed increased SWS and decreased REM sleep. Further details of his research are outlined below.

The Control of SWS. The **raphé nuclei** (pronounced ra-fay, from the Greek word meaning "seam") are located in a thin strip that runs along the midline in the caudal (toward the tail) portion of the reticular formation (see **Figure 9.17**). Cats with intact raphé nuclei sleep 14 to 15 hours per day. Damage to the raphé nuclei produced a "sleepless" cat (Jouvet & Renault, 1966). Cats with 80 to 90 percent damage to the raphé nuclei will show complete insomnia for 3 or 4 days. Over time there will be a partial recovery of sleep, but cats with substantial raphé nuclei damage never sleep more than 2.5 hours per day.

One of the neurotransmitters in the raphé nuclei is serotonin. Jouvet (1969) administered parachlorophenylalanine (PCPA), a drug that decreases serotonin levels, to cats. Cats receiving PCPA did not sleep for over 40 hours, and it took 10 days for the sleep time of these cats to return to normal (see **Figure 9.18**). Injections of tryptophan, an amino acid that is a precursor of serotonin, restored normal sleep patterns within a few minutes in cats that had previously received PCPA. The normal pattern of sleep following a tryptophan injection lasted 6 to 10 hours, which was followed by a resumption of continuous wakefulness until the effects of PCPA on serotonin levels wore off. Jouvet (1974) also noted that damage to the raphé nuclei lowered the overall level of serotonin in the brain. Further, he observed that the amount of serotonin loss following raphé nuclei damage was highly correlated with the amount of sleep loss; that is, the less serotonin produced following raphé nuclei damage, the less the cats slept. On the basis of his research, Jouvet concluded that activation of the serotonergic raphé nuclei initiates and maintains SWS.

Although no one has challenged his assertion that the raphé nuclei are responsible for the *maintenance* of SWS, subsequent research indicates that Jouvet may have reached too far in drawing the conclusion that the raphé nuclei *initiate* SWS. One indication that the raphé nuclei are not responsible for initiating SWS is that stimulation of the raphé nuclei does not cause an awake animal to go to sleep (Kostowski et al., 1969). Stimulation of structures in the **basal forebrain region**, an area located anterior to the hypothalamus and including the preoptic area (see **Figures 9.17** and **9.19**), has been shown to induce sleep in an awake cat (Szymusiak & McGinty, 1986). Additionally, damage to these basal forebrain structures has been shown to produce sleeplessness in cats. Have you ever laid in bed feeling really tired, knowing that if you could only fall asleep you would sleep for hours? Blame your basal forebrain region!

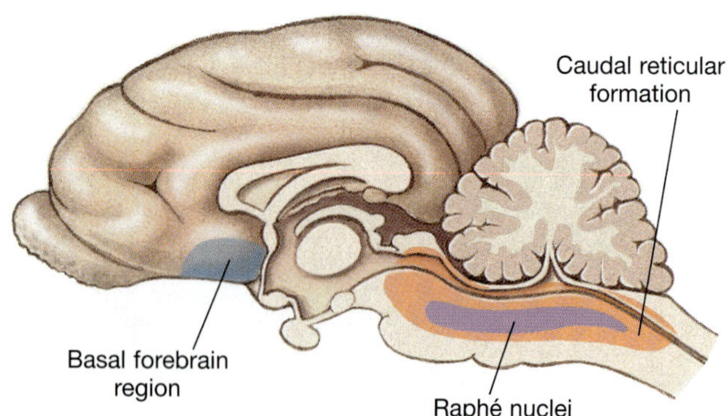

Figure 9.17 Sagittal plane view of the cat brain, showing the location of several structures (the basal forebrain region, the raphé nuclei, and the caudal reticular formation) that play an important role in sleep. The basal forebrain initiates SWS, while raphé nuclei maintains SWS. The caudal reticular formation initiates REM sleep.

➤ *What type of sleep do the raphé nuclei regulate? (p. 282)*

raphé nuclei A thin strip of neurons that runs along the midline in the caudal portion of the reticular formation; maintains SWS.

basal forebrain region An area located anterior to the hypothalamus and including the preoptic area that initiates SWS.

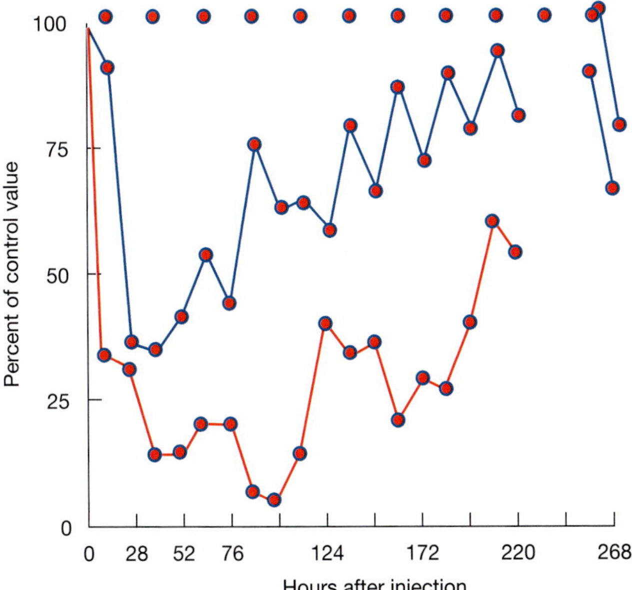

Figure 9.18 Serotonin and SWS. The effects of administration of parachlorophenylalanine (PCPA) on total SWS time (upper solid line) and serotonin levels (lower solid line) relative to cats not receiving PCPA (controls; dashed line).
From Jouvet, 1969.
➤ *By how many hours is the sleep of cats with substantial raphé nuclei damage reduced? (p. 282)*

Have you noticed that you tend to become more sleepy when the weather is hotter? As we learned in Chapter 7, thermoreceptors in the skin transmit temperature information to the preoptic area of the brain. Benedek, Obal, Lelkes, and Obal (1982) found that warming the preoptic area of cats produced drowsiness and the EEG synchrony characteristic of SWS—more evidence that activation of basal forebrain structures initiates SWS.

The Control of REM Sleep. We have learned that the locus coeruleus is responsible for cortical arousal and behavioral alertness (see **p. 275–276**). Jouvet (1967) was incorrect again when he suggested that the locus coeruleus also governs REM sleep. He based this conclusion on research indicating that electrical stimulation of the locus coeruleus in cats produced the desynchronized EEG pattern characteristic of REM sleep, and that damage to the locus coeruleus resulted in an absence of REM sleep.

More recent research (Hobson, 1989) has shown that locus coeruleus activity is associated with an absence of REM sleep, and that REM sleep occurs when the locus coeruleus is not active. Hobson suggested that activity in the locus coeruleus inhibits REM sleep. Decreased locus coeruleus activity removes the inhibition of the **caudal reticular formation**, which then initiates REM sleep (refer to **Figure 9.17**).

Acetylcholine is one of the neurotransmitters of the caudal reticular formation. Stimulating the caudal reticular formation of cats with cholinergic agonists produces immediate and prolonged REM sleep (Qualtrochi et al., 1989; Shiromani et al., 1986), whereas administration into other brain areas does not produce REM sleep (Baghdoyan et al., 1984). Also, cholinergic agonists increase the amount of REM sleep time in human subjects, whereas cholinergic antagonists decrease REM sleep time (Sitaram, Moore, & Gillin, 1978). Damage to the caudal reticular formation in humans also has been associated with an absence of REM sleep (Lavie et al., 1984).

Recordings of brain activity during REM sleep reveal a pattern of activity called PGO waves. **PGO waves** (for pons, geniculate, occipital) are brief bursts of neural activity that begin in the pons, are then transmitted to the lateral geniculate nuclei, and continue on to the

caudal reticular formation Area within reticular formation that produces REM sleep.

PGO waves Brief bursts of neural activity that begin in the pons, are transmitted to the lateral geniculate nuclei, and continue on to the occipital lobe; occur just prior to the onset of REM sleep and continue throughout the REM sleep period.

Figure 9.19 The basal forebrain region and sleep. Stimulation of the basal forebrain region causes a cat that is awake and alert (left panel) to fall asleep (right panel).
➤ *What might prevent basal forebrain stimulation from initiating sleep? (p. 282)*

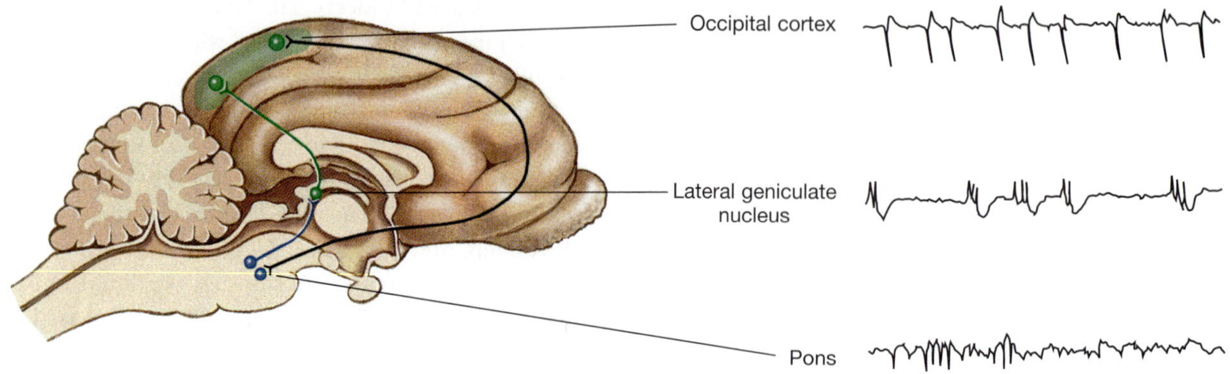

Figure 9.20 PGO waves and REM sleep. PGO waves that occur during REM sleep originate in the pons and are then conducted to the lateral geniculate nucleus and finally to the occipital lobe.

➤ *In what stage of sleep are PGO waves observed? (p. 283)*

occipital lobe (see **Figure 9.20**). The PGO wave occurs just prior to the onset of REM sleep, and PGO waves continue throughout the REM sleep period. Activity in the caudal reticular formation begins prior to the observation of PGO waves and may act to initiate both PGO waves and REM sleep (Lydic, McCarley, & Hobson, 1987). The visual images in the dreams that occur during REM sleep are probably the result of activity in the occipital lobe that occurs during PGO waves. (Recall from Chapter 2 that the primary function of the occipital lobe is the analysis of visual information.)

Before You Go On

What do you think misled Jouvet to conclude that the raphé nuclei initiate sleep and that the locus coeruleus is responsible for regulating REM sleep?

Dreams

One of the stories that I remember from attending Sunday school is of Joseph describing two of his dreams to his brothers. Even before telling his brothers of his dreams, Joseph was hated by them because their father, Jacob, favored him over his 11 brothers. Describing the first dream, Joseph said: "Listen to the dream I had. We were in the field tying up sheaves of wheat, when my sheaf got up and stood up straight. Yours formed a circle around mine and bowed down to it." Of the second dream, Joseph told his brothers, "I had another dream, in which I saw the sun, the moon, and the eleven stars bowing down to me." The meaning of both of Joseph's dreams was clear to his brothers: They were a prophecy of his brothers becoming subservient to him. The brothers were so upset over Joseph's dreams that they sold him to the Ishmaelites, who then took Joseph to Egypt. (But don't worry—the story has a happy ending. Curious? Read Genesis Chapter 37 to find out what happens to Joseph.)

The reaction of Joseph's brothers to his dreams reflects the significance invested in dreams throughout history. Seventy passages in the Bible describe dreams. The ancient Babylonians wrote their dreams on clay tablets as early as 5000 B.C. The Egyptians built temples to Serapis, the god of dreams. Francis of Assisi was rebuffed by the Pope until the Pope dreamed of a sign that led him to believe in the genuineness of Francis.

What do we know about our dreams? Until about 25 years ago, the only way to study dreams was to rely on people's recollections, or self-reports. Because self-reports can be unreliable (for example, due to perceptual biases or forgetting), the validity of the recollections was always in question. Sleep researchers (e.g., Dement, 1974) now have established more scientific ways of investigating dreams. If you participated in such an investigation, you would be awakened at various times during the night and asked whether you have been dreaming. If you have been dreaming, the researchers would ask questions about the content of your dream.

The Content of Our Dreams. A **dream** is an altered state of consciousness in which remembered images and fantasies are temporally confused with external reality. Dreams usually take place in familiar settings and are about objects or events in the dreamer's life (refer to **Figure 9.21**). Misfortune is more likely to be a part of our dreams than success. Although it would seem reasonable

---

dream An altered state of consciousness in which remembered images and fantasies are temporally confused with external reality.

to expect sex to be a common theme in our dreams, only 1 percent of dreams involve overt sexual activity. People we know are the most common characters in our dreams; bizarre creatures and monsters rarely appear.

People have about four to six dreams each night (Dement, 1969). The first dream usually begins after about 90 minutes of sleep. The dreams last about as long as the scenes would in real life, and we experience a total of about 1 to 2 hours of dream time each night. As we learned earlier, most, but not all, dreams occur during REM sleep. Dement found that those subjects who were awakened during REM sleep reported 70 percent of the time that they had been dreaming, whereas subjects awakened during SWS reported 30 percent of the time that they had been dreaming. The quality of the dreams experienced in REM sleep also differs from those experienced during SWS. Most SWS dreams seem to consist of a single thought, image, conversation, or emotion, as contrasted with the storylike aspect of REM dreams.

THE FAR SIDE
By GARY LARSON
"The golden arches! The golden arches got me!"

Figure 9.21 The meaning of a dream. Our dreams typically are about objects or events in our lives. In this Far Side cartoon, the cow's dream about a restaurant with golden arches is definitely relevant to the cow's life.

➤ *What is the definition of a dream? (p. 284)*

Perhaps you, like many people, believe that you do not dream. However, Faraday's (1974) research clearly shows that all people will at least sometimes report dreaming if awakened during REM sleep. Dement and Kleitman (1957) observed that the ability to recall a dream decreases the longer the sleep researcher waits after REM sleep to awaken the subject. So it would make sense that the reason people say they do not dream is due to a lack of recall rather than an absence of dreaming.

We said earlier that dreams are an example of an altered state of consciousness. How is a dream experience different from experiences that occur during a waking state? Dreams differ from conscious experiences in two significant ways. First, the setting of a dream can change instantaneously. For example, you might dream one second about sailing in a lake and the next about climbing a mountain, settings that might be separated by hours or days in the waking state. Second, our dreams can be set in the present, past, or future, and can move freely among these; we are, of course, stuck in the present in our waking experiences (until H. G. Wells's time machine is perfected!).

The Function of Our Dreams. We've described what a dream is and what happens in a dream state, but why do we dream? Several different theories have been proposed to explain the reasons for our dreams.

A Psychoanalytic View of Dreams. Sigmund Freud (1900/1953), in his classic work *Interpretation of Dreams*, suggested that dreams represent an acceptable release of sexual and aggressive instincts. According to Freud, the part of the unconscious that contains unacceptable desires—the id—wants to express these needs but the ego finds them unacceptable. In Freud's view, the actual events that happen during a dream (the **manifest content**) are symbolic of unconscious wishes or desires that the ego refuses to allow to be expressed in the waking state (the **latent content**). Dreams thus allow the inhibited id impulses to be expressed, without requiring the ego to acknowledge the existence of the unacceptable desires.

Among most psychologists who are not psychoanalysts, interest in Freud's view of dreams is mostly historical (Cartwright, 1978). Other psychologists, although accepting Freud's idea that dreams serve a psychological function, suggest a different function for dreams than the release of unconscious id desires. We next examine the cognitive, or mentalistic, perspective of the function of dreams.

---

manifest content According to the psychoanalytic theory, the actual events that happen during a dream.

latent content According to the psychoanalytic theory, the symbolic content of a dream.

A Cognitive View of Dreams. Cognitive psychologists have suggested that dreams are a way of dealing with life's problems (Antrobus, 1991; Domhoff, 1996). Dreams not only involve everyday experiences but typically occur just prior to the onset of important events. For example, you might dream about starting a new job the night before you accept the position. Dreams can thus be viewed as a sort of safe preview of stressful events. (Perhaps the cow in **Figure 9.21** knew he was headed for the butcher shop!)

The **cognitive perspective** also suggests that dreams may help to store certain memories and to discard or forget other memories. There is evidence that REM sleep enhances the consolidation or storage of recent experiences (Scrima, 1982). We will examine the role of sleep in memory consolidation in Chapter 14. The cognitive view, like the Freudian view, remains mostly unproven (Foulkes, 1985).

Activation Synthesis Theory. Allan Hobson and Robert McCarley (1977) proposed that dreams have no inherent meaning. Instead, according to the **activation synthesis theory**, dreams are a mental interpretation of the neural activity that occurs during sleep. One type of neural activity occurring during REM sleep is the inhibition of the motor system; commonly, people dream of being chased, locked up, or tied up. According to Hobson and McCarley, these dreams are the brain's interpretation of the suppression of muscle tension that occurs during REM sleep.

Another characteristic of REM sleep is the activation of the vestibular system (see Chapter 7). Because the vestibular system is responsible for the maintenance of balance, stimulation of the vestibular organs while we are lying down would be expected to create sensations of falling or floating, which are indeed frequent themes of dreams. Further, the activation of the sexual organs that occurs during REM sleep would explain . . . well you get the picture!

Hobson (1988) suggests that there is a reason that REM sleep and dreaming do not occur throughout the night. According to Hobson, neurons in the pons initiate REM sleep. These neurons fire in unrestrained bursts, much like a machine gun. Pontine neurons do not contain unlimited "ammunition" and must "reload" before refiring. A depletion of acetylcholine (ACh), the neurotransmitter or ammunition for these neurons, has been shown to be associated with the end of a period of REM sleep. The next period of REM begins when the neurons are reloaded with ACh. Drugs that stimulate cholinergic neurons have been shown to increase REM sleep and dreaming (Gillin et al., 1985), whereas cholinergic antagonists have been shown to reduce REM sleep and dreaming. (In case you've forgotten, cholinergic neurons are those that use acetyl*choline* as a neurotransmitter.) Of the three views that we have presented, the activation synthesis hypothesis currently has the most experimental support.

Lucid Dreams. You are sitting in your biological psychology class when the professor asks whether anyone has any questions. You raise your hand; when the professor calls on you and everyone turns around to see who is asking the question, you realize that you are not wearing a stitch of clothing! But wait, you say—I'm in bed with my pajamas on! This experience, called a **lucid dream**, occurs when we are conscious of our dream state (Gackenbach & LaBerge, 1988). The lucid dream has two components: The content of the dream (the biological psychology class) and the consciousness or awareness that we are dreaming (the "But wait!").

Because you are aware that you are dreaming, you might wonder whether you are really asleep during a lucid dream. Research by Stephen LaBerge and his associates (LaBerge, 1981; Gackenbach, 1983) indicates that many lucid dreams begin with the high level of cortical activity that occurs at the beginning of an REM sleep period. The level of cortical activity and lucidity declines over the course of an REM sleep period, and the lucid dream ends either when the dream continues but our awareness that we are dreaming fades, or when we awaken.

If we are conscious of the experience, how do we know that we are dreaming? Gackenbach and LaBerge (1988) suggest that one way to tell that we are indeed dreaming and not awake is the inconsistency of the dream content with reality. For example, the presence of your deceased aunt in a dream might be a clue that you are dreaming. And you know that you might go to an early class in your pajamas, but you'd *never* go without anything on!

LaBerge (1980) observed that about 85 percent of his subjects experienced some lucid dreaming. Other estimates range from 47 percent (Blackmore, 1983) to 100 percent (Gackenbach et al., 1983). Further, Gackenbach and Bosveld (1983) examined the differences between lucid and nonlucid dreams. The emotional impact of a lucid dream has been shown to be more intense than the impact of a nonlucid dream (Gackenbach & Bosveld, 1983). Sexual activity is a common theme; people report experiencing intense orgasms during lucid dreams.

One of the most interesting aspects of lucid dreaming is that we are able to learn to experience lucid dreams

---

cognitive perspective The view that dreams help solve everyday problems and may help to store certain memories and to discard other memories.

activation synthesis theory The view that dreams are a mental interpretation of the neural activity that occurs during sleep.

lucid dream A dream in which the person is conscious that he or she is dreaming.

(Gackenbach & LaBerge, 1988) and thus control dream content. If you realize that you are dreaming, you can reduce the emotional impact of exposing yourself in class. LaBerge (1981) described his control of a lucid dream:

> I am crossing a bridge over an abyss. When I look into the depths I am afraid to continue. My companion, behind me, says, "You know, you don't have to go this way. You can go back the way you came," and points back down an immense distance. But then it occurs to me that if I became lucid I would not need to fear the height. As I realize that I am dreaming, I'm able to master my fear—I cross the bridge and awaken." (p. 48)

Teaching people how to dream lucidly at will may lessen the negative experience of repetitive nightmares or other extreme anxiety-provoking dreams.

Before You Go On

After she falls asleep, exhausted from her afternoon in Paris, Sheila dreams that she is in the Louvre and that the Mona Lisa is trying to tell her something. She tries to move closer, but a guard sees her approach the painting and begins to chase her. She runs and runs but can't seem to get away. Give a brief interpretation of her dream from the cognitive view and the activation synthesis hypothesis.

Section Review

- SWS is maintained by the raphé nuclei.
- Structures in the basal forebrain region, including the preoptic area, appear to initiate SWS.
- The caudal reticular formation initiates REM sleep. Decreased activity in the locus coeruleus removes the inhibition of the caudal reticular formation, beginning REM.
- PGO waves are brief bursts of neural activity that begin in the pons, are transmitted to the lateral geniculate nucleus, and then to the occipital lobe.
- The first PGO wave immediately precedes the onset of REM sleep, and PGO waves continue throughout REM.
- In a dream, remembered images and fantasies are temporarily confused with external reality.
- Dreams are more likely to occur during REM sleep than SWS.
- Freud believed that dreams allow a person to express inhibited impulses.
- The cognitive theory suggests that dreams represent a means of solving problems we may be facing in our lives.
- The activation synthesis theory proposes that a dream is a mental interpretation of the neural activity that occurs during REM sleep.
- A lucid dream occurs when we are aware that we are dreaming.

APPLICATION

Causes and Treatment of Sleep Disorders

Shortly after returning to school for the spring semester, Walter saw an ad for a ski trip to Colorado over spring break. He had never been skiing but thought it would be fun to try, and the trip was being sponsored by the student government, so it was reasonably priced. The only drawback was that he'd have to share a room with several other students. After much thought, Walter decided to go. The first night at the ski lodge started okay. Walter had a great dinner and talked about college with his roommates when he returned to the room. Walter was surprised to learn that Paul, one of the other students, was also a psychology major. About 1 A.M., everyone turned in for the night, ready to hit the slopes the next morning. Walter had just about fallen asleep when he heard a horrible shrill and piercing sound. It was his fellow psychologist, Paul, snoring very loudly. Walter was surprised that none of his other roommates were awakened by the deafening noise. As he watched Paul, Walter noticed that he stopped breathing for perhaps 30 to 40 seconds, then gasped for air, and finally emitted a loud snore. Walter listened awhile and decided to try to sleep. He tossed and turned for what seemed like hours, unnerved as much when Paul stopped breathing as when he gasped for air. He must have finally fallen asleep, because he did wake up in the morning, but he was exhausted. Paul probably did not feel much better, but was used to waking tired. Walter realized that he had to spend several more nights in the room with Paul and hoped that someone in the lodge had earplugs. ■

Paul suffers from **sleep apnea**, a repeated interruption of sleep caused by the cessation of breathing (apnea). Individuals with sleep apnea fall asleep and then stop breathing. The cessation of breathing, caused by an obstruction of airflow in the throat, can last for up to a minute. The obstruction occurs when the muscles

sleep apnea A sleep disorder characterized by repeated interruptions of sleep caused by the cessation of breathing (apnea).

in the upper throat relax, causing the airway in the back of the mouth to close. The person will make a loud snorting sound as he or she gasps for air. The cycle of stopped breathing followed by gasping for air may occur up to several hundred times each night. It is no wonder that Walter was unnerved by Paul's sleep apnea and that he had such difficulty sleeping in the same room.

Sleep apnea is a serious problem that not only disrupts sleep but can cause death. Bliwise and colleagues (1988) suggested that sleep apnea is a major cause of death in the elderly. Successful treatment of sleep apnea involves keeping the air passage open. This is most often accomplished by using a small compressor that delivers a steady stream of air through a mask worn over the nose (probably *not* an item available at the lodge!). This treatment eliminates the obstruction by keeping the air passage open throughout the night (Palca, 1989).

Sleep apnea is one example of a sleep disorder. Sleep disorders fall into two broad categories: insomnia, or not enough sleep (which includes sleep apnea), and hypersomnia, or getting too much sleep. Our discussion will focus on the characteristics, causes, and treatments of several different disorders in these categories.

Insomnia

From time to time, you have probably experienced difficulty going to sleep. Like Walter, you toss and turn for what seems like hours, then finally fall asleep. When you awaken the next morning at your usual time, you still feel tired. After a few restless nights, you might begin to think that you have a sleeping problem. Unless you, too, have a roommate with sleep apnea, it is certainly possible that you suffer from **insomnia**, a long-term inability to obtain adequate sleep. This inability can involve (1) taking a long time to fall asleep, (2) frequent waking during the night, and/or (3) awakening several hours before the normal rising time.

Insomnia is a fairly common problem. Dement (1986) suggested that "if we include all of its forms, insomnia is probably the most common medical problem." About 35 percent of adults complain of insomnia at some time in any given year, and it is a persistent problem for about 15 to 30 percent of the population (Fredrickson, 1987). Not all people are equally likely to suffer from insomnia. Insomnia is more prevalent in older adults and women (Coleman, 1986). People who are widowed, divorced, or separated also are more likely to report insomnia than married or single people.

Interestingly, insomnia is often a misperception. Most individuals complaining of chronic insomnia actually require only about 30 minutes to fall asleep, and they frequently sleep as much as other people. In one study, Weitzman (1981) looked at the EEG records of people who reported that they slept very little if at all. Weitzman found that these patients usually slept for 6 or 7 hours a night.

A number of factors can cause insomnia. Psychological problems such as anxiety or depression are an important contributor (Soldatos & Kales, 1986). Individuals who are anxious about their daily problems often have difficulty falling asleep. Some people worry so much about being unable to fall asleep that they have greater difficulty doing so, creating a vicious, self-perpetuating cycle. Depressed people usually have no trouble falling asleep, but suffer from early morning wakefulness. Other causes of insomnia include an environment that is excessively noisy, an uncomfortable bed, or new surroundings.

Drugs can also cause insomnia (see Chapter 5). Stimulants such as caffeine or nicotine can make it quite difficult to go to sleep. Individuals often consume alcohol or take a sedative to fall asleep. However, excessive use of alcohol can actually lead to insomnia (Johnson, Burdick, & Smith, 1970), notwithstanding the other negative effects of long-term alcohol use.

The use of sedatives is a popular way of treating insomnia. However, a sedative reduces the time needed to fall asleep by an average of only 15 minutes, and the total extra sleep time produced by a sleeping pill is only about half an hour (Mendelson, 1990). Further, some sedatives enable people to fall asleep, but some wear off before morning and cause the person to awaken early (Kales et al., 1983). Other sedatives may last too long, causing sleepiness for part of the next day. Still other sedatives reduce REM sleep time, which causes the person to awaken still tired (Gottesmann, 1996). The benzodiazepine *Zolpidem* does not appear to disrupt the natural progression and duration of sleep stages and, thus, has become a popular treatment for insomnia (Besset et al., 1995).

There are certainly dangers to using sedatives to treat insomnia. Long-term use of sedatives can actually cause greater difficulty sleeping; as the body becomes tolerant to the drug, the person is forced to continue its use just to fall asleep. Another undesirable effect of the repeated use of sleeping medication is **drug-dependent insomnia**, which is a disturbance of sleep that occurs when a person attempts to sleep without the medication or takes a lower-than-normal dose. The insomnia produced by withdrawal from

insomnia A sleep disorder characterized by a long-term inability to obtain adequate sleep; symptoms include taking a long time to fall asleep, frequent waking during the night, and/or awakening several hours before the normal rising time.

drug-dependent insomnia A sleep disorder that occurs when a person attempts to sleep without previously used sleep medication or takes a lower-than-normal dose.

sleeping medication is perceived as worse than the insomnia that was experienced before the medication was initially taken, and it can develop after as few as three nights of taking sleeping medication (Kales et al., 1979). Given that (1) most people who complain of insomnia grossly underestimate the time they actually sleep, (2) sleeping medication only reduces the average time to go to sleep from 30 minutes to 15 minutes and increases the time slept by 30 minutes, and (3) rebound insomnia will be experienced after the sleeping medication is taken, the use of sleeping medication would generally appear to be ill-advised.

Insomnia caused by chronic underlying problems such as anxiety or depression can be treated along with the psychopathology (Soldatos & Kales, 1986). By contrast, brief, minor insomnia can often be overcome without extensive therapy. Lilie and Rosenberg (1990) offered the following suggestions. First, try to awaken and go to sleep at the same time each day. It is very difficult to establish a regular sleep-wake cycle if you awaken or go to sleep at different hours (think about Sheila's jet lag). Second, avoid a room that is too warm or too noisy. Third, read something pleasant or relaxing or take a warm bath, or get a massage prior to going to sleep. Do not take stimulants such as caffeine or nicotine, especially in the evenings. Fourth, do not use alcohol or sedatives to help you fall asleep. Finally, if you still can't fall sleep, don't lie in bed worrying about not being able to sleep. Instead, get up and read, work, or watch television until you feel drowsy.

Hypersomnia

In contrast to insomnia, people who suffer from **hypersomnia** get too much sleep. No such thing you say? Read on!

One type of hypersomnia is **narcolepsy**. The main characteristic of narcolepsy is a sudden, uncontrollable sleep attack, usually initiated by monotonous activity, which is caused by a dysfunction in the locus coeruleus that leads to an intrusion of REM sleep into wakefulness. The sleep attacks usually last 2 to 4 minutes but can last as long as 15 minutes. After these brief bouts of sleeping, the individual will awaken feeling refreshed. The danger of this disorder is that the sleep attacks can occur at any time, and come without warning. A narcoleptic could thus fall asleep while crossing the street, driving a car, flying an airplane, or operating heavy machinery; think of how your activities would be restricted if it were possible that you could fall asleep anytime.

There are three additional symptoms sometimes observed in people with narcolepsy: cataplexy, sleep paralysis, and hallucinations. Individuals with narcolepsy can show a sudden, complete lack of muscle tone called **cataplexy**. During a cataplectic attack, the person will suddenly wilt and then fall to the ground. While on the ground, the person will lie paralyzed, unable to move for several seconds to several minutes. It seems that whatever causes sleep attacks can also elicit the loss of muscle tone characteristic of REM sleep.

Cataplexy, exhibited by most, but not all, narcoleptics is almost always elicited by intense circumstances such as being in a highly emotional state or engaging in very strenuous physical activity.

Sleep paralysis is a brief paralysis that occurs when the narcoleptic is going to sleep or awakening. The paralysis often can be interrupted by touching the person or saying his or her name. Sleep paralysis is not as common as cataplexy; only 20 percent of narcoleptics experience this symptom.

Recall that most dreams occur during REM sleep. Some narcoleptics also dream or experience hallucinations. As you might imagine, hallucinations are often unpleasant, alarming, and sometimes terrifying. Hallucinations can occur during sleep paralysis when the person is going to sleep or awakening.

As we mentioned earlier, narcolepsy appears to be a disorder involving an intrusion of REM sleep into wakefulness. Analysis of EEG records has revealed that most narcoleptic patients show REM sleep patterns during their sleep attacks (Wilson et al., 1973). Narcoleptic patients enter REM directly from a waking state (see **Figure 9.22**). The REM sleep lasts from 10 to 20 minutes. If the narcoleptic remains asleep, there follows a slow progression through Stages 1 through 4 of SWS.

Genetics plays a major role in narcolepsy. Dement (1974) reported that the incidence of narcolepsy among relatives of someone with the disorder is 60 times higher than in the general population. Also, there is a specific antigen, called HLA-DR2, found in the blood of most narcoleptics. Biologists have bred a line of narcoleptic dogs (Foutz et al., 1979); these dogs show abnormal functioning in the locus coeruleus, the area of the brain that inhibits REM sleep (Miller et al., 1990). It is likely that dysfunction in the locus coeruleus causes an intrusion of REM sleep into the waking state.

What can a person with narcolepsy do to stay awake? Two different approaches are used in the treatment of

---

hypersomnia A sleep disorder characterized by too much sleep.

narcolepsy A sleep disorder characterized by a sudden, uncontrollable sleep attack, usually initiated by monotonous activity; can also include cataplexy, sleep paralysis, and hallucinations.

cataplexy A sudden, complete lack of muscle tone; one symptom of narcolepsy.

sleep paralysis A brief paralysis that occurs when the narcoleptic is going to sleep or awakening.

narcolepsy (Kales, Soldatos, & Kales, 1981): drug treatment and behavior modification. Catecholamine agonists such as amphetamine (see Chapter 5) can be given to keep the narcoleptic patient awake. The drugs probably work by activating noradrenergic receptors in the locus coeruleus, an effect that would inhibit REM sleep. Antidepressant drugs such as imipramine (Tofranil) (see Chapter 5) appear to reduce the narcoleptic symptoms of cataplexy, sleep paralysis, and hallucinations. These antidepressant drugs increase activity in neurons in which serotonin, norepinephrine, and dopamine are the neurotransmitters. (The effects of different drugs on different systems suggest that the structures that produce the sleep attacks are different from the structures that produce the other symptoms of narcolepsy.) Usually, both types of drugs are administered in the treatment of narcolepsy. As we have discussed, monotonous activities such as driving an automobile can cause the narcoleptic to fall asleep. Changing behavior so that monotonous activities are avoided can reduce the likelihood of experiencing a sleep attack. People susceptible to cataplexy can learn to control the intensity of their emotions in order to reduce the likelihood of an attack.

REM without atonia A sleep disorder characterized by a failure to lose muscle tone during REM, which results in high levels of motor activity during REM sleep.

Another disorder associated with REM sleep is REM sleep behavioral disorder or **REM without atonia** (Schenck et al., 1986). Individuals afflicted with REM without atonia do not lose muscle tone during REM. In fact, they are quite active during REM sleep and may even act out their dreams, which can result in very unpleasant consequences. The following case illustrates this danger:

> I was a halfback playing football, and after the quarterback received the ball from the center he lateraled it sideways to me and I'm supposed to go around end and cut back over tackle and—this is very vivid—as I cut back over tackle there is this big 280-pound tackle waiting, so I, according to football

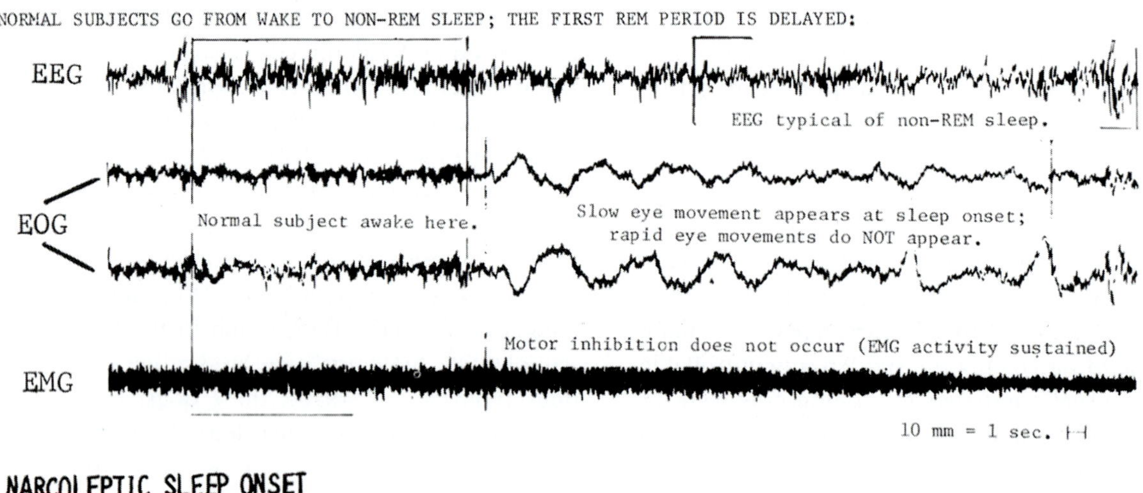

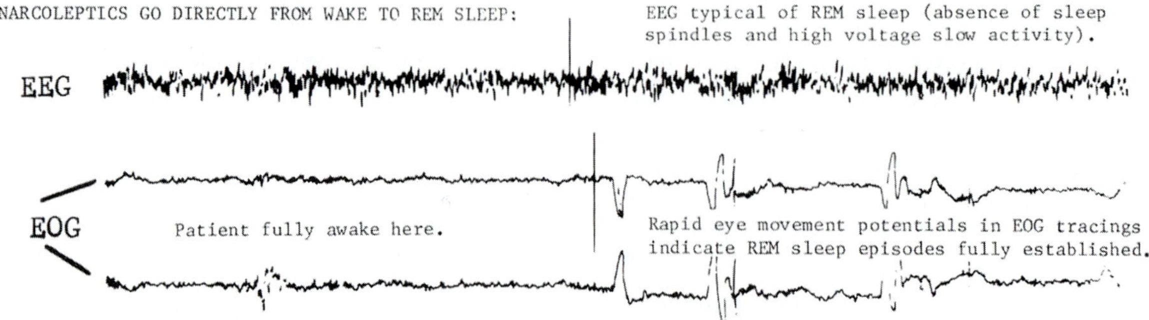

Figure 9.22 Narcolepsy and sleep onset. (a) In normal sleep, individuals first enter SWS prior to REM sleep. (b) Persons with narcolepsy can enter REM sleep from the waking state.

➤ *What is the significance of the sleep differences between normal and narcoleptic persons? (p. 289)*

> rules, was to give him my shoulder and bounce him out of the way, supposedly, and when I came to I was standing in front of our dresser and I had knocked lamps, mirrors and everything off the dresser, hit my head against the wall and my knee against the dresser. (Schenck et al., 1986, p. 294)

Jouvet (1972) reported a similar disorder in cats. He lesioned the brains of cats in the area caudal to the dorsolateral pons. Lesions in this area produce cats that will, in the absence of external stimulation, carry out different behaviors during REM sleep periods. For example, a cat "may attack unknown enemy or play with an absent mouse" (Jouvet, 1972).

What causes REM without atonia? Lesions of the dorsolateral pons have been shown to disrupt the neural connection from the dorsolateral pons to the magnocellular nucleus in the medial medulla (Sakai, 1980). The magnocellular nucleus is active during REM sleep (Kanamori, Sakai, & Jouvet, 1980) and lesions of this area also produce REM without atonia (Schenkel & Siegel, 1989). These observations suggest that the neural connection between the dorsolateral pons and the magnocellular nucleus is involved in the inhibition of muscle tone during REM sleep, and that failure of this area to function properly produces REM without atonia.

Slow-Wave Sleep Disorders. You should not confuse REM without atonia with sleepwalking. REM without atonia is a disorder of REM sleep in which dreams are acted out. By contrast, **sleepwalking**, or **somnambulism**, occurs during SWS and is not related to dreaming. Sleepwalking is most often seen in children, who usually outgrow the problem. In a typical episode, a child gets out of bed and walks around his or her room for up to a half hour. The child usually will walk in a poorly coordinated manner but may engage in such activities as opening a door or going to the bathroom. While sleepwalking, the child is not responsive to others and will either return to his or her bed and continue sleeping or awaken in a confused state. When the child awakens, he or she will have no recollection of having sleepwalked. The only treatment for sleepwalking involves implementing appropriate safety measures such as locking windows and doors.

Night terrors, or ***pavor nocturnus***, is an abrupt awakening from SWS accompanied by intense autonomic nervous system arousal and feelings of panic. A person experiencing a night terror typically lets out a piercing cry, sits upright in bed, and stares into space. The panic fades quickly, and the person will then go back to sleep. A night terror should not be confused with a nightmare, which is an anxiety-induced dream. A person who experiences night terrors will not recall any dream. Night terrors are most common in children, especially ages 3 to 8, and are usually temporary; treatment is generally not necessary.

Nocturnal enuresis, or bedwetting, is another SWS disorder. The ability to control the bladder during the night develops as a child matures; most children by age 4 or 5 do not wet the bed. One way to treat chronic bedwetting is through the use of a commercial device that establishes an association between bladder tension and awakening. When the child begins to wet, an alarm rings and awakens the child. The purpose of this procedure is to form an association between the need to urinate and the alarm. With repeated trials, the child will awaken rather than wet the bed. This treatment, which represents one type of conditioning, usually is effective, although relapse occurs in approximately 25 percent of children (Johnson, 1981). Reconditioning occurs quickly upon retreatment and often cures bedwetting permanently. For more on conditioning, see Chapter 14 (learning).

Before You Go On

What is the difference between REM without atonia and sleepwalking?

What is the difference between night terrors and nightmares?

Section Review

- There are two major classes of sleep disorders: insomnia, or failing to get enough sleep, and hypersomnia, or getting too much sleep.
- One example of insomnia is sleep apnea, which occurs when an obstruction in the windpipe causes a cessation of breathing (apnea) during sleep.
- A person with insomnia may take a long time to get to sleep, awaken frequently during the night, and/or awaken several hours before normal rising time.
- Anxiety and depression are major causes of insomnia, along with stimulating drugs and noisy or unfamiliar environments.

sleepwalking (or **somnambulism**) Movement during SWS, such as getting out of bed and walking.

night terrors (or ***pavor nocturnus***) An abrupt awakening from SWS accompanied by intense autonomic nervous system arousal and feelings of panic.

nocturnal enuresis (or **bedwetting**) An SWS disorder characterized by an inability to control the bladder during sleep.

- Narcolepsy, a type of hypersomnia, is characterized by sudden, uncontrollable sleep attacks that can last from 2 to 15 minutes.
- Narcolepsy appears to result from damage to the locus coeruleus, which allows REM sleep to occur in the waking state.
- Other symptoms of narcolepsy include cataplexy, a complete loss of muscle tone initiated by intense circumstances; sleep paralysis, a brief paralysis that occurs when the person is going to sleep or awakening and is accompanied by high levels of anxiety; and hallucinations.
- Disorders of SWS include sleepwalking or somnambulism, walking around while still asleep for up to 30 minutes; night terrors (*pavor nocturnus*), an abrupt awakening from SWS accompanied by intense autonomic nervous system arousal and feelings of panic; and nocturnal enuresis or bedwetting.

Chapter Review

Critical Thinking Questions

1. Heather is planning a trip from California to Australia. Describe the biological consequences she is likely to experience as a result of her trip (the time difference is 11 hours). What might Heather do to minimize the effects of jet lag?
2. Swen lives in northern Finland. During the winter, he experiences several days with no sunlight. What might be the effects of these "endless nights"? How might Swen avoid or alleviate these effects?
3. Carolyn dreamed that she was being chased by a lion. Interpret Carolyn's dream from the activation synthesis perspective.

Vocabulary Questions

1. ________________ is a pattern of mood changes based on the seasons.
2. People who are most alert in the morning are called ________________; people who are most alert in the evening are referred to as ________________.
3. The sleep-wake cycle that occurs in the absence of external time cues is called a ________________.
4. Two examples of phase-sequence problems are ________________ and ________________.
5. When we are awake, the active EEG pattern is called ________________ activity, and the relaxed EEG pattern is called ________________ activity.
6. The area within the reticular formation responsible for cortical activity and behavioral alertness is the ________________.
7. The two distinct EEG patterns observed during Stage 2 sleep are ________________ and ________________.
8. Stages 1 through 4 sleep are also called ________________.
9. The ________________, located in a thin strip along the midline of the reticular formation, control the length of slow-wave sleep; REM sleep is controlled by the ________________.
10. A ________________ is an altered state of consciousness in which remembered images and fantasies are temporarily confused with external reality.
11. According to the ________________ theory, dreams are a way of dealing with life's problems.
12. A repeated interruption of sleep caused by the cessation of breathing is called ________________.
13. The main characteristic of ________________ is sudden, uncontrollable sleep attacks.
14. The maintenance of muscle tone during REM sleep is called ________________.
15. The inability to control the bladder during the night is called ________________ ________________ or ________________.

Review Questions

1. A change in biological functioning that occurs over a 24-hour period is called a
   a. circadian cycle.
   b. circannual pattern.
   c. circular pattern.
   d. cyclical rhythm.
2. The circadian rhythm is controlled by
   a. the pineal gland.
   b. the suprachiasmatic nucleus.
   c. the reticular formation.
   d. the phases of the moon.
3. Zeitgeber means
   a. sleep giver.
   b. time taker.
   c. time giver.
   d. sleep taker.

4. In rotating shift workers, a ________________ is more manageable than a ________________.
   a. night shift, swing shift
   b. phase-delay shift, phase-advance shift
   c. day shift, swing shift
   d. phase-advance shift, phase-delay shift
5. The part of the brain that controls arousal is the
   a. pineal gland.
   b. reticular activating system.
   c. frontal lobe.
   d. cerebellum.
6. The five levels of sleep are
   a. alpha, beta, theta, delta, and gamma.
   b. Stage 1, Stage 2, Stage 3, Stage 4, and REM sleep.
   c. alpha, beta, theta, delta, and REM.
   d. Stage 1, Stage 2, Stage 3, Stage 4, and delta.
7. Most of our dreams occur during
   a. Stage 1 sleep.
   b. Stage 3 sleep.
   c. Stage 4 sleep.
   d. REM sleep.
8. The idea that we need sleep to restore our biological resources is called
   a. the restorative theory.
   b. the evolutionary perspective.
   c. the cognitive theory.
   d. the activation synthesis hypothesis.
9. We dream because we need to express our unconscious desires, according to the
   a. cognitive theory.
   b. activation synthesis hypothesis.
   c. evolutionary theory.
   d. psychoanalytic theory.
10. According to the ________________, dreams are a mental interpretation of the neural activity that occurs during sleep.
   a. cognitive theory
   b. activation synthesis hypothesis
   c. evolutionary theory
   d. psychoanalytic theory
11. We are said to be having a ________________ when we are conscious of our dream state.
   a. flashback
   b. Freudian slip
   c. hallucination
   d. lucid dream
12. The long-term inability to obtain adequate sleep is called
   a. caffeine overload.
   b. insomnia.
   c. hypersomnia.
   d. narcolepsy.
13. Three symptoms observed in narcoleptics, in addition to the sleep attacks, are
   a. cataplexy, sleep paralysis, and hallucinations.
   b. cataplexy, lucid dreams, and REM sleep.
   c. insomnia, sleep paralysis, and hallucinations.
   d. insomnia, lucid dreams, and hallucinations.
14. Sleepwalking and night terrors both occur during
   a. slow-wave sleep.
   b. REM sleep.
   c. the waking state.
   d. lucid dreams.

Suggested Readings

DEMENT, W. C. (1992). *The sleepwatchers.* Stanford, CA: Stanford Alumni Association.

HORNE, J. (1988). *Why we sleep: The function of sleep in humans and other animals.* Oxford: Oxford University Press.

MOORCROFT, W. H. (1993). *Sleep, dreaming, and sleep disorders* (2nd ed.). Lanham, MD: University Press of America.

MOORE-EDE, M. C., SULZMAN, F. M., & FULLER, C. A. (1982). *The clocks that time us: Physiology of the circadian timing system.* Cambridge, MA: Harvard University Press.

WEBB, W. (1992). *Sleep: The gentle tyrant* (2nd ed.). Boston, MA: Anker Publishing.

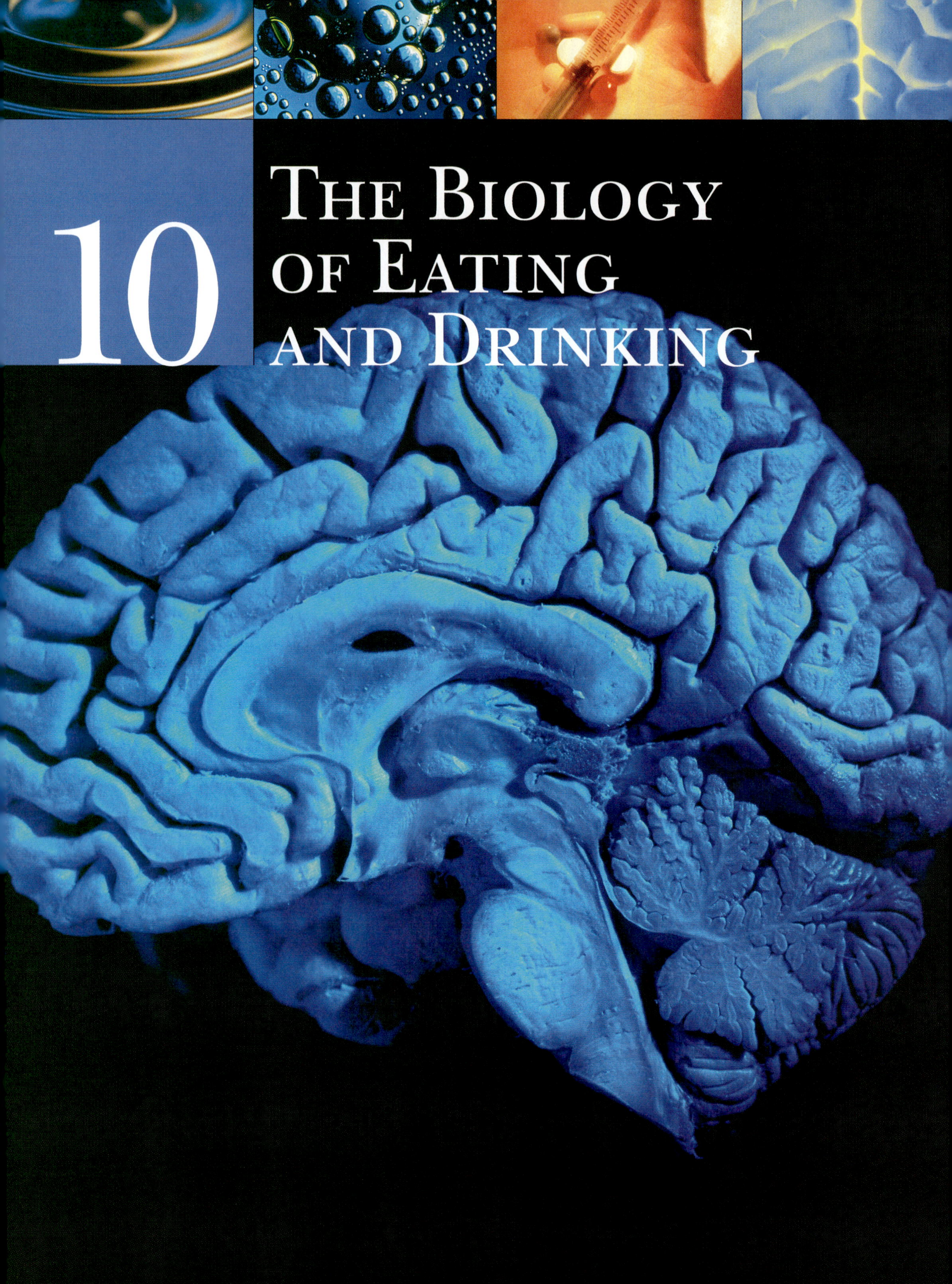

10 The Biology of Eating and Drinking

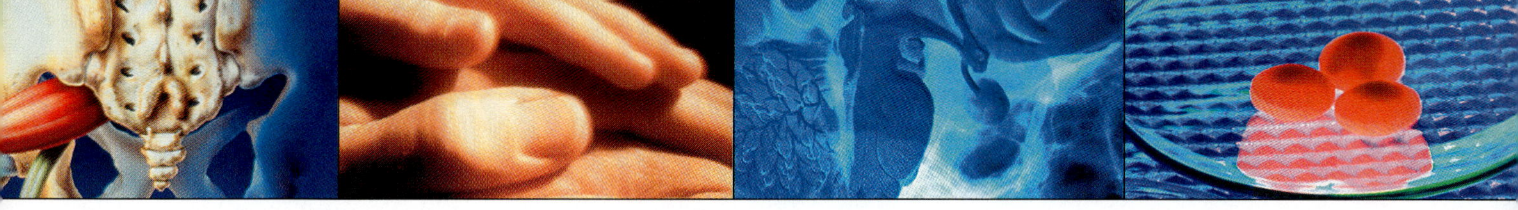

Ever Tried to Eat Just One Potato Chip?

For some time, Chris has noticed that his clothes have been getting tighter and tighter. Unless he loses weight, he will probably have to buy a new wardrobe, the last thing he can afford right now. On several occasions, Chris has tried to diet to lose some weight, without success.

On his first try, he avoided his favorite eating places and declared pizza and beer, two of his favorites, to be off-limits. Chris did okay for a few days, but then was pressured by friends to go out to dinner to celebrate a birthday. How could he refuse? He promised himself that he would only eat a salad, but when he entered the Italian restaurant, the aroma wafting from the kitchen made him realize that he was starving—because of his diet, he hadn't eaten all day! He ended up eating a large bowl of spaghetti, sharing almost half a pepperoni pizza, and drinking three glasses of beer. "Oh well," he thought the next morning. "So much for that diet" and headed for Dunkin' Donuts.

His next attempt, three weeks later, was prompted by his girlfriend's comment about his beer belly. Two days later, he went home for Thanksgiving and his mother, who not only was a great cook but also felt that all of her children were malnourished, insisted that he have a second helping of turkey and dressing. It was no use dieting at home, and he conveniently "forgot" about the diet upon returning to school.

After Christmas break and another round of his mother's delicious holiday cooking, Chris made losing weight a New Year's resolution. He avoided high-calorie foods for about a week and even lost a few pounds. But then he went to a big Super Bowl party. At first, he avoided the goodies, but after an hour or so he could no longer resist. He tried to satisfy his craving with a few potato chips, but before he realized it, he had eaten almost half a bowl. After half a bowl of chips, he was of course thirsty, so he had a beer. He gave up and joined the festivities wholeheartedly, consuming a large chunk of submarine sandwich, a nachos, and more beers.

The next day, Chris realized that he had to do something different to lose weight. A weight-loss center? Too expensive if he really wanted to join, and he'd probably just gain the weight back as soon as he stopped going. Exercise? In January, with 2 feet of snow on the ground? He sighed and headed to the candy machine. ■

◀ The hypothalamus is less than one cubic centimeter in size.

Before You Begin

Why does Chris find it so hard to stick to a diet?

What is it about food that he finds so satisfying?

What changes does he need to make to lose weight?

In this chapter, we will answer these and the following questions:

- What biological processes make Chris hungry when he enters the restaurant and thirsty after he eats the chips?
- What processes satisfy his hunger and thirst?
- How are his hunger for the chips and his thirst for the beer related physiologically?
- What central nervous system structure or structures control his eating and drinking behavior?
- What mechanism made him feel full after his first helping of Thanksgiving dinner?
- What are the psychological and biological bases of eating disorders such as anorexia nervosa and bulimia, and how can they be treated?

Eating

Why do we eat? We humans, especially those of us in developed countries where food is plentiful, do not usually think about it in this way, but the ability to survive depends on the effectiveness of the biological systems controlling eating, the means by which an organism obtains energy. These systems must protect against starvation by initiating eating when an animal needs food. On the flip side, these systems must suppress eating when the animal is full, or **satiated**, to prevent excessive weight gain, which can lead to metabolic disturbances that can threaten the animal's health as well as expose the animal to additional risks of predators. (Have you ever tried to move quickly after Thanksgiving dinner?) The control mechanisms that govern eating behavior lie within the central nervous system (Logue, 1991), but information gathered from peripheral biological systems plays an important role in the maintenance of an adaptive body weight.

But before we learn about these central and peripheral systems, we must learn about the processes they control. The following section, which covers the body's energy needs and digestion, will show you what happens to Chris's body when he consumes that plate of spaghetti; we will then move on to discuss the neural and nonneural mechanisms that control when he starts and stops eating, as well as how much.

Your Body's Energy Needs and the Digestive Process

The operation of all bodily functions requires energy. There are three nutritional substances that can be converted to energy—carbohydrate, fat, and protein. The normal animal has only limited reserves of these, so food is consumed to correct any depletion and restore energy to the level necessary for optimal physiological functioning. When Chris puts a forkful of spaghetti into his mouth, he chews it, breaking it up into a small mass appetizingly called a bolus, with the enzymes in saliva beginning the breakdown of carbohydrates. When he swallows the bolus, it passes through the esophagus into the stomach, where stomach acid and enzymes continue the digestion process with the breakdown of proteins. The food then passes to the small intestine where most digestion occurs. Enzymes break down the food into smaller components that can be absorbed by the small intestine (see **Figure 10.1**). (Anything not absorbed by the small intestine passes into the large intestine in preparation for elimination—you get the picture!) For example when carbohydrates, now in the form of glucose, are absorbed by the small intestine, Chris's blood glucose level rises. Then insulin is released from the pancreas, speeding up the absorption of glucose into the liver cells where it is converted into glycogen and stored. Stored glycogen can be later converted back to glucose and distributed to the cells to supply energy for cell metabolism. Any excess glucose is stored as fat in a type of tissue called adipose tissue.

The metabolism of nutrients is illustrated in **Figure 10.2**. Energy nutrients (carbohydrates, fats, proteins) are broken down into simpler compounds (glucose, fatty acids, amino acids). The simpler compounds can be used to generate energy or to form essential body compounds such as protein and nucleic acids. Any excess energy can be stored as fat, which can be made available in the case of future energy needs.

Animals monitor nutritional levels and regulate food intake to correct any nutritional deficiencies. Kissileff (1971) observed that animals increase their food intake to meet the higher nutritional energy needs of a cold environment (fat makes good insulation, and shivering uses up a lot of calories!). Also, Janowitz and Grossman (1949) showed that animals fed a nonnutritive substance will increase total food intake to maintain a constant caloric level. In the next section, we begin our discussion of the central nervous system's control of food intake.

---

satiated A feeling of fullness.

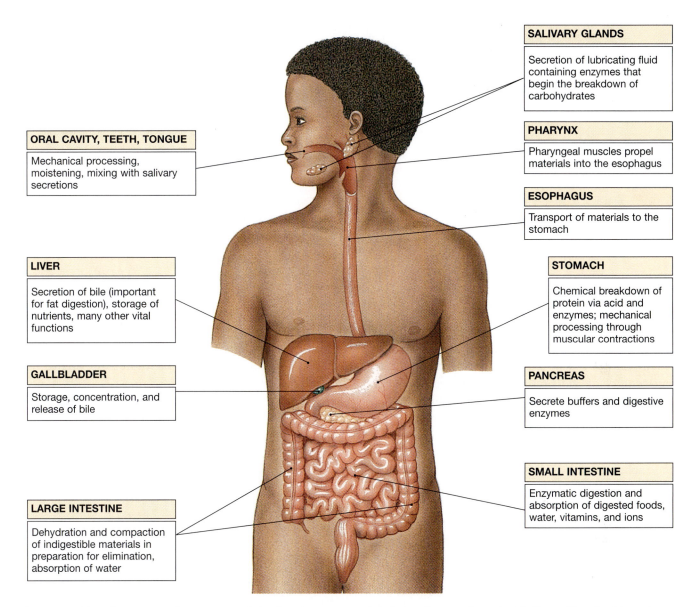

SALIVARY GLANDS
Secretion of lubricating fluid containing enzymes that begin the breakdown of carbohydrates

ORAL CAVITY, TEETH, TONGUE
Mechanical processing, moistening, mixing with salivary secretions

PHARYNX
Pharyngeal muscles propel materials into the esophagus

ESOPHAGUS
Transport of materials to the stomach

LIVER
Secretion of bile (important for fat digestion), storage of nutrients, many other vital functions

STOMACH
Chemical breakdown of protein via acid and enzymes; mechanical processing through muscular contractions

GALLBLADDER
Storage, concentration, and release of bile

PANCREAS
Secrete buffers and digestive enzymes

SMALL INTESTINE
Enzymatic digestion and absorption of digested foods, water, vitamins, and ions

LARGE INTESTINE
Dehydration and compaction of indigestible materials in preparation for elimination, absorption of water

Figure 10.1 Digestive system. The structures of the digestive system and their functions are shown in this figure. When food is swallowed it passes through the stomach into the small intestine, where it is absorbed.

➤ *Where in the digestive system does digestion begin? (p. 296)*

Before You Go On

Describe what happened to the potato chips Chris ate at the Super Bowl party from the time he put them in his mouth, using the terms: bolus, breakdown, absorption, and glycogen.

Historical View of the Role of the Hypothalamus in Hunger and Satiety

Early research suggested that one area of the hypothalamus, the **lateral hypothalamus (LH),** controls the initiation of eating, or feeding behavior, and another, the **ventromedial hypothalamus (VMH),** controls the inhibition of eating, or satiety (see **Figure 10.3**). This view is now known to be an oversimplification, with recent studies showing that two fiber tracts, rather than two localized structures, control the initiation of eating and the inhibition of eating. We first look at the historical view of the role of the hypothalamus in hunger and satiety, followed by a description of a more contemporary view.

lateral hypothalamus (LH) An area in the hypothalamus involved in hunger and the initiation of eating.

ventromedial hypothalamus (VMH) An area in the brain involved in satiety and the suppression of eating.

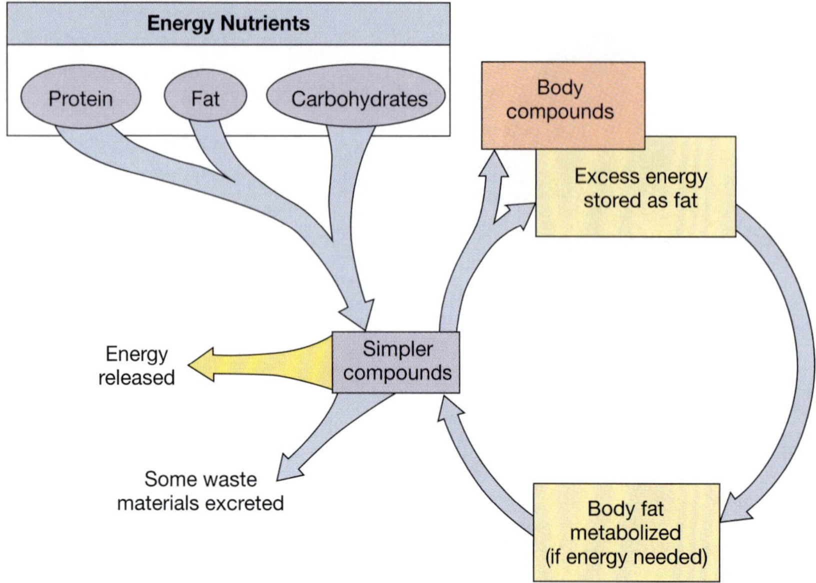

Figure 10.2 Energy nutrients. The carbohydrates, fats, and proteins can be either converted to energy or broken down into simpler compounds (glycogen, fatty acids, amino acids). The simpler compounds can be used to generate energy or to form essential body compounds such as muscles and bones. Any excess energy can be stored as fat, which can be made available in the case of future nutritional deficiency.

➤ *What factor has the most influence on the amount of food consumed during a meal? (p. 296)*

LH-Lesion Syndrome. The pioneering research of Anand and Brobeck (1951) suggested that the "feeding center" of the brain was located in the lateral hypothalamus. After the lateral hypothalamus was destroyed, a rat that had not eaten for some time (for example, 24 hours) and was presumably **deprived** (the clinical term for "hungry"), immediately stopped eating (**aphagia**) and drinking (**adipsia**) and died within a week. This pattern of behavioral change is called the **LH-lesion syndrome**. However, Teitelbaum and Epstein (1962) discovered that with appropriate treatment, some LH-lesioned animals would regain their normal eating habits and to a lesser extent regain drinking behaviors.

Teitelbaum and Epstein (1962) identified four stages in the animals' recovery from surgery; **Table 10.1** summarizes the stages. In Stage I, the animal will neither eat nor drink; to survive, it must be force-fed through a tube connected to the stomach. The rat enters Stage II approximately 20 days after surgery. During this stage, it eats palatable food but is not able to regulate food intake to meet its needs. It will not eat dry food and will not drink. During Stage III, which begins about 40 days after surgery, the ability to regulate food intake to meet nutritional needs reappears. The rat will eat dry food if hydrated but still will not drink water. A large percentage of LH-lesioned rats die before reaching Stage IV, but those who survive this long will start drinking water again.

deprived Being hungry or without food.

aphagia A failure to eat.

adipsia A failure to drink.

LH-lesion syndrome The pattern of behavior, aphagia and adipsia, that follows damage to the lateral hypothalamus.

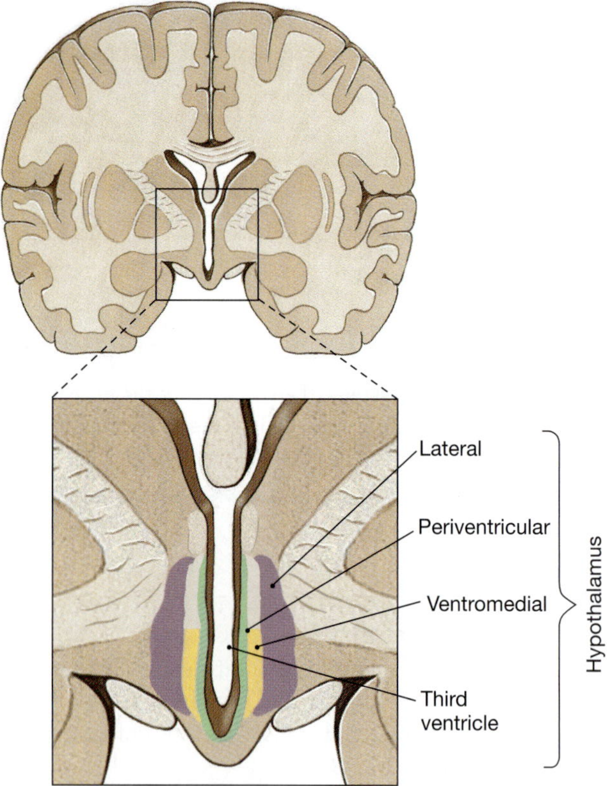

Figure 10.3 The hypothalamus and eating behavior. A coronal plane view showing the location of three structures (lateral hypothalamus, paraventricular nucleus, and ventromedial hypothalamus) that control eating behavior.

➤ *What happens to eating behavior when the lateral hypothalamus is destroyed? (p. 298–299)*

Table 10.1 ■ Stages of Recovery in Animals with the LH-Lesion Syndrome

	Stage I: Adipsia/Aphagia	Stage II: Adipsia/Anorexia	Stage III: Adipsia/Dehydration-Adipsia	Stage IV: "Recovery"
Eats wet palatable foods	No	Yes	Yes	Yes
Regulates food intake and body weight on wet palatable foods	No	No	Yes	Yes
Eats dry foods (if hydrated)	No	No	Yes	Yes
Drinks water; survives on dry food and water	No	No	No	Yes

Source: Teitelbaum, P., & Epstein, A. M. (1962). The lateral hypothalamic syndrome: Recovery of feeding and drinking after lateral hypothalamic lesions. *Psychological Review, 69*, 74–90.

Even an animal that survives to Stage IV still has a number of problems. First, although it will drink while eating (**prandial drinking**), it does not drink without eating even when deprived of water. Second, the animal is extremely sensitive to the quality of its food: it will not consume any food that does not taste good. Finally, it never regains the weight lost during the initial stages of the disorder but eats only enough food to maintain its postoperative weight. **Figure 10.4** compares the physical appearance and body weight of an aphagic rat (part c) and a normal rat (part b).

The pattern of recovery of eating and drinking in the LH-lesioned animals resembles the sequence of the development of eating and drinking in normal animals (Teitelbaum, Cheng, & Rozin, 1969). Newborn rats drink milk (essentially a wet food) but refuse water, a pattern of behavior that resembles Stage II. A slightly older animal will eat dry food and drink water while eating, but it will not drink without eating even after it has been deprived of water, a pattern resembling Stage III. This recovery of eating and drinking following LH lesions suggests that the brain possesses sufficient flexibility to use neurons other than the LH to initiate eating and drinking behavior. Teitelbaum's recovery data also tells us something important about the eating disorder anorexia nervosa, which we will discuss later in this chapter.

VMH-Lesion Syndrome. Hetherington and Ranson (1942) found that destruction of the VMH produced a dramatic increase in rats' food intake; the weight of VMH-lesioned rats rose rapidly to double or even quadruple that of normal rats. This pattern of behavioral change is called the **VMH-lesion syndrome**, and the excessive intake of food is called **hyperphagia**. The VMH-lesion syndrome occurs in two stages (Brobeck,

prandial drinking Drinking while eating.

VMH-lesion syndrome The pattern of behavior, hyperphagia and finickiness, that follows damage to the ventromedial hypothalamus.

hyperphagia The excessive intake of food.

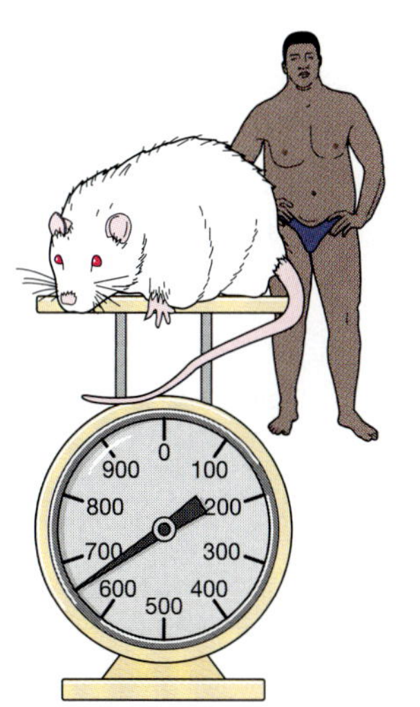

Figure 10.4 Comparison of hyperphagic, normal, and aphagic rats. Before a lesion of the lateral or ventromedial hypothalamus, these rats weighed the same. In their present condition, the hyperphagic rat (a) weighs 650 grams, the normal rat (b) weighs 175 grams, and the aphagic rat (c) weighs 100 grams.
➤ *Does a lesion of the VMH produce hyperphagia or aphagia? (p. 299)*

Tepperman, & Long, 1943). The dynamic stage is characterized by a steady increase in food intake, reaching four times the normal level over the first 10 to 20 days following surgery. The hyperphagic rat shows a steady increase in weight, which peaks at two to four times the normal weight about 40 days following surgery. **Figure 10.4** compares both the physical appearance and the body weight of a hyperphagic rat (part a) and a normal rat (part b). Weight stabilizes during the static stage. It seems that once the new weight becomes stabilized, lesioned animals consume only enough food to maintain it. Bray and Gallagher (1975) reported a similar change in the eating behavior of human patients who experienced a pathology (for example, tumor or disease) in the VMH area. These patients, like the rats, developed hyperphagia and obesity.

Teitelbaum (1955) observed that, in addition to being hyperphagic and obese, VMH-lesioned rats are very finicky eaters. They will not eat any bad-tasting food such as stale chow or food mixed with bitter-tasting quinine (which nonlesioned rats will eat, although just a little), but they will eat a greater amount of sweet-tasting or highly palatable food than normal rats. The VMH-lesioned rats become less willing to work for food as their weight increases (Miller, Bailey, & Stevenson, 1950), and the obese rat is considerably less motivated to obtain food than is the normal rat. In addition, Gladfelter and Brobeck (1962) found that the VMH-lesioned animal is less active than a nonlesioned animal in a quiet environment, but more active in a noisy one (for example, during the time when the animals are tended). These results suggest that the environment is more influential in determining the level of activity in VMH-lesioned animals than it is in nonlesioned ones.

The Cephalic Reflex. When a human or nonhuman animal is exposed to food, it exhibits a set of responses that prepares it to digest, metabolize, and store the food once it has been consumed. These internal preparatory responses are called **cephalic reflexes** (Powley, 1977). A reflex is said to be cephalic (cephalic = brain) when input to the brain originates in the head region, output to the periphery is sent to the autonomic nervous system and endocrine system, and the central nervous system mediates the input and output. Cephalic reflexes are elicited by the taste and smell of food, and include the secretion of saliva in the mouth, gastric juices in the stomach, pancreatic enzymes in the small intestine, and insulin into the bloodstream. The intensity of these cephalic responses is directly related to the palatability of food: the more palatable the food, the greater the cephalic responses and the larger the amount of food that is consumed. **Table 10.2** presents a summary of cephalic response magnitudes as a function of the sensory characteristics of different foods.

The lateral hypothalamus appears to be involved in this cephalic reflexive regulation of eating. The smell or taste of food or even the sight of food activates the LH (see **Figure 10.5**). The lateral hypothalamus receives direct input from the olfactory and gustatory systems

cephalic reflexes A set of responses that prepare an animal to digest, metabolize, and store food that is controlled by the central nervous system.

Table 10.2 ▪ Cephalic Response Amplitude as a Function of Sensory Quality of Food

Cephalic Responses and Afferent Stimuli	Foods Compared	Subjects
Salivary secretion:		
Sight of food	Pickled plum > orange > apple > biscuits (approx.: 6:3.4:1.2:1)	Man (Japanese)
Sight and smell of food	Banana split or pizza > unappealing pizza (approx.: 7:1)	Man
Gastric secretion:		
Sham feeding	Self-selected meal > hospital meal > gruel (approx.: 1.8:1.4:1)	Man
Sham feeding	Meat > milk > bread (approx.: 7:6:1)	Dog
Sham feeding	Fish > meat (approx.: 1.8:1)	Man (Russian)
Sham feeding	Meat > milk > bread (approx.: 2.2:2:1)	Dog
Exocrine pancreas secretion:		
Sight and smell of food	Usual French breakfast > forced beefsteak at breakfast (approx.: 4:1)	Man (French)
Sham feeding	Pard dog food > rat chow	Rat

Source: Powley, T. L. (1977). The ventromedial hypothalamic syndrome, satiety, and a cephalic phase hypothesis. *Psychological Review, 84,* 89–126.

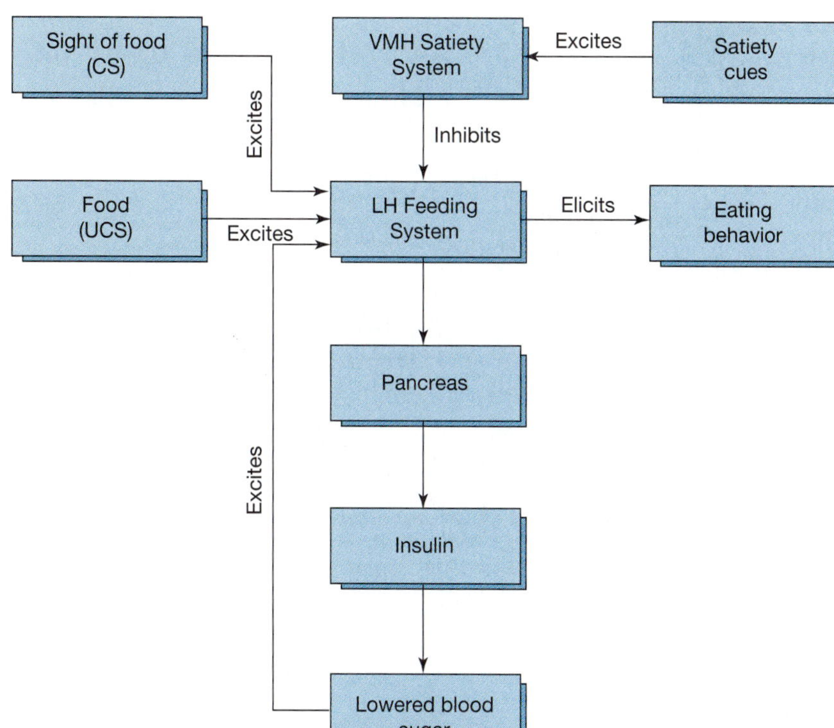

Figure 10.5 Hypothalamic-cephalic feeding system. The sight of food (CS), the smell or taste of food (UCS), or both can activate the LH feeding system, which then elicits eating. Stimulation of the lateral hypothalamus also causes the pancreas to release insulin, which acts to lower blood glucose level. The lowered blood glucose level continues the stimulation of the lateral hypothalamus. Eating will continue until the satiety cues activate the VMH satiety system, which in turn inhibits the LH feeding system and causes eating behavior to end. ➤ *Which area of the hypothalamus is involved in regulation of the cephalic reflex. (p. 300)*

(Norgren, 1970; Pfaff & Pfaffman, 1969), and the intensity of the response to this input is directly related to the palatability of food (Burton, Mora, & Rolls, 1975). One reason that more palatable foods are eaten in greater amounts than are less palatable foods is that more palatable foods generate a greater cephalic response. In addition, activation of the lateral hypothalamus enhances the cephalic reflexes. In a positive feedback loop (see **p. 123–125** in Chapter 4), these cephalic responses maintain the activation of the feeding system (Anand, Chhina, & Singh, 1962), which in turn maintains eating behavior.

Although this cycle explains the increased ability of palatable foods to stimulate eating, we must look to an additional set of responses (which also have been identified as cephalic) for an explanation of the active rejection of food. Doty (1967) found that taste cues could also elicit a rejection reflex consisting of ejection, gagging, and vomiting. The rejection reflex is produced by unpalatable food (for example, quinine) and is the result of stimulation of the feeding system in the presence of unpalatable foods (Robinson & Mishkin, 1968).

Powley (1977) proposed that one major function of the VMH satiety system is to control the intensity of the cephalic responses to food (refer to **Figure 10.5**). Satisfaction of nutritional needs leads to the activation of the VMH, which inhibits the LH and, thus, stops eating. According to Powley, the destruction of the VMH satiety system eliminates VMH inhibition and causes an exaggeration of cephalic responses to food. In a VMH-lesioned animal, palatable foods produce a heightened preparatory response, thereby increasing food intake; unpalatable foods increase the cephalic rejection response and cause an increased avoidance of unpleasant foods. Powley argues that this exaggeration of the cephalic responses to food is responsible for both the excessive eating and the finickiness about food exhibited by VMH-lesioned animals.

Several studies have demonstrated this greater cephalic responding in VMH-lesioned rats. Strubbe and Steffens (1975) measured insulin release in VMH-lesioned and normal rats beginning within the first minute of feeding and found that the insulin response of VMH-lesioned animals was four times faster than the response of normal animals. Weingarten and Powley (1977) reported a significantly larger secretion of gastric acid in VMH-lesioned animals than in normal animals; Rozkowska and Fonberg (1973) found a greater salivary response in VMH-lesioned rats as compared to normal rats. Also, Weingarten and Powley (1977) compared food intake and weight gain in VMH-lesioned and nonlesioned animals exposed to two diets. One of these diets (Purina rat pellets) elicited a minimal level of cephalic responding; the other (Pard dog food) produced a high level of cephalic responding. Although none of the animals overate or gained weight on the Purina diet, the VMH-lesioned animals became hyperphagic and gained weight over a 2-week period when switched to the Pard diet. When returned to the Purina diet, these animals reduced their intake and stopped gaining weight. These results suggest that one reason VMH-lesioned animals overeat is that they are overresponsive to palatable foods.

Comparative Psychology Applied to Eating Behavior. Our discussion suggests that VMH-lesioned animals have a heightened preference for palatable foods and overeat because of an overresponsive cephalic reaction to food. But what does the behavior of obese, VMH-lesioned rats have to do with human eating behavior? Recall from Chapter 1 that in comparative psychology, researchers compare the behavior of humans with that of other animals. In an extensive study, Stanley Schachter (1971) did just that. He compared the eating habits of obese and normal-weight subjects (humans and nonhuman animals) by conducting an extensive review of the results of studies investigating (1) the effect of a VMH-lesion in animals and (2) the behavioral characteristics of obese humans, who were college students at Columbia University. (Schachter defined obesity as a weight 15 percent above the norm established by the Metropolitan Life Insurance Company for a specific height and weight.) First, Schachter presented the comparisons of habits in the form of a "batting average," a ratio of the number of studies that showed differences to the total number of studies conducted. For example, Schachter found that 9 out of 9 studies (or .100) found that VMH-lesioned animals ate more than nonlesioned animals and that 2 out of 3 studies (or .67) found that obese human subjects ate more than normal-weight human subjects. Second, he expressed the average percentage difference between the behavior of obese and normal subjects as a "fat" to "normal" (F/N) ratio. The results of Schachter's analysis are presented in **Table 10.3**. For example, Schachter found VMH-lesioned animals ate (on the average) 1.19 times more than nonlesioned animals and that obese human subjects ate (on the average) 1.66 times more than did normal-weight human subjects.

Table 10.3 ■ Eating Habits of Animals and Humans

	Batting Average		F/N ratio	
	Animals	Humans	Animals	Humans
Amount of food eaten	9/9	2/3	1.19	1.66
Number of meals per day	4/4	3/3	0.85	0.92
Amount eaten per meal	2/2	5/5	1.34	1.29
Speed of eating	1/1	1/1	1.28	1.26
Good taste	5/6	2/2	1.45	1.42
Bad taste	3/4	1/2	0.76	0.84

Note: Batting average refers to number of studies showing a difference to all studies conducted; F/N refers to ratio of fat to normal behavior.

Source: Schachter, S. (1971). Some extraordinary facts about obese humans and rats. *American Psychologist, 26*, 129–144. Copyright 1971 by the American Psychological Association. Reprinted by permission.

Schachter's analysis suggests that, compared to their normal counterparts, both hyperphagic animals and obese humans eat more food during a day, eat fewer meals per day, eat more per meal, eat faster, like good-tasting food more, dislike bad-tasting food more, and are less motivated to expend unusual effort to obtain food. Furthermore, obese humans and hyperphagic rats continue to eat with a full stomach (a procedure called **preloading**); normal-weight animals and humans will generally not eat with a full stomach, unless perhaps their mothers offer them seconds at Thanksgiving! Note that the F/N ratios in many cases are nearly identical in human and nonhuman animals.

The hyperphagic animal and the obese human also share a number of characteristics unrelated to eating: compared to their normal-weight counterparts, both are more emotional (or in the ratio case, measure as more reactive to threatening or challenging stimuli), exhibit greater sensitivity to pain, and are more responsive to non-food-related stimuli. The remarkable similarities of eating habits across the board in obese humans and hyperphagic animals led Schachter to conclude that the physiological locus of human obesity must also lie in the ventromedial area of the hypothalamus.

Before You Go On

Describe the components of the cephalic reflex that caused Chris to feel hungry when he entered the restaurant.

Beyond the Hypothalamus: Current Views on the Control of Eating Behavior

Two lines of evidence led a researcher named Edward Stricker to question the idea that the lateral hypothalamus solely controls feeding behavior and the ventromedial hypothalamus solely controls satiety.

The Nigrostriatal Feeding System. Recall from Chapter 8 that the **nigrostriatal pathway** is a dopaminergic system (uses dopamine as a neurotransmitter) that

preloading A procedure that reduces food intake as a result of food being placed in the stomach prior to food being available.

nigrostriatal pathway A fiber tract that begins in the substantia nigra, ends in the basal ganglia, and initiates eating behavior.

originates in the substantia nigra, passes through the lateral hypothalamus, and proceeds to the basal ganglia (see **Figure 10.6**). This pathway is involved in the control of voluntary behavior; eating and drinking, although essential to an organism's survival, are considered voluntary behavior. Stricker (1983) destroyed parts of the nigrostriatal bundle in the basal ganglia, while leaving intact the neurons in the lateral hypothalamus. Rats with these lesions showed aphagia and adipsia even though the lateral hypothalamus was not damaged. Thus, destruction of the nigrostriatal pathway *outside of* the LH produced all of the symptoms of the LH-lesion syndrome. As Stricker confirmed in a 1990 study, the LH-lesion syndrome results from the interruption of this pathway (see **Figure 10.6**).

The second line of evidence casting doubt on hypothalamic theory was assembled by Neve, Kozlowski, and Marshall. In a 1982 study, they observed a compensatory increase in the functioning of the other dopaminergic neurons in the nigrostriatal system following LH lesions. These investigators proposed that the compensatory response allows the recovery from LH lesions described earlier in this chapter.

You should not conclude from the above discussion that the lateral hypothalamus has no specific role in feeding behavior. Research has indicated that direct electrical stimulation of the LH elicits feeding behavior. Further, Stanley, Anderson, Grayson, and Leibowitz (1989) found that hungry animals show a higher level of **neuropeptide Y (NPY)** in the LH. As animals eat, the level of NPY declines. As we will learn later (see **p. 310**), the internal changes associated with deprivation (hunger) are detected in the LH and surrounding area, which serves to activate the nigrostriatal pathway and initiate eating behavior.

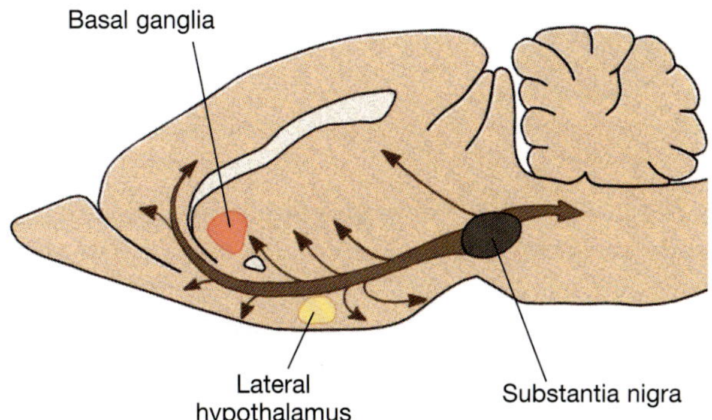

Figure 10.6 The nigrostriatal feeding system in the rat brain. The nigrostriatal pathway originates in the substantia nigra, passes through the lateral hypothalamus, and ends at the basal ganglia.
➤ *What type of behavior is controlled by this pathway? (p. 303)*

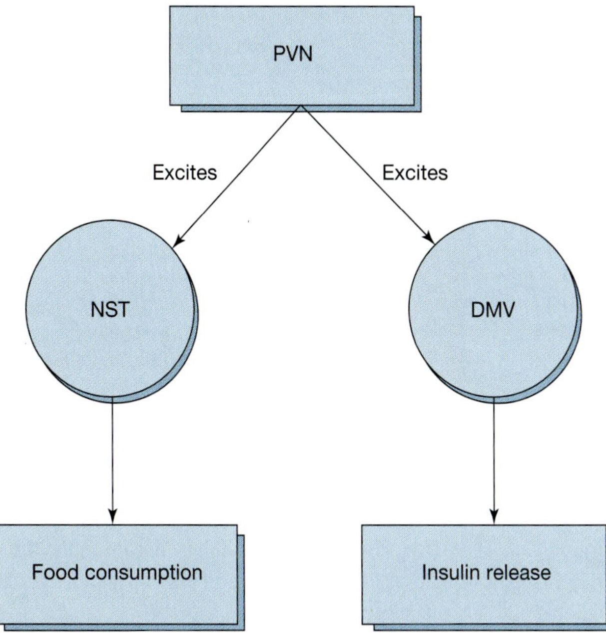

Figure 10.7 The paraventricular satiety system. Fibers from the paraventricular nucleus travel through the outer edges of the ventromedial nucleus to the nucleus of the solitary tract (NST) and the dorsal motor nucleus of the vagus (DMV).
➤ *In what part of the brain are the NST and DMV located? (p. 303)*

The Paraventricular Satiety System. In that same 1990 study, Stricker found that, like the lateral hypothalamus, the ventromedial hypothalamus does not act alone to promote satiety, but it instead is part of a more extensive neural system that regulates this behavior.

Some studies (Kirchgessner & Sclafani, 1988; Leibowitz et al., 1985) suggest that damage to the **paraventricular nucleus (PVN)** of the hypothalamus (refer to **Figure 10.3**) can result in the VMH-lesion syndrome. Fibers from the PVN travel through the outer edges of the ventromedial nucleus en route to two structures in the medulla: the nucleus of the solitary tract (NST) and the **dorsal motor nucleus of the vagus** (**DMV**; see **Figure 10.7**). Both structures are involved in food intake and metabolism: the NST influences the amount of food consumed, especially the intake of foods high in carbohydrates (Chris's pizza and

---

neuropeptide Y (NPY) A peptide neurotransmitter in the lateral hypothalamus involved in hunger and eating behavior.

paraventricular nucleus (PVN) An area of the hypothalamus that is involved in satiety and the suppression of eating.

dorsal motor nucleus of the vagus (DMV) A group of neurons in the medulla that regulates insulin release by the parasympathetic nervous system.

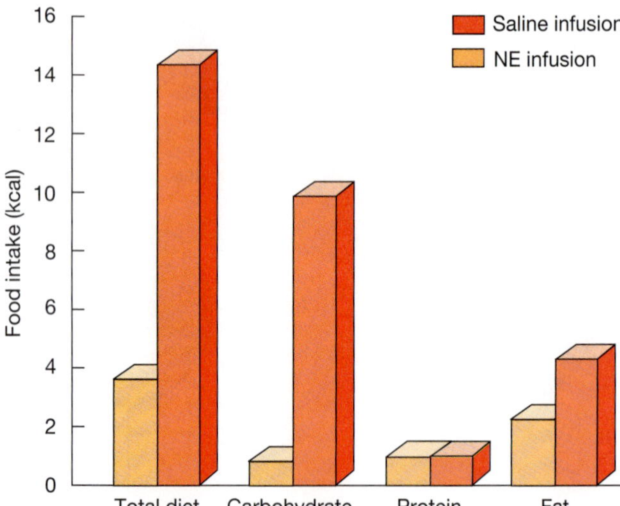

Figure 10.8 The effect on eating behavior of norepinephrine (NE) injected into the PVN. NE increased consumption of carbohydrates and fat, but not protein.

➤ *Why does stimulation of the PVN result in increased consumption? (p. 204)*

spaghetti), and the DMV regulates insulin release by the parasympathetic nervous system.

It appears that damage to the fiber tracts of the NST and DMV from the PVN or VMH is what is producing the behavioral characteristics of the VMH-lesion syndrome. Sclafani (1971) observed that lesions lateral to the VMH produced overeating, a result that Gold, Jones, Sawchenko, and Kapatos (1977) attributed to the destruction of efferent connections from the VMH and the PVN. Lesions that sever PVN connections to the NST and the DMV without damaging the VMH also produce overeating (Kirchgessner & Sclafani, 1988).

What do you think would happen if the paraventricular nucleus were stimulated directly? Leibowitz, Weiss, Yee, and Tretter (1985) wanted to find out, so they injected norepinephrine (NE) directly into the PVN and observed increased consumption of carbohydrates and fats, but not proteins (see **Figure 10.8**). Drugs (e.g., clonidine) that activate certain adrenergic (norepinephrine) receptors also produce overeating when injected into the PVN, whereas drugs that block these adrenergic receptors (e.g., AMPT) suppress eating (Yee, MacLow, Chan, & Leibowitz, 1987). In fact, Yee, MacLow, Chan, and Leibowitz found that continuous injection of clonidine into the PVN caused rats to become fat, whereas continuous administration of AMPT led to a loss of weight.

One would expect that stimulation of receptors in the nigrostriatal pathway would lead to increased consumption, but why does stimulation of receptors in the PVN produce eating? According to Wellman, Davies, Morien, and McMahon (1993), descending fibers from the PVN inhibit the feeding reflexes elicited by the two aforementioned medulla structures—the NST and the DMV. Several researchers (Kow & Pfaff, 1989; Wellman et al., 1993) suggest that the PVN actually contains two classes of adrenergic receptors: α_1-adrenergic receptors and α_2-adrenergic receptors. Input to the PVN can thus have one of two effects. First, activation of the α_1-adrenergic receptors excites the PVN and results in the suppression of eating (see **Figure 10.9a**). Studies have shown that feeding is suppressed by α_1-adrenergic agonists such as phenylephrine (Wellman & Davies, 1991) and amidephrine (Morien, McMahon, & Wellman, 1993). Second, stimulation of the α_2-adrenergic receptors inhibits the PVN and results in an increased intake of food (see **Figure 10.9b**). Studies have shown that eating behavior is enhanced by α_2-adrenergic agonists such as norepinephrine (Goldman, Marino, & Leibowitz, 1985) and inhibited by α_2-adrenergic antagonists such as idazoxan (Alexander et al., 1993) and yohimbine (Berlan et al., 1991).

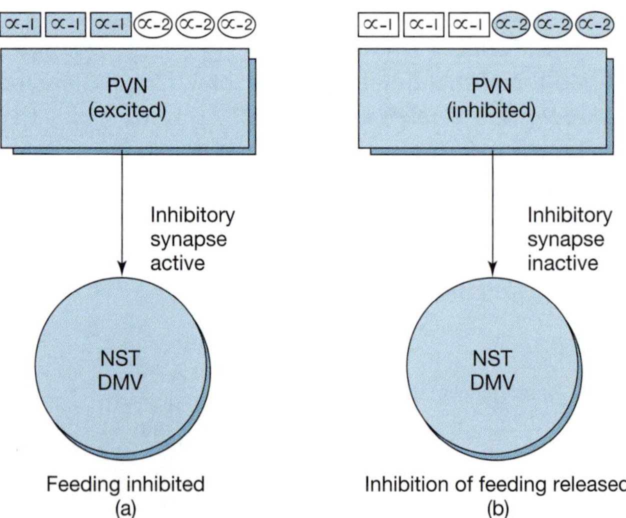

Figure 10.9 The role of the paraventricular nucleus of the hypothalamus in feeding and satiety. (a) When α_1-adrenergic receptors are stimulated, the PVN is excited and inhibits activity in the nucleus of the solitary tract (NST) and dorsal motor nucleus of the vagus (DMV), suppressing eating behavior. (b) When α_2-adrenergic receptors are stimulated, the PVN is inhibited, which releases the inhibition of the NST and the DMV, resulting in an increased intake of food.

➤ *Do adrenergic receptors inhibit or stimulate eating behavior? (p. 305)*

Why would the PVN contain two types of adrenergic receptors? Animals are reluctant to consume novel foods, an instinct that protects them from consuming food that would make them ill. The avoidance of novel foods is called **ingestional neophobia** (Domjan, 1976), a response you may have seen in babies presented with strained vegetables for the first time. As the food becomes more familiar, this response fades and consumption of the avoided food increases. (Unless, of course, the strained vegetable was spinach, which will most likely end up on the floor instead of in the baby's mouth—can you blame her?) Thus, the α_1-adrenergic receptors suppress the eating of a novel food, and, upon repeated presentation of the food, the α_2-adrenergic receptors release the inhibition of eating behavior.

Norepinephrine is not the only neurotransmitter that stimulates neurons in the PVN and VMH. Serotonergic receptors (see Chapter 4) also are located in this area of the brain and, like the α_1-adrenergic receptors, inhibit consumption of food, especially carbohydrates. Researchers have reported that injection of serotonin (5-HT) into either the PVN or the VMH suppresses the consumption of carbohydrates (Leibowitz, Weiss, & Suh, 1990), whereas drugs that either inhibit the synthesis of 5-HT or block 5-HT receptors increase food consumption, especially carbohydrates (Saller & Stricker, 1976; Stallone & Nicolaidis, 1989).

Many drugs that have adrenergic or serotonergic action have an important influence on eating and weight control. Adrenergic agonists such as amphetamine or serotonergic agonists such as fenfluramine have a strong anorexic (appetite suppressing) effect and have been used in the treatment of obesity (Bray, 1992). This effect of these drugs seems to be the result of their excitatory influence on the PVN (see **Figure 10.9a**), which acts to suppress or prevent eating.

Perhaps you have heard of the drug **fen-phen**. This drug actually is composed of two different drugs: **fenfluramine**, a serotonergic agonist, and **phentermine**, a dopaminergic agonist. Both drugs were approved by the Federal Drug Administration (FDA) as appetite suppressants in the treatment of obesity: phentermine in 1959 and fenfluramine in 1973. In the early 1990s, the two drugs were combined as fen-phen. Research (Atkinson et al., 1997; Weintraub et al., 1992) found that fen-phen, when combined with behavioral management techniques, produced significant, long-term weight loss in most obese patients. The success of fen-phen in treating obesity led to its skyrocketing use. However, the FDA had never approved the use of these two drugs together, and some patients developed serious medical problems after long-term use of fen-phen. The Mayo Clinic reported in the August 28, 1997 issue of the *New England Journal of Medicine* that 24 patients had developed heart valve disease after taking fen-phen. Other reports of heart valve disease following the use of fen-phen, even in patients with no prior symptoms of heart disease, led the FDA in 1997 to recommend that patients stop taking fen-phen. Both drugs have subsequently been removed from the market. Hopefully, a new and safe drug treatment for obesity will be forthcoming.

The brain cannot control feeding on its own. The control mechanisms of the central nervous system that initiate and suppress eating must rely on other biological systems for information regarding the nutritional condition of the rest of the body. For example, Chris's nigrostriatal pathway may have initiated the eating of the spaghetti and the pizza, but it was his olfactory system smelling the food that made him realize he needed something to eat. In the following sections, we will learn how information from other parts of the body reaches the central nervous system to let Chris know when he is hungry and when it is time to stop eating.

Before You Go On

Describe the nigrostriatal pathway and explain why early researchers mistakenly concluded that the lateral hypothalamus was the feeding center.

Describe the paraventricular satiety system and explain why early researchers mistakenly concluded that the ventromedial hypothalamus was the satiety center.

Compare the effects of PVN α_1-adrenergic receptors and α_2-adrenergic receptors on feeding behavior.

Section Review

- The main function of eating is to regulate energy balance and maintain an optimal body weight.
- Destruction of the lateral hypothalamus has been found to produce a loss of appetite and a loss of weight.
- Damage to the ventromedial hypothalamus has been found to cause overeating and obesity.

---

ingestional neophobia A reluctance to consume novel foods.

fen-phen A drug that is composed of fenfluramine and phentermine.

fenfluramine A serotonergic agonist that has a strong anorexic effect.

phentermine A dopaminergic agonist that has a strong anorexic effect.

- When a human or nonhuman animal eats palatable foods, the act of eating stimulates internal changes (salivation, gastric juice release, insulin release); these cephalic responses are detected by the lateral hypothalamus, which acts to maintain eating behavior.
- The VMH controls the intensity of these cephalic reflexes, with damage to the VMH leading to an enhanced feeding response.
- Obese humans and VMH-lesioned animals exhibit similar feeding behaviors (finickiness with regard to taste, inability to inhibit eating, and extreme sensitivity to environmental cues).
- Recent research has shown that the lateral hypothalamus is one part of the nigrostriatal feeding system. Activation of any part of the nigrostriatal pathway leads to an increase in eating behavior.
- The ventromedial hypothalamus system is one part of a satiety system that controls the suppression or prevention of eating behavior.
- Descending fibers from the PVN travel to the nucleus of the solitary tract (NST), which elicits eating, especially of carbohydrates, and to the dorsal motor nucleus of the vagus (DMV), which elicits secretion of insulin.
- Activation of α_1-adrenergic receptors stimulates the paraventricular nucleus (PVN) of the hypothalamus to inhibit feeding behavior and insulin release.
- Stimulation of α_2-adrenergic receptors inhibits the PVN and results in increased food intake.

Nonneural Control of Eating Behavior

As we have already learned, an organism's ability to survive depends on the maintenance of an adequate energy balance and an optimal body weight. Energy balance is regulated on a short-term, meal-to-meal basis; control of body weight occurs on a long-term, day-to-day basis. Any depletion detected by these regulatory systems produces the perceptual experience of hunger, leading the organism to eat to satisfy its needs (Logue, 1991). But what exactly is hunger? What internal changes, when detected, are perceived as hunger? We turn our attention to these questions next.

Peripheral Cues

Two classes of peripheral cues, oral sensations and stomach contractions, have been associated with hunger and eating. These cues also have been proposed as being associated with satiety and the suppression of eating. So ignore the rumbling in your stomach and read on to find out why you think a trip to the snack bar will make it stop.

Oral Cues. The taste quality of food does not initiate eating, but does appear to control the continuation of eating. The chips that Chris simply could not stop eating serve as a good example of the influence of taste on feeding behavior. The effect of oral sensations on the maintenance of feeding was shown in a study by Snowden (1969). Snowden implanted a tube into rats' stomachs. The technique, developed by Teitelbaum and Epstein (1962), is illustrated in **Figure 10.10**. The idea was to train the rat to press a bar to deliver food directly to its stomach. The rat eventually learned to do this, although the training was slow when compared to rats fed through the mouth, and oral supplements had to be used during training. The animal lost weight during training and never returned its preoperative weight. Once the animal had learned to bar-press to receive food, the bar-pressing responses were brief, and the amount eaten at a meal was small. The presence of hunger caused these rats to initiate feeding, but in the absence of oral cues, they did not maintain eating.

Oral signals are also involved in the suppression of food intake. Janowitz and Grossman (1949) cut a rat's esophagus, bringing the cut end out of the animal. The animal ate, but the swallowed food fell to the ground. The meal consumed by the esophagotomized animal was only slightly larger than a normal meal. But the suppression of eating was short-lived: the esophagotomized animal soon resumed eating. Because there were no additional satiety signals, eating was resumed once the oral cues were no longer present.

Stomach Cues. Cannon (1934) suggested that stomach contractions signaled the presence of hunger and initiated eating. In a classic experiment, Cannon and Washburn (1912) had normal human subjects swallow a balloon that recorded stomach contractions. They found a close relationship between the presence of stomach contractions and the subjects' subjective experience of hunger. However, later evidence has indicated that gastric factors do not play a significant role in the initiation of eating. Tsang (1938) found that removing rats' stomachs did not alter the daily intake of food, although they did eat more frequently and their meals were smaller. The same observation is true of human patients whose stomachs have been removed for medical reasons. These results suggest that information coming from the stomach is not what makes human and nonhuman animals hungry. So it isn't the grumbling in your stomach that spurs the trip to the snack bar; read on to find out why your body thinks it needs that burger and fries.

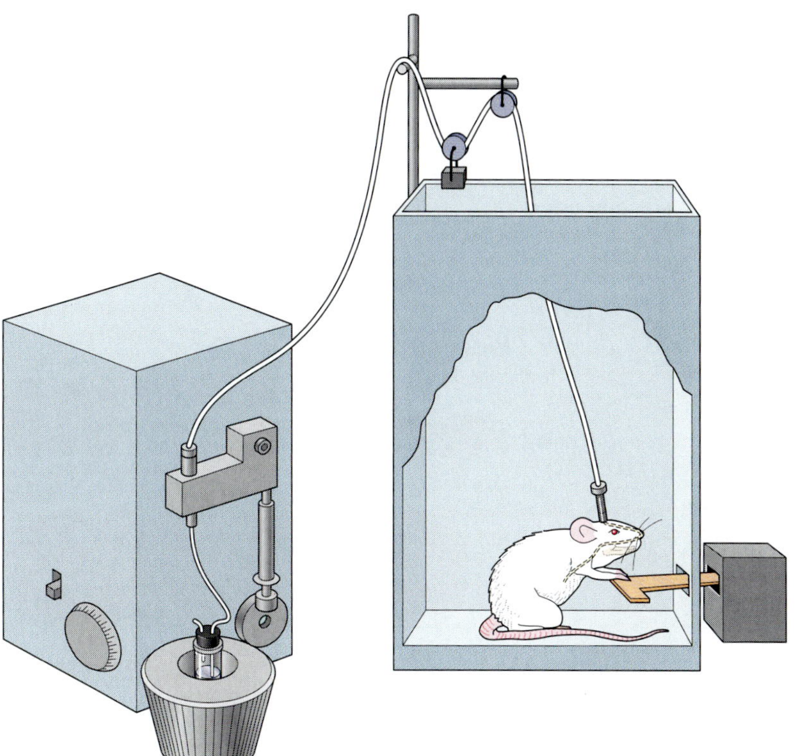

Figure 10.10 The apparatus used to administer intragastric self-injection by the rat. When the rat presses the bar, the pipetting machine delivers the liquid diet through the tube directly into the rat's stomach.

➤ *Why was it difficult to train this rat to press the bar? (p. 306)*

What is your first cue to stop eating? You might say "I'm full," and indeed a full stomach has been identified as one stimulus that inhibits eating. Preloading a rat's stomach by putting food directly into its stomach produces a significant reduction in eating. As discussed earlier, although the breakdown of food occurs in the mouth, the stomach, and the small intestine, the metabolism of the nutrients cannot occur until the nutrients are absorbed into the blood and distributed to the cells. The suppression of eating occurs before absorption, indicating that short-term inhibition does not depend on metabolic changes.

Two events occur in the stomach that cause the rat to stop eating. First, the presence of food distends the stomach, and this distention suppresses eating by activating pressure detectors. Berkun, Kessen, and Miller (1952) injected either a liquid food or saline (salt solution) directly into the stomachs of hungry rats. Regardless of which substance was used, these animals consumed less than animals with empty stomachs. Second, there are nutrient detectors in the stomach. Janowitz and Hollander (1953) found that when liquid food, rather than saline, was injected into the stomach, a smaller volume was needed to suppress eating.

Evidence suggests that the paraventricular satiety system, which receives input from the gastric region via the vagus nerve, is involved in the suppression of eating produced by preloading the stomach. Sharma, Anand, Dua, and Singh (1961) observed electrical activity in the VMH area when a balloon in the stomach was filled with water. The researchers concluded that the pressure and nutrient detectors within the stomach are responsible for activating the VMH area, which in turn suppresses eating.

Research by Deutsch (Deutsch, 1983; Deutsch & Gonzales, 1980) provides more information about how gastric factors contribute to the inhibition of eating. Deutsch and Gonzales (1980) allowed rats that had been deprived for 15 hours to consume a high-calorie liquid diet for 30 minutes and then removed 5 mL of the contents of rats' stomach through an implanted tube. When permitted to eat again, the rats ate only enough to compensate for the calories contained in the 5 mL that had been removed. Interestingly, Deutsch (1983) reported that the compensation occurred only when the animals were familiar with the food. According to Deutsch, feedback from the metabolic consequences of a particular food allows the brain to recognize the nutritional value of the signals coming from the stomach. Without this information, the animal will not be able to recognize when to stop eating on the basis of cues coming from the stomach. So you are more likely to overeat a new food that your brain has never before "digested."

Before You Go On

If, as you have learned, stomach contractions do not make you hungry, what do you think is the function of these contractions?

Metabolic Cues

Okay, so it was the delicious taste of spaghetti and pizza that kept Chris eating, and the fullness of his stomach that made him stop. But if it isn't cues from the stomach growling, how did he realize he was hungry and needed to start eating? The evidence indicates that a deficiency in energy-rich substances such as sugar and fat provides the hunger signal. The CNS, detecting these deficiencies, initiates eating.

Glucostatic Theory. In 1953, Jean Mayer proposed that low levels of blood **glucose** produce the sensation of hunger by stimulating specialized **glucoreceptors** in the lateral hypothalamus (Mayer, 1953). The administration of **insulin**, a hormone that lowers blood glucose levels, was found to initiate eating in nonhuman animals (Mackay, Callaway, & Barnes, 1940) and to induce sensations of hunger in human subjects. A high blood glucose level stimulates the pancreas to release insulin. Insulin lowers blood glucose by removing it from the bloodstream and storing it as glycogen in the liver and muscle, or converting it to fat (see **Figure 10.11**). You may know someone who needs injections of insulin because of a chronic medical condition. This condition, in which too little insulin is manufactured by the pancreas, causing chronically high blood glucose levels, is called **diabetes mellitus**.

Louis-Sylvestre and Le Magnen (1980) continuously measured blood glucose levels in rats and found that blood glucose levels fell several minutes prior to each meal. This finding provides additional evidence of a correlation between blood glucose level and the initiation of eating, but does not prove that there is a causative relationship (i.e., that a lowered blood glucose level initiates eating). Campbell and Smith (1990) went a step further and demonstrated that a fall in blood glucose levels is the actual cause of eating (see **Figure 10.12**). They injected small amounts of glucose into rats' veins whenever a fall in blood glucose was anticipated; these injections actually prevented the rats from eating.

glucose A sugar (dextrose) used in energy metabolism.

glucoreceptors Specialized receptors that monitor glucose levels.

insulin A hormone secreted by the pancreas that lowers blood glucose levels.

diabetes mellitus A chronic medical condition in which too little insulin is manufactured by the pancreas, causing high blood glucose levels.

glucagon A hormone secreted by the pancreas that increases blood glucose levels.

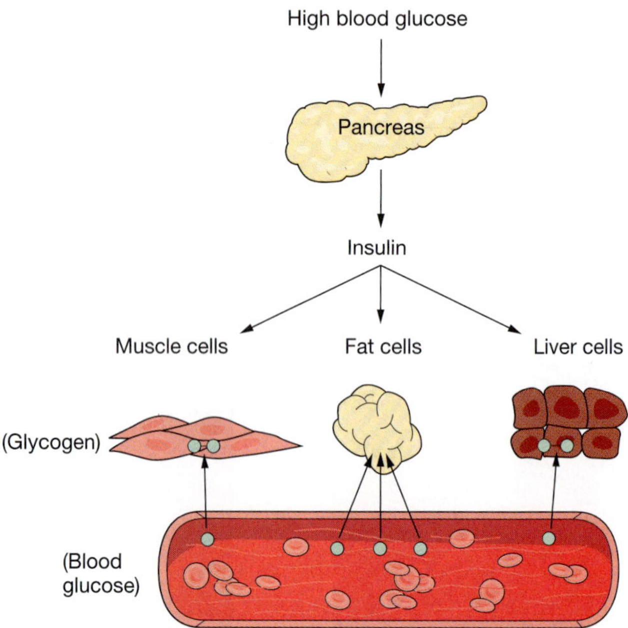

Figure 10.11 Influence of insulin on blood glucose level. Heightened blood glucose level (hyperglycemia) stimulates the pancreas to release insulin, which lowers blood glucose by removing it from the bloodstream and storing it as glycogen in the liver and muscle, or as fat.

➤ *Why would administration of insulin increase food intake? (p. 308)*

In a study by Judith Rodin (1986), human subjects ate a piece of cake made with the sugar glucose or a piece of fruit containing the sugar fructose. Glucose produces a strong insulin release and a large drop in blood sugar. An equally sweet amount of fructose causes a weak insulin release and a small drop in blood sugar. The subjects who consumed the cake (glucose) ate more than did the subjects who ate the fruit (fructose). These findings suggest that if you are on a diet, but simply must have something to eat, a piece of fruit is a better choice than a piece of cake because of the type of sugar (in addition to the obvious health benefit of the fruit—lower in fat, higher in nutrients).

Mayer's glucostatic theory also applies to satiety; he suggested that the increase in blood glucose that follows food intake activates glucoreceptors that suppress eating. Other research has shown that injections of **glucagon**, a pancreatic hormone that increases blood glucose levels (an effect opposite that of insulin) produce a rapid decrease in both stomach contractions and reported hunger in human subjects (Stunkard, Van Itallie, & Reis, 1955); glucagon injections also suppress food intake in deprived animals (Mayer, 1955). **Figure 10.13** presents a diagram of the influence of glucagon on blood glucose level.

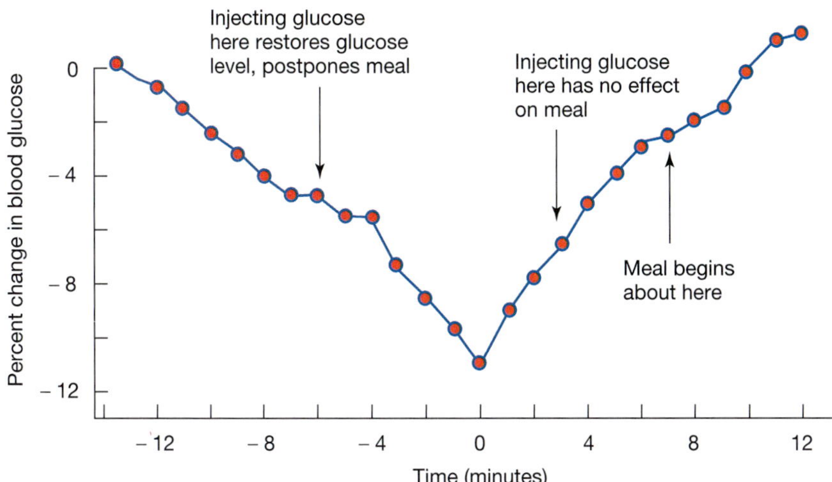

Figure 10.12 Illustration showing the relationship between a fall in blood sugar level and eating behavior. The blood sugar level falls to a low level approximately 7 minutes before a meal. Injecting glucose before, but not after, the blood sugar level reaches its low level suppresses eating.
➤ *What is glucoprivation? (p. 309–310)*

As you might have expected, the paraventricular satiety system responds to the increase in blood glucose by suppressing eating. Anand, Chhina, and Singh (1962) found that a rise in the blood glucose level coincided with increased electrical activity in the VMH area and with the suppression of eating. But where are the satiety glucoreceptors located? Stricker, Rowland, Saller, and Friedman (1977) injected insulin in the VMH of rats, producing hypoglycemia (low blood glucose). A subsequent injection of glucose or fructose produced satiety and inhibited eating. Because fructose cannot cross the blood-brain barrier (see Chapter 4), the animal should have remained hungry after fructose injections if the glucoreceptors were located in the brain. So the glucoreceptors for satiety are located somewhere else. But where?

Maurcio Russek (1971) proposed that the satiety glucoreceptors are located in the liver. Russek injected glucose into either the hepatic portal vein (the blood supply to the liver) or the jugular vein (the blood supply to the brain) in a food-deprived dog. Administration of glucose into the hepatic portal vein suppressed eating, but administration into the jugular vein had no effect on eating.

Challenges to the glucostatic theory. If the glucostatic theory is correct, why do individuals with diabetes mellitus overeat despite high blood glucose levels? The explanation is that the untreated diabetic cannot convert glucose to energy. Recall that insulin promotes the entry of glucose into the body's cells for subsequent metabolism. Two years after he initially proposed the glucostatic theory, Mayer revised his model, suggesting that the availability of glucose for metabolism rather than its quantity in the bloodstream determines the presence of hunger (Mayer, 1955). So when glucose is either not present or unavailable for use, the lack of glucose deprives the cells of energy, a state

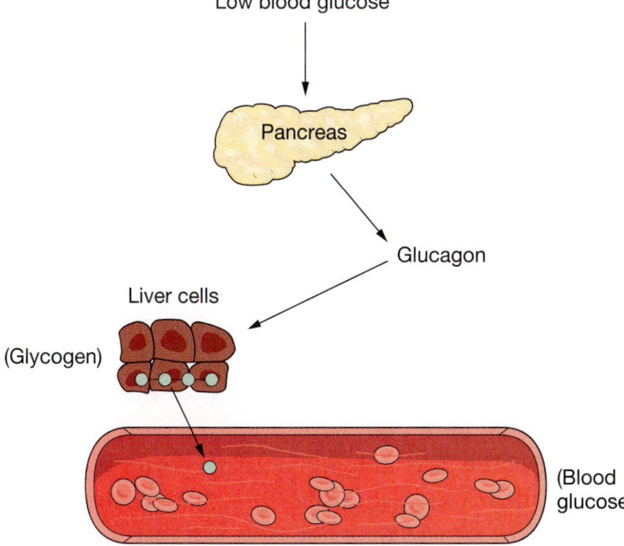

Figure 10.13 Influence of glucagon on blood sugar level. When blood glucose level is low (hypoglycemia), glucagon is released from the pancreas. Glucagon converts glycogen into glucose and then releases it into the bloodstream for use as an energy source.
➤ *Why would administration of glucagon suppress food intake? (p. 308)*

referred to as **glucoprivation**, which serves as a hunger signal and ultimately, leads to eating.

In 1969, Smith and Epstein tested Mayer's revised glucostatic theory. They injected rats with the substance 2-deoxy-D-glucose (2-DG), a form of glucose that cannot be metabolized. Smith and Epstein found that although their blood glucose levels remained high, rats injected with 2-DG overate. These animals, like diabetics, were both hungry and hyperglycemic (i.e., they had high blood sugar).

So a fall in blood sugar level caused Chris to begin eating the pizza, but what caused his blood sugar level to fall? One possibility is deprivation; yet, animals often eat when the level of deprivation is not sufficient to cause a depletion in the availability of nutritional resources. (Do you think Chris's body really needed the pizza and spaghetti?) In a 1990 study, Campbell and Smith showed that the fall in blood sugar that precedes eating was caused by a brief, 50 percent rise in insulin secretion from the pancreas. This increased insulin release preceded both the decrease in blood sugar level and the initiation of eating. Campbell and Smith suggested that signals from the brain caused the pancreas to release insulin, which lowered blood sugar levels and resulted in eating. Back to the central nervous system!

Recall that in his initial report, Mayer (1953) suggested that the glucoreceptors that respond to decreases in blood sugar are located in the lateral hypothalamus. More recent evidence (Ritter, Slusser, & Stone, 1981; Tordoff, Rawson, & Friedman, 1991) suggests that these glucoreceptors are located in the liver and in the hindbrain, but not in the hypothalamus. Tordoff, Rawson, and Friedman (1991) observed that an injection of 2,5-AM (2,5 anhydro-D-mannitol), a drug that interferes with glucose metabolism in the liver, caused rats to begin eating. Because 2,5-AM cannot cross the blood-brain barrier, this drug must have acted on the liver, not the hypothalamus. They also found that the effect of 2,5-AM on eating was eliminated if the branch of the vagus nerve that serves the liver was severed. Thus, the liver detects the availability of glucose, which is reduced as a result of 2,5-AM administration, and then transmits this information, via the vagus nerve, to the brain.

Ritter, Slusser, and Stone (1981) injected some silicone grease into the cerebral aqueduct (talk about something slipping your mind!), which blocked any transfer of cerebrospinal fluid between the third and fourth ventricles. These researchers then injected 5-TG, a drug with effects similar to 2-DG, into one of two areas. Ritter, Slusser, and Stone found that administration of 5-TG into the fourth ventricle, which is surrounded by the hindbrain, stimulated eating. By contrast, injection of 5-TG into the third ventricle, which is surrounded by the hypothalamus, did not elicit eating.

So once Mayer revised his glucostatic theory, he was partially correct—glucoreceptors in the liver and in the hindbrain detect a decrease in blood glucose level, or the reduced availability of glucose. This message is then sent to the nigrostriatal feeding system, activating this system and eliciting eating behavior. Similarly, an increase in blood sugar stimulates the glucoreceptors in the liver, which then send the message to the paraventricular satiety system. Support for this view is provided by a study by Schmitt (1973), which found that an infusion of glucose into the liver increased neural activity in the VMH. The paraventricular satiety system continues to inhibit eating as long as blood sugar levels are above threshold level for hunger.

Before You Go On

Compare and contrast the effects of glucagon and insulin on blood glucose levels.

How do you know that glucoreceptors are located in the liver and not in the brain?

Lipostatic Theory. A decreased level of **lipids**, or free fatty acids, can also cause hunger (Ritter, Brenner, & Yox, 1992; Ritter & Taylor, 1989, 1990). Ritter and her colleagues reported that injections of mercaptoacetate, which blocks an animal's ability to metabolize fatty acids without affecting glucose levels, produced an increase in food consumption. The unavailability of fatty acids as a source of energy is called **lipoprivation**.

The increased food intake produced by administration of mercaptoacetate can be eliminated by administration of capsaicin, which is a neurotoxin found in red peppers that destroys fine-diameter unmyelinated peripheral nervous system axons that carry information from internal organs to the brain (Ritter, Brenner, & Yox, 1992), or by cutting the vagus nerve at the point where it enters the abdominal cavity (Ritter & Taylor, 1990). These observations suggest that the receptors that detect low availability of fatty acids are located in

---

glucoprivation A condition in which glucose is either not present or unavailable for use.

lipid (or fatty acids) Fat that can be used in energy metabolism.

lipoprivation The unavailability of fatty acids as a source of energy.

the abdominal cavity and that information about hunger is carried by fine-diameter unmyelinated neurons from this area to the brain.

The paraventricular satiety system also appears to be sensitive to the level of fat stored in the adipose tissue. According to some researchers (Bender, 1992; Hubey & Martin, 1992), a protein in fat tissue, called **adipose satiety factor**, acts to suppress eating. To demonstrate the inhibitory effect of adipose satiety factor, Hubey and Martin (1992) overfed rats by injecting food into their stomachs. They then extracted the adipose satiety factor from the fat tissue from these rats and injected it into rats fed a normal quantity of food. The intake of the normally fed rats decreased for 12 hours.

Hormonal Satiety Cues. The neuropeptide hormone **cholecystokinin (CCK)** also may serve as a satiety sensor, monitoring the amount of food intake and inhibiting eating once a sufficient amount has been consumed. When food enters the duodenum, the intestinal mucosa secrete CCK. This intestinal hormone limits the rate at which food passes from the stomach into the small intestine, ensuring proper digestion. Cholecystokinin also has been suggested to produce satiety and inhibit eating; injections of CCK have been found to decrease food intake in both human and nonhuman animals (Kisseloff et al., 1981; Marley, 1982).

Two separate mechanisms of CCK action have been proposed. According to the first model, activation of peripheral CCK receptors in the stomach and small intestine stimulates the vagus nerve, which transmits this satiety message to the hypothalamus through the nucleus of the solitary tract. Two lines of research seem to provide evidence for this peripheral satiety mechanism. First, several studies (Crawley & Kiss, 1985; Kulkosky, Breckenridge, Krinsky, & Woods, 1976) have found that severing the vagus nerve blocks the satiety effect of CCK. Second, drugs that antagonize the effect of CCK on peripheral CCK receptors have been observed to increase food intake in already satiated rats as well as to slow the satiating effect of food intake in these rats (Dourish, Rycroft, & Iversen, 1989).

The second way in which CCK may produce satiety is through activation of CCK receptors in the brain. Receptors sensitive to CCK are found in the ventromedial hypothalamus as well as in the paraventricular nucleus of the hypothalamus (Hill et al., 1987). To demonstrate that CCK released from the peripheral organs activates CCK receptors in the brain, Dourish, Rycroft, and Iversen (1989) administered a drug that specifically antagonizes the functioning of the CCK receptors in the brain and observed that CCK brain receptors became insensitive to peripheral CCK released during eating. Food intake increased in animals that previously had been partially satiated, and the animals ate for a longer period. These researchers then turned the experiment around, selectively antagonizing the action of the peripheral CCK receptors; there was a smaller effect than when the functioning of the brain CCK receptors was blocked. These observations seem to suggest that CCK produces satiety through activation of both peripheral and brain CCK receptors.

However, the effect of CCK on eating may be the result of nausea rather than satiety. Deutsch and Hardy (1977) found that animals developed a **conditioned aversion** to a flavor paired with CCK. (A **flavor aversion** is an avoidance of a specific flavor that has been paired with any treatment that produces illness.) Further, Moore and Deutsch (1985) observed that the inhibitory effect of CCK on eating was decreased by an injection of an antiemetic, a drug that suppresses nausea. Stricker and Verbalis (1991) reported that the same neurochemical, oxytocin, was released from the posterior pituitary following drug-induced nausea, such as that produced by lithium chloride, and administration of CCK. These observations suggest that nausea rather than satiety causes CCK to suppress eating.

Before You Go On

Describe how energy balance (levels of glucose and fatty acids) is maintained on a short-term basis.

Using what you have learned about glucoprivation and lipoprivation, explain why fad diets that eliminate consumption of a particular type of nutrient probably will not work.

Environmental Influences on Eating Behavior

We have learned that peripheral cues, such as oral sensations and stomach contractions, and metabolic cues, such as levels of glucose and fatty acids, are associated

---

adipose satiety factor A protein in fat tissue that acts to suppress eating.

cholecystokinin (CCK) A neuropeptide hormone limiting the rate at which food passes from the stomach into the small intestine that may serve as a satiety sensor.

conditioned aversion The ability of an environmental event, usually a flavor, to elicit an avoidance of that event as a result of the pairing of that event with illness.

flavor aversion The aversion to a flavor in food or drink that develops as a result of conditioning.

Figure 10.14 Conditioned hunger. Attractive foods can elicit a strong insulin response and intense hunger. Only a strong conditioned satiety response could enable a person to resist the temptation to eat pastries like the ones seen in the bakery's window.
➤ *Where in the central nervous system does the sight of your favorite food provoke the greatest response? (p. 312)*

with hunger and satiety. But do we have to be deprived or begin eating to become hungry, or eat sufficient amounts of food to resolve nutritional needs to feel satiated? We next describe evidence that stimuli in our environment can make us feel hungry or satiated.

Conditioned Hunger. Has seeing a cream puff in the window of the local bakery (see **Figure 10.14**) or a piece of carrot cake on a dessert tray ever made you feel hungry, even if you've just eaten a full meal? Burton, Mora, and Rolls (1975) found that the sight of an animal's most preferred food (mine is strawberry cheesecake) produced the greatest activity in the lateral hypothalamus, whereas the sight of an unpalatable food did not elicit any response. Often, the mere thought of some delectable food is sufficient to initiate hunger. What mechanism is responsible for this **conditioned hunger**?

An animal's motivation to eat is intensified during eating because the aforementioned cephalic responses (salivation, gastric secretions, and so on—see **p. 300**) elicited by food stimulate the nigrostriatal feeding system and maintain eating until the satiety cues inhibit eating (Powley, 1977). Palatable foods produce greater cephalic responses and cause the animal to eat more than do unpalatable foods. These greater cephalic responses can become conditioned.

conditioned hunger The ability of an environmental event to produce hunger as a result of conditioning.

conditioned satiety The ability of an environmental event to produce satiety as a result of conditioning.

Conditioning involves pairing a novel stimulus (sight of a bakery) with a biologically significant stimulus (taste of strawberry cheesecake) a sufficient number of times for the novel stimulus to elicit the same behavior (conditioned response) that had orginally only been elicited by the biologically significant stimulus (unconditioned response). In Pavlov's view the sight of the bakery is called the conditioned stimulus and the taste of the strawberry cheesecake is called the unconditioned stimulus. See Chapter 14 for a further discussion of conditioning.

Weingarten and Powley (1977) found that in rats a light and tone (conditioned stimulus), after having been paired with a high-fat food (unconditioned stimulus), developed the capacity to stimulate the release of gastric acid (conditioned response). Furthermore, Booth, Coons, and Miller (1969) observed that a light (conditioned stimulus) paired with LH stimulation (unconditioned stimulus) produced hypoglycemia (decreased blood glucose) as the conditioned response, and administration of novocaine to the LH area blocked the hypoglycemic conditioned response. Rodin (1986) conducted a study with human subjects and found that the presence of food or even the thought of food elicited the release of insulin from the pancreas and produced feelings of hunger. These results suggest that environmental cues associated either with palatable foods or with LH stimulation can elicit the cephalic feeding responses.

The research of Stanley Schachter, discussed earlier in this chapter, underscores the importance of environmental cues in initiating eating by obese humans. Additionally, Weingarten and Powley (1977) found that VMH-lesioned animals showed greater conditioned responding than did nonlesioned rats. On the basis of Schachter's observation of greater responsivity to food-related cues in obese humans, such a comparatively stronger conditioned response in humans would be expected. As predicted, Spitzer and Rodin (1987) observed that obese humans show a stronger insulin response to food-related cues than do individuals of normal weight.

Conditioned Satiety. Susan eats two bites of chocolate ice cream and feels "full." How can two bites of ice cream produce satiety? The **conditioned satiety** response is likely responsible for Susan's behavior. Booth (1985) proposed that stimuli that occur at the end of a meal become associated with the nutritional changes that occur after eating (for example, glucagon release in response to food in the stomach). These conditioned stimuli come to elicit a conditioned satiety response, thus producing a short-term inhibition of eating. The unconditioned nutritional changes maintain the inhibition until the next meal. The observation that human and nonhuman animals stop eating before the nutritional effects of eating occur supports the idea that classical conditioning is involved in producing satiety.

Several studies have documented the development of a conditioned satiety response. Booth (1972) gave rats experience with both a dilute and a rich diet. A different flavor was associated with each diet. At the beginning of the experiment, animals ate an equal amount of each diet and displayed an equivalent preference for each flavor. During the course of the study, the animals ate less of the rich diet and more of the dilute diet. Booth proposed that a greater conditioned satiety response (for example, glucagon release from a little food in the stomach) was produced by the rich diet than by the dilute diet because the rich diet produced a stronger unconditioned satiety effect (greater increase in blood sugar following eating). In support of this theory, Booth found that when the flavor associated with the rich diet was switched to the dilute diet, the rats ate small amounts of both diets and lost weight; if the flavor associated with the dilute diet was switched to the rich diet, the animals ate large amounts of both diets and gained weight. Booth, Lee, and McAleavey (1976) observed a similar phenomenon in human subjects. The results of these studies again support the idea that conditioned satiety plays a role in the regulation of food intake.

Animals other than humans typically eat only a single type of food at a time; this enables them to learn the flavors that are linked to satiation. The wide variety of different foods eaten during a meal is partly responsible for the high level of overeating seen in humans. Support for this conclusion is provided by a study by Le Magnen (1981). He observed that rats at mealtime ate more when allowed access to four different-flavored foods than if they were given only a single food—that is, a single flavor. We might be able to regulate our eating more easily if we were to limit the number of different kinds of foods that we consume in a single meal.

Figure 10.15 Food aversion. Food aversion results when an illness is associated with the consumption of a certain food.
➤ *In the case of food aversion, is the food the conditioned stimulus, the unconditioned stimulus, or the conditioned response? (p. 313)*

Flavor Aversion Learning. I have a friend who avoids walking down the supermarket aisle where tomato sauce is displayed; he says that even the sight of cans of tomatoes makes him ill. My oldest son once got sick after eating string beans, and now he refuses to touch them. I once became nauseous several hours after eating at a local restaurant, and I have not returned there since. Almost all of us have some food that we will not eat or a restaurant that we avoid (see **Figure 10.15**). Often the reason for this behavior is that at some time we experienced illness after eating a particular food or dining at a particular place, and we learned to associate the food or the place with the illness through the classical conditioning process. Such an experience creates a conditioned aversion to the taste (or smell or sight) of the food or to the place where the food was consumed.

The classic research of John Garcia and his associates (Garcia, Kimeldorf, & Hunt, 1957; Garcia, Kimeldorf, & Koelling, 1955) demonstrated that animals learn to avoid a flavor associated with illness. Although rats have a strong preference for saccharin and will consume large quantities even when nondeprived, Garcia and his colleagues discovered that an animal will not subsequently drink saccharin if illness followed its consumption. In their studies, rats, after consuming saccharin, were made ill by agents such as x-ray irradiation or lithium chloride; the rats subsequently avoided the taste. Flavor aversion learning is quite rapid, with significant avoidance observed after only a single trial.

You hate asparagus; your roommate likes asparagus, but cannot stand the taste of broccoli (one of your favorites). Does a person's dislike for a particular food reflect the establishment of a flavor aversion? Informally questioning the students in my biological psychology class last year, I found that many of them had had an experience in which illness followed eating a certain food and that these students chose to no longer eat that food. If you have a particular food that you avoid eating, perhaps you too can identify the cause of your aversion to this food. In a more formal investigation, Garb and Stunkard (1974) questioned 696 subjects about their food aversions and reported that 38 percent of the subjects had at least one strong food aversion. The researchers found that 89 percent of the people reporting a strong food aversion could identify a specific instance in which they became ill after eating the food, refusing to consume it thereafter. Even though most often the illness did not begin until several hours after consumption of the food, these people still avoided the food in the future. Also, Garb and Stunkard's survey indicated that the subjects were more likely to develop aversions between the ages of 6 and 12 than at any other age.

More systematic experimentation has documented the establishment of food aversions in people (Logue, 1985). In one study, Bernstein (1978) found that children in the early stages of cancer acquired an aversion to a distinctively flavored Mapletoff ice cream (maple and black walnut flavor) consumed before toxic chemotherapy targeting the gastrointestinal (GI) tract. Instead of eating Mapletoff ice cream, these children now preferred either to play with a toy or to eat another flavor ice cream. By contrast, children who had received the toxic therapy to the GI tract without eating the Mapletoff ice cream, as well as children who had been given the Mapletoff ice cream before toxic chemotherapy not involving the GI tract, continued to eat the Mapletoff ice cream. Bernstein and Webster (1980) reported similar results in adults: cancer patients receiving radiation therapy typically showed a loss of appetite and weight (Morrison, 1976). Perhaps the association of hospital food with illness could be reduced by presenting radiation therapy prior to meals, a procedure that might lead to greater eating and a better chance of recovery.

Before You Go On

After a full meal at your favorite restaurant, you are walking down the street when you pass your favorite ice cream shop. Suddenly, your mouth begins to water and you really feel the need for a double chocolate fudge ice cream cone. Describe the role of classical conditioning in producing your hunger response.

Describe how, once you take your first bite of the ice cream cone, your CCK might object to your having any more.

Section Review

- Food deprivation lowers blood sugar and free fatty acid levels, which serve as stimuli motivating the search for and then consumption of food.
- The taste quality of food, although not initiating eating, controls the continuation of eating.
- The more palatable the food, the greater the physiological response and the larger the quantity of food that is consumed.
- Environmental cues can elicit a conditioned hunger response and serve to stimulate eating, with cues associated with more palatable foods producing a stronger conditioned hunger response.
- During eating, internal nutritional changes (increased glucose and adipose satiety factor, CCK release) produced by food are detected by receptors in the duodenum, liver, and hindbrain.
- A message is then sent to the paraventricular satiety system, which acts to suppress eating.
- Cues produced by the consumption of food become associated with these internal nutritional changes and are able to elicit a conditioned satiety response.
- The level of satiety is influenced by the nutritional value of food: the greater nutritional value, the stronger the satiety and the smaller the quantity of food consumed.
- More nutritional foods produce a stronger conditioned satiety response that can suppress eating behavior even before the unconditioned nutritional effects of the food have been experienced.

set-point theory The view that animals maintain upper and lower limits of their body weight.

critical set-point The critical level of stored fat that either activates or inhibits food-seeking behaviors.

Long-Term Regulation of Body Weight

We have learned how an animal maintains an adequate balance of energy-providing glucose and fatty acids on a short-term, meal-to-meal basis, and how hunger and satiety can become conditioned responses. Recall that, in order to survive, the animal must also maintain an optimal body weight. Next we move on to see how body weight is regulated on a long-term basis.

Set-point Theory

Animals can maintain a constant body weight throughout their lifetime when given a free-feeding diet. Findings by Keesey and Powley (1986) suggest that each animal has a critical level of stored fat, called the **critical set point**. When the animal's stored fat falls below this set point, the nigrostriatal activates food-seeking behaviors. This system will remain active until the animal's body weight returns to its set point. Similarly, once the amount of stored body fat increases past the critical set point, the paraventricular satiety system is activated and further eating is inhibited. (This is the simple explanation of why Chris has such

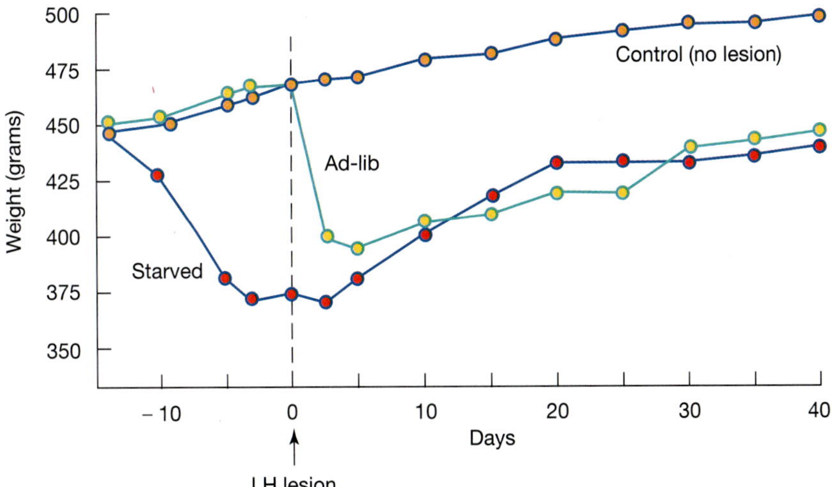

Figure 10.16 Influence of preoperative starvation on the LH-lesion syndrome. Animals deprived prior to lesioning of the LH do not lose weight following lesioning, but instead regain weight to the level seen in nondeprived LH-lesioned animals.

➤ *What is the set-point theory? (p. 314–315)*

trouble losing weight—his body's set point is higher than the weight he would like to achieve on his diet.)

Normal animals deprived of food for several days will regain the lost weight when provided access to food. The animal does not eat enough at one time to regain the lost weight but instead gains weight slowly over several days. Short-term satiety may temporarily inhibit eating, but the animal will eventually regain the lost weight by eating more frequently.

Keesey and Powley (1986) proposed that the set point is lowered by destruction of the feeding system, such as by lesioning the LH. To activate the nigrostriatal feeding system in LH-lesioned animals, body weight must drop to a level lower than that of a normal animal. In one study (Powley & Keesey, 1970), animals that were deprived of food and underweight before lesioning the LH area exhibited no additional weight loss as the result of the LH lesions, but instead regained weight to the level seen in nondeprived LH-lesioned rats (see **Figure 10.16**). Thus, LH lesioning appears to reduce the animal's set point rather than directly cause aphagia. Aphagia appears to be a side effect of the lowered set point induced by the lesion.

Damage to the paraventricular satiety system appears to establish a new and higher critical set point. The VMH-lesioned animal becomes obese because it eats until it has stored enough fat to satisfy the new higher set point. This hypothesis also explains Hoebel and Teitelbaum's finding (1966) that VMH-lesioned rats did not subsequently overeat if they were made obese by force-feeding prior to surgery (**Figure 10.17**). According to the set-point theory, fat stores of these obese rats already were at or above the higher critical set point, and thus following VMH lesioning, their satiety systems inhibited further eating.

The Role of Metabolism in Eating and Satiety

What is the role of metabolic rate in the control of eating and the regulation of body weight? A person's metabolic rate, which is the sum of all the chemical and phys-

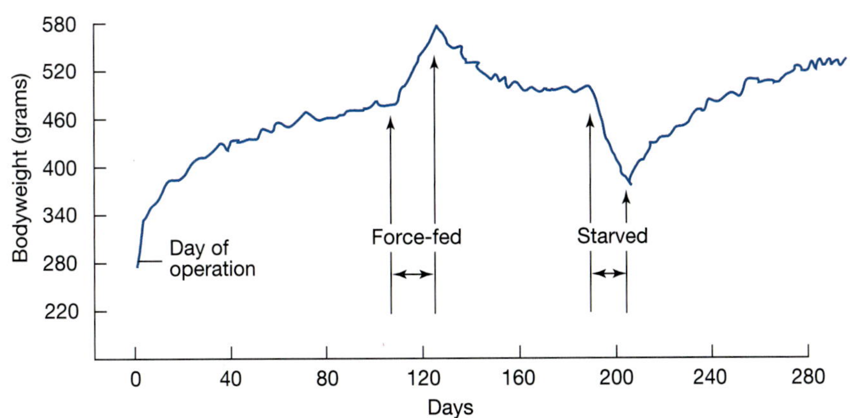

Figure 10.17 Influence of preoperative force-feeding and post-operative starvation on the VMH-lesion syndrome. VMH-lesioned animals gain weight if force-fed and lose weight if deprived, but return to previous weight after force-feeding or deprivation is ended.

➤ *Why do VMH-lesioned animals gain weight when force-fed, but lose that weight when returned to normal diet? (p. 315)* ical processes that are occurring within the person at a particular moment in time, appears to be genetically influenced. Roberts, Savage, Coward, Chew, and Lucas (1988) measured the metabolic rate of 18 infants at ages 3 months and 1 year. Despite eating the same amount of food, the babies of overweight mothers generated 21 percent less energy (had a lower metabolism rate) at 3 months than the babies of normal-weight mothers. At 1 year, the babies with the lower metabolism at 3 months had become overweight compared to the babies with the higher metabolism.

To Diet or Not to Diet?

Obese individuals often go on a diet to lose weight. These individuals find losing weight difficult, and almost always gain back any weight they may have lost (Agras et al., 1996). The difficulty losing weight and the inability to keep the weight off is caused at least partially by metabolic differences between obese and normal-weight people.

A metabolic disturbance produces elevated levels of insulin in both obese humans (Solomon, Ensinck, & Williams, 1968) and hyperphagic rats (Frohman, Goldman, & Bernardis, 1972), causing them to be in a constant state of hunger. As long as the food is tasty, their hunger usually causes them to eat whatever is placed before them; however, their obesity often prevents them from working for food if it is not easily available. If the hyperphagic rat is prevented from becoming fat, it will be as motivated to work for food as a normal animal (Sclafani & Kluge, 1974).

Freidman and Stricker (1976) suggested that the hyperphagic animal eats because food is its only available source of energy. The elevated insulin level found in the hyperphagic rat promotes the storage of digested food as glycogen and fat, while preventing the obese animal from effectively using its fat reserves as an energy source.

In hyperphagic rats that have been kept at normal weight, an elevation in blood insulin level and subsequent weight gain occurs shortly after VMH destruction, although the normal-weight VMH-lesioned rats have lower blood insulin levels than do obese lesioned animals (Tannenbaum, Paxinos, & Bindra, 1974). These nonobese VMH-lesioned animals continue to gain weight even on a restricted diet: their elevated levels of insulin cause them to store more of their ingested food as fat than normal animals (Han & Liu, 1966).

Typically, obese people quickly regain weight they have lost by dieting (Agras et al., 1996). Given that nonobese VMH-lesioned animals store more food as fat than nonlesioned animals, the weight gain seen in obese individuals after the cessation of dieting may reflect an inherent tendency of obese people to store more of their ingested food as fat than people of normal weight. Thus, unless the obese person's food intake is severely restricted, additional methods must be used to maintain weight loss.

To Exercise or Not to Exercise?

Jean Mayer (1978) suggested that exercise must be an integral part of a successful weight-reduction program. He compared many obese adolescents and adults to static-stage hyperphagic animals: having reached their maximal weight, they eat only enough to maintain it. Obese people are typically less active than their normal-weight counterparts. Exercise enables obese individuals to use their excess calories rather than store them as fat. Mayer reported the successful implementation in a large city public school system of a weight-loss program involving diet and exercise. The obese children were placed on a balanced but not restrictive diet and were given psychological counseling on how to improve their dress, their walk, and their general appearance. They attended special physical education classes and followed an independent exercise program during weekends and holidays. Mayer found improvement in the majority of the children enrolled in his program: their activity increased, and they lost weight. More recent studies (Epstein et al., 1995; Jeffrey & Wing, 1995) continue to find exercise to be associated with both an initial weight loss and the maintenance of that weight loss among both adults and children.

Why does exercise influence the success of weight-loss programs? The influence of exercise on metabolic level appears to be a big factor. Lissner, Odell, D'Agostino, and Stokes (1991) found that dieting sharply lowered the metabolic rate of 18 women. The effect of this decrease in metabolic rate produced by dieting counteracts any weight loss that would otherwise result from the restriction of food intake. These researchers found that combining dieting and moderate physical exercise produced an increase in metabolic rate and led to significant weight loss, which was maintained as long as the women continued to exercise.

Before You Go On

Describe what happens when (1) an animal's fat stores fall below its critical set point and (2) an animal's stores increase past its critical set point.

APPLICATION

The Origin and Treatment of Two Eating Disorders

Our society admires the "thin" and scorns the "heavy." Social psychologists (Rodin & Salovey, 1989; Schwartz, 1984) have found that obese people are generally considered unattractive by others, not only because of their physical appearance but also because of what others perceive as a lack of self-control. Obese children are cruelly tormented by their peers. Although the scorn experienced by the obese adult is more subtle, it is generally obvious that others think poorly of them. The obese person is frequently discriminated against at school and at work. "Fat people" jokes are the mainstay of many comedians. Our culture's obsession with thinness has contributed to the prevalence of two eating disorders: anorexia nervosa and bulimia. ■

Anorexia Nervosa

Some people will go to extraordinary lengths to avoid being overweight. A close family friend, for example, diets constantly, even though she is quite thin. She perceives herself as fat, always needing to lose several pounds to be attractive. Someone once said "you can never be too rich or too thin." But those who suffer from **anorexia nervosa**, a psychological disorder that is considered to be a consequence of our society's obsession with thinness (Bruch, 1980), are far too thin. Although people with anorexia frequently are slightly overweight before the onset of their illness, they rarely are obese and sometimes are thin. Once they become ill, people with anorexia lose an average of 35 percent of their body weight, often weighing as little as 60 to 80 pounds (see **Figure 10.18**). And even after anorexics lose 35 percent of their body weight, they still feel fat—they look in the mirror and still see a fat person. Anorexics are preoccupied with food and with not becoming fat; they seem unaware of hunger and feel full after only several bites. Occasionally they may binge eat, but then usually attempt to purge the ingested food. Anorexia nervosa occurs most commonly among adolescent girls and young women (Yates, 1989).

The significant weight loss exhibited by patients with anorexia produces a variety of physiological effects, including the loss of menstrual cycles, cardiac arrhythmias, and extremely low blood pressure. As a result, the mortality rate from the disorder is approximately 5 percent (Hsu, 1986). The singer Karen Carpenter was a well-known victim of anorexia.

Figure 10.18 Anorexia nervosa. The extreme thinness of this woman is typical of those who suffer from anorexia.

➤ *Why is anorexia so difficult to treat?* *(p. 318)*

According to Hilde Bruch (1980), the fear of becoming fat is the major force precipitating anorexia. Bruch's therapeutic approach is to deemphasize the importance of body size for the patient's self-esteem and to enhance feelings of self-worth and self-initiative. Bruch has found that changes in self-esteem can lead to the resumption of normal eating behavior.

Other investigators have suggested that anorexia is caused by a physiological or chemical disturbance (Bemis, 1978). One very indirect piece of evidence for this view is that people with anorexia share the attribute with rats with lateral hypothalamic damage of diminished food intake and self-starvation to the point of

anorexia nervosa An eating disorder in which adolescent girls or young women diet and lose as much as 35% of their body weight and yet still feel fat.

death. Further, there is a strong genetic predisposition for anorexia (Holland, Sicotte, & Treasure, 1988).

Although the exact origin of anorexia remains unknown, there are treatments available. Behavior therapy has been used with some success (Agras & Kraemer, 1984). In one study, Garfinkel, Kline, and Stancer (1973) rewarded hospitalized patients for eating (for example, by giving them a weekend pass or an opportunity to socialize with friends). Their patients gained 20 to 30 pounds during the 2 to 10 weeks of treatment.

The use of some medications also has shown promise as a treatment for anorexia (Hoffman & Halmi, 1993). Hoffman and Halmi (1993) reported that the serotonergic agonist fluoxetine (Prozac) has been useful in promoting weight gain during the initial treatment for anorexia. As we will discuss in Chapter 15, people with anorexia often also suffer from depression and serotonergic agonists have been found to be effective in the treatment of depression. The antidepressant effect of serotonergic agonists, rather than their appetite suppressant effect, is most likely responsible for the increase in weight when used in the treatment of anorexia, as serotonergic agonists act to decrease weight in obese persons. The serotonergic agonists have not been effective in changing the attitudes of people with anorexia about weight, and thus these medications have not been successful in preventing relapse, with an accompanying loss of weight.

Because it is so difficult to change a person's body image, anorexia nervosa is considered to be an especially difficult disorder to treat (Hoffman & Halmi, 1993). Many researchers are searching for a long-term effective treatment for anorexia. We can only hope that such a treatment is not too far off.

Bulimia

Shannon had known for some time that she had a problem, but until last night, she had been able to hide it from her parents. Her mother had occasionally commented on her sweet tooth or on the empty bag of cookies that had been left inadvertently in her room, but Shannon had, for the most part, been able to hide her binge eating. Shannon's usual routine was to consume a bag of chips and several candy bars or a half gallon of ice cream that she had hidden in the freezer at a time when she knew her parents would be out of the house. She would then make herself vomit the food. Shannon hated the routine, but she became anxious after eating the food and felt relieved after vomiting. Shannon had always locked the bathroom door before sticking her finger down her throat, but she forgot to last night. She wasn't aware of her mother's presence until she turned away from the toilet and saw the horror on her mother's face. At first, she tried to deny that anything was wrong, but she finally admitted that she had a problem. Shannon knew that she needed to be helped and agreed to find a counselor, but she was still angry with herself for forgetting to lock the bathroom door. ■

Shannon suffers from an eating disorder called **bulimia**. Bulimia is characterized by recurrent episodes of binge eating, followed by purging, most often via induced vomiting. Other methods of purging include the use of laxatives, excessive exercise, and/or dieting. As with anorexia, the vast majority of people with bulimia are young women. In binge eating, vast quantities of food are consumed, even thousands of calories at a time. A "meal" consisting of a whole fried chicken, a jar of peanut butter, a giant bag of potato chips, an entire loaf of bread, and a gallon of ice cream would not be unusual for someone with bulimia.

Binging and purging can result in a variety of physiological changes. Repeated vomiting can erode tooth enamel, produce chronic inflammation of the esophagus, and cause a loss of potassium, which in turn may produce cardiac arrhythmias and cardiac arrest.

What causes bulimia? Like anorexia, bulimia involves a distortion of body image (Powers et al., 1987). Unlike people with anorexia, who are too successful at dieting, people with bulimia are unsuccessful at controlling their food intake; they may diet from guilt after purging but when the diet ultimately fails, they binge again (Heatherton & Baumeister, 1991). Also in contrast to anorexia, people with bulimia recognize the abnormality of their eating behavior and hide it from others. Because there are fewer outward physical signs of a problem (bulimics do not have the severe weight loss that anorexics do) and because they are so secretive, bulimia is harder to recognize. Some researchers have identified a connection between depression and bulimia. Although bulimia can lead to depression, depression may also be a cause of the abnormal eating behavior, as people with bulimia tend to have a family history of affective (depressive) disorders (Logue, 1991).

Another possible cause of bulimia is a hormonal imbalance. People with bulimia have been found to secrete abnormally low levels of the hormone cholecystokinin (CCK) in response to a meal (Geracioti & Liddle, 1988). Recall that CCK secretion inhibits eating. Geracioti &

bulimia An eating disorder that is characterized by recurrent episodes of binge eating, followed by purging and induced vomiting.

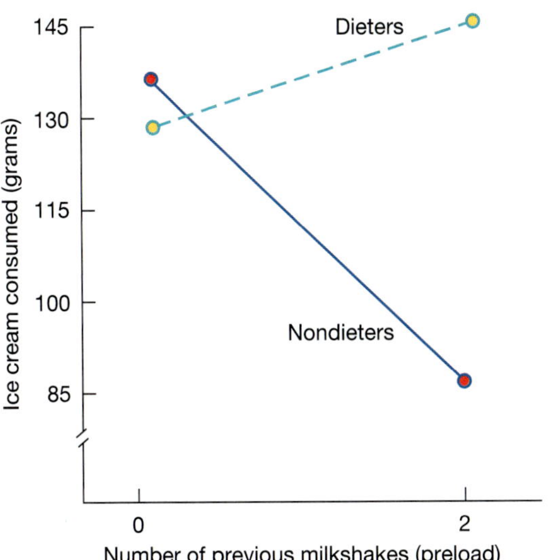

Figure 10.19 The influence of preloading on the amount consumed by restrained (dieting) and unrestrained (nondieting) subjects. Consumption of two milkshakes (preloading) reduced subsequent consumption in unrestrained eaters but actually increased consumption in restrained eaters.

➤ *Why is bulimia harder to recognize than anorexia? (p. 318)*

Liddle found that in people with bulimia, peak CCK levels after a standard meal were half of those of control subjects. Low levels of CCK may have lessened the normal inhibition of eating and thereby produced extreme binging.

Bulimia usually begins following a period of stringent dieting (Ruderman & Grace, 1988), and research has reported that dieting can lead to binge eating (Hibscher & Herman, 1977; Polivy & Herman, 1985; Ruderman, 1986). (Remember Chris's spaghetti and half a pizza at his favorite restaurant?) Hibscher and Herman (1977) studied the causes of binge eating in restrained eaters (dieters) versus unrestrained eaters (nondieters). If the restrained eater, who can normally inhibit eating, eats even a small amount of food, inhibition of eating is reduced; the restrained eater will then consume even greater amounts than the unrestrained eater. In another study, one group of subjects, composed of dieters and nondieters, was initially asked to drink two milkshakes. Another group, also consisting of dieters and nondieters, did not drink the milkshakes. Both groups were then asked to taste three flavors of ice cream. In nondieters (unrestrained eaters), preloading with the milkshakes acted to reduce subsequent consumption of ice cream (see **Figure 10.19**). With the dieters (restrained eaters), it was a different story. If they did not drink the milkshakes, the dieters were able to limit consumption of the ice cream, eating less than the nondieters. However, preloading in the dieters led to the largest amount of ice cream consumed. These results suggest that the dieter consumes larger quantities of food once eating begins, whereas the nondieter is able to respond to satiety cues and control eating. Ruderman (1986) also observed that even a slight reduction in control can lead to binge eating in restrained eaters. It is likely that the guilt over losing control over eating, the propensity for binging as a result of dieting, and diminished satiety cues contribute to the tendency to develop the disorder of bulimia.

How can bulimia be treated? The person with bulimia initially experiences anxiety when confronted with forbidden food. This fear motivates eating to distract from negative feelings. Binging serves to increase these negative emotions, and purging seems to be the only effective way to reduce the anxiety resulting from eating. Hoage (1989) reported that forced exposure to forbidden foods and prevention of purging represents a viable approach to treating bulimia. Anxiety over eating is eliminated as a result of consuming forbidden food and then not purging. Hoage found that after such conditioning, patients were less likely to binge and purge.

The use of serotonergic agonists is another promising approach. We learned earlier in the chapter that the serotonergic agonist drug fenfluramine was effective in reducing eating and promoting weight loss in obese humans. Hoffman and Halmi (1993) and Kennedy and Goldbloom (1991) reported that fenfluramine reduced both binging and vomiting in patients with bulimia, and Ayuso-Gutierrez, Palazon, and Ayuso-Mateos (1994) reported that another serotonergic agonist, fluvoxamine (Luvox), also had the same effect. As we will learn in Chapter 15, serotonergic agonists enhance mood in depressed persons; as with anorexia nervosa, the reason that these drugs are helpful in treating bulimia may be this mood improvement. Hoffman and Halmi (1993) observed that drug therapy for bulimia was most effective when combined with a cognitive-behavioral treatment that modified eating habits and used diet and exercise to manage weight. (As was noted earlier, fenfluramine is no longer being prescribed as an appetite suppressant; fluvoxamine is still being prescribed as an antidepressant, with no apparent coronary disease resulting from its use.)

Before You Go On

How do society's values affect the eating behavior of adolescent girls and young women?

Section Review

- Set-point therapy proposes that the nigrostriated feeding system controls the lower limit of weight and the paraventricular satiety system controls the upper limit of weight.
- Metabolic rate appears to be influenced by inheritance.
- Obese individuals tend to have a lower metabolic rate than normal-weight people; a similar difference exists between VMH-lesioned and nonlesioned rats.
- The obese person and the hyperphagic rat also have elevated insulin levels that cause more food to be stored as fat even on a restricted diet.
- Exercise, which increases metabolic rate, is needed in combination with dieting to lower weight in obese individuals.
- Anorexia nervosa is an eating disorder characterized by self-starvation and a distorted body image.
- Two factors that contribute to the development of anorexia are genetic predisposition and social pressure; lateral hypothalamic damage may also be involved in anorexia, but the direct physiological cause is unknown.
- Bulimia is characterized by recurrent episodes of binge eating followed by purging.
- Dieting makes an individual vulnerable to binge eating.
- A lower level of the hormone CCK in some people with bulimia may act to intensify the level of binging.
- Anxiety over gaining weight elicits purging, and the reinforcing aspects of purging and the fear of eating fattening foods may contribute to the establishment of the binge-purge cycle.
- Serotonergic agonists have shown some promise in treating bulimia and, to a lesser extent, anorexia.

Drinking

Kim's friends say that she is addicted to nuts. Her favorites are cashew nuts, but almost any kind will do. Kim often wonders why she becomes so thirsty after eating nuts. When she saw that cashew nuts were on sale today, Kim stuffed several dozen into a bag and added them to her shopping cart. When she reached her car, Kim could not resist—she removed the nuts from her shopping bag so she could have a few as she drove home. These nuts were quite salty and tasted especially good, so by the time she got home, the bag was empty. As she unloaded the groceries, Kim noticed that she had become very thirsty. Suddenly she could think of nothing but how thirsty she was. When she opened the fridge to put the milk away, a can of ice-cold juice beckoned. Kim grabbed it, opened it, and guzzled it down. The juice tasted great, and her thirst was quickly gone. Now she could put away the rest of the groceries. ■

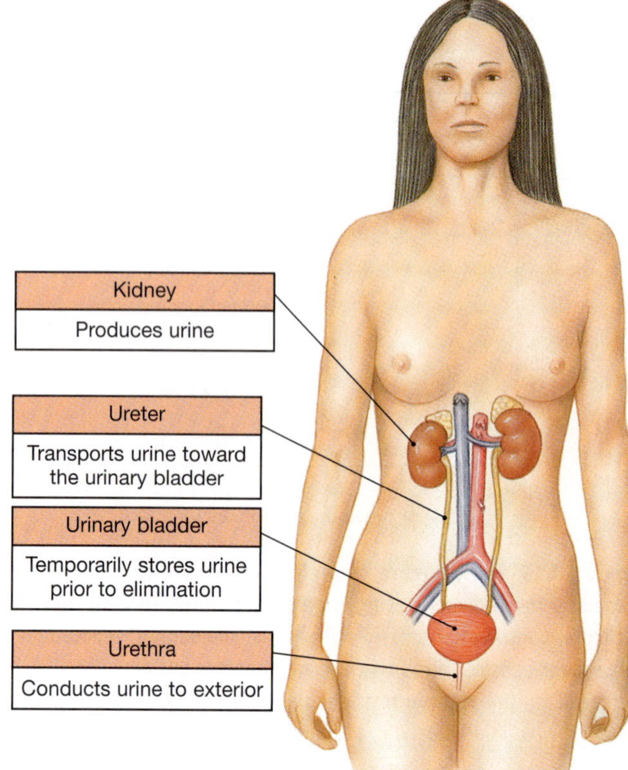

Figure 10.20 Urinary system. Structures of the urinary system and their functions are shown in this figure. The kidneys excrete excess water by converting it into urine and then having urine transported to the exterior.

➤ *What happens to excess bodily fluids? (p. 320)*

Why did Kim become thirsty from eating salty cashew nuts? Why was her thirst so urgent? For the answers to these absorbing questions, read on!

Your Body's Fluid Needs

Your body maintains a constant level of fluid within each cell (intracellular fluid) and outside each cell (extracellular fluid). The extracellular fluid is composed of the blood plasma and the interstitial fluids that surround each cell. Approximately two-thirds of our body's fluid is inside the cells; the other one-third is outside the cells in the interstitial fluid (26%) and blood (7%). The maintenance of this constant fluid level is essential for effective metabolic functioning; any change activates compensatory mechanisms that restore optimal fluid levels. Usually, you drink more water than you need; and your kidneys excrete the excess (see **Figure 10.20**). If your fluid level is lower than it should be, internal changes are activated that decrease the amount of water contained in urine. In addition, specific brain receptors are stimulated, creating the sensation of thirst that, in turn, causes you to drink water in order to restore the optimal level of fluid (Logue, 1991).

Thirst

Several different conditions can produce thirst and motivate drinking behavior. Thirst often is caused by a biological need, but like hunger, it can also be the result of a psychological need.

The "Dry Mouth" Theory. In 1934, Walter Cannon proposed that we become thirsty and drink when our mouth is dry. Although a dry mouth may cause us to drink, it does not regulate the amount we drink. Only a few sips of water eliminate a dry mouth, but we usually drink much more to satisfy our thirst. In addition, neither removal of the salivary glands (which causes a permanently dry mouth) nor administration of drugs that cause excessive salivation have any influence on the amount of water consumed when thirsty. Factors other than a dry mouth thus appear to determine the amount of water we drink.

Osmotic Thirst. Body fluids contain a small amount of sodium chloride (salt). Increases in the amount of sodium chloride (as when Kim eats the nuts) affect the extracellular body fluids first so that the concentration of sodium chloride outside the cell becomes greater than the concentration inside the cell (see **Figure 10.21a**). This greater salt concentration creates a higher level of osmotic pressure outside than inside the cell; water moves out of the cell to equalize the osmotic pressure (see **Figure 10.21b**). This decrease in water dehydrates the cell and activates processes that restore normal intracellular water levels. Sometimes, internal conservation by the kidney can be effective in returning the intracellular fluid level to normal, but it is often necessary to increase fluid intake to restore internal fluid balance. Thus, increased sodium chloride levels in the extracellular fluid is detected, producing **osmotic thirst**. (Recall from Chapter 4 that osmosis is the movement of fluid across a membrane that tends to equalize concentrations of solutes.)

Verney's (1947) classic experiment investigated the changes that occur when salt is injected into the bloodstream. He discovered that salt injections cause the posterior pituitary to secrete **antidiuretic hormone (ADH)**, which causes the kidneys to retain more fluid. Verney also noted that the salt injections cause rats to drink excessive amounts of water. Verney's results demonstrate that increased salt concentration in the blood produces both an internal conservation of the water that is already present in the body and a behavioral response that introduces additional fluid.

Why does salt cause ADH release and thirst? Verney (1947) suggested that the heightened osmotic pressure, caused by increased extracellular salt concentration, stimulates special receptors located in the hypothalamus. These **osmoreceptors,** as they are called, produce the sensation of thirst and initiate the release of ADH from the posterior pituitary.

---

osmotic thirst A condition of thirst due to increased osmotic pressure in the intracellular fluid.

antidiuretic hormone (ADH) A hormone secreted by the posterior pituitary that causes the kidneys to retain more fluid.

osmoreceptors Specialized receptors that monitor osmotic pressure in the intracellular fluid.

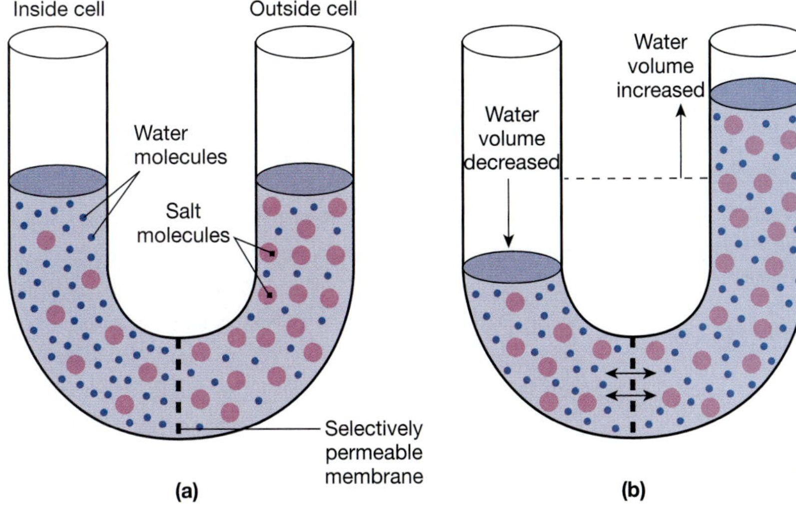

Figure 10.21 Osmotic thirst. (a) Eating salty foods increases the salt concentration in the extracellular fluid, which causes osmotic pressure in the extracellular fluid to be greater than in the intracellular fluid. (b) The greater osmotic pressure in the extracellular fluid draws fluid from the intracellular fluid leading to equal salt concentrations and osmotic pressure in the intracellular and extracellular fluids. As a result the cell becomes dehydrated.

➤ *Is osmotic thirst caused by a low level of intracellular fluid or a low level of extracellular fluid? (p. 321)*

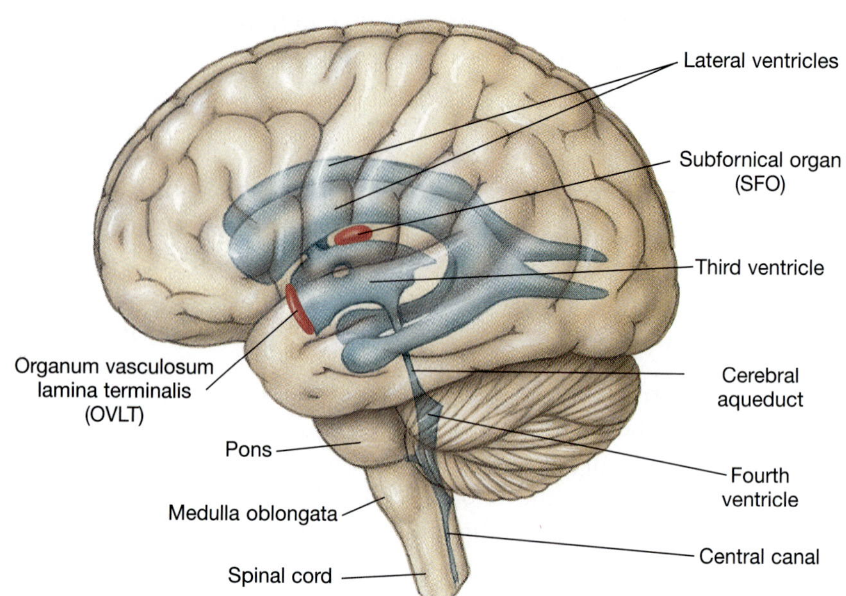

Figure 10.22 A sagittal plane view of the two structures (subfornical organ and organum vasculosum lamina terminalis) that control drinking behavior. Receptors located in the subfornical organ and organum vasculosum lamina terminalis detect angiotensin and increased osmotic pressure, and produces thirst and drinking.
➤ *Why are the SFO and the OVLT more sensitive to changes in salt concentration than the lateral preoptic area of the hypothalamus? (p. 322)*

Early studies suggested that the osmoreceptors were located in the lateral preoptic area (LPO) of the hypothalamus (Blass & Epstein, 1971; Peck & Novin, 1971). Lesioning the LPO eliminated the ADH release and the drinking response to injections of hypertonic saline, which means a solution with a salt concentration greater than blood. Hypertonic saline injected directly into the LPO caused the release of ADH; as we have already seen, ADH release increases water retention by the kidneys. However, the amount of drinking produced by injections of hypertonic saline into the LPO is relatively small. Animals in these studies drank only a few milliliters of water following hypertonic saline injection into the LPO. By contrast, intravenous injection of hypertonic saline produced consumption of great quantities of water. This observation suggests that most osmoreceptors must be located in an area other than the LPO. This makes sense when you consider that the LPO lies inside the blood-brain barrier; the LPO would not be an ideal site to detect changes caused by increased salt ingestion, because salt will not cross the blood-brain barrier. The osmoreceptors would more likely be found outside of the blood-brain barrier.

More recent research (Stricker & Verbalis, 1988) points to a highly vascularized area of the brain that borders the third ventricle as the site of most osmoreceptors (refer to **Figure 10.22**). This area contains two important structures: the **subfornical organ (SFO)** and the **organum vasculosum lamina terminalis (OVLT)**. These areas lie outside the blood-brain barrier and thus would be sensitive to changes in the concentration of salt. A number of studies have shown that destruction of these structures impairs an animal's normal response to hypertonic saline. For example, Hosutt, Rowland, and Stricker (1981) reported that injections of hypertonic saline did not induce drinking in animals with SFO lesions, and Thrasher, Keil, and Ramsay (1982) found a reduced response to hypertonic saline after the OVLT was destroyed. In both studies, extremely high doses of hypertonic saline did elicit drinking following lesioning. The most reasonable interpretation of these results is that osmoreceptors are located in several structures in these brain areas, and the magnitude of responding depends on the combined influence of all brain osmoreceptors.

subfornical organ (SFO) A structure that lies outside the blood-brain barrier and monitors changes in the concentration of salt in the bloodstream and loss of extracellular fluid.

organum vasculosum lamina terminalis (OVLT) A structure that lies outside the blood-brain barrier and monitors changes in the concentration of salt in the bloodstream and loss of extracellular fluid.

hypovolemic thirst A condition of thirst that occurs when extracellular fluid is lost.

Hypovolemic Thirst. A second type of thirst, **hypovolemic thirst**, occurs when extracellular fluid is lost. Several circumstances can lead to loss of extracellular fluid: (1) sweating during exercise (sweat is salty because both salt and fluids are lost when we sweat), (2) diarrhea induced by illness, (3) bleeding as the result of an injury, and (4) heavy menstrual flow. Like osmotic thirst, the effect of hypovolemic thirst is the activation of internal changes that cause water retention and increased water intake.

When hypovolemia exists, the decreased volume of extracellular fluid lowers blood pressure. This lowered blood pressure (detected by baroreceptors in the heart) stimulates the posterior pituitary gland to release ADH, which increases water retention by the kidneys. In addition, the lowered blood pressure stimulates autoreceptors in the kidneys to release an enzyme called renin. Renin causes the blood protein angiotensinogen to be converted into the hormone **angiotensin**. (There are several forms of angiotensin. The only form that affects thirst is angiotensin II. For the sake of simplicity, we will use angiotensin here to refer to angiotensin II.) Angiotensin, in turn, stimulates the adrenal cortex to release **aldosterone**, a hormone that causes increased salt and water retention by the kidney. **Figure 10.23** diagrams these changes that occur in response to lowered blood pressure.

Loss of extracellular fluid not only increases fluid conservation, it also produces thirst. Early physiological evidence suggested that angiotensin activates neurons in the preoptic and anterior areas of the hypothalamus that detect volumetric thirst and motivate drinking. To demonstrate the influence of angiotensin on drinking, Epstein, Fitzsimmons, and Rolls (1970) injected angiotensin into the preoptic and anterior hypothalamic areas of rats. They found that drinking occurred in response to administration of angiotensin even in satiated animals. Furthermore, increasing the quantity of injected angiotensin caused the rats to drink more. These results suggest that under natural conditions, the amount of fluid that we drink corresponds to the amount lost, because the level of angiotensin released varies depending on the extent to which extracellular fluid is depleted.

Loss of bodily fluids creates not only hypovolemic thirst, but also a craving for substances such as salt that are lost as a result of hypovolemia. Animals

angiotensin A hormone converted from angiotensinogen by the enzyme renin that acts to stimulate the adrenal cortex to release aldosterone.

aldosterone A hormone released by the adrenal cortex that causes increased water and salt retention.

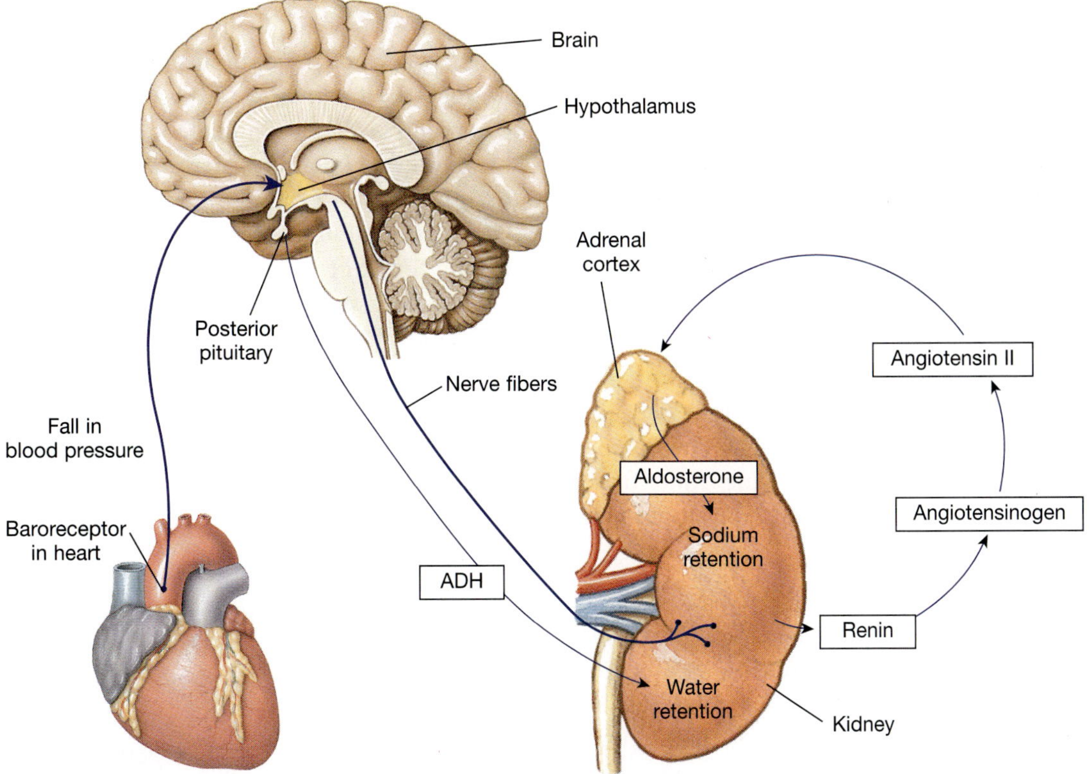

Figure 10.23 Hormonal changes initiated by a drop in blood pressure detected by heart baroreceptors (receptors that detect changes in blood pressure). Stimulation of the hypothalamus causes the posterior pituitary to secrete ADH and the kidney to release renin. Renin secretion results in the conversion of angiotensinogen into angiotensin. Angiotensin then stimulates the adrenal cortex to secrete aldosterone. ADH increases fluid retention, whereas aldosterone increases sodium retention.

➤ *What causes salt cravings? (p. 323–324)*

deprived of sodium chloride develop a preference for salty-tasting solutions. These animals prefer salty fluids to salty foods (Bertino & Tordoff, 1988). The hormones aldosterone and angiotensin both contribute to this salt craving. Stricker (1983) found that aldosterone injections increased desire for salty foods, and Dalhouse, Langford, Walsh, and Barnes (1986) reported increased consumption of salty fluids following angiotensin injections. Further, the combined effects of aldosterone and angiotensin produce greater salt craving than either hormone alone (Sakai & Epstein, 1990).

A Common Neural Circuit. Osmotic and hypovolemic thirst often occur together, and evidence points to a common neural circuit mediating both. Recall the discussion of the role of the subfornical organ (SFO) and organum vasculosum lamina terminalis (OVLT) in osmotic thirst. These two areas also appear to be involved in hypovolemic thirst. Simpson, Epstein, and Camardo (1978) provided evidence for an involvement of the subfornical organ in volumetric drinking. These researchers injected angiotensin into the SFO and observed increased fluid consumption. Also, lesioning this area reduced hypovolemic thirst. Similarly, Buggy and Johnson (1977) reported that lesions of the OVLT reduced angiotensin-induced drinking.

The subfornical organ sends neural input to the **nucleus medianus**, an area that lies near the anterior and ventral part of the third ventricle. This area of the brain appears to be involved in both osmotic and hypovolemic thirst. Several studies (Gardiner & Stricker, 1985; Mangiapane et al., 1983) have reported that following lesioning of the nucleus medianus, administration of hypertonic saline did not elicit drinking. Similarly, injections of polyethylene glycol, a large molecule that cannot cross capillary membranes and produces thirst by drawing fluid from inside the cell, did not produce drinking in animals with nucleus medianus lesions.

A Good Meal Can Make You Thirsty. Most of us drink during meals (Kraly, 1990). The food we eat does create thirst, as water is diverted from the rest of the body to the stomach and small intestine to be used in the digestive process. This movement of fluid causes hypovolemia, and the secretion of angiotensin elicits drinking (Nose et al., 1986).

Any salt in a meal will also lead to cellular dehydration and osmotic thirst. Le Magnen and Tallon (1966) determined that the change in osmotic pressure produced by a meal governs the amount we drink; the greater the change, the more we drink.

Food containing protein is especially dehydrating. Fitzsimmons and Le Magnen (1969) demonstrated that rats on a carbohydrate diet consumed equal quantities of food and water, whereas rats on a protein diet consumed 1.47 times as much water as food. Although these results suggest that we drink as much as we need to compensate for the dehydrating effect of a meal, drinking during a meal—other than to eliminate a dry mouth and convert water into urea—is probably learned. This conclusion was supported by a study (Oakley & Toates, 1969) that showed that animals learn to drink a sufficient amount of fluid before eating to prevent dehydration. It seems that we can anticipate impending thirst and drink enough to counteract future dehydration.

Satiation of Thirst

The factors that cause us to stop drinking have not been as clearly defined as those that cause us to start drinking. In all probability, rigid controls over the suppression of drinking are not as important as those that control the production of thirst; as we have discussed, any excess water can be readily eliminated. Evidence suggests that the amount of ingested water plays an important role in the inhibition of drinking. The mouth is thought to be like a meter: after a sufficient amount has been drunk, further fluid intake is suppressed. However, this oral meter is not a perfect regulatory device.

To study the importance of oral factors, Bellows (1939) cut a dog's esophagus, bringing the cut end out of the animal. The esophagotomized animal drank, but the swallowed water fell to the ground. (Sound familiar? See the study by Janowitz and Grossman on esophagotomized rats, **p. 306**). Bellows discovered that his esophagotomized dogs drank twice as much water as their bodies needed before they stopped drinking. This result suggests that oral factors do contribute to the suppression of drinking but that other factors are also involved.

One other important factor in the inhibition of drinking seems to be the presence of water in the stomach. Rolls, Wood, and Rolls (1980) placed water into the stomach of monkeys through a tube, a procedure that enabled these experimenters to bypass oral factors. The results showed that drinking is suppressed when water is in the stomach. By contrast, injections of isotonic saline, a solution that matches the body's own level of sodium chloride, did not suppress drinking. This study suggests that the stomach contains recep-

---

nucleus medianus A group of neurons that lie near the anterior and ventral part of the third ventricle that mediate both osmotic and hypovolemic thirst.

tors that monitor water intake and signal whether or not fluid needs have been met.

Other studies have suggested that receptors in the liver also play a role in regulating fluid consumption. For example, Kozlowski and Drzewreki (1973) infused fluid into the hepatic portal vein, which takes fluid from the stomach to the liver, and reported decreased fluid intake.

Satiety for salt consumption also occurs in salt-deprived animals, but the stomach does not appear to contain receptors for detecting ingested salt (Mook, 1969). Instead, the liver appears to contain receptors that detect the presence of sodium in the blood. Tordoff, Schulkin, and Freidman (1987) injected a hypertonic saline solution into the hepatic portal vein (blood supply to the liver) of sodium-deprived rats. This treatment significantly reduced drinking. By contrast, a salt solution injected into the jugular vein, which does not go directly to the liver, did not affect subsequent drinking.

The liver appears to send the salt satiety message to the brain via the vagus nerve. Smith and Jerome (1983) cut the branch of the vagus nerve connecting the liver to the brain and found that animals showed an increased water consumption presumably because of the absence of the satiety cues needed to inhibit drinking.

Research has indicated that suppression of drinking is the function of the parainfundibular hypothalamic area of the brain. Witt et al. (1952) reported that lesions in the parainfundibular hypothalamus produce polydipsia, or excessive water intake. When functioning of the parainfundibular hypothalamus is disrupted, inhibition of drinking is extremely difficult and large amounts of fluid are ingested.

Before You Go On

Why did the nuts make Kim so thirsty?

Describe how the ice-cold juice satiated Kim's thirst.

Section Review

- Ingestion of salty foods causes an increased salt concentration in the extracellular water and causes fluid to move from the inside to the outside of the cell.
- Cellular dehydration results from the movement of water out of the cell and causes osmotic thirst.
- Loss of extracellular fluid lowers blood pressure, leads to increased levels of angiotensin and aldosterone in the blood, and causes hypovolemic thirst.
- Angiotensin increases water retention, and aldosterone increases salt retention.
- Receptors located in areas adjacent to the third ventricle (subfornical organ and organum vasculosum lamina terminalis) appear to detect angiotensin in the blood and increased osmotic pressure, and in response produce thirst and drinking; neurons in this area also produce a craving for salt.
- Ingestion of fluid activates satiety receptors for water in both the stomach and the liver, whereas satiety receptors for salt are found only in the liver.
- Messages from the satiety receptors in the liver and stomach travel to the parainfundibular hypothalamus to produce satiety and suppress drinking behavior.

Chapter Review

Critical Thinking Questions

1. John has gained 20 pounds in the last few months. He believes that his habit of eating while watching sports on television is responsible for his weight gain. Could he be right? Provide a mechanism that could cause overeating while watching television. Suggest several alternative explanations for John's weight gain. What could John do to lose weight?
2. Karen has just run a marathon. She is extremely exhausted and very thirsty. Describe two biological processes that contribute to her thirst. What might she have done prior to the race to prevent her extreme thirst after the race? What should Karen do now to eliminate her thirst?
3. Susan is extremely thin. She never seems hungry, and when she does eat, she only eats a little. You are very concerned about her health. Suggest several possible causes of Susan's physical appearance and eating habits. Do you have any suggestions that might help Susan?

Vocabulary Questions

1. ________________ is the refusal to eat; ________________ is the refusal to drink.
2. An excessive intake of food is called ______________.
3. The ________________ originates in the substantia nigra, passes through the lateral hypothalamus, and proceeds to the basal ganglia, and is involved in control of feeding behavior.
4. The ________________ originates in the paraventricular nucleus of the hypothalamus, passes through the ventromedial nucleus, and proceeds to two hindbrain structures, and is involved in control of satiety.

5. The idea that a low level of blood glucose stimulates glucoreceptors to produce the sensation of hunger is known as the ________________ theory.
6. The deprivation of energy from cells due to a lack of glucose is known as ________________.
7. According to the ________________ theory, a decreased level of fatty acids can cause hunger.
8. A protein in fat tissue, called ________________, acts to suppress eating.
9. The neuropeptide hormone ________________, which limits the rate at which food passes from the stomach into the small intestine, may also serve as a satiety sensor.
10. According to the ________________ theory, each individual organism has a weight that it actively maintains, either by initiating eating behavior when weight falls below this point, or by suppressing eating behavior when weight rises past this point.
11. Psychological hunger, also called ________________, occurs when the sight of a favorite food elicits hunger even when you are full.
12. A combination of ________________ and ________________ has been found to be the most successful way to lose weight and keep it off.
13. A person who goes on binges of overeating and then induces vomiting to get rid of the food suffers from ________________.
14. ________________ is the result of an imbalance in the level of solutes such as sodium chloride across a cell membrane.
15. Secretion of the hormone ________________ by the posterior pituitary gland causes the kidneys to retain more fluid.
16. Suppression of drinking is the function of the ________________ area of the brain.
17. Excessive water intake is called ________________; a lack of water intake is called ________________.

Review Questions

1. The three nutritional substances that can be converted to energy by the body are
   a. glucose, fat, and protein.
   b. glucose, carbohydrates, and milk.
   c. meat, dairy, and vegetables.
   d. fat, carbohydrates, and insulin
2. Preloading is
   a. packing the car the day before a vacation.
   b. continuing to eat with a full stomach.
   c. eating an extra-large meal when it is known that no food will be available for a long time.
   d. eating several small meals one after the other.
3. The two hindbrain structures that are part of the paraventricular satiety system are the
   a. substantia nigra and the ventromedial nucleus.
   b. substantia nigra and the cerebellum.
   c. nucleus of the solitary tract and the cerebellum.
   d. nucleus of the solitary tract and the dorsal motor nucleus of the vagus.
4. Cephalic reflexes include
   a. the secretion of saliva, the production of gastric juices, and the release of insulin into the bloodstream.
   b. hissing, spitting, and scratching.
   c. blinking, twitching, and dizziness.
   d. eye movements, breathing, and swallowing.
5. The ________________, rather than the ________________, determines the amount of food that will be consumed at one feeding.
   a. taste of food; level of nutrient depletion
   b. level of nutrient depletion; taste of food
   c. palatability of food; activity level
   d. metabolism; palatability of food
6. An individual who has high levels of blood glucose but is unable to utilize the glucose because of a lack of insulin has a disorder called
   a. diabetes mellitus.
   b. anorexia nervosa.
   c. bulimia.
   d. hypoglycemia.
7. ________________ removes glucose from the blood; ________________ increases blood glucose levels.
   a. Glucagon; insulin
   b. Glycogen; insulin
   c. Insulin; glycogen
   d. Insulin; glucagon
8. The presence of food in the stomach activates ________________, which suppresses eating behavior.
   a. baroreceptors
   b. pressure receptors
   c. glucoreceptors
   d. hormones
9. When we avoid a food that has previously made us ill we are said to be exhibiting
   a. common sense.
   b. a conditioned aversion.
   c. avoidance.
   d. a conditioned stimulus.

10. A person who loses 35 percent of body weight, is preoccupied with food, and eats very little is suffering from
    a. bulimia.
    b. hypoglycemia.
    c. adipsia.
    d. anorexia nervosa.
11. A person who consumes large amounts of food, which is then purged, is suffering from
    a. hypoglycemia.
    b. adipsia
    c. anorexia nervosa.
    d. bulimia.
11. A person with anorexia nervosa shares qualities with a
    a. VMH-lesioned rat.
    b. PVN-lesioned rat.
    c. LH-lesioned rat.
    d. SO-lesioned rat.
13. The thirst produced by increased sodium chloride levels in extracellular fluid is called ____________; the thirst produced by a decreased volume of extracellular fluid is called ____________.
    a. dry mouth; hypovolemic thirst
    b. hypovolemic thirst; osmotic thirst
    c. osmotic thirst; dry mouth
    d. osmotic thirst; hypovolemic thirst
14. Osmoreceptors are located in the
    a. lateral preoptic area of the hypothalamus.
    b. subfornical organ and the organum vasculosum lamina terminalis.
    c. ventromedial hypothalamus.
    d. paraventricular nucleus.

Suggested Readings

BRAY, G.A., BROUCHARD, C. & JAMES, P.T. (1997). *The handbook of obesity.* New York: Dekker.

KEESEY, R. E., & POWLEY, T. L. (1986). The regulation of body weight. *Annual Review of Psychology, 37,* 109–134.

LE MAGNEN, J. (1992). *Neurobiology of feeding and nutrition.* San Diego: Academic Press.

LOGUE, A. W. (1991). *The psychology of eating and drinking* (2nd ed.). New York: Freeman.

STRICKER, E. M. (1990). *Handbook of behavioral neurobiology. Vol. 10. Neurobiology of food and fluid intake.* New York: Plenum Press.

WALSH, B. T. (1988). Eating disorders. Washington, DC: American Psychiatric Press.

11 Sexual Development and Behavior

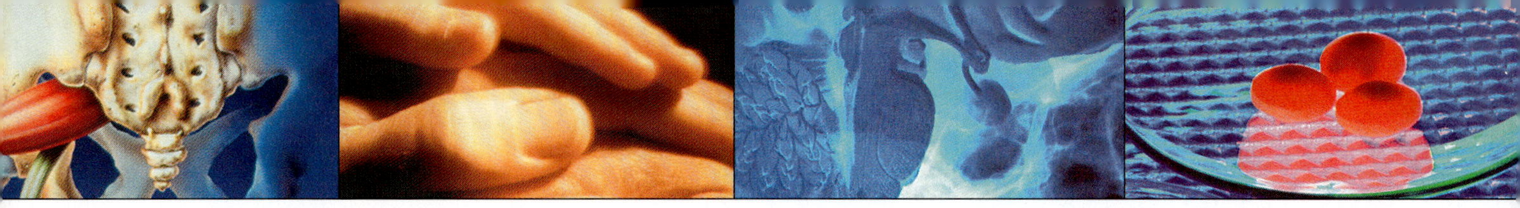

The Pleasures of Sex

In high school, Paula dreamed of marriage and children. After graduation, she worked as a waitress in a local restaurant. Paula met Doug one day when he came into the restaurant for lunch. He quickly became a regular, coming in for talk more than food; their relationship grew, and they were married the next year.

Their first years of marriage were happy. Doug's promotion to supervisor at the automobile plant allowed them to buy a small house. Soon their first child, Ryan, was born; Sarah followed in 2 years.

Then Doug lost his job. Doug has worked at several part-time jobs during the past year but has not found a full-time job. Bills have mounted, and Paula has returned to her job as a waitress. Doug has become very moody. The warmth and closeness of their early years of marriage have been replaced with arguments about finances.

Since Doug became unemployed, their sex life has also changed, and not for the better. Even though Paula had been prepared by her mother to view sex as an unpleasant necessity, Paula found to her surprise that she thoroughly enjoyed sex with Doug. Doug was a gentle and considerate, yet passionate lover. But now his interest in sex has decreased; the frequency of their lovemaking has dropped to once or twice a month. The warm caresses and foreplay that had once preceded intercourse have become perfunctory and mechanical. On several occasions they have started to make love but had to stop when Doug was unable to maintain an erection.

Paula no longer experiences pleasure during sex; in fact, she has actually come to dread it. She tried to talk to Doug about it, but he refused to admit there was a problem or even discuss it. Desperate to talk about her feelings, she has thought of discussing her problem with her best friend. She has even gone over the conversation in her mind, but she is not certain that she could overcome her embarrassment at sharing something so intimate. ■

◀ Of the roughly 200 million sperm in an ejaculation, only about 100 reach the egg.

Before You Begin

What biological process(es) determined that Paula and Doug's first child would be a boy and their second a girl?

Why does Paula find sex so pleasurable, whereas her mother did not?

Why did Doug's interest in sex decline after he lost his job?

In this chapter, we will help you answer these and the following questions:

- When does sexual development begin?
- What is the biological basis of sexual arousal and intercourse?
- What effect do hormones have on sexual arousal in males? In females?
- What psychological processes motivate sexual behavior?
- Is there a biological basis for sexual preference?

Sexual Development

We learned in Chapters 1 and 3 that at conception the human zygote or fertilized egg has 23 pairs of chromosomes for a total of 46. Paula and Doug's son received one member of each pair from Paula and the other from Doug. The members of each pair of Ryan's chromosomes are similar, with one exception; one pair, called the sex chromosomes, is different. There are two types of sex chromosomes: X and Y. Doug (along with all other human males) has one X chromosome and one Y chromosome in each somatic cell in his body; Paula (and all other human females) has two X chromosomes in each somatic cell. Recall from Chapter 1 that the sperm and the egg are not somatic cells, but gametes, with half the usual number of chromosomes. So each of Paula's eggs has a single X chromosome, but Doug's sperm can have either an X or Y chromosome. Ryan received one X chromosome from Paula and a Y chromosome from Doug. Sarah received an X chromosome from each parent (see **Figure 11.1**). Thus, Ryan's sex was determined at the time of conception by Doug's sperm: the sperm that fertilized Paula's egg carried a Y chromosome, producing a boy; if the egg had been fertilized by a sperm carrying an X chromosome, Ryan would have been a girl.

The Development of the Sexual Reproductive System

Interestingly, regardless of its genetic makeup, the fertilized egg, or zygote, is sexually dimorphic (di = two; morph = form); that is, it is capable of developing either as a male or as a female. Whether the zygote develops as a male or as a female depends on the activity of a **sex-determining gene** located in the middle of the short arm of the Y chromosome (Gubay et al., 1990). This sex-determining gene controls both the physical and the behavioral aspects of sexual development.

At 6 weeks of development, the human embryo has formed crude, primordial reproductive structures. No sexual differentiation is visible at this time and embryologists describe this as the "indifferent state" (Mange & Mange, 1998; see **Figure 11.2**). Among these primitive structures are two sets of ducts known as the **Wolffian system** and the **Müllerian system**, a pair of simple gonads, and early genital structures with vaguely familiar, noncommital names, such as genital tubercle, urogenital groove, urethral folds, and labioscrotal swellings. The Wolffian system will later form some of the male reproductive structures, and the

sex-determining gene The gene on the short arm of the Y chromosome that controls the sex of an individual member of a species.

Wolffian system Forerunner of parts of the male reproductive system consisting of ducts that later form the seminal vesicles, vas deferens, and prostate.

Müllerian system Forerunner of parts of the female reproductive system that later form the uterus and upper part of vagina, and fallopian tubes.

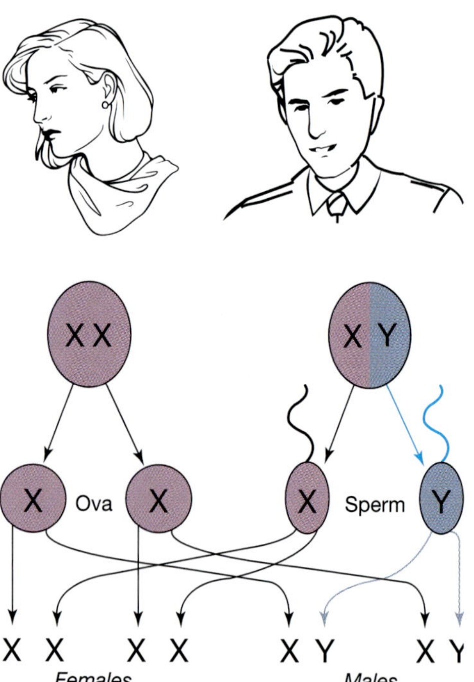

Figure 11.1 The genetic transmission of biological sex. The biological sex of a person depends on whether the sperm cell that fertilizes the ovum carries an X or a Y chromosome.

➤ *Which parent determines the sex of the offspring? (p. 330)*

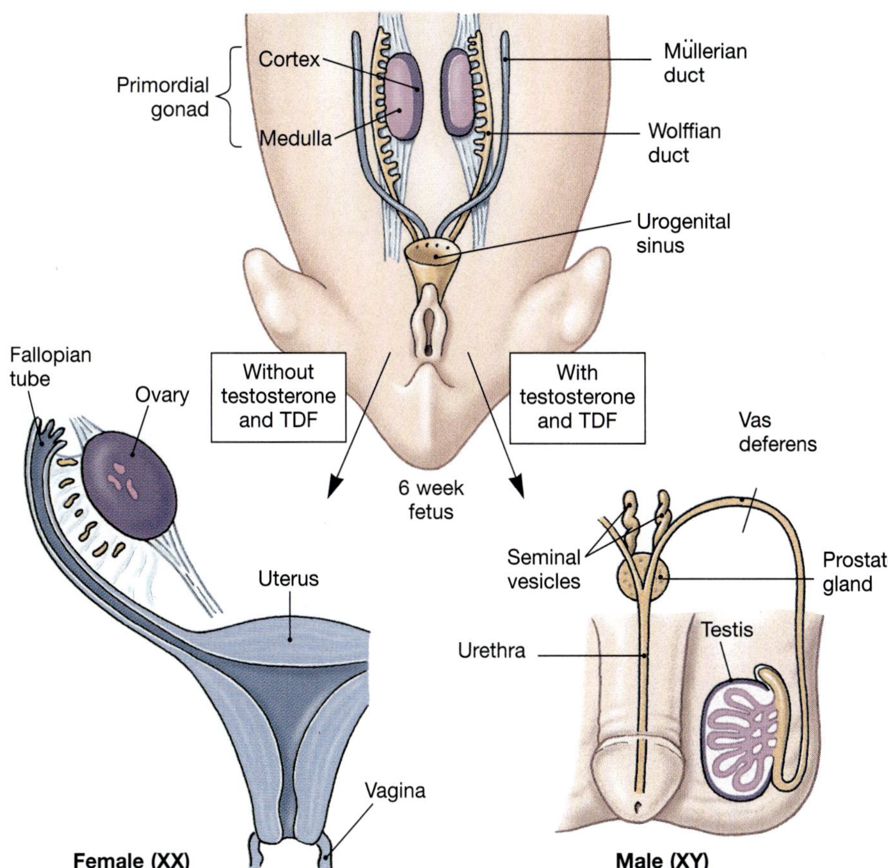

Figure 11.2 Development of sex organs. Changes occur in the undifferentiated reproductive system (top) at 6 weeks that produce the reproductive system of either a female (left) or male (right).
➤ *What hormones determines whether the male or the female reproductive system develops? (p. 331)*

Müllerian system, some of the female structures. At six weeks, the primitive gonad is neither testis nor ovary, but the medulla (or inner core) of each gonad has the potential to develop into a male testis, and the cortex (or outer core) has the potential to develop into a female ovary. The early genital structures will undergo a transition into the familiar male or female external anatomy.

During the sixth week of embryonic development, the sex-determining gene on the short arm of the Y chromosome produces an enzyme called **testis-determining factor** (**TDF**; Koopman et al., 1991). The testis-determining factor causes the undifferentiated gonads to become testes, which later secrete testosterone and manufacture sperm. The Wolffian ducts mature into the seminal vesicles and prostate gland, which produce the fluid in which sperm cells are ejaculated, and the vas deferens, the passage through which the sperm cells travel from the testis to the urethra. While the Wolffian system is developing into these male reproductive structures, the Müllerian system is degenerating as a result of the **Müllerian-inhibiting substance**, which is a hormone released by the testes that helps prevent the development of the female reproductive system. Testosterone released from the embryonic testis beginning in the seventh week is responsible for the development of the male's external sex organs (refer to **Figure 11.2**).

If the testis-determining factor is not present, which is the case in a female embryo, the gonads become ovaries, which secrete estrogen and progesterone and manufacture eggs. The Müllerian ducts mature into the internal portions of a female reproductive system: the uterus and upper part of the vagina; and the fallopian tubes, through which ova travel from the ovaries to the uterus. There is no Wolffian-inhibiting substance in the female; it is the absence of testosterone that leads to the development of the female's external sex organs (refer to **Figure 11.2**).

How do we know that it is the presence of the Y chromosome, and not the absence of a second X chromosome, that causes the embryo to develop as a male? Good question! Koopman and colleagues (1991), who wanted to answer this question, conducted a study in which the segment of the Y chromosome containing the sex-determining gene was placed onto one of the X chromosomes of a female mouse, which caused the male reproductive system to develop in this genetically female mouse, indi-

---

testis-determining factor (TDF) The enzyme that causes the undifferentiated gonads to become testes.

Müllerian-inhibiting substance A hormone released by the testes that prevents the development of the female reproductive system.

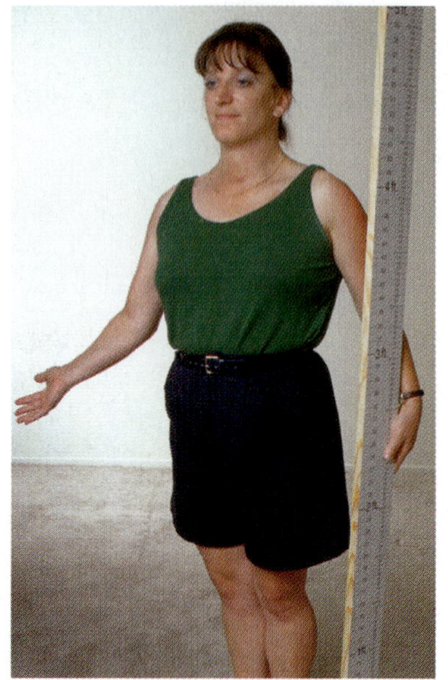
(a)

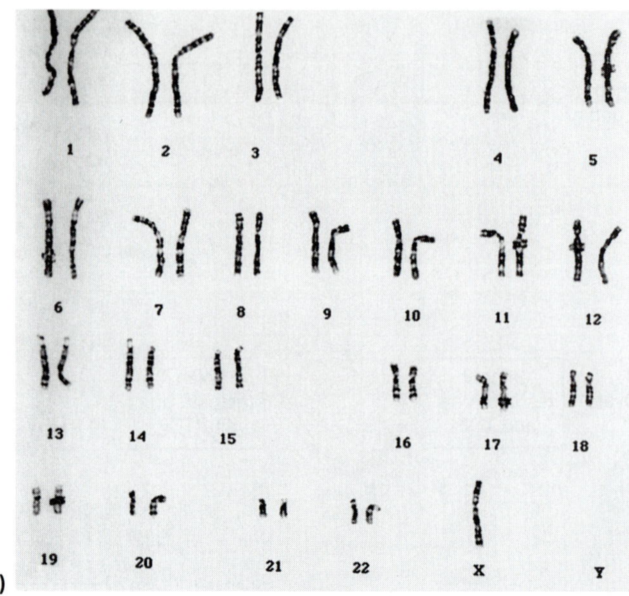

(b)

Figure 11.3 Turner's syndrome. (a) Individual; (b) karyotype of the chromosomes of an individual. Note the single X chromosome at the lower right of the karyotype.

➤ *Why are individuals with Turner's syndrome infertile? (p. 332)*

cating that it is the Y chromosome that causes the development of the male reproductive system.

The study of individuals with **Turner's syndrome** (see **Figure 11.3**) provides further support for the critical role of the Y chromosome in determining biological sex. Turner's syndrome is a condition in which a person is born with only one X chromosome, but no other sex chromosome, usually the result of a defect in the father's sperm (Knebelmann et al., 1991). If the absence of a second X chromosome determined male sexual development, the male reproductive system should develop someone with only one X chromosome. However, in persons with Turner's syndrome, the female reproductive system develops, to a point; because two X chromosomes are needed for the ovaries to produce ova, individuals with Turner's syndrome are infertile (incapable of having children).

Additional evidence of the critical role of the Y chromosome comes from cases in which a male has two X chromosomes and no Y chromosome or cases in which a female has an X and a Y chromosome, each of which happens in around 1 in 20,000 people. How could this happen? The answer lies in the crossover process (Kelly, 1991). Recall from Chapter 1 that crossing over occurs when a segment of one member of a chromosome pair is exchanged with a segment from its partner during meiosis, the process by which sperm and eggs are formed. If the sex-determining gene on the Y chromosome is transferred to the X chromosome during crossing over, this sperm will carry an X chromosome that produces testis-determining factor, resulting in a biological male with two X chromosomes (remember Koopman et al.'s mouse?). The fertilization of an egg by a sperm with the Y chromosome that lost the sex-determining gene will result in the development of a biological female with one X and one Y chromosome. It should be noted that both are very rare events (Mange & Mange, 1998).

Turner's syndrome A condition in which a person is born with only one X chromosome, but no other sex chromosome; the female reproductive system develops in persons with Turner's syndrome.

Before You Go On

Explain the following statement: "The occurrence of an XX male or an XY female cannot be attributed to any defect in the mother's egg."

The Development of a Male or Female Brain

We know that the brains of males and females are different, but what effect does biological sex have on the brain, the part of the body of most interest to us as biological psychologists? The hormones released by the anterior pituitary gland and by the gonads, as well as the hormones that stimulate the hypothalamus to produce sexual responsivity, are different for males and females.

This suggests that differences in the brains of males and females are responsible for differences in the control of sex hormones and of sexual behavior. What process is responsible for the development of these differences? A number of research studies (Harris & Levine, 1965; Gorski, 1985) suggest that the presence of testosterone in the prenatal or early postnatal period is responsible for the development of a masculinized brain. In the absence of testosterone, a female brain develops.

The Importance of Testosterone. Pfeiffer's classic 1936 study provides convincing evidence for the influence of testosterone on the sexual development of the brain. When Pfeiffer removed the testes of neonatal male rats and the ovaries of neonatal female rats, both genetic males and females exhibited a female cyclic pattern of gonadotrophic hormone release as adults. In contrast, transplantation of the testes into neonatal male and female rats that had their gonads removed caused these animals to exhibit a male pattern of gonadotrophic hormone release. (As we will discover later in this chapter, the levels of the female sex hormones estrogen and progesterone change dramatically over the course of a 28-day cycle, whereas there are only slight changes in the male sex hormone testosterone over that same time period.)

The transplantation of ovaries into male neonatal rats whose gonads had been removed had no influence on the pattern of gonadotrophic hormone release (because it is the presence or absence of testosterone that is the key to sexual differentiation). The results of this study, and many similar studies that have followed, provide strong evidence that early postnatal exposure to testosterone causes the brain of a male to develop, and that in the absence of testosterone, the brain of a female develops.

The prenatal or early postnatal exposure to testosterone determines not only whether the hormonal cycle typical of males or females emerges, but also the behavioral responsivity of these animals to sexual hormones. The presence of testosterone early in development is necessary to produce a brain that will respond to the influence of testosterone. If testosterone is not present early in development, the brain of the adult male will not respond to this sex hormone. To demonstrate the effect of early exposure to testosterone on the brain, Phoenix, Goy, Gerald, and Young (1959) first injected testosterone into pregnant guinea pigs (yes, in this case, the subjects were literally, not just figuratively, guinea pigs!). The ovaries of the female offspring of these testosterone-treated guinea pigs were removed shortly after birth. Phoenix and his colleagues then administered testosterone to these female guinea pigs once they had matured. The treated female guinea pigs exhibited a significantly greater number of male-like mounting behaviors than were observed in adult female guinea pigs that had not been exposed to testosterone during the prenatal period. This result suggests that the prenatal exposure of female guinea pigs to testosterone produced a brain that would cause these animals to exhibit a male-typical pattern of sexual behavior (the mounting behavior; see **Figure 11.4**) in response to later exposure to testosterone. These guinea pigs also appeared to exhibit decreased female-typical sexual behavior (the **lordosis** or copulatory posture in which the female raises her hindquarters to facilitate penile intromission by the male; see **Figure 11.4**) following administration of estrogen.

So prenatal or early postnatal exposure to testosterone can increase the male-like behaviors and decrease the female-like behaviors of a genetic female. What do you think would happen to males who were not exposed to testosterone early in development? To demonstrate the effect of such a lack of exposure, Grady, Phoenix, and Young (1965) castrated male cats shortly after birth (without testes, testosterone is not produced). They reported that when these cats were given injections of testosterone as adults, they failed to exhibit normal male sexual behavior. Further, injections of estrogen produced greater female-typical sexual behavior in these male cats as compared to male cats that had not been castrated (and thus had been exposed to testosterone during brain development).

A Critical Period of Development. As we have seen, the prenatal and early postnatal period is a critical, period during which testosterone influences the development of the brain. After this time, exposure to testosterone will have no effect. To determine when

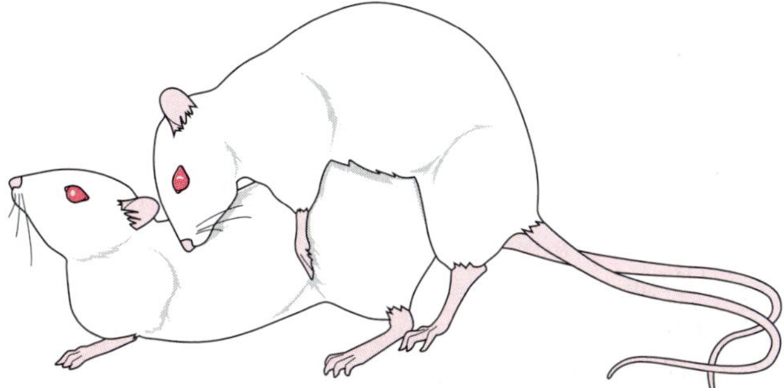

Figure 11.4 Copulation in rats. The female rat raises her hindquarters (lordosis), which facilitates penile intromission by the male rat, which is exhibiting characteristic mounting behavior. ➤ *What is the effect of castration on these male-typical and female-typical sexual behaviors? (p. 333)*

lordosis A female-receptive posture in which the hindquarters are raised, which facilitates penile intromission by the male.

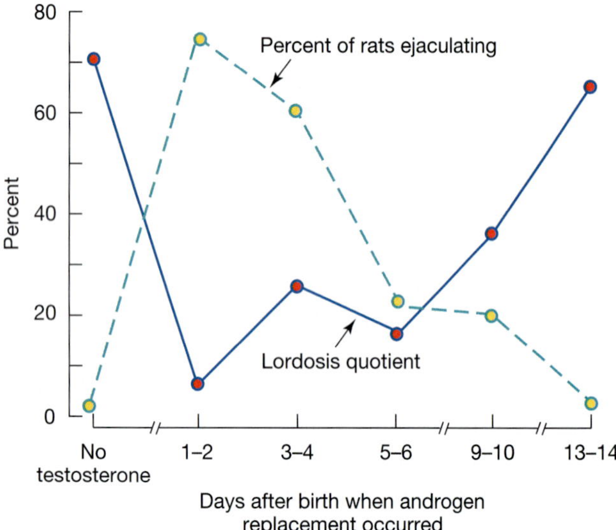

Figure 11.5 The critical period for sexual development of the brain of rats. Administering testosterone to neonatally castrated rats within 2 days of birth produced adult sexual responsivity to testosterone, as indicated by ejaculatory response. The effect of testosterone decreased over the 14 days following birth. After this critical period, neonatally castrated rats not only were unresponsive to testosterone as adults but also showed a female sexual response, as measured by the lordosis quotient, or the percent that the female stands still and assumes a posture that aids intromission. ➤ *What is the effect of testosterone administration after the end of the critical period? (p. 333–334)*

the critical period ends, Beach, Noble, and Orndoff (1969) castrated male rats shortly after birth and then exposed them to testosterone at different times in their first 14 days of life. These researchers reported that if testosterone was administered within 4 days after birth, the rats would, as adults, show normal male sexual behavior following exposure to testosterone (see **Figure 11.5**). The influence of testosterone administration decreased rapidly as the time between castration and testosterone administration increased. After 14 days, testosterone had little effect, and testosterone administered to these rats as adults did not elicit any male sexual behavior.

Testosterone administered to neonatally castrated rats also decreased female-like behavior as compared to neonatally castrated rats that were not exposed to testosterone during the critical period. If testosterone was administered during the critical period of the sexual development of the brain (1 to 6 days following birth), castrated male rats, as adults, did not exhibit female sexual behavior (refer to **Figure 11.5**). In contrast, female sexual behavior was exhibited if testosterone was not administered postnatally or when it was given 13 or 14 days after birth.

Structural Differences in the Brain. So exposure to testosterone early in development produces a male brain, whereas the absence of testosterone during early development results in a female brain. But what exactly is the difference between a male brain and a female brain? Some specific structural differences in the medial preoptic area, an area of the hypothalamus, that controls male sexual behavior, have been noted. Gorski, Gordon, Shryne, and Southam (1978) found that the medial preoptic area is 6 times larger in male rats than female rats (see **Figure 11.6**). Similarly, Swaab and Fliers (1985) reported that this area of the hypothalamus is 2.5 times larger in human males than in females.

Exposure to testosterone during the critical period appears to be directly responsible for these differences. Jacobson and Gorski (1981) found that in the male rat the size and number of neurons in the preoptic area increased during the time from birth to 10 days, corresponding with the aforementioned critical period of brain development. In another study, Toran-Allerand (1984) removed the brains of newborn mice and exposed selected slices of the hypothalamus maintained in culture to testosterone. Toran-Allerand observed significantly greater neural development in the tissue samples exposed to testosterone, with greater growth of new axons and dendrites as well as more extensive branching of existing axons and dendrites.

The Influence of Estradiol. Testosterone is not the only hormone that influences brain development. Development of a male-like brain also can result from exposure to other hormones such as androstenedione, estradiol, and diethylstilbestrol (Kelly, 1991). Why would hormones other than testosterone produce a male-like brain? The answer lies in the chemical similarities of testosterone and **estradiol**, which is one type of the female sex hormone estrogen, present in the mature female's bloodstream. When testosterone crosses the blood-brain barrier, enzymes in the cells of the brain add a benzene ring (⬡) to each molecule of testosterone, converting testosterone to estradiol. According to Kelly (1991), it is estradiol, rather than testosterone, that is actually responsible for masculinization of the brain.

You might be wondering why the estradiol circulating in Paula's blood did not masculinize the brain of her daughter. **Alpha-fetoprotein**, a protein synthe-

Estradiol Hormone thought to be responsible for masculinization of the brain; a benzene ring (⬡) is added to each molecule of testosterone by an enzyme in the brain, converting testosterone to estradiol.

alpha-fetoprotein A protein synthesized by the fetal liver and present in the bloodstream of both male and female fetuses that deactivates circulating estradiol by binding to it.

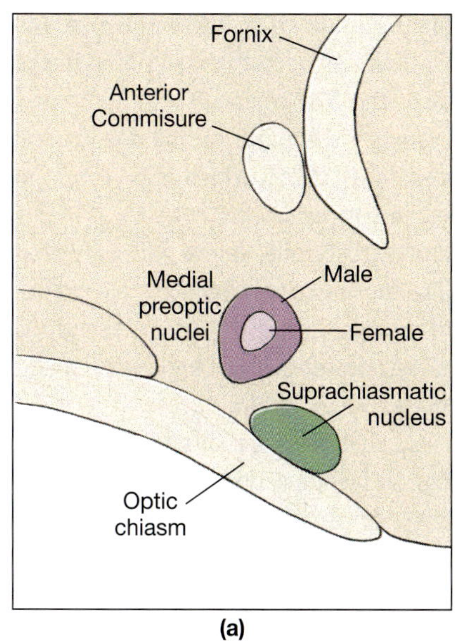

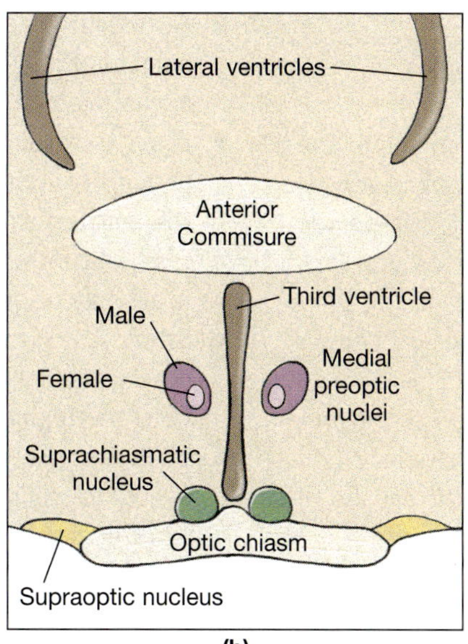

Figure 11.6 Biological differences in the brains of male and female rats. The medial preoptic area of the hypothalamus is significantly smaller in the brain of the female rat than the male rat. (a) Sagittal plane view; (b) coronal plane view.

➤ *What hormone(s) is (are) responsible for the structural differences in male and female brains? (p. 334–335)*

sized by the fetal liver and present in the bloodstream of both male and female fetuses, deactivates the circulating estradiol by binding to it (Plapinger, McEwen, & Clemens, 1993). Once deactivated, estradiol cannot masculinize the developing brain. Testosterone is not affected by alpha-fetoprotein; therefore, the testosterone manufactured by fetal testicles enters the brain of the male offspring and is converted to estradiol.

A Range of Sex-Typical Behaviors? You might at this point have the impression that the brain is either completely male-like or completely female-like. There is, however, strong evidence that intermediate levels of both masculinization and feminization occur (Kelly, 1991). The normal variations in masculinization and feminization are responsible for the range of sexual behaviors seen among normal males and females.

How might intermediate levels of masculinization and feminization occur? According to Kelly (1991), there is considerable variability in the amounts of testosterone to which a developing fetus is exposed. Exposure to lower levels of testosterone early in development will decrease the male-like characteristics of the brain and increase the female-like characteristics. Early exposure to lower levels of testosterone also will decrease male-typical hormonal cycles and sexual behaviors, and increase those typical of the female.

A study by vom Saal and Bronson (1980) links the level of early exposure to testosterone to the degree of masculinization or feminization of the brain. After examining the level of testosterone in the blood of mouse fetuses and in the amniotic fluid surrounding them, vom Saal and Bronson reported that testosterone levels differed depending on the positioning of the fetus in the uterus. A female mouse fetus will have a higher concentration of testosterone in its blood and amniotic fluid when it is between two male mice than when it is between a male and female or between two female mice. Vom Saal and Bronson reported that, as adults, the female mice positioned between the two males displayed erratic changes in female-typical hormonal changes, began to mate later, and ceased bearing young earlier than did adult female mice that developed between two females.

A similar effect is observed when a male mouse is positioned between two female mice in utero. Vom Saal and Bronson reported that in such mice, the testes were smaller and weighed less, and the dosage of testosterone necessary to produce sexual responsivity in a castrated male was higher compared to male mice positioned between two males. These observations support the idea that variations in sexual hormone cycles and sexual behavior among males and females may reflect, at least in part, differences in levels of exposure to testosterone during the prenatal period.

Before You Go On

Using what you have learned about genetics, hormones, and the development of the central nervous system, describe the development of Paula and Doug's son, Ryan, from the moment the sperm fertilized the egg until the moment the doctor proclaimed "it's a boy!"

Using what you have learned about genetics, hormones, and the development of the central nervous system, describe the development of Paula and Doug's daughter, Sarah, from the moment the sperm fertilized the egg until the moment the doctor proclaimed "it's a girl!"

Section Review

- The sex-determining gene located on the middle of the short arm of the Y chromosome determines an individual's biological sex: if the gene is present, the person develops as a male; if it is absent, the person develops as a female.
- At 6 weeks the embryo is capable of developing as either a male or a female.
- The presence of the sex-determining gene causes the production of the enzyme testis-determining factor, which in turn causes the undifferentiated gonads of the embryo to become testes.
- Testosterone released from the testes causes the Wolffian system to develop into parts of the mature male reproductive system, and Müllerian-inhibiting substance, also released from the testes, causes the Müllerian system to degenerate.
- In the absence of testis-determining factor, the Müllerian system develops into part of the mature female reproductive system.
- Testosterone produced by the male testes in the prenatal or early postnatal period also acts to masculinize the brain.
- The male brain controls the male-typical hormonal cycles and behavior.
- The absence of testosterone in the female during the prenatal or early postnatal period results in the development of a female brain.
- The female brain controls the female-typical hormonal cycle and behavior.
- The critical period for the development of the male brain ends shortly after birth, after which the presence of testosterone has no effect.
- Testosterone acts on the brain to increase the size and number of neurons, as well as neural connections, in the medial preoptic area of the hypothalamus.
- When testosterone reaches the brain during the critical period, it is converted to estradiol, which is one form of the female sex hormone estrogen.
- Estradiol, rather than testosterone, is the hormone that is actually responsible for masculinizing the male brain.
- Estradiol present in females during the critical period is deactivated by alpha-fetoprotein, which prevents females from developing a masculinized brain.
- There is strong evidence that there are intermediate levels of both masculinization and feminization of the brain, which result from varying levels of testosterone present during the critical period and is responsible for the range of sexual behaviors seen in normal male and female populations.

Human Sexual Behavior

So far we have learned about the effect of testosterone levels, primarily in nonhuman animals, but there are many other factors that also affect sexual behavior. When we think of sexual behavior, we usually think about what in clinical terms is referred to as the human sexual response, the physiological changes that occur when a male or a female is sexually aroused. When we are sexually stimulated, we are very much aware of some of the biological structures involved, and perhaps not so concerned at that moment with exactly how they work, or how our hormones and psychological factors contribute to sexual arousal. But all of these are essential aspects of sexual behavior, as you will see shortly.

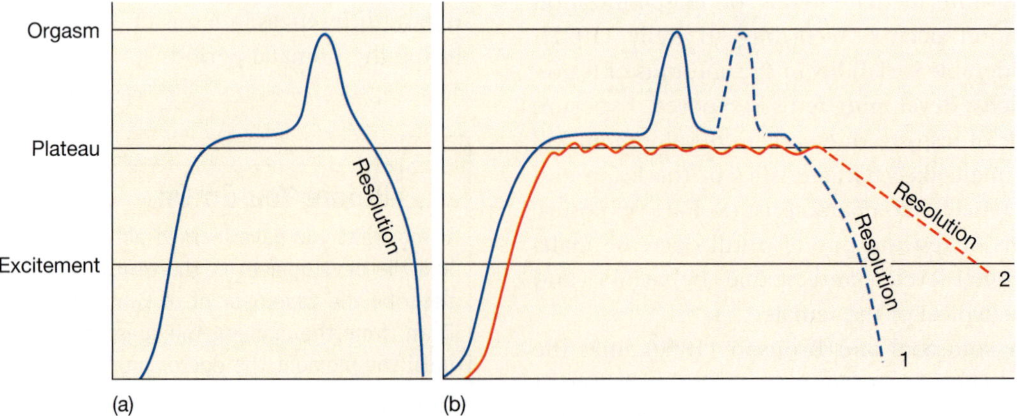

Figure 11.7 Masters and Johnson's four phases of the human sexual response. (a) Male sexual response; (b) two patterns seen in females; in pattern 1, the female experiences one or more orgasms, and in pattern 2, she does not experience an orgasm.

➤ *Does a female always experience all four phases of the human sexual response? (p. 338)*

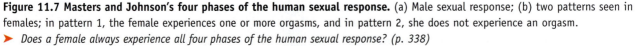

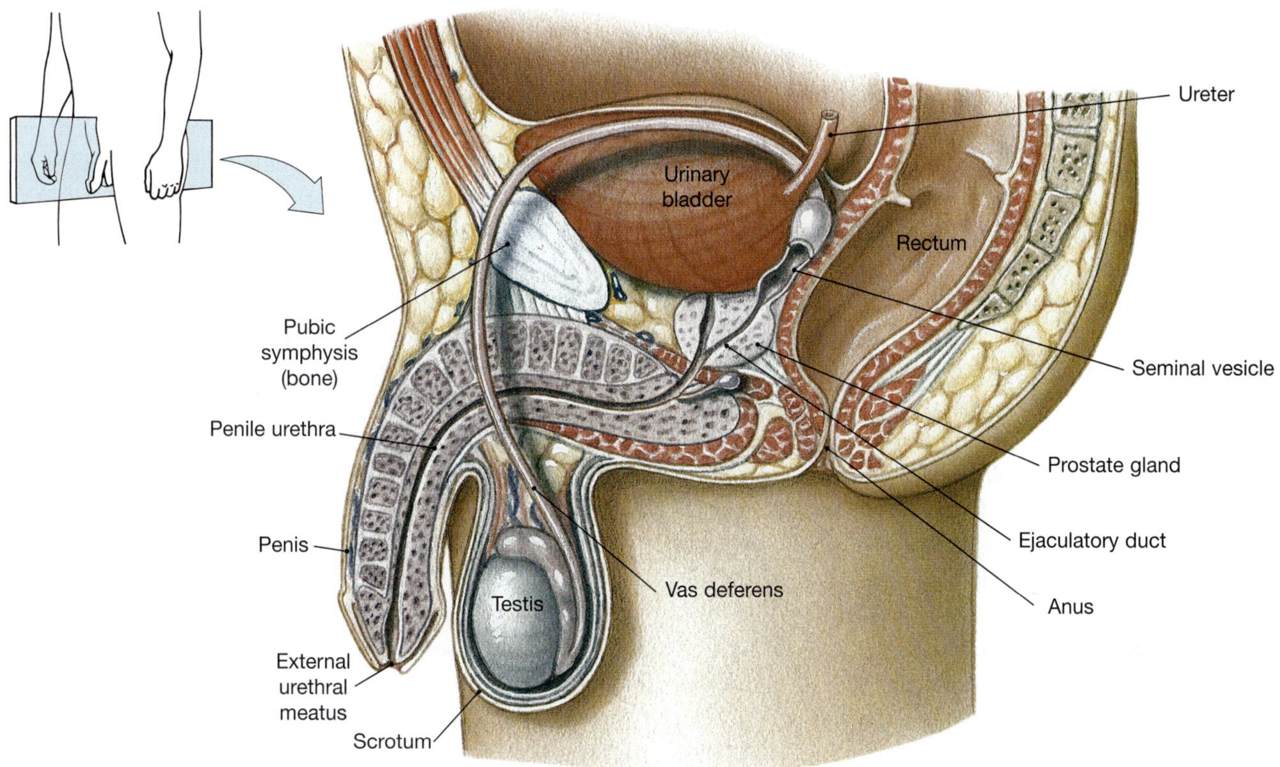

Figure 11.8 Male reproductive system. The major structures (penis, testis) in the male reproductive system are shown.
➤ *Where in the male's body does vasocongestion occur? (p. 337)*

The Physiology of Sexual Behavior

Masters and Johnson (1966) reported observations of the physiological changes occurring during sexual behavior in 382 women and 312 men. More than 10,000 cycles of sexual arousal and orgasm were recorded over a period of 12 years to provide a clear picture of the human sexual response.

According to Masters and Johnson's research, there are four phases in the human sexual response: excitement, plateau, orgasm, and resolution (see **Figure 11.7**). Although different physiological changes occur during each phase, there is no detectable shift from one phase to another; the sexual response is a continuous process. Masters and Johnson's phase distinction is merely a model used to describe the changes that occur.

Stages of the Male Sexual Response. The male becomes aroused during the excitement phase. Within a few seconds after stimulation, the penis (see **Figure 11.8**) fills with blood to produce a penile erection; the increased blood flow to the pelvic area of both males and females is due to a dilation of the blood vessels called **vasocongestion**. Other physiological changes that occur in some males during the excitement phase include nipple erection and sexual flush.

If the sexual stimulation persists, sexual arousal intensifies during the plateau phase. The physiological changes that began in the excitement phase continue and intensify. In addition, generalized muscle tension develops, and breathing, pulse rate, and blood pressure rise. As the tension necessary for orgasm is established, the male reaches the peak of sexual arousal.

The male's **orgasm**, which is the climax of the sexual response, occurs in two stages. In the first stage, the male senses the inevitability of ejaculation when the vas deferens, the seminal vesicles, and the prostate contract (refer to **Figure 11.8**). **Myotonia**, this rhythmic contraction of muscles of the male genital organs, forces the ejaculate into the urethra. In the second stage, the urethra and the penis contract rhythmically, at intervals of 0.8 seconds, forcing the semen out of the urethra. In this second

vasocongestion Dilation and filling of the blood vessels.
orgasm The climax of the sexual response.
myotonia Contraction of certain muscles during orgasm.

phase, as the sex organs contract, the intensely pleasurable aspects of orgasm are experienced.

After orgasm, the male slowly returns to the nonaroused state in the resolution phase. The most significant aspect of the resolution phase is a loss of sexual responsivity. In this refractory phase, males usually cannot be sexually aroused and are often incapable of having an erection. The length of the resolution phase varies, both within and between men, lasting only a few minutes for some and up to 24 hours for others.

Stages of the Female Sexual Response. Several patterns of sexual response are found in females. Although most females show the same pattern of sexual response as males (excitement, plateau, orgasm, resolution), some do not experience distinct plateau and orgasm phases exhibiting instead a series of sustained orgasms (see **Figure 11.7**). Other patterns include a move from excitement to orgasm without any plateau phase or a shift from plateau to resolution without an orgasm.

When a female is sexually stimulated, she, like the male, experiences profound physiological changes. During the excitement phase, these changes include vasocongestion of the blood vessels in the clitoris and seepage of fluid through the vaginal walls (see **Figure 11.9**). This fluid provides the vaginal lubrication necessary for intercourse. In addition, contraction of muscles around the nipple (myotonia) causes the female's nipples to become erect, and vasocongestion causes them to swell. This vasocongestion also enlarges the clitoris in a way that is analogous to the erection of the male's penis. The sexual flush begins, and heart rate and blood pressure increase.

Vasocongestion and myotonia reach their peak during the plateau phase. This intensified physiological response reflects a high level of sexual arousal in response to continued sexual stimulation. The physiological changes taking place in the plateau phase produce both the subjective feeling of sexual arousal and the tension necessary for the orgasmic experience. Some women mistake the intense arousal experienced during the plateau stage for an orgasm.

The physiological changes, specifically the intense muscle contractions, that occur during a female's orgasm resemble those that occur in the male. During the female's orgasm, her genital organs contract rhythmically at approximately 0.8-second intervals. A mild orgasm may have three or four contractions, whereas a very strong, prolonged orgasm may have a dozen contractions.

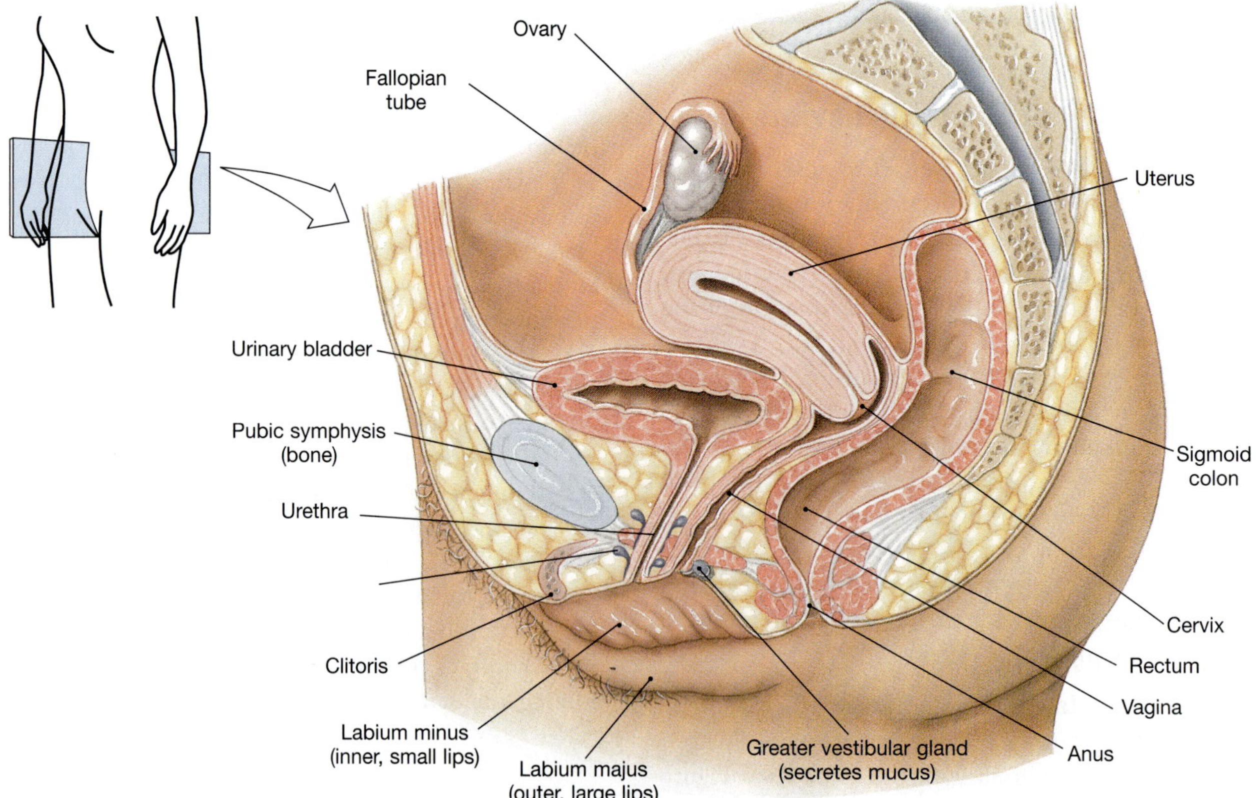

Figure 11.9 Female reproductive system. The major structures (clitoris, vagina, ovary) in the female reproductive system are shown.
➤ *Where in the female's body does myotonia occur? (p. 338)*

Although the male's ejaculation provides him with evidence of his orgasm, the female has no such concrete evidence, although she may be able to feel the contraction of the muscles around the vaginal entrance. Hyde (1994) described the female orgasm as a "spreading sensation that begins around the clitoris and then spreads outward through the whole pelvis."

Following an orgasm, a female enters the resolution phase, during which the level of arousal diminishes. However, unlike the male, no refractory period follows orgasm. With sufficient stimulation, a female can experience another orgasm right away.

Before You Go On

Compare and contrast the stages of the male sexual response and the female sexual response.

Why do you think the stages of the female sexual response are so much more variable than those of the male sexual response?

Which stage(s) of the human sexual response seem(s) to be missing from Doug and Paula's relationship since he lost his job?

Section Review

- The four phases of the human sexual response are excitement, plateau, orgasm, and resolution.
- Vasocongestion of the genitals occurs in both males and females in the excitement phase.
- Males always experience all four phases of the human sexual response, with a loss of sexual responsivity (refractory period) during the resolution phase that varies from a few minutes to up to 24 hours.
- Myotonia is the rhythmic contraction of muscles throughout the body that occurs during orgasm, which contributes to sexual pleasure.
- Most females show the same pattern of sexual response as males, but some experience multiple orgasms, move from excitement to orgasm, or do not experience an orgasm; females do not experience a refractory period during the resolution phase.

Biological Systems Controlling Sexual Behavior

The ability to experience the four stages of the human sexual response depends in part on the effective functioning of certain biological processes, which involve both hormonal and neural systems. The effect of these biological systems is twofold: first, they provide a general sensitivity to sexually related environmental cues; second, they produce sexual arousal and motivate behaviors.

Hormonal Influence in Males. The male sex hormone **testosterone** plays a significant role in producing the arousal necessary for sexual behavior. Testosterone is manufactured in the Leydig cells of the testes. This production is controlled by the hypothalamus, which releases gonadotrophic-releasing hormone into the hypophyseal portal system (see Chapter 2) and stimulates the anterior pituitary to manufacture and release luteinizing hormone into the bloodstream. Luteinizing hormone acts to stimulate the testes to produce and subsequently release testosterone into the bloodstream. In mammalian adults, the level of testosterone fluctuates slightly (see Chapter 9), but the adult male, human or nonhuman, remains sensitive to those environmental events, such as the presence of a receptive female, that can initiate sexual behavior.

The importance of testosterone becomes apparent when it is eliminated, as in **castration** (removal of the testes). Because they are the site of the manufacture and release of testosterone, when the testes are removed, testosterone levels plummet. The loss of testosterone typically renders a male less able or completely unable to be sexually aroused, leading to the conclusion that testosterone has a significant influence on sexual motivation, or the desire to engage in sexual activity.

The rapidity of the loss of sexual motivation after castration varies considerably among members of a species. Davidson (1966) discovered that although most rats lost their sexual interest within a few weeks after castration, some male rats remained sexually motivated for as long as 5 months. Following castration, humans also show a variable loss of sexual drive and behavior (Money & Ehrhardt, 1972). Bremer (1959) observed 157 Norwegian males who had agreed to be castrated to reduce the lengths of their prison terms for sex-related offenses. His findings documented this variability: 49 percent showed rapid asexualization, or loss of sexual motivation; 18 percent lost their interest within a year; and the remaining third of the males continued to experience sexual motivation for several years. The data for male rats and male humans are quite comparable if we consider the differential life spans of each species: the average life span of a rat is approximately 2

testosterone The male sex hormone manufactured in the Leydig cells of the testes.

castration The removal of the testes in males and the ovaries in females.

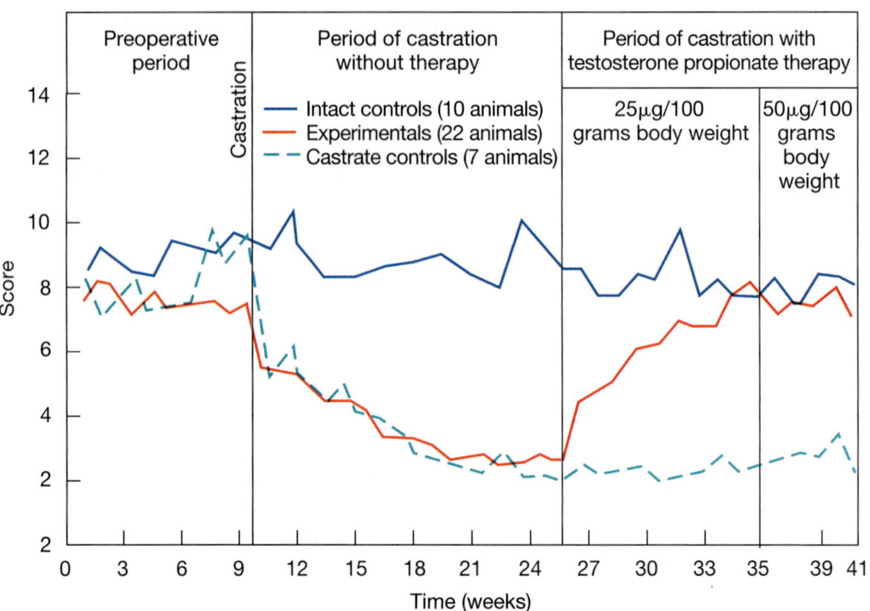

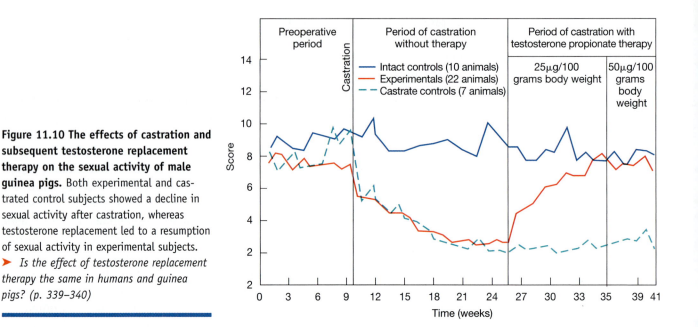

Figure 11.10 The effects of castration and subsequent testosterone replacement therapy on the sexual activity of male guinea pigs. Both experimental and castrated control subjects showed a decline in sexual activity after castration, whereas testosterone replacement led to a resumption of sexual activity in experimental subjects.
➤ *Is the effect of testosterone replacement therapy the same in humans and guinea pigs? (p. 339–340)*

years, so that a rat retaining sexual motivation 5 months after castration is comparable to a human retaining motivation for several years.

Why does the loss of sexual motivation vary so greatly? A male's sexual history seems to be one critical factor. Hart (1968) reported that when compared with other castrated rats, those who were mature and sexually experienced prior to castration had the slowest decline in sexual interest. Beach's (1969) study with dogs and Rosenblatt's (1965) research with cats support these findings.

If the loss of testosterone eliminates sexual motivation, then it would make sense that administration of testosterone would restore it. Administering testosterone to castrated human and nonhuman males does indeed produce a rapid return of sexual responsivity. In a study by Grunt and Young (1952), male guinea pigs typically showed a gradual reduction in sexual behavior during 16 weeks following castration (**see Figure 11.10**). Subsequent injections of testosterone produced a steady increase in sexual motivation that reached the level of uncastrated control animals approximately 6 to 9 weeks after the administration of testosterone began. Castrated control animals that did not receive testosterone injections showed no resumption of sexual behavior. Similar results have been observed following replacement therapy in castrated human males (Money, 1961).

An interesting result of Grunt and Young's study is that doubling the effective dose of testosterone did not increase sexual motivation. Bermant and Davidson (1974) made a similar observation in castrated men. Apparently, a critical level of testosterone is necessary to produce sexual motivation. Once this critical level is reached, additional testosterone has no effect on sexual motivation.

Hormonal Influence in Females. As we have just learned, barring surgical intervention, the levels of sex hormones in males fluctuate slightly. In contrast, the level of female sex hormones changes dramatically but pretty regularly during the **estrus cycle** in nonhuman mammals and during the **menstrual cycle** in humans and some other primates. Levels of the hormone **estrogen** are high in the middle of each cycle, but low at the beginning and end of the cycle. For most mammals, female sexual arousal and behavior occur only when the level of estrogen is high; the intense sexual arousal that most female mammals exhibit during this period is called estrus, or more commonly, **heat**. However, human females and females of some other primate species respond sexually throughout the menstrual cycle, indicating that the hormone estrogen does not play the same major role in sexual motivation that it does in other species.

The estrus and menstrual cycles are divided into two phases: the follicular phase and the luteal phase. In human females, each phase lasts approximately 14 days. However, the timing of ovulation varies from individual to individual, and even from cycle to cycle in the same individual, which is why the contraceptive method of

estrus cycle A cycle of changes in the level of female sex hormones found in nonhuman mammals.

menstrual cycle A cycle of changes in the level of female sex hormones found in humans and some other primates.

estrogen The female sex hormone produced by the Graafian follicle and corpus luteum.

heat A period of intense sexual arousal found when estrogen levels peak in estrus animals.

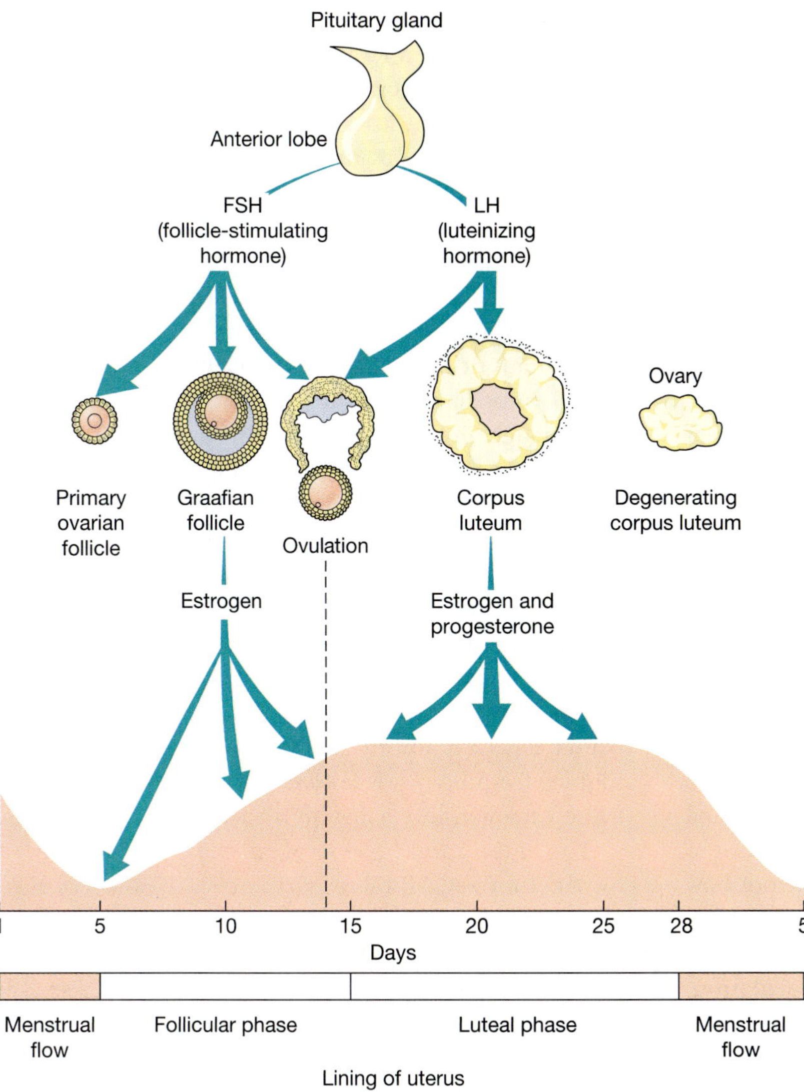

Figure 11.11 Changes that occur in the pituitary hormones, ovaries, and uterine wall during the menstrual cycle. The width of the arrows is proportional to the level of the hormone at that time of the cycle, and their direction shows the cause-effect relationships.

From E. P. Volpe (1979).

➤ *What functions do the Graafian follicle serve? (p. 341)*

avoiding intercourse when ovulation occurs, called the rhythm method, has such a high failure rate. At the beginning of the follicular phase, the anterior pituitary gland begins secreting **follicle-stimulating hormone (FSH)** (see **Figure 11.11**), which causes (1) one or several ovarian follicles, the small spheres of cells surrounding the ovum (egg) within the ovary, to grow into a mature Graafian follicle, (2) the ovum to mature, and (3) the Graafian follicle to secrete estrogen.

The released estrogen has three different effects. First, in a negative feedback loop, high levels of estrogen inhibit further release of FSH. Second, it stimulates the anterior pituitary to release a second hormone, called **luteinizing hormone (LH)**. Thus, as estrogen levels rise, FSH concentrations fall and LH concentrations rise. Finally, estrus animals experience intense sexual arousal when the estrogen level peaks.

Toward the end of the follicular phase, the follicle containing the mature ovum becomes embedded in the surface of the ovary. When the LH level is highest, the walls of the follicle rupture, pushing the egg through the wall of the ovary into the fallopian tube. The release of the egg is called ovulation (see **Figure 11.11**).

After ovulation, the luteal phase begins. LH causes the ruptured follicle to become a corpus luteum or "yellow body" (see **Figure 11.11**). The corpus luteum begins to secrete estrogen and a second sex hormone, **progesterone**. The secreted estrogen and progesterone prepare the lin-

---

follicle-stimulating hormone (FSH) A hormone secreted by the anterior pituitary gland that causes one or several ovarian follicles to grow into a mature Graafian follicle, the ovum to mature, and the Graafian follicle to secrete estrogen.

luteinizing hormone (LH) In females, a hormone secreted by the anterior pituitary gland that causes ovulation and the ruptured follicle to become the corpus luteum. In males, LH stimulates testosterone secretion.

progesterone A female sex hormone manufactured by the corpus luteum.

ing of the uterus for implantation of a fertilized egg. This preparation involves the growth of the **endometrium**, the inner lining of the uterus. If fertilization does occur, the corpus luteum continues to secrete estrogen and progesterone to maintain the endometrium until the placenta takes on this task in the third month. However, if the ovum is not fertilized, the uterine lining is reabsorbed in estrus animals or expelled in menstrual animals; expulsion of the uterine lining is known as **menstruation** (or the "period").

Another effect of progesterone is the inhibition of LH release (another negative feedback loop). If the egg has been fertilized, progesterone will continue to be secreted. If the egg has not been fertilized, secretion of progesterone will stop. When progesterone production ceases, the luteal phase ends and the next cycle (secretion of FSH, etc.) begins.

What is the effect of all these physiological changes on the female's sexual behavior? There are three ways to assess the influence of sex hormones on female sexual arousal and sexual behavior: (1) by correlating the incidence of sexual behavior with changes in hormonal levels, (2) by administering hormones during periods when they are absent in the body, and (3) by removing the ovaries and observing the subsequent effect on sexual behavior. Considered together, the results of the use of these three techniques will give you a good idea of how sexual hormones affect sexual behavior in the female.

As we have discussed, in estrus (nonhuman) females, estrogen levels peak just before ovulation. This peak has been shown to correspond to a defined period of sexual receptivity that lasts for several days before ovulation. The receptive female secretes vaginal pheromones, hormones (chemicals) that are released into the physical environment, which make her attractive to males. Once a male is attracted to her, the estrus female will readily accept his advances, and sexual activity will ensue. When the female is not in heat, she does not produce pheromones and thus does not attract males. If any male mistakenly makes sexual advances outside the estrus period, the female will resist his attempts to copulate.

Further evidence linking estrogen levels and sexual behavior comes from studies in which estrogen was administered at a time in the estrus cycle when it was normally low. For example, Beach (1947) found that estrogen injections in female rats will produce a period of intense sexual receptivity identical to that which normally occurs before ovulation. The female's sexual motivation lasts as long as the estrogen level remains high. By contrast, surgical removal of the ovaries, called **ovariectomy**, produces a rapid, permanent loss of sexual receptivity (recall that estrogen is secreted by the Graafian follicles and corpus luteum in the ovaries). Beach reported that this loss of sexual motivation could be reversed by administering estrogen replacement therapy.

Although the influence of estrogen on sexual receptivity is not as significant in females of many nonhuman primate species as it is in estrus animals, it is still important. Females of many primate species will engage in sexual activity throughout the entire cycle (Ford & Beach, 1951), but the highest incidence of sexual activity occurs during the few days before ovulation. In 1943, Young and Orbison observed that female chimpanzees moved toward the males and exhibited the sexual presentation posture more frequently just prior to ovulation. Genital swelling and the secretion of vaginal pheromones, two other effects of high estrogen levels, also increase the male primate's attraction to the female, contributing to the higher frequency of sexual activity during periods when estrogen levels are high.

The importance of estrogen can also be seen in ovariectomized female primates. Beach (1958) reported that removal of the ovaries produced a complete loss of sexual activity in most nonhuman female primates, although a few showed infrequent sexual activity. Estrogen replacement can reverse this loss,

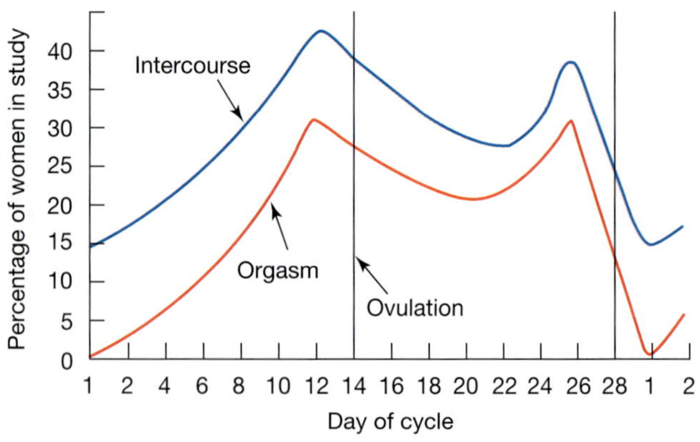

Figure 11.12 Percentage of women engaging in sexual intercourse during the female menstrual cycle. Sexual activity increases at the same time that estrogen increases up to the middle of the cycle, and then the incidence of sexual intercourse declines as estrogen declines. Note the rapid rise in sexual activity at the end of the cycle.

➤ *How does the relationship between estrogen level and the occurrence of sexual behavior differ in estrus and menstrual animals? (p. 342–343)*

endometrium The mucous inner lining of the uterus.
menstruation The expelling of the uterine lining.
ovariectomy The surgical removal of the ovaries.

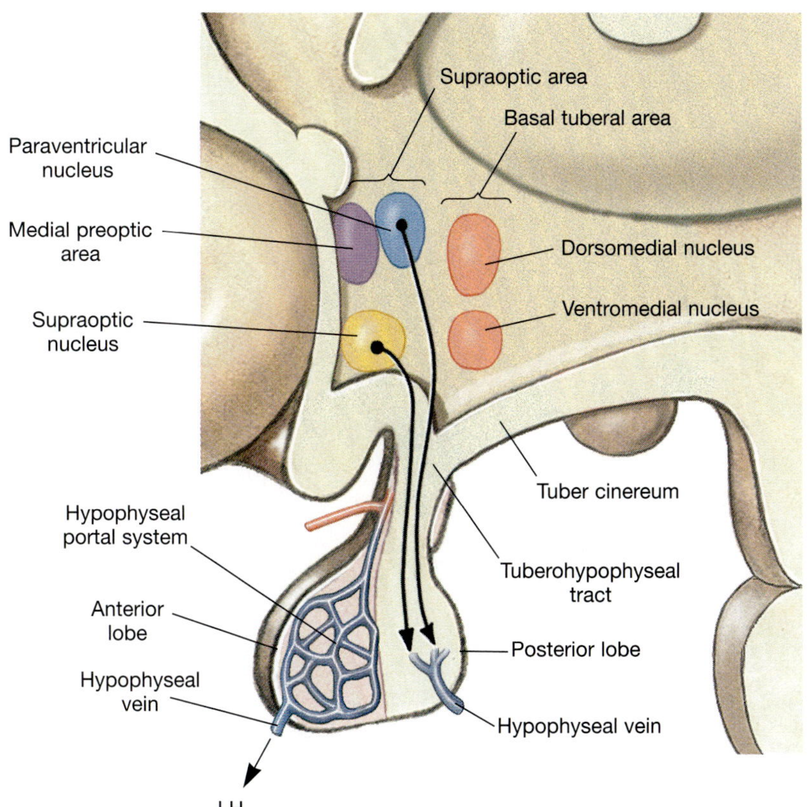

Figure 11.13 Important structures in the hypothalamus and the pituitary gland. Hormones produced in the hypothalamus are released into the hypophyseal portal system and travel to the anterior pituitary gland where they influence production of pituitary hormones.
➤ *How does the hypothalamus affect the manufacture and release of testosterone? (p. 344)*

but some females do not completely regain sexual receptivity even with estrogen therapy.

Estrogen affects the human female's sexual activity, but its effect is clearly less significant and more variable than in nonhuman female primates (Money & Ehrhardt, 1972). Udry and Morris's (1968) study of human sexual behavior found a sharp increase in reported sexual activity between the end of menstruation and ovulation (recall that ovulation occurs around the middle of the cycle, the 14-day mark; see **Figure 11.12**). Udry and Morris also noted that women showed increased sexual activity just before menstruation. Although it is unclear why this second increase occurs, one possible answer is that a drop in progesterone during the premenstrual period may make some women tense and irritable, and this increased arousal may be misinterpreted as sexual desire.

Although sexual behavior occurs less frequently at some times in the cycle than others, it does occur throughout the cycle. Obviously, factors other than estrogen influence human female sexual behavior; for many women, sexual motivation is not diminished by removal of the ovaries or by the onset of menopause, a natural ceasing of estrogen production by the ovaries. After a hysterectomy-ovariectomy or during menopause, women often receive testosterone therapy. Testosterone acts to increase a woman's sexual responsivity. The reason testosterone has this effect (and the reason testosterone is prescribed) is that prior to menopause women secrete an adrenal androgen hormone similar to testosterone called **androstenedione**. Androstenedione, produced continuously in low levels by the adrenal gland, affects the level of a woman's sexual motivation and frequency of sexual behavior. Removal of the adrenal gland produces a lack of or a sharp decrease in androstenedione and a subsequent reduction in sexual motivation, whereas sexual motivation is reinstated by testosterone therapy (Michael, 1980). Further, drugs that block androgen production produce a decrease in sexual activity (Berlin & Meinecke, 1981).

Why are estrus animals only responsive for a limited time during the cycle, whereas humans and many nonhuman primates are responsive continuously? The evolution of an increased sensitivity to androstenedione gives females a hormonal basis for experiencing sexual responsivity throughout the menstrual cycle. Many primatologists (Hrdy, 1979) believe that the evolution of continuous sexual

---

androstenedione An androgen produced continuously in low levels by the adrenal gland, accounting for continued sexual receptivity in post-menopausal women.

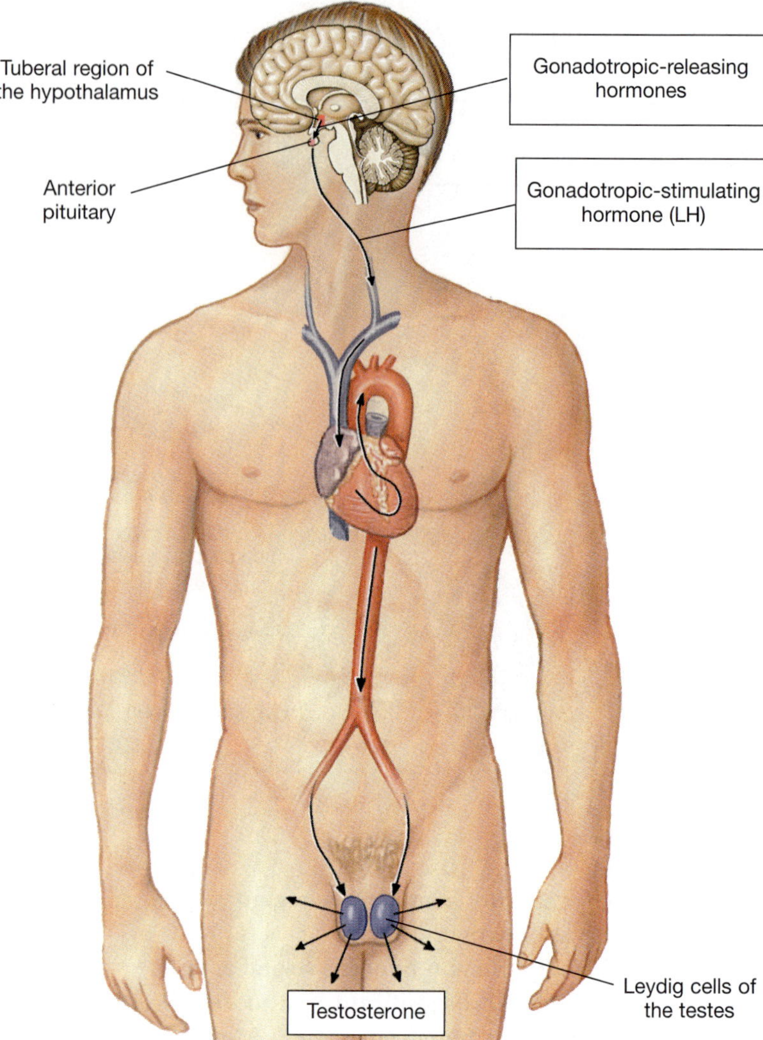

Figure 11.14 Influence of the hypothalamus on the production and release of testosterone. Stimulation of the tuberal region of the hypothalamus causes the release of gonadotrophic-releasing factor, which causes the anterior pituitary to secrete luteinizing hormone (LH). LH then travels through the bloodstream to stimulate the Leydig cells of the testes to manufacture and release testosterone.

➤ *Where in the central nervous system are testosterone-sensitive receptors located? (p. 344–345).*

responsivity enabled some nonhuman primates (for example, gibbons) and humans to establish stable pair bonding. Evolutionary theory holds that the stability of pair bonds promotes the care and protection of the young, but it is also what makes "breaking up so hard to do."

Before You Go On

Explain how castration affects a male's sexual motivation.

Explain why the rhythm method of contraception has such a high failure rate, using what you have learned about the stages of the menstrual cycle.

medial preoptic area A group of neurons in the anterior hypothalamus that contains testosterone-sensitive receptors.

Neural Influence in Males. Testosterone alone does not directly produce sexual behavior. Several areas of the central nervous system contribute to sexual behavior, including the hypothalamus, the amygdala, and the cerebral cortex.

The hypothalamus influences sexual behavior in two ways: (1) it indirectly stimulates the manufacture and release of testosterone, and (2) it elicits sexual behavior. Stimulation of the tuberal region of the hypothalamus (see **Figure 11.13**) causes the release of gonadotrophic-releasing hormones that are then transmitted to the anterior pituitary gland. The gonadotrophic-releasing hormones cause the anterior pituitary to secrete luteinizing hormone and follicle-stimulating hormone into the bloodstream. Luteinizing hormone stimulates the Leydig cells of the testes, while follicle-stimulating hormone is responsible for the manufacture and release of testosterone (see **Figure 11.14**).

The **medial preoptic area** is located in the anterior part of the hypothalamus (see **Figures 11.6** and **11.13**), and acts to elicit sexual behavior in males. This area of the hypothalamus contains receptors that are stimulated by testosterone to produce sexual responsivity (Kelly, 1991). Bloch, Butler, and Kohlert (1996) reported that electrical stimulation of the medial preoptic area increased male-typical mounting sexual behavior, and that this area of the brain became active during sexual behavior (Heeb & Yahr, 1996). Destruction of the medial preoptic area had the opposite effect (McGinness, Williams, & Lumia, 1996; Meisel & Sachs, 1994). Similar results were observed by Roeder and Mueller (1969) in human males; hypothalamic lesions decreased the activity of convicted male sex offenders. In another study, the sex drive of men with a long history of a sexual interest in children (pedophilia) declined following hypothalamic lesions (Whalen, 1977).

Remember the castration studies cited earlier? In those studies, testosterone was injected into the bloodstream. To determine whether testosterone administration affected the hypothalamus, Davidson (1980) injected testosterone directly into the anterior hypothalamus of castrated rats and reported a resumption of sexual motivation. Heimer and Larsson (1966/1967) found that testosterone replacement therapy did not reinstate sexual arousal in animals with anterior hypothalamic lesions, suggesting that the destruction of the anterior hypothalamus makes males insensitive to the presence of testosterone, and thus renders them unable to respond to sexual stimulation. (These earlier studies suggested that the key area in the hypothalamus eliciting sexual behavior was the anterior hypothalamus; more recent studies have narrowed it down to the neurons in the medial preoptic area.)

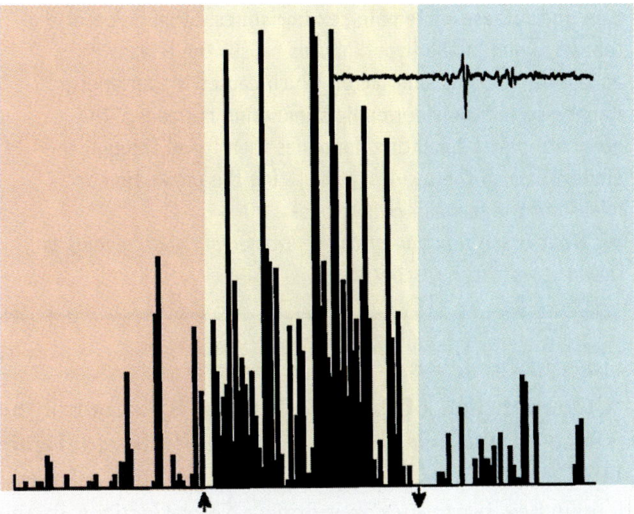

Figure 11.15 Activity in the medial amygdaloid nucleus of a male rat before (pink), during (yellow), and after (blue) being exposed to a receptive female rat. Exposure to a receptive female increases the level of activation in the medial amygdaloid.

➤ *How does the presence of a receptive female rat activate the medial amygdaloid nucleus? (p. 345–346)*

Dopamine is one neurotransmitter in the medial preoptic area. Sexual behavior has been associated with the release of dopamine in the medial preoptic area (Hull et al., 1993). Dopamine is not released by the presence of a receptive female in castrated male rats (Hull et al., 1997), which provides further evidence of the importance of the medial preoptic area in eliciting male sexual behavior.

The medial preoptic area of the anterior hypothalamus can elicit sexual behavior only after two conditions have been met. First, testosterone must be present. Second, the presence of a receptive female must be detected. Testosterone-sensitive neurons react to the presence of testosterone, but how does the medial preoptic area recognize that a receptive female is present? Several other brain structures provide feedback to the medial preoptic area regarding the presence of a receptive female.

Special receptors in the olfactory bulbs, collectively called the **vomeronasal organ**, can detect the presence of pheromones released by a receptive female. The vomeronasal organ sends information about a receptive female to the medial amygdaloid nucleus (Pfaff, 1997). The presence of a receptive female has been shown to activate the medial amygdaloid nucleus (see **Figure 11.15**; Minerbo et al., 1994). Stimulation of the medial amygdaloid nucleus has been shown to elicit sexual behavior in male rats, even in the absence of a receptive female (Garritano et al., 1996). So how might the medial amygdaloid nucleus influence sexual behavior? Good question! The answer lies in the direct neural connection between the medial amygdaloid nucleus and the medial preoptic area. This connection allows the detection of the presence of a receptive female to be passed to the medial preoptic area.

But how exactly does the medial preoptic area act to elicit sexual behavior? Axons from the medial preoptic area project to the ventral midbrain via the medial forebrain bundle. Recall from Chapter 5 that the medial forebrain bundle is part of the mesotelencephalic reinforcement system. Activity in the tegmentostriatal pathway of the mesotelencephalic reinforcement system is stimulated by the presence of reinforcing stimuli; that is, the presence of a receptive female activates this system. The ventral midbrain sends information from the

---

vomeronasal organ Specialized sensory receptors in the olfactory bulbs that can detect the presence of pheromones released by a receptive female.

medial preoptic area to the basal ganglia, which acts to initiate male-typical copulatory sexual behavior.

The cortex also plays an important role in a male's sexual behavior. Beach (1958) suggested that the cortex serves several functions, including: (1) organization of the motor responses involved in sexual activity; (2) detection of the sexual content of sensory information; and (3) storage of the memories of past sexual experiences. The failure of the cortex to function properly can lead to either a misdirected sexual response or a failure to engage in sexual behavior.

The effects of cortical damage on sexual behavior in males depend on the area and the extent of the damage. Large neocortical lesions, especially in the frontal cortex, can result in a decline in sexual activity (Beach, Zitrin, & Jaynes, 1955). The more extensive the lesion, the greater the loss of sexual responsivity.

The effects of cortical damage also vary among the different species. For example, comparable destruction in cats and rats produces greater loss of sexual behavior in the cats. Nonhuman primates and human males with cortical damage experience an even greater loss of sexual behavior than is seen in cats.

One cortical area crucial to normal sexual behavior is the temporal lobe, which receives sensory information and analyzes this information to determine the availability of an appropriate sexual partner. When the temporal cortex operates properly, animals, including humans, exhibit sexual behavior only toward appropriate partners. However, malfunctions in the temporal lobe can result in sexual behavior toward unnatural objects (for example, a member of another species or an inanimate object). The disruptive effect of a malfunction in the temporal lobe on the sexual behavior of male monkeys was demonstrated in a classic experiment by Klüver and Bucy (1939). They discovered that nonhuman male primates, following removal of the temporal lobe, mounted and attempted to copulate with many inappropriate objects, including members of another primate species and inanimate objects.

Human males with temporal lobe damage also have shown aberrant sexual behaviors. In 1955, Terzian and DalleOre reported that men with temporal-lobe damage exhibited a strong sexual response to inappropriate objects. Also, Kolarsky, Freund, Machek, and Polak (1967) found a strong relationship between sexual disorders, such as fetishism, transvestitism, and voyeurism, and temporal lobe dysfunction.

Neural Influence in Females. The hypothalamus and the cortex also serve important functions in sexual receptivity and sexual behavior in females, both human and nonhuman.

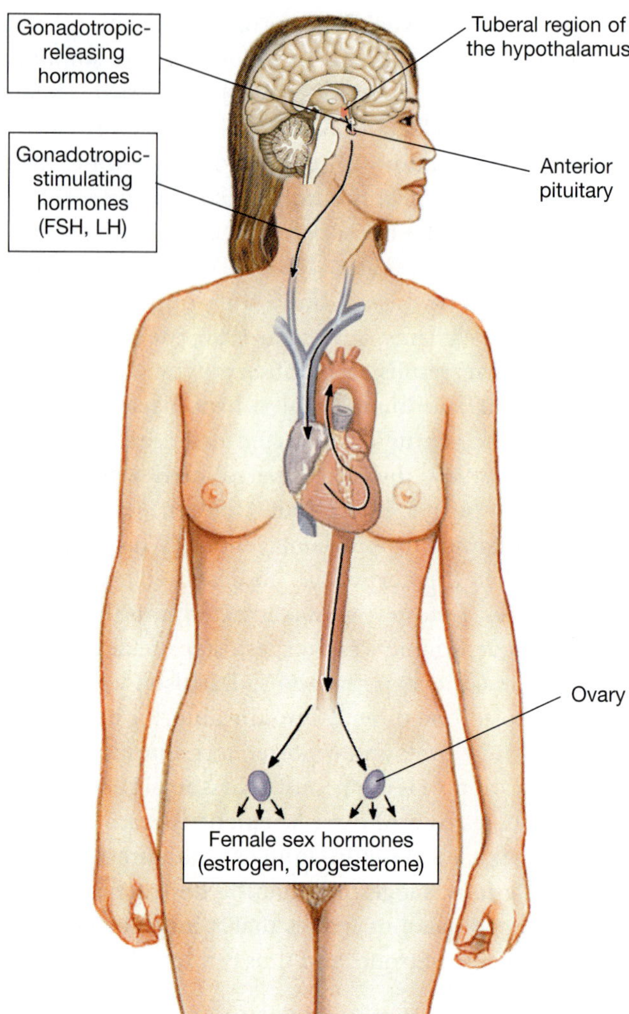

Figure 11.16 Influence of the hypothalamus on the production and release of female sex hormones. Stimulation of the tuberal region of the hypothalamus causes the release of gonadotrophic-releasing factor, which causes the anterior pituitary to secrete gonadotrophic-stimulating hormones. The gonadotrophic-stimulating hormones then travel through the bloodstream to the ovaries, stimulating the production and release of the female sex hormones.

➤ *What is the function of the ventromedial hypothalamus in sexual receptivity? (p. 347)*

One function of the hypothalamus is to control the release of the female sex hormones (refer to **Figure 11.16**). As in males, hypothalamic control of the release of female sex hormones is indirect. Neural activity in the basal tuberal area of the hypothalamus causes the secretion of the gonadotrophic-releasing factor, which stimulates the anterior pituitary gland, causing the release of the gonadotrophic-stimulating hormones into the bloodstream (Harris, 1955). The gonadotrophic-stimulating hormones in turn cause the ovaries to produce and release the female sex hormones (see **Figure 11.16**).

To test the role of the hypothalamus, Sawyer (1960) lesioned the basal tuberal hypothalamic region (see **Figure 11.13**) of cats and rabbits; as a result, both sex hormone production and sexual activity were completely eliminated. Estrogen replacement therapy reinstated sexual motivation but not hormonal production, supporting the role of the basal tuberal hypothalamic region in the release of gonadotrophic-stimulating hormones.

If estrogen replacement therapy reinstates sexual motivation in animals with lesions in the basal tuberal area, a different hypothalamic area must be responsible for the influence of estrogen on sexual behavior. Many studies indicate that this area is the ventromedial hypothalamus (VMH) (see **Figure 11.13**). Pleim and Barfield (1988) injected estrogen directly into the ventromedial hypothalamus of female cats whose ovaries had been removed and noted an intense sexual response in previously nonresponsive cats. Pfaff and Sakuma (1979) observed that electrical stimulation of the ventromedial hypothalamus increased sexual behavior in female rats, whereas sexual behavior was eliminated following lesioning of the ventromedial hypothalamus. Loss of sexual responding after lesioning reflects the inability of these animals to detect the presence of the hormone estrogen, which is responsible for sexual arousal. The presence of estrogen-sensitive receptors in the ventromedial hypothalamus would account for the lack of response to administration of estrogen in animals with ventromedial hypothalamic lesions.

Axons from the ventromedial hypothalamus project to the periaqueductal gray of the midbrain, which in turn projects to the spinal cord. According to Pfaff (1997), the neural message from the ventromedial hypothalamus, activated by the presence of estrogen, elicits the female-typical lordosis response.

The medial preoptic area also appears to be involved in eliciting sexual behavior in females. Stimulation of the medial preoptic area produces female-typical behavior (Bloch, Butler, & Kohlert, 1996), and activity in the medial preoptic area increases during sexual behavior in female rats (Heeb & Yahr, 1996). Activity in the medial preoptic area activates the tegmentostriatal pathway (in females by the same mechanism described for males on **p. 344–345**. Sexual behavior has been shown to increase the activity of dopaminergic neurons in the nucleus accumbens of female rats (Pfaus et al., 1995), which explains why sexual behavior is so pleasurable. As was discussed earlier in the chapter, the medial preoptic area is significantly smaller in females than males, although the implication of this difference is not readily apparent.

Earlier in the chapter, we learned that neocortical lesions either reduced or disrupted male sexual behavior, suggesting that the cortex has a facilitative role in male sexual behavior. In contrast, the influence of the cortex on nonhuman female sexual behavior appears to be primarily inhibitory. Clemens, Wallen, and Gorski (1967) observed that sexual activity increased when the cortical functioning of female rats was chemically suppressed.

Why is the role of the cortex in sexual activity different in nonhuman male and female animals? One reason is that the nonhuman male's sexual behavior requires more sensory and motor coordination than that of the female. In addition, a male's sexual arousal relies heavily on the sight and smell of a receptive female, whereas a nonhuman female's sexual arousal depends very heavily on her hormonal state.

The cortex also appears to provide some organization of female sexual behavior in nonhuman animals. For example, the sexual response of cortically lesioned female rats, rabbits, cats, and dogs is not as integrated as that of their nonlesioned counterparts (Ford & Beach, 1951). The sexual behavior of these lesioned animals is sufficiently organized to permit copulation, but they do not show the orderly sequence of sexual behavior seen in nonlesioned animals. There are no comparable data for the role of the cortex in the sexual behavior of female nonhuman primates and humans.

Before You Go On

Compare and contrast the role of the central nervous system (specifically, the hypothalamus and cortex) in the sexual behavior of males and females.

Psychological Processes Governing Sexual Activity

Sexual arousal and behavior are controlled not only by biological factors, but also by psychological processes. One such psychological process is classical conditioning. In this form of learning, about which you will learn more in Chapter 14, environmental stimuli acquire the ability to elicit sexual arousal and to motivate sexual behavior. Consider the following example to illustrate the conditioning of sexual arousal.

You are sitting with your significant other in front of a warm glowing fire, listening to your favorite music. You might have been sexually aroused and have received sexual satisfaction in a situation such as this

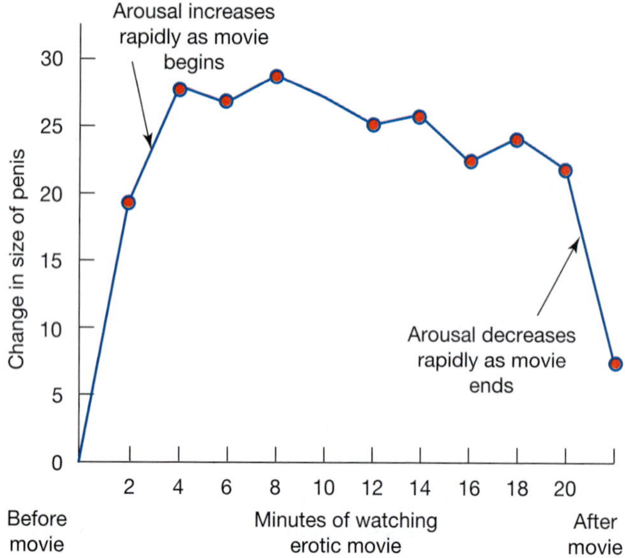

Figure 11.17 The sexual arousal of males watching an erotic movie. Sexual arousal increases rapidly when the movie begins and declines quickly after the movie ends.

➤ *What nonvisual erotic stimuli can produce sexual arousal? (p. 348)*

before. As a result of these past associations, you might become sexually aroused in this setting. However, if you have never been aroused and experienced satisfaction in a similar setting in the past, the setting alone may not produce sexual arousal. You or your partner might have to take more active measures.

The Influence of Erotic Stimuli. Another example of an environmental stimulus is sexually explicit material such as films or photographs. Howard, Reifler, and Liptzin (1971) showed male subjects an erotic movie and simultaneously recorded changes in penis size as a measure of sexual arousal (see **Figure 11.17**). During the first few minutes of the film, most of the males showed a rapid increase in penis size. Most subjects' sexual arousal continued throughout the entire 20-minute movie and decreased rapidly when the movie ended. When Geer, Morokigg, and Greenwood (1974) showed females an erotic movie, most of the women responded with rapid vasocongestion of the clitoris, and their sexual arousal also continued until the movie ended.

Sexual arousal can also result from exposure to nonvisual stimuli. In a study by Heiman (1975), listening to explicit, romantic material produced intense sexual arousal in both male and female college students, whereas nonexplicit material had no effect.

In addition to producing sexual arousal, exposure to sexually arousing stimuli may also motivate sexual activity. For example, Cattell, Kawash, and DeYoung (1972) found that exposing males to erotic slides not only produced sexual arousal but also motivated sexual intercourse once the men returned home to their wives. Note that erotic material does not induce sexual arousal in everyone. Some people find sexually explicit material disgusting, and to others it is boring (Griffitt, May, & Veitch, 1974).

Acquired Sexual Motives. We have seen that either auditory or visual presentation of sexually explicit material can produce sexual arousal. But how? Because all people do not become aroused when viewing or hearing sexually explicit stimuli, it is possible that, like the romantic setting described earlier, these events develop the ability to elicit sexual arousal through conditioning. An **acquired sexual motive** is a learned sexual response to a stimulus that occurs as a result of a conditioning experience. Direct support for this view is provided by studies that have paired neutral stimuli with sexual arousal. These studies indicate that neutral stimuli, when paired with sexual arousal in both nonhuman animals (Domjan, 1994; Domjan et al., 1986) and humans (Rachman, 1966), become able to produce sexual arousal and motivate sexual behavior.

Domjan and his colleagues (Domjan et al., 1986) investigated conditioning of sexual arousal in the male Japanese quail. These researchers presented a red light on the approach of a receptive female quail. The continued pairing of the red light with the arrival of the receptive female resulted in the male quail becoming excited by the presentation of the red light. Further, the presence of the red light led the male quail to more readily copulate with a receptive female quail. The male quail even developed a preference for the area of the cage where the red light was presented. A similar conditioning of preferences for an area associated with a receptive female has been found in male rats (Schwartz, 1956).

Rachman (1966) instructed male subjects to view pictures of nude females together with pictures of women's shoes. After several conditioning trials, the male subjects in Rachman's study exhibited sexual arousal when the pictures of the shoes were presented without the pictures of the women. While the origins of shoe fetishes may lie in conditioning experiences, the sexual arousal in Rachman's study is not an exam-

---

acquired sexual motive A stimulus in the physical environment becomes able to produce the physical changes associated with sexual arousal as a result of conditioning.

ple of a fetish, where a person can only experience satisfaction in the presence of the fetish object.

Imagination and reminiscence appear to play an important role in the strength of sexual arousal produced by a particular stimulus. When people replay a satisfying sexual experience in their minds, the ability of the conditioned stimulus to produce sexual arousal is enhanced. Recall the example of you and your significant other sitting by the fire, and imagine that on the following day, you visualize what happened. By replaying in your mind the arousal and pleasure, the setting that you experienced may in the future elicit greater sexual arousal.

Before You Go On

Using what you have learned about conditioning, describe how recalling a satisfying sexual experience with Doug could cause Paula to become sexually aroused.

Section Review

- The male's ability to be aroused depends on the presence of the sex hormone testosterone.
- Sexual responsivity is controlled by estrogen in estrus animals and the adrenal androgen androstenedione in some nonhuman female primates and in humans.
- The tuberal region of the hypothalamus governs hormone secretion.
- The medial preoptic area of the anterior hypothalamus in males and the ventromedial hypothalamus in females elicit sexual behavior.
- The vomeronasal organ of the olfactory bulb detects the presence of a pheromone secreted by a receptive female, and sends this information to the medial amygdaloid nucleus and then on to the medial preoptic area.
- In the male, the cortex (1) organizes the motor responses involved in sexual activity; (2) detects the sexual content of sensory information; and (3) stores memories of past sexual experiences.
- The temporal lobe of the cortex identifies a sexually appropriate partner, thereby releasing sexual behavior. The cortex appears to organize the nonhuman female sexual response and inhibit nonhuman female sexual behavior, although its influence in human females is unknown.
- The medial preoptic area, via the medial forebrain bundle, projects to the ventral midbrain, which sends information to the basal ganglia, the area responsible for the integration of male-typical sexual behavior.
- The ventromedial hypothalamus projects to the periaqueductal gray of the midbrain, which in turn projects to the spinal cord, which elicits the female-typical lordosis response.
- Environmental stimuli such as an attractive partner or shoes can develop the capacity to produce sexual arousal (an acquired sexual motive) through the classical conditioning process.

Sexual Preference

Heterosexual people engage in sexual activity with people of the opposite sex (hetero = different), whereas homosexual people engage in sexual activity with same-sex partners (homo = same). Research (Laumann, Gagnon, Michael & Michaels, 1994) suggests that the homosexuality rate is 3–4 percent in men and 1 percent in women. Biological psychologists have proposed several different biological explanations of this difference in sexual preference. One view suggests a genetic basis for sexual preference. In this study, Kallman (1952) reported a 100 percent concordance rate among the identical twins (two persons with 100% of their genes in common; see Chapter 3). If one identical twin was homosexual, the other twin was invariably also homosexual; if one identical twin was heterosexual, the other was invariably also heterosexual. Among fraternal twins (or twins with at most 50% of their genes in common), the concordance rate was only 10 percent, which is no different than one would find with any pair of siblings (brothers or sisters born at different times who also have at most 50% of their genes in common). Some recent studies (Bailey & Bell, 1993; Buhrich, Bailey, & Martin, 1991) have also found that the concordance rate for homosexuality among relatives is higher than among unrelated individuals, although the concordance rate for identical twins was lower (approximately 50 percent) than the 100 percent reported by Kallman. However, other researchers (Eckert et al., 1986; Heston & Shields, 1968; King & McDonald, 1992) have failed to find concordance rates for homosexuality among relatives above the level found in the general population. From an evolutionary standpoint, one could argue that natural selection would quickly eliminate a homosexual gene, given that most homosexuals will have no children. On the other hand, a homosexual might enhance his or her own genetic success by assisting in the reproductive efforts of his or her siblings, who share with the homosexual a common genetic base.

A second biological theory proposes that a hormonal imbalance produces homosexual behavior. Some

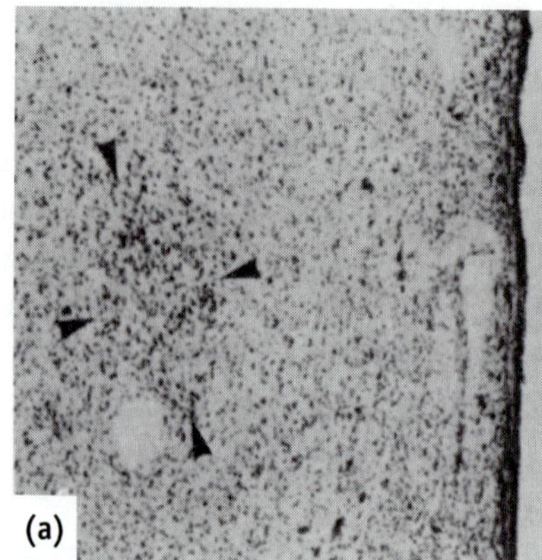

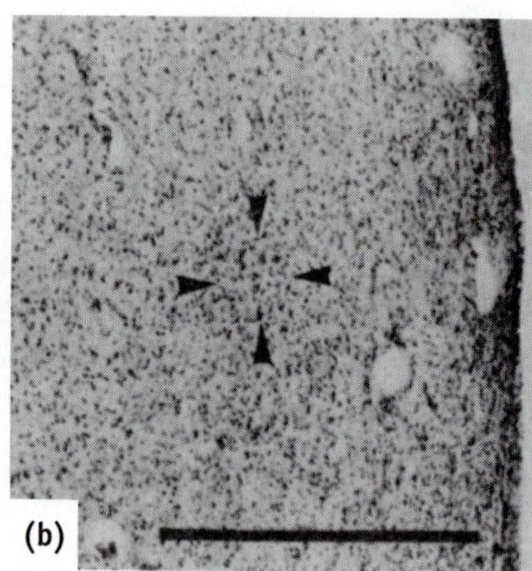

Figure 11.18 The interstitial nucleus 3 ($INAH_3$) in (a) male heterosexuals and (b) homosexual males. The $INAH_3$ is 2 times larger in the heterosexual male than the homosexual male in these photographs.

From Levay, 1991.

➤ *What is the size of $INAH_3$ in heterosexual women? (p. 350)*

have suggested that a lower-than-normal level of testosterone is responsible for male homosexuality (Hyde, 1994). However, other research (Money, 1980) has found no hormonal difference between homosexual males and heterosexual males. Some psychiatrists have attempted unsuccessfully to treat homosexuality with testosterone injections. Although the injections did not alter sexual preference, they did sometimes increase sex drive. Surprised? You shouldn't be—remember what we learned earlier about administration of testosterone **(p. 339–340)**. A study by Loraine and colleagues (1971) suggested that homosexual women had higher testosterone levels and lower estrogen levels than heterosexual women. However, the results of this study have not been replicated. Furthermore, because testosterone merely increases sexual arousal, it is unclear how a high testosterone level and lower estrogen level would influence the sexual preference of homosexual women.

Yet another approach suggests that there are structural differences in the brains of heterosexuals and homosexuals. Simon LeVay (1991) performed postmortem measurements of the volumes of four cell groups of the anterior hypothalamus of heterosexual and homosexual males and found that the volume of one area (interstitial nucleus 3 or $INAH_3$) was twice as large in heterosexual males as in homosexual males (see **Figure 11.18**). As we learned earlier (see **p. 334–335**), the anterior hypothalamus is larger in heterosexual men than in heterosexual women. LeVay suggested that a larger $INAH_3$ area is associated with sexual attraction to women and a smaller $INAH_3$ area is associated with attraction to men.

LeVay (1994) does not assume that the group of $INAH_3$ neurons in the anterior hypothalamus is the sexual orientation center, but rather suggests that it is an important part of the neural pathway governing sexual behavior. Support for LeVay's view can be found in the Allen and Gorski (1992) discovery that the anterior commissure, a fiber tract connecting the right and left hemispheres, is one-third larger in homosexual men than heterosexual men, which is the same difference found between heterosexual men and women. Gladue (1994) captures these findings best when he states, "The emerging neuroanatomical picture is that, in some brain areas, homosexual men are more likely to have female-typical neuroanatomy than are heterosexual men."

What process might lead to such structural brain differences between heterosexuals and homosexuals? If you have been paying attention, you probably guessed "hormones." It has indeed been suggested that prenatal exposure to testosterone contributes to homosexuality in females and a lack of exposure to testosterone contributes to homosexuality in males.

Adrenogenital syndrome occurs when the adrenal glands secrete too much androstenedione, resulting in genetically female humans with masculinized genitals. Money, Schwartz, and Lewis (1984) observed 30 young women with this condition, called adrenogenital syndrome, and found that 11 (37 percent) of these females described themselves as homosexual or bisexual. Twelve (40 percent) of the women said they were heterosexuals and 7 (23 percent) would not discuss their sexual preference. This study seems to suggest that early fetal exposure to androstenedione may influence human sexual preference. However, two things should be noted: (1) the number of individuals in this study was extremely small and (2) adrenogenital

---

adrenogenital syndrome A condition that occurs when the adrenal glands secrete too much androstenedione, resulting in genetically female humans with masculinized genitals.

syndrome is a rare disorder that most homosexual women do not have.

So the presence of testosterone during early fetal development produces individuals with the genetic makeup of a female and the sexual organs of a male. On the flip side, what would happen if a genetic male were insensitive to testosterone? Individuals with **androgen insensitivity syndrome** do not have testosterone receptors in the brain and are therefore insensitive to testosterone. Genetic males with this disorder develop external female genitalia (Money & Ehrhardt, 1972; see **Figure 11.19**). Money, Schwartz, and Lewis (1984) studied 15 young men with androgen insensitivity and reported feminization of the external genitalia. However, only 2 of these individuals had any sexual contact and none reported a homosexual preference.

The research on adrenogenital syndrome and androgen insensitivity syndrome points out an important difference between biological sex and sexual preference. A male can have the genitalia of a female as a result of androgen insensitivity, but not be attracted to men. Similarly, a woman can have the genitalia of a male, as a result of adrenogenital syndrome, but not be attracted to women. At this time, there is not sufficient evidence to support the view that early exposure to testosterone in females or a lack of early exposure to testosterone in males is a cause of homosexuality.

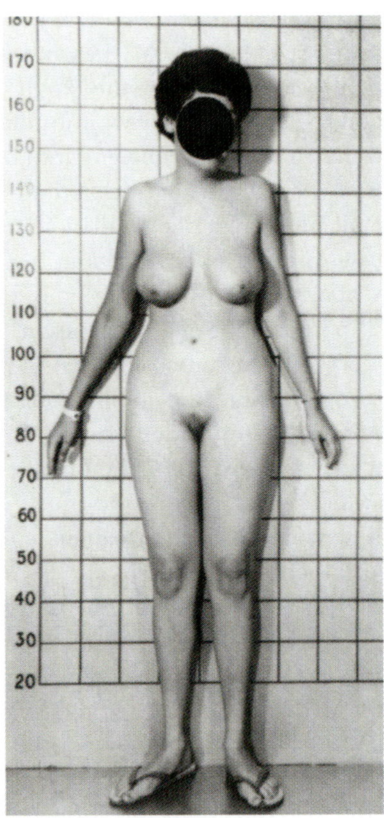

Figure 11.19 Androgen insensitivity syndrome. This picture shows the feminization that occurs in an adult genetic male with androgen insensitivity syndrome.

➤ *What is adrenogenital syndrome? (p. 350)*

Before You Go On

Construct an experiment that would prove whether sexual preference is determined by genetics, hormone levels, and/or structural differences.

APPLICATION

Treatment of Sexual Dysfunction

Many people can "fail to perform" due to temporary states such as anxiety or depression. It is important to note that these experiences do not reflect a sexual dysfunction, which is a chronic failure to obtain sexual satisfaction. Sexual dysfunction is a complex phenomenon. Masters and Johnson (1970) reported that organic factors cause about 10 to 20 percent of cases. Psychological problems are thought to account for the rest. We will briefly describe several forms of **sexual dysfunction** and their organic causes, and then we will discuss Masters and Johnson's (1970) suggested treatment for this disorder.

Masters and Johnson found **erectile dysfunction**, or **impotence**, to be the most common form of male sexual dysfunction. Masters and Johnson reported that 245, or 54 percent, of the 448 males in their study suffered from a chronic inability to have an erection sufficient to achieve penetration, although most had been able to engage in intercourse on at least one occasion. Erectile failure can occur as a result of serious illness such as coronary disease, Parkinson's disease, multiple sclerosis, or diabetes mellitus; damage to the lower spinal cord area controlling erectile functions; and

---

androgen insensitivity syndrome A condition in which genetic males do not have testosterone receptors in the brain, are therefore insensitive to testosterone, and develop external female genitalia.

sexual dysfunction The failure to obtain sexual satisfaction.

erectile dysfunction (impotence) A chronic inability to have an erection sufficient to achieve penetration.

severe stress or fatigue. Drugs can also cause sexual dysfunction (Long, 1984). For example, alcohol and opiates appear to impair erectile function. Anticholinergic drugs, primarily used in treating peptic ulcers and glaucoma, can produce erectile dysfunction by inhibiting the parasympathetic nerves that normally produce an erection.

Premature ejaculation, the second most common form of male sexual dysfunction, was experienced by 186, or 41 percent, of the study's males. Masters and Johnson defined premature ejaculation as the inability 50 percent of the time to delay ejaculation until his partner achieves orgasm. Premature ejaculation can result from antiadrenergic drugs—medicines normally prescribed to treat hypertension and other vascular disorders—that block the sympathetic nerves that normally inhibit an ejaculation. Unusual sensitivity around the opening of the penile glands also can lead to premature ejaculation.

Retarded ejaculation, or the inability to ejaculate, is the third major form of sexual dysfunction in males. Some males with this dysfunction can ejaculate with manual stimulation, whereas others cannot. Although Masters and Johnson found this to be a rare disorder (affecting only 17, or 4 percent of their male patients), others (Kaplan, 1974) believe that it is fairly common. Parkinson's disease has been associated with retarded ejaculation.

Orgasmic dysfunction, the inability to experience an orgasm, is by far the most prevalent form of sexual dysfunction in females. Masters and Johnson found that 342, or 91 percent, of the 371 female patients in their study were unable to experience an orgasm. The majority of these women, 56 percent, never had an orgasm; the others were able to experience an orgasm only under certain conditions.

Masters and Johnson reported that 29, or 9 percent, of the sexual dysfunctions of their female patients were caused by involuntary contractions of the muscles surrounding the vagina. In this condition, known as **vaginismus**, the muscle contractions cause the entrance to the vagina to close, thereby preventing intercourse. Severe illness or fatigue can contribute to orgasmic dysfunction, and some disorders of the reproductive system can contribute to vaginismus.

Treatment for sexual dysfunction can take one of two forms: biological or psychological. In many patients, sexual dysfunction can be eliminated by treating the organic cause. For example, for a diabetic, insulin can manage both the diabetes and the sexual dysfunction. In other cases, drugs can be used to treat the sexual dysfunction. Perhaps you have heard about the drug Viagra (sildenafil). Viagra inhibits cyclic guanosine monophosphate in the corpus cavernosum, which is a body of erectile tissue in the penis. The inhibition of guanosine monophosphate increases the penile response to stimulation. Clinical studies have shown Viagra to be a safe and effective treatment for erectile dysfunction (Goldstein et al., 1998). Goldstein and his colleagues administered Viagra for 24 weeks to 532 men with erectile dysfunction. During the last 4 weeks of the study, the men receiving Viagra were able to have intercourse successfully on 69 percent of their attempts compared to only 22 percent in men receiving a placebo. However, there are side effects of Viagra use, most notably headaches and flushing. As Viagra was only approved by the Food and Drug Administration in 1998, it is too soon to tell whether it really is the miracle drug many believe it to be.

The psychological approaches aimed at establishing effective sexual functioning, are called **sex therapy**. In the initial stages of sex therapy, a patient is given factual information about human sexuality and the organic cause(s) of a particular sexual dysfunction. This information will correct many misconceptions a person may have concerning sexuality; the elimination of these misperceptions and a better understanding of his or her disorder can enhance sexual functioning. Sensate-focus exercises in which a patient learns to provide his or her partner with sensual pleasure other than intercourse, are an important part of Masters and Johnson's program. The exercises are structured to provide patients with successful sexual experiences and to eliminate anxiety and the expectation of failure. To accomplish these goals, patients are instructed not to engage in any unassigned sexual activity. Then, therapists instruct patients to touch their partners in a nongenital area; the patients experience the pleasure of being intimate with their partners without the stress of impending intercourse. Having succeeded in these initial touching exercises, patients are instructed to gradually add more sexual contact to increase their pleasure.

---

premature ejaculation The inability 50 percent of the time to delay ejaculation until his partner achieves orgasm.

retarded ejaculation The inability to ejaculate during sexual intercourse.

orgasmic dysfunction The inability to experience an orgasm or the ability to experience an orgasm only under certain conditions.

vaginismus Muscle contractions that cause the entrance to the vagina to close, thereby preventing intercourse.

sex therapy A set of procedures aimed at establishing effective sexual functioning.

The treatment of sexual dysfunction is often quite successful. Masters and Johnson (1970) reported that 65 to 90 percent of their patients experienced an absence of symptoms following therapy. A 5-year follow-up study of 225 patients reported that only 7 percent again became dysfunctional. Other psychologists (Cole, 1985; Crowe, Gillan, & Golombook, 1981) have also reported the successful treatment of sexual dysfunction, which suggests that sex therapy can result in long-lasting behavioral change.

Before You Go On

Do you think that Doug's sexual dysfunction has a biological or psychological basis?

Section Review

- Three biological theories have been offered to explain differences in sexual preference: a genetic predisposition, a hormonal imbalance, and brain differences.
- The concordance rates for homosexuals are higher among relatives in some studies, but not in others.
- No difference in hormonal levels between heterosexuals than homosexuals has been consistently found.
- The interstitial nucleus ($INAH_3$) of the anterior hypothalamus has been shown to be larger in heterosexual than homosexual men.
- Adrenogenital syndrome occurs when the adrenal gland secretes too much androstenedione and a genetic female human has masculinized genitals.
- Androgen insensitivity syndrome occurs when a genetic male develops female genitalia due to an absence of testosterone receptors in the brain.
- Sexual dysfunctions in males include erectile dysfunction, premature ejaculation, and retarded ejaculation.
- Females may experience such sexual dysfunctions as orgasmic dysfunction and vaginismus.
- Organic factors such as serious illness or neurological damage, as well as the use of certain drugs, cause 10 to 20 percent of sexual dysfunction.
- Sex therapy employs sensate-focus exercises to provide sensual pleasure without as well as specific techniques to modify specific sexual dysfunction.

Chapter Review

Critical Thinking Questions

1. Charlotte became ill during her pregnancy and her adrenal glands secreted abnormally high levels of androgens. Her medical problem was eventually brought under control. Assuming that Charlotte's offspring is a genetic female, what impact might the prenatal androgen exposure have on her daughter's development?
2. Simone has often been referred to as a tomboy, but can be quite feminine when she wishes. She also is attracted to males. Suggest a possible reason for Simone's rough-and-tumble character.
3. Many persons find sexual activity to be extremely pleasurable. Describe the physiological changes that occur during sexual activity. Indicate the similarities and differences in the physiology of sexual activity of males and females. What biological system might be responsible for the pleasurable quality of sexual activity?

Vocabulary Questions

1. The gene on the Y chromosome responsible for determining an individual's biological sex is called the ________________.
2. The presence of the ________________ causes the undifferentiated gonads of the embryo to become testes.
3. In the absence of testis-determining factor, the ________________ system matures into a female reproductive system.
4. In the absence of ________________, a female brain develops.
5. Estradiol present in females during development is deactivated by ________________ to prevent females from developing a masculinized brain.
6. The four phases of the human sexual response are ________________, ________________, ________________, and ________________.

7. The male's ability to become aroused depends on the presence of the sex hormone ________________; the female's ability to become aroused depends on the presence of the sex hormone ________________.
8. The ________________ released by the anterior pituitary gland stimulates the ovaries to release female sex hormones.
9. The ________________ appears to organize the female sexual response and inhibit female sexual behavior.
10. ________________ engage in sexual activity with individuals of the opposite sex; ________________ engage in sexual activity with individuals of the same sex.
11. Females may experience such sexual dysfunctions as ________________ dysfunction and ________________.
12. ________________ exercises provide sensual pleasure without intercourse.

Review Questions

1. If the sex-determining gene is present, the individual develops as a ________________; if it is absent, the individual develops as a ________________.
   a. male, female
   b. female, male
   c. XX, XY
   d. XXY, XYY
2. Testosterone released from the testes causes the ________________ to develop into the mature male reproductive system.
   a. Müllerian system
   b. Wolffian system
   c. penis
   d. pituitary gland
3. The presence of ________________ in the prenatal and early postnatal period is responsible for the development of a masculinized brain.
   a. testosterone
   b. estrogen
   c. progesterone
   d. androstenedione
4. The medial preoptic area of the hypothalamus is
   a. more than twice as large in men as in women.
   b. more than twice as large in women as in men.
   c. responsible for sex drive.
   d. six times larger in female rats than in male rats.
5. Vasocongestion of the genitals occurs in both males and females in the ________________ phase, and myotonia occurs during the ________________ phase.
   a. resolution, excitement
   b. plateau, resolution
   c. orgasm, plateau
   d. excitement, orgasm
6. The hypothalamus releases gonadotrophic-releasing hormones, which in turn stimulate the anterior pituitary gland to release luteinizing hormone, which acts on the
   a. ovaries to produce androstenedione.
   b. ovaries to increase sex drive.
   c. testes to produce testosterone.
   d. penis to increase sex drive.
7. The period of intense sexual responsivity in females occurs
   a. at the beginning of the estrus cycle.
   b. just prior to ovulation.
   c. just after ovulation.
   d. at the end of the estrus cycle.
8. Removal of the ________________ in an estrus animal ________________ sexual behavior.
   a. ovaries, increases
   b. testes, increases
   c. ovaries, decreases
   d. testes, decreases
9. The three functions of the cortex in the male are to
   a. organize motor responses, detect sexual content of sensory information, and store memories of past sexual experiences.
   b. organize motor responses, approach a potential partner, and store memories of past sexual experiences.
   c. detect sexual content of sensory information, approach a potential partner, and organize motor responses.
   d. detect sexual content of sensory information, detect pheromones, and organize motor responses.
10. The reinforcing and pleasurable aspects of sexual activity reflect the activation of the ________ by sexual stimuli.
   a. pituitary gland
   b. hypothalamus
   c. sex organs
   d. tegmentostriatal pathway

11. The presence of a receptive female causes the release of ________________ in the male's medial preoptic area.
    a. norepinephrine
    b. serotonin
    c. GABA
    d. dopamine

12. The presence of a receptive female activates the ________________.
    a. central septum
    b. medial amygdala
    c. dorsal hippocampus
    d. ventral pons

13. The three theories of the basis for sexual preference are
    a. genetic predisposition, hormonal balance, and structural differences.
    b. genetic predisposition, hormonal balance, and social experiences.
    c. hormonal balance, structural differences, and social experiences.
    d. hormonal balance, genetic predisposition, and social experiences.

14. Sexual dysfunctions in males include
    a. orgasmic dysfunction, vaginismus, and premature ejaculation.
    b. erectile dysfunction, premature ejaculation, and retarded ejaculation.
    c. erectile dysfunction, orgasmic dysfunction, and vaginismus.
    d. premature ejaculation, retarded ejaculation, and orgasmic dysfunction.

Suggested Readings

Gerall, A. A., Moltz, H., & Wald, I. L. (1992). *Handbook of behavioral neurobiology: Vol. 11. Sexual differentiation.* New York: Plenum.

Masters, W., & Johnson, V. (1966). *Human sexual response.* Boston: Little, Brown.

Masters, W., & Johnson, V. (1970). *Human sexual inadequacy.* Boston: Little, Brown.

Money, J., & Ehrhardt, A. A. (1972). *Man & woman. Boy & girl.* Baltimore, MD: Johns Hopkins University Press.

Nelson, R. J. (1995). *An introduction to behavioral endocrinology.* Sunderland, MA: Sinauer.

12 The Biology of Emotion and Stress

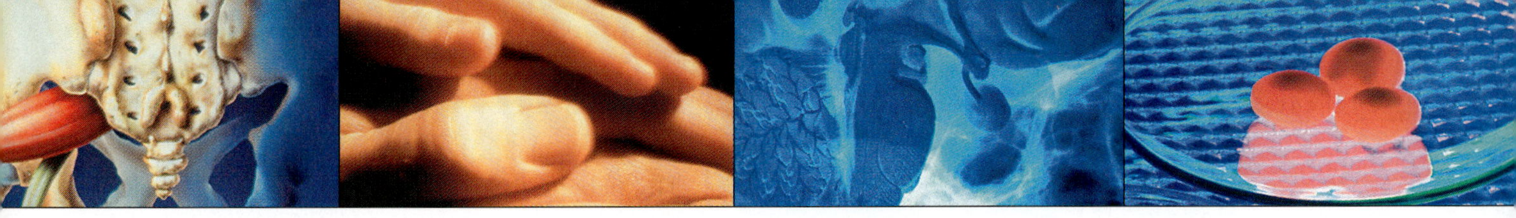

An Irreplaceable Loss

After Stuart's mother died, when he was 7, his father raised him alone. Stuart had a very special relationship with his father, and they shared many memorable times together. Every Saturday afternoon in the summer they would go to a baseball game. On Sundays, they would go sailing on the nearby lake. In the winter, there was always a basketball game or a movie. Even just taking a walk or a bike ride with his father in the park near their home was fun. Stuart and his father maintained their wonderful relationship even after his father remarried when Stuart was 15.

One day when Stuart was a junior in college, he was in the middle of a lab exercise when his roommate Tim walked in. Stuart immediately knew that something was wrong just by looking at Tim's face. When Tim told Stuart that his stepmother had called with the news that his father had suffered a heart attack, Stuart's hands started to shake and his knees felt weak. He rushed to the nearest telephone, his hands shaking so much that he could hardly punch in the numbers.

As soon as he heard his stepmother's voice, he knew that his father had died. He managed to give her some words of comfort and told her that he'd be on the next flight home, but as soon as he hung up the phone, his body shook with sobs and he barely made it back to his room. Stuart threw himself on his bed, clenched his fists, and pounded his pillow. His world had never seemed so bleak. ■

◀ Despair can suppress the immune system and lead to an increased risk of illness.

Before You Begin

What is the physiological basis of Stuart's shaking hands and wobbly knees?

What part(s) of the brain is (are) responsible for Stuart's feelings of happiness when he spends time with his father and grief when he learns of his death?

In this chapter, we will help you answer these and the following questions:

- What exactly is an emotion, and what process do we go through when experiencing one?
- When Stuart pounds his pillow, what type of aggression is he experiencing? What other types are there?
- Can the news of his father's death be considered a stressor?
- What can Stuart do to mitigate the effects of the stress imposed by his father's death?

His father's death triggered an intense emotional response in Stuart. If we asked him, Stuart would probably say that he was badly hurt, in almost intolerable pain. Although Stuart's pain is quite different from the sensory type of pain that was discussed in Chapter 7, it is very real and has a strong physiological basis. In this chapter, we will examine the physiological basis of Stuart's feelings of loss, as well as the joy he will eventually be able to recapture from his memories of the good times with his father.

What Is Emotion?

Have you ever been happy when you received an A on a difficult examination, or surprised when your parents showed up at your dorm room unexpectedly? Perhaps your best friend criticized your new sweater, causing you to feel angry or hurt. Although each of these situations is different, all share a common characteristic: the experience of the event caused you to have an emotional response. We feel many different and varied emotions: rage, disgust, fear, joy, annoyance, sorrow, anger, grief, terror, happiness, surprise, and amazement are all common emotions experienced by us from time to time.

What is an emotion? An **emotion** is a feeling that differs from an individual's normal state. Emotions have three central features (Carlson & Hatfield, 1992). The first is a change in physiological arousal, which can range from slight to intense. The second is an affective or feeling component. This refers to the name you give your feelings. Further, all emotions are either pleasant or unpleasant. For example, you feel "good" when you are praised and "bad" when you are criticized. Third, feeling an emotion motivates us to behave. The behavior that occurs depends on the emotion (Ekman, 1984; Lazarus, 1993). For example, we may become aggressive when we are angry, and the emotion of fear usually motivates escape behavior.

emotion A feeling that differs from an individual's normal state; a change in physiological arousal; an affective component; and a behavioral response.

Three Theories of Emotion

What biological process determines whether we feel happiness or sorrow? Three major theories—the James-Lange theory, the Cannon-Bard theory, and the Schachter theory—have been proposed to explain the nature of emotion. The first two theories emphasize the role of physiological processes in emotional experience; the third theory suggests that cognitive processes are the determining factor.

The James-Lange Theory

Independently, William James (1884) and Carl Lange (1885/1922) proposed that the physiological changes that occur when we encounter an event produce the emotions that we experience (see **Figure 12.1**). The kinds of visceral changes (for example, increased or decreased heart rate) and somatic changes (for example,

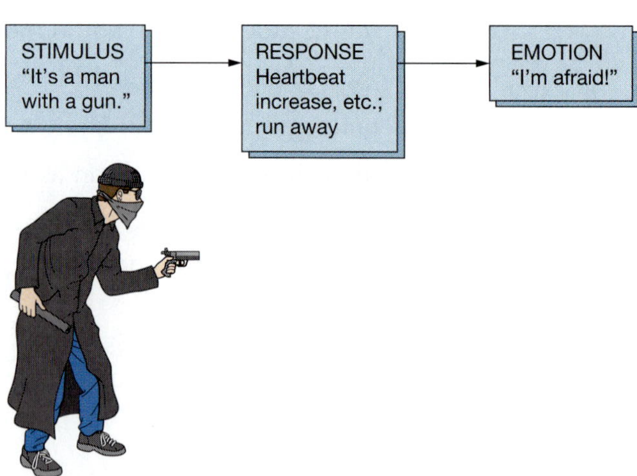

Figure 12.1 The James-Lange theory of emotion. In the figure, you perceive a man with a gun. The recognition of man with a gun causes you to respond physiologically. Your biological response allows you to recognize that you are frightened.

➤ *According to the James-Lange theory, how can we experience so many different emotions? (p. 359)*

increased or decreased muscle tension) depend on the event; different situations cause different internal physiological responses. According to the **James-Lange theory** of emotion, we interpret these physiological changes to determine how we feel. The visceral and somatic responses enable us to experience different emotions.

Consider the following contrasting examples to illustrate the James-Lange theory. Your instructor announces that you will have an examination next week; this frightens you. Alternately your instructor postpones a scheduled exam, giving you another week to study, so you feel relieved. According to the James-Lange theory, the announcement that you will have an exam causes increased heart rate, elevated blood pressure, and increased respiration rate; the announcement that the examination is to be postponed causes your heart rate to slow down, your blood pressure to decline, and your respiration rate to decrease. These different internal responses cause the differing emotions of fright and relief.

Some evidence suggests that subtle physiological differences exist between several emotional states. In one important study, Ax (1953) found that when we are afraid, our internal response is different from when we are angry. According to Ax, the adrenal medulla releases epinephrine and norepinephrine when we experience both anger and fear. However, more epinephrine than norepinephrine is released when we are frightened, whereas more norepinephrine than epinephrine is released when we are angry. The effects of norepinephrine and epinephrine differ slightly. For example, norepinephrine increases diastolic blood pressure (pressure when the heart is relaxed and filling with blood), whereas epinephrine increases systolic blood pressure (pressure when the heart is pumping blood).

Wolf and Wolff (1947) reported that when human subjects were angered, their stomach linings became red and inflamed because of increased stomach motility, increased secretion of gastric juices, and dilation of the blood vessels. By contrast, the subjects' stomach linings appeared pale during periods of anxiety or depression, because of decreased stomach motility, decreased secretion of gastric juices, and constriction of the blood vessels. Shagass and Malmo (1954) and Malmo, Kohlmeyer, and Smith (1956) observed a correlation between anger and increased tension in the forearm area. In more recent research, Ekman, Levenson, and Friesen (1983) found that skin temperature increased more with anger than with fear or anxiety, and Frey and Langsmith (1986) observed that tears of sadness contained more protein than tears shed when chopping raw onions.

Walter Cannon (1927) suggested several problems with the James-Lange theory. First, emotional experiences can occur even when there is total isolation of the viscera from

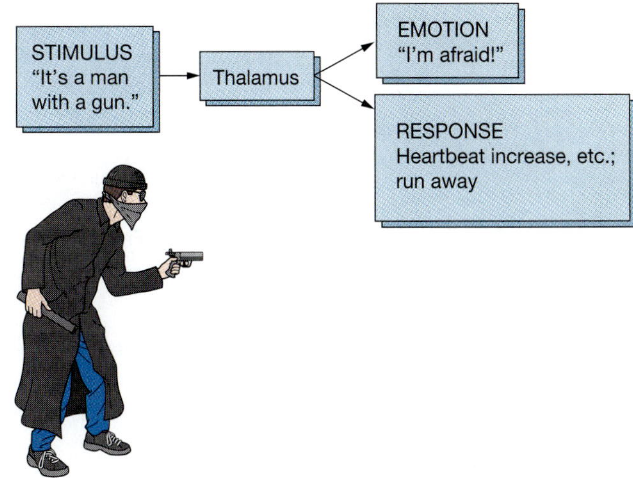

Figure 12.2 The Cannon-Bard theory of emotion. According to the Cannon-Bard view, noticing the man with the gun activates the thalamus. The message from the thalamus is sent simultaneously to both the cortex and the autonomic nervous system. Stimulation of the cortex produces the perception of fright, and the physiological arousal necessary to cope with the man with the gun occurs when the autonomic nervous system is aroused. ➤ *According to Papez and MacLean, what is wrong with the above illustration? (p. 360)*

the central nervous system. This separation prevents the communication of any visceral response to an event to the central nervous system; if James and Lange were correct, this should eliminate the experience of emotions. Cannon cited several studies that showed that emotional feeling was unchanged following spinal cord destruction in dogs (Sherrington, 1900), cats (Cannon, Lewis, & Britton, 1927), and humans (Dana, 1921). More recent observations of spinal cord-injured patients (Chwalisz, Diener, & Gallagher, 1986; Lowe & Carroll, 1985) similarly reveal no evidence of lessened emotional experience. These observations suggest that feedback from peripheral physiological systems is not necessary for emotional experiences.

Second, Cannon argued that we cannot sense the subtle physiological differences between emotional states. For example, there is only one sensory fiber from the viscera for every ten sensory fibers from skeletal motor neurons, and therefore, Cannon argued, we are unaware of most visceral functioning.

Third, Cannon argued that the visceral changes that take place following exposure to an event are too slow, and emotional responses occur too quickly for visceral changes to determine emotional responses.

James-Lange theory of emotion The view that the interpretation of the physiological changes that occur in response to a specific event determines how we feel.

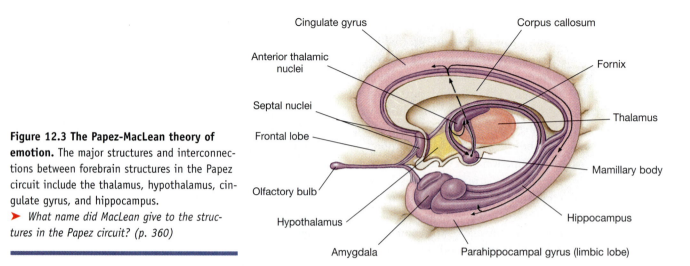

Figure 12.3 The Papez-MacLean theory of emotion. The major structures and interconnections between forebrain structures in the Papez circuit include the thalamus, hypothalamus, cingulate gyrus, and hippocampus.

➤ *What name did MacLean give to the structures in the Papez circuit? (p. 360)*

Cannon's arguments and the research he conducted led him to formulate an alternative theory of emotion, which is the topic of the next section.

Before You Go On

According to the James-Lange theory, what physiological changes caused Stuart to experience grief over his father's death?

The Cannon-Bard Theory

Walter Cannon (1927) and Philip Bard (1934) proposed that visceral changes, somatic changes, and the emotional experience occur at the same time (refer to **Figure 12.2**). According to this view, experiencing an event stimulates the thalamus, a major part of the forebrain located above the hypothalamus (see Chapter 2). Activation of the thalamus simultaneously stimulates both the cortex, which produces the perception of the emotion, and the rest of the body, which produces the internal changes and motor responses associated with that emotion. Although significant evidence supports the **Cannon-Bard theory** of emotionality, the thalamus is not the only area controlling emotional expression. First, Papez in 1937 and later MacLean in 1949 showed that the hypothalamus and the limbic system are also involved in the emotional response to an event.

Papez (1937) proposed that emotional experiences are mediated by a system of interconnected forebrain structures (see **Figure 12.3**). The major structures in the Papez circuit include the thalamus, hypothalamus, cingulate gyrus, and hippocampus. Several lines of evidence suggested to Papez that these structures are involved in emotion. First, activation of structures in the Papez circuit elicits strong emotional responses. Second, lesions of the mammallary bodies of the hypothalamus produce docile, emotionless monkeys.

Paul MacLean (1949) revised and expanded Papez's theory. MacLean named Papez's circuit the limbic system (from the latin word *limbus* meaning "border"), because it forms a border around midbrain structures. He compared the relative size of the cerebral cortex and limbic system in several different animal species and noted that the relative size of the cerebral cortex is greater in primates than in cats and greater in cats than in rabbits (see **Figure 12.4**). By contrast, the relative size of the limbic system in each species is approximately the same. MacLean concluded that the limbic system, or Papez-MacLean circuit, must control the primitive functions shared by all mammalian species.

MacLean suggested that there were three separate circuits in the limbic system, encompassing the amygdala, the hippocampus, the cingulate gyrus, the septum, the hypothalamus, and the thalamus. The first circuit includes the amygdala and the hippocampus and is involved in survival. The importance of this circuit is indicated by the observation that damage to the medial amygdala leads to an excessively tame, unaggressive, and emotionally unresponsive animal (Fonberg, 1965), whereas destruction of the central amygdala produces a very aggressive and extremely emotionally responsive one (Wood, 1958).

Stimulating specific neurons in the amygdala has been found to trigger specific emotions. For example, activation of the medial amygdala causes anger (see **Figure 12.5**) and motivates aggressive behavior in cats (Ursin & Kaada, 1960), dogs (Fonberg, 1965), and

---

Cannon-Bard theory of emotion The view that an event activates the thalamus simultaneously stimulating both the cortex, which produces the perception of the emotion, and the rest of the body, which produces the internal changes and motor responses associated with that emotion.

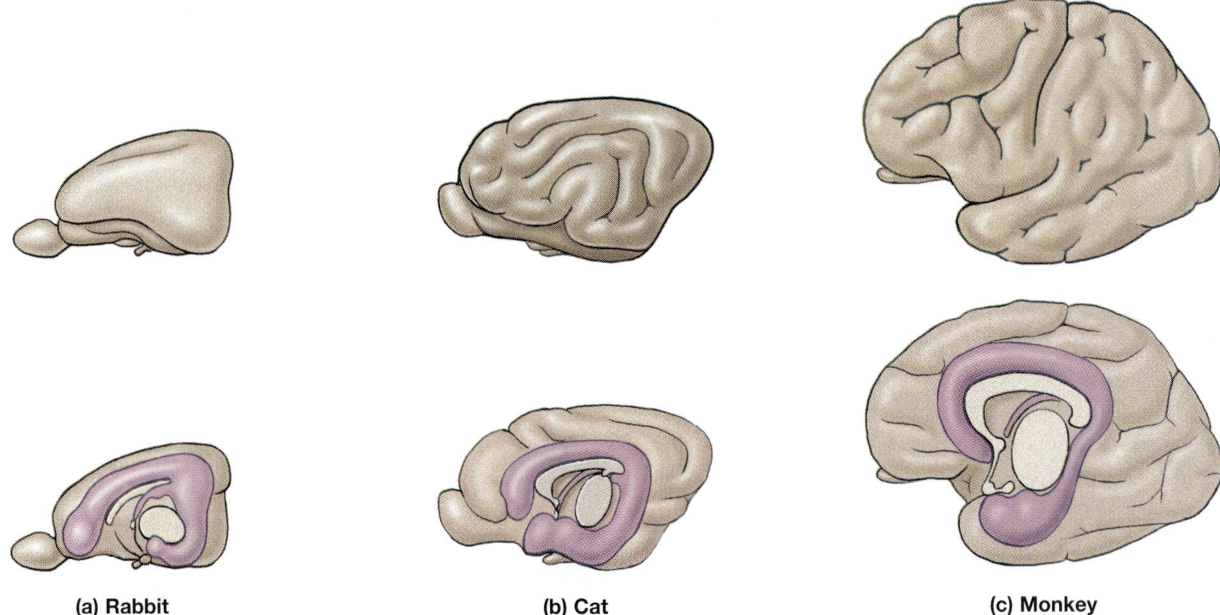

Figure 12.4 The brains of (a) rabbit, (b) cat, and (c) monkey. Top diagrams present a lateral surface view of the cerebral cortex of each animal and the bottom diagrams show the medial surface with the limbic system darkened.

➤ *What is the significance of the relative sizes of the limbic systems of these animals? (p. 360)*

humans (Sweet, Ervin, & Mark, 1969). Activation of the central amygdaloid nucleus produces fear in cats (Schreiner & Kling, 1953), rats (Galef, 1970), dogs (Fonberg, 1965), and primates (Kling, Dicks, & Gurwitz, 1968). Although stimulation of the amygdala has been shown to produce fear in humans (Hitchcock, 1979), the precise area has not been established.

MacLean's second circuit includes the cingulate gyrus, the septum, and some neurons in the hypothalamus. According to MacLean, stimulation of this circuit produces pleasure, especially sexual pleasure. As we discussed in Chapter 5, many researchers have discovered that stimulation of certain brain structures (especially the tegmentostriatal pathway that includes the lateral hypothalamus, the medial forebrain bundle, the ventral tegmental area, and the nucleus accumbens) is extremely reinforcing and is responsible for the pleasurable quality of some emotions.

Figure 12.5 Anger. Stimulation of the medial amygdala elicits anger and motivates aggressive actions in monkeys.

➤ *What is the effect of damage to the medial amygdala? (p. 360)*

The third circuit in MacLean's model consists of parts of the hypothalamus and the anterior thalamus. According to MacLean, this circuit is involved in the control of cooperative social behaviors that aid the survival of a species.

So according to the James-Lange theory, emotions are caused by distinctive visceral responses. According to the Papez-MacLean model, activation of a specific neural system can produce a specific emotion. But what about those cases in which we are aroused but cannot use our internal state to recognize how we feel? Under these circumstances, cognitive processes can provide the information necessary to label our emotional state, which leads us to our third model, formulated by Stanley Schachter.

Before You Go On

Which of the three circuits in the Papez-MacLean model was activated when Stuart received the news of his father's death?

Schachter's Cognitive Approach

In 1964, Schachter proposed a cognitive theory of emotion. **Schachter's cognitive approach** argues that when we become aware of internal tension or arousal, we seek to identify the cause of the arousal, and unless we know why we are aroused, we will attribute our arousal to the prevailing environmental conditions, which in **Figure 12.6**, for example, is the sight of a man with a gun. In another example, if you are internally aroused (or excited) at a party where those around you are having a good time, you attribute your arousal to the party and assume that you are also having a good time. If you experience similar arousal while studying in anticipation of a difficult exam, you might attribute your arousal to fear of not performing well on the test. An important aspect of Schachter's theory is his idea that internal arousal need not actually be produced by a particular environment but only experienced in that setting, opening up the possibility that we may misattribute our arousal to our environment, when in reality, another factor produced it. You might not be having a good time at the party, if the exam has been on your mind.

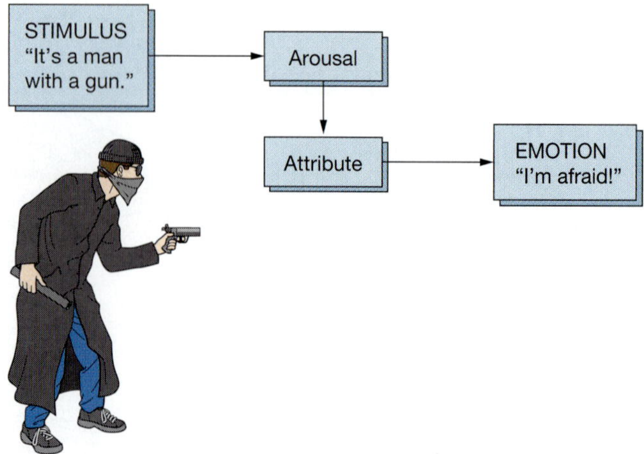

Figure 12.6 Schachter's cognitive view of emotion. In this view, you first notice that you are physiologically aroused. If you do not know why you are aroused, you interpret your arousal according to prevailing environmental conditions. In this case, you interpret your arousal as being caused by the man with the gun, and thereby conclude that you are afraid.

➤ *According to Schachter's theory, is it possible that something other than the man with the gun made you afraid? (p. 362)*

The Classic Schachter-Singer Study. Schachter and Singer's classic study (1962) demonstrates the vital role of cognitions in producing emotional experiences. Schachter and Singer informed subjects that the study in which they were participating was intended to evaluate the effects of a vitamin compound on visual skills. One group of subjects was injected with adrenalin (epinephrine), a drug that produces a state of internal arousal. A second group received a placebo injection. Schachter and Singer told some subjects in each group that the side effects of the "vitamin" would cause trembling hands, pounding hearts, and warm flushed faces—in fact, these are some symptoms produced by epinephrine. Other subjects in each group were informed that the side effects would include numbness, itching, and a slight headache—symptoms different from those actually produced by epinephrine. Still other subjects in each group were not told anything about the side effects of the "vitamin."

In the second phase of the study, each subject waited with a confederate (an accomplice of the researcher), believed to be another subject, for the experiment to begin. This phase required the confederate and the subject to answer a questionnaire, parts of which were designed to assess the subjects' emotional responses. Each confederate acted in one of two ways while completing the questionnaire: the confederate either displayed euphoria (for example, threw paper airplanes, shot paper wads, and played with a hula hoop) or displayed anger (complained about having to complete the questionnaires and finally shredded the forms and bolted from the testing room).

How did each actual subject report feeling after witnessing the confederate's behavior? Consistent with Schachter's cognitive approach, none of the subjects who received the placebo injection were emotionally affected by the confederate's behavior (see **Figure 12.7**). The confederate's action was not sufficient to produce internal arousal, and without arousal the subjects had no reason to be influenced by the confederate's behavior. On the other hand, the subjects who received the epinephrine were internally aroused and needed an explanation for their arousal. As predicted, subjects told of epinephrine's true side effects attributed their arousal to the "vitamin" injection and were not influenced by the confederate's behavior. But subjects who had been injected with epinephrine and either misinformed or uninformed about its effects would need to attribute their unexplained arousal to the environment, in this case confederate's behavior. Schachter and Singer reported that these subjects did report feeling more euphoric or angry than other subjects after viewing the confederates' euphoric or angry behavior.

Schachter's cognitive approach The view that if we are unable to identify the cause of physiological arousal, the arousal will be attributed to the prevailing environmental conditions.

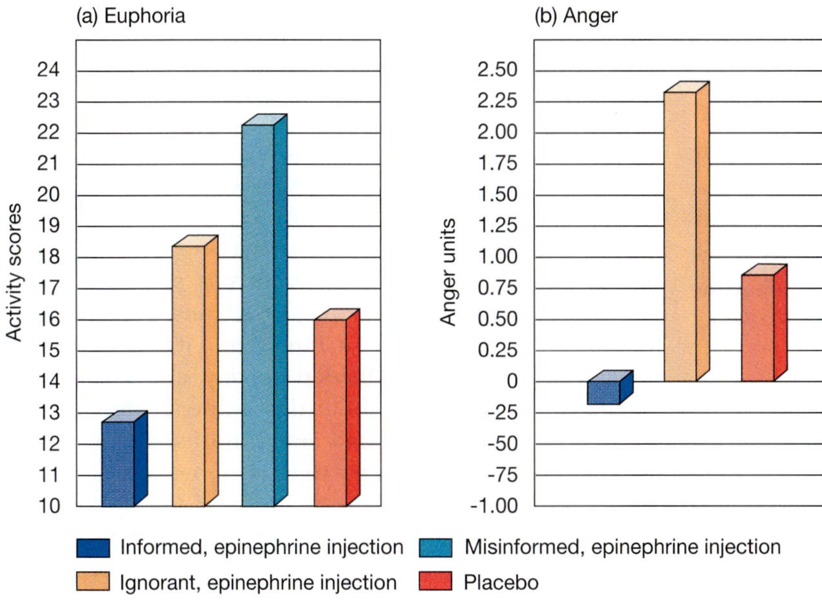

Figure 12.7 The outcome of Schachter and Singer's study on the attribution of emotions. Subjects who were misinformed or uninformed about the cause of their arousal felt either angry or euphoric, depending on the actions of the confederate. Other subjects were not affected by the confederate's action.

➤ *Why weren't the test subjects who received the placebo affected by the confederate's behavior? (p. 362)*

Although many psychologists (Reisenzein, 1983) have criticized Schachter and Singer's study because of several problems with their methods, other experiments (Zillman, 1986), often using different procedures, have supported their conclusions. We will describe one such study next.

Are You in Love? Imagine yourself going on a first date. Although you know little about your date, you have been anxiously anticipating the evening. As the hour approaches, your palms start to sweat and your heart begins to pound. When you finally meet, you find that your mouth is dry and you feel tense. What caused all of this physiological upheaval? These are all symptoms of apprehension or anxiety, but you may attribute these feelings to "being in love."

In an interesting test of the importance of adversity in producing the emotion of love, Dutton and Aron (1974) asked their male subjects to cross a long, narrow, flexible suspension bridge that spans a gorge and river in a park in Vancouver, British Columbia (see **Figure 12.8**). This experience was quite frightening; the wooden plank swayed while the subjects crossed 200 feet above rocks and rapids. After crossing the bridge, the men met a very attractive woman experimenter who questioned them about their experiences. The woman approached the men either immediately after their participation, when they were still aroused by their fearful experience, or 10 minutes later, when their arousal had diminished. After the interview, the woman gave the subjects her telephone number and indicated they could call her to learn more about the study. Dutton and Aron assumed that if the men were attracted to the woman, they would call her. They found that 65 percent of the subjects in the arousal condition—those approached immediately after crossing the bridge—telephoned the woman, compared to only 30 percent in the nonaroused condition.

Misattribution of arousal also affects emotions other than love. Studies indicate that the misattribution of arousal can explain the increased anger in hot environments (Anderson, 1987), the increased enjoyment of a commercial following an arousing scene on television (Gattes & Cantor, 1982), the increased sexual passion that follows an intense argument or frightening experience (Palace, 1995), and the increased edge experienced by successful athletes during competition (Raglin, 1992).

Figure 12.8 Are you in love? After crossing this long, narrow, flexible suspension bridge spanning a gorge and river in a park in Vancouver, British Columbia, male subjects met an attractive woman experimenter. When the woman approached the male subjects immediately after they crossed the bridge, many of them attributed their arousal to the female experimenter and not to crossing the bridge.

➤ *What is misattribution of arousal? (p. 363)*

These studies demonstrate that cognitive processes play a significant role in the interpretation of emotions.

We have seen that both physiological and psychological processes influence how we experience emotions. These emotions, in turn, have a powerful influence on our actions. When you feel happy, you might give a loved one a hug; when you feel angry, you might yell at that same loved one. Perhaps no other behavior is influenced as much by our emotions as aggressive behavior. We will next look at the influence of two emotions, anger and fear, on aggressive behavior.

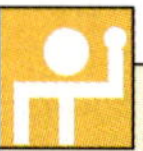

Before You Go On

You are rock climbing with a group of friends when you suddenly find yourself trapped on a ledge with a member of the group on whom you have a tremendous crush. Your heart is pounding, and your stomach is churning—is it fear, or the fact that your crush is holding on to you to keep you from falling?

Section Review

- An emotion is a feeling that differs from the normal affective state.
- The three attributes of an emotion are (1) change in physiological arousal, (2) an affective response, and (3) the capacity to motivate a specific behavior.
- According to the James-Lange theory of emotion, an event causes a distinctive physiological response, and we interpret our internal physiological changes to determine how we feel.
- According to the Cannon-Bard theory, each emotion-causing event activates the thalamus, which stimulates the cortex and viscera, so that visceral changes and emotional experience occur at the same time.
- According to the Papez-MacLean model, which proposes that it is the limbic system that influences our emotional response to an event, one neural circuit, which includes the amygdala and hippocampus, controls survival; a second neural circuit, which includes the cingulate gyrus, the septum, and some areas of the hypothalamus, is involved in the experience of pleasure; and a third circuit, which includes part of the hypothalamus and anterior thalamus, controls cooperative social behavior.
- Schachter's cognitive theory proposes that when we notice that we are internally aroused and do not know why we are aroused, we will attribute our arousal to the prevailing environmental conditions.

Emotions and Aggressive Behavior

Phillip has become increasingly worried about his wife, Darla, and her inability to control her temper. She becomes angry at their two daughters and will punish them severely for even the slightest misbehavior. During a recent flare-up with the girls over some spilled cereal, Darla was spanking Tara, the eldest of the two, very hard and screamed at Phillip when he tried to intervene. When it was all over, Darla's anger subsided quickly, and Phillip was able to talk with her about the incident. She seemed to recognize that she had acted too harshly and told Phillip that she would try to control her temper when disciplining the girls.

Phillip had begun to notice Darla's inability to control her temper after a recent promotion to a vice president at the bank, which requires her to establish a more efficient procedure for evaluating loan applications. Along with her new job responsibilities, she seems to have a never-ending set of complaints from loan applicants, and usually comes home tired and irritable.

Tonight Phillip's world seemed to come apart. The girls were especially quarrelsome, fighting over coloring books and bickering over which television show to watch. Phillip saw Darla's anger building, and when their 5-year-old daughter, Jamie, refused to go to bed, Darla snapped. Her face turned red, and she struck Jamie's arm violently. Jamie began to scream, and Phillip knew immediately that his daughter was seriously injured. Darla appeared to be frozen, and then ran from the room sobbing. At the emergency room, the x-rays revealed that Jamie's arm was broken. Afraid that Darla might be prosecuted for child abuse, Phillip told the doctor that his daughter had fallen off a swing in their backyard. He was ashamed of his lie, but was relieved that the doctor did not question him further. ■

In this section of the chapter, we will discuss the causes of aggressive behavior such as Darla's, which has caused intense physical and psychological pain for her family. Our discussion will reveal that the inability to control anger may reflect dysfunction in specific brain structures. Other psychological and biological causes of aggressive behavior will be discussed as well.

A Definition of Aggression

We often refer to behavior such as Darla's as aggressive. But what exactly do we mean by that? **Table 12.1** presents a very diverse list of behaviors that can be consid-

Table 12.1 ■ Samples of Potentially Aggressive Behaviors

1.	A Boy Scout helping an old lady across the street accidently trips and she sprains her ankle.
2.	An assassin attempts to kill the President but the shot misses.
3.	A housewife knocks a flowerpot off the fifth-story window ledge and it hits a passerby.
4.	A farmer kills a chicken for dinner.
5.	In a debate, one person belittles another's qualifications.
6.	A soldier presses a button that fires a nuclear missile and kills thousands of people he cannot even see.
7.	A police officer trying to break up a riot hits a rioter on the head with a club and knocks him unconscious.
8.	A cat stalks, catches, tosses around, and eventually kills a mouse.
9.	A wife accuses her husband of having an affair and he retorts that after living with her anyone would have an affair.
10.	A frightened boy, caught stealing but trying to escape, shoots his discoverer.
11.	One child takes away a toy from another, making him cry.
12.	A man unable to get into his locked car kicks in the side of the door.
13.	A man pays $.25 to beat an old car with an iron bar, which he does vigorously.
14.	A football player blocks another player from behind (clipping) and breaks his leg.
15.	A businessman hires a professional killer to "take care of" a business rival.
16.	A woman carefully plots how she will kill her husband, then she does so.
17.	Two students get into a drunken brawl and one hits the other with a beer bottle.
18.	A businessman works vigorously to improve his business and drive out the competition.
19.	On the Rorschach inkblot test, a hospitalized mental patient is scored as being highly aggressive, although he has never actually harmed anyone.
20.	A young boy talks a lot about how he is going to beat up others, but never does it.
21.	A hired killer successfully completes his job.

Adapted from: Beck, R.C. (1990). *Motivation: Theories and principles*. (3rd ed.). Englewood Cliffs, NJ: Prentice-Hall.

ered aggressive. An energetic executive trying to drive out competitors seems quite different from a mugger who stabs a victim during a robbery; yet, both behaviors can be considered aggressive.

Can a single definition of aggression encompass all of the behaviors presented in **Table 12.1**? Psychologists have struggled for years with this problem. The most frequent definition is that **aggression** is behavior motivated by the intent to harm a living being or, under some conditions, an inanimate object (Klein, 1982). Thus, any behavior that has such malicious intent is considered aggressive (see **Figure 12.9**).

How can we infer intent from observing behavior? We might try to determine someone's intent from verbal behavior. For example, Phillip might ask Darla why she struck their daughter. However, verbal reports may not represent an accurate indication of intent; we are unlikely to tell others about our deliberately aggressive acts. Also, because animals have no verbal behavior, we cannot use it to detect their intent. Moyer (1976, 1983) suggested an indirect way of assessing intent. According to Moyer, we can infer intent by observing the persistence of an animal's or human's "destructive acts toward the same or similar stimulus objects at different times." In our example, Moyer would consider Darla's hitting her children as aggressive because she does it repeatedly to both of her children.

Are All Aggressive Acts Alike?

Many different behaviors can be considered aggressive, and aggressive acts can occur in a variety of situations. But is all aggressive behavior alike? In 1976, Moyer presented a detailed analysis of aggression, in which he outlined eight types of aggression: (1) irritable, (2) sex-related, (3) fear-induced, (4) predatory, (5) maternal, (6) intermale, (7) instrumental, and

aggression A behavior motivated by the intent to harm a living being or, under some conditions, an inanimate object.

Figure 12.9 Aggression. In this Shoe cartoon, the pitcher is attempting to decide how to best pitch to a strong batter. Determined not to give the batter a hit, the pitcher decides to throw at the batter's head, definitely an aggressive act.

➤ *If there were no thought bubble in the final frame of the above cartoon, how, according to Moyer, might you infer the pitcher's intent? (p. 366)*

(8) territorial. **Table 12.2** presents a brief description of each. Each type of aggression is characterized by a different pattern of aggressive behavior. For example, although an animal's natural prey and an unfamiliar male conspecific (another male of the same species) both release aggressive behavior, the form of the animal's predatory response is quite different from the form of its aggressive response toward the conspecific male. Further, each type of aggressive behavior is controlled by a different genetic mechanism. Popova, Nikulina, and Kulikov (1993) found that selective breeding for reduced levels of one type of aggression did not influence the other types.

Table 12.2 ■ Eight Types of Aggression

Type	Description
Fear-induced	An animal cornered and unable to escape from danger becomes aggressive.
Instrumental	An animal emits an aggressive behavior to obtain a desired goal.
Intermale	A male threatens and then attacks a strange male of the same species.
Irritable	A frustrated or angry animal attacks another animal or object.
Maternal	A mother assaults a perceived threat to her young.
Predatory	An animal stalks, catches, and kills its natural prey.
Sex-related	A male becomes aggressive when encountering sex-related stimuli.
Territorial	An animal defends its territory against intrusion.

Moyer (1976) suggested that in nonhuman animals the motivational system differs for each type of aggression. This is explained in part by the existence in nonhuman animals of separate biological systems for each form of aggression, with the exception of instrumental aggression (means to an end). In addition, a specific releasing stimulus exists for each form of aggression, but the effectiveness of a particular releasing stimulus depends on the efficient functioning of the relevant physiological systems. For example, a releasing stimulus for predatory aggression (e.g., the presence of the prey) will not trigger predatory behavior unless the neural circuits in the lateral hypothalamus that control predatory aggression are functioning effectively (Flynn, 1972).

Humans, on the other hand, do not appear to have different releasing stimuli or behavior patterns for different types of aggression. Consider a male debater who belittles an opponent's qualifications (example 5 in **Table 12.1**). This aggression could be one of several different types of aggression, including instrumental aggression (contending for a woman's attention), fear-induced aggression (fear of the opponent's attack), and irritable aggression (anger at the opponent over an incident just before the debate). These observations indicate that in humans, different motives can produce the same form of aggressive behavior.

In this chapter, we will look closely at two of the eight forms of aggressive behavior: irritable aggression and fear-induced aggression. Our discussion will focus on the specific neural and hormonal systems that control each type, and will explore their powerful influence on

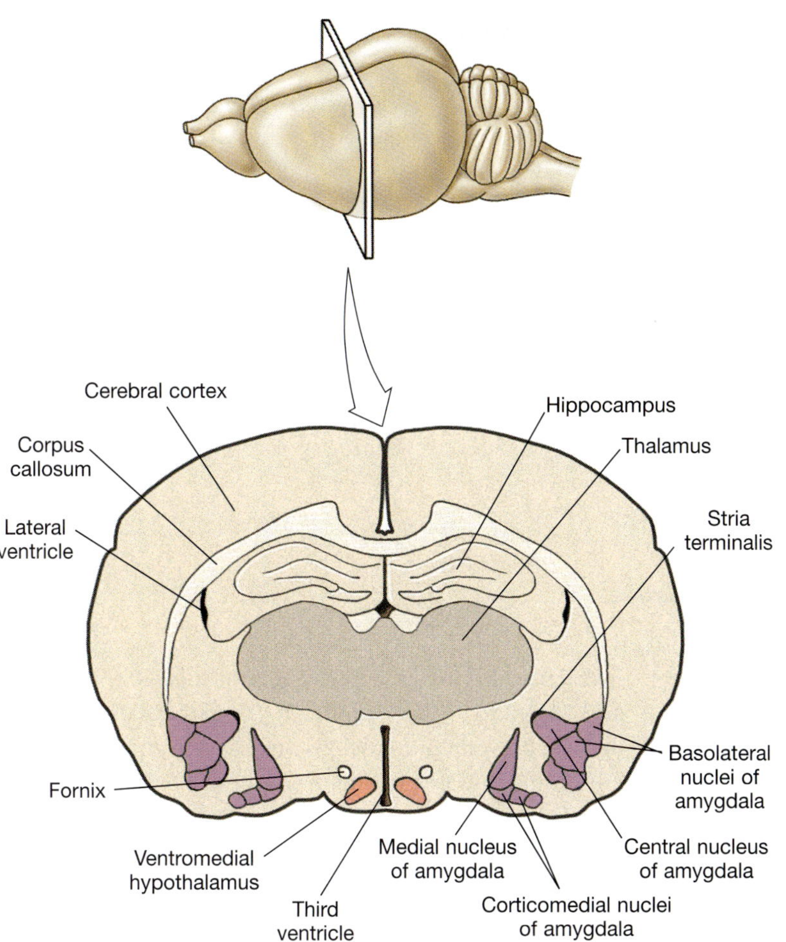

Figure 12.10 The key structures in the amygdala of the rat brain related to aggressive behavior. This coronal plane view shows the stria terminalis, central nucleus, basolateral nuclei, medial nucleus, and corticomedial nuclei of the amygdala.

➤ *Which structure in the amygdala seems to excite irritable aggressiveness? (p. 368)*

our actions. Because it is the most frequently observed and studied type of human aggression, we will begin our discussion with irritable aggression.

Before You Go On

Phillip and Darla are walking back to their car after an evening at the movies, when a man runs up and grabs Darla's purse. As Darla screams "Stop, thief!," Phillip chases after the purse snatcher, catches him, and throws him to the ground. According to Moyer's theory, which type of aggressive behavior was exhibited by the purse snatcher? By Darla? By Phillip?

Irritable Aggression

Several weeks ago, I took my family to a restaurant for dinner. Although the restaurant was not crowded, the service was terrible. We waited for almost an hour just to have our order taken and an equally long time before our dinner was finally served. To top it off, our waiter was completely inattentive to our requests. By the end of dinner, I was in a foul mood. I usually leave a good tip, but on this occasion, I left no tip and indicated my displeasure to the manager. My behavior exemplifies **irritable aggression**. Perhaps you have acted aggressively in a similarly annoying situation.

Irritable aggression is elicited by two emotions. Inability to achieve a goal (eat dinner) produces the emotion of frustration; exposure to physically or psychologically painful events (being ignored by the waiter) produces the emotion of anger. In mild form, irritable aggression involves an overt display of annoyance or a halfhearted threat (my omission of a tip and talk with the manager), whereas extreme cases of irritable aggression involve destructive, uncontrollable rage (Darla's fracturing her daughter's arm).

Several central nervous system structures have been identified as having an influence on the control of irritable aggression. Some brain systems arouse irritable aggressive behavior, and others inhibit it. Several hormones also appear to play a role in the expression of irritable aggression.

---

irritable aggression An aggressive response to annoying situations (either an inability to achieve a goal or exposure to physically or psychologically painful events).

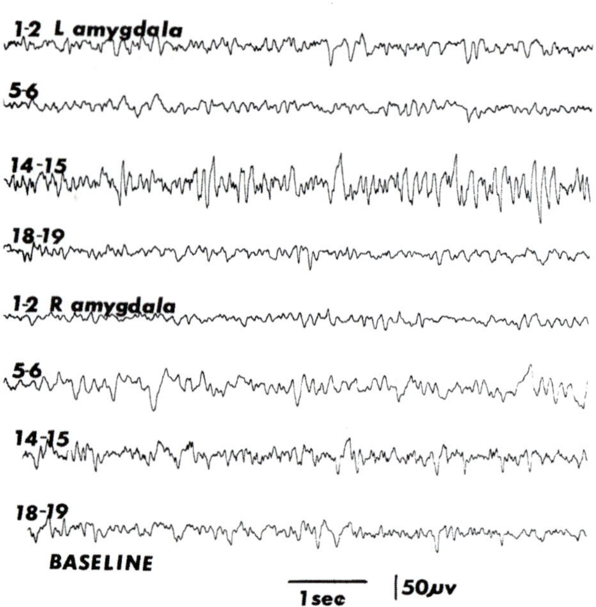

Figure 12.11 Electrical activity of a teenage girl who had smothered a baby whose crying annoyed her. The electrical activity was recorded in four sites in the right and left amygdala before, during, and after a tape of a baby crying. Note the intense activity recorded from electrodes 14–15 of the right and left amygdala that began when crying started and ended when the crying stopped. The crying had no effect on other areas of the amygdala.

➤ *What is the name of the surgical treatment that this girl underwent? (p. 368)*

Neural Influence. The classic research by Klüver and Bucy (1937) showed that destruction of the temporal lobes in male monkeys produced an inability to respond to threatening cues and demonstrated that the temporal lobes are involved in the initiation of irritable aggression. On the basis of this study, some surgeons (Terzian & DalleOre, 1955) removed the temporal lobes of excessively aggressive people. Although this surgical treatment did reduce irritable aggression, it also produced negative side effects, including socially inappropriate sexual activity, compulsive orality, decreased ability to recognize people, and memory deficits. These behavioral effects have been called the **Klüver-Bucy syndrome**. In place of this radical surgical procedure, other, more limited treatments that produce a reduction of irritable aggressiveness are now used. (Note that any psychosurgical procedure is extreme and is recommended only when other treatments have proven ineffective.) More recent research (Engel, 1992) has confirmed that aggressive behavior is associated with intense activity in the temporal lobes.

Another brain area that appears to influence the excitation and suppression of irritable aggressiveness is the amygdala (refer to Chapter 2; see **Figure 12.10**). The amygdala is divided into five functional areas: the stria terminalis, the central nucleus, the basolateral nuclei, the medial nucleus, and the corticomedial nuclei. The area of the amygdala that seems to excite aggressiveness is the medial nucleus. In support of this view, MacLean and Delgado (1953) reported that stimulation of the medial amygdaloid nucleus in cats produced intense emotional and behavioral arousal that included hissing, growling, claw extension, and pupillary dilation, but not the attempt to escape. Shibata, Yamameto, and Ueki (1982) reported similar effects of medial amygdaloid stimulation in rats; Fonberg (1965) observed that stimulation of the medial amygdaloid nucleus aroused irritable aggressiveness in dogs, and damage to this area produced tameness and a lack of irritable aggressiveness.

Another indication that the amygdala plays an important role in irritable aggressiveness in humans is the observation that seizures (or excessive neural activity) in the amygdala have been associated with extremely violent behavior. During a seizure, the amygdala is extremely active, and irritable aggressiveness can be intense. Mark and Ervin (1970) have demonstrated a positive relationship between activity in the amygdala that occurs during a seizure and the occurrence of hostility in humans.

The following case history provides a vivid illustration of the role of the amygdala in producing irritable aggression. Mark and Ervin (1970) reported the case of a teenage girl who behaved as a model child except for occasional, extremely destructive acts initiated by circumstances that annoyed her. For example, being criticized for playing records too loudly caused her to strike others. The girl was finally institutionalized when she smothered a baby because the crying annoyed her. Mark and Ervin implanted electrodes in her amygdala and recorded activity before, during, and after the presentation of a recording of a baby's crying. They found that the crying evoked intense, localized activity in the amygdala (see **Figure 12.11**) as well as the experience of intense anger.

Klüver-Bucy syndrome A disorder produced by damage to the temporal lobes that is characterized by socially inappropriate sexual activity, compulsive orality, decreased ability to recognize people, and memory deficits.

A surgical treatment that has benefited this girl, and others like her whose extreme irritable aggression can be linked to an amygdaloid malfunction, is an **amygdalectomy**. This psychosurgery procedure destroys selected neurons in the amygdala. Mark and Ervin (1970) reported that following this surgery, their patient was released and experienced no further attacks.

Other clinical observations also suggest that amygdalectomy is an effective treatment for excessive aggression in some people. For example, Ramamurthi (1988) found that of a group of 603 hostile people who had received amygdala lesions, 70% showed a marked reduction in irritable aggression. Narabayaski (1972) lesioned the amygdala in 51 hostile people and reported that 85 percent showed a significant reduction in irritable aggression. Some psychologists (Valenstein, 1980) have claimed that the effects of amygdalectomy on aggression are short-lived. One of Valenstein's patients exhibited apathy and listlessness, but not a lack of aggressiveness. According to Valenstein, the presence of apathy could have been misinterpreted as an absence of violent behavior.

Irritable aggressive behavior has also been shown to be influenced by the hypothalamus in nonhuman animals. Stimulation of the anterior lateral hypothalamus produced irritable aggression in rats (Panksepp & Trowill, 1969). Further, Brutus, Shaikh, Edinger, and Siegel (1986) found that stimulation of one brain area (either the pyriform cortex, which is an area in the medial temporal lobe, or the amygdala) lowered the threshold for eliciting aggression from another brain area (the anterior hypothalamus).

The ventromedial hypothalamus (see **Figure 12.10**) functions to suppress irritable aggressive behavior, and intense irritability has been observed following ventromedial lesions in rats (Grossman, 1972). Hyperirritability also has been reported in humans who have tumors in the ventromedial hypothalamic area (Wheatley, 1944). Sclafani's research (1971) indicates that the ventromedial hypothalamus inhibits irritable aggressive behavior in rats by directly suppressing activity of the anterior lateral hypothalamus. Sclafani cut the neural connections between these two areas and reported a hyperirritability identical to that produced by ventromedial lesions.

Disease and Irritable Aggression. A number of diseases have been found to intensify levels of irritability, hostility, and overt aggressiveness. Two diseases—brain tumors and epilepsy—are described next to document the influence of disease on irritable aggression.

The case of Charles Whitman is perhaps the best-known example of aggression caused by a brain tumor. Whitman was an extremely violent young man whose anger slowly intensified over a period of years. When his anger finally peaked, he killed his wife and mother, and then took a high-powered rifle with several hundred rounds of ammunition to the tower at the University of Texas in Austin. Whitman killed a receptionist, barricaded the tower's door, and within 90 minutes killed 14 people and wounded 24 others before he was killed. An autopsy revealed a malignant tumor in the area of the medial amygdaloid nucleus (Sweet, Ervin, & Mark, 1969). Other investigators (for example, Malamud, 1967) have reported cases in which extremely violent persons were found to have temporal lobe or amygdaloid tumors. Temporal lobe damage caused by viral encephalitis also has been associated with aggression (Greer, Lyons-Crew, Mauldini & Brown, 1989).

We discussed earlier the association between seizures initiated in the amygdala and irritable aggression. Williams (1969) observed that intense anger or rage is also likely to follow epileptic activity in the anterior temporal lobe. Similarly, Monroe (1970) also reported that aggressive behavior usually followed intense spontaneous activity in the temporal lobe. However, most people with epilepsy, rather than being angry and violent after a seizure, become frightened or depressed. The reason for these different behavioral responses is unknown, but it is thought that past experience may affect an individual's reaction to a seizure.

Brain Activity and Irritable Aggression. Abnormal EEG (or cortical) activity has also been associated with violence. Bayrakal (1965) reported that of 200 problem children, 100 had abnormal EEGs. Among these 100 children, most showed disturbances in activity in the temporal lobe and related subcortical areas as well as a typical behavioral pattern: poor impulse control, inadequate social adaptation, and irritable aggression in the form of hostility. Monroe (1970) reported that 50 to 60 percent of children with behavioral problems show EEG disturbances, compared with 5 to 15 percent of children without any behavioral problems.

Individuals who commit violent crimes are also likely to have abnormal EEG patterns (Bonkalo, 1967). Knott (1965) found that compared with the general population, psychopaths show a significantly greater number of EEG abnormalities. Yoshii, Ishiwara, and Tani (1963) observed similar differences between juvenile delinquents and the rest of the population.

Hormonal Influence on Irritable Aggression. Several types of evidence support the view that the male sex hormone testosterone affects irritable aggression. First, researchers (Archer, 1991; Dabbs et al., 1995;

---

amygdalectomy A psychosurgical procedure that destroys selected neurons in the amygdala; used to treat extreme aggressiveness.

Dabbs & Morris, 1990) have found a positive correlation between the level of testosterone and the level of aggressive behavior. For example, Dabbs and Morris (1990) reported that a high testosterone level in 4,462 male U.S. military veterans was related to a variety of antisocial behaviors including having had past trouble with parents, teachers, and classmates; being assaultive toward other adults; and going AWOL in the military. Further, Dabbs and colleagues (1995) found that males convicted of violent crimes (for example, murder) had higher testosterone levels than did males convicted of nonviolent crimes (for example, burglary).

Second, males of most species engage in more aggressive fighting and threatening behavior than do females, and this behavior is not simply intermale aggression. For example, male domestic animals, such as the bull and the stallion, are as aggressive with people who handle them as they are with other males of their own species (Moyer, 1976). With regard to humans, men commit a significantly greater number of violent crimes than do women (Archer & Lloyd, 1985; Eagly, 1987; Maccoby & Jacklin, 1980).

Third, castrating male human and nonhuman animals reduces the incidence of irritable aggression. (Recall from Chapter 11, that castration leads to an absence of testosterone.) Many studies have shown that domestic animals are docile following castration. Studies in human males have noted that castration of sex offenders can also reduce their level of aggressiveness.

Finally, administration of testosterone has been shown to reinstate the antisocial behaviors of castrated male human and nonhuman animals. Wagner, Beaving, and Hutchinson (1980) observed an increase in aggressive behavior of castrated mice following testosterone replacement (see **Figure 12.12**); cessation of testosterone administration led to a reduced level of aggressiveness. A similar effect of replacement therapy has been found in castrated human males. For example, Hawke (1950) noted that testosterone injections reinstated aggressive behaviors including attacking children, instigating fights, breaking windows, and destroying property. The irritable aggression decreased when testosterone was no longer administered.

Some researchers suggest that the female sex hormone estrogen enhances irritable aggression in females. Kohler (1925) observed that sexually receptive female chimpanzees (those with elevated levels of estrogen) became aggressive when approached by a sexually motivated male, and Michael (1969) reported increased aggressiveness in sexually receptive female rhesus monkeys as well as in baboons. In addition, Michael reported that estrogen injections significantly increased the frequency of irritable aggressive behavior displayed by female rhesus monkeys and baboons.

In contrast to estrogen, progesterone, another female sex hormone, appears to inhibit irritable aggression. Irritability of women during the premenstrual period—part of what is called the **premenstrual syndrome (PMS)**—has been attributed to the drop in progesterone level that occurs at this time. Many researchers have reported that many women show increased irritable aggression during the premenstrual period (Deuster, Adera, South-Paul, 1999; Van Goozen, Frijda, Wiegant, Endert, & Van de Poll, 1996). For example, Van Goozen, Frijda, Wiegant, Endert, and Van de Poll (1996) exposed 58 women to an aversive anger-provoking situation. Significantly higher systolic

premenstrual syndrome Irritability in human females during the premenstrual period that has been attributed to a drop in progesterone level.

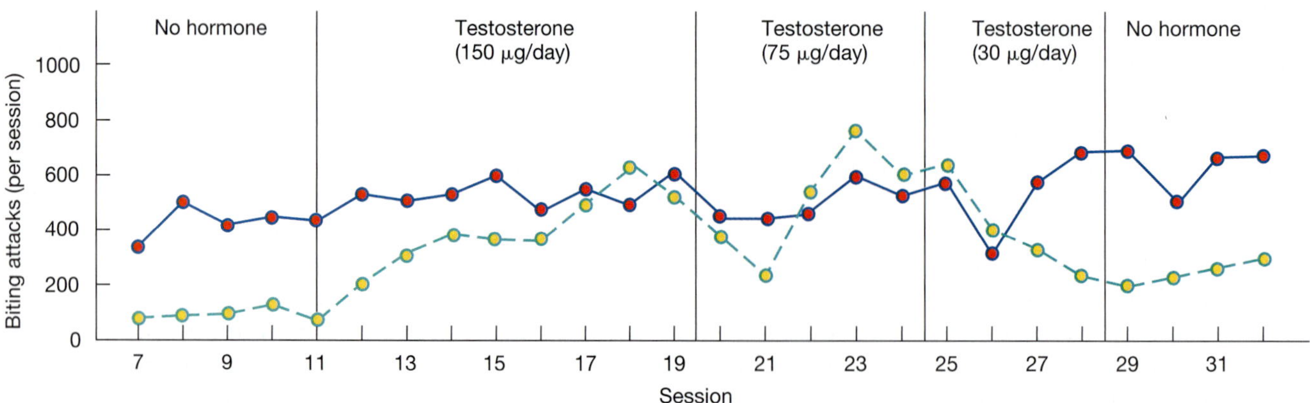

Figure 12.12 The effects of testosterone replacement on aggressive behavior in castrated mice. The solid line shows that testosterone has no effect in noncastrated mice; the dashed line illustrates the occurrence of aggressive behavior toward a target following testosterone replacement.

➤ *What hormones affect irritable aggression in females? (p. 370)* blood pressure and intensity of anger were noted for women in the premenstrual phase than at other times in the menstrual cycle, but only for those (approximately 50%) who had reported suffering from premenstrual emotional lability and irritation prior to the study. Documenting additional support for the relationship between PMS and aggression, Dalton (1961) noted that 49 percent of reported crimes committed by women occurred during the offenders' premenstrual period. (The premenstrual period accounts for only 25 percent of the menstrual cycle.) Female vervet monkeys also show a heightened irritability during the premenstrual period (Rapkin, Pollack, Raleigh, Stone, & McGuire, 1995).

There is evidence that administration of progesterone can decrease the level of irritable aggression that often occurs during the premenstrual period. For example, Dalton (1964) found that the administration of progesterone decreased premenstrual hostility and aggressiveness. In addition, Hamburg, Moos, and Yalom (1968) reported that women who took oral contraceptives containing progesterone showed much less premenstrual irritability than women who did not take them.

Serotonin and Irritable Aggression. We learned earlier that high testosterone level is associated with aggressive behavior. Does this relationship mean that testosterone activates the amygdala to produce irritable aggression? Paul Bernhardt (1997) suggests that testosterone alone does not produce irritable aggression. Bernhardt observed that successful businessmen and male athletes who are not any more aggressive than their less successful counterparts have higher testosterone levels; that is, testosterone level is correlated with success of a man's actions as well as his level of aggressive behavior. According to Bernhardt, high testosterone levels promote dominance-seeking behaviors in males. When attempts at dominance fail, the male experiences the emotion of frustration. If serotonin levels in the amygdala are low, which probably is true in a male whose dominance-seeking behaviors are unsuccessful, failure causes an extremely negative emotional frustration reaction and an intense aggressive response. In other words, high testosterone levels promote dominance-seeking behavior and low serotonin levels produce aggression when the dominance-seeking behaviors fail.

There is considerable evidence that low levels of serotonin are associated with irritable aggression in both nonhuman primate males (Higley et al., 1996; Mehlman et al., 1995) and human males (Coccaro et al., 1994; Virkkunen et al., 1996). The primate studies were conducted in a natural environment. In these studies, young juvenile male monkeys that had low 5-hydroxyindoleacetic acid (5-HIAA) levels, a metabolite of serotonin, showed high levels of risk-taking behavior, which included high levels of

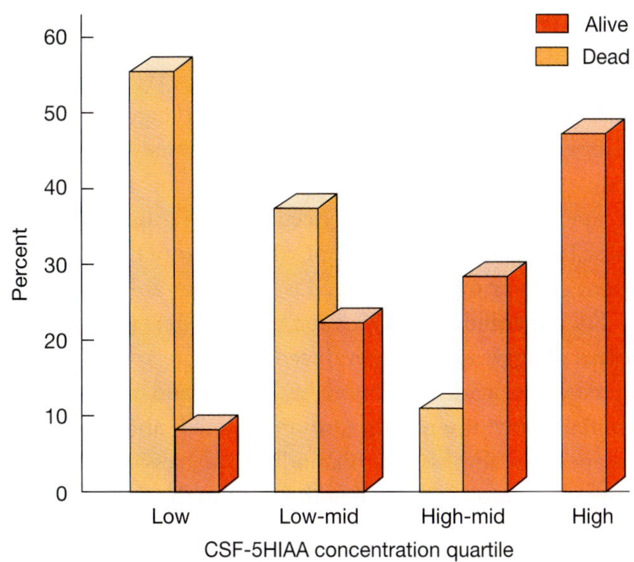

Figure 12.13 Serotonin level and survival rate. The illustration shows the percentage of male monkeys in a natural environment who survive to age 6 as a function of 5-HIAA in the cerebrospinal fluid at age 2.

➤ *Why is serotonin level related to the level of risk-taking behavior? (p. 371)*

aggressive behavior directed toward male monkeys that were older and larger than themselves. Another high risk-taking behavior exhibited by the males with low 5-HIAA was leaping off tall trees. Mehlman and colleagues (1995) observed that the juvenile monkeys with low 5-HIAA levels showed low levels of social competence, which likely lead to their failed dominance-seeking behavior. Unfortunately, the life span of a young male monkey with low 5-HIAA levels is usually very brief. Higley and colleagues (1996) found that most of the low 5-HIAA male monkeys died before the age of 6 (see **Figure 12.13**). By contrast, these researchers noted that all male monkeys with high 5-HIAA levels survived to the age of 6.

Low serotonin levels are also associated with irritable aggression in human males. Coccaro and colleagues (1994) found that in men with personality disorders, low levels of 5-HIAA in cerebrospinal fluid was associated with high levels of impulsive or irritable aggression. In another study, Virkkunen, Eggert, Rawlings, and Linnoila (1996) found that men who were convicted of violent crimes and had low serotonin levels were most likely to commit another violent act when released from prison.

As we have learned (and already knew from reading the newspaper and viewing the evening news), irritable aggression is the most prevalent form of human aggression. We will next examine another type of aggression, fear-induced aggression, to illustrate the diversity of emotions that can produce aggressive behavior.

Fear-Induced Aggression

A cornered animal can be quite dangerous. When human and nonhuman animals are exposed to dangerous environmental conditions, the intense, internal emotional state of fear is aroused. Fear motivates the attempt to escape, but aggression often occurs if the escape response fails. This aggressive behavior continues until the aversive event ends or until the animal is no longer able to fight.

Such **fear-induced aggression** clearly differs from other forms of aggression. Fear-induced aggressive behavior is a defensive reaction exhibited by human and nonhuman animals only when they are threatened and perceive escape to be impossible. Fear-induced aggression involves intense autonomic arousal and defensive threat display. If the threat is unsuccessful, a vicious attack ensues. Thus, the aggressive behavior of a cornered or captured animal is a final, last-ditch effort to escape a perceived life-threatening situation. Animals who feel cornered exhibit an extremely intense aggressive response, which can lead to the injury or death of the perceived source of the danger. The worst thing you can do is to make an animal perceive that it has no means of escape. Under these conditions, you are likely to be attacked by even a normally nonaggressive animal.

Klüver and Bucy's classic study (1937) of rhesus monkeys indicated that fearfulness was significantly reduced by lesions of the temporal lobes. In another study, Franzen and Myers (1973) found that a lesion of either the anterior third of the temporal lobes or the prefrontal cortex eliminated fear-induced aggression in rhesus monkeys.

Joseph LeDoux and his colleagues (LaBar et al., 1995; LeDoux, 1995; LeDoux et al., 1988) have shown that stimulation of the central amygdaloid nucleus and the basal amygdaloid nuclei elicits fear. In one study, LeDoux, Iwata, Cicchetti, and Reiss (1988) observed that stimulation of the central and basal amygdala produced an increased startle reaction to a visual stimulus in rats. This increased fear response was evidenced by both freezing and flinching responses. Other research has shown that lesions of the central and basal areas of the amygdala impair the acquisition of a fear response. Campbeau and Davis (1995) and Young and Leaton (1996) found that damage to these two areas of the amygdala disrupted a rat's learning to escape from a painful electric shock stimulus.

fear-induced aggression An aggressive behavior that is a defensive reaction exhibited only when an animal is threatened and perceives escape to be impossible; involves intense autonomic arousal and defensive threat display; if the threat is unsuccessful, a vicious attack ensues.

The amygdala also influences the experience of fear in humans. LaBar and colleagues (1998) observed an increased blood flow to the amygdala when human subjects were presented a light stimulus that had previously been associated with shock. Further, LaBar, LeDoux, Spencer, and Phelps (1995) found that a tone associated with a loud noise produced a weak autonomic nervous system response in humans who had undergone a surgical procedure in which the amygdala and surrounding tissues on one side of their brains were lesioned to treat severe epileptic seizures. Although damage to this area of the brain impaired their autonomic response, these individuals still knew that the tone predicted the loud noise.

We have learned that stimulation of the central and basal amygdala elicits the emotion of fear. Activation of these areas of the amygdala also can produce increased fear-induced aggressive behavior. For example, Fonberg (1965) found that stimulation of the central amygdaloid nucleus produced aggressive behavior in confined dogs. Similarly, Anand and Dua (1956) reported that arousal of the central nucleus and the dorsal section of the basal nucleus motivated fear-induced aggression in cats.

Destruction of these excitatory amygdaloid areas produces a fearless animal that will not show fear-induced aggressive behavior when in danger. There is strong evidence that lesions of these excitatory areas lead to an absence of both fear and fear-induced aggression in threatening situations in many animal species, such as cats (Schreiner & Kling, 1953), wild Norway rats (Wood, 1958), dogs (Fonberg, 1965), and primates (Kling, Dicks, & Gurwitz, 1968).

Blanchard and Blanchard's (1972) observations of the behavior of albino rats following amygdalectomy provide a dramatic illustration of the importance of the amygdala in motivating fear and fear-induced aggression. A normal albino rat that sees a cat will freeze and remain immobile as long as the cat is present, but an amygdalectomized rat shows no fear of cats. One of Blanchard and Blanchard's amygdalectomized rats climbed on the cat's head and nibbled its ear. Even after being attacked and released by the cat, the rat attached itself to the cat's back.

Evidence also indicates that the amygdala has an important influence on fear-induced aggression in humans. Hitchcock (1979) reported that stimulation of the medial amygdala produced fear and fear-induced aggressive reactions; Kaada (1972) observed that destruction of the medial amygdala reduced fear and fear-induced aggressiveness. Heath (1964) found that fear (and fear-induced aggression) and anger (and irritable aggression) could be elicited by stimulating the same anatomical location. Moyer (1976) suggests that one likely reason for this finding is that the amygdala centers that control fear-induced aggression and irritable aggression are anatomically very close to each other. The specific areas of the amygdala that affect fear-induced aggression in people have not been identified.

The ventral portion of the basal amygdaloid nuclei and the lateral nucleus of the amygdala appear to play an inhibitory role in fear-induced aggression. Fonberg (1965, 1968) reported that stimulation of these amygdaloid areas inhibits both fear and fear-induced aggressive behavior in cats and in dogs.

Another brain area that inhibits fear-induced aggression is the septal area, located in the limbic system (Albert & Walsh, 1984). Brady and Nauta (1955) found that septal lesions in rats produced an increased tendency to escape and an aggressive response to threat. Schnurr (1972) found that mice with lesions in the anterior septal areas showed both intense attempts to escape danger and vigorous biting when restrained.

So far, we have seen that both physiological and psychological processes determine how we feel and act. Some emotional responses are mild, whereas others can be quite intense. Intense emotions, such as Darla's anger and frustration with her children, are often evoked by stressful environmental events (her new responsibilities at work). In the next sections, we will discuss our emotional response to these events, and how we can best cope with stressful events in our lives.

Before You Go On

What evidence is there that irritable aggression and sex-related aggression are closely related?

List the various areas of the amygdala involved in aggression and give the function of each.

Section Review

- Aggression is defined as actions of a human or nonhuman animal that are intended to harm another animal or person.
- According to Moyer, there are eight forms of aggressive behavior, including fear-induced, instrumental, intermale, irritable, maternal, predatory, sex-related, and territorial.
- In both human and nonhuman animals, each form of aggression, with the exception of instrumental aggression, appears to have a particular physiological basis.
- Irritable aggression is an impulsive aggressive reaction elicited by anger and frustration, which can be directed toward the source of the annoyance or be displaced to another animate or inanimate object.
- The irritable aggressive reaction can be mild or can involve intense autonomic arousal and vicious attack behavior.
- Neural systems located in the temporal lobes, the medial amygdala, and the anterior lateral hypothalamus initiate irritable aggressive behavior.
- The ventromedial hypothalamus inhibits irritable aggressive behavior.
- Malfunctions in the excitatory areas of the temporal lobe and amygdala have been related to extremely violent behavior in humans; surgical destruction of these areas has been an effective treatment for hostile and destructive behavior.
- High levels of testosterone promote dominance-seeking behaviors, and if serotonin levels in the amygdala are low, failure of the dominance-seeking behaviors produces intense aggressiveness.
- Estrogen has been associated with irritable aggression.
- Progesterone appears to suppress irritable aggression.
- Fear-induced aggression occurs when an animal is cornered with no possible escape, and involves intense autonomic arousal and defensive threat display. If the threat is unsuccessful, a vicious attack ensues.
- A number of central nervous system areas, especially the temporal lobes and several areas of the amygdala (the central amygdaloid nucleus and the basal amygdaloid nucleus), elicit fear and fear-induced aggressive behavior.
- The ventral portion of the basal amygdaloid nucleus, the lateral amygdaloid nuclei, and septal area inhibit fear-induced aggression.

Stress

During our lives, we experience many different environmental events. One class of events—called stressors—can place unusual demands on us. A **stressor** is any event that either strains or overwhelms our ability to adjust to our environment (Taylor, 1996). Physiological stressors include extreme cold or heat, invasion of dangerous microorganisms, and physical injury, whereas the death of a relative or friend, an impending examination, and being fired from a job are examples of psychological stressors. However, stressors are not always negative; for example, the anticipation of that first date we discussed earlier can be as stressful as an approaching deadline. Consider the following example. On Monday, my dean calls to request a report about recent faculty accomplishments by Friday. Knowing how difficult it can be to get information from faculty on such short notice, I immediately send an e-mail to the psychology department fac-

stressor Any event that either strains or overwhelms our ability to adjust to our environment.

ulty. The deadline for the report draws near, and several faculty members still have not yet responded. I am beginning to feel pressure to get the report completed and am sure the tension will increase as Friday approaches and necessary information is still missing.

Pressure can be defined as an expectation (by yourself or others) to behave in a specific way within a particular time frame; a deadline that produces pressure is one example of a stressor. Other examples of stressors are conflict, the inability to satisfy two or more incompatible motives (having to decide whether or not to talk to the faculty who have not responded), and frustration, the obstruction of achievement of a goal (the missing information needed for the report).

Significant psychological and physiological changes, or the stress response, occur when we encounter a stressor. These biological and behavioral responses determine whether we are able to adapt to the stressful experiences in our lives. Our reactions to stressors are sometimes effective, and sometimes not.

The physiological consequences of experiencing a stressor are closely related to psychological processes. In other words, our perception of a stressful event influences our physiological response to a stressor. Jay Weiss and his associates (Weiss, 1972; Weiss, Stone, & Harrell, 1970) discovered that shocks that could not be controlled by the subject produced a stronger physiological reaction than did controllable shocks of equal duration and intensity. Similarly, unpredictable shocks caused a greater physiological response than shocks administered at predictable times. These results suggest that an event is more likely to provoke a physiological response when it is perceived as uncontrollable or unpredictable.

Before You Go On

After a long, frustrating day at the office, and after being stuck in traffic for an hour, Darla walks through the front door to be greeted by the dog, who is so happy to see her that he makes a mess on the floor, and by her daughters, who are fighting over markers (they are both rainbow-colored from head to toe). Phillip, who has just beat Darla through the door, sees that she is about to boil over and sends her upstairs for a relaxing bath while he makes dinner. List all of the potential stressors in this scenario.

---

general adaptation syndrome (GAS) A pattern of physiological responses to a physiological or psychological stressor.

alarm reaction The first stage in the GAS that is characterized by intense sympathetic nervous system arousal.

Our Biological Reaction to Stressors

According to Hans Selye (1956), we exhibit a general pattern of internal biological changes when we are exposed to a stressor (refer to **Figure 12.14**). Selye called this physiological stress response the **general adaptation syndrome (GAS)**. Selye observed that all stressors, regardless of whether they are physiological or psychological, produce the general adaptation syndrome.

In Selye's view, any event that taxes our ability to adjust will activate the general adaptation syndrome. There are three stages in the general adaptation syndrome: (1) the alarm reaction, (2) resistance, and (3) exhaustion.

The Alarm Reaction. You start to give a speech in front of your class. During the speech you notice that your voice quavers, your mouth is dry, your palms are sweating, and your hands are shaking. These biological responses are part of the **alarm reaction**.

When you are exposed to a stressor, your sympathetic nervous system is aroused (see **Figure 12.14**), resulting in (1) increased respiration rate, which enhances oxygen intake; (2) increased heart rate, which allows more oxygen to be pumped; (3) release of stored red blood cells from the spleen to carry the increased oxygen; (4) redistribution of blood supply from the skin and viscera to the brain and muscles; (5) increased glycogen conversion into glucose (sugar) and then glucose release from the liver (the brain and muscles use this released glucose as an energy source); (6) secretion of epinephrine and norephinephrine from the adrenal medulla into the bloodstream; (7) dilation of the pupils which enhances visual ability; and (8) activation of the reticular formation.

Why do stressful experiences cause these physiological responses? In 1915, Walter Cannon referred to these internal changes as our emergency reaction. This emergency reaction mobilizes our resources and prepares us for "fight or flight," enabling us to cope behaviorally with stressful experiences.

Although the alarm reaction generally allows for effective coping, it can be impairing. Many people "freeze" when confronted with an emergency such as an impending accident; their intense internal responses prevent them from helping victims of the event. The inability to recall information for examinations is another example of an impairing stressor-produced reaction. An extreme stressor may even cause death.

Although it may seem like an eternity when you are standing up in front of the class, the alarm reaction only lasts for a relatively short time, several minutes to several hours. When the stressor ends, the parasympathetic nervous system takes over, enabling us to restore our physiological reserves to prestressor levels. For example, the parasympathetic nervous system increases the digestive

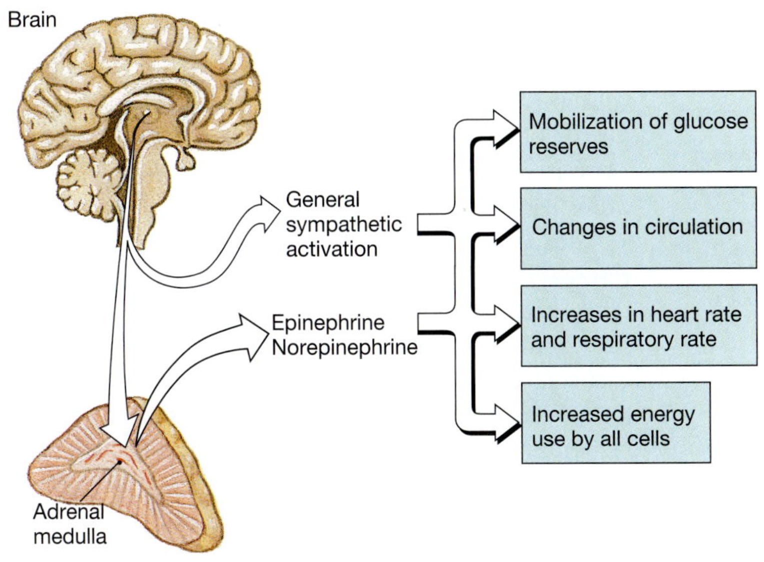

ALARM PHASE

"Fight or Flight" Immediate short-term responses to crises

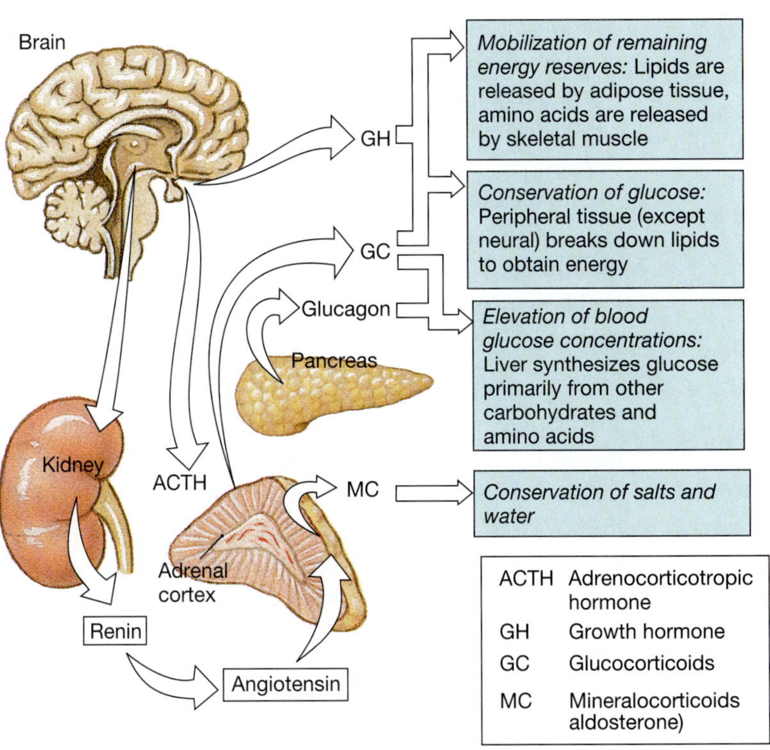

ACTH	Adrenocorticotropic hormone
GH	Growth hormone
GC	Glucocorticoids
MC	Mineralocorticoids aldosterone)

RESISTANCE PHASE

Long-term metabolic adjustments occur

Causes may include:
— Exhaustion of lipid reserves
— Inability to produce glucocorticoids
— Failure of electrolyte balance
— Cumulative structural or functional damage to vital organs

EXHAUSTION PHASE

Collapse of vital systems

Figure 12.14 The general adaptation syndrome. Diagram showing the internal physiological changes initiated by a stressor during the alarm stage, the stage of resistance, and the stage of exhaustion.

➤ *What conditions promote a change from the alarm stage to the stage of resistance? (p. 376)* process, returning glycogen quickly to prestress levels. However, if the stressor continues, we enter the second phase of the general adaptation syndrome, in which we mobilize all of our physiological resources to cope with the stressor.

The Stage of Resistance. In the **stage of resistance**, a prolonged stressor continues the activation of the hypothalamus that began in the alrm phase, which causes an increased release of adrenocorticotrophic-stimulating hormone (ACTH) from the anterior pituitary gland (see **Figure 12.14**). ACTH released into the bloodstream continues to cause the manufacture and release of glucocorticoid hormones from the adrenal cortex.

Glucocorticoid hormones (hydrocortisone, corticosterone, cortisol) allow an animal to remain mobilized in its fight against a continued stressor by stimulating the conversion of nonsugars (fats, proteins) to sugars and enhancing the rate of glycogen storage in the liver (see **Figure 12.14**). This provides us with the continued energy needed to cope with the stressor. In addition, glucocorticoid hormones increase the effectiveness of epinephrine and norepinephrine, thereby allowing us to continue to respond even with diminished epinephrine and norepinephrine levels. The glucocorticoid hormones act like a tune-up for an automobile, which allows its engine to run more efficiently and to use less gas; the glucocorticoid hormones enable your body to use energy more effectively and thus to require less food.

During the resistance stage, the internal systems described above are activated, and all physiological systems not directly involved in stress resistance are inhibited. A prolonged stressor causes decreased secretion of the thyroid-stimulating hormone (TSH) and the growth hormone (GH). Sexual and reproductive physiology are also inhibited. For males, a prolonged stressor produces a decrease in sperm and testosterone levels. A suppressed menstrual cycle (or suppressed estrus in nonhuman mammals), failure to ovulate, increased miscarriage, and reduced lactation are the consequences for females of a prolonged stressor.

The glucocorticoid hormones described above also antagonize the body's inflammatory processes. This suppression of the inflammatory system (1) delays the growth of new tissue around a wound or foreign substance in the skin, (2) inhibits antibody formation, (3) decreases white blood cell formation, and (4) reduces the effectiveness of the thymus gland and other lymphoid tissues.

Thus, glucocorticoid hormones provide the resources needed to cope with stressful events but simultaneously antagonize your body's defense against a stressor. Consequently, the introduction of additional stressors such as a virus can result in an illness that could have been resisted if your body had not been so busy responding to the original stressor. Additional stressors may even result in death.

Many studies have shown that stressors can reduce the ability to fight illness. For example, Cohen, Tyrell, and Smith (1991) determined the level of life stress for 394 healthy subjects and then administered nasal drops containing one of five different viruses. These researchers found that the subjects reporting higher stress showed greater rates of infection for all five viruses. Similarly, Jemmott and colleagues (1983) reported that during periods of academic stress (for example, during the final examination periods) the level of immune system response, as indicated by the secretion of immunoglobulin A antibody (IgA), was reduced and the incidence of illness increased. Other researchers (Sapolsky, 1996; Shapiro, 1996) have even reported a link between stress and the common cold.

The Stage of Exhaustion. If the stressor continues indefinitely, an animal will eventually deplete all of its physiological resources and enter the **stage of exhaustion**. When no resources remain, all of the body's defense systems fail and the animal dies. So there is a measure of truth to the idea that stress can kill you.

Diseases of Adaptation. Long-term exposure to a stressor can wreak havoc on the body. Selye labeled diseases produced by the stress response **diseases of adaptation**. (Note: These are different from illnesses caused by external factors such as viruses, which are themselves considered stressors—see **p. 373**.) These diseases include essential hypertension (high blood pressure with no known physiological cause), gastric or peptic ulcers (small holes in the stomach or upper part of the small intestine caused over time by excessive secretion of hydrochloric acid), and colitis (inflammation of the mucous membrane of the colon). Stress reactions are capable of causing each of these illnesses and are also capable of intensifying their severity. Let's examine ulcers as an example of a disease of adaptation.

---

stage of resistance The second phase of the GAS, in which we mobilize all of our physiological resources to cope with a prolonged stressor.

stage of exhaustion The last stage of the GAS, in which a stressor that continues indefinitely depletes all physiological resources, resulting in a failure of all the body's defense systems, and eventually death.

diseases of adaptation Illnesses caused by the body's coping with stressors, which include essential hypertension, gastric or peptic ulcers, and colitis.

Mahl's (1949) experiment shows that a psychological stressor can cause increased hydrochloric acid (HCl) secretion. He convinced eight premedical students to swallow a balloon that allowed him to measure HCl secretion. HCl levels were measured on nonstressful days and on the day of an extremely important exam determining admission to medical school. Mahl found HCl secretion much higher just prior to the exam in six of the eight students as compared to control days. The two students who did not have high HCl secretion appeared not to have been stressed by anticipation of the exam. One student had already been admitted to medical school, and the other student had only average grades and did not expect to be admitted. The results of this study demonstrate that psychological stressors can increase HCl secretion.

In a study that revealed a link between stressors and ulcers, Sawrey, Conger, and Turrell (1956) required hungry rats to cross a grid floor that delivered a shock in order to receive food. These rats experienced conflict: according to our definition on **p. 373**, the conflicting motives were hunger and fear of shock. In order to isolate the effect of conflict, the researchers used a number of controls: (1) some hungry animals were shocked at a time other than when food was presented, so their two motives (hunger, fear of shock) did not conflict; (2) others were shocked after they had been fed, so they were not hungry when they were shocked; (3) another group received no shock when they were hungry; and (4) still other rats received no shock at all. Sawrey, Conger, and Turrell found that although both the shock and hunger stressors led to ulcers, rats that experienced conflict had the most severe ulcers.

Weiss (1968) suggested that the inability to control stress is a major cause of ulcers. To examine the influence of control, Weiss delivered shocks to two groups of monkeys. One group could escape shock by jumping onto a platform; the other group could not control the shock, which terminated independently of their behavior. Monkeys in the noncontrol shock condition group received the same number of shocks for the same amount of time as did the monkeys in the control shock condition group. Weiss discovered that monkeys unable to control shock developed ulcers, whereas those in control (able to escape shock) did not.

Wait a minute! If the rats in the Sawrey, Conger, and Turrell study had control over whether they received the shock (they could have gone hungry), why did they develop ulcers, whereas the monkeys in the Weiss study who had control did not develop ulcers? Gray (1972) suggested that the most severe ulcers developed in the Sawrey, Conger, and Turrell study because the conflict over both motives (hunger and shock) is greater than over just one of the motives (hunger or shock). It also is likely that perceived control is less in conflict than in nonconflict situations.

Before You Go On

Phillip, Darla, and the girls are finally sitting down to dinner when Jamie knocks her glass over, spilling the milk and breaking the glass. Darla perceives this as a stressor. Describe a possible pattern of biological reactions, using the three stages of the general adaptation response.

Explain how stress might cause Darla to develop an ulcer.

How Do you Cope with Stressors?

Experiencing stress is part of our lives. As students, your exams provide frequent stressful experiences. Although some of you may develop symptoms of a physical illness as a result of taking exams, most of you will not. Why do some people develop stress-related illnesses and others do not? Evidence indicates that different people respond differently to the same stressor. Some people have an intense alarm reaction to a stressor that causes only a low or moderate physiological reaction in others. These responsivity differences influence disease development; the more we respond physiologically to a stressor, the more apt we are to develop a stress-related illness. We next examine the evidence supporting the idea that how we respond to a stressor influences our susceptibility to disease.

Type A Behavior Pattern

You have a paper due tomorrow. You have worked hard for the past several weeks but have not completed the project. Because you really need a good grade, you plan on staying up all night to finish. A friend calls to ask you a question. Annoyed by the call, you snap at your friend not to bother you until after tomorrow and hang up on her. You will probably later regret having been so abrupt, but you need to get the paper done. ■

Why were you so tense about the paper and so rude to your friend? If you acted in this manner, you are exhibiting some aspects of the type A behavior pattern.

Two California cardiologists, Meyer Friedman and Ray Rosenman (Friedman & Rosenman, 1974), noted that many of their cardiac patients were very impatient. Looking closely at these patients, Friedman and Rosenman also observed that they showed an excessive competitive drive, high aggressiveness, and an intense sense of time urgency. Friedman and Rosenman called this set of characteristics the **type A behavior pattern**. You were probably tense about the paper due to your sense of time urgency, and rude to your friend because of your annoyance at being interrupted. By contrast, individuals with type B behavior pattern are relatively relaxed, patient, easy going, and amicable.

Suspecting that the type A behavior pattern might be important in the development of coronary disease, Friedman and Rosenman examined 3,000 individuals over an $8\frac{1}{2}$-year period. After controlling for (or taking into account) risk factors such as obesity, smoking, and hypertension, they reported that those with type A behavior pattern were twice as likely to have a heart attack as type Bs (see **Figure 12.15**).

Other researchers have found the type A behavior pattern to be related to coronary disease. For example, type As show more severe narrowing of coronary arteries than type Bs (Blumenthal et al., 1978). Dembroski and colleagues (1985) noted that people with type A behavior pattern have enhanced coronary arteriosclerosis (thickening and hardening of the arteries of the heart). Based on a number of research findings, a review panel of the National Heart, Lung, and Blood Institute concluded that the type A behavior pattern is significantly associated with an increased risk of heart disease (Cooper, Detrie, & Weiss, 1981).

Why are type As at greater risk for coronary disease? The answer to this question begins with the fact that type As are significantly more reactive to stressors than type Bs (Krantz & Manuck, 1984). In one important study, Dembroski, MacDougall, and Shields (1977) showed that people with type A behavior pattern showed higher heart rate and increased blood pressure during a task that measured reaction times to visually presented stimuli than type B subjects. Friedman, Byers, Diamant, and Rosenman (1975) reported that, when exposed to a challenging task, type As displayed higher norepinephrine levels. Lyness (1993) found that when challenged or threatened with a loss of control, type As show significantly higher pulse rates and blood pressure, which are both indications of sympathetic nervous system activation. By contrast, Lyness observed no differences between type As and Bs in situations than are neither challenging nor threatening.

Glass (1977) suggested that this greater stressor-induced release of norepinephrine in type As plays an important role in the development of coronary disease. Several studies (Eliot 1979; Haft, 1974) demonstrate that norepinephrine release can accelerate arterial damage, enhance thrombus (blood clot) formation, and produce cardiac arrhythmias, providing strong support for Glass's view. Further, Hicks, Kilcourse, and Sinnott (1983) found that type As smoke more, sleep less, and drink more caffeinated drinks than do type Bs. Unfortunately, all of the above behaviors are associated with increased risk of coronary disease.

You might wonder why all people with type A behavior do not develop coronary disease, and why people without type A behavior do develop coronary disease. In fact, some studies (Houston & Snyder, 1988; Matthews & Haynes, 1986) have not found type A behavior pattern to be a risk factor in coronary disease. Some of the inconsistencies may result from the difficulty of identifying people with type A behavior pattern (Dimsdale, 1988). Not all people show extreme levels of all of the behaviors associated with the type A behavior pattern. For example, a person can be easygoing yet competitive. The fact that physiological and psychological differences between type As and type Bs do not occur in all situations is a second

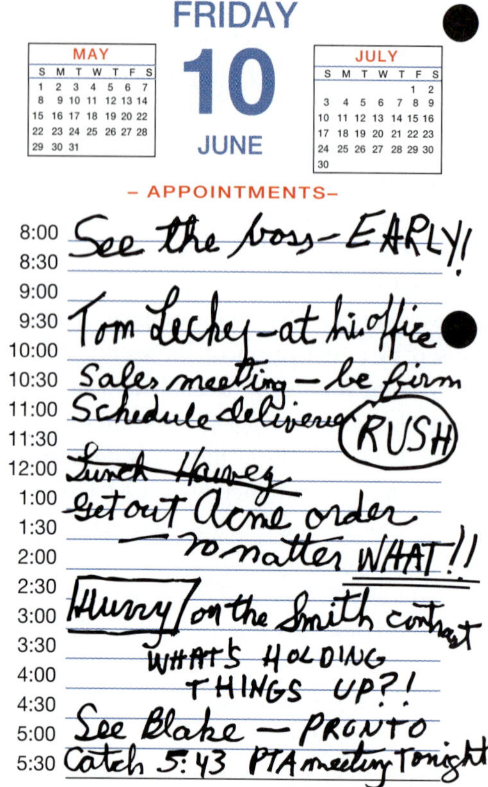

Figure 12.15 Type A behavior pattern. Type A people are very impatient and experience an extreme sense of time urgency. These feelings can be vividly seen in the June 10 page of the appointment book shown above. The owner of the appointment book died of a heart attack several days later.

➤ *In addition to impatience and an intense sense of time urgency, what behaviors do type As exhibit? (p. 377)*

type A behavior pattern A set of behaviors that includes an excessive competitive drive, high aggressiveness, and an intense sense of time urgency.

possible explanation. Glass (1977) reported that his subjects showed the type A behavior pattern (competitiveness, impatience, and hostility) and extreme physiological responsivity only when given a challenging task or when exposed to an uncontrollable stressor. In nonstressful circumstances, he found no differences between the two types of individuals.

A final factor producing inconsistent results is that, as we have already learned, exposure to intense and prolonged stressors can lead to disease. Many individuals with coronary disease who do not show type A behavior may have experienced extremely stressful events for prolonged periods of time.

A number of investigators (Jiang et al., 1996; Miller et al., 1996; Williams, 1989, 1993) have suggested that quick-tempered anger may be the critical aspect of the type A behavior pattern causing coronary disease. These studies showed a high correlation between anger and heart disease. In one study (Williams, 1989), Duke University law students were followed over a 25-year period. Those who reacted with anger to even little things were five times as likely to die by middle age than their less-anger-prone classmates. In fact, Dembroski and colleagues (1985) reported that the potential for hostility or suppressed anger was the only attribute of type A behavior pattern that was related to coronary disease. Many researchers (Jiang et al., 1996; Miller et al., 1996) now believe that the hostility and anger associated with type A behavior pattern is the single most important risk factor for coronary disease.

So people differ in terms of their responsivity to stressors, and the potential for hostility makes people susceptible to coronary disease. Yet, there are many people who, despite being exposed to extreme stressors, cope well both behaviorally and biologically. Why are some people able to thrive in the face of aversive events?

The Concept of Hardiness. The concept of **hardiness** may explain why some individuals thrive despite being raised in extremely dysfunctional circumstances, whereas others fail, even in the most advantageous environments. According to Suzanne Kobasa and her colleagues (Kobasa, 1979, 1990; Kobasa, Maddi, & Zola, 1983; Kobasa et al., 1994; Oulette-Kobasa & Pucetti, 1983), hardy people are less responsive biologically to stressors than other people. Further, hardy individuals cope better with stressors than others do.

What makes hardy people react differently to stressors than nonhardy ones? A number of studies (Kobasa, 1990) indicate that hardiness reduces the negative impact of stressors. People with the trait of hardiness differ from other people in three important ways. First, hardy people show a higher level of commitment than nonhardy people. This commitment leads to greater involvement in tasks and a greater tendency to perceive these tasks as meaningful. Second, the hardy person views change as a challenge rather than a burden or threat. Finally, hardy individuals have a greater sense of control over events in their lives than other people.

These characteristics of hardiness can be seen in a study by Kobasa (1979), who studied 837 middle- and upper-level executives who worked at a large Chicago utility company. Some of these executives had become physically ill following a stressful event (for example, divorce, job transfer, death of a close friend, inferior job performance evaluation) in the previous 3-year period, whereas other executives had not become ill following the experience of comparable stressors. Kobasa found that the hardy executives (those who did not become ill after the stressor) had a strong feeling of control over life events, had a stronger sense of commitment to specific goals, and viewed job changes as a challenge rather than a threat.

Before You Go On

Is Darla a type A or a type B person? What about Phillip? What about you?

What are the three characteristics of hardiness? Do you consider yourself a hardy or nonhardy individual?

Section Review

- A stressor is an event that either strains or overwhelms our ability to adjust to our environment.
- Our biological and behavioral responses to stressors determine whether we are able to adapt to the stressful experience.
- One type of stressor, conflict, occurs when it is not possible to satisfy two or more competing motives.
- Another type of stressor, frustration, occurs when the ability to reach a goal is blocked.
- Pressure, a third type of stressor, is experienced when a person is expected to behave in a particular way within a particular time frame.
- According to Selye, the general adaptation syndrome is a pattern of internal changes (alarm reaction, stage of resistance, stage of exhaustion) that occurs when we are exposed to a physiological or psychological stressor.

hardiness An ability to cope effectively with stressors due to a high level of commitment, a perception that change is a challenge rather than a burden or threat, and a sense of control over events.

- The alarm reaction, the first stage of the general adaptation syndrome, consists of cortical arousal, produced by stimulation of the reticular activating system, and activation of the sympathetic nervous system, mobilizing our resources and allowing us to cope behaviorally with stressful experiences.
- The alarm stage lasts for several minutes to several hours, and stops if our experience of the stressor stops.
- When the stressor ends, the parasympathetic nervous system becomes dominant, enabling us to restore our biological reserves to prestressor levels.
- If the stressor continues, we enter the stage of resistance, in which high levels of glucocorticoid hormones are released by the adrenal cortex, providing the energy needed to cope with long-term stressors.
- Our inflammatory system is also suppressed by the release of glucocorticoid hormones in the stage of resistance, reducing the body's ability to defend against stressors.
- Exposure to a new stressor at the resistance stage can cause disease that would not have occurred if the body had not already been coping with the first stressor.
- If the stressor continues indefinitely, the body's resources eventually will be depleted, and the stage of exhaustion begins, which may eventually lead to death.
- Our reaction to stress can lead to diseases of adaptation, including essential hypertension, ulcers, and colitis.
- People with a set of characteristics called type A behavior pattern show an excessive competitive drive, high aggressiveness, great impatience, and an intense sense of time urgency, as well as a stronger biological reaction to stressors than do individuals with type B behavior patterns.
- One aspect of the type A behavior pattern, the potential for hostility, has been associated with a heightened susceptibility to heart disease.
- Hardiness is the ability to cope effectively with stressful events.
- According to Kobasa, hardy persons are better able to cope with stressors, because they show a higher level of commitment to goals, view change as a challenge rather than a threat, and have a greater sense of control over events in their lives.

cognitive appraisal A procedure to evaluate cognitively the impact of an event by determining whether a stressor represents a serious threat to your well-being, an interesting new challenge, or little or no threat.

stress inoculation A procedure designed to alter the cognitive appraisal process by recognizing situations that are stressful, linking the behavioral responses to the situations, understanding that reactions to stressors are determined by the appraisal of the situation, and then learning new ways to appraise the situation.

APPLICATION

Management of the Stress Response

Is there any way to modify our response to stressors to avoid the negative physical and psychological consequences? Fortunately, the answer is yes. There are a number of methods available to reduce stress responses to acceptable levels (Rosenthal & Rosenthal, 1985; Woolfolk & Lehrer, 1984). Some of these methods directly antagonize the stress responses, and others decrease the perceived aversiveness of stressful experiences. The use of these procedures by stress-sensitive people can reduce susceptibility to physical or psychological disease or to curtail disease that has already developed. We end the chapter by examining in some detail one successful method of stress management.

Richard Lazarus (Lazarus, 1993; Lazarus & Lazarus, 1994) suggested that exposure to a stressor causes people to evaluate cognitively the impact of the event on their life. Lazarus called this evaluation **cognitive appraisal**. Cognitive appraisal can either increase or decrease reactions to stressors.

Lazarus suggested that there are two stages in the cognitive appraisal process. The first stage is an evaluation of the degree to which environmental events represent a threat or challenge (see **Figure 12.16**). Lazarus called this stage primary appraisal. Primary appraisal could indicate that a stressor represents (a) a serious threat to an individual's well-being, (b) an interesting new challenge, or (c) little or no threat. Lazarus has shown that the physiological reaction to an event can either be intensified (if the event is viewed as more threatening) or reduced (if the event is viewed as less threatening) by the cognitive appraisal process.

After determining whether the stressor represents a challenge or threat, people then evaluate their ability to respond to the situation. In this stage of cognitive appraisal, called secondary appraisal, people determine whether they have the resources to cope with the stressor. They try the coping method determined by the secondary appraisal process and evaluate its success. The success of both primary and secondary appraisal determines the strength or intensity of the stress response. Failure to adapt to the stressor may lead either to additional attempts to cope with the stressor or to withdrawal from it.

Can people learn to alter the steps of the cognitive appraisal process so that they can cope more effectively with stressors? Donald Meichenbaum (1985) developed a three-stage procedure that modifies a person's cognitive appraisal process and enhances the ability to cope with stress, which he calls **stress inoculation**. In stage one, called the educational stage, the person learns to recog-

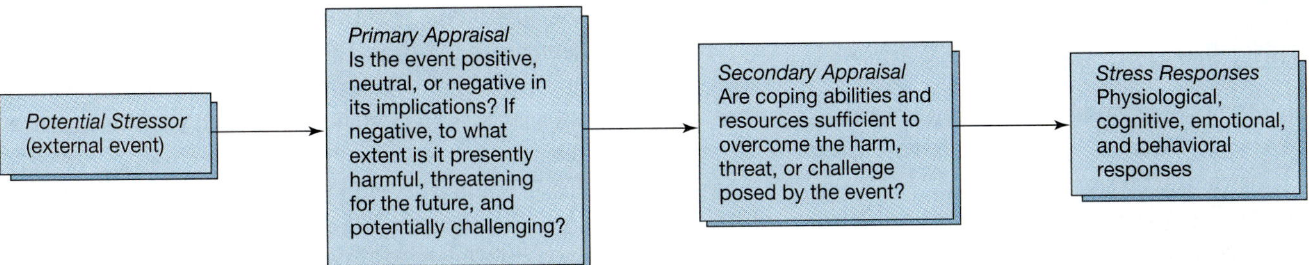

Figure 12.16 The cognitive appraisal process. According to Lazarus, exposure to a stressful event leads the individual to evaluate whether the stressor represents a threat or a challenge (primary appraisal). After the primary appraisal stage, the person determines whether he or she has the capacity to cope with the stressor (secondary appraisal). Following the evaluation of the stressor, the individual responds biologically and psychologically to the event.

From Kolb & Whishaw, 1996.

➤ *What is stress inoculation? (p. 380–381)*

nize situations that are stressful and to link their behavioral responses to the situations. For example, an individual could learn that violent actions follow criticism by another person. The educational stage also involves learning that reactions to stressors are determined by the appraisal of the situation. In our example, the individual would discover that criticism is appraised as a threat to self-esteem and that attack has been developed as a coping response to that threat. In the last part of the educational stage, the individual learns new ways to appraise the situation, called cognitive reappraisal. In our example, the individual could learn to view criticism as a constructive attempt to help rather than as an attack on self-esteem.

The second stage of stress inoculation involves rehearsal. In this stage, the individual practices the new ways of appraising the situation (cognitive reappraisals) by verbalizing them. Some examples of phrases designed to reduce the physiological reaction to stressors include "I can work out a plan to handle this" or "It's not worth it to get so angry." The rehearsal stage also involves practicing muscle relaxation to reduce physiological arousal.

In the application stage, cognitive reappraisals are used in actual stressful situations. **Table 12.3** presents some examples of cognitive reappraisals, called coping self-statements, that can be used before, during, and after stressful experiences.

Stress inoculation has proven to be quite successful. Novaco (1985) reported that appraising irritating situations constructively rather than becoming angry or violent significantly reduced physiological reactions to the stressful events. Similarly, Meichenbaum (1977) reported that anxious people can cope effectively with frightening situations by developing adaptive coping self-statements to be used when confronted by these events. In a recent application of stress inoculation training, Ross and Berger (1996) found that stress inoculation reduced the pain experienced by athletes during rehabilitation following knee surgery. ■

Table 12.3 ■ Examples of Coping Self-Statements

Preparation
I can develop a plan to deal with it.
Just think about what I can do about it. That's better than getting anxious.
No negative self-statements, just think rationally.
Confrontation
One step at a time; I can handle this situation.
This anxiety is what the doctor said I would feel; it's a reminder to use my coping exercises.
Relax; I'm in control. Take a slow deep breath. Ah, good.
Coping
When fear comes, just pause.
Keep focus on the present; what is it I have to do?
Don't try to eliminate fear totally; just keep it manageable.
It's not the worst thing that can happen.
Just think about something else.
Self-reinforcement
It worked; I was able to do it.
It wasn't as bad as I expected.
I'm really pleased with the progress I'm making.

From: Meichenbaum, D. H. (1977). *Cognitive behavior modification: An integrative approach*. New York: Plenum.

Before You Go On

Phillip announces that unless Darla gets some help he wants a divorce. Create a scenario describing her response to this potential stressor, using the steps of the cognitive appraisal process.

Section Review

- Cognitive appraisal, the evaluation of the impact of an event, can either increase or decrease a person's physiological reaction to a stressor.
- The first stage of cognitive appraisal, primary appraisal, involves determining whether a stressor is a challenge or a threat.
- The second stage of cognitive appraisal, secondary appraisal, involves determining whether personal resources are adequate to cope with the stressor.
- The application of both primary and secondary appraisal determined the strength of the stress response.
- Stress inoculation is a three-stage procedure designed to enhance a person's ability to respond positively to stressors.
- The educational stage involves the recognition of stressors, identification of behavioral responses used to cope with stressful events, and cognitive reappraisal.
- Cognitive reappraisals are practiced in the rehearsal stage.
- In the application stage, cognitive reappraisals are applied to real-life situations.

Chapter Review

Critical Thinking Questions

1. Joan has just ended a long-term dating relationship. She is feeling quite sad and cannot stop crying. Explain the basis of Joan's emotional response to the end of this relationship using the three theories of emotion (James-Lange, Cannon-Bard, Schachter).
2. It has been several months and Joan is still quite upset. What physiological changes might have taken place over the last few months? What are the dangers if Joan is continued to be troubled by the end of the dating relationship? How might Joan cope better with this situation?
3. Joan has just learned that her ex-boyfriend is currently dating her best friend. What emotions might this knowledge produce in Joan? How might she respond to this information? What factors might cause her response to be an aggressive one?

Vocabulary Questions

1. An ________________ is a feeling that differs from an individual's normal state.
2. According to the ________________ theory, we experience visceral changes, somatic changes, and the emotional experience simultaneously.
3. The area of the brain responsible for the expression of anger and aggression is the ________________.
4. According to the ________________ theory, when we notice we are internally aroused, we will attribute our arousal to prevailing environmental conditions.
5. The most frequently observed type of aggression is ________________ aggression.
6. The ________________ and the ________________ are thought to influence aggressive behavior.
7. Aggressive behavior elicited by danger is called ________________.
8. A ________________ is any event that strains or overwhelms our ability to adjust to our environment.
9. According to Selye, diseases produced by the physiological stress response are called ________________.
10. The characteristic of the type A behavior pattern that may be critical to the development of coronary disease is ________________.
11. Stressors are perceived as a challenge rather than a threat due to ________________.
12. The cognitive evaluation of the impact of an event on one's life is called ________________.
13. Meichenbaum's method of altering the cognitive appraisal process to cope more effectively with stress is called ________________.

Review Questions

1. According to the James-Lange theory, we experience
   a. the physiological changes, then the emotion.
   b. the emotion, then the physiological changes.
   c. the physiological changes and the emotion simultaneously.
   d. differing emotional responses to stressors depending on our hardiness.
2. The major structures in the Papez circuit include the
   a. thalamus, frontal lobe, parietal lobe, and hippocampus.
   b. frontal lobe, midbrain, and brainstem.
   c. thalamus, hypothalamus, cingulate gyrus, and hippocampus.
   d. thalamus, hypothalamus, cerebellum, and amygdala.

3. According to MacLean, there are three separate circuits in the limbic system responsible for
   a. anger, worry, and euphoria.
   b. survival, pleasure, and cooperative social behaviors.
   c. anger, survival, and pleasure.
   d. anger, worry, and survival.
4. Behavior motivated by the intent to harm a living being or inanimate object is
   a. stress.
   b. anger.
   c. aggression.
   d. burnout.
5. According to Moyer's model, there are ________________ types of aggression.
   a. three
   b. six
   c. five
   d. eight
6. The hormones ________________ and ________________ are thought to stimulate aggressive behavior.
   a. testosterone; estrogen
   b. testosterone; progesterone
   c. estrogen; progesterone
   d. norepinephrine; progesterone
7. The ________________ area of the amygdala has been implicated in irritable aggression.
   a. central
   b. medial
   c. basal
   d. ventral
8. High levels of ____________ promote dominance seeking behaviours, and if ____________ levels in the amygdala are low, failure of dominance seeking behaviors produces intense aggressiveness.
   a. testosterone, dopamine
   b. estrogen, dopamine
   c. testosterone, serotonin
   d. estrogen, serotonin
9. The defensive reaction exhibited by an animal when it perceives that there is no escape is called
   a. irritable aggression.
   b. fear-induced aggression.
   c. instrumental aggression.
   d. territorial aggression.
10. The three stages of the general adaptation syndrome are
    a. the alarm reaction, the defensive reaction, and the exhaustion phase.
    b. the defensive reaction, the resistance phase, and the exhaustion phase.
    c. the defensive reaction, the resistance phase, and death.
    d. the alarm reaction, the resistance phase, and the exhaustion phase.
11. The characteristics of the type A behavior pattern are
    a. an excessive competitive drive, high aggressiveness, and an intense sense of time urgency.
    b. obsessive-compulsive behavior, instrumental aggression, and a severe response to stressors.
    c. patience, friendliness, and joie de vivre.
    d. high aggressiveness, an excessive competitive drive, and caffeine addiction.
12. A person who is less responsive biologically to stressors is said to exhibit
    a. the type B behavior pattern.
    b. hardiness.
    c. luck.
    d. stress inoculation.
13. The two stages of cognitive appraisal are
    a. primary appraisal and stress.
    b. secondary appraisal and stress.
    c. primary appraisal and post-traumatic stress disorder.
    d. primary appraisal and secondary appraisal.
14. The three stages of stress inoculation are
    a. the educational stage, rehearsal, and application.
    b. cognitive reappraisal, rehearsal, and performance.
    c. the educational stage, adjustment, and application.
    d. cognitive reappraisal, application, and rejection.

Suggested Readings

Aggleton, J. (Ed.). (1992). *The amygdala: Neurobiological aspects of emotion, memory, and mental dysfunction.* New York: Wiley-Less.

LeDoux, L. (1995). *The emotional brain.* New York: Simon & Schuster.

Moyer, K. E. (1983). The physiology of motivation: Aggression as a model. In C. James Scheirer & Anne M. Rogers (Eds.), *G. Stanley Hall Lecture Series* (Vol. 3). Washington, DC: American Psychological Association.

Stan, N. L., Leventhal, B., & Travasso, T. (Eds.). (1990). *Psychological and biological approaches to emotion.* Hillsdale, NJ: Erlbaum.

Taylor, S. (1996). *Health psychology* (3rd ed.). New York: McGraw-Hill.

13 Lateralization and Language

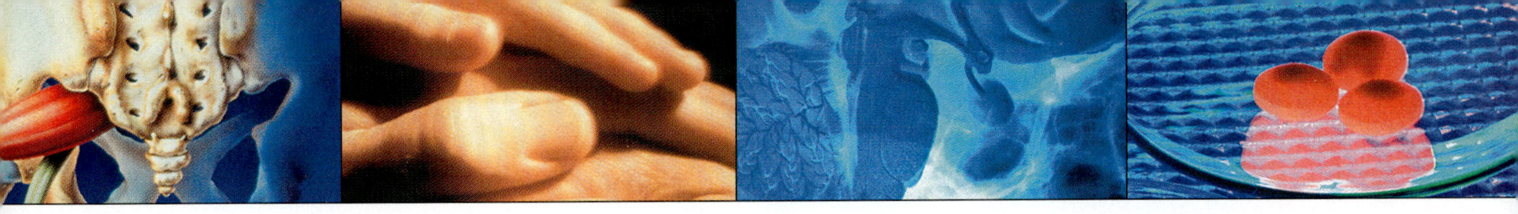

An Unexpected Stroke

John was in his room, engrossed in studying for finals, when the phone rang. John knew that something was wrong as soon as he heard his father's voice. John's grandmother, who was 74, had suffered a stroke and was in the hospital.

John was close to his grandmother, and the news of her illness was upsetting. She was expected to live, but she was paralyzed on the right side of her body and could not speak, although she seemed to understand what was said to her. Her doctor indicated that it might be weeks or even months before they knew whether the deficits would be permanent. Grandma was resting comfortably, and the doctors were hopeful that she would not suffer from another stroke.

During the next 5 days, John's thoughts turned often to his grandmother, making studying difficult. He started for home as soon as he finished his last exam, and he had plenty of time to think during the long drive. One friend had told him that his grandmother's disabilities might be permanent. Another friend, a premedical student, told him that his grandmother's stroke must have occurred on the left side of her brain; if it had occurred on the right, the left side of her body would have been paralyzed and her speech unaffected.

◀ The auditory receptors are sensitive enough to hear a pin drop to the ground.

As he neared the hospital, he wondered, would his grandmother recognize him? Would she understand him? Would she be able to speak? What awaited John behind the door to her room? ■

Before You Begin

What happened to John's grandmother's brain that impaired her movement and language abilities?

What part of her brain was damaged, and why did the injury produce these specific impairments in functioning?

In this chapter, we will help you answer these and the following questions:

- What is language?
- Is language unique to humans?
- What areas of the brain are responsible for production and understanding of language?
- What do split-brain studies show about the way in which the two cerebral hemispheres function?
- How is lateralization between hemispheres studied in humans?
- Which functions differ between the two cerebral hemispheres?
- Why does brain lateralization exist?
- What is the relationship between lateralization and handedness?
- What is aphasia? What types of aphasias exist? What are their effects?
- What is apraxia? Alexia? Agnosia? What characteristics distinguish these similiar-sounding disorders, and what do they have in common with other communicative disorders?
- What causes language disorders, and how can they be treated?

Language

Mickey and Gil, both 2 years old, are playing with bubbles on Mickey's front porch on a warm summer afternoon. Their mothers dip little plastic wands into the jar of bubble soap and blow out streams of bubbles, which the two little boys delightedly chase after and pop. Gil suddenly seizes the jar of soap, spilling it and covering both himself and the porch floor with a sticky mess.

Gil's mother takes him inside the house to clean him up. As they go, Mickey observes to his mother, "Gil spill bubboo." He then thinks for a moment before chattily adding a further comment: "Mickey no spill bubboo."

Mickey, age 2, is able to produce original sentences that clearly express his thoughts; he is also able to vary his sentences in understandable ways. He does this spontaneously, limitlessly, and continuously. What aspects of the human brain are responsible for this miraculous ability to communicate, which all normal children possess, mostly untaught? Read on to discover what is known about what may be the uniquely human ability to express ourselves using words, as well as to understand what is being said to us, even when it is expressed imperfectly (how did you know Mickey meant "bubbles"?).

What is language? When you compare Mickey's first attempts at talking to the smooth flow of words emanating from the podium in your biological psychology class, you can begin to appreciate the complexity of this form of communication we call language. **Language** is a system of words, word meanings, and rules for combining words into phrases and sentences. For example, take the sentence, *The dog bit the man.* You can understand it because you know the meanings of the individual words—*dog, bit,* and *man,* and because you understand the grammatical structure of the English language: You know that the sentence is about a dog who did something to a man. Each of the thousands of human languages has its own system for arranging sounds into meaning. Any human being can learn to communicate in any human language.

To appreciate the important role that language plays in our lives try to ask your roommate if he or she would like to go out for pizza without saying a word (and no writing!). This will make obvious the first of the three functions of language: communication of ideas. This allows people to work and play together and form social bonds. A second, less obvious function is that language facilitates the thinking process. Although thought can occur without language, the system of interrelated symbols and rules that make up language greatly enhances our ability to learn concepts and solve problems. For example, nonhuman animals can understand the structure of their environment without the use of language (Dickinson, 1989); however, our use of language allows us to have greater opportunities (going out for pizza) than are available to nonhuman animals. Third, language allows us to write down our experiences and ideas, thus helping us retain knowledge of past events as well as overcome the limitations of our memory system.

Before You Go On

What aspects of your life would be different if humans did not have language? What aspects would be the same?

language A system of words, word meanings, and rules for combining words into phrases and sentences.

The Structure of Language

Spoken language is made up of four main structural units: phonemes, morphemes, phrases, and sentences.

Phonemes. The simplest functional element of spoken language is a **phoneme**, or speech sound. For example, the word *bone* contains three phonemes: the *b* sound, the long *o* sound, and the *n* sound. The word *light* also contains three: the *l*, the long *i*, and the *t*. Each language uses a different number of phonemes. English is comprised of 45 basic sounds; languages can have as few as 15 or as many as 85 (Mills, 1980). Because different languages use different numbers of sounds, people who have learned one language often cannot discriminate between phonemes that do not exist in their language. (Written language has graphemes rather than phonemes. Graphemes are the written letters of a language that represent the sounds of a language.)

Morphemes. The smallest meaningful unit of language is a **morpheme**. A morpheme is the simplest combination of sounds, or phonemes, that has meaning. Words are examples of morphemes. So are prefixes and suffixes. For example, the word *unavailable* contains three morphemes, *un*, *avail*, and *able*.

Phrases and Sentences. Words are rarely used alone in language. Instead, we combine words into a phrase. A **phrase** is two or more related words that, when combined, express a single thought. We then put two or more phrases together to form a sentence. A **sentence** is two or more phrases that convey an assertion, question, wish, command, or exclamation. For example, the sentence *The couple bought the house* consists of two major phrases: the noun phrase *the couple* and the verb phrase *bought the house*.

Rules of Language Usage

Phonemes cannot be combined in just any order to form words, nor can words be randomly combined to form phrases or phrases randomly combined into a sentence. *Fnag* is not an English word, although all its phonemes occur in English, nor is *dog cat fish* an English phrase. Rules govern how phonemes are grouped to form words and how words are combined to form phrases and sentences. Language structure can be divided into two categories: phonology and syntax.

Phonology. Not all possible phoneme combinations are permissible in a particular language. **Phonology,** the study of the sound system of a language, prescribes how phonemes can be combined into morphemes. Each language places its own restriction on how phonemes can be combined.

Syntax. Words cannot be randomly combined into phrases or phrases into sentences. Rules of **syntax** indicate the acceptable ways that words can be combined into meaningful phrases and sentences. No speaker of Standard English would say, *Table is back on the* or *Newspaper the read I.*

Before You Go On

Write a sentence in any language in which you are fluent. Describe how the four main units of language work together to produce that sentence.

The Meaning of Language

Syntax tells us how to combine words into phrases and sentences. Syntax does not, however, tell us the meaning of these word combinations. How do we determine the meaning of a sentence? The study of **semantics**, or the linguistic analysis of the meaning of language, provides an answer. A sentence contains a "doer" (the agent) and a something or someone that is "done-to" (the object). Consider the sentence *The boy hit the ball.* In this sentence the boy, the agent, does something to the ball. How do we know that this is the meaning of the sentence? According to Bever (1970), one approach that we can use to analyze meaning is the "first-noun-phrase-did-it" strategy. Using this strategy, a sentence is assumed to be in the active voice; the first noun phrase is assumed to be the agent and the second noun phrase is assumed to be the object. In other words, the sentence means that the boy (the agent) did something to the ball (the object). This strategy works much of the time, because most of our sentences are in the active voice. Because the sentence *The boy hit the ball* is in the active voice, Bever's strategy works and the sentence is understood.

What if we change the sentence to *The ball was hit by the boy*? This sentence in the passive voice has a different syntax than the other sentence, but the same meaning. If we use the "first-noun-phrase-did-it" strategy, we would mis-

---

phoneme The simplest functional speech sound.

morpheme The smallest meaningful unit of language.

phrase A group of two or more related words that expresses a single thought.

sentence Two or more phrases that convey an assertion, question, command, wish, or exclamation.

phonology The study of the sound system that prescribes how phonemes can be combined into morphemes.

syntax The system of rules for combining the various units of speech.

semantics The meaning of language.

interpret the sentence. Fortunately, some clues indicate that a sentence is not in the active voice. For example, the words *was* and *by* indicate that the sentence is in the passive voice and therefore the "first-noun-phrase-did-it" strategy is not appropriate. Although it takes longer to understand a sentence in the passive voice (Slobin, 1966), recognizing when sentences are in the passive voice prevents us from misinterpreting these sentences.

Before You Go On

What are the two essential parts of a sentence?

Why does it take longer to understand a sentence in the passive voice than in the active voice?

An Instinctive View of Language

Noam Chomsky (1965, 1975, 1987) was impressed with how easily young children learned their native language, and presented what he called an instinctive view of human language acquisition. He described the universal sequence of language development from nonsense sounds to the generation of complex sentences and, on the basis of these observations, suggested that children are born with a language-generating mechanism that he called the **language acquisition device (LAD)**. The LAD "knows" the universal aspects of language. This knowledge allows children to readily grasp the syntax relevant to their native language. In Chomsky's view, however, this biological preparedness does not result in automatic language acquisition; a child must be exposed to language to learn it. Usually, parents eager for their child to start talking provide more than adequate exposure ("say 'ma-ma'").

Chomsky's view received a considerable amount of support during the 1960s and 1970s (Dodd & White, 1980). For example, Eric Lenneberg (1967, 1969) argued that language acquisition is an innate, species-specific characteristic and that its expression depends only on physical maturation and minimal exposure to language. According to Lenneberg, language is acquired in a fixed order and at a particular rate. Lenneberg found that nonsense jargon (lengthy, fluent speech that makes little or no sense) is always followed by one-word speech, which develops into the use of two-word structures, followed by telegraphic speech, and then the use of complex sentences. Language is acquired in the same sequence, even when maturation is abnormally delayed, as in the case of children with Down syndrome, only at a slower rate.

language acquisition device (LAD) An innate mechanism that allows children to readily grasp the syntax relevant to their native language with minimal experience.

Although only minimal exposure is necessary for language to be acquired, the earlier the experience the better. Johnson and Newport (1989) evaluated the ability of Korean and Chinese immigrants to accurately identify 276 sentences as being grammatically correct or incorrect. Each immigrant had been living in the United States for approximately 10 years. Even though the length of exposure to English was the same for all the immigrants, Johnson and Newport found that those immigrants who arrived before age 8 understood grammar as well as native speakers. The accuracy declined to approximately 80 percent when the age at immigration was 11 to 15 years and to approximately 75 percent when the age at immigration was 17 to 39 years. Although individuals who immigrate to the United States after age 8 can master basic words and how to use them, the results of Johnson and Newport's study suggests that these immigrants are unlikely to become as fluent as individuals born in the United States in producing and comprehending subtle grammatical differences.

Before You Go On

What is the significance of Chomsky's view of language acquisition? Relate this view to the age at which most students in the United States are exposed to a second language.

The Anatomy of Language

Okay, so it didn't work—after 5 minutes of playing charades, you've broken down and used language to ask your roommate to go out for pizza. After thinking about it briefly, she asks what you want on your pizza. Your question and your roommate's response are just one of many linguistic interactions that people have every day. How is your roommate able to respond to your question? She must hear and understand your words, decide on an answer, and produce that answer—all in a split second. What brain structures allow you to understand and respond to your friend's question? The following model of language organization provides us with the beginning of an answer to this question.

Norman Geschwind (1970, 1979) proposed that the comprehension of spoken language is the function of Wernicke's area (see **Figure 13.1a**) in the left hemisphere of the brain. Recall from Chapter 1 that the German physician Karl Wernicke first recognized the significance of this brain area in 1874 (see **p. 9** and **Figure 1.5**). Wernicke's area is located in the dorsal part of the left temporal lobe in the posterior superior temporal gyrus.

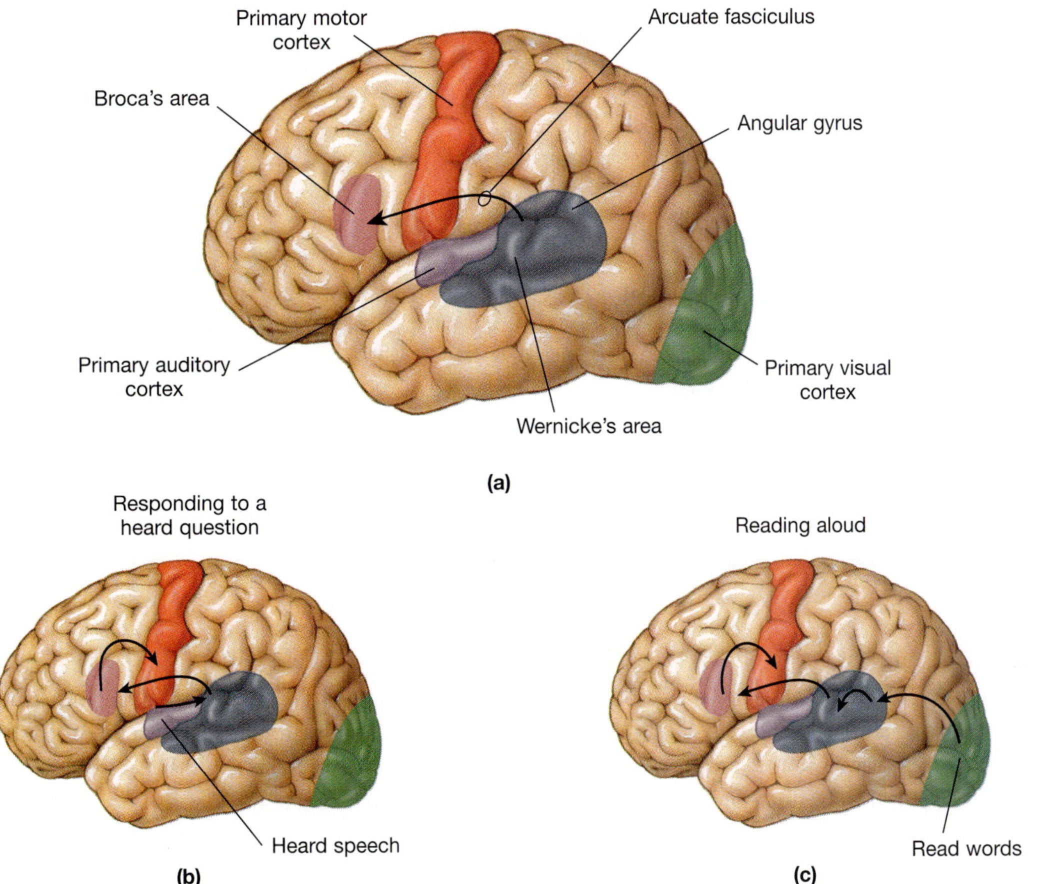

Figure 13.1 The Geschwind model of language. (a) The location of key areas in language comprehension and speech production. (b) The neural route from hearing a question to responding verbally to that question. (c) The neural route for reading a word and then reading aloud that word.
➤ *Outline the route of the visual and auditory response to reading this question aloud. (p. 386–389)*

Geschwind suggests that once the meaning of spoken language is understood, Wernicke's area generates a representation of a verbal response. This representation could be an auditory neural image of the response. The neural representation of the verbal response is then transferred to the **arcuate fasciculus**, which is a bundle of fibers that connects Wernicke's area with Broca's area (refer to **Figure 13.1b**).

Again, in Chapter 1 we alluded to the significance of Broca's area for speech as first demonstrated by the French physician, Paul Broca, in 1861 (see **pp. 8–9** and **Figure 1.5**). Broca's area is located in the left frontal area in the posterior third frontal convolution anterior to the primary motor cortex (see **Figure 13.1a**).

Language can be communicated through visual modalities (reading/writing) as well as through verbal modalities (speaking/listening). According to Geschwind's model, the secondary visual cortex and the **angular gyrus** are responsible for comprehension of the written word (see **Figure 13.1c**). Located within the parietal lobe, the angular gyrus borders the left occipital lobe and has connections to Wernicke's area. Damage to the connection between the angular gyrus and Wernicke's area has been associated with impairment in the ability to comprehend written words. This observation suggests that Wernicke's area is important for comprehension of both spoken and written language.

Before You Go On

How does the Wernicke-Geschwind theory explain language production?

arcuate fasciculus A bundle of nerve fibers that connects Wernicke's area with Broca's area.

angular gyrus An area within the parietal lobe that borders the left occipital lobe and has connections to Wernicke's area, which is involved in the comprehension of the written word.

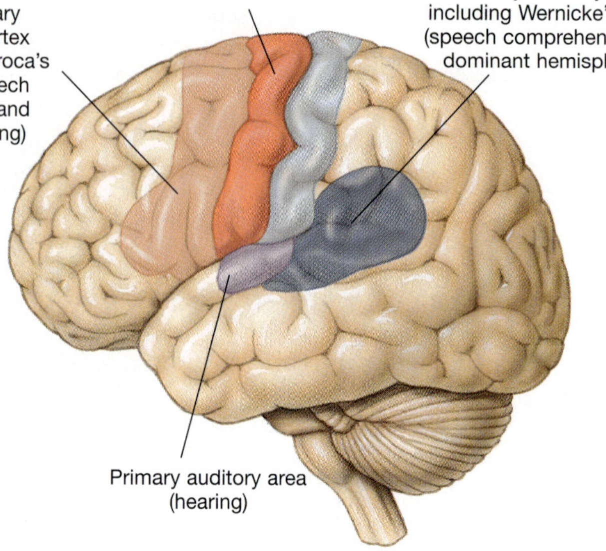

Figure 13.2 Brain structures controlling sound detection, speech comprehension, and speech planning and sequencing. Sounds are detected in the primary auditory cortex; the meaning of sounds are recognized in the secondary auditory cortex; and a verbal response is planned and sequenced in the premotor cortex, which includes Broca's area.

➤ *What is the specific role of Wernicke's area in language? (pp. 389–390)*

More recent research (Damasio, 1995; Davis, 1993) suggests that areas beyond Wernicke's area are important in the comprehension of speech. The syntactic and semantic comprehension of language is the responsibility of the secondary auditory cortex, which is located in the superior and middle temporal gyrus (including Wernicke's area) and the **temporoparietal cortex** (including the supramarginal gyrus and the angular gyrus; see **Figure 13.2**). Damage to these areas may produce what is called neologistic jargon. **Jargon** is lengthy, fluent speech that makes little or no sense, and a **neologism** is a word that is invented by the speaker. The presence of neologistic jargon in utterances following damage to the superior and middle temporal gyrus and the temporoparietal cortex points to an important role for these areas in language comprehension (Perecman & Brown, 1981).

Geschwind's model of the functions of Broca's area has also been challenged by subsequent research. Several neuroscientists (Damasio, 1995; Dronkers, Redfern, & Shapiro, 1993) argue that Broca's area alone is responsible only for the planning and sequencing of speech sounds. Damage limited to Broca's area may produce initial mutism followed by an apraxia of speech, or a great difficulty in the production of speech (Damasio, 1995). Individuals with apraxia of speech have difficulty in the selection and sequencing of speech sounds. Damage to the **premotor area**, which is anterior to the primary motor cortex and includes Broca's area, results in agrammatic (or nongrammatical) and awkward speech (Damasio, 1995; refer to **Figure 13.1a**). As we will see later in the chapter, agrammatic and awkward speech are the primary symptoms associated with Broca's aphasia (see **p. 8–9** in Chapter 1).

A child reads aloud from a book. According to Geschwind's model, Wernicke's area mediates between visual input (reading the words) and motor output (saying the words). However, more recent evidence indicates that written words processed in the visual cortex can go directly to the premotor area without first being transferred to the temporoparietal cortex for phonological analysis and the anterior inferior frontal cortex for semantic analysis (see **Figure 13.3**; Peterson et al., 1988).

There also is evidence that not all auditory input is processed using the same circuitry. Peterson and colleagues (1988) observed that spoken nonsense syllables and meaningful words are analyzed by separate pathways: a repetition response to nonsense syllables can be sent from the temporoparietal cortex directly to the premotor area, whereas a verbal response to a meaningful word requires routing from the temporoparietal cortex to the anterior inferior frontal cortex for semantic analysis prior to transfer to the premotor area (see **Figure 13.3**).

---

temporoparietal cortex An area that includes the supramarginal gyrus and the angular gyrus which is involved in the syntactic and semantic comprehension of language.

jargon Lengthy, fluent speech that makes little or no sense.

neologism A word invented by a speaker.

premotor area Area anterior to the primary motor cortex including Broca's area, damage to which results in agrammatic and awkward speech.

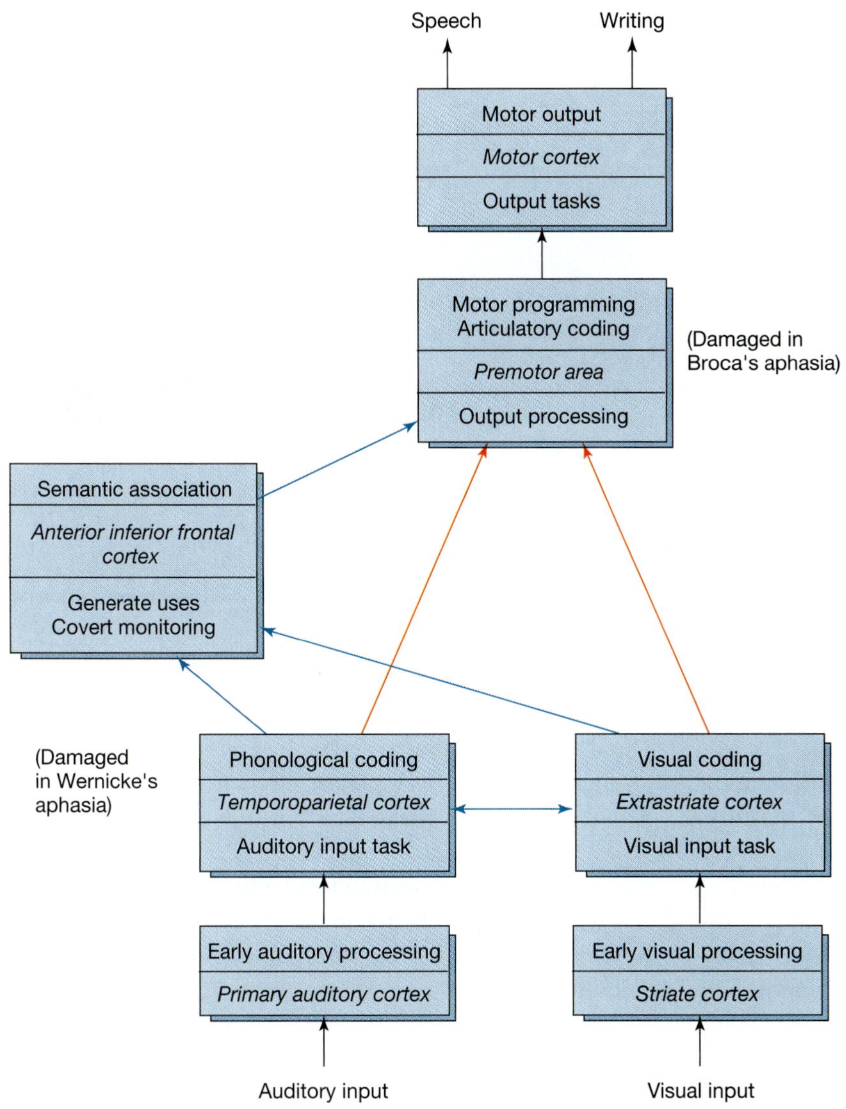

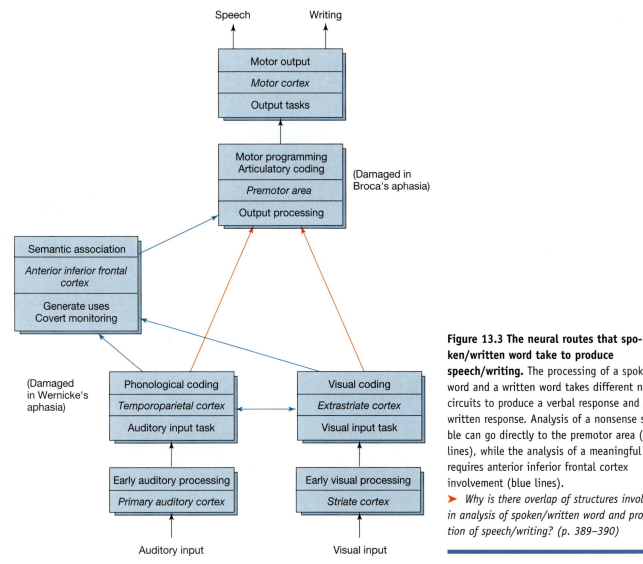

Figure 13.3 The neural routes that spoken/written word take to produce speech/writing. The processing of a spoken word and a written word takes different neural circuits to produce a verbal response and a written response. Analysis of a nonsense syllable can go directly to the premotor area (red lines), while the analysis of a meaningful word requires anterior inferior frontal cortex involvement (blue lines).

➤ *Why is there overlap of structures involved in analysis of spoken/written word and production of speech/writing? (p. 389–390)*

Before You Go On

You and your roommate go to the pizza parlor. It's crowded, and they're running short on menus, so you have to share one. You pick it up and begin reading options aloud to your roommate. Describe the path of all visual and auditory input involved, beginning with your seeing the words on the page, and ending with your roommate comprehending your spoken morphemes.

APPLICATION

Teaching Chimpanzees Language

A primate can use sounds to express a variety of different emotional states in a manner that other primates understand and to which they respond. Observations of vervet monkeys in Kenya (Seyfarth, Cheney, & Marler, 1980) reveal both the sophistication of primates' vocalizations and the reactions of other primates to these vocalizations. For example, the vervet monkeys made distinctive alarm calls when they spotted predators. The sight of a leopard caused them to emit a series of short, tonal calls. The sight of an eagle elicited a low-pitched grunt. The reaction to a snake consisted of a series of high-pitched "chutters." Each of these calls elicited a different response from vervet monkeys nearby: They ran for cover when hearing the eagle-alarm call; they looked down when hearing the snake-alarm call. These observations indicate that primates can communicate through vocalizations; however, these vocalizations are not language. Can primates learn to use language to communicate?

Early investigations suggested that primates could not learn language. Winthrop and Luella Kellogg (1933) raised the baby chimpanzee Gua in their home with their infant son, Donald. Despite many attempts to teach Gua to speak, the chimp never uttered any English words, although she did learn to obey certain commands. Cathy and Keith Hayes (1951) were somewhat more successful in teaching the chimpanzee Vicki to speak. Vicki learned to say three words—*papa, mama,* and *cup.* Yet, these words were acquired only after a long period of training, which included manipulating the chimp's lips.

Compared with the Kelloggs and the Hayes, Beatrice and Allen Gardner (1971) were much more successful in teaching language to the chimp Washoe. The Gardners believed that an intellectual impairment was not responsible for earlier failures to teach chimpanzees language; instead, they suggested that these failures were caused by the chimpanzees' physical inability to produce the complex vocalizations necessary for speech. So instead of trying to teach Washoe to speak English, they taught her American Sign Language. Washoe lived in a trailer in the Gardners' backyard and during all her waking hours had the companionship of one or two people who talked to her only in sign language. After 4 years of training, Washoe had learned over 200 signs and was able to combine them into sentences, such as *Please tickle more* or *Give me sweet drink.*

Did Washoe learn to use language to communicate? The Gardners think so. Washoe's "language" certainly seemed to have many of the characteristics of human language. First, it appeared to make sense. For example, Washoe used the sign for *cat* to point out a cat and the sign for *dog* to identify a dog. Second, Washoe's verbalizations appeared to be in sentence form. Third, sentences created by Washoe seemed to be structured according to the rules of grammar; the sentence *Please tickle more* illustrates Washoe's mastery of syntax. Finally, Washoe apparently responded to questions. For example, if the Gardners asked in sign language the question, "Who pretty?," Washoe answered, "Washoe."

Techniques other than sign language also have been used to teach primates to communicate. Duane Rumbaugh and colleagues (Rumbaugh & Gill, 1976; Savage-Rumbaugh, Rumbaugh, & Boysen, 1980) taught chimpanzees to use language with the aid of a computer. To obtain what they wanted, the chimpanzees had to press the keys that corresponded to specific words. For example, the chimpanzee Lana learned to send the following message, "Please machine make movie period." Two other chimpanzees, Austin and Sherman, even learned to communicate with each other through the computer. For example, Rumbaugh and his colleagues sometimes gave either Austin or Sherman food; the "unfed" chimpanzee had to ask the "fed" chimpanzee for food. Austin and Sherman learned to ask each other for food and for many other things.

Despite the fact that primates appear to use language to communicate, many psychologists do not believe that primates are capable of learning language. Herbert Terrace (1979), for example, teaching American Sign Language to a chimpanzee named Nim Chimpsky, noted some important differences between Nim's use of language and human language. An intense, directed effort was required to teach Nim even very simple signs, whereas children do not need to be taught language; they learn to talk simply by being in an environment where language is used. Also, Terrace found no evidence that Nim could create unique, grammatically correct sentences. According to Terrace, the chimpanzee did not learn the creative aspect of language; that is, she did not know how to use rules to create an infinite number of new and complex sentences. Instead, Terrace argued that the chimpanzee's multiword sentences merely imitated the order used by the trainer. Reviewing the transcripts of communications of Washoe and several other chimpanzees, Terrace concluded that these animals also were unable to generate syntactically correct novel combinations of signs. Terrace also noted that few of Nim's statements were spontaneous; most of them were in response to a human's statement. This lack of spontaneous speech is quite different from human speech.

Figure 13.4 Photograph of Kanzi, a bonobo chimpanzee, pressing symbols that represent specific words. Kanzi has learned to press appropriate symbols to answer a question.
➤ *Has Kanzi really learned a language? (p. 393)*

Other psychologists (Marx, 1980; Pate & Rumbaugh, 1983; Thompson & Church, 1980) have supported Terrace's view. They reported that although their chimpanzees were able to learn the meaning of many symbols, the chimps were unable to link them together into meaningful sentences. Further, Rumbaugh (1990) reported that although his chimpanzees would respond when symbols were arranged in a familiar order, the chimps were unable to respond correctly to a new order of symbols. These observations suggest that chimpanzees, unlike humans, are unable to generate or understand new linguistic units.

One might think that the research shows that no primates are able to learn language. However, more recent studies by Sue Savage-Rumbaugh and Duane Rumbaugh (Savage-Rumbaugh et al., 1992) suggests that the chimpanzee species *Pan paniscus,* also known as the pygmy chimpanzee or the bonobo chimpanzee, may be able to learn language. *Pan paniscus,* although related to the common chimpanzee species (*Pan troglodytes*), shows social behavior more typical of humans than do other chimpanzees. For example, *Pan paniscus* forms long-lasting attachments. Further, the female bonobo is sexually responsive throughout her menstrual cycle, and the male bonobo shares responsibility for infant care with its female mate. Most other chimpanzee species are promiscuous, and the females are only responsive during estrus and males contribute little to child-rearing.

The Rumbaughs first tried to teach a female bonobo, Mata, to respond by pressing symbols on a board that represented specific words. Although Mata was unable to learn to use the symbols, her infant son, Kanzi, quickly mastered the task (see **Figure 13.4**). Both Kanzi and his sister, Mulika, were able to use the symbols to request objects. They could also use the symbols to describe past events. Perhaps most important, Savage-Rumbaugh and colleagues (1992) reported that Kanzi and Mulika were able to construct new requests using original combinations of symbols. Interestingly, Kanzi also has shown an ability to understand spoken English and can respond even to original commands such as "go to the refrigerator and get out a tomato."

Why might Kanzi and Mulika have been able to master language when other chimpanzees apparently were not able to do so? Savage-Rumbaugh and colleagues (1992) suggest several reasons. First, bonobos may have better language capabilities than other chimpanzees. Yet, Kanzi and Mulika's mother was not able to learn to use the symbols. Second, Kanzi and Mulika were exposed to language early in life by observing and then imitating language. Perhaps this early observational and imitation experience promotes better language acquisition than does the formal training used with other chimpanzees. Although the behavior of Kanzi and Mulika seems to suggest that some primates can learn language, the same kind of optimism was generated by earlier research. Deacon (1996) suggests that the distinctive feature of language is not the ability to use symbols to stand for objects, but the creation of a system of symbols whose meaning lies in their relation to each other and not to any concrete reality. For example, humans can use language to imagine what could have been or what might lie in the future. Only future research will tell whether humans alone possess this use of language. ■

Before You Go On

What would be the significance of primates being able to acquire language?

Section Review

- Language is a system of words, word meanings, and the rules for combining words into phrases and sentences.
- The three functions of language are the communication of ideas, the facilitation of thought, and the recording of ideas in written form.
- Spoken language is made up of phonemes (sounds), morphemes (words), phrases, and sentences.
- Phonology is the study of the sound system of language that prescribes how phonemes can be combined into morphemes.
- Syntax dictates the acceptable ways that morphemes (words) can be combined into phrases or phrases into sentences.
- Semantics is the study of the meaning of language.
- Noam Chomsky suggested that children are born with a language-generating mechanism called the language acquisition device (LAD) and are thus instinctively prepared for the development of language skills.
- According to Geschwind's model of language production, Wernicke's area comprehends spoken language and sends a neural representation of the verbal response to the arcuate fasciculus and on to Broca's area, which is responsible for expression of a verbal response.
- Geschwind's model assumes that the secondary visual cortex and the angular gyrus are responsible for the comprehension of the written word. Input from the angular gyrus is transferred to the premotor area via Wernicke's area for a verbal response.
- More recent research shows that the secondary auditory cortex, which includes Wernicke's area and the angular gyrus, is involved in speech perception, whereas the premotor area, which includes Broca's area, is responsible for speech programming and sequencing.
- The processing of the written word begins in the angular gyrus and can be transferred directly to the premotor area for a verbal response, or to the anterior inferior frontal cortex for further analysis prior to transfer to the premotor cortex.
- Primates have been taught sign language and can use signs in sentences. Some psychologists believe that these primates communicate with language and therefore argue that language is not limited to humans. However, other psychologists believe that primates are not actually using language but are merely imitating behavior that has been reinforced by their trainers.

Hemispheric Lateralization

In the last several chapters, we have discussed such important functions as hunger, thirst, sleep, and vision as if they originated in the brain as a whole, or as if the two cerebral hemispheres were mirror images of each other. Other structures that exist in twos, such as our ears or our eyes, do indeed perform work this way.

However, as you learned in the early chapters of this text and as our chapter-opening vignette suggests, there are major differences, in both structure and function, between the two hemispheres (see Chapter 1, lateralization of function and Chapter 2, cerebral hemispheres). Severe impairments can result from damage to a part of one cerebral hemisphere, even if the other hemisphere remains intact, and numerous studies have shown that some functions differ between hemispheres in most people. One of these functions is language, which has two components: expression, more commonly in the form of speech, and perception, or understanding what is being said. This differentiation of functions is called **hemispheric lateralization**.

Recall from Chapter 2 that the cerebral cortex is divided into two hemispheres, which are connected by a series of cerebral commissures. The largest of these is the corpus

hemispheric lateralization The differentiation of functions in the right and left hemispheres.

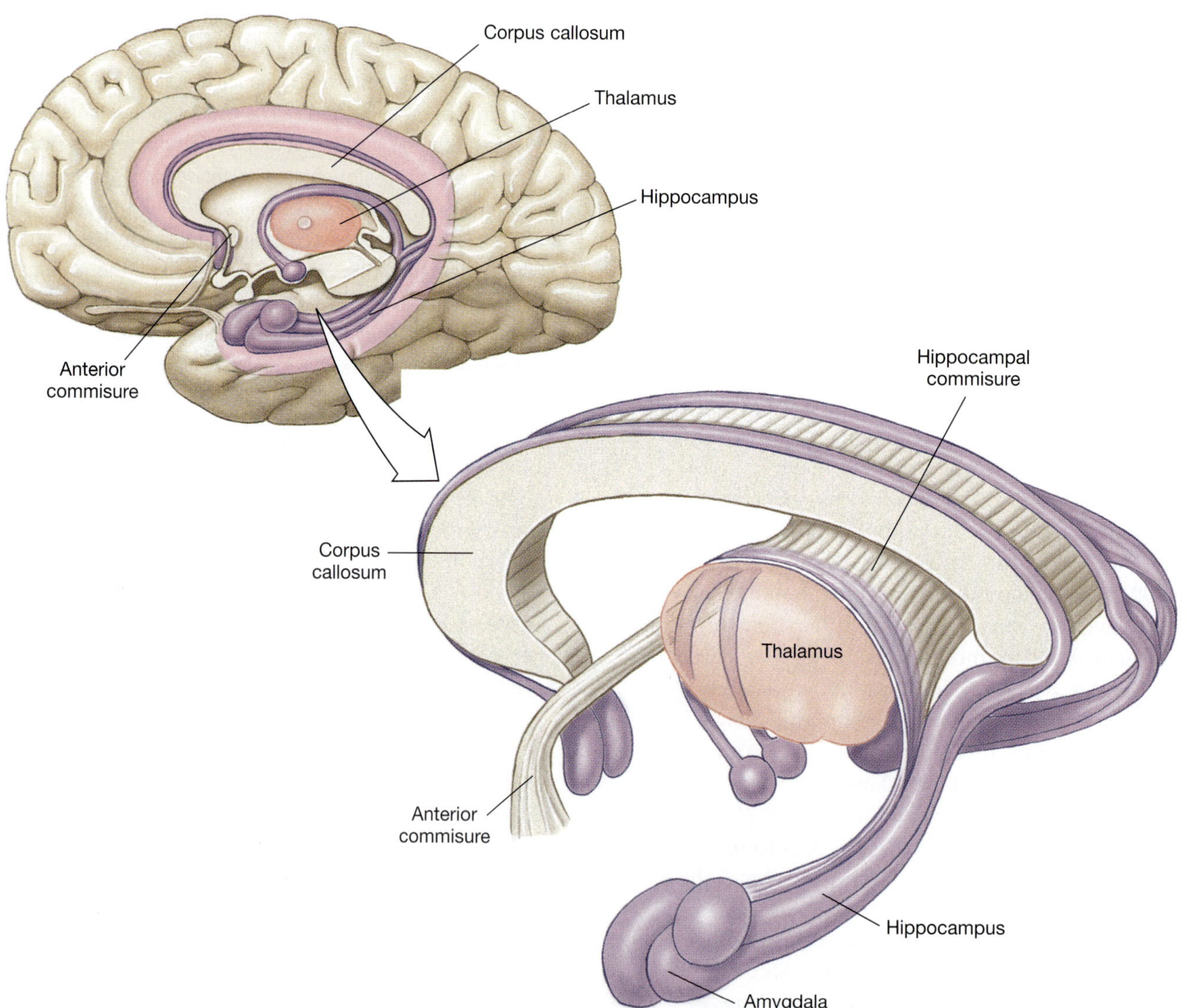

Figure 13.5 Three-dimensional illustration of the corpus callosum, anterior commissure, and hippocampal commissures. A sagittal plane view (top left) shows the location of these structures in the brain. The corpus callosum, anterior commissures, and hippocampal commissures allow information to be exchanged between the right and left hemispheres.

Adapted from Nieuwenhuys, 1988.

➤ *What is the function of the cerebral commissures? What happens if they are damaged? (pp. 394–396)* callosum (see **Figure 13.5**). The commissures are composed of the axons of neurons carrying information from one hemisphere to the other, and most information exchange between the two hemispheres takes place here. Curious as to the nature of the lateralization of function between the two cerebral hemispheres, a researcher named Roger Sperry conducted a series of experiments on cats in the 1950s in which he severed the commissures, as well as the optic chiasm, eliminating most communication between the two hemispheres. This technique, called the **split-brain preparation**, is the subject of the next section.

Split-Brain Studies in Cats

Sperry reported that "split-brain" cats, those in whom the cerebral commissures and optic chiasm had been cut, showed no evidence that information stored in one hemisphere was available to the other hemisphere. (Hippocampal commissures connecting the two hemispheres are not affected by the split-brain procedure, and they provide for some exchange of information, which we will discuss later.) Further, behaviors learned by one hemisphere could not be performed by the other hemisphere. In fact, "split-brain" animals could learn different behaviors in each hemisphere, suggesting the cats functioned as if they had two separate "brains" (Myers & Sperry, 1953, 1958; Sperry, Stamm, & Mimer, 1956). One of Sperry's studies is described next.

Myers and Sperry (1953) trained cats to perform a discrimination task between visual stimuli with a patch over one eye. (In a discrimination task, responding to one visual stimulus, such as a round light, is rewarded, whereas responding to the other visual stimulus, such as a square light, is not.) In experimental animals whose cerebral commissures and optic chiasm had been cut, the use of the patch limited visual information to one hemisphere. By contrast, despite the patch, visual information was available to both hemispheres in control animals, cats with (1) intact cerebral commissures and optic chiasm or (2) either the cerebral commissures or optic chiasm cut but not both (for a review of the optic chiasm in humans, refer to **Figure 13.6**). Myers and Sperry reported that experimental and control animals learned the visual discrimination at the same rate and to an equal level of performance (see **Figure 13.7a**). After the initial training, the patch was then switched to the other eye. Although the transfer of the patch did not affect performance in control animals, Myers and Sperry found that switching the patch had a profound effect on the performance of experimental subjects. Following the switch, the performance of experimental animals declined to a chance level (see **Figure 13.7b**). Subsequent relearning of the visual discrimination by experimental animals revealed no evidence of any prior learning: the experimental animals relearned the task at the same rate as naive subjects [compare the curves in part b (top and bottom)].

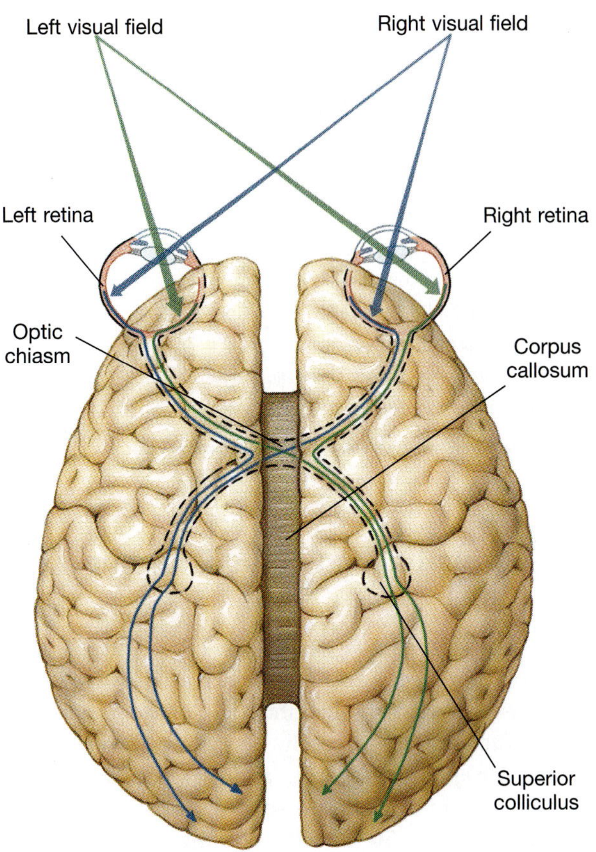

Figure 13.6 The route of visual input from the right and left visual fields to the right and left hemispheres. Input from the right (or left) visual field goes to both hemispheres when the optic chiasm is intact.

➤ *Trace the route of visual input from the right visual field to both eyes and then into the cerebral cortex. (p. 395)*

Sperry's research suggests that each hemisphere can process information independently. Sperry also was interested in extending his observations to humans. As we will see in the next section, a physician named Joseph Bogen gave him this opportunity.

Before You Go On

What was the purpose of Sperry's experiments with cats? Summarize their results.

split-brain preparation A surgical procedure that severs the cerebral commissures and the optic chiasm (only in animals), eliminating most communication between the two hemispheres.

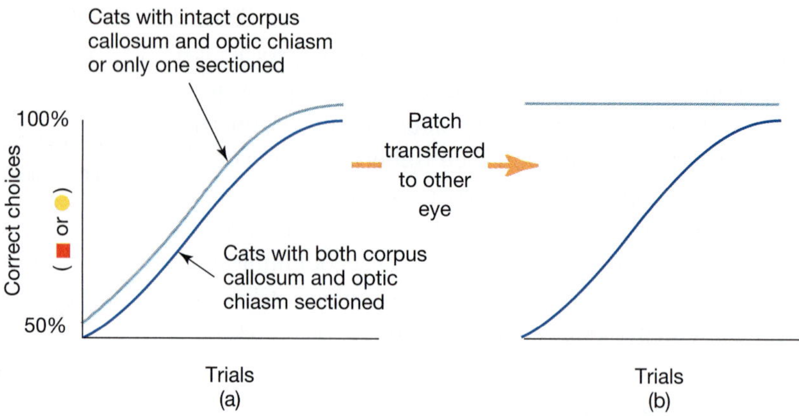

Figure 13.7 Performance on a simple visual discrimination task by subjects in Myers and Sperry's (1953) split-brain study.
(a) Experimental and control animals learned a visual discrimination task at the same rate and to an equal final performance level.
(b) Switching the patch to the other eye following training lowered performance to chance levels and led to slow reacquisition of discrimination in experimental cats but had no influence on the performance of the control animals.
➤ *How do the above results show that separate memories can be stored in each hemisphere? (p. 395)*

The Cutting of the Corpus Callosum in Humans

Sue has a seizure disorder. Before each of her seizures, she experiences a feeling of extreme dread. Then, as she enters what is called the tonic phase of a seizure, her muscles contract intensely. Her body becomes rigid; this lasts for about 15 seconds, and then she starts to jerk violently during the clonic phase of a seizure. The convulsions last for about 30 seconds, with the intensity of muscle contractions slowly diminishing. After the seizure is over, Sue usually sleeps for several hours.

Sue's seizures began when she was a young child. Her parents took her to a neurologist, who recognized her symptoms and ordered an electroencephalogram (EEG). The EEG recordings revealed abnormal activity in Sue's temporal lobes. After ruling out a tumor or other disease as the cause of the seizures, Sue's neurologist concluded that she had epilepsy and prescribed Dilantin, a central nervous system depressant that acts as an anticonvulsant. Sue has responded well to the drug, and her seizures are now fewer and far less severe. ■

In the 1960s, some of Joseph Bogen's patients were suffering from grand mal, or widespread convulsive, seizures like those described in the above vignette; unlike Sue, these patients were not helped by standard drug treatments (Bogen, 1977). EEG recordings indicated that the seizures of these patients, like all grand mal seizures, originated in a specific cortical area and then spread to the same area on the contralateral (opposite) side of the brain. As the activity continued to bounce from one hemisphere to the other, it intensified until the grand mal seizure occurred. Earlier attempts to treat epilepsy by severing sections of the corpus callosum had not produced reliable success (Van Wagenen & Herren, 1940). However, Sperry's split-brain research suggested to Bogen that disconnecting the hemispheres was worth pursuing as a treatment for severe epilepsy. Bogen reasoned that if the cerebral commissures were completely severed, then the spread of the neural activity between hemispheres would be prevented, and the intensity of the seizures would be lessened. Bogen developed a surgical procedure called a **commissurotomy**, in which the cerebral commissures are cut. Commissurotomies have been performed on over 100 individuals for whom drug therapy was not an effective option, and are indeed an effective treatment for grand mal seizures. This procedure controls the severity of seizures without seriously compromising the individual's normal functioning; Bogen reported that following surgery, his patients' emotional and intellectual functioning did not appear to be significantly impaired, a finding confirmed by Sperry's subsequent research.

commissurotomy A surgical procedure in which the cerebral commissures are cut; it is an effective treatment for grand mal seizures.

Before You Go On

How does split-brain surgery relieve seizures? What does this treatment suggest about the way the two halves of the brain work together?

Split-Brain Studies with Humans

Sperry's research (1974, 1985) using Bogen's patients suggests that the two hemispheres of the human brain do indeed have different functions: Language and analytical functions are lateralized to (located in) the left cortical hemisphere, whereas nonverbal, visual-spatial functions are lateralized to the right cortical hemisphere.

Left-Hemisphere Language Functions. Sperry studied the behavior of some of Bogen's split-brain patients to investigate hemispheric lateralization. He used a special piece of equipment called a tachistoscope to study the functioning of each hemisphere. With the tachistoscope, information can be presented very briefly (for 1 second or less) either to the right visual field or to the left visual field. (A visual field is that portion of the visual world to the right or left of the point of fixation.) You will recall from Chapter 6 that information presented to the right visual field is transmitted to the left hemisphere, whereas stimuli presented to the left visual field is transmitted to the right hemisphere (refer to **Figures 6.5** and **13.6**). (Note: Unlike the experimental animals, the optic chiasm in the human split-brain subjects remained intact.)

In Sperry's studies, the subjects were seated at a table. A partition was placed in the middle of the table so that visual stimuli were presented by the tachistoscope to only one visual field at a time. Different stimuli were then shown to split-brain subjects, who were asked to verbally identify each object. When the information was presented to the right visual field (the left hemisphere), the normal and split-brain subjects accurately and rapidly identified the object. For example, if a picture of a fork were flashed in the right visual field, the person would identify the object by saying *fork.* However, although normal subjects could verbally identify objects shown in the left visual field (the right hemisphere), split-brain subjects could not (see **Figure 13.8**). A central finding of Sperry's research was that a particular split-brain subject could verbally identify an object when it was presented in the right visual field but could not identify that same object if it was presented in the left visual field.

In an interesting variation of the above research, a split-brain subject is shown the word *heart.* The *he* part of the word is presented in the left visual field (to the right hemisphere) and the *art* part is shown in the right visual field (to the left hemisphere). What would the split-brain subject report seeing? Sperry found that a subject would verbally report seeing only the word *art* (see **Figure 13.9**).

Why did a split-brain report seeing *art,* but not *he*? The left hemisphere is more active than the right when a normal individual with intact cerebral commissures is engaged in verbal activities. For example, blood flow is greater in the left than in the right hemisphere during verbal tasks (Papanicaloau et al., 1988). Further, the increase in neural activity, as measured by an fMRI, is greater for the left hemisphere than the right when an unimpaired person is engaged in a verbal task (Roland, 1993). All of these observations suggest that the ability to name objects is a function of the left hemisphere alone and explains why John's grandmother could not speak following a stroke affecting her left hemisphere. Although the split-brain subject described in the above study could not verbalize it, he or she could point to the word *he* with the left hand; we will find out why in the next section.

Right-Hemisphere Language Functions. Sperry's research suggests that the left hemisphere controls speech functions. But what, if any, role does the right

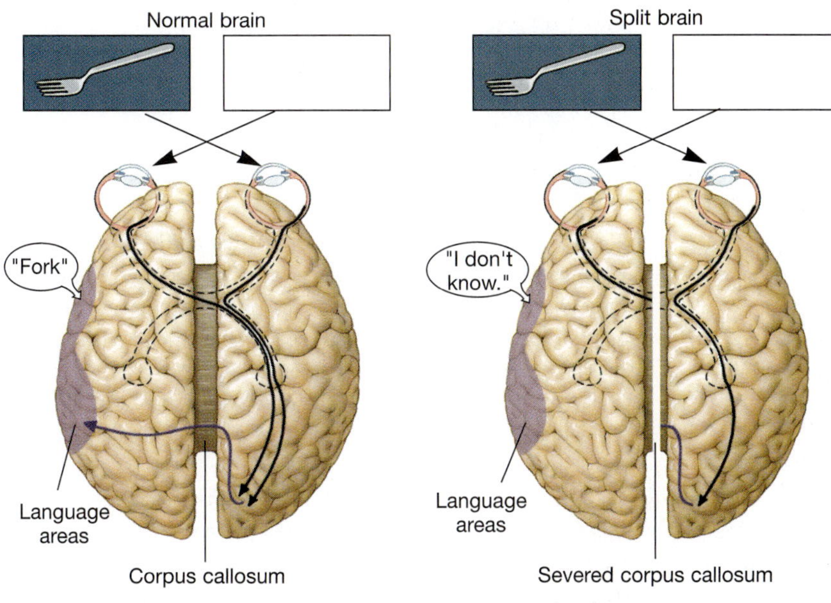

Figure 13.8 The difference between normal and split-brain patients. When a fork is presented to the left visual field of the normal subject (a), the person can verbally identify the object as a fork. However, the same object presented to the left visual field of a split-brain subject (b) cannot be identified.

➤ *Why can't the split-brain patient verbally identify the fork presented to the right hemisphere? To answer the question, trace the route of visual input in the split-brain patient.* *(p. 397)*

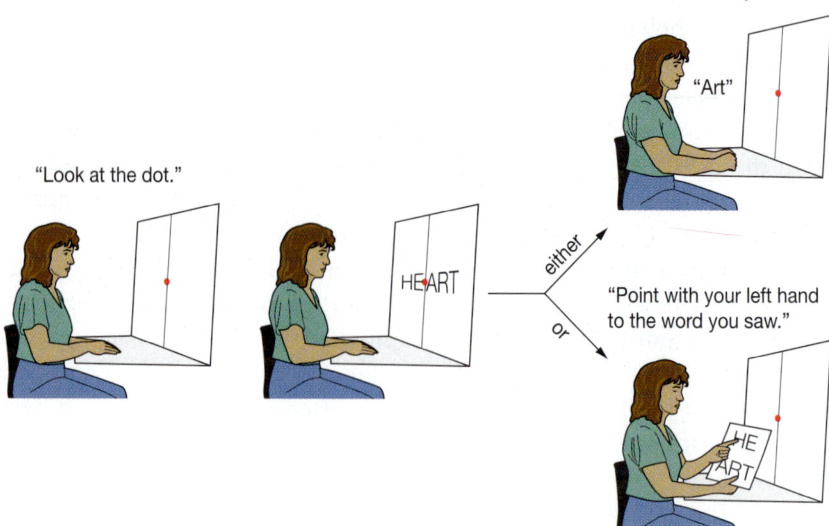

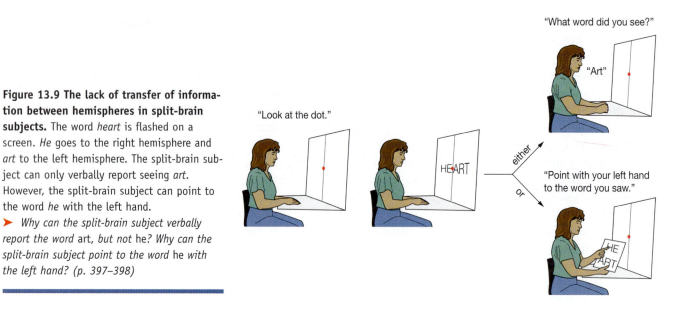

Figure 13.9 The lack of transfer of information between hemispheres in split-brain subjects. The word *heart* is flashed on a screen. *He* goes to the right hemisphere and *art* to the left hemisphere. The split-brain subject can only verbally report seeing *art*. However, the split-brain subject can point to the word *he* with the left hand.

➤ *Why can the split-brain subject verbally report the word* art, *but not* he*? Why can the split-brain subject point to the word* he *with the left hand? (p. 397–398)*

hemisphere play in language? The ever-curious Sperry and his associate, Michael Gazzaniga, conducted several studies to answer this question (Gazzaniga, 1967, 1977, 1983, 1995; Gazzaniga, LeDoux, & Wilson, 1977; Gazzaniga & Sperry, 1967). Before we proceed, recall from Chapter 8 that most axons of the lateral corticospinal tract cross over at the medulla level, so that even in split-brain patients the right hemisphere controls voluntary motor functions on the left side of the body, and the left hemisphere controls motor functions on the right side of the body.

In one experiment, Gazzaniga (1983) showed split-brain subjects a picture of a specific object (say a bolt) to either the right or the left visual field. Subjects were then asked to reach under a curtain with the left hand and select this object from among several other objects (refer to **Figure 13.10**). Gazzaniga found that split-brain subjects were able to pick out the correct object with the left hand, which is under right-hemisphere control, when the object was shown to the left visual field (right hemisphere). By contrast, when the object was shown to the right visual field (left hemisphere), the split-brain subjects were unable to pick out the object with their left hand. Interestingly, the subject could not verbally identify the object selected by the left hand and would deny that any object had been seen. These results indicate that although the right hemisphere cannot name objects, it can understand the meaning of a word. Later research suggests that the right hemisphere can comprehend vocabulary at the level of a 13-year-old child and sentence structure at the level of a 5-year-old child (Code & Rowley, 1987).

Even though it is not central to speech production, the right hemisphere does have an important function in language (Ornstein, 1997). The right hemisphere appears to influence the comprehension of subtle figurative aspects of language. In one study, Bottini and colleagues (1994) observed that the right hemisphere was active when people determine the moral of one of Aesop's fable, but was not active when superficial aspects of the fable were being judged. A similar activation of the right hemisphere was found when indi-

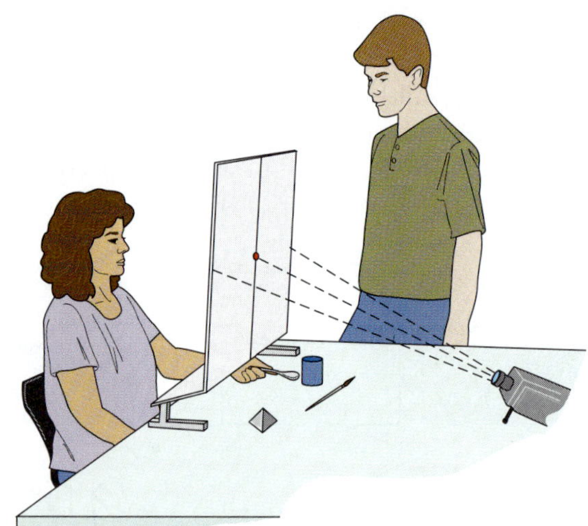

Figure 13.10 An apparatus used to test the abilities of split-brain patients. The tachistoscope presents objects to the left or to the right hemisphere. The subject's task is to reach under the screen and retrieve the object shown on the screen with either the left or the right hand. If the object is presented only to the left visual field (to the right hemisphere), the split-brain patient can select the correct object with the left hand but not with the right hand. Adapted from Gazzaniga, 1967.

➤ *Why can the split-brain patient choose the correct item with the right hand but not name the object presented to the left visual field? (p. 398)* viduals were judging metaphors (Brownell et al., 1990). Ornstein (1997) argues that without the ability to recognize the figurative aspects of language, the person with right hemisphere damage has difficulty understanding complex human discourse.

Ornstein (1997) also suggests that the right hemisphere provides an understanding of the context of language. Consider the ambiguous sentence "We saw her duck." This sentence could mean either that we saw a type of animal or we saw a person lower her head, with the meaning determined by context. Obviously, a person can recognize the words in an ambiguous sentence, but not appreciate its meaning without an appropriate frame of reference (context). People with right-hemisphere damage have difficulty recognizing context and thereby, the rich meaning of language.

The right hemisphere also governs the emotional expression of language. Shapiro and Danly (1985) found that individuals with right-hemisphere damage speak with less expression and inflection than do people without brain damage. Tucker (1981) reported that people with right-hemisphere damage have difficulty interpreting the emotional tone of other people's speech. For example, they would not be able to tell whether Sue was sad or angry when she described her experience with epilepsy.

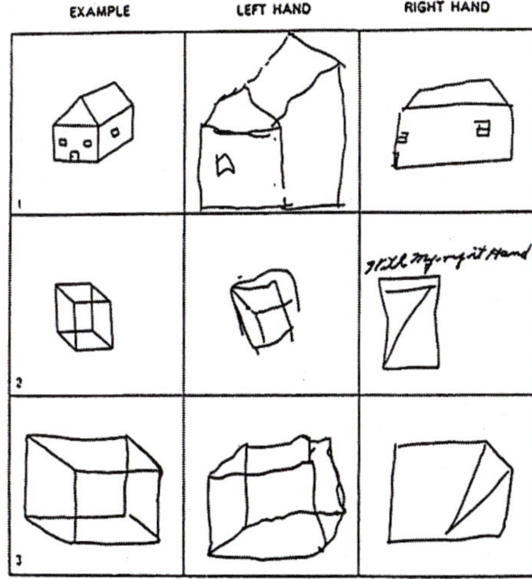

Figure 13.11 The drawings of a split-brain patient. The split-brain patient is asked to reproduce the three designs seen in the left column. When using the right hand, the split-brain patient's drawings bear little resemblance to the actual object; in contrast, the drawings made by the left hand look fairly similar to the actual objects. (The drawings were made by three right-handed persons, and artwork by the nondominant hand is less than perfect.)
➤ *Why do drawings done with their left hand by split-brain patients resemble the actual object, but not if the right hand is used? (p. 399)*

Right-Hemisphere Use of Visual-Spatial Information. As you may already have guessed, visual-spatial abilities, the coordination of visual and motor functions, appear to be lateralized in the right hemisphere. (Remember the ability of the left hand to identify objects presented to the right hemisphere?) The right hemisphere enables us to recognize and react to complex visual stimuli. Once again, the best way to evaluate this function is when it is absent. Individuals with right-hemisphere damage have trouble recognizing faces. They also have problems finding their way between physical locations in their environment.

In a study that provides further evidence for right-hemisphere control of visual-spatial activities, Gazzaniga and Sperry (1967) instructed split-brain subjects either to draw an object or to assemble blocks into a specific design. The subjects could reproduce an object or assemble blocks correctly with their left hand (right hemisphere) but not with their right hand (left hemisphere). **Figure 13.11** shows the difference in drawings produced by the right and the left hemispheres.

Jerre Levy and her colleagues (Levy, 1985; Levy, Trevarthen, & Sperry, 1972) also studied the lateralization of visual-spatial abilities. In this line of research, split-brain subjects are asked to focus on the center of a screen and are then shown a *chimeric face*, which is composed of one half of one person's face and the other half of another person's face (see **Figure 13.12a**). The split-brain subjects are then shown the two whole (nonchimeric) faces corresponding to the two halves of the chimeric face, and asked to identify the face they had previously seen. When verbally identifying the face, split-brain subjects will name the face presented to the right visual field (left hemisphere; refer to **Figure 13.12b**). By contrast, when split-brain subjects are asked to point to the face they had previously seen, they will point to the face presented to the left visual field (right hemisphere; see **Figure 13.12c**).

We learned earlier that the increase in brain activity is greater in the left hemisphere than in the right when a person with intact cerebral commissures is engaged in a verbal task. Based on what you have learned so far, which hemisphere do you think would be more active during performance of a spatial task? Roland (1993) observed a greater increase in neural activity in the right hemisphere in normal people during spatial tasks such as block design or puzzles, providing further support for the concept of hemispheric lateralization.

Other differences in function between the two hemispheres have been observed. For example, the right hemisphere is more active than the left hemisphere when

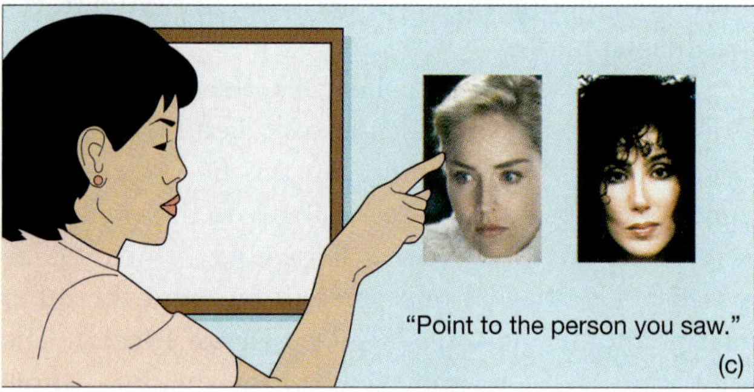

Figure 13.12 Hemispheric differentiation of the processing of visual information. A split-brain subject is shown a composite picture of two different faces (a). When asked to name the face previously seen, the split-brain subject will name the face on the right visual field (b). By contrast, when asked to point to the face seen, the split-brain subject will point to the face on the left visual field. ➤ *Why does the split-brain subject name the face presented to the right visual field, but point to the face shown to the left visual field? (p. 399)*

you listen to music (refer to **Figure 13.13**). There are many other important differences in function between the two hemispheres, too numerous to be mentioned here; see **Table 13.1** for a summary of the lateralization of function between the right and left hemispheres.

Before You Go On

Which half of your cerebral hemisphere is most active when you are reading a book? When you are looking intently at a friend's face? When you are listening to music?

Do We Have Two Brains?

Sperry's work suggests that our two cerebral hemispheres have many different functions. But do we have two brains? Sperry's own words best describe his answer to this question with regard to his split-brain patients:

> Each hemisphere . . . has its own . . . private sensations, perceptions, thoughts, and ideas, all of which are cut off from the corresponding experiences in the opposite hemisphere. Each left and right hemisphere has its own private chain of memories and learning experiences that are inaccessible to recall by the other hemisphere. In many respects each disconnected hemisphere appears to have a separate "mind of its own." (Sperry, 1974)

Thus far we have described in some detail the operation of the brain(s) in split-brain persons. But in unimpaired people the connection between them allows the two hemispheres to work together rather than independently. According to Levy (1985), the integration of the activities of the two hemispheres allows for higher mental processes than could be achieved by the two hemispheres working independently. And it is this integration that allows the expression of creativity and intelligence distinctively characteristic of humans.

The importance of hemispheric cooperation can be seen in individuals who fail to develop a corpus callosum. In most people, the corpus callosum develops during the first 5 to 10 years of life, and it is one of the last brain structures to mature. Like other central nervous system structures, the corpus callosum develops mainly through the retention of some axons and the atrophy of others (refer to the discussion of cell death and the establishment of synaptic connections during the prenatal period on **p. 85** in Chapter 3). This selection process normally results in functional neural connections between the two hemispheres. In a very few individuals, for some unknown reason, the corpus callosum fails to mature and establish synaptic connections between the two hemispheres. Observations of these people show them to be different in most respects from the split-brain subjects of the above studies (Chiarello, 1980). In contrast to split-brain patients, despite the lack of a functional corpus callosum, these individuals can verbally identify objects presented to either the right or left visual field. In all likelihood, humans are able to compensate to some extent for the lack of a corpus callosum by using other connections (anterior cerebral commissures, hippocampal commissures).

However, individuals without a developed corpus callosum do exhibit some language and motor impair-

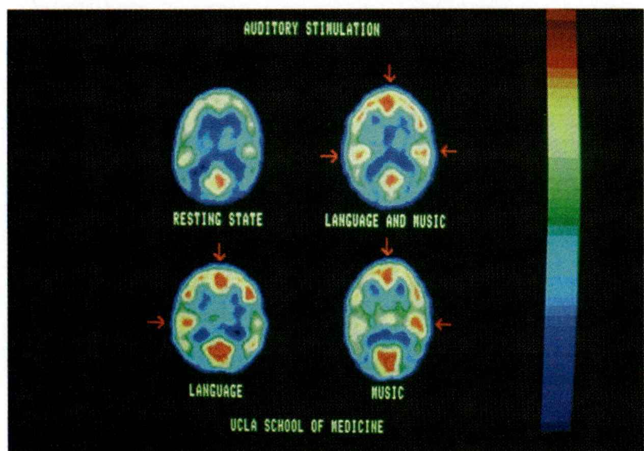

Figure 13.13 PET scans showing differences in hemispheric functioning. The left hemisphere shows more activity when language is processed, whereas the right hemisphere shows more activity when music is processed.

➤ *How do the above PET scans demonstrate hemispheric lateralization? (pp. 399–400)*

ments. For example, Sanders (1989) observed that these individuals have greater difficulty understanding passive voice sentences (e.g., the ball was hit by the bat) than normal individuals. They also tend to be slow and clumsy at motor tasks (Sauerwein et al., 1981). For example, they have difficulty coordinating their two hands to tie their shoelaces. This motor impairment may be the result of conflicting information from each hemisphere. Such conflict is resolved when the two hemispheres can readily communicate with each other.

Before You Go On

What do individuals who have not developed a corpus callosum tell us about the way the two halves of our brains work together?

Why Does Hemispheric Lateralization Exist?

We have learned that the left hemisphere is lateralized for language content and the right hemisphere is lateralized for the figurative and emotional aspects of language and visual-spatial activities. Why did hemispheric lateralization evolve?

Sperry (1985) proposed that each hemisphere controls a different type of thinking. The left hemisphere interprets experiences in a logical, analytical fashion, much as a computer processes information. It detects conspicuous features of events and interprets experiences in an orderly, sequential fashion. Language, a left-hemisphere function, is structured sequentially and lends itself to such analytical interpretation.

Sperry suggests that the right hemisphere operates in a more complex, or synthetic mode. It views experiences

Table 13.1 ■ Lateralization of Function of the Left and Right Hemispheres

Function	Left Hemisphere	Right Hemisphere
Visual system	Letters, words	Complex geometric patterns Faces
Auditory system	Language-related sounds	Nonlanguage environmental sounds Music
Somatosensory system		Tactile recognition of complex patterns Braille
Movement	Complex voluntary movement	Movements in spatial patterns
Memory	Verbal memory	Nonverbal memory
Language	Phonetic Semantic Syntactic Arithmetic	Emotional Intonation Pragmatic Prosody
Spatial processes		Geometry Sense of direction Mental rotation of shapes

Note: Functions of the respective hemispheres are predominantly mediated by one hemisphere in right-handed people.

Source: Adapted from Kolb, B., & Whishaw, I. Q. (1996). *Fundamentals of human neuropsychology* (4th ed.). New York: Freeman.

in their totality rather than interpreting isolated units, a type of thinking referred to as synthetic (from synthesize, "to combine"). For example, the right hemisphere recognizes a ball as a specific object rather than as a collection of curved lines. The Gestalt view of perception (Rock & Palmer, 1990), which argues that "the whole is different from the sum of its parts," suggests the importance of the synthetic mode of thinking.

To understand the distinction between the two modes of thinking, consider the difference between the word *cup* and the object *cup*. The word *cup* exists as three separate letters that are recognized as a word by a sequential analysis of the letters (analytical—left hemisphere). By contrast, the object *cup* cannot be broken down into its constituent elements and exists only as the stimulus configuration of a cup (synthetic—right hemisphere).

Stephen Kosslyn (1987) conducted research to evaluate the validity of Sperry's idea that each hemisphere has a different mode of thinking. Kosslyn presented a series of stimuli to the left or right visual fields of normal college students. (It is assumed that visual stimuli presented to one visual field will go more strongly to the contralateral hemisphere.) The stimuli consisted of a dot either on or off the outline of a blob. **Figure 13.14** shows four sample stimuli. There were two kinds of tasks in this study. The first task involved judging whether the dot was on or off the line. The second task involved judging whether the dot was nearer or farther than 2 millimeters from the outline of the blob. The first task requires an analytic mode of thinking to detect whether or not the dot is on the line. By contrast, the second task requires a synthetic mode of thinking to determine whether the dot is nearer or farther than 2 millimeters from the blob. Kosslyn found that judgments were more rapid for the first task (on-off line) if the stimulus was presented to the right visual field (to the left hemisphere), whereas judgments were better for the second task (distance from the line) if the visual stimulus was presented to the left visual field (to the right hemisphere).

Studies of the Japanese language provide additional evidence for different modes of thinking by the left and right hemispheres. There are two forms of Japanese written language: *Kanji*, which is based on Chinese ideographs with one symbol conveying an entire idea; and *Kana*, which is based on phonetic symbols and can be used for writing foreign words, such as scientific terms. Researchers have found that Japanese children and adults process the phonetic-based Kana in the left hemisphere and the picture-based Kanji in both the left and right hemispheres (Shibazaki, 1983; Shimada & Otsuka, 1981).

My experience has shown me that a task is sometimes accomplished more efficiently when two individuals separately do part of the work and then later combine the product of their efforts. Hellige (1993) suggests that hemispheric lateralization exists for a similar reason; that is, to allow parallel processing of information and to provide a means of hemispheric sharing of that information. For example, the left hemisphere usually is dominant for processing the phonetic, syntactic, and semantic aspects of language, whereas the right hemisphere is usually dominant for processing intonational and pragmatic aspects of language. Both aspects of language are equally important, but it is more efficient to process the different aspects of language separately, and then combine the information through the cerebral commissures that connect the two hemispheres. Thus, when we are listening to someone, the left hemisphere processes the phonetic content of the message and the right hemisphere processes the intonation of the message. Think of how many ways John could interpret the following statement by his grandmother's doctor: "She is improving." Depending on the tone of the doctor's voice, the statement could be interpreted as (a) "She is improving, but will never be the same," or (b) "She has made great progress toward a full recovery." Information from both hemispheres is required to understand what the doctor is really saying.

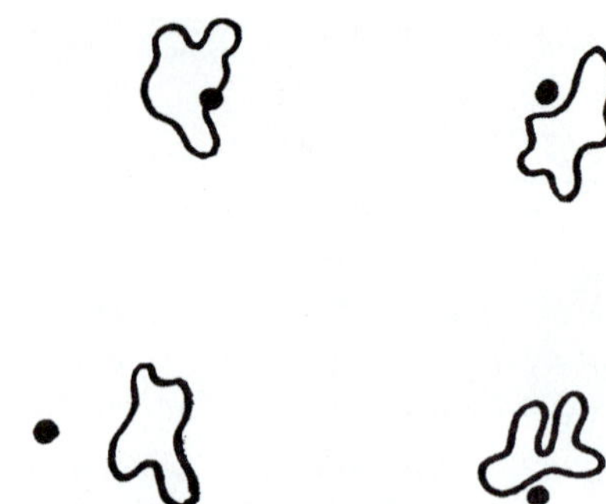

Figure 13.14 Sample of stimuli used in Kosslyn's (1987) study. The stimuli were presented to the right or the left visual field. Subjects were then asked to indicate whether the dot was on or off the line or whether the dot was more than 2 millimeters from the line.

➤ *How does this task assess synthetic versus analytic functioning? (p. 402)*

Before You Go On

What does Kosslyn's blob experiment suggest about the way each half of the brain processes information?

Handedness

So the left hemisphere is dominant for many aspects of language (phonetics, syntax, semantics) and controls motor functioning in the right side of the body. So why doesn't everyone write with their right hand? Which hemisphere is dominant for the aspects of language in the 10 percent of the population who are left-handed? Although almost all right-handed people show left hemisphere dominance for language, approximately 70 percent of left-handed people show left-hemisphere dominance (Rasmussen & Milner, 1975). The remaining left-handed individuals show either equal dominance (15 percent) or right-hemisphere dominance (15 percent).

Despite the left-hemisphere dominance for language in the majority of left-handed persons, Satz (1980) reported that damage to the right hemisphere impairs language to a greater degree than is seen in right-handed persons. This finding points to the greater right hemisphere influence in left-handed persons. The corpus callosum is approximately 10 percent thicker in left-handed than in right-handed persons (Habib et al., 1991). It is likely that the greater thickness of the corpus callosum in left-handed persons promotes more communication between hemispheres and leads to the greater influence of language by the right hemisphere seen in left-handed people.

What causes a person to be left-handed? Genetics appears to be an important factor, as left-handedness runs in families. Geschwind and Galaburda (1985) suggest that hormones as well as genetics may contribute to left-handedness. According to Geschwind and Galaburda, the higher levels of testosterone in males may delay the maturation of the left hemisphere, resulting in greater influence of language by the right hemisphere. The fact that left-handedness is more common in males than females supports Geschwind and Galaburda's view. Further, damage to the left hemisphere early in development has been associated with a shift from left-hemisphere to right-hemisphere dominance (Maratsos & Matheny, 1994). It should be noted that handedness and language are not causally related, but that similar processes affect both handedness and language.

So far we have learned that a large area of the left hemisphere, especially the temporal lobe, is involved in language comprehension and expression. But what happens when such an area is damaged? In the next section, we turn our attention to the types of communicative disorders that occur following damage to specific areas of the brain.

Before You Go On

Recall from the chapter-opening vignette that John's grandmother's stroke caused paralysis on her right side, and the loss of the ability to speak. Why can't you tell from the above information whether she is right-handed or left-handed?

Section Review

- The corpus callosum, the largest of the cerebral commissures, consists of a large number of axons that link the two cerebral hemispheres together and allow them to communicate.
- Lateralization is the differentiation of function between the two hemispheres.
- The left hemisphere processes the phonetic, syntactic, and semantic aspects of language.
- The right hemisphere interprets the intonational, emotional, and pragmatic aspects of language.
- Visual-spatial functions are controlled by the right cerebral hemisphere.
- According to Sperry, the left hemisphere interprets experiences in a logical, analytical fashion.
- Also according to Sperry, the right hemisphere operates in a more complex, synthetic mode, interpreting experiences in their totality rather than as isolated units.
- Hemispheric lateralization may exist to allow for the parallel processing of information by the two hemispheres in their different modes, and the subsequent sharing of information.
- Virtually all right-handed persons and 70 percent of left-handed persons show left-hemisphere dominance for language.
- Thirty percent of left-handed persons show either equal dominance (15 percent) or right-hemisphere dominance (15 percent).

Communicative Disorders: The Aphasias

Friday started like any other day. Ken was using the money he earned from his job at a convenience store to help pay for college. He arrived for work at 6 P.M. and was scheduled to work until midnight.

At 8:00 P.M., two young men entered the store. Most of his customers came in, got what they wanted, and left. When the young men had been wandering through the store for several minutes, he started to become concerned that they might be trying to steal something. When he approached them and asked if he could help them find something, one of the men pulled a gun and demanded all the money in the register.

When he went back behind the counter, Ken set off the silent alarm. He then took the money from the register as calmly as he could, and handed it over. The man with the gun seemed nervous and ordered Ken to lie on the floor. Suddenly, Ken heard a police siren and then several loud noises, and then every-

thing went black. He awakened in a hospital bed, in intense pain. He tried to speak, but all he could say was "pain."

Ken had been shot three times. The doctor explained to his parents that two of the bullets caused only minor damage, but the third bullet damaged an area on the front part of the left side of his brain that affects language. It was difficult to know the extent of the damage; his speech might return to normal in a few days or be impaired forever. ■

Communicative disorders are impairments in speech, hearing, and/or language. Some communicative disorders that could result from neurological damage include aphasia, an acquired impairment in the use of language; apraxia of speech, an inability to plan and sequence movements involved in speech production (see **p. 236** and Chapter 8); auditory verbal agnosia, an inability to identify spoken words but not other auditory stimuli (see **p. 205** and Chapter 7); alexia, an inability to read; and agraphia, an inability to write. (The term *dyslexia* is used to describe difficulty comprehending written language, and the term *dysgraphia* is used to describe difficulty producing written language.)

aphasia An acquired impairment of language caused by damage to the areas of the brain involved in receiving (understanding) and/or expressing (producing) language.

Ken is showing symptoms of **aphasia**, an acquired impairment of language (see Chapters 1 and 2) caused by damage to the areas of the brain involved in receiving (understanding) and/or expressing (producing) language. The impairment produced by aphasia is limited to language. The disorder of aphasia leaves nonverbal processes such as reasoning and memory intact, so a person with aphasia should be able to use nonverbal communication. For example, Ken might greet you at the door with a smile, obviously recognizing you, but not be able to say hello. People with aphasia, however, may show additional, non-language-related impairments resulting from damage to brain structures other than those controlling language.

A number of neurological disorders, such as schizophrenia and Alzheimer's disease, involve language impairments; however, the language deficits associated with these disorders are secondary to the primary characteristics of the disease, so it would be inaccurate to describe someone with schizophrenia or Alzheimer's disease as having aphasia. Aphasia differs from those other disorders in several ways (Davis, 1993). First, the language disturbances caused by aphasia are qualitatively different from the language disturbances caused by schizophrenia or Alzheimer's disease. Second, the treatments for aphasia and other disorders differ. In this chapter, we will discuss language impairments caused by aphasia; the language

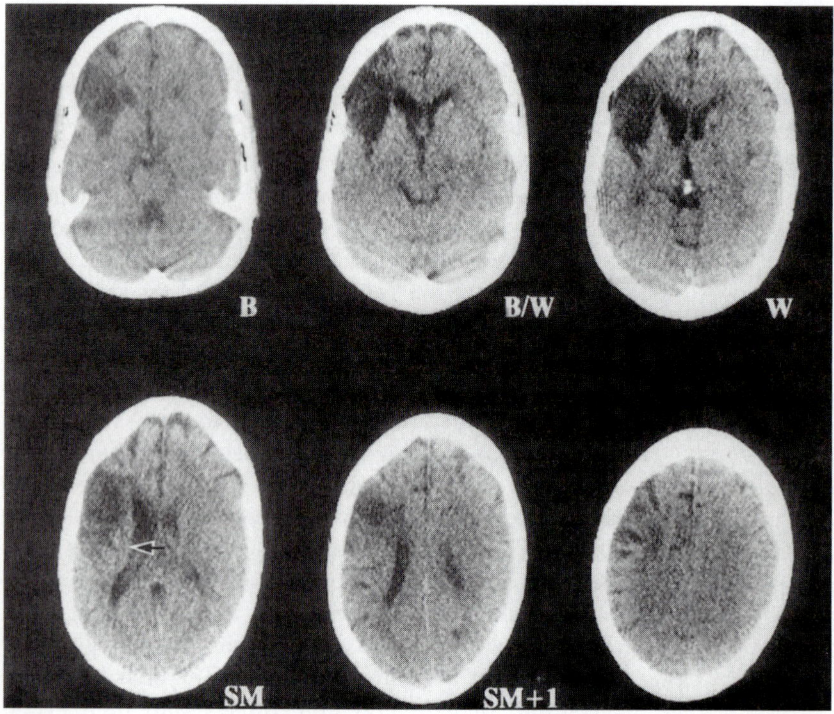

Figure 13.15 CT scans of patient with Broca's aphasia. Damage to the anterior left hemisphere can be clearly seen in the darkened area in the anterior area of the left hemisphere in the above CAT scans.

➤ *Why would damage to the anterior left hemisphere lead to Broca's aphasia? (p. 405)*

impairments caused by schizophrenia and Alzheimer's disease will be discussed in the next two chapters.

There are two major classes of aphasia: fluent aphasia and nonfluent aphasia (Davis, 1993). The major deficiencies associated with **fluent aphasia** are an inability to understand the language of others and a decreased meaningfulness of speech production. By contrast, the major deficiency associated with **nonfluent aphasia** is difficulty producing fluent, well-articulated, and self-initiated speech. There are a number of different subtypes in each category. Not only do the behaviors characteristic of each type of aphasia differ, but the site of brain damage that causes each type differs as well.

Nonfluent Aphasias

Ken suffers from nonfluent aphasia, which as we just learned is a difficulty producing fluent, well-articulated, and self-initiated speech. There are three types of nonfluent aphasias: Broca's aphasia, global aphasia, and transcortical motor aphasia.

Broca's Aphasia. Broca's aphasia is the most prevalent type of nonfluent aphasia. In 1861, Paul Broca proposed that this language disorder was caused by a lesion (or dysfunction) in the left frontal lobe area rostral to the base of the primary motor cortex (see **Figure 13.15**). The primary attribute of **Broca's aphasia** is an inability to initiate well-articulated conversational speech. Mohr (1980) referred to damage limited to Broca's area as "baby Broca's aphasia," or as we will learn later in the chapter, apraxia of speech. More widespread damage including areas adjacent to Broca's area produces "big Broca's aphasia," characterized by slow, labored, and telegraphic or **agrammatical** (speech that missing grammatical morphemes, such as articles—a, the—and verb tense endings), intonation (the melody of language), stress patterns (the emphasis on syllables and words), and misarticulation (problems in the production of speech sounds). A person with Broca's aphasia also has poor handwriting (see **Figure 13.16**); in addition, the written communication the person produces resembles his or her speech. The person also has **anomia**, or difficulty selecting the correct word for either written or spoken language. Although the individual with Broca's aphasia has extreme difficulty initiating speech that can be easily understood by others, his or her comprehension of the speech of others is relatively intact. In other words, the person with Broca's aphasia can understand the language of others but cannot communicate well.

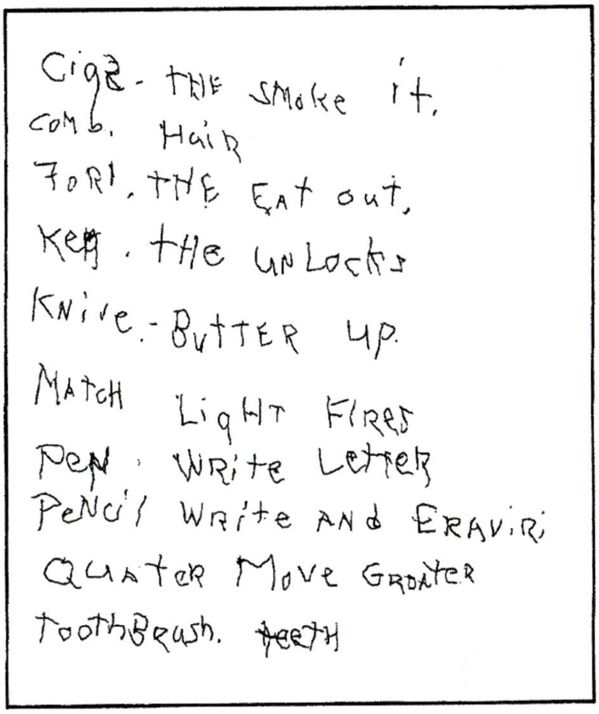

Figure 13.16 A sample of the writing from a patient with Broca's aphasia. The person with Broca's aphasia is asked to describe in writing what one does with the 10 test objects (cigarette, comb, fork, key, knife, match, pen, pencil, quarter, toothbrush). The poor handwriting and agrammatical writing can be clearly seen in this sample.

➤ *Why does a person with Broca's aphasia show similar defects in speech and writing? (p. 405)*

The following example illustrates the communication problems associated with this disorder. **Figure 13.17** is from the **Western Aphasia Battery** (Kertesz, 1982), a test used to diagnose aphasia and determine its severity.

fluent aphasia A communicative disorder characterized by an inability to understand the language of others.

nonfluent aphasia A communicative disorder characterized by great difficulty producing fluent, well-articulated, and self-initiated speech.

Broca's aphasia A communicative disorder caused by damage to the area in the left frontal lobe area rostral to the base of the primary motor cortex that produces an inability to initiate well-articulated conversational speech.

agrammatical A deficiency in grammar.

anomia A difficulty selecting the correct word for either written or spoken language.

Western Aphasia Battery A test used to diagnose aphasia and determine its severity.

Figure 13.17 Photograph from the Western Aphasia Battery. The patient is asked to describe what is happening in the picture; his or her response can be used to diagnose the presence of specific types of aphasia.

➤ *What are the primary characteristics of Broca's aphasia? (p. 405)*

When asked to describe what is going on in the picture, one patient diagnosed with Broca's aphasia gave the following verbal response:

> Ah ______ ah ______ picnic ______ ah ______ ah [pikae], [pukae], hamburgers, girl, boy [rikacksin] up period. Uh ______ uh interest book uh man period. Uh / [tirmad] / coke girl period. Man uh [Kot] book period. Ah ______ fishing good period. Uh ______ nice flag. Uh trees uh excellent period. Uh house uh house uh house fine fine house. Car separate. Waving sailboat ah ah [sud], [sudei] sailboat period. That's all. (From an interview by Byrne, 1987)

It is quite obvious from this language sample that the patient is having an extremely difficult time communicating her thoughts. This individual had suffered a stroke that left her with a severe language disorder. Prior to her stroke, she had been able to speak fluently.

Global Aphasia. People suffering from **global aphasia** experience a severe depression of all language functioning. They demonstrate poor speech comprehension and have difficulty repeating words or remembering names. Speech may be limited to a jargon (nonsense) phrase that is repeated in all contexts or to a phrase that is used in an inappropriate way. Words are rarely used in a functional or meaningful way. The limited functional speech does not mean that people with global aphasia cannot communicate at all; they can, for example, communicate their feelings and wishes to others through facial, vocal, or other physical gestures.

In addition to an inability to produce meaningful language, people with global aphasia do not understand the language of others. The characteristics of global aphasia suggest that damage extends beyond Broca's area. In fact, global aphasia occurs as a result of both anterior (including Broca's area) and posterior (including Wernicke's area) lesions. Although the person with global aphasia cannot understand language, the limited speech is why global aphasia is categorized as a nonfluent aphasia.

Transcortical Motor Aphasia. The person with **transcortical motor aphasia** usually does not initiate speech and often must be strongly encouraged to speak. When the person does speak, his or her speech is nonfluent and usually agrammatical. Utterances typically consist of only one or two words, and complete sentences are very rare. In contrast to the sparseness of self-initiated speech, the person with transcortical motor aphasia can fluently repeat long and complex sentences. Like the person with Broca's aphasia, the person with transcortical motor aphasia has relatively good language comprehension. Transcortical motor aphasia is caused by damage to the premotor cortical areas anterior and superior to Broca's area. The relatively intact language comprehension reflects the lack of damage to the arcuate fasciculus and Wernicke's area.

Although the other characteristics differ, the fluency of speech production is impaired in all three types of aphasia we have just described. We next examine fluent aphasias, those in which there is no impairment in the fluency of speech production.

global aphasia A communicative disorder characterized by severe depression of all language functioning due to damage to both anterior (including Broca's area) and posterior (including Wernicke's area) language areas.

transcortical motor aphasia A communicative disorder caused by damage to the premotor cortical areas anterior and superior to Broca's area that causes sparse self-initiated speech.

Before You Go On

What characteristics do all the nonfluent aphasias have in common? In what general ways do they differ?

How could a patient with a nonfluent aphasia communicate?

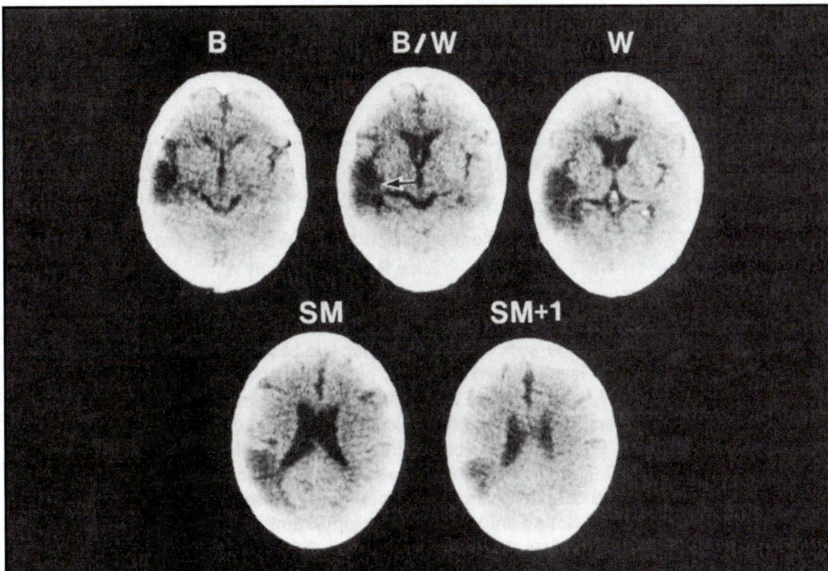

Figure 13.18 CT scans of patient with Wernicke's aphasia. Damage to the posterior left hemisphere can be clearly seen in the posterior area of the left hemisphere in the above CT scans.

➤ *Why would damage to the posterior left hemisphere lead to Wernicke's aphasia? (p. 407)*

Fluent Aphasias

The four types of fluent aphasias include Wernicke's aphasia, conduction aphasia, anomic aphasia, and transcortical sensory aphasia.

Wernicke's Aphasia. Damage to the posterior portion of the superior and middle left temporal gyrus and the left temporoparietal cortex produces a language disorder called **Wernicke's aphasia** (see **Figure 13.18**). Unlike the nonfluency of the patient with Broca's aphasia, the person with Wernicke's aphasia can speak fluently. However, even though syntactic structure is preserved, the meaningfulness of speech is decreased. The person with Wernicke's aphasia produces jargon, leaving out key words, substituting words, and including extra words.

A person with Wernicke's aphasia may also substitute verb tenses or have difficulty using the correct pronoun or preposition. This kind of speech is **paragrammatic**; that is, it involves the use of inappropriate morphemes in speech. For example, the person with Wernicke's aphasia may say *to you* rather than *for you* or *he* rather than *she.* A person with this type of aphasia might also substitute or transpose sounds; for example, the patient may say *pork* for *fork* or *pesnal* for *pencil.* Attempts to repeat something are quite dissimilar to the original speech.

Here's how a patient with Wernicke's aphasia describes the picnic scene shown in **Figure 13.17**:

> The boys and the girls are having a picnic. The son is flying the kase—the take. They all live in the garage. The keys are floating in the lake. The page of the flag. This is the home of the grass, the car—the home. This is the home of the home. See the oak in the creed. See the oak in the chair, the oak tree, the ocean—the animal—the trees are in the apple—is the sky in the apple. This is terrible. The trees live up in the mountain. (From an interview by Byrne, 1987)

Now reread the paragraph, pretending that you have not seen **Figure 13.17**. Would you be able to figure out what is being described?

The patient with Wernicke's aphasia does not always know that his or her speech is unintelligible and is surprised by the puzzled looks of people with whom he or she is talking. These puzzled looks may be all the patient has to go by, for someone with Wernicke's aphasia not only has a decrease in meaning of speech, but also has difficulty understanding the language of others. Additionally, reading comprehension is poor and writing is unintelligible (see **Figure 13.19**).

The symptoms of Wernicke's aphasia demonstrate the importance of language; without language, people are cut off from their social environment. People with Wernicke's aphasia have difficulty understanding the language of others and communicating their thoughts to others. However, once they are convinced that their speech is unintelligible, persons with Wernicke's aphasia, like other aphasics, can communicate with facial expressions or motor gestures.

Wernicke's aphasia A communicative disorder caused by damage to the posterior portion of the superior and middle temporal gyrus and the temporoparietal cortex that produces an inability to comprehend language.

paragrammatic The use of inappropriate morphemes in speech.

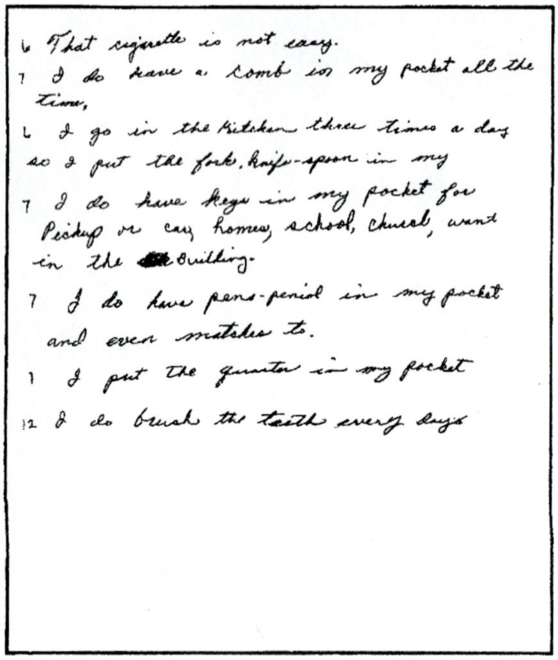

6 That cigarette is not easy.
7 I do have a comb in my pocket all the time,
6 I go in the Kitchen three times a day so I put the fork, knife-spoon in my
7 I do have keys in my pocket for Pickup or car, homes, school, church, want in the Building.
7 I do have pens-pencil in my pocket and even matches to.
1 I put the quarter in my pocket
12 I do brush the teeth every days

Figure 13.19 A sample of the writing from a patient with Wernicke's aphasia. The person with Wernicke's aphasia is asked to describe in writing what one does with the 10 test objects (cigarette, comb, fork, key, knife, match, pen, pencil, quarter, toothbrush). The normal form but impaired meaning in the writing can be clearly seen in this sample.

➤ *Why does a person with Wernicke's aphasia show similar defects in speech and writing? (p. 388–390)*

Conduction Aphasia. A patient with **conduction aphasia** has great difficulty repeating verbal information. The level of impairment depends on the length of the phrase to be repeated. With short, familiar phrases, the person's repetition may be accurate or there may be a single phonemic paraphasia. (A **paraphasia** is an error in speaking, and a phonemic paraphasia is the substitution of a similar sounding word for the verbal stimulus. Saying *pike* instead of *pipe* would be an example of a phonemic paraphasia.) With longer, less familiar phrases, the number of phonemic paraphasias may increase until the patient's speech contains none of the previously spoken words. Although repetition is impaired in a person suffering from conduction aphasia, language comprehension is relatively good and conversational speech is only mildly impaired.

Wernicke (1874) suggested that damage to the arcuate fasciculus causes conduction aphasia. Because the arcuate fasciculus connects language comprehension with speech production, it seemed reasonable to assume that damage to the arcuate fasciculus would lead to conduction aphasia (see **Figure 13.1**). More recent evidence obtained from CT scans shows that damage to the left temporoparietal region, above and below the Sylvian fissure (which includes the arcuate fasciculus), causes conduction aphasia (Damasio, 1995), but damage limited to the arcuate fasciculus does not appear to be associated with this disorder (Perecman & Brown, 1981). Conduction aphasia could reflect a short-term memory problem, which would explain the repetition impairment, or a deficiency in the selection of phonemes during speech production, which would explain the paraphasias.

Anomic Aphasia. Earlier in the chapter (see **p. 405**), we learned that a difficulty selecting the correct word for written or spoken language is called anomia. In all likelihood, you have at one time or another experienced anomia. For you, like most people, anomia occurs only occasionally. However, individuals with **anomic aphasia** have consistent difficulty finding names and often substitute indefinite nouns and pronouns for substantive words. The impairment in language with anomic aphasia can be seen vividly in the following description by a 27-year-old patient:

> When you get into the car, close your door. Put your feet on those two things on the floor. So, all I have to do is pull . . . I have to put my . . . I'm just gonna do it the way I'm thinking of right now. You just put your thing which I know of which I cannot say right now but I can make a picture of it . . . you put it in . . . on your . . . inside the thing that turns the car on. You put your foot on the thing that makes the, uh, stuff come on. It's called the, uh. . . . (Davis, 1993, p. 20)

The person with anomic aphasia has good language comprehension and speech is fluent and grammatical, but the absence of key words makes it difficult to know that the above description is about driving a car. Verbal communication is possible for people with anomic aphasia, but only in situations in which the context indicates the specific words to which the indefinite words, such as *thing*, refer.

Goodglass and Kaplan (1979) suggest that identification of a dysfunction in a specific brain structure that pro-

---

conduction aphasia A communicative disorder caused by damage to the temporoparietal region above and below the Sylvian fissure, including the arcuate fasciculus, which produces a difficulty repeating verbal information.

paraphasia An error in speaking.

anomic aphasia A communicative disorder characterized by consistent difficulty finding names.

duces anomic aphasia is not possible. Instead, they argue that damage to multiple posterior language areas causes anomic aphasia. The areas involved in anomic aphasia are the same as those involved in Wernicke's aphasia, the posterior portion of the superior and middle left temporal gyrus and the left temporoparietal cortex. Therefore, it has been suggested that anomic aphasia may be a mild form of Wernicke's aphasia (Brookshire, 1997).

Transcortical Sensory Aphasia. The last type of fluent aphasia is **transcortical sensory aphasia**. An individual with this form of aphasia experiences impairments similar to those experienced by someone with Wernicke's aphasia (fluent speech, poor comprehension, anomia), except for an unusual ability to repeat verbal stimuli. The most salient aspect of transcortical sensory aphasia is **echolalia**, which is a repetition of something someone has just said. Thus, this disorder causes people to endlessly repeat a question instead of answering it. Lesions posterior to Wernicke's area around the anterior boundary of the occipital lobe have been associated with transcortical sensory aphasia (Damasio, 1981). Goodglass and Kaplan (1979) suggest that speech production is separated from intention and meaning in the language of people with transcortical sensory aphasia. This separation causes them to repeat questions rather than respond to them. **Table 13.2** presents a summary of the characteristics of each of the aphasias we have described.

Before You Go On

Compare the communication problems faced by a patient with fluent aphasia with those of a patient with nonfluent aphasia.

Describe a conversation between one patient with Broca's aphasia and another with anomic aphasia.

Section Review

- An aphasia is an acquired impairment of language caused by damage to the areas of the brain that control language functioning.
- Nonfluent aphasia can be one of three types: Broca's aphasia, global aphasia, and transcortical motor aphasia.
- The primary characteristics of Broca's aphasia, in which the left frontal lobe area rostral to the base of the primary motor cortex is damaged, are the inability to initiate well-articulated, conversational speech and agrammatism.
- In global aphasia, in which anterior and posterior language areas of the left frontal lobe are damaged, there is a severe depression of all language functioning.
- In transcortical motor aphasia, in which areas anterior and superior to Broca's area are damaged, speech is nonfluent and agrammatical and naming is poor, but comprehension is relatively intact, and there is fluent repetition.
- Fluent aphasia can be one of four types: Wernicke's aphasia, conduction aphasia, anomic aphasia, and transcortical sensory aphasia.
- In Wernicke's aphasia, in which the posterior portion of the superior and middle left temporal gyrus and the left temporoparietal cortex is damaged, speech is fluent, but comprehension, repetition, and naming are all poor.
- The primary characteristic of conduction aphasia, caused by damage to the left temporoparietal region, is difficulty repeating verbal information (poor repetition).
- The primary characteristic of anomic aphasia, in which the posterior portion of the superior and middle left temporal gyrus and the left temporoparietal cortex is damaged, is consistent difficulty finding names for objects.
- In transcortical sensory aphasia, in which the area posterior to Wernicke's area is damaged, comprehension and naming are poor, but speech is fluent, and repetition is exceptional, causing the person to repeat what is said (echolalia).

Other Communicative Disorders

Communicative disorders other than aphasia include apraxia, agnosia, alexia, and agraphia. Each of these impairments can occur with aphasia or alone. We first look at the motor speech disorder of apraxia.

Apraxia of Speech

A dysfunction in the frontal lobe area responsible for the planning and sequencing of speech production limited to Broca's area will produce a disorder called apraxia of speech. (Recall from Chapter 8 that *apraxia* is a serious impairment in the ability to organize voluntary move-

---

transcortical sensory aphasia A communicative disorder caused by damage to an area posterior to Wernicke's area around the anterior boundary of the occipital lobe, which is similar to Wernicke's aphasia (fluent speech, poor comprehension, anomia), except for an unusual ability to repeat verbal stimuli.

echolalia A repetition of something someone has just said.

Table 13.2 ■ Site of Lesion and Characteristics of Different Fluent and Nonfluent Aphasias

Disorder	Site of Lesion	Spontaneous Speech	Speech comprehension	Repetition	Naming
Broca's aphasia	Left frontal cortex rostral to base of motor cortex	Nonfluent	Relatively intact	Poor	Poor
Global aphasia	Anterior and posterior language areas	Nonfluent	Poor	Poor	Poor
Transcortical motor aphasia	Areas anterior and superior to Broca's area	Nonfluent	Relatively intact	Intact	Poor
Wernicke's aphasia	Posterior part of the superior and middle left temporal gyrus and left temporoparietal cortex	Fluent	Poor	Poor	Poor
Conduction aphasia	Temporoparietal region, above and below posterior Sylvian fissure	Fluent	Relatively intact	Poor	Intact
Anomic aphasia	Posterior part of the superior and middle left temporal gyrus and left temporoparietal cortex	Fluent	Relatively intact	Intact	Poor
Transcortical sensory aphasia	Posterior to Wernicke's area around boundary of occipital lobe	Fluent	Poor	Intact	Poor

ment.) An individual with apraxia of speech is unable to voluntarily control the movement of the muscles necessary for speech production. There is no muscle weakness and no difficulty using the lips, tongue, or pharynx for such nonspeaking purposes as chewing and swallowing food. The impairment associated with this disorder becomes evident only when the person starts to speak: he or she has great difficulty producing the correct sound for a specific word. For example, a person with apraxia of speech might say *spork* instead of *fork.*

Wertz, LaPointe, and Rosenbek (1984) identified several types of articulation errors in individuals with apraxia of speech. Although incorrect sounds are substituted for correct sounds, most of the phoneme substitutions resemble the correct sound. The failure to articulate the correct sound is not consistent; the person may articulate a given phoneme correctly on one occasion and then substitute another phoneme for the same phoneme on another occasion.

Context has an important influence on whether the correct sound is produced. For example, the person with apraxia of speech may articulate correctly the *d* sound in *dishes* when the same phoneme is repeated in the phrase *Don did the dishes,* but misarticulate the same sound when contrasting phonemes occur, as in the phrase *Don bought the dishes.* Further, the person is more likely to articulate sounds correctly in a natural setting than in an artificial setting. As an example, the patient may articulate *good-bye* correctly when she says it spontaneously upon leaving, but not when she is asked to say *good-bye.* The person is aware of the misarticulations and may become upset by the failure to say the correct sound.

Apraxia of speech most often occurs in conjunction with Broca's aphasia. Damage to the brain generally extends beyond the boundaries of Broca's area. A patient with apraxia of speech and Broca's aphasia will have difficulty articulating sounds and will produce agrammatic speech. (The agrammatism is a characteristic of aphasia, not apraxia.) The following is an attempt by a patient with Broca's aphasia and apraxia of speech to describe the attempted assassination of President Ronald Reagan:

> Um . . . Reagan . . . um . . . President . . . Reagan . . . shod . . . was . . . um . . . yesterday . . . um . . . um . . . New Yoak Cidy . . . uh . . . hospidal . . . be oh-kay . . . nod bad. . . . (Brookshire, 1992, p. 278)

This selection clearly shows that the patient is misarticulating words as well as leaving out function words such as articles, conjunctions, and prepositions. These omissions give the speech a "telegraphic" character accentuated by incorrect sound articulations.

Auditory-Verbal Agnosia

A person suffering from *agnosia* is unable to identify an object using a specific sensory modality, but the object can be recognized through other modalities (see Chapters 6 and 7). Sensory deficits with agnosia can be limited to language. For example, a person with an **auditory-verbal agnosia**, or **pure word deafness**, cannot identify spoken words because he or she does not recognize them as meaningful, but can recognize other auditory stimuli such as bells and whistles. In addition, auditory-verbal agnosia does not affect reading comprehension; in other words, the person cannot say the word dog when he hears it spoken, but he can read it perfectly or even read the word aloud perfectly. Damage that severs the connections between the primary auditory cortex and the secondary auditory cortex in both hemispheres is associated with auditory-verbal agnosia. A **visual-verbal agnosia** is an inability to recognize printed words, but not spoken words. (Both auditory-verbal agnosia and visual-verbal agnosia are quite rare.) This disorder results from damage that isolates the visual cortex from cortical language areas.

Alexia and Agraphia

Over a century ago, Dejerine (1891) discovered that damage to the angular gyrus, an area of the cerebral cortex located in the posterior parietal lobe (see **Figure 13.1**), was associated with an inability to read (**alexia**) and an inability to write (**agraphia**). Reading and writing require integration of input from the visual, auditory, and body senses (somatosenses). One of the reasons deaf people rarely achieve more than a fourth-grade reading level is their inability to associate written symbols with sounds (King & Quigley, 1985). The angular gyrus receives information from each of these senses, making it ideally suited to control reading and writing (Benson & Greenberg, 1969). Damage to the angular gyrus would be expected to lead to reading and writing deficits.

An individual who loses the ability to read and write is said to suffer from alexia with agraphia. You might think that damage that causes a person to be unable to read would always cause the person to be unable to write. However, in 1892 Dejerine noted that one of his patients could not read but had no difficulty writing. This patient suffered from what we now call **pure alexia**, or alexia without agraphia. Dejerine's patient had lost the ability to read following a lesion to the left occipital lobe and the posterior end of the corpus callosum. The patient could still write but could not read his own writing! More recent investigations (Damasio & Damasio, 1992) indicate that lesions that disconnect the angular gyrus from visual input lead to pure alexia.

As we learned in Chapter 6, a person with visual agnosia cannot recognize objects and thus cannot give the names for them. By contrast, the person with pure alexia can identify and name objects but cannot read. Bilateral damage to the secondary visual cortex produces visual agnosia, whereas pure alexia occurs when the angular gyrus does not receive input from the visual cortex.

Dyslexia

Unlike those with alexia, people who have **dyslexia** can read, but they have difficulty with reading. Dyslexia can become apparent when a child is learning to read (developmental dyslexia) or can be caused when people who already know how to read sustain brain damage (acquired dyslexia).

There are a number of different types of dyslexia. For example, someone with word-form dyslexia does not immediately recognize words but, if given sufficient time to sound out the words, is able to read. By contrast, someone with phonological dyslexia can identify familiar words but is unable to sound out unfamiliar ones even if given plenty of time.

There are two methods of reading—whole-word reading and phonetic reading. We recognize a specific word by its shape with whole-word reading; we read a word by sounding out its letters with phonetic reading. Whole-word reading is used with familiar words, and phonetic reading is used with unfamiliar words. People with word-form dyslexia have impaired whole-word reading; people with phonological dyslexia have impaired phonetic reading.

---

auditory-verbal agnosia (pure word deafness) A communicative disorder characterized by an inability to recognize spoken words as meaningful due to damage that severs the connections between the primary auditory cortex and the secondary auditory cortex in both hemispheres.

visual-verbal agnosia A communicative disorder characterized by an inability to recognize printed words, that results from damage isolating the visual cortex from cortical language areas.

alexia A communicative disorder characterized by an inability to read caused by damage to the angular gyrus.

agraphia A communicative disorder characterized by an inability to write caused by damage to the angular gyrus.

pure alexia (alexia without agraphia) A communicative disorder characterized by an inability to read, caused by lesions that disconnect the angular gyrus and visual input.

dyslexia A communicative disorder characterized by difficulty with reading caused by damage to the area of the brain where sounds and symbols are associated.

Table 13.3 ▪ Site of Lesion and Characteristics of Apraxia, Auditory-Verbal Agnosia, Alexia/Dyslexia, and Agraphia/Dysgraphia

Disorder	Site of Lesion	Characteristics
Apraxia of speech	Third frontal convolution anterior to primary motor cortex (Broca's area)	Inability to voluntarily sequence speech production
Auditory-verbal agnosia	Connections from primary auditory cortex and the secondary auditory cortex	Inability to identify spoken words as being meaningful
Alexia/dyslexia	Connections from primary visual cortex to the angular gyrus	An inability to read/ difficulty reading
Agraphia/dysgraphia	Inferior parietal lobe and superior temporal lobe	An inability to write/ difficulty writing

Recent research (Demb, Boynton, & Heeger, 1998; Shaywitz et al., 1998) using fMRIs have revealed differences in brain activity between people with dyslexia and control subjects. Shaywitz and colleagues (1998) found that people with dyslexia show less activity in posterior regions of the brain than do people without dyslexia, and Demb and colleagues (1998) observed less activation of the visual cortex in people with dyslexia than control subjects. The lower level of neural activity in the posterior areas of the brain, which is the area of the brain where sounds (auditory) and symbols (visual) are associated, undoubtedly is related to the difficulty with reading seen in people with dyslexia.

Dysgraphia

We learned earlier that people with agraphia cannot write but still can read. As with reading, the impairment may be a difficulty in writing (**dysgraphia**) rather than an inability to write (agraphia). Difficulty using visually based writing (or visually imaging whole words) is found in people with orthographic dysgraphia; these individuals can spell out regular words such as *won* that sound the way they are spelled (where phonetics can be used) but not irregular words such as *one* (where pronunciation of the entire word must be in memory). By contrast, someone with phonological dysgraphia can write familiar words such as *car*, but cannot write unfamiliar words such as *automobile* that must be sounded out phonetically.

Benson and Geschwind (1985) reported that orthographic and phonological dysgraphia have different biological bases; damage to the inferior parietal lobe is associated with orthographic dysgraphia, whereas damage to the superior temporal lobe is associated with phonological dysgraphia. These observations suggest that different neural circuits mediate whole-word writing and phonetic writing. A similar separation of cerebral control exists for whole-word reading and phonetic reading. **Table 13.3** presents a summary of the characteristics of apraxia of speech, alexia/dyslexia, and agraphia/dysgraphia.

We have learned that there are a number of different types of language disorders and that many of them share similar characteristics. When someone walks into a doctor's office with a language disorder, how does the doctor know the difference between Wernicke's aphasia and conduction aphasia? Broca's aphasia and transcortical motor aphasia? What causes these types of damage? The next section examines the causes, diagnosis, and incidence of the various types of language disorders.

Before You Go On

What do the disorders of alexia and agraphia tell us about reading and writing as distinct from speaking and listening?

Causes, Diagnosis, and Incidence of Communicative Disorders

Causes

The causes of aphasia are quite varied; many of them are similar to the causes of brain damage described in Chapter 2 (see **p. 45–46**). We learned from the chapter-opening vignette that John's grandmother developed aphasia following a stroke (see Chapter 2). Strokes, or cerebrovascular accidents, represent the third leading cause of

---

dysgraphia A communicative disorder characterized by difficulty in writing.

death in the United States (Caplan, 1988). Brain damage caused by a stroke is the most typical cause of aphasia.

Head trauma represents another major cause of aphasia. The vignette describing Ken's gunshot wound illustrates the effect of such an injury. Aphasia results when such objects as bullets damage the language areas. A closed-head injury (which can result from a motorcycle or automobile accident) blows received during a fight, or a fall from a high place also can cause aphasia.

Several insidious processes can cause aphasia. A tumor within a language area represents one insidious cause of aphasia. As the tumor grows, more areas of the brain are affected and the language impairment becomes more severe. Although the tissue of the brain is generally resistant to infection, aphasia can result from an infection. Exposure to toxic substances represents another insidious process that may lead to aphasia. Long-term exposure to heavy metals (lead, mercury) or certain chemical compounds can slowly damage the brain, including the language areas, and can produce a gradual onset of aphasic symptoms.

Metabolic disorders such as hypoglycemia and thyroid disorders can cause central nervous system dysfunction and aphasia. Aphasia can also be caused by nutritional deficiencies. Obstructive hydrocephalus (literally "water head," but the water is really cerebrospinal fluid) that produces increasing intracranial pressure is yet another cause of aphasia (see **p. 47** in Chapter 3).

Diagnosis

One might think that determining whether a person suffers from Broca's or Wernicke's aphasia would be a simple matter. In truth, many individuals with language impairments cannot be easily placed into a single category. One reason for this difficulty is that the person may have multiple or extensive lesions that produce symptoms of several different forms of aphasia. Also, the aging process may produce language impairments characteristic of more than one type of aphasia.

Darley (1982) argued that classifying patients may focus too much attention on differences rather than similarities between them. Treatment approaches should be associated with specific behaviors rather than with a specific diagnosis. For example, the same treatment for naming difficulties would be appropriate for a patient with either Broca's aphasia or Wernicke's aphasia, even though in other respects treatments for those two types of aphasia would be different. (See the Application section on **p. 414–415** for more on the treatment of language disorders.)

Incidence

Benson's (1979) evaluation of individuals with language impairments suggests that a diagnosis of the type of aphasia can be made in only about half of aphasia patients, so the incidence of each type of this disorder is unclear. In those patients with a clear diagnosis, Benson found that 65 percent were evenly distributed among Broca's, Wernicke's, and anomic aphasias. Benson reported that about 10 percent of the diagnoses were of global and conduction aphasias. The remaining 25 percent of diagnosed aphasias included transcortical aphasias and modality-specific disorders such as auditory agnosia or pure word deafness (an impaired recognition of auditory stimuli) and alexia.

Before You Go On

An adult has a stroke. Testing reveals that his speech is fluent, his comprehension is relatively intact, and he has no trouble naming objects shown to him on flash cards, but he has trouble repeating phrases said to him. What type of aphasia is he suffering from?

Section Review

- Apraxia of speech, the loss of voluntary control of the muscles necessary for speech production, most commonly occurs in conjunction with Broca's aphasia because damage is not generally limited to Broca's area.
- In auditory-verbal agnosia, also called pure word deafness, the patient cannot identify spoken words but can recognize other auditory stimuli.
- Visual-verbal agnosia is the inability to recognize the printed word without impairment of comprehension of speech.
- The inability to read is called alexia, and the inability to write is called agraphia; when they occur together, as is most common, the disorder is called alexia with agraphia.
- There are several types of dyslexia, defined as great difficulty in reading. In word-form dyslexia, the person does not immediately recognize words but can read them if given sufficient time to sound them out; in phonological dyslexia, the person can identify familiar words but cannot sound out unfamiliar ones.
- There are many causes of language disorders: strokes; head trauma; insidious processes such as disease, tumor, or exposure to toxic substances; and metabolic disorders.
- In practice, the different types of language disorders may not be well differentiated and can be difficult to distinguish from one another.

APPLICATION

Treatment Approaches for Aphasia

Speech-language pathologists provide treatment to improve the communication skills of persons who have aphasia and other types of language disorders. There are two schools of thought regarding the nature of aphasia, each of which calls for a different treatment (Brookshire, 1997). Some researchers believe that aphasia is the loss of language and that language needs to be retaught. Others believe that aphasia is an access problem; that is, the language is still there but cannot be retrieved.

Those who believe aphasia to be a disorder of retrieval advocate a *stimulation approach* to treatment. Hildred Schuell and her colleagues (1964) argued that sensory stimulation is the only method available for making complex events happen in the brain and that auditory stimulation is crucial in the retrieval of language processes. Use of other skills, such as reading and writing, in the treatment of aphasia are also encouraged, but the main component of treatment is intensive auditory stimulation. According to the stimulation approach, responses should be elicited, not forced or corrected. If a response is not elicited, the patient is given more stimulation to retrieve the response, but the client is not corrected or given information about why a response is inadequate.

Auditory stimulation tasks can involve listening, speaking, or both. Listening tasks include performing "point to" tasks, where the therapist says a word and asks the patient to point to the correct word or object in a grouping; following verbal directions by the therapist to perform a task; and providing answers to yes/no questions. Speaking tasks (which also, obviously, involve listening) involve repeating words spoken by the therapist; completing a phrase begun by the therapist, who provides the first sound, first syllable, or meaning; engaging in verbal association, in which the therapist provides a word and the patient comes up with another via free association, opposites, or rhyming, depending on instructions; responding to words given by the therapist with definitions or appropriate sentences; and retelling stories read aloud by the therapist (see **Figure 13.20**).

Figure 13.20 Auditory stimulation. An aphasic patient is provided therapy by a speech language pathologist.

➤ *What is the prognosis likely to be for this patient with aphasia? (p. 414–415)*

Those who believe that aphasia results from a loss of language and that language needs to be relearned promote a programmed approach (Costelle, 1977), in which behavior-modification techniques are used to teach language. The activities themselves may not differ significantly from those used with the sensory stimulation approach. Programmed therapy focuses on particular goals (sentence production), specifies the stimuli that are to be used (pictures), and indicates how a response is to be recorded (latency of response and completeness of sentence). The therapist provides feedback to the patient by indicating whether each response is correct or incorrect.

A programmed approach to treatment involves three steps. First, baseline measures are obtained to show the response rate of the behavior that is to be changed. Second, *behavior-modification* procedures are applied, with reinforcement and punishment used to change the rate of performance of the baseline behavior. The third step in the programmed approach is to extend the situations that elicit speech. In this step, the therapist attempts to transfer the behavior from the highly structured clinical setting to more spontaneous and natural situations. This may involve altering reinforcement schedules and types of reinforcement to make these contingencies more like the ones the patient will find in the "real world."

In clinical practice it is not uncommon for practitioners to use some combination of the stimulation and the programmed approach (Brookshire, 1997). How effective are treatment programs for aphasia? Spontaneous recovery of language functioning occurs in many aphasic individuals. Most of the spontaneous recovery of language functioning occurs within the first 3 months following brain damage, although some recovery may continue for an additional several months. The spontaneous improvement in language function may be misinterpreted as a response to treatment. To show treatment effectiveness, patients must experience greater recovery of language than would be expected to result from spontaneous recovery alone. Recent studies of treatment effectiveness indicate that language recovery is enhanced following treatment for aphasia (Brookshire, 1997). One large-scale clinical study found that patients undergoing treatment showed greater improvement than did patients who were in a nontreatment control condition (Poeck, Huber, & Willmes, 1989). This study reported that 78 percent of the patients receiving immediate treatment showed significant improvement in language skills, whereas only 48 percent improved when treatment was delayed for 4 months.

For many adults with aphasia, language skills may not improve even with therapy. Many others, however, do improve. The improvements many adults experience following treatment suggests that language skills impaired by brain damage can be recovered, or relearned, which brings us to the topics covered by the next chapter, learning and memory.

Before You Go On

Compare and contrast the two views of the nature of aphasia, noting how they influence treatment approaches.

Section Review

- Some researchers, who believe that aphasia is a difficulty in accessing intact language functions, advocate the stimulation approach to treatment, in which auditory stimulation in the form of listening and speaking tasks is used to improve the retrieval of language.
- Other researchers believe that aphasia reflects a loss of language, and advocate the programmed approach to relearn language.
- It has been shown that recovery is enhanced in many patients who undergo treatment in the first several months after damage.

Chapter Review

Critical Thinking Questions

1. Susan has especially good verbal skills but cannot draw, whereas Carolyn is an accomplished artist but is not very articulate. Discuss evidence that suggests that the differences in Susan's and Carolyn's abilities reflect hemispheric differences.
2. Richard rushed to the hospital upon learning that his wife had had a stroke. When he arrived at the hospital, Richard learned that the stroke had damaged the superior part of his wife's left temporal lobe. Based on what you have learned, what changes in his wife's language abilities is Richard likely to notice?
3. Walter was shot last year. His wounds have since healed, but he continues to experience difficulty initiating well-articulated conversational speech. Walter has no problem understanding others, but he often omits function words and others have difficulty understanding him. What area of Walter's brain was likely damaged in the shooting?

Vocabulary Questions

1. The simplest functional unit of a language is a speech sound, also called a ________________.
2. The simplest meaningful unit of language is a ________________.
3. In any language, ________________ dictates how phonemes can be combined into morphemes.
4. The rules of ________________ dictate how words are combined into meaningful phrases.
5. The bundle of fibers that connects Wernicke's area and Broca's area is the ________________.
6. The axons that connect the two halves of the cerebral cortex make up the cerebral ________________.
7. The point at which the right and left optic nerves intersect is called the ________________.
8. The division of labor between the two cerebral hemispheres is referred to as ________________.
9. An acquired impairment of language is an ________________.

10. Difficulty comprehending spoken and written speech is referred to as ________________.
11. Difficulty producing well-articulated speech is referred to as ________________.
12. Speech that omits function words such as conjunctions, articles, and prepositions is ________________.
13. A person who cannot voluntarily program the muscles necessary for speech suffers from ________________.
14. A person who has difficulty reading suffers from ________________.

Review Questions

1. How many phonemes does the word *dish* contain?
   a. one
   b. two
   c. three
   d. four
2. How many morphemes does the word *distrust* contain?
   a. one
   b. two
   c. three
   d. four
3. Which of the following is an example of a noun phrase?
   a. swims quickly
   b. is able
   c. the little boy
   d. to commit an error
4. Commissurotomy is an effective treatment for patients with uncontrollable grand mal seizures because it
   a. removes the seizure focus area of the brain.
   b. prevents seizure activity from intensifying.
   c. increases the effectiveness of drug therapy.
   d. obstructs the onset of seizure activity.
5. The purpose of Sperry's experimental split-brain preparation was to
   a. prevent serious grand mal seizures.
   b. investigate the visual system of cats.
   c. block communication between hemispheres.
   d. allow for cross-cuing within the brain.
6. Sperry's research with cats showed that
   a. the cerebral hemispheres can process information separately.
   b. epilepsy originates in the corpus callosum.
   c. visual discrimination is located in the right hemisphere.
   d. split-brain subjects can no longer learn to perform new tasks.
7. The tachistoscope is used to
   a. present stimuli to both halves of the cortex simultaneously.
   b. present stimuli to only one visual field at a time.
   c. observe the language behavior of split-brain patients.
   d. distinguish between split-brain and normal subjects.
8. The right cerebral hemisphere cannot name objects, but it can
   a. use the right hand to select objects.
   b. verbally identify objects in the left visual field.
   c. govern most other language skills.
   d. understand the meaning of a word.
9. People with right-hemisphere damage often have difficulty
   a. speaking clearly and understanding what they hear.
   b. understanding the emotional content of speech.
   c. both reading and writing.
   d. repeating back what they hear.
10. A person who has difficulty finding his way from one physical location to another has probably suffered damage to
    a. his corpus callosum.
    b. his right hemisphere.
    c. Broca'a area.
    d. Wernicke's area.
11. A person who has difficulty coordinating her two hands to tie her shoelaces might have
    a. suffered damage to her left hemisphere.
    b. undergone split-brain surgery.
    c. failed to develop a corpus callosum.
    d. learned to employ cross-cuing.
12. Which of the following is an example of a synthetic mode of thinking?
    a. Defining the word *ball.*
    b. Writing and reading the word *ball.*
    c. Recognizing different spherical objects as balls.
    d. Comparing the heights and widths of two different balls.
13. Most of the brain structures that are important in language comprehension are located in the
    a. left occipital lobe.
    b. left frontal lobe.
    c. left temporal lobe.
    d. corpus callosum.
14. Broca's aphasia is characterized by
    a. poor writing, but normal oral articulation.
    b. poor articulation, but relatively intact comprehension.
    c. poor articulation and poor comprehension.
    d. poor comprehension, but normal writing.

15. A person with transcortical motor aphasia usually cannot
    a. initiate speech.
    b. repeat long, complex sentences.
    c. understand speech.
    d. read and write.
16. A characteristic of Wernicke's aphasia is
    a. paraphrasia.
    b. dyslexia.
    c. paragrammatic speech.
    c. all of the above.
17. A person who refers to a door as "the thing that opens" is exhibiting a sign of
    a. apraxia of speech.
    b. anomia.
    c. agraphia.
    d. alexia.

Suggested Readings

BROOKSHIRE, R. H. (1997). *An introduction to neurogenic communication disorders* (5th ed.). St. Louis, MO: Mosby-Year Book.

DAMASIO, A. R., & DAMASIO, H. (1992). Brain and language. *Scientific American, 267,* 60–67.

GESCHWIND, N., & GALBURDA, A. M. (1987). *Cerebral lateralization: Biological mechanisms, associations, and pathology.* Cambridge, MA: MIT Press.

HELLIGE, J. B. (1993). *Hemispheric asymmetry.* Cambridge, MA: Harvard University Press.

ORNSTEIN, R. (1997). *The Right Mind.* San Diego: Harcourt Brace.

SPRINGER, S. P., & DEUTSCH, G. (1993). *Left brain, right brain* (4th ed.). New York: W. H. Freeman.

14 The Biology of Learning and Memory

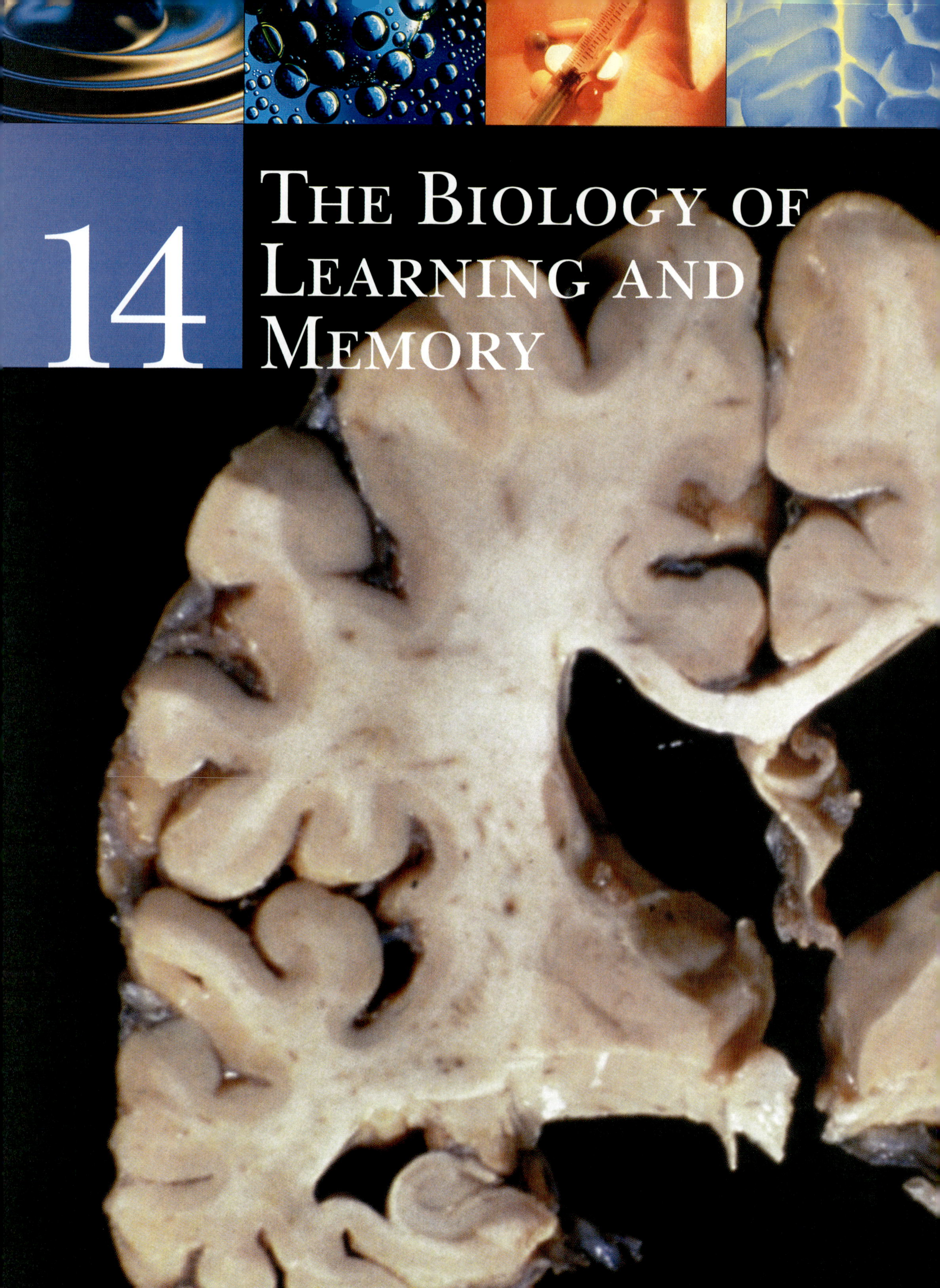

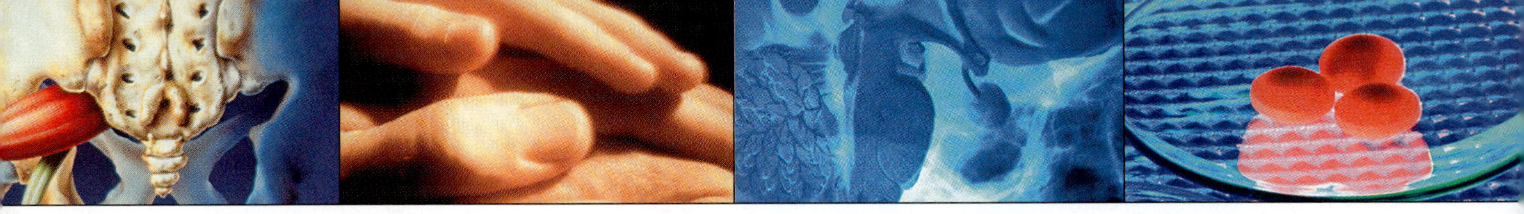

A Fleeting Memory

Todd and his wife, Helen, were shopping in a local mall when a man approached them with a friendly greeting. The man chatted with Todd and Helen briefly and went on his way. After the man left, Todd asked Helen who he was, and she identified him as a neighbor, Bill Jones, who several months ago had moved into a house down the block.

When Helen told him that he frequently talked with this neighbor, Todd became upset. Helen sighed, and knew Todd would ask her again about Bill Jones the next time he saw him. When they arrived home, Todd received a phone call from his aunt, informing him of his uncle's death. Todd, immediately struck with intense grief, cried for almost an hour over the loss. Yet, after being distracted by the doorbell, Todd no longer remembered his uncle's death. He experienced the same intense grief when Helen reminded him of the phone call, as if he was hearing the news for the first time.

Todd's memory has not always been this bad. His problem began after an accident a year ago. While working at a construction site, Todd was hit in the head by a falling beam. Although he was unconscious for only a few minutes, the accident completely altered his life. Todd can still recall events that occurred before the injury, but new thoughts, once they leave his consciousness, are lost. He's lost the ability to learn anything new; he reads the newspaper and promptly forgets what he's read, or even the month or the year. He feels trapped in the present, with no idea of what has just happened. ■

◀ Extensive neural atrophy leads to substantive enlargement of cerebral ventricles.

Before You Begin

What caused Todd's severe memory impairment?

What parts of his brain were affected by the accident?

Why can Todd remember Helen, his wife, but not his neighbor, whom he's known for several months?

Is there anything that can be done to improve Todd's memory?

In this chapter, we will help you answer these and the following questions:

- What is learning?
- What is memory?
- What is the relationship between learning and memory?
- How is the memory of Bill Jones's name stored in Helen's brain?
- What physical changes take place in the brain when a memory is stored?
- What brain structures are involved in the storage and retrieval of memories?
- How do these structures work together?
- What conditions improve the chances that a specific memory will be retained?

In this chapter, we will discuss the biological bases of learning and memory, or how the central nervous system, when functioning properly, allows you to, among other things, read the words on this page and recall them when your instructor springs a surprise quiz. **Learning** is a change in our behavior that occurs as a result of our experiences; **memory** is the capacity to retain and retrieve those experiences. We begin with a brief introduction to learning and memory, followed by a detailed examination of the neural processes that change as a result of an experience, allowing the formation of memories that Todd wants so desperately to experience again.

---

learning A change in our behavior that occurs as a result of our experiences.

memory The capacity to retain and retrieve past experiences.

habituation A decrease in the innate responsiveness to a specific stimulus as a result of repeated experience.

sensitization An increase in the innate reactivity to a stimulus following exposure to an intense event.

Pavlovian conditioning A type of learning in which a novel stimulus becomes able to elicit an instinctive response as the result of having been paired with an instructive stimulus.

Types of Learning

Consider the following scenarios, each of which illustrates one of four kinds of learning.

1. You select a shirt from your closet, remove it from its hanger, and put it on. At first you notice the feel of the fabric against your skin, but after awhile you no longer are aware of this sensation (although you are pretty sure that you are wearing a shirt).

2. You are studying intently for an exam and your roommate quietly enters your room. She walks up behind you and touches you on the shoulder to get your attention. You jump out of your chair as if you had been shot out of a cannon.

3. You are having dinner with an attractive partner. The lights are dim, soft music is playing, and candles are flickering on the table. In this romantic setting, you become sexually aroused.

4. You and a group of friends take a road trip to a nearby casino. You stop at the first open 25-cent slot machine and, with your first quarter, win $325.

The first scenario illustrates a type of learning called **habituation**, a decrease in the innate responsiveness to a specific stimulus as a result of repeated experience. Thus, you initially react to the feel of the fabric of your shirt, but with continued exposure to your clothing, you no longer feel the fabric. The benefit of this type of learning is rather obvious—imagine what it would be like if you were constantly aware of the feeling of your clothes, jewelry, and so forth touching your skin—you would hardly be able to read the words on this page, much less learn anything from them.

The second scenario illustrates **sensitization**, an increase in the innate reactivity to a stimulus following exposure to an intense event. Studying for an examination is an intense event. While aroused for studying, your sensitivity to other stimuli is heightened. Thus, you show an increased startle reaction to your roommate's touch. Another less obvious example that may seem more like common sense than the result of sensitization is an increased reluctance to eat new foods when you are ill.

The third example illustrates **Pavlovian conditioning**, a type of learning first studied by Ivan Pavlov at the beginning of the 20th century. Pavlov was a Russian physiologist who studied the process governing digestion. He discovered that dogs exhibit several reflexive reactions to having food placed in their mouths. (Believe it or not, this really is related to your romantic dinner—read on!)

Figure 14.1 Operant conditioning. Gambling provides a vivid picture of the powerful effect that reinforcement has on human behavior. As seen in this photo, the possibility of winning can lead people to play the slot machine.
➤ *Why do people spend hours pulling the lever on a slot machine? (p. 421)*

For example, Pavlov noted that his dogs salivated and secreted gastric juices when fed. According to Pavlov, the function of these reflexive responses is to aid in the digestion process. Pavlov then made a very important discovery. After some experiences with food being placed in their mouths, Pavlov noticed that the dogs secreted saliva and stomach juices simply when they saw the food or when food was placed in their dishes. Pavlov concluded that his dogs had learned new behaviors, because he had not observed these responses during the dogs' first exposure to the sight of food.

To explain his observations, Pavlov suggested that both animals and humans possess instinctual or *unconditioned reflexes.* An unconditioned reflex consists of two components: the **unconditioned stimulus (UCS)** (in this case, the taste of food), which involuntarily elicits the **unconditioned response (UCR)** (the dog's saliva or gastric juice response). As the result of repeated pairings of the environmental event (the sight of the food) and the unconditioned stimulus, the environmental event acts as a **conditioned stimulus (CS)**, becoming able to elicit the learned or **conditioned responses (CR)** (saliva or gastric juice secretion) on its own, without the UCS.

In our example, as a result of the previous association of the attractive person with sexual pleasure (UCS), the partner becomes a conditioned stimulus that can elicit sexual arousal as the conditioned response. Other examples of Pavlovian conditioning include fear (CR) of driving at night in the rain (CS) as a result of pain experienced after an automobile accident; feeling nauseous (CR) when seeing a particular food (CS) that previously made you ill; and lowering your head (CR) when going down the stairs to the basement (CS) because of an earlier bump on the head.

Our fourth example illustrates **operant conditioning**. Operant conditioning can involve learning how to behave to obtain **reinforcement** (the coins flowing from the slot machine; see **Figure 14.1**) or how to behave to avoid **punishment**. Reinforcers are events or activities (the jackpot) that increase the frequency of the behavior that precedes the event or activity (putting the quarter in and pulling the lever). Other instances of operant behavior producing reinforcement include fishing (when a person can freely cast) and dating (when the individual can ask out as many people as he or she wants).

Punishers are events or activities that decrease the frequency of the behavior that precedes the event or activity. Examples of the use of punishers include loss of privileges for a child who refuses to do his or her homework; a verbal reprimand for a habitually late worker; a fine for driving 80

---

unconditioned stimulus (UCS) A stimulus that is innately able to elicit an instinctive response.

unconditioned response (UCR) An innate reaction to the unconditioned stimulus.

conditioned stimulus (CS) A stimulus that becomes able to elicit an instinctive response as a result of having been previously paired with the unconditioned stimulus.

conditioned response (CR) A learned reaction to the conditioned stimulus.

operant conditioning A type of learning in which a response either produces reinforcement or avoids punishment.

reinforcement An event that increases the frequency of behavior that preceded the event.

punishment An event that decreases the behavior that precedes the event.

in a 55-mile-per-hour zone; and not being allowed to play in a baseball game for missing a practice. In each of the above examples, the purpose of the punisher is to decrease the future occurrence of the undesirable behavior.

B. F. Skinner (1938) conducted extensive investigations of the influence of reinforcement on behavior, using a simple structured environment. This environment, called an operant chamber, is an enclosed box with a small bar on the inside wall. When the bar is pressed, reinforcement is dispensed. The operant chamber has been modified to accommodate many different animal species. For example, when pigeons are being studied, a key for pecking replaces the bar press used for rats and some other species.

The concept of contingency is a central aspect of Skinner's theory. A **contingency** is a specified relationship between behavior and reinforcement. According to Skinner, the environment determines contingencies between behavior and reinforcement, and people must perform the appropriate behavior to obtain reinforcement. Other researchers (Campbell & Church, 1969) have shown that animals are sensitive to contingencies between behavior and punishment, and that behavior is suppressed as a result of the behavior having been previously punished.

Now that you know what learning is, we will go on to describe several views of memory storage and retrieval, the process that allows you to remember what you have learned. Later in the chapter, we will examine the biological changes that occur during learning that allow the formation of memories.

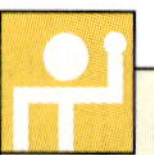

Before You Go On

You are driving nervously through an intersection in which you recently experienced an accident when you hear the sound of a car horn, which causes you to slam on the brakes. Which type(s) of learning are you exhibiting?

What are the main differences among habituation, sensitization, Pavlovian conditioning, and operant conditioning?

contingency The specified relationship between a behavior and its reinforcement or punishment.

Atkinson-Shiffrin model The view that an experience is sequentially stored in the sensory register, the short-term store, and then the long-term store.

sensory register In the Atkinson-Shiffrin model, the initial storage site where a memory is held for a very brief time without modification.

short-term store In the Atkinson-Shiffrin model, a temporary facility where information is held prior to being stored in permanent memory.

Section Review

- The four types of learning are habituation, sensitization, Pavlovian conditioning, and operant conditioning.
- Habituation produces a decreased innate reaction to an event as a result of repeated exposure to that event.
- Sensitization is the increase in response to other events following exposure to an intense event.
- Pavlovian conditioning establishes an association between an event and emotional and physical responses.
- Operant conditioning is the acquisition of voluntary behaviors that produce reinforcement or avoid punishment.

Models of Memory Storage and Retrieval

The Atkinson-Shiffrin Model

According to Atkinson and Shiffrin, there are three stages in the storage of information: sensory register, the short-term store, and the long-term store (Atkinson & Shiffrin, 1971). Consider what happens when you look up your study partner's telephone number. The **Atkinson-Shiffrin model** proposes that external input (the telephone number) is initially stored in the **sensory register** for a very brief time, usually one-half to one second (see **Figure 14.2**). The information contained in the sensory register is an initial impression of the external environment. Experiences stored in the sensory register are exact duplicates of external stimuli (the seven numbers on the page of the directory); however, not all information in the external environment is stored in the sensory register (you do not store all of the phone numbers on the page). According to the Atkinson-Shiffrin model, information decays rapidly after leaving the sensory register and is lost unless transferred into the short-term store (you are probably going to have to look up the phone number again the next time you need to call).

The Atkinson-Shiffrin model proposes that the **short-term store** is a temporary storage facility for our experiences. Memories can remain in the short-term store for 5, 10, 15 seconds, or even longer. The length of time that information remains in the short-term store depends on two variables. First, input such as the phone number must be rehearsed, or repeated, in order to be held in the short-term store. Without rehearsal, the phone number can be lost before it is stored in a meaningful way. Rehearsal also serves to

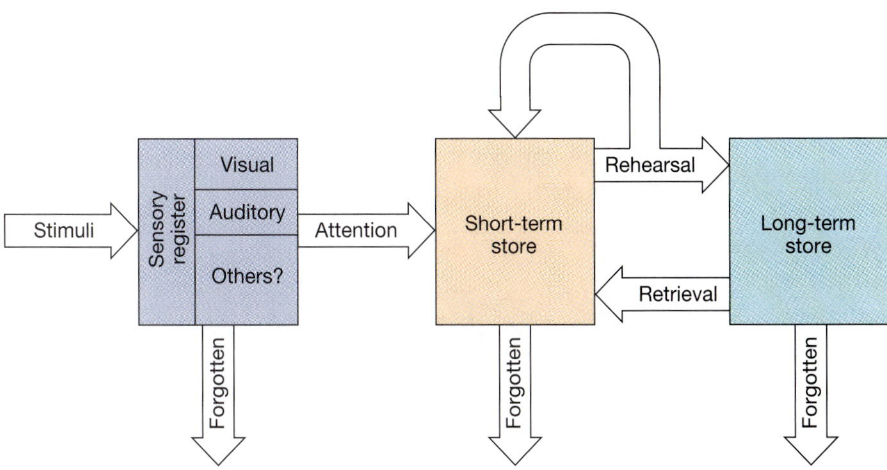

Figure 14.2 The Atkinson-Shiffrin three-stage model of memory storage. Initially, experiences are stored in the sensory register. The interpretation and organization of experiences occur in the second stage of memory storage, when memories enter the short-term store. In the final stage, long-term store, memory enters the permanent (or almost permanent) memory.

➤ *What events trigger short-term storage of memories? Long-term storage? (p. 422–423)*

organize information in the short-term store, enhancing the likelihood that you will be able to recall the phone number later. Second, only a limited amount of information can be retained in the short-term store. When new information enters the short-term store (your roommate bursting in yelling the score of the big game), old information (the phone number) will be "bumped out," unless the short-term store has enough room for both the old and the new information. Rehearsal can prevent the game score from "bumping" the telephone number from the short-term store.

Most information contained in the short-term store is transferred into the **long-term store**, the site of permanent memory storage. Although Atkinson and Shiffrin (1971) suggested that information can be lost from the long-term store because of decay, the issue of whether information is ever lost from long-term memory has not been settled. Most research indicates that information that gets into the long-term store stays there permanently (Spear & Riccio, 1994). However, some research suggests that decay does cause some memories to be lost.

Storage of the telephone number in the long-term store does not guarantee that you will be able to recall it tomorrow or the next week. Two processes may hinder recall of information from the long-term store. First, the presence of other memories in the long-term store may prevent recollection of a particular experience; this failure to recall a specific memory because of the presence of other memories in the long-term store is called **interference**. Second, failure to recall a memory from the long-term store may result from the absence of a specific stimulus that can trigger the retrieval of the memory (Underwood, 1983). People use notable aspects of an event, called **memory attributes**, to help them remember an event. For example, a friend's visit may remind you of a past experience with this friend. Or, returning to a place you have not been for several years may cause you to remember something you once did there. Your friend's presence or the place you revisited is the memory attribute that enables you to retrieve the memory of your earlier experiences. A memory attribute can even be an internal stimulus, such as an emotion (Bower, 1981). For example, you might remember a grandparent's death when you are sad because the emotion of sadness is the memory attribute for your grandparent's funeral. You also would be likely to remember that painful day every time you passed the funeral home. In the absence of these environmental events, the memory of your grandparent's death is less likely to be recalled.

The Atkinson-Shiffrin model suggests that the analysis or organization of an experience can occur even after the memory is transferred to the long-term store. When a memory is retrieved from the long-term store to the short-term store, it can receive additional processing. This processing may facilitate later recall of the experience. Processing can also alter the memory, making it more logical or appealing. Thus, memories that have been retrieved and further processed may not accurately reflect the actual experience (Loftus, 1991). For example, your memory of your grandparent's funeral, especially if you were very young when the death occurred, may have been shaped more by recollections of family members than the exact circumstances of the funeral.

---

long-term store The site of permanent memory storage.

interference An inability to recall a specific memory because of the presence of other memories.

memory attribute A salient aspect of an event that can stimulate memory retrieval.

Alternatives to the Atkinson-Shiffrin Model

Two significant alternatives to the Atkinson-Shiffrin model have been proposed. Baddeley (1986) presented one alternative, the rehearsal systems approach. He argued that memories are transferred directly from the sensory register to permanent or long-term storage. Experiences can be retained in sensory systems for analysis, which is the function of the working memory. According to Baddeley, **working memory** possesses the attributes of the short-term store; that is, it has a limited capacity and duration, and rehearsal serves to enhance organization and increase retrieval. Later in the chapter, when we discuss the memory consolidation process, we will look at evidence that indicates that permanent memory storage occurs very soon (within a few seconds) after an experience.

In a completely different conceptualization of the processing of information, Craik and Lockhart (1972) argued that, rather than existing in different storage levels, memories differ in the extent to which they have been processed. They suggest that the more completely a memory is processed, the more likely it is that the memory will be remembered at a later time. Craik and Lockhart's view is not necessarily inconsistent with Baddeley's view or with the Atkinson-Shiffrin model, but may simply describe different aspects of the storage of our experiences.

Before You Go On

Using what you have learned about the Atkinson-Shiffrin model, indicate where in the three-stage model you think Todd's memory deficit originates.

Section Review

- The Atkinson-Shiffrin model proposes that the three stages of memory storage are the sensory register, the short-term store, and the long-term store.
- The sensory register is the initial storage site.
- The short-term store rehearses and organizes experiences.
- The long-term store is the site of permanent memory storage.
- An alternative model of memory storage, the rehearsal systems approach, argues that memories are transferred directly from the sensory register to long-term storage.
- In yet another view, memories are seen as differing only in the extent to which they have been processed, not in storage level.

working memory A memory that is actively being processed by rehearsal.

episodic memory The memory of an event experienced at a particular time and place.

semantic memory The memory of knowledge concerning the use of language, and the rules, formulas, or algorithms for the development of concepts or solutions to problems.

Types of Memories

Episodic Versus Semantic Memories

Now you have an idea of how memories are stored. But are all memories alike? Is recalling a place you have visited the same as remembering that telephone numbers are made up of seven digits? Endel Tulving (1983) suggested that there are two types of long-term memories: episodic and semantic. An **episodic memory** consists of information about temporally related events, such as an event that you experienced at a particular time and place, whereas a **semantic memory** contains information about words and symbols, and the rules, formulas, or algorithms for the development of concepts or solutions to problems. For example, your memory that you ate pancakes for breakfast is an episodic memory, whereas your memory that the sentence "I ate pancakes for breakfast" is constructed with a noun and a verb is a semantic memory.

Tulving (1983) has found that the recollection of memories from the episodic system is deliberate and often requires conscious effort, whereas recall of information contained in the semantic system is automatic, occurring without conscious knowledge. Although we can be aware of knowledge contained in both memory systems, we interpret episodic memories as part of our personal past and semantic memories as part of the impersonal present. Thus, we use the term *remember* when referring to episodic memories and the term *know* to describe semantic memories. When you say that you have learned something, such as how to conjugate a verb, you are likely referring to semantic memory. According to Tulving, semantic memories are retrieved unchanged, whereas episodic memories are often changed on retrieval, making the episodic memory system much more vulnerable to distortion than is the semantic system.

Tulving emphasized that the difference between episodic and semantic memory is greater than just the different types of information stored in each memory; he argued that the episodic memory system is anatomically distinct from the semantic memory system. As you may have guessed from the above discussion of retrieval and as we will discover later in the chapter when we discuss the anatomical basis of memory, episodic memories are more susceptible than semantic memories to interference. **Table 14.1** lists the important differences between episodic and semantic memory.

Before You Go On

You are walking home from the library looking at the stars when all of a sudden the trick that helped you learn the names of the planets pops into your head, along with the image of your teacher, Mr. Albertson, reciting "my very educated mother just served us nine pickles" in front of your third-grade class. Is this an example of episodic memory or semantic memory?

Procedural Versus Declarative Memories

I have not been on a bicycle in many years. Still, I'm fairly certain that I remember how to ride one because as a child, I had many experiences riding bicycles. Because of the storage of these bicycle-riding experiences in the long-term store, I could probably hop on one and ride it today, although I might be a bit wobbly. My stored memories of bicycle riding is an example of a procedural memory.

According to Squire (1986), **procedural memory** is skill memory (see **Table 14.2**). Procedural memories are not accessible to conscious awareness; instead, evidence of a procedural memory can be gained only through observations of performance. For example, you may not be able to describe how to play Mozart's Piano Sonata in C major, but you can demonstrate your ability to do so. These memories represent knowledge of how to do things, such as play a piano, tie shoelaces, or knit, that are stored as a result of operant conditioning experiences. Procedural memories also can represent emotional reactions to environmental events, such as becoming fearful before driving over a high bridge or sad when thinking of a deceased friend. These emotional reactions are stored as a result of Pavlovian conditioning.

Table 14.1 ■ Characteristics of Episodic Memory and Semantic Memory

Episodic Memory	Semantic Memory
Stores events	Stores ideas or concepts
Organized temporally	Organized conceptually
Based on personal belief	Based on social agreement
Reported as remembrance	Reported as knowledge
Access is deliberate	Access is automatic
Affect relatively important	Affect relatively unimportant
Very susceptible to amnesia	Relatively nonsusceptible to amnesia
Stored late in childhood	Stored early in childhood

Source: Adapted from Tulving, E. (1983). *Elements of episodic memory*. Oxford: Clarendon Press/Oxford University Press.

Table 14.2 ■ Characteristics of Declarative Memory and Procedural Memory

Procedural Memory	Declarative Memory
Stores skills and procedures	Stores facts, episodes, and data
Is learned incrementally	Can be learned in a single trial
Contained within processing systems	Available to many processing systems
Information is modality specific	Information is modality general
Phylogenetically primitive	Phylogenetically late
Ontogenetically early	Ontogenetically late
Preserved in amnesia	Impaired in amnesia
Inaccessible to conscious recollection	Accessible to conscious recollection

Source: Adapted from Squire, L. R. (1986). The neuropsychology of memory. In P. Marler & H. Terrace (Eds.), *The biology of learning. Berlin: Springer-Verlag.*

In contrast to procedural memory, **declarative memory** is memory of facts. For example, you can learn and can store the fact that your favorite television show is on at 8:30 P.M. on Tuesday. The time and day of the television show is a fact and is stored as a declarative memory (see **Table 14.2**). Other examples of declarative memory include how to spell *dissociate* and the date of your parents' anniversary.

We are consciously aware of declarative memories. According to Squire (1986), a declarative memory can exist as a verbal thought or as a nonverbal image. Thus, you are verbally aware of when your favorite television show can be seen, whereas knowledge of the route to school can exist as a nonverbal image. A declarative memory can be formed in a single experience; however, practice can enhance the ability to recall a declarative memory. Like episodic memories, declarative memories are more susceptible to interference than are procedural memories.

procedural memory Skill memory or the memory of a highly practiced behavior.

declarative memory Factual memory or the memory of specific events.

Squire (1986) also suggests that whereas procedural memories are phylogenetically primitive (can be found in simple invertebrates), declarative memories are phylogenetically recent (can be found in advanced vertebrate species). This observation suggests that declarative and procedural memories are anatomically distinct, a view that we will explore later in the chapter when the anatomical basis of behavior is discussed. Further, Squire proposes that procedural memories are stored early in ontogenetic development, across a person's lifetime, whereas declarative memories are stored late in ontogenetic development. A similar distinction was noted by Tulving for semantic memories (stored early in childhood) and episodic memories (stored late in childhood). Thus, you can remember how to ride a tricycle, but not remember the event experienced at 4 of learning to ride the tricycle, or you can know how to construct a sentence, but not recall when you learned how to do so.

Before You Go On

Try to describe, from memory, how to drive your car or ride a bike. Why is this task so difficult?

Section Review

- Episodic memory is memory of past events that is organized temporally and recalled deliberately.
- Semantic memory is memory of ideas or concepts that is organized conceptually and recalled automatically.
- Declarative memory is memory of facts and is accessible to conscious thought.
- Procedural memory is skill memory and is not accessible to conscious thought.

The Memory Consolidation Process

Hebb's Cell Assemblies

How exactly is your study partner's telephone number represented at the cellular level in your central nervous system? According to Donald Hebb (1949), experiencing an event activates a neural circuit in the central nervous system. The activity *reverberates*, or continues to circulate, even after the termination of the event. Hebb suggested that one function of this reverberatory activity is to act as a temporary store and retain a record of an event until it can be consolidated into a permanent memory. He referred to such a circuit as a **cell assembly** (see **Figure 14.3**).

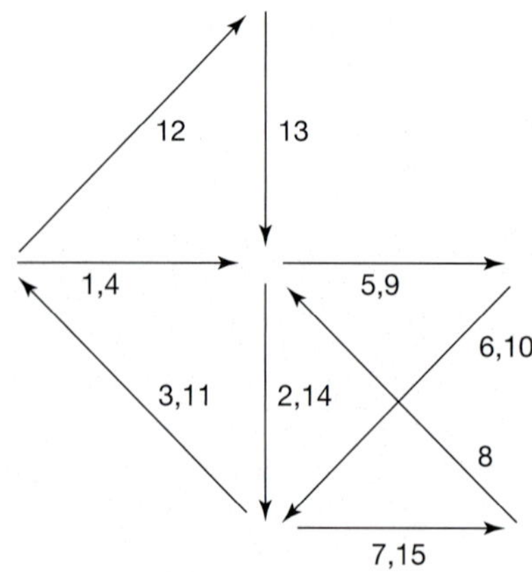

Figure 14.3 Hebb's cell assembly. This particular circuit consists of nine pathways that fire in the sequence labeled on the circuit. Activity reverberates in this cell assembly and provides the basis for the memory of that event.

➤ *What would happen if one of the pathways failed to function? (p. 426–427)*

In Hebb's view, physiological changes in a cell assembly that occur following an event represent the permanent record of the event. Because these physiological changes occur relatively slowly, the **reverberatory activity** must be maintained until the storage process is completed. If reverberatory activity is disrupted, the consolidation process stops, and no further physiological changes take place. (Can you see how this fits with the Atkinson-Shiffrin model?)

According to Hebb, the cell assembly is the basic unit of memory. Simple psychological processes, such as reflexive behaviors, are controlled by a single cell assembly; more complex processes, such as voluntary behaviors, are governed by interconnected cell assemblies. Cell assemblies become interconnected as a *phase sequence* when they are activated at the same time. Hebb (1972) described how cell assemblies become connected and control complex processes:

> Cell assemblies that are active at the same time become interconnected. Common events in the child's environment establish assemblies, and then when these events occur together the assemblies become con-

cell assembly A number of neurons that become active at the same time; this neural circuit serves as the site of permanent memory.

reverberatory activity The continued reactivation of a neural circuit for a time following an experience.

nected (because they are active together). When the baby hears footsteps, let us say, an assembly is excited; while this is still active, "footsteps assembly" becomes connected with the "face assembly" and the "being-picked-up assembly." (Hebb, 1972, p. 67)

Hebb (1949) suggested that the strength of a memory depends on the amount of time that the stimulus was initially experienced. Disruption of reverberatory activity early in the consolidation process leads to a weak or nonexistent permanent memory of an event. However, disruption late in the consolidation process usually has little impact: the permanent physiological changes have almost been completed, the permanent memory is strong, and recall of the event is probable. (Again, can you see how this fits with the Atkinson-Shiffron model?)

In summary, the three main tenets of Hebb's model are as follows: (1) reverberatory neural activity follows an event, (2) this activity is essential for the storage of a memory into a permanent form, and (3) reverberatory neural activity is followed by physiological changes representing the permanent record of an event. In the following sections, we discuss the work of later researchers who have attempted to find empirical evidence supporting Hebb's theory.

Support for the Existence of Reverberatory Circuits. Some evidence supports Hebb's (1949) cell-assembly model. For example, Burns (1958) isolated a section of cortical tissue by cutting its neural connections to other parts of the brain. Next, he electrically stimulated selected areas of the isolated neural tissue and recorded bursts of neural activity in the area of the stimulation. The neural activity continued for up to 30 minutes following termination of the electrical stimulation, depending on its intensity. Reverberation seems to be the most reasonable explanation for the continued neural activity following stimulation, but Burns went a step further, providing more direct evidence of reverberation. He reasoned that if all the neurons in the circuit were stimulated simultaneously, then the sustained activity would stop when all the neurons were in the refractory period. To test this hypothesis, Burns delivered a single intense shock to the center of the isolated cortical tissue. As predicted, he noted initial activity throughout the neural tissue followed by complete cessation of neural activity.

Other studies (Verzeano et al., 1970; Verzeano & Negishi, 1960) have also supported Hebb's model. In both of these studies, electrodes were implanted close together (30 to 200 micrometers apart) and arranged in a row to record electrical activity in adjacent neurons. Brain stimulation produced neural activity that began with the stimulated neurons and continued sequentially in adjacent neurons. Furthermore, the activity occurred in recurring waves of neural impulses throughout the neural circuit. Verzeano and his associates also observed that the pattern of neural activity depended on the stimulus presented, implying that different reverberatory circuits are activated by different events. It is possible that the activation of different neural circuits by different events accounts for our ability to remember more than one phone number, for example.

Before You Go On

Describe how your study partner's telephone number is recorded in your central nervous system, using Hebb's cell-assembly model. Do you think that the telephone number would be represented by a single cell assembly or more than one?

Is Reverberatory Activity Essential for Memory Storage?

If the encoding of an event in the long-term store requires reverberatory activity, disruption of activity in the neural circuit early in the consolidation of a memory should prevent encoding of the event as a memory. Duncan's (1949) study provided evidence that seemed to support the critical role of reverberating activity in memory consolidation.

Duncan (1949) trained rats to actively avoid electric shock in a device called a shuttle box. In an active-avoidance task, the animal makes an overt response to avoid being punished. The shuttle box is a two-chamber apparatus; the animal learns to jump over a hurdle from one chamber to the other to avoid a painful event. In Duncan's study, each animal received one avoidance learning trial per day for 18 days. After each training trial, rats in eight experimental groups received an electroconvulsive shock (ECS). The time lapse between the end of the training trial and the ECS varied from 20 seconds to 14 hours. A control group of rats did not receive the ECS. Because electroconvulsive shock produces intense, widespread neural activity, Duncan hypothesized that reverberatory activity in neural circuits would be disrupted, and thus have a negative impact on memory consolidation. Duncan further hypothesized that the shorter the interval between the training trial and the ECS, the lower the subsequent recall of the experi-

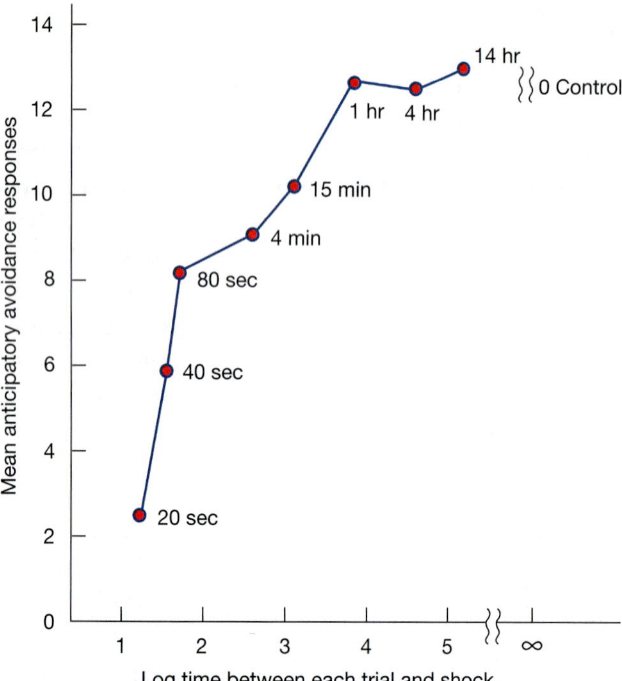

Figure 14.4 Active-avoidance performance as a function of the interval between avoidance training and presentation of ECS. Anticipatory runs are trials in which shock is avoided. The results of this study suggest that the amnesic influence of electroconvulsive shock declines as the interval between training and electroconvulsive shock increases.

➤ *What happens when ECS is administered shortly after a learning trial? When ECS does not immediately follow the learning trial? (p. 427–428)*

ence (less of the memory would have a chance to be stored). As he predicted, Duncan found that the longer the interval between training trial and ECS, the higher the level of memory recall as indicated by avoidance performance (see **Figure 14.4**). The reduced memory following ECS treatment is called **retrograde amnesia**, which is an inability to recall events that precede a traumatic event. Duncan assumed that the retrograde amnesia resulted from the disruption of memory consolidation caused by the ECS-induced termination of reverberatory activity. The results of Duncan's study suggested that consolidation occurs slowly: avoidance performance was impaired even when several hours passed between training and ECS.

Following Duncan's initial observations, several studies (Leukel, 1957; Ransmeier, 1953; Thompson & Dean, 1955) observed the effects of ECS on retention in a variety of tasks. Leukel and Ransmeier used a maze-learning paradigm, and Thompson and Dean employed a visual discrimination task. All of these studies reported that ECS produced deficits in the retention of a response. Retrograde amnesia following ECS was also reported in human subjects (Cronholm & Molander, 1958; Flesher, 1941; Williams, 1950; Zubin & Barrera, 1941).

However, these early studies contained significant methodological flaws. Because electroconvulsive shocks are an aversive event, using multiple ECS presentations may have led inadvertently, through Pavlovian conditioning, to the association of the aversive properties of ECS with the environment in which ECS was presented. The aversive qualities of this environment may have impaired subsequent performance (failure to exhibit an avoidance response) of the learned response. Poor performance attributed to the absence of a permanent memory may, in fact, reflect avoidance of the situation in which ECS was received. The positive correlation between performance and the length of time between the learning trial and ECS, which had been attributed to greater memory consolidation, may instead result from a lesser degree of aversive conditioning caused by the delay between the end of the training trial and ECS.

Miller and Coons (1955) showed that ECS does indeed have aversive properties and that multiple ECSs can lead to an increased avoidance response time. Miller and Coons first trained rats to run down an alley to obtain food, and then delivered electric shock (a less-intense electrical shock than ECS that is painful, but does not produce convulsions) to them while they ate. Electroconvulsive shocks were then administered to some rats at various intervals following the electrical shock. If ECS does indeed disrupt consolidation of the shock experience, then on a subsequent trial the rats should have forgotten that they were shocked and run quickly to the food. However, if ECS has aversive properties, time to respond should instead increase because of a reluctance to reach the food and receive the ECS. Miller and Coons reported that rats given ECS after being shocked showed greater avoidance behavior than did rats that received shocks but not ECS. Further, the longer the interval between the shock and the ECS, the shorter the delay in going after the food.

Studies employing ECS after the 1950s have used a single ECS to minimize aversive conditioning. Experiments have also employed passive avoidance tasks, those where not responding prevents the painful stimulus, in contrast to the active avoidance tasks in which the subject was required to overtly respond to

---

retrograde amnesia The inability to recall events that preceded a traumatic event.

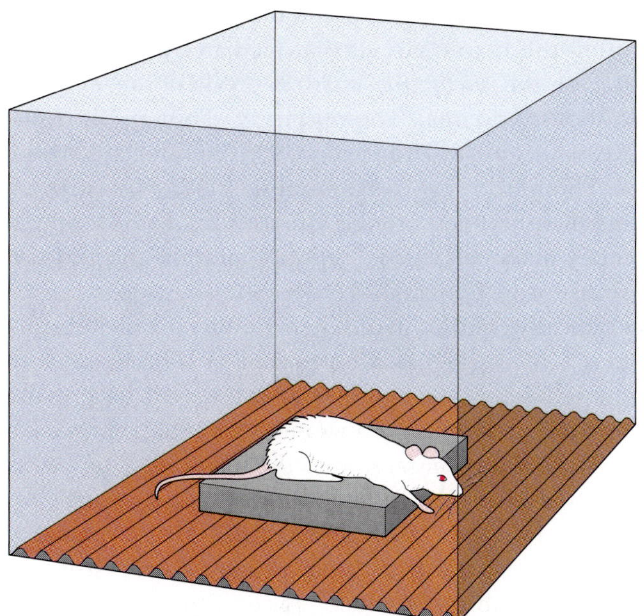

Figure 14.5 Step-down apparatus used for training passive-avoidance response. When the animal steps off the platform, it receives electric footshock. The degree of reluctance to step off the platform indicates the level of conditioning of the passive-avoidance response.

➤ *How is avoidance performance measured in the step-down apparatus? (p. 429)*

avoid the shock. (In a passive avoidance task, any aversive qualities of ECS would lead to a subject taking a longer time to make an avoidance response.) If ECS induces memory deficits, then the use of the single ECS will result in decreased performance; but if ECS causes aversive conditioning, then the result will be greater performance. Studies using single-trial passive avoidance tasks have reported that ECS induces memory deficits only when administered very soon after passive avoidance training (Chorover & Schiller, 1965; Lewis, 1969).

Chorover and Schiller (1965) used a step-down apparatus to train rats to passively avoid electric shock. This step-down apparatus consisted of a chamber with a grid floor and a small wooden platform in the middle of the chamber (see **Figure 14.5**). Rats that stepped off the platform were shocked. After receiving a shock, rats in the experimental groups received ECS. Chorover and Schiller varied the interval between the termination of the shock and delivery of the ECS from 3 to 60 seconds. Rats in the control groups either received shock without ECS or neither shock nor ECS. When tested the next day, control group rats that had not received ECS after training refused to step off the platform, demonstrating that they remembered being shocked in the apparatus (see **Figure 14.6**). The control group rats that had received neither shock nor ECS the previous day readily stepped off the platform. Rats that received ECS within 10 seconds after passive avoidance training stepped off the platform as quickly as the control animals, suggesting that the presentation of ECS after training disrupted consolidation of the memory of the shock. Chorover and Schiller found ECS to be ineffective when presented more than 10 seconds after training (refer to **Figure 14.6**), implying that memory consolidation occurs within a matter of seconds. Thus, the longer gradients following ECS observed in other studies were caused by processes other than the failure to consolidate.

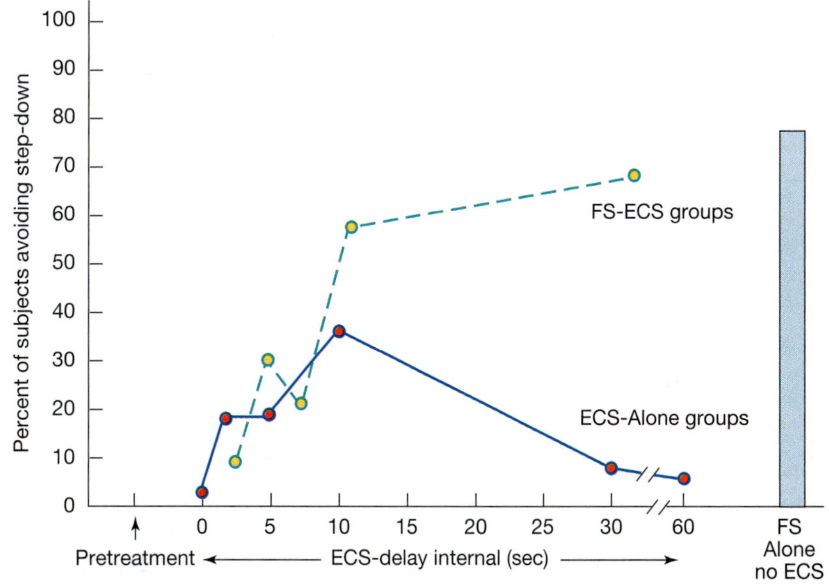

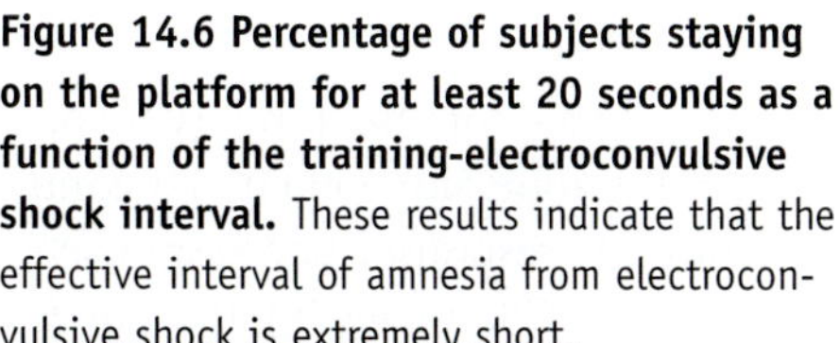

Figure 14.6 Percentage of subjects staying on the platform for at least 20 seconds as a function of the training-electroconvulsive shock interval. These results indicate that the effective interval of amnesia from electroconvulsive shock is extremely short.

➤ *Chorover and Schiller found that both control group rats and rats that received ECS 10 seconds after training readily stepped off the platform. What does this finding suggest? (p. 429)*

A number of studies suggest that memories are consolidated in a fraction of a second (Lewis, 1979; Miller & Springer, 1973). Furthermore, these studies indicate that one function of working memory is to organize or expand the stored memory, which later enhances the ability to retrieve the memory, and that ECS affects not the consolidation or storage of a memory but rather the retrieval of the memory.

Misanin, Miller, and Lewis (1968) provided evidence that ECS interferes with memory retrieval rather than memory storage. They trained rats to passively avoid shock in the step-down apparatus. Twenty-four hours after initial training, some subjects were shown a light, which had signaled the onset of shock during passive avoidance training, followed by an ECS. Other rats received only the light or only the ECS. Both groups of rats were tested for retention of original passive avoidance 24 hours later. The authors reported that ECS produced retrograde amnesia when it followed the light, whereas the rats that received only the light CS or only the ECS remembered their original training and passively avoided the shock. Because consolidation of the memory of the passive avoidance response had most certainly been completed within 24 hours, the retrograde amnesia could not have resulted from disruption of memory consolidation. Instead, Misanin, Miller, and Lewis suggested that there are two kinds of memory systems: active and passive. The active memory system corresponds to the working memory; the passive memory system, to the permanent long-term store. According to this view, retrograde amnesia can be produced only when a memory is active; that is, ECS can interfere with retrieval, but only when the memory of an event is being actively recalled. In the view of Misanin, Miller, and Lewis, the light reactivated the memory of original training, and the ECS produced interference and subsequent amnesia.

Before You Go On

Using what you have learned so far about memory, do you think that Todd's memory problem is one of storage or retrieval? How could you prove it?

Conditioning of Neural Circuits

So we have seen that Hebb's reverberatory neural circuits do exist, but this neural activity affects memory retrieval rather than memory consolidation. What about the third part of Hebb's theory: Are new neural circuits established as a result of experiencing a specific event?

Richard F. Thompson and his associates have identified the neural circuit that mediates the conditioning of the *nictitating membrane,* called the eyeblink response (Krupa, Thompson, & Thompson, 1993; Krupa, Weng, & Thompson, 1996; Steinmetz, Lavond, & Thompson, 1989; Thompson, 1989). The nictitating membrane is a tough inner eyelid that is found in many mammals, birds, reptiles, amphibians and fish (but not in humans). The eyeblink response can be classically conditioned. When an unconditioned stimulus (UCS), such as a puff of air or a brief shock to the skin below the eye, threatens the animal's eye, the nictitating membrane in some vertebrates moves laterally from the nasal side to the temporal side, covering the eye (the unconditioned response, UCR). When the UCS is paired with a neutral stimulus (for example, a light or tone), the neutral stimulus becomes able to elicit a conditioned eyeblink response (CR); in other words, the neutral stimulus becomes a conditioned stimulus (CS). Eyeblink conditioning proceeds slowly, taking as many as 100 CS–UCS pairings for the CS to elicit the CR on 50 percent of the trials.

Thompson (1989) paired a tone (CS) with a corneal air puff (UCS) to a rabbit's eye. He reported that two neural circuits mediate a rabbit's nictitating membrane response. The first neural circuit begins when the 5th cranial nerve (trigeminal nerve) is activated by a corneal air puff. The neural impulse is then sent to the sensory trigeminal nucleus and on to the accessory abducens, an area in the pons that contains the motor nuclei controlling the blinking of the eye (see the blue path in **Figure 14.7**). Activation of this neural circuit produces a fast-acting response (the rabbit's eye closes quickly). A second neural circuit begins with activation of the 5th cranial nerve; the neural impulses pass through the inferior olive nucleus and the Purkinje cells of the cerebellar cortex to the lateral interpositus nucleus of the cerebellum, and on to the red nucleus before reaching the accessory abducens and the motor nuclei that produce the nictitating membrane response (see red path in **Figure 14.7**). Activation of this neural circuit produces a slow-acting nictitating membrane response (the rabbit's eye closes slowly).

Following repeated pairings of the tone (CS) and corneal air puff (UCS), the tone alone elicited a conditioned nictitating membrane response. The response to the CS is slower than to the UCS, suggesting that the CS is activating the slower-developing neural circuit (see the green path in **Figure 14.7**).

Thompson's research also confirms that the CS is indeed stimulating the longer neural circuit. Prior to conditioning, the tone had no effect on the eyeblink

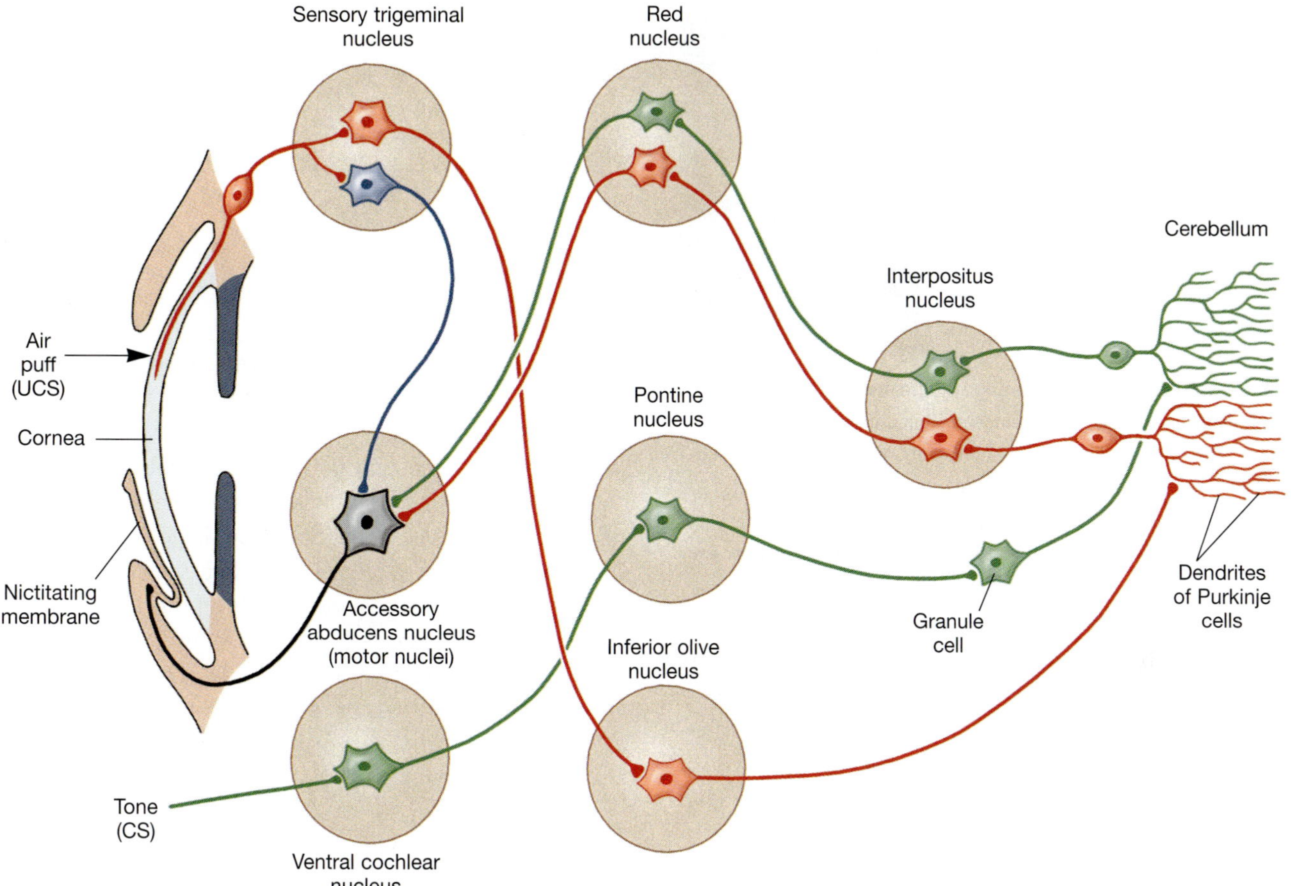

Figure 14.7 The two neural circuits that mediate the influence of tone (CS) and corneal air puff (UCS) on the nictitating membrane response. The UCS activates a direct route between sensory (trigeminal nucleus) and motor (accessory abducens nucleus) neurons and an indirect route through the inferior olive nucleus, cerebellum (interpositus nucleus and dendrites of Purkinje cell), and red nucleus before reaching the motor nuclei controlling the nictitating membrane response. The pairing of CS and UCS produces simultaneous activity in the pontine nucleus and the inferior olive nucleus and allows the CS to activate the longer neural circuit eliciting the nictitating membrane response.

Adapted from Thompson, 1994.

➤ *Trace the pathway that allows the CS to activate the longer neural circuit, eliciting the nictitating membrane response. (p. 430–432)*

response. Conditioning establishes and then strengthens a neural circuit between the sensory receptors that detect the tone (CS) and the muscles that produce the nictitating membrane response (CR). This circuit begins with the detection of the tone in the ventral cochlear nucleus. The message is then sent to the pontine nucleus and then on to lateral interpositus of the cerebellum. From the lateral interpositus nucleus, the input goes to the red nucleus, the accessory abducens, and finally the motor nuclei that activate the nictitating membrane response.

Thompson and his colleagues found that destruction of the longer neural circuit eliminated a previously conditioned nictitating membrane response but did not affect the ability of the corneal air puff to elicit the unconditioned nictitating membrane response. These results indicate that the shorter neural circuit remained functional; that is, the UCS could still activate the nictitating membrane response through its direct connection with the accessory abducens nucleus (see the blue path in **Figure 14.7**). Once the longer neural circuit has been destroyed, reconditioning of the nictitating membrane response is impossible.

By what process is the CS connected to the neural circuit for the eyeblink response? Steinmetz, Lovand, and Thompson (1989) paired direct electrical stimulation of the pontine nucleus (CS) with activity in the inferior olive nucleus (UCS). Following CS–UCS pairings, stimulation of the pontine nucleus activated the same responses as did activity in the inferior olive nucleus. The simultaneous activity of the pontine nucleus (stimulated by the CS) and the inferior olive nucleus (stimulated by the UCS) appears to be responsible for enabling this CS to activate the neural circuit.

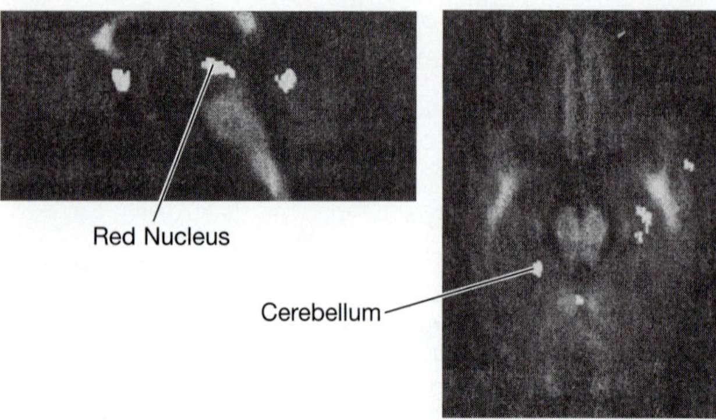

Figure 14.8 Eyeblink conditioning in humans. PET scans show areas of increased activity in the cerebellum and the red nucleus during the conditioning of an eyeblink response in human subjects.
➤ *What role does the cerebellum play in eyeblink conditioning? (p. 432)*

The **lateral interpositus nucleus of the cerebellum** is central to the conditioning of the nictitating membrane response. Krupa, Thompson, and Thompson (1993) found no evidence of conditioning when the lateral interpositus nucleus was cooled, so that the transmission of neural signals was slowed in this area of the brain. Despite repeated CS–UCS pairings, the CS did not elicit the nictitating membrane response. Nor would the CS elicit a nictitating membrane response after the effects of the cooling ended, indicating that conditioning had not taken place. Once the effects of the cooling wore off, conditioning proceeded at a rate comparable to that seen in subjects with no previous experience. These researchers also found that cooling the red nucleus prevented the CS from eliciting the CR, but did not prevent conditioning. After the effects of cooling the red nucleus ended, the CS elicited the nictitating membrane response without the need for further CS–UCS pairings. These results indicate that the neural circuit must be fully functional for the CS to elicit the nictitating membrane response, but that the lateral interpositus nucleus of the cellebellum is the area in the central nervous system where the conditioning of the nictitating membrane takes place.

Research with humans suggests a comparable neural circuit responsible for eyeblink conditioning. Logan and Gratton (1995) found that neural activity, measured with PET scans, revealed increased activity in the cerebellum and red nucleus during the conditioning of an eyeblink response (see **Figure 14.8**). Further, Woodruff-Pak, Papka, and Ivry (1996) reported that people with damage to the cerebellum show impaired eyeblink conditioning.

lateral interpositus nucleus of the cerebellum The area of the brain where the conditioning of the eyeblink response takes place.

Before You Go On

What do Thompson's experiments suggest about the relationship between learning and memory?

Section Review

- Donald Hebb proposed that experiencing an event activates a neural circuit, or cell assembly, in the central nervous system.
- Reverberatory activity in the cell assembly is thought to be responsible for consolidating permanent memory.
- Simple processes are controlled by single cell assemblies; complex processes require multiple assemblies.
- The strength of a memory depends on the amount of time the initial experience or stimulus is available.
- Subsequent testing of Hebb's model has suggested that reverberatory circuits do exist, but that memory appears to consolidate very quickly and the reverberatory circuit plays a role in the retrieval of memory, not in consolidation.
- Research examining the eyeblink response in rabbits has shown that specific neural circuits can be modified by experience. The circuit for a conditioned eyeblink response begins in the ventral cochlear nucleus, goes to the pontine nucleus and lateral interpositus nucleus and Purkinje cells of the cerebellum, then to the red nucleus, the accessory abducens, and finally the motor nuclei that activate the nictitating membrane response.
- The lateral interpositus nucleus of the cerebellum is the area where the conditioning of the eyeblink response takes place.

The Cellular Basis of Learning and Memory

I spent much of my childhood hoping that the Brooklyn Dodgers would win a World Series over the New York Yankees. My prayers were finally answered in 1955. I can still remember that series, especially Johnny Padres's brilliant pitching in the seventh game.

What physical changes occurred in my brain that have allowed these memories to be stored for over 40 years? What process now enables me to retrieve the memory of a World Series played in 1955? In the next sections, we will examine the physical processes that provide the basis for permanent memory storage and retrieval.

Many biological psychologists (Agranoff, 1980; Dunn, 1980) have suggested that a change in the structure of the nucleic acids (RNA and DNA; see Chapter 1) provides the mechanism for the storage of memories; this view is called the **nucleotide rearrangement theory**. Other researchers (Hawkins, Kandel, & Seigelbaum, 1993; Lynch, 1986) have proposed that learning produces changes in neural responsiveness, a view called the **cellular modification theory**. These changes can reflect either enhanced functioning of existing neural circuits or the establishment of new neural connections. We will briefly examine both views in the following sections.

Nucleotide Rearrangement Theory

Biological psychologists have found the nucleotide rearrangement theory attractive for several reasons. First, because the DNA molecule is an innate blueprint for instinctive behaviors, it seems reasonable to believe that it could also store acquired behaviors. Second, DNA possesses sufficient complexity to store the vast amount of information learned over a lifetime.

Two approaches have been used to test the nucleotide rearrangement view of memory storage. Some studies have measured biochemical changes associated with learning, whereas others have utilized a more active approach, attempting to inhibit changes in nucleotides.

Chemical Changes Associated with Learning. Many studies have evaluated whether learning produces quantitative or qualitative changes in RNA. (Because the manufacture of RNA is controlled by DNA [see Chapter 1], changes in RNA are believed to reflect changes in DNA.) Rats, like humans and most other mammals, have a preferred, or dominant, paw or limb that they use to reach for objects. Hyden and Egyhazi (1964) found that rats forced to reach for food with their nonpreferred paw showed a significant increase in cortical RNA in the hemisphere opposite to the nonpreferred paw, compared with control rats allowed to reach with their preferred paw. Qualitative changes in the RNA of the experimental subjects were also observed by Hyden and Egyhazi (1964), who found changes in the ratios of nucleotide bases (the building blocks of RNA and DNA) in the experimental subjects, but not in the control subjects.

Other studies have attempted to identify a specific protein change following learning. (Because protein synthesis is controlled by RNA, altered protein synthesis is believed to reflect nucleotide alteration). George Ungar and associates (Ungar, Galvan, & Clark, 1968) identified a protein thought to be associated with fear. To identify this protein, rats were shocked when they entered a dimly lit chamber. These animals, which naturally prefer dark places, subsequently avoided the dark chamber. Analysis of the rats' brains revealed a protein not present in untrained rats. Ungar and his associates named the protein "scotophobin," after the Greek word for "fear of the dark." However, a number of researchers (DeWied, Sarantakis, & Weinstein, 1973; Miller, Small, & Berk, 1975) found that the effects of scotophobin are nonspecific; that is, scotophobin decreases emotionality, and it is the decreased emotionality, rather than a specific fear of darkness, that accounts for the avoidance of the dark chamber.

Inhibition of RNA Synthesis. If the nucleotide rearrangement theory is accurate, one effect of drugs that temporarily impair or prevent RNA synthesis should be to block memory storage. Many studies have indeed reported that inhibition of RNA synthesis results in memory impairment (Flexner & Flexner, 1968; Quartermain, 1976).

Flood and associates (1973) found that the RNA inhibitor anisomycin, a drug that inhibits protein synthesis, is an effective amnesic agent, even with few exposures. **Figure 14.9** shows the results of their study in which mice were trained to avoid electric shock passively. The level of training was manipulated by varying shock intensity; the greater the intensity of shock, the higher the training strength. The mice in each training level condition also received one, two, or three successive injections of anisomycin. The first injection was given 15 minutes before training; the subsequent injections were given at 2-hour intervals after training. Flood and colleagues found that the greater the number of injections, the greater amnesia of the avoidance training. Furthermore, at a high level of training, three injections were needed to produce any amnesia, indicating that with stronger training, protein synthesis must be inhibited for a longer period to produce forgetting. Flood and colleagues (1975) observed a similar influence of training strength and length of protein inhibition on the level of forgetting of an active avoidance response.

---

nucleotide rearrangement theory The view that a permanent change in DNA and RNA occurs as a result of learning.

cellular modification theory The view that learning permanently enhances the functioning of existing neural circuits or establishes new neural connections.

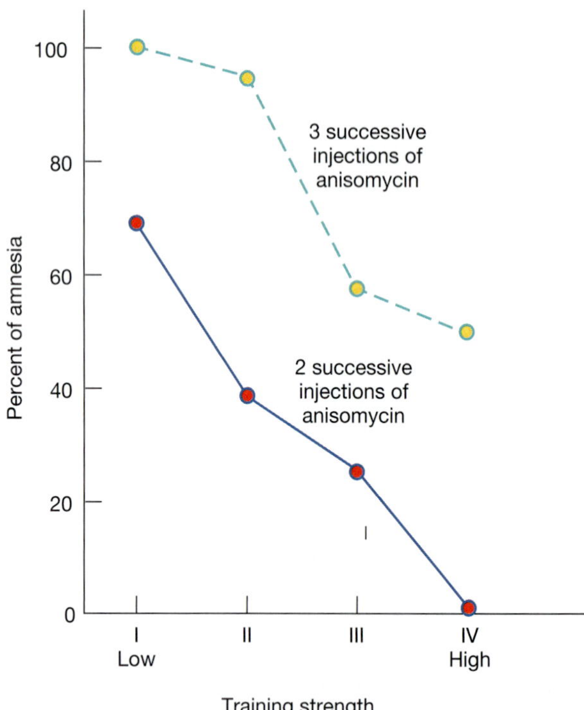

Figure 14.9 The percentage of mice showing amnesia as a function of level of training and the number of injections of anisomycin, a protein inhibitor. The amnesic effect of anisomycin was increased with a higher number of injections but reduced with additional training.

➤ *What would you expect to happen if more injections of anisomycin preceded training? If more training trials were given? (p. 433)*

Before You Go On

If the nucleotide rearrangement theory is correct, what implications does gene therapy (the intentional manipulation of DNA) have for human learning and memory?

Cellular Modification Theory

Just as experience can alter RNA-controlled protein synthesis within neurons, it can also enhance the synaptic responsivity in existing or new neural circuits. Structural changes also underlie the strengthening of neural circuits that occurs as a result of experience (remember Hebb's cell-assembly model?). We will first examine the effect of experience on synaptic responsivity, followed by a discussion of the structural changes that result from experience.

Learning in *Aplysia Californica*. Eric Kandel and his associates have investigated changes in synaptic responsivity following learning in the sea slug *Aplysia californica* (Abrams, Karl, & Kandel, 1991; Dale, Schacher, & Kandel, 1988; Edmonds et al., 1990; Eliot et al., 1991; Hawkins, Kandel, & Siegelbaum, 1993). This simple shell-less marine mollusk has three external organs—the gill, the mantle, and the siphon (see **Figure 14.10**)—that retract or withdraw when either the mantle or the siphon is touched. This defensive withdrawal response can be either sensitized or habituated as a result of experience.

Repeated presentations of a weak tactile stimulus decreases the strength of the defensive withdrawal reac-

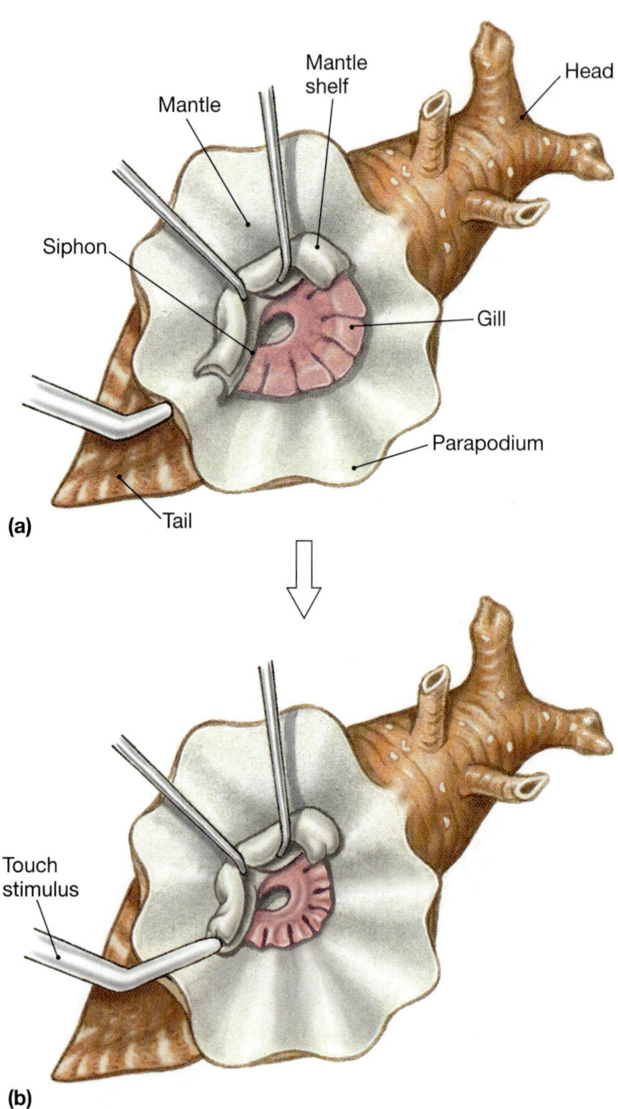

Figure 14.10 *Aplysia californica*. In this shell-less marine mollusk, touching either the siphon or the mantle elicits a defensive retraction of the three external organs—the gill, the mantle, and the siphon. (a) The external organs are relaxed and (b) withdrawn.

➤ *What is the adaptive value of the Aplysia's external organs? (p. 434)*

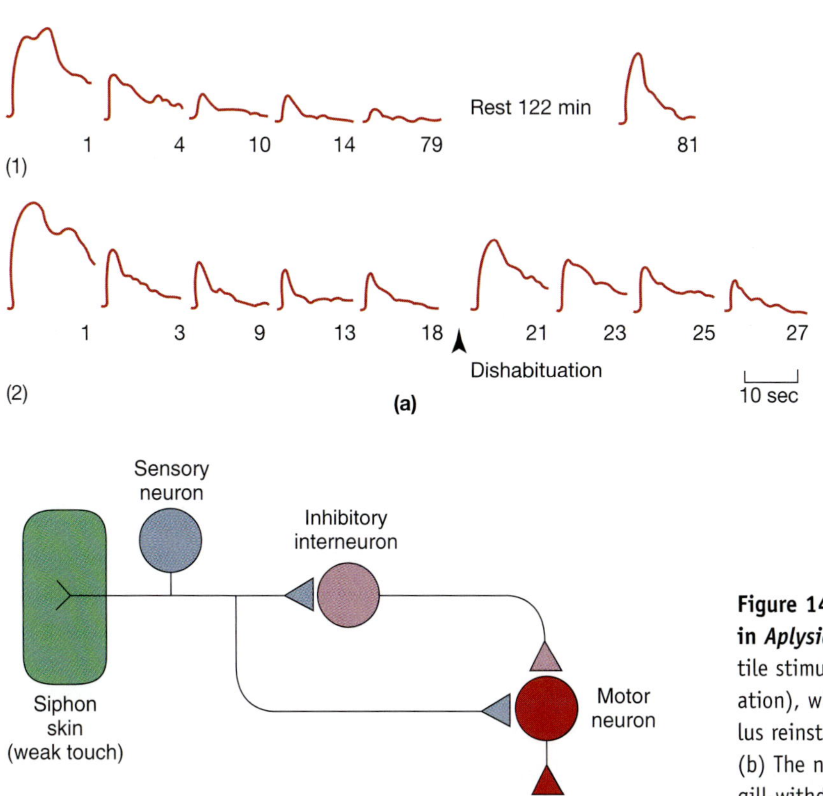

Figure 14.11 Habituation of the gill withdrawal response in *Aplysia californica*. (a) Repeated exposure to a weak tactile stimulus leads to a reduced withdrawal reaction (habituation), whereas either a rest period or another tactile stimulus reinstates the withdrawal reaction (dishabituation). (b) The neural circuit that mediates the habituation of the gill-withdrawal response includes the sensory neuron, an inhibitory interneuron, and the motor neuron.

➤ *What is the mechanism for habituation? (p. 435)*

tion (see **Figure 14.11a**). This decreased responding is caused by habituation, which as we learned earlier in the chapter is a type of learning characterized by a diminished innate reaction to a stimulus as a result of repeated stimulus presentations. Habituation of the *Aplysia*'s defensive response is stimulus specific, which means that any change in the location of the touch will produce a normal-strength withdrawal response.

In contrast to the decreased response caused by habituation to a weak touch, the presentation of an electric shock to the tail prior to touching the siphon of the *Aplysia* will produce an increased defensive reaction. This increased response to touching the siphon is caused by sensitization, which, as we learned earlier, is an increase in the innate reactivity to a stimulus following exposure to an intense stimulus. Unlike habituation, which occurs in response to a specific stimulus, the effect of a sensitizing stimulus is nonspecific. Following exposure to an electric shock, any stimulus, even a weak one, will elicit a strong defensive reaction.

The *Aplysia*'s defensive reaction can be conditioned. For example, Carew, Hawkins, and Kandel (1983) paired a light touch to the mantle or siphon (CS) with a strong electric shock to the tail (UCS). These investigators reported that following repeated pairings of the light touch (CS) with electric shock (UCS), the light touch alone elicited the withdrawal response (CR).

Conditioning in the *Aplysia* is controlled by the same variables that affect all conditioned responses, such as the time between the CS and the UCS and the intensity of the UCS. When the CS precedes the UCS by a short time (.5 sec.), conditioning proceeds rapidly (Hawkins, Carew, & Kandel, 1986). By contrast, the CR does not develop if the CS precedes the UCS by 2, 5, or 10 seconds or if the UCS precedes the CS (backward conditioning). Further, the CS produces the same conditioned response as the unconditioned withdrawal response to the UCS (Hawkins et al., 1989).

Hawkins, Kandel, and Siegelbaum (1993) proposed that the habituation of the *Aplysia*'s defensive reaction lowers responsivity of the synapses between the sensory and motor neurons involved (see **Figure 14.11b**). This decreased synaptic responsivity reflects a decreased Ca^{++} ion influx into the cell and a reduced neurotransmitter release from the presynaptic membrane of the sensory neuron. In other words, habituation translates into decreased neurotransmitter release at the synapse.

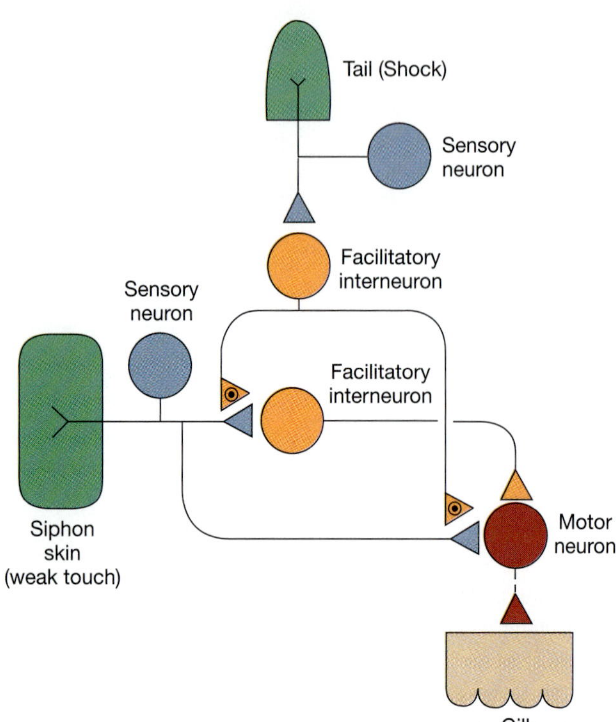

Figure 14.12 Sensitization of the gill withdrawal response in *Aplysia californica*. Exposure to an intense electric shock leads to an increased withdrawal reaction to a weak tactile stimulus (sensitization). The neural circuit that mediates the sensitization of the gill-withdrawal response includes the sensory neuron, a facilitatory interneuron, and the motor neuron.

➤ *What is the mechanism for sensitization? (p. 436)*

Similarly, sensitization and conditioning increases the responsivity of the synapses between the sensory-motor neurons of the *Aplysia*'s defensive reflex (Hawkins, Kandel, & Siegelbaum, 1993; see **Figures 14.12** and **14.13**). The increased synaptic responsivity is the result of increased neurotransmitter release from the sensory neuron and increased activity in the motor neuron, which is caused by presynaptic facilitation (refer to Chapter 4).

Kandel and his associates have identified the mechanism of synaptic facilitation in *Aplysia.* Some of the interneurons modulating the defensive reflex are serotonergic (Glanzman et al., 1989). Serotonin (5-HT) released from a facilitatory interneuron increases the duration of the action potential in the sensory neuron by prolonging the closure of K^+ ion channels (refer to **Figure 14.14**; Eliot et al., 1991). You will recall from Chapter 4 that during an action potential, there is increased movement of K^+ ions out of the cell. With reduced K^+ ion movement out of the cell as a result of the closed K^+ ion channels, the duration of the action potential increases. The prolonged action potential leads to greater Ca^{++} ion movement into the presynaptic membrane of the sensory neuron, thereby allowing increased neurotransmitter release into the synapse between the sensory and motor neurons.

Earlier we said that pairing a touch (CS) with a tail shock (UCS) leads to conditioning of the defensive response. Apparently, the CS produces the same increase in synaptic responsivity as does a sensitizing stimulus (Hawkins, Kandel, & Siegelbaum, 1993). Serotonin released from the facilitatory interneuron causes a decreased K^+ ion movement from the sensory neuron (Eliot et al., 1989). This decreased movement of K^+ ions increases the duration of the action potential in the sensory neuron, increases Ca^{++} ion influx into the cell membrane of the sensory neuron, and enhances neurotransmitter release from the sensory neuron. The effect of greater neurotransmitter release is an increased strength of the conditioned withdrawal response.

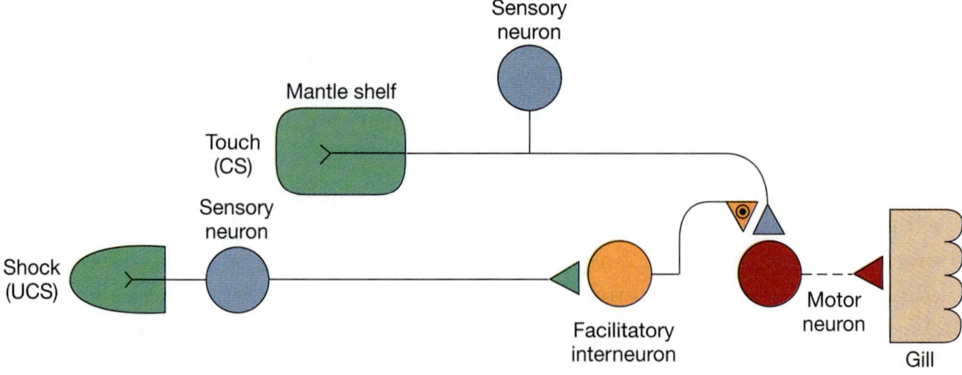

Figure 14.13 Classical conditioning in *Aplysia californica*. The pairing of tactile stimulation of the mantle (CS) with shock stimulation of the tail (UCS) leads to the conditioning of the withdrawal response to the CS. The neural circuit that mediates the conditioning of the gill-withdrawal response includes the sensory neuron, an facilitatory interneuron, and the motor neuron.

➤ *What is the mechanism for Pavlovian conditioning? (p. 436)*

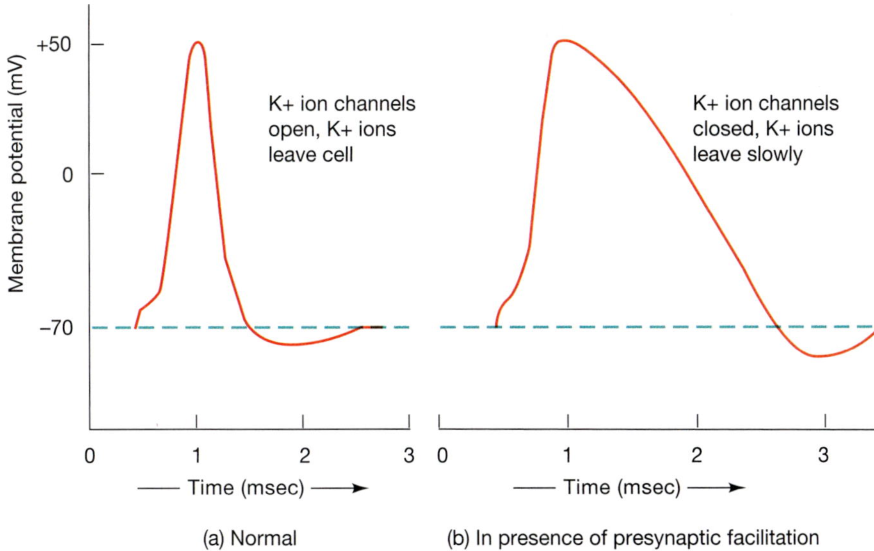

Figure 14.14 The changes in K⁺ ion movement that occur during an action potential. The typical sequence of ion movement is shown on the left; the slower exit of K⁺ ions from inside the cell caused by presynaptic facilitation is seen on the right.
➤ *How could a prolonged action potential play a role in memory storage and retrieval? (p. 436–437)*

Conditioning can lead not only to greater neurotransmitter release but also to an increased number of synaptic connections. Next we discuss the research of Gary Lynch (Lynch, 1986; Lynch & Baudry, 1984), who has examined the structural changes that occur following conditioning.

Structural Changes and Experience. Lynch found not only that experience enhances the entry of Ca^{++} into the nerve cell, but that the Ca^{++} ions activate a dormant enzyme called **calpain**. Calpain breaks down the protein **fodrin**, which makes up the coating around the dendrites. The breakdown of the dendrite's coating exposes more of the dendrite to stimulation from other neurons; that is, as the coating breaks down, the neuron becomes more sensitive. With continued experience, the breakdown process continues, resulting in even greater sensitivity of the neuron.

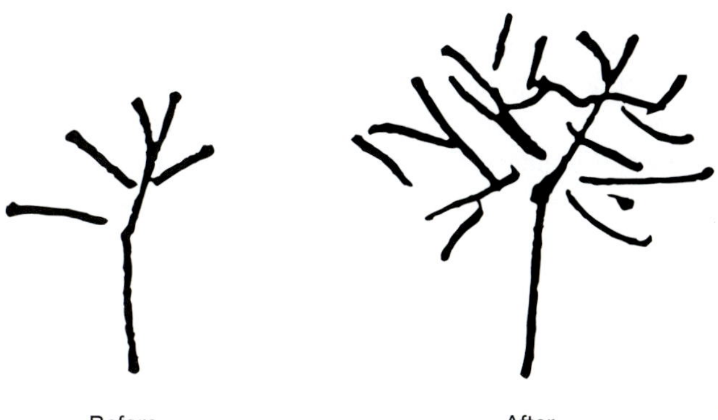

Figure 14.15 Arborization of dendrites. Continued experience increases neural connections via breakdown of the dendritic coating.
➤ *What chemical reaction is responsible for arborization? (p. 437)*

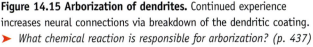

Lynch (1986) also suggested that the breakdown of cellular coating allows the dendrites to change shape and spread out, leading to the establishment of new neural connections (see **Figure 14.15**). In Lynch's view, this arborization of the dendrites results in the establishment of new neural connections, which represents the biological basis of learning.

These neuronal changes are also the neural basis of memory. Lynch and Baudry (1984) trained rats to find food in an eight-arm radial maze (see **Figure 14.16**). The procedure used in this study involved placing food reinforcement in all eight arms. The rats' task on each trial was to visit each of the arms only once. When a rat returned to a previously visited arm, it received no food. The rats quickly learned the task; they remembered which arms they had visited and which arms they still could visit to receive reinforcement. Lynch and Baudry then implanted a pump in the rat's brain that could infuse a chemical called leupeptin into the lateral ventricle. This chemical inhibits the breakdown of fodrin, thereby preventing the establishment of new neural connections. These researchers found that the animals that received leupeptin entered the arms of the radial maze randomly, recalling nothing of their past learning experience, whereas control animals that did not receive leupeptin showed good recall of the prior experiences.

Recall from Chapter 3 that synaptic connections are formed by the attraction of the filopodia to neurotrophins released by target cells during the prenatal

calpain A dormant enzyme that breaks down the protein fodrin.

fodrin A protein makes up the coating around the dendrites.

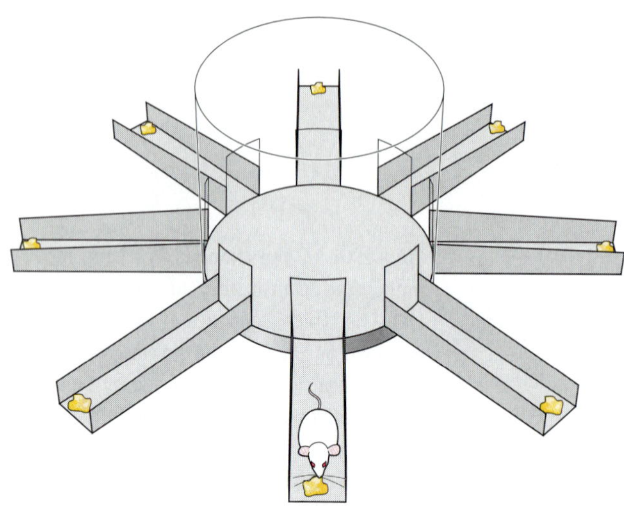

Figure 14.16 Eight-arm radial maze used to study spatial memory. In studies of spatial memory, reinforcement (food) is placed in the arms of the maze and rats are required to visit each of these arms without returning to a previously visited arm.

➤ *What effect does administration of leupeptin have on performance of this task? (p. 437)*

development of the nervous system. A similar process seems to allow for the establishment of new synaptic connections formed as a result of experience. Murphy and Regan (1998) reported that neural cell adhesion molecules (NCAMs), one type of neurotrophin, are produced both during the development of the nervous system and beginning 6 to 8 hours after learning in both chicks and rats. New dendrites are formed during the time that NCAMs are present, and are associated with the strengthening of existing or establishing new neural pathways that allow for the storage and retrieval of experiences.

We have discussed research suggesting that experience alters RNA and produces changes in neural responsivity. You might think that the nucleotide rearrangement theory and the cellular modification theory present antagonistic views of memory consolidation; however, the two theories are not necessarily mutually exclusive. The ability to recall past experiences may be the result of structural changes in the nervous system that are controlled by RNA and DNA. If this is true, then analysis of the biological changes that occur after learning takes place should reveal both nucleotide rearrangements and structural neural modifications.

We have discovered that learning leads to changes in neuronal structure and function. But it is a quantum jump from clusters of neurons and sprouting dendrites to the processes that allow us to remember our past. Further, it is clear that memories are not stored in any specific location in the brain. The noted psychologist Karl Lashley (1950) searched and failed to locate the **engram**, or the physical representation of a memory. Lashley trained rats to run through a maze to obtain reward, and then lesioned parts of the rats' association cortices. Despite removing parts of the cortex, Lashley found that the rats retained at least some memory of their past experience. It is clear that many questions remain about how we remember our past. The investigation of the nature of memory is at the frontier of neuroscience. Providing answers to our questions will be the task of the next generation of neuroscientists.

engram The physical representation of a memory.

Before You Go On

Could the nucleotide rearrangement theory and the cellular modification theory both be true? What evidence would be needed to show this?

Section Review

- According to the nucleotide rearrangement theory, learning causes changes in DNA and RNA.
- Evidence for the nucleotide rearrangement theory arises from two research findings: that both qualitative and quantitative changes in RNA follow learning, and that inhibition of RNA synthesis produces memory impairment.
- The cellular modification theory argues that learning can modify the responsivity of specific neurons as well as produce structural changes in neurons.
- Work with *Aplysia californica* has demonstrated that habituation, sensitization, and conditioning can result from specific chemical reactions at the synapse level; habituation produces a decreased neurotransmitter release, whereas both sensitization and conditioning increase neurotransmitter release.
- Experience causes the coating of dendrites to break down, resulting in arborization, or the establishment of new connections between neurons. This structural change appears to underlie the permanent storage of experiences.

The Anatomy of Learning and Memory

So now you know a little about how learning occurs at the level of the neurons and synapses, and that memories are stored throughout the brain. But do some parts of the brain play a greater role in the storage and retrieval of memories than others? What happens if these areas are damaged? Larry Squire and his colleagues (Squire, 1987;

Squire, Shimamura, & Amaral, 1989; Squire & Zola-Morgan, 1988; Zola-Morgan & Squire, 1993) have developed a model detailing the structures involved in memory (see **Figure 14.17**). According to Zola-Morgan and Squire (1993), information that is initially processed in the sensory areas of the cortex is sent first to structures in the medial temporal lobe for further processing. Key structures in the **medial temporal lobe** include the hippocampus and surrounding cortical areas (perirhinal, entorhinal, and parahippocampal cortices). Projections from these medial temporal lobe structures then convey information to the **mediodorsal thalamus**, where the information receives still further processing. Following analysis by the mediodorsal thalamus, information is relayed to the frontal lobe.

The frontal lobe plays a crucial role in the planning, execution, and control of behavior. Zola-Morgan and Squire (1993) suggest that the medial temporal lobe structures and the mediodorsal thalamus jointly establish long-term memory, and that connections between these structures and the frontal lobe provide a route by which memories can influence behavior. This model proposes that the structures in the medial temporal lobe and the mediodorsal thalamus are involved in memory. We will next look at several studies that provide evidence supporting Zola-Morgan and Squire's model.

Medial Temporal Lobe

The Case of H.M. In 1953, patient H.M. had his medial temporal lobes (including the hippocampus, amygdala, and surrounding cortical tissue) removed as a treatment for severe epilepsy. Although the operation alleviated his epilepsy, this success proved quite costly. Although H.M. remained pleasant and good-humored after the operation, he suffered from severe memory impairment. H.M. is very cooperative, and many researchers (Corkin et al., 1997; Corkin et al., 1981; Milner, 1970; Scoville & Milner, 1957) have examined the details of his memory disorder for the past 40 years.

The most profound deficit is H.M.'s **anterograde amnesia** (ante = in front of), or an inability to recall events that have occurred since the operation (remember Todd from the chapter-opening vignette?). For example, on each visit to the hospital, H.M. has to be reintroduced to his doctors. His amnesia results from his failure to permanently store those experiences. H.M. also shows retrograde amnesia for events that took place in the several years leading up to his operation but can clearly remember events older than this.

> H.M. is fully aware of the extent of his memory impairment: "Every day is alone in itself, whatever enjoyment I've had, and whatever sorrow I've had. . . . Right now, I'm wondering. Have I done or said anything amiss? You see, at this moment everything looks clear to me, but what happened just before? That's what worries me. It's like waking from a dream; I just don't remember." (Milner, 1970, p. 37)

medial temporal lobe A brain area containing the hippocampus and surrounding cortical areas (the perirhinal, entorhinal, and parahippocampal cortices) that are involved in the storage of experiences.

mediodorsal thalamus A brain structure that plays a key role in the storage of experiences.

anterograde amnesia The inability to recall events that occur after some disturbance to the brain.

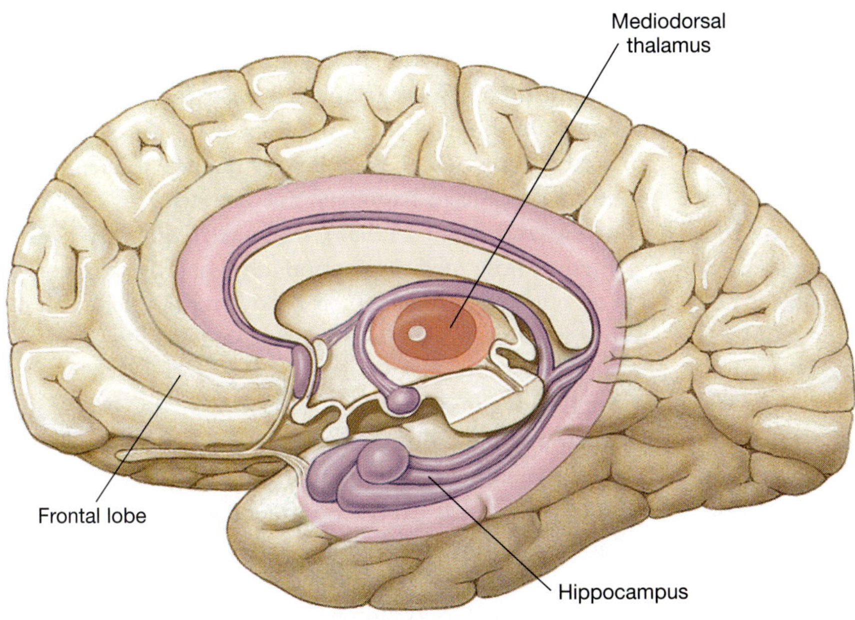

Figure 14.17 Sagittal plane view of key structures for memory storage and retrieval. Information is sent from sensory areas in the cortex to the medial temporal lobe (hippocampus and adjacent areas) and then to the mediodorsal thalamus (MD) for further processing.

➤ *What is the function of the connections between the memory structures located deep within the brain and the frontal lobe? (p. 439)*

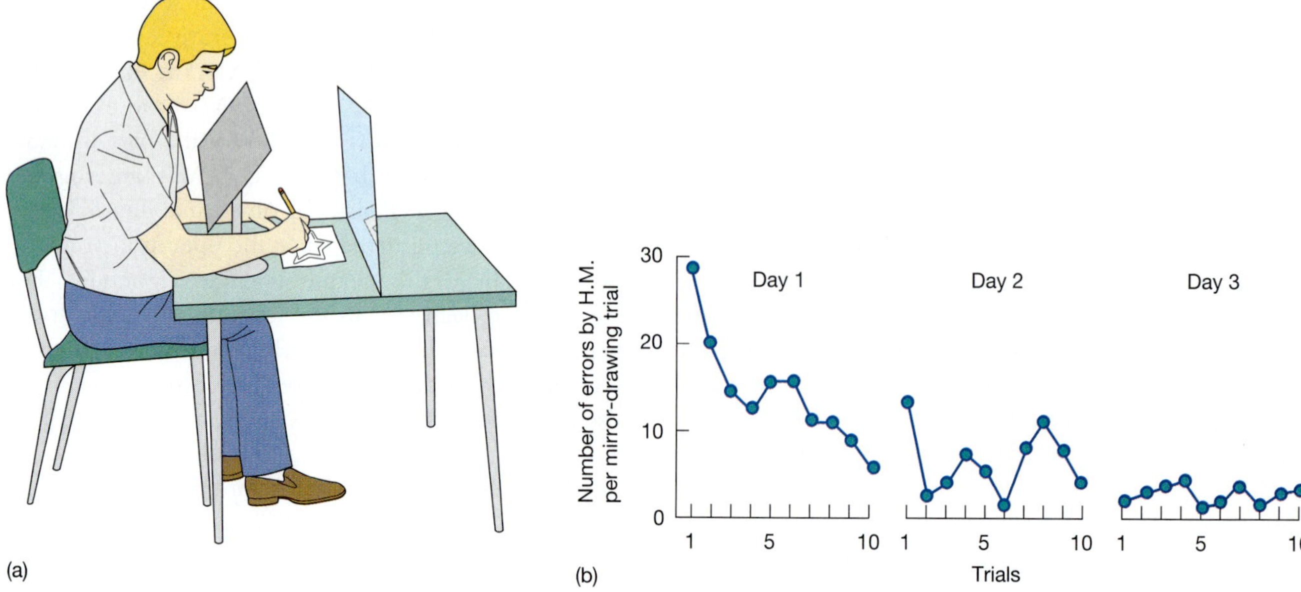

Figure 14.18 The mirror drawing task. (a) In this illustration, a patient traces a star seen in a mirror. (b) H.M. made fewer errors during each day of training, and his improvement was retained over 3 days of training.

➤ *How could H.M.'s performance on the mirror-tracing task improve during training if he cannot remember having performed this task from one day to the next? (p. 440)*

Although H.M. does suffer from severe memory impairment, some areas of his memory remain intact. Squire (1987) suggested that although H.M. cannot store declarative memories (see **p. 425**), he can store and recall procedural memories (see **p. 425**). Further, even though recent episodic memories (see **p. 424**) are lost, semantic memories (see **p. 424**) are not affected by medial temporal lobe damage. Although H.M.'s language ability was not affected by the operation and he can still read and write, his speech contains no words introduced into the English language since his surgery (Gabrieli, Cohen, & Corkin, 1988). For example, H.M. defined "flower child" as "a young person who grows flowers." The failure to learn new words further reflects his inability to store new facts (declarative memories).

Brenda Milner (1965) has conducted many studies evaluating H.M.'s memory. Her work clearly shows that H.M. can acquire new skills (procedural memories). In one study, H.M. participated in a mirror drawing task (see **Figure 14.18a**). The task involves tracing an object while looking at it in a mirror, without looking down at your hand or the paper. This task is difficult (try it!), because it involves drawing in a direction opposite to the one indicated by the visual stimulus (the reflection in the mirror), and requires practice. On this task, H.M.'s performance improved over a series of trials; he made fewer errors on each subsequent trial (see **Figure 14.18b**). As can be seen from **Figure 14.18b**, his improvement was maintained over several days of training (three days are shown), indicating that a memory of the task was formed. Although H.M.'s performance improved, he could not remember participating in the task from one day to the next.

How could H.M. become more adept at tracing the figure but have no recollection of having previously drawn it? Tracing the figure is a visuomotor skill that involves procedural memory. As suggested by Squire, procedural memories appear to be unaffected by damage to the medial temporal lobe. By contrast, awareness of having traced the figure is an episodic memory; episodic memory storage does appear to be affected by damage to the medial temporal lobe.

Other cases of amnesia following damage to the medial temporal lobe area have been documented. For example, Scoville and Milner (1957) examined eight psychiatric patients whose medial temporal lobes had been removed in an attempt to reduce their behavioral problems. All of these patients showed severe anterograde amnesia.

The Importance of the Hippocampus. Removal of the medial temporal lobe damages a number of other structures, including the hippocampus, amygdala, and surrounding cortical areas. Considerable evidence (Zola-Morgan & Squire, 1993) indicates that the hippocampus is the key memory structure in the medial temporal lobe. Lesions to the hippocampus (including the dentate gyrus and the subicular complex) and surrounding areas (perirhinal, entorhinal, and parahippocampal cortices) produce deficits in the retention of a simple visual discrimination (Squire, Zola-Morgan, & Chen, 1988) and performance on a delayed matching-to-sample task (Alvarez-Royo et al., 1992; Overman, Ormsby, & Mishkin, 1991).

In a delayed matching-to-sample task, a subject is shown a stimulus (called the sample) and then, after varying time intervals, is shown the sample and a second stimulus. The subject is then asked which of the two stimuli is the sample shown previously. Subjects with hippocampal damage can match the sample if the retention interval is short but not if the retention interval is long. The level of memory impairment is influenced by the extent of hippocampal area damage. Although damage limited to the hippocampus produces some memory impairment, greater deficits are seen when the hippocampus and surrounding cortical tissue are damaged (Clower et al., 1991).

Zola-Morgan, Squire, and Amaral (1986) examined the memory of patient R.B., a 52-year-old man with a history of coronary disease. R.B. suffered a cardiac arrest, which caused a temporary loss of blood to the brain (anoxia) and resulted in brain damage. The brain damage produced profound anterograde amnesia. Five years after his cardiac arrest, R.B. died. Histological examination of his brain revealed a significant degeneration of hippocampal tissue (see **Figure 14.19**). Damage to the hippocampus also has been linked to memory deficits in other patients (Squire, Amaral, & Press, 1990; Victor & Agamanolis, 1990). For example, Squire, Amaral, and Press (1990) performed a high-resolution MRI on several patients with severe memory impairment and observed significant reduction in the size of the hippocampus in each case. The recent use of MRI scans on H.M. also shows that most of the hippocampus and all of the entorhinal and parahippocampal cortices are absent bilaterally in H.M. (Corkin et al., 1997; see **Figure 14.20**).

Although the amygdala of patient H.M. was also removed as a result of his surgery, this area of the brain does not appear to play a crucial role in H.M.'s amnesia (Zola-Morgan & Squire, 1993). Evidence for this lack of involvement is the observation that damage limited to the amygdala produces no memory deficit in primates (Zola-Morgan, Squire, & Amaral, 1989), although, as you recall from Chapter 12, the amygdala plays a central role in the emotions of anger and fear.

H.M. was unable to store new declarative memories, but he was able to retrieve declarative memories acquired prior to his surgery, an observation that supports the idea that the hippocampus is involved in the storage of declarative memories, but is not the site of those memories. Several researchers (Gabrieli, 1998; Tulving, 1998) point to the frontal and temporal lobes as the site of storage of declarative memories. Gabrieli (1998) suggests that "knowledge in a domain (e.g., for pictures or words, living or manufactured objects) is distributed over a specific, but extensive neural network." Activation of a specific neural network allows us to remember a past experience. In support of this view, PET scan studies (Nyberg, Cabeza, & Tulving, 1996; Tulving & Markowitsch, 1997) reveal that the frontal and temporal lobes of both hemispheres become active during the retrieval of past events.

Our discussion indicates that the hippocampus (including dentate gyrus and subicular complex) and surrounding structures (perirhinal, entorhinal, and parahippocampal cortices) are critical to the storage of

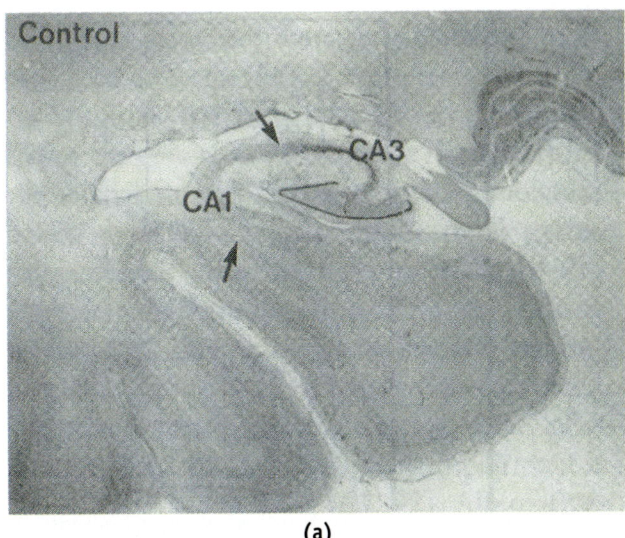

(a)

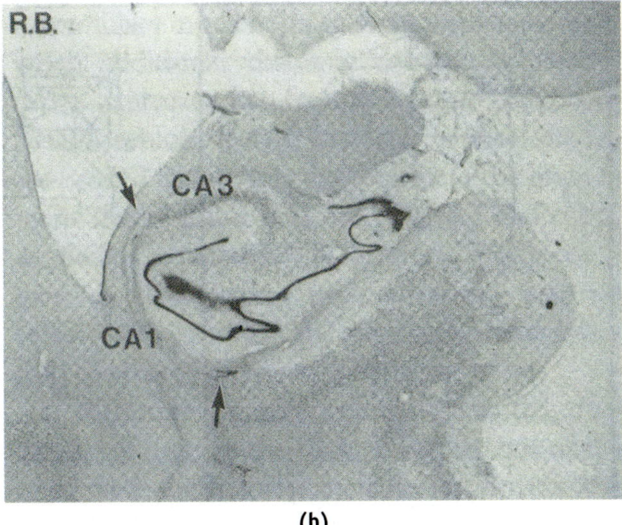

(b)

Figure 14.19 Two different photographs of the hippocampus. (a) Normal hippocampal structures. (b) The degeneration of hippocampal pyramidal cells of field CA1 caused by anoxia in patient R.B.

➤ *What effects did degeneration of the neurons in the hippocampus of patient R.B. have on his memory? (p. 441)*

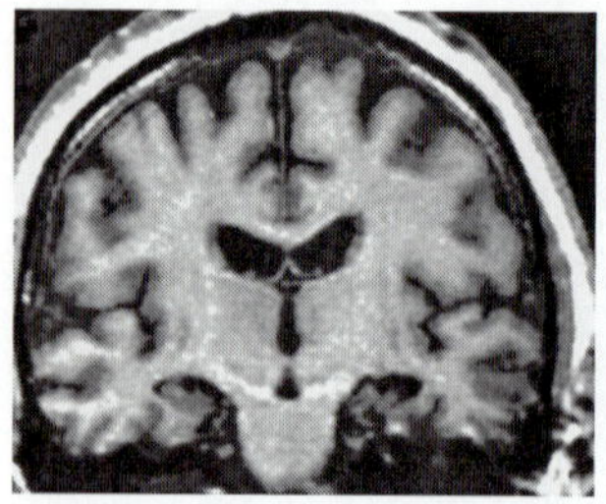

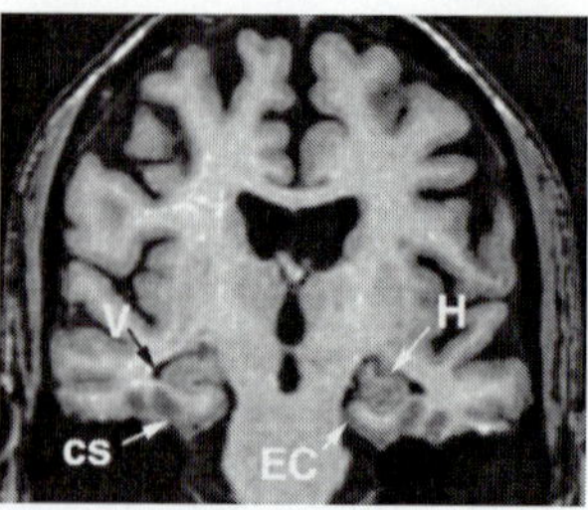

Figure 14.20 The hippocampus of H.M. The hippocampus (H) and entorhinal cortex (EC) are present in the brain of a normal subject (right), but absent bilaterally in the brain of H.M. (left).
➤ *What were the consequences of bilateral removal of H.M.'s hippocampus? (p. 441)*

new declarative memories. Studies of neural activity in the hippocampus have shown that experience can modify the functioning of hippocampal neurons. We next turn our attention to this area of research.

Long-Term Potentiation in the Hippocampus. Our previous discussion indicated that experience can change synaptic responsivity in the sensory neurons controlling the defensive withdrawal reaction of *Aplysia* (see **p. 434–435**). Can such changes be found in the nervous system of more advanced species? Considerable research shows that experience modifies neural activity in specific hippocampal pathways of rats (Hawkins, Kandel, & Seigelbaum, 1993). A brief, intense series of electrical impulses to the afferent neurons leading to one of three pathways into the hippocampus causes increased synaptic responsivity when a test stimulus is later applied to the same neural pathway. The three pathways are the perforant fiber, mossy fiber, and Schaffer collateral fiber pathways. This increased neural responsivity, which takes the form of an increase in the amplitude and duration of excitatory postsynaptic potentials (EPSPs) to the test stimulus, is called **long-term potentiation (LTP)**. The summation of EPSPs from several neurons is referred to as a *synaptic wave.* **Figure 14.21** shows a synaptic wave generated in response to a test stimulus before and after exposure to an intense potentiating stimulation. As you can see from the figure, the synaptic wave is as strong at 96 hours as it is at 1 hour following the intense electrical stimulation, hence the name "long-term."

The most widely studied hippocampal pathway is the **perforant fiber pathway** (see **Figure 14.22**). Neurons in this pathway begin in the entorhinal cortex and connect to the granule cells in the dentate gyrus. A brief series of intense stimuli (usually five bursts of 100 Hz is sufficient) to the entorhinal cortex produces an increased reactivity of the neurons in the dentate gyrus. Other pathways that have been shown to sustain LTP include the **mossy fiber pathway**, which begins in the granule cells in the dentate gyrus and connects with the pyramidal cells in the CA_3 field of the hippocampus, and the **Schaffer collateral fiber pathway**, which begins in the hippocampal pyramidal cells of

long-term potentiation (LTP) An increased neural responsivity, which takes the form of an increase in the amplitude and duration of excitatory postsynaptic potentials (EPSPs), that follows a brief, intense series of electrical impulses to neural tissue.

perforant fiber pathway A hippocampal pathway that begins in the entorhinal cortex and connects to the granule cells in the dentate gyrus.

mossy fiber pathway A hippocampal pathway that begins in the granule cells in the dentate gyrus and connects with the pyramidal cells in the CA_3 field of the hippocampus.

Schaffer collateral fiber pathway A hippocampal pathway that begins in the hippocampal pyramidal cells of field CA_3 and connects with the pyramidal cells of field CA_1 of the hippocampus.

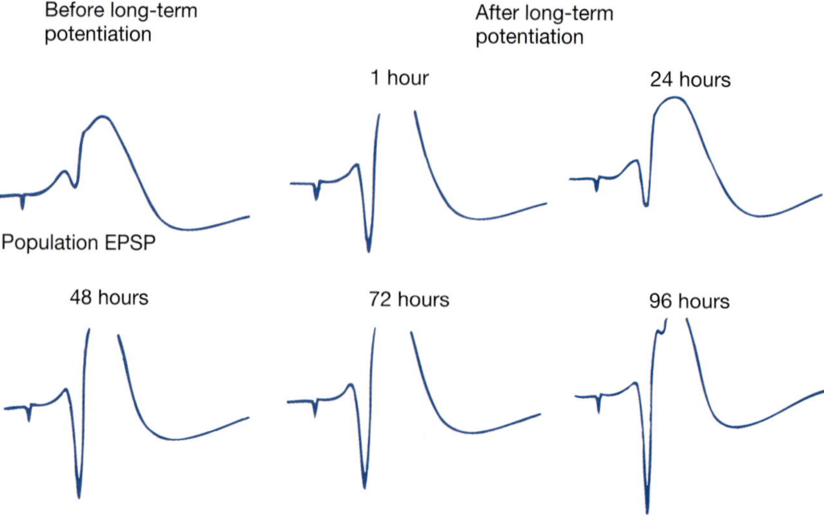

Figure 14.21 Summated EPSPs from the dentate gyrus before and after presentation of a potentiating stimulus. Notice that increased synaptic responsivity persists for 96 hours following exposure to intense electrical stimulation.
From Berger, 1984.
➤ *How does the long-term potentiation phenomenon help us understand the physiological basis of learning and memory? (p. 442–444)*

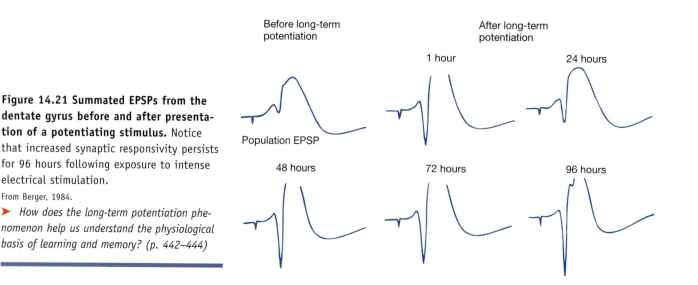

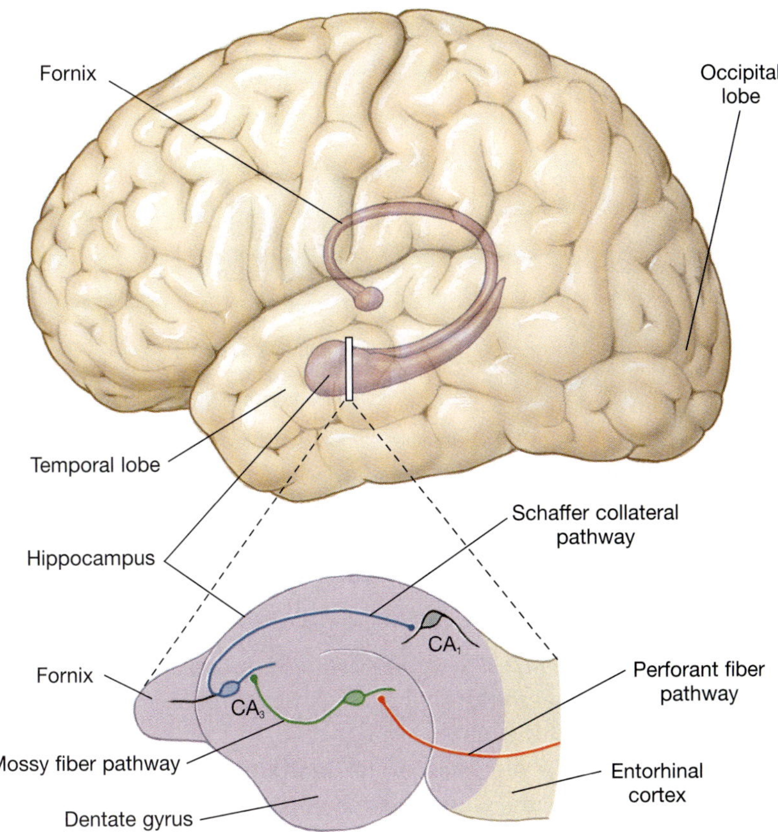

Figure 14.22 Sagittal plane view of three neural circuits in the hippocampus. The perforant pathway begins in the entorhinal cortex and synapses in the dentate gyrus; the mossy fiber pathway begins in the dentate gyrus and synapses on hippocampus CA_3 field; and the Schaffer pathway begins in hippocampal field CA_3 and synapses on hippocampal CA_1 field.

From Kandel et al., 1991.

➤ *Why does long-term potentiation affect the separate pathways in the hippocampus individually? (p. 434 & 443)*

field CA_3 and connects with the pyramidal cells of field CA_1 of the hippocampus.

Long-term potentiation has several key characteristics. First, a brief sensitizing stimulus is sufficient to produce it. This demonstrates that neurons in the hippocampus have the ability to change synaptic responsivity following a single event. Second, the change in synaptic responsivity associated with LTP is confined to a specific neural pathway. For example, intense stimulation of the neurons in the perforant pathway increases the synaptic responsivity of neurons in that pathway but not in other hippocampal pathways. This characteristic of LTP allows an experience to alter responsivity only in relevant neural pathways. Third, long-term potentiation can be produced by a single stimulus or by the convergence of stimuli that individually would not produce LTP but together can modify synaptic responsivity. Analysis of an experience requires input from multiple sources; the ability of several inputs to produce LTP shows that convergence of input to a specific pathway can modify synaptic responsivity. Fourth, LTP can last days or weeks, a finding that indicates that LTP is not a temporary change in synaptic responsivity.

The increased synaptic responsivity of hippocampal neurons can be conditioned, an observation that increases the validity of the view that changes in neural activity underlie learning and memory. Kelso and Brown (1986) implanted stimulating electrodes into different fibers of one hippocampal pathway. They then simultaneously presented a weak stimulus through one stimulating electrode and a strong stimulus through a second stimulating electrode. (The weak stimulus by itself was not capable of producing LTP, whereas the strong stimulus by itself was.) Following pairing of the weak and strong stimuli, the weak stimulus alone was capable of producing LTP. The presentation of a weak stimulus through another electrode that had not been paired with the strong stimulus did not produce LTP.

What process is responsible for the change in synaptic responsivity associated with LTP? LTP appears to occur as a result of modification in the functioning of the NMDA (N-methyl, D-aspartate) receptor (Liao, Hessler, & Malinow, 1995). The **NMDA receptor** is sensitive to the neurotransmitter glutamate. The presence of glutamate alone at the NMDA receptor is not sufficient to produce an action potential. Magnesium (Mg^{++}) ions block the ion channels of the NMDA receptors, so glutamate cannot open them (see **Figure**

NMDA receptor A receptor site that is sensitive to the neurotransmitter glutamate.

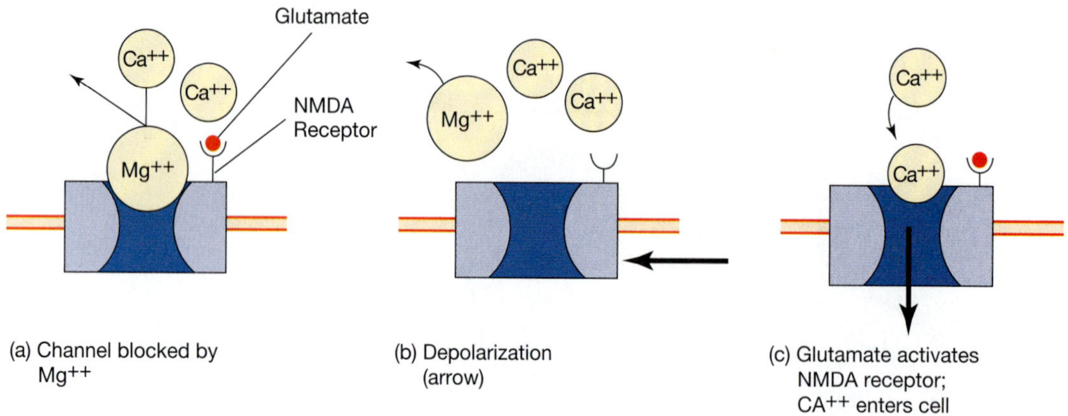

Figure 14.23 Ion changes at the NMDA receptor that result in LTP. As seen in (a), glutamate cannot activate NMDA due to presence of Mg^{++} ions in the channel. Depolarization of the postsynaptic membrane as a result of activation of non-MNDA receptors causes Mg^{++} ions to leave the channel (b). In (c), glutamate can activate the NMDA receptor, and Ca^{++} ions can enter the ion channel.

➤ *What is the role of the NMDA receptor in long-term potentiation? (p. 443–444)*

14.23). For the NMDA receptor to be activated, the receptor site must already have been partially depolarized by nearby EPSPs when the glutamate reaches the postsynaptic membrane. Activation of non-NMDA hippocampal receptors depolarizes the postsynaptic membrane of the NMDA receptors and removes Mg^{++} ions from the ion channels. If glutamate is then present at the NMDA receptor sites, Ca^{++} ions can enter the now-open channels. Remember our discussion of calpain and changes in the postsynaptic membrane? Calpain release is activated by the influx of Ca^{++} ions into NMDA receptors, altering the structure of the postsynaptic membrane. The alteration of the postsynaptic membrane is responsible for LTP and increased synaptic responsivity.

Can it be shown that LTP is involved in the learning of new behavior? Several lines of evidence support an involvement of LTP in learning. First, LTP has been found in single cells in the hippocampus following spatial learning in rats (Izquierdo, 1995). Single-cell recordings reveal long-term changes in neural reactivity as the result of a spatial learning experience. Second, the injection of the drugs that block NMDA receptors have been shown to impair spatial learning (Davis, Butcher, & Morris, 1992; Fin et al., 1995). Animals receiving drugs that block NMDA receptors repeatedly go to arms where food is not located or fail to return consistently to places where food is located. These results suggest that changes in synaptic responsivity in the NMDA receptors in the hippocampus, or LTP, are central to the ability of an animal to learn about its spatial environment.

Our discussion so far indicates that LTP is produced by changes in postsynaptic responsivity. Research has provided evidence that LTP also results from changes in presynaptic responsivity, specifically increased presynaptic neurotransmitter release. Several studies (Bliss et al., 1986; Malgaroli & Tsien, 1992; Malinow, 1991) have reported increased glutamate release following exposure to a potentiating stimulus.

How could increases in presynaptic neurotransmitter release be maintained over time? One likely mechanism involves a substance, called a **retrograde messenger**, that is sent from the postsynaptic membrane to the presynaptic membrane to maintain neurotransmitter release. Several lines of evidence indicate that nitric oxide (NO) is a retrograde messenger for LTP. Garthwaite, Charles, and Chess-Williams (1988) found that activation of NMDA receptors causes the release of NO from the postsynaptic membrane, and O'Dell, Hawkins, Kandel, and Arancio (1991) injected NO into hippocampal neurons and observed increased release of glutamate from the presynaptic membrane.

In summary, an intense stimulus can produce increased synaptic reactivity in the hippocampus via presynaptic and postsynaptic mechanisms, called long-term potentiation (LTP). As a result of LTP, there is increased postsynaptic responsivity as well as enhanced neurotransmitter release from the presynaptic membrane. The increased presynaptic neurotransmitter release maintains LTP until the permanent changes on the NMDA receptors can occur.

---

retrograde messenger A chemical that is sent from the postsynaptic membrane to the presynaptic membrane to maintain neurotransmitter release.

Before You Go On

Describe the plight of H.M. in your own words. What does this case imply about the role of memory?

What evidence suggests that damage to the medial temporal lobe affects declarative and episodic memory but leaves procedural and semantic memory unimpaired?

What parallels exist between synaptic responsivity in *Aplysia* and long-term potentiation in rats?

The Role of the Mediodorsal Thalamus

So far, we have seen the effects on memory of damage to several structures in the medial temporal lobe. Damage to the mediodorsal thalamus has also been associated with profound memory impairment (Aggeton & Mishkin, 1985; Horel & Misantone, 1976; Zola-Morgan, Squire, & Amaral, 1989). Horel and Misantone observed that destruction of the mediodorsal thalamus affected the ability of primates to distinguish new from familiar objects. By contrast, mediodorsal thalamic lesions had no influence on the retention of a simple visual discrimination. In other words, the mediodorsal thalamus appears to be involved, like the medial temporal lobe, in the memory of facts (declarative memories) but not skills (procedural memories). However, damage limited to the mediodorsal thalamus produces mild memory deficits, not severe amnesia like that observed following hippocampal damage (Aggeton & Mishkin, 1985). More severe memory loss is observed when both the mediodorsal thalamic nuclei and its surrounding structures are damaged.

Memory impairments have also been observed in humans following damage to the mediodorsal thalamic nuclei. Von Cramon, Hebel, and Schuri (1985) studied seven patients who had severe memory impairments following medial thalamic infarctions, or anoxia to the medial portion of the thalamus. The researchers used a CT scan to identify which areas were damaged by the loss of oxygen. All of these patients showed considerable damage to the mediodorsal thalamus and surrounding tissue.

Anoxia is not the only cause of memory-related damage to the brain. Severe memory impairment also is frequently observed in chronic alcoholics. This memory loss was first described by the Russian neurologist Sergei Korsakoff in 1889. His patients failed to recall past events; if an event recurred, these individuals showed no evidence of having previously experienced it. This disorder is now called **Korsakoff's syndrome**.

Korsakoff's syndrome is caused by a thiamine deficiency that results from the inadequate intake of nonalcoholic nutrients. Thiamine (vitamin B_1) is needed to metabolize glucose, and a deficiency in thiamine leads to the atrophy of brain cells, especially in the mediodorsal thalamus (Squire, Amaral, & Press, 1990).

Like H.M., individuals with Korsakoff's syndrome show profound anterograde amnesia. For example, a person with Korsakoff's syndrome could not recall what he or she had for breakfast, even if only a short period of time intervened between breakfast and the attempt to recall the experience of breakfast.

The memory impairment in Korsakoff's syndrome involves a loss of declarative but not procedural memory. For example, Sidman, Stoddard, and Mohr (1968) trained a patient with Korsakoff's syndrome to select a square containing the image of a circle from among seven other squares containing ellipses of various shapes. Even after several minutes of working on other tasks, the patient could select the appropriate stimulus. These observations show that this particular patient could remember the correct response. However, although the patient continued to respond appropriately, he soon forgot the words for what he had learned. When asked during training what he was doing, he replied that he was choosing the circle. However, after several minutes, he could no longer verbally describe his actions. These results suggest that the patient retained knowledge of the contingency between behavior and reinforcement (procedural memory), but forgot exactly what he was doing (declarative memory). In a similar study, individuals with Korsakoff's syndrome could remember previously acquired contingencies between behavior and outcomes, but could not recall the logic behind their actions (El-Wakil, 1975).

Although patients with damage to the mediodorsal thalamic nuclei show memory deficits similar to those seen in medial temporal lobe patients, individuals with damage to the medial temporal lobe differ in some ways from individuals with mediodorsal thalamic nuclei damage. Patients like H.M., with medial temporal lobe damage, are aware of their memory deficits. By contrast, Korsakoff's syndrome patients, and others with mediodorsal thalamic nuclei damage, are unaware of their memory loss. These individuals will confabulate, or make up stories, to fill in the gaps in their memories. Further, emotion is intact following medial temporal lobe damage, whereas patients tend to be emotionally flat and apathetic after damage to the mediodorsal thalamus. The confabulation and lack of insight in patients with Korsakoff's syndrome is probably due to damage to the prefrontal cortex (Moscovitch, 1992;

Korsakoff's syndrome A disorder, usually seen in chronic alcoholics, caused by a thiamine deficiency that results from the inadequate intake of nonalcoholic nutrients and is characterized by profound anterograde amnesia and impaired insight.

Shimamura, Janowsky, & Squire, 1990). The mediodorsal thalamus projects to the prefrontal cortex, and individuals with Korsakoff's syndrome show impairments like those seen following damage to the prefrontal cortex.

As we have seen, damage to the areas controlling memory can occur as a result of many conditions: chronic alcoholism, strokes or other conditions limiting blood flow to key structures in the brain, and head trauma from accidents such as the one described in the chapter-opening vignette. In the next section you will discover that profound loss of memory also can occur in patients with Alzheimer's disease, a progressive, debilitating disorder, for which there is no cure.

Before You Go On

Do you think Todd suffered mediodorsal thalamic damage or medial temporal lobe damage?

Contrast the effects of mediodorsal thalamic damage with the effects of medial temporal lobe damage.

Section Review

- Information is first processed in the sensory areas of the cortex and then sent to the medial temporal lobe for further processing.
- Projections from the medial temporal lobe structures convey information to the mediodorsal thalamus for additional processing.
- In the medial temporal lobe, key areas responsible for memory are the hippocampus and surrounding structures, which are intricately connected to the frontal lobe.
- Damage to the medial temporal lobe causes anterograde amnesia, or an inability to recall events subsequent to the damage, limited to episodic and declarative memory.
- Long-term potentiation, or increased synaptic responsivity, can be produced by a single stimulus or a series of stimuli.
- LTP is confined to the single pathway that receives the stimulus, and it may last for days or weeks.
- LTP may result from presynaptic facilitation as well as from increased postsynaptic responsivity.
- Damage to the mediodorsal thalamus is associated with anterograde amnesia and with Korsakoff's syndrome.
- The mediodorsal thalamus projects to the prefrontal cortex, and individuals with damage to the mediodorsal thalamus, like those with prefrontal lobe damage, confabulate and show a lack of insight.

APPLICATION

Alzheimer's Disease

Greg has found it increasingly difficult to care for his wife, Beth. His children have urged him to place her in a nursing home. Greg and Beth have been married for 45 years, and the thought of being away from her torments him. Beth's problems began several years ago, just after Greg retired. They had purchased a new camper with all the amenities and looked forward to traveling to all the places around the country they had always wanted to see. At first, Beth simply seemed unusually forgetful. She would park her car at the mall and be unable to find it, or she would get lost on the way home from their daughter's house across town. In addition, Beth became unusually anxious; when their son got married, Beth needed a tranquilizer to calm her enough to go to the wedding.

Over the next few years, Beth's forgetfulness worsened. She soon lost all recollection of recent events. When a neighbor asked her what she wore to her son's wedding, Beth could not remember. She had difficulty understanding questions; for example, when Greg asked her if she wanted to go to the movies, she responded that she enjoyed seeing *Gone with the Wind*. Beth also talked a lot but made little sense.

After much urging, Beth consented to go to the doctor. Because a standard physical exam revealed no pathology that could account for her symptoms, the physician strongly urged further tests and indicated that he suspected Alzheimer's disease. Beth did not understand the implications of the doctor's tentative diagnosis, but Greg knew enough about Alzheimer's to be terrified.

Neurological and neuropsychological tests supported the diagnosis. Greg was told that Beth would continue to deteriorate, her memory would become progressively worse, and eventually she would become unresponsive. Greg knew that Beth's condition was likely to get bad, but he was not prepared for the day when she no longer recognized him or their children.

Beth suffers from dementia of the Alzheimer's type (DAT), or Alzheimer's disease. **Dementia** is a loss of or impairment in a person's mental functioning. The term *dementia* comes from two Latin words meaning "away" and "mind." Dementia is not a specific disease but instead is a set of symptoms related to impairment in mental functioning. The following areas are affected: language (for example, anomia or word-finding problems as we saw in Chapter 13), memory (for example, forgetting an appointment), visuospatial orientation (for example, becoming lost in a

dementia A loss of or impairment in a person's mental functioning.

familiar area), and judgment (for example, the failure to wear a coat in extremely cold weather).

Several conditions can lead to dementia, and **Alzheimer's disease** or **dementia of Alzheimer's type**, is the most common. First described by physician Alois Alzheimer in 1907, its symptoms can become apparent as early as age 40, but are more likely to occur at more advanced ages. About 5 percent of the general population over age 65, and 20 percent over age 85, suffers from Alzheimer's disease (Johansson & Zarit, 1997). Alzheimer's disease is more likely to occur in women, perhaps because women live longer than men (Gallagher-Thompson & Thompson, 1995). Dementia of the Alzheimer's type is characterized by a gradual onset and, at later stages, a progressive deterioration of mental functioning. Alzheimer's ultimately is a fatal disease, with the course of the illness running from 6 to 12 years (Cummings & Benson, 1983).

Stages of Alzheimer's Disease

For diagnostic purposes, dementia of the Alzheimer's type can be divided into three stages according to severity of deficits in functioning (refer to **Table 14.3**). Mild anterograde amnesia characterizes Stage I, also called early or mild Alzheimer's disease. For example, the person with Stage I Alzheimer's disease will forget where he or she left the car keys or parked the car. In Stage II, also called middle or moderate Alzheimer's disease, the person begins to lose memory of all recent events. The person with Stage III, also called late or severe Alzheimer's disease, cannot recognize family members or remember distant events, such as those that happened in childhood. The amnesia associated with Alzheimer's disease is different from that of Korsakoff's syndrome. The patient with Alzheimer's disease loses semantic and procedural as well as episodic and declarative memories.

Language functioning is also impaired, and this impairment worsens as the disease progresses. As seen in **Table 14.3**, language impairment in Stage I involves *anomia*, or name-finding problems, reduced word frequency (for example, fewer words are used to answer a question), and vague or unclear words used in conversation. Comprehension and repetition appear to be generally good at this stage. In Stage II, comprehension is significantly reduced. Also, jargon, words, or paraphasias, become prominent, anomia is pronounced, with many words needed to identify objects, and conversation makes little sense. Language in Stage III is lost completely; the person becomes mute and unresponsive.

Other characteristics of Alzheimer's disease include changes in personality (from apathetic, anxious, and

Alzheimer's disease (or **dementia of the Alzheimer's type**) A type of dementia that is characterized by progressive neurological degeneration and a profound deterioration of mental functioning.

Table 14.3 ■ Characteristics of the Three Stages in the Progression of Dementia of the Alzheimer's Type (DAT)

	Other Terms	Intelligence	Personality	Language
Stage I	Early	Forgetful	Apathetic	Usually comprehends
	Mild	Disoriented	Anxious	Vague words in talk
		Careless	Irritable	Naming may be impaired
Stage II	Middle	Recent events	Restless	Comprehension reduced
	Moderate	forgotten		Paraphasias, jargon
		Math skills		Irrelevant talk
		reduced		Naming becomes wordy
				Poor self-monitoring
Stage III	Late	Recent events	Unresponsive	Unresponsive
	Severe	fade fast	Withdrawn	Mute
		Remote memory		
		impaired		
		Family not		
		recognized		

Source: Adapted from Davis, G. A. (1993). *A survey of adult aphasia and related language disorders* (2nd ed.). Boston: Allyn & Bacon. Adapted with permission.

irritable in Stage I to restless in Stage II and withdrawn and unresponsive in Stage III), loss of visuospatial orientation, and poor judgment.

Persons with Alzheimer's disease usually remain in good physical health until the later stages of the disease, when their ability to participate in physical activities declines dramatically and they become increasingly susceptible to illnesses such as pneumonia (Gallagher-Thompson & Thompson, 1995).

The Cellular Basis of Alzheimer's Disease

A conclusive diagnosis of Alzheimer's disease requires identification of distinct neurological changes in the brain, which can only be confirmed by direct examination of brain tissue (Damasio, Van Hoesen, & Hyman, 1990). The brains of persons with Alzheimer's disease are characterized by the presence of neurofibrillary tangles and senile plaques. **Neurofibrillary tangles** are unusual triangular and looped fibers in the cytoplasm of nerve cells (see **Figure 14.24**). **Senile plaques** are granular deposits of **amyloid beta protein** and the remains of degenerated dendrites and axons of nerve fibers, which increase in number as the disease progresses.

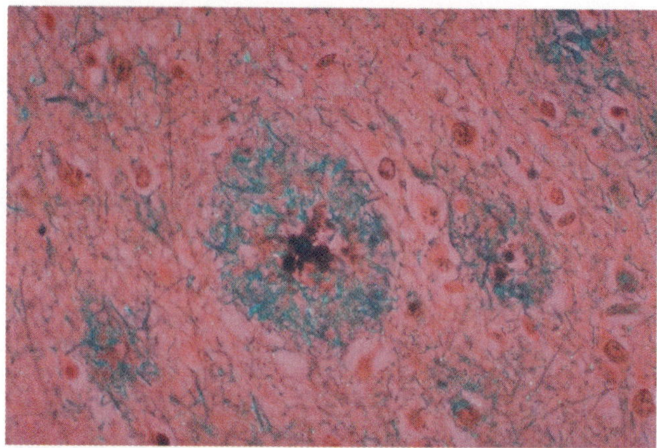

Figure 14.24 Photograph of the brain tissue from a 69-year-old man with Alzheimer's disease. The neurofibrillary tangles appear as twisted fibers that make the cells seem blackened. Senile plaques (large masses) contain amyloid protein and degenerated axons and dendrites. The neurofibrillary triangles are seen as dark squiggles.

➤ *What behavioral changes are associated with Alzheimer's disease? (p. 447–448)*

Amyloid beta protein deposits are thought to cause degeneration of neural fibers and disruption of neural connections within specific areas of the brain. As would be expected from the memory deficits of Alzheimer patients, senile plaques become pronounced in the granular layers II and IV of the inferior temporal lobe; both of these layers have connections to the hippocampus. Senile plaques also form in the temporal lobe, especially Wernicke's area, causing the language impairment found in Alzheimer patients. Further, senile plaques are found in the posterior association regions of the cerebral cortex and pyramidal layers III and V of the parietotemporal lobe, in the areas controlling memory and language.

Persons with Down syndrome (see Chapter 3) who live to middle age are very likely to develop Alzheimer's disease (Selkoe, 1991). As persons with Down syndrome are susceptible to serious cardiac and respiratory diseases, reaching middle age used to be uncommon. Medical advances, however, have increased the life expectancy of someone born with Down syndrome today to 55 (Strauss & Eyman, 1996). Postmortem examinations of the brains of Down syndrome patients with Alzheimer's disease reveal significant accumulation of senile plaques and neurofibrillary tangles. Some senile plaques and neurofibrillary tangles are also found in the brains of Down syndrome patients who have died in their teens or twenties. Down syndrome is caused by the presence of three copies of chromosome 21; this is the same chromosome that mutates to produce amyloid beta protein. This observation provides further evidence that amyloid protein plays a critical role in producing Alzheimer's disease.

Degeneration of Neural Pathways

Biological psychologists have found that neural tissue degeneration in Alzheimer patients occurs in those cholinergic neurons that originate in the basal forebrain and synapse in the neocortex and in those that begin in the medial septal area and synapse in the hippocampus (Coyle, Price, & DeLong, 1983). The degeneration of cholinergic neurons significantly decreases the levels of acetylcholine, choline acetyltransferase (the enzyme that stimulates acetylcholine synthesis), and acetylcholinesterase (the enzyme that deactivates acetylcholine). The reduced levels of ACh, choline acetyltransferase, and acetylcholinesterase further suppress cholinergic transmission.

neurofibrillary tangles Unusual triangular and looped fibers in the cytoplasm of nerve cells.

senile plaques Granular deposits of amyloid beta protein and the remains of degenerated dendrites and axons of nerve fibers in the brain.

amyloid beta protein A protein that accumulates in the neural tissue and is thought to cause the degeneration of neural fibers and disruption of neural connections within specific areas of the brain characteristic of Alzheimer's disease.

An impaired cholinergic system has been shown to lead to memory deficits in nonhuman animals (Rauch & Raskin, 1984). Evidence that decreased cholinergic transmission contributes to memory impairment is also provided by studies that find memory deficits following administration of cholinergic antagonists (Deutsch, 1983; Givens & Olton, 1990). Deutsch (1983) reported that cholinergic antagonists eliminated hippocampal theta activity and impaired spatial learning. Givens and Olton (1990) directly injected cholinergic blockers into the medial septal nucleus and found reduced release of acetylcholine in the hippocampus during spatial learning and a subsequent impairment in spatial memory.

If cholinergic transmission is impaired in Alzheimer patients, would administration of cholinergic agonists be helpful? One cholinergic agonist, tacrine (Cognex), has been prescribed to Alzheimer patients since the early 1990s. Cognex blocks the reuptake of acetylcholine, prolonging its activity at the synapse, and clinical trials with Cognex report improvement in 20 to 30 percent of patients with Alzheimer's disease (Farde et al., 1992). However, the average degree of improvement was modest, and in some cases effectiveness decreased with continued use.

The failure of cholinergic agonists to successfully treat the memory deficits associated with Alzheimer's disease suggests that these cognitive impairments may be caused at least in part by the degeneration of other types of neurons. Hyman, Van Hoesen, and Damasio (1987) observed degeneration of neurons that secrete norepinephrine, serotonin, and glutamate in Alzheimer patients. Especially significant may be the degeneration of glutamate neurons. (Recall our earlier discussion of the involvement of glutamate in LTP in the hippocampus.) Hyman, Van Hoesen, Damasio, and Barnes (1984) observed degeneration of the glutamate-secreting neurons in the perforant pathway, a major pathway involved in memory that begins in the entorhinal cortex and synapses in the dentate gyrus. Further, Hyman, Van Hoesen, and Damasio (1987) found an 83 percent reduction of glutamate in the dentate gyrus, an important structure for memory storage. Degeneration of this structure probably contributes to the anterograde amnesia seen in Alzheimer patients.

Genetics and Alzheimer's Disease

We learned earlier that Down syndrome is associated with Alzheimer's disease, an observation suggesting a link between chromosome 21 and Alzheimer's disease. The relationship between Down syndrome and Alzheimer's disease has led to the discovery of a gene on chromosome 21 linked to early-onset Alzheimer's disease (Goate et al., 1991). The presence of this gene has been associated with increased amyloid beta protein production. A gene on chromosome 14 also has been shown to be related to increased levels of amyloid beta protein and early-onset Alzheimer's disease (Citron et al., 1997; Sherrington et al., 1995). Other researchers (Corder et al., 1993; Strittmatter & Roses, 1996) have identified a gene, called apolipoprotein E or ApoE, on chromosome 19 that is associated with increased amyloid beta protein levels and late-onset Alzheimer's disease. There are several forms of ApoE, the most common being ApoE2, ApoE3, and ApoE4. Everyone has two copies of the ApoE gene, but those with one or two copies of ApoE4 have a much greater risk of developing late-onset Alzheimer's disease. The mechanism by which the ApoE gene, or other genes associated with Alzheimer's disease, increases the risk of this disease is not currently known, but will certainly be an area of significant inquiry.

Treatment of Alzheimer's Disease

What can be done to treat a person with Alzheimer's disease? At this time, there is no cure, but several interventions do seem to be helpful. Mnemonic techniques can enhance memory in the early stages of the disease (Wilson & Evans, 1996). *Mnemonics* are memory aids that improve the storage and retrieval of information. They rely on associative processes to link events. For example, suppose an Alzheimer patient has difficulty remembering where he or she has left the car keys. The keys could be put in the same place every day, allowing the patient to associate the keys with that place. Reality orientation programs that enable Alzheimer patients to maintain awareness of who and where they are seem somewhat beneficial as well. Support groups can help families learn more about the disease and about methods of caring for the Alzheimer patient.

We learned earlier that amyloid beta protein deposits may play a role in causing Alzheimer's disease. Selkoe (1992) suggested that oxidation of amyloid beta proteins may be responsible for producing the amnesic effect. Carney and Floyd (1991) found that protein oxidation is greater in older than in younger gerbils, and that memory is poorer in older than in younger gerbils. Carney and Floyd administered a drug that inactivates the chemicals that oxidize proteins and observed that spatial memory in older gerbils improved to the level seen in young gerbils. On the basis of this research, Selkoe suggests that future treatment of Alzheimer's disease might include methods of inhibiting the oxidization of amyloid beta proteins or of preventing the entry of these proteins into cerebral tissue.

Before You Go On

What stage of Alzheimer's is Beth in?

Based on what you have learned about the cellular, neurochemical, and genetic bases of Alzheimer's, propose a new method of treatment for this disease.

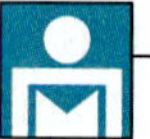

Section Review

- Alzheimer's disease is a progressive impairment in mental functioning that includes deficits in language, memory, visuospatial orientation, and judgment.
- Alzheimer's disease can be divided into three stages, according to the severity of the symptoms: Stage I, Stage II, and Stage III.
- Stage I Alzheimer's disease is characterized by mild forgetfulness and disorientation, sometimes accompanied by anxiety.
- Stage II Alzheimer's disease is characterized by greater forgetfulness of recent events, reduced comprehension of language, and paraphasias.
- Stage III Alzheimer's disease is characterized by severe memory loss, nonrecognition of family members, unresponsiveness, and complete loss of language skills.
- The neurological changes present in Alzheimer patients are neurofibrillary tangles and senile plaques as well as progressive degeneration of cholinergic neurons that originate in the basal forebrain and synapse in the neocortex and those that begin in the medial septal area and synapse in the hippocampus.
- Research into Alzheimer's disease is ongoing, and several genetic links have been discovered, but there is currently no cure for this disease.

Chapter Review

Critical Thinking Questions

1. Sheryl was in an automobile accident but has no recollection of the event. What process may be responsible for Sheryl's inability to recall the accident?
2. Lori has difficulty remembering where she parked her car or what she had to eat this morning. Yet, she can readily recall the plot of a movie that she saw as a child. Explain possible reasons for Lori's ability to remember some experiences but not others.
3. Bill's grandmother suffered a stroke last week. The stroke caused considerable bilateral damage to the medial temporal lobe and surrounding areas. What memory impairments might Bill's grandmother experience as a result of the stroke? What memory functioning might remain intact?

Vocabulary Questions

1. A change in behavior that results from experience is ________________.
2. The first stage of memory is the storage of experiences in the ________________.
3. The repetition of experiences in order to transfer them to long-term memory is ________________.
4. Memory of an event experienced at a particular time or place that is accessed deliberately is ________________ memory.
5. Knowledge of facts as opposed to skills is referred to as ________________ memory.
6. Hebb's simple physical unit of memory is referred to as a ________________.
7. Amnesia for events that happen after an injury to the nervous system is called ________________ amnesia.
8. The process of creating an enhanced defensive reaction in response to a stimulus is referred to as ________________.
9. Increased neural responsivity to a test stimulus is called ________________.
10. A form of severe memory impairment seen in chronic alcoholics is called ________________.

Review Choice Questions

1. The pairing of the bell (________________) with food (________________) allows the bell to elicit saliva (________________).
   a. UCS, CS, CR
   b. CS, UCS, CR
   c. CS, UCS, UCR
   d. UCS, CS, UCR

2. The three stages of the Atkinson-Shiffrin model are
   a. sensory register, long-term potentiation, and long-term memory.
   b. sensory register, short-term memory, and long-term memory.
   c. cell assembly, short-term memory, and working memory.
   d. rehearsal, memory consolidation, and memory transfer.
3. Remembering your mother's birthday by recalling how you celebrated it last year is an example of the use of
   a. memory attributes.
   b. memory transfer.
   c. memory consolidation.
   d. rehearsal.
4. According to Craik and Lockhart, long-term memories are memories that are
   a. stored for the longest time.
   b. the result of long-term potentiation.
   c. the most elaborated.
   d. the most thoroughly processed.
5. Remembering how to wash dishes is an example of
   a. procedural memory.
   b. declarative memory.
   c. semantic memory.
   d. episodic memory.
6. Hebb's memory consolidation theory is based on the idea that reverberatory activity
   a. must precede the event to be remembered.
   b. is necessary for retrieval of information from memory.
   c. results in permanent physiological changes.
   d. is responsible for long-term potentiation.
7. You go to your friend's house and notice a strong smell of garlic. After a while, the smell becomes less noticeable. This is an example of
   a. habituation.
   b. sensitization.
   c. consolidation.
   d. long-term potentiation.
8. What change in the neuron represents the structural basis of learning and memory?
   a. lengthening of the dendrites
   b. arborization of the dendrites
   c. toughening of the cell wall
   d. release of fodrin
9. H.M. could recall ________________ memories, but not ________________ memories.
   a. procedural, semantic
   b. procedural, episodic
   c. declarative, semantic
   d. declarative, episodic
10. Sensory information that is processed in the neocortex is sent next to the
    a. mediodorsal thalamus.
    b. frontal cortex.
    c. medial temporal lobe.
    d. amygdala.
11. An important characteristic of long-term potentiation is that
    a. long-term stimulation is necessary to produce it.
    b. it occurs only in the mediodorsal thalamus.
    c. it is not a conditioned response but rather occurs naturally.
    d. the associated change in receptivity occurs in only a single pathway.
12. Patients with mediodorsal damage, such as that caused by Korsakoff's syndrome, differ from patients with medial temporal lobe damage in that they
    a. can describe what they are doing.
    b. are unaware of their memory deficit.
    c. can learn new tasks.
    d. retain their emotions intact.
13. Patients with Alzheimer's disease show impairments in
    a. language.
    b. memory.
    c. judgment.
    d. all of the above.
14. There is a progressive deterioration of the ________________ neurotransmitter system in Alzheimer patients.
    a. adrenergic
    b. serotonergic
    c. cholinergic
    d. dopaminergic

Suggested Readings

Cohen, N. J., & Eichenbaum, H. (1993). *Memory, amnesia, and the hippocampal system.* Cambridge, MA: MIT Press.

Martinez, J. L. & Kesner, R. P. (1998). Learning and memory: A biological view. (3rd ed.). New York: Academic Press.

Rose, S. P. (1992). *The making of memory: From molecules to mind.* New York: Anchor Books/Doubleday.

Selkoe, D. J. (1992). Aging brain, aging mind. *Scientific American, 267,* 134–142.

Zola-Morgan, S., & Squire, L. R. (1993). Neuroanatomy of memory. *Annual Review of Neuroscience, 16,* 547–563

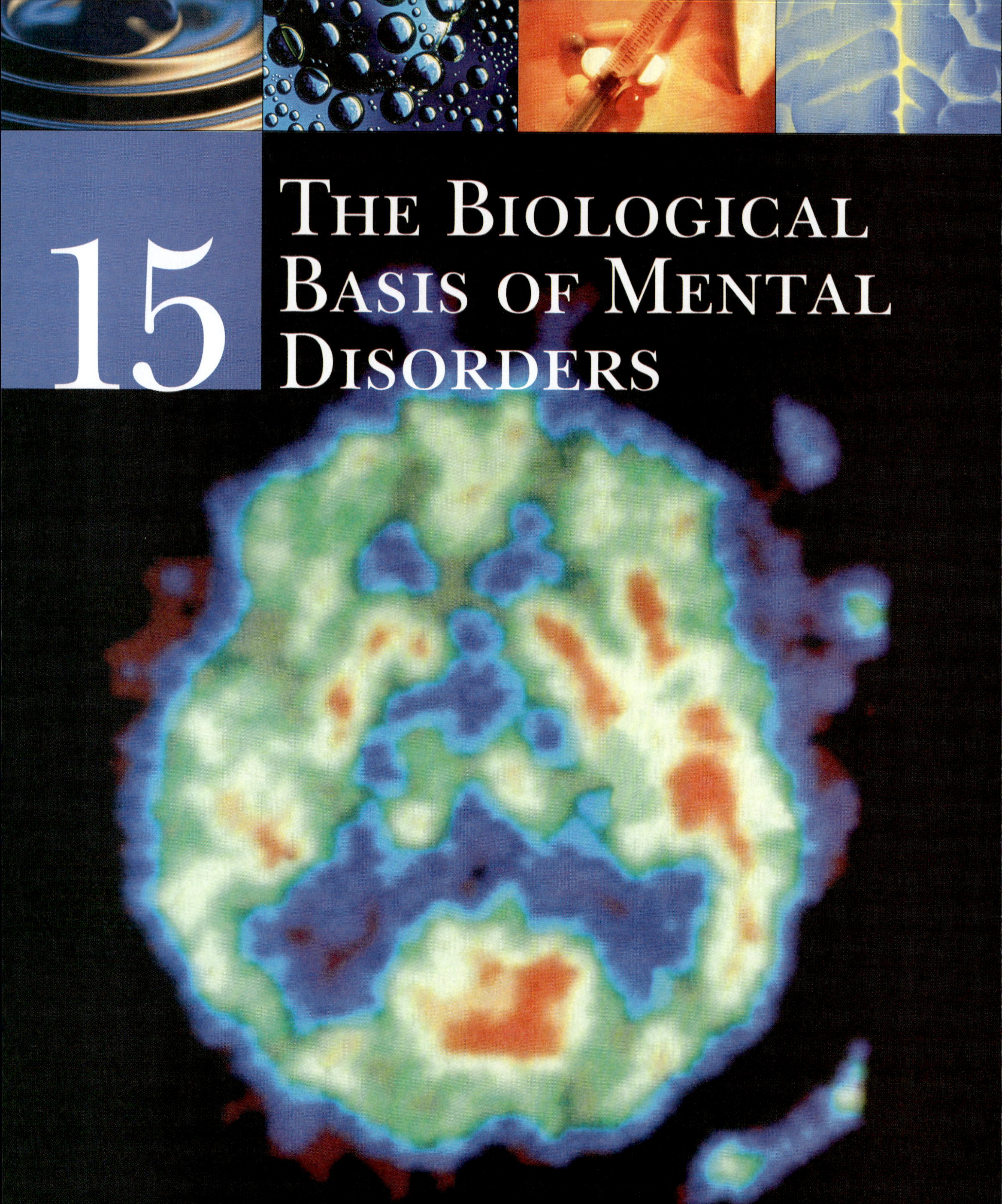

15 The Biological Basis of Mental Disorders

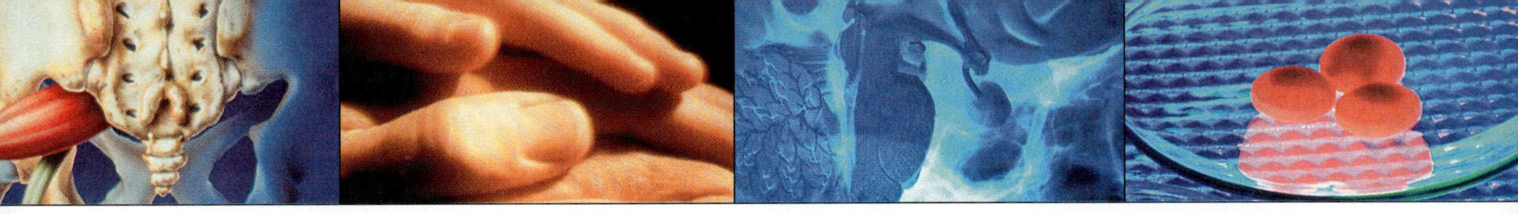

A Feeling of Hopelessness

Today is Rose's fortieth birthday, and she would seem to have all the necessary ingredients for happiness. She and her husband, Sidney, who was recently promoted to executive vice president of his company, have a large home in an exclusive neighborhood. To celebrate her birthday, Sidney bought Rose a new Mercedes. Rose and Sidney have three children who also are very successful: their oldest son, on the Dean's list at the State University; their daughter, a high school basketball star; the youngest, a son, president of the junior class.

Rose looks back fondly on their earlier years. She married Sidney the summer after she graduated from high school, supporting them with a secretarial job while Sidney earned his college degree. She continued to work after their first child was born. When she became pregnant again, Rose jumped at the chance to quit her job and devote herself full-time to her family.

She enjoyed her children's early years; helping with homework, chauffeuring them to their varied activities, and providing comfort and security made her feel important. These feelings have faded as her children have come to need her less and less, being replaced, starting about a year ago, with apathy and sadness. Over the past two months, with the approach of her birthday, these feelings have intensified. She feels useless, unneeded, and helpless as well.

Rose realizes that she does not have the training to get a job and develop her own life now that her children are grown. The thought of going to college after so long an absence from school terrifies her. Rose has been a wife and mother for so long that she has no idea of who she is.

Unable to cope with her feelings, Rose has begun to isolate herself from others and has lost interest in leisure activities that she used to enjoy. Her appetite has dwindled and she has lost 10 pounds during the past month. Rose has also had trouble sleeping; it seems to take forever for her to fall asleep, and she is restless, often waking in the middle of the night unable to fall back to sleep. Sidney, very concerned about his wife's welfare, has suggested that she see their family physician. Rose just replies, "What good would that do?" and thinks about ending it all. ■

◀ PET scan detects the level of activity in different parts of the brain by measuring the absorption of injected 2-deoxyglucose.

Before You Begin

What is the biological basis of Rose's depression?

What can her family do to help her?

Would seeing her physician "do any good"?

In this chapter, we will help you answer these and the following questions:

- Are all types of depression the same?
- What is bipolar disorder, and how can it be treated?
- Could genetics and/or experience have played a role in the development of Rose's depression?
- What is the brain amine theory of affective disorder?
- How is Rose's depression affecting her sleep cycle?
- What are the symptoms of schizophrenia, and what causes them?
- Does schizophrenia run in families?
- Why are there so many different treatments for schizophrenia?

Affective Disorders

A close friend announces that she is quitting school. You try to talk her out of it, but her mind is made up. You are so upset by the news that you are tempted to skip class, but you go because the instructor is due to return your last test. You get the test back, and you got an A! The good grade not only raises your spirits but prompts you to think positively about the future. As we described in Chapter 11, both your sadness over your friend's departure and joy about your good grade are two emotions that everyone experiences at one time or another. Usually, these moods are part of a healthy emotional life. However, there are times when our emotional states interfere with our normal, daily functioning. Such an impairment in functioning may reflect an **affective disorder**, the persistence of high levels of one of two mood states—depression or mania. (Recall that *affect* means "feeling.") There are two major classes of affective disorders. **Depressive disorders** occur when depression is the only mood state present. By contrast, bipolar disorders involve both mania and depression. Depressive disorders occur with much greater frequency than do bipolar disorders in the general population (Sarason & Sarason, 1993). We will describe the general characteristics of depression and mania as well as discuss the biological causes of these affective disorders.

Depression

Martin Seligman (1975) has described **depression**, an affective disorder in which a profound sense of sadness is the central attribute, as the "common cold of psychopathology." No one is immune to despair; each of us has become depressed following a disappointment or failure. Usually, these feelings fade over time. Wallace's (1956) classic account of the behavior of tornado victims in Worcester, Massachusetts, illustrates the typical healing power of time. Wallace noted that although the residents of Worcester functioned well immediately after a tornado hit their town, they were extremely distraught 24 to 48 hours after the disaster: they wandered about aimlessly or just sat in the rain (see **Figure 15.1**). Within several days, most residents showed no evidence of their previous depression and were able to undertake the task of rebuilding their town. For some, however, the feelings of helplessness persisted, and they were unable to resume the normal tasks of daily life.

Holden (1986) found that 6 percent of the population will be depressed in any given 6-month period. Kessler and colleagues (1994) reported that 21.3 percent of women and 12.7 percent of men suffer from severe depression at least once during their lives. Many other studies (Culbertson, 1997) also have found a two-to-one ratio gender difference in the rate of experiencing depression. People who are depressed, such as Rose in our opening story, are unable to cope with life's stressors; their clinical disturbance prevents them from experiencing the pleasures available to nondepressed people. Further, Maj and colleagues (1992) found that about 75 percent of individuals who experience a major depressive episode will have another within 5 years, and Holden (1986) reported that people who experience recurrent periods of depression will spend a fifth of their lives hospitalized, with 20 percent of these long-term sufferers being totally disabled by their depression and unable to work again.

Characteristics of Depression. The American Psychiatric Association's *Diagnostic and Statistical Manual* (*DSM-IV*; 1994) identifies 10 symptoms of depression: (1) depressed mood; (2) diminished interest or pleasure in activities; (3) weight loss, or change in appetite; (4) insomnia or hypersomnia; (5) agitation; (6)psychomotor retardation; (7) fatigue or loss of energy; (8) feelings of worthlessness or guilt; (9) diminished

---

affective disorder A psychiatric disorder characterized by one or two mood states—depression or mania.

depressive disorder A type of affective disorder in which depression is the only mood state present.

depression A pervasive feeling of intense sadness or loss that continues for some time.

Figure 15.1 Depression. Natural disasters such as a tornado can be extremely distressing. The despair produced by the devastation of their homes can be seen in the faces of the victims of this disaster.

➤ *What are the ten characteristics of depression? (p. 454–455)*

ability to think or concentrate; and (10) recurrent thoughts of death, including suicidal ideation. The two types of affective disorders involving depression are (1) major depression and (2) dysthymia.

Major Depression. Remember Rose from our chapter-opening vignette? In all likelihood, she is suffering from **major depression**, which is characterized by depressed mood of at least 2 weeks' duration, as well as the other symptoms just described: weight loss or change in appetite, problems in sleeping, fatigue, agitation or lethargy, difficulty concentrating, feelings of hopelessness, and thoughts of suicide. A depressive disorder is intense and incapacitating; if she does not get help, Rose may completely lose interest in the world around her and may indeed be tempted to end it all. The relative frequencies of the symptoms of major depression are shown in **Figure 15.2**.

How long can Rose expect to remain depressed? The length of a major depression is difficult to predict. The person may be depressed for only a few weeks or for as long as 6 months. Once the depressive episode has ended, previous patterns of acting and feeling usually return. However, about half of all people who experience one major depressive episode will experience another one (Sarason & Sarason, 1993). This second episode will usually occur within 2 years of the first. Canero (1985) found that people who experience recurrent episodes have, on average, seven major depressive episodes in their lifetimes.

Dysthymia. Although people with major depression tend to experience a rapid onset of intense symptoms as described above, others can experience less intense symptoms of depression off and on for many years. During this time, these individuals are depressed for more days than not and they have bad days and not so bad days. When depressed, they feel that way for most of the day. This kind of chronic depression is called **dysthymia**, which comes from the Greek words dys (bad) and thymos (mind). The person with dysthymia experiences several of the symptoms of depression, such as difficulty with eating, sleeping, or concentration, and may also suffer from low self-esteem and feelings of hopelessness. This form of depression tends to be less incapacitating than major depression, and most individuals with this type of depressive disorder do not seek help; instead, they try to live as well as they can with their distress, considering it a personality trait "I'm a sad person" rather than a disorder.

Before You Go On

Compare and contrast major depression and dysthymia.

Mania

Mania is an exaggeration of the rush of excitement and joy you experienced when your instructor handed you that test with the big red "A" on it. The American

major depression A type of depressive disorder that is characterized by an intense, debilitating depressed mood of at least 2 weeks' duration.

dysthymia A chronic depressive disorder in which the symptoms wax and wane for years, but are less intense than those of major depression.

mania An elevated, expansive, or irritable mood and inflated self-esteem or grandiosity.

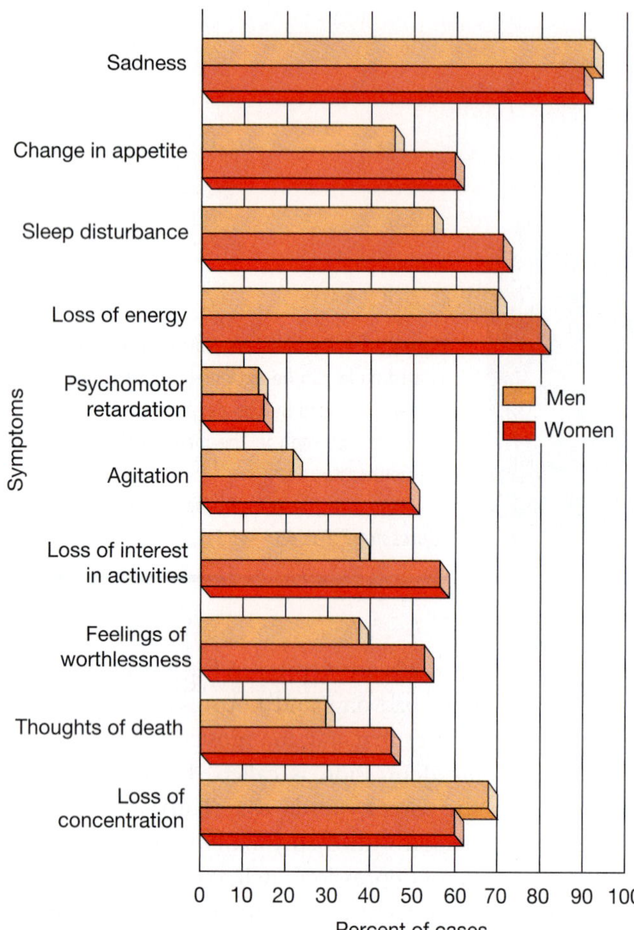

Figure 15.2 The symptoms of depression. This figure shows the percentage of men and women suffering from major depression who exhibit each of the symptoms of depression.

Adapted from Sarason & Sarason, 1993.

➤ *On average, how many episodes of severe depression will a person who suffers from major depression experience in his or her lifetime? (p. 455)*

Psychiatric Association's *DSM-IV* lists eight symptoms of a manic episode: (1) an elevated, expansive, or irritable mood; (2) inflated self-esteem or grandiosity; (3) decreased need for sleep; (4) increased or pressured speech; (5) flight of ideas or racing thoughts; (6) distractibility; (7) increased activity or psychomotor agitation; and (8) excessive involvement in pleasurable activities that have a high potential for painful consequences (e.g., unrestrained buying sprees or sexual indiscretions). The symptoms of mania typically first appear during adolescence or young adulthood (Roy-Byrne et al., 1985). Mania usually does not occur alone, but is instead generally one element of a cycle of mood swings referred to as a bipolar disorder.

Bipolar Disorder

A bipolar disorder exists when a person experiences alternating episodes of mania and depression. There are two types of bipolar disorders: (1) bipolar disorder and (2) cyclothymia.

Bipolar Disorder. Although a person must experience only one manic episode and one major depressive episode for a diagnosis of **bipolar disorder** to be made, episodes of mania and depression typically continue throughout the person's lifetime. A number of prominent individuals throughout history are thought to have suffered from bipolar depression (see **Figure 15.3**). Only a very small percentage of people exhibit only the mania phase of bipolar depressive disorder (Goodwin & Jamison, 1987). About 1 percent of the population suffers from bipolar disorder, and it is equally common in males and females.

What factors influence the likelihood that a person will experience recurrent manic and/or depressive episodes? Ambelas and George (1986) have identified three factors; the probability of recurrent episodes is higher if (1) the individual was young at the time of the first episode, (2) the first episode was precipitated by a minor stressor, and (3) a close family member has some kind of affective disorder.

Cyclothymia. Similar to the relationship between major depression and dysthymia, the affective disorder **cyclothymia** (cylo = cycle) is similar to bipolar disorder except that the episodes of mania and depression are less intense. The milder form of mania, referred to as **hypomania**, may involve any or all of the symptoms of mania, except that occupational or social functioning is not impaired (Sarason & Sarason, 1993). Functioning may be impaired during the depressive phase of cyclothymia, but not as severely as in major depression.

For a diagnosis of cyclothymia to be made, a person must exhibit symptoms for at least 2 years. The symptoms of cyclothymia usually first appear during adolescence or early adulthood. Cyclothymia is equally prevalent in females and males, and individuals with cyclothymia are likely to develop bipolar disorder later in life.

---

bipolar disorder A type of bipolar disorder that is characterized by episodes of mania and depression that typically continue throughout one's lifetime.

cyclothymia A type of bipolar disorder that is characterized by less intense episodes of mania and depression than is seen with bipolar disorder.

hypomania A milder form of mania in which occupational or social functioning is not impaired.

Figure 15.3 Bipolar disorder. President Theodore Roosevelt is thought to have suffered from the mania (left panel) and depression (right panel) characteristic of bipolar disorder.

➤ *What three factors influence the probability of recurrent manic-depressive episodes? (p. 456)*

Biological Basis of Affective Disorders

How exactly is Rose's central nervous system affected by her depression? Are there structural differences? Metabolic changes? Is the central nervous system affected by the different affective disorders? Read on for the answers to these questions.

Metabolic Activity in the Brain. During Rose's depressive episodes, she has difficulty initiating voluntary behavior, problems concentrating, and withdraws socially. These symptoms suggest that cortical activity may be lower during her depressive episodes. On the other hand, the primary attributes of mania—increased activity, unusual talkativeness, and rapid speech—suggest that abnormally high cortical activity may be present during a manic episode.

Measurements of overall brain activity, as shown by PET scans, confirm that activity in the brain is lower than normal during a depressive episode and higher than normal during a manic episode (see **Figure 15.4**). Although depression is associated with reduced metabolic activity throughout the brain, differences are especially apparent in the left hemisphere (Starkstein & Robinson, 1994). Specifically, decreased activity in the left frontal cortex appears to be particularly associated with the depressed mood (Davidson, 1992).

So mood state is correlated with metabolic activity in the brain. But what biological systems in the brain could be responsible for the dysfunctional metabolic

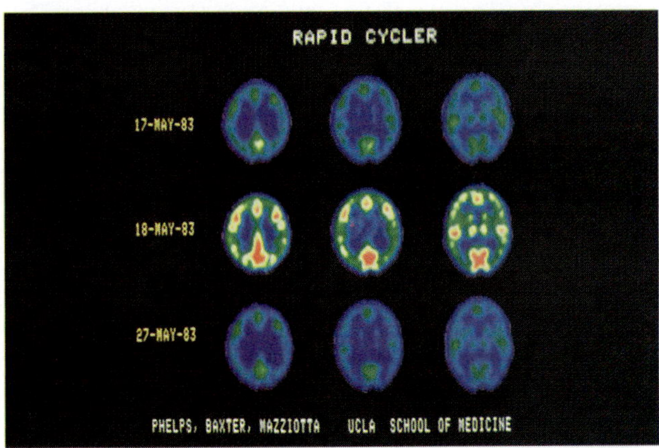

Figure 15.4 PET scans of a patient who experienced rapid and substantial changes in mood over a 10-day period. The patient was depressed, and metabolic activity low, on May 17. A hypomanic mood was experienced on May 18, and metabolic activity in the brain increased. By May 27, the patient was again depressed and metabolic activity low. The greatest metabolic activity is seen as red followed by yellow, green, and blue.

➤ *In which hemisphere are differences in activity especially noticeable during a depressive episode? (p. 457)*

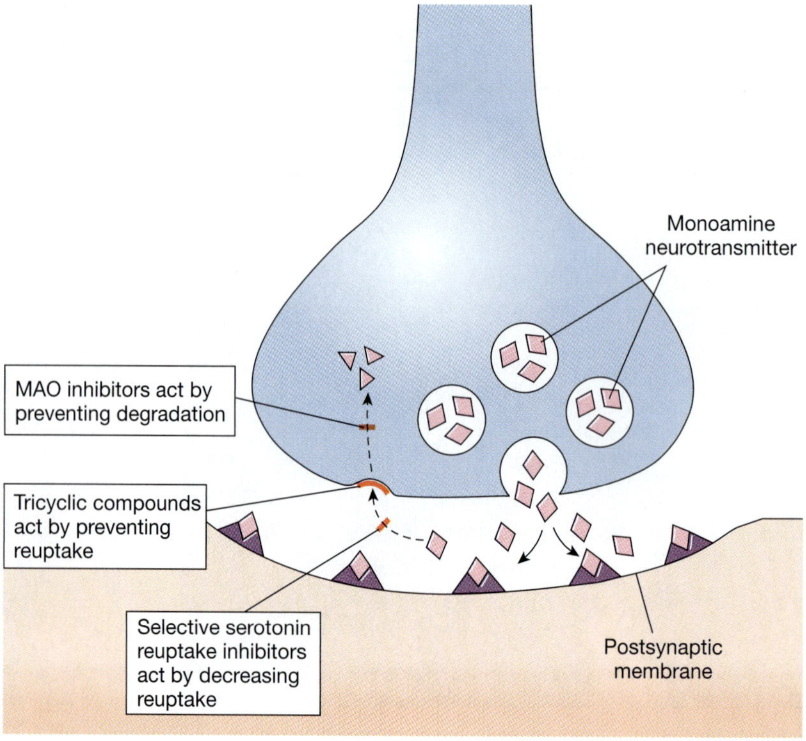

Figure 15.5 The effect of antidepressant drugs tricyclic compounds, MAO inhibitors, and selective serotonin reuptake inhibitors. Tricyclic compounds block the reuptake of monoamines into the presynaptic membrane; monoamine oxidase (MAO) inhibitors prevent the breakdown of monoamines by monoamine oxidase; and selective serotonin reuptake inhibitors (SSRIs) decrease the reuptake of monoamines.
➤ *What is the brain amine theory of affective disorders? (p. 458)*

activity and thus, the occurrence of affective disorders? We now turn our attention to examining evidence that disorders in several neurotransmitter systems are involved in producing depressive and manic mood states.

Brain Amine Theory of Affective Disorders. Many researchers (Bunney & Davis, 1965; Schildkraut, 1965, 1978) have suggested that disturbances in the functioning of the amine chemical transmitter systems in the brain (the catecholamines and indoleamines, see Chapter 4) are involved in affective disorders. The two particular amine transmitter substances that have been implicated are norepinephrine (a catecholamine) and serotonin (an indoleamine). The theory that abnormal levels of norepinephrine and serotonin are at least partially responsible for producing affective disorders is called the **brain amine theory of depression**.

Early studies pointed to a deficiency in amine levels in depressed individuals (Depue & Evans, 1976). For example, Ashcroft, Crawford, and Eccleston (1966) found that the level of a serotonin metabolite, 5-hydroxyindole acetic acid (5HIAA), was lower than normal in patients with major depression, which would suggest that levels of serotonin were low as well. (A metabolite is a compound produced by the process of metabolism, in this case, the metabolism of serotonin). Several other studies, such as the one conducted by Maas, Dekirmenjian, and Fawcett (1971) found a lower-than-normal level of a norepinephrine metabolite (3-methoxy-4-hydroxyphenylethylene glycol, or MHPG) in the cerebrospinal fluid, plasma, and urine of patients with major depression. In addition, Bunney, Goodwin, and Murphy (1972) found that urinary levels of norepinephrine metabolites increased as patients with bipolar disorder became manic and decreased when they became depressed.

Drugs that decrease brain amine levels have been found to induce depressive behavior. For example, Lemieux, Davignon, and Genest (1956) reported that reserpine, a drug prescribed for hypertension that reduces the levels of both serotonin and norepinephrine, produced depression. By contrast, drugs that elevate brain amine levels decrease depressive symptoms.

The effects of antidepressant drugs (see Chapter 4) also suggest that an amine deficiency plays a part in depression. Two classes of drugs—tricyclic compounds and monoamine oxidase (MAO) inhibitors—increase brain amine levels and alleviate the symptoms of depression for many depressed individuals. The tricyclic compounds increase levels of norepinephrine in the brain by interfering with its reuptake after the neuron fires (see #2 in **Figure 5.1 [p. 133]** and **Figure 15.5**). Davis, Klerman, and Schildkraut (1967) found the tricyclic drugs effective in the treatment of some cases of depression. The MAO

brain amine theory of depression A theory that abnormal levels of norepinephrine and serotonin are at least partially responsible for producing affective disorders.

inhibitors increase levels of norepinephrine and serotonin by preventing their breakdown, thus prolonging their effectiveness during neural transmission (refer to #2 in **Figure 5.1 [p. 133]** and **Figure 15.5**). Davis, Klerman, and Schildkraut (1967) reported that the MAO inhibitor phenylzine was often effective in alleviating depression.

Although tricyclic compounds and MAO inhibitors are still prescribed in the treatment of depression, a depressed person is now most likely to receive a **selective serotonin reuptake inhibitor (SSRI)**, such as fluoxetine (Prozac) and sertraline (Zoloft). In fact, Prozac is now the most widely prescribed psychiatric drug (Holden, 1996). The SSRIs act to relieve depressive symptoms by decreasing the reuptake of serotonin (see #2 in **Figure 5.1 [p. 133]** and **Figure 15.5**), thereby increasing serotonin levels.

Why are SSRIs used more than the tricyclic compounds and MAO inhibitors? SSRIs have more predictable effects and less serious side effects than do the tricyclic compounds and MAO inhibitors (Feighner et al., 1991). The side effects of SSRIs are generally mild nausea or headache. By contrast, the tricyclic compounds may produce dizziness, drowsiness, blurred vision, rapid heart rate, dry mouth, and excessive sweating. These side effects can be so severe that the depressed person stops taking the medication or reduces it to an ineffective dose. MAO inhibitors interact with tyramine, an amino acid found in fermented foods, and produce an increase in blood pressure that is sometimes fatal. Because so many foods contain tyramine, such as cheese, wine, and pickles, MAO inhibitors are used with extreme care and only in patients who do not respond to other antidepressant medications (Thase, Trivedi, & Rush, 1995).

Additional support for the role of the brain amines is provided by research evaluating the effect of lithium carbonate on patients with bipolar disorder. Recall that Bunney, Goodwin, and Murphy (1972) observed that levels of norepinephrine metabolites in the urine increased during episodes of mania. Because lithium carbonate decreases brain levels of norepinephrine, it should provide an effective treatment of mania (Frazer & Winokur, 1977). The clinical effectiveness of lithium carbonate seems well established (Solomon et al., 1995). For example, Prien, Caffey, and Klett (1973) conducted a double-blind study to evaluate the influence of lithium on patients with bipolar disorder. Some patients received lithium; others were given a placebo treatment. This 2-year study indicated that the group treated with the placebo displayed a strong tendency to stop treatment and be hospitalized. By contrast, the group treated with lithium carbonate showed a significant reduction in manic episodes. Lithium carbonate also has been shown to reduce the intensity of depressive episodes in people with bipolar disorder. Other studies (Dunner, Stallone, & Fieve, 1976) have shown that lithium carbonate decreases the frequency of both depressive and manic episodes.

Our discussion to this point suggests that decreased levels of norepinephrine and serotonin are associated with depression and increased levels with mania. However, more recent research (Gold, Goodwin, & Chrousos, 1988) suggests that the earlier studies, which measured norepinephrine levels by fluorometric assay of the norepinephrine metabolite MHPG, may not have provided an accurate view of the biochemical basis of affective disorders. More recent studies using a more sensitive mass spectroscope to assay MHPG levels have reported that patients with major depression show either normal or increased cerebrospinal fluid levels of norepinephrine (Christensen et al., 1980; Post et al., 1984). Other studies have found increased plasma norepinephrine levels in patients with major depression (Lake et al., 1982; Siever et al., 1984). Mass spectroscopic measurements have also revealed that depressed patients show increased norepinephrine metabolite levels (Linnoila et al., 1982). Additionally, antidepressant drugs that successfully reduce depressive symptoms have also been shown to produce decreased levels of cerebrospinal and plasma MHPG (Linnoila et al., 1982).

How can we reconcile these seemingly conflicting results? Resolution begins with a discussion of the functioning of the locus coeruleus, an area of the brain located in the pons and connected to the hypothalamus, hippocampus, and cerebral cortex. The locus coeruleus is a major site for the synthesis of norepinephrine. Electrical stimulation of the locus coeruleus has been shown to produce intense arousal, hypervigilance, and suppression of exploratory activity in primates (Aston-Jones, Foote, & Bloom, 1984). Exposure to threatening situations increases activity in the locus coeruleus, whereas activity in the locus coeruleus decreases during sleep, grooming, and feeding.

The behaviors (intense arousal, hypervigilance, and suppressed exploration) seen when the locus coeruleus is stimulated are similar to those seen in a depressed person, which suggests that excessive activity in the locus coeruleus may be involved in depression. In support of this view, researchers (Campbell et

---

selective serotonin reuptake inhibitor (SSRI) A class of drugs that act by decreasing the reuptake of serotonin by the presynaptic membrane.

al., 1979; Murphy, Aulakh, & Garrick, 1986) have reported that antidepressant drugs decrease the rate of firing of neurons in the locus coeruleus. Further, Nielsen and Braestrup (1977) found that antidepressants reduced the level of norepinephrine metabolite MHPG in the brain.

So why did earlier studies report that decreased norepinephrine levels were associated with depression? Heninger and Charney (1987) have suggested that people with long-standing depression may become hypersensitive to norepinephrine, and that the body's regulatory mechanisms may have adapted by decreasing production of norepinephrine to compensate for the increased sensitivity. Increased sensitivity will lead to increased activity in the locus coeruleus and to prolonged depression. According to this theory, the therapeutic influence of antidepressants results from increasing responsivity of noradrenergic receptors; this increased responsivity may decrease activity in the locus coeruleus and thereby ameliorate the depression. In other words, early in depression, the locus coeruleus may be very active due to increased epinephrine levels, but as the depression becomes prolonged, the locus coeruleus remains active due to heightened sensitivity to norepinephrine.

Acetylcholine, GABA, and Depression

Norepinephrine and serotonin are not the only neurotransmitters that have been implicated in depression. Acetylcholine and GABA also have been investigated as possible contributors. Several researchers (Davis et al., 1976; Janowsky et al., 1980) have suggested that patients with major depression may have hyperresponsive cholinergic systems. (Recall that cholinergic refers to synapses that utilize acetylcholine as a neurotransmitter.) Acetylcholine stimulates certain receptors in the locus coeruleus, increasing the activity of this brain area and thus producing depression. One line of evidence supporting this view is the observation that cholinergic agonists can produce depression.

Gamma-aminobutyric acid (GABA) is yet another neurotransmitter that appears to be involved in depression. Many depressed patients have been found to have low cerebrospinal fluid and plasma GABA levels (Berrettini et al., 1982; Petty & Schlesser, 1981). Further, administration of progabide, a GABA agonist, has been shown to have antidepressant effects (Morselli et al., 1980). GABA inhibits the firing of the locus coeruleus (Aston-Jones, Foote, & Bloom, 1984), so a decrease in GABA levels would increase activity in the locus coeruleus, producing depression.

Before You Go On

A person has decreased levels of norepinephrine, serotonin, and acetylcholine, and increased levels of GABA. Based on what you have learned, would you expect this person to exhibit symptoms of depression or mania?

Why do you think that a particular antidepressant drug can be effective for one patient but not for another?

Section Review

- The two types of affective disorders, depressive disorder and bipolar disorder, are characterized by one or two extreme mood states: depression and mania.
- Symptoms of depression include diminished mood, diminished pleasure in activities, and feelings of worthlessness or guilt.
- Symptoms of mania include an elevated, expansive, or irritable mood and inflated self-esteem or grandiosity.
- There are two kinds of depressive disorders: dysthymia, which is a chronic, low level of depression, and major depression, which involves many of the same symptoms as dysthymia except symptoms are more intense and the onset is more likely to be sudden.
- Bipolar disorder consists of alternating episodes of depression and mania, and can be one of two types: cyclothymia or bipolar disorder.
- In cyclothymia, the episodes of mania and depression are less intense but are likely to last longer than in bipolar disorder.
- Brain activity is lower than normal during a depressive mood state and higher than normal during a manic mood state.
- The differences in brain activity during a depressive episode are most apparent in the left hemisphere, especially the left frontal cortex.
- High levels of activity in the locus coeruleus produce intense arousal, hypervigilance, and suppression of exploratory activity.
- Antidepressant drugs (tricyclic compounds, MAO inhibitors, SSRIs), which are noradrenergic and serotonergic agonists, reduce the rate of firing of neurons in the locus coeruleus and enhance mood.
- Acetylcholine stimulates certain receptors in the locus coeruleus, and administration of cholinergic agonists can produce depression.
- The neurotransmitter gamma-aminobutyric acid (GABA) inhibits the firing of neurons in the locus coeruleus, and levels of this neurotransmitter may be abnormally low in depressed patients.

Causes of Affective Disorders

There is considerable evidence that both family history, or genetics, and experience influence the development of affective disorders.

The Role of Genetics. One common method of identifying the genetic basis of a particular characteristic, such as depression, is the twin study. Identical twins are so called because they have identical genes; identical or monozygotic twins as they are also known, are formed when, for some unknown reason, the fertilized egg, or zygote splits in two (mono = one). Fraternal twins (also called dizygotic twins) are less similar genetically; fraternal twins are formed when two different eggs or zygotes are fertilized by two different sperm (di = two). As you might already have figured out, fraternal twins will share some of the same genes because they share the same parents, but will be no more similar genetically than brothers and sisters born separately. The rate at which any characteristic of interest occurs in both twins is called the **concordance rate**. If the concordance rate is much higher in identical twins than in fraternal twins, there is a strong likelihood that there is a genetic basis for the characteristic.

Rosenthal (1970), who summarized a number of studies that examined concordance rates for bipolar disorder, reported that the concordance rate for identical twins ranged from 50 to 100 percent (see **Table 15.1**). This means that if one twin has bipolar disorder, the likelihood that the other twin will also have this disorder is between 50 and 100 percent. The concordance rate for fraternal twins ranged from 0 to 40 percent; most studies reported from 20 to 30 percent. The concordance rate for first-degree relatives, such as parent and child, is between 10 and 20 percent; this indicates that an individual has an increased risk of developing bipolar disorder if a close relative suffers from it. In comparison, the likelihood that two nonrelated persons will both develop bipolar disorder is 1 to 2 percent.

Genetic factors also appear to contribute to major depression. Gershon, Bunney, Leckman, Van Eerdewegh, and DeBauche (1976) found that the concordance rate for major depression for identical twins was 54 percent, whereas the concordance rate for first-degree relatives was 17 percent. Other studies (Pauls et al., 1992; Tsuang & Faraone, 1990) also have reported that the concordance rate for identical twins is approximately 50 percent. By contrast, Tsuang and Faraone (1990) found that the concordance rate among fraternal twins was about 20 percent.

Adoption studies (DiLalla et al., 1996; Wender et al., 1986) have provided further evidence of a genetic influence on affective disorders. One problem with studying the concordance rate between first-degree relatives such as parents and children is that, in addition to sharing many of the same genes, they share the same environment. An adopted child does not share the same environment as his or her biological parents, so the concordance rate between the adopted child and the biological parents is a truer measure of the influence of genetics. By the same token, the concordance rate between an adopted child and his or her parents is a truer measure of the influence of the environment. The adoption studies show that the difference in concordance rates between identical and fraternal twins remains even when the twins were raised apart (DiLalla et al., 1996).

So genetic factors appear to contribute to both major depression and bipolar disorder. Is the genetic

concordance rate The rate at which any characteristic occurs among relatives.

Table 15.1 ■ Concordance Rates for Bipolar Depression in Monozygotic (Identical) and Dizygotic (Fraternal) Twins

	Monozygotic Twins		Dizygotic Twins	
Study	Pairs	Concordance Rate	Pairs	Concordance Rate
Luxenburger, 1930	4	75.0	13	0.0
Rosanoff et al., 1934–1935	23	69.6	67	16.4
Kallmann, 1952	27	92.6	55	23.6
Slater, 1953 (only manic-depressive)	7	57.1	17	23.5
Other affective disorders	1	0.0	13	18.8
Dafonseca, 1959	21	71.4	39	38.5
Harvaid and Hauge, 1965	10	50.0	39	2.6

Source: Adapted from Rosenthal, D. (1970). *Genetic theory and abnormal behavior*. New York: McGraw-Hill. Reprinted by permission of The McGraw-Hill Companies.

contribution greater for one than the other? To evaluate the risk for both bipolar disorder and major depression, Rice and his colleagues (Rice et al., 1987) interviewed the relatives of 612 individuals with symptoms of a mood disorder who were hospitalized in one of five psychiatric facilities. The sample consisted of 2,225 parents, siblings, children, and spouses of the patients. On the basis of their interviews, the researchers found that 1 percent of the relatives of persons with major depression showed symptoms of this disorder, and 5 percent of the relatives of persons with bipolar disorder showed symptoms of this disorder. These researchers interpreted these results as suggesting that the genetic contribution is 5 times higher for bipolar disorder than for major depression. Other researchers (Winokur et al., 1995) compared relatives of persons with bipolar disorder and relatives of persons with major depression. They found that the correlation for bipolar disorder is higher among relatives than is the correlation for major depression.

Researchers have attempted to identify the particular gene or genes responsible for the inheritance of an affective disorder. Some research (Winokur & Clayton, 1967) has pointed to a dominant gene on the X chromosome as responsible for the inheritance of bipolar disorder. Recall that the X chromosome is one of the two chromosomes that determine gender; the Y chromosome is the other (see Chapter 1). If this view is correct, then male offspring of normal mothers, but fathers with bipolar disorder should not develop this disorder, because they receive a Y chromosome, not an X chromosome from their fathers. Winokur, Clayton, and Reich (1969) investigated the family history of people with bipolar disorder and found no instances in which both father and son had been diagnosed with bipolar disorder. The researchers also evaluated father-daughter pairs and found a 13 percent concordance rate (one of the daughter's two X chromosomes comes from the father); mother-offspring pairs (mother-son and mother-daughter) had a 17 percent concordance rate (the mother always passes one X chromosome). These results support the idea that genes located on the X chromosome are responsible for the transmission of bipolar disorder. However, other researchers (Goetzl et al., 1974; Hays, 1976) have reported instances of father-son pairs diagnosed with bipolar disorder. In a more recent study, Baron and colleagues (1987) presented evidence pointing to an X chromosome locus for bipolar disorder in Sephardic Jews (descendants of Jews who settled mainly in Spain, Portugal, and North Africa), but not for other populations.

Other chromosomes also have been suggested as the location of the gene responsible for the transmission of affective disorders. One research study (Egeland et al., 1987), which examined the occurrence of bipolar disorder in a large, extended Amish family, pointed to an abnormality on the short arm of chromosome 11. However, other research (Hodgkinson et al., 1987; Detera-Waldleigh et al., 1988) has not supported Egeland and colleagues' results. Although inheritance clearly contributes to affective disorders, the genetic mechanism responsible for that contribution has not yet been identified. An intense search for the genetic basis of depression continues (Berrettini et al., 1997).

Before You Go On

Give a possible reason for the conflicting results of the studies searching for the genetic mechanism involved in the transmission of affective disorders.

How would you go about determining whether there is a genetic basis of Rose's depression?

The Role of Experience. We have already looked at the role of inheritance in contributing to the biochemical abnormalities found in depressed persons; we next examine evidence that certain experiences can cause these biochemical changes.

The research of Jay Weiss and his associates (Weiss et al., 1981; Weiss et al., 1985) has suggested that repeated exposure to uncontrollable events may be responsible for the brain amine changes observed in depressed persons. These researchers have found that when rats are exposed to a series of inescapable shocks, they show a pattern of behavior, called **learned helplessness**, that includes early-morning wakefulness, decreased feeding, decreased sexual drive, decreased grooming, and a lack of voluntary responding in a variety of situations—all of these are symptoms of depression.

What biochemical changes occur following uncontrollable stress such as that experienced by the rats in Weiss's experiments? Several studies (Hughes et al., 1984; Lehnert et al., 1984) observed isolated decreases in norepinephrine in the locus coeruleus following prolonged exposure to inescapable shocks. The decreased norepinephrine level presumably reflects increased sensitivity to norepinephrine. We learned earlier that antidepressant drugs decreased

---

learned helplessness A pattern of behavior that includes early-morning wakefulness, decreased feeding, decreased sexual drive, decreased grooming, and a lack of voluntary behavior in a variety of situations produced by exposure to a series of uncontrollable events.

the rate of firing of neurons in the locus coeruleus (Murphy, Aulakh, & Garrick, 1986) and that antidepressants reduced the level of norepinephrine metabolite MHPG in the brain (Nielsen & Braestrup, 1977). If the analogy between learned helplessness and depression is valid, antidepressant drugs should decrease learned helplessness and reduce activity in the locus coeruleus. In support of this view, Weiss and Simpson (1986) reported that administration of antidepressant drugs decreased locus coeruleus activity and eliminated the behavioral deficits seen following exposure to inescapable shocks. These results suggest that uncontrollable events produce heightened activity in the locus coeruleus, which is manifested as the behavioral changes associated with depression.

The generalization from studies of brain amine activity following exposure to uncontrollable events in animals to major depression in humans may be premature. One reason is that there does not appear to be a perfect correspondence between neurotransmitter levels and depression. Although antidepressant drugs alter neurochemical transmission in less than a day, it typically takes at least 2 weeks for the depressive mood to improve. Further, Bright and Everitt (1992) reported that antihypertensive drugs that alter catecholamine activity do not produce depression.

Before You Go On

Why do you think that antidepressant drugs, which alter neurotransmitter levels so quickly, take as long as 2 weeks to exert their effects on mood state?

Sleep and Depression

One of the symptoms of depression described earlier in the chapter (see **p. 454**) is either insomnia or hypersomnia. Recall from our discussion of REM sleep in Chapter 9 that the frequency and length of REM sleep increases during the latter half of the sleep cycle, and that the circadian rhythm regulates the onset, pattern, and termination of sleep. The research of several investigators (Gillin & Borbely, 1985; Vogel et al., 1980; Wehr & Goodwin, 1983) indicates that many people with depression show a disturbance in the typical sleep cycle: REM sleep occurs earlier than normal in the sleep period, and total sleeping time is shortened (see **Figure 15.6**). Depressed persons also experience greater difficulty falling asleep and are more easily awakened during sleep (remember Rose?).

What might be responsible for these sleep disturbances? Gold, Goodwin, and Chrousos (1988) suggest that REM sleep occurs earlier in the night to compensate for the hyperarousal of the locus coeruleus experienced during the day. (As we learned in Chapter 9, REM sleep is associated with reduced locus coeruleus activity.) Supporting this view is the observation that administration of antidepressant drugs that reduce overall locus coeruleus activity during the day either restores the normal REM sleep pattern or delays the onset of REM sleep (Hartmann & Cravens, 1973; Kupfer & Bowers, 1972).

What would happen if a depressed person whose sleep-wake cycle is disturbed went to bed and woke up earlier than normal? Wehr, Wirz-Justice, Goodwin,

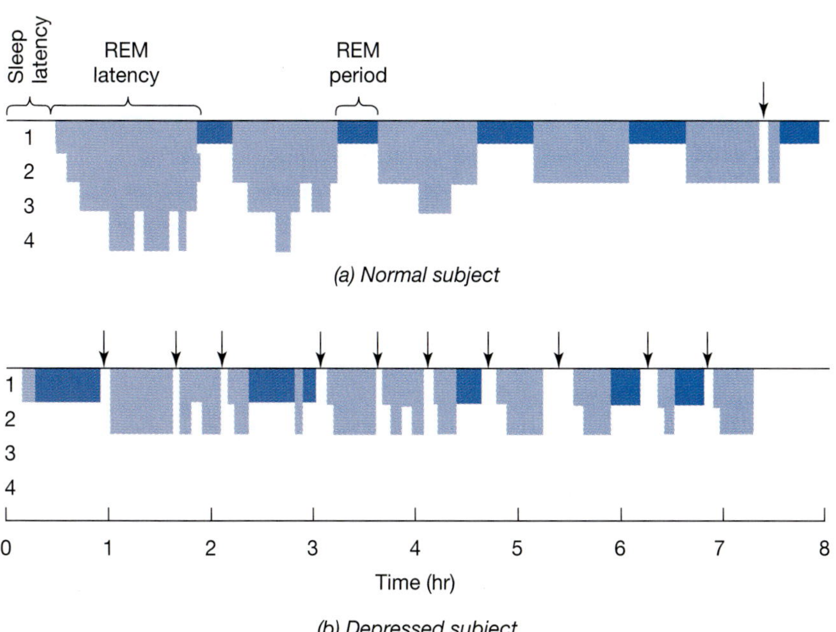

Figure 15.6 Depression and REM sleep. (a) The sleep pattern characteristic of nondepressed person and (b) the sleep pattern seen in many depressed persons in which REM occurs earlier in sleep and the duration of sleep is shortened.

➤ *Why does REM sleep occur earlier in the cycle in depressed persons? (p. 463)*

Duncan, and Gillin (1979) discovered that such advancement of the sleep-wake cycle by several hours (i.e., going to sleep at 5 P.M. and waking at 2 A.M.) alleviated the symptoms of depression. These researchers found that as the depressed patients' sleeping patterns changed, their mood improved. Another study found that depression can be alleviated by waking a depressed person whenever he or she begins the REM phase of sleep (Vogel et al., 1990). The effectiveness of this treatment develops slowly, with mood improving over the course of several weeks.

Weitzman, Kripke, Goldmacher, McGregor, and Nogeire (1970) found that the disturbed sleep response of many depressed people can be produced in nondepressed people by shifting the onset of sleep from 10 P.M. to 10 A.M. An experimentally altered sleep-wake cycle has been shown to elicit depression, hostility, and suicidal thoughts in some healthy individuals (Cutler & Cohen, 1979).

According to Wehr, Wirz-Justice, Goodwin, Duncan, and Gillin (1979), a disturbance in the circadian rhythm of some depressed people causes certain biological changes that initiate REM sleep earlier in the sleep cycle, thus causing the altered sleep pattern. In support of this view, Wehr, Muscettola, and Goodwin (1980) discovered that the normal changes in body temperature and motor activity during the circadian cycle took place 3 hours earlier in some depressed subjects.

This relationship between an advanced sleep-awake cycle and depression may be influenced by genetic factors (Giles, Roffwarg, & Rush, 1978; Giles et al., 1987). Giles, Roffwarg, and Rush (1987) have shown that first-degree relatives of depressed persons have a greater likelihood of experiencing phase-advanced REM than do relatives of nondepressed persons. This greater concordance rate is found even when the relative of the depressed person has not experienced a depressive episode. Further, those family members of depressed persons who exhibited the shortest REM latency were the most likely to become depressed later (Giles et al., 1988). Newborns whose mothers have a history of depression are more likely to show phase-advanced REM sleep patterns than are infants of mothers without a history of depression.

Advancing the time of REM sleep, although related to depression in some people, is only one of many biochemical factors that appear to be involved in producing depression. Not all depressed people show a sleep disturbance, and an altered sleep-wake cycle does not always produce depression in nondepressed people. This observation provides further evidence that there is more than one biochemical process involved in depression.

Before You Go On

Explain why certain antidepressant drugs might delay the onset of REM sleep.

Section Review

- Twin studies show that the risk of two people developing an affective disorder increases as the closeness of their genetic relationship increases.
- The genetic contribution appears to be much higher for bipolar disorder than for major depression.
- Investigators have identified several possible locations of the gene for affective disorders, but no genetic mechanism has yet been identified.
- Exposure to uncontrollable events may be one factor responsible for the increased locus coeruleus activity associated with depression.
- The administration of antidepressant drugs has been shown to decrease locus coeruleus activity and eliminate the behavioral deficits seen following exposure to uncontrollable events.
- In depressed persons who experience a disturbance in the typical waking-sleeping cycle, REM sleep occurs earlier than normal, and total sleep time is shortened.
- REM sleep may occur earlier to compensate for the hyperarousal of the locus coeruleus during the day.
- Antidepressants that reduce locus coeruleus activity restore the normal REM sleep pattern.
- Advancement of the wake-sleep cycle by several hours has been shown to alleviate depression in some patients.

APPLICATION

A Biochemical Marker for Depression

Many persons with major depression have been shown to suffer from **hypercortisolism**, an abnormally high or hypersecretion of cortisol from the adrenal cortex (Gold, Goodwin, & Chrousos, 1988). According to Gold, Goodwin, and Chrousos

hypercortisolism An abnormally high or hypersecretion of cortisol from the adrenal cortex.

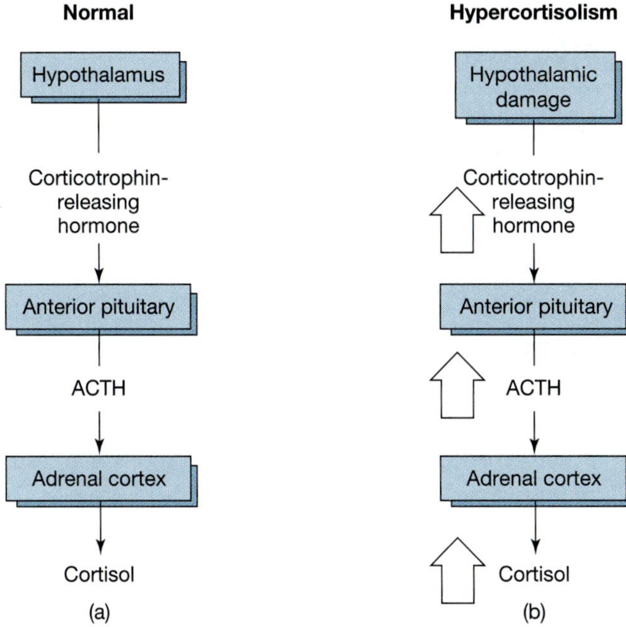

Figure 15.7 Hypercortisolism. (a) Activation of the hypothalamus in a normal person leads to the release of corticotrophin-releasing hormone, which acts to release ACTH from the anterior pituitary. ACTH in turn acts to release cortisol from the adrenal cortex. (b) Damage to hypothalamus results in an increased level of corticotrophin-releasing hormone, which results in an increased ACTH release from the anterior pituitary. The increased ACTH release in turn causes increased cortisol release from the adrenal cortex.

➤ *What is the biochemical marker of depression? (p. 464–465)*

(1988), dysfunctions in several central nervous system structures cause the hypercortisolism seen in patients with major depression. First, the anterior pituitary gland of these patients secretes elevated amounts of adrenocorticotrophic-stimulating hormone (ACTH), which in turn causes the excessive cortisol secretion (see **Figure 15.7**; Numeroff, Wilderlor, & Bisette, 1984). But what causes the excessive ACTH secretion? A dysfunction in the hypothalamus leads to elevated levels of hypothalamic corticotrophin-releasing hormone, which results in increased ACTH secretion (refer to **Figure 15.7**). Evidence of this dysfunction can be found in the increased levels of corticotrophin-releasing hormone in the cerebrospinal fluid of depressed persons (Numeroff, Wilderlov, & Bisette, 1984).

Further evidence of a failure in the adrenal-pituitary system (the connection between ACTH from the anterior pituitary on the cortisol release from the adrenal cortex) is the abnormal response of depressed patients on the **dexamethasone suppression test**. When nondepressed persons are given dexamethasone, a synthetic glucocorticoid hormone, ACTH and cortisol secretion is suppressed (see **Figure 15.8**). By contrast, dexamethasone does not suppress ACTH and cortisol release in many persons with major depression. An abnormal response on the dexamethasone suppression test is considered to be a neuroendocrine marker of major depression (Whybrow, Akiskal, & McKinney, 1984).

The effects of hypercortisolism can be severe, producing many of the symptoms associated with depression. For example, administration of ACTH in the ventricles of the brain of rats produces decreased sexual drive (Sirinathsinghji et al., 1983) and decreased willingness to explore unfamiliar surroundings (Swerdlow et al., 1986).

dexamethasone suppression test A test to determine whether administration of dexamethasone suppresses ACTH and cortisol secretion.

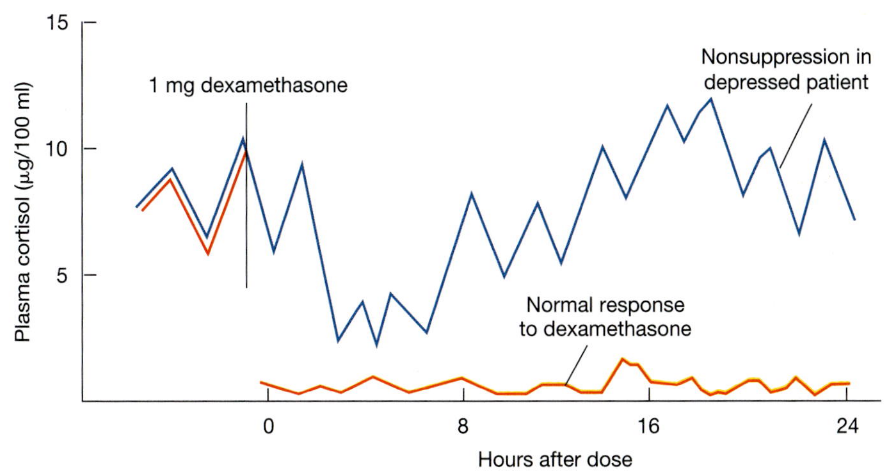

Figure 15.8 The dexamethasone suppression test. Administration of dexamethasone to nondepressed people suppresses the secretion of cortisol from adrenal cortex, whereas dexamethasone does not suppress cortisol release in depressed persons.

➤ *Why do depressed person's fail the dexamethasone suppression test? (p. 465)*

Additional support for the involvement of the adrenal-pituitary system in major depression comes from patients suffering from anorexia nervosa. Hypercortisolism is often seen in anorexic patients (Gold, Gwirtsman, & Avgerinos, 1986; Hotta et al., 1986), many of whom have strong family histories of major depression and suffer from depression themselves (Cantwell et al., 1977; Winokur, March, & Mendels, 1980).

We learned earlier that excessive activity in the locus coeruleus is associated with depression. In addition to its effects on ACTH levels, corticotrophin-releasing hormone also increases the firing of neurons in the locus coeruleus (Valentino, Foote, & Aston-Jones, 1983). Gold, Goodwin, and Chrousos (1988) suggest that continued exposure to stressors may not only produce hypercortisolism and anorexia but also heighten activity in the locus coeruleus, which leads to depression.

Not all patients with major depression show the same pattern of symptoms (see **p. 455–456**). Some depressed persons are hyperphagic rather than anorexic and show hypersomnia rather than insomnia. Gold, Goodwin, and Chrousos (1988) suggest that these atypical symptoms of depression are caused by a pathological suppression of the corticotrophin-releasing hormone and the locus coeruleus-norepinephrine system. In this view, long-term exposure to stressors causes the inactivation of these two systems and results in major depression characterized by hyperphagia and hypersomnia. Supporting this view is the observation of large decreases in cerebrospinal fluid corticotrophin-releasing hormone (Kling et al., 1986) and cerebrospinal fluid MHPG (Kling, 1989) following repeated exposure to stressors.

Before You Go On

Describe the sequence of events that lead to hypercortisolism, beginning with the hypothalamus and including the terms hypothalamic corticotrophin-releasing hormone, anterior pituitary, ACTH, adrenal cortex, and cortisol.

hallucinations Sensory experiences that occur in the absence of environmental stimuli.

schizophrenia A serious disabling psychiatric disorder that is characterized by a loss of contact with reality and disturbances in perception, emotion, cognition, and motor behavior.

Section Review

- Hypercortisolism is an elevated cortisol secretion.
- A dysfunction in the hypothalamus produces elevated levels of corticotrophin-releasing factor, which increase ACTH secretion and stimulate the locus coeruleus.
- Hypercortisolism and increased locus coeruleus activity are associated with major depression.
- Anorexia also is correlated with both hypercortisolism and major depression.
- Some depressed persons exhibit the atypical symptoms of hyperphagia, hypersomnia, and suppression of both the hypothalamus-corticotrophin-releasing system and locus coeruleus-norepinephrine system.

Schizophrenia

The Voices. Testing one, two, testing one. Checking out the circuits: "What hath God wrought. Yip di mina di zonda za da boom di yaidi yoohoo." By this time the voices had gotten very clear. At first I'd had to strain to hear or understand them. They were soft and working with some pretty tricky codes. Snap-crackle-pops, the sound of the wind with blinking lights and horns for punctuation. In the beginning it seemed mostly nonsense, but as things went along they made more and more sense. Once you hear the voices, you realize they've always been there. It's just a matter of being tuned to them. The voices weren't much fun in the beginning. But later the voices could be very pleasant. They'd often be the voices of someone I loved, and even if they weren't I could talk too, asking questions about this or that and getting reasonable answers. There were very important messages that had to get through somehow. More orthodox channels like phone and mail had broken down. (Vonnegut, 1975, pp. 136–137)

Hallucinations, or sensory experiences in the absence of environmental stimuli, such as those described in the preceding paragraph, are one symptom of **schizophrenia**. The narrator of the above paragraph is a young man who suffers from auditory hallucinations. A serious disabling mental disorder, schizophrenia is characterized by a loss of contact with reality and disturbances in perception, emotion, cognition, and motor behavior. This disorder is almost always associated with severe disruption of personal, social, and occupational functioning. People with schizophrenia usually have impaired social skills and few friends; academic performance can be impaired, and difficulty is often experienced obtaining and keeping a job.

The behaviors that characterize schizophrenia were first described in 1883 by Emil Kraepelin, who called the disorder **dementia praecox**, from the Latin terms meaning "premature mental deterioration." According to Kraepelin, the symptoms of dementia praecox included delusions, hallucinations, attention deficits, and bizarre motor behavior. Kraepelin believed that the illness began in adolescence and involved an irreversible mental deterioration.

Eugene Bleuler in 1911 renamed this syndrome schizophrenia, from the Greek words *schizein*, meaning "to split," and *phren*, meaning "head." His rationale for changing the name of the disorder was based on three observations. First, the deterioration does not always begin in adolescence but can begin late in life. Second, some individuals' mental functioning improves rather than deteriorates after the disorder is diagnosed. Finally, Bleuler believed that the disorder reflected a splitting of the psyche's functions; that is, the person with schizophrenia experiences a dissociation of thought, emotion, and perception. Don't confuse schizophrenia with "split personality" or multiple personality disorder. The person with multiple personality disorder has two or more distinct personalities; the person with schizophrenia has a single, rather unusual personality.

Symptoms of Schizophrenia

There are four categories of symptoms of schizophrenia: (1) disturbances in thought, (2) disturbances in perception, (3) disturbances in movement, and (4) disturbances in affect.

Disorders of Thought. Schizophrenia causes disturbances in formal thought processes. Tangentiality, the inability to stick to one topic, is one example of a disturbance in thought form; people with schizophrenia will often shift from one idea to another within a single sentence. Making up a meaningless word, or neologism, is another formal thought disturbance. Others include the use of many rhyming words, the persistent use of particular words or ideas, and long pauses before completing a thought. All of these formal thought problems can make it very difficult to understand the communications of people with schizophrenia.

Disturbances in the content of thought are also associated with schizophrenia. Such disturbances are called **delusions**, or beliefs that have no basis in reality. Delusions of persecution, or a belief that others are trying to harm, are common among people with schizophrenia. Other common delusions are (1) that an external source is inserting thoughts into their minds; (2) that their thoughts either are being broadcast to others or are being stolen by an external force; and (3) that others are making them feel or act in a specific fashion.

People with schizophrenia often do not understand why they may have been hospitalized or what is wrong with them. Such lack of insight, another problem in thought content, is found in 97 percent of all people with schizophrenia (Sartorius, Shapiro, & Jablonsky, 1974).

A person does not necessarily need to experience all of these symptoms to be diagnosed with schizophrenia. For example, many people with schizophrenia do not experience delusions (Lucas, Sansbury, & Collins, 1962) and some people with schizophrenia have no problems with formal thought processes (Andreasen, 1994).

Disorders of Perception. Not only are the thought processes of people with schizophrenia likely to be disordered, but so is the way they view the world. The most dramatic perceptual distortions are the aforementioned hallucinations, which are commonly auditory—hearing a voice, hearing other people's thoughts, or hearing two other voices carrying on a conversation. Other types of hallucinations involve seeing, feeling, smelling, or tasting things that are not present. Hallucinations seem to occur in about 75 percent of cases of schizophrenia (Sartorius, Shapiro, & Jablonsky, 1974).

Motor Disturbances. People with schizophrenia may show high levels of motor excitement, pacing constantly or flailing their limbs. They may also experience catatonic stupors or immobility, remaining in unusual positions, such as on one leg, for long periods of time (see **Figure 15.9**). Other motor disturbances include strange facial expressions or repetitive motor actions such as head rubbing or paper tearing.

Affective Symptoms. The final kind of symptom associated with schizophrenia is affective (i.e., involves emotion). People with schizophrenia exhibit one of two mood disorders. Some people exhibit a blunted or flat affect, showing little or no emotional responsivity. Even traumatic events, like the death of a family member, elicit no emotional response in these individuals. Other people with schizophrenia demonstrate inappropriate affect; that is, their emotional reactions are not suited to

---

dementia praecox A mental disorder described by Emil Kraepelin that included delusions, hallucinations, attention deficits, and bizarre motor behavior, now known as schizophrenia.

delusions Distorted thought processes that leads to erroneous beliefs.

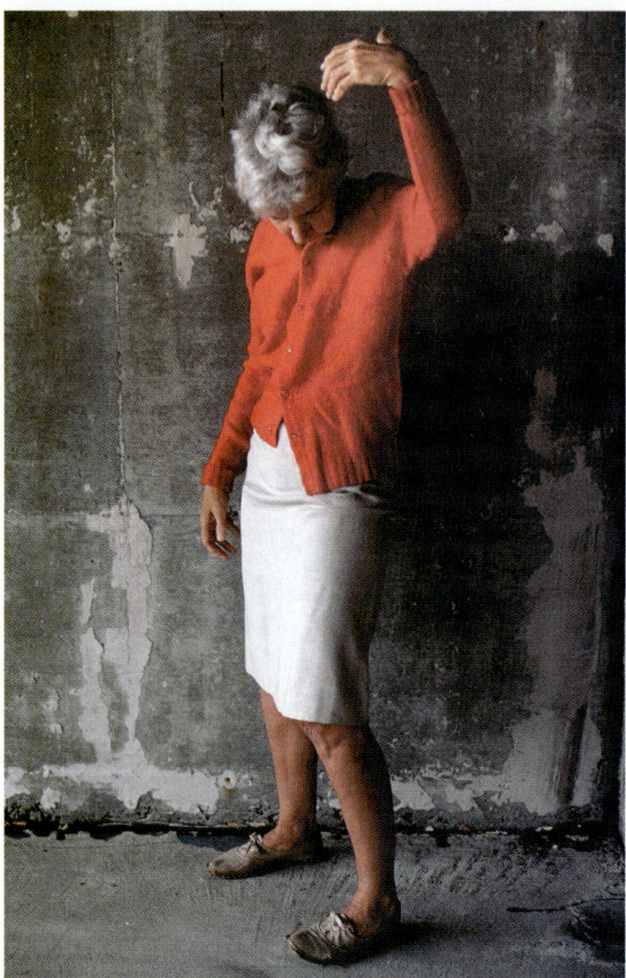

Figure 15.9 Motor disturbance of schizophrenia. This woman shows the rigidity and bizarre posture characteristic of some people with schizophrenia.

➤ *What are two other types of motor disturbances experienced by persons with schizophrenia? (p. 467)*

the context in which they occur. For example, a person may laugh when told that a friend has died or become angry when told he or she looks nice. Blunted or flat affect occurs in about two-thirds of cases of schizophrenia; inappropriate affect is less common (Sartorius, Shapiro, & Jablonsky, 1974).

positive symptoms of schizophrenia Symptoms that are characterized by behaviors in excess of normal behaviors including disorders of thought and perception.

negative symptoms of schizophrenia Symptoms that are characterized by an absence of normal behaviors, including disorders of affect and movement.

prodromal phase The first phase of schizophrenia in which the person becomes socially withdrawn.

active phase The second phase of schizophrenia in which the more obvious symptoms of schizophrenia appear.

residual phase The third phase of schizophrenia in which some recovery of functioning occurs.

Positive Versus Negative Symptoms

The symptoms of schizophrenia also can be categorized into positive and negative symptoms (Andreasen, 1991). **Positive symptoms of schizophrenia** are characterized by behaviors in excess of normal behaviors, and include disorders of thought (delusions) and of perception (hallucinations); **negative symptoms of schizophrenia** are characterized by an absence of normal behaviors and include disorders of affect (blunted affect) and movement (poverty of speech, lack of voluntary motor behavior, and social withdrawal).

Course of the Schizophrenic Disorder

There are three stages of the schizophrenic disorder: (1) the prodromal phase, (2) the active phase, and (3) the residual phase (Bootzen & Acocella, 1988). In the **prodromal phase**, the person becomes socially withdrawn. School or work performance declines in this stage. The onset is usually in adolescence or early adulthood. This stage may be very brief, or symptoms may develop gradually over a long period. In the **active phase**, the more acute symptoms of schizophrenia appear, such as delusions, hallucinations, or any of the other symptoms described in the previous section. A recovery of some functioning occurs in the **residual phase**. The person may return to the social isolation of the prodromal phase, or continue to experience some of the other negative symptoms of schizophrenia without the positive symptoms.

What happens after the residual phase? Blueler (1978) found that 10 percent of people who experienced a schizophrenic episode remained in the residual phase, while 25 percent recovered completely. Sixty-five percent alternated between the residual and active phase.

Who is most likely to recover from schizophrenia? Lehman and Cancro (1985) found that the prognosis is best when (1) the person was psychologically healthy before the symptoms appeared, (2) the symptoms appeared suddenly, (3) life events precipitated the disorder, and (4) the symptoms first occurred later in life.

Before You Go On

A patient with schizophrenia hears voices telling him that his life is in danger; he alternates between pacing and catatonia, and between hysterical laughter and unresponsiveness. Categorize these symptoms according to the four types you have learned, then regroup them as positive or negative symptoms.

Section Review

- Schizophrenia is a serious psychiatric disorder characterized by disturbances in thought, perception, motor behavior, and feelings.
- Positive symptoms of schizophrenia include delusions (false systems of belief) and hallucinations (false sensory experiences).
- Negative symptoms of schizophrenia include catatonia (complete immobility) and flat or blunted affect.
- The three stages of the schizophrenic disorder include the prodromal phase, the active phase, and the residual phase.
- In the prodomal phase, the person becomes socially withdrawn.
- In the active phase, the more obvious symptoms of schizophrenia appear, such as delusions or hallucinations.
- Recovery of some functioning occurs in the residual phase.

Biological Basis of Schizophrenia

We have learned that schizophrenia is a very serious debilitating disorder. Two biological causes have been proposed: one focuses on biochemical disturbances and the other on brain damage. We will first examine the biochemistry of schizophrenia, followed by a discussion of brain damage and schizophrenia.

The Biochemistry of Schizophrenia. Many biological psychologists (Losonczy, Davidson, & Davis, 1987; Meltzer & Stahl, 1976; Nauta & Domesick, 1981) have suggested that a disturbance in the functioning of the mesocortical dopamine system (see Chapters 5 and 14) is responsible for producing the positive symptoms of schizophrenia (delusions and hallucinations). The mesocortical system begins in the ventral tegmental area and projects to several forebrain regions of the cortex and limbic system (entorhinal cortex, suprarhinal, and anterior cingulate cortex; lateral and medial frontal cortex). The **dopamine hypothesis of schizophrenia** states that either an excess of dopamine or an increased sensitivity to this neurotransmitter in the mesocortical dopamine system produces the positive symptoms of schizophrenia.

Like many other important scientific breakthroughs (remember Olds and Milner's research on the biological basis of reinforcement), the discovery that dopaminergic neurons are involved in schizophrenia was made by accident. In 1950, French surgeon Henri Laborit noticed that antihistamine drugs reduced the anxiety of his patients without producing mental confusion. Based on Laborit's observations, French chemist Paul Charpentier developed the drug chlorpromazine, and tested it on animals, noting that it had a sedative effect. Laborit then reported that chlorpromazine also had a calming effect in humans. Chlorpromazine (brand name Thorazine) was administered to people with a number of mental disorders, but only for those people with schizophrenia was chlorpromazine an effective treatment (Delay & Deniker, 1952), alleviating or eliminating the hallucinations and delusions experienced by these patients. Administration of chlorpromazine and other antipsychotic drugs such as haloperidol has become an integral part of the treatment of schizophrenia.

In 1967, Avid Carlsson reported findings that suggested a link between chlorpromazine, dopaminergic transmission, and schizophrenia. As Carlsson observed and as we learned in Chapter 5 (see **p. 133–134**), chlorpromazine acts as a dopamine antagonist by blocking postsynaptic dopaminergic receptor sites (see #1 in **Figure 5.2** [**p. 134**] and **Figure 15.10**). This effect of chlorpromazine supports the dopamine hypothesis of schizophrenia. The effectiveness of chlorpromazine as a

dopamine hypothesis of schizophrenia The view that either an excess of dopamine or an increased sensitivity to this neurotransmitter in the mesocortical dopamine system produces the positive symptoms of schizophrenia.

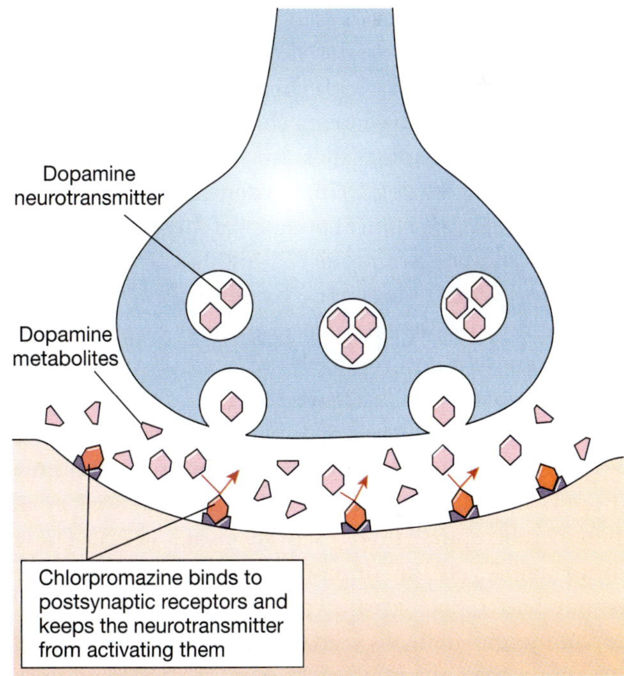

Figure 15.10 The effect of chlorpromazine on dopaminergic transmission. Chlorpromazine, a dopaminergic antagonist, blocks dopaminergic transmission by attaching to receptor sites.

➤ *Does chlorpromazine act as an agonist or an antagonist? (p. 469)*

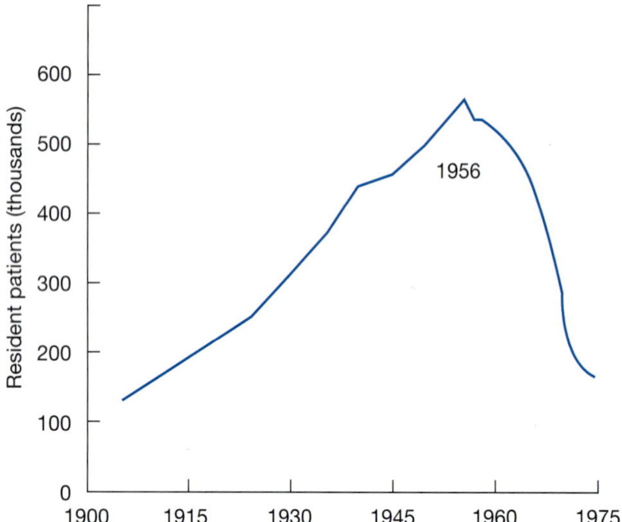

Figure 15.11 The success of biological treatment of schizophrenia. The resident population of psychiatric institutions increased steadily from 1900 to 1956, when chlorpromazine and other antipsychotic drugs were introduced.

➤ *Why did the use of chlorpromazine and other antipsychotic drugs have such a dramatic influence on the resident population of psychiatric institutions? (p. 469–470)*

treatment for schizophrenia is responsible in large part for the tremendous decline in the number of patients in mental health institutions (see **Figure 15.11**).

Further support for the dopamine hypothesis has come from studies in which chlorpromazine and other antipsychotic drugs have been shown to bind selectively to dopamine receptor sites in vitro (Cohen, 1981; Creese, Burt, & Snyder, 1976; Snyder, 1976). These studies showed that the clinical potency of these drugs (their ability to alleviate symptoms) is highly correlated with their affinity for D_2 dopamine receptor sites; that is, the more tightly a drug binds to dopamine receptors, the more effective it is in reducing the positive symptoms of schizophrenia (refer to **Figure 15.12**).

Abnormally high levels of dopamine metabolites have been found in the plasma of people with schizophrenia (Bowers et al., 1980; Pickar et al., 1984) as well as in their cerebrospinal fluid (Sedvall et al., 1974). These abnormal levels of dopaminergic metabolites are assumed to reflect greater activity at the synapses of dopaminergic neurons and/or a greater number of dopamine receptors at each synapse. In fact, postmortem studies have revealed twice as many D_3 and D_4 receptors in subjects with a history of schizophrenia than in normal subjects (Gurevich et al., 1997; Murray et al., 1995), whereas D_1 receptors are lower than in normal subjects (Okubo et al., 1997). Murray and colleagues (1995) found greater concentrations of D_4 receptors in the nucleus accumbens, whereas Gurevich and colleagues (1997) reported greater D_3 receptors in the nucleus accumbens and neostriatum (caudate nucleus and putamen; see **Figure 15.13**). Further, Cross, Crow, and Owen (1981) found a positive correlation between the number of D_4 receptors and the severity of the subject's previous hallucinations and delusions.

Drugs that increase dopamine activity in the central nervous system, especially amphetamine and cocaine, can produce the positive symptoms of schizophrenia in people without this disorder (Janowsky & Risch, 1979; Snyder, 1972). The occurrence of amphetamine or cocaine psychosis as a result of chronic administration of these drugs provides additional support for the dopamine hypothesis of schizophrenia. Use of amphetamines has also been shown to exacerbate positive symptoms in people already diagnosed with schizophrenia.

Our discussion to this point has shown that drugs that block dopaminergic activity reduce the positive symptoms of schizophrenia, whereas drugs that increase dopamine levels in the brain produce or exaggerate positive symptoms. So why is it still called the dopamine *hypothesis*? Because in addition to the supportive evidence, there is considerable evidence that is inconsistent with the dopamine hypothesis. For example, not all people with schizophrenia show improvement in positive symptoms following treatment with chlorpromazine or other dopamine-blocking drugs (Baldessarini, 1995). Perhaps as many as 30 percent of patients do not respond to Thorazine. Recently, the antipsychotic drug clozapine (Clozaril) has been found to be clinically effective even in patients who have been unresponsive

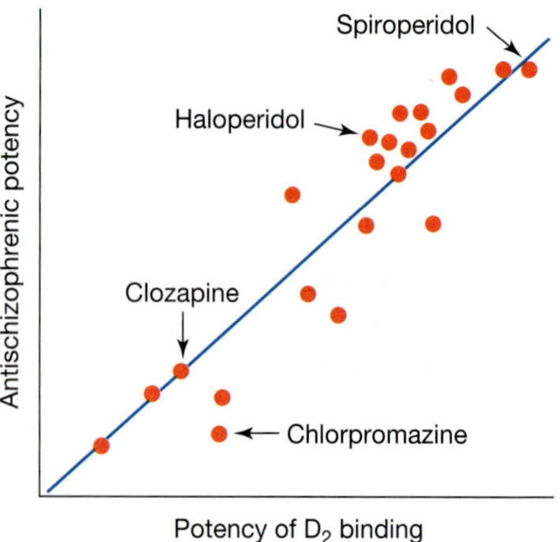

Figure 15.12 Clinical potency. The therapeutic potency of antischizophrenic drugs is positively correlated with the ability of each drug to bind with dopamine (D_2) receptors.

➤ *Which of the drugs shown has the highest clinical potency? (p. 470)*

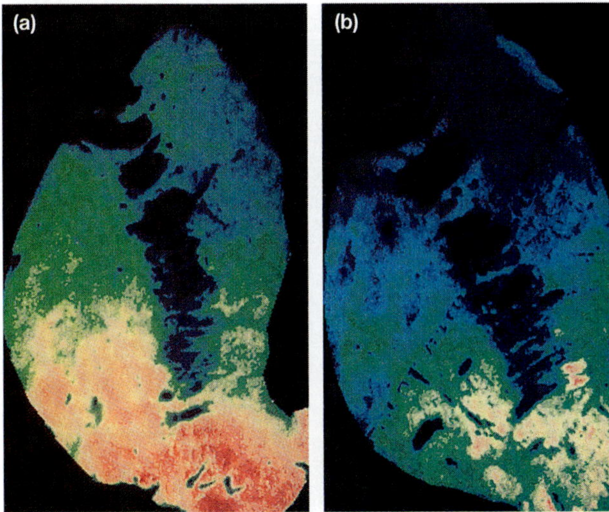

Figure 15.13 Concentrations of D_3 receptors in the neostriatum. Postmortem studies show greater concentrations of D_3 receptors in the caudate nucleus and putamen of persons with schizophrenia (a) than persons without nonschizophrenia (b).
➤ *What is the significance of greater concentrations of D_3 receptors in the brains of persons with schizophrenia to the dopamine hypothesis of schizophrenia? (p. 470)*

to chlorpromazine treatment (Pilowsky et al., 1992). Clozapine is a weak blocker of D_2 receptor sites, but a much more effective blocker of D_4 and 5-HT receptors (Kerwin, 1996).

Recent research (Benes et al., 1996; Tsai et al., 1995) also has reported lower-than-normal levels of the neurotransmitters GABA and glutamate in the brains of persons with schizophrenia. Akbarian and colleagues (1996) also found that the glutamate receptors have an altered form. We learned in Chapter 5 that the drug phencyclidine (PCP) can induce schizophrenia-like symptoms in humans. Jentsch and colleagues (1997) observed schizophrenia-like behaviors in primates treated with PCP; symptoms were reversed with a dopamine-blocking antipsychotic drug. The mechanism of action of PCP involves the NMDA glutamate receptor, which provides further evidence of an involvement of glutamate neurotransmitter in schizophrenia.

So what role does the neurotransmitter dopamine play in schizophrenia? Heinrichs (1993) suggests that "schizophrenia may be a dopamine-related illness, but this relationship has not yet emerged as the neurological key to the disorder. Dopamine transmission may be a peripheral, or minor component of the pathological mechanism itself. The nature of this mechanism remains elusive and indistinct." Undoubtedly, the search for the means by which antipsychotic drugs alleviate the positive symptoms of schizophrenia will continue. This knowledge will help clarify the role of dopamine, and other neurotransmitters, in producing the symptoms of schizophrenia, and will likely contribute to the development of drugs that are even more effective in treating this illness.

What about the negative symptoms of schizophrenia (flat or blunted affect, social withdrawal, etc.)? Although antipsychotic drugs may reduce some negative symptoms in some patients, a substantial number of patients do not show any improvement in negative symptoms following drug treatment (Willerman & Cohen, 1990). This observation suggests that excessive dopamine is not responsible for the negative symptoms of schizophrenia. What, then, is responsible? One hypothesis has suggested that brain damage, especially to the frontal lobes, is responsible for producing the negative symptoms of schizophrenia. We next turn our attention to brain damage as a possible cause of schizophrenia.

Before You Go On

Compare and contrast the brain amine theory of affective disorders and the dopamine hypothesis of schizophrenia.

Brain Damage and Schizophrenia. A number of MRI studies (Andreason, 1988, 1994; Kelsoe et al., 1988; Shelton & Weinberger, 1986) have shown that the cerebral ventricles of many patients with schizophrenia are enlarged (see **Figure 15.14**). Larger spaces would imply that there is less brain matter, and indeed this enlargement has been attributed to smaller-than-normal neurons (Selemon, Rajkowska, & Goldman-Rakic, 1995) and the loss of neurons in the structures that surround the cerebral ventricles (Pfefferbaum et al., 1990; Suddath et al., 1989). These structures include the thalamus, basal ganglia, and hippocampus. All of these areas have important cognitive or motor functions.

Postmortem examinations of the brains of people with schizophrenia have revealed differences in specific neural structures as compared to normal individuals and to people with other psychiatric disorders. These studies have found that people with schizophrenia show lower tissue densities (fewer neurons) in the cerebral cortex (Benes, Davidson, & Bird, 1986), the dorsomedial nucleus of the thalamus (Pakkenberg, 1990), the hippocampus (Altshuler et al., 1990), and the entorhinal cortex, parahippocampal

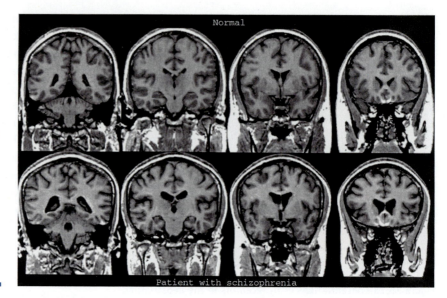

Figure 15.14 MRI scans of a normal subject (a) and a patient with schizophrenia (b). The patient with schizophrenia has an almost nonexistent corpus callosum as well as enlarged lateral ventricles.

➤ *Which neural structures of schizophrenics are different from those of normal individuals and of people with other psychiatric disorders? (p. 471–472)*

cortex, and cingulate cortex (Shapiro, 1993). Further, Benes and Bird (1987) reported that neurons in the cerebral cortex and the hippocampus were connected in a more disorganized fashion than is found in people without schizophrenia (see **Figure 15.15**). The disorientation of hippocampal neurons has been found in both the right and left hemispheres (Conrad et al., 1991).

The disorganization of neurons in the cerebral cortex and the hippocampus may be due to a failure of normal neural development (see Chapter 3). In support of this view, the disorganization of the hippocampus in the person with schizophrenia is much like that seen in mutant mice with disordered neurogenesis in the hippocampus (Scheibel & Conrad, 1993). Further, Akbarian and colleagues (1996) found in a postmortem examination of the prefrontal cortex of schizophrenics evidence that abnormal neuron migration had occurred during the fetal period. Abnormal amounts of the neurotrophins that guide cell migration have been found in the brains of people with schizophrenia (Honer et al., 1997; Poltorak et al., 1997), an observation that would explain the disorganized orientation of neurons in the cerebral cortex and hippocampus.

Brain-imaging techniques (CT, MRI, and PET scans—see **pp. 64 to 67** in Chapter 2) also have been used to identify particular kinds of brain damage in people with schizophrenia. For example, Bogerts (1989) found a loss of neural tissue in the frontal and anterior

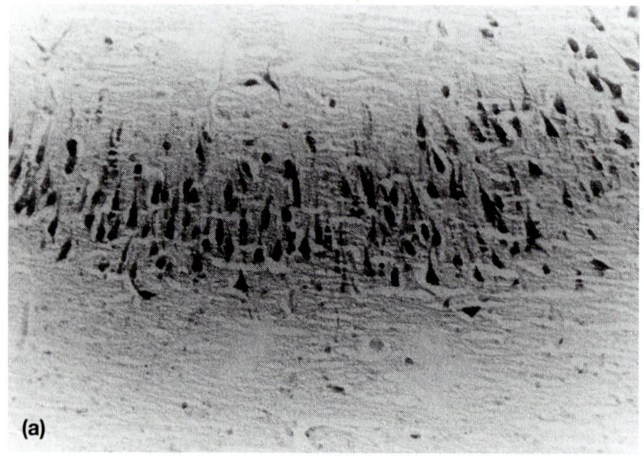

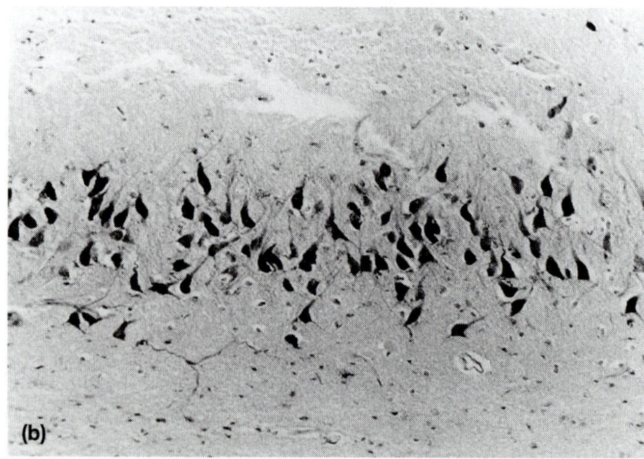

Figure 15.15 The disorganized brain of the schizophrenic. (a) The arrangement of hippocampal cells in normal subject and (b) in a patient with schizophrenia. The hippocampal cells are arranged in a more haphazard, disorganized fashion in the patient with schizophrenia.

➤ *What does the disorientation of the brain of the schizophrenic say about the origin of this disorder? (p. 472)*

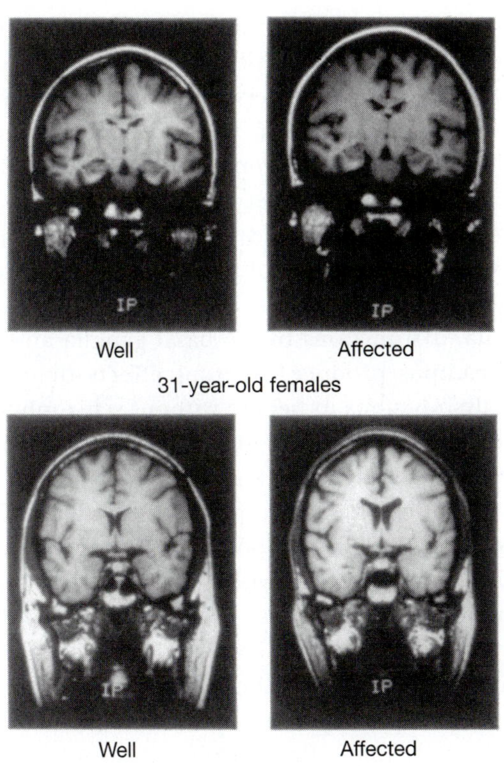

Figure 15.16 MRI scans showing brain differences in identical twins, one twin has schizophrenia (right side) and the other does not (left side). One prominent difference is the enlarged ventricles in the twin with schizophrenia.

➤ *What is another difference between discordant identical twins? (p. 473)*

temporal lobes as well as in the hypothalamus when CT scans of 54 patients with schizophrenia were compared with those of age-matched control subjects. Suddath, Christison, Torrey, Casanova, and Weinberger (1990) compared the MRI scans of 15 sets of identical twins that were discordant for schizophrenia (one twin had schizophrenia and the other did not). They reported that the twin who had schizophrenia showed larger lateral and third ventricles and a smaller anterior hippocampus than the twin who did not have schizophrenia (see **Figure 15.16**).

Measurements of the metabolic activity in the brain using the PET scan have revealed decreased metabolic activity in the cerebral cortex, most notably in the prefrontal cortex (see Chapter 2 and **Figure 15.17**), a condition called **hypofrontality** (Buchsbaum, 1990). Hypofrontality is thought to explain the negative symptoms of schizophrenia (Heinrichs, 1993). Damage to the prefrontal cortex in people with no history of schizophrenia has been associated with motivational difficulties, poverty in the content of speech, flattening of affect, social withdrawal, and cognitive impairments (Heinrichs, 1990). Sound familiar? They should—they are the negative symptoms of schizophrenia described earlier in the chapter. Thus, it is not surprising that several researchers (Andreasen et al., 1990; Goldman-Rakic, 1991) have concluded that the negative symptoms of schizophrenia reflect prefrontal cortex deficits.

Cohen and Servan-Schreiber (1992) suggested that reduced activity in the mesocortical dopamine neurons in the prefrontal cortex caused by brain damage may be associated with the cognitive deficits experienced by people with schizophrenia. These cognitive deficits are characterized by a difficulty in shifting between strategies when attempting to solve problems. When faced with a new task, the person with schizophrenia will continue to give previously correct responses, failing to shift to new, correct responses. For example, the subject will guess c again if c was the correct answer to the previous question.

Several lines of research have suggested that deficits in dopaminergic activity in the prefrontal cortex are responsible not only for the cognitive impairments associated with schizophrenia but for the negative symptoms as well. Performance on cognitive tasks is impaired following destruction of the mesocortical dopaminergic neurons in the prefrontal cortex of

hypofrontality The view that impaired functioning of the prefrontal lobes causes the negative symptoms of schizophrenia.

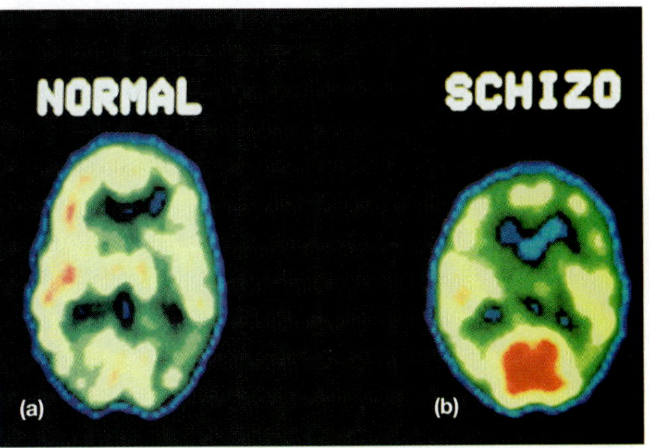

Figure 15.17 PET scans showing differences in metabolic activity in the brain of a normal person (a) and a patient with schizophrenia (b). The normal person shows a much higher level of metabolic activity, especially in the prefrontal cortex.

➤ *Do people with schizophrenia show increased or decreased metabolic activity in the brain? (p. 473)* monkeys (Oades, 1981; Simon, Scatton, & Moal, 1980). Brozoski, Brown, Rosvold, and Goldman (1979) found that the level of this cognitive impairment was equal to the impairment observed when the entire prefrontal area was ablated. These authors also reported that administration of dopamine agonists following destruction of the mesocortical dopamine neurons restored cognitive functioning in their primate subjects. Additionally, Weinberger, Berman, and Illowsky (1988) found that in the cerebrospinal fluid of people with schizophrenia, levels of homovanillic acid, a dopamine metabolite, were highly correlated with levels of activity in the prefrontal cortex during performance of a cognitive task; the lower the level of the dopamine metabolite, the greater the cognitive impairment. The metabolic hypofrontality seen in people with schizophrenia has been shown to be reversible by the administration of dopamine agonists (Geraud et al., 1987).

Our discussion to this point suggests that the negative symptoms of schizophrenia are caused by brain damage, especially to the prefrontal cortex. Hypofrontality in people with schizophrenia reflects decreased metabolism in the prefrontal cortex and is associated with deficits in the mesocortical dopaminergic neurons.

There is, however, strong evidence that argues against the conclusion that damage to the prefrontal lobes is central to the disorder of schizophrenia. Although the negative symptoms of schizophrenia may occur following frontal lobe damage, the same behaviors can be seen following damage to other parts of the brain (Andreason et al., 1991; Heinrichs, 1990). Further, negative symptoms have also been observed in people who have suffered from depression (Sommers, 1985), strokes (Heilman, Bowers, & Valenstein, 1985) and dementia (Joynt & Shoulson, 1985). These observations seem to imply that the negative symptoms are not specific to the disorder of schizophrenia or to frontal lobe brain damage.

We have learned that neither the dopamine hypothesis nor the hypofrontality theory provides a complete explanation of schizophrenia. So what exactly do we know about the biological basis of schizophrenia? Nancy Andreasen (1994) suggests that several different brain structures are dysfunctional, and together they produce the disorder of schizophrenia. The effect of a dysfunction in a single area may be quite different from its effect when accompanied by dysfunctions in other areas. For example, the basal ganglia of people with schizophrenia appears to be dysfunctional, causing excess dopamine activity in this area of the brain (Wong, Gjedde, & Wagner, 1986). The primary function of the basal ganglia is the integration of voluntary motor responses (refer to Chapter 8). However, schizophrenia typically is not a disorder primarily of movement, but more often of motivation, emotion, and cognition. The hippocampus of people with schizophrenia also appears to be dysfunctional (Suddath et al., 1990). Damage to the hippocampus is associated with memory loss (refer to Chapter 14), yet schizophrenia is not a disorder of memory. It is possible that among people with schizophrenia, dysfunctions in the basal ganglia and in the hippocampus produce different effects than do the same dysfunctions in people without schizophrenia.

Heinrichs (1993) presents a different view of schizophrenia. He suggests that the various brain structures mentioned in the previous sections (frontal lobes, basal ganglia, hippocampus) may be dysfunctional in some people with schizophrenia, but that the abnormalities in these structures is secondary to the disorder of schizophrenia. According to Heinrichs, the "neuropathological smoking gun" that causes schizophrenia has not been found. Heinrichs also suggests that what is called schizophrenia may not be a single disorder but instead several related ones, citing the observation that some patients show dysfunctions in the prefrontal cortex whereas others do not and that dopamine antagonists help some people with schizophrenia but not others. Heinrichs suggests that further research is needed to identify the neural structure or structures responsible for producing schizophrenia.

Before You Go On

Heinrichs has hired you to identify the neural structure or structures responsible for producing schizophrenia, and your report is due tomorrow. Using what you have learned so far in this chapter, propose a biological basis for schizophrenia.

Section Review

- The dopamine hypothesis of schizophrenia states that either excessive levels of dopamine or increased sensitivity to dopamine in the mesocortical dopamine system is responsible for producing the positive symptoms of schizophrenia.
- Support for the dopamine hypothesis includes the observation of abnormally high levels of dopamine metabolites in people with schizophrenia and the fact that Thorazine

and other antipsychotic drugs that reduce dopamine levels are often successful in alleviating the positive symptoms of schizophrenia.

- Administration of dopamine agonists such as amphetamine and cocaine can produce positive symptoms of schizophrenia, providing further support for the dopamine hypothesis.
- Not all patients with schizophrenia show improvement in positive symptoms following treatment with Thorazine or other D_2 receptor blocking drugs. The antipsychotic drug clozapine, which is a weaker blocker of D_2 receptors but is a more effective blocker of D_4 and 5-HT receptors than Thorazine, has been found to be clinically effective in Thorazine-resistant patients. Therefore, the biochemical basis of the positive symptoms of schizophrenia remains unclear.
- People with schizophrenia have fewer and smaller neurons in the cerebral cortex, the dorsomedial thalamus, the hippocampus, and the entorhinal cortex, parahippocampal cortex, and cingulate cortex. Further, neurons in the cerebral cortex and the hippocampus are connected in a disorganized fashion, which may be due to a failure of normal neural development.
- Decreased activity in the prefrontal cortex, called hypofrontality, has been suggested as a cause of the negative symptoms of schizophrenia.
- Destruction of the mesocortical dopaminergic system, which influences activity in the prefrontal cortex, has been shown to produce deficits on cognitive tasks whereas administration of dopamine agonists restores cognitive functioning.
- The negative symptoms of schizophrenia also are associated with other disorders that do not involve frontal lobe damage; thus the neural basis of the negative symptoms of schizophrenia remains unknown.

Causes of Schizophrenia

Because schizophrenia is so common, affecting about 1.5 percent of the United States population (Carpenter & Buchanan, 1994), as well as severely debilitating to the sufferer and to the sufferer's family, scientists have devoted a great deal of effort to trying to understand the causes of this disorder. There is now significant evidence that genetic factors and exposure to viral agents during the prenatal period affect the likelihood of developing schizophrenia. We begin our discussion by examining the role of inheritance in schizophrenia.

Genetics and Schizophrenia. Two approaches, both of which we introduced earlier in the chapter in the discussion of affective disorders, have been used to evaluate the possible role of inheritance in the development of schizophrenia: studies examining the occurrence of the disorder in families and the search for one or more genetic markers. Twin studies (Barnes, 1987; Gottesman, 1991) have found that the concordance rate is much higher for identical than for fraternal twins; that is, the likelihood that a twin of someone with schizophrenia will also develop this disorder is much higher if the twin is identical rather than fraternal. In fact, Farmer, McGuffin, and Gottesman (1987) reported that the concordance rate for identical twins was more than five times higher than for fraternal twins.

As seen in **Figure 15.18**, the risk of developing schizophrenia seems to be directly related to the closeness of the relationship between the individual and the person with schizophrenia, which reflects the similarities in their genes (Gottesman, 1991). As you can see from the figure, the more distant the familial relationship, the less the risk.

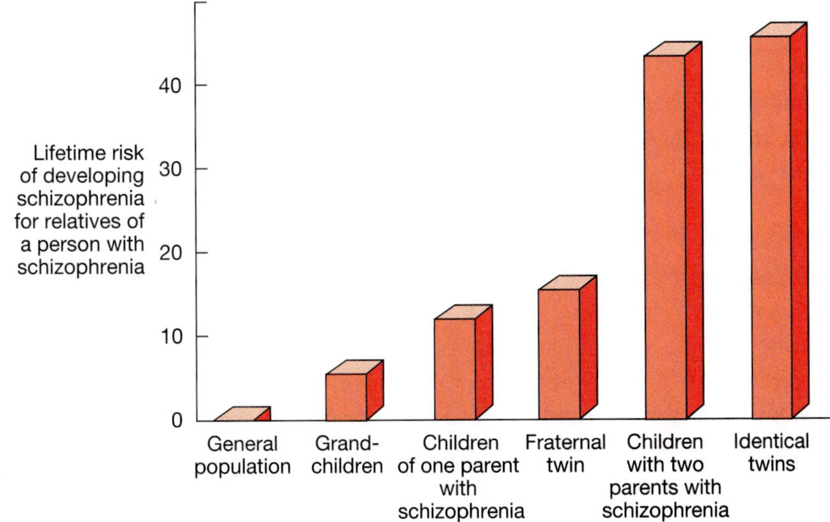

Figure 15.18 The risk of developing schizophrenia as a function of family relationship. As seen in the figure, the risk increases as genetic similarity increases.

➤ *Is the risk of developing schizophrenia higher for a cousin of someone with this disorder than for a sibling? (p. 475)*

Figure 15.19 Inheritance of schizophrenia. Each of the Genain quadruplets—Nora, Iris, Myra, and Hester—developed schizophrenia in their 20s, although the extent of their schizophrenia differed, suggesting a joint influence of inheritance and environment in the development of this disorder.
➤ *What differences might lead the Genain quadruplets to differ in their degree of adjustment? (p. 476–477)*

The results of adoption studies support the theory of a genetic contribution to schizophrenia (Gottesman, 1991; Plomin et al., 1997) by showing that the likelihood of an adopted child developing schizophrenia is greater if one or both biological parents had schizophrenia than if neither parent had this disorder. By contrast, the risk of developing schizophrenia is not increased by having an adopted parent diagnosed with schizophrenia (Gottesman, 1991). Further, the approximately 1-in-2 chance of one twin developing schizophrenia when an identical twin has this disorder remains, even when the two twins are reared apart (Plomin et al., 1997). This higher risk provides clear and conclusive evidence for a genetic contribution to schizophrenia.

The most interesting, and widely reported, case study in the inheritance of schizophrenia is that of the Genain quadruplets (see **Figure 15.19**). (The name *Genain* is actually a pseudonym from the Greek words meaning "dire birth.") All four girls developed symptoms of schizophrenia when they were in their 20s. The National Institute of Mental Health (NIMH) sponsored much of the research of the sisters over the course of their illnesses; their first names, Nora, Iris, Myra, and Hester, were also pseudonyms given by NIMH to protect their privacy. When they were born in 1930, the quadruplets were celebrities. As young children, they performed song-and-dance routines in their hometown. As they grew to young adulthood, they began to show behaviors characteristic of schizophrenia. One of the twins dropped out of high school and all had trouble holding jobs. Nora, the oldest quadruplet, was first hospitalized for schizophrenia at age 21. Iris was hospitalized 7 months later. When the other two sisters, Myra and Hester, were diagnosed with schizophrenia in 1955, all four sisters spent the next 3 years being studied at NIMH.

The quadruplets have a number of family members who have suffered from psychiatric disorders. Their father's behavior was often described as bizarre—he showed considerable hostility toward many people and refused to allow the quadruplets to play with other children. Other family members—their father's brother, mother, and paternal uncle—had been hospitalized with "nervous breakdowns."

Although all four sisters suffered from schizophrenia, they differed in terms of the severity of their schizophrenic episodes and the course of the disorder. Rosenthal's (1963) initial report on the Genain quadruplets showed Nora and Myra to be the more functional sisters. After leaving NIMH, Myra went to business school, worked as a secretary, and married and had children, and Nora worked for at least 7 years, mostly in government training programs. The other two quadruplets, Hester and Iris, spent more than 15 years hospitalized in a state mental institution.

A follow-up study in 1981 at NIMH found the quadruplets to be normal in terms of their CT scans, but the quadruplets differed from individuals without schizophrenia on their PET scans (see **Figure 15.20**). All the Genain quadruplets showed heightened activity in the visual areas of the brain when they were resting with their eyes closed, suggesting that they were hallucinating. The fact that the Genain quadruplets also showed less alpha wave activity (see Chapter 9), which appears when people relax and their minds go blank, than is seen in persons without schizophrenia provides further evidence of hallucinations. The PET scans of Myra and Nora were closer to the PET scans of persons who do not have schizophrenia than those found in Hester and Iris. This result is predictable from the better adjustment of Myra and Nora, as is the fact that Myra and Nora received much less antipsychotic medication than did their sisters.

Our discussion suggests that what is inherited is only a susceptibility or predisposition to developing schizophrenia. The concordance rate for identical twins is only 48 percent, a result that indicates that the presence of a particular gene is not by itself sufficient to produce schizophrenia. Factors other than inheritance appear to contribute to the development of schizophrenia.

The second method demonstrating a genetic involvement is to try to locate the gene or genes responsible for producing the disorder. Several studies (Bassett et al., 1988; Sherrington et al., 1995) have reported that some people with schizophrenia have an abnormality in the long arm of chromosome 5. However, other research (Kennedy et al., 1988; St. Claire et al., 1989) has failed to observe an abnormality on this chromosome. Several recent studies (DeAngelis, 1997; Lander & Kruglyak, 1995) have sug-

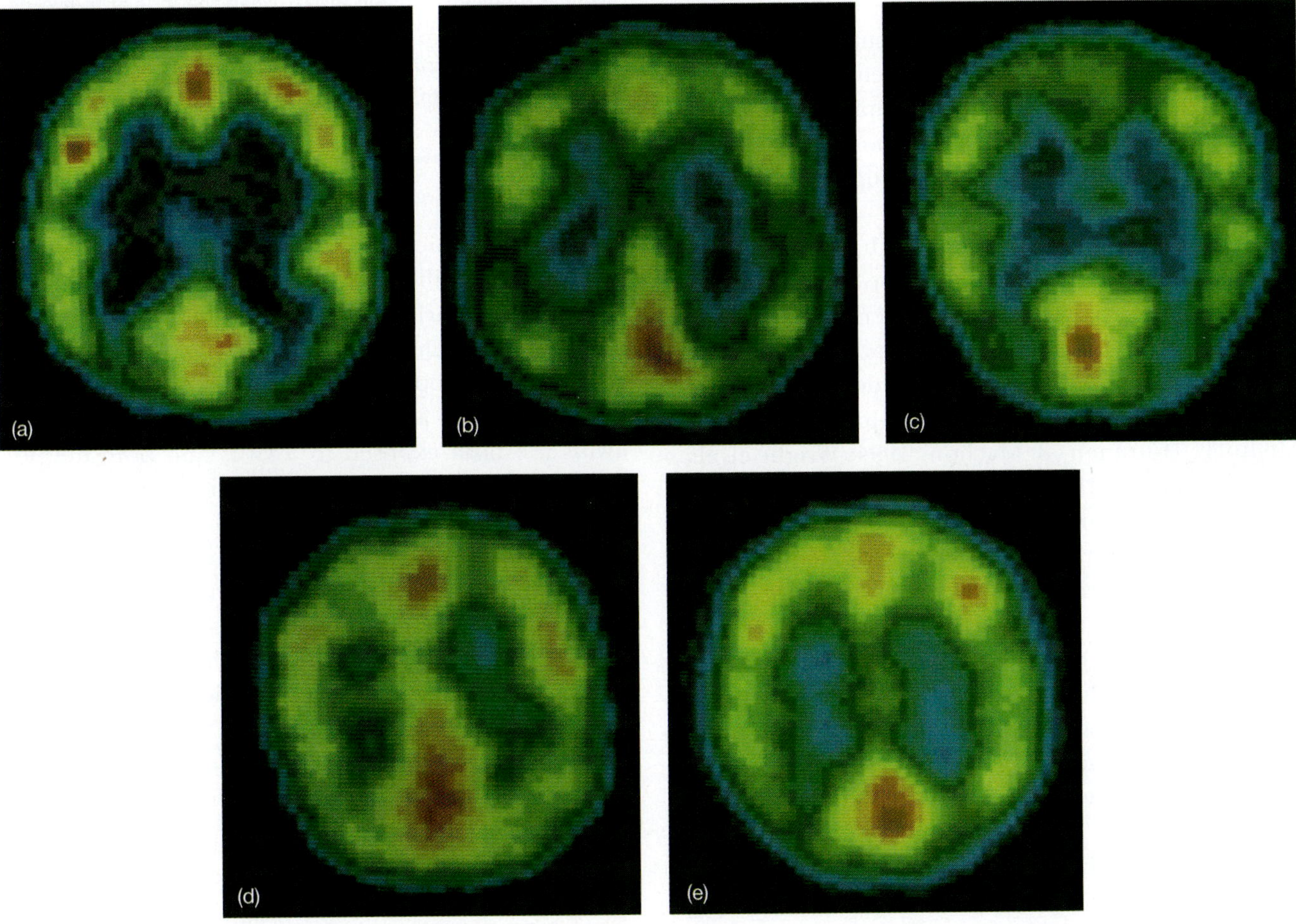

Figure 15.20 PET scans of the Genain quadruplets. All of the Genain sisters showed greater activity in the visual areas of the brain when resting with their eyes closed than is seen in people without schizophrenia, but the PET scans of Myra (b) and Nora (c) were closer to normal (a) than those of Hester (d) and Iris (e).

➤ *Why were the PET scans of Myra and Nora more like those of people without nonschizophrenia than those of Hester and Iris? (p. 477)* gested that genes on chromosomes 6 and 22 contribute to the risk of developing schizophrenia. Research in this area is only in the initial stages, and the search for the gene or genes controlling schizophrenia will likely continue to reveal more about the inheritance of this disorder.

Before You Go On

Why do you think that adoption study data on schizophrenia might be skewed in favor of the biological influence rather than the environmental influence? (Hint: The adoptive parents are considered the environmental influence.)

A Viral Infection and Schizophrenia. A number of researchers (Barr, Mednick, & Munk-Jorgensen, 1990; Waddington, 1993) have proposed that exposure to a viral infection during the second trimester of pregnancy contributes to the development of schizophrenia. The disorientation seen in the arrangement of neurons in the brain of someone with schizophrenia that we described earlier in the chapter supports the idea that something happens during fetal development that leads to schizophrenia.

There is considerable evidence that a viral infection is the culprit causing the disorientation of the neurons of people with schizophrenia. First, when there is a flu epidemic, fetuses who are in the middle trimester show an increased risk of developing schizophrenia (Barr, Mednick, & Munk-Jorgensen, 1990; Mednick, Huttunen, & Machon, 1994; Wright et al., 1995). **Figure 15.21** clearly shows that when a fetus is in the second trimester of pregnancy, the risk of developing schizophrenia is proportional to the level of influenza; the risk is low when the influenza level was low, moderate when the influenza level was moderate, and high when the influenza level was great. Second, the decline in infectious disease rate is highly correlated with a decline in risk of developing schizophrenia (Eagles, 1991). Third, the fall-winter flu season coincides with a greater risk of fetuses who are in the middle trimester later developing schizophrenia (McGrath, Welham, & Pemberton, 1995; Torrey et al., 1996). The relationship between being in the middle trimester of pregnancy during the flu season and later developing schizophrenia is true for both the northern hemisphere (Torrey et al., 1996) and the southern hemisphere (McGrath, Welham, & Pemberton, 1995). However, it is not true for tropical climates in which there are no seasonal changes (Bradbury & Miller, 1985).

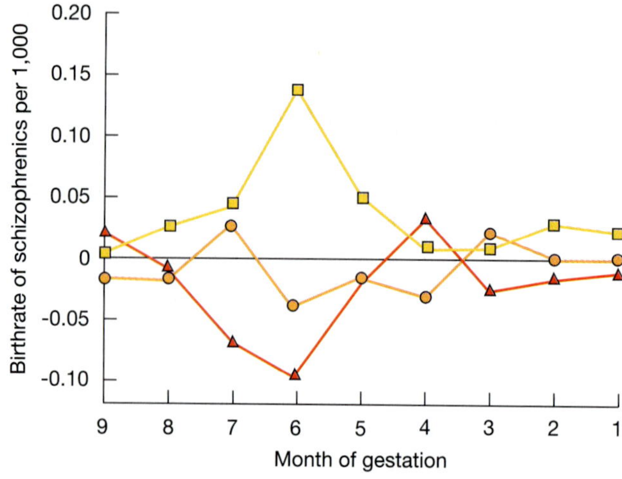

Figure 15.21 Exposure to the flu and the rate of schizophrenia. The influence of three levels of flu influenza on the mean schizophrenia birthrate per 1,000 as a function of the month of exposure. The rate of schizophrenia is highest when the influenza rate was high during the sixth month of gestation (yellow line), moderate when the influenza rate was medium (orange line), and lowest when the influenza level was low (red line).

➤ *How would exposure to the flu during the second trimester of pregnancy be a contributing factor to the development of schizophrenia? (p. 478)*

Genetics clearly plays a crucial role in the development of schizophrenia, perhaps by creating a vulnerability to developing schizophrenia following prenatal exposure to a virus. Yet even when two identical twins are both exposed to a virus and both develop schizophrenia, the severity of their disorder can differ. As we learned earlier, two of the Genain quadruplets showed much more severe forms of this disorder than their other two sisters. Further, even among identical twins who are both exposed to a virus, one twin may develop schizophrenia while the other twin does not. Stressors have been implicated as an important source of these differences (Mirsky & Duncan, 1986). Identifying strategies to reduce the stress reactions of individuals at risk for developing schizophrenia is currently underway (Hafner, 1998).

Before You Go On

If the concordance rate for schizophrenia is only 48 percent among identical twins, why do you think all four Genain quadruplets developed the disorder?

Section Review

- Twin studies provide evidence that some people may be genetically predisposed to developing schizophrenia.
- Family studies show that the risk of developing schizophrenia is directly related to the degree to which someone is genetically related to someone else who has schizophrenia; the more distant the genetic relationship, the less the risk.
- Adoption studies have shown that the likelihood that an adopted child will develop schizophrenia is greater if a biological parent has schizophrenia than if the biological parents do not have this disorder.
- Several studies have identified chromosome sites as possible locations of the gene for schizophrenia, but none of these studies has been replicated successfully.
- Exposure to a viral infection during the second trimester of pregnancy is a likely contributor to the development of schizophrenia.

Chapter Review

Critical Thinking Questions

1. Susan broke up with her boyfriend several weeks ago. She refuses to leave her house, does not want to see anyone, and is convinced that her life is over. Is Susan depressed? Discuss the biological processes that might be contributing to Susan's behavior. What might be done to help Susan feel better?
2. Twin and adoption studies have been used to evaluate the contribution of genes to the development of depression and schizophrenia. Discuss the strengths and weaknesses of these approaches. What method would provide convincing evidence for a genetic contribution to the development of behavior disorders?
3. Anthony has been diagnosed with schizophrenia. Describe the symptoms of this disorder. What biological processes have been shown to be associated with schizophrenia? Evaluate what we know about the relationship between these processes and the symptoms of schizophrenia.

Vocabulary Questions

1. An impairment in functioning caused by the persistence of high levels of depression or mania of a certain period of time is called an ________________.
2. ________________ involve both mania and depression.
3. ________________ is characterized by depressed mood of at least 2 weeks' duration; the experience of less intense depressive symptoms off and on for many years is called ________________.
4. The milder form of mania that occurs in a patient with cyclothymia is called ________________.
5. The theory that abnormal levels of neurotransmitters are at least partially responsible for producing affective disorders is called the ________________.
6. Excessive activity in the ________________, a major site for the synthesis of norepinephrine, may be involved in depression.
7. The genetic contribution is significantly higher for ________________ than for major depression.
8. ________________ is an abnormally high secretion of cortisol from the adrenal cortex.
9. In depressed persons, REM sleep occurs ________________ than normal in the sleep cycle, and total sleeping time is ________________.
10. ________________ are sensory experiences in the absence of environmental stimuli.
11. Disturbances in the content of thought are referred to as ________________.
12. The delusions and hallucinations experienced by schizophrenics are often referred to as ________________ symptoms.
13. The prominent symptoms of schizophrenia appear in the ________________ phase.
14. The drug ________________ acts as a dopamine antagonist, blocking postsynaptic dopaminergic receptor sites.
15. Decreased metabolic activity in the prefrontal regions of the cerebral cortex is called ________________.
16. The more distant the familial relationship between a person with schizophrenia and a relative, the ________________ the risk of the relative developing the disorder.

Review Questions

1. The following are among the ten characteristics of depression:
   a. depressed mood, change in appetite, and sleep disturbances
   b. blunt affect, change in appetite, and insomnia
   c. disordered thought processes, fatigue, inability to concentrate
   d. hallucinations, delusions, and psychomotor agitation
2. The following are among the eight symptoms of a manic episode:
   a. inflated self-esteem, delusions, and hallucinations
   b. decreased need for sleep, blunt affect, and distractibility
   c. delusions, hallucinations, and blunt affect
   d. increased speech, an elevated mood, and flights of fancy
3. The two types of bipolar disorder are
   a. dysthymia and cyclothymia.
   b. bipolar disorder and cyclothymia.
   c. mania and depression.
   d. schizophrenia and hypofrontality.
4. During depressive episodes, cortical activity
   a. increases, then decreases.
   b. decreases, then increases.
   c. decreases.
   d. increases.
5. The tricyclic compounds and monoamine oxidase inhibitors provide clinical relief by
   a. increasing levels of norepinephrine in the brain.
   b. decreasing levels of norepinephrine in the brain.
   c. increasing levels of dopamine in the brain.
   d. decreasing levels of dopamine in the brain.
6. The comparison of the occurrence of a disorder in two related individuals is called the
   a. concordance rate.
   b. twin study.
   c. gene theory.
   d. adoption study.
7. The brain amine changes observed in depressed persons may be caused by
   a. loss of a job.
   b. repeated exposure to uncontrollable events.
   c. loss of a spouse.
   d. amphetamine.
8. The response of a normal person to the dexamethasone suppression test would be
   a. suppression of ACTH and cortisol secretion.
   b. no effect on ACTH and cortisol secretion.
   c. increased ACTH and cortisol secretion.
   d. suppression of ACTH and dexamethasone secretion.
9. The treatment of the sleep disturbances associated with depression is to
   a. wake the person when he or she enters slow-wave sleep.
   b. phase delay the sleep cycle by several hours.
   c. phase advance the sleep cycle by several hours.
   d. kick the person when he or she begins to snore.
10. Schizophrenia is characterized by
    a. loss of contact with reality and disturbances in thought, perception, motor behavior, and emotions.
    b. alternation of depressive and manic episodes.
    c. multiple personalities.
    d. an inflated sense of self-worth.
11. The affective symptoms of schizophrenia can include
    a. mania or depression.
    b. joy or sorrow.
    c. blunt or inappropriate affect.
    d. positive symptoms.
12. The negative symptoms of schizophrenia include
    a. poor social skills and inability to function in society.
    b. lack of voluntary motor behavior and excessive speech.
    c. blunted affect and excessive voluntary motor behavior.
    d. blunted affect and poverty of speech.
13. The three stages of the schizophrenic disorder include
    a. the preliminary phase, the active phase, and the residual phase.
    b. the preliminary phase, the active phase, and the dormant phase.
    c. the prodromal phase, the active phase, and the dormant phase.
    d. the prodromal phase, the active phase, and the residual phase.
14. The idea that an excess of dopamine or increased sensitivity to dopamine produces the positive symptoms of schizophrenia is called the
    a. dopamine hypothesis of schizophrenia.
    b. neurotransmitter hypothesis of schizophrenia.
    c. brain amine theory of schizophrenia.
    d. brain amine theory of mental disorders.
15. Drugs that increase dopamine activity in the central nervous system can produce
    a. the negative symptoms of schizophrenia.
    b. the positive symptoms of schizophrenia.
    c. depression.
    d. bipolar disorder.
16. According to one view, the negative symptoms of schizophrenia are caused by
    a. excessive levels of dopamine.
    b. overindulgence in drugs.
    c. brain damage.
    d. stress.

17. Adoption studies show that the likelihood of an adopted child developing schizophrenia is
    a. greater if neither biological parent had the disorder.
    b. greater if neither adoptive parent had the disorder.
    c. greater if one or more adoptive parents had the disorder.
    d. greater if one or more biological parents had the disorder.
18. Exposure to a viral infection during the _______________ trimester of pregnancy is a likely contribution ot the development of schizophrenia.
    a. first
    b. second
    c. third
    d. none of the above

Suggested Readings

DEPREE, R. A., & IACONO, W. G. (1989). Neurobehavioral aspects of affective disorders. *Annual Review of Psychology, 40,* 457–492.

GOTTESMAN, I. I. (1991). *Schizophrenia genesis: The origins of madness.* New York: W. H. Freeman.

HEINRICHS, R. W. (1993). Schizophrenia and the brain. *American Psychologist, 48,* 221–233.

McKENNA, P. J. (1994). *Schizophrenia: From mind to molecule.* Washington, DC: American Psychiatric Press.

STRANGE, P. G. (1992). *Brain biochemistry and brain disorders.* Oxford, England: Oxford University Press.

GLOSSARY

ablation Experimental destruction of specific neurons in the nervous system; also called lesioning.

absolute refractory period The time following the repolarization of the membrane potential that the neuron is insensitive to further stimulation.

accommodation The change of the shape of the lens to focus a particular image.

acetylcholine (ACh) A neurotransmitter that is synthesized from acetyl CoA and choline; occurs only in the presence of the enzyme choline acetyltransferase.

acetylcholinesterase (AChE) An enzyme present in the synaptic cleft that quickly deactivates ACh after it is released and binds to the postsynaptic membrane.

acquired sexual motive A stimulus in the physical environment becomes able to produce the physical changes associated with sexual arousal as a result of conditioning.

across-fiber pattern coding Type of coding in which information about a stimulus is determined by the pattern of neural impulses carried by two or more neurons.

actin The thin protein myofilament found in muscle fiber.

action potential The changes that occur within the neuron upon receipt of information about a stimulus.

activation synthesis theory The view that dreams are a mental interpretation of the neural activity that occurs during sleep.

active phase of schizophrenia The second phase in which the more obvious symptoms of schizophrenia appear.

addiction A pattern of behavior characterized by an overwhelming involvement with securing and then using a drug despite adverse consequences of drug use and with a significant likelihood of relapse after quitting or withdrawal.

adipose satiety factor A protein in fat tissue that acts to suppress eating.

adipsia A failure to eat.

adrenogenital syndrome A condition that occurs when the adrenal glands secrete too much androstenedione, resulting in genetically human females with masculinized genitals.

affective disorder A psychiatric disorder characterized by one of two mood states—depression or mania.

afferent neuron A neuron that sends messages from the sensory receptors to the central nervous system.

aggression A behavior motivated by the intent to harm a living being or, under some conditions, an inanimate object.

agonists Drugs that mimic or enhance the activity of a neurotransmitter.

agrammatical A deficiency in grammar.

agraphia A communicative disorder characterized by an inability to write caused by damage to the angular gyrus.

alarm reaction The first stage in the GAS that is characterized by intense sympathetic nervous system arousal.

alar plate A zone of cells of the dorsal portion of the neural tube that develops into the sensory neurons and interneurons of the dorsal horn of the spinal cord.

alcohol (ethyl alcohol) A powerful depressant produced by the fermentation of certain grains and fruits; allows the neurotransmitter GABA to bind more readily or more tightly to the GABA receptor sites.

alcoholism A dependence on alcohol.

aldosterone A hormone released by the adrenal cortex that causes increased salt retention.

alexia A communicative disorder characterized by an inability to read; caused by damage to the angular gyrus.

all-or-none law The principle that once threshold is reached, an action potential will be the same regardless of the intensity of the original stimulus.

alpha activity (or alpha waves) An EEG pattern of waves that are larger and more synchronized (8 and 12 Hz) than those of beta activity and that occurs when an individual is relaxed with eyes closed.

alpha-fetoprotein A protein synthesized by the fetal liver and present in the bloodstream of both male and female fetuses that deactivates circulating estradiol by binding to it.

alpha motor neuron Motor neuron with a long axon that leaves the ventral root of the spinal cord or brainstem and synapses with individual muscle fibers.

alzheimer's disease (or dementia of Alzheimer's type) A type of dementia characterized by progressive neurological degeneration and a profound deterioration of mental functioning.

amacrine cell Type of retinal neuron that receives neural messages from the bipolar cells and synapses with and inhibits both bipolar and ganglion cells.

amphetamine A class of stimulant drugs typically used to prevent sleep or to suppress appetite that increase the release of norepinephrine and dopamine by blocking their reuptake.

ampulla Enlarged area in each semicircular canal.

amygdala A structure in the limbic system located at the base of the temporal lobe that controls anger, fear, and aggressive behavior.

amygdalectomy A psychosurgery procedure that destroys selected neurons in the amygdala to treat extreme aggressiveness.

amyloid beta protein A protein that accumulates in the neural tissue and is thought to cause degeneration of neural fibers and disruption of neural connections within specific areas of the brain.

amyotrophic lateral sclerosis A degenerative neuromuscular disease that impairs the control of most voluntary muscles and is caused by the degeneration of the corticospinal and corticobulbar tracts and the anterior horns of the spinal cord.

analgesia Pain relief.

androgen insensitivity syndrome A condition in which genetic males do not have testosterone receptors in the brain, and are therefore insensitive to testosterone, and develop external female genitalia.

androstenedione An androgen produced continuously in low levels by the adrenal gland.

anencephaly A neural tube defect that results when the brain or a major part of it fails to develop.

angiotensin II A hormone converted from angiotensinogen by the enzyme renin that acts to stimulate the adrenal cortex to release aldosterone.

angular gyrus An area within the parietal lobe that borders the left occipital lobe and has connections to Wernicke's area, which is involved in the comprehension of the written word.

annulospiral endings Sensory receptors that surround the central part of the intrafusal muscle fiber.

anomia A difficulty selecting the correct word for either written or spoken language.

anomic aphasia A communicative disorder characterized by consistent difficulty finding names.

anorexia A loss of appetite.

anorexia nervosa An eating disorder in which adolescents or young women diet and lose as much as 35 percent of their body weight and yet still feel fat.

antagonists Drugs that block the activity of a neurotransmitter.

anterior Toward the front end.

anterior pituitary gland The part of the pituitary that manufactures and secretes releasing hormones.

anterograde amnesia The inability to recall events that occur after some disturbance to the brain.

anterograde degeneration The breakdown of the axon from the site of damage to the presynaptic terminals.

anterolateral system Somatosensory pathways that begin in the spinal cord and project information about temperature and pain to the brainstem reticular formation and the primary somatosensory cortex.

antianxiety drugs A class of sedative-hypnotic drugs that are often used to reduce nervousness, anxiety, or fear.

antidiuretic hormone (ADH) A hormone secreted by the posterior pituitary that causes the kidneys to retain more fluid.

antipsychotic drugs (major tranquilizers) A class of sedative-hypnotic drugs that are used in the treatment of psychosis, and to calm stroke victims and other agitated individuals, by blocking postsynaptic dopamine and serotonin receptors.

aphagia A failure to eat.

aphasia An acquired impairment of language that is caused by damage to the areas of the brain involved in receiving (understanding) and/or expressing (producing) language.

apraxia A disorder of movement that is characterized by problems in performing purposeful movements.

apraxia of speech A disorder characterized by a great difficulty in the selection and sequencing of speech due to damage limited to Broca's area of the left frontal lobe.

arachnoid mater The thin weblike sheet of tissue that is the middle layer of meninges.

arcuate fasciculus A bundle of nerve fibers that connects Wernicke's area with Broca's area.

astrocyte The star-shaped glial cell that provides physical support for a neuron, transports nutrients into and waste products out of the neuron, regulates blood flow, and guides neural development.

Atkinson-Shiffrin three-stage model of memory The view that an experience is sequentially stored in the sensory register, the short-term store, and then the long-term store.

auditory agnosia An inability to recognize language and nonlanguage sounds due to bilateral damage to the secondary auditory cortex.

auditory nerve (vestibulocochlear nerve or the eighth cranial nerve) The nerve formed when fibers from the cochlear nerve and vestibular nerve merge.

auditory-verbal agnosia (pure word deafness) A communicative disorder characterized by an inability to recognize spoken words as meaningful due to damage that severs the connections between the secondary auditory cortex and from the primary auditory cortex in both hemispheres.

autonomic nervous system The division of the peripheral nervous system containing the nerves that regulate the functioning of internal organs.

autoradiography Injection of radioactive chemicals into the bloodstream and subsequent analysis of neural tissue to determine where a specific chemical is found in the nervous system.

autoreceptors The inhibitory action of a neurotransmitter on the receptor sites on the presynaptic membrane, which acts to decrease further neurotransmitter release.

axon The long, relatively thick fiber that transmits neural impulses away from the neural cell body.

axon hillock The junction between the soma and axon where all input is summed up and, if threshold is reached, the action potential is generated.

axoxonic A neuron with no axons.

ballistic movement Movement that occurs rapidly and is not dependent on sensory feedback.

barbiturates A class of sedative-hypnotic drugs that are derivatives of barbituric acid and act by enhancing the binding of GABA neurotransmitter on certain GABA receptor sites.

basal forebrain region An area located anterior to the hypothalamus and including the preoptic area that initiates SWS.

basal ganglia Area of the forebrain close to the thalamus that integrates movement and controls postural adjustments and muscle tone; consists of the caudate nucleus, putamen, and globus pallidus.

basal plate A zone of cells of the ventral portion of the neural tube that develops into motor neurons and interneurons of the ventral horn of the spinal cord and the sympathetic and parasympathetic nervous systems.

basilar membrane A membrane in the organ of Corti to which the auditory receptors are attached by Deiter's cells.

basket cells Neurons that inhibit surrounding Purkinje cells to produce continuous movement in a specific muscle and prevent movement in opposing muscles.

behavior An action of an organism.

behavior genetics The study of how inheritance affects the behavior of a specific species.

Bell-Magendie law The principle that the dorsal root carries sensory information to the spinal cord and the ventral root conveys commands to the muscles.

benzodiazepines A class of antianxiety drugs that includes Librium, Valium, and Xanax; these drugs act by facilitating the binding of GABA neurotransmitter to specific GABA receptor sites.

beta activity (or beta waves) A rapid desynchronized EEG pattern of small voltage changes (18 to 24 Hz) that occurs when an individual is awake and active.

binocular depth cues Depth cues provided by comparing the images received by each of the two eyes.

biological psychology The discipline that investigates the influence of biological systems on behavior.

bipolar cells Neurons that form the middle layer of the retina.

bipolar disorder A type of affective disorder that is characterized by episodes of mania and depression that typically continue throughout one's lifetime.

blobs Blob-shaped clusters of neurons in the primary visual cortex that are sensitive to specific colors.

blood-brain barrier A barrier formed by the tight joints in the endothelial walls that surround the capillaries and by astroglia cells that limits the flow of certain substances between the bloodstream and the brain.

bradykinesia A movement disorder in which a person shows a slowness of initiating movement.

brain The division of the central nervous system located within the vertebrate skull that interprets sensory messages and determines the appropriate behavioral response to that sensory message.

brain amine theory of depression A theory that abnormal levels of norepinephrine and serotonin are at least partially responsible for producing affective disorders.

brightness Intensity of light stimulus.

Broca's aphasia A communicative disorder caused by damage to the area in the left frontal lobe rostral to the base of the primary motor cortex that produces an inability to initiate well-articulated conversational speech.

Broca's area An area in the posterior third frontal convolution of the left frontal lobe rostral to the base of the primary motor cortex that is involved in speech production.

bulimia An eating disorder characterized by recurrent episodes of binge eating, followed by purging.

caffeine A stimulant found in various plants that increases alertness and decreases fatigue by increasing glutamate release.

calpain A dormant enzyme that breaks down the protein fodrin.

Cannon-Bard theory of emotion The view that an event activates the thalamus simultaneously stimulating both the cortex, which produces the perception of the emotion, and the rest of the body, which produces the internal changes and motor responses associated with that emotion.

carbidopa Drug that prevents the destruction by enzymes in the intestine and plasma and conversion of L-dopa in the PNS.

castration The removal of the testes in males and the ovaries in females.

cataplexy A sudden, complete lack of muscle tone; one symptom of narcolepsy.

caudal Toward the tail.

caudal reticular formation Area within reticular formation that produces REM sleep.

caudate nucleus A long curving structure that is part of the basal ganglia.

cell assembly A number of neurons that become active at the same time; this neural circuit serves as the site of permanent memory.

cell-autonomous differentiation A process whereby neurons develop without outside influence.

cell membrane Structure that controls the flow of substances into and out of the neuron.

cellular modification theory The view that learning permanently enhances the functioning of existing neural circuits or establishes new neural connections.

center-off, surround-on ganglion cells Type of ganglion neurons that are stimulated when the surround is illuminated.

center-on, surround-off ganglion cells Type of ganglion neurons that are stimulated when the center of the receptive field is illuminated.

central canal The chamber of the ventricular system that runs through the spinal cord.

central nervous system (CNS) The division of the nervous system that analyzes the significance of sensory information, decides how to respond to that information, and sends the message to execute that response to the peripheral nervous system.

central sulcus The deep groove that separates the anterior and posterior halves of the cerebral cortex.

cephalic reflexes A set of responses controlled by the central nervous system that prepare an animal to digest, metabolize, and store food.

cephalization The fusion of many ganglion pairs to form an increasingly larger and more complex brain.

cerebellum Area of the brain located behind and beneath the cerebral cortex that develops neural motor programs and coordinates skilled movements.

cerebral commissures The fiber tracts that connect the two hemispheres of the brain.

cerebral cortex Structure in the forebrain that processes sensory information, controls thinking and decision making, stores and retrieves memories, and initiates motor responses.

cerebral palsy A congenital motor disorder characterized by postural instability and extraneous movement.

cerebrospinal fluid The clear fluid contained in the ventricular system and arachnoid space that supports and protects the CNS and provides it with nutrients.

cerveau isolé preparation Surgical procedure in which the cerebral cortex is isolated from the rest of the brain by a transection between the inferior colliculus and superior colliculus, which produces continuous sleep and an inability to be awakened.

cholecystokinin (CCK) A neuropeptide hormone limiting the rate at which food passes from the stomach into the small intestine that may serve as a satiety sensor.

cholinergic Synaptic transmission involving ACh as the neurotransmitter.

chorda tympani A branch of the seventh cranial nerve that conveys taste information from the posterior tongue and the palate and throat to the nucleus of the solitary tract.

choroid plexus The rich network of blood vessels in the ventricles that manufactures the cerebrospinal fluid.

chromatolysis The breakdown of the cell body following damage to the axon.

chromosome The structure in a cell containing genes or the units of inheritance.

ciliary muscles The muscles that control the shape of the lens.

cingulate gyrus A structure in the limbic system involved in positive and negative emotional responses.

circadian cycle A change in biological and behavioral functioning that occurs over a 24-hour period.

circadian rhythm The intrinsic process that controls the 24-hour cycle.

climbing fibers Neurons that have an inhibitory influence on the cerebellum, allowing it to reset quickly and to respond to new incoming information.

cocaine A stimulant extracted from the leaves of the coca plant that produces increased alertness and decreased fatigue by triggering the release and blocking the reuptake of norepinephrine and dopamine.

cochlea The snail-shaped structure in the inner ear, composed of the vestibular duct and the tympanic duct, that contains the auditory receptors.

cochlear nerve Nerve formed by neurons that synapse with the afferent dendrites of the auditory receptors.

cochlear nuclei Neurons in the medulla that receive neural messages from the auditory receptors via the auditory nerve.

coding A specific pattern of neural activity that contains information about stimuli in the physical environment.

cognitive appraisal A procedure to evaluate cognitively the impact of an event by determining whether a stressor represents a serious threat to your well-being, an interesting new challenge, or little or no threat.

collateral sprouting A process by which neighboring neurons of a degenerating neuron sprout new axonal endings to connect to the receptor sites left vacant by the degenerated neuron.

color constancy The perception that the color of an object remains the same even under different lighting conditions.

commissurotomy A surgical procedure in which the cerebral commissures are cut that is an effective treatment for grand mal seizures.

comparative psychology The comparative study of the behavior of different species of animals.

complex cells Neurons in the primary visual cortex that are very sensitive to a line stimulus oriented in a particular direction, which can appear anywhere in the receptive field.

component direction-selective neurons Neurons in the primary visual cortex (Area V1) that detect the movement of an object in one plane—horizontal, vertical, or oblique.

computerized axial tomography (CT) A technique that produces a static image of the brain by shooting a narrow beam of x-rays from all angles to produce a cross-sectional view of the brain; the resulting image is commonly referred to as a CT scan.

conception The moment of fertilization of an egg by a sperm.

concordance rate The extent to which a trait is shared by both members of a twin pair.

conditioned hunger The ability of an environmental event to produce hunger as a result of conditioning.

conditioned response (CR) A learned reaction to the conditioned stimulus.

conditioned satiety The ability of an environmental event to produce satiety as a result of conditioning.

conditioned stimulus (CS) A stimulus that becomes able to elicit an instinctive response as a result of having previously been paired with the unconditioned stimulus.

conduction aphasia A communicative disorder caused by damage to the temporoparietal region, above and below the Sylvian fissure, which includes the arcuate fasciculus, that produces a difficulty repeating verbal information.

cone Type of photoreceptor concentrated in the central region of the retina that is responsible for the acuity of daytime vision.

congenital Present at birth.

connexons Specialized protein channels that allow ions to move across gap junctions.

constructional apraxia A difficulty drawing pictures or assembling objects.

contingency The specified relationship between a behavior and reinforcement or punishment.

contralateral control The process by which one side of the brain controls the movement on the opposite side of the body.

contralateral neglect A disturbance in the ability to respond to visual, auditory, or somatosensory stimuli on one side of the body due to damage to the contralateral posterior parietal cortex.

cornea Transparent outer layer of the eye.

coronal plane A view of a structure from the front.

corpus callosum The largest of the cerebral commissures that are composed of the axons of neurons carrying most information that is exchanged between the two hemispheres.

cortical plate A layer of daughter cells between the intermediate and marginal layers that develops into the neurons and glial cells of the cerebral cortex.

corticobulbar tract Group of neurons originating mostly in the primary motor cortex involved in the control of the movement of the face and tongue.

corticospinal tracts Two motor pathways that originate in the pyramidal cells of the primary motor cortex and are involved in the control of precise voluntary movements of the fingers, hands, and arms as well as the trunk, legs, and feet.

cranial nerve A group of neurons that directly link sensory receptors to the brain, and the brain to certain muscles.

crista Structure in the ampulla that contains vestibular receptor cells.

critical set point The critical level of stored fat that either activates or inhibits food-seeking behaviors.

crossing over The process of exchange of genetic material between chromosomes during meiosis.

cupula Gelatinous mass in the crista in which the vestibular receptor cells are embedded.

cyclothymia A type of bipolar disorder that is characterized by less intense episodes of mania and depression than is seen with bipolar disorder.

declarative memory Factual memory or the memory of specific events.

deep cerebellar nuclei Group of neurons that project to the ventral lateral thalamus, the red nucleus, the descending reticular formation, and the alpha motor neurons of the spinal cord to correct movements in progress.

delta activity (or delta waves) An EEG pattern during deep sleep that is characterized by synchronized waves that are larger in amplitude (1 to 4 Hz) than theta waves.

delusions Beliefs that are not based in reality.

dementia A loss of or impairment in a person's mental functioning.

dementia praecox A mental disorder described by Emil Kraepelin that included delusions, hallucinations, attention deficits, and bizarre motor behavior.

dendrites Thin, widely branching projections from the cell body of a neuron that receive neural impulses.

dendrodendritic transmission Communication between axoxonic neurons, from the dendrites of one neuron and the dendrites of another neuron.

deoxyribonucleic acid (DNA) A large, two-stranded molecule that contains the genetic blueprint of the entire organism and controls the production of RNA.

depolarization The reduction in the charge across the neural cell membrane by a stimulus.

depressants A class of psychoactive drugs that act on the central nervous system to slow down mental and physical functioning.

depression An intense feeling of sadness or loss.

depressive disorder A type of affective disorder in which depression is the only mood state present.

dexamethasone suppression test A test to determine whether administration of dexamethasone suppresses ACTH and cortisol secretion.

diabetes mellitus A chronic medical condition in which too little insulin is manufactured in the pancreas, causing high blood glucose levels.

diencephalon The embryonic division of the forebrain that becomes the thalamus, the hypothalamus, and several visual structures.

differentiation The creation of different cell types.

diffusion The tendency of molecules to move from areas of higher concentration to areas of lower concentration.

diseases of adaptation Illnesses caused by the body's coping with stressors; include essential hypertension, gastric or peptic ulcers, and colitis.

diurnal animals Animals that are awake during the day and asleep at night.

doctrine of specific nerve energies The theory that the message detected by the nervous system is determined by the nerve carrying the message.

dominant gene A gene that determines the presence of a physical or psychological characteristic, regardless of whether it is present in one or both members of a gene pair.

dopamine (DA) A neurotransmitter that is produced from the amino acid tyrosine.

dopamine hypothesis of schizophrenia The view that either an excess of dopamine or an increased sensitivity to this neurotransmitter in the mesocortical dopamine system produces the positive symptoms of schizophrenia.

dopaminergic Synaptic transmission involving dopamine as the neurotransmitter.

dorsal Toward the back.

dorsal column-medial lemniscal system Somatosensory pathways that begin in the spinal cord and project information about touch and proprioception to the primary somatosensory cortex.

dorsal column nuclei (DCN) Neurons in the medulla that receive neural messages about touch via the dorsal column-medial lemniscal system.

dorsal motor nucleus of the vagus (DMV) A group of neurons in the medulla that regulates insulin release by the parasympathetic nervous system.

Down syndrome A genetic disorder caused by the presence of three copies of chromosome 21; characterized by altered facial features, decreased mental functioning, and abnormalities in several internal organs.

dream An altered state of consciousness in which remembered images and fantasies are temporally confused with external reality.

drug dependent insomnia A sleep disorder that occurs when a person attempts to sleep without taking previously used sleep medication or takes a lower-than-normal dose.

dura mater The thick, tough, and flexible outermost layer of the meninges.

dysgraphia A communicative disorder characterized by difficulty in writing.

dyslexia A communicative disorder characterized by difficulty with reading that is caused by damage to the area of the brain where sounds and symbols are associated.

dysthymia A type of depressive disorder in which the symptoms wax and wane for years, but are less intense than in major depression.

echolalia A repetition of something someone has just said.

ectoderm The outermost layer of the embryo, which will become the nervous system.

efferent neuron A neuron that sends messages from the central nervous system to the muscles, glands, and organs.

electrical synapses The junction between the dendrites of one neuron and the dendrites of another neuron where localized depolarization or hyperpolarization moves across the gap junction.

electroencephalogram (EEG) A graphical record of the electrical activity of the cerebral cortex.

electrostatic pressure The attraction of opposite-polarity (+/-) molecules and the repulsion of same-polarity (+/+ or -/-) molecules.

embryo The developmental stage for the first 8 weeks after conception.

emotion A feeling that differs from an individual's normal state; a change in physiological arousal; an affective component; and a behavioral response.

encephalé isolé preparation A surgical procedure that transects the brain at the level of the spinal cord and has no effect on normal sleep-awake cycles.

endocrine system A system consisting of cells that release hormones into the bloodstream, where they are carried to distant target areas.

endoderm The innermost layer of the embryo, which will become the gut, lungs, and liver.

endometrium The membrane that lines the uterus.

endorphins Naturally occurring peptides with opiate-like effects.

engram The physical representation of a memory.

enzymatic degradation Deactivation of neurotransmitter molecules by an enzyme in the synapse.

epinephrine A hormone produced by the adrenal medulla and released into the bloodstream.

episodic memory The memory of an event experienced at a particular time and place.

equipotentiality The idea that all neurons within a particular brain area share equally in determining a specific function.

erectile dysfunction (impotence) A chronic inability to have an erection sufficient to achieve penetration.

estradiol Hormone thought to be responsible for masculinization of the brain; a benzene ring (⬡) is added to each molecule of testosterone by an enzyme in the brain, converting testosterone to estradiol.

estrogen The female sex hormone produced by the Graafian follicle and corpus luteum.

estrus cycle A cycle of changes in the level of female sex hormones found in nonhuman mammals.

ethology The study of the behavior of animals in their natural environments.

evolution The process by which succeeding generations of animals change in both physical appearance and behavior.

excitatory postsynaptic potential (EPSP) The depolarization produced by neurotransmitter molecules acting on the receptor sites on the postsynaptic membrane.

experimental allergic encephalomyelitis A neurological disorder with symptoms resembling multiple sclerosis that is produced when myelin proteins are injected into the bloodstream of laboratory animals.

extension Movement of a limb away from the body.

extensor muscle Muscle that produces movement of a limb away from the body.

extrafusal muscle fiber Muscle fiber that is controlled by an alpha motor neuron.

false transmitter A drug that prevents the neurotransmitter from binding to the receptor sites by attaching to the receptor sites on the postsynaptic membrane.

fast pain (prickling pain) Type of pain carried over myelinated Type A fibers that quickly reach the spinal cord.

fast-twitch muscle Muscle fiber that contracts rapidly, but tires quickly.

fear-induced aggression An aggressive behavior that is a defensive reaction exhibited only when an animal is threatened and perceives escape to be impossible; involves intense autonomic arousal and defensive threat display; if the threat is unsuccessful, a vicious attack ensues.

fenfluramine A serotonergic agonist that has a strong anorexic effect.

fen-phen A drug that is composed of fenfluramine and phentermine.

fertilization The fusion of the egg and the sperm.

fetal alcohol syndrome A disorder produced by exposure to alcohol during prenatal development; characterized by low birth weight and diminished height, distinctive facial features, mental retardation, and behavioral problems (hyperactivity and irritability).

fetus The developmental stage beginning at 8 weeks and continuing for the remainder of the pregnancy.

filopodia Spinelike extensions from the growth cone that pull the axon to the target cell.

flavor aversion The aversion to a flavor in food or drink that develops as a result of conditioning.

flexion Movement of a limb toward the body.

flexor muscle Muscle that produces movement of a limb toward the body.

fluent aphasia A communicative disorder characterized by an inability to understand the language of others.

fodrin A protein that makes up the coating around the dendrites.

follicle-stimulating hormone (FSH) A hormone secreted by the anterior pituitary that causes one or several ovarian follicles to grow into a mature Graafian follicle, the ovum to mature, and the Graafian follicle to secrete estrogen.

forebrain The division of the brain containing the basal ganglia, the cerebral cortex, the hypothalamus, the limbic system, and the thalamus.

fovea The central region of the retina where a light stimulus is focused.

fragile X syndrome A disorder caused by a fragile gene at one site on the large arm of the X chromosome that can cause the X chromosome to break; individuals with this disorder have an abnormal facial appearance and mental retardation.

free-nerve endings Skin receptors located just below the skin in both hairy and hairless skin that detect temperature and pain stimuli.

free-running rhythm A 25-hour sleep-wake cycle that occurs in the absence of external time cues.

frequency theory of pitch The view that the entire basilar membrane vibrates at the frequency of a given sound.

frontal lobe The lobe in the anterior-most part of the cerebral cortex that is responsible for higher mental processes and the control of movement.

functional MRI (fMRI) The fMRI utilizes high-powered, rapidly oscillating magnetic fields and powerful computation to measure cerebral blood flow in the brain and obtain an image of the neural activity in a specific area of the brain.

gamma-aminobutyric acid (GABA) A neurotransmitter that is synthesized from glutamic acid when the enzyme glutamic acid decarboxylase removes a carboxyl group.

gamma motor neuron A neuron that synapses with the intrafusal muscle fibers to produce continuous muscle tension.

ganglia Nerve cells that are grouped together and that show specialization of function.

ganglion cells Neurons that form the outermost layer of the retina.

gap junction The narrow space between the dendrite of one neuron and the dendrite of another neuron.

gate-control theory of pain The view that sensory input from pain receptors will produce the perception of pain only if the message first passes through a "gate" located in the spinal cord and lower brainstem structures.

gene The structure that provides the blueprint for the development and function of the physical and psychological characteristics of a species.

general adaptation syndrome (GAS) A pattern of physiological responses to a stressor; all stressors, regardless of whether they are physiological or psychological, produce the general adaptation syndrome.

genetics Study of heredity or inheritance.

glial cell A type of nervous system cell that provides a support function.

global aphasia A communicative disorder characterized by severe depression of all language functioning and due to damage to both anterior (including Broca's area) and posterior (including Wernicke's area) language areas.

globus pallidus An area shaped like a globe with very pale markings that is part of the basal ganglia.

glucagon A hormone secreted by the pancreas that increases blood glucose levels.

glucoprivation A condition in which glucose is either not present or unavailable for use.

glucoreceptors Specialized receptors that monitor glucose levels.

glucose A sugar (dextrose) used in energy metabolism.

Golgi tendon organs Receptors located among the fibers of tendons that measure the total amount of force exerted by the muscle on the bone to which the tendon is attached.

gray matter The cell bodies of neurons.

growth cone The swollen end of the developing neuron from which an axon emerges.

guidepost cells Cells that direct the growth of the axon toward the target cell.

habituation A decrease in the innate responsiveness to a specific stimulus as a result of repeated experience.

hair cells The auditory, vestibular, gustatory, and olfactory receptors.

hallucinations Sensory experiences that occur in the absence of environmental stimuli.

hardiness An ability to cope effectively with stressors due to a high level of commitment, a perception that change is a challenge rather than a burden or threat, and a sense of control over events.

heat A period of intense sexual arousal found when estrogen levels peak in estrus animals.

hemispheric lateralization The differentiation of functions in the right and left hemispheres.

heroin (diacetylmorphine) A powerful semisynthetic narcotic that is made by adding acetic anhydride to morphine.

heterozygous A term describing a gene pair in which the two members of the gene pair are different.

higher-order hypercomplex cells Neurons in the primary visual cortex that respond to stimuli of specific sizes and shapes.

hindbrain The division of the brain just above the spinal cord that contains the medulla oblongata, the pons, the cerebellum, and the raphe system.

hippocampus Structure in the limbic system that controls memory storage and retrieval.

homozygous A term describing a gene pair in which the members of the gene pair are alike.

horizontal cell Type of retinal neuron that receives neural messages from the photoreceptors and synapses with and has an inhibitory influence on the bipolar cells.

horizontal plane A view of a structure from above.

hormones Chemicals produced by the endrocrine glands that are circulated widely throughout the body via the bloodstream.

hue Wavelength of light stimulus measured in nanometers (nm or billionth of a meter).

Huntington's disease A neurological disorder caused by a defect in a gene on the short arm of chromosome 4 that destroys neurons in the cerebral cortex and basal ganglia and is characterized by a slow, progressive deterioration of motor control, cognition, and emotion.

hydrocephalus A blockage of the flow of cerebrospinal fluid.

hypercomplex cells Neurons in the primary visual cortex that respond to visual stimuli of a particular orientation and a specific length in a particular location within the receptive field.

hypercortisolism An abnormally high secretion of cortisol from the adrenal cortex.

hyperphagia The excessive intake of food.

hyperpolarization The increase in the charge across the cell membrane.

hypersomnia A sleep disorder characterized by too much sleep.

hypofrontality The view that impaired functioning of the prefrontal lobes causes the negative symptoms of schizophrenia.

hypomania A milder form of mania in which occupational or social functioning is not impaired.

hypophyseal portal system The arterial capillary link from the hypothalamus to the anterior pituitary gland.

hypothalamus Structure in the forebrain that detects need states and controls pituitary hormone production and release.

hypovolemic thirst A condition of thirst that occurs when extracellular fluid is lost.

Ia fibers Axons from the annulospiral endings that enter the dorsal root of the spinal cord and synapse with alpha motor neurons.

Ib fibers Axons of the Golgi tendon organs that extend to the spinal cord, where they synapse with small interneurons that inhibit alpha motor neurons.

incus (anvil) The bone of the middle ear attached to the malleus and stapes.

induction A process whereby neurons rely on the influence of other cells to determine their final form.

inferior Below a structure.

inferior colliculus Area of the tectum of the midbrain that receives neural messages from both the cochlear nuclei and superior olivary nucleus; responsible, with the superior colliculus, for coordination of the visual and auditory senses.

ingestional neophobia A reluctance to consume novel foods.

inhibitory postsynaptic potential (IPSP) The hyperpolarization produced by neurotransmitter molecules acting on the receptor sites on the postsynaptic membrane.

insomnia A sleep disorder characterized by a long-term inability to obtain adequate sleep; symptoms include taking a long time to fall asleep, frequent waking during the night, and/or awakening several hours before the normal rising time.

insulin A hormone secreted by the pancreas that lowers blood glucose levels.

interference An inability to recall a specific memory because of the presence of other memories.

intermediate layer The layer of cells that forms between the ventricular and marginal layers of the developing nervous system.

intermediate-twitch muscle Muscle fiber that contracts at a rate somewhere between that of fast-twitch and slow-twitch muscles.

interneuron A neuron that connects a sensory and a motor neuron or communicates with other neurons.

intrafusal muscle fiber Muscle fiber within muscle spindle surrounded by annulospiral endings.

invertebrate An animal without a backbone.

ionotrophic receptor A receptor whose ion channels are changed directly by the action of the neurotransmitter.

iris Bands of muscles covered by the colored portion of the eye.

irritable aggression An aggressive response to annoying situations (either an inability to achieve a goal or exposure to physically or psychologically painful events).

James-Lange theory of emotion The view that the interpretation of the physiological changes that occur in response to a specific event determines how we feel.

jargon Lengthy, fluent speech that makes little or no sense.

jet lag The fatigue and sleep disturbance caused by traveling across several time zones.

K complex A single large negative wave (upward spike) followed by a single large positive wave (downward spike) seen during Stage 2 sleep.

Klüver-Bucy syndrome A disorder produced by damage to the temporal lobes that is characterized by socially inappropriate sexual activity, compulsive orality, decreased ability to recognize people, and memory deficits.

Korsakoff's syndrome A disorder, usually seen in chronic alcoholics, caused by a thiamine deficiency that results from the inadequate intake of nonalcoholic nutrients and is characterized by profound anterograde amnesia and impaired insight.

labeled-line coding Type of coding in which information about the stimulus is determined by the nerve carrying that message.

lamellae The thin membranes contained in the outer segment of a photoreceptor.

language A system of words, word meanings, and rules for combining words into phrases and sentences.

language acquisition device (LAD) An innate mechanism that allows children to readily grasp the syntax relevant to their native language with minimal experience.

lark Individual who is active and alert in the morning and becomes drowsy and inattentive in the evening.

latent content According to the psychoanalytic theory, the symbolic content of a dream.

lateral Away from the midline.

lateral cervical nucleus (LCN) Neurons in the medulla that receive neural messages about touch via the lemniscal tract.

lateral corticospinal tract Group of neurons originating in the primary motor cortex whose axons cross over to synapse with those alpha motor neurons in the spinal cord that control movement of the fingers, hands, arms, lower legs, and feet.

lateral geniculate nucleus of the thalamus The neurons of the thalamus that receive neural impulses via synapses from the axons of the ganglion cells of the retina.

lateral hypothalamus (LH) An area in the hypothalamus involved in hunger and the initiation of eating.

lateral inhibition The enhancement of the contrast between a light stimulus and its surround by the inhibition of the bipolar cells adjacent to the active photoreceptors, which allows the detection of the edges of a light stimulus.

lateral interpositus of the cerebellum The area of the brain where the conditioning of the eyeblink response takes place.

lateralization of function The differentiation of the functions of the two hemispheres of the brain.

lateral reticulospinal tract Motor pathway that originates in the medullary reticular formation and synapses with those alpha motor neurons of the spinal cord that activate the flexor muscles of the legs.

lateral sulcus The deep groove that separates the temporal from the frontal and parietal lobes of the cerebral cortex.

learned helplessness A pattern of behavior that includes early morning wakefulness, decreased feeding, decreased sexual drive, decreased grooming, and a lack of voluntary behavior in a variety of situations produced by exposure to a series of uncontrollable events.

learning A change in behavior that occurs as a result of experiences.

lens A series of transparent, onion-like layers of tissue that change shape to focus images.

levodopa (l-dopa) Precursor of dopamine that is converted by dopaminergic neurons into dopamine.

LH-lesion syndrome The pattern of behavior, aphagia and adipsia, that follows damage to the lateral hypothalamus.

light therapy The use of intense broad-spectrum light to reduce melatonin release and produce increased activity and enhanced mood in individuals with seasonal affective disorder.

limb apraxia A difficulty purposefully moving a limb caused by damage to the left parietal lobe or the corpus callosum.

limbic system The part of the forebrain, consisting of a group of structures that forms a border around midbrain structures, that controls emotional expression and the storage and retrieval of memories.

lipid (or fatty acids) Fat that can be used in energy metabolism.

lipoprivation The unavailability of fatty acids as a source of energy.

locus coeruleus The group of neurons within the reticular formation that plays a central role in determining the levels of cortical activity and behavioral alertness.

longitudinal fissure The deep groove that separates the right and left hemispheres.

long-term potentiation (LTP) An increased neural responsivity, which takes the form of an increase in the amplitude and duration of excitatory postsynaptic potentials (EPSPs), that follows a brief, intense series of electrical impulses to neural tissue.

long-term store The site of permanent memory storage.

lordosis A female-receptive posture in which the hindquarters are raised, which facilitates penile intromission by the male.

loudness Perception of the amplitude of a sound wave, measured in decibels (db).

lucid dream A dream in which the person is conscious that he or she is dreaming.

luteinizing hormone (LH) A hormone secreted by the anterior pituitary that causes ovulation and the ruptured follicle to become the corpus luteum. In males, LH stimulates testosterone secretion.

lysergic acid diethylamide (LSD) A powerful synthetic hallucinogenic drug that acts by stimulating serotonergic receptors.

magnetic resonance imaging (MRI) A technique that produces a static image of the brain by first passing a strong magnetic field through the brain, followed by a radio wave, and measuring the radiation emitted from hydrogen molecules.

magnocellular layers The bottom two layers of the primary visual cortex.

major depression A type of depressive disorder that is characterized by an intense, debilitating depressed mood, of at least 2 weeks' duration.

malleus (hammer) The bone of the middle ear that is attached to the tympanic membrane and the incus.

mania An intense episode of excitement and enthusiasm.

manifest content According to the psychoanalytic theory, the actual events that happen during a dream.

marginal layer The outermost layer of the developing nervous system to which daughter cells migrate.

marijuana A psychedelic drug obtained from a mixture of crushed leaves, flowers, stems, and seeds of the hemp plant (cannabis sativa) that acts by stimulating THC receptors.

mass action The idea that a specific function is shared by all the neurons of a particular region of the brain.

medial Toward the midline.

medial forebrain bundle (MFB) A group of nerve fibers located in the limbic system considered part of the brain's reinforcement system.

medial geniculate nucleus A group of neurons in the thalamus that receives neural impulses from the inferior colliculus.

medial lemniscus A ribbon-like band of fibers in the dorsal column-medial lemniscal system that convey neural messages from the lateral cervical nucleus and the dorsal column nuclei to the ventrobasal complex.

medial preoptic area A group of neurons in the anterior hypothalamus that contain testosterone-sensitive receptors.

medial reticulospinal tract Motor pathway that originates in the pontine reticular formation and synapses with those spinal alpha motor neurons that activate the extensor muscles of the legs.

medial temporal lobe A brain area containing the hippocampus and surrounding cortical areas (the perirhinal, entorhinal, and parahippocampal cortices) that are involved in the storage of experiences.

mediodorsal thalamus A brain structure that plays a key role in the storage of experiences.

medulla oblongata Hindbrain structure located just rostral to the spinal cord that controls functions such as respiration and heart rate that are essential to life.

meiosis The formation of gametes.

Meissner's corpuscles Skin receptors located in the elevations (papillae) of the dermis found only in hairy skin cells of the epidermis that detects low-frequency vibrations.

melatonin Hormone secreted from the pineal gland that has a sedative effect; high levels of melatonin reduce activity and produce fatigue.

memory The capacity to retain and retrieve past experiences.

memory attribute A salient aspect of an event, the presence of which can lead to retrieval of the past event.

meninges The three layers of tissue between the skull and the brain and the vertebral column and the spinal cord.

menstrual cycle A cycle of changes in the level of female sex hormones found in humans and some other primates.

menstruation The expelling of the uterine lining.

Merkel's disks Skin receptors located in the base of epidermis near the sweat ducts that are sensitive to pressure.

mescaline The hallucinogenic ingredient found in peyote that acts by stimulating serotonergic receptors.

mesencephalon The embryonic division that becomes the midbrain.

mesoderm The middle layer of the embryo, which will form the connective tissue, muscle, and blood and blood vessels.

mesotelencephalic reinforcement system The brain reinforcement system that contains the tegmentostriatal pathway and the nigrostriatal pathway.

metabotrophic receptor A receptor whose ion channels are changed by a second messenger.

metencephalon The embryonic division of the hindbrain that becomes the pons and the cerebellum.

methadone A narcotic drug that binds to opiate receptor sites, alleviates the craving for heroin, and prevents the withdrawal symptoms that otherwise would result from not taking heroin.

microdialysis A technique for identifying the neurotransmitter in a specific area of the nervous system by measuring the chemical constituents of blood and other body fluids.

microglia A type of glial cell that removes dead neurons.

microsleep A very brief period of sleep in which the subject is awake but EEG patterns resemble Stage 1 sleep.

midbrain A division of the central nervous system that contains the tectum and the tegmentum.

monoamine A class of neurotransmitters that contain an amine group (NH_2); includes norepinephrine, dopamine, and serotonin.

monoamine oxidase An enzyme that acts to deactivate norepinephrine, dopamine, and serotonin.

monoamine oxidase (MAO) inhibitors A class of drugs that increase levels of norepinephrine, dopamine, and serotonin by preventing enzymatic deactivation.

monocular depth cues Depth cues provided by each eye individually including relative size, overlap, relative texture, relative height, linear perspective, relative brightness, and relative motion.

monosynaptic stretch reflex A reflex in which only one synapse exists between the sensory receptor and motor neuron.

morpheme The smallest meaningful unit of language.

morphine An extremely potent natural narcotic that is the main alkaloid compound found in opium.

mossy fiber pathway A hippocampal pathway that begins in the granule cells in the dentate gyrus and connects with the pyramidal cells in the CA_3 field of the hippocampus.

mossy fibers Neurons that have an inhibitory influence on the cerebellum, allowing it to reset quickly and to respond to new incoming information.

motion sickness Feelings of dizziness and nausea that occur when the body is moved passively without motor input.

motor end plate The flattened area of the extrafusal muscle fiber where the motor neuron and muscle fiber synapse.

motor neuron Specialized neuron that carries messages from the central nervous system to muscles.

motor unit The alpha motor neuron and all the muscle fibers that it controls.

movement A change in place or position.

Müllerian-inhibiting substance A hormone released by the testes that prevents the development of the female reproductive system.

Müllerian system The female reproductive system consisting of the ovary, uterus and upper part of vagina and fallopian tubes.

multiple sclerosis A progressive neurological disorder caused by the degeneration of the myelin covering the axons of the nervous system by the immune system.

muscle fiber Long and slender muscle cell that produces movement.

muscle spindle A structure embedded within the extrafusal muscle fiber that enables the CNS to contract a muscle to counteract the stretching of the muscle fiber containing the muscle spindle.

muscle tone The resting tension of skeletal muscle caused by activity of gamma motor neurons.

myasthenia gravis A neuromuscular disorder in which the body produces antibodies that destroy the cholinergic receptors at the neuromuscular junctions; the major symptom is muscular fatigue that occurs after muscles have been exercised.

myelencephalon The embryonic division of the hindbrain that becomes the medulla.

myelin A fatlike substance that surrounds and insulates certain neurons.

myofibril Cylindrical structure within a muscle fiber.

myofilament The two components of myofibrils, myosin and actin.

myosin The thick protein myofilament found in muscle fiber.

myotonia Contraction of certain muscles of the genital organs during orgasm.

naltrexone An opiate antagonist that binds to opiate receptor sites and blocks the action of heroin and other opiates.

narcolepsy A sleep disorder characterized by a sudden, uncontrollable sleep attack, usually initiated by monotonous activity; can also include cataplexy, sleep paralysis, and hallucinations.

narcotics Opiate drugs that produce analgesia, sedation, and a sense of well-being.

negative afterimage The lingering sensation of a color that is experienced after staring at its complementary color for some time.

negative feedback loop The release of a substance acts to inhibit its subsequent release.

negative symptoms of schizophrenia Symptoms that are characterized by an absence of normal behaviors and include disorders of affect and movement.

neologism Making up a meaningless word.

neostriatum Phylogenetically newer part of basal ganglia that contains the caudate nucleus and putamen, which receive sensory input from the thalamus, the substantia nigra, and the primary motor cortex, and sends messages to the paleostriatum.

nerve A bundle of neurons.

neural crest A specialized group of cells that migrate away from the neural tube to form several types of tissue, including the sensory and autonomic neurons of the peripheral nervous system.

neural folds The lateral edges of the neural plate.

neural groove The space formed when the neural folds push up.

neural impulse The transmission of a message by means of an axon projecting from each neural cell body.

neural plate The thickened ectoderm layer of an embryo.

neural tube The closed space that is formed when the neural folds meet and close the neural groove.

neurofibrillary tangles Unusual triangular and looped fibers in the cytoplasm of nerve cells.

neurogenesis The formation of new neurons.

neuromodulators A class of chemicals, including the endorphins, that control the amount of neurotransmitter released at the presynaptic membrane.

neuromuscular junction The point of connection between an alpha motor neuron and its extrafusal muscle fiber.

neuron An individual nerve cell, with the main components being the dendrites, soma or cell body, axon, and presynaptic terminal.

neuropeptide Y (NPY) A peptide neurotransmitter in the lateral hypothalamus involved in hunger and eating behavior.

neuropsychology The study of the behavioral effects of brain damage in humans.

neuroscience Study of the nervous system.

neurotransmitter Chemicals stored in the synaptic vesicles that are released into the synaptic cleft and transmit messages to other neurons.

neurotransmitter reuptake Return of the neurotransmitter to the vesicles in the presynaptic membrane.

neurotrophins The chemicals released by target cells that attract the filopodia of a developing neuron.

nicotine A stimulant found in the leaves of the tobacco plant that produces increased alertness and decreased fatigue by activating cholinergic receptors and by increasing the release of dopamine.

night terrors (or *pavor nocturnus*) An abrupt awakening from SWS accompanied by intense autonomic nervous system arousal and feelings of panic.

nigrostriatal pathway A group of nerve fibers, beginning in the substantia nigra and projecting to the neostriatum, that play a role in memory consolidation and eating behavior.

NMDA receptor A receptor site that is sensitive to the neurotransmitter glutamate.

nocturnal animals Animals that sleep during the day and are awake at night.

nocturnal enuresis (or bedwetting) A SWS disorder characterized by an inability to control the bladder during sleep.

node of Ranvier The unmyelinated space between the myelinated segments (collectively called the myelin sheath) of an axon.

nonbarbiturate sedative-hypnotic drugs A class of sedative-hypnotic drugs that are not derived from barbituate acid, but have the same mode of action as barbiturates.

nonfluent aphasia A communicative disorder characterized by a great difficulty producing fluent, well-articulated, and self-initiated speech.

nonvisual photoreceptor Type of photoreceptor that detects the daily dawn-dusk cycle.

noradrenergic Synaptic transmission involving norepinephrine as the neurotransmitter.

norepinephrine (NE) A neurotransmitter, sometimes called noradrenalin, that is produced from the amino acid tyrosine.

nucleotide rearrangement theory The view that a permanent change in DNA and RNA occurs as a result of learning.

nucleus The part of a cell containing DNA, the genetic blueprint; or a group of neural cell bodies in the central nervous system.

nucleus accumbens (NA) Structure in the tegmentostriatal reinforcement system containing dopamine and opiate receptors; the NA produces pleasurable feelings.

nucleus medianus A group of neurons that lie near the anterior and ventral part of the third ventricle that mediate both osmotic and hypovolemic thirst.

nucleus of the solitary tract (NST) A group of neurons in the medulla that receive information from the taste receptors and influence the amount of food consumed, especially the intake of foods high in carbohydrates.

nystagmus Rapid side-to-side movements of the eyes caused by inconsistent information from the visual and vestibular systems.

occipital lobe The lobe located in the posterior most part of the cerebral cortex responsible for the analysis of visual stimuli.

odors Airborne molecules of volatile substances that are detected by olfactory receptors.

off ganglion cell Type of ganglion neuron that is inhibited by amacrine cells in the presence of light and excited by the termination of light stimulus due to removal of inhibition from amacrine cells.

olfactory bulbs Paired structures at the base of the brain that contain mitral cells, which receive information about odor from the olfactory receptors.

olfactory epithelium The mucous membrane located in the top rear of the nasal passage that is lined by olfactory receptors.

olfactory tract Fiber bundle formed by axons of the mitral cells of the olfactory bulb, which project to the primary olfactory cortex.

oligodendrocyte The type of glial cell that myelinates certain neurons in the central nervous system.

on ganglion cell Type of ganglion neuron that is excited by bipolar cells in response to a light stimulus.

on-off ganglion cell Type of ganglion neuron that is excited by a bipolar cell when a light stimulus is present and released from inhibition by an amacrine cell when the light stimulus is removed.

operant conditioning A type of learning in which a response either produces reinforcement or avoids punishment.

opiates Drugs, such as heroin and morphine, that produce decreased perception of pain and a strong sense of emotional well-being.

opium A natural opiate that comes directly from the opium poppy.

opponent-process theory of color vision The view that there are six stimuli that operate in opposing pairs: blue-yellow, green-red, and white-black. A different receptor cell exists for each member of an opponent pair, so there are six types of color receptors.

opsin The protein component of photopigment.

optic chiasm The place where the two optic nerves meet.

optic disk The point at the back of the eye where the axons from the ganglion cells come together; also called the blind spot, because an object focused at this point cannot be seen.

optic nerves The two nerves formed by the axons of ganglion after leaving the optic disk.

optic tracts The fiber tracts, or second cranial nerves, that are formed by the axons of the ganglion cells leaving the optic chiasm.

organ of Corti The structure within the cochlea that contains the basilar membrane, the hair cells, and the tectorial membrane.

organum vasculosum lamina terminalis (OVLT) A structure that lies outside the blood-brain barrier and monitors changes in the concentration of salt in the bloodstream and loss of extracellular fluid.

orgasm The climax of the sexual response.

orgasmic dysfunction The inability to experience an orgasm or the ability to experience an orgasm only under certain conditions.

osmoreceptors Specialized receptors that monitor osmotic press in the intracellular fluid.

osmotic thirst A condition of thirst due to increased osmotic pressure in the intracellular fluid.

otoliths Calcium carbonate crystals located atop a gelatinous mass in the vestibular sacs.

oval window The membrane that divides the middle and inner parts of the ear.

ovariectomy The surgical removal of the ovaries.

owl Individual who is drowsy and inattentive in the morning, and active and alert in the evening.

Pacinian corpuscles The largest of the skin receptors, found in dermis layer of both hairy and hairless skin, that detect high-frequency vibrations.

paleostriatum Phylogenetically older part of basal ganglia that contains the globus pallidus, which receives information from the neostriatum and sends messages to the thalamus and then on to the primary motor cortex and brainstem structures controlling movement.

pallidotomy Psychosurgery treatment for Parkinson's disease that lesions the posterior and ventral globus pallidus and reduces tremors, rigidity, and bradykinesia.

papillae Small, visible bumps on the tongue that contain taste buds.

paragrammatic The use of inappropriate morphemes in speech.

paraphasia An error in speaking; a phonemic paraphasia is the substitution of a similar sounding word for the verbal stimulus.

parasympathetic nervous system A division of the autonomic nervous system that is activated by conditions of recovery or termination of stressors.

paraventricular nucleus (PVN) An area of the hypothalamus that is involved in satiety and the suppression of eating.

parietal lobe The lobe in the cerebral cortex located between the central sulcus and the occipital lobe responsible for the analysis of somatosensory stimuli.

Parkinson's disease A degenerative neurological disorder characterized by difficulty integrating voluntary movement, rigidity of the limbs caused by increased muscle tone, and muscle tremors, due to degeneration of those dopamine-producing cells of the substantia nigra that synapse with the basal ganglia.

parvocellular layers The top four layers of the primary visual cortex.

patellar tendon reflex A type of reflex in which a tap on the tendon of the knee stretches the muscles that extend the leg, causing the leg to kick outward.

pattern direction-selective neurons Neurons located in the middle-temporal (MT) cortex that combine the information coming from the primary visual cortex to recognize the exact direction in which an object is moving.

Pavlovian conditioning A type of learning in which a novel stimulus becomes able to elicit an instinctive response as the result of having been paired with a stimulus that was innately able to elicit the same instinctive response.

perforant fiber pathway A hippocampal pathway that begins in the entorhinal cortex and connects to the granule cells in the dentate gyrus.

periaqueductal gray (PAG) An area of the midbrain that is the origin of a descending fiber tract that synapses with inhibitory interneurons in the lower brainstem and spinal cord to block messages about pain.

peripheral nervous system (PNS) The division of the nervous system that detects environmental information, transmits that information to the central nervous system, and executes decisions by the central nervous system.

peyote A psychedelic drug obtained from the peyote cactus plant.

PGO waves Brief bursts of neural activity that begin in the pons, are transmitted to the lateral geniculate nuclei, and continue on to the occipital lobe; occur just prior to the onset of REM sleep and continue throughout the REM sleep period.

phase-advance shift A schedule that requires a worker to start on the late shift and then rotate to an earlier shift, which acts to shorten the day.

phase-delay shift A schedule in which a worker is rotated to a later shift each week, which acts to lengthen the day.

phencyclidine (PCP) A powerful synthetic hallucinogenic drug sometimes known as angel dust that, when used for long periods of time, can lead to permanent neurological damage.

phenothiazine A class of antipsychotic drugs that includes chlorpromazine (Thorazine).

phentermine A dopaminergic agonist that has a strong anorexic effect.

phenylketonuria (PKU) A genetic disorder involving the absence of an enzyme needed to breakdown phenylalanine; the resulting buildup of phenylalanine can lead to mental retardation.

pheromone A hormone that is released into the physical environment rather than the bloodstream that influences the behavior of another animal.

phoneme The simplest functional speech sound.

phonology The study of the sound system that prescribes how phonemes can be combined into morphemes.

photopigment The chemical molecules embedded in the lamellae that are responsible for the detection of light.

photoreceptors The receptors located at the rear of the eye that transduce light into a neural impulse.

phrase A group of two or more related words that express a single thought.

phrenology The view that mental functioning is related to the size and the integrity of specific areas of the brain.

physical dependence A state of physical need for a drug.

physiological psychology The study of the relationship between the nervous system and behavior by surgically, electrically, or chemically influencing specific nervous system structures.

pia mater The thin membrane that adheres closely to the surface of the brain and is the innermost layer of the meninges.

pinna The outer, visible portion of the ear.

pitch Perception of the frequency of a sound wave, measured in hertz (Hz).

pituitary gland A gland located just ventral to the hypothalamus that is responsible for secretion of adrenocorticotrophic-stimulating hormone (ACTH), follicle-stimulating hormone (FSH), growth hormone (GH), luteinizing hormone (LH), protectin (PRC), thyroid-stimulating hormone (TSH), oxytocin, and antidiuretic hormone and is divided into two segments: the anterior pituitary gland and the posterior pituitary gland.

place theory of pitch The view that different sounds activate the nerve fibers at different locations on the basilar membrane.

polysynaptic reflexes A reflex with one or more interneurons between the sensory and motor neurons.

pons Hindbrain structure located superior to the medulla that relays sensory information to the cerebellum and thalamus.

positive feedback loop The release of a substance that acts to promote its further release.

positive symptoms of schizophrenia Symptoms that are characterized by behaviors in excess of normal behaviors, and include disorders of thought and perception.

positron emission topography (PET) Measurement of metabolic activity of a specific structure in the nervous system in order to determine neural functioning.

posterior Toward the rear end.

posterior nuclei Group of neurons in the thalamus that receive information about temperature and pain via the anterolateral system.

posterior parietal cortex Area in the posterior part of the parietal cortex that integrates input from the visual, auditory, and somatosensory systems and relays it to the primary motor cortex.

posterior pituitary gland The part of the pituitary gland, considered an extension of the hypothalamus, that produces and releases oxytocin and antidiuretic hormone; also called the neurohypophysis.

postsynaptic membrane The outer surface of a target cell that receives messages from the presynaptic membrane.

prandial drinking Drinking while eating.

precentral gyrus Area in the posterior part of the frontal lobe that contains the primary motor cortex; the control center for movement.

prefrontal cortex Area in the anterior part of the frontal lobe that controls complex intellectual functions.

prefrontal lobotomy Surgical procedure that severs the connections of the prefrontal cortex to the rest of the brain.

preloading A procedure in which food is placed in the stomach prior to food being available.

premature ejaculation The inability 50% of the time to delay ejaculation until his partner achieves orgasm.

premenstrual syndrome Irritability in human females during the premenstrual period that has been attributed to a drop in progesterone level.

premotor area Area anterior to the primary motor cortex that includes Broca's area; damage results in agrammatic and awkward speech.

premotor cortex An area in the frontal lobe that receives input mostly from the visual cortex and is involved in the planning and sequencing of voluntary movements.

presynaptic facilitation The enhanced release of neurotransmitters from the presynaptic membrane caused by the action of another neuron.

presynaptic inhibition The prevention of the release of a normal amount of neurotransmitter from the presynaptic membrane, despite the occurrence of an action potential, caused by the action of another neuron.

presynaptic membrane The outer surface of the presynaptic terminal, which is the site of release of neurotransmitter into the synaptic cleft.

presynaptic terminal A swelling at the end of the axon.

primary auditory cortex The area of the temporal lobe on the inside of the lateral (Sylvian) fissure that detects characteristics of sounds (frequency, amplitude, complexity) from the neural impulses originating from the auditory receptors.

primary gustatory cortex An area located just ventral and rostral to the area representing the tongue in the somatosensory cortex that recognizes the qualities of a taste stimulus.

primary motor cortex Area in the precentral gyrus of the frontal lobe that initiates voluntary movements.

primary olfactory cortex Area in the pyriform cortex of the limbic system that detects the emotional character of an odor.

primary somatosensory cortex Area in the anterior part of the parietal lobe that detects characteristics of tactile stimulation (touch, temperature, pain, and proprioception).

primary visual cortex (Area V1) Area in the occipital lobe of the cerebral cortex that receives neural impulses via synapses with lateral geniculate nucleus neurons; responsible for detection of features contained in light stimuli.

procedural memory Skill memory or the memory of a highly practiced behavior.

prodromal phase of schizophrenia The first phase in which the person becomes socially withdrawn.

progesterone The female sex hormone manufactured by the corpus luteum.

proprioceptive system Somatosense that monitors body position and movement, acts to maintain body position, and insures the accuracy of intended movements.

prosencephalon The embryonic division that becomes the forebrain.

prosopagnosia An impaired ability to recognize faces following damage to the inferior prestriate area and adjacent portions of the inferotemporal cortex.

psychedelics (hallucinogens) A class of drugs that produce profound alterations in a person's state of consciousness.

psychoactive drug A drug that changes the way a person thinks, feels, perceives, or acts.

psychological dependence The intense craving for a drug.

psychopharmacology The study of the effects of psychoactive drugs on behavior.

psychophysiology The study of the relationship between behavior and physiology through the analysis of the physiological responses of human subjects engaged in various activities.

punishment An event that decreases the occurrence of the inappropriate behavior.

pupil Opening in the iris through which light passes.

pure alexia (alexia without agraphia) A communicative disorder characterized by an inability to read, but not to write, that is caused by severing the connection between the angular gyrus from the primary visual cortex.

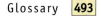

Purkinje cells Neurons in the cerebellum that remain active until a movement is completed.

pursuit movement The smooth eye movements that occur when the eyes follow a moving object.

putamen An oval-shaped structure that is part of the basal ganglia.

pyramidal cells Large pyramid-shaped neurons in the primary motor cortex.

radial glial cells The glial cells that guide the migration of daughter cells during the embryonic development of the nervous system.

raphé nuclei A thin strip of neurons that runs along the midline in the caudal portion of the reticular formation; maintains SWS.

rapid eye movement (REM) sleep The phase of sleep in which the EEG pattern resembles the awake state, the eyes move rapidly behind their closed lids, and muscle tone is absent.

rate law The principle stating that the greater the stimulus intensity, the faster rate of neural firing (up to the maximum rate possible for that neuron).

receptive field The part of the visual field to which a particular neuron is sensitive.

recessive gene A gene that can determine the presence of a specific physical or behavioral characteristic only when that gene is present in both members of a gene pair.

red nucleus Structure in the tegmentum that controls basic body and limb movements.

reflex A simple, automatic response to a sensory stimulus.

regeneration The regrowth of a neuron and the reestablishment of its connections to other neurons.

rehabilitation The process of developing compensatory behaviors that substitute for lost functions.

reinforcement An event that increases the frequency of behavior that preceded the event.

relative refractory period The time following the absolute refractory period during which the neuron can be stimulated only by an event of greater intensity than is normally required to activate the neuron.

REM without atonia A sleep disorder characterized by a failure to lose muscle tone during REM, which results in high levels of motor activity during REM sleep.

Renshaw cell An inhibitory interneuron excited by a collateral branch of an alpha motor neuron that causes an alpha motor neuron to stop firing, preventing excessive contraction of the muscle fiber.

repolarization The process of recovery of the resting membrane potential.

residual phase of schizophrenia The phase in which recovery of some functioning occurs.

resting membrane potential The difference in polarity between the inside and the outside of the cell membrane when the neuron is at rest.

retarded ejaculation The inability to ejaculate during sexual intercourse.

reticular activating system (RAS) A diffuse, interconnected network of neurons originating in the hindbrain and extending through the midbrain that produces cortical arousal and behavioral alertness.

reticular formation Network of neurons in the tegmentum that controls arousal and consciousness.

retina The interior lining at the back of the eye comprised of three layers of neurons.

retinal The lipid component of photopigment that is synthesized from Vitamin A.

retinohypothalamic tract Fiber tract that conveys information about the daily dawn-dusk cycle to the SCN.

retrograde amnesia The inability to recall events that preceded a traumatic event.

retrograde degeneration The progressive breakdown of the axon between the site of the break and the cell body.

retrograde messenger A chemical that is sent from the postsynaptic membrane to the presynaptic membrane to maintain neurotransmitter release.

reverberatory activity The continued reactivation of a neural circuit for a time following an experience.

rhodopsin The photopigment found in rods, which consists of rod opsin and retinal.

rhombencephalon The embryonic division that becomes the hindbrain.

ribonucleic acid (RNA) A large, single-stranded molecule that controls the manufacture of proteins, which in turn regulates cell functioning.

rod Type of photoreceptor concentrated at the periphery of the retina that is responsible for night vision.

rod opsin The form of opsin found in rods.

rostral Toward the head.

round window The membrane that, along with the oval window, maintains the movement of fluid of the inner ear through the cochlea as long as the stapes vibrates in response to sound waves.

rubrospinal tract Motor pathway that originates in the red nucleus and crosses over to synapse in the spinal cord with those alpha motor neurons that control movement of the hands (but not the fingers), as well as the lower arms, lower legs, and feet.

Ruffini's corpuscles Skin receptors located just below the skin that detect low-frequency vibrations.

saccadic movements The rapid jerky movements of the eye from one point to another as the physical environment is scanned.

saccule Sacs in the vestibule that contain vestibular receptors.

sagittal plane A view of a structure from the side.

saltatory conduction The propagation of an action potential from node to node along myelinated axons.

sarcomere Functional unit of the myofibril, consisting of an overlapping band of thick myosin myofilaments and thin actin myofilaments.

satiated A feeling of fullness.

saturation The purity of a light stimulus.

Schachter's cognitive approach The view that if we are unable to identify the cause of physiological arousal, the arousal will be attributed to the prevailing environmental conditions.

Schaffer collateral fiber pathway A hippocampal pathway that begins in the hippocampal pyramidal cells of field CA_3 and connects with the pyramidal cells of field CA_1 of the hippocampus.

schizophrenia A serious disabling psychiatric disorder that is characterized by a loss of contact with reality and disturbances in perception, emotion, cognition, and motor behavior.

Schwann cell The type of glial cell that myelinates certain neurons in the peripheral nervous system.

seasonal affective disorder An affective disorder characterized by elevated levels of melatonin, fatigue, and depression as a result of fewer hours of daylight during winter.

second messenger Chemical changes, produced inside the cell by a neurotransmitter, that lead to ion channel changes.

secondary auditory cortex The area of the temporal lobe surrounding the primary auditory cortex where the perception of pitch, loudness, and timbre occurs.

secondary motor cortex Area in the frontal lobe that plans and sequences voluntary movements and includes the supplementary motor area and the premotor cortex.

secondary somatosensory cortex An area of the cortex that is lateral and slightly posterior to the primary somatosensory cortex and is responsible for the perception of touch, temperature, pain, and proprioception.

secondary visual cortex The area that detects the shape, color, movement, and depth of a light stimulus.

sedative-hypnotic drugs A class of drugs that at low doses have a calming (sedative) influence; higher doses have a sleep-inducing hypnotic effect.

selective serotonin reuptake inhibitor (SSRI) A class of drugs that act by decreasing the reuptake of serotonin by the presynaptic membrane.

semantic memory The memory of knowledge concerning the use of language, and the rules, formulas, or algorithms for the development of concepts or solutions to problems.

semantics The meaning of language.

semicircular canals Three fluid-filled structures in the cochlea that detect rotation of the head.

senile plaques Granular deposits of amyloid beta protein and the remains of degenerated dendrites and axons of nerve fibers.

sense The ability of the nervous system to receive and react to environmental stimuli.

sensitization An increase in the innate reactivity to a stimulus following exposure to an intense event.

sensory neuron Specialized neuron that detects information from the outside world.

sensory register In the Atkinson-Shiffrin model, the initial storage site where a memory is held for a very brief time as an exact duplicate of the event.

sentence Two or more phrases that convey an assertion, question, command, wish, or exclamation.

serotonergic Synaptic transmission involves serotonin as the neurotransmitter.

serotonin (5-HT) A neurotransmitter that is synthesized from the amino acid tryptophan.

set-point theory The view that animals maintain upper and lower limits of their body weight.

sex-determining gene The gene on the short arm of the Y chromosome that controls the sex of an individual member of a species.

sex therapy A set of procedures aimed at establishing effective sexual functioning.

sexual dysfunction The failure to obtain sexual satisfaction.

short-term store In the Atkinson-Shiffrin model, a temporary facility where information is held prior to being stored in permanent memory.

simple cells Neurons in the primary visual cortex that respond to lines (edges) in a specific part of the visual field that have a specific orientation (line-tilt).

sine-wave gratings The alternating lighter and then darker intensities found in a light stimulus.

skeletal muscle Muscle that produces movement in the physical environment.

skull The outer bony covering that protects the brain.

sleep apnea A sleep disorder characterized by repeated interruptions of sleep caused by the cessation of breathing (apnea).

sleep paralysis A brief paralysis that occurs when someone with narcolepsy is about to go to sleep or has just awakened.

sleep spindle A 1- to 2-second burst of activity of 12 to 14 Hz that occurs during Stage 2 of sleep.

sleepwalking (or somnambulism) Movement during SWS, such as getting out of bed and walking.

slow pain (burning and aching pain) Type of pain propagated by unmyelinated Type C fibers that slowly reach the spinal cord.

slow-twitch muscle Muscle fiber that contracts slowly, but fatigues slowly.

slow-wave sleep (SWS) The phase of sleep in which theta and delta activity occurs.

smooth muscle Muscle that controls internal organs.

sodium-potassium pump A process that actively transports sodium ions out of the cell and potassium ions into the cell, expelling three Na^+ ions for every two K^+ ions that it brings back into the cell.

soma Cell body of the neuron.

somatic nervous system The division of the peripheral nervous system containing sensory receptors that detect environmental stimuli and motor nerves that activate skeletal muscles.

somatosense Skin sensations of touch, pain, temperature, and proprioception.

spatial summation The combined influence of many neurotransmitter released at different locations on the postsynaptic membrane at a particular moment in time.

spina bifida A neural tube defect that results when some part of the neural folds fail to close.

spinal cord The division of the central nervous system located within the vertebrate spinal column that receives sensory messages from and sends motor commands to the peripheral nervous system. Some sensory messages are sent to the brain and some motor commands originate in the brain.

spinal nerve A group of neurons that send messages to and from the brain through the spinal cord.

spinal reflex A reflex in which afferent sensory input enters the spinal cord and then directly innervates an efferent motor neuron.

spinocerebellar system Somatosensory pathways that begin in the spinal cord and project proprioceptive information to the cerebellum.

spinothalamic tract Somatosensory pathway that begins in the spinal cord and projects information about temperature and pain to the primary somatosensory cortex.

spiral ganglion cells Neurons that receive neural messages from auditory receptors.

split-brain preparation A surgical procedure that severs the cerebral commissures and the optic chiasm (only in animals), eliminating most communication between the two hemispheres.

stage of exhaustion The last stage of the GAS, in which a stressor that continues indefinitely depletes all physiological resources, resulting in a failure of all of the body's defense systems and eventually death.

stage of resistance The second phase of the GAS in which our physiological resources are mobilized to cope with a prolonged stressor.

stapes (stirrup) The bone of the middle ear attached to the incus and the oval window.

stereotaxic apparatus A surgical instrument that allows a neuroscientist to lesion a specific region of the brain.

stimulants A class of drugs that produce alertness by enhancing the functioning of the sympathetic nervous system and the reticular activating system.

stimulus-bound behavior The motivation of behavior by prevailing environmental conditions.

stress inoculation A procedure to alter the cognitive appraisal process by recognizing situations that are stressful, linking the behavioral responses to the situations, understanding that reactions to stressors are determined by the appraisal of the situation, and then learning new ways to appraise the situation.

stressor Any event that either strains or overwhelms our ability to adjust to our environment.

striated muscle Another name for skeletal muscle originating from its striped appearance caused by the overlapping bands of thick myosin myofilaments and thin actin myofilaments.

subarachnoid space Space between arachnoid mater and pia mater that is filled with cerebrospinal fluid.

subfornical organ (SFO) A structure that lies outside the blood-brain barrier and monitors changes in the concentration of salt in the bloodstream and loss of extracellular fluid.

substance P Neurotransmitter released by sensory pain receptors when an animal is exposed to a painful event.

substantia nigra Structure in the tegmentum that is involved in the integration of voluntary movements.

subventricular layer A layer of daughter cells between the intermediate and marginal layers that become either glial cells or interneurons.

superior Above a structure.

superior colliculus Structure in the tectum that receives neural impulses from the fibers of the mammalian optic tract and projects to parts of the parietal and temporal lobes; responsible for attention to visual stimuli and coordination of eye movements.

superior olivary nucleus Group of neurons in the medulla that receive neural messages from the cochlear nuclei.

supplementary motor area An area in the frontal lobe that receives input from the posterior parietal cortex and the somatosensory cortex and is involved in the planning and sequencing of voluntary movements.

suprachiasmatic nucleus (SCN) An area located above the optic chiasm in the medial hypothalamus that is responsible for the control of circadian cycle.

supraesophageal ganglia A primitive brain, formed by the fusion of several ganglion pairs.

sympathetic nervous system A division of the autonomic nervous system that is activated by challenging or dangerous situations.

synapse The point of contact between a neuron and its target; includes the presynaptic membrane, the synaptic cleft, and the postsynaptic membrane.

synaptic cleft The space between the presynaptic and the postsynaptic membranes.

synaptic vesicles Sacs within the presynaptic terminal that contain neurotransmitters.

syntax The system of rules for combining the various units of speech.

target cells The cells with which neurons establish synaptic connections.

taste buds A cluster of 20 to 50 taste receptors that lie either near or within the papillae.

tectorial membrane A membrane in the organ of Corti in which the outer hair cells are embedded.

tectospinal tract Motor pathway that originates in the superior colliculi, synapses with those spinal alpha motor neurons that control upper trunk (shoulder) and neck movement, and coordinates head and trunk movements, especially the visual tracking of stimuli.

tectum Structure in the midbrain that controls simple reflexes and orienting eye and ear movements.

tegmentostriatal pathway A group of nerve fibers that detects reinforcement-related stimuli in the lateral and preoptic areas of the hypothalamus and transmits the information through the MFB to the ventral tegmental area (VTA) and then on to the nucleus accumbens (NA), septum, and prefrontal cortex.

tegmentum Division of the midbrain that contains the substantia nigra, the red nucleus, and the reticular formation.

telencephalon The embryonic division of the forebrain that becomes the cerebral cortex, the basal ganglia, the hippocampus, the amygdala, and the olfactory bulb.

temporal lobe The lobe of the cerebral cortex that is ventral to the lateral sulcus and is responsible for the analysis of auditory stimuli.

temporal summation The combined effects of neurotransmitter release over time.

temporoparietal cortex An area that includes the supramarginal gyrus and the angular gyrus which is involved in the syntactic and semantic comprehension of language.

tendon Strong band of connective tissue linking muscle to bone that causes the movement of bones.

testis-determining factor (TDF) The enzyme that causes the undifferentiated gonads to become testes.

testosterone The male sex hormone manufactured in the Leydig cells of the testes.

thalamotomy Psychosurgery treatment for Parkinson's disease that lesions the ventrolateral thalamus and relieves tremors and improves rigidity, but not bradykinesia.

thalamus Structure in the forebrain that relays information from the sensory receptors to the cerebral cortex.

theta activity (theta waves) An EEG pattern during light sleep that is characterized by synchronized waves that are larger in amplitude (4 to 7 Hz) than beta and alpha waves.

threshold The level of cell membrane depolarization that is required for an action potential to occur.

timbre The purity of a sound; the combination of frequencies that gives each sound its characteristic quality.

tolerance The reduced effects of a drug as a result of repeated use.

transcortical sensory aphasia A communicative disorder caused by damage to an area posterior to Wernicke's area around the anterior boundary of the occipital lobe that is similar to Wernicke's aphasia (fluent speech, poor comprehension, anomia), except for an unusual ability to repeat verbal stimuli.

transcortical motor aphasia A communicative disorder caused by damage to the premotor cortical areas anterior and superior to Broca's area that produces sparse self-initiated speech.

transduction The process of converting physical energy into a neural impulse.

transmitter-gated ion channels Ion channels that are sensitive to the presence of a specific neurotransmitter.

transneuronal degeneration Damage to neurons with which a degenerating neuron has synaptic connections.

tricyclic compounds A class of drugs that increase brain norepinephrine, and to a lesser extent dopamine and serotonin, by interfering with neurotransmitter reuptake.

tumor An abnormal proliferation of glial cells and meninges cells.

Turner's syndrome A condition in which a person is born with only one X chromosome, but no other sex chromosome; the female reproductive system develops in persons with Turner's syndrome.

tympanic membrane The membrane that divides the outer and middle parts of the ear; also called the eardrum.

type A behavior pattern A set of behaviors that include an excessive competitive drive, high aggressiveness, and an intense sense of time urgency.

umami receptor A taste receptor sensitive to the presence of glutamate and other amino acids.

unconditioned response (UCR) An innate reaction to the unconditioned stimulus.

unconditioned stimulus (UCS) A stimulus that is innately able to elicit an instinctive response.

utricle Sacs in the vestibule that contain vestibular receptors.

vaginismus Muscle contractions that cause the entrance to the vagina to close, thereby preventing intercourse.

vagusstoff Loewi's term for the chemical that acts to decrease heart rate.

vasocongestion Dilation of the blood vessels.

ventral Toward the belly.

ventral corticospinal tract Group of neurons originating in the primary motor cortex whose axons do not cross over; these neurons synapse with those alpha motor neurons that control the movement of the trunk and upper legs.

ventral posteriomedial thalamic nucleus A group of neurons that receive taste information from the nucleus of the solitary tract and then project that information to the primary gustatory cortex.

ventral tegmental area (VTA) Structure in the tegmentostriatal reinforcement system that projects to the nucleus accumbens.

ventricles The four chambers of the ventricular system in the brain.

ventricular layer The innermost layer of the developing nervous system whose cells divide to become daughter cells.

ventricular system A series of hollow interconnected chambers in the brain and spinal cord that contain cerebrospinal fluid.

ventrobasal (VB) complex Neurons in the thalamus that receive information about touch and proprioception via the dorsal column-medial lemniscal system and about temperature and pain via the anterolateral system.

ventromedial hypothalamus (VMH) An area in the brain involved in satiety and the suppression of eating; it contains estrogen-sensitive receptors.

ventromedial tracts Four motor pathways originating in different parts of the subcortex that control movements of the trunk and limbs; includes the vestibulospinal, tectospinal, lateral reticulospinal, and medial reticulospinal tracts.

vertebral column The outer bony covering that protects the spinal cord; also called the spine or backbone.

vertebrate An animal with a protective covering over its spinal cord and brain.

vestibular ganglion The bipolar neurons that receive input from the vestibular receptors.

vestibular nerve The axons of the vestibular ganglion cell bodies.

vestibular nuclei That part of the medulla that synapses with most vestibular nerve fibers.

vestibule (vestibular sacs) Structure in the vestibular system that detects passive head movement.

vestibulospinal tract Motor pathway that originates in the vestibular nuclei of the brainstem, synapses with those alpha motor neurons in the spinal cord that produce lower trunk and leg movement, and plays a central role in the control of posture.

visual agnosia Following bilateral damage to the inferotemporal cortex, the inability to name an object when it is presented visually but not when it is presented in another modality.

visual field deficit An inability to see objects placed in a particular part of the visual field caused by damage to a portion of one of the cerebral hemispheres.

visual photoreceptor Type of photoreceptor that codes the features of a light stimulus.

visual-verbal agnosia A communicative disorder characterized by an inability to recognize printed words, but not spoken words, that results from damage that isolates the visual cortex from cortical language areas.

vitreous humor A clear, jelly-like substance that fills the posterior cavity of the eye.

VMH-lesion syndrome The pattern of behavior, hyperphagia and finickiness, that follows damage to the ventromedial hypothalamus.

voltage-gated ion channels Ion channels that are sensitive to changes in the cell membrane potential.

vomeronasal organ Specialized sensory receptors in the olfactory bulbs that can detect presence of pheromones released by a receptive female.

Wernicke's aphasia A communicative disorder caused by damage to the posterior portion of the superior and middle temporal gyrus and the temporoparietal cortex that produces an inability to comprehend language.

Wernicke's area An area in the dorsal part of the left temporal lobe in the posterior superior temporal gyrus that is involved in speech perception.

Western Aphasia Battery A test used to diagnose aphasia and determine its severity.

white matter Myelinated axons of nerve fibers.

withdrawal The unpleasant, sometimes painful symptoms that occur when the effects of a drug end.

withdrawal reflex The automatic withdrawal of a limb from a painful stimulus.

Wolffian system The male reproductive system consisting of the testes, seminal vesicles, and vas deferens.

working memory A memory that is actively being processed by rehearsal.

Xanax (alprozolam) The most frequently used benzodiazepine.

X ganglion cells Small retinal ganglion cells that project to the parvocellular layers of the primary visual cortex.

Y ganglion cells Large retinal ganglion cells that project to the magnocellular layers of the primary visual cortex.

Young-Helmholz trichromatic theory The view that there are three different sets of fibers (receptors) in the eye: one that responds to blue, a second to green, and a third to red.

zeitgebers The external time cues that reset an animal's biological clock every 24 hours.

zygote A single cell formed when the sperm fertilizes the egg.

REFERENCES

Abrams, T. W., Karl, K. A., & Kandel, E. R. (1991). Biochemical studies of stimulus convergence during classical conditioning in aplysia: Dual regulation of adenylate cyclase by Ca^{2+}/calmodulin and transmitter. *Journal of Neuroscience, 11,* 2655–2665.

Adamec, R. E. (1991). The role of the temporal lobe in feline aggression and defense. *Psychological Record, 41,* 233–253.

Aggleton, J. P., & Mishkin, M. (1985). Mammillary-body lesions and visual recognition in monkeys. *Experimental Brain Research, 58,* 190–197.

Agnew, H. W., Jr., Webb, W. B., & Williams, R. L. (1967). Comparison of stage four and 1-REM sleep deprivation. *Perceptual and Motor Skills, 24,* 851–858.

Agranoff, B. W. (1980). Biochemical events mediating the formation of short-term and long-term memory. In Y. Tsukada and B. W. Agranoff (Eds.), *Neurobiological basis of learning and memory.* New York: Wiley.

Agras, W. S., & Kraemer, H. C. (1984). The treatment of anorexia: Do different treatments have different outcomes? *Public Association of Research on Nervous and Mental Disorders, 62,* 193–207.

Agras, W. S., Berkowitz, R. I., Arnow, B. A., Telch, C. F., et al. (1996). Maintenance following a very-low-calorie diet. *Journal of Consulting and Clinical Psychology, 64,* 610–613.

Akabas, M. H., Dodd, J., & Al-Awqati, Q. (1988). A bitter substance induces a rise in intracellular calcium in a subpopulation of rat taste cell. *Science, 242,* 1047–1049.

Akbarian, S., Kim, J. J., Potkin, S. G., Hetrick, W. P., Bunney, W. E., Jr., & Jones, E. G. (1996). Maldistribution of interstitial neurons in prefrontal white matter of the brains of schizophrenic patients. *Archives of General Psychiatry, 53,* 425–436.

Akerstedt, T. (1990). Psychological and psychophysiological effects of work. *Scandinavian Journal of Work and Environmental Health, 16* (Suppl. 1), 5–16.

Akerstedt, T., & Froberg, J. E. (1976). Interindividual differences in circadian pattern of catecholamine excretion, body temperature, performance, and subjective arousal. *Biological Psychology, 4,* 277–292.

Albert, D. J., & Walsh, M. L. (1984). Neural systems and the inhibitory modulation of agonistic behavior: A comparison of mammalian species. *Neuroscience and Biobehavioral Reviews, 8,* 5–24.

Albuquerque, E. X., Rash, J. E., Mayer, R. F., & Satterfield, J. R. (1976). An electrophysiological and morphological study of the neuromuscular junction in patients with myasthenia gravis. *Experimental Neurology, 51,* 536–563.

Aldrich, M. S., Alessi, A. G., Beck, R. W., & Gilman, S. (1987). Cortical blindness: Etiology, diagnosis, and prognosis. *Annuals of Neurology, 21,* 149–158.

Alexander, J. T., Cheung, W. K., Dietz, C. B., & Leibowitz, S. F. (1993). Meal patterns and macronutrient intake after peripheral and PVN injections of the α-2-receptor antagonist idazoxan. *Physiology and Behavior, 53,* 623–630.

Allen, L. S., & Gorski, R. A. (1992). Sexual orientation and the size of the anterior commissure in the human brain. *Proceedings of the National Academy of Sciences, 89,* 7199–7202.

Allen, S. J., Dawbarn, D., & Wilcock, G. K. (1988). Morphometric immunochemical analysis of neurons in the nucleus basalis of Meynert in Alzheimer's disease. *Brain Research, 454,* 275–281.

Alloy, C. R., Acocella, J., & Bootzin, R. R. (1996). *Abnormal psychology: Current perspectives* (7th ed.). New York: McGraw-Hill.

Altshuler, L. L., Casanova, M. F., Goldberg, T. E., & Kleinman, J. E. (1990). The hippocampus and parahippocampus in schizophrenia, suicide, and control brains. *Archives of General Psychiatry, 47,* 1029–1034.

Alvarez-Royo, P., Clower, R. P., Zola-Morgan, S., & Squire, L. R. (1991). Stereotaxic lesions of the hippocampus in monkeys: Determination of surgical coordinates and analysis of lesions using magnetic resonance imaging. *Journal of Neuroscience Methods, 38,* 223–232.

Ambelas, A., & George, M. (1986). Predictability of course of illness in manic patients with positive life events. *Journal of Nervous and Mental Disease, 1974,* 693–695.

American Psychiatric Association. (1994). *Diagnostic and statistical manual of mental disorders* (4th ed.). Washington, DC: Author.

American Psychological Association. (1992). Ethical principles of psychologists and code of conduct. *American Psychologist, 47,* 1597–1611.

Amoore, J. E. (1963). Stereochemical theory of olfaction. *Nature, 198,* 271–272.

Amyes, E. W., & Nielsen, J. M. (1955). Clinicopathologic study of vascular lesions of the anterior cingulate region. *Bulletin of the Los Angeles Neurological Societies, 20,* 112–130.

Anand, B. K., & Brobeck, J. R. (1951). Hypothalamic control of food intake in rats and cats. *Yale Journal of Biology and Medicine, 24,* 123–140.

Anand, B. K., Chhina, G. S., & Singh, B. (1962). Effect of glucose on the activity of hypothalamic "feeding centers." *Science, 138,* 597–598.

Anand, B. K., & Dua, S. (1956). Electrical stimulation of the limbic system of the brain ("visceral brain") in the waking animal. *Indian Journal of Medicinal Research, 44,* 107–119.

Anch, A. M., Browman, C. P., Milter, M. M., & Walsh, J. K. (1988). *Sleep: A scientific perspective.* Englewood Cliffs, NJ: Prentice Hall.

Anderson, C. A. (1989). Temperature and aggression: The ubiquitous effects of heat on the occurrence of human violence. *Psychological Bulletin, 106,* 74–96.

Anderson, C. D. (1981). Expression of affect and physiological response in psychosomatic patients. *Journal of Psychosomatic Research, 25,* 143–149.

Anderson, S. W., Damasio, H., Jones, R. D., & Tranel, D. (1991). Wisconsin Card Sorting Test performance as a measure of frontal lobe damage. *Journal of Clinical Experimental Neuropsychology, 13,* 909–922.

Andreasen, N. C. (1988). Brain imaging: Applications in psychiatry. *Science, 239,* 1381–1388.

Andreasen, N. C. (1991). Assessment issues and the cost of schizophrenia. *Schizophrenia Bulletin, 17,* 475–481.

Andreasen, N. C. (1994). Changing concepts of schizophrenia and the historical fallacy. *American Journal of Psychiatry, 151,* 1405–1407.

Andreasen, N. C., Flaum, M., Swayze, V. W., Tyrrell, G., & Arndt, S. (1990). Positive and negative symptoms in schizophrenia. *Archives of General Psychiatry, 47,* 615–621.

Antrobus, J. (1991). Dreaming: Cognitive processes during cortical activation and high afferent thresholds. *Psychological Review, 98,* 96–212.

Archer, J. (1991). The influence of testosterone in human aggression. *British Journal of Psychology, 82,* 1–28.

Archer, J., & Lloyd, B. B. (1985). *Sex and gender.* New York: Cambridge University Press.

Arendt, J. (1994). Clinical perspectives for melatonin and its agonists. *Biological Psychiatry, 35,* 1–2.

Arendt, J., Aldhous, M., English, J., & Marks, V. (1987). Some effects of jet lag and their alleviation by melatonin. *Ergonomics, 30,* 1379–1393.

Argamaso, S. M., Boggs, B. R., & Foster, R. G. (1992). Effects of retinal degeneracy on locomotor rhythms in mice: Circadian and molecular analysis of *rd/rd* and *rds/rds* mutants. *Society for Research in Biological Rhythms Abstracts, 3,* 71.

Asanuma, H. (1989). *The motor cortex.* New York: Raven Press.

Aschoff, J., & Wever, R. (1976). Human circadian rhythms: A multioscillatory system. *Federation Proceedings, 35,* 2326–2332.

Aserinsky, E., & Kleitman, N. (1953). Regularly occurring periods of eye motility, and concomitant, during sleep. *Science, 118,* 273–274.

Ashcroft, G., Crawford, T., & Eccleston, E. (1966). 5-Hydroxyindole compounds in the cerebrospinal fluid of patients with psychiatric or neurological disease. *Lancet, 2,* 1049–1052.

Aston-Jones, G. (1985). Behavioral functions of locus coeruleus derived from cellular attributes. *Physiological Psychology, 13,* 118–126.

Aston-Jones, G., & Bloom, F. E. (1981). Activity of norepinephrine-containing locus coeruleus neurons in behaving rats anticipates fluctuations in the sleep-waking cycle. *Journal of Neuroscience, 1,* 876–886.

Aston-Jones, G., Foote, S. L., & Bloom, F. E. (1984). Anatomy and physiology of the locus coeruleus neurons: Functional implications. In M. G. Ziegler & C. R. Lake (Eds.), *Norepinephrine. Frontiers of clinical neuroscience* (Vol. 2, pp. 92–116). Baltimore: Williams & Wilkins.

Atkinson, R. C., & Shiffrin, R. M. (1971). The control of short-term memory. *Scientific American, 225,* 82–90.

Atkinson, R. L., Blank, R. C., Schumacker, D., Dhurandhar, N. V., et al. (1997). Long-term drug treatment of obesity in a private setting. *Obesity Research, 5,* 578–586.

Avenet, P., Hofmann, F., & Lindemann, B. (1988). Transduction in taste receptor cells requires cAMP-dependent protein kinase. *Nature, 331,* 351–354.

Avenet, P., & Lindemann, B. (1989). Perspectives of taste perception. *Journal of Membrane Biology, 112,* 1–8.

Ax, A. F. (1953). The physiological differentiation between fear and anger in humans. *Psychosomatic Medicine, 15,* 433–443.

Axel, R. (1995, October). The molecular logic of smell. *Scientific American,* 154–159.

Ayuso-Gutierrez, J. L., Palazon, M., & Ayuso-Mateos, J. L. (1994). Open trial of fluvoxamine in the treatment of bulimia nervosa. *Internal Journal of Eating Disorders, 15,* 245–249.

Baddeley, A. D. (1986). *Working memory.* Oxford: Oxford University Press.

Baghdoyan, H. A., Rodrigo-Angulo, M. L., McCarley, R. W., & Hobson, J. A. (1984). Site-specific enhancement and suppression of desynchronized sleep signs following cholinergic stimulation of three brainstem regions. *Brain Research, 306,* 39–52.

Bailey, J. M., & Bali, A. P. (1993). Familiality of female and male homosexuality. *Behavioral Genetics, 23,* 313–322.

Baldessarini, R. J. (1995). Drugs and the treatment of psychiatric disorders: Depression and mania. In J. G. Hardman, L. E. Limbird, P. B. Molinoff, R. W. Ruddon, & A. G. Gilman (Eds.), *Goodman and Gilman's the pharmacological basis of therapeutics* (9th ed., pp. 399–430). New York: McGraw-Hill.

Baldessarini, R. J. (1995). Drugs and the treatment of psychiatric disorders: Psychosis and anxiety. In J. G. Hardman, L. E. Limbird, P. B. Molinoff, R. W. Ruddon, & A. G. Gilman (Eds.), *Goodman and Gilman's the pharmacological basis of therapeutics* (9th ed., pp. 399–430). New York: McGraw-Hill.

Ballard, P. A., Tetrud, J. W., & Langston, J. W. (1985). Permanent human parkinsonism due to 1-methyl-4-phenyl-1,2,3,6-tetrahydropyridine (MPTP). *Neurology, 35,* 949–956.

Ballinger, J. C. (1991). Long-term pharmacologic treatment of panic disorder. *Journal of Clinical Psychiatry, 52,* 18–23.

Barnes, D. M. (1987). Biological issues in schizophrenia. *Science, 235,* 430–433.

Baron, M., Risch, N., Hamburger, R., Mandel, B., Kushner, S., Newman, M., Drumer, D., & Belmaker, R. H. (1987). Genetic linkage between X-chromosome markers and bipolar affective illness. *Nature, 326,* 289–292.

Baron, M. S., Vitek, J. L., Bakay, R. A. E., et al. (1996). Treatment of advanced Parkinson's disease by posterior Gpi pallidotomy: 1-year results of a pilot study. *Annals of Neurology, 40,* 355–366.

Bard, P. (1934). On emotional expression after decortication with some remarks on certain theoretical views. *Psychological Review, 41,* 309–329.

Barr, C. E., Mednick, S. A., & Munk-Jorgensen, P. (1990). Exposure to influenza epidemics during gestation and adult schizophrenia. *Archives of General Psychiatry, 47,* 869–874.

Bartoshuk, L. M. (1988). Taste. In R. C. Atkinson, R. J. Herrnstein, G. Lindzey, & R. D. Luce (Eds.), *Stevens's handbook of experimental psychology: Perception and motivation* (Vol. 1). New York: Wiley.

Bartoshuk, L. M. (1991). Taste, smell, and pleasure. In R. C. Bolles (Ed.), *The hedonics of taste* (pp. 15–28). Hillsdale, NJ: Erlbaum.

Bartoshuk, L. M. (1993). Genetic and pathological taste variation: What can we learn from animal models and human disease? In D. Chadwick, J. Marsh, and J. Goode (Eds.), *The molecular basis of smell and taste transduction* (pp. 251–267). New York: Wiley.

Bartoshuk, L. M., & Beauchamp, G. K. (1994). Chemical senses. *Annual Review of Psychology, 45,* 419–449.

Bartoshuk, L. M., Fast, K., Karrer, T. A., Marino, S., Price, R. A., & Reed, D. A. (1992). PROP supertasters and the perception of sweetness and bitterness. *Chemical Senses, 17,* 594.

Bartoshuk, L. M., Gentile, R. L., Moskowitz, H. R., & Meiselman, H. L. (1974). Sweet taste induced by miracle fruit (*Synsephalum dulcificum*). *Physiology and Behavior, 12,* 449–456.

Basbaum, A. I., & Fields, H. L. (1984). Endogenous pain control systems: Brainstem spinal pathways and endorphin circuitry. *Annual Review of Neuroscience, 7,* 309–338.

Bassett, A. S., McGillivray, B. C., Jones, B. D., & Pantzar, J. T. (1988). Partial trisomy chromosome 5 cosegretating with schizophrenia. *Lancet, 1,* 799–801.

Baumgardner, T. L., Green, K. E., & Reiss, A. L. (1994). A behavioral neurogenetics approach to developmental disabilities: Gene-brain-behavior associations. *Current Opinion in Neurology, 7,* 172–178.

Bayrakal, S. (1965). The significance of electroencephalographic abnormality in behavior-problem children. *Canadian Psychiatric Association Journal, 10,* 387–392.

Beach, F. A. (1947). A review of physiological and psychological studies of sexual behavior in mammals. *Psychological Review, 27,* 240–307.

Beach, F. A. (1958). Normal sexual behavior in male rats isolated at fourteen days of age. *Journal of Comparative and Physiological Psychology, 51,* 37–38.

Beach, F. A. (1969). It's all in your mind. *Psychology Today, 3,* 33–35.

Beach, F. A., Noble, R. G., & Orndoff, R. K. (1969). Effects of perinatal androgen treatment on responses of male rats to gonadal hormones in adulthood. *Journal of Comparative and Physiological Psychology, 68,* 490–497.

Beach, F. A., Zitrin, A., & Jaynes, J. (1955). Neural mediation of mating in male cats: II. Contribution of the frontal cortex. *Journal of Experimental Zoology, 130,* 381–401.

Beckstead, R. M., Morse, J. R., & Norgren, R. (1980). The nucleus of the solitary tract in the monkey: Projections to the thalamus and brainstem nuclei. *Journal of Comparative Neurology, 190,* 259–282.

Békésy, Von G. (1947). The variation of phase along the basilar membrane with sinusoidal vibrations. *Journal of the Acoustical Society of America, 19,* 452–460.

Békésy, Von G. (1960). *Experiments in hearing.* New York: McGraw-Hill.

Bellows, R. T. (1939). Time factors in water drinking in dogs. *American Journal of Physiology, 125,* 87–97.

Bemis, K. M. (1978). Current approaches to the etiology and treatment of anorexia nervosa. *Psychological Bulletin, 85,* 593–617.

Bender, J. (1992, June). *Characterization of cholecystokinin, bombesin, fenfluramine and an endogenous factor from fed pig plasma according to criteria of satiety.* Paper presented at the Conference of the Society for the Study of Ingestive Behavior, Princeton, NJ.

Benedek, G., Obal, F., Lelkes, Z., & Obal, F. (1982). Thermal and chemical stimulation of the hypothalamus heat detectors: The effects on the EEG. *Acta Physiologica Hungaria, 60,* 27–35.

Benes, F. M., & Bird, E. D. (1987). An analysis of the arrangement of neurons in the cingulate cortex of schizophrenic patients. *Archives of General Psychiatry, 44,* 608–616.

Benes, F. M., Davidson, J., & Bird, E. D. (1986). Quantitative cytoarchitectural studies of the cerebral cortex of schizophrenics. *Archives of General Psychiatry, 43,* 31–35.

Benes, F. M., Vincent, S. L., Marie, A., & Khan, Y. (1996). Up-regulation of $GABA_A$ receptor binding on neurons of the prefrontal cortex in schizophrenic subjects. *Neuroscience, 75,* 1021–1031.

Benson, D. F. (1979). Aphasia. In K. M. Heilman & E. Valenstein (Eds.), *Clinical neuropsychology.* New York: Oxford University Press.

Benson, D. F., & Geschwind, N. (1985). Aphasia and related disorders: A clinical approach. In M. M. Mesulum (Ed.), *Principles of behavioral neurology.* Philadelphia: Davis.

Benson, D. F., & Greenberg, J. (1969). Visual form agnosia. *Archives of Neurology, 20,* 82–89.

Berkun, M. M., Kessen, M. L., & Miller, N. E. (1952). Hunger-reducing effects of food by stomach fistula versus food by mouth measured by a consummatory response. *Journal of Comparative and Physiological Psychology, 45,* 550–554.

Berlan, M., Galitzky, J., Riviere, D., Foureau, M., Tran, M. A., Flores, R., Louvet, J. P., Houin., G., & Lafontan, M. (1991). Plasma catcholamine levels and lipid mobilization induced by yohimbine in obese and nonobese women. *International Journal of Obesity, 15,* 305–315.

Berlin, F. S., & Meinecke, C. F. (1981). Treatment of sex offenders with antiandrogenic medication: Conceptualization, review of treatment modalities, and preliminary findings. *American Journal of Psychiatry, 138,* 601–607.

Bermant, G., & Davidson, J. M. (1974). *Biological bases of sexual behavior.* New York: Harper & Row.

Bernhardt, P. C. (1997). Influence of serotonin and testosterone in aggression and dominance: Convergence with social psychology. *Current Directions in Psychological Science, 2,* 44–48.

Bernstein, I. L. (1978). Learned taste aversions in children receiving chemotherapy. *Science, 200,* 1302–1303.

Bernstein, I. L., & Webster, M. M. (1980). Learned taste aversions in humans. *Physiology and Behavior, 25,* 363–366.

Berrettini, W. H., Ferraro, T. N., Goldin, L. R., Detera-Wadleigh, S. D., Choi, H., Muniec, D., Guroff, J. J., Kazuba, D. M., Nurnberger, J. I., Jr., Hsieh, W. T., Hoehe, M. R., & Gershon, E. S. (1997). A linkage study of bipolar illness. *Archives of General Psychiatry, 54,* 27–35.

Berrettini, W. H., Nurnberger, J. I. Jr., Hare, T., Gershon, E. S., & Post, P. M. (1982). Plasma and CSF GABA in affective illness. *British Journal of Psychiatry, 141,* 483–487.

Berry, D. S., & Pennebaker, J. W. (1993). Nonverbal and verbal emotional expression and health. *Psychotherapy and Psychosomatics, 59,* 11–19.

Bertino, M., & Tordoff, M. G. (1988). Sodium depletion increases rats' preferences for salted food. *Behavioral Neuroscience, 102,* 565–573.

Besset, A., Tafti, M., Villemin, E., Borderies, P., & Billiard, M. (1995). Effects of zolpidem on the architecture and cyclical structure of sleep in poor sleepers. *Drugs and Experimental Clinical Research, 21,* 161–169.

Bever, T. G. (1970). The cognitive basis for linguistic structures. In J. R. Hayes (Ed.), *Cognition and development of language.* New York: Wiley.

Bickford, E. W. (1985). *Human circadian rhythms: A review.* (Lighting Research Institute Project 88 DR NEMA2). Morris Plains, NJ: Lighting Research Institute.

Blackmore, S. (1983). *Beyond the body.* London: Granada.

Blaha, C. D., & Phillips, A. G. (1990). Application of in vivo electrochemistry to the measurement of changes in dopamine release during intracranial self-stimulation. *Journal of Neuroscience Methods, 34,* 125–133.

Blanchard, D. C., & Blanchard, R. J. (1972). Innate and conditioned reactions to threat in rats with amygdaloid lesions. *Journal of Comparative and Physiological Psychology, 81,* 281–290.

Blass, E. M., & Epstein, A. N. (1971). A lateral preoptic osmosensitive zone for thirst. *Journal of Comparative and Physiological Psychology, 76,* 378–394.

Bleuler, E. (1911). *Dementia praecox oder gruppe der schizophrenien. [Dementia praecox or the group of schizophrenias*]. Leipzig: F. Deuticke.

Bliss, T. V. P., Douglas, R. M., Errington, M. L., & Lynch, M. A. (1986). Correlation between long-term potentiation and release of endogenous amino acids from dentate gyrus of anesthetized rats. *Journal of Physiology, 377,* 391–408.

Bliwise, D. L., Bliwise, N. G., Partinen, M., Pursley, A. M., & Dement, W. C. (1988). Sleep apnea and mortality in an aged cohort. *American Journal of Public Health, 78,* 544–547.

Bloch, G. J., Butler, P. C., & Kohlert, J. G. (1996). Galanin microinjected into the medial preoptic nucleus facilitates female- and male-typical sexual behaviors in the female rat. *Physiology and Behavior, 59,* 1147–1154.

Bloom, F. E., & Lazerson, A. (1988). *Brain, mind, and behavior* (2nd ed.). New York: Freeman.

Blumenthal, J. A., Williams, R., King, Y., Schanberg, S. M., & Thompson, L. W. (1978). Type A behavior and angiographically documented coronary disease. *Circulation, 58,* 634–639.

Bogen, J. E. (1977). Educational implications of recent research on the human brain. In M. C. Wittrock (Ed.), *The human brain.* Englewood Cliffs, NJ: Prentice-Hall.

Bogerts, B. (1989). The role of limbic and paralimbic pathology in the etiology of schizophrenia. *Psychiatry Research, 29,* 255–256.

Bonkalo, A. (1967). Electroencephalography in criminology. *Canadian Psychiatric Association Journal, 12,* 281–286.

Booth, D. A. (1972). Conditioned satiety in the rat. *Journal of Comparative and Physiological Psychology, 81,* 457–471.

Booth, D. A. (1977). Satiety and appetite are conditioned reactions. *Psychosomatic Medicine, 39,* 76–81.

Booth, D. A. (1985). Food-conditioned eating preferences and aversions with interoceptive elements: Conditioned appetites and satieties. *Annals of the New York Academy of Sciences, 443,* 22–41.

Booth, D. A., Coons, E. E., & Miller, N. E. (1969). Blood glucose responses to electrical stimulation of the hypothalamic feeding area. *Physiology and Behavior, 4,* 991–1001.

Booth, D. A., Lee, M., & McAleavey, C. (1976). Acquired sensory control of satiation in man. *British Journal of Psychology, 67,* 137–147.

Bootzin, R. R., & Acocella, J. R. (1988). *Abnormal psychology: Current perspectives* (5th ed.). New York: Random House.

Bothwell, M. (1995). Functional interactions of neurotrophins and neurotrophin receptors. *Annual Review of Neuroscience, 18,* 223–255.

Bottini, G., Corcoran, R., Sterzi, R., Paulesu, E., Schenone, P., Scarpa, P., Frackowiak, R. S. J., & Frith, C. D. (1994). The role of the right hemisphere in the interpretation of figurative aspects of language: A positron emission tomography activation study. *Brain, 117,* 1241–1253.

Bower, G. H. (1981). Mood and memory. *American Psychologist, 36,* 129–148.

Bowers, M. B., Jr., Heninger, G. R., Sternberg, D., & Meltzer, H. Y. (1980). Clinical processes and central dopaminergic activity in psychotic disorders. *Community Psychopharmacology, 4,* 177–183.

Bozarth, M. A., & Wise, R. A. (1981). Heroin reward is dependent on a dopaminergic substrate. *Life Science, 29,* 1881–1886.

Bozarth, M. A., & Wise, R. A. (1983). Neural substrates of opiate reinforcement. *Progress in Neuropharmacology and Biological Psychiatry, 7,* 569–575.

Bradbury, T. N., & Miller, G. A. (1985). Season of birth in schizophrenia: A review of evidence, methodology, and etiology. *Psychological Bulletin, 98,* 569–594.

Brady, J. V. (1961). Motivational-emotional factors and intracranial self-stimulation. In D. E. Sheer (Ed.), *Electrical stimulation of the brain* (pp. 413–430). Austin: University of Texas Press.

Brady, J. V., & Nauta, W. J. H. (1955). Subcortical mechanisms in emotional behavior: The duration of affective changes following septal forebrain lesions in the albino rat. *Journal of Comparative and Physiological Psychology, 48,* 412–420.

Bray, G. A. (1992). Pathophysiology of obesity. *American Journal of Clinical Nutrition. 55,* 488–494.

Bray, G. A., & Gallagher, T. F., Jr. (1975). Manifestations of hypothalamic obesity in man: A comprehensive investigation of eight patients and a review of the literature. *Medicine, 54,* 301–330.

Bray, G. M., Villegas-Perez, M. P., Vidal-Sanz, M., & Aguayo, A. (1987). The use of peripheral nerve grafts to enhance neuronal survival, promote growth and permit terminal reconnections in the central nervous system of adult rats. *Journal of Experimental Biology, 132,* 5–19.

Bregman, B. S., Kunkel-Bagden, E., Reier, P. J., Dai, H. N., McAtee, M., & Gao, D. (1993). Recovery of function after spinal cord injury: Mechanisms underlying transplant-mediated recovery of function after spinal cord injury in newborn and adult rats. *Exploring Neurology, 123,* 3–16.

Bregman, B. S., Kunkel-Bagden, E., Schnell, L., Dai, H. N., Gao, D., & Schwab, M. E. (1995). Recovery from spinal cord injury mediated by antibodies to neurite growth inhibitors. *Nature, 378,* 498–501.

Bremer, F. (1937). L'Activite cerebrale au cours du sommeil et de la narcose: Contribution 3 l'etude de mecanisme du sommeil. *Bulletin de l'Academie Royale de Medecine de Belgique 2,* 68–86.

Bremer, J. (1959). *Aesexualization.* New York: MacMillan.

Bright, R. A., & Everitt, D. E. (1992). Beta-blockers and depression. Evidence against an association. *Journal of the American Medical Association, 267,* 1783–1787.

Brinkman, C. (1984). Supplementary motor area of the monkey's cerebral cortex: Short- and long-term deficits after unilateral ablation and the effects of subsequent callosal section. *Journal of Neuroscience, 4,* 918–929.

Britt, M. D., & Wise, R. A. (1983). Ventral tegmental site of opiate reward: Antagonism by a hydrophilic opiate receptor blocker. *Brain Research, 258,* 105–108.

Brobeck, J. R., Tepperman, J., & Long, C. N. H. (1943). Effects of experimental obesity upon carbohydrate metabolism. *Yale Journal of Biology and Medicine, 15,* 893–904.

Broca, P. (1861). Remarques sur le siege de la faculte du langage articule, suives d'une observation d'aphemie (perte de la parole). *Bulletin de la Societe Anatomique, 36,* 330–357.

Brookshire, R. H. (1992). *Introduction to neurogenic communication disorders* (4th ed.). St. Louis: Mosby.

Brookshire, R. H. (1997). *Introduction to neurogenic communication disorders* (5th ed.). St. Louis: Mosby.

Brown, P. K., & Wald, G. (1964). Visual pigments in single rods and cones of the human retina. *Science, 144,* 145–151.

Brownell, H. H., Simpson, T. L., Bihrle, A. M., Potter, H. H., & Gardner, H. (1990). Appreciation of metaphoric alternative word meanings by left and right brain-damaged patients. *Neuropsychologia, 28,* 173–184.

Brozoski, T. J., Brown, R. M., Rosvold, H. E., & Goldman, P. S. (1979). Cognitive deficit caused by regional depletion of dopamine in prefrontal cortex of rhesus monkey. *Science, 205,* 929–932.

Bruch, H. (1980). Preconditions for the development of anorexia nervosa. *American Journal of Psychoanalysis, 40,* 169–172.

Brutus, M., Shaikah, M.D., Edinger, H., & Siegel, A. (1986). Effects of experimental temporal lobe seizures upon hypothalamically elicited aggressive behavior in the cat. *Brain Research, 26,* 53–63.

Buck, L., & Axel, R. (1991). A novel multigene family may encode odorant receptors: A molecular basis for odor recognition. *Cell, 65,* 175–187.

Buggy, J., & Johnson, A. K. (1977). Preoptic-hypothalamic periventricular lesions: Thirst deficits and hypernatremia. *American Journal of Physiology, 233,* R44–R52.

Buhrich, N., Bailey, J. M., & Martin, N. G. (1991). Sexual orientaion, sexual identity, and sex-dimorphic behavior in male twins. *Behavior Genetics, 21,* 75–96.

Bunney, W. E., Jr., & Davis, J. M. (1965). Norepinephrine in depressive reactions: A review. *Archives of General Psychiatry, 13,* 483–494.

Bunney, W. E., Goodwin, F. K., & Murphy, D. L. (1972). The "switch process" in manic-depressive illness. *Archives of General Psychiatry, 27,* 312–317.

Burchiel, K. J. (1995). Thalamotomy for movement disorders. *Neurosurgical Clinics of North America, 6,* 55–71.

Burns, B. D. (1958). *The mammallian cerebral cortex.* London: Arnold.

Burton, M. J., Mora, F., & Rolls, E. T. (1975). Visual and taste neurons in the lateral hypothalamus and substantia innominata: Modulation of responsiveness by hunger. *Journal of Physiology, 252,* 50–51.

Buschbaum, M. S. (1990). The frontal lobes, basa ganglia, and temporal lobes as sites for schizophrenia. *Schizophrenia Bulletin, 16,* 379–389.

Bushnell, M. C., Goldberg, M. E., & Robinson, D. L. (1981). Behavioral enhancement of visual responses in monkey cerebral cortex: I. Modulation in posterior cortex related to selective visual attention. *Journal of Neurophysiology, 46,* 755–772.

Byrne, M. E. (1988). Turn-taking and requesting in conversational discourse of normal adults and adults with nonfluent aphasia. Pennsylvania State University. Unpublished doctoral dissertation.

Cadelli, D. S., & Schwab, M. E. (1991). Myelin-associated inhibitors of neurite outgrowth and their role in CNS regeneration. *Annals of the New York Academy of Sciences, 633,* 234–240.

Caggiula, A. R., & Szechtman, H. (1972). Hypothalamic stimulation: A biphasic influence on the copulation of the male rat. *Behavioral Biology, 7,* 591–598.

Cain, W. S. (1982). Odor identification by males and females: Predictions versus performance. *Chemical Senses, 7,* 129–142.

Cain, W. S. (1988). Olfaction. In R. C. Atkinson, R. J. Herrnstein, G. Lindzey, & R. D. Luce (Eds.), *Stevens' handbook of experimental psychology: Vol. 1. Perception and motivation.* New York: Wiley.

Calford, M. B., Graydon, M. L., Huerta, M. F., Kaas, J. H., & Pettigrew, J. D. (1985). A variant of the mammalian somatotopic map in a bat. *Nature, 313,* 477–479.

Campbeau, S., & Davis, M. (1995). Involvement of the central nucleus and basolateral complex of the amygdala in fear conditioning measured with fear-potentiated startle in rats trained concurrently with auditory and visual conditioned stimuli. *Journal of Neuroscience, 15,* 2301–2311.

Campbell, B. A., & Church, P. M. (1969). *Punishment and aversive behavior.* New York: Appleton-Century-Crofts.

Campbell, I. C., Gallagher, D. W., Hamburg, M. A., Tallman, J. F., & Murphy, D. L. (1985). Electrophysiological and receptor studies in rat brain: Effects of clorgyline. *European Journal of Pharmacology, 111,* 355–364.

Campbell, L. A., & Smith, F. J. (1990). Transient declines in blood glucose signal meal initiation. *International Journal of Obesity, 14* (Suppl. 3), 15–33.

Cancro, R. (1985). Schizophrenic disorders. In H. I. Kaplan and B. J. Sadock (Eds.), *Comprehensive textbook of psychiatry,* (4th Ed). Baltimore: Williams & Wilkins.

Cannon, W. B. (1915). *Bodily changes in pain, hunger, fear, and rage: An account of recent researches into the function of emotional excitement.* New York: Appleton-Century-Crofts.

Cannon, W. B. (1927). The James-Lange theory of emotion. *American Journal of Psychology, 39,* 106–124.

Cannon, W. B. (1934). Hunger and thirst. In E. Murchison (Ed.), *A handbook of general experimental psychology.* Worcester, MA: Clark University Press.

Cannon, W. B., Lewis, J. T., & Britton, S. W. (1927). The dispensability of the sympathetic division of the autonomic nervous system. *Boston Medical Surgery Journal, 197,* 514.

Cannon, W. B., & Washburn, A. L. (1912). An explanation of hunger. *American Journal of Physiology, 29,* 441–454.

Cantwell, D. P., Sturzenberger, S., Burroughs, J., Salkin, B., & Green, J. K. (1977). Anorexia nervosa: An affective disorder? *Archives of General Psychiatry, 34,* 1087–1093.

Caplan, L. R. (1988). *Stroke, CIBA clinical symposia.* Summit, NJ: CIBA Pharmaceutical Company.

Carew, T. J., Hawkins, R. D., & Kandel, E. R. (1983). Differential classical conditioning of a defensive withdrawal reflex in *Aplysia californica. Science, 219,* 397–420.

Carlson, J. C., & Hatfield, E. (1992). *Psychology of emotion.* Fort Worth: Harcourt Brace & Jovanovich.

Carlsson, A. (1967). Recent studies on the mode of action of antidepressant drugs. *Naunyn Schmiedebergs Archives of Experimental Pathology and Pharmacology, 257,* 115–117.

Carney, J. M., & Floyd, R. A. (1991). Protection against oxidative damage to CNS by alpha-phenyl-tert-butyl nitrone (PBN) and other spin-trapping agents: A novel series of nonlipid free radical scavengers. *Journal of Molecular Neuroscience, 3,* 47–57.

Caroscio, J. T., Mulvihill, M. N., Sterling, R., & Abrams, B. (1987). Amyotrophic lateral sclerosis: Its natural history. *Neurology Clinician, 5,* 1–8.

Carpenter, W. T., & Buchanan, R. W. (1994). Schizophrenia. *New England Journal of Medicine,* 330, 681–690.

Carr, G. D., & White, N. (1984). The relationship between stereotype and memory improvement produced by amphetamine. *Psychopharmacology, 82,* 203–209.

Carr, G. D., & White, N. (1986). Anatomical dissociation of amphetamine's rewarding and aversive effects: An intracranial microinjection study. *Psychopharmacology, 39,* 340–346.

Carroll, C. R. (1989). *Drugs in modern society* (2nd ed.). Dubuque, IA: Wm. C. Brown.

Cartwright, R. D. (1978). Happy endings for our dreams. *Psychology Today, 12,* 66–76.

Cattell, R. B., Kawash, G. F., & De Young, G. E. (1972). Validation of objective measures of ergic tension: Response of the sex urge to visual stimulation. *Journal of Experimental Research in Personality, 6,* 76–83.

Caviness, V. S., Jr., & Sidman, R. L. (1973). Time of origin of corresponding cell classes in the cerebral cortex of normal and reeler mutant mice: An autoradiographic analysis. *Journal of Comparative Neurology 148,* 141–152.

Chang, V. C., Mark, G. P., Hernandez, L., & Hoebel, B. G. (1988). Extracellular dopamine increases in the nucleus accumbens following rehydration or sodium repletion. *Society for Neuroscience Abstracts, 14,* 527.

Chase, T. N., Wexler, N. S., & Barbeau, A. (1979). *Advances in neurology: Vol. 23. Huntington's disease.* New York: Raven.

Chen, G., Li, S., & Jiang, C. (1986). Clinical studies on neurophysiological and biochemical basis of acupuncture analgesia. *American Journal of Chinese Medicine, 14,* 86–95.

Chen, J., Paredes, W., & Gardner, E. L. (1994). *Delta⁹-Tetrahydrocannabinol's enhancement of nucleus accumbens dopamine resembles that of reuptake blockers rather than releasers—Evidence from in vivo microdialysis experiments with 3-methoxytyramine.* Paper presented at the annual meeting of College Problems in Drug Dependence, Palm Beach, FL.

Cheney, P. D. (1985). Role of cerebral cortex in voluntary movements. A review. *Physical Therapy, 65,* 624–635.

Chiarello, C. (1980). A house divided? Cognitive functioning with callosal agenesis. *Brain and Language, 11,* 128–158.

Chomsky, N. (1965). *Aspects of the theory of syntax.* Cambridge, MA: M.I.T. Press.

Chomsky, N. (1968). *Language and mind.* New York: Harcourt Brace Jovanovich.

Chomsky, N. (1975). *Reflections on language.* New York: Pantheon.

Chomsky, N. (1987). Language in a psychological setting. *Sophia Linguistic Working Papers in Linguistics, No. 22,* (pp. 322–323). Sophia University, Tokyo.

Chorover, S. L., & Schiller, P. H. (1965). Short-term retrograde amnesia in rats. *Journal of Comparative and Physiological Psychology, 59,* 73–78.

Christensen, N.J., Vestergaard, P., Sorensen, T., & Rafaelsen, O.J. (1980). Cerebrospinal fluid adrenaline and noradrenaline in depressedfluid adrenaline and noradrenaline in depressed patients. patients. *Acta Psychiatrica Scandinavica, 61,* 178–182.

Church, W. H., Justice, J. B., Jr., & Byrd, L. D. (1987). Extracellular dopamine in rat striatum following uptake inhibition by cocaine, nomifensine and benztropine. *European Journal of Pharmacology, 139,* 345–348.

Chusid, J. G. (1985). *Correlative neuroanatomy and functional neurology* (19th ed.). Los Alto, CA: Lange Medical Publications.

Chwalisz, K., Diener, E., & Gallagher, D. (1988). Autonomic arousal feedback and emotional experience: Evidence from spinal cord injury. *Journal of Personality and Social Psychology, 54,* 820–828.

Citron, M., Westaway, D., Xia, W., Carlson, G., Diehl, T., Levesque, G., Johnson-Wood, K., Lee, M., Seubert, P., Davis, A., Kholodenko, D., Motter, R., Sherrington, R., Perry, B., Yao, H., Strome, R., Lieberburg, I., Rommens, J., Kim, S., Schenk, D., Fraser, P., St. George Hyslop, P., & Selkoe, D. J. (1997). Mutant presenilins of Alzheimer's disease increase production of 42-residue amyloid beta-protein in both transfected cells and transgenic mice. *Nature Medicine, 3,* 67–72.

Claes, S., VanZand, K., Legius, E., Dom, R., Malfroid, M., Baro, F., Godderis, J., & Cassiman, J. J. (1995). Correlations between triplet repeat expansion and clinical features in Huntington's disease. *Archives of Neurology, 52,* 749–753.

Clarke, D. J. et al. (1988). Human fetal dopamine neurons grafted in a rat model of Parkinson's disease: Ultrastructural evidence for synapse formation using tyrosine hydroxylase immunocytochemistry. *Experimental Brain Research, 73,* 115–126.

Clarke, P. B. S., Hommer, D. W., Pert, A., & Skirboll, L. R. (1985). Electrophysiological actions of nicotine on substantia nigra single units. *British Journal of Pharmacology, 85,* 827–835.

Clemens, L. G., Wallen, K., & Gorski, R. (1967). Mating behavior: Facilitation in the female rat after cortical application of potassium chloride. *Science, 157,* 1208–1209.

Clower, R., Alvarez-Royo, P., Zola-Morgan, P., & Squire, L. R. (1991). Recognition memory impairment in monkeys with selective hippocampal lesions. *Society for Neuroscience Abstracts, 17,* 338.

Coccaro, E. F., Silverman, J. M., Klar, H. M., Horvath, T. B., & Siever, L. J. (1994). Familial correlates of reduced central serotonergic system function in patients with personality disorders. *Archives of General Psychiatry, 51,* 318–324.

Code, C., & Rowley, D. (1987). Age and aphasia type: The interaction of sex, time since onset and handedness. *Aphasiology, 1,* 339–346.

Cohen, B. M. (1981). Dopamine receptors and antipsychotic drugs. *McLean Hospital Journal, 1,* 95–115.

Cohen, J. D., & Servan-Schreiber, D. (1992). Context, cortex, and dopamine: A connectionist approach to behavior and biology in schizophrenia. *Psychological Review, 99,* 45–77.

Cohen, S. (1960). Purification of a nerve-growth promoting protein from the mouth salivary gland and its neurocytotoxic antiserum. *Proceedings of the National Academy of Science, 46,* 302–311.

Cohen, S. (1985). *Substance abuse problems.* New York: Haworth Press.

Cohen, S., Tyrell, D., & Smith, A. (1991). Psychological stress and susceptibility to the common cold. *The New England Journal of Medicine, 235,* 606–612.

Colangelo, W., & Jones, D. G. (1982). The fetal alcohol syndrome: A review and assessment of the syndrome and its neurological sequelae. *Progress in Neurobiology, 19,* 271–314.

Cole, M. (1985). Sex therapy—A critical appraisal. *British Journal of Psychiatry, 147,* 337–351.

Coleman, R. M. (1986). *Wide awake at 3:00 A.M.: By choice or by chance?* New York: Freeman.

Conrad, A. J., Abebe, T., Austin, R., Forsythe, S., & Scheibel, A. B. (1991). Hippocampal pyramidal cell disarray in schizophrenia as a bilateral phenomenon. *Archives of General Psychiatry, 48,* 413–417.

Coons, E. E., & Cruce, J. A. F. (1968). Lateral hypothalamus: Food and current intensity in maintaining self-stimulation of hunger. *Science, 159,* 1117–1119.

Cooper, T., Detrie, T., & Weiss, S. M. (1981). Coronary prone behavior and coronary heart disease: A critical review. *Circulation, 63,* 1199–1215.

Corder, E. H., Saunders, A. M., Strittmatter, W. J., Schmechel, D. E., Gaskell, P. C., Small, G. W., Roses, A. D., Haines, J. L., & Pericak-Vance, M. A. (1993). Gene dose of apolipoprotein E type 4 allele and the risk of Alzheimer's disease in late onset families. *Science, 261,* 921–923.

Corkin, S., Amaral, D. G., Gonzalez, R. G., Johnson, K. A., & Hyman, B. T. (1997). H. M.'s medial temporal lobe lesion: Findings from magnetic resonance imaging. *Journal of Neuroscience, 17,* 3964–3979.

Corkin, S., Sullivan, E. V., Twitchell, T. E., & Grove, E. (1981). The amnesic patient H. M.: Clinical observations and test performance 28 years after operation. *Society for Neuroscience Abstracts, 7,* 235.

Corso, J. F. (1973). Hearing. In B. B. Wolman (Ed.), *Handbook of general psychology* (pp. 348–381). Englewood Cliffs, NJ: Prentice-Hall.

Corwin, J. T., & Warchol, M. E. (1991). Auditory hair cells: Structure, function, development, and regeneration. *Annual Review of Neuroscience, 14,* 301–333.

Cosgrove, G. R., & Eskander, M. D. (1998). Thalamotomy and pallidotomy. Available at: http://neurosurgery.mgh.harvard.edu/pallidt.htm.

Costello, J. (1977). Programmed instruction. *Journal of Speech and Hearing Disorders, 42,* 3–28.

Cotman, C. W., & Nieto-Sampedro, M. (1984). Cell biology of synaptic plasticity. *Science, 225,* 1287–1294.

Coulombe, D., & White, N. (1982). The effect of post training hypothalamic self-stimulation on sensory preconditioning in rats. *Canadian Journal of Psychology, 36,* 57–66.

Courtney, S., Ungerleider, L., Keil, K., & Haxby, J. (1996). Object and spatial visual working memory activate separate neural systems in human cortex. *Cerebral Cortex, 6,* 39–49.

Coyle, J. T., Price, D. L., & DeLong, M. R. (1983). Alzheimer's disease: A disorder of cortical cholinergic innervation. *Science, 219,* 1184–1190.

Craik, F. I. M., & Lockhart, R. S. (1972). Levels of processing: A framework for memory research. *Journal of Verbal Learning and Behavior, 11,* 671–684.

Crawley, J. N., & Kiss, J. Z. (1985). Paraventricular nucleus lesions abolish the inhibtion if feeding induced by systemic cholecystokinin. *Peptides, 6,* 927–935.

Creese, I., Burt, D. R., & Snyder, S. H. (1976). Dopamine receptor binding predicts clinical and pharmacological potencies of antischizophrenic drugs. *Science, 192,* 481–483.

Crider, R. (1986). *Phencyclidine: Changing abuse patterns, Phencyclidine: An update,* Ed. Doris Clouet (National Institute on Drug Abuse Monograph 64, pp. 163–173). Washington, DC: U.S. Government Printing Office.

Cronholm, B., & Molander, L. (1958). Influence of an interpolated ECS on retention of memory material. *University of Stockholm Psychological Laboratory Reports,* 61.

Cross, A. J., Crow, T. J., & Owen, F. (1981). 3H-Flupenthixol binding in post-mortem brains of schizophrenics: Evidence for a selective increase in dopamine D_2 receptors. *Psychopharmacology, 74,* 122–124.

Crowe, M. J., Gillan, D., & Golombook, S. (1981). Form and content in the conjoint treatment of sexual dysfunction: A controlled study. *Behavior Research and Therapy, 19,* 47–54.

Culbertson, F. M. (1997). Depression and gender: An information review. *American Psychologist, 52,* 25–31.

Cummings, J. L., & Benson, D. (1983). *Dementia: A clinical approach.* Boston: Butterworths.

Cutler, N. R., & Cohen, H. B. (1979). The effect of one night's sleep loss on mood and memory in normal subjects. *Comprehensive Psychiatry, 20,* 61–66.

Czeisler, C. A., Moore-Ede, M.C., & Coleman, R. M. (1982). Rotating shift work schedules that disrupt sleep are improved by applying circadian principles. *Science, 217,* 460–463.

Dabbs, J. M., Jr., Carr, T. S., Frady, R. L., & Riad, J. K. (1995). Testosterone, crime, and misbehavior among 692 male prison inmates. *Personality and Individual Differences, 18,* 627–633.

Dabbs, J. M., & Morris, R. (1990). Testosterone, social class, and antisocial behavior in a sample of 4,462 men. *Psychological Science, 1,* 209–211.

Dale, N., Schacher, S., & Kandel, E. R. (1988). Long-term facilitation in aplysia involves increase in transmitter release. *Science, 239,* 282–285.

Dalhouse, A. D., Langford, H. G., Walsh, D., & Barnes, T. (1986). Angiotensin and salt appetite: Physiological amounts of angiotensin given peripherally increase salt appetite in the rat. *Behavioral Neuroscience, 100,* 597–602.

Dalton, K. (1961). Menstruation and crime. *British Medical Journal, 3,* 1752–1753.

Dalton, K. (1964). *The premenstrual syndrome.* Springfield, IL: Thomas.

Damasio, A. R. (1990). Category-related recognition defects as a clue to the neural substrates of knowledge. *Trends in Neurosciences, 13,* 95–98.

Damasio, A. R., & Damasio, H. (1992). Brain and language. *Scientific American, 267,* 88–95.

Damasio, A. R., Van Hoesen, G. W., & Hyman, B. T. (1990). Reflections on the selectivity of neuropathological changes in Alzheimer's disease. In M. F. Schwartz (Ed.), *Modular deficits in Alzheimer-type dementia* (pp. 83–100). Cambridge, MA: Bradford/MIT Press.

Damasio, H. (1981). Cerebral localization of the aphasias. In M. T. Sarno (Ed.), *Acquired aphasia.* New York: Academic Press.

Damasio, H. (1995). *Human brain anatomy in computerized images.* New York: Oxford University Press.

Dana, C. L. (1921). The anatomic seat of the emotions: A discussion of the James-Lange theory. *Archives of Neurological Psychiatry (Chicago), 6,* 634–639.

Darley, F. L. (1982). *Aphasia.* Philadelphia: Saunders.

Davidson, J. M. (1966). Characteristics of sex behavior in male rats following castration. *Animal Behavior, 14,* 266–272.

Davidson, J. M. (1980). Hormones and sexual behavior in the male. In D. T. Krieger & J. C. Hughes. *Neuroendocrinology.* Sunderland, MA: Sinauer Associates.

Davidson, R. J. (1992). Emotion and affective style: Hemispheric substrates. *Psychological Science, 3,* 39–43.

Davis, G. A. (1993). *A survey of adult aphasia and related language disorders* (2nd ed). Englewood Cliffs, NJ: Prentice-Hall.

Davis, J. M., Klerman, G., & Schildkraut, J. (1967). Drugs used in the treatment of depression. In L. Efron, J. O. Cole, D. Levine, & J. R. Wittenborn, *Psychopharmacology, A review of progress.* Washington, DC: U.S. Clearinghouse of Mental Health Information.

Davis, K. L., Hollister, L. E., Overall, J., Johnson, A., & Train, K. (1976). Physostigmine: Effects on cognition and affect in normal subjects. *Psychopharmacology (Berlin), 51,* 23–27.

Davis, S., Butcher, S. P., & Morris, R. G. M. (1992). The NMDA receptor antagonist D-2-amino-5-phosphopentanoate (D-AP5) impairs spatial learning and LTP *in vivo* at intracerebral concentrations comparable to those that block LTP *in vitro. Journal of Neuroscience, 12,* 21–34.

Daw, N. W. (1968). Colour-coded ganglion cells in the goldfish retina: Extension of their receptive fields by means of new stimuli. *Journal of Physiology (London), 197,* 567–592.

Deacon, T. W. (1996). *The making of language.* Edinburgh: Edinburgh University Press.

Deacon, T., Schumacher, J., Dinsmore, J., Thomas, C., Palmer, P., Kott, S., Edge, A., Penney, D., Kassissieh, S., Dempsey, P., & Isacson, O. (1997). Histological evidence of fetal pig neural cell survival after transplantation into a patient with Parkinson's disease. *Nature Medicine, 3,* 350–353.

DeAngelis, T. (1997, January). Chromosomes contain clues on schizophrenia. *APA Monitor,* p. 26.

Dejerine, J. (1891). Sur un cas de cecite verbale avec agraphia, suivi d'autopsie. *Comptes Rendus des Seances de la Societe de Biologie et de Ses Filiales, 3,* 197–201.

Delay, J., & Deniker, P. (1952). Le traitement des psychoses par une methode neurolytique derivee d'hibernotheraphie; le 4560 RP utilisee seul un cure prolongee et continuee. *Comptes Rendus Congres des Medecins Alienistes et Neurologistes de France et des Pays de Langue Francaise, 50,* 497–502.

DeLong, M., & Strick, P. L. (1974). Motor functions of the basal ganglia: Single unit activity during movement. In F. O. Schmidt & F. G. Worden (Eds.), *The neurosciences: The third study program* (pp. 319–326). Cambridge, MA: MIT Press.

Demarest, M. (1981, July 6). Cocaine: Middle-class high. *Time, 118,* 56.

Demb, J. B., Boynton, G. M., & Heeger, D. J. (1998). Functional magnetic resonance imaging of early visual pathways in dyslexia. *Journal of Neuroscience, 18,* 6939–6951.

Dembroski, T. M., MacDougall, J. M., & Shields, J. L. (1977). Physiologic reactions to social challenge in persons evidencing the Type A coronary-prone behavior pattern. *Journal of Human Stress, 3,* 2–10.

Dembroski, T. M., MacDougall, J. M., Williams, R. B., Haney, T. L., & Blumenthal, J. A. (1985). Components of Type A, hostility, and anger-in: Relationship to angiographic findings. *Psychosomatic Medicine, 47,* 219–233.

Dement, W. C. (1969). The biological role of REM sleep. In A. Kales (Ed.), *Sleep physiology and pathology.* Philadelphia: Lippincott.

Dement, W. C. (1974). *Some must watch while some must sleep.* New York: W. H. Freeman.

Dement, W. C. (1986). Normal sleep, disturbed sleep, transient and persistent insomnia. *Acta Psychiatrica Scandinavica Supplement, 74,* 41–46.

Dement, W. C., & Kleitman, N. (1957). Cyclic variations in EEG during sleep and their relation to eye movements, body motility, and dreaming. *Electroencephalography and Clinical Neurophysiology, 9,* 673–690.

Depue, R. A., & Evans, R. (1976). *The psychobiology of the depressive disorders: Implications for the effects of stress.* New York: Academic Press. (Original work published 1662)

Descartes, R. (1650). *Les passions de l'ame,* Amersterdam.

Descartes, R. (1956). *Discourse on method* (L. J. Lafleur, Trans.). Indianapolis: Bobbs-Merrill. (Original work published 1637)

Descartes, R. (1972). *Treatise of man* (T. S. Hall, Trans.). Cambridge, MA: Harvard University Press. (Original work published in 1662)

DeSimone, J. A., Heck, G. L., & Bartoshuk, L. M. (1980). Surface active taste modifiers: A comparison of the physical and psychophysical properties of gymnemic acid and sodium lauryl sulfate. *Chemical Senses, 5,* 317–330.

Detera-Wadleigh, S. D., Berrettini, W. H., Goldin, L. R., Boorman, D., Anderson, S., & Gershon, E. S. (1987). Close linkage of c-Harvey-ras-1 and the insulin gene to affective disorder is ruled out in three North American pedigrees. *Nature, 325,* 808–809.

Deuster, P. A., Adera, T., & South-Paul, J. (1999). Biological, social, and behavioral factors associated with premenstrual syndrome. *Archives of Family Medicine, 8,* 122–128.

Deutsch, J. A. (1983). The cholinergic synapse and the site of memory. In J. A. Deutsch (Ed.), *The physiological basis of memory.* New York: Academic Press.

Deutsch, J. A., & Gonzalez, M. F. (1980). Gastric nutrition content signals satiety. *Behavioral and Neural Biology, 30,* 113–116.

Deutsch, J. A., & Hardy, W. T. (1977). Cholecystokinin produces bait shyness in rats. *Nature, 266,* 196.

De Valois, R. L., Albrecht, D. G., & Thorell, L. G. (1982). Spatial frequency selectivity of cells in macaque visual cortex. *Vision Research, 22,* 545–559.

De Valois, R. L., & De Valois, K. K. (1975). Neural coding of color. In E. C. Carterette & M. P. Friedman (Eds.), *Handbook of perception: Seeing* (Vol. 5, pp. 117–166). Orlando, FL: Academic Press.

De Valois, R. L., & De Valois, K. K. (1988). *Spatial vision.* New York: Oxford University Press.

De Wied, D., Sarantakis, D., & Weinstein, B. (1973). Behavioral evaluation of peptides related to scotophobin. *Neuropharmacology, 12,* 1109–1115.

DeYoe, E. A., & Van Essen, D. C. (1988). Concurrent processing streams in monkey visual cortex. *Trends in Neuroscience, 11,* 219–226.

Dichgans, J. (1984). Clinical symptoms of cerebellar dysfunction and their topodiagnostic significance. *Human Neurobiology, 2,* 269–279.

DiChiara, G., Acquas, E., & Tanda, G. (1996). Ethanol as

a neurochemical surrogate of conventional reinforcers: The dopamine-opiod link. *Alcohol, 13,* 13–17.

Dickinson, A. (1989). Expectancy theory in animal conditioning. In S. B. Klein & R. R. Mowrer (Eds.), *Contemporary learning theories: Pavlovian conditioning and the states of traditional learning theory* (pp. 279–308). Hillsdale, NJ: Erlbaum.

DiLalla, D. L., Carey, G., Gottesman, I. I., & Bouchard, T. J., Jr. (1996). Heritability of MMPI personality indicators of psychopathology in twins reared apart. *Journal of Abnormal Psychology, 105,* 491–499.

DiMarzo, V., Fontana, A., Cadas, H., Schinelli, S., Cimino, G., Schwartz, J. C., & Piomelli, D. (1994). Formation and inactivation of endogenous cannabinoid anandamide in central neurons. *Nature, 372,* 686–691.

Dimsdale, J. E. (1988). A perspective on Type A behavior and coronary disease. *New England Journal of Medicine, 318,* 110–112.

Dodd, D. H., & White, R. M. (1980). *Cognition: Mental structures and processes.* Boston: Allyn & Bacon.

Domhoff, G. W. (1996). *Finding meaning in dreams: A quantitative approach.* New York: Plenum Press.

Domjan, M. (1976). Determinants of the enhancement of flavored water intake by prior exposure. *Journal of Experimental Psychology: Animal Behavior Processes, 2,* 17–27.

Domjan, M. (1994). Formulation of a behavior system for sexual conditioning. *Psychonomic Bulletin and Review, 1,* 421–428.

Domjan, M., Lyons, R., North, N. C., & Bruell, J. (1986). Sexual Pavlovian conditioned approach behavior in male Japanese quail (*Coturnix coturnix japonica*). *Journal of Comparative Psychology, 100,* 413–421.

Doty, R. (1967). Neural organization of deglutition. In C. F. Code (Ed.), *Handbook of physiology* (Sec. 6, Vol. 4). Washington, DC: American Physiological Society.

Dourish, C. T., Rycroft, W., & Iversen, S. D. (1989). Postponement of satiety by blockade of brain cholecystokinin (CCK-8) receptors. *Science, 245,* 1509–1511.

Drachman, D. B., Adams, R. N., & Josifer, L. F. (1982). Functional activities of autoantibodies to acetylcholine receptors and the clinical severity of myasthenia gravis. *New England Journal of Medicine, 307,* 769–775.

Dray, A. (1980). The physiology and pharmacology of mammalian basal ganglia. *Neurobiology, 14,* 221–335.

Dronkers, N. F., Redfern, B., & Shapiro, J. K. (1993). Neuroanatomic correlates of production deficits in severe Broca's aphasia. *Journal of Clinical and Experimental Neuropsychology, 15,* 59–60.

Duncan, C. P. (1949). The retroactive effect of electroshock on learning. *Journal of Comparative and Physiological Psychology, 42,* 32–44.

Dunn, A. J. (1980). Neurochemistry of learning and memory: An evaluation of recent data. *Annual Review of Psychology, 31,* 343–390.

Dunner, D. L., Stallone, F., & Fieve, R. F. (1976). Lithium carbonate and affective disorders: A double-blind study of prophylaxis of depression in bipolar illness. *Archives of General Psychiatry, 33,* 117–120.

Dunnett, S. B., & Bjorklund, A. (1987). Mechanisms of function of neural grafts in the adult mammalian brain. Journal of *Experimental Biology, 132,* 265–289.

Dutton, D. G., & Aron, A. P. (1974). Some evidence for heightened sexual attraction under conditions of high anxiety. *Journal of Personality and Social Psychology, 30,* 510–517.

Dykens, E. M., Hodapp, R. M., & Leckman, J. F. (1994). *Behavior and development in fragile X syndrome.* Thousand Oaks, CA: Sage.

Dykes, R. W. (1983). Parallel processing of somatosensory information: A theory. *Brain Research Reviews, 6,* 47–115.

Eagles, J. M. (1991). Is schizophrenia disappearing? *British Journal of Psychiatry, 158,* 834–835.

Eagly, A. H. (1987). *Sex differences and social behavior: A social-role interpretation.* Hillsdale, NJ: Erlbaum.

Eckert, E. D., Bouchard, T. J., Bohlen, J., & Heston, L. L. (1986). Homosexuality in monozygotic twins reared apart. *British Journal of Psychiatry, 148,* 421–425.

Edmonds, B., Klein, M., Dale, N., & Kandel, E. R. (1990). Contribution of two types of calcium channels to synaptic transmission and plasticity. *Science, 250,* 1142–1147.

Edwards, J. S., & Palka, J. (1971). Neural regeneration: Delayed formation of central contacts by insect sensory cells. *Science, 172,* 591–594.

Egeland, J. A., Gerhard, D. S., Pauls, D. L., Sussex, J. N., Kidd, K. K., Allen, C. R., Hostetter, A. M., & Housman, D. E. (1987). Bipolar affective disorders linked to DNA markers on chromosome 11. *Nature, 325,* 783–787.

Ekman, P. (1984). Expression and the nature of emotion. In K. Scherer & P. Ekman (Eds.), *Approaches to emotion.* Hillsdale, NJ: Erlbaum.

Ekman, P., Levenson, R. W., & Friesen, W. V. (1983). Autonomic nervous system activity distinguishes among emotions. *Science, 221,* 1208–1210.

Eliot, L. S., Blumenfeld, H., Edmonds, B. W., Kandel, E. R., & Siegelbaum, S. A. (1991). Imaging [Ca] transients at Aplysia sensorimotor synapses: Contribution of direct and indirect modulation to presynaptic facilitation. *Society of Neuroscience Abstracts, 17,* 1485.

Eliot, L. S., Dudai, Y., Kandel, E. R., & Abrams, T. W. (1989). Ca^{2+} calmodulin sensitivity may be common to all forms of neural adenylate cyclase. *Proceedings of the National Academy of Sciences U.S.A., 86,* 9564–9568.

Eliot, L. S., Schachter, S., Kandel, E. R., & Hawkins, R. D. (1989). Pairing-specific, activity-dependent facilitation of *Aplysia* sensory-motor neuron synapses in isolated culture. *Society of Neuroscience Abstracts, 15,* 482.

Eliot, R. S. (1979). *Stress and the major cardiovascular disorders.* Mount Kisco, NY: Futura.

El-Wakil, F. W. (1975). Unpublished master's thesis, University of Massachusetts, Amherst.

Engel, J., Jr. (1992). Recent advances in surgical treatment of temporal lobe epilepsy. *Acta Neurologica Scandinavica (Supplementum), 140,* 71–80.

Engen, T. (1982). *The perception of odors.* New York: Academic Press.

Enna, S. J., & Gallagher, J. P. (1983). Biochemical and electrophysiological characteristics of mammalian GABA receptors. *International Review of Neurobiology, 24,* 181–212.

Epstein, A. N., Fitzsimmons, J. T., & Rolls, B. J. (1970). Drinking induced by injection of angiotensin into the brain of the rat. *Journal of Physiology, 210,* 457–474.

Epstein, L. H., Valoski, A. M., Vara, L. S., McCurley, J., Wisniewski, L., Kalarchian, M. A., Klein, K. R., & Shrager, L. R. (1995). Effects of decreasing sedentary behavior and increasing activity on weight change in obese children. *Health Psychology, 14,* 109–115.

Ervin, F. R., Mark, V. H., & Stevens, J. R. (1969). Behavioral and affective responses to brain stimulation in man. In J. Zubin & C. Shagass (Eds.), *Neurological aspects of psychopathology.* New York: Grune & Stratton.

Eslinger, P. J., & Grattan, L. M. (1993). Frontal lobe and frontal-striatal substrates for different forms of human cognitive flexibility. *Neuropsycholgia, 31,* 17–28.

Ettenberg, A., Pettit, H. O., Bloom, F. E., & Koob, G. F. (1982). Heroin and cocaine intravenous self-administration in rats: Mediation by separate neural systems. *Psychopharmacology, 78,* 204–209.

Evans, K. R., & Vaccarino, F. J. (1989). Effects of microinjections of amphetamine and morphine into the caudate and nucleus accumbens on feeding: Interactions with sweetness. Cited in S. B. Klein & R. R. Mowrer (Eds.), *Contemporary learning theories: Instrumental conditioning and the impact of biological constraints on learning* (pp. 111–142). Hillsdale, NJ: Erlbaum.

Faraday, A. (1974). *The dream game.* New York: Harper & Row.

Farbman, A. I. (1994). The cellular basis of olfaction. *Endeavour, 18,* 2–8.

Farde, L., Nordstrom, A. C., Wiesel, F. A., Paccli, S., Halldin, C., & Sedvall, G. (1992). Positron emission tomographic analysis of central D_1 and D_2 dopamine receptor occupancy in patients treated with classical neuroleptics and clozapine. Relation to extrapyramidal side effects. *Archives of General Psychiatry, 49,* 538–544.

Farmer, A. E., McGuffin, P., & Gottesman, I. I. (1987). Twin concordance for DSM-III schizophrenia. Scrutinizing the validity of the definition. *Archives of General Psychiatry, 44,* 634–641.

Feeney, D. M. (1987). Human rights and animal welfare. *American Psychologist, 42,* 593–599.

Feighner, J. P., Gardner, E. A., Johnston, J. A., Batey, S. R., Khayrallah, M. A., Ascher, J. A., & Lineberry, C. G. (1991). Double-blind comparison of bupropion and fluoxetine in depressed outpatients. *Journal of Clinical Psychiatry, 52,* 329–335.

Fernandez, E., & Turk, D. C. (1992). Sensory and affective components of pain: Separation and synthesis. *Psychological Bulletin, 112,* 205–217.

Fin, C., da Cunha, C., Bromberg, E., Schmitz, P. K., Bianchin, M., Medina, J. H., & Izquierdo, I. (1995). Experiments suggesting a role for nitric oxide in the hippocampus in memory processes. *Neurobiology of Learning and Memory, 63,* 113–115.

Fitzsimmons, J. T., & Le Magnen, J. (1969). Eating as a regulatory control of drinking in the rat. *Journal of Comparative and Physiological Psychology, 67,* 273–283.

Flesher, D. (1941). L'amnesia refrogada dropo l'eltroshiek: Contributo allo studio della patogenesi della amnesia in genere. *Schweiz Archives Neurologia Psychiatry, 48,* 1–28.

Flexner, L. B., & Flexner, J. B. (1968). Intracerebral saline: Effect on memory of trained mice treated with puromycin. *Science, 159,* 330–331.

Flood, J. F., Bennett, E. L., Orme, A. E., & Rosenzweig, M. R. (1975). Relation of memory formation to controlled amounts of brain protein synthesis. *Physiology and Behavior, 15,* 97–102.

Flood, J. F., Bennett, E. L., Rosenzweig, M. R., & Orme, A. E. (1973). The influence of duration of protein synthesis inhibition on memory. *Physiology and Behavior, 15,* 97–102.

Flourens, P. J. M. (1965). Pierre Jean Marie Flourens on the functions of the brain (M. D. Boring, Trans.). In R. J. Herrnstein & E. G. Boring (Eds.), *A source book in the history of psychology.* Cambridge, MA: Harvard University Press. (Original work published 1824)

Flynn, J. P. (1972). Patterning mechanisms, patterning reflexes, and attack behavior in cats. In J. K. Cole & D. D. Jensen (Eds), *Nebraska symposium of motivation.* Lincoln: University of Nebraska Press.

Fonberg, E. (1965). Effect of partial destruction of the amygdaloid complex on the emotional-defensive behavior of dogs. *Bulletin de l'Academic Polanaise des Sciences. Cl. II., 13,* 429–431.

Fonberg, E. (1968). The role of the amygdaloid nucleus in animal behaviour. *Progress in Brain Research, 22,* 273–281.

Ford, C., & Beach, F. (1951). *Patterns of sexual behavior.* New York: Harper & Row.

Foster, R. G. (1992). Photoreceptors and circadian systems. *Current Directions in Psychological Science, 2,* 34–39.

Foulkes, D. (1985). *Dreaming: A cognitive-psychological analysis.* Hillsdale, NJ: Erlbaum.

Foutz, A. S., Mitler, M. N., Cavalli-Sforva, G. L., & Dement, W. C. (1979). Genetic factors in canine narcolepsy. *Sleep, 1,* 413–421.

Franzen, E. A., & Myers, R. E. (1973). Neural control of social behavior: Prefrontal and anterior temporal cortex. *Neuropsychologia, 11,* 141–157.

Frazer, A., & Winokur, A. (1977). Therapeutic and pharmacological aspects of psychotropic drugs. In A. Frazer & A. Winokur (Eds.), *Biological bases of psychiatric disorders.* New York: Spectrum.

Fredrickson, P. A. (1987). The relevance of sleep disorders medicine to psychiatric practice. *Psychiatric Annals, 17,* 91–100.

Freed, C. R., Breeze, R. E., Rosenberg, N. L., Schneck, S. A., Kriek, E., Qie, J., Lone, T., Zhang, Y., Snyder, J. A., Wells, T. H., Ramiq, L. O., Thompson, L., Mazziotta, J. C., Huang, S. C., Grafton, S. T., Brooks, D., Sawle, G., Schroten, G., & Ansari, A. A. (1992). Survival of implanted fetal dopamine cells and neurologic improvement 12 to 46 months after transplantation for Parkinson's disease. *New England Journal of Medicine, 327,* 1549–1555.

Freud, S. (1953). The interpretation of dreams. In J. Strachey (Ed.), *The standard edition of the complete psychological works of Sigmund Freud* (Vols. 4 and 5). London: Hogarth Press. (Original work published in 1900)

Frey, W. H., & Langseth, M. (1986). *Crying: The mystery of tears.* New York: Winston Press.

Friedman, M., Byers, S. O., Diamant, J., & Rosenman, R. H. (1975). Plasma catecholamine response of coronary-prone subjects (Type A) to a specific challenge. *Metabolism, 4,* 205–210.

Friedman, M., & Rosenman, R. H. (1974). *Type A behavior and your heart.* New York: Knopf.

Friedman, M. I., & Stricker, E. M. (1976). The physiological psychology of hunger: A physiological perceptive. *Psychological Review, 83,* 409–431.

Friedmann, J., Globus, G., Huntley, A., Mullaney, D., Naitoh, P., & Johnson, L. (1977). Performance and mood during and after gradual sleep reduction. *Psychophysiology, 14,* 245–250.

Fritsch, G., & Hitzig, E. (1960). On the electrical excitability of the cerebrum. In G. Von Bonin (Trans.), *Some papers on the cerebral cortex.* Springfield, IL: Charles C. Thomas. (Original work published 1870)

Frohman, L. A., Goldman, J. K., & Bernardis, L. L. (1972). Metabolism of intravenously injected 14C-glucose in weanling rats with hypothalamic obesity. *Metabolism, 21,* 799–805.

Fultan, J. F., & Jacobsen, C. F. (1935). The functions of the frontal lobes: A comparative study in monkeys, chimpanzees, and man. *Advances in Modern Biology, 4,* 113–123.

Gabrieli, J. D. E. (1998). Cognitive neuroscience of human memory. *Annual Review of Psychology, 49,* 87–115.

Gabrieli, J. D. E., Cohen, N. J., & Corkin, S. (1988). The impaired learning of semantic knowledge following bilateral medial temporal-lobe resection. *Brain and Cognition, 7,* 157–177.

Gackenbach, J., & Bosveld, J. (1989, October). Take control of your dreams. *Psychology Today,* 27–32.

Gackenbach, J., & LaBerge, S. (1988). *Conscious mind, sleeping brain: Perspectives on lucid dreaming.* New York: Plenum.

Gage, F. H., & Fisher, L. J. (1991). Intracerebral grafting: A tool for the neurobiologist. *Neuron, 6,* 1–12.

Galef, B. G. (1970). Target novelty elicits and directs shock-associated aggression in wild rats. *Journal of Comparative and Physiological Psychology, 71,* 87–91.

Galli-Resta, L., & Maffei, L. (1988). Spontaneous impulse activity of rat retinal ganglion cells in prenatal life. *Science, 242,* 90–91.

Gallistel, C. R., Shizgal, P., & Yeomans, J. (1981). A portrait of the substrate for self-stimulation. *Psychological Review, 88,* 228–273.

Galvani, L. (1791). De viribus electricitatis in motu muscalari commentarius. Translated by M. G. Foley as Luigi Galvani: Commentary on the effects of electricity on muscular motion. Norwalk, CT: Burndy Library, 1953.

Garb, J. J., & Stunkard, A. J. (1974). Taste aversions in man. *American Journal of Psychiatry, 131,* 1204–1207.

Garcia, J., Kimeldorf, D. J., & Hunt, E. L. (1957). The use of ionizing radiation as a motivating stimulus. *Psychological Review, 68,* 383–395.

Garcia, J., Kimeldorf, D. J., & Koelling, R. A. (1955). Conditioned aversion to saccharin resulting from exposure to gamma radiation. *Science, 122,* 157–158.

Gardiner, T. W., & Stricker, E. M. (1985). Impaired drinking responses of rats with lesions of nucleus medianus: Circadian dependence. *American Journal of Physiology, 248,* R224–R230.

Gardner, B. J., & Gardner, R. A. (1971). Two-way communication with an infant chimpanzee. In A. M. Schrier & F. Stolnitz (Eds.), *Behavior of nonhuman primates: Modern research trends* (pp. 117–184). New York: Academic.

Garfinkel, P. E., Kline, S. A., & Stancer, H. C. (1973). Treatment of anorexia nervosa using operant conditioning techniques. *Journal of Nervous and Mental Disease, 157,* 428–433.

Garritano, J., Martinez, C. , Grossman, K., Intemann, P., Merritt, K., Pfoff, R., & Smock, T. (1996). The output of the hippocampus is inhibited during sexual behavior in the male rat. *Experimental Brain Research, 111,* 35–40.

Garthwaite, J., Charles, S. L., & Chess-Williams, R. (1988). Endothelium-delivered relaxing factor release on activation of NMDA receptors suggests role as intercellular messenger in the brain. *Nature, 336,* 385–388.

Gazzaniga, M. S. (1967, August). The split brain in man. *Scientific American,* pp. 24–29.

Gazzaniga, M. S. (1977). Consistency and diversity in brain organization. *Annals of the New York Academy of Sciences, 30,* 415–423.

Gazzaniga, M. S. (1983). Right hemisphere language following brain bisection. *American Psychologist, 38,* 525–537.

Gazzaniga, M. S. (1985). *The social brain: Discovering the networks of the mind.* New York: Basic Books.

Gazzaniga, M. S. (1995). Consciousnesss and the cerebral hemispheres. In M. S. Gazzaniga (Ed.), *The cognitive neurosciences.* Cambridge, MA: MIT Press.

Gazzaniga, M. S., & LeDoux, J. E. (1978). *The integrated mind.* New York: Plenum.

Gazzaniga, M. S., LeDoux, J. E., & Wilson, D. H. (1977). Language, praxis, and the right hemisphere: Clues to some mechanisms of consciousness. *Neurology, 27,* 1144–1147.

Gazzaniga, M. S., & Sperry, R. W. (1967). Language after section of the cerebral hemispheres. *Brain, 90,* 131–148.

Geer, J. H., Morokigg, P., & Greenwood, P. (1974). Sexual arousal in women: The development of a measurement device for vaginal blood volume. *Archives of Sexual Behavior, 3,* 559–564.

Georgopoulous, A. P., Taira, M., & Lukashin, A. (1993). Cognitive neurophysiology of the motor cortex. *Science, 260,* 47–52.

Geracioti, T. D. Jr., & Liddle, R. A. (1988). Impaired cholecystokinin secretion in bulimia nervosa. *New England Journal of Medicine, 319,* 683–688.

Geraud, G., Arne-Bes, M. C., Guell, A., & Bes, A. (1987). Reversibility of hemodynamic hypofrontality in schizophrenia. *Journal of Cerebral Blood Flow Metabolism, 7,* 9–12.

Gerra, G., Marato, A., & Caccacari, R. (1995). Clonidine and opiate receptor antagonists in the treatment of heroin addiction. *Journal of Substance Abuse Treatment, 12,* 35–41.

Gershon, E. S., Bunney, W. E., Leckman, J. F., Van Eerdewegh, M., & DeBauche, B. (1976). The inheritance of affective disorders: A review of data and hypotheses. *Behavior Genetics, 6,* 227–261.

Geschwind, N. (1970). The organization of language and the brain. *Science, 170,* 940–944.

Geschwind, N. (1979). Specializations of the human brain. *Scientific American, 241,* 180–199.

Geschwind, N., & Galaburda, A. M. (1985). Cerebral lateralization: Biological mechanisms, associations, and pathology: I. A hypothesis and a program for research. *Archives of Neurology, 42,* 428–459.

Gessa, G. L., Muntoni, F., Collu, M., Vargiu, L., & Mereu, G. (1985). Low doses of ethanol activate dopaminergic neurons in the ventral tegmental area. *Brain Research, 348,* 201–204.

Ghez, C. (1985). Voluntary movement. In E. R. Kandel & J. H. Schwartz (Eds.), *Principles of neural science* (2nd ed. pp. 487–501). New York: Elsevier.

Ghez, C., & Fahn, S. (1985). The cerebellum. In E. R. Kandel & J. H. Schwartz (Eds.), *Principles of neural science* (2nd ed., pp. 502–522). New York: Elsevier.

Ghez, C., Hening, W., & Gorden, J. (1991). Organization of voluntary movement. *Current Opinions in Neurobiology, 1,* 664–671.

Gilbert, P. L., Harris, M. J., McAdams, L. A., & Jeste, D. V. (1995). Neuroleptic withdrawal in schizophrenic patients. *Archives of General Psychiatry, 52,* 173–188.

Giles, D. E., Biggs, M. M., Rush, A. J., & Roffwarg, H. P. (1988). Risk factors in families of unipolar depression. I. Psychiatric illness and reduced REM latency. *Journal of Affective Disorders, 14,* 51–59.

Giles, D. E., Roffwarg, H. P., & Rush, A. J. (1987). REM latency concordance in depressed family members. *Biological Psychiatry, 22,* 910–914.

Gillin, J. C., & Borbely, A. A. (1985). Sleep: A neurobiological window on affective disorders. *Trends in Neurosciences, 8,* 537–542.

Gillin, J., Sitaram, N., Janowsky, D., et al. (1985). Cholinergic mechanisms in REM sleep. In A. Wauquier, J. M. Monti, & M. Radulovacki (Eds.), *Sleep: Neurotransmitters and neuromodulators.* New York: Raven Press.

Givens, B. S., & Olton, D. S. (1990). Cholinergic and GABAergic modulation of medial septal area: Effect on working memory. *Behavioral Neuroscience, 104,* 849–855.

Gladfelter, W. E., & Brobeck, J. R. (1962). Decreased spontaneous locomotor activity in the rat inducted by hypothalamic lesions. *American Journal of Physiology, 203,* 811–817.

Gladue, B. A. (1994). The biopsychology of sexual orientation. *Current Directions in Psychological Science, 3,* 150–154.

Glanzman, D. L., Mackey, S. L., Hawkins, R. D., Dyke, A. M., Lloyd, P. E., & Kandel, E. R. (1989). Depletion of serotonin in the nervous system of *Aplysia* reduces the behavioral enhancement of gill withdrawal as well as the heterosynaptic facilitation produced by tail shock. *Journal of Neuroscience, 9,* 4200–4213.

Glass, D. C. (1977). *Behavior patterns, stress, and coronary disease.* Hillsdale, NJ: Erlbaum.

Gleason, K. K., & Reynierse, J. H. (1969). The behavioral significance of pheromones in vertebrates. *Psychological Bulletin, 71,* 58–73.

Gluck, M. A., & Myers, C. E. (1995). Representation and association in memory: A neurocomputational view of hippocampal function. *Current Direction in Psychological Science, 4,* 23–29.

Goate, A., Chartier-Harlin, M. C., Mullan, M., Brown, J., Crawford, F., Fidani, L., Giuffra, L., Haynes, A., Irving, N., James, L., Mant, R., Newton, P., Rooke, K., Roques, P., Talbot, C., Pericak-Vance, M., Roses, A., Williamson, R., Rossor, M., Owen, M., & Hardy, J. (1991). Segregation of a missense mutation in the amyloid precursor protein gene with familial Alzheimer's disease. *Nature, 349,* 704–706.

Goeders, N. E., Lane, J. D., & Smith, J. E. (1984). Self-administration of methionine enkephalin into the nucleus accumbens. *Pharmacology, Biochemistry, and Behavior, 20,* 451–455.

Goetzl, U., Green, R., Whybrow, P., & Jackson, R. (1974). X-linkage revisited. *Archives of General Psychiatry, 31,* 665–671.

Gold, P. W., Goodwin, F. K., & Chrousos, G. P. (1988). Clinical and biochemical manifestations of depression: Relation to the neurobiology of stress. *New England Journal of Medicine, 319,* 413–420.

Gold, P. W., Gwirtsman, H, Avgerinos, P. C., Nieman, L. K., Gallucci, W. T., Kaye, W., Jimerson, D., Ebert, M., Rittmaster, R., & Loriaux, D. L., et al. (1986). Abnormal hypothalamic-pituitary-adrenal function in anorexia nervosa. Pathophysiologic mechanisms in underweight and weight-corrected patients. *New England Journal of Medicine, 22,* 1335–1342.

Gold, R. M., Jones, A. P., Sawchenko, P. E., & Kapatos, G. (1977). Paraventricular area: Critical focus of a longitudinal neurocircuitry mediating food intake. *Physiology and Behavior, 18,* 1111–1119.

Goldman, C. K., Marino, L., & Leibowitz, S. F. (1985). Postsynaptic alpha 2-noradrenergic receptors mediate feeding induced by paraventricular nucleus injection of norepinephrine and clonidine. *European Journal of Pharmacology, 115,* 11–19.

Goldman, D. (1955). Treatment of psychotic states with chlorpromazine. *Journal of the American Medical Association, 157,* 1274–1278.

Goldman, M. S., & Kelly, P. J. (1992). Symptomatic and functional outcome of stereotactic ventralis lateralis thalamotomy for intention tremor. *Journal of Neurosurgery, 77,* 223–229.

Goldman-Rakic, P. S. (1991). Prefrontal cortical dysfunction in schizophrenia: The relevance of working memory. In B. Caroll (Ed.), *Psychopathology and the brain* (pp. 1–23). New York: Raven Press.

Goldstein, A. (1976). Opioid peptide (endorphins) in pituitary and brain. *Science, 193,* 1081–1086.

Goldstein, A. (1994). *Addiction: From biology to drug policy.* (pp. 179–189). New York: W. H. Freeman.

Goldstein, I., Lue, T. F., Padma-Nathan, H., Rosen, R. C., Steers, R. C., & Wicker, P. A. (1998). Oral sildenafil in the treatment of erectile dysfunction. Sildenafil Study Group. *New England Journal of Medicine, 338,* 1397–1404.

Goodglass, H., & Kaplan, E. (1979). Assessment of cognitive deficit in the brain-injured patient. In M. S. Gazzaniga (Ed.), *Handbook of behavioral neurology* (Vol. 2, pp. 3–22). New York: Plenum.

Goodwin, F. K., & Jamison, K. R. (1987). Bipolar disorders. In R. E. Hales & A. J. Frances (Eds.), *American Psychiatric Association annual review* (Vol. 6). Washington DC: American Psychiatric Association.

Goodman, I. J., & Brown, J. L. (1966). Stimulation of positively and negatively reinforcing sites in the avian brain. *Life Sciences, 5,* 693–704.

Gorski, R. A. (1985). The 13th J.A.F. Stevenson memorial lecture. Sexual differentiation of the brain: Possible mechanisms and implications. *Canadian Journal of Physiology and Pharmacology, 63,* 577–594.

Gorski, R. A., Gordon, J. H., Shryne, J. E., & Southam, A. M. (1978). Evidence for a morphological sex difference within the medial preoptic area of the rat brain. *Brain Research, 148,* 333–346.

Gottesmann, C. (1996). The transition from slow-wave sleep to paradoxical sleep: Evolving facts and concepts of the neurophysiological processes underlying the intermediate stage of sleep. *Neurosciences Biobehavioral Research, 20,* 367–387.

Gottesman, I. I. (1991). *Schizophrenia genesis.* New York: W. H. Freeman.

Gouras, P. (1968). Identification of cone mechanisms in monkey ganglion cells. *Journal of Physiology (London), 199,* 533–538.

Grady, K. L., Phoenix, C. H., & Young, W. C. (1965). Role of developing rat testis in differentiation of the neural tissues mediating mating behavior. *Journal of Comparative and Physiological Psychology, 59,* 176–182.

Gray, J. A. (1972). The psychophysiological nature of introversion-extroversion: A modification of Eysenek's theory. In V. D. Nebylitsyn & J. A. Gray (Eds.), *Biological basis of individual behavior.* New York: Academic Press.

Greenlee, M. W., Lang, H. J., Mergner, T., & Seeger, W. (1995). Visual short-term memory of stimulus velocity in patients with unilateral posterior brain damage. *Journal of Neuroscience, 15,* 2287–2300.

Greer, M. K., Lyons-Crews, M., Mauldin, L. B., & Brown, F. R. III (1989). A case study of the cognitive and behavioral deficits of temporal lobe damage in herpes simplex encephalitis. *Journal of Autism and Developmental Disorders, 19,* 317–326.

Griffitt, W., May, J., & Veitch, R. (1974). Sexual stimulation and interpersonal behavior: Heterosexual evaluative responses, visual behavior, and physical proximity. *Journal of Personality and Social Psychology, 30,* 367–377.

Groos, G., & Hendricks, J. (1982). Circadian rhythms in electrical discharge of rat suprachiasmatic neurons recorded *in vitro. Neuroscience Letters, 34,* 283–288.

Gross, C.G., & Sergent, J. (1992). Face recognition. *Current Opinions in Neurobiology, 2,* 156–61.

Grossman, S. P. (1972). The ventromedial hypothalamus and aggressive behaviors. *Physiology and Behavior, 9,* 721–725.

Grunt, J. A., & Young, W. C. (1952). Differential reactivity of individuals and the response of the male guinea pig to testosterone proprionate. *Endocrinology, 51,* 237–248.

Gubbay, J., Collignon, J., Koopman, P., Capel, B., Economou, A., Munsterberg, A., Vivian, N., Goodfellow, P., & Lovell-Badge, R. (1990). A gene mapping to the sex-determining region of the mouse Y chromosome is a member of a novel family of embryonically expressed genes. *Nature, 346,* 245–250.

Guerin, G. F., Goeders, N. E., Dworkin, S. I., & Smith, J. E. (1984). Intracranial self-administration of dopamine into the nucleus accumbens. *Society for Neuroscience Abstracts, 10,* 1072.

Guidotti, A., Ferrero, P., Fujimoto, M., Santi, R. M., & Costa, E. (1986). Studies on endogenous ligands (endocoids) for the benzodiazepine/beta carboline binding sites. *Advances in Biochemical Pharmacology, 41,* 137–148.

Guidotti, A., Forchetti, C. M., Corda, M. G., Konkel, D., Bennett, C. D., & Costa, E. (1983). Isolation, characterization, and purification to homogeneity of an endogenous polypeptide with agonistic action on benzodiazepine receptors. *Proceedings of the National Academy of Sciences, 80,* 3531–3535.

Gunston, G. D., Burkimsher, D., Malan, H., & Sive, A. A. (1992). Reversible cerebral shrinkage in kwashiorkor: An MRI study. *Archives Disabled Child, 67,* 1030–1072.

Gurevich, E. V., Bordelon, Y., Shapiro, R. M., Arnold, S. E., Gur, R. E., & Joyce, J. N. (1997). Mesolimbic dopamine D_3 receptors and use of antipsychotics in patients with schizophrenia. *Archives of General Psychiatry, 54,* 225–232.

Guthrie, J. P., Ash, R. A., & Bendapudi, V. (1995). Additional validity evidence for a measure of morningness. *Journal of Applied Psychology, 80,* 186–190.

Habib, M., Gayraud, D., Oliva, A., Regis, J., Salamon, G., & Khalil, R. (1991). Effects of handedness and sex on the morphology of the corpus callosum: A study with brain magnetic resonance imaging. *Brain and Cognition, 16,* 41–61.

Hafner, H. (1998). Neurodevelopmental disorder and psychosis: One disease or major risk factor? *Current Opinion in Psychiatry, 11,* 17–18.

Haft, J. I. (1974). Cardiovascular injury induced by sympathetic catecholamines. *Progress in Cardiovascular Diseases, 17,* 73–86.

Hall, Z. (1992). *An introduction to molecular neurobiology.* Sanderland, MA: Sinauer Associates.

Hamburg, D. A., Moos, R. H., & Yalom, I. D. (1968). Studies of distress in the menstrual cycle and postpartum period. In R. P. Michael (Ed.), *Endocrinology and human behavior.* London: Oxford University Press.

Hamburger, V. (1958). Regression versus peripheral control of differentiation in motor hypoplasia. *American Journal of Anatomy, 102,* 365–410.

Hamburger, V. (1975). Cell death in the development of the lateral motor column of the chick embryo. *Journal of Comparative Neurology, 160,* 535–546.

Han, P. W., & Liu, A. C. (1966). Obesity and impaired growth of rats force fed 40 days after hypothalamic lesions. *American Journal of Physiology, 211,* 229–231.

Harris, G. W., (1955). *Neural control of the pituitary gland.* London: Edward Arnold.

Harris, G. W. & Levine, S. (1965). Sexual differentiation of the brain and its experimental control. *Journal of Physiology, 181,* 379–400.

Hart, B. (1968). Role of prior experience on the effects of castration on sexual behavior of male dogs. *Journal of Comparative and Physiological Psychology, 66,* 719–725.

Hartmann, E. L. (1973). *The functions of sleep.* Westford, MA: Murray Printing Company.

Hartmann, E. L. , & Cravens, J. (1973). The effects of long-term administration of psychotrophic drugs on human sleep. IV. The effects of chlorpromazine. *Psychopharmacologia, 33,* 203–218.

Hartline, H. K. (1949). Inhibition of activity of visual receptors by illuminating nearby retinal areas in the *Limulus* eye. *Federation Proceedings, 8,* 69.

Hassler, R., & Riechert, T. (1954). Indikationen und Lokalisations methode der gezielten him operationen. *Nervenarzt, 25,* 441.

Hatten, M. E. (1990). Riding the glial monorail: A common mechanism for glial-guided neuronal migration in different regions of the developing mammalian brain. *Trends in Neuroscience, 13,* 179–184.

Hauri, P. (1979). What can insomniacs teach us about the functions of sleep? In R. Drucker-Colin, M. Shkurovich, & M. B. Sterman (Eds.), *The functions of sleep* (pp. 251–271). New York: Academic.

Hawke, C. C. (1950). Castration and sex crimes. *American Journal of Mental Deficiency, 55,* 220–226.

Hawkins, R. D., Carew, T. J., & Kandel, E. R. (1986). Effects of interstimulus interval and contingency on classical conditioning of the *Aplysia* siphon withdrawal reflex. *Journal of Neuroscience, 6,* 1695–1701.

Hawkins, R. D., Greene, W., & Kandel, E. R. (1998). Classical conditioning, differential conditioning, and second-order conditioning of the *Aplysia* gill-withdrawal reflex in a simplified mantle organ preparation. *Behavioral Neuroscience, 112,* 636–645.

Hawkins, R. D., Kandel, E. R., & Seigelbaum, S. A. (1993). Learning to modulate transmitter release: Themes and variations in synaptic plasticity. *Annual Review of Neuroscience, 16,* 625–665.

Hawkins, R. D., Lalevic, N., Clark, G. A., & Kandel, E. R. (1989). Classical conditioning of the Aplysia siphon-withdrawal reflex exhibits response specificity. *Proceedings of the National Academy of Sciences, USA, 86,* 7620–7624.

Hayes, K. J., & Hayes, C. (1951). The intellectual development of a home-raised chimpanzee. *Proceedings of the American Philosophical Society, 95,* 105–109.

Hays, P. (1976). Etiological factors in manic-depressive psychoses. *Archives of General Psychiatry, 33,* 1187–1188.

He, S., Cavanagh, P., & Intiligator, J. (1996). Attentional resolution and the locus of visual awareness. *Nature, 383,* 334–337.

Heath, R. G. (1964). Pleasure response of human subjects to direct stimulation of the brain: Physiologic and psychodynamic considerations. In R. G. Heath (Ed.), *The role of pleasure in behavior.* New York: Harper & Row.

Heatherton, T. F., & Baumeister, R. F. (1991). Binge eating as escape from self-awareness. *Psychological Bulletin, 110,* 86–108.

Hebb, D. O. (1949). *The organization of behavior.* New York: Colley.

Hebb, D. O. (1972). *Textbook of psychology* (3rd ed.). Philadelphia: Saunders.

Heeb, M. M., & Yahr, P. (1996). C-fos immunoreactivity in the sexually dimorphic area of the hypothalamus and related brain regions of male gerbils after exposure to sex-related stimuli or performance of specific sexual behaviors. *Neuroscience, 72,* 1049–1071.

Heffner, H. E., & Masterton, R. B. (1990). Sound localization in mammals: Brainstem mechanisms. In M. Berkley & W. Stebbins (Eds.), *Comparative perception, Vol. 1: Discrimination.* New York: Wiley.

Heilman, K. M., Bowers, D., & Valenstein, E. (1985). Emotional disorders associated with neurological diseases. In K. Heilman & E. Valenstein (Eds.), *Clinical neuropsychology* (pp. 377–402). New York: Oxford University Press.

Heiman, J. R. (1975). The psychology of erotica: Women's sexual arousal. *Psychology Today, 8,* 90–94.

Heimer, L., & Larsson, K. (1966/1967). Impairment of mating behavior in male rats following lesions in the preoptic-anterior hypothalamic continuum. *Brain Research, 3,* 248–263.

Heinrichs, R. W. (1990). Variables associated with Wisconsin Card Sorting Test performance in neuropsychiatric patients referred for assessment. *Neuropsychiatry, Neuropsychology, and Behavioral Neurology, 3,* 107–112.

Heinrichs, R. W. (1993). Schizophrenia and the brain. *American Psychologist, 48,* 221–233.

Hellige, J. B. (1993). Unity of thought and action: Varieties of interaction between the left and right cerebral hemispheres. *Current Directions in Psychological Science, 2,* 21–25.

Helmholtz, H. von (1852). On the theory of compound colors. *Philosophical Magazine, 4,* 519–534.

Helmholtz, H. von (1954). *On the sensations of tone as a physiological basis for the theory of music.* (A. J. Ellis, Trans.). New York: Dover. (Original work published 1863)

Heninger, G. R., & Charney, D. S. (1987). Mechanism of action of antidepressant treatments: Implications for the etiology and treatment of depressive disorders. In H. V. Meltier (Ed.), *Psychopharmacology: The third generation of progress.* (pp. 535–544). New York: Raven.

Hering, E. (1878). *Zur lehre vom lichtsinne.* Vienna: Gerold.

Heston, L., & Shields, J. (1968). Homosexuality in twins: A family study and a registry study. *Archives of General Psychiatry, 18,* 149–160.

Hetherington, A. W., & Ranson, S. W. (1942). Effect of early hypophysectomy on hypothalamic obesity. *Endocrinology, 31,* 30–34.

Heydt, R. von der, Peterhans, E., & Duersteler, M. R. (1992). Periodic-pattern-selective cells in monkey visual cortex. *Journal of Neuroscience, 12,* 1416–1434.

Hibscher, J. A., & Herman, C. P. (1977). Obesity, dieting and the expression of "obese" characteristics. *Journal of Comparative and Physiological Psychology, 91,* 374–380.

Hicks, R. A., Kilcourse, J., & Sinnott, M. A. (1983). Type A-B behavior and caffeine use in college students. *Psychological Reports, 52,* 338.

Higley, J. D., Mehlman, P. T., Higley, S. B., Fernald, B., Vickers, J., Lindell, S. G., Taub, D. M., Suomi, S. J., & Linnoila, M. (1996). Excessive mortality in young free-ranging male nonhuman primates with low cerebrospinal fluid 5-hydroxyindoleacetic acid concentrations. *Archives of General Psychiatry, 53,* 537–543.

Hill, D. R., Campbell., N. J., Shaw, T. M., & Woodruff, G. N. (1987). Autographic localization and biochemical characterization peripheral type CCK receptors in rat CNS usin highly selective nonpeptide CCK antagonists. *Journal of Neuroscience, 7,* 2967–2976.

Hill, D. W., Hill, L., Fields, K. L., & Smith, J. C. (1993). Effects of jet lag on factors related to sport performance. *Canadian Journal of Applied Physiology, 18,* 91–103.

Hitchcock, E. (1979). Amygdalotomy for aggression. In M. Sandler (Ed.), *Psychopharmacology of aggression.* New York: Raven Press.

Hoage, C. M. (1989). The use of in-session eating in the outpatient treatment of bulimia nervosa. In L. M. Hornyah & E. K. Baker (Eds.), *Experimental therapies for eating disorders* (pp. 60–77) New York: Guilford Press.

Hobson, J. A. (1988). *The dreaming brain.* New York: Basic Books.

Hobson, J. A. (1989). *Sleep.* New York: Scientific American Library.

Hobson, J. A., & McCarley, R. W. (1977). The brain as a dream state generator: An activation-synthesis hypothesis of the dream process. *American Journal of Psychiatry, 134,* 1335–1348.

Hodge, M. (1991). Assessing early speech motor function. *Clinical Communicative Disorders, 1,* 69–85.

Hodgkinson, S., Sherrington, R., Gurling, H., Marchbanks, R., Reeders, S., Mallet, J., McInnis, M., Petursson, H., & Brynjolsson, J. (1987). Molecular genetic evidence for heterogeneity in manic depression. *Nature, 325,* 805–806.

Hoebel, B. G. (1969). Feeding and self-stimulation: Neural regulation of food and water intake. *Annals of the New York Academy of Sciences, 157,* 758–778.

Hoebel, B. G., & Teitelbaum, P. (1966). Weight regulation in normal and hypothalamic hyperphagic rats. *Journal of Comparative and Physiological Psychology, 61,* 189–193.

Hoffman, L., & Halmi, K. (1993). Psychopharmacology in the treatment of anorexia nervosa and bulimia nervosa. *Psychiatric Clinics of North America, 16,* 767–778.

Hoffman, M. A., & Swaab, D. F. (1994). The human hypothalamus: Comparative morphometry and photoperiodic influences. *Progress in Brain Research, 93,* 133–147.

Holden, C. (1986). Depression research advances: Treatment lags. *Science, 233,* 723–726.

Holland, A., Sicotte, N., & Treasure, J. (1988). Anorexia nervosa, evidence for a genetic basis. *Journal of Psychosomatic Research, 32,* 561–571.

Hollander, E., Simeon, D., & Gorman, J. M. (1994). Anxiety disorders. In R. E. Hales & S. C. Yudofsky (Eds.), *Textbook of psychiatry* (2nd ed., pp. 495–563). Washington, DC: American Psychiatric Press.

Honer, W. G., Falkai, P., Young, C., Wang, T., Xie, J., Bonner, J., Hu, L., Boulianne, G. L., Luo, Z., & Trimble, W. S. (1997). Cingulate cortex synaptic terminal proteins and neural cell adhesion molecules in schizophrenia. *Neuroscience, 78,* 99–110.

Horel, J. A., & Misantone, L. G. (1976). Visual discrimination impaired by cutting temporal lobe connections. *Science, 193,* 336–338.

Horne, J. A., & Wilkinson, S. (1985). Chronic sleep reduction: Daytime vigilance performance and EEG measures of sleepiness, with particular reference to "practice" effects. *Psychophysiology, 22,* 69–78.

Hosutt, J. A., Rowland, N., & Stricker, E. M. (1981). Impaired drinking responses of rats with lesions of the subfornical organ. *Journal of Comparative and Physiological Psychology, 95,* 104–113.

Hotta, M., Shibasaki, T., Masuda, A., Imaki, T., Demura, H., Ling, N., & Shizume, K. (1986). The responses of plasma adrenocorticotropin and cortisol to corticotropin-releasing hormone (CRH) and cerebrospinal fluid immunoreactive CRH in anorexia nervosa patients. *Journal of Clinical Endocrinology Metabolism, 62,* 319–324.

Houston, B. K. & Snyder, C. R. (1988). *Type A behavior: Research, theory, and intervention.* New York: Wiley.

Howard, J. L., Reifler, C. B., & Liptzin, M. B. (1971). Effects of exposure to pornography. In *Technical Report of the Commission on Obscenity and Pornography* (Vol. VIII). Washington, DC: U.S. Government Printing Office.

Howlett, A. C., Bidaut-Russell, M., Devane, W. A., Laurence, S. M., Johnson, M. R., & Herkenham, M. (1990). The cannaboid receptor: Biochemical, anatomical and behavioral characterization. *Trends in Neurosciences, 13,* 420–424.

Hrdy, S. B. (1979). Infanticide among animals: A review, classification, and examination of the implications for the reproductive strategies of females. *Ethology and Sociobiology, 1,* 13–40.

Hubel, D. H., & Wiesel, T. N. (1962). Receptive fields, binocular interaction, and functional architecture in the cat's visual cortex. *Journal of Physiology, 160,* 106–154.

Hubel, D. H. & Wiesel, T. N. (1965). Binocular interaction in striate cortex of kittens reared with artificial squint. *Journal of Neurophysiology, 28,* 1041–1059.

Hudspeth, A. J. (1983). Mechanoelectrical transduction by hair cells in the acousticolateralis sensory system. *Annual Review of Neuroscience, 6,* 187–215.

Hudspeth, A. J. (1992). Hair-bundle mechanics and a model for mechanoelectrical transduction by hair cells. *Society of General Physiologists Series, 47,* 357–370.

Hughes, A. J. (1997). Drug treatment of Parkinson's disease in the 1990s: Achievements and future possibilities. *Drugs, 53,* 195–205.

Hughes, C. W., Kent, T. A., Campbell, J., Oke, A., Croskill, H., & Preskorn, S. H. (1984). Central blood flow and cerebrovascular permeability in an inescapable shock (learned helplessness) animal model of depression. *Pharmacology, Biochemistry, and Behavior, 21,* 891–894.

Hughes, H. C., Nozawa, G., & Kitterle, F. (1996). Global precedence, spatial frequency channels, and the statistics of natural images. *Journal of Cognitive Neuroscience, 8,* 197–230.

Hughes, J., Smith, T. W., Kosterlitz, H. W., Fothergill, L. A., Morgan, B. A., & Morris, H. R. (1975). Identification of two related pentapeptides from the brain with potent opiate agonist activity. *Nature, 258,* 577–579.

Hull, E. M., Du, J., Lorrain, D. S., & Matuszewich, L. (1997). Testosterone, preoptic dopamine, and copulation in male rats. *Brain and Research Bulletin, 44,* 327–333.

Hull, E. M., Eaton, R. C., Moses, J., & Lorrain, D. (1993). Copulation increases dopamine activity in the medial preoptic area of male rats. *Life Sciences, 52,* 935–940.

Hulsey, M. G., & Martin, R. J. (1992). An anorectic agent from adipose tissue of overfed rats: Effects on feeding behavior. *Physiology and Behavior, 52,* 1141–1149.

Humphrey, P. P. A., Hartig, P., & Hoyer, D. (1993). A proposed new nomenclature for 5-HT receptors. *Trends in Pharmacological Sciences, 14,* 233–236.

Huntington, G. (1872). On chorea. *Medical Surgical Reporter, 26,* 317–321.

Hurd, Y. L., Kehr, J., & Ungerstedt, U. (1988). *In vivo* microdialysis as a technique to monitor drug transport: Correlation of extracellular cocaine levels and dopamine overflow in the rat brain. *Journal of Neurochemistry, 51,* 1314–1316.

Hurd, Y. L., & Ungerstedt, U. (1989). Cocaine: An *in vivo* microdialysis evaluation of its acute action on dopamine transmission in rat striatum. *Synapse, 3,* 48–54.

Hsu, L. K. (1986). The treatment of anorexia. *American Journal of Psyciatry, 143,* 573–581.

Hyde, J. S. (1994). *Understanding human sexuality.* New York: McGraw Hill.

Hyden, H., & Egyhazi, E. (1964). Changes in RNA content and base composition in cortical neurons of rats in a learning experiment involving transfer of handedness. *Proceedings of the National Academy of Sciences, 52,* 1030–1035.

Hyman, B. T., Van Hoesen, G. W., & Damasio, A. R. (1987). Alzheimer's disease: Glutamate depletion in the hippocampal perforant pathway zone. *Annuals of Neurology, 22,* 37–40.

Hyman, B. T., Van Hoesen, G. W., Damasio, A. R., & Barnes, C. L. (1984). Alzheimer's disease: Cell-specific pathology isolates the hippocampal formation. *Science, 225,* 1168–1170.

Iacono, R. P., Shima, F., Lonser, R. R., Kuniyoshi, S., Maeda, G., & Yamada, S. (1995). The results, indications, and physiology of posteroventral pallidotomy for patients with Parkinson's disease. *Neurosurgery, 36,* 1118–1127.

Inouye, D., & Kawamura, H. (1979). Persistence of circadian rhythmicity in mammalian hypothalamic "island" containing the suprachiasmatic nucleus. *Proceedings of the National Academy of Sciences (USA), 76,* 5961–5966.

Ivarson, C., de Ribauprene, Y., & de Ribauprene, F. (1988). Influence of auditory localization cues on the neuronal activity in the auditory thalamus of the cat. *Journal of Neurophysiology, 59,* 586–606.

Izquierdo, I. (1995). Role of the hippocampus, amygdala, and entorhinal cortex in memory storage and expression. In J. L. McGaugh, F. Bermudez-Rattoni, & R. A. Prado-Alcala (Eds.), *Plasticity in the central nervous system* (pp. 41–56). Mahwah, NJ: Erlbaum.

Jackson, J. H. (1870). A study of convulsions. In J. Taylor (Ed.), *Selected writings of John Hughlings Jackson* (1932), (pp. 8–36). New York: Basic Books.

Jacobs, B. L. (1987). How hallucinogenic drugs work. *American Scientist, 75,* 386–392.

Jacobson, C. D., & Gorski, R. A. (1981). Neurogenesis of the sexually dimorphic nucleus of the preoptic area in the rat. *Journal of Comparative Neurology, 196,* 519–529.

Jacobson, M. (1991). *Developmental neurobiology.* New York: Plenum Press.

James, W. (1884). What is an emotion? *Mind, 9,* 188–205.

Janowitz, H. D., & Grossman, M. I. (1949). Some factors affecting the food intake of normal dogs and dogs with esophagostomy and gastric fistula. *American Journal of Physiology, 159,* 143–148.

Janowitz, H. D., & Hollander, F. (1953). Effect of prolonged intragastric feeding on oral ingestion. *Federation Proceedings, 12,* 72.

Janowsky, D. S., & Risch, C. (1979). Amphetamine psychosis and psychotic symptoms. *Psychopharmacology, 65,* 73–77.

Janowsky, D. S., Risch, C., Parker, D., Huey, L., & Judd, L. (1980). Increased vulnerability to cholinergic stimulation in affective-disorder patients. *Psychopharmacology Bulletin, 16,* 29–31.

Jarvik, M. E., & Schneider, N. G. (1992). Nicotine. In J. H. Lowinson, P. Ruiz, R. B. Millman, & J. G. Langrod (Eds.), *Substance abuse: A comprehensive textbook* (2nd ed., pp. 247–266). Baltimore: Williams & Wilkins, 1992.

Jeffrey, R. W., & Wing, R. R. (1995). Long-term effects of interventions for weight loss using food provision and monetary incentives. *Journal of Consulting and Clinical Psychology, 63,* 793–796.

Jemmott, J. B. III, Borysenko, J. Z., Borysenko, M., McClelland, D. C., Chapman, R., Meyer, D., & Benson, H. (1983). Academic stress, power motivation, and decrease in secretion rate of salivary secretory immunoglobulin A. *Lancet, 1,* 1400–1402.

Jenner, P. (1990). Parkinson's disease: Clues to the cause of cell death in the substantia nigra. *Seminars in the Neurosciences, 2,* 117–126.

Jenner, P., Schapira, A. H. V., Marsden, C., et al. (1992). New insights into the cause of Parkinson's disease. *Neurology, 42,* 2241–2250.

Jentsch, J. D., Redmond, D. E., Jr., Elsworth, J. D., Taylor, J. R., Youngren, K. D., & Roth, R. H. (1997). Enduring cognitive deficits and cortical dopamine dysfunction in monkeys after long-term administration of phencyclidine. *Science, 277,* 953–955.

Jessell, T. M. (1991). Cell migration and axon guidance. In E. R. Kandel, J. H. Schwartz, & T. M. Jessell (Eds.), *Principles of neural science* (3rd ed., pp. 908–928). Norwalk, CT: Appleton & Lange.

Jiang, W., Babyak, M., Krantz, D. S., Waugh, R. A., Coleman, R. E., Hanson, M. M., Frid, D. J., McNulty, S., Morris, J. J., O'Connor, C. M., & Blumenthal, J. A. (1996, June 5). Mental stress-induced myocardial ischemia and cardiac events. *Journal of the American Medical Association, 275,* 1651–1656.

Johansson, B., & Zarit, S. H. (1997). Early cognitive markers of the incidence of dementia and mortality: A longitudinal population-based study of the oldest old. *Internal Journal of Geriatric Psychiatry, 12,* 53–59.

Johansson, F., Malm, J., Nordh, E., & Hariz, M. (1997). Usefulness of pallidotomy in advanced Parkinson's disease. *Journal of Neurology and Neurosurgical Psychology, 62,* 125–132.

Johnson, J. S., & Newport, E. L. (1989). Critical period effects in second language learning: The influence of maturational state on the acquisition of English as a second language. *Cognitive Psychology, 21,* 60–99.

Johnson, L. C. (1982). Sleep deprivation and performance. In W. B. Webb (Ed.), *Biological rhythms, sleep, and performance* (pp. 111–141). New York: Wiley.

Johnson, L. C., Burdick, J. A., & Smith, J. (1970). Sleep during alcohol intake and withdrawal in the chronic alcoholic. *Archives of General Psychiatry, 22,* 406–418.

Jones, B. E., Bobillier, P., & Jouvet, M. (1969). Effets de la destruction des neurons contenant des catecholamines du mesencephale sur le cycle veille-sommeils du chat. *Comptes Rendus de la Societe de Biologie (Paris), 163,* 176–180.

Jouvet, M. (1967). The states of sleep. *Scientific American, 216,* 62–72.

Jouvet, M. (1969). Biologic amines and the states of sleep. *Science, 163,* 32–41.

Jouvet, M. (1972). The role of monoamines and acetylcholine-containing neurons in the regulation of the sleep-waking cycle. *Ergebnisse der Physiologie, 64,* 166–307.

Jouvet, M. (1974). Monoaminergic regulation of the sleep-waking cycle in the cat. In F. O. Schmitt & F. G. Worden (Eds.), *The neurosciences: Third study program* (pp. 499–508). Cambridge, MA: MIT Press.

Jouvet, M., & Renault, J. (1966). Insomnie persistante apres lesions des noyaux du raphe chez le chat. *Comptes Rendus de la Societe de Biologie (Paris), 160,* 1461–1465.

Joynt, R. J., & Shoulson, I. (1985). Dementia. In K. Heilman and E. Valenstein (Eds.), *Clinical neuropsychology* (pp. 453–480). New York: Oxford University Press.

Julien, R. M. (1998). *A primer of drug action* (8th ed.). New York: Freeman.

Kaada, B. R. (1972). Stimulation and regional ablation of the amygdaloid complex with reference to function representations. In B. E. Eleftheriou (Ed.), *The neurobiology of the amygdala.* New York: Plenum.

Kaas, J. H., Nelson, R. J., Sur, M., & Merzenich, M. M. (1981). Organization of somatosensory cortex in primates. In F. O. Schmitt, F. G. Worden, G. Adelman, & S. G. Dennis (Eds.), *The organization of the cerebral cortex* (pp. 237–261). Cambridge, MA: MIT Press.

Kales, A., Scharf, M. B., Kales, J. D., & Soldatos, C. R. (1979). Rebound insomnia: A potential hazard following withdrawal of certain benzodiazepines. *Journal of the American Medical Association, 241,* 1692–1695.

Kales, A., Soldatos, C. R., Bixler, E. O., & Kales, J. D. (1983). Early morning insomnia with rapidly eliminated benzodiazepines. *Science, 220,* 95–97.

Kales, A., Soldatos, C. R., & Kales, J. D. (1981). Sleep disorders: Evaluation and management in the office setting. In S. Arieti (Ed.), *American handbook of psychiatry* (2nd ed., pp. 423–454). New York: Basic Books.

Kallman, F. J. A. (1952). A comparative twin study of the genetic aspects of male homosexuality. *Journal of Nervous Systems and Mental Diseases, 115,* 101–107.

Kanamori, N., Sakai, K., & Jouvet, M. (1980). Neuronal activity specific to paradoxical sleep in the ventromedial medullary reticular formation of unrestrained cats. *Brain Research, 189,* 251–255.

Kandel, E. R., Siegelbaum, S. A., & Schwartz, J. H. (1991). Synaptic transmission. In E. R. Kandel, J. H. Schwartz, & T. M. Jessell (Eds.), *Principles of neural science* (3rd ed., pp. 123–134).

Norwalk, CT: Appleton & Lange.

Kaplan, H. S. (1974). *The new sex therapy.* New York: Brunner/Mazel.

Katsuki, Y. (1961). Neural mechanism of auditory sensation in cats. In W. A. Rosenblith (Ed.), *Sensory Communication,* Cambridge, MA: MIT Press.

Kauer, J. S. (1987). Coding in the olfactory system. In T. E. Finger & W. L. Silver (Eds.), *Neurobiology of taste andsmell* (pp. 205–231). New York: Wiley.

Kauer, J. S. (1988). Real-time imaging of evoked activity in local circuits of the Salamander olfactory bulb. *Nature, 331,* 166–168.

Keesey, R. E., & Powley, T. L. (1986). The regulation of body weight. *Annual Review of Psychology, 37,* 109–133.

Kellogg, W. N., & Kellogg, L. A. (1933). *The ape and the child.* New York: McGraw-Hill.

Kelly, D. D. (1991). Sexual differentiation of the nervous system. In E. R. Kandel, J. H. Schwartz, & T. M. Jessell (Eds.), *Principles of neural science* (3rd ed., pp. 959–973). New York: Elsevier.

Kelso, S. R., & Brown, T. H. (1986). Differential conditioning of associative synaptic enhancement in hippocampal brain slices. *Science, 232,* 85–87.

Kelsoe, J. R., Jr., Cadet, J. L., Pickar, D., & Weinberger, D. R. (1988). Quantitative neuroanatomy in schizophrenia: A controlled magnetic resonance imaging study. *Archives of General Psychiatry, 45,* 533–541.

Kendrick, K. M., & Baldwin, B. A. (1987). Cells in temporal cortex in conscious sheep can respond preferentially to the sight of faces. *Science, 236,* 448–450.

Kennedy, J. L., Giuffra, L. A., Moises, H. W., Cavalli-Sforza, L. L., Pakstis, A. J., Kidd, J. R., Castiglione, C. M., Sjogren, B., Wetterberg, L., & Kidd, K. K. (1988). Evidence against linkage of schizophrenia to markers on chromosome 5 in a northern Swedish pedigree. *Nature, 336,* 167–170.

Kennedy, S. H., & Goldbloom, D. S. (1991). Current perspectives on drug therapies for anorexia nervosa and bulimia nervosa. *Drugs, 41,* 367–377.

Kerr, D. I. B., & Ong, J. (1995). GABA receptors. *Pharmacological Therapeutics, 67,* 187–246.

Kertesz, A. (1982). *Western aphasia battery.* New York: Grimes Stratton.

Kerwin, R. (1996). Imaging studies of neuroleptic occupancy. *Journal of Clinical Psychiatry, 57,* 315–316.

Kessler, R. C., McGonagle, K. A., Zhao, S., Nelson, C. B., Hughes, M., Eshleman, S., Wittchen, H. U., & Kendler, K. S. (1994). Lifetime and 12-month prevalence of DSM-III-R psychiatric disorders in the United States. *Archives of General Psychiatry, 51,* 8–19.

Keynes, R. J., & Cook, G. M. (1992). Repellent cues in axon guidance. *Current Opinion in Neurobiology, 2,* 55–59.

King, C., & Quigley, S. (1985). *Reading and deafness.* San Diego: College-Hill Press.

King, G. R., & Ellinwood, E. H., Jr. (1992). Amphetamines and other stimulants. In J. H. Lowinson, P. Ruiz, R. B. Millman, & J. G. Langrod (Eds.), *Substance abuse: A comprehensive textbook* (2nd ed., pp. 247–266). Baltimore: Williams & Wilkins.

King, M., & McDonald, E. (1992). Homosexuals who are twins: A study of 46 probands. *British Journal of Psychiatry, 160,* 407–409.

Kinnamon, S. C., Dionne, V. E., & Beam, K. G. (1988). Apical localization of K^+ channels in taste cells provides the basis for sour taste transduction. *Proceedings of the National Academy of Sciences, U.S.A., 85,* 7023–7027.

Kirchgessner, A. L., & Sclafani, A. (1988). PVN-hindbrain pathway involved in the hypothalamic hyperphagia-obesity syndrome. *Physiology and Behavior, 42,* 517–528.

Kissileff, H. R. (1971). Unpublished data cited by J. Le Magnen, Advances in studies on the physiological control and regulation of food intake. In E. Stellar & J. M. Sprague, *Progress in Physiological Psychology* (Vol. 4). New York: Academic Press.

Kissileff, H. R., Pi-Sunyer, F. X., Thornton, J., & Smith, G. P. (1981). C-terminal octapeptide of cholecystokinin decreases food intake in man. *The American Journal of Clinical Nutrition, 34,* 154–160.

Klein, S. B. (1982). *Motivation: Biosocial approaches.* New York: McGraw-Hill.

Klein, S. B. (1996). *Learning: Principles and applications* (3rd ed). New York, McGraw-Hill.

Kling, A., Dicks, D., & Gurwitz, E. M. (1968). Amygdalectomy and social behavior in a caged-group of vervets (*C. aethiops*). *Proceedings of the 2nd International Congress of Primateology,* Atlanta, GA.

Klüver, H., & Bucy, P. C.(1937). "Psychic blindness" and other symptoms following bilateral temporal labectomy in rhesus monkeys. *American Journal of Psychology, 119,* 352–353.

Klüver, H., & Bucy, P. C. (1939). Preliminary analysis of functions of the temporal lobe in rhesus monkeys. *Archives of Neurology and Psychiatry, 42,* 979–1000.

Knebelmann, B., Boussin, L., Guerrier, D., Legeai, L., Kahn, A., Josso, N., & Picard, J. Y. (1991). Anti-Müellerian hormone Bruxelles: A nonsense mutation associated with the persistent Muellerian duct syndrome. *Proceedings of the National Academy of Sciences, USA, 88,* 3767–3771.

Knott, J. R. (1965). Electroencephalograms in psychopathic personality and murders. In W. Wilson (Ed.), *Applications of electroencephalography in psychiatry.* Durham, NC: Duke University Press.

Kobasa, S. C. (1979). Stressful life events, personality, and health: An inquiry into hardiness. *Journal of Personality and Social Psychology, 37,* 1–11.

Kobasa, S. C. (1990). Stress-resistant personality. In R. E. Ornstein & D. Swencionir (Eds.), *The healing brain* (pp. 219–230). New York: Guilford Press.

Kobasa, S. C., Maddi, S. R., Puccetti, M. C., & Zola, M. A. (1994). Effectiveness of hardiness, exercise, and social support as resources against illness. In A. Steptoe & J. Wardle (Eds.), *Psychosocial processes and health* (pp. 247–260). Cambridge, England: Cambridge University Press.

Kobasa, S. C., Maddi, S. R., & Zola, M. A. (1983). Type A and hardiness. *Journal of Behavioral Medicine, 6,* 41–51.

Kobatake, E., & Tanaka, K. (1994). Neuronal selectivities to complex object features in the ventral visual pathway of the macaque cerebral cortex. *Journal of Neurophysiology, 71,* 856–867.

Koch, H. (1982). Drugs most frequently used in office-based practice. National Ambulatory Medical Care Survey. National Center for Health Statistics Advance Data, no. 12.

Kohler, W. (1925). *The mentality of apes.* London: Routledge & Kegan Paul.

Kolarsky, A., Freund, K., Machek, J., & Polak, O. (1967). Male sexual deviation: Association with early temporal damage. *Archives of General Psychiatry, 17,* 735–743.

Kolb, B. (1995). *Brain plasticity and behavior.* Mahwak, NJ: Erlbaum.

Kolb, B., & Whishaw, I. Q. (1996). *Human neuropsychology* (4th ed.). New York: Freeman.

Koob, G. F. (1992). Drugs of abuse: Anatomy, pharmacology and function of reward pathways. *Trends in Pharmacological Science, 13,* 177–184.

Koob, G. F., Pettit, H. O., Ettenberg, A., & Bloom, F. E. (1984). Effects of opiate antagonists and their quaternary derivatives on heroin self-administration in the rat. *Journal of Pharmacology and Experimental Therapeutics, 229,* 481–487.

Koolhaas, J. M., Van den Brink, T. H. C., Roozendaal, B., & Boorsma, F. (1990). Medial amygdala and aggressive behavior: Interaction between testosterone and vasopressin. *Aggressive Behavior, 16,* 223–229.

Koopman, P., Gubbay, J., Vivian, N., Goodfellow, P. N., & Lovell-Badge, R. (1991). Male development of chromosomally female mice transgenic for SRY. *Nature, 351,* 117–121.

Kordower, J. H., Freeman, T. B., Snow, B. J., Vingerhoets, F. J., Mufson, E. J., Sanberg, P. R., Hauser, B. A., Smith, D. A., Nauert, G. M., & Perl, D. P. (1995). Neuropathological evidence of graft survival and striatal reinnervation after transplantation of fetal mesencephalic tissue in a patient with Parkinson's disease. *New England Journal of Medicine, 332,* 1118–1124.

Kordower, J. H., Rosenstein, J. M., Collier, T. J., Burke, M. A., Chen, E. Y., Li, J. M., Martel, L., Levey, A. E., Mufson, E. J., Freeman, T. B., & Olanow, C. W. (1996). Functional fetal nigral grafts in a patient with Parkinson's disease: Chemoanatomic, ultrastructural and metabolic studies. *Journal of Comparative Neurology, 370,* 203–230.

Kosslyn, S. M. (1987). Seeing and imaging in the cerebral hemispheres: A computational approach. *Psychological Review, 94,* 148–175.

Kostowski, W., Giacalone, E., Garattini, S., & Valzelli, L. (1969). Electrical stimulation of midbrain raphé: Biochemical, behavioral, and bioelectrical effects. *European Journal of Pharmacology, 7,* 170–175.

Kow, L.-M., & Pfaff, D. W. (1989). Responses of hypothalamic paraventricular neurons in vitro to norepinephrine and other feeding-relevant agents. *Physiology and Behavior, 46*, 265–271.

Kozlowski, S., & Drzewiecki, K. (1973). The role of osmoreception in portal circulation in control of water intake in dogs. *Acta Physiologica Polonica, 24*, 325–330.

Kraepelin, E. (1923). *Textbook of psychiatry.* New York: Macmillan. (Original work published 1883)

Kraly, F. S. (1990). Drinking elicited by eating. In A. N. Epstein & A. Morrison (Eds.), *Progress in psychobiology and physiological psychology* (Vol. 14). New York: Academic Press.

Krantz, D. S., & Manuck, S. B. (1984). Acute psychophysiologic reactivity and cardiovascular disease: A review and methodologic critique. *Psychological Bulletin, 96*, 435–464.

Krupa, D. J., Thompson, J. K., & Thompson, R. F. (1993). Localization of a memory trace in the mammillian brain. *Science, 260*, 989–991.

Krupa, D. J., Weng, J., & Thompson, R. F. (1996). Inactivation of brainstem motor nuclei blocks expression but not acquisition of the rabbit's classically conditioned eyeblink response. *Behavioral Neuroscience, 110*, 219–227.

Kuffler, S. W. (1953). Discharge patterns and functional organization of mammalian retina. *Journal of Neurophysiology, 16*, 37–68.

Kulklosky, P. J., Breckenridge, C., Krinsky, R., & Woods, S. C. (1976). Satiety elicited by the C-terminal octapeptide of cholecystokinin-pancreozymin in normal and VMH-lesioned rats. *Behavioral Biology, 18*, 227–234.

Kunkel-Bagden, E. & Bregman, B. S. (1990). Spinal cord transplants enhance the recovery of locomotor function after spinal cord injury at birth. *Exploring Brain Research, 81*, 25–34.

Kunkel-Bagden, E., Dai, H. N., & Bregman, B. S. (1993). Methods to assess the development and recovery of locomotor function after spinal cord injury in rats. *Experimental Neurology, 119*, 153–164.

Kupfer, D. J, & Bowers, M. B. Jr. (1972). REM sleep and central monoamine oxidase inhibition. *Psychopharmacologia, 27*, 183–190.

Kurihara, K. (1987). Recent progress in taste receptor mechanisms. In Y. Kawamura & M. R. Kare (Ed.), *Umami: A basic taste.* New York: Dekker.

LaBar, K. S., Gatenby, J. C., Gore, J. C., LeDoux, J. E., & Phelps, E. A. (1998). Human amygdala activation during conditioned fear acquisition and extinction: A mixed-trial fMRI study. *Neuron, 20*, 937–945.

LaBar, K. S., LeDoux, J. E., Spencer, D. D., & Phelps, E. A. (1995). Impaired fear conditioning following unilateral temporal lobectomy in humans. *Journal of Neuroscience, 15*, 6846–6855.

Labbe, A., Firl, A., Jr., Mufson, E. J., & Stein, D. G. (1983). Fetal tissue implant: Reduction of cognitive deficits in rats with frontal cortex lesions. *Science, 221*, 470–472.

La Berge, S. (1980). Lucid dreaming as a learnable skill: A case study. *Perceptual and Motor Skills, 51*, 1039–1042.

La Berge, S. P. (1981, January). Lucid dreaming: Directing the action as it happens. *Psychology Today*, 48–57.

La Berge, S., & Dement, W. (1982). Voluntary control of respiration during REM sleep. *Sleep Research, 11*, 107.

Laborit, H. (1950). La therapeutique neuro-vegetate du choc et de la maladie post-traumatique. *Press Medicale, 58*, 138–140.

Laguzzi, R., & Adrien, J. (1980). Effets des antagonistes de la serotonine sur le cycle veille-sommeil au rat. *Journal de Physiologie et Pathalogie, 76*, 20A.

Lague, L., Raiguel, S., & Orban, G. A. (1993). Speed and direction selectivity of macaque middle temporal neurons. *Journal of Neurophysiology, 69*, 19–39.

Lake, C. R., Pickar, D., Ziegler, M. G., Lipper, S., Slater, S., & Murphy, D. L. (1982). High plasma norepinephrine levels in patients with major affective disorder. *American Journal of Psychiatry, 139*, 1315–1318.

Lander, E., & Kruglyak, L. (1995). Genetic dissection of complex traits: Guidelines for interpreting and reporting linkage studies. *Nature Genetics, 11*, 241–247.

Lange, C. (1922). *The emotions.* Baltimore: Williams & Wilkins. (Original work published 1885)

Larsson, J., Gulyas, B., & Roland, P. E. (1996). Cortical representation of self-paired finger movement. *Neuroreport, 7*, 463–468.

Lashley, K. S. (1950). In search of the engram. In *Symposium of the Society for Experimental Biology* (Vol. 4). New York: Cambridge University Press.

Lashley, K. S. (1963). *Brain mechanisms and intelligence.* New York: Dover Publications. (Original work published 1929)

Lavie, P., Pratt, H., Scharf, B., Peled, R., & Brown, J. (1984). Localized pontine lesion: Nearly total absence of REM sleep. *Neurology, 34*, 1118–1120.

Lavine, R., Buchsbaum, M. S., & Poncy, M. (1976). Auditory analgesia: Somatosensory evoked response and subjective pain rating. *Psychophysiology, 13*, 140–148.

Lawrence, D. G., & Kuypers, G. J. M. (1968). The functional organization of the motor system in the monkey: I. The effects of bilateral pyramidal lesions. *Brain, 91*, 1–14.

Lazarus, R. S. (1993). From psychological stress to the emotions: A history of changing outlooks. *Annual Review of Psychology, 44*, 1–21.

Lazarus, R. S., & Lazarus, B. N. (1994). *Passion and reason: Making sense of our emotions.* New York: Oxford University Press.

LeDoux, E. (1995). Emotion: Clues form the brain. *Annual Review of Psychology, 46*, 209–235.

LeDoux, J. E., Iwata, J., Cicchetti, P., & Reis, D. J. (1988). Different projections of the central amygdaloid nucleus mediate autonomic and behavioral correlates of conditioned fear. *Journal of Neuroscience, 8*, 2517–2529.

Lehman, H. E., & Cancro, R. (1985). Schizophrenia: Clinical features. In H. I. Kaplan & B. J. Saddock, *Comprehensive textbook of psychiatry* (4th ed., Vol. 1). Baltimore: Williams & Wilkins.

Lehnert, H., Reinstein, D. K., Strowbridge, B. W., & Wurtman, R. J. (1984). Neurochemical and behavioral consequences of acute, uncontrollable stress: Effects of dietary tyrosine. *Brain Research, 303*, 215–223.

Leibowitz, S. F., Weiss, G. F., & Suh, J. S. (1990). Medial hypothalamic nuclei mediate serotonin's inhibitory effect on feeding behavior. *Pharmacology, Biochemistry, and Behavior, 37*, 735–742.

Leibowitz, S. F., Weiss, G. F., Yee, F., & Tretter, J. B. (1985). Noradrenergic innervation of the paraventricular nucleus: Specific role in control of carbohydrate ingestions. *Brain Research Bulletin, 14*, 561–567.

Leiner, H. C., Leiner, A. L., & Dow, R. S. (1989). Reappraising the cerebellum: What does the hindbrain contribute to the forebrain? *Behavioral Neuroscience, 103*, 998–1008.

Le Magnen, J. (1981). The metabolic basis of dual periodicity of feeding in rats. *Behavioral and Brain Sciences, 4*, 561–607.

Le Magnen, J., & Tallon, S. (1966). La pariodicite spontance de la prise d'aliments ad libitum du rat blanc. *Journal of Physiology, (Paris), 58*, 323–349.

Lemieux, G., Davidson, A., & Genest, J. (1956). Depressive states during rauwolfia therapy for arterial hypertension. *Canadian Medical Association Journal, 74*, 522–526.

Lenneberg, E. H. (1967). *Biological foundations of language.* New York: Wiley.

Lenneberg, E. H. (1969). On explaining language. *Science, 164*, 635–643.

Leukel, F. A. (1957). A comparison of the effects of ECS and anesthesia on acquisition of the maze habit. *Journal of Comparative and Physiological Psychology, 50*, 300–306.

LeVay, S. (1991). A difference in hypothalamic structure between heterosexual and homosexual men. *Science, 253*, 1034–1037.

LeVay, S. (1994, March). Quoted in D. Nimmons, Sex and the brain. *Discover*, pp. 64–71.

Levi-Montalcinci, L. (1951). Selective growth-stimulating effects of mouth sarcomas on the sensory and sympathetic nervous system of chick embryos. *Journal of Experimental Zoology, 341*, 149–152.

Levine, K. (1993, February 8). Drug approved for treating appetite loss in AIDS patients. *Drug Topics.*

Levy, J. (1985, May). Right brain, left brain: Fact and fiction. *Psychology Today*, pp. 38–44.

Levy, J., Trevarthen, C., & Sperry, R. W. (1972). Perception of bilateral chimeric figures following hemispheric disconnection. *Brain, 95*, 61–78.

Lewis, D. J. (1969). Sources of experimental amnesia. *Psychological Review, 76*, 461–472.

Lewis, D. J. (1979). Psychology of active and inactive memory. *Psychological Bulletin, 86*, 1054–1083.

Liao, D., Hessler, N. A., & Malinow, R. (1995). Activation of postsynaptically silent synapses during pairing-induced LTP in CA1 region of hippocampal slice. *Nature, 375*, 400–404.

Liddell, F. D. K. (1982). Motor vehicle accidents (1973–6) in a cohort of Montreal drivers.

Journal of Epidemiological Community Health, 36, 140–145.

Liepmann, H. (1900). Das krankheitsbild der apraxia. *Monatsschr Psychiatric Neurologic, 1,* 11–18.

Lilie, J. K., & Rosenberg, R. P. (1990). Behavioral treatment of insomnia. *Progress in Behavior Modification, 25,* 152–177.

Lindsley, D. B. (1951). Emotion. In S. S. Stevens (Ed.), *Handbook of experimental psychology* (pp. 473–516). New York: Wiley.

Lindsley, D. B. (1958). The reticular system and perceptual discrimination. In H. H. Jasper (Ed.), *Reticular formation of the brain* (pp. 513–534). Boston: Little, Brown.

Lindsley, D. B., Bowden, J., & Magoun, H. W. (1949). Effect upon EEG of acute injury to the brainstem activating system. *Electroencephalogy Clinical Neurophysiology, 1,* 475–486.

Lindvall, O., Sawle, G., Widner, H., Rothwell, J. C., Bjorklund, A., Brooks, D., Brundin, P., Frackowiak, R., Marsden, C. D., & Odin, P. (1994). Evidence for long-term survival and function of dopaminergic grafts in progressive Parkinson's disease. *Annals of Neurology, 35,* 172–180.

Linnoila, M., Karoum, F., Calil, H. M., Kopin, I. J., & Potter, W. Z. (1982). Alteration of norepinephrine metabolism with despramine and zimelidine in depressed patients. *Archives of General Psychiatry, 39,* 1025–1028.

Lino, A., Silvy, S., Condorelli, C., & Rusconi, H. C. (1993). Melatonin and jet lag: Treatment schedule. *Biological Psychiatry, 34,* 587.

Linseman, M. A., & Harding, S. (1990). Intracerebroventricular morphine enhances alcohol consumption by rats. *Pharmacology, Biochemistry, and Behavior, 36,* 405–408.

Lipton, D. S., Brewington, V., & Smith, M. (1993). Acupuncture treatment for drug abuse: A technical review. *Journal of Substance Abuse Treatment, 10,* 569–576.

Lissner, L., Odell, P. M., D'Agostino, R. B., Stokes, J. III, et al. (1991). Variability of body weight and health outcomes in the Framington population. *New England Journal of Medicine, 324,* 1839–1844.

Livingstone, M., & Hubel, D. (1988). Segregation of form, color, movement and depth: Anatomy, physiology, and perception. *Science, 240,* 740–749.

Loewi, O. (1921). Uber humorale Ubertragbeit Herznervenwirkung. *Archives fuer die Gesamte Physiologie des Menschen und der Tiere, 189,* 239–262.

Loftus, E. F. (1991). Made in memory. In G. Bower (Ed.), *The psychology of learning and motivation* (Vol. 27, pp. 187–212). Orlando, FL: Academic.

Logan, C. G., & Gratton, S. T. (1995). Functional anatomy of human eyeblink conditioning determined with regional cerebral glucose metabolism and positron-emission tomography. *Proceedings of the National Academy of Sciences, USA, 92,* 7500–7504.

Logue, A. W. (1985). Conditioned food aversion learning in humans. *Annals of the New York Academy of Sciences, 443,* 316–329.

Logue, A. W. (1991). *The psychology of eating and drinking* (2nd ed.). New York: Freeman.

Long, J. W. (1984). *Clinical management of prescription drugs.* New York: Harper Collins.

Loraine, J. A., Adampopoulous, D. A., Kirkhan, K. E., Ismail, A. A., & Dove, G. A. (1971). Patterns of hormone excretion in male and female homosexuals. *Nature, 234,* 552–554.

Losonczy, M. F., Davidson, M., & Davis, K. L. (1987). The dopamine hypothesis of schizophrenia. In H. Y. Meltzer (Ed.), *Psychopharmacology: The third generation of progress* (pp. 715–726). New York: Raven Press.

Louis-Sylvestre, J., & Le Magnen, J. (1980). A fall in blood glucose level precedes meal onset in free-feeding rats. *Neuroscience and Biobehavioral Reviews, 4,* 13–16.

Lovick, T. A. (1997). The medullary raphe nuclei: A system for integration and grain control in autonomic and somatomotor responsiveness. *Experimental Physiology, 82,* 31–41.

Lowe, J., & Carroll, D. (1985). The effects of spinal injury on the intensity of emotional experience. *British Journal of Clinical Psychology, 24,* 135–136.

Lucas, C., Sanbury, P., & Collins, J. G. (1962). A social and clinical study of delusions in schizophrenia. *Journal of Mental Health, 108,* 747–758.

Luce, G. (1971). *Body time.* New York: Pantheon.

Lydic, R., McCarley, R. W., & Hobson, J. A. (1987). Serotonin neurons and sleep. II: Time course of dorsal raphe discharge, PGO waves, and behavioral states. *Archives of Italian Biology, 126,* 1–28.

Lynch, G. (1986). *Synapses, circuits, and the beginnings of memory.* Cambridge: MIT Press.

Lynch, G., & Baudry, M. (1984). The biochemistry of memory: A new and specific hypothesis. *Science, 224,* 1057–1063.

Lyness, S. A. (1993). Predictors of differences between Type A and B individuals in heart rate and blood pressure reactivity. *Psychological Bulletin, 114,* 266–295.

Maas, J. W., Dekirmenjian, H., & Fawcett, J. (1971). Catecholamine metabolism, depression and stress. *Nature, 230,* 330–331.

Maccoby, E. E., & Jacklin, C. N. (1980). Sex differences: A rejoiner and reprise. *Child Development, 51,* 964–980.

Mackay, E. M., Callaway, J. W., & Barnes, R. H. (1940). Hyperalimentation in normal animals produced by protamine insulin. *Journal of Nutrition, 20,* 59–66.

Macdonald, R. L., Weddle, M. G., & Gross, R. A. (1986). Benzodiazepine, b-carbonline, and barbiturate actions on GABA responses. *Advances in Biochemical Psychopharmacology, 41,* 67–78.

MacLean, P. D. (1949). Psychosomatic disease and the "visceral brain": Recent developments bearing on the Papez theory of emotion. *Psychosomatic Medicine, 11,* 338–353.

MacLean, P. D. (1977). The triune brain in conflict. *Psychotherapy and Psychosomatics, 28,* 207–220.

MacLean, P. D., & Delgado, J. M. R. (1953). Electrical and chemical stimulation of frontotemporal portion of limbic system in the waking animal. *Electroencephalography and Clinical Neurophysiology, 5,* 91–100.

Mahl, G. F. (1949). Anxiety, HCl secretion and peptic ulcer etiology. *Psychosomatic Medicine, 11,* 30–44.

Maj, M., Veltro, F., Pirozzi, R., Lobrace, S., & Magliano, L. (1992). Pattern of recurrence of illness after recovery from an episode of major depression: A prospective study. *American Journal of Psychiatry, 149,* 795–800.

Majewska, M. D., Harrison, N. L., Schwartz, R. D., Barker, J. L., & Paul, S. M. (1986). Steroid hormone metabolites are barbiturate-like modulators of the GABA receptors. *Science, 232,* 1004–1007.

Major, R., & White, N. (1978). Memory facilitation by self-stimulation reinforcement mediated by the nigrostriatal bundle. *Physiology and Behavior, 20,* 723–733.

Malamud, N. (1967). Psychiatric disorders with intracranial tumors of the limbic system. *Archives of Neurology, 17,* 113–123.

Malgaroli, A., & Tsien, R. W. (1992). Glutamate-induced long-term potentiation of the frequency of miniature synaptic currents in cultured hippocampal neurons. *Nature, 357,* 134–139.

Malinow, R. (1991). Transmission between pair of hippocampal slice neurons: Quantal levels, oscillations, and LTP. *Science, 252,* 722–724.

Malmo, R. B., Kohlmeyer, W., & Smith, A. A. (1956). Motor manifestations of conflict in interview. *Journal of Abnormal Social Psychology, 52,* 268–271.

Mangiapane, M. L., Thrasher, T. N., Keil, L. C., Simpson, J. B., & Ganong, W. F. (1983). Deficits in drinking and vasopressin secretion after lesions of the nucleus medianus. *Neuroendocrinology, 37,* 73–77.

Maratsos, M., & Matheny, L. (1994). Language specificity and elasticity: Brain and clinical syndrome studies. *Annual Review of Psychology, 45,* 487–516.

Marge, E. J. & Marge, A. P. (1998) *Basic human genetics.* (2nd ed). Sunderland, MA: Sinauer.

Margules, D. L., & Stein, L. (1967). Neuroleptics versus tranquilizers: Evidence from animal behavior studies of mode and site of action. In H. Brill et al. (Eds.), *Neuropsychopharmacology* (pp. 108–120). Amsterdam: Elsevier.

Margules, D. L., & Stein, L. (1969). Cholinergic synapses of a periventricular punishment system in the medial hypothalamus. *American Journal of Physiology, 217,* 475–480.

Marley, P. D., Emson, P. C., & Rehfeld, J. F. (1982). Effect of 6-hydroxydopamine lesions of the medial forebrain bundle on the distribution of cholecystokinin in rat forebrain, *Brain Research, 252,* 382–385.

Mark, V. H., & Ervin, F. R. (1970). *Violence and the brain.* New York: Harper & Row.

Marks, W. B., Dobelle, W. H., & MacNichol, E. F. (1964). Visual pigments of single primate cones. *Science, 143,* 1181–1183.

Marsden, C. D. (1984). Motor disorders in basal ganglia disease. *Human Neurobiology, 2,* 245–250.

Martens, H., Klein, T., Rizzo, III, J. F., Shanahan, T. L., & Czeisler, C. A. (1992). Light-induced melatonin suppression in a blind man. *Society for Research in Biological Rhythms Abstracts, 3,* 58.

Martin, J. H., & Jessell, T. M. (1991). Development as a guide to the regional anatomy of the brain. In E. R. Kandel, J. H. Schwartz, & T. M. Jessell (Eds.), *Principles of neural science* (3rd ed., pp. 296–308). Norwalk, CT: Appleton & Lange.

Martini, F. H. (1998). *Fundamentals of anatomy and physiology* (4th ed). Upper Saddle River, NJ: Prentice-Hall.

Marx, J. L. (1980). Ape-language controversy flares up. *Science, 207,* 1330–1333.

Masters, W., & Johnson, V. (1966). *Human sexual response.* Boston: Little, Brown.

Masters, W., & Johnson, V. (1970). *Human sexual inadequacy.* Boston: Little, Brown.

Matthews, K. A., & Haynes, S. G. (1986). Type A behavior pattern and coronary risk: Update and critical evaluations. *American Journal of Epidemiology, 123,* 923–960.

Mayer, J. (1953). Genetic, traumatic, and environmental factors in the etiology of obesity. *Psychological Review, 33,* 472–508.

Mayer, J. (1955). Regulation of energy intake and body weight: The glucostatic theory and the lipostatic hypothesis. *Annals of the New York Academy of Science, 63,* 15–43.

Mayer, J. (1978). *Overweight: Causes, cost and control.* Englewood Cliffs, NJ: Prentice-Hall.

McCaul, K. D., & Malott, J. M. (1984). Distraction and coping with pain. *Psychological Bulletin, 95,* 516–533.

McCormick, D. A. (1989). Acetylcholine: Distribution, receptors, and actions. *Seminars in the Neurosciences, 1,* 91–101.

McCormick, D. A., & Bal, T. (1994). Sensory gating mechanisms of the thalamus. *Current Opinions in Neurobiology, 4,* 550–556.

McDonald, E. R., Wiedenfeld, S. A., Hillel, A., Carpenter, J. L., et al. (1994). Survival in amyotrophic lateral sclerosis: The role of psychological factors. *Archives of Neurology, 51,* 17–23.

McEnvoy, J. (1992). Fragile X syndrome: A brief overview. *Educational Psychology in Practice, 8,* 146–149.

McGinnis, M. Y., Williams, G. W., & Lumia, A. R. (1996). Inhibition of male sex behavior by androgen receptor blockade in preoptic area or hypothalamus, but not amygdala or septum. *Physiology and Behavior, 60,* 783–789.

McGrath, J., Welham, J., & Pemberton, M. (1995). Month of birth, hemisphere of birth and schizophrenia. *British Journal of Psychiatry, 167,* 783–785.

Mednick, S. A., Huttunen, M. O., & Machon, R. A. (1994). Prenatal influenza infections and adult schizophrenia. *Schizophrenia Bulletin, 20,* 263–267.

Mehlman, P. T., Higley, J. D., Faucher, I., Lilly, A. A., Taub, D. M., Vickers, J., Suomi, S. J., & Linnoila, M. (1995). Correlation of CSF 5-HIAA concentration with sociality and the timing of emigration in free-ranging primates. *American Journal of Psychiatry, 152,* 907–913.

Meichenbaum, D. (1977). *Cognitive-behavior modification: An integrative approach.* New York: Plenum.

Meichenbaum, D. (1985). *Stress inoculation training.* New York: Pergamon Press.

Meijer, J. H., & Rietveld, W. J. (1989). Neurophysiology of the suprachiasmatic circadian pacemaker in rodents. *Physiological Reviews, 69,* 671–707.

Meijer, J. H., van der Zee, E. A., & Dietz, M. (1988). Glutamate phase shifts circadian activity rhythms in hamsters. *Neuroscience Letters, 86,* 177–183.

Meijmann, T., van der Meer, O., & van Dormolen, M. (1993). The after-effects of night work on short-term memory performance. *Ergonomics, 36,* 37–42.

Meisel, R. L., & Sachs, B. D. (1994). The physiology of male sexual behavior. In E. Knobil & J. D. Neill (Eds.), *The physiology of reproduction (2nd ed., Vol. 1,* pp. 3–105). New York: Raven.

Meltzer, H. Y., & Stahl, S. M. (1976). The dopamine hypothesis of schizophrenia: A review. *Schizophrenia Bulletin, 2,* 19–76.

Melzack, R., & Wall, P. D. (1965). Pain mechanisms: A new theory. *Science, 150,* 971–979.

Menco, B. P. M., Bruch, R. C., Dau, B., & Danho, W. (1992). Ultrastructural localization of olfactory transduction components: The G protein subunit G_{olf} and type III adenylyl cyclase. *Neuron, 8,* 441–453.

Mendelson, J. (1966). The role of hunger in T-maze learning for food by rats. *Journal of Comparative and Physiological Psychology, 62,* 341–353.

Mendelson, J. (1967). Lateral hypothalamic stimulation in satiated rats: The rewarding effects of self-induced drinking. *Science, 157,* 1077–1079.

Mendelson, W. B. (1987). *Human sleep: Research and clinical care.* New York: Plenum Press.

Mereu, G., Yoon, K-W.P., Boi, V., Gessa, G. L., Naes, L., & Westfall, T. C. (1987). Preferential stimulation of ventral tegmental area dopaminergic neurons by nicotine. *European Journal of Pharmacology, 141,* 395–400.

Merigan, W. H., & Maunsell, J. H. (1993). How parallel are the primate visual pathways? *Annual Review of Neuroscience, 16,* 369–402.

Merzenich, M. M., Knight, P. L., & Roth, G. L. (1975). Representation of cochlea within primary auditory cortex in the cat. *Journal of Neurophysiology, 61,* 231–249.

Meyers, R. (1942). The modification of alternating tremor, rigidity, and festination by surgery of the basal ganglia. *Research Public Association Research Nervous Mental Disorders, 21,* 692–665.

Michael, R. P. (1969). Effects of gonadal hormones on displaced and direct aggression in pairs of rhesus monkeys of opposite sex. In S. Garattini & E. B. Sigg (Eds.), *Aggressive behaviour.* New York: Wiley.

Michael, R. P. (1980). Hormones and sexual behavior in the female. In D. T. Krieger & J. C. Hughes (Eds.), *Neuroendocrinology.* Sunderland, MA: Sinauer Associates.

Miczek, K. A., Thompson, M. L., & Shuster, L. (1986). Analgesia following defeat in an aggressive encounter development of tolerance and changes in opioid receptors. *Annal of the New York Academy of Science, 467,* 14–29.

Miller, J. D., Faull, K. F., Bowersox, S. S., & Dement, W. C. (1990). CNS monoamines and their metabolites in canine narcolpesy: A replication study. *Brain Research, 509,* 169–171.

Miller, N. E. (1985). The value of behavioral research on animals. *American Psychologist,* 40, 423–440.

Miller, N. E., Bailey, C. J., & Stevenson, J. A. F. (1950). Decreased "hunger" but increased food intake resulting from hypothalamic lesions. *Science, 112,* 256–259.

Miller, N. E., & Coons, E. E. (1955). Conflict versus consolidation of memory to explain "retrograde amnesia" produced by ECS. *American Psychologist, 10,* 394.

Miller, R. R., Small, D., & Berk, A. M. (1975). Information content of rat scotophobin. *Behavioral Biology, 15,* 463–472.

Miller, R. R., & Springer, A. D. (1973). Amnesia, consolidation and retrieval. *Psychological Review, 80,* 69–79.

Miller, T. Q., Smith, T. W., Turner, C. W., Guijarro, M. L., & Hallet, A. J. (1996). A meta-analytic review of research on hostility and physical health. *Psychological Bulletin, 119,* 322–348.

Mills, C. B. (1980). Effects of context on reaction time to phonemes. *Journal of Verbal Learning and Verbal Behavior, 19,* 75–83.

Milner, B. (1965). Memory disturbance after bilateral hippocampal lesions. In P. Milner & S. Glickman (Eds.), *Cognitive processes and the brain* (pp. 97–111). Princeton, NJ: Van Nostrand.

Milner, B. (1970). Memory and the temporal regions of the brain. In K. H. Pribram & D. E. Broadbent (Eds.), *Biology of memory* (pp. 29–50). New York: Academic.

Minerbo, G., Albeck, D., Goldberg, E., Lindberg, T., Nakari, M., Martinez, C., Garritano, J., & Smock, T. (1994). Activity of peptidergic neurons in the amygdala during sexual behavior in the male rat. *Experimental Brain Research, 97,* 444–450.

Mirsky, A. F., & Duncan, C. C. (1986). Etiology and expression of schizophrenia: Neurobiological and psychosocial factors. *Annual Review of Psychology, 37,* 291–319.

Misanin, J. R., Miller, R. R., & Lewis, D. J. (1968). Retrograde amnesia produced by electroconvulsive shock after reactivation of a consolidated memory trace. *Science, 160,* 554–555.

Mistlberger, R., Bergmann, B., & Rechtshaffen, A. (1987). Period-amplitude analysis of rat electroencephalogram: Effects of sleep deprivation and exercise. *Sleep, 10,* 508–522.

Moghaddam, B., & Bunney, B. S. (1989). Differential effect of cocaine on extracellular dopamine levels in rat medial prefontal cortex and nucleus accumbens: Comparison to amphetamine. *Synapse, 4,* 156–161.

Mohr, J. P. (1980). Revision of Broca aphasia and the syndrome of Broca's area infarction and its implications in aphasia theory. In R. H. Brookshire (Ed.), *Clinical Aphasiology Conference Proceedings.* Minneapolis: BRK.

Money, J. (1961). Components of eroticism in man: The hormones in relation to sexual morphology and sexual drive. *Journal of Nervous and Mental Diseases, 132,* 239–248.

Money, J. (1980). *Love and love sickness.* Baltimore: Johns Hopkins University Press.

Money, J., & Ehrhardt, A. (1972). *Man and woman, boy and girl.* Baltimore: Johns Hopkins University Press.

Money, J., Schwartz, M., & Lewis, V. G. (1984). Adult erotosexual status and fetal hormonal masculinization and demasculinization: 46,XX congenital virilizing adrenal hyperplasia and 46,XX androgen-insensitivity syndrome compared. *Psychoendocrinology, 9,* 405–414.

Monroe, R. R. (1970). *Episodic behavioral disorders: A psychodynamic and neurophysiologic analysis.* Cambridge, MA: Harvard University Press.

Mook, D. (1969). Some determinants of preference and aversion in the rat. *Annals of the New York Academy of Sciences, 157,* 1158–1170.

Moorcroft, W. H. (1987). An overview of sleep. In J. Gackenback (Ed.), *Sleep and dreams* (pp. 3–29). New York: Garland.

Moore, B. O., & Deutsch, J. A. (1985). An antiemetic is antidotal to the satiety effects of cholecystokinin. *Nature, 315,* 321–322.

Moore, R. Y. (1982). The suprachiasmatic nucleus and the organization of a circadian system. *Trends in Neurosciences, 5,* 404–407.

Moore, R. Y., & Card, J. P. (1985). Visual pathways and the entrainment of circadian rhythms. *Annals of the New York Academy of Sciences, 453,* 123–133.

Moore, R. Y., Card, J. P., & Riley, J. N. (1980). The suprachiasmatic hypothalamic nucleus: Neuronal ultrastructure. *Neuroscience Abstract, 6,* 758.

Moore, R. Y., & Eichler, V. B. (1972). Loss of a circadian adrenal corticosterone rhythm following suprachiasmatic lesions in the rat. *Brain Research, 42,* 201–206.

Moore-Ede, M. C. (1993). *The twenty-four hour society.* Reading, MA: Addison-Wesley.

Moore-Ede, M. C., Sulzman, F. M., & Fuller, C. A. (1982). *The clocks that time us.* Cambridge, MA: Harvard University Press.

Morien, A., McMahon, C., & Wellman, P. J. (1993). Effects on food and water intake of the alpha 1-adrenoceptor agonists amidephrine and SK&F-89748. *Life Sciences, 53,* 169–174.

Morley, J. E. (1982). The ascent of cholecystokinin (CCK)—From gut to brain. *Life Sciences, 30,* 479–493.

Morrison, S. D. (1976). Control of food intake in cancer cachexia: A challenge and a tool. *Physiology and Behavior, 17,* 705–714.

Morselli, P. L., Bossi, L., Henry, J. F., & Bartholini, G. (1986). On the therapeutic action of SL 76002, a new GABA-mimetic agent: Preliminary observations in neuropsychiatric disorders. *Brain Research Bulletin, 5,* 411–414.

Moruzzi, G., & Magoun, H. W. (1949). Brain stem reticular formation and activation of the EEG. *Electroencephalography and Clinical Neurophysiology, 1,* 455–473.

Moscovitch, M. (1992). Memory and working-with-memory: A component process model based on modules and central systems. *Journal of Cognitive Neuroscience, 4,* 257–267.

Movshon, A. (1990). Visual processing of moving images. In H. Barlow, C. Blakemore, & M. Weston-Smith (Eds.), *Images and understanding: Thoughts about images; ideas about understanding* (pp. 122–137). New York: Cambridge University Press.

Movshon, J. A., Adelson, E. H., Gizzi, M. S., & Newsome, W. T. (1985). The analysis of moving visual patterns. In C. Chagas, R. Gattass, & C. Gross (Eds.), *Pattern recognition mechanisms* (pp. 117–151). New York: Springer.

Moyer, K. E. (1976). *The psychobiology of aggression.* New York: Harper & Row.

Moyer, K. E. (1983). The physiology of motivation: Aggression as a model. In C. J. Scheier & A. M. Rogers (Eds.), *G. Stanley Hall lecture series* (Vol. 3). Washington, DC: American Psychological Association.

Mucha, R. F., van der Kooy, D., O'Shaughnessy, M., & Bucenieks, P. (1982). Drug reinforcement studies by the use of place conditioning in rat. *Brain Research, 243,* 91–105.

Mullaney, D. J., Kripke, D. F., Fleck, P. A., & Johnson, C. C. (1983). Sleep loss and nap effects of sustained continuous performance. *Psychophysiology, 20,* 643–651.

Muller, J. (1833–1840). *Handbuch der Physiologie des Menschen fur Vorlesungen,* 2 vols. Coblenz: Holscher.

Mundinger, F., Riechert, T., & Disselhoff, J. (1970). Long-term results of stereotaxic operations on extrapyramidal hyperkinesia (excluding parkinsonism). *Confin Neurology, 32,* 71–78.

Murphy, D. L., Aulakh, C. S., & Garrick, N. A. (1986). How antidepressants work: Cautionary conclusions based on clinical and laboratory studies of the longer-term consequences of antidepressant drug treatment. *Ciba Foundation Symposium, 123,* 106–125.

Murphy, K. J., & Regan, C. M. (in press). Contributions of cell adhesion molecules to altered synaptic weightings during memory consolidation. *Neurobiology of Learning and Memory.*

Murray, A. M., Hyde, T. M., Knable, M. B., Herman, M. M., Bigelow, L. B., Carter, J. M., Weinberger, D. R., & Kleinman, J. E. (1995). Distribution of putative D_4 dopamine receptors in postmortem striatum from patients with schizophrenia. *Journal of Neuroscience, 15,* 2186–2191.

Murray, J. B. (1986). Marijuana's effect on human cognitive functions, psychomotor functions, and personality. *Journal of General Psychology, 113,* 23–55.

Myers, J. J., & Sperry, R. W. (1985). Interhemispheric communication after section of the forebrain commissures. *Cortex, 21,* 249–260.

Myers, R. E., & Sperry, R. W. (1953). Interocular transfer of a visual form discrimination habit in cats after section of the optic chiasma and corpus callosum. *American Association of Anatomists: Abstracts of Papers from Platform,* p. 351.

Myers, R. E., & Sperry, R. W. (1958). Interhemispheric communication through the corpus callosum. Mnemonic carry-over between the hemispheres. *Archives of Neurology and Psychiatry, 80,* 298–303.

Nahas, G. G. (1984). Pharmacologic and epidemiologic aspects of alcohol and cannabis. *New York State Journal of Medicine, 84,* 599–604.

Narabayaski, H. (1972). Stereotaxic amygdalotomy. In B. Eleftheriou (Ed.), *The neurobiology of the amygdala.* New York: Plenum.

National Parkinsonian Foundation (1998, April). Parkinson's disease: An overview. (http://www.pdf.org/disease.htm).

Nauta, W., & Domesick, V. B. (1981). Ramifications of the limbic system. In S. Matthysse (Ed.), *Psychiatry and the biology of the human brain* (pp. 165–188). New York: Elsevier North Holland.

Nauta, W. J. H., & Feirtag, M. (1986). *Fundamental neuroanatomy.* New York: W. H. Freeman.

Nelson, R. J., Badura, L. L., & Goldman, B. D. (1990). Mechanisms of seasonal cycles of behavior. *Annual Review of Psychology, 41,* 81–108.

Nemeroff, C. B., Widerlov, E., Bissette, G., Walleus, H., Karlsson, I., Eklund. K., Kilts, C. D., Loosen, P. T., & Vale, W. (1984). Elevated concentrations of CSF corticotrophin-releasing factor-like immunoreactivity in depressed patients. *Science, 226,* 1342–1344.

Neve, K. A., Kozlowski, M. R., & Marshall, J. F. (1982). Plasticity of neostriatal dopamine receptors after nigrostriatal injury: Relationship to recovery of sensorimotor functions and behavioral supersensitivity. *Brain Research, 244,* 33–44.

Newsome, W. T., Britten, K. H., & Movshon, J. A. (1989). Neuronal correlates of a perceptual decision. *Nature, 341,* 52–54.

Nichols, C. S., & Russell, R. M. (1990). Analysis of animal rights literature reveals the underlying motives of the movement: Ammunition for counter offense by scientists. *Endocrinology, 127,* 985–989.

Nicol, S. E., & Gottesman, I. I. (1983). Clues to the genetics and neurobiology of schizophrenia. *American Scientist, 71,* 398–404.

Nielsen, M., & Braestrup, C. (1977). Chronic treatment with desipramine caused a sustained decrease of 3, 4-dihydroxyphenylglycol-sulphate and total 3-methoxy-4-hydroxyphenylglycol in the rat brain. *Archives of Pharmacology, 300,* 87–92.

Norgren, R. (1970). Gustatory responses in the hypothalamus. *Brain Research, 21,* 63–77.

Nose, H., Morita, M., Yawata, T., & Morimoto, T. (1986). Continuous determination of blood volume on conscious rats during water and food intake. *Japanese Journal of Physiology, 36,* 215–218.

Novaco, R. W. (1985). Anger and its therapeutic regulation. In M. Chesney & R. Rosenman (Eds.), *Anger and hostility in cardiovascular and behavioral disorders.* Washington, DC: Hemisphere.

Nyberg, L., Cabeza, R., & Tulving, E. (1996). PET studies of encoding and retrieval: The HERA model. *Psychonomic Bulletin and Review, 3,* 135–148.

Oades, R. D. (1981). Impairments of search behaviour in rats after haloperidol treatment, hippocampal or neocortical damage suggest a mesocorticolimbic role in cognition. *Biological Psychology, 12,* 77–85.

Oakley, K., & Toates, F. M. (1969). The passage of food through the guts of rats and its uptake of fluid. *Psychonomic Science, 16,* 225–226.

O'Brien, D. F. (1982). The chemistry of vision. *Science, 218,* 961–966.

O'Dell, T. J., Hawkins, R. D., Kandel, E. R., & Arancio, O. (1991). Tests of the roles of two diffusible substances in long-term potentiation: Evidence for nitric oxide as a possible early retrograde messenger. *Proceedings of the National Academy of Sciences, USA, 88,* 11285–11289.

Okubo, Y., Suhara, T., Suzuki, K., Kobayashi, I., Inoue, O., Terasaki, O., Someya, Y., Sassa, T., Sudo, Y., Matsushima, E., Iyo, M., Tateno, Y., & Toru, M. (1997). Decreased prefrontal dopamine D_1 receptors in schizophrenia revealed by PET. *Nature, 385,* 634–636.

Olds, J. (1962). Hypothalamic substrates of reward. *Psychological Review, 42,* 554–604.

Olds, J., & Milner, P. (1954). Positive reinforcement produced by electrical stimulation of septal area and other regions of rat brain. *Journal of Comparative and Physiological Psychology, 47,* 419–427.

Olney, J. W. (1994). New mechanisms in excitatory transmitter neurotoxicity. *Journal of Neural Transmission Supplement, 43,* 47–51.

O'Malley, S., Jaffe, A., Chang, G., & Schottenfeld, R. S. (1996). Six-month follow-up of naltrexone and psychotherapy for alcohol dependence. *Archives of General Psychiatry, 53,* 217–224.

Oppenheim, R. W. (1991). Cell death during development of the nervous system. *Annual Review of Neuroscience, 14,* 453–501.

Orban, G., Dupont, P., Vogels, R., De, B. B., Bormans, G., & Mortelmans, L. (1996). Task dependency of visual processing in the human visual system. *Behavioral Brain Research, 76(1–2),* 215–223.

Oulette-Kobasa, S. C., & Pucetti, M. C. (1983). Personality and social resources in stress resistance. *Journal of Personality and Social Psychology, 45,* 836–850.

Overman, W. H., Ormsby, G., & Mishkin, M. (1990). Picture recognition vs. picture discrimination learning in monkeys with medial temporal removals. *Experimental Brain Resources, 79,* 18–24.

Pakkenberg, B. (1990). Pronounced reduction of total neuron number in mediodorsal thalamic nucleus and nucleus accumbens in schizophrenics. *Archives of General Psychiatry, 47,* 1023–1028.

Palace, E. M. (1995). Modification of dysfunctional patterns of sexual response through autonomic arousal and false physiological feedback. *Journal of Consulting and Clinical Psychology, 63,* 604–615.

Palca, J. (1989). Sleep researchers awake to possibilities. *Science, 245,* 351–352.

Panksepp, J. (1969). Electrically induced affective attack from the hypothalamus of the albino rat. *Psychonomic Science, 16,* 118–119.

Panksepp, J. (1986). The neurochemistry of behavior. *Annual Review of Psychology, 37,* 77–107.

Panskepp, J., & Trowill, J. (1969). Electrically induced affect attack from the hypothalamus of the male rat. *Psychonomic Science, 16,* 118–119.

Papanicolaou, A.C., Moore, B.D., Deutsch, G., Levin, H.S., & Eisenberg, H.M. (1988). Evidence for right-hemisphere involvement in recovery from aphasia. *Archives of Neurology, 45,* 1025–1029.

Papez, J. W. (1937). A proposed mechanism of emotion. *Archives of Neurology and Psychiatry, 38,* 725–743.

Parkinson, L. (1817). *An essay on shaking palsy.* London.

Parlee, M. B. (1982). Changes in moods and activation levels during the menstrual cycle in experimentally naive subjects. *Psychology of Women Quarterly, 7,* 119–131.

Parrent, A. G., Lozano, A. M., Postrovsky, J. O., & Tasker, R. R. (1992). Central pain in the absence of functional sensory thalamus. *Stereotactic Functional Neurosurgery, 59,* 9–14.

Pauls, D. L., Morton, L. A., & Egeland, J. A. (1992). Risks of affective illness among first-degree relatives of bipolar I old-order Amish probands. *Archives of General Psychiatry, 49,* 703–708.

Paulson, H. L., & Fischbeck, K. H. (1996). Trinucleotide repeats in neurogenetic disorders. *Annual Review of Neuroscience, 19,* 79–107.

Pate, J. L., & Rumbaugh, D. H. (1983). The language-like behavior of Lana chimpanzee: Is it merely discrimination learning and paired-associate learning? *Animal Learning and Behavior, 11,* 134–138.

Peck, J. W., & Novin, D. (1971). Evidence that osmoreceptors mediating drinking in rabbits are in the lateral preoptic region. *Journal of Comparative and Physiological Psychology, 74,* 134–147.

Penfield, W. (1975). *The mystery of mind.* Princeton, NJ: Princeton University Press.

Penfield, W., & Jasper, H. (1954). *Epilepsy and the functional anatomy of the brain.* Boston: Little, Brown.

Perecman, E., & Brown, J. W. (1981). Phonemic jargon: A case report. In J. W. Brown (Ed.), *Jargonaphasia.* New York: Academic Press.

Perischetti, F., Srinidhi, J., Kanaley, L., Ge, P., Myers, R. H., D'Arrigo, K., Barnes, G. T., McDonald, M. E., Vonsattel, J. P., Gusella, J. F., & Bird, E. D. (1994). Huntington's disease CAG trinucleotide repeats in pathologically confirmed post-mortem brains. *Neurobiology of Disease, 1,* 159–166.

Perkins, K. A., Epstein, L. H., & Pastor, S. (1990). Changes in energy balance following smoking cessation and resumption of smoking in women. *Journal of Clinical and Consulting Psychology, 58,* 121–125.

Peterson, S. E., Fox, P. T., Posner, M. I., Mintun, M. A., & Raichle, M. E. (1988). PET studies of the cortical anatomy of single-word processing. *Nature, 331,* 585–589.

Petty, F., & Schlesser, M. A. (1981). Plasma GABA in affective illness. A preliminary investigation. *Journal of Affective Disorders, 3,* 339–343.

Pfaff, D. W. (1997). Hormones, genes, and behavior. *Proceedings of the National Academy of Sciences (USA), 94,* 14213–14216.

Pfaff, D. W., & Pfaffmann, C. (1969). Olfactory and hormonal influences on the basal forebrain on the male rat. *Brain Research, 15,* 137–156.

Pfaff, D. W., & Sakuma, Y. (1979). Deficit in the lordosis reflex of female rats caused by lesions in the ventromedial nucleus of the hypothalamus. *Journal of Physiology, 288,* 203–210.

Pfaus, J. G., Damsma, G., Wenkstern, D., & Fibiger, H. C. (1995). Sexual activity increases dopamine transmission in the nucleus accumbens and striatum of female rats. *Brain Research, 693,* 21–30.

Pfefferbaum, A., Lim, K. O., Rosenbloom, M., & Zipursky, R. B. (1990). Brain magnetic resonance imaging: Approaches for investigating schizophrenia. *Schizophrenia Bulletin, 16,* 453–476.

Pfeiffer, C. A. (1936). Sexual differences of the hypophysis and their determination by the gonads. *American Journal of Anatomy, 58,* 195–226.

Phillips, A. G., Blaha, C., & Fibiger, H. (1989). Neurochemical correlates of brain stimulation reward measured by *ex vivo* and *in vivo* analyses. *Neuroscience and Biobehavioral Reviews, 13,* 99–104.

Phillips, A. G., & Fibiger, H. C. (1989). Neuroanatomical bases of intracranial self-stimulation: Untangling the Gordian knot. In J. M. Leibman & S. J. Cooper (Eds.), *The neuropharmacological basis of reward* (pp. 66–105). Oxford: Clarendon.

Phoenix, C. W., Goy, R. W., Gerald, A. A., & Young, W. C. (1959). Organizing action of prenatally administered testosterone proprionate on the tissue mediating mating behavior in the female guinea pig. *Endocrinology, 65,* 369–382.

Pickar, D., Labarca, R., Linnoila, M., Roy, A., Hommer, D., Everett, D., & Paul, S. M. (1984). Neuroleptic-induced decrease in plasma homovanillic acid and antipsychotic activity in schizophrenic patients. *Science, 225,* 954–957.

Pilowsky, L. S., Costa, D. C., Ell, P. J., Murray, R. M., Verhoeff, N. P., & Kerwin, R. W. (1992). Clozapine, single photon emission tomography, and the D_2 dopamine receptor blockade hypothesis of schizophrenia. *Lancet, 340,* 199–202.

Plapinger, L., McEwen, B. S., & Clemens, C. E. (1993). Ontogeny of estradiol-binding sites in the rat brain: II. Characteristics of a neonatal binding macromolecule. *Endocrinology, 93,* 1129–1139.

Pleim, E. T. , & Barfield, R. J. (1988). Progesterone versus estrogen facilitation of female sexual behavior by intracranial administration to female rats. *Hormones and Behavior, 22,* 150–159.

Plomin, R., DeFries, J. C., McClearn, G. E., & Rutter, M. (1997). *Behavioral genetics.* New York: Freeman.

Poeck, K., Huber, W., & Willmes, K. (1989). Outcome of intensive language rehabilitation in aphasia. *Journal of Speech and Hearing Disorders, 54,* 471–479.

Poggio, G. F. (1990). Cortical neural mechanisms of stereopsis studied with dynamic random-dot stereograms. *Cold*

Spring Harbor Symposium Quantitative Biology, 55, 749–758.

Poggio, G. F., & Poggio, T. (1984). The analysis of stereopsis. *Annual Review of Neuroscience, 7,* 379–412.

Poggio, T. (1984). Vision by man and machine. *Scientific American, 250,* 106–116.

Pohl, W. (1973). Dissociation of spatial discrimination deficits following frontal and parietal lesions in monkeys. *Comparative and Physiological Psychology, 82,* 227–239.

Polivy, J., & Herman, C. P. (1985). Dieting and binging: A causal analysis. *American Psychologist, 40,* 193–201.

Poltorak, M., Wright, R., Hemperly, J. J., Torrey, E. F., Issa, R., Wyatt, R. J., & Freed, W. J. (1997). Monozygotic twins discordant for schizophrenia are discordant for N-CAM and L1 in CSF. *Brain Research, 751,* 152–154.

Pons, T. P., Garraghty, P. E., Friedman, D. P., & Mishkin, M. (1987). Physiological evidence for serial processing in somatosensory cortex. *Science, 237,* 417–420.

Popova, N. K., Nikulina, E. M., & Kulikov, A. V. (1993). Genetic analysis of different kinds of aggressive behavior. *Behavioral Genetics, 23,* 491–497.

Post, R. M., Ballenger, J. C., Uhde, T., & Bunney, W. (1984). Efficacy of carbamazepine in manic-depressive illness: Implications for underlying mechanisms. In R. M. Post & C. Ballenger (Eds.), *Neurobiology of mood disorders.* Baltimore: Williams & Wilkins.

Power, P. S., Schulman, R. G., Gleghorn, A. A., & Prange, M. E. (1987). Perceptual and cognitive abnormalities in bulimia. *American Journal of Psychiatry, 144,* 1456–1460.

Powley, T. L. (1977). The ventromedial hypothalamic syndrome, satiety, and a cephalic phase hypothesis. *Psychological Review, 84,* 89–126.

Powley, T. L., & Keesey, R. E. (1970). Relationship of body weight to the lateral hypothalamic feeding syndrome. *Journal of Comparative and Physiological Psychology, 70,* 25–36.

Prien, R. F., Caffey, E. M., Jr., & Klett, C. J. (1973). Prophylactic efficacy of lithium carbonate in manic-depressive illness. *Archives of General Psychiatry, 28,* 337–341.

Puce, A., Allison, T., Gore, J. C., & McCarthy, G. (1995). Face-sensitive regions in human extrastriate cortex studied by functional MRI. *Journal of Neurophysiology, 74,* 1192–1199.

Purdy, D. (1983). Birth Defects. *Current Health, 2,* 12–13.

Purves, D., & Lichtman, J. W. (1985). *Principles of neural development.* Sunderland, MA: Sinauer.

Qualtrochi, J. J., Mamelak, A. N., Madison, R. D., Macklis, J. D., & Hobson, J. A. (1989). Mapping neuronal inputs to REM sleep induction sites with carbachol fluorescent microspheres. *Science, 245,* 984–986.

Quartermain, D. (1976). The influence of drugs on learning and memory. In M. R. Rosenzweig & E. L. Bennet (Eds.), *Neural mechanisms of learning and memory* (pp. 508–520). Cambridge, MA: MIT Press.

Rachman, S. (1966). Sexual fetishism: An experimental analogue. *Psychological Record, 16,* 293–296.

Raglin, J. S. (1992). Anxiety and sport performance. In J. O. Holloszy (Ed.), *Exercise and sports sciences reviews* (Vol. 20). Baltimore: Williams & Wilkins.

Ralph, M. R., Foster, R. G., Davis, F. C., & Menaker, M. (1990). Transplanted suprachiasmatic nucleus determines circadian period. *Science, 247,* 975–978.

Ramamurthi, B. (1988). Stereotactic operation in behaviour disorders. Amygdalotomy and hypothalamotomy. *Acta Neurochir Supplementum (Wien), 44,* 152–157.

Raming, K., Krieger, J., Strotman, J., Boekhoff, I., Kubick, S., Baumstark, C., & Breer, H. (1993). Cloning and expression of odorant molecules. *Nature, 361,* 353–356.

Ramón y Cajal, S. (1894). La fine strucure des centres nerveux. *Proceedings Royal Society London, 55,* 444–468.

Ramón y Cajal, S. (1911). *Histologie du Systeme Nerveux de l'Homme & des Vertebres,* Vol. 2. L. Azoulay (Trans.). Paris: Maloine. Republished in 1955. Madrid: Instituto Ramon y Cajal.

Ransmeier, R. E. (1953). *The effects of convulsion, hypoxia, hypothermia, and anesthesia on retention in the master.* Unpublished doctoral dissertation, University of Chicago.

Rapkin, A. J., Pollack, D. B., Raleigh, M. J., Stone, B., & McGuire, M. T. (1995). Menstrual cycle and social behavior in vervet monkeys. *Psychoneuroendocrinology, 20,* 289–297.

Rapoport, S. I., & Robinson, P. J. (1986). Tight-junctional modification as the basis of osmotic opening of the blood-brain barrier. *Annals of the New York Academy of Sciences, 481,* 250–267.

Rasmussen, T., & Milner, B. (1975). Clinical and surgical studies of the cerebral speech areas in man. In K. J. Zulch, O. Creutzfeldt, & G. C. Galbraith (Eds.), *Cerebral localization* (pp. 238–257). Berlin: Springer-Verlag.

Rauch, S. L., & Raskin, L. A. (1984). Cholinergic mediation of spatial memory in the preweanling rat: Application of the radial arm maze paradigm. *Behavioral Neuroscience, 98,* 35–43.

Ray, O., & Ksir, C. (1996). *Drugs, society, and human behavior* (7th ed.). St. Louis: Mosby.

Redfern, P. A. (1970). Neuromuscular transmission in new-born rats. *Journal of Physiology (London), 209,* 701–709.

Redmond, D. E., Jr., Naftolin, F., Collier, T. J., Leranth, C., Robbins, R. J., Sladek, C. D., Roth, R. H., & Sladek, J. R., Jr. (1988). Cryopreservation, culture, and transplantation of human fetal mesencephalic tissue into monkeys. *Science, 242,* 768–771.

Reedy, F. E. J., Bartoshuk, L. M., Miller, I. J. J., Duffy, V. B., Lucchina, L., & Yanagisawa, K. (1993). Relationships among papillae, taste pores, and 6-n-propylthiouracil (prop) suprathreshold taste sensitivity. *Chemical Senses, 18,* 618–619.

Reeves, T. M., & Smith, D. C. (1987). Reinnervation of the dentate gyrus and recovery of alternation behavior following entorhinal cortex lesions. *Behavioral Neuroscience, 101,* 179–189.

Reisenzein, R. (1983). The Schachter theory of emotion: Two decades later. *Psychological Bulletin, 94,* 239–264.

Ressler, K. J., Sullivan, S. L., & Buck, L. B. (1994). A molecular dissection of spatial patterning in the olfactory system. *Current Opinion in Neurobiology, 4,* 588–596.

Reynolds, D. V. (1969). Surgery in the rat during electrical analgesia induced by focal brain stimulation. *Science, 164,* 444–445.

Rice, J., Reich, T., Andreasen, N. C., Endicott, J., VanEerdewegh, M., Fishman, R., Hirschfeld, R. M. A., & Klerman, G. L. (1987). The familial transmission of bipolar illness. *Archives of General Psychiatry, 44,* 441–447.

Richelson, E. (1996). Preclinical pharmacology of neuroleptics: Focus on new generation compounds. *Journal of Clinical Psychiatry, 57,* 4–11.

Richter, C. P. (1967). Psychopathology of periodic behavior in animals and man. In J. Zubin & H. F. Hunt (Eds.), *Comparative psychopathology* (pp. 205–227). New York: Grune & Stratton.

Ritter, R. C., Brenner, L., & Yox, D. P. (1992). Participation of vagal sensory neurons in putative satiety signals from the upper gastrointestinal tract. In S. Ritter, R. C. Ritter, & C. D. Barnes (Eds.), *Neuroanatomy and physiology of abdominal vagal afferents.* Boca Raton, FL: CRC Press.

Ritter, R. C., Slusser, P. G., & Stone, S. (1981). Glucoreceptors controlling feeding and blood glucose: Location in the hindbrain. *Science, 213,* 451–453.

Ritter, S., & Taylor, J. S. (1989). Capsaicin abolishes lipoprivic but not glucoprivic feeding in rats. *American Journal of Physiology, 256,* R1232–R1239.

Ritter, S., & Taylor, J. S. (1990). Vagal sensory neurons are required for lipoprivic but not glucoprivic feeding in rats. *American Journal of Physiology, 258,* R1395–R1401.

Roberts, D. C. S., & Koob, G. F. (1982). Disruption of cocaine self-administration following 6-OHDA lesions of the VTA in rats. *Pharmacology, Biochemistry, and Behavior, 17,* 901–904.

Roberts, D. C. S., & Zito, K. A. (1987). Interpretation of lesion effects on stimulant self-administration. In M. A. Bozarth (Ed.), *Methods of assessing the reinforcing properties of abused drugs* (pp. 87–103). New York: Springer-Verlag.

Roberts, S. B., Savage, J., Coward, W. A., Chew, B., & Lucas, A. (1988). Energy expenditure and intake in infants born to lean and overweight mothers. *New England Journal of Medicine, 318,* 461–466.

Robinson, B. W., & Mishkin, M. (1968). Alimentary responses to forebrain stimulation in monkeys. *Experimental Brain Research, 4,* 330–336.

Rock, I., & Palmer, S. (1990, December). The legacy of Gestalt psychology. *Scientific American,* 84–90.

Rodin, J. (1986). Aging and health: Effects of the sense of control. *Science, 233,* 1271–1276.

Rodin, J., & Salovey, P. (1989). Health psychology. *Annual Review of Psychology, 40,* 533–579.

Roeder, F., & Mueller, D. (1969). The stereotaxic treatment of pedophilic homosexuality. *German Medical Monthly* (English Language Monthly), *14*, 265–271.

Roelink, H., Augsburger, A., Heemskerk, J., Korzh, V., Norlin, S., Ruiz i Altaba, A., Tanabe, Y., Placzek, M., Edlund, T., Jessell, T. M. et al. (1994). Floor plate and motor neuron induction by vhh-1, a vertebrate homolog of hedgehog expressed by the notochord. *Cell, 76*, 761–775.

Roffwarg, H. P., Munzio, J. N., & Dement, W. C. (1966). Ontogenic development of the human sleep-dream cycle. *Science, 152*, 604–619.

Roland, P. E. (1993). *Brain activation.* New York: Wiley-Liss.

Rolls, B. J., Wood, R. J., & Rolls, R. M. (1980). Thirst: The initiation, maintenance, and termination of drinking. In J. M. Sprague & A. N. Epstein (Eds.), *Progress in psychology and physiological psychology.* New York: Academic Press.

Roos, K. P. (1986). Length, width, and volume changes in osmotically stressed myocytes. *American Journal of Physiology, 251*, H1373–H1378.

Rose, J. E., Brugge, J. F., Anderson, D. J., & Hind, J. E. (1967). Phase-locked response to low-frequency tones in single auditory nerve fibers of the squirrel monkey. *Journal of Neurophysiology, 30*, 769–793.

Rosenblatt, J. S. (1965). Effect of experience on sexual behavior in cats. In F. Beach (Ed.), *Sex and behavior.* New York: Wiley.

Rosenthal, D. (Ed.). (1963). *The Genain quadruplets: A case study and theoretical analysis of heredity and environment in schizophrenia.* New York: Basic Books.

Rosenthal, D. (1970). *Genetic theory and abnormal behavior.* New York: McGraw-Hill.

Rosenthal, N. E., Saek, D. A., James, S. P., Parry, B. G., Mendelson, W. B., Tamarking, I., & Wehr, T. A. (1985). Seasonal affective disorder and psychotherapy. *Annals of the New York Academy of Sciences, 453*, 260–269.

Rosenthal, T. L. & Rosenthal, R. H. (1985). Clinical stress management. In D. H. Barlow (Ed.), *Clinical handbook of psychological disorders: A step-by-step treatment manual.* (pp. 145–202). New York: Guilford Press.

Ross, M. J., & Berger, R. S. (1996). Effects of stress inoculation training on athletes' postsurgical pain and rehabilitation after orthopedic injury. *Journal of Consulting and Clinical Psychology, 64*, 406–410.

Routtenberg, A., & Lindy, J. (1965). Effects of the availability of rewarding septal and hypothalamic stimulation on bar-pressing for food under conditions of deprivation. *Journal of Comparative and Physiological Psychology, 60*, 158–161.

Roy, A., DeJong, J., Linnoila, M. (1989). Cerebrospinal fluid monoamine metabolites and suicidal behavior in depressed patients. *Archives of General Psychiatry, 46*, 609–612.

Roy-Byrne, P. P., Post, R. M., Uhde, T. W., Porcu, T., & Davis, D. (1985). The longitudinal course of recurrent affective illness: Life chart data from research patients at the NIMH. *Acta Psychiatrica Scandinavica Supplementum, 71*, 3–34.

Rozkowska, E., & Fonberg, E. (1973). Salivary reactions after ventromedial hypothalamic lesions in dogs. *Acta Neurobiologica Experimentalis, 33*, 553–562.

Ruderman, A. J. (1986). Dietary restraint: A theoretical and empirical review. *Psychological Review, 99*, 247–262.

Ruderman, A. J., & Grace, P. S. (1988). Bulimics and restrained eaters: A personality comparison. *Addictive Behavior, 13*, 359–368.

Rumbaugh, D. M. (1990). Comparative psychology and the great apes: Their competency in learning, language, and numbers. *Psychological Record, 40*, 15–39.

Rumbaugh, D. M., & Gill, R. V. (1976). The mastery of language-type skills by the chimpanzee (Pan). *Annals of the New York Academy of Sciences, 280*, 562–578.

Rusak, B., & Groos, G. (1982). Suprachiasmatic stimulation phase shifts rodent circadian rhythms. *Science, 215*, 1407–1409.

Russek, M. (1971). Hepatic receptors and the neurophysiological mechanisms controlling feeding behavior. In S. Ehrenpreis (Ed.), *Neurosciences research* (Vol. 4). New York: Academic Press.

Rutherford, W. (1886). A new theory of hearing. *Journal of Anatomy and Physiology, 21*, 166–168.

Sacks, O. (1985). *The man who mistook his wife for a hat and other clinical tales.* New York: Harper Collins.

Saitoh, K., Maruyama, N., & Kudoh, M. (1981). Sustained response of auditory cortex units in the cat. In Y. Katsuki, R. Norgren, & M. Sato. (Eds.), *Brain mechanisms of sensation.* New York: Wiley.

Sakai, K. (1980). Some anatomical and physiological properties of pontomesencephalic tegmental neurons with special reference to the PGO waves and postural atonia during paradoxical sleep in the cat. In J. A. Hobson & M. A. Brazier (Eds.), *The reticular formation revisited.* New York: Raven Press.

Sakai, R. R., & Epstein, A. N. (1990). Dependence of adrenalectomy-induced sodium appetite on the action of angiotensin II in the brain of the rat. *Behavioral Neuroscience, 104*, 167-176.

Saller, C. F., & Stricker, E. M. (1976). Hyperphagia and increased growth in rats after intraventricular injection of 5,7-kihydroxytryptamine. *Science, 192*, 385–387.

Sanders, R. J. (1989). Sentence comprehension following agenesis of the corpus callosum. *Brain and Language, 37*, 59–72.

Sapolsky, B. M. (1996). Why stress is bad for your brain. *Science, 273*, 749–750.

Sarason, I. G., & Sarason, B. R. (1993). *Abnormal psychology* (7th ed.). Upper Saddle River, NJ: Prentice-Hall.

Sartorius, N., Shapiro, R., & Jablonsky, A. (1974). The international pilot study of schizophrenia. *Schizophrenia Bulletin, 2*, 21–35.

Satz, P. (1980). Incidence of aphasia in left-handers: A test of some hypothetical models of cerebral speech organization. In J. Herron (Ed.), *Neuropsychology of left-handedness.* New York: Academic Press.

Sauerwein, H. C., Lassonde, M. C., Cardu, B., & & Geoffroy, G. (1981). Interhemispheric integration of sensory and motor functions in agenesis of the corpus callosum. *Neuropsychologia, 19*, 445–454.

Savage-Rumbaugh, E. S., Rumbaugh, D. M., & Boysen, S. (1980). Do apes use language? *American Scientist, 68*, 49–61.

Savage-Rumbaugh, E. S., Sevcik, R. A., Brakke, K. E., & Rumbaugh, D. M. (1992). Symbols: Their communicative use, communication, and combination by bonobos (*Pan panicus*). In L. P. Lipsitt & C. Rovee-Collier (Eds.), *Advances in infancy research* (Vol. 7, pp. 221–278). Norwood, NJ: Ablex.

Sawrey, W. L., Conger, J. J., & Turrell, E. S. (1956). An experimental investigation of the role of psychological factors in the production of gastric ulcers in rats. *Journal of Comparative and Physiological Psychology, 49*, 457–461.

Sawyer, C. H. (1960). Reproductive behavior. In J. Field (Ed.), *Handbook of physiology. Section 1: Neurophysiology* (Vol. II). Washington, DC: American Psychological Society.

Schachter, S. (1964). The interaction of cognitive and physiological determinants of emotional state. In L. Berkowitz (Ed.), *Advances in experimental social psychology* (Vol. 1). New York: Academic Press.

Schachter, S. (1971). Some extraordinary facts about obese humans and rats. *American Psychologist, 26*, 129–144.

Schachter, S., & Singer, J. E. (1962). Cognitive, social, and physiological determinants of emotional state. *Psychological Review, 69*, 379–399.

Scharf, B. (1975). Audition. In B. Scharf (Ed.), *Experimental sensory psychology.* Glenview, IL: Scott-Foresman.

Scheibel, A. B., & Conrad, A. S. (1993). Hippocampal dysgenesis in mutant mouse and schizophrenic man: Is there a relationship? *Schizophrenia Bulletin, 19*, 21–33.

Schenck, C. H., Bundlie, S. R., Ettinger, M. G., & Mahowald, M. W. (1986). Chronic behavioral disorders of human REM sleep: A new category of parasomnia. *Sleep, 9*, 293–308.

Schenck, C. H., & Mahowald, M. W. (1992). Motor dyscontrol in narcolepsy: Rapid-eye-movement (REM) sleep without atonia and REM sleep behavior disorder. *Annals of Neurology, 32*, 3–10.

Schenkel, E., & Siegel, J. M. (1989). REM sleep without atonia after lesions of the medial medulla. *Neuroscience Letters, 98*, 159–165.

Schildkraut, J. J. (1965). The catecholamine hypothesis of affective disorders: A review of supporting evidence. *American Journal of Psychiatry, 122*, 509–522.

Schildkraut, J. J. (1978). The biochemistry of affective disorders: A brief summary. In A. M. Nicholi, Jr. (Ed.), *The Harvard guide to modern psychiatry.* Cambridge, MA: Harvard University Press.

Schildkraut, J. J., Green, A. I., & Mooney, J. J. (1985). Affective disorders: Biochemical aspects. In H. I. Kaplan & B. J. Sadock (Eds.), *Comprehensive textbook of psychiatry/IV.* Baltimore: Williams & Wilkins.

Schiller, P. H. (1996). On the specificity of neurons and visual areas. *Behavioural Brain Research, 76,* 21–35.

Schlaadt, R., & Shannon, P. T. (1990). *Drugs* (3rd ed.). Upper Saddle River, NJ: Prentice-Hall.

Schmitt, M. (1973). Influences of hepatic portal receptors on hypothalamic feeding and satiety centers. *American Journal of Physiology, 225,* 1089–1095.

Schnapf, J. L., & Baylor, D. A. (1987). How photoreceptor cells respond to light. *Scientific American, 256,* 40–47.

Schneider-Helmert, D., & Spinweber, C. L. (1986). Evaluation of L-tryptophan for treatment of insomnia: A review. *Psychopharmacology, 89,* 1–7.

Schnell, L., & Schwab, M. E. (1993). Sprouting and regeneration of lesioned corticospinal tracts in the adult rat spinal cord. *European Journal of Neuroscience, 5,* 1156–1171.

Schnurr, R. (1972). Localization of septal rage syndrome in Long Evans rats. *Journal of Comparative and Physiological Psychology, 81,* 291–296.

Schoenlein, R. W., Peteanu, L. A., Mathies, R. A., & Shank, C. V. (1991). The first step in vision: Femtosecond isomerization of rhodopsin. *Science, 254,* 412–421.

Schotzinger, R. J., & Landis, S. C. (1988). Cholinergic phenotype developed by noradrenergic sympathetic neurons after innervation of a novel cholinergic target in vivo. *Nature, 335,* 637–639.

Schreiner, L., & Kling, A. (1953). Behavioral changes following rhinencephalic injury in the cat. *Journal of Neurophysiology, 16,* 643–658.

Schuell, H. H., Jenkins, J. J., & Jimenez-Pabon, E. (1964). *Aphasia in adults.* New York: Harper & Row.

Schwartz, J. C., Giros, B., Martres, M.-P., & Sokoloff, P. (1992). The dopamine receptor family: Molecular biology and pharmacology. *Seminars in the Neurosciences, 4,* 99–108.

Schwartz, J. H. (1991). The cytology of neurons. In E. R. Kandel, J. H. Schwartz, & T. M. Jessell (Eds.), *Principles of neural science* (3rd ed., pp. 37–48). Norwalk, CT: Appleton & Lange.

Schwartz, M. (1956). Instrumental and consummatory measures of sexual capacity in the male rat. *Journal of Comparative and Physiological Psychology, 49,* 328–333.

Schwartz, R. (1984). Body weight regulation. *University of Washington Medicine, 10,* 16–20.

Schwartz, W. J., & Gainer, H. (1977). Suprachiasmatic nucleus: Use of 14C-labeled deoxyglucose uptake as a functional marker. *Science, 197,* 1089–1091.

Sclafani, A. (1971). Neural pathways involved in the ventromedial hypothalamic lesion syndrome in the rat. *Journal of Comparative and Physiological Psychology, 77,* 70–96.

Sclafani, A., & Kluge, L. (1974). Food motivation and body weight levels in hypothalamic hyperphagic rats: A dual lipostat model of hunger and appetite. *Journal of Comparative and Physiological Psychology, 86,* 28–46.

Scott, T. R., & Plata-Salaman, C. R. (1991). Coding of taste quality. In T. V. Getchell (Ed.), *Smell and taste in health and disease* (pp. 345–368). New York: Raven Press.

Scoville, W. B., & Milner, B. (1957). Loss of recent memory after bilateral hippocampal lesions. *Journal of Neurology, Neurosurgery, and Psychiatry, 20,* 11–21.

Scrima, G. (1982). The narcoleptic approach paradigm (NAP) for the direct study of dreams and dream sleep. *International Journal of Neuroscience, 16,* 69–73.

Sedvall, G., Fyro, B., Nyback, H., Wiesel, F. A., & Wode-Helgodt, B. (1974). Mass fragmentometric determination of homovanillic acid in lumbar cerebrospinal fluid of schizophrenic patients during treatment with antipsychotic drugs. *Journal of Psychiatric Research, 11,* 75–80.

Seeman, P., & Lee, T. (1975). Antipsychotic drugs: Direct correlation between clinical potency and presynaptic action of dopamine neurons. *Science, 188,* 1217–1219.

Seil, F. J., Kelly III, J. M., & Leiman, A. C. (1974). Anatomical organization of cerebral neocortex in tissue culture. *Experimental Neurology, 45,* 435–450.

Selemon, L. D., Rajkowska, G., & Goldman-Rakic, P. S. (1995). Abnormally high neuronal density in the schizophrenic cortex. A morphometric analysis of prefrontal area 9 and occipital area 17. *Archives of General Psychiatry, 52,* 805–818.

Seligman, M. E. P. (1975). *Helplessness: On depression, development, and death.* San Francisco: Freeman.

Selkoe, D. J. (1991). The molecular pathology of Alzheimer's disease. *Neuron, 6,* 487–498.

Selkoe, D. J. (1992). Aging brain, aging mind. *Scientific American, 267,* 60–67.

Selye, H. (1956). *The stress of life.* New York: McGraw-Hill.

Sem-Jacobson, C. W. (1968). *Depth-electrographic stimulation of the human brain and behavior: From fourteen years of studies and treatment of Parkinson's disease and mental disorders with implanted electrodes.* Springfield, IL: Thomas.

Seyfarth, R. M., Cheney, D. L., & Marler, P. (1980). Monkey responses to three different alarm calls: Evidence of predator classification and semantic communication. *Science, 210,* 801–803.

Shagass, C., & Malmo, R. B. (1954). Psychodynamic themes and localized muscle tension during psychotherapy. *Psychosomatic Medicine, 16,* 295–313.

Shapiro, A. P. (1996). *Hypertension and stress: A unified concept.* Mahwah, NJ: Erlbaum.

Shapiro, B. E., & Danly, M. (1985). The role of the right hemisphere in the control of speech prosody in propositional and affective contexts. *Brain and Language, 25,* 19–36.

Shapiro, C. M. (1982). Energy expenditure and restorative sleep. *Biological Psychology, 15,* 229–239.

Shapiro, R. M. (1993). Regional neuropathology in schizophrenia: Where are we? Where are we going? *Schizophrenia Research, 10,* 187–239.

Sharma, K. N., Anand, B. K., Dua, S., & Singh, D. (1961). Role of stomach in regulation of activities of hypothalamic feeding centers. *American Journal of Physiology, 201,* 593–598.

Shatz, C. J. (1992). The developing brain. *Scientific American, 267,* 60–67.

Shaywitz, S. E., Shaywitz, B. A., Pugh, K. R., Fulbright, R. K., Constable, R. T., Mencl, W. E., Shankweiler, D. P., Liberman, A. M., Skudlarski, P., Fletcher, J. M., Katz, L., Marchione, K. E., Lacadie, C., Gatenby, C., & Gore, J. C. (1988). Functional disruption in the organization of the brain for reading in dyslexia. *Proceedings of the National Academy of Sciences USA, 95,* 2636–2641.

Shelton, R. C., & Weinberger, D. R. (1986). X-ray computed tomography studies in schizophrenia: A review and synthesis. In H. A. Nasvallack & D. R. Weinberger (Eds.), *The neurology of schizophrenia* (pp. 207–250). Amsterdam: Elsevier Science.

Sherrington, C. S. (1900). Experiments on the value of vascular and visceral factors for the genesis of emotion. *Proceedings of the Royal Society (London), B, 66,* 390–403.

Sherrington, C. S. (1906). *The integrative action of the nervous system.* New Haven, CT: Yale University Press.

Sherrington, R., Brynjolfsson, J., Petursson, H., Potter, M., Dudleston, K., Barraclough, B., Wasmuth, J., Dobbs, M., & Gurling, H. (1988). Localization of a susceptibility locus for schizophrenia on chromosome 3. *Nature, 336,* 164–167.

Sherrington, R., Rogaev, E. I., Liang, Y., Rogaeva, E. A., Levesque, G., Ikeda, M., Chi, H., Lin, C., Li, G., Holman, K., Tsuda, T., Mar, L., Foncin, J. F., Bruni, A. C., Montesi, M. P., Sorbi, S., Rainero, I., Pinessi, L., Nee, L., Chumakov, I., Pollen, D., Brookes, A., Sanseau, P., Polinsky, R. J., Wasco, W., DaSilva, H. A. R., Haines, J. L., Pericak-Vance, M. A., Tanzi, R. E., Roses, A. D., Fraser, P. E., Rommens, J. M., & St. George-Hyslop, P. H. (1995). Cloning of a gene bearing missense mutations in early-onset familial Alzheimer's disease. *Nature, 375,* 754–760.

Shibata, S., Yamamoto, T. Y., & Ueki, S. (1982). Differential effects of medial, central, and basolateral amygdaloid lesions on four models of experimentally-induced aggression in rats. *Physiology and Behavior, 28,* 289–294.

Shibazaki, M. (1983). Development of hemispheric function in hiraganda, kanji, and figurative processing for normal children and mentally retarded children. *Japanese Journal of Special Education, 21,* 1–9.

Shimada, M., & Otsuka, A. (1981). Functional hemisphere differences in kanji processing in Japanese. *Japanese Psychological Review, 24,* 472–489.

Shimamura, A. P., Janowsky, J. S., & Squire, L. R. (1990). Memory for the temporal order of events in patients with frontal lobe lesions and amnesic patients. *Neuropsychologia, 28,* 803–813.

Shiromani, P. J., Siegel, J. M., Tomaszewski, K. S., & McGinty, D. J. (1986). Alterations in blood pressure and REM sleep after pontine carbachol microinfusion. *Experimental Neurology, 91,* 285–292.

Shutts, D. (1982). *Lobotomy: Resort to the knife.* New York: Van Nostrand Reinhold.

Siddiqui, A., & Shah, B. H. (1997). Neonatal androgen manipulation differentially affects the development of monoamine systems in rat cerebral cortex, amygdala, and hypothalamus. *Brain Research Developmental Brain Research, 98,* 247–252.

Sidman, M., Stoddard, L. T., & Mohr, J. P. (1968). Some additional quantitative observations of immediate memory in a patient with bilateral hippocampal lesions. *Neuropsychologia, 6,* 245–254.

Siever, L. J., Uhde, T. W., Jimerson, D. C., Lake, C. R., Silberman, E. R., Post, R. M., & Murphy, D. L. (1984). Differential inhibitory noradrenergic responses to clonidine in 25 depressed patients and 25 normal control subjects. *American Journal of Psychiatry, 141,* 733–741.

Sigman, M. (1995). Nutrition and child development: More food for thought. *Current Directions in Psychological Science, 4,* 52–55.

Silinsky, E. M. (1989). Adenosine derivatives and neuronal function. *Seminars in the Neurosciences, 1,* 155–165.

Simon, H., Scatton, B., & Moal, M. L. (1980). Dopaminergic A10 neurons are involved in cognitive functions. *Nature, 286,* 150–151.

Simpson, J. B., Epstein, A. N., & Camardo, J. S. (1978). The localization of dipsogenic receptors for angiotensin II in the subfornical organ. *Journal of Comparative and Physiological Psychology, 92,* 581–608.

Sinclair, D. (1981). *Mechanisms of cutaneous sensation.* Oxford, England: Oxford University Press.

Sirinathsinghji, D. J., Rees, L. H., Rivier, J., & Vale, W. (1983). Corticotropin-releasing factor is a potent inhibitor of sexual receptivity in the female rat. *Nature, 305,* 232–235.

Sitaram, N., Moore, A. M., & Gillin, J. C. (1978). Experimental acceleration and slowing of REM ultradian rhythm by cholinergic agonist and antagonist. *Nature, 274,* 490–492.

Sjostrom, M., Frieden, J., & Ekblom, B. (1987). Endurance—What is it? Muscle morphology after an extremely long distance run. *Physiologica Scandinavica, 130,* 513–520.

Skinner, B. F. (1938). *The behavior of organisms: An experimental analysis.* New York: Appleton-Century-Crofts.

Slobin, D. I. (1966). Grammatical transformations and sentence comprehension in childhood and adulthood. *Journal of Verbal Learning and Verbal Behavior, 5,* 219–227.

Smith, G. P., & Epstein, A. N. (1969). Increased feeding in response to decreased glucose utilization in the rat and monkey. *American Journal of Physiology, 217,* 1083–1087.

Smith, G. P., & Jerome, C. (1983). Effects of total and selective abdominal vagotomies on water intake in rats. *Journal of the Autonomic Nervous System, 9,* 259–271.

Smith, K. R. (1974). The problem of stimulation deafness. II. Histological changes in the cochlea as a function of tonal frequency. *Journal of Experimental Psychology, 37,* 304–317.

Snowden, C. T. (1969). Motivation, regulation and the control of meal parameters with oral and intragastric feeding. *Journal of Comparative and Physiological Psychology, 69,* 91–100.

Snyder, A. Z., Abdullaev, Y. G., Posner, M. I., & Raichle, M. E. (1995). Scalp electrical potentials reflect regional cerebral blood flow responses during processing of written words. *Proceedings of the National Academy of Sciences USA, 92,* 1689–1693.

Snyder, S. H. (1972). Catecholamines in the brain as mediators of amphetamine psychoses. *Archives of General Psychiatry, 27,* 169–179.

Snyder, S. H. (1976). The dopamine hypothesis of schizophrenia: Focus on the dopamine receptor. *American Journal of Psychiatry, 133,* 197–202.

Snyder, S. H. (1984). Drug and neurotransmitter receptors in the brain. *Science, 224,* 22–31.

Snyder, S. H. (1986). *Drugs and the brain.* New York: Scientific American Books.

Snyder, S. H., Banerjee, S. P., Yamamura, H. I., & Greenberg, D. (1974). Drugs, neurotransmitters and schizophrenia. *Science, 184,* 1243–1253.

Snyder, S. H., & D'Amato, R. J. (1986). MPTP: A neurotoxin relevant to the pathophysiology of Parkinson's disease. *Neurology, 36,* 250–258.

Soldatos, C. R., & Kales, A. (1986). Treatment of sleep disorders. In R. M. Berlin & C. R. Soldatos (Eds.), *Sleep disorders in psychiatric practice.* Orlando, FL: Rylandic.

Solomon, D. A., Keitner, G. I., Miller, I. W., Shea, M. T., & Keller, M. B. (1995). Course of illness and maintenance treatments for patients with bipolar disorder. *Journal of Clinical Psychiatry, 56,* 5–13.

Solomon, S. S., Ensinck, J. W., & Williams, R. H. (1968). Effect of starvation on plasma immunoreactive insulin and nonsuppressible insulin-like activity in normal and obese humans. *Metabolism, 17,* 528.

Sommers, A. (1985). "Negative symptoms": Conceptual and methodological problems. *Schizophrenia Bulletin, 11,* 364–379.

Spear, N. E., & Riccio, D. C. (1974). *Memory: Phenomena and principles.* Boston: Allyn & Bacon.

Sperry, R. W. (1974). Lateral specialization in the surgically separated hemispheres. In F. O. Schmitt & F. G. Worden (Eds.), *The neurosciences Third Study Program* (pp. 5–19). Cambridge, MA: MIT Press.

Sperry, R. W. (1982). Some effects of disconnecting the cerebral hemispheres. *Science, 217,* 1223–1226.

Sperry, R. W. (1985). Changed concepts of brain and consciousness: Some value implications. *Zygon, 20,* 41–57.

Sperry, R. W., Stamm, J., & Miner, N. (1956). Relearning tests for interocular transfer following division of optic chiasm and corpus callosum in cats. *Journal of Comparative and Physiological Psychology, 49,* 529–533.

Spitzer, L., & Rodin, J. (1981). Human eating behavior: A critical review of studies in normal weight and overweight individuals. *Appetite: Journal for Intake Research, 2,* 293–329.

Spyraki, C., Fibiger, H. C., & Phillips, A. G. (1982). Dopaminergic substrates of amphetamine-induced place preference conditioning. *Brain Research, 253,* 185–193.

Squire, L. R. (1986). Mechanisms of memory. *Science, 232,* 1612–1619.

Squire, L. R. (1987). *Memory and brain.* New York: Oxford University Press.

Squire, L. R., Amaral, D. G., & Press, G. A. (1990). Magnetic resonance measurements of hippocampal formation and mammillary nuclei distinguish medial temporal lobe and diencephalic amnesia. *Journal of Neuroscience, 10,* 3106–3117.

Squire, L. R., Shimamura, A. P., & Amaral, D. G. (1989). Memory and the hippocampus. In J. H. Byrne & W. O. Berry (Eds.), *Neural modes of plasticity: Experimental and theoretical approaches.* San Diego: Academic.

Squire, L. R., & Zola-Morgan, S. (1988). Memory: Brain systems and behavior. *Trends in Neuroscience, 11,* 170–175.

Squire, L. R., Zola-Morgan, S., & Chen, K. (1988). Human amnesia and animal models of amnesia: Performance of amnesic patients on tests designed for the monkey. *Behavioral Neuroscience, 11,* 210–221.

Stallone, D., & Nicolaidis, S. (1989). Increased food intake and carbohydrate preference in the rat following treatment with the serotonin antagonist metergoline. *Neuroscience Letters, 102,* 319–324.

Standaert, D. G., & Young, A. B. (1996). Treatment of central nervous system degenerative disorders. In J. G. Hardman, L. E. Limbird, P. B. Molinoff, R. W. Ruddon, & A. G. Gilman (Eds.), *Goodman & Gilman's the pharmacological basis of therapeutics* (9th ed., pp. 503–513). New York: McGraw-Hill.

Stanford, L. R. (1987). Conduction velocity variations minimize conduction time differences among retinal ganglion cell axons. *Science, 238,* 358–360.

Stanley, B. G., Anderson, K. C., Grayson, M. H., & Leibowitz, S. F. (1989). Repeated hypothalamic stimulation with neuropeptide Y increases daily carbohydrate and fat intake and body weight gain in female rats. *Physiology and Behavior, 46,* 173–177.

Stark, P., & Boyd, E. S. (1963). Effects of cholinergic drugs on hypothalamic self-stimulation response rates of dogs. *American Journal of Physiology, 205,* 745–748.

Starkstein, S. E., & Robinson, R. G. (1994). Neuropsychiatric aspects of stroke. In C. E. Coffey, J. L. Cummings, M. R. Lovell, & G. D. Pearlson (Eds.), *The American Psychiatric Press textbook of geriatric neuropsychiatry* (pp. 457–477).

St. Clair, D., Blackwood, D., Muir, W., Baillie, D., Hubbard, A., Wright, A., & Evans, H. J. (1989). No linkage of chromosome 5q11-q13 markers to schizophrenia in Scottish families. *Nature, 339,* 305–309.

Stebbins, W. C., Miller, J. M., Johnsson, L. G., & Hawkins, J. E. (1969). Ototoxic hearing loss and cochlear pathology in the monkey. *Annals of Otology, Rhinology and Laryngology, 78,* 1007–1026.

Stein, L. (1969). Chemistry of purposive behavior. In J. T. Tapp (Ed.), *Reinforcement and behavior* (pp. 328–355). New York: Academic.

Stein, L., & Wise, C. D. (1969). Release of norepinephrine from the hypothalamus and amygdala by rewarding medial forebrain bundle stimulation and amphetamine. *Journal of Comparative and Physiological Psychology, 67,* 189–198.

Stein, L., & Wise, C. D. (1973). Amphetamine and noradrenergic reward pathways. In E. Usdin & S. H. Snyder (Eds.), *Frontiers in catecholamine research.* New York: Pergamon.

Steinmetz, J. E., Lavond, D. G., & Thompson, R. F. (1989). Classical conditioning in rabbits using pontine nucleus stimulation as a conditioned stimulus and inferior olive stimulation as an unconditioned stimulus. *Synapse, 3,* 225–233.

Stephan, F. K., & Zucker, I. (1972). Circadian rhythms in drinking behavior and locomotor activity of rats are eliminated by hypothalamic lesion. *Proceedings of the National Academy of Sciences, USA, 69,* 1583–1586.

Steriade, M. (1996). Arousal: Revisiting the reticular activating system. *Science, 272,* 225–226.

Strauss, D., & Eyman, R. K. (1996). Mortality of people with mental retardation in California with and without Down Syndrome. *American Journal of Mental Retardation, 100,* 643–653.

Stricker, E. M. (1983). Brain neurochemistry and the control of food intake. In E. Satinoff & P. Teitelbaum (Eds.), *Handbook of behavioral neurobiology: Vol. 6. Motivation.* New York: Plenum Press.

Stricker, E. M. (1990). *Handbook of behavioral neurobiology.* New York: Plenum.

Stricker, E. M., Rowland, N., Saller, C. F., & Friedman, M. I. (1977). Homeostasis during hypoglycemia: Central control of adrenal secretion and peripheral control of feeding. *Science, 196,* 79–81.

Stricker, E. M., & Verbalis, J. G. (1987). Central inhibitory control of sodium appetite in rats: Correlation with pituitary oxytocin secretion. *Behavioral Neuroscience, 101,* 560–567.

Stricker, E. M., & Verbalis, J. G. (1991). Caloric and noncaloric controls of food intake. *Brain Research Bulletin, 27,* 299–303.

Strittmatter, W. J., & Roses, A. D. (1996). Apolipoprotein E and Alzheimer's disease. *Annual Review of Neuroscience, 19,* 53–77.

Stromberg, I., Almquist, P., Bygdeman, M., Finger, T. E., Gerhardt, G., Granholm, A. C., Mahalik, T. J., Seiger, A., Olson, C., & Hoffer, B. (1989). Human fetal mesencephalic tissue grafted to dopamine-denervated striatum of athymic rats: Light and electron-microscopical histochemistry and in vivo chronoamperometric studies. *Journal of Neuroscience, 9,* 614–624.

Strubbe, J. H., & Steffens, A. B. (1975). Rapid insulin release after ingestion of a meal in the unanesthetized rat. *American Journal of Physiology, 229,* 1019–1022.

Stunkard, A. J., Van Itallie, T. B., & Reis, B. B. (1955). The mechanism of satiety: Effect of glucagon on gastric hunger contractions in man. *Proceedings for Society of Experimental Biology and Medicine, 89,* 258–261.

Suddath, R. L., Casanova, M. F., Goldberg, T. E., Daniel, D. G., Kelsoe, J. R., Jr., & Weinberger, D. R. (1989). Temporal lobe pathology in schizophrenia: A quantitative magnetic resonance imaging study. *American Journal of Psychiatry, 146,* 464–472.

Suddath, R. L., Christison, G. W., Torrey, E. F., Casanova, M. F., & Weinberger, D. R. (1990). Anatomical abnormalities in the brains of monozygotic twins discordant for schizophrenia. *New England Journal of Medicine, 322,* 1616.

Sudhof, T. C. (1995). The synaptic vesicle: A cascade of protein-protein interactions. *Nature, 375,* 645–653.

Sudzak, P. D., Glowa, J. R., Crawley, J. N., Schwartz, R. D., Skolnick, P., & Paul, S. M. (1986). A selective imidazobenzodiazepine antagonist of ethanol in the rat. *Science, 234,* 1243–1247.

Susser, E. S., & Lin, S. P. (1992). Schizophrenia after prenatal exposure to the Dutch Hunger winter of 1944–1945. *Archives of General Psychiatry, 49,* 983–988.

Sutter, M. I., & Schreiner, C. E. (1991). Physiology and topography of neurons with multipeaked tuning curves in cat primary auditory cortex. *Journal of Neurophysiology, 65,* 1207–1226.

Svennilson, E., Torvik, A., Lowe, R., & Leksell, L. (1960). Treatment of Parkinsonism by stereotactic thermal lesions in the pallidal region. *Acta Psychiatry Scandinavia, 35,* 358–377.

Swaab, D. F., & Fliers, E. (1985). A sexually dimorphic nucleus in the human brain. *Science, 228,* 1112–1115.

Sweet, W. H., Ervin, F., & Mark, V. H. (1969). The relationship of violent behavior to focal cerebral disease. In S. Garattini & E. B. Sigg (Eds.), *Aggressive behavior.* New York: Wiley.

Swerdlow, N. R., Geyer, M. A., Vale, W. W., & Koob, G. F. (1986). Corticotropin-releasing factor potentiates acoustic startle in rats: Blockade by chloriazepoxide. *Psychopharmacology (Berlin), 88,* 147–152.

Szymusiak, R., & McGinty, D. (1986). Sleep-related neuronal discharge in the basal forebrain of cats. *Brain Research, 370,* 82–92.

Tanabe, T., Iino, M., & Takagi, S. G. (1975). Discrimination of odors in olfactory bulb, pyriform-amygdaloid areas, and orbitofrontal cortex of the monkey. *Journal of Neurophysiology, 38,* 1284–1296.

Tanaka, K. (1993). Neuronal mechanisms of object recognition. *Science, 262,* 685–688.

Tandan, R., & Bradley, W. G. (1985). Amyotrophic lateral sclerosis: Part I. Clinical features, pathology, and ethical issues in management. *Annals of Neurology, 18,* 271–281.

Tannenbaum, G. A., Paxinos, G., & Bindra, D. (1974). Metabolic and endocrine aspects of the ventromedial hypothalamic syndrome in the rat. *Journal of Comparative and Physiological Psychology, 86,* 404–413.

Tasker, R. R., & Kiss, Z. H. (1995). The role of the thalamus in functional neurosurgery. *Neurosurgical Clinics in North America, 6,* 73–104.

Taylor, S. E. (1996). *Health psychology* (3rd ed.). New York: Random House.

Teitelbaum, P. (1955). Sensory control of hypothalamic hyperphagia. *Journal of Comparative and Physiological Psychology, 48,* 156–163.

Teitelbaum, P., Cheng, M. F., & Rozin, P. (1969). Stages of recovery and development of later hypothalamic control of food and water intake. *Annals of the New York Academy of Sciences, 157,* 848–860.

Teitelbaum, P., & Epstein, A. N. (1962). The lateral hypothalamic syndrome: Recovery of feeding and drinking after lateral hypothalamic lesions. *Psychological Review, 69,* 74–90.

Tepas, D. I. (1982). Work/sleep time schedules and performance. In W. B. Webb (Ed.), *Biological rhythms, sleep and performance.* New York: Wiley.

Terrace, H. S. (1979). *Nim.* New York: Knopf.

Terzian, H., & DalleOre, G. D. (1955). Syndrome of Klüver and Bucy reproduced in man by bilateral removal of the temporal lobes. *Neurology, 5,* 378–380.

Tessier-Lavique, M., & Goodman, C. S. (1996). The molecular biology of axon guidance. *Science, 274,* 1123–1133.

Thase, M. E., Trivedi, M. H., & Rush, A. J. (1995). MAOIs in the contemporary treatment of depression. *Neuropsychopharmacology, 12,* 185–219.

Thompson, C. R., & Church, R. M. (1980). An explanation of the language of a chimpanzee. *Science, 208,* 313–314.

Thompson, R., & Dean, W. A. (1955). A further study on the retroactive effects of ECS. *Journal of Comparative and Physiological Psychology, 48,* 488–491.

Thompson, R. F. (1989). A model system approach to memory. In P. R. Solomon, G. R. Goethals, C. M. Kelley, & B. R. Stephens (Eds.), *Memory: interdisciplinary approaches.* New York: Springer-Verlag.

Thompson, R. F., Clark, G. A., Donegan, N. H., Lavond, D. G., Lincoln, J. S., Madden, J., Mamounas, L. A., Mauk, M. D., McCormick, D. A., & Thompson, J. K. (1984). Neuronal substrates of learning and memory: A "multiple-trace" view. In G. Lynch, J. L. McGaugh, & N. M. Weinberger (Eds.), *Neurobiology of learning and memory* (pp. 137–164). New York: Guilford.

Thrasher, T. N., Keil, L. C., & Ramsay, D. J. (1982). Lesions of the organum vasculosum of the lamina terminalis (OVLT) attenuate osmotically induced drinking and vasopressin secretion in the dog. *Endocrinology, 110,* 1837–1839.

Tootell, R. B., Silverman, M. S., Switkes, E., & De Valois, R. L. (1982). Deoxyglucose analysis of retinotopic organization in primate striate cortex. *Science, 218,* 902–904.

Tootell, R. B., & Taylor, J. B. (1995). Anatomical evidence for MT and additional cortical visual areas in humans. *Cerebral Cortex, 5,* 39–55.

Toran-Allerand, C. D. (1984). On the genesis of sexual differentiation of the central nervous system: Morphogenetic consequences of steroidal exposure and possible role of alpha-fetoprotein. *Progressive Brain Research, 61,* 63–98.

Tordoff, M. G., Rawson, N., & Friedman, M. I. (1991). 2,5-Anhydro-D-mannitol acts in liver to initiate feeding. *American Journal of Physiology, 261,* R283–R288.

Tordoff, M. G., Schulkin, J., & Friedman, M. I. (1987). Further evidence for hepatic control of salt intake in rats. *American Journal of Physiology, 253,* R444–R449.

Torrey, E. F., Rawlings, R. R., Ennis, J. M., Merrill, D. D., & Flores, D. S. (1996). Birth seasonality in bipolar disorder, schizophrenia, schizoaffective disorder and stillbirths. *Schizophrenia Research, 21,* 141–149.

Träskmann, L., Asberg, M., Bertilsson, L., & Sjostrand, L. (1981). Monoamine metabolites in CSF and suicidal behavior. *Archives of General Psychiatry, 38,* 631–636.

Travis, J. (1994). Glia: The brain's other cells. *Science, 266,* 970–972.

Tsai, G., Passini, L. A., Slusher, B. S., Carter, R., Baer, L., Kleinman, J. E., & Coyle, J. T. (1995). Abnormal excitatory neurotransmitter metabolism in schizophrenic brains. *Archives of General Psychiatry, 52,* 829–836.

Tsang, Y. C. (1938). Hunger motivation in gastrectomized rats. *Journal of Comparative Psychology, 26,* 1–17.

Tsuang, M. T. (1976). Lithium therapy: Practical aspects. *Discovery of the Nervous System, 37,* 282–285.

Tsuang, M. T., & Faraone, S. V. (1990). *The genetics of mood disorders.* Baltimore, MD: Johns Hopkins University Press.

Tsuang, M. T., Lyons, M. J., & Faraone, S. V. (1990). Heterogeneity of schizophrenia. Conceptual models and analytic strategies. *British Journal of Psychiatry, 156,* 17–26.

Tucker, D. M. (1981). Lateral brain function, emotion, and conceptualization. *Psychological Bulletin, 89,* 19–46.

Tulving, E. (1983). *Elements of episodic memory.* Oxford: Clarendon Press/Oxford University Press.

Tulving, E. (1998). Brain/mind correlates of human memory. In M. Sabourin, F. Criak, & M. Robert (Eds.), *Advances in psychological science: Vol. 2. Biological and cognitive aspects* (pp. 441–460). Hove, East Sussex, UK: Psychology Press.

Tulving, E., & Markowitsch, H. J. (1997). Memory beyond the hippocampus. *Current Opinion in Neurobiology, 7,* 209–216.

Tunturi, A. R. (1953). A difference in representation of auditory signals for the left and right ears in the isofrequency contours of right middle ectosylvian auditory cortex in the dog. *American Journal of Physiology, 168,* 712–727.

Turek, F. W. (1985). Circadian neural rhythms in mammals. *Annual Review of Physiology, 47,* 49–64.

Udani, P. M. (1992). Protein energy metabolism (PEM), brain and various facets of child development. *Indian Journal of Pediatrics, 59,* 165–186.

Udry, J. R., & Morris, N. M. (1968). Distribution of coitus in the menstrual cycle. *Nature, 220,* 593–596.

Ulrich, R. S. (1984). View through a window may influence recovery from surgery. *Science, 224,* 420–421.

Underwood, B. J. (1983). *Attributes of memory.* Glenview, IL: Scott, Foresman.

Ungar, G., Galvan, L., & Clark, R. H. (1968). Chemical transfer of learned fear. *Nature, 217,* 1259–1261.

Vaccarino, F. J., Bloom, R. E., & Koob, G. F. (1985). Blockade of nucleus accumbens opiate receptors attenuates intravenous heroin reward in the rat. *Psychopharmacology, 86,* 37–42.

Vaccarino, F. J., Schiff, B. B., & Glickman, S. E. (1989). Biological view of reinforcement. In S. B. Klein & R. R. Mowrer (Eds.), *Contemporary learning theories: Instrumental conditioning and the impact of biological constraints on learning* (pp. 111–142). Hillsdale, NJ: Erlbaum.

Valenstein, E. S. (1973). *Brain control.* New York: Wiley.

Valenstein, E. S. (1980). *The psychosurgery debate: Scientific, legal, and ethical perspectives.* San Francisco: W. H. Freeman.

Valenstein, E. S. (1986). *Great and desperate cures: The rise and decline of psychosurgery and other radical treatments for mental illness.* New York: Basic Books.

Valenstein, E. S., Cox, V. C., & Kakolewski, J. W. (1969). The hypothalamus and motivated behavior. In J. T. Tapp (Ed.), *Reinforcement and behavior* (pp. 242–285). New York: Academic.

Valentino, R. J., Foote, S. L., & Aston-Jones, G. (1983). Corticotropin-releasing factor activates noradrenergic neurons of the locus coeruleus. *Brain Research, 270,* 363–367.

Van Goozen, S. H., Frijda, N. H., Wiegant, V. M., Endert, E., & Van de Poll, N. E. (1996). The premenstrual phase and reactions to aversive events: A study of hormonal influences on emotionality. *Psychoneuroendocrinology, 21,* 479–497.

Van Wagenen, W. P., & Herren, R. Y. (1940). Surgical division of commissural pathways in the corpus callosum. *Archives of Neurology and Psychiatry, 44,* 740–759.

Verney, E. B. (1947). The antidiuretic hormone and the factors which determine its release. *Proceedings of Royal Society, 135,* 25–106.

Verzeano, J., Laufer, M., Spear, S., & McDonald, S. (1970). The activity of neuronal networks in the thalamus of the monkey. In K. H. Pribram & D. E. Broadbent (Eds.), *Biology of memory* (pp. 239–272). New York: Academic.

Verzeano, M., & Negishi, K. (1960). Neuronal activity in cortical and thalamic networks. *Journal of General Physiology, 43* (Suppl.), 177.

Victor, M., & Agamanolis, J. (1990). Amnesia due to lesions confined to the hippocampus: A clinical-pathological study. *Journal of Cognitive Neuroscience, 2,* 246–257.

Virkkunen, M., Eggert, M., Rawlings, R., & Linnoila, M. (1996). A prospective follow-up study of alcoholic violent offenders and fire setters. *Archives of General Psychiatry, 53,* 523–529.

Vogel, G. W., Buffenstein, A., Minter, K., & Hennessey, A. (1990). Drug effects on REM sleep and on endogenous depression. *Neuroscience Biobehavioral Review, 14,* 49–63.

Vogel, G. W., Vogel, F., McAbee, R. S., & Thurmond, A. J. (1980). Improvement of depression by REM sleep deprivation. New findings and a theory. *Archives of General Psychiatry, 37,* 247–253.

Volpicelli, J. R., Alterman, I., Hayashida, M., & O'Brien, C. P. (1992). Naltrexone in the treatment of alcohol dependence. *Archives of General Psychiatry, 49,* 876–880.

Volpicelli, J. R., O'Brien, C. P., Alterman, A. I., & Hayashida, M. (1990). Naltrexone and the treatment of alcohol dependence. Initial observation. In L. D. Reid (Ed.), *Opioids, bulimia, and alcohol abuse and alcoholism.* New York: Springer-Verlag.

vom Saal, F. S., & Bronson, F. H. (1980). *In utero* proximity of female mouse fetuses to males: Effect on reproductive performance during later life. *Biology of Reproduction, 22,* 777–780.

Von Cramon, D. Y., Hebel, N., & Schuri, U. (1985). A contribution to the anatomical basis of thalamic amnesia. *Brain, 108,* 993–1008.

Vonnegut, M. (1975). *The eden express.* New York: Bantam.

Waddington, J. L. (1993). Neurodynamics of abnormalities in cerebral metabolism and structure of schizophrenia. *Schizophrenia Bulletin, 19,* 55–69.

Wagner, G., Beaving, L., & Hutchinson, R. (1980). The effects of gonadal hormone manipulations on aggressive target-biting in mice. *Aggressive Behavior, 6,* 1–7.

Wald, G. (1950). Eye and camera. *Scientific American, 183,* 32–41.

Wald, G. (1968). Molecular basis of visual excitation. *Science, 162,* 230–239.

Waldvogel, J. A. (1990). The bird's eye view. *American Scientist, 78,* 342–353.

Wallace, A. F. C. (1956). *Tornado in Worchester: An explanatory study of individual and community behavior in an extreme situation.* Washington: National Academy of Sciences, National Research Council (Publication 392, Disaster Study No. 3).

Wallman, J., & Pettigrew, J. D. (1985). Conjugate and disjunctive saccades in two avian species with contrasting oculomotor strategies. *Journal of Neuroscience, 5,* 1418–1428.

Waterhouse, B. D., Sessler, F. M., Cheng, J. T., Woodward, D. J., Azizi, S. A., & Moises, H. C. (1988). New evidence for a gating action of norepinephrine in central neuronal circuits of mammalian brain. *Brain Research Bulletin, 21,* 425–432.

Watkins, L. R., & Mayer, D. J. (1982). Involvement of spinal opioid systems in footshock-induced analgesia by naloxone is possible only before induction of analgesia. *Brain Research, 242,* 309–326.

Webb, W. B. (1975). *Sleep: The gentle tyrant.* Englewood Cliffs, NJ: Prentice-Hall.

Webb, W. B. (1988). An objective behavioral model of sleep. *Sleep, 11,* 488–496.

Webb, W. B., & Agnew, H. W. (1970). Sleep stage characteristics of long and short sleepers. *Science, 163,* 146–147.

Webb, W. B., & Cartwright, R. D. (1978). Sleep and dreams. In M. R. Rosenzweig & L. W. Porter (Eds.), *Annual review of psychology* (Vol. 29). Palo Alto, CA: Annual Reviews.

Wehr, T. A., & Goodwin, F. K. (1983). *Circadian rhythms in psychiatry.* Pacific Grove, CA: Boxwood Press.

Wehr, T. A., Muscettola, G., & Goodwin, F. K. (1980). Urinary 3-methoxy-Y-hydroxyphenylglycol circadian rhythm: Early timing (phase-advance) in manic-depressives compared with normal subjects. *Archives of General Psychology, 37,* 257–263.

Wehr, T. A., Wirz-Justice, A., Goodwin, F. K., Duncan, W., & Gillin, J. C. (1979). Phase advance of the circadian sleep-wake cycle as an antidepressant. *Science, 206,* 710–713.

Weibel, D., Cadelli, D. S., & Schwab, M. E. (1994). Regeneration of lesioned rat optic nerve fibers is improved after neutralization of myelin-associated neurite growth inhibitors. *Brain Research, 642,* 259–266.

Weinberger, D. R., Berman, K. F., & Illowsky, B. P. (1988). Physiological dysfunction of dorsolateral prefrontal cortex in schizophrenia. III. A new cohort and evidence for a monoaminergic mechanism. *Archives of General Psychiatry, 45,* 609–615.

Weingarten, H., & Powley, T. L. (1977). Cited in T. L. Powley. The ventromedial hypothalamic syndrome, satiety, and a cephalic phase hypothesis. *Psychological Review, 84,* 89–126.

Weinrad, R. M., & O'Brien, C. P. (1997). Naltrexone in the treatment of alcoholism. *Annual Review of Medicine, 48,* 477–487.

Weintraub, M., Sundaresan, P. R., Schuster, B., Ginsberg, C., Madam, A., Stein, E. C., & Byrne, L. (1992). Long-term weight control study. II (weeks 34 to 104). And open-label study of continous fenfluramine plus phentermine versus targeted intermittent medication, caloric restriction, and exercise. *Pharmacology Therapeutics, 51,* 595–601.

Weiss, J. M. (1968). Effects of coping on stress. *Journal of Comparative and Physiological Psychology, 65,* 251–260.

Weiss, J. M. (1972). Psychological factors in stress and disease. *Scientific American, 226,* 104–113.

Weiss, J. M., Goodman, P. A., Losito, P. G., Corrigan, S., Charry, J., & Bailey, W. (1981). Behavioral depression produced by an uncontrolled stressor: Relation to norepinephrine, dopamine, and serotonin levels in various regions of the rat brain. *Brain Research Review, 3,* 167–205.

Weiss, J. M., & Simpson, P. G. (1986). Depression in an animal model: Focus on the locus coeruleus in antidepressants and receptor function. In D. L. Murphy (Ed.), *Antidepressant and receptor functions* (pp. 191–209). Chichester: Wiley.

Weiss, J. M., Simpson, P. G., Ambrose, M. J., Webster, A., & Hoffman, L. J. (1985). Chemical basis of behavioral depression. In E. Katkin & S. Manuck (Eds.), *Advances in behavioral medicine* (Vol. 1, pp. 233–275). Greenwich: JAI Press.

Weiss, J. M., Stone, E. A., & Harrell, N. (1970). Coping behavior and brain norepinephrine in rats. *Journal of Comparative and Physiological Psychology, 72,* 153–160.

Weitzman, E. D. (1981). Sleep and its disorders. *Annual Review of Neuroscience, 4,* 381–418.

Weitzman, E. D., Kripke, D. F., Goldmacher, D., McGregor, T., & Nogeire, C. (1970). Acute reversal of the sleep-waking cycle in man. *Archives of Neurology, 22,* 483–489.

Wellman, P. J., & Davies, B. T. (1991). Suppression of feeding induced by phenylephrine microinjections within the paraventricular hypothalamus in rats. *Appetite, 17,* 121–128.

Wellman, P. J., & Davies, B. T. (1991). Reversal of phenylpropanol-amine anorexia in rats by alpha 1-receptor antagonist benoxacthian. *Pharmacology, Biochemistry, and Behavior, 38,* 905–908.

Wellman, P. J., Davies, B. T., Morien, A., & McMahon, L. (1993). Modulation of feeding by hypothalamic paraventricular nuclues α-1 and α-2-adrenergic receptors. *Life Sciences, 53,* 669–679.

Wender, P. H., Kety, S. S., Rosenthal, D., Shulsinger, G., Otrmann, J., & Lunde, I. (1986). Psychiatric disorders in the biological and adoptive families of adopted individuals with affective disorders. *Archives of General Psychiatry, 43,* 932–929.

Wernicke, C. (1874). *Der Aphasische Symptomenkomplex.* Breslau, Poland: M. Cohn & Weigert.

Wertz, R. T., LaPointe, L. L., & Rosenbek, J. C. (1984). *Apraxia of speech in adults: The disorder and its management.* Orlando, FL: Grune & Stratton.

Westerink, B. H. C., Tuntler, J., Damsma, G., Rollema, H., & De Vries, J. B. (1987). The use of tetrodotoxin for the characterization of drug-enhanced dopamine release in conscious rats studied by brain dialysis. *Naunyn-Schmiedeberg's Archives of Pharmacology, 336,* 502–507.

Wever, E. C. (1949). *Theory of hearing.* New York: Wiley.

Wexler, N. S., Rose, E. A., & Housman, D. E. (1991). Molecular approaches to hereditary diseases of the nervous system: Huntington's disease as a paradigm. *Annual Review of Neuroscience, 14,* 503–529.

Whalen, R. (1977). Brain mechanisms controlling sexual behavior. In F. Beach (Ed.), *Human sexuality in four perspectives.* Baltimore: Johns Hopkins University Press.

Wheatley, M. D. (1944). The hypothalamus and affective behavior in cats. *Archives of Neurology and Psychiatry, 52,* 296–316.

Whybrow, P. C., Akiskal, H. S., & McKinney, W. T. (1984). *Mood disorders: Toward a new psychobiology.* New York: Plenum Press.

Whytt, R. (1768). The works of Robert Whytt, M.D. (3rd ed., published by his son). Edinburgh: Balfour, Auld, and Smellie.

Wictorin, K., Brundin, P., Gustavii, B., Lindovall, O., & Bjorklund, A. (1990). Reformation of long axon pathways in adult rat central nervous system by human forebrain neuroblasts. *Nature, 347,* 556–558.

Wilford, B. B. (1981). *Drug abuse: A guide for the primary care physician.* Chicago: American Medical Association.

Willerman, C., & Cohen, D. B. (1990). *Psychopathology.* New York: McGraw-Hill.

Williams, D. (1969). Neural factors related to habitual aggression. *Brain, 92,* 503–520.

Williams, M. (1950). The effects of experimentally induced needs upon retention. *Journal of Experimental Psychology, 23,* 506–522.

Williams, R. (1993). *Anger kills.* New York: Times Books.

Williams, R. B. (1989). *The trusting heart: Great news about Type A behavior.* New York: Timesbooks.

Williams, R. W. & Herrup, K. (1988). The control of neuron number. *Annual Review of Neuroscience, 11,* 423–453.

Wilska, A. (1935). Eine methode zur bestimmung der horschwellenamplituden der tromenfells bei verscheideden frequenzen. *Skandinavisches Archives fur Physiologie, 72,* 161–165.

Wilson, R., Raynal, D., Guilleminault, C., Zarcone, V., & Dement, W. B. (1973). REM sleep latencies in daytime sleep recordings of narcoleptics. *Sleep Research, 2,* 166.

Wilson, R. S., & Evans, D. A. (1996). How clearly do we see our memories? *Journal of the American Geriatric Society, 44,* 93–94.

Winkour, G., & Clayton, P. (1967). Family history studies: I. Two types of affective disorders separated according to genetic and clinical factors. In J. Wortis (Ed.), *Recent advances in biological psychiatry* (Vol. 9). New York: Plenum Press.

Winkour, G., Clayton, P. J., & Reich, T. (1969). *Manic-depressive illness.* St. Louis: Mosby.

Winn, P. (1995). The lateral hypothalamus and motivated behavior: An old syndrome reassessed and a new perspective gained. *Current Directions in Psychological Science, 4,* 182–187.

Winn, P., Williams, S. F., & Herberg, L. J. (1982). Feeding stimulated by very low doses of damphetamine administered systemically or by microinjection into the striatum. *Psychopharmacology, 78,* 336–341.

Winokur, A., March, V., & Mendels, J. (1980). Primary affective disorder in relatives of patients with anorexia nervosa. *American Journal of Psychiatry, 137,* 695–698.

Winokur, G. Coryell, W., Keller, M., Endicott, J., & Leon, A. (1995). A family study of manic-depressive (bipolar I) disease. Is it a distinct illness separable from primary unipolar depression? *Archives of General Psychiatry, 52,* 367–373.

Wise, R. A. (1966). Addictive drugs and brain stimulation reward. *Annual Review of Neuroscience, 19,* 319–340.

Wise, R. A. (1988). Psychomotor stimulant properties of addictive drugs. *Annals of the New York Academy of Sciences, 537,* 228–234.

Wise, R. A., & Rompre, P. O. (1989). Brain dopamine and reward. *Annual Review of Psychology, 40,* 191–225.

Witt, D. M., Keller, A. D., Batsel, H. I., & Lynch, J. R. (1952). Absence of thirst and resultant syndrome associated with anterior hypothalamectomy in the dog. *American Journal of Physiology, 171,* 780.

Wolf, S., & Wolff, H. G. (1947). *Human gastric function* (2nd ed.). New York: Oxford University Press.

Wong, D. F., Gjedde, A., & Wagner, H. N. (1986). Quantification of neuroreceptors in the living human brain. Irreversible binding of ligands. *Journal of Cerebral Blood Flow Metabolism, 6,* 137–146.

Wong, D. F., Gjedde, A., & Wagner, H. N. Jr., Dannals, R. F., Douglass K. H., Links, J. M., & Kuhar, M. J. (1986). Quantification of neuroreceptors in the living human brain. II. Inhibition studies of receptor density and affinity. *Journal of Cerebral Blood Flow Metabolism, 6,* 147–153.

Wong, D. F., Wagner, H. N., Jr., Dannals, R. F., Links, J. M., Frost, J. J., Ravert, H. T., Wilson, A. A., Rosenbaum, A. E., Gjedde, A., Douglass, K. H., Petronis, J. D., Folstein, M. F., Toung, J. K. T., Burns, H. D., & Kuhar, M. J. (1984). Effects of age on dopamine and serotonin receptors measured by positron tomography in the living human brain. *Science, 226,* 1393–1396.

Wong-Riley, M. (1979). Changes in the visual system of monocularly sutured or enucleated cats demonstrable with cytochrome oxidase histochemistry. *Brain Research, 171,* 11–28.

Wood, C. D. (1958). Behavioral changes following discrete lesions of temporal lobe structures. *Neurology, 8,* 215–220.

Woodruff-Pak, D. S., Papka, M., & Ivry, R. B. (1996). Cerebellar involvement in eyeblink classical conditioning in humans. *Neuropsychology, 10,* 443–458.

Woolfolk, R. L., & Lehrer, P. M. (1984). Clinical stress reduction: An overview. In R. L. Woolfolk & P. M. Lehrer (Eds.), *Principles and practice of stress management* (pp. 1–11). New York: Guilford Press.

Word, C. D. (1958). Behavioral changes following discrete lesions of temporal lobe structures. *Neurology, 8,* 215–220.

Wright, P., Takei, N., Rifkin, L., & Murray, R. M. (1995). Maternal influenza, obstetric complications, and schizophrenia. *American Journal of Psychiatry, 152,* 1714–1720.

Yahr, M. D. (1987). Parkinsonianism. In G. Adelman (Ed.), *Encyclopedia of neuroscience.* Boston: Birkhauser.

Yanagisawa, K., Bartoshuk, L. M., Karrer, T. A., et al. (1992). Anesthesia of the chorda tympani nerve: Insights into a source of dysgeusia. *Chemical Senses, 17,* 724.

Yang, B. (1979). The research in the forecast of acupunture anesthesia. In *National symposia of acupunture and moxibustion and acupuncture anesthesia.* Beijing, China.

Yates, A. (1989). Current perspectives on the eating disorders: I. History, psychological and biological aspects. *Journal of the American Academy of Child and Adolescent Psychiatry, 28,* 813–828.

Yau, K. W. (1991). Calcium and light adaptation in retinal photoreceptors. *Current Opinion in Neurobiology, 1,* 252–257.

Yee, F., MacLow, C., Chan, I. N., & Leibowitz, S. F. (1987). Effects of chronic paraventricular nucleus infusion of clonidine and alpha-methyl-para-tyrosine on macronutrient intake. *Appetite, 9,* 127–138.

Yoshii, N., Ishiwara, T., & Tani, K. (1963). Juvenile delinquents and their abnormal EEGs 14 and 6 per second positive spikes pattern. *Medical Journal of Oska University, 14,* 61–66.

Youdin, M. B. H., & Riederer, P. (1997). Understanding Parkinson's disease. *Scientific American, 276,* 52–59.

Young, A. B. (1995). Huntington's disease: Lessons from and for molecular neuroscience. *The Neuroscientist, 1,* 51–58.

Young, B. J., & Leaton, R. N. (1996). Amygdala central nucleus lesions attenuate acoustic startle stimulus-evoked heart rate changes in rats. *Behavioral Neuroscience, 110,* 228–237.

Young, M. P., & Yamane, S. (1992). Sparse population coding of faces in the inferotemporal cortex. *Science, 256,* 1327–1331.

Young, T. (1802). On the theory of light and colours. *Philosophical Transactions of the Royal Society of London, 92,* 12–48.

Young, W. C., & Orbison, W. D. (1943). Changes in selected features of behavior in pairs of oppositely sex chimpanzees during the sexual cycle and after ovariectomy. *Journal of Comparative Psychology, 37,* 107–143.

Zeki, S. (1993). *A view of the brain.* London: Blackwell Scientific Publications.

Zillman, D. (1986). Effects of prolonged consumption of pornography. Background paper for *The Surgeon General's workshop on pornography and public health,* June 22–24. Report prepared by E. P. Mulvey & J. L. Haugaard and released by Office of the Surgeon General on August 4, 1986.

Zola-Morgan, S., & Squire, L. R. (1986). Memory impairment in monkeys following lesions limited to the hippocampus. *Behavioral Neuroscience, 100,* 155–160.

Zola-Morgan, S., & Squire, L. R. (1993). Neuroanatomy of memory. *Annual Review of Neuroscience, 16,* 547–563.

Zola-Morgan, S., Squire, L. R., & Amaral, D. G. (1986). Human amnesia and the media temporal region: Enduring memory impairment following a bilateral lesion limited to field CA1 of the hippocampus. *Journal of Neuroscience, 6,* 2950–2967.

Zola-Morgan, S., Squire, L. R., & Amaral, D. G. (1989). Lesions of the hippocampal formation but not lesions of the fornix or the mammillary nuclei produce long-lasting memory impairment in monkey. *Journal of Neuroscience, 9,* 897–912.

Zubin, J., & Barrera, S. E. (1941). Effect of electric convulsive therapy on memory. *Proceedings for the Society of Experimental Biology, 48,* 596–597.

Acknowledgements

Photographs

Top Row of Chapter Opening Photos (1) Miles Ertman, Masterfile Corporation; **(2)** Audra Geras, Masterfile Corporation; **(3)** Garry Black, Masterfile Corporation; **(4)** David Muir, Masterfile Corporation; **(5)** Damir Frkovic, Masterfile Corporation; **(6)** Bob Anderson, Masterfile Corporation; **(7)** David Muir, Masterfile Corporation; **(8)** Bob Anderson, Masterfile Corporation.

Chapter 1 Chapter opening photo Biophoto Associates, Photo Researchers, Inc.; **Figure 1.6 (bottom)** Ed Reschke; **Figure 1.7** Srulik Haramaty, Phototake, NYC; **Figure 1.8** Marka, Custom Medical Stock Photo, Inc.; **Figure 1.9** SIU, Visuals Unlimited; **Figure 1.10** Michael Driscoll, Yerkes Primate Center; **Figure 1.11** Custom Medical Stock Photo, Inc.; **Figure 1.14(a)** M. Abbey, Photo Researchers, Inc.; **Figure 1–14(b)** Hal Beral, Visuals Unlimited; **Figure 1.20** Yoav Levy, Phototake NYC; **Figure 1.21** Richard T. Nowitz, Phototake NYC.

Chapter 2 Chapter opening photo Scott Camazine, Photo Researchers, Inc. **Figure 2.4** Fred Hossler, Visuals Unlimited; **Figure 2.14** Barts Medical Library, Phototake NYC; **Figure 2.28** Michael Abbey/Science Source, Photo Researchers, Inc.; **Figure 2.29(top right)** Cajal Institute; **Figure 2.29(bottom right)** Cajal Institute; **Figure 2.30(b)** Jerome Yeats, Photo Researchers, Inc.; **Figure 2.31** Scott Camazine, Photo Researchers, Inc.; **Figure 2.32** Yoav Levy, Phototake NYC; **Figure 2.34** Wellcome Dept. of Cognitive Neurology/SPL, Photo Researchers, Inc.

Chapter 3 Chapter opening photo Petit Format/Nestle/Science Source, Photo Researchers, Inc. **Figure 3.10** Growth cone courtesy of E. Welnhofer and C. S. Cohan. © Wiley-Liss 1997; **Figure 3.14(a)** CNRI/Science Photo Library/Science Source, Photo Researchers, Inc.; **Figure 3.14(b)** Hattie Young/Science Photo Library, Photo Researchers, Inc.; **Figure 3.15** Dr. A. F. Streissgath.

Chapter 4 Chapter opening photo Synaptek Scientific Products Inc./Science Photo Library, Photo Researchers, Inc.

Chapter 5 Chapter opening photo CNRI/Science Photo Library, Photo Researchers, Inc. **Figure 5.3** Charles Prietner, Visuals Unlimited; **Figure 5.6** Gregory G. Dimijian, Photo Researchers, Inc.; **Figure 5.7** National Library of Medicine; **Figure 5. 9** Will McIntyre, Photo Researchers, Inc.; **Figure 5.11** R. Konig/Jacana, Photo Researchers, Inc.; **Figure 5.12** E. R. Degginger, Photo Researchers, Inc.; **Figure 5.13(a-e)** Scientific Office of Sandoz, Ltd., Triangle, (1955–1956). *The Sandoz Journal of Medical Science, 2,* 117–124, Annotations, *The History of LSD 25.*

Chapter 6 Chapter opening photo Bruce Rowell, Masterfile Corporation; **Figure 6.3** Ed Reschke, Peter Arnold, Inc.; **Figure 6.22(a)** Mary Clare Reynolds, Photophile; **Figure 6.22(b)** Rachel Epstein, Stuart Kenter Associates; **Figure 6.22©** Photophile; **Figure 6.22(d)** Photophile; **Figure 6.29** © Josef Albers Foundation/Yale University Press.

Chapter 7 Chapter opening photo Prof. P. Motta, Dept. of Anatomy, University "La Sapienza," Rome/Science Photo Library/Photo Researchers, Inc.; **Figure 7.3** Ward's Natural Science Establishment, Inc.; **Figure 7.4(b)** Prof. P. Motta, Dept. of Anatomy, University "La Sapienza," Rome/Science Photo Library/Photo Researchers, Inc.; **Figure 7.17(d)** Frederic H. Martini; **Figure 7.22(a)** Will & Deni McIntyre, Photo Researchers, Inc.; **Figure 7.22(b)** Yoav Levy, Phototake NYC.

Chapter 8 Chapter opening photo CNRI, Phototake NYC; **Figure 8.2(a)** Frederic H. Martini; **Figure 8.2(b)** G.W. Willis, M.D., Biological Photo Service; **Figure 8.2©** G.W. Willis, M.D., Biological Photo Service; **Figure 8.6** Don Fawcett/Science Source, Photo Researchers, Inc.; **Figure 8.21** L. O'Shaughnessy, Leslie O'Shaughnessy Studios; **Figure 8.24** Joseph R. Siebert, Ph.D., Custom Medical Stock Photo, Inc.; **Figure 8.25** National Library of Medicine; **Figure 8.26** Dr. Olle Lindvall, M.D.

Chapter 9 Chapter opening photo Tom Brewster, Phototake NYC; **Figure 9.3** W. J. Schwartz and H. Gainer (1977). Suprachiasmatic nucleus: Use of 14C labeled deoxyglucose uptake as a functional marker. *Science, 197,* 1089–1091; **Figure 9.12(left)** Stanford University News Service; **Figure 9.12 (right)** Stanford University News Service.

Chapter 10 Chapter opening photo Manfred Kage, Peter Arnold, Inc.; **Figure 10.14** M. Antman, The Image Works; **Figure 10.15** Michael Newman, PhotoEdit; **Figure 10.18** Wm. Thompson, Index Stock Imagery, Inc.

Chapter 11 Chapter opening photo David M. Philips, Visuals Unlimited; **Figure 11.3(a)** Rachel Epstein, Stuart Kenter Associates; **Figure 11.3(b)** Custom Medical Stock Photo, Inc.; **Figure 11.18(a)** From S. Levay (1991). A difference in hypothalamic structure between heterosexual and homosexual men. *Science, 253,* 1035. © American Association for the Advancement of Science. Reprinted with permission. Also reprinted by permission of the author; **Figure 11.19** Howard W. Jones, Jr., M.D.

Chapter 12 Chapter opening photo Joel Benard, Masterfile Corporation; **Figure 12.5** Jim Amos, Photo Researchers, Inc.; **Figure 12.8** Capilano Suspension Bridge and Park.

Chapter 13 Chapter opening photo Rachel Epstein, Stuart Kenter Associates; **Figure 13.4** Yerkes Primate Center © Yerkes Primate Lab Emory University; **Figure 13.12(left)** Paramount/Courtesy the Kobal Collection. Photo by Takashi Seida; **Figure 13.12(right)** MGM/Courtesy the Kobal Collection; **Figure 13.13** Dr. John Mazziotta et al./Neurology/Science Photo Library, Photo Researchers, Inc.; **Figure 13.15** Dr. M. A. Naeser; **Figure 13.18** Dr. M. A. Naeser; **Figure 13.20** Charles Gupton, Stock Boston.

Chapter 14 Chapter opening photo D. Miller, Peter Arnold, Inc.; **Figure 14.1** Bonnie Kamin, PhotoEdit; **Figure 14.8** C. G. Logan; **Figure 14.19(a)** Larry R. Squire, Ph.D; **Figure 14.19(b)** Larry R. Squire, Ph.D; **Figure 14.20(a)** Suzanne H. Corkin; **Figure 14.20(b)** Suzanne H. Corkin; **Figure 14.24** Cecil Fox/Science Source, Photo Researchers, Inc.

Chapter 15 Chapter opening photo Dr. Monty Buchsbaum, Peter Arnold, Inc.; **Figure 15.1** Lionel Delevingne, Stock Boston; **Figure 15.3(left)** Archive Photos; **Figure 15.3(right)** Stock Montage, Inc./Historical Pictures Collection; **Figure 15.4** Lewis R. Baxter, Jr., M. D.; **Figure 15.9** Grunnitus, Monkmeyer Press; **Figure 15.13(a)** Dr. E. V. Gurevich; **Figure 15.13(b)** Dr. E. V. Gurevich; **Figure 15.14** Dr. Nancy C. Andreason; **Figure 15.15(a)** Dr. Arnold Scheibel; **Figure 15.15(b)** Dr. Arnold Scheibel; **Figure 15.16** Dr. E. Fuller Torrey and Dr. Weinberger, National Institute of Mental Health; **Figure 15.17** NIH/Science Source, Photo Researchers, Inc.; **Figure 15.19** Monte S. Buchsbaum, M.D., Mount Sinai School of Medicine, New York, NY; **Figure 15.20(a-e)** Monte S. Buchsbaum, M.D., Mount Sinai School of Medicine, New York, NY.

Cartoons, Figures, and Tables

Chapter 1 Figure 1.1 The Granger Collection; **Figure 1.2** National Library of Medicine; **Figure 1.3** Adapted from F. Martini (1998). *Fundamentals of Anatomy and Physiology,* 4th ed., p. 418. Upper Saddle River, NJ; Prentice Hall. © Prentice Hall. Reprinted with permission; **Figure 1.4** The Francis A. Countway Library of Medicine, Boston, Massachusetts; **Figure 1.5** Adapted from F. Martini (1998). *Fundamentals of Anatomy and Physiology,* 4th ed., p.447. Upper Saddle River, NJ; Prentice Hall. © Prentice Hall. Reprinted with permission; **Figure 1.6(top)** Adapted from F. Martini (1998). *Fundamentals of Anatomy and Physiology,* 4th ed., p.447. Upper Saddle River, NJ; Prentice Hall. © Prentice Hall. Reprinted with permission; **Figure 1.12** Adapted from F. Martini (1998). *Fundamentals of Anatomy and Physiology,* 4th ed., p. 1116. Upper Saddle River, NJ; Prentice Hall. © Prentice Hall. Reprinted with permission; **Figure 1.15** Adapted from L. A. Borradaile &

F. A. Potts (1961). *The Invertebrata: A manual for use of students.* Cambridge: Cambridge University Press. Reprinted by permission of Cambridge University Press; **Figure 1.16** Adapted from L. A. Borradaile & F. A. Potts (1961). *The Invertebrata: A manual for use of students.* Cambridge: Cambridge University Press. Reprinted by permission of Cambridge University Press; **Figure 1.17** Adapted from T. Smock (1999). *Physiological Psychology,* p.181. Upper Saddle River, NJ; Prentice Hall. © Prentice Hall. Reprinted with permission; **Figure 1.18** Michael J. Timmons; **Figure 1.19** From A. Barasa (1960). Forma, Grandezza e densita dei neuroni della corteccia cerebrale in mammiferi di gran-dezza corporea differente. *Zeitschrift für Zellforschung, 53,* 69-89.

Chapter 2 Figure 2.1 From T. Smock (1999). *Physiological Psychology: A Neuroscience Approach,* p. 12. Upper Saddle River, NJ; Prentice Hall. © Prentice Hall. Reprinted with permission; **Figure 2.2** Adapted from from F. Martini (1998). *Fundamentals of Anatomy and Physiology,* 4th ed., p. 371. Upper Saddle River, NJ; Prentice Hall. © Prentice Hall. Reprinted with permission; **Figure 2.3** Adapted from F. Martini (1998). *Fundamentals of Anatomy and Physiology,* 4th ed., p. 21. Upper Saddle River, NJ; Prentice Hall. © Prentice Hall. Reprinted with permission; **Figure 2.4** Adapted from F. Martini (1998). *Fundamentals of Anatomy and hPysiology,* 4th ed., p. 398. Upper Saddle River, NJ; Prentice Hall. © Prentice Hall. Reprinted with permission; **Figure 2.5** Adapted from F. Martini (1998). *Fundamentals of Anatomy and Physiology,* 4th ed., p. 398. Upper Saddle River, NJ; Prentice Hall. © Prentice Hall. Reprinted with permission; **Figure 2.6** From F. Martini (1998). *Fundamentals of Anatomy and Physiology,* 4th ed., p. 374. Upper Saddle River, NJ; Prentice Hall. © Prentice Hall. Reprinted with permission; **Figure 2.7** Adapted from E.R. Kandel (1991). Nerve cells and behavior. In E.R. Kandel, J. Schwartz, & T.M. Jessell (Eds.), *Principles of Neural Science, 3rd ed.* © 1991 by Appleton & Lange. Reprinted by permission; **Figure 2.8** Adapted from F. Martini (1998). *Fundamentals of Anatomy and Physiology,* 4th ed., p. 377. Upper Saddle River, NJ; Prentice Hall. © Prentice Hall. Reprinted with permission; **Figure 2.9** Adapted from F. Martini (1998). *Fundamentals of Anatomy and Physiology,* 4th ed., p. 149. Upper Saddle River, NJ; Prentice Hall. © Prentice Hall. Reprinted with permission; **Figure 2.10** From Delanney, et al. (1989). Adapted from *General Biology,* Revised Edition. © 1961 by Holt, Rinehart and Winston and renewed 1989 by Willis H. Johnson & Louis E. Delanney. Reproduced by permission of the publisher. This material may not be reproduced, stored in a retrieval system, or transmitted in any form or by any means without the prior written permission of the publisher; **Figure 2.11** From F. Martini (1998). *Fundamentals of Anatomy and Physiology,* 4th ed., p. 418. Upper Saddle River, NJ; Prentice Hall. © Prentice Hall. Reprinted with permission; **Figure 2.12** Adapted from adapted from F. Martini (1998). *Fundamentals of Anatomy and Physiology,* 4th ed., p. 450. Upper Saddle River, NJ; Prentice Hall. © Prentice Hall. Reprinted with permission; **Figure 2.13** Adapted from F. Martini (1998). *Fundamentals of Anatomy and Physiology,* 4th ed., p. 189. Upper Saddle River, NJ; Prentice Hall. © Prentice Hall. Reprinted with permission; **Figure 2.15** From F. Martini (1998). *Fundamentals of Anatomy and Physiology,* 4th ed., p. 419. Upper Saddle River, NJ; Prentice Hall. © Prentice Hall. Reprinted with permission; **Figure 2.16** Adapted from F. Martini (1998). *Fundamentals of Anatomy and Physiology,* 4th ed., p. 435. Upper Saddle River, NJ; Prentice Hall. © Prentice Hall. Reprinted with permission; **Figure 2.17** Adapted from P.D. MacLean (1977). The triune brain in conflict. *Psychotherapy and Psychosomatics, 28,* 208. Reprinted by permission of S. Karger AG; **Figure 2.18** Adapted from F. Martini (1998), *Fundamentals of Anatomy and Physiology.* 4th ed., p. 465. Upper Saddle River, NJ; Prentice Hall. © Prentice Hall. Reprinted with permission; **Figure 2.19** Adapted from F. Martini (1998). *Fundamentals of Anatomy and Physiology,* 4th ed., p. 470. Upper Saddle River, NJ: Prentice Hall. © Prentice Hall. Reprinted with permission; **Figure 2.20** From T. Smock (1999). *Physiological Psychology: A Neuroscience Approach,* p. 171. Upper Saddle River, NJ; Prentice Hall. © Prentice Hall. Reprinted with permission; **Figure 2.21** From T. Smock (1999). *Physiological Psychology: A Neuroscience Approach,* p. 182. Upper Saddle River, NJ; Prentice Hall. © Prentice Hall. Reprinted with permission; **Figure 2.22** Adapted from F. Martini (1998). *Fundamentals of Anatomy and Physiology,* 4th ed., p. 604. Upper Saddle River, NJ; Prentice Hall. © Prentice Hall. Reprinted with permission; **Figure 2.23** Adapted from F. Martini (1998). *Fundamentals of Anatomy and Physiology,* 4th ed., p. 464. Upper Saddle River, NJ; Prentice Hall. © Prentice Hall. Reprinted with permission; **Figure 2.24** From R. Nieuwenhuys, J. Voogd, & C. Van Huijzen (1988). *The Human Central Nervous System,* 3rd ed. Berlin: Springer-Verlag. Reprinted by permission of Springer-Verlag & Dr. Rudolf Nieuwenhuys; **Figure 2.25** From F. E. Bloom & A. Lazerson (1985). *Brain, Mind, and Behavior.* New York: Freeman © 1985. ©1988 by Educational Broadcasting Corporation. Used with permission by W.H. Freeman and Co.; **Figure 2.26** Adapted from W. Penfield & T. Rasmussen (1950). *The Cerebral Cortex of Man: A Clinical Study of Localization of Function.* New York: MacMillan. © 1950 by Penfield & Rasmussen. Reprinted with the permission of Macmillan Library Reference USA, a division of Ahsuog, Inc.

Chapter 3 Figure 3.1 From F. Martini (1998). *Fundamentals of Anatomy and Physiology,* 4th ed., p. 122. Upper Saddle River, NJ; Prentice Hall. © Prentice Hall. Reprinted with permission; **Figure 3.2** Adapted from F. Martini (1998). *Fundamentals of Anatomy and Physiology,* 4th ed., p. 379. Upper Saddle River, NJ; Prentice Hall. © Prentice Hall. Reprinted with permission; **Figure 3.3** From F. Martini (1998). *Fundamentals of Anatomy and Physiology,* 4th ed., p. 454. Upper Saddle River, NJ; Prentice Hall. © Prentice Hall. Reprinted with permission; **Figure 3.6** Adapted from J.H. Martin & T.M. Jessell (1991). Development as a guide to the regional anatomy of the brain. In E.R. Kandel, J. Schwartz, & T.M. Jessell (Eds.), *Principles of Neural Science,* 3rd ed. © 1991 by Appleton & Lange. Reprinted by permission; **Figure 3.7** From W.M. Cowan (1979). Figure by Tom Prentiss as appeared in The development of the brain. *Scientific American,* September 1979. Reprinted by permission of the illustrator; **Figure 3.8** Adapted from P. Rakic (1972). Mode of cell migration to the superficial layers of fetal monkey neocortex. *Journal of Comparative Neurology, 145,* 6-84. Adapted by permission of Wiley-Liss, Inc., a subsidiary of John Wiley & Sons, Inc.; **Figure 3.9** From N. Zecevic & P. Rakic (1976). Differentiation of Purkinje cells and their relationships to other components of developing cerebellar cortex in man. *Journal of Comparative Neurology, 167,* 27-48. Adapted by permission of Wiley-Liss, Inc., a subsidiary of John Wiley & Sons, Inc.; **Figure 3.11** Adapted from T.M. Jessell (1991). Cell migration and axon guidance. In E.R. Kandel, J. Schwartz, & T.M. Jessell (Eds.), *Principles of Neural Science,* 3rd Ed. © 1991 by Appleton & Lange. Reprinted by permission; **Figure 3.12** Adapted from P.H. Taghert, M.J. Bastiani, R.K. Ho, & C.S. Goodman (1982). Guidance of pioneer growth cones: Filopodia contacts and coupling revealed with an antibody to Lucifer Yellow. *Developmental Biology, 94,* 397. Reprinted by permission of Academic Press Inc. & Professor C.S. Goodman; **Figure 3.13** From T. Smock (1999). *Physiological Psychology: A Neuroscience Approach,* p. 368. Upper Saddle River, NJ; Prentice Hall. © Prentice Hall. Reprinted with permission; **Figure 3.16** Adapted from A.M. Schneider & Tarshis (1995). *Elements of Physiological Psychology.* New York: McGraw-Hill. Reprinted by permission of The McGraw-Hill Companies, Inc.

Chapter 4 Figure 4.1 From T. Smock (1999). *Physiological Psychology: A Neuroscience Approach,* p. 55. Upper Saddle River, NJ; Prentice Hall. © Prentice Hall. Reprinted with permission; **Figure 4.2** Adapted from F. Martini (1998). *Fundamentals of Anatomy and Physiology,* 4th ed., p. 69. Upper Saddle River, NJ; Prentice Hall. © Prentice Hall. Reprinted with permission; **Figure 4.3** From F. Martini (1998). *Fundamentals of Anatomy and Physiology,* 4th ed., p. 73. Upper Saddle River, NJ; Prentice Hall. © Prentice Hall. Reprinted with permission; **Figure 4.5** From F. Martini (1998). *Fundamentals of Anatomy and Physiology,* 4th ed., p. 77. Upper Saddle River, NJ; Prentice Hall. © Prentice Hall. Reprinted with permission; **Figure 4.6** From F. Martini (1998). *Fundamentals of Anatomy and Physiology,* 4th ed., p. 82. Upper Saddle River, NJ; Prentice Hall. © Prentice Hall. Reprinted with permission; **Figure 4.7** Adapted from F. Martini (1998). *Fundamentals of Anatomy and Physiology,* 4th ed., p. 391. Upper Saddle River, NJ; Prentice Hall. © Prentice Hall. Reprinted with permission; **Figure 4.8** Adapted from J. Eccles (1977). *The Understanding of The Brain,* 2nd Ed. New York: McGraw-Hill. Reprinted with permission of The McGraw-Hill Companies; **Figure 4.9** From F. Martini (1998). *Fundamentals of Anatomy and Physiology,* 4th ed., p. 393. Upper Saddle River, NJ; Prentice Hall. © Prentice Hall. Reprinted with permission; **Figure 4.10** From F. Martini (1998). *Fundamentals of Anatomy and Physiology,* 4th ed., p. 395. Upper Saddle River, NJ; Prentice Hall. © Prentice Hall. Reprinted with permission; **Figure 4.11** Adapted from F. Martini (1998). *Fundamentals of Anatomy and Physiology,* 4th ed., p. 398. Upper Saddle River, NJ;

Prentice Hall. © Prentice Hall. Reprinted with permission; **Figure 4.13** From T. Smock (1999). *Physiological Psychology: A Neuroscience Approach*, p. 90. Upper Saddle River, NJ; Prentice Hall. © Prentice Hall. Reprinted with permission; **Figure 4.14** From F. Martini (1998). *Fundamentals of Anatomy and Physiology*, 4th ed., p. 404. Upper Saddle River, NJ; Prentice Hall. © Prentice Hall. Reprinted with permission; **Figure 4.15** From F. Martini (1998). *Fundamentals of Anatomy and Physiology*, 4th ed., p. 406. Upper Saddle River, NJ; Prentice Hall. © Prentice Hall. Reprinted with permission; **Figure 4.16** Adapted from T. Smock (1999). *Physiological Psychology: A Neuroscience Approach*, p. 143. Upper Saddle River, NJ; Prentice Hall. © Prentice Hall. Reprinted with permission; **Figure 4.18** From T. Smock (1999). *Physiological Psychology: A Neuroscience Approach*, p. 119. Upper Saddle River, NJ; Prentice Hall. © Prentice Hall. Reprinted with permission; **Figure 4.19** From F.C. Sauer (1935). Mitosis in the neural tube. *Journal of Comparative Neurology, 62*; 377-405. © 1935. Reprinted with permission of John Wiley & Sons, Inc.; **Figure 4.24** From T. Smock (1999). *Physiological Psychology: A Neuroscience Approach*, p. 119. Upper Saddle River, NJ; Prentice Hall. © Prentice Hall. Reprinted with permission; **Figure 4.25** Adapted from F. Martini (1998). *Fundamentals of Anatomy and Physiology*, 4th ed., p. 593. Upper Saddle River, NJ; Prentice Hall. © Prentice Hall. Reprinted with permission. **Table 4.1** Adapted from N.R. Carlson (1988). Foundations of *Physiological Psychology*. Boston: Allyn & Bacon. Reprinted by permission of Allyn & Bacon.

Chapter 5 Figure 5.8 (Cartoon) GARFIELD © 1989 Paws, Inc. Reprinted with permission of UNIVERSAL PRESS SYNDICATE. All rights reserved; **Figure 5.14** Adapted from J. Olds (1958). Self-stimulation experiments and differentiated rewards. In H.H. Jasper, L.S. Proctor, R.S. Knighton, W.C. Noshav, and R.T. Costello (Eds.) *Reticular Formation of the Brain*. Boston: Little Brown. © 1958 by Little, Brown and Company. Reprinted by permission of Lippincott Williams & Wilkins; **Figure 5.19** Adapted from J.R. Volpicelli, C.P. O'Brien, A.I. Alterman, & M. Hayashida (1990). Naltrexone and the treatment of alcohol-dependence. Initial observations. In L.D. Reid (Ed.), *Opioids, Bulimia and Alcohol Abuse and Alcoholism.* Reprinted by permissions of Springer-Verlag Publishers and the author. **Table 5.2** Adapted from O.S. Ray & C. Ksir (1996). *Drugs, Society and Human Behavior.*, 7th Ed. © 1996 by Mosby-Year Book, Inc. New York: Springer-Verlag. Reprinted by permission of W. B. Saunders Company; **Table 5.3** From C.O. Byer & L.W. Shainberg (1995). *Living Well: Health In Your Hands,* 2nd ed. Sudbury, MA: Jones and Bartlett Publishers. www.jbpub.com. Reprinted with permission.

Chapter 6 Figure 6.1 Adapted from G. Wald 1950. Eye and camera. *Scientific American, 183,* 33. Reprinted by permission of the Estate of Eric Mose; **Figure 6.2** From F. Martini (1998). *Fundamentals of Anatomy and Physiology,* 4th ed., p. 560. Upper Saddle River, NJ; Prentice Hall. © Prentice Hall. Reprinted with permission; **Figure 6.3** From F. Martini (1998). *Fundamentals of Anatomy and Physiology,* 4th ed., p. 560. Upper Saddle River, NJ; Prentice Hall. © Prentice Hall. Reprinted with permission; **Figure 6.5** From F. Martini (1998). *Fundamentals of Anatomy and Physiology,* 4th ed., p. 557. Upper Saddle River, NJ; Prentice Hall. © Prentice Hall. Reprinted with permission; **Figure 6.6** Adapted from F. Martini (1998). *Fundamentals of Anatomy and Physiology,* 4th ed., p. 569. Upper Saddle River, NJ; Prentice Hall. © Prentice Hall. Reprinted with permission; **Figure 6.7** Adapted from F. Martini (1998). *Fundamentals of Anatomy and Physiology,* 4th ed., p. 569. Upper Saddle River, NJ; Prentice Hall. © Prentice Hall. Reprinted with permission; **Figure 6.9** Adapted from F. Martini (1998). *Fundamentals of Anatomy and Physiology,* 4th ed., p. 569. Upper Saddle River, NJ; Prentice Hall. © Prentice Hall. Reprinted with permission; **Figure 6.11** From F. Martini (1998). *Fundamentals of Anatomy and Physiology,* 4th ed., p. 563. Upper Saddle River, NJ; Prentice Hall. © Prentice Hall. Reprinted with permission; **Figure 6.12** Adapted from F. Martini (1998). *Fundamentals of Anatomy and Physiology,* 4th ed., p. 566. Upper Saddle River, NJ; Prentice Hall. © Prentice Hall. Reprinted with permission; **Figure 6.13** From M. Tessler-Laviqne (1991). Phototransduction and information process in the retina. In E.R. Kandel, J. Schwartz, and T.M. Jessell (Eds.), *Principles of Neural Science,* 3rd Ed. © 1991 by Appleton & Lange. Reprinted by permission; **Figure 6.14** From James Egleson (1972). Contour and Contrast by F. Ratliff. *Scientific American, 226,* 94; **Figure 6.15** Adapted from S. W. Kuffler (1953). Discharge patterns and functional organization of the mammalian retina. *Journal of Neurophysiology, 16,* 106–154. Reprinted by permission of Lippincott Williams & Wilkins; **Figure 6.16** Adapted from D. Hubell & T.N. Wiesel (1962). Receptive field, binocular interaction and function architecture in the cat's visual cortex. *Journal of Physiology, 160,* 106-154. Reprinted by permission of The Physiological Society; **Figure 6.17** Adapted from D. Hubell & T.N. Wiesel (1962). Receptive field, binocular interaction and function architecture in the cat's visual cortex. *Journal of Physiology, 160,* 106-154. Reprinted by permission of The Physiological Society; **Figure 6.18** Adapted from D. Hubell & T.N. Wiesel (1962). Receptive field, binocular interaction and function architecture in the cat's visual cortex. *Journal of Physiology,* 160, 106-154. Reprinted by permission of The Physiological Society; **Figure 6.19** From R.L. DeValois & D.D. DeValois (1988). *Spatial Vision.* New York: Oxford University Press. © 1988 by Oxford University Press, Inc. Used by permission of Oxford University Press; **Figure 6.20** From R.L. DeValois & D.D. DeValois (1988). *Spatial Vision.* New York: Oxford University Press © 1988 by Oxford University Press, Inc. Used by permission of Oxford University Press; **Figure 6.21** Examples of complex that inferotemporal cortical neurons can learn to respond. Courtesy of Keiji Tanaka; **Figure 6.24** From D. Fernald (1997). *Psychology.* Upper Saddle River, NJ; © Prentice Hall. Reprinted with permission; **Figure 6.25** From F. Martini (1998). *Fundamentals of Anatomy and Physiology,* 4th ed., p. 567. Upper Saddle River, NJ; Prentice Hall. © Prentice Hall. Reprinted with permission; **Figure 6.28** Adapted from R.L. DeValois. & K.K. DeValois (1975). Neural coding or color. In E. C. Charterette & M.P. Friedman (Eds.), *Handbook of Perception V. Seeing* (p. 130). New York: Academic Press. Reprinted by permission of Academic Press.

Chapter 7 Figure 7.2(a) Adapted from F. Martini (1998). *Fundamentals of Anatomy and Physiology,* 4th ed., p. 571. Upper Saddle River, NJ; Prentice Hall. © Prentice Hall. Reprinted with permission; **Figure 7.2(b)** From F. Martini (1998). *Fundamentals of Anatomy and Physiology,* 4th ed., p. 571. Upper Saddle River, NJ; Prentice Hall. © Prentice Hall. Reprinted with permission; **Figure 7.3** From F. Martini (1998). *Fundamentals of Anatomy and Physiology,* 4th ed., p. 578. Upper Saddle River, NJ; Prentice Hall. © Prentice Hall. Reprinted with permission; **Figure 7.4(a)** Adapted from N. R. Carlson (1994). Psycholgoy and Behavior, 5th ed. Boston: Allyn & Bacon. Reprinted by permission of Allyn & Bacon. **Figure 7.5** From A. James Hudspeth (1988). Adapted with permission, from the *Annual Review of Biophysics and Biophysical Chemistry, 17,* 100. © 1988 by Annual Reviews. www.annualreviews.org. Also reprinted with permission of the author; **Figure 7.6** From F. Martini (1998). *Fundamentals of Anatomy and Physiology,* 4th ed., p. 580. Upper Saddle River, NJ; Prentice Hall. © Prentice Hall. Reprinted with permission; **Figure 7.7** Adapted from F. Martini (1998). *Fundamentals of Anatomy and Physiology,* 4th ed., p. 584. Upper Saddle River, NJ; Prentice Hall. © Prentice Hall. Reprinted with permission; **Figure 7.8** Adapted from G. Von Békésy (1960). *Experiments in Hearing.* New York: McGraw-Hill. Reprinted by permission of The McGraw-Hill Companies; **Figure 7.9** Adapted from A. R. Tunturi. (1952). A difference in representation of auditory signals for the left and right ears in the isofrequency contours of right middle ectosylvian auditory cortex in the dog. *American Journal of Physiology, 168,* 712-727. Reprinted by permission of the American Physiological Society; **Figure 7.10** From T. Milner (1977). How much distraction can you hear? *Stereo Review.* Reprinted by permission; **Figure 7.13** Adapted from F. Martini (1998). *Fundamentals of Anatomy and Physiology,* 4th ed., p. 575. Upper Saddle River, NJ; Prentice Hall. © Prentice Hall. Reprinted with permission; **Figure 7.14** From F. Martini (1998). *Fundamentals of Anatomy and Physiology,* 4th ed., p. 525. Upper Saddle River, NJ; Prentice Hall. © Prentice Hall. Reprinted with permission; **Figure 7.15** From: from F. Martini (1998). *Fundamentals of Anatomy and Physiology,* 4th ed., p. 575. Upper Saddle River, NJ; Prentice Hall. © Prentice Hall. Reprinted with permission; **Figure 7.16** Adapted from F. Martini (1998). *Fundamentals of Anatomy and Physiology,* 4th ed., p. 576. Upper Saddle River, NJ; Prentice Hall. © Prentice Hall. Reprinted with permission; **Figure 7.17** From F. Martini (1998). *Fundamentals of Anatomy and Physiology,* 4th ed., p. 543. Upper Saddle River, NJ; Prentice Hall. © Prentice Hall. Reprinted with permission; **Figure 7.18** Adapted from A. B. Vallbo & R. S. Johnson (1984). Properties of cutaneous mechanic receptors in the human hand related to touch sensation. *Human Neurobiology 3,* 6, 8. Reprinted by permission of Springer-Verlag Publishing; **Figure 7.19** Adapted from G. Somjen. *Sensory Coding in the Mammalian Nervous*

System. New York: Plenum. Reprinted by permission of Plenum Publishing Corporation and George Somjen; **Figure 7.20** Adapted from F. Martini (1998). *Fundamentals of Anatomy and Physiology*, 4th ed., pp. 494, 499. Upper Saddle River, NJ: Prentice Hall. © Prentice Hall. Reprinted with permission; **Figure 7.23** Adapted from: from F. Martini (1998). *Fundamentals of Anatomy and Physiology*, 4th ed., p. 549. Upper Saddle River, NJ; Prentice Hall. © Prentice Hall. Reprinted with permission; **Figure 7.24** Adapted from L. M. Bartoshuk (1993). Genetic and pathological taste variation: What we can learn from animal models and human disease? In D. Chadwick, J. Marsh, & J. Goode (Eds.), *The Molecular Basis of Smell and Taste Transduction.* Permission is granted on behalf of the Ciba Foundation; **Figure 7.25** Adapted from J. Dodd & V.F. Castellucci (1991). Smell and taste: The Chemical Senses. In E.R. Kandel, J. Schwartz, & T.M. Jessell (Eds.), *Principles of Neural Science*, 3rd Ed. © 1991 by Appleton & Lange. Reprinted by permission; **Figure 7.26** Adapted from D. Ottoson (1983). *Physiology of the Nervous System.* Reprinted by permission of Macmillan Press Ltd.

Chapter 8 Figure 8.2 From F. Martini (1998). *Fundamentals of Anatomy and Physiology*, 4th ed., p. 136. Upper Saddle River, NJ; Prentice Hall. © Prentice Hall. Reprinted with permission; **Figure 8.3** From Mark R. Rosenzweig & Arnold L. Lieman (1989). *Physiological Psychology*, 2nd Ed. Reprinted by permission of the authors; **Figure 8.4** Adapted from F. Martini (1998). *Fundamentals of Anatomy and Physiology*, 4th ed., p. 278. Upper Saddle River, NJ; Prentice Hall. © Prentice Hall. Reprinted with permission; **Figure 8.5** Adapted from F. Martini (1998). *Fundamentals of Anatomy and Physiology*, 4th ed., p. 284. Upper Saddle River, NJ; Prentice Hall. © Prentice Hall. Reprinted with permission; **Figure 8.6** Adapted from F. Martini (1998). *Fundamentals of Anatomy and Physiology*, 4th ed., p. 286. Upper Saddle River, NJ; Prentice Hall. © Prentice Hall. Reprinted with permission; **Figure 8.7** From F. Martini (1998). *Fundamentals of Anatomy and Physiology*, 4th ed., p. 288-89. Upper Saddle River, NJ; Prentice Hall. © Prentice Hall. Reprinted with permission; **Figure 8.8** From F. Martini (1998). *Fundamentals of Anatomy and Physiology*, 4th ed., p. 435. Upper Saddle River, NJ; Prentice Hall. © Prentice Hall. Reprinted with permission; **Figure 8.9** Adapted from J. Gordon (1991). Spinal mechanisms of motor coordination. In E.R. Kandel, J. Schwartz, & T.M. Jessell (Eds.), *Principles of Neural Science*, 3rd ed. © 1991 by Appleton & Lange. Reprinted by permission; **Figure 8.11** Adapted from J. Gordon (1991). Spinal mechanisms of motor coordination. In E.R. Kandel, J. Schwartz, & T.M. Jessell (Eds.) *Principles of Neural Science*, 3rd ed. © 1991 by Appleton & Lange. Reprinted by permission; **Figure 8.12** Adapted from J. Gordon (1991). Spinal mechanisms of motor coordination. In E.R. Kandel, J. Schwartz, and T.M. Jessell (Eds.) *Principles of Neural Science,* 3rd ed. © 1991 by Appleton & Lange. Reprinted by permission; **Figure 8.13** From D. E. Silverthorn (1988). Human Physiology: An Integrated Approach, p. 373. Upper Saddle River, NJ; Prentice Hall. © Prentice Hall. Reprinted with permission; **Figure 8.14** Adapted from F. Martini (1998). *Fundamentals of Anatomy and Physiology*, 4th ed., p. 434. Upper Saddle River, NJ; Prentice Hall. © Prentice Hall. Reprinted with permission; **Figure 8.15(top)**. Adapted from T. Smock (1999). *Physiological Psychology: A Neuroscience Approach*, p. 232. Upper Saddle River, NJ; Prentice Hall. © Prentice Hall. Reprinted with permission; **Figure 8.15(bottom)** Adapted from F. Martini (1998). *Fundamentals of Anatomy and Physiology*, 4th ed., p. 449. Upper Saddle River, NJ; Prentice Hall. © Prentice Hall. Reprinted with permission; **Figure 8.16** Adapted from C. Brinkman (1984). Supplementary motor area of the monkey's cerebral cortex: Short-and long-term deficits after unilateral ablation and the effects of subsequent callosal section. *Journal of Neuroscience, 4*, 925. Reprinted by permission of the Society for Neuroscience; **Figure 8.17** Adapted from F. Martini (1998). *Fundamentals of Anatomy and Physiology*, 4th ed., p. 499. Upper Saddle River, NJ; Prentice Hall. © Prentice Hall. Reprinted with permission; **Figure 8.19** From F. Martini (1998). *Fundamentals of Anatomy and Physiology*, 4th ed., p. 472. Upper Saddle River, NJ; Prentice Hall. © Prentice Hall. Reprinted with permission; **Figure 8.20** From T. Smock (1999). *Physiological Psychology: A Neuroscience Approach*, p. 247. Upper Saddle River, NJ; Prentice Hall. © Prentice Hall. Reprinted with permission; **Figure 8.22** From T. Smock (1999). *Physiological Psychology: A Neuroscience Approach*, p. 236. Upper Saddle River, NJ; Prentice Hall. © Prentice Hall. Reprinted with permission.

Chapter 9 Figure 9.1 From R. Coleman (1986). *Wide Awake At 3:00 A.M.: By Choice or By Chance?* © 1986 by Richard Coleman. New York: W. H. Freeman and Co. Used with permission of W.H. Freeman and Co.; **Figure 9.2** Adapted from J. W. Kalat (1998). *Biological Psychology*, 6th ed. © 1998. Reprinted with permission of Wadsworth Publishing, a division of International Thomson Publishing; **Figure 9.4** Adapted from J. Aschoff (1969). Desychronization and resynchronization of human circadian rhythms. *Aerospace Medicine, 40*, 844-849. Reprinted by permission of Aviation Space and Environmental Medicine; **Figure 9.6** Adapted from M. Moore-Ede, F.M. Sulzman, & C.A. Fuller (1982). *The Clocks that Time Us.* Cambridge, MA: Harvard University Press. Reprinted by permission of Martin Moore-Ede; **Figure 9.9** Adapted from H. W. Magoun (1954). *Brain Mechanism and Consciousness.* Oxford: Blackwell Scientific, Ltd. Reprinted by permission of Blackwell Scientific Ltd.; **Figure 9.10** Adapted from R. Y. Moore (1979). With permission from the *Annual Review of Neuroscience, 2*, 113–168. © 1979 by *Annual Reviews.* www.annualreviews. org. Also reprinted by permission of the author; **Figure 9.11** From G. Aston-Jones & F.F. Bloom (1981). Activity of norepinephrine containing locus coeruleus neurons in behaving rats anticipating fluctuations in sleep-waking cycle. *The Journal of Neuroscience, 1*, 882. Reprinted by permission of the Society for Neuroscience; **Figure 9.13** From J. A. Horne (1988). *Why We Sleep: The Functions of Sleep in Humans and Other Mammals.* Oxford: Oxford University Press. Reprinted by permission of Oxford University Press; **Figure 9.14** Adapted from E. Hartman (1967). *The Biology of Dreaming.* Springfield, Illinois: Charles C. Thomas Publisher, Ltd. Courtesy of Charles C. Thomas Publisher, Ltd. **Figure 9.15** Adapted from H. Zepelin and A. Rechtschaffen (1974). Mammalian sleep, longevity, and energy metabolism. *Brain, Behavior, and Evolution, 10*, 428-430. Reprinted by permission of S. Karger AG; **Figure 9.16** Adapted from H.P. Roffwarg et al. (1966). Ontogenetic development of the human sleep-dream cycle. *Science, 152*, 608. © 1966 American Association for the Advancement of Science; Reprinted with permission; **Figure 9.18** From M. Jouvet (1969). Biogenic amines and the status of sleep. *Science, 163*, 34. © 1966 American Association for the Advancement of Science; Reprinted with permission; **Figure 9.19** Adapted from M.B. Sterman & C.D. Clementem (1962). Forebrain inhibitory mechanism: Sleep patterns induced by basal forebrain stimulation in the behaving cat. *Experimental Neurology, 6*, 107. Reprinted by permission of Academic Press; **Figure 9.20** From J. Allan Hobson (1989). *Sleep.* San Francisco: W. H. Freeman and Co. Used with permission of W.H. Freeman and Co.; **Figure 9.21** (Cartoon) THE FAR SIDE © 1982 FARWORKS, INC. Used by permission. All rights reserved; **Figure 9.22** Adapted from W. Dement, C. Guilleminault, & V. Zarcone (1975). The pathologies of sleep: A case series approach. In D. B. Tower (Ed.), *The Nervous System (Vol. 2): The Clinical Neurosciences.* New York: Raven Press. Reprinted by permission of the author. **Table 9.1** From B. Wallace (1993). Day persons, night persons, and variability in hypnotic susceptibility. *Journal of Personality and Social Psychology, 64*, 827-833. © 1993 by the American Psychological Association. Reprinted with permission.

Chapter 10 Figure 10.1 From F. Martini (1998). *Fundamentals of Anatomy and Physiology*, 4th ed., p. 863. Upper Saddle River, NJ; Prentice Hall. © Prentice Hall. Reprinted with permission; **Figure 10.2** Adapted from E. N. Whitney & May Hamilton (1977). *Understanding Nutrition,* © 1977. Reprinted with permission of Wadsworth Publishing, a division of Thomson Learning; **Figure 10.3** Adapted from T. Smock (1999). *Physiological Psychology: A Neuroscience Approach*, p. 340. Upper Saddle River, NJ; Prentice Hall. © Prentice Hall. Reprinted with permission; **Figure 10.6** From Cooper, et al. (1970). *The Biochemical Basis of Neuropharmacology*, 7th ed. New York: Oxford University Press. © 1970, 1974, 1978, 1982, 1986, 1991, 1996 by Oxford University Press, Inc. Used by permission of Oxford University Press, Inc.; **Figure 10.8** Adapted from S.F. Leibowitz, et al. (1985). Noradrenergic innervation of the paraventricular nucleus: specific role in the control of carbohydrate ingestions. *Brain Research Bulletin, 14*, 561-567. © 1985 with permission from Elsevier Science; **Figure 10.11** Adapted from E. N. Whitney and May Hamilton (1977). *Understanding Nutrition.* © 1977. Reprinted with permission of Wadsworth Publishing, a division of Thomson Learning; **Figure 10.12** Adapted from C. A. Campbell & F. A. Smith (1990). Systemic factors in the control of food intake: Evidence for patterns as signals. E. Em. Stricker (Ed.), *Handbook of Behavioral Neurobiology, 10. © 1990.* Reprinted by permission of Plenum Publishing Corporation; **Figure 10.13**

Adapted from E. N. Whitney & M. Hamilton (1977). *Understanding Nutrition.* © 1977. Reprinted with permission of Wadsworth Publishing, a division of Thomson Learning; **Figure 10.16** Adapted from T. L. Powley & R. E. Keesey (1970). Relationship of body weight to the lateral hypothalamic feeding syndrome. *Journal of Comparative and Physiological Psychology, 70,* 30. © 1970 by the American Psychological Association. Reprinted with permission; **Figure 10.17** Adapted from B. G. Hoebel & P. Teitelbaum (1966). Weight regulation in normal and hypothalamic hyperphagic rats. *Journal of Comparative and Physiological Psychology, 61,* 191. © 1966 by the American Psychological Association. Reprinted with permission; **Figure 10.19** Adapted from J. A. Hibscher & C.P. Herman (1977). Obesity, dieting and the expression of obese characteristics. *Journal of Comparative and Physiological Psychology, 91,* 377. © 1977 by the American Psychological Association. Reprinted with permission; **Figure 10.20** From F. Martini (1998). *Fundamentals of Anatomy and Physiology,* 4th ed., p. 962. Upper Saddle River, NJ; Prentice Hall. © Prentice Hall. Reprinted with permission; **Figure 10.21** Adapted from F. Martini (1998). *Fundamentals of Anatomy and Physiology,* 4th ed., p. 75. Upper Saddle River, NJ; Prentice Hall. © Prentice Hall. Reprinted with permission; **Figure 10.22** Adapted from F. Martini (1998). *Fundamentals of Anatomy and Physiology,* 4th ed., p. 449. Upper Saddle River, NJ; Prentice Hall. © Prentice Hall. Reprinted with permission; **Figure 10.23** From N.R. Carlson (1982). *Psychology of Behavior,* 2nd ed. Boston: Allyn & Bacon. Reprinted by permission of Allyn & Bacon; **Table 10.2** From T. L. Powley, (1977). *Psychological Review, 84,* 89-126. © 1977 by the American Psychological Association. Reprinted by permission of the American Psychological Association and the author; **Table 10.3** From S. Schachter (1971). Some extrordinary facts about obese humans and rats. *American Psychologist, 26,* 133. © 1971 by the American Psychological Association. Reprinted by permission of the American Psychological Association and the author.

Chapter 11 **Figure 11.1** From T. Smock (1999). *Physiological Psychology: A Neuroscience Approach,* p. 284. Upper Saddle River, NJ; Prentice Hall. © Prentice Hall. Reprinted with permission; **Figure 11.2** From T. Smock (1999). *Physiological Psychology: A Neuroscience Approach,* p. 285. Upper Saddle River, NJ; Prentice Hall. © Prentice Hall. Reprinted with permission; **Figure 11.5** Adapted from F. A. Beach, R. G. Noble, & R. K. Orndoff (1969). Effects of perinatal androgen treatment on responses of male rats to gonadal hormones in adulthood. *Journal of Comparative and Physiological Psychology, 68,* 493. © 1969 by the American Psychological Association. Reprinted by permission; **Figure 11.6** Adapted from R. A. Gorski et al. (1978). Evidence for a morphological sex difference with the medial preoptic area of the brain. *Brain Research, 148,* 333-346, © 1978, with permission from Elsevier Science; **Figure 11.7** Adapted from W. Masters & V. Johnson (1966). *Human Sexual Response.* Boston: Little, Brown and Company; **Figure 11.8** From F. Martini (1998). *Fundamentals of Anatomy and Physiology,* 4th ed., p. 1039. Upper Saddle River, NJ; Prentice Hall. © Prentice Hall. Reprinted with permission; **Figure 11.9** From F. Martini (1998). *Fundamentals of Anatomy and Physiology,* 4th ed., p. 1055. Upper Saddle River, NJ; Prentice Hall. © Prentice Hall. Reprinted with permission; **Figure 11.10** From J. A. Grant & D. C. Young (1952). Differential reactivity of individuals and the response of the male guinea pig to testosterone proporonate. *Endocrinology, 51,* p. 237-248. © The Endocrine Society. Reprinted by permission of The Endocrine Society; **Figure 11.11** From E. P. Volpe (1979). *Man, Nature, and Society,* 2nd Ed., © 1975, 1979 by Wm C. Brown Company Publishers. Reprinted by permission of The McGraw-Hill Companies; **Figure 11.12** Adapted from J. R. Udry & N. M. Morris (1968). Distribution of coitus in the menstrual cycle. *Nature, 220,* 594. Reprinted with permission from *Nature* and the author. © 1968 Macmillan Magazines Limited; **Figure 11.13** Adapted from C. R. Noback & J. R. Demarest (1972). *The Nervous System: Introduction and Review.* New York: McGraw-Hill. Reprinted by permission of Charles Norback; **Figure 11.15** From *Experimental Brain Research, 97,* 447, figure #7. New York: Springer-Verlag, Inc. © Dr. David S. Albeck, Ph. D, Rockefeller University.

Chapter 12 **Figure 12.3** From F. Martini (1998). *Fundamentals of Anatomy and Physiology,* 4th ed., p. 464. Upper Saddle River, NJ; Prentice Hall. © Prentice Hall. Reprinted with permission; **Figure 12.4** From P.D. MacLean (1954). Studies on limbic system ("visceral brain") and their bearing on psychosomatic problems. In E. D. Wittkower & R. A. Clegharn (Eds.), *Recent Developments in Psychosomatic Medicine.* Philadelphia: Lippincott. Reprinted by permission of Lippincott Williams & Wilkins; **Figure 12.9** (Cartoon) Jeff MacNelly, Tribune Media Services, Inc. © Tribune Media Services, Inc. All Rights Reserved. Reprinted with permission; **Figure 12.10** From G. Paxinos & C. Watson (1982). *The Brain in Stereotaxic Coordinates.* Sydney: Academic Press; **Figure 12.11** V. H. Mark & F. R. Ervin (1970). *Violence and the Brain.* Harper & Row: New York; **Figure 12.12** Adapted from G. Wagner, L. Beauving, & R. Hutchinson (1980). The effects of gonadal hormone manipulations on aggressive target-biting in mice. *Aggressive Behavior, 6,* 4. Reprinted by permission of Wiley-Liss, Inc., a division of John Wiley & Sons Inc.; **Figure 12.13** Adapted from J. D. Higley, P. T. Mehlman, S. B. Highley, B. Ferguson, J. Vickers, S. G. Lindell, D. M. Taub, S. J. Suomi, & M. Linnoila. (1996). *Archives of General Psychiatry,* 53, 540; **Figure 12.14** Adapted from F. Martini (1998). *Fundamentals of Anatomy and Physiology,* 4th ed., p. 631. Upper Saddle River, NJ; Prentice Hall. © Prentice Hall. Reprinted with permission; **Figure 12.16** From S. Taylor (1996). *Health Psychology, 3rd ed.*. New York: McGraw-Hill. Reprinted by permission of The McGraw-Hill Companies; **Table 12.1** From R.C. Beck (1990) *Motivation: Theories and Principles* 3rd ed., Englewood Cliffs, NJ: Prentice Hall. © 1990. Adapted by permission of Prentice-Hall Inc., Upper Saddle River, NJ.

Chapter 13 **Figure 13.1** From Geschwind (1979). Adapted figure by Carol Donner as appeared in Specializations in the human brain. *Scientific American, 241,* 190. Reprinted by permission of the illustrator; **Figure 13.3** Adapted from S. E. Peterson, P. T. Fox, M. I. Posner, M. Minton, & M. E. Raichle (1988). *Nature, 331,* 588. Reprinted with permission from *Nature* and the author. © 1988 Macmillan Magazines Limited; **Figure 13.5** Adapted from R. Nieuwenhuys (1988). *The Human Central Nervous System,* 3rd ed. Reprinted by permission of Springer-Verlag and the author Dr. Rudolff Nieuwenhuys; **Figure 13.7** R.E. Myers & R.W. Sperry (1953) Interocular tranfer of a visual form discrimination habit in cats after section of the optic shiasma and corpus callosum. *American Association of Anatomists: Abstracts of Papers from Platform,* p. 35.; **Figure 13.10** Adapted from M.S. Gazzaniga (1967). The split brain in man. *Scientific American,* p. 27. Reprinted by permission of the Estate of Eric Mose; **Figure 13.11** Adapted from M. S. Gazzaniga (1967). The split brain in man. *Scientific American,* p. 24-29. Reprinted by permission of Dr. Michael S. Gazzaniga; **Figure 13.12** Adapted from J. Levy, C. Trevarthen & R. W. Sperry (1972). Perception of bilateral chimeric figures following hemispheric deconnexion, *Brain, 95,* 68. Reprinted by permission of Professor Jerre Levy; **Figure 13.14** From S. M. Kosslyn (1987). Seeing and imaging in the cerebral hemispheres: A computational approach. *Psychological Review, 94,* 164. © 1987. Reprinted by permission of Professor Stephen M. Kosslyn; **Figure 13.16** From R. H. Brookshire (1997). *Introduction to Neurogenic Communication Disorders,* 5th ed. St. Louis: Mosby-Year Books. Reprinted by permission of W. B. Saunders Company; **Figure 13.17** The Psychological Corporation; **Figure 13.19** From R. H. Brookshire (1997). *Introduction to Neurogenic Communication Disorders,* 5th ed. St. Louis: Mosby-Year Books. Reprinted by permission of W. B. Saunders Company; **Table 13.1** Adapted from B. Kolb & I. Q. Whishaw (1996). *Fundamentals of Human Neuropsychology,* 4th ed. New York: W. H. Freeman and Co. © 1980, 1985, 1990, 1996 by W. H. Freeman and Co. Used with permission.

Chapter 14 **Figure 14.2** Adapted from R. C. Atkinson, & R. M. Shiffrin (1968). Human memory: A proposed system and its control processes. In K. W. Spence & J. T. Spence (Eds.), *The Psychology of Learning and Motivation, Advances In Research & Theory,* (Vol. 1, p. 93). New York: Academic. Reprinted by permission of Academic Press; **Figure 14.3** From D. O. Hebb (1949). *The Organization of Behavior.* New York: John Wiley. Reprinted by permission; **Figure 14.6** From S. L. Chorover & P. H. Schiller (1965). Short-term retrograde amnesia in rats. *Journal of Comparative and Physiological Psychology, 59,* 76. © 1965. Reprinted by permission of the American Psychological Association and Professor Stephen Chorover; **Figure 14.7** From R. F. Thompson (1994). Adapted with permission from the *Annual Review of Neuroscience, 17.* © 1994, by Annual Reviews. www.annualreviews.org. Also reprinted by permission of the author; **Figure 14.9** From J.F. Flood et al. (1973). The influence of duration of protein synthesis inhibition on memory. *Physiology and Behavior, 10,* 555–562. J.F. Flood, E.L. Bennett, M.R. Rosenzweig, and A.E. Orme (Eds.). © 1973 with permission from Elsevier Science; **Figure 14.10** From T. Smock (1999). *Physiolog-*

ical Psychology: A Neuroscience Approach, p. 375. Upper Saddle River, NJ; Prentice Hall. © Prentice Hall. Reprinted with permission; **Figure 14.11** From T. Smock (1999). *Physiological Psychology: A Neuroscience Approach,* p. 376. Upper Saddle River, NJ; Prentice Hall. © Prentice Hall. Reprinted with permission; **Figure 14.12** From T. Smock (1999). *Physiological Psychology: A Neuroscience Approach,* p. 377. Upper Saddle River, NJ; Prentice Hall. © Prentice Hall. Reprinted with permission; **Figure 14.13** From R. D. Hawkins, T. W. Abrams, T. J. Carew, & E. R. Kandel (1983). A cellular mechanism of classical conditioning in *Aplysia*: Activity dependent amplification of presynaptic facilitation. *Science, 219,* 400–405; **Figure 14.17** Adapted from L. R. Squire (1986). The neuropsychology of memory. In P. Marler & H. Terrace (Eds.), *The Biology of Learning.* Reprinted by permission of Springer-Verlag and the author; **Figure 14.18(b)** From B. Milner (1965). Memory disturbances after bilateral hippocampal lesions. In P. Milner and S. Glickman (eds.) *Cognitive Processes and the Brain;* **Figure 14.21** From T. W. Berger (1984). *Science,* 224, 627-630. © 1984 American Association for the Advancement of Science. Reprinted with permission; **Figure 14.22** From E. R. Kandel (1991). Cellular mechanisms of learning and the biological basis of individuality. In E. R. Kandel, J. H. Schwartz & T. M. Jessel (Eds.), *Principles of Neural Science.* © 1991 by Appleton Lange. Reprinted with permission; **Table 14.3** From G. A. Davis (1993). *A Survey of Adult Aphasia and Related Language Disorders,* 2nd ed. Boston: Allyn & Bacon. All rights reserved. Adapted by permission.

Chapter 15 **Figure 15.2** From I.G. Sarason & B.R. Sarason (1993). *Abnormal Psychology,* 7th ed. Adapted by permission of Prentice-Hall, Inc., Upper Saddle River, NJ; **Figure 15.6** From J.C. Gillin & A.A. Borbely (1985). Sleep: A neurobiological window on affective disorders, In J. C. Gillin & A. A. Borbely, *Trends in Neurosciences, 8,* 537-542, © 1985. With permission from Elsevier Science; **Figure 15.8** Adapted from O. Lingjaede (1983). The biochemistry of depression. *Acta Psychiatrica Scandinavica Supplementum, Munksgaard Scientific Journal, 69,* 44. © 1983 Munksgaard International Publishers Ltd. Copenhagen, Denmark. Reprinted by permission; **Figure 15.11** From T. Smock (1999). *Physiological Psychology: A Neuroscience Approach,* p. 441. Upper Saddle River, NJ; Prentice Hall. © Prentice Hall. Reprinted with permission; **Figure 15.12** Adapted from P. Seeman, T. Lee, M. Chan-Wong, & K. Wong (1996). Antipsychotic drug doses and neuroleptic/dopamine receptors, *Nature, 261,* 717-719. Reprinted with permission from *Nature* and the author. © 1996 Macmillan Magazines Limited; **Figure 15.18** From Irving I. Gottesman (1991). *Schizophrenia Genesis.* New York: W. H. Freeman and Co. © 1991 by Irving I. Gottesman. Used with permission of W. H. Freeman and Co.; **Figure 15.21** From C. Barr, S. Mednick & P. Munk-Jorgensen. (1990). Exposure to influenza epidemics during gestation and adult schizophrenia, *Archives of General Psychiatry, 47,* 873. © 1990 American Medical Association. Reprinted by permission; **Table 15.1** Adapted from D. Rosenthal (1970). *Genetic Theory and Abnormal Behavior.* New York: McGraw-Hill. Reprinted by permission of The McGraw-Hill Companies.

Name Index

Subject Index